PARRY and GRANT

ENCYCLOPAEDIC DICTIONARY OF INTERNATIONAL LAW

Second Edition

Edited by
JOHN P. GRANT and J. CRAIG BARKER

2004
Oceana Publications, Inc.
Dobbs Ferry, New York

Library of Congress Control Number: 2003113178

ISBN 0-379-21449-0

Manufactured in the United States of America on acid-free paper.

**Dedicated to
the memory of Clive Parry
(13 July 1917 to 10 September 1982)
whose legacy to international legal scholarship lives on.**

TABLE OF CONTENTS

PREFACE

What the term "Encyclopaedic Dictionary of International Law" lacks in elegance it compensates for as an accurate description of both the genesis and continuing object and purpose of this work. The first edition, published in 1986, was a union of two separate projects: one, started by the late Professor Clive Parry at the University of Cambridge, was essentially an encyclopaedia of international law in English and in short compass; the other, started by one of the current editors and a group of international lawyers teaching at Scottish law schools, was more in the nature of a dictionary of international law. When these two projects were put together in the early 1980s, the result was truly a dictionary plus or an encyclopaedia minus: an encyclopaedic dictionary.

The present editors remain convinced of the utility of this approach. A dictionary of international law properly so called (and there are some) tells a reader what a term or concept means, but says nothing about the context in which that term or concept is used in international law, nor about its effect. On the other hand, an encyclopaedia of international law tells the reader all, or more than, he or she needs to know about the context and effect of areas (not terms and concepts) of the law; but, being often of great length and broadly grouped under headings, may not provide quick and easy access to the information the reader seeks. And given the predilection of legal scholars, including international legal scholars, for describing and analyzing and commenting on terms and concepts without defining them, there is, it is submitted, a need for a work that defines terms and concepts, locates them in the appropriate subject area of international law and briefly explains their effect.

This *Encyclopaedic Dictionary* is intended to embrace mainstream international law—what might be called the law of peace and the law of war. As international law expands horizontally, and as new subject areas appear and new sub-disciples are established with a vocabulary of their own, it becomes increasingly difficult for any individual or group to master the terminology of the whole of contemporary international law. The editors believe that their selection for inclusion in this work reflects the needs of the generalist rather than the specialist.

This edition includes more material on human rights and humanitarian law and international organizational law than the first edition. The digests of World Court and arbitral cases have been updated and expanded. The principal, especially multilateral, treaties are noted and referenced. Considerations of space have kept the biographies of leading figures in international law limited to those whose writings have singled them out. Bibliographical references, too, have had to be kept to a minimum necessary to enable a reader to delve beyond the entries in this work.

While each entry is intended to be self-contained, with reference material and citations in full, entries are also cross-referenced with related terms or cases by the simple expedient of using **bold** text. Because they are referred to frequently, there are no citations to the United Nations Charter, the Statute of the International Court of Justice and the Vienna Convention on the Law of Treaties, the texts of all three being appended in the Documents section of this work. For other reasons, there are no citations in the text of entries to European Union and European Community treaties: see Guidance on Use and Citations, following. The Table of Abbreviations contains only reference material actually used in the *Encyclopaedic Dictionary* and no acronyms; these now appearing as entries. In citing treaties, the editors have gone first to four principal sources: the *Consolidated Treaty Series*, the *League of Nations Treaty Series*, the *United Nations Treaty Series* and *International Legal Materials*.

The editors have many to thank for their assistance and support. Three Lewis & Clark School of Law students devoted a semester to drafting entries for this work; all the drafts were impeccably researched and well written, and the editors express their gratitude to Derily Bechthold, Jennifer Gannett and Yumi Minagawa; their legal futures are bright. The first undersigned received considerable assistance from the staff at the Boley Law Library at Lewis & Clark School of Law, particularly research librarian Wendy Hitchcock, the finder of the unfindable. The second undersigned would like to thank his research students, Graham Melling and Yitiha Simbeye, for frequent and helpful discussions of ideas, and Professor Sandy Ghandhi for his continual support and assistance. Both the editors bow in awe at the expertise of Bruce Williamson and Sean Slater from the Lewis & Clark School of Law computing service, whose talents allowed for the creation of a mechanism for the easy transfer of data between the editors and between the editors and the publishers.

The principal contacts at Oceana Publications Inc., Senior Vice-President Susan De Maio and production editor JoAnn Mitchell, invariably acted with the professionalism one expects from a major law publisher; but, perhaps more importantly, they were a joy to deal with. What can one say about family support? Certainly, Elaine Sutherland, the wife of the first undersigned, being a legal scholar herself, knew exactly what any writer needs: constant encouragement, copious nutritional sustenance and compulsion to have a life beyond the immediate task. Kim Barker, the wife of the second undersigned, has provided all of the above as well as caring for the young Barkers, Megan and Mackenzie, who themselves provided the delights and distractions which ensured the balance to maintain sanity on a project such as this.

Dr. Samuel Johnston is reputed to have replied to a lady who enquired why, in his Dictionary, he had defined a pastern as the knee of a horse: "Ignorance ma'am! Sheer ignorance." The editors of this dictionary, bearing full responsibility for any errors, offer, in advance, the same defense.

John P. Grant,
Portland, Oregon

J. Craig Barker,
Reading, England
September 2003

TABLE OF ABBREVIATIONS

A.C.	Appeal Cases (UK)
A.D.	Annual Digest and Reports of Public International Law Cases 1919-49 (*see I.L.R.*)
A.J.I.L.	American Journal of International Law
A.J.I.L. Supp.	American Journal of International Law Supplement
Am. U. J. Int'l L. & Poly	American University Journal of International Law and Policy
Annuaire	Annuaire de l'Institut de Droit International
Bevans	Treaties and Other International Agreements of the US 1776-1949
B.Y.I.L.	British Yearbook of International Law
C./Cd./Cmd./Cmnd.	Command Papers (UK)
C.F.R.	Code of Federal Regulations (US)
Ch.	Chancery Reports (UK)
Colum. J. Transnat'l. L.	Columbia Journal of Transnational Law
Col. L. Rev.	Columbia Law Review
Cor. L.Q.	Cornell Law Quarterly
C Rob.	C. Robinson's Admiralty Reports (English)
C.T.S.	Consolidated Treaty Series, 1648-1919
Duke L.J.	Duke Law Journal
Edw.	Edwards' Admiralty Reports (English)
E.H.R.R.	European Human Rights Reports
E.T.S.	European Treaty Series
Ex. D.	Exchequer Division Reports (English)
F.	Federal Reporter (Second Series) (US)
Fed. Reg.	Federal Register (US)
Fed.	Federal Reporter (US)
Ga. J. Int'l & Comp. L.	Georgia Journal of International and Comparative Law
G.A.O.R.	(UN) General Assembly Official Records
GA Res.	(UN) General Assembly Resolution
Hague Recueil	Hague Academy of International Law, Recueil des Cours
Hansard	House of Commons/Lords, Official Reports

Harv. Int'l L.J.	Harvard International Law Journal
Harv. L. Rev.	Harvard Law Review
Hudson, Int. Leg.	Hudson, International Legislation
Hum. Rts. L.J.	Human Rights Law Journal
I.C.J.	International Court of Justice
I.C.J. Rep.	International Court of Justice, Reports of Judgments, Advisory Opinions and Orders 1947/8- (*see P.C.I.J. Rep.*)
I.C.J. Yearbook	International Court of Justice Yearbook
I.C.L.Q.	International and Comparative Law Quarterly
I.L.C. Yearbook	International Law Commission Yearbook
I.L.M.	International Legal Materials
I.L.R.	International Law Reports 1950- (see *A.D.*)
Indian J. Int. L.	Indian Journal of International Law
Iowa L. Rev.	Iowa Law Review
K.B.	King's Bench (now Queen's Bench) Reports (UK)
L.N.O.J.	League of Nations Official Journal
L.N.T.S.	League of Nations Treaty Series, 1920-45
L.Q.R.	Law Quarterly Review (UK)
Moore, Int. Arb.	Moore, History and Digest of International Arbitrations to which the United States has been a Party (1898)
N.Y	New York Reports (US)
N.Y.S.	West's New York Supplement (USA)
O.J.	Official Journal of the European Community
I Oppenheim	Oppenheim, International Law, Vol. I (Peace; 9th ed. by Jennings and Watts, 1992, unless otherwise stated)
II Oppenheim	Oppenheim, International Law, Vol. II (Disputes, War and Neutrality; 7th ed. by Lauterpacht, 1952, unless otherwise stated)
P.	Prize Court Reports/Probate Reports (UK); Pacific Reporter (US)
P.C.I.J. Rep.	Permanent Court of International Justice; Ser. A, B and A/B: Judgments, Orders and Advisory Opinions; Ser. C: Acts and Documents relating to Judgments and Advisory Opinions; Ser. D: Statute and Rules of the Court; Ser. E: Annual Report; Ser. F: General index (*see I.C.J. Rep.*)

Pet.	Peter's United States Reports (US)
P.D.	Probate Division Reports (UK)
Q.B.	Queen's Bench Reports (UK)
Res.	Resolution
R.I.A.A.	(UN) Reports of International Arbitral Awards
S.C.O.R.	(UN) Security Council Official Records
SC Res.	(UN) Security Council Resolution
State Dept. Bull.	Department of State Bulletin (US)
T.G.S.	Transactions of the Grotius Society
T.I.A.S.	Miller, Treaties and other International Acts of the United States of America (1945-)
U.N.	United Nations
U.N.C.I.O. Docs.	United Nations Conference on International Organization Documents
UN Doc.	United Nations Document
U.N.J.Y.B.	United Nations Juridical Yearbook
U.N.T.S.	United Nations Treaty Series, 1946-
U.S.	United States Reports (Supreme Court)
U.S.C. /U.S.C.A.	United States Code/United States Code Annotated.
U.S.T.	United States Treaties and other International Agreements, 1950-
Ves. Jun.	Vesey Juniors Chancery Reports (UK)
Va. J.Int'l L.	Virginia Journal of International Law
Wall	Supreme Court Reports (US)
Wheat.	Supreme Court Reports (US)
Yale L.J.	Yale Law Journal
Yb. Com. Arb.	Yearbook of Commercial Arbitration

GUIDANCE ON USE AND CITATIONS

It is the intention of the editors that no detailed guidance should be required for those using this *Encyclopaedic Dictionary of International Law.* To facilitate the location of entries, an extensive but simple system of cross-references has been employed. Within entries, **bold** denotes a related substantive entry.

Because of the frequency of their citation, and the general familiarity with their location and content, no references have been given in this work for the following agreements:

United Nations Charter of 26 June 1945

Statute of the International Court of Justice of 26 June 1945

Vienna Convention on the Law of Treaties of 22 May 1969

The texts of these instruments are appended to this *Encyclopaedic Dictionary.*

The International Court of Justice's Rules of Court 1978 are in *17 I.L.M. 1286 (1978)*, with the latest text available on the ICJ website: <www.icj-cij.org>.

The Treaties establishing the European Community and European Union have been subject to frequent amendment. The principal texts are as follows:

Treaty on European Union (consolidated text): *Official Journal of the European Community C 324* of 24 December 2002.

Treaty establishing the European Community (consolidated text): *Official Journal of the European Community C 325* of 24 December 2002.

The texts of these Treaties are available online at: <http://europa.eu.int/eur-lex/en/>.

A

Aaland Islands Case *(1920) L.N.O.J. Spec. Supp. No. 3.* During the union between Sweden and Finland, the Aaland Islands formed part of the administrative division of Finland, but were ceded to Russia by the Treaty of 17 September 1809 *(60 C.T.S. 457)*. By the Convention of 30 March 1856, annexed to the Treaty of Paris between Russia and France and Great Britain *(114 C.T.S. 405)*, Russia was constrained to declare that the islands should not be fortified. Upon the attainment of independence by Finland, the question of their status and future fell to be considered by the Council of the League of Nations which, the PCIJ not having then been set up, referred *inter alia* "the present position with regard to international obligations concerning the demilitarisation of the Aaland Islands" to an *ad hoc* Committee of Jurists. While stating that "the existence of international servitudes, in the true technical sense of the term, is not generally admitted," the Committee of Jurists expressed the view that the provisions of the Convention of 1856 had been "laid down in European interests. They constituted a special international status relating to military considerations for the Aaland Islands. It follows that until [they] are . . . replaced, every State interested has the right to insist on compliance with them." *See* Padelford and Andersson, The Aaland Islands Question, *33 A.J.I.L. 465 (1939)*.

abandonment (of territory) *See derelictio*.

ablegatus An early term, translated into envoy, signifying a diplomatic representative of a level below that of ambassador. *See Satow's Guide to Diplomatic Practice* (5th ed.), 84.

absence (in voting) The absence of a State when a vote is taken in an organ of an international organisation can raise problems. One authority confidently asserts that "[i]t would seem to be safe to conclude that in general absence would be treated in the same way as an abstention": Amerasinghe, *Principles of International Law of International Organizations* (1996), 153. *See* **abstention (in voting)**. Certainly, the justification for not equating abstention with a negative vote does not apply to absence given that absence presents no opportunity to cast a negative vote. However, absence may be unchallengeable, at least by the absent State, where it is estopped by some breach of a constituent instrument occasioned by that absence, as, *e.g.*, the failure of a permanent member of the Security Council to "be represented at all times at the seat of the Organisation" (art. 28(1) of the UN Charter).

absolute consent, principle of In relation to the amendment of the constitutions of international organizations, this principle requires unanimity on the part of all members. Thus, *e.g.*, art. 48 of the Treaty on European Union permits amendments to enter into effect only after a unanimous vote in the European Council and unanimous ratification by all the member States. *See* Amerasinghe, *Principles of the International Law of International Organizations* (1996), 413.

absorption An international organization may cease to exist through absorption by another, *e.g.*, the International Bureau of Education was assimilated into UNESCO in 1969. *See* Sands and Klein, *Bowett's Law of International Institutions* (5th ed.), 526.

abstention (in voting) Abstention by a State in voting in an organ of an international organization can give rise to significant legal problems. "At one time abstentions were apparently counted as negative votes, thus, among other things, preventing unanimity. But now it would seem that, firstly, abstention is not regarded as preventing unanimity, as is shown by the provisions of many constitutional instruments; secondly, that abstinence is regarded as a failure to vote, which means that the abstainer is not regarded as 'present and voting'; and, thirdly, that in the SC when under Article 27(3) of the Charter the concurring votes of the permanent members are required for a decision, abstention on the part of a permanent member is not regarded as the absence of a concurring vote": Amerasinghe, *Principles of International Law of International Organizations* (1996), 151. The ICJ has offered an explanation for this tacit amendment to the clear wording of art. 27(3) in the ***Namibia Advisory Opinion 1971 I.C.J. Rep. 16*** at 22: "However, the proceedings of the Security Council extending over a long period supply abundant evidence that presidential rulings and the positions taken by members of the Council, in particular its permanent members, have consistently and uniformly interpreted the practice of voluntary abstention by a permanent member as not constituting a bar to the adoption of resolutions. By abstaining, a member does not signify objection to the approval of what is being proposed; in order to prevent the adoption of a resolution requiring unanimity of the permanent members, a permanent member has only to cast a negative vote." The justification for abstention being treated as not equivalent to a **veto** does not apply so easily where a permanent member is absent when a vote is taken, and the validity of resolutions adopted in the absence of a permanent member is not finally resolved. See Goodrich, Hambro and Simons, *Charter of the United Nations* (3rd ed.), 231; Stone, *Legal Controls of International Conflict* (2nd imp. revised), 204-212; Kelsen, *Recent Trends in the Law of the United Nations* (1951), 927-936; de Arechaga, *Voting and the Handling of Disputes in the Security Council* (1978). *See also* **absence (in voting)**.

Abu Dhabi Arbitration Properly styled *Petroleum Development (Trucial Coast) Ltd. v. Sheikh of Abu Dhabi (1951) 18 I.L.R. 144,* this proceeding arose out of a dispute as to whether the contract between the parties, dated 1939, which purported to vest the sole rights of oil exploration and exploitation in the Sheikh's territories in the claimants, comprehended the subsoil of the sea-bed adjacent to the territorial waters of Abu Dhabi, with respect to which area the Sheikh had in 1949, following the issue of a proclamation laying exclusive claim to it, granted a fresh concession to a rival company. The contract providing for arbitration of differences and that it was to be considered to be based "on goodwill and sincerity of belief" and to be interpreted "in a fashion consistent with reason," the Arbitrator, Lord Asquith, *held* its proper law to be, rather than any system of municipal law, "principles rooted in the good sense and common practice of . . . civilized nations—a sort of 'modern law of nature,'" according to which it would be "a most artificial refinement to read back into the contract the implication of a doctrine [i.e. the **continental shelf** doctrine] not mooted till seven years later [i.e. in the **Truman Proclamation**, 1945]." He described the continental shelf doctrine as lacking "definitive status" because of "so many ragged ends and unfilled blanks, so much that is merely tentative and exploratory." *See* the *Qatar Arbitration*.

abuse of rights, doctrine of An abuse of rights "occurs when a state avails itself of its right [under international law] in an arbitrary manner in such a way as to inflict upon another state an injury which cannot be justified by a legitimate consideration of its own advantage": *I Oppenheim 407*. The doctrine is expressly recognized in art. 3 of the Montevideo Convention on the Rights and Duties of States 1933 *(165 L.N.T.S 19)*, which provides that the exercise of the rights set out in the Convention "has no other limitation than the exercise of the rights of other States according to international law"; and in art. 87(2) of the UN Convention on the Law of the Sea 1982 *(1833 U.N.T.S. 3)*, which provides that the freedom of the high seas "shall be exercised by all States with due regard for the interests of other States in their exercise of the freedom of the high seas." The doctrine has likewise been recognized and applied in a number of judicial and arbitral proceedings (see Whiteman, *Digest of International Law*, Vol. 1 (1963), 224-30); and in one arbitration, the ***Trail Smelter Arbitration** (1941) 3 R.I.A.A. 1905*, the tribunal declared that "no State has the right to use its territory in such a manner as to cause injury or damage . . . in or to the territory of another or the properties or persons therein." See also ***German Interests in Polish Upper Silesia Case** (1926) P.C.I.J. Ser. A. No. 7; **Free Zones Case** (1930) P.C.I.J. Ser. A., No. 24; **Corfu Channel** Case 1949 I.C.J. Rep. 22; **Anglo-Norwegian Fisheries Case** 1951 I.C.J. Rep. 116; **Lake Lanoux Arbitration** (1957) 24 I.L.R. 140.*

For some writers, the doctrine is a general principle of law recognized by civilized nations (under art. 36(2) of the ICJ Statute): Lauterpacht, *The Function of Law in the International Community* (1933), 286-306. Others regard it as a general principle of international (customary) law: Kiss, *L'abus de droit en droit international*, (1953), 193-6. For yet others, it is nothing more than the application of the principle of good faith to the exercise of rights: Cheng, *General Principles of Law as applied by International Courts and Tribunals* (1953), 121-36. The operation of the doctrine is clearly not free from difficulty: "There is no legal right, however well established, that could not, in some circumstances, be refused recognition on the ground that it has been abused. The doctrine of abuse of rights is therefore an instrument which . . . must be wielded with studied restraint": Lauterpacht, *The Development of International Law by the International Court* (1958), 164. *I Oppenheim 408* states that "the extent of the application of the still controversial doctrine of the prohibition of the abuse of rights is not at all certain."

Académie de Droit International de la Haye See **Hague Academy of International Law**.

acceptance Acceptance is "the international act so named whereby a State establishes on the international plane its consent to be bound by a treaty": Vienna Convention on the Law of Treaties 1969, art. 2(1)(b). "The consent of a State to be bound by a treaty is expressed by acceptance or approval under conditions similar to those which apply to ratification": art. 14(2). "Unless the treaty otherwise provides, instruments of ratification, acceptance, approval or accession establish the consent of a State to be bound by a treaty upon: (a) their exchange between the contracting States; (b) their deposit with the depositary; or (c) their notification to the contracting States or to the depositary, if so agreed": art. 16. *See* Aust, *Modern Treaty Law and Practice* (2000), 87-8.

accession Accession, sometimes also referred to as adherence or adhesion, is the term used to connote the method whereby a State which has not signed a treaty may subsequently become a party to it. In terms of art. 2(1)(b) of the Vienna Convention on the Law of Treaties 1969, accession "mean[s] . . . the international act so named whereby a State establishes on the international plane its consent to be bound by a treaty." Art. 15 provides: "The consent of a State to be bound by a treaty is expressed by accession when: (a) the treaty provides that such consent may be expressed by that State by means of accession; (b) it is otherwise established that the negotiating States were agreed that such consent may be expressed by that State by means of accession; or (c) all the parties have subsequently agreed that such consent may be expressed by that State by means of accession." Art. 16

provides: "Unless the treaty otherwise provides, instruments of . . . accession establish the consent of a State to be bound by a treaty upon: (a) their exchange between the contracting States; (b) their deposit with the depositary; or (c) their notification to the contracting States or to the depositary, if so agreed." *See Satow's Guide to Diplomatic Practice* (5th ed.), 276-82; Aust, *Modern Treaty Law and Practice* (2000), 88-90.

accord In French, *accord* is the equivalent of *agrément* (or agreement in English). The term is, however, sometimes used in English, signifying an agreement of a greater or less degree of informality. Cf. McNair, *Law of Treaties* (2nd ed.), 24.

accretion In international law, this is a generic term for methods by which a State may acquire title to territory through the gradual operations of nature and requiring no formal acts of appropriation, *e.g.*, alluvial deposits at the mouths of rivers, significant changes in the course of rivers: *The Anna 5 C. Rob. 373 (1805);* **Island of Palmas Case *(1928) 2 R.I.A.A. 829** at 839. If a river is a boundary between States, accretion will alter the boundary with the erosion and deposit of soil: *Louisiana v. Mississippi 282 U.S. 458 (1931). See I Oppenheim 696.* Cf. **alluvion, avulsion**.

Achille Lauro Incident In October 1985, the Italian cruise ship Achille Lauro was seized by four members of the Palestinian Liberation Front, who killed an American citizen, Leon Klinghoffer, and held the passengers and crew captive on demands for the Israeli release of 50 Palestinian prisoners. They surrendered after two days in exchange for a guarantee of safe passage. US warplanes intercepted an Egyptian airliner on which they were seeking their escape and the airliner was forced to land in Sicily. Italy refused US demands for the extradition of the four terrorists and insisted on prosecuting them itself. *See* Cassese, *Terrorism, Politics and Law: The Achille Lauro Affair* (1989).

ACOPS *See* **Advisory Committee on Protection of the Sea**.

acquiescence A factor in the formation of customary international law and prescriptive rights whereby consent to a rule is not in the form of positive statements or action, but takes the form of "silence or absence of protest in circumstances which . . . demand a positive reaction in order to preserve a right": MacGibbon, The Scope of Acquiescence in International Law, *(1954) 31 B.Y.I.L. 143-86* at 182. *See* **The Lotus Case *(1927) P.C.I.J., Ser. A, No. 10;* Anglo-Norwegian Fisheries Case *1951 I.C.J. Rep. 116** at 139. In treaty law, under art. 20(5) of the Vienna Convention on the Law of Treaties 1969, "a reservation is considered to have been accepted by a State if it shall have raised no objection to the reservation by the end of a period of twelve months after it was notified of the reservation or by the date on which it expressed its consent to be bound by the treaty, whichever is later." In relation to acquisitions of territory, acquiescence refers to the conduct of a State competing for title or the State with former title to the territory; cf. **recognition**. *See* **Grisbadarna Arbitration *(1909) 11 R.I.A.A. 155;* Island of Palmas Case *(1928) 2 R.I.A.A. 829;* Frontier Land Case *1959 I.C.J. Rep. 209. And see* Bowett, Estoppel before International Tribunals and its Relation to Acquiescence, *(1957) 33 B.Y.I.L. 176.*

acquired (or vested) rights This term is used to connote private rights, acquired either by nationals or by aliens, under the existing law of a given State which, according to traditional international law, do not cease on a change of sovereignty, and in the event of **State succession** must be respected by the successor State: **German Settlers in Poland Case *(1923) P.C.I.J. Ser. B, No. 6.** In contemporary international law, the prevailing opinion is that private rights, whether arising from **concession contracts** or other sources, cannot be regarded as acquired rights: they are protected only to the extent to which the new sovereign consents. However, private rights do not automatically fall with the change of sovereign; and acquired rights are presumed to be as little affected as possible by the change, absent specific measures to alter or rescind these rights: *I Oppenheim 2.* Thus, by virtue of the right to permanent sovereignty over natural wealth and resources, the successor State may, for reasons of public utility, security or the national interest, cancel such rights provided that prompt, adequate and effective compensation is paid to the beneficiary: Resolutions on **Permanent Sovereignty** over Natural Resources 1962 (G.A. Res. 1803 (XVII) and 1973 (G.A. Res. 3171 (XXVIII)). *See generally* O'Connell, *State Succession in Municipal Law and International Law* (1967), Chaps. 6 and 10; Kaeckenbeeck, The Protection of Vested Rights in International Law, *(1950) 27 B.Y.I.L. 1*; Rosenne, The Effect of Change of Sovereignty upon Municipal Law, *(1950) 27 B.Y.I.L. 267. See also* **expropriation.**

Acquisition of Polish Nationality, Advisory Opinion on the Question of *(1923) P.C.I.J. Ser. B, No. 7.* On the League of Nations' Council's request of 7 July 1923 as to whether the interpretation of art. 4 of the Polish Minorities Treaty of 28 June 1919 *(225 C.T.S. 412)* respecting the nationality of persons formerly of German nationality born in Polish territory was within the competence of the League, and, if so, what the precise interpretation was, on 15 September 1923 the Court *advised* (unanimously) that the League was competent. The minorities régime established by the Treaty and placed under the guarantee of the League embraced all inhabitants of non-Polish origin, whether Polish nationals or not. Further, the stipulations of art. 4 attributing Polish nationality to persons born of parents habitually resident in the territory concerned were to be taken to refer only to such residence at the dates of such persons' births and not to require residence also at the date of coming into force of the Treaty.

acquisition of territory *See* **territory, acquisition of.**

acquisitive prescription *See* **prescription, acquisitive.**

act A term "usually denoting a multilateral treaty which establishes rules of law or a régime, such as the Act of Algeciras of 7 April 1906 [relating to the affairs of Morocco: *201 C.T.S. 39*]. A *Final Act* has been defined as 'a formal statement or summary of the proceedings of a congress or conference, enumerating the treaties or related treaty instruments drawn up as a result of its deliberations' [Satow, *Diplomatic Practice* (5th ed.), 260]. . . . The term *General Act* is now usually employed when the instrument which enumerates the several treaties or conventions resulting from a conference itself becomes a treaty, these treaties or conventions being either embodied in it or annexed to it. Instances are the General Acts of the Berlin Conference of 1885 [respecting the Congo: *165 C.T.S. 485*] and of the Brussels Conference of 1890 [relating to the African Slave Trade: *173 C.T.S. 293*] and the General Act signed at Geneva on 26 September 1928 for the Pacific Settlement of International Disputes *[93 L.N.T.S. 343]*": McNair, *Law of Treaties* (2nd ed.), 234. The Vienna Convention on the Law of Treaties 1969 makes no specific mention of the term "act."

act of State, doctrine of (1) "This is to the effect that the courts of one state do not, as a rule, question the validity or legality of the official acts of another sovereign state or the official or officially avowed acts of its agents, at any rate insofar as those acts involve the exercise of the state's public authority, purport to take effect within the sphere of the latter's own jurisdiction and are not in themselves contrary to international law": *I Oppenheim 365-6.* The classical, and founding, expression of this doctrine is that of Chief Justice Fuller in *Underhill v. Hernandez 168 U.S. 250 (1897)*: "Every sovereign state is bound to respect the independence of every other sovereign, and the courts of one country will not sit in judgment on the acts of another government done within its own territory." The practice of States differs, and it may be concluded that customary international law does not require a State to recognize the validity of acts of State of a foreign State: *Anglo-Iranian Oil Co. v. Jaffrate (1953) 20 I.L.R. 316, Anglo-Iranian Co. v. SUPOR (1955) 22 I.L.R. 19; Anglo-Iranian Co. v. Idemitsu Kosan Kabushiki Kaisha (1953) 20 I.L.R. 305. But see Buttes Gas & Oil Co. v. Hammer, (1981) 3 W.L.R. 787.* In *Banco Nacional de Cuba v. Sabbatino 367 U.S. 398 (1964)* the US Supreme Court, in declining to pass upon the legality of the Cuban sugar expropriation of 1960, restated the doctrine: "rather than laying down or reaffirming an inflexible and all-encompassing rule in this case, we decide only that the Judicial Branch will not examine the validity of a taking of property within its own territory by a foreign sovereign, extant and recognized by this country at the time of suit, in the absence of treaty or other unambiguous agreement regarding controlling legal principles, even if the complaint alleges that the taking violates customary international law." This decision prompted the so-called Hickenlooper (or **Sabbatino**) **amendment** to the Foreign Assistance Act of 1961 (S. 620(e)(2) of the Act, as amended *22 U.S.C. 2370 (e)(2))*, providing that U.S. courts are to decline to render a decision giving effect to the principles of international law in property claims, based on confiscations after January 1, 1950, by an act in violation of the principles of international law. *See* **sovereign immunity**.

(2) As a corollary of (1) above, the rule that "[a]ll servants or agents (or former servants or agents, of a foreign state are immune from legal proceedings in respect of acts done by them on behalf of the foreign state. The reason is that such proceedings indirectly implead the state . . . [and]. . . would be likely to involve delicate issues of international politics, which would make them unsuitable for adjudication by municipal courts": Akehurst, *A Modern Introduction to International Law*, (7th ed.), 122. This rule admits of exceptions, particularly in respect of **crimes against peace, war crimes** and **crimes against humanity.** Under art. 6 of the Statute of the Nuremberg **International Military Tribunal** 1945 *(82 U.N.T.S. 278)*, liability extended to "leaders, organizers, accomplices" many of whom were, almost by definition, former officials of the German State; "He who violates the laws of war cannot obtain immunity while acting in pursuance of the authority of the State if the State in authorizing action moves outside its competence under international law": *In re Goering and others (1946) 13 I.L.R. 203* at 221-2. *See also* the ***Rainbow Warrior Case***. The jurisdiction of the **International Criminal Court** stipulates for no defense based on official, or former official, capacity: art. 27 of the Rome Statute 1998 *((1998) 37 I.L.M. 999)*.

(3) In UK constitutional law, "an act of the Executive as a matter of policy performed in the course of its relations with another state, including its relations with the subjects of that state, unless they are temporarily within the allegiance of the crown": Wade, Act of State in English Law, *(1934) 15 B.Y.I.L. 98* at 103: "an exercise of sovereign power" which "cannot be challenged, controlled or interfered with by municipal courts. Its sanction is not that of law, but that of sovereign power, and, whatever it be, municipal courts must accept it, as it is, without question": *Salaman v. Secretary of State for India [1906] 1 K.B. 613* at 639 *per* Fletcher Moulton L.J. Such a defense is not available against a British subject (*Nissan v. Attorney-General [1970] A.C. 179*), nor against any alien resident in British territory (*Johnstone v. Pedlar [1921] 2 A.C. 262).*

(4) The term is sometimes used to connote acts attracting **State responsibility**. Art. 12 of the Draft Articles on State Responsibility 2001 *(UN Doc. A/56/10 Chap. IV.E.1)* declares that there is a breach of an international obligation "when an act of that State" is disconform to the obligation. In this context, however, the term is not one of art. *See* Crawford, *The International Law Commission's Articles on State Responsibility* (2002), 159.

act of war   The expression "act of war" acquired a quasi-technical significance primarily by reason of the stipulation of art. 16(1) of the League of Nations Covenant that "[s]hould any Member of the League resort to war in disregard of its covenants under Articles 12, 13 or 15, it shall *ipso facto* be deemed to have committed an act of war *(un acte de guerre)* against all other Members of the League. . . ." By contrast, arts. 12, 13 and 15 do not speak in terms of an "act of war," but rather of "resort to war" and of "go[ing] to war." Nevertheless the Committee of Jurists consulted by the League Council following the Corfu Incident of 1923 was asked: "Are measures of coercion which are not meant to constitute acts of war consistent with the terms of Articles 12 to 15 when . . . taken . . . without prior recourse to the procedure laid down in these Articles?" The Committee answered that "[c]oercive measures . . . not intended to constitute acts of war . . ." might or might not be consistent with arts. 12-15. From this it would seem to follow that an act of war is either intended by the actor State to bring about a condition of war or, though not so intended, may be regarded by the State against which it is directed as having done so. If a declaration of war is not "a mere challenge to be accepted or refused at pleasure but puts the other party also in a state of war" (*The Eliza Ann (1813) 1 Dods. 244* at 299, *per* Lord Stowell), an act of war not intended as a tacit declaration may be broadly described as being a challenge of this sort in terms of international law as it stood before the adoption of the Charter of the UN. Under Chapter VII of the Charter, collective enforcement measures to maintain or restore international peace and security are predicated, not upon an act of war or resort to war, but on a "threat to the peace, breach of the peace or act of aggression": art. 39. Likewise, the right of **self-defense** is exercisable, not upon and act of war or resort to war, but on an "armed attack": art. 51.

***ad hoc* judge**   In the International Court of Justice in a contentious case, "[i]f the Court includes upon the Bench a judge of the nationality of one of the parties, any other party may choose a person to sit as judge": art. 31(2) of the ICJ Statute. "If the Court includes . . . no judge of the nationality of the parties each of these parties may proceed to choose a judge. . . .": art. 31(3). *See also* arts. 7 and 8 of the Rules of Court 1978. A State entitled to appoint an *ad hoc* judge is not obliged to do so: ***Temple of Preach Vihear Case* 1962 *I.C.J. Rep. 6*. While the institution of judges *ad hoc* has been criticized as detracting from the true international character of the Court and as potentially disruptive of the unity of the bench, it is better regarded as justified as increasing the judicial resources available to the Court and as necessary in contemporary world politics: Rosenne, *Law and Practice of the International Court* (1985), vol. 1, 205 *et seq*. The Court has also permitted the appointment of *ad hoc* judges in advisory opinions: ***Western Sahara Case* 1975 *I.C.J. Rep. 12*. For a list of judges *ad hoc*, see the current *I.C.J. Yearbook*, Chapter I(II).

***ad referendum*, signature**   The Vienna Convention on the Law of Treaties 1969, art. 12(2)(b), recognizes the practice of signature of treaties *ad referendum*, i.e. subject to confirmation, and provides that, for purposes of the rule therein laid down as to when the consent of a State to be bound by a treaty is expressed by the signature of its representative, "the signature *ad referendum* of a treaty by a representative, if confirmed by his State, constitutes a full signature of the treaty." Cf. **ratification**.

adherence (or adhesion)   These terms, applicable to treaties, are now regarded as synonymous with **accession**.

ADIZ   *See* **air defense identification zones**.

administering authority   (1) The authority designated by a trusteeship agreement as being responsible for the administration of a United Nations **trust territory**, and which, under art. 81 of the Charter, "may be one or more States or the Organization itself." Italy (in respect of Somalia, 1950-60) was the only administering authority not to have been at the relevant time a member of the United Nations. There are no administering authorities, the last remaining trust territory having achieved independence (as Palau) in 1994. *See* **trusteeship system**.

(2) The member of the UN with responsibilities for the administration of territories whose peoples have not yet attained a full measure of self-government is also sometimes referred to as the administering authority (or State, or power) in relation to such territories. *See* Chapter XI of the UN Charter, titled "Declaration Regarding Non-Self-Governing Territories."

Administrative Committee on Co-ordination The Administrative Committee on Co-ordination (ACC), formerly the Coordination Committee, was created by a Res. 13(III) of the UN Economic and Social Council of 21 September 1946, which established as its task "to ensure the fullest and most effective implementation of the agreements entered into between the United Nations and the Specialized Agencies." The ACC has now been renamed the **Chief Executives Board**, with an expanded mandate and responsibility for the 27 organizations in the UN system.

Administrative Decision No. V *(U.S. v. Germany) (1924) 7 R.I.A.A. 119*. Differences having arisen between the German and American members of the US-Germany Mixed Claims Commission, established under an Agreement of 10 August 1922 over the principles to be observed by the Commission regarding the nationality of claims, *held* by the Commission (*per* Parker, Umpire) that the jurisdiction of the Commission was not based upon general rules of international law or practice relating to nationality of claims, but was related to Germany's obligations under the Treaty of Berlin 1921, and those obligations were established with reference to claims impressed with American nationality on the date when the loss, damage or injury occurred and on the date when the Treaty of Berlin became effective; a subsequent change in nationality did not therefore operate so as to discharge Germany's obligations.

Administrative Tribunal of the UN, Effect of Awards Case *1954 I.C.J. Rep. 47*. By a resolution of 9 December 1953, the UN General Assembly requested of the ICJ an advisory opinion on the following questions: 1. "Having regard to the Statute of the United Nations Administrative Tribunal [etc] has the General Assembly the right on any grounds to refuse to give effect to an award of compensation . . . in favour of a staff member of the United Nations, whose contract of service has been terminated without his assent?" 2. "If the answer . . . is affirmative, what are the principal grounds upon which the General Assembly could lawfully exercise such a right?" On 13 July 1954, the Court *advised* (9 to 3) that the General Assembly had no such right because "[w]hen the Secretary-General concludes a contract of service . . . he engages the legal responsibility of the Organization. . . . If he terminates the contract of service . . . and this . . . results in a dispute which is referred to the Administrative Tribunal, the parties to the dispute are the staff member . . . and the United Nations Organization, and these parties will become bound by the judgment. . . . It follows that the General Assembly, as an organ of the United Nations, must likewise be bound."

administrative tribunals In international organizations, there are tribunals established to determine disputes arising from the relationship between international civil servants and the institutions in which they are employed, such tribunals being "essential to ensure the efficient working of the Secretariat, and to give effect to the paramount consideration of securing the highest standards of efficiency, competence and integrity": ***Administrative***

Tribunal of the U.N., Effect of Awards Case 1954 I.C.J. Rep. 47 at 57. Tribunals have been established by the UN (UNAT), which covers also employment disputes in a small number of Specialized Agencies, and pension disputes in others, the ILO (ILOAT), which covers also employment disputes in most of the European-based Specialized Agencies, the World Bank, the International Monetary Fund, OECD and NATO, and a number of other institutions. The juridical status of UNAT is described by the ICJ in the *Administrative Tribunal of the UN Case, supra* at 53: "the tribunal is established, not as an advisory organ or a mere subordinate committee of the General Assembly, but as an independent and truly judicial body pronouncing final judgments without appeal within the limited field of its functions." *See* Sands and Klein, *Bowett's Law of International Institutions* (5th ed.), 416-29; Amersinghe, *Documents on International Administrative Tribunals* (1989); Amersinghe, *The Law of the International Civil Service* (2nd ed.).

admissibility This term refers to the requirements laid down by customary international law or by treaty (*e.g.*, as to **nationality of claims**, or **exhaustion of local remedies**) which an applicant before an international tribunal must fulfill if the tribunal, although it has jurisdiction to hear the case, is to be able to go on to determine the merits. An objection to the admissibility of a complaint will be of a preliminary character as, if successful, it will prevent the tribunal proceeding to hear the case on the merits; but the circumstances of a particular case may require the determination of the issue of admissibility to be joined with the hearing on the merits.

In the jurisprudence of the ICJ, "admissibility" is "a plea that the tribunal should rule the claim to be inadmissible on some ground other than the ultimate merits": Fitzmaurice, *The Law and Procedure of the International Court of Justice* (1986), Vol. 1, 438, who, contrasting this plea with a challenge to the jurisdiction, described admissibility as "a plea that the tribunal itself is incompetent to give any ruling at all." Admissibility may be challenged on grounds of nationality of claims, exhaustion of local remedies or undue delay. *See **Ambatielos Case** (Preliminary Objection) 1952 I.C.J. Rep. 28*; ***Nottebohm Case** (Preliminary Objection) 1953 I.C.J. Rep. 122*; ***Military and Paramilitary Activities in and against Nicaragua** (Jurisdiction and Admissibility) 1984 I.C.J. Rep. 169; **Lockerbie Cases** (Preliminary Objections) 1998 I.C.J. Rep. 9*. However, the distinction between a **preliminary objection** based on admissibility and one based on jurisdiction is not clear cut: "[n]either jurisprudence nor doctrine displays any certainty or unanimity over the categorization of preliminary objections, which have become characterized by ever increasing sophistication and subtlety. All that can be deduced from experience, including some diplomatic experience, is that this is an individual matter to be appreciated in the light of each case": Rosenne, *Procedure in the International Court: A Commentary on the 1978 Rules of the International Court of Justice* (1983), 162.

"Admissibility," used to connote the criteria which must be satisfied before an individual can invoke the complaints, sometimes referred to as the petition or communications, procedure under **human rights** agreements, has become a term of art in that context. Thus, art. 3 of the Optional Protocol to the International Covenant on Civil and Political Rights 1966 *(999 U.N.T.S. 171)* provides that "[t]he [Human Rights] Committee shall consider inadmissible any communication under the present Protocol which is anonymous, or which it considers to be an abuse of the right of submission of such communications or to be incompatible with the provisions of the Covenant"; and art. 5(2) provides that "[t]he Committee shall not consider any communication from any individual unless it is ascertained that: (a) The same matter is not being examined under another procedure of international investigation or settlement; (b) The individual has exhausted all available domestic remedies." *See also* art. 14(7)(a) of the International Convention on the Elimination of All

Forms of Racial Discrimination 1966 *(660 U.N.T.S. 195)*; art. 22(5) of the Torture Convention 1984 *(1465 U.N.T.S. 85)*; arts. 2-4 of the Optional Protocol of 15 October 1999 the Convention on the Elimination of All Forms of Discrimination Against Women *(39 I.L.M. 281 (2000))*; art. 35 of the European Convention on Human Rights and Fundamental Freedoms 1950, as amended by Protocol 11 *(213 U.N.T.S. 221, as amended; E.T.S. No. 5, as amended by E.T.S. No. 155))*; arts. 46-47 of the American Convention on Human Rights 1969 *(9 I.L.M. 673 (1970))* and art. 46 of the African Charter on Human and Peoples' Rights 1981 *(21 I.L.M. 58 (1982))*. *See generally* Tardu, *Human Rights: The International Petition System* (1979); Hannun, *Guide to International Human Rights Practice* (2nd ed.).

admission (to an international organization) The constituent instruments of international organizations invariably contain provisions relating to the admission of new members beyond the ambit of the **original members**, setting out both conditions and a procedure for admission. Thus, the UN Charter requires applicants for admission to be "peace-loving States which accept the obligations contained in the present Charter and, in the judgment of the Organization, are able and willing to carry out these obligations" (art. 4(1)); and admission is effected by "a decision of the General Assembly upon the recommendation of the Security Council" (art. 4(2)). *See* the ***Admission of a State to Membership of the United Nations, Conditions for, Case* 1948 I.C.J. Rep. 57; *Admission of a State to the United Nations, Competence of the General Assembly for, Case* 1950 I.C.J. Rep. 4**. *See* Amerasinghe, *Principles of the Institutional Law of International Organizations* (1996), 105-15; Sands and Klein, *Bowett's Law of International Institutions* (5th ed.), 534-41.

Admission of a State to the United Nations, Competence of the General Assembly for, Case 1950 I.C.J. Rep. 4. By resolution dated 22 November 1949, the UN General Assembly requested of the ICJ an advisory opinion on the following questions: "Can the admission of a State to membership in the United Nations pursuant to Article 4, paragraph (2), of the Charter, be effected by a decision of the General Assembly when the Security Council has made no recommendation for admission by reason of the candidate failing to obtain the requisite majority or of the negative vote of a Permanent Member upon a resolution so to recommend?" Observing that the question called upon it to interpret art. 4(2) of the Charter and holding itself competent so to do pursuant to art. 96 of the Charter and art. 65 of its Statute, the Court on 3 March 1950 *advised* (12 to 2) in the negative, declaring the wording of the article to be clear and that any holding that the General Assembly might admit a new member in the absence of a recommendation of the Security Council would be to deprive the latter organ of an important power entrusted to it and "almost nullify [its role] in the exercise of one of the essential functions of the Organization."

Admission of a State to Membership of the United Nations, Conditions for, Case 1948 I.C.J. Rep. 57. By resolution dated 17 November 1947, the UN General Assembly requested of the ICJ an advisory opinion on the following question: "Is a Member of the United Nations which is called upon, in virtue of Article 4 of the Charter, to pronounce itself by its vote, either in the Security Council or in the General Assembly, on the admission of a State to membership . . . juridically entitled to make its consent . . . dependent on conditions not expressly provided by . . . the said Article? In particular, can [it], while it recognizes the conditions set forth in that provision to be fulfilled by the State concerned, subject its affirmative vote to the additional condition that other States be admitted . . . together with that State?" On 28 May 1948, the Court, observing that the request could not be construed as referring to the actual vote, the reasons for which, entering into a mental process, were obviously subject to no control, nor to a member State's freedom of expressing its opinion, and could "only relate to the statements made by a Member concerning the vote it proposes to give," *advised* (9 to 6) on both questions negatively on the ground that the conditions for new membership laid down in art. 4 are exhaustive.

admitted member(s)   Within international organizations, there are invariable two classes of members, **original members** and admitted members. *See, e.g.*, arts. 3 and 4 of the UN Charter. *See* **admission (to an international organization)**. *See* Sands and Klein, *Bowett's Law of International Institutions* (5th ed.), 534.

adoption   Adoption is the term used in the law of treaties to denote the agreement of the parties as to what the text of a proposed treaty shall be, a process not necessarily identical either with the authentication of that text or its acceptance as binding. The Vienna Convention on the Law of Treaties 1969, art. 9, provides: "(1) The adoption of the text of a treaty takes place by the consent of all the States participating in its drawing up except as provided in paragraph 2. (2) The adoption of the text of a treaty at an international conference takes place by the vote of two-thirds of the States present and voting, unless by the same majority they shall decide to apply a different rule."

adoption, doctrine of   The doctrine, otherwise called the doctrine of **transformation**, to the effect that "rules of international law are not to be considered as part of English law except in so far as they have already been adopted and made part of our law by the decisions of the judges, or by Act of Parliament, or long established custom," in contrast to "the doctrine of incorporation which says that the rules of inter national law are incorporated into English law automatically and considered to be part of English law unless they conflict with an Act of Parliament": *Trendtex Trading Corporation v. Central Bank of Nigeria [1977] Q.B. 529* at 533 *per* Lord Denning M.R., who, having accepted the doctrine of adoption without question in *R. v. Secretary of State for the Home Department, ex parte Thakrar [1974] Q.B. 684* at 701, changed his view in the instant case: "Otherwise I do not see that our courts could ever recognise a change in the rules of international law." *See also* **incorporation, incorporation**.

Advisory Committee on Protection of the Sea (ACOPS)   One of the world's first environmental NGOs, ACOPS has its seat in London, usefully also the headquarters of the IMO, and encourages international agreements to reduce marine pollution in all its aspects, from oil and land-based sources, as well other aspects of degradation of the coastline and marine environment. *See* <www.acops.org>.

advisory opinion   "The [International] Court [of Justice] may give an advisory opinion on any legal question at the request of whatever body may be authorized by or in accordance with the Charter of the United Nations to make such a request": art. 65(1) of the ICJ Statute. The General Assembly and the Security Council are authorized to request advisory opinions: art. 96(1) of the UN Charter. Under art. 96(2), ECOSOC, the Trusteeship Council, the Interim Committee of the General Assembly, the Committee for Applications for the Review of Judgments of the UN Administrative Tribunal, and all but one of the **Specialized Agencies** (the exception being the Universal Postal Union) have been authorized by the General Assembly to request advisory opinions, as has the International Atomic Energy Agency. Advisory opinions are of their nature not binding in law, though they may establish principles of law that are followed in subsequent actings, opinions and cases.

The ICJ is not obliged to give an advisory opinion; the wording of art. 65(1) of the Statute leaves the Court a discretion. The Court has indicated that it will only decline a request to give an advisory opinion if there exist "compelling reasons" to do so: ***Western Sahara***

Opinion 1975 I.C.J. Rep. 12. It appears that, as long as a request is framed in terms capable of judicial examination, the Court will give an opinion; it is immaterial that the request may have been politically motivated or couched in abstract terms: ***Admission of a State to the United Nations Opinion 1948 I.C.J. Rep. 57.*** However, it appears that the Court will not give an advisory opinion where the request concerns a matter which is essentially a contentious dispute between States or concerns essentially factual matters and a State concerned refuses to co-operate, thereby making it "very doubtful whether there would be available to the Court materials sufficient to enable it to arrive at any judicial conclusion upon the question of fact"; ***Eastern Carelia Case (1923) P.C.I.J., Ser. B, No. 5.*** Cf. ***Interpretation of the Peace Treaties Opinion 1950 I.C.J. Rep. 65.*** Nor will the Court give an advisory opinion where the request by a Specialized Agencies falls outside the scope of its activities: ***Legality of the Use by a State of Nuclear Weapons in Armed Conflict 1996 I.C.J. Rep. 292.***

For a list of advisory opinions from 1922 see current *I.C.J. Yearbook,* Chapter VII (II). *And see* Hudson, *The Permanent Court of International Justice* (rev. ed, 1943), 483-524; Keith, *The Extent of the Advisory Jurisdiction of the International Court of Justice* (1971); Pratap, *The Advisory Jurisdiction of the International Court* (1972); Pomerace, *The Advisory Function of the International Court in the League and U.N. Eras* (1973); Fitzmaurice, *Law and Procedure of the International Court* (1985); Rosenne, *Law and Practice of the International Court* (3rd ed.).

Aegean Sea Continental Shelf Case *1978 I.C.J. Rep. 3.* By an application dated 10 August 1976 specifying as the basis of jurisdiction the General Act of Geneva, 1928 *(93 L.N.T.S. 343)* coupled with the so-called Brussels Communique of 31 May 1973, the Government of Greece requested the ICJ to determine the boundary of the continental shelf with Turkey and the rights of the parties within their respective spheres, simultaneously requesting the indication of interim measures of protection prohibiting both exploratory activities within the disputed areas as well as further military measures which might endanger peaceful relations. By its order of 11 September 1976, the Court *found* (12 to 1) that the circumstances were not such as to require interim measures, unilateral action by Turkey consisting simply in seismic exploration neither creative of new rights nor involving appropriation of natural resources, and it being impossible to presume that either party would fail to heed its obligations of peaceful settlement or the recommendations of the Security Council in the matter: *1976 I.C.J. Rep. 3.* By its judgment of 19 December 1978 the Court *held* (12 to 2) that it lacked jurisdiction to hear the merits, the Brussels Communique, an unsigned communication to the press by the prime ministers of the parties not constituting an unconditional commitment to submit the dispute to the Court.

aequo et bono *See **ex aequo et bono**.*

Aerial Incident at Lockerbie Cases *See **Lockerbie Cases**.*

Aerial Incident of July 27, 1955 (Preliminary Objections) *(Israel v. Bulgaria) 1959 I.C.J. Rep. 127.* Following the shooting-down of an El-Al airliner, which had strayed into Bulgarian airspace on a flight from Vienna to Tel Aviv on July 27 1955 and failure to settle the matter by negotiation, Israel made an application invoking art. 36 of the ICJ Statute. Israel had accepted the ICJ's compulsory jurisdiction, and Bulgaria had similarly accepted the jurisdiction of the PCIJ in 1921. Israel argued that art. 36(5) of the PCIJ Statute meant that when Bulgaria became a member of the UN in 1955, and therefore a party to the ICJ Statute, its acceptance of the jurisdiction of the PCIJ was transferred to the ICJ. *Held* (12 to 4) that the ICJ did not have jurisdiction because Bulgaria had not accepted the jurisdiction of the Court in terms of art. 36(2). The Declaration of 1921 had lapsed before Bulgaria's admission to the UN since it was not a signatory to the Charter. The purpose of the transfer provision of art. 36(5) was to regulate the position of signatories to the Charter in the light of the impending dissolution of the PCIJ, which ceased to exist in 1946. Declarations of submission to its compulsory jurisdiction, not transferred by their signatory States being signatory to the Charter, lapsed, and were not revived by later admission to membership of the UN. Other applications by the UK and US were withdrawn.

aerial incidents A number of occurrences involving aircraft have led to cases before the ICJ and, while not all have proceeded to a judgment on the merits, they have, often through the pleadings of the parties, helped establish principles to be observed by States accidentally overflown before they take action. *See Aerial Incident of 7 October 1952 (USA v. USSR) 1956 I.C.J. Rep. 9; Aerial Incident of 10 March 1953 (USA v. Czechoslovakia) 1953 I.C.J. Rep. 6; Aerial Incident of 4 September 1954 (USA v. USSR) 1958 I.C.J. Rep. 158; Aerial Incident of 7 November 1954 (USA v. USSR) 1959 I.C.J. Rep. 276;* **Aerial Incident of 27 July 1955** *(Israel v. Bulgaria) 1959 I.C.J. Rep. 127; Aerial Incident of 27 July 1955 (USA v. Bulgaria) 1960 I.C.J. Rep. 146; Aerial Incident of 27 July 1955 (UK v. Bulgaria) 1959 I.C.J. Rep. 264; Aerial Incident of 3 July 1988 (Iran v. USA); Aerial Incident of 10 August 1999 (Pakistan v. India) 2000 I.C.J. Rep. 12. See also* the **Lockerbie Cases**.

On 10 May 1984, the Assembly of ICAO approved an amendment to the Chicago Convention on International Civil Aviation 1944 *(15 U.N.T.S. 295)* in an endeavor to clarify the rules applicable in such incidents *(23 I.L.M. 705 (1984))*. The amendment took the form of the insertion of a new art. 3 bis, (a) recognizing that every State must refrain from resorting to the use of weapons against civil aircraft in flight and that, in case of interception, the lives of persons on board and the safety of aircraft must not be endangered (this provision not being interpreted as modifying in any way the rights and obligations of States set forth in the UN Charter); (b) recognizing that every State, in the exercise of its sovereignty, is entitled to require the landing of a civil aircraft flying above its territory without authority or if there are reasonable grounds to conclude that it is being used for any purpose inconsistent with the aims of the convention, and for this purpose may resort to any appropriate means consistent with relevant rules of international law including the Chicago Convention and specifically (a) above; (c) obliging every civil aircraft to comply with an order given in conformity with (b) above; and (d) requiring each contracting State to take appropriate measures to prohibit the deliberate use of any civil aircraft registered in that State or operated by an operator with its principal place of business or permanent residence in that State for any purpose inconsistent with the aims of the Convention.

aerial piracy *See* **hijacking (of aircraft)**

aerial warfare The rules of aerial warfare are mainly not specific to that mode of hostilities, and there is no general treaty on the matter. However, the Hague Rules of Aerial Warfare adopted by a Commission of Jurists on 29 February 1923 *(17 A.J.I.L. Supp. 245 (1923)*; with commentary *(32 A.J.I.L. Supp. 12 (1938))*, while not adopted in binding form, are persuasive, and are reflected in many military law manuals. *Inter alia*, terror bombing is prohibited (art. 22); targets must be of a military nature (art. 24(1) and (2)) and steps must be taken to avoid as far as possible the destruction of hospitals, cultural and historic monuments, museums and churches (art. 25); undefended targets should not be attacked (art. 26). How far modern technology facilitates and how far it impedes adherence to such principles is moot. *See generally*, Spaight, *Air Power and War Rights* (3rd ed.).

affiliate members "The **World Tourism Organisation** has a special category of membership: affiliate membership, which is open to international bodies, both inter-governmental and non-governmental, concerned with specialised interests in tourism as well as to commercial bodies and associations whose activities are related to the aims of the organisation or fall within its competence. [Constitution of the World Tourism Organization, art. 7(1)]": Schermers & Blokker, *International Institutional Law* (3rd ed), 118-9.

African Charter on Human and Peoples' Rights Drafted within the framework of the OAU, the African Charter on Human and Peoples' Rights was adopted on 17 June 1981: *OAU DOC. CAB/LEG/67/3 Rev.5*; *21 I.L.M. 58 (1982)*. It contains, in Part I, an enumeration of fairly standard rights to be guaranteed to individuals, plus a number of duties required of individuals (arts. 27-29). An African Commission on Human and Peoples' Rights is established, in Part II, "to promote . . . rights and ensure their protection in Africa" (art. 30). In its monitoring role, the Commission may hear "communications" from a State party alleging a violation by another State party (arts. 47-54) or from individuals and groups, including recognized **NGO**s (arts. 55-9). Special provision is made for "serious and massive violations" of human rights (art. 58). Monitoring in the Commission is also effected through biennial reports from States parties (art. 62). In its work, the Commission is instructed to "draw inspiration" from a wide range of international instruments in addition to the African Charter (art. 60). A Protocol to the African Charter was adopted in 1998 *(OAU DOC. LRG/AFHPR/PROT(III))*, establishing an African Court on Human and Peoples' Rights, modelled on the old European Court of Human Rights and the Inter-American Court of Human Rights. When operational, this Court of 11 judges (art. 10) will hear cases referred by the Commission, a complainant State and a State complained against (art. 5) and, exceptionally, by individuals and groups (art. 6). *See* Umozurike, *The African Charter on Human and Peoples' Rights* (1997); Evans and Murray, *The African Charter on Human and Peoples' Rights* (2002). *See* <www.achpr.org>.

African Charter on the Rights and Welfare of the Child The African Children's Charter was established under the aegis of the **OAU** in July 1990 *(OAU DOC. CAB/LEG/24.9/49)* and came into effect on 28 November 1999. Modeled on the Convention on the Rights of the Child (*see* **Child, Convention on the Rights of the**), a global UN instrument, and intended as a supplement to the **African Charter on Human and Peoples' Rights**, it is the first regional human rights agreement specifically for children. The rights set out in Part I include mainly economic, social and cultural rights, and also a number of civil and political rights. Enforcement of the Charter is through a Committee of Experts on the Rights and Welfare of the Child (art. 32), which receives three-yearly reports from parties (art. 43), as well as communications from individuals and groups (art. 44), investigates compliance and reports regularly to the OAU Assembly (art. 45).

African Economic Community Established under the auspices of the **OAU** by the Abaju (Nigeria) Treaty of 3 June 1991 *(31 I.L.M. 1241 (1992))*, the major characteristic of the AEC, as compared with similar communities, is that it is prospective in nature. It will have a real existence only after a 6-stage process of variable duration to proceed over nearly 40 years (art. 6), during which it will coordinate and assimilate the achievements of the regional economic communities in Africa (art. 88).

African Union The African Union was established by the Constitutive Act signed by 53 African States at Lomé, Togo, on 11 July 2000, which came into force on 26 May 2001 (text at *OAU DOC. CAB/LEG/23.15*). The union is a further development of the **OAU** and is partly designed to promote the evolution of the **African Economic Community;** and it is loosely modeled on the European Union. Art. 3 sets out 14 broadly-drawn objectives, including "political and socio-economic integration," defense and the promotion of peace, human rights, sustainable development and health. It operates under a number of principles, emphasizing sovereign equality, respect for borders, prohibition on the use of force, peaceful resolution of disputes, non-interference in another member's internal affairs and democracy: art. 4. The Union has a right to intervene in a member State only in respect war crimes, genocide and crimes against humanity: art. 4(h).

The supreme organ of the African Union is the Assembly consisting of the heads of State and government (or their accredited representatives) of the members: art. 6. It determines the common policies of the Union and decides matters referred up from subordinate bodies (art. 9); and does so by "consensus or, failing which, by a two-thirds majority": art 7(1). More specific functions are assigned to the Executive Council, a ministerial body (art. 10(1)), meeting regularly and dealing with, *inter alia*, foreign trade, energy, food production, water and environmental protection: art. 13(1). Specialized Technical Committees have been established in 7 areas of the Unions activities: art. 14. It is envisaged that a Pan-African Parliament (art. 17), a Court of Justice (art. 18, and an African Central Bank, Monetary Fund and Investment Bank (art. 19) will all be established in the fullness of time by protocol to the Constitutive Act. *See* <www.africa-union.org>.

Agenda for Peace Following the Security Council meeting of Heads of State and Government in January 1992, the UN Secretary-General was asked to prepare an "analysis and recommendations on ways of strengthening and making more efficient within the framework and provisions of the Charter the capacity of the United Nations for preventive diplomacy, for peacemaking and peace-keeping": *UN Doc. S/23500*. Secretary-General Boutros-Ghali's report, titled An Agenda for Peace *(UN Doc. A/47/277—S/24111)* and dated 17 June 1992, defined and explained the concepts of **preventive diplomacy, peacemaking** and **peace-keeping** (and also the new concept of **post-conflict peace-building**) in the context of post-Cold War (mainly internal) conflicts. On the occasion of the 50th anniversary of the UN, Boutros-Ghali produced a Supplement to an Agenda for Peace *(UN Doc. A/50/60—S/1995/1)*, dated 3 January 1995), amplifying some of the points made in 1992 in the light of States' reactions to the Agenda and practice and experience in the intervening years.

aggression This term first acquired technical significance by reason of the stipulation of art. 10 of the Covenant of the League of Nations that members undertook "to respect and preserve as against external aggression the territorial integrity and existing political independence of all Members." It was adopted by the UN Charter, art. 1(1) specifying as a first purpose of the Organization "[t]o maintain international peace and security, and to that end: to take effective measures for the prevention and removal of threats to the peace, and for the suppression of acts of aggression and other breaches of the peace"; and art. 39 providing that "[t]he Security Council shall determine the existence of any threat to the peace, breach of the peace or act of aggression and shall make recommendations or decide what measures shall be taken . . . to maintain or restore international peace and security." Meanwhile, the Charters of the International Military Tribunals *(82 U.N.T.S. 279)* had designated the planning, preparation, initiation of or engagement in a "war of aggression" as a "crime against peace" within the jurisdiction of those tribunals. The work of four successive Special Committees of the General Assembly, going over again to some extent the ground covered by various bodies in the time of the League, resulted ultimately in G.A. Res. 3314 (XXIX) of 14 December 1974, approving by consensus an elaborate definition of aggression as "the use of armed force by a State against the sovereignty, territorial integrity or political independence of another State, or in any other manner inconsistent with the Charter . . .": art. 1. "The first use of armed force . . . shall constitute *prima facie* evidence of an act of aggression," although the Security Council may determine that such use of force does not amount to aggression, as where "the acts concerned or their consequences are not of sufficient gravity": art. 2. Art. 3 itemizes qualifying acts, and art. 4 empowers the Security Council to "determine that other acts constitute aggression under the provisions of the Charter." A major proviso is contained in art. 7, in which the definition of aggression is expressly declared not to prejudice "the right to self-determination, freedom, and independence, as derived from the Charter, of peoples forcibly deprived of that right . . . nor the right of these peoples to struggle to that end and to seek and receive support." *See generally* Stone, *Aggression and World Order* (1958); Ferencz, *Defining International Aggression* (1975).

Ago, Roberto 1902-94. Professor at Catania, Genoa, Milan and Rome. Member and subsequently chairman, ILC 1956-1979; Judge, ICJ 1979-91. Works include "The Internationally Wrongful Act of the State, Source of International Responsibility," eight reports to the ILC, 1969-1979 and *Teoria del diritto internazionale privato* (1934).

agréation, agreément *Agréation* or *agreément* is the process or act of consent by the receiving State to the appointment of the head of a diplomatic mission, art. 4 of the Vienna Convention on Diplomatic Relations 1961 *(500 U.N.T.S. 95)* providing: "1. The sending State must make certain that the *agreément* of the receiving State has been given for the person it proposes to accredit as head of the mission to that State. 2. The receiving State is not obliged to give reasons to the sending State for a refusal of *agreément*." According to art. 7, "the sending State may freely appoint the members of the staff of the mission. In the case of military, naval or air attachés, the receiving State may require their names to be submitted beforehand, for its approval." However, "[t]he receiving State may at any time and without having to explain its decision, notify the sending State that the head of the mission or any members of the diplomatic staff of the mission is *persona non grata* or that any other member of the staff of the mission is not acceptable": art. 9(1). *See Satow's Guide to Diplomatic Practice* (5th ed.), Chap. 12.

agreement, international The Vienna Convention on the Law of Treaties 1969, art. 1(a), provides that, for its purposes, "'treaty' means an international agreement concluded between States in written form and governed by international law, whether embodied in a single instrument or in two or more related instruments and whatever its particular designation." "In its restricted sense, the term 'agreement' means an agreement intended to have an obligatory character but usually of a less formal or significant nature than a treaty or convention. Like treaties and conventions, agreements in this sense may be concluded between heads of State, between States, or between governments. . . . While it can be used for multilateral treaties—for example the Agreement regarding the Status of Forces of Parties to the North Atlantic Treaty of 19 June 1951 [*199 U.N.T.S. 67]*—it is more commonly used for bilateral treaties of a fairly routine nature. . . . The designation 'agreement' is . . . given to a treaty which is in the form of a single instrument and which generally differs from a 'convention' in that it deals with a narrower or less permanent subject-matter. Sometimes agreements are concluded between a government department in one country and a government department in another. It depends on the circumstances whether such 'interdepartmental agreements' are binding under international law or whether they are merely private law contracts": *Satow's Guide to Diplomatic Practice* (5th ed.), 242-3. "The term '*de facto* agreement' has been used—not, I think, by lawyers—and appears to denote an international agreement which will be effective in spite of the fact that, legally speaking, a necessary party has not signed it; for instance, the Treaty of 22 May 1926, recording that the neutralization of Belgium had come to an end . . . and the Trieste Agreement of 5 Oct. 1954, called a Memorandum of Understanding *[235 U.N.T.S. 99]*": McNair, *Law of Treaties* (2nd ed.), 24 n.

aide-mémoire In diplomatic practice, a summary of a conversation, "often a detailed statement of facts, and of arguments based thereon, not differing essentially from a Note, except that it does not begin and end with a formula of courtesy and need not be signed": *Satow's Guide to Diplomatic Practice* (5th ed.), 45.

air defense identification zones Zones so designated have been established by various States, based loosely on art. 11 of the **Chicago Convention** on Civil Aviation 1944 *(15 U.N.T.S. 295)*, for air traffic control and security purposes. The best known are ADIZ, established by the US and extending more than half way across the Atlantic and Pacific, and CADIZ, the Canadian equivalent, covering both the Atlantic and polar areas. In these areas, air traffic intending to land in the US or Canada respectively must identify themselves on entry, and conform to ground control direction, though over the high seas (cf. **airspace**). These claims have seemingly been acquiesced in, and it should be noted that they are not claims to sovereign rights. *See* Murchison, *The Contiguous Air Space Zone in International Law* (1955).

air navigation Since the recognition, by art. 1 of the International Convention for the Regulation of Aerial Navigation, Paris, 1919 *(11 L.N.T.S. 172)*, of the principle that "every State has complete and exclusive sovereignty over the **airspace** above its territory," the legal basis of international air navigation has necessarily been treaty. As to the evolution of the doctrine of sovereignty of the air, see Cooper, The International Air Navigation Conference in Paris, *19 J. Air Law and Commerce 12 (1952)*. The Paris Convention established (art. 2) a conventional freedom of innocent passage in time of peace, subject (art. 3) to the right of any State to designate prohibited areas for military reasons or in the interest of public safety and (art. 15) to designate the route to be followed by an aircraft overflying without landing. This régime, amended in some respects by the Protocol of 1929 *(137 L.N.T.S. 11)*, was replaced by that of the **Chicago Convention** on International Civil Aviation 1944 *(15 U.N.T.S. 295)*. This Convention, which similarly affirms the principle of State sovereignty over the airspace above its territory and territorial sea (art. 1) and which applies only to civil aircraft (art. 3(a)), lays down in Part I (arts. 1-42) a code of the general principles of air navigation. These include principles governing non-scheduled flights (art. 5), scheduled services (arts. 5-6), and the reservation of *cabotage* (art. 7). Overflight by pilotless aircraft without special authorization is prohibited (art. 8), and States may establish reasonable prohibited areas and even, exceptionally, impose complete prohibitions for military or safety reasons on a basis of non-discrimination (art. 9). Arts. 10-16 relate to the application to foreign aircraft of national laws respecting customs, sanitation, immigration, landing charges, etc., and arts. 17-21 with registration and nationality of aircraft (*see* **aircraft, nationality**). Arts. 22-28 deal with principles to facilitate air navigation (customs, accident and distress, industrial property, navigation services); and arts. 29-36 with standard conditions to be fulfilled with respect to aircraft. Chapter VI (arts. 37-42) provide for international standards and recommended practices dealing with some of these matters, as also other miscellaneous aspects of air transport (formalities, aircraft in distress, accident investigation, documentation, radio, cargo restrictions, photography, airworthiness certificates and personnel licensing etc.) which are updated periodically in the Annexes to the Convention. *See generally* Cheng, *The Law of International Air Transport* (1962); Shawcross and Beaumont, *Air Law* (5th ed.).

air pollution In terms of art. 1 of the Convention on Long-Range Transboundary Air Pollution, adopted at Geneva on 13 November 1979 *(1302 U.N.T.S. 217)*, air pollution "means the introduction by man, directly or indirectly, of substances or energy into the air resulting in deleterious effects of such a nature as to endanger human health, harm living resources and ecosystems and material property and impair or interfere with amenities and other legitimate uses of the environment." This Convention, which was adopted under the aegis of the Economic Commission for Europe, provides in art. 3: "The Contracting Parties, within the framework of the present Convention, shall by means of exchanges of information, consultation, research and monitoring, develop without undue delay policies and strategies which shall serve as a means of combating the discharge of air pollutants, taking into account efforts already made at national and international levels." The Convention, with 49 parties, establishes an Executive Body representing all the contracting States, through which 8 Protocols have been added to the Convention identifying specific obligations or measures.

Problems of air pollution are most strongly experienced in Europe; hence the 1979 Convention. However, there exists in customary law a general prohibition against a State using its territory, or permitting the use of its territory, in such a way as to cause damage in a neighboring State: *Trail Smelter Case (1941) 3 R.I.A.A. 1905,* a case involving damage to crops in the State of Washington, U.S.A., by noxious sulphur fumes from a smelter in British Columbia, Canada. Art. 212 of the UN Convention on the Law of the Sea 1982 *(1833 U.N.T.S. 3)* contains a general obligation on States to adopt laws and regulations to control marine pollution from or through the atmosphere. *See* Okowa, *State Responsibility for Transboundary Air Pollution in International Law* (2001).

Air Transport Services Agreement Arbitration (USA v. France) (1963) 38 I.L.R. 182. Questions arose as to the flying rights granted by France to the USA under a bilateral Air Transport Services Agreement of 27 March 1946 and in particular whether those rights included rights for a US airline (PAA) to fly via Paris to Beirut, Ankara and Istanbul, and on to Tehran. *Held* by the Arbitration Tribunal established under Article X of the 1946 Agreement (Reuter, de Vries and, as third Arbitrator, Ago), that on an interpretation of the terms of the 1946 Agreement in their context and in the light of the negotiating history, the Ankara, Istanbul and Tehran stops were not included in the general path of the route allowing a service to Paris and beyond via points in "the Near East"; nor, in particular, were they included in the region designated "the Near East"; the conduct of the French authorities from May 1955 onwards had given rise to an implicit agreement under which a right for PAA to serve Tehran via Paris and Beirut had been established; and the conduct of the parties, confirmed in an Exchange of Notes concluded in 1960, had given rise to an agreement under which American carriers had acquired the right to serve Istanbul and Ankara via Paris, but without commercial rights between Paris and those stops.

air warfare *See* **aerial warfare**.

aircraft sabotage To address the then growing problem of the deliberate destruction of aircraft by international terrorist groups, the Convention for the Suppression of Unlawful Acts against the Safety of Civil Aviation was concluded at Montreal on 23 September 1971 *(974 U.N.T.S. 177)*. Under the Convention, the principal offence is "to place or cause to be placed on an aircraft in service, by any means whatsoever, a device or substance which is likely to destroy that aircraft, or to cause damage to it which renders it incapable of flight, or to cause damage which is likely to endanger its safety in flight" (art. 1(1)(c)). Liability extends beyond the perpetrator to those who attempt the offences and to accomplices (art. 1(2)(a) and (b)). The Convention applies to both international and domestic flights (art. 4(2)), but does not apply to aircraft used for military, customs or police services (art. 4(1)).

The State of registration of an aircraft on board which an offence has been committed, the State on whose territory the offence occurs, the State where the aircraft lands with the offender still on board, and the State in which a lessee of an aircraft has his principal place of business or his permanent residence are bound by the Convention to take measures to establish their jurisdiction in these circumstances (art. 5(1)). A Contracting State may extradite an offender but, if it does not, it is obliged "without exception and whether or not the offence was committed within its territory," to try the case itself (art. 7). The offence is deemed to be an extraditable offence in extradition treaties already existing between Contracting States and must be included in future extradition treaties (art. 8(1)); if there is no extradition treaty in force between two Contracting States, the Convention itself can be used as such in respect of the offence (art. 8(2)). The extradition provisions apply to offenders found in any Contracting State notwithstanding the limitation in art. 5(1). *See* the *Lockerbie Cases*; *Lockerbie Trial*.

aircraft, nationality The **Chicago Convention** on International Civil Aviation of 7 December 1944 *(15 U.N.T.S. 295)* provides (art. 17) that "[a]ircraft have the nationality of the State in which they are registered," and (art. 18) that "[a]n aircraft cannot be validly registered in more than one State, but its registration may be changed from one State to another," as well as (art. 19) that "[t]he registration or transfer of registration of aircraft in any contracting State shall be made in accordance with its laws and regulations." The Convention, which, incidentally, is expressed (art. 3) not to apply to State, including military, customs and police, aircraft, imposes no requirement of national ownership as a qualification for registration, as did the Aerial Navigation Convention of 1919, (art. 7) *(11 L.N.T.S. 172)*. While it falls to each State to determine its own rules for granting nationality to aircraft, these rules must be reported to ICAO, and ICAO and other States may require details of the registration and ownership of any particular aircraft (art. 21). *See* **State aircraft**. *See* Honig, *The Legal Status of Aircraft* (1956).

airspace In common parlance, the airspace of a State lies above its land and sea territory, and is subject to its exclusive jurisdiction. Thus, "[t]he contracting States recognize that every State has complete and exclusive sovereignty over the airspace above its territory": art. 1, **Chicago Convention** on International Civil Aviation 1944 *(15 U.N.T.S. 295)*; "For the purposes of this Convention the territory of a State shall be deemed to be the land areas and territorial waters adjacent thereto under the sovereignty, suzerainty, protection or mandate of such State" (art. 2). "The sovereignty of a coastal State extends to the air space over the territorial sea as well as to its bed and subsoil": art. 2(2), UN Convention on the Law of the Sea 1982 *(1833 U.N.T.S. 3)*; among the freedoms of the high seas, exercisable also in the **exclusive economic zone**, is "freedom of overflight": art. 87(1)(b).

However, the term "airspace" has not been defined in international law by case or treaty. Latterly, some States have claimed to exercise control in the airspace over the high seas proximate to their territory (*see* **air defense identification zones**). The vertical limit of State sovereignty is uncertain. The main positions are (i) no limit (*see* **Bogota Declaration**), (ii) the height to which a subjacent State can in physical fact exert its control, (iii) the height to which the most potent States can exercise their actual control, (iv) the height at which no molecules of gaseous air are found (variable, c. 100-1,000 miles depending on definition of 'no'), (v) the height at which aerodynamic lift ceases entirely and centrifugal force takes over (the Von Karman line, c.52 miles), (vi) the height to which an aircraft depending only on aerodynamic lift, not speed, can fly (c.25 miles), vii) a variable height depending on the type of flight instrumentality involved, spacecraft during landing and takeoff being permitted transit through "airspace" under the sovereignty of the State *qua* aviation. (For full tabulation, see *Report to the National Aeronautics and Space Adminis-*

tration on the Law of Outer Space, American Bar Foundation, 1960, reprinted in "Legal Problems of Space Exploration," *U.S. Senate Doc. 26, 87th Congress, 1st Session, 1961*).

State practice has developed under which the transit of a satellite in orbit is acquiesced in, while overflight by a plane even at extreme heights is viewed as an aerial intrusion. All discussions on the law of outer space assume a vertical limit to State sovereignty. *See* **Outer Space Treaty**. *See* Cheng, *The Law of International Air Transport* (1962); Johnson, *Rights in Air Space* (1965); Wassenbergh, *Public International Air Transportation Law in a New Era* (1989).

Aix-la-Chapelle, Congress of In fact the third congress held at Aix-la Chapelle (the other two being in 1668 and 1748), the title is commonly given to the conference of the European Powers (Austria, France, Great Britain, Prussia and Russia) in October-November 1818 to discuss the modalities of the withdrawal of the army of occupation from France and consequent relations with France. It was notable for the adoption of the Procés-verbal of Conference of 21 November 1818 *(69 C.T.S. 385)* adding Ministers-Resident to the classification of diplomatic agents laid down at the **Congress of Vienna**.

Alabama Claims Arbitration *(U.S. v. Great Britain)* (1872) *Moore, Int. Arb., 653*. The Treaty of Washington 1871 *(143 C.T.S. 145)* provided (art. 1) for the arbitration of the claims of the United States arising out of the depredations of the *Alabama* and other vessels permitted to be built or fitted out in Great Britain for the Confederate cause during the American Civil War. Art. 6 stipulated that the arbitrators should apply to any arbitration the rules of neutral conduct, subsequently known as the Three Rules of Washington (*see* **Washington, Three Rules of**) set out in the Treaty, requiring that a neutral State should use "due diligence" to prevent fitting out of hostile expeditions within its territory. Holding the requisite degree of diligence to be proportionate to "the risks to which either of the belligerents may be exposed, from a failure to fulfil the obligations of neutrality" (instead of, for instance, to the means of surveillance available to the neutral), the Tribunal of 5 arbitrators (Sir A. Cockburn, the British member, dissenting) *held* Great Britain to be at fault, disallowing, however, the American claim in respect of the costs of pursuit of the Confederate cruisers as indistinguishable from the general expenses of the war and, equally, the claim in respect of the prospective earnings of vessels destroyed by them, these being but speculative. A lump sum of $15.5 million in gold was awarded which was subsequently distributed among individual claimants by a domestic American tribunal. This arbitration confirmed that a State, *in casu* Great Britain, could not invoke its domestic law, *in casu* the absence of any legal prohibition on fitting out vessels for the confederate forces, as a justification for the breach of an international obligation.

ALADI *See* **Latin American Integration Association**.

Alaska Boundary Arbitration *(Great Britain v. U.S.A.)* *(1903) 15 R.I.A.A. 481*. This boundary dispute between the parties was submitted to arbitration by the Convention of 24 January 1903 *(192 C.T.S. 336)*. The tribunal determined the boundary in accordance with the maxim that a boundary should be easy to distinguish and difficult to cross, in this case having regard to a mountain divide. The award, delivered on 20 October 1903, was accepted in an Exchange of Notes of 25 March 1905 *(198 C.T.S. 189)*. *See also* the ***British-Guiana-Venezuela Boundary Arbitration***.

Alexandrowicz, Charles Henry 1902-74. Austro-Hungarian, subsequently British, national. Professor Madras, 1951-61; Sydney, 1961-8. Founder, **Grotian Society**. Works include *World Economic Agencies, Law and Practice* (1962); *An Introduction to the*

History of the Law of Nations in the East Indies (1967); *The Law of Global Communications* (1971); *The Law-Making Functions of the Specialised Agencies of the United Nations* (1973).

Algeciras, Act of General Act of the International Conference at Algeciras relating to the Affairs of Morocco, signed 7 April 1906 *(201 C.T.S. 39)*. Terminated by the Final Declaration of 29 October 1956 *(263 U.N.T.S. 165)*, recognizing the independence of Morocco.

alien In strictness, the term alien belongs to the common law rather than international law, denoting a non-subject, or non-citizen, as opposed to a subject, or citizen. Such a non-subject/citizen was originally assumed to be the subject/citizen of some other sovereign. But even in English law the distinction between subject and alien, based as it was on **allegiance,** came to be blurred by the drawing of a further distinction in time of war between alien *ami* (or friend) and alien enemy on the basis of domicile rather than allegiance or nationality. Cf. McNair and Watts, *Legal Effects of War*, (2nd ed.), Chaps. 2 and 3. This usage is, however, still distinct from that whereby, in the Anglophone literature of international law, the word alien is employed to denote simply the national of any other State in the context of **State responsibility**, as in the expressions admission of, expulsion of, treatment of, or protection of aliens, which have been used for more than a century by such textbooks as *Westlake* (1st ed. 1904) and *Oppenheim* (1st ed. 1905).

alienability The quality of being capable of transfer. All territory, including territorial rights, is alienable, with the caveat that territorial waters can only be alienated along with the adjoining territory. *See I Oppenheim 463, 488.* Cf. **appurtenance.**

aliens, admission "By customary international law no state can claim the right for its nationals to enter into, and reside on, the territory of a foreign state. The reception of aliens is a matter of discretion, and every state is, by reason of its territorial supremacy, competent to exclude aliens from the whole, or any part, of its territory. States may, however, by treaty confer on each other's nationals a right to enter their territories, especially in treaties of commerce and friendship, which often entitle the foreign nationals concerned not merely to enter the state but to establish themselves in business there. . . . Since a state need not receive aliens at all, it can receive them only under certain conditions": *I Oppenheim 897-9. See* Goodwin-Gill, *International Law and the Movement of Persons between States* (1992), Part 1; Plender, *International Migration Law* (2nd ed.).

aliens, expulsion All States have the general right to expel aliens, but a state must not abuse its right by proceeding in an arbitrary manner. "The right of States to expel aliens is generally recognized. . . . On the other hand . . . the need for the expelling State not to act arbitrarily especially in the case of expulsion of an alien who has been residing within the expelling State for some length of time, and has established his means of livelihood there, justifies the home State of the expelled individual, by virtue of its right of protection over citizens abroad, in making diplomatic representations to the expelling State, and asking for the reasons for the expulsion." *I Oppenheim 691-2. See also* Goodwin-Gill, *International Law and the Movement of Persons between States* (1992), Part III.

aliens, treatment of "When a State admits into its territory foreign investments or foreign nationals, whether natural or juristic persons, it is bound to extend to them the protection of the law and assumes obligations concerning the treatment to be afforded them. These obligations, however, are neither absolute nor unqualified": ***Barcelona Traction Case (Second Phase)*** *1970 I.C.J. Rep. 32* at 46. Cf. ***Mallen Claim (1927)*** *4 R.I.A.A. 173.*

Generally speaking, in its treatment of aliens a State must comply with a minimum international law standard, but if the standard of the local administration of justice is higher than this, the alien is entitled to the benefits of the higher standard: *Neer Case (1926) 4 R.I.A.A. 61*; *Faulkner Case (1926) 4 R.I.A.A. 70*; *Roberts Case (1926) 4 R.I.A.A. 80*; *Swinney Case (1926) 4 R.I.A.A. 100. See also* **denial of justice.**

allegiance   Allegiance is, strictly, a term of English law, derived from feudal notions, and connoting the duty owed by the individual to his lord or sovereign as the correlative of his claim of protection upon such superior. Until displaced by the statutory scheme of nationality and citizenship introduced by the British Nationality Act 1948, the concept of permanent allegiance lay at the root of the status of a British subject—of British nationality. Temporary allegiance, equally, characterized and comprised the duty of the non-subject or alien present within the State or otherwise constructively a subject towards the latter: Cf. *R. v. Lynch [1903] 1 K.B. 444*; *Joyce v. Director of Public Prosecutions [1946] A.C. 347*. As a common law term and concept, the notion of allegiance has of course passed into the law of the United States and of some other (particularly Commonwealth) States with common law roots. It may possibly belong naturally to other municipal systems with feudal origins. Its increasing use by Anglophone writers to describe the duty owed by any individual to any State, though natural, has little justification. It is also said that aliens admitted to a State "owe a duty of modified allegiance to the local sovereign": O'Connell, *International Law* (1965), 762.

alliance   "Alliances are arrangements between two or more states whereby they agree to co-operate militarily in respect of their conduct in relation to one or more third states (although the term 'alliance' may sometimes be used in a wider sense, covering co-operation for various, non-military purposes). The arrangements are usually embodied in a treaty of alliance. Although in theory an alliance may be for the purpose of attacking a third state, and such offensive alliances have been known, an alliance for such a purpose would now be unlawful. More common, and entirely lawful, are alliances for purposes of common defense in the event of an attack by a third state. Such defensive alliances may be either general alliances, against any possible enemy, or particular alliances, against one or more specific enemies. Further, they may be either permanent or for a limited period of time only": *I Oppenheim 1318*. The prohibition in art. 2(4) of the UN Charter on the use of force, except in **self-defense** (art. 51) and the superiority of Charter provisions and norms over other treaty obligations (art. 103) means that any treaty establishing an offensive, as opposed to a defensive, alliance is impermissible. For the main examples of alliances, see **ANZUS; Baghdad Pact; NATO; SEATO.**

alluvion   A method by which a State may acquire title to territory added to the seashore or a river bank through the operations of nature, and requiring no formal act of appropriation. *See The Anna 5 C. Rob. 373 (1805)*; *Island of Palmas Case (1928) 2 R.I.A.A. 829* at 839. If a river is a boundary between States, the boundary will alter with the erosion and deposit of soil: *See Louisiana v. Mississippi 282 U.S. 485 (1931). See I Oppenheim 697*. Cf. **accretion, avulsion.**

Alston, Philip   1950- . Professor of Law and Foundation Director of the Centre for International and Public Law at the Australian National University (1989-95); Professor of International Law at the European University Institute (1997-). His works include *The United Nations and Human Rights: A Critical Appraisal* (1992, 2nd ed. 2001); *International Human Rights in Context: Law, Politics, Morals* (with Steiner, 1996, 2nd ed. 2000); *Peoples' Rights* (2001).

alternat "The *alternat* consisted in this, that in the copy of the document or treaty which was destined to each separate Power, the names of the head of that state and his plenipotentiaries were given precedence over the others, and his plenipotentiaries' signatures were also attached before those of the other signatories. Thus each Power occupied the place of honour in turn": *Satow's Guide to Diplomatic Practice* (5th ed.), 24.

ambassador The title of ambassador is that traditionally given to a diplomatic agent of the highest class in inter-State relations, the *Réglement sur le rang entre les agents diplomatiques* adopted at the Congress of Vienna on 19 March 1815 *(64 C.T.S. 1)* dividing *employés diplomatiques* into three classes of which the first was "Celle des ambassadeurs, légats ou nonces" who alone "ont . . . le caractare representatif." The Vienna Convention on Diplomatic Relations 1961 *(500 U.N.T.S. 95)* avoids the term ambassador, speaking only (art. 1(a)) of the "head of the mission." Though heads of most diplomatic missions continue to be styled ambassadors, that title is occasionally conferred, as it has been in the past, on persons on special rather than permanent mission, or "at large," and is employed also simply to designate a domestic rank in the diplomatic services of some States. It is less commonly used for the designation of delegates to organs of international organizations, and never for that of representatives of such organizations. The head of a diplomatic mission of one Commonwealth country in another is usually styled "High Commissioner."

Ambatielos Arbitration (1951) *12 R.I.A.A. 83*. This arbitration under the terms of the Declaration annexed to the Treaty of 16 July 1926 *(61 L.N.T.S. 15)*, and the Treaty of 10 November 1886 *(168 C.T.S. 283)*, which were held by the ICJ in the *Ambatielos Case* to create an obligation to submit to arbitration binding upon the United Kingdom, arose out of the diplomatic support by Greece of a claim by M. Ambatielos, a Greek national, founded originally on a complaint against the judgment of an English court of first instance in favor of the British Board of Trade for possession of certain vessels delivered under a contract of sale in respect of which Ambatielos was adjudged to be in default. The defense to the action was in effect that the delivery dates had not been kept, but the claimant had, on grounds of Crown privilege, been refused discovery of official papers which might have sustained this argument. He had, equally, been refused leave by the Court of Appeal to call an oral witness instead, on the grounds that such a witness could have been called in the court below, but was not so called. The Arbitration Commission had principally to deal with the questions raised by the United Kingdom of undue delay (some 30 years) in the presentation of the claim and of non-exhaustion of local remedies, the individual claimant having neglected to appeal to the House of Lords, the ultimate court of appeal available to him. *Held* in its Award dated 6 March 1951 for Greece on the first question, there being "no rule of international law which lays down a time-limit in regard to prescription, except in the case of special agreements to that effect . . ."; but against Greece in the matter of exhaustion of remedies.

Ambatielos Case *(Greece v. United Kingdom) 1952 I.C.J. Rep. 28; 1953 I.C.J. Rep. 10*. In connection with the claim of M. Ambatielos (*see **Ambatielos Arbitration***), Greece in 1951 invoked the jurisdiction of the ICJ on the basis of the Treaty of Commerce and Navigation of 16 July 1926 *(61 L.N.T.S. 15)*, art. 29 whereof stipulated for the reference of disputes etc. to the "arbitration" of the PCIJ (for which the ICJ was to be construed as substituted by virtue of art. 37 of the latter's Statute), requesting the Court to adjudge that the United Kingdom was under an obligation to join in the submission of the claim to arbitral settlement under the Treaty of 10 November 1886 *(168 C.T.S. 283)* between the parties, to which a Protocol providing for such settlement was annexed, or under the Treaty of 1926, to which a Declaration touching arbitration was similarly annexed; or alternatively that Greece was entitled to seize the Court of the merits of the claim. Upon a preliminary objection on the part of the United Kingdom to the jurisdiction, the Court *held* (13 to 2) that, having regard to the date at which the claim arose (1921) and to the fact that the Treaty of 1926 could not be construed to have retroactive effect, it was indeed without jurisdiction on the merits. But it also *held* (10 to 5) that it had jurisdiction to decide as to the existence of any obligation of the United Kingdom to submit to the arbitration of the difference, *qua* a difference as to the validity of the claim insofar as it was based on the Treaty of 1886, by reason of the terms of the Declaration, which was to be considered part of the Treaty of 1926 and therefore subject to the provisions of art. 29 of the latter. In further proceedings, the Court *held* (10 to 4) that the case was one in which Greece was to be construed as presenting the claim of a private person on the basis of the Treaty of 1886 by reason of the scope and effect of the most-favored-nation clause in art. X thereof taken together with other treaties (and notably art. 10 of the Anglo-Bolivian Treaty of 1 August 1911 *(214 C.T.S. 181))*, reserving the right of diplomatic protection in cases of denial of justice, and by reason equally of a divergence of views as to the stipulation for free access to the courts in art. 15(3) of the 1886 Treaty, which could be reasonably argued to be infringed by a refusal of disclosure such as had been made in relation to the instant claim.

Ambrose Light *(1885) 25 Fed. 408*. A US naval vessel on 24 April 1885, sighted on the high seas a vessel, the *Ambrose Light*, which flew a strange flag, which subsequently hoisted a Colombian flag, and which was carrying armed soldiers and a quantity of arms. The ship's papers purported to commission her as a Colombian warship, and were signed by persons involved in insurrection against the Government of Colombia. The vessel was engaged upon a hostile expedition against the Colombian port of Cartagena and was designed to assist in the blockade and siege of that port by the rebels. The vessel was seized and brought to a US port for condemnation in prize. *Held* by a US Federal Court, that as at the time of the seizure the insurgents had not been recognized by either the Government of Colombia or any other Government as entitled to exercise belligerent rights, the vessel had been lawfully seized, as bound upon an expedition technically piratical; but as the US Government had subsequently, on the basis of facts in existence at the time of the seizure, by necessary implication recognized the insurgent forces as a government *de facto* in a state of war with Colombia and entitled to belligerent rights, the vessel could not be condemned for acts of war which that recognition authorized.

amendment The Vienna Convention on the Law of Treaties 1969, Part IV, is entitled "Amendment and Modification of Treaties," laying down in art. 39 the "general rule regarding the amendment of treaties" to the effect that a "treaty may be amended by agreement between the parties. The rules laid down in Part II [with respect to the 'Conclusion and Entry into Force of Treaties'] apply to such an agreement except in so far as the treaty may otherwise provide"; and in art. 40 a detailed régime for the "amendment of multilateral treaties," elaborating the general principle that amendment requires the consent of all parties. *See* Aust, *Modern Treaty Law and Practice* (2000), Chap. 15.

American Convention on Human Rights 1969 *(1144 U.N.T.S. 123)*. This Convention was the culmination of Latin-American developments in human rights that had commenced with the adoption of the Inter-American Charter of Social Guarantees and the American Declaration of the Rights and Duties of Man, commonly styled the **Bogotá Declaration,** (Resolutions XXIX and XXX respectively) at the Ninth International Conference of American States. The Convention was adopted on 22 November 1969, came into force on 18 July 1978 and currently has 24 parties. The Convention guarantees civil and political rights (Chap. II) and economic, social and cultural rights (Chap. III). It is possible for a State to suspend the operation of the Convention "in time of war, public danger, or other emergency that threatens [its] independence or security," but eleven articles are declared to be incapable of suspension: art. 27.

The Convention establishes an Inter-American Commission on Human Rights and an Inter-American Court of Human Rights to oversee its implementation: art. 34. The Commission, the successor to an identically-named predecessor which was established in 1959 to oversee the operation of the American Declaration of the Rights and Duties of Man, has seven members: art. 34. The Commission can consider petitions from individuals and groups alleging violation of the Convention: art. 44. The Commission can only consider communications from other State parties if the State against which the complaint is raised has recognized that right: art. 45(1). Once the Commission has determined the admissibility of the petition or communication (*see* arts. 46 and 47), it seeks a friendly settlement: art. 48(1)(f).

If no such settlement is reached the Commission draws up a report setting out the facts and stating its conclusions. Within three months of the transmission of the report to the State concerned, the Commission or the complaining State may refer the matter to the Inter-American Court of Human Rights. Alternatively the Commission may, by the vote of an absolute majority of its members, set out its opinion and make recommendations to the State concerned regarding the remedying of any violation: art. 51. The Court has seven judges (art. 52); and there is provision for the appointment of an *ad hoc* judge (art. 55(2)-(4)). Only States parties to the Convention and the Commission have the right to submit a case to the Court: art. 61(1). However, the Court does not have jurisdiction unless the State complained against has recognized that jurisdiction: art. 62. If the Court finds a violation of the Convention, it may rule, if appropriate, that the consequences be remedied and that fair compensation be paid: art. 63(1). The court is empowered, "in cases of extreme gravity and urgency, and when necessary to avoid irreparable damage to persons," to adopt provisional measures: art. 63(2). The States and the organs of the OAS may consult the Court over issues of interpretation: art. 64. A judgment of the Court is final and not subject to appeal, though the Court may be asked to interpret a judgment: art. 67. *See* Davidson, *The Inter-American Court of Human Rights* (1992); Buergenthal and Shelton, *Protecting Human Rights in the Americas* (4th ed.): Davidson, *The Inter-American Human Rights System* (1996); Harris and Livingstone, *The Inter-American System of Human Rights* (1998).

American Society of International Law Founded in 1906 and incorporated by Act of Congress in 1950, the American Society of International Law is the premier membership organization in the United States dedicated to advancing the study and use of international law. It is a non-political forum for debate and discussion and an educational institution concerning issues of international law and relations. It publishes the *American Journal of International Law* (since 1906), one of the world's leading journals on international law; *International Legal Materials* (since 1962), an invaluable and timely collection of documents; a bi-monthly *ASIL Newsletter*; and, online, *ASIL Insights*, commentaries on "the law behind the headlines," and *International Law in Brief*, abstracts of current developments. *See* <www.asil.org>.

Amnesty International An independent world-wide human rights **NGO**, established in the UK in 1961, which initially focused on prisoners of conscience. It has subsequently extended its mission to research and action on preventing and ending grave abuses of the rights to physical and mental integrity, freedom of conscience and expression, and freedom from discrimination, within the context of promoting all human rights. Amnesty International opposes torture and capital punishment in all cases and without reservation. It seeks observance throughout the world of the UN **Universal Declaration of Human**

Rights, through individual members and adoption groups. The latter groups work for prisoners of conscience and human rights in countries other than their own, the countries being balanced geographically and politically to ensure impartiality. Amnesty International has consultative status with the United Nations (ECOSOC), and the Council of Europe, is recognized by UNESCO, has relations with a number of other intergovernmental organizations. *See* <www.amnesty.org>.

Amos, Sheldon 1835-1886; English jurist with a career in teaching and colonial administration, best known for his works on international law: *Lectures on International Law* (1873); editor of Manning's *Commentaries on the Law of Nations* (1875); and *Political and Legal Remedies for War* (1880).

angary This term has an ancient lineage, being derived from the *jus angariae*—the right of transport; it was mentioned "in the *Digest*, in the Code, in the *de Jure Maritimo* of Locenius, and in the Treatise of Stypmanus on the Hanseatic Maritime Laws": *per* the Court in *Ministre de la Marine v. Cie Franco-Tunisienne d'Armement (1946) 13 I.L.R. 238*. It is a "right of belligerents to destroy, or use, in case of necessity, for the purpose of offence and defence, neutral property on their territory, or on enemy territory, or on the open sea": *II Oppenheim 761-4*. Lauterpacht defines it thus: "In time of war a State is entitled to requisition the property of neutral subjects": Angary and the Requisition of Neutral Property, *(1950) 27 B.Y.I.L. 455-9*. The difference between angary and requisition was explained in the (successful) argument of Norway in the following terms: angary ". . . relates to neutral property temporarily within the State and not belonging to or associated with the national domain, such as a neutral ship within a belligerent port, while (the right of requisition) relates within the territory of the State": *Requisition of Shipbuilding Contracts Case (Norway v. United States) (1922) 1 I.L.R. 189* at 191.

Anglo-French Continental Shelf Case *(United Kingdom v. France) (1977), (1978) 18 R.I.A.A. 3, 271.* The UK and France disputed the **continental shelf** boundary between them in the central and western areas of the English Channel and out into the Southwestern Approaches in the Atlantic. The parties differed as to the applicable rules of law and as to the way the applicable rules should be applied to the particular facts. By an Agreement signed on 10 July 1975, the parties agreed to submit the issue to arbitration. The Court of Arbitration was asked to determine, "in accordance with the rules of international law applicable in the matter as between the Parties," the course of the continental shelf boundary between the United Kingdom (including the Channel Islands) and France in the area westward of 30 minutes west of the Greenwich Meridian as far as the 1000 meter isobath. Both States were parties to the Geneva Convention on the Continental Shelf 1958 *(499 U.N.T.S. 82)*, but France contended it had not entered into force between them by reason of the UK's refusal to accept certain French reservations, particularly to art. 6, whereby France, *inter alia*, refused to accept the principle of equidistance in certain areas, including the Bay of Granville (Channel Islands area).

Held (unanimously, with Judge Briggs appending a separate declaration on certain points of law) that the following should be the boundaries: in the English Channel, a median line giving full effect to all islands; in the South-Western Approaches, a median line giving half effect to the Scilly Islands; in the area north and northwest of the Channel Islands, a twelve-mile enclave boundary. The Court found itself not competent to decide the boundary east and south of the Channel Islands.

The Court ruled (i) Art. 12 of the 1958 Convention authorized France to make its consent to be bound subject to reservations to articles other than 1, 2 and 3, as to which reservations were specifically prohibited. By its ratification, the UK gave its consent to France being a party subject to such reservations, and its statement that it was "unable to accept" the French reservations to art. 6 was not intended to prevent entry of the Convention into force between them. (ii) Art. 6 does not formulate the equidistance rule and special circumstances rule as two separate rules, but as a combined rule which gives expression to the norm that, failing agreement, the boundary is to be determined by equitable principles. The method of delimitation in any case, whether under the Convention or customary law, is to be determined in the light of geographical and other relevant circumstances and of the norm that delimitation must be in accord with equitable principles. In the present case, the customary rules "lead to much the same result as the provisions of Article 6." (iii) The presence of the Channel Islands close to the French Coast, if given full effect in delimitation, would result in substantially decreasing the area of French shelf. This is *prima facie* a circumstance of inequity to be redressed. (iv) The projection of the Scilly Islands into the Atlantic is an element of distortion and a special circumstance under Article 6. Since the Scillies extend twice as far from the UK mainland as does the Island of Ushant from the French mainland, the Scillies were given only half effect in determining the equidistance line. Subsequently, the UK asked the Court to correct errors of a technical nature in parts of the boundary and the drawing thereof on the Boundary-Line Chart, and the Court found this application admissible and agreed to rectify the boundary north and west of the Channel Islands as requested, but rejected the request for rectification of the boundary in the South-Western Approaches.

Anglo-Iranian Oil Co. Case *(U.K. v. Iran) 1951 I.C.J. Rep. 89.* The proceedings in this case were initiated by an application to the ICJ in virtue of the right of diplomatic protection, the United Kingdom having adopted the dispute of a British corporation, the Anglo-Iranian Oil Co. Ltd., with Iran arising from the nationalization of the company's undertaking in Iran. Following the application, the applicant State requested the indication, pursuant to art. 41 of the Court's Statute, of provisional measures for the preservation of its rights. The Court *granted* this request (10 to 2), stating that "the indication of such measures in no way prejudges the jurisdiction of the Court to deal with the merits." Upon a preliminary objection to the jurisdiction in the merits to the effect that Iran's Declaration of Acceptance of the Optional Clause was restricted to disputes arising out of treaties entered into after the date of such acceptance (19 September 1932) and that the instant dispute did not so arise, the Court *held* (9 to 5) that it had no jurisdiction, rejecting in particular the British submissions (1) that the concessionary contract entered into by the company and Iran in 1933 as an incident of the settlement of an earlier dispute of a like nature had a "double character" and constituted in effect also a treaty between Iran and the United Kingdom; and (2) that a treaty between the parties of a date subsequent to 1932 could be spelled out by putting together various establishment treaties entered into with third States by Iran after that date and most-favoured-nation clauses in the Treaties with Great Britain of 4 March 1857 *(116 C.T.S. 329)* and 9 February 1903 *(192 C.T.S. 375).*

Anglo-Norwegian Fisheries Case *(U.K. v. Norway) 1951 I.C.J. Rep. 116.* This case, begun by an application referring to the Declarations of Acceptance of the Optional Clause in art. 36(2) of the ICJ Statute by the United Kingdom and Norway, asked the Court "(a) to declare the principles of international law to be applied in defining the baselines, by reference to which the Norwegian Government is entitled to delimit a fisheries zone, extending to seaward 4 miles from those lines and exclusively reserved for its own nationals, and to define the said base-lines in so far as it appears necessary, in the light of the arguments of the Parties, in order to avoid further legal difficulties between them; (b) to award damages to the . . . United Kingdom in respect of . . . interferences . . . with British fishing vessels outside the zone which . . . the Norwegian Government [may be] entitled to reserve for its nationals." The legitimacy of a 4-mile limit was not in dispute between the parties, but the United Kingdom objected to the measurement of this from base-lines otherwise than across the mouths of bays of a length exceeding 10 miles and drawn between points which were sometimes "low-tide elevations" (drying rocks).

In *holding* (10 to 2) that the method of delimitation employed in the Norwegian Royal Decree of 12 July 1935 was not contrary to international law (so that, incidentally, no question of damages arose) the Court: (1) found that the coastal zone involved in the dispute was "of a very distinctive configuration" being very broken or indented, for the greater part of its length protected by an island fringe or 'skjaergaard,' and so high as to be generally visible from a long distance," the inhabitants "deriv[ing] their livelihood essentially from fishing"; (2) similarly found that "for the purpose of measuring the breadth of the territorial sea, it is the low-watermark as opposed to the high-watermark . . . which has been generally adopted in the practice of States"; (3) held that "geographical realities" required that the relevant low-watermark in the region under discussion was that of the 'skjaergaard' rather than that of the mainland; (4) held also that, of the three methods canvassed for the application of the low-watermark rule, that of the **tracé parallele,** following the sinuosities of the coast, was inapplicable to so indented a coast, and that the **arcs-of-circles** method was not obligatory in law; (5) and that the rule confining the use of straight base-lines to cases where they do not exceed ten miles in length "although . . . adopted by certain States both in their national law and in their treaties and conventions, and [in] certain arbitral decisions . . . has not acquired the authority of a general rule of international law"; (6) and finally found that the base-lines actually selected by Norway had not "violated international law," such having not departed appreciably from the general direction of the coast, having legitimately taken into account peculiar local economic interests, and having conformed to a traditional pattern of delimitation conferring something in the nature of an historic title generally tolerated by other States. The principles of the judgment, and to a great extent its language, were adopted in the Geneva Convention on the Territorial Sea etc. 1958 *(516 U.N.T.S. 205),* arts. 3-5, and were reproduced in the UN Convention on the Law of the Sea 1982 *(1833 U.N.T.S. 3),* arts. 5-7.

animus disponendi The intention to renounce sovereignty over territory. Cf. *animus occupandi.*

animus occupandi The intention on the part of a State to acquire and retain sovereignty over territory; an essential element of acquisition of title to territory by occupation. *See Island of Palmas Case (1928) 2 R.I.A.A. 829*; *Clipperton Island Case (1931) 2 R.I.A.A. 1105*; *Eastern Greenland Case (1933) P.C.I.J. Ser. A/B, No. 53*; *Frontier Land Case 1959 I.C.J. Rep. 209*; *Minquers and Ecrehos Case 1953 I.C.J. Rep. 47. See* **occupation**.

Annan, Kofi 1938- . Ghanian-born career international civil servant who entered the UN system in 1962. Seventh Secretary-General of the UN, 1997- . Nobel Prize laureate with the UN itself, 2001. Author of reports on renewing the UN (1997), peace and development in Africa (1998), a millennium report (2000) and a call to action on the HIV/AIDS pandemic (2001).

annexation The acquisition of title to territory (*scil.* previously under the sovereignty of another State) by a unilateral act of appropriation by a conqueror State subsequent to subjugation: "At no period did conquest alone and *ipso facto* make the conquering state the sovereign of the conquered territory. . . . Conquest was only a mode of acquisition if the conqueror, after having firmly established the conquest, and the state of war having come to an end, then formally annexed the territory": *I Oppenheim 699.* When, in June 1945, the

Allies assumed "supreme authority with respect to Germany, including all the powers possessed by the German Government, High Command and any state, municipal, or local government or authority," they expressly declared that the assumption of these powers "does not effect the annexation of Germany": Whiteman, *Digest of International Law*, Vol. 1 (1963), 325. As it is now accepted that the use of force, except in self-defense, is contrary to international law, so the fruits of an illegal use of force cannot stand in law. So, after the "Six Day War" in June 1967 when Israel invaded the Sinai Peninsula, the West Bank of the Jordan, the Golan Heights and the unoccupied parts of Jerusalem, the Security Council, in Res. 242 (XXII), called for the "withdrawal of Israeli armed forces from territories occupied in the recent conflict" and emphasised "the inadmissibility of the acquisition of territory by war." Annexation remains important only as a basis of titles to territory acquired when it was permissible. Cf. **debellatio.** *See generally* Jennings, *The Acquisition of Territory in International Law* (1963), Chap. 4.

In British constitutional law and practice, the term "annexation" is employed to connote the incorporation of territory within the dominion of the Crown, or within a particular part thereof, irrespective of its prior status. For a modern example, see the Island of Rockall Act 1982, under which, from 10 February 1972, "the Island of Rockall (of which possession was formally taken in the name of Her Majesty on 18th September 1955 in pursuance of a Royal Warrant dated 14th September 1955 addressed to the Captain of Her Majesty's Ship Vidal) shall be incorporated into that part of the United Kingdom known as Scotland and shall form part of the District of Harris in the County of Inverness, and the law of Scotland shall apply accordingly."

Antarctic Treaty 1959 *(402 U.N.T.S. 71)* This treaty was adopted after the International Geophysical Year to ensure continued freedom of scientific research and to ensure that Antarctica was used only for peaceful purposes. The treaty was signed on 1 December 1959, entered into force on 23 June 1961 and currently has 44 parties. Antarctica, defined in art. 6 as the area south of 60° South latitude, "including all ice shelves," is to be used for peaceful purposes only. "There shall be prohibited, *inter alia*, any measures of a military nature, such as the establishment of military bases and fortifications, the carrying out of military manoeuvers, as well as the testing of any type of weapons" (art. 1); also expressly prohibited are "nuclear explosions in Antarctica and the disposal there of radio-active waste material" (art. 5(1)). The treaty is without prejudice to any Contracting Party's position regarding any previously-asserted claims to territorial sovereignty in Antarctica: art. 4(1). "No acts or activities taking place while the present treaty is in force shall constitute a basis for asserting, supporting or denying a claim to territorial sovereignty in Antarctica or create any rights of sovereignty in Antarctica. No new claim, or enlargement of an existing claim, to territorial sovereignty in Antarctica shall be asserted while the present treaty is in force": art. 4(2). "Scientific personnel . . . and members of the staffs accompanying any such persons, shall be subject only to the jurisdiction of the Contracting Party of which they are nationals": art. 8(1). Each party "shall have the right to designate observers to carry out any inspection provided for by the present Article" (art. 7(1)); "[e]ach observer . . . shall have complete freedom of access at any time to any or all areas of Antarctica" (art. 7(2)), ". . . including all stations, installations and equipment within these areas, and all ships and aircraft at points of discharging or embarking cargoes or personnel in Antarctica" (art. 7(3)). Each party must inform the other parties in advance of all expeditions by its ships or nationals and all expeditions organized in its territory, and all stations occupied by its nationals: art. 7(5). Contracting Parties conducting substantial scientific activity in Antarctica attend periodic consultative meetings (art. 9(1) and (2)): there are 27 such Parties; they are referred to as Consulting Parties and have a predominant role in decision-making; there are 17 Acceding Parties.

A lacuna in this regime, relating to the environment and natural resources of Antarctica, has been remedied over the years by Agreed Measures for the Conservation of Antarctic Fauna and Flora 1964, and by four international instruments: Convention on the Conservation of Antarctic Seals of 1 June 1972 (*1080 U.N.T.S. 175*); Convention on the Conservation of Antarctic Marine Living Resources of 20 May 1980 *(19 I.L.M. 837 (1980))*; Convention on the Regulation of Antarctic Mineral Resource Activities of 2 June 1988 *(27 I.L.M. 859 (1988))*; and Protocol on Environmental Protection to the Antarctic Treaty of 4 October 1991 (*30 I.L.M. 1455 (1991)). See* Auburn, *Antarctic Law and Politics* (1982); Francioni and Scovazzi, *International Law for Antarctica* (1987); Bush, *Antarctica and International Law* (3 vols, 1982-8).

Anzilotti, Dionisio   1867-1960. Italian law professor; Assistant Secretary-General, League of Nations, 1920-2; Judge of the PCIJ 1922-39. Works include: *Teoria General della Responsabilita dello Stato nel Diritto Internazionale* (1902); *Il Diritto Internazionale dei Giudizi Interni* (1905); *Corso di Diritto Internazionale* (1st ed. 1912-5; 3rd ed. 1928, trans. into French and German).

ANZUS   An acronym for the tripartite security arrangements between Australia, New Zealand and the USA based on the security treaty between those States signed at San Francisco on 1 September 1951 *(131 U.N.T.S. 83)*. ANZUS is a collective self-defense organization modeled on **NATO**. The ANZUS Agreement pre-dated **SEATO** which, until its dissolution in 1977, deprived ANZUS of much of its defense significance. The principal difference between ANZUS and NATO lies in the obligation to render assistance in the event of aggression: in NATO the obligation is automatic, while in ANZUS the obligation is weaker. *See also* the Agreements on Mutual Defense Assistance concluded in 1951 and 1952 between the USA and respectively Australia and New Zealand *(132 U.N.T.S. 297* and *178 U.N.T.S. 315). See* generally Starke, *The ANZUS Treaty Alliance* (1965).

apartheid   This term, originally the Afrikaans name for the policy of racial segregation pursued by the Government of the Republic of South Africa, may be said to have become a term of art in treaty law by reason of its employment in the International Convention on the Elimination of All Forms of Racial Discrimination 1966 *(660 U.N.T.S. 195)* art. 3, and its elaborate definition in the International Convention on the Suppression and Punishment of the Crime of Apartheid 1973 *(1015 U.N.T.S. 243)*. In terms of the latter, art. 2, "the crime of apartheid" includes denial of life and liberty of person, deliberate imposition of living conditions calculated to cause physical destruction in whole or in part, legislative or other measures calculated to deny political, social and human rights, measures designed to segregate groups along racial lines, or exploitation or persecution for the purpose of establishing and maintaining domination by one racial group over another. Apartheid attracts international criminal liability (art. 3), though, absent its characterization as a crime against humanity, it is not subject to the jurisdiction of the **International Criminal Court**.

Applicability of Article VI, Section 22, of the Convention on the Privileges and Immunities of the United Nations   *1989 I.C.J. Rep. 177.* By resolution dated 24 May 1989, the Economic and Social Council of the United Nations requested of the ICJ an advisory opinion on "the question of the applicability of Article VI, Section 22, of the Convention on the Privileges and Immunities of the United Nations *[1 U.N.T.S. 15]* in the case of Dumitru Mazilu, *Rapporteur* of the Sub-Commission on the Prevention of Discrimination and Protection of Minorities of the Commission on Human Rights." The Sub-Commission had instructed Mazilu, a Romanian citizen, to prepare a report on "Human Rights and Youth." Romanian officials denied him a travel permit to attend the 1987 meeting of the Sub-Commission at which he was to present his report. In addition, these authorities intimated that any intervention by the UN Secretariat would be deemed interference in Romania's internal affairs. The Romanian government contended that the Convention did not consider *rapporteurs* as experts on missions for the UN; that anything more than functional immunities and privileges did not apply; that those privileges and immunities started to apply only at the point when the expert departed on a journey related to his mission; and that, in a country of which he is a national, an expert had privileges and immunities only with respect to the actual activities relating to his mission. On 15 December 1989, after deciding that it had jurisdiction, the Court *advised* (unanimously) that Art. VI, Section 22, of the Convention on the Privileges and Immunities of the United Nations was applicable to Mazilu as a special *rapporteur*. *See* also the ***Special Rapporteur Opinion***.

Applicability of the Obligation to Arbitrate under Section 21 of the United Nations Headquarters Agreement of 26 June 1947 *1988 I.C.J. Rep. 12.* By resolution dated 2 March 1988, the General Assembly requested an advisory opinion on the following question: ". . . is the United States of America, as a party to the Agreement between the United Nations and the United States of America regarding the Headquarters of the United Nations, under an obligaedtion to enter into arbitration in accordance with Section 21 of the Agreement?" The resolution had been adopted in response to the passage of the (US) Foreign Relations Authorization Act, Title X of which imposed certain restrictions on the Palestinian Liberation Organization, including a prohibition against the establishment and maintenance of PLO facilities and offices within US jurisdiction. The UN Secretary-General invoked the dispute-settlement procedures contained in Section 21 of the Agreement, asserting that the Headquarters Agreement *(11 U.N.T.S. 11)* allowed the PLO to maintain offices. The USA notified the UN that it was unwilling to participate in dispute settlement procedures because it had yet to conclude that a dispute existed between it and the UN. On 26 April 1988, after having determined that a dispute indeed existed, the Court *advised* (unanimously) that the USA was obligated under Section 21 of the UN Headquarters Agreement to permit arbitration of the dispute between itself and the UN.

applicant In proceedings in the ICJ in contentious cases, the plaintiff State is referred to as the applicant, art. 40(1) of the Court's Statute providing that proceedings are to be initiated by "written application," the term "application" and "applicant State" also being used in the Rules of Court of 1978 (art. 38(1)-(3) and (5)). Cf. **respondent**. The European Convention on Human Rights 1950 *(606 U.N.T.S. 267; E.T.S. Nos. 5 and 155)* also uses the term "applicant" to refer to an individual bringing a case against a State for an infraction of the Convention under art. 35.

Application of the Convention on the Prevention and Punishment of the Crime of Genocide (Croatia v. Yugoslavia) *See **Genocide Convention Cases***.

application of treaty, provisional Art. 25 of the Vienna Convention on the Law of Treaties 1969 provides: "1. A treaty or part of a treaty is applied provisionally pending its entry into force if: (a) the treaty itself so provides; or (b) the negotiating States have in some other manner so agreed. 2. Unless the treaty otherwise provides or the negotiating States have otherwise agreed, the provisional application of a treaty or part of a treaty with respect to a State shall be terminated if that State notifies the other States between which the treaty is being applied provisionally of its intention not to become a party to the treaty."

approval The Vienna Convention on the Law of Treaties 1969, art. 2(1)(b), defines a number of terms, including approval as "the international act so named whereby a State establishes on the international plane its consent to be bound by a treaty." "The consent of a State to be bound by a treaty is expressed by . . . approval under conditions similar to those which apply to ratification": art. 14(2). "Unless the treaty otherwise provides, instruments of . . . approval . . . establish the consent of a State to be bound by a treaty upon: (a) their exchange between the contracting States; (b) their deposit with the depositary; or (c) their notification to the contracting States or to the depositary, if so agreed": art. 16.

appurtenance   This principle links maritime territory to the land-mass of a State in such a way that neither can be acquired, or alienated, without the other. In terms of the UN Convention on the Law of the Sea 1982 (*1833 U.N.T.S. 3*), a State has rights in its **continental shelf** "throughout the natural prolongation of its land territory to the outer edge of the continental margin . . ." (art. 76(1)), and such exclusive rights "do not depend on occupation, effective or notional, or on any express proclamation." These rights are conferred because "the submarine areas concerned may be deemed to be actually part of the territory over which the coastal State already has dominion—in the sense that, although covered with water, they are a prolongation or continuation of that territory, an extension of it under the sea": ***North Sea Continental Shelf Cases*** *1969 I.C.J. Rep. 3* at 22. *See also* Judge McNair in the ***Anglo-Norwegian Fisheries Case*** *1951 I.C.J. Rep. 116* at 160: "[t]he possession of [maritime] territory is not optional, not dependent upon the will of the State, but compulsory." *See also* ***Grisbådarna Arbitration*** *(1909) 11 R.I.A.A 155.*

Arab Charter on Human Rights   The Council of the Arab League established the Arab Charter on Human Rights on 15 September 1994 (in Res. 5437; reprinted in *18 Hum. Rts. L.J. 151 (1992)*). The Charter is premised on the distinctiveness and unity of the Arab world (Preamble) and contains a fairly standard enumeration of civil and political rights, though expressed somewhat differently from global and other regional instruments, and some economic, social and cultural rights: Part II. In times of "public emergency which threatens the life of the nation," a party may derogate from many of these rights: art. 4. Emphasis is laid on **self-determination** and the condemnation of "racism, Zionism, occupation and foreign domination": art. 1, the whole of Part I. A Committee of Experts on Human Rights of 7 is established to oversee the Charter (art. 40), which fulfils its function by the scrutiny of and comment on three-yearly reports from the States party: art. 41.

Arab League   The Arab League was established by the Pact of the League of Arab States of 22 March 1945 *(70 U.N.T.S. 237)* "to draw closer the relations between member States and co-ordinate their political activities with the aim of realizing a close collaboration between them, to safeguard their independence and sovereignty, and to consider in a general way the affairs and interests of the Arab countries": art. 2. The founding members of the Arab League were: Egypt, Iraq, Lebanon, Saudi-Arabia, Syria, Transjordan (Jordan) and Yemen; Algeria, Bahrain, Comoros, Djibouti, Kuwait, Libya, Mauritania, Morocco, Oman, Palestine, Qatar, Somalia, Sudan, Tunisia and the United Arab Emirates have subsequently been admitted to membership.

A Council consisting of all the members was established with the function of "realizing the purpose of the League and of supervising the execution of the agreements concluded between the member States": art. 3. Voting in the Council is generally by majority, in which case any decision is binding only on those members that accept it (art. 7), though unanimity is required in certain instances, *e.g.*, measures to repel aggression against a member (art. 6). Committees of the Council are responsible for the major areas of the Council's responsibility; and the Arab League has established 10 specialized organizations, modeled on the UN Specialized Agencies.

Additionally, the Council is empowered, on application of disputing members, to provide arbitration and mediation facilities: art. 5. Where a member is subject to aggression or the threat thereof the Council "shall determine the necessary measures to repel this aggression": art. 6. Members are obliged to refrain from the use of force for the settlement of disputes (art. 5), and to "respect the form of government obtaining in the other States of the League . . . and not to take any action tending to change that form" (art. 8). The members are empowered to establish "among themselves, closer collaboration and stronger bonds than those provided for in the present Pact" by concluding agreements, which are not binding on other members (art. 9). The Arab League qualifies as a regional arrangement within the meaning of Chapter VIII of the UN Charter. *See* Macdonald, *The League of Arab States* (1965). *See* <www.leagueofarabstates.org>.

Aramco Arbitration *(1958) 27 I.L.R. 117.* This proceeding, properly styled *Saudi Arabia v. Arabian American Oil Co. (ARAMCO)*, arose out of a dispute as to the meaning of art. 1 of the Concession Agreement of 1933, as amended, which provided that the company had "the exclusive right . . . to explore, prospect, drill for, extract, treat, manufacture, transport, deal with, carry away and export petroleum. . . ." Aramco entered into agreements with regular purchasers whereby the purchasers could themselves transport oil from certain Arabian outlets. In 1954, the Saudi Arabian Government entered into an agreement with Aristotle Onassis to establish a private company, Saudi Arabian Maritime Tankers Co., Ltd. (SATCO), which was to transport Arabian oil. Aramco objected to SATCO tankers receiving priority in transporting oil, and invoked the arbitration provision of art. 31 of the Concession Agreement.

Held that "the agreement of the Parties [of February 1955 to submit the dispute to arbitration] does not relate to one single system of law. In so far as the Tribunal is empowered to determine the law to be applied, it will do so by resorting to the general doctrine of Private International Law"; that a concession agreement has a "double character . . .; it involves, first, a state act and, second, rights of ownership vested in the concessionaire"; that the rules of Moslem law "clearly demonstrate that the oil Concession of Aramco has a contractual character"; that "[t]he Concession Agreement is thus the fundamental law of the Parties and the Arbitration Tribunal is bound to recognize its particular importance owing to the fact that it fills a gap in the legal system of Saudi Arabia with regard to the oil industry. The Tribunal holds that the concession has the nature of a constitution which has the effect of conferring acquired rights on the Contracting Parties. By reason of its very sovereignty within its territorial domain, the State possesses the legal power to grant rights which it forbids itself to withdraw before the end of the Concession. . . ."; that it seemed "certain that no agreement between the Parties would have been reached if the concessionary Company had not been able to obtain the guarantee of an exclusive right of transportation by sea and of exportation of its oil and products with freedom to exercise its right at its discretion"; that "there is an inescapable conflict between the two Concessions [to Aramco and SATCO]"; and that "the ports of every State must be open to foreign merchant vessels and can only be closed when the vital interests of the State so require."

Arbitral Award by The King of Spain of 23 December 1906 *(Honduras v. Nicaragua) 1960 I.C.J. Rep. 192.* By virtue of an agreement reached on 21 July 1957, Honduras and Nicaragua submitted to the ICJ a dispute over the validity of an arbitral award handed down on 23 December 1906 by the King of Spain fixing part of the boundary between Honduras and Nicaragua, pursuant to a treaty between the two countries concluded on 7 October 1894 and to be in force for a period of ten years. *Held* (14 to 1) that the award was valid and binding and that Nicaragua was under an obligation to give effect to it. The Court found that (i) the requirements of the 1894 Treaty had been complied with when in October 1904 the King of Spain was designated as arbitrator; (ii) in the absence of any provision in the treaty regarding the date of its entry into force, the intention of the parties was that it should come into force on the date of exchange of ratifications (24 December 1896), even though certain provisions were to be implemented earlier, and that therefore the King of Spain's acceptance of his designation as arbitrator occurred while the treaty was in force; (iii) Nicaragua's conduct in the context of the arbitration left it no longer open to Nicaragua to rely on either of the two previous points as a ground for asserting the nullity of the award; (iv) by express declaration and by conduct Nicaragua had recognized the award as valid and it was no longer open to it to challenge the validity of the award; (v) apart from repeated acts of recognition by Nicaragua, the award would still have to be recognized as valid since the King of Spain did not exceed the authority conferred upon him, no essential error having the effect of rendering the award a nullity could be discerned, and there was no lack or inadequacy of the reasons given by the arbitrator in support of his conclusions; and (vi) there were no omissions, contradictions or obscurities in the award such as to make it incapable of execution.

arbitration Arbitration was used in the Greek city-states and was occasionally resorted to in medieval times: *see* Ralston, *International Arbitration from Athens to Locarno* (1926). The provisions in the Jay Treaty of 1794 between the US and Great Britain *(52 C.T.S. 243)* led to an increased use of arbitration internationally. Further impetus was given by the Hague Convention for the Pacific Settlement of International Disputes 1899 *(187 C.T.S. 410)*, as revised by the Convention of 1907 *(205 C.T.S. 277),* which established the **Permanent Court of Arbitration**. *See* Rosenne, *The Hague Peace Conferences of 1989 and 1907 and International Arbitration* (2001). Mixed Arbitral Tribunals were established after the First World War to deal with claims by nationals of the Allied and Associated Powers against the three Central Powers. While there has been a suggestion that resort to arbitration has declined since the mid-20th century, "states have continued to regard arbitration as an appropriate way of handling certain types of dispute": Merrills, *International Dispute Settlement* (3rd ed.), 116.

Submission to arbitration is a voluntary act on the part of a State, and may be general or *ad hoc*. The submission to arbitration, whether in a treaty or in respect of a particular dispute, is contained in a compromissory clause (or ***compromis***). *See* Carlston, *The Process of International Arbitration* (1946): Simpson and Fox, *International Arbitration: Law and Practice* (1959); Stuyt, *Survey of International Arbitrations* (1972); Wetter, *The International Arbitral Process Public and Private* (1979); Merrills, *supra*, Chap. 5.

Arbitration, Permanent Court of *See* **Permanent Court of Arbitration**.

archipelagic sea lanes Within **archipelagic waters**, an **archipelagic State** may designate sea lanes and air routes thereabove for the continuous and expeditious passage of foreign ships and aircraft: UN Convention on the Law of the Sea 1982 *(1833 U.N.T.S. 3)*, art. 53(1). Such sea lanes are to all normal routes used for international navigation or overflight (art. 53(4)). Traffic separation schemes may be established within "narrow channels" in archipelagic waters (art. 53(6)). All ships and aircraft have the right, cumbersomely referred to as archipelagic sea lane passage, to follow these sea lanes "in normal mode solely for the purpose of continuous, expeditious and unobstructed transit between one part of the high seas or exclusive economic zone and another part of the high seas or exclusive economic zone" (art. 53(3)); and the Convention further qualifies this right by requiring **innocent passage** (art. 52(1)). *See* Brown, *The International Law of the Sea* (1994), Vol. 1, 118-23; Churchill and Lowe, *The Law of the Sea* (3rd ed.), Chap. 6.

archipelagic State Part IV of the UN Convention on the Law of the Sea 1982 *(1833 U.N.T.S. 3)* which bears the cross-title "archipelagic states," defines an "archipelagic state" as "a State constituted wholly by one or more archipelagos and may include other islands," and an "archipelago" as "a group of islands, including parts of islands, interconnecting waters and other natural features which are so closely interrelated that such islands, waters and other natural features form an intrinsic geographical, economic and political entity, or which historically have been regarded as such" (art. 46). This Part of the Convention goes on to prescribe a special rule as to the drawing by an archipelagic State for the purpose of delimiting its waters of straight baselines embracing "the main islands and an area in which the ratio of . . . water to . . . land . . . is between 1 to 1 and 9 to 1" (art. 47); and to permit the designation of **archipelagic sea lanes** and air routes to be followed by foreign vessels and aircraft through or above its "**archipelagic waters**" and the adjacent territorial sea (art. 53). *See* Brown, *International Law of the Sea* (1994), Vol. 1, 106-14; Churchill and Lowe, *The Law of the Sea* (3rd ed.), Chap. 6.

archipelagic waters The waters enclosed by baselines drawn by archipelagic States in conformity with the rules promulgated by the UN Convention on the Law of the Sea 1982 *(1833 U.N.T.S. 3)*, art. 47, are archipelagic waters, subject to the sovereignty of the **archipelagic State** "regardless of their depth or distance from the coast" (art. 49(1)), but open to innocent passage by ships and aircraft (art. 52(1)) through any **archipelagic sea lanes** that might be established (art. 53). Their status, not being identical to that of the internal waters, territorial sea or international straits, is best described as *sui generis*: Brown, *International Law of the Sea* (1994), Vol. 1, 114. *See* Churchill and Lowe, *The Law of the Sea* (3rd ed.), Chap. 6.

archives, diplomatic and consular The Vienna Convention on Diplomatic Relations 1961 *(500 U.N.T.S. 95)* does not anywhere define diplomatic archives or documents. However, art. 1(1)(k) of the Vienna Convention on Consular Relations 1963 *(596 U.N.T.S. 261)* defines consular archives to include "all the papers, documents, correspondence, books, films, tapes and registers of the consular post together with the ciphers and codes, the card-indexes and any article of furniture intended for their protection or safekeeping." "In practice, this wide definition has been applied by analogy to the Vienna Diplomatic Convention, on the basis that given the wider immunities generally given to diplomatic missions, it would be absurd for a narrower construction of the term 'archives' to be applied to diplomatic archives than to consular archives": Denza, *Diplomatic Law* (2nd ed.), 162.

Art. 24 of the 1961 Convention provides that "[t]he archives and documents of the missions shall be inviolable at any time and wherever they may be." The protection required of diplomatic archives by the terms of the Vienna Convention went beyond that previously required under customary international law: "the expression 'inviolable' was deliberately chosen by the International Law Commission to convey both that the receiving must abstain from any interference through its own authorities and that it owes a duty of protection of the archives in respect of unauthorized interference by others": Denza, *supra*, 160. Art. 33 of the 1963 Convention provides that "[t]he consular archives and documents shall be inviolable at all times and wherever they may be." Article 61 of the same Convention provides further that "[t]he consular archives and documents of a consular post headed by an honorary consular officer shall be inviolable at all times and wherever they may be provided that they are kept separate from other papers and documents and, in particular, from the private correspondence of the head of a consular post and of any person working with him, and from the materials, books or documents relating to their profession or trade."

archives, State The Vienna Convention on Succession of States in Respect of State Property, Archives and Debts of 7 April 1983 *(22 I.L.M. 306 (1983))* makes detailed provision for succession, without compensation, to State archives needed for normal administration of, or relating exclusively or principally to the territory to which the succession of States relates (arts. 19 to 31). In addition, a **newly independent State** obtains title to archives which "belonged to the territory" (art. 28). Furthermore, the predecessor State is to make available material which "bears upon title to the territory" and "of interest to" or "connected with the interests of" the territory (arts. 27, 28, 30, 31). The provisions of the Convention may be displaced by agreement, but such agreements are not to infringe the right of the peoples of the States concerned to development, to information about their history and about their cultural heritage. The operation of some of these provisions may in any event be limited by art. 25 (preservation of the integral character of groups of State archives).

arcs-of-circles A method "which is constantly used for determining the position of a point or object at sea, is a new technique in so far as it is a method for delimiting the territorial sea. This technique was proposed by the United States delegation at the 1930 Conference for the codification of international law. . . . It is not obligatory by law": *Anglo-Norwegian Fisheries Case 1951 I.C.J. Rep. 116* at 129. "'T' being the breadth of the territorial sea . . . the line all the points of which are at a distance of T miles from the nearest point on the coast . . . may be obtained by means of a continuous series of arcs of circles drawn with a radius of T miles from all points on the coast line. The outer limit of the territorial sea is formed by the most seaward arcs. In the case of a rugged coast, this line, although undulating, will be less of a zigzag than if it followed all the sinuosities of the coast, because circles drawn from those points on the coast where it is most deeply indented will not usually affect the outer limit of the seaward arcs. In the case of a straight coast, or if the straight baseline method is followed, the arcs of circles method produces the same result as the strictly parallel line": Commentary on the ILC Draft Articles Concerning the Law of the Sea, art. 6 (which became art. 6 of the Geneva Convention on the Territorial Sea and the Contiguous Zone 1958 *(516 U.N.T.S. 205)* without change), *[1956] 2 I.L.C. Yearbook, 268*. As to the fact that the arcs-of-circles method was "well known long before 1930" and that it is more appropriately called the method of the **envelope line**, see Shalowitz, *Shore and Sea Boundaries* (1962), Vol. 1, 73, 171.

Arctic While some States bordering the Artic region, *e.g.*, Canada and the USSR, have at some times made **sector claims** to the region, it seems that any territorial claims to the Arctic lack validity because (a) sector claims themselves have no foundation in international law (*I Oppenheim 693*); (b) the Arctic, being merely frozen high seas, is not subject to national appropriation (UN Convention on the Law of the Sea 1982 (*1833 U.N.T.S. 3*), art. 89); and (c) the Arctic ice sheets do not have the status of islands (under the UN Convention, art. 121).

Arechaga, Eduardo Jimenez de 1918-94. Uruguayan, Professor, Montevideo, 1946-69; member, ILC 1961-69; judge, ICJ 1970-79, President 1976-79. Works include: *Introducción al Derecho* (1948); *La estipulación en favor de terceros Estados en el Derecho Internacional* (1955); *Curso de Derecho International Público* (two vols., 1959).

Argentina-Chile Frontier Case *(1966) 38 I.L.R. 10*. In 1902, an arbitration award determined certain parts of the common boundary between Argentina and Chile. The boundary in part of the sector between what were later established as Boundary Posts 16 and 17 was described as following the River Encuentro to a peak called Cerro de la Virgen. During the course of demarcating the boundary in accordance with the award, it became evident that the River Encuentro did not have its source on the slopes of Cerro de la Virgen. The dispute between the two States regarding the application of the award along that stretch of the frontier was referred to Queen Elizabeth II as arbitrator. A Court of Arbitration appointed in 1965 was asked to determine, on the proper interpretation and fulfillment of the award, the course of the boundary between Boundary Posts 16 and 17 to the extent, if any, that in that sector it had remained unsettled since the 1902 Award. *Held* by the Court of Arbitration that the geographical error in the award only affected that part of the boundary where it was impossible to apply the award on the ground, and it was to that part of the boundary that the Court must restrict its interpretation and fulfillment of the award; evidence of effective administration over the disputed areas was in principle relevant to the question of whether the boundary was or had become settled or unsettled, but was in practice inconclusive; in interpreting an arbitral award it was the arbitrator's intentions which were in question, and stricter rules in respect of the preparatory work and subsequent conduct of the parties should be applied; where an instrument lays down that a boundary must follow a river, and that river divides into two or more channels, the boundary must normally follow the major channel; the essence of the award was that the arbitrator intended to make the boundary follow the major channel of the Encuentro until it began markedly to deviate from the direction of Cerro de la Virgen, at which point the boundary must leave the river and follow a line towards Cerro de la Virgen in a manner as far as possible consistent with the general practice of the award. The Court then prescribed in detail the course of the boundary in the disputed sector.

Armed Activities on the Territory of the Congo Cases *(Democratic Republic of Congo v. Burundi, Rwanda, and Uganda) 2001 I.C.J. 3, 6.* On 23 June 1999, the Democratic Republic of Congo (DRC) instituted proceedings against Burundi, Uganda and Rwanda respectively for armed aggression committed in violation of the U.N. Charter and the Charter of the Organization of African Unity (OAU). In its application against Uganda, the DRC based jurisdiction on declarations made under art. 36(2) of the ICJ Statute. In its Application against Rwanda and Burundi, the DRC based jurisdiction on art. 36(1) of the ICJ Statute, the Torture Convention 1984 (*1465 U.N.T.S. 85*) and the Montreal Convention for the Suppression of Unlawful Acts Against the Safety of Civil Aviation 1971 (*974 U.N.T.S. 177*); and also on art. 38(5) of the Rules of Court in respect of consent to jurisdiction yet to be given. The DRC accused Ugandan, Rwandan, and Burundian troops of invading Congolese territory, and of violating, *inter alia*, Congolese sovereignty. The DRC requested the Court to adjudge and declare that Burundi, Uganda and Rwanda were guilty of acts of aggression; that they had violated and continued to violate the 1949 Geneva Conventions and their 1977 Additional Protocols; that their forcible action against the Inga hydroelectric dam and their severance of electricity had resulted in deaths in Kinshasa and surrounding areas; and the shooting down of a Congo Airlines Boeing 727 on 9 October 1998 led to the deaths of 40 civilians and violated international aviation law. The DRC also requested that the Court order the withdrawal of these troops and an award of compensation. On 19 June 2000, the DRC, in its case against Uganda, filed a request for the indication of provisional measures, stating that the resumption of fighting between the armed troops of Uganda and another foreign army had resulted in damages to the Congolese territory and population. On I July 2000, the Court (unanimously) *indicated* provisional measures against Uganda, requiring the parties to refrain from further armed action, to comply with the strictures of the UN Charter and the OAS Charter and to ensure full respect for human rights and humanitarian law in the zone of conflict: *2000 I.C.J. Rep. 111.* On 30 January 2001, the Court ordered the discontinuance of the proceedings against Rwanda and Burundi at the request of the parties. The case against Uganda remains on the Court's list.

On 28 May 2002, the DRC filed an application instituting proceedings against Rwanda for "massive, serious and flagrant violations of human rights and international humanitarian law" resulting "from acts of armed aggression . . . in flagrant violation of the sovereignty and territorial integrity of the [DRC], as guaranteed by the United Nations and OAU

Charters." The DRC sought the immediate withdrawal of Rwanda forces from its territory and the payment of its Statute as a matter of urgency. On 10 July 2002, the Court *declined* (unanimously) to indicate provisional measures as it did not have the *prima facie* jurisdiction necessary to indicate those provisional measures requested by the Congo: *2002 I.C.J. Rep. forthcoming.*

armed conflict A term which has gained currency in an attempt to avoid the technicalities attaching to the concept of **war**. "In its Judgment in the **Wimbledon Case** (1923) the [PCIJ] described the Polish-Russian War of 1920-21 as an 'armed conflict' *([P.C.I.J. Ser. A, N]o. 1,* p.28) and, in the four Geneva Conventions of 1949 for the Protection of War Victims, their scope is defined as extending to "all cases of declared war or of any other armed conflict which may arise between two or more of the High Contracting Parties, even if the state of war is not recognised by one of them" (Art. 2 of Conventions I-IV *[75 U.N.T.S. 3 et seq]*). Similarly, in the Hague Convention of 1954 on the Protection of Cultural Property in the Event of Armed Conflict, this description is employed in the title and text of the Convention (Arts. 4 and 19 *[249 U.N.T.S. 215])*": Schwarzenberger, *International Law as Applied by International Courts and Tribunals*, Vol.2, *The Law of Armed Conflict* (1968), 1-2. *See also* the **Fundamental Rules of International Humanitarian Law in Armed Conflicts**.

armed forces The Réglement respecting the Laws and Customs of War on Land annexed to the Hague Convention of 29 July 1899 *(187 C.T.S. 429)* provides that the *forces armées* or armed forces of belligerents may consist in combatants and non-combatants, both categories being entitled on capture to treatment as prisoners of war (art. 1(3)). To this extent, therefore, the expression "armed forces" may be said to be one of art; however, it is not used elsewhere in the Réglement or in the revision thereof annexed to Hague Convention Respecting the Laws and Customs of War 1907 *(205 C.T.S. 277)*, though its meaning is obvious enough. It is employed, moreover, in the 1949 Geneva Conventions, both in the titles of the First *(75 U.N.T.S. 31)* and Second *(75 U.N.T.S. 85* " Conventions (those for the amelioration of the condition of the wounded, sick, etc. "in armed forces in the field," and "of armed forces at sea"), as well as in their substantive provisions: *e.g.*, Convention I, arts. 12, 13(1), (3) ("regular armed forces") and (4); and equally in Convention III *(75 U.N.T.S. 135)* respecting prisoners of war (art. 4), and Convention IV *(75 U.N.T.S. 287)* relative to Civilian Persons (art. 3(1)). For the purposes of Protocol I of 1977 to the 1949 Geneva Conventions *(1125 U.N.T.S. 3)*, art. 43 provides: "The armed forces of a Party to a conflict consist of all organized armed forces, groups and units which are under a command responsible to that Party for the conduct of its subordinates, even if that Party is represented by a government or an authority not recognized by an adverse Party. Such armed forces shall be subject to an internal disciplinary system which, *inter alia*, shall enforce compliance with the rules of international law applicable in armed conflict."

armed neutralities Armed neutralities may no longer play any part in the laws of war. Their genesis and history are explained in *II Oppenheim 629-31* thus: "In 1780, during the war between Great Britain on the one hand, and her American colonies, France, and Spain on the other, Russia sent a circular to Great Britain, France, and Spain, in which she proclaimed the following five principles: (1) that neutral vessels should be allowed to navigate from port to port of belligerents, and along their coasts; (2) that enemy goods on neutral vessels, contraband excepted, should not be seized by belligerents; (3) that, with regard to contraband, Articles 10 and 11 of the Treaty of 1766 between Russia and Great Britain *[43 C.T.S. 365]* should be applied in all cases; (4) that a port should only be considered blockaded if the blockading belligerent had stationed vessels there, so as to create an obvious danger for neutral vessels entering the port; (5) that these principles should be applied in the proceedings and judgments on the legality of prizes. In July 1780 Russia entered into a treaty with Denmark *[47 C.T.S. 345]*, and in August 1780 with Sweden *[47 C.T.S. 356]*, for the purpose of enforcing those principles by equipping a number of men-of-war. Thus the [First] 'Armed Neutrality' made its appearance. In 1781 the Netherlands, Prussia, and Austria, in 1782 Portugal, and in 1783 the Two Sicilies joined the league. France, Spain, and the United States of America accepted its principles without formally joining. [I]n the treaties of peace the principles of the 'Armed Neutrality' were not mentioned. This league had no direct practical consequences, since Great Britain retained her former standpoint. Moreover, some of the States that had joined it acted contrary to some of the principles when they themselves went to war. . . . Nevertheless, the First Armed Neutrality has proved of great importance, because its principles furnished the basis of the Declaration of Paris of 1856 [see **Paris, Declaration of**]. But although Russia had herself acted in defiance of the principles of the First Armed Neutrality, she called a Second Armed Neutrality into existence in 1800. . . . [She] concluded treaties with Sweden, Denmark, and Prussia *[55 C.T.S. 411, 425, 427]* by which [it] became a fact. It lasted only a year on account of the assassination of the Emperor Paul of Russia on March 23, and the defeat of the Danish fleet by Nelson on April 2, 1801, in the battle of Copenhagen. Nevertheless, the Second Armed Neutrality likewise proved of importance, for it led to a compromise in the 'Maritime Convention . . . between Great Britain and Russia . . . to which Denmark and Sweden acceded *[56 C.T.S. 105]*. By Article 3 of this treaty, Great Britain recognized, as far as Russia was concerned, the rules that neutral vessels might navigate [between enemy ports] and that blockades must be effective. In the same article Great Britain forced Russia to recognize the rule that enemy goods on neutral vessels might be seized, and did not recognize the immunity of neutral vessels under convoy from visit and search. . . ."

armistice   The Regulations annexed to the Hague Convention with respect to the Laws and Customs of War by Land of 29 July 1899 *(187 C.T.S. 429)* provide (art. 36) that an armistice suspends military operations by mutual agreement between the belligerent parties. An armistice is either general or local (art. 37). It must be notified in due time to the competent authorities and to the troops (art. 38). What relations *(rapports)* are permissible between the parties and with the population of the theatre of war affected are matters of agreement (art. 39). Any serious violation by one party gives the other the right of denunciation and even of recommencement of hostilities at once in case of urgency (art. 40). But an infraction by an individual confers upon the aggrieved party only the right of demanding punishment of the offender and an indemnity (art. 41). This code of rules, repeated without change in the 1907 revision of the Convention *(205 C.T.S. 277)*, is regarded as very incomplete, by the editor of *II Oppenheim 547* "so that gaps must be filled from the old customary rules."

This work distinguishes between suspensions of arms (local and very temporary armistices), and general and partial armistices, the first of which categories is apparently included in that of local armistices by the Hague Regulations. "While this is not *necessarily* so (nor, historically, even usually so), the modern tendency is for the general (as distinct from the merely local) armistice to be used towards the end of the war, and as a step towards its termination. Indeed . . . the armistice has tended in some respects to move forward to the old place of the treaty of peace. It follows, insofar as this becomes so, that the negotiation for an armistice tends to go beyond military matters, and the negotiators usually include high personnel other than those of the armed forces": Stone, *Legal Controls of International Conflict* (2nd imp., revised), 636. In a clear reference to local and general armistices, art. 15 of the Geneva Convention on the Amelioration of the Condition of the Sick and Wounded in Armed Forces in the Field 1949 *(75 U.N.T.S. 31)* provides that, "[w]henever circumstances permit, an armistice or suspension of fire shall be arranged . . . to permit the removal, exchange and transport of the wounded left on the battlefield."

arms and flags, national Art. 20 of the Vienna Convention on Diplomatic Relations 1961 *(500 U.N.T.S. 95)* stipulates that a diplomatic mission and its head "shall have the right to use the flag and emblem of the sending State on the premises of the mission including the residence . . . and on his means of transport." Art. 29 of the Vienna Convention on Consular Relations 1963 *(596 U.N.T.S. 261)* similarly provides that "[t]he sending State shall have the right to the use of its national flag and coat-of-arms . . . on the building occupied by the consular post and at the entrance door thereof, on the residence of the head of the . . . post and on his means of transport when used on official business," regard being had in the exercise of this right "to the laws, regulations and usages of the receiving State."

arms control, limitation *See* **disarmament**.

Armstrong Cork Company Case *(US v. Italy) (1953) 14 R.I.A.A. 159.* In 1940, the Armstrong Cork Company, incorporated in the USA, purchased a quantity of cork in Algeria. The cork was consigned to the claimants and placed on board an Italian ship, the *Maria*, bound for New York. On 6 June 1940, the Italian Government, in contemplation of war, published an Order recalling to Italian ports all Italian merchant ships. The *Maria* accordingly diverted to Naples where it arrived on 9 June 1940. The cork was unloaded and placed in the shipping company's store. In 1941, the Italian Ministry of Foreign Trade gave the shipping company authority to sell the cork and to use the proceeds to meet storage and other charges. The claimant company sought compensation under art. 78(4) of the 1947 Peace Treaty with Italy *(49 U.N.T.S. 126)*, which concerned situations where, as a result of the war, property in Italy had been injured or damaged. *Held* by the Italian-US Conciliation Commission that the claim was without basis in art. 78(4) of the Treaty of Peace since the act attributable to the Italian Government (namely the Order of 6 June 1940) preceded the declaration of war on 10 June 1940 and, after war was declared, no measure was taken with regard to the cork which could be considered in international law a war measure. In subsequent proceedings in 1957 the claimant company obtained compensation from the US Foreign Claims Settlement Commission *(26 I.L.R. 685)*.

arrangement A term usually denoting an international instrument of a less formal kind, often used for instruments recording technical, practical matters. While frequently adopted for instruments which do not establish legal rights and obligations (*e.g.*, often in the form of a "Memorandum of Arrangements"), this is essentially a matter to be determined in the light of the parties' intentions which may, in particular circumstances, treat "arrangement" as equivalent to "treaty" or "agreement."

Arrest Warrant Case *(Democratic Republic of the Congo v. Belgium) 2002 I.C.J. Rep. 3.* On 17 October 2000, the Democratic Republic of Congo (DRC) instituted proceedings against Belgium regarding an international arrest warrant issued on 11 April 2000 by a Belgian judge against Abdoulaye Yerodia Ndombasi, the DRC's Minister of Foreign Affairs. The arrest warrant sought Ndombasi's detention and extradition to Belgium as a result of his alleged violations of international humanitarian law. The DRC based the Court's jurisdiction on the fact that "Belgium has accepted the Court's jurisdiction and [that], to the extent necessary, the present Application signifies acceptance of that jurisdiction by the Democratic Republic of Congo." The DRC claimed that Belgium violated its sovereignty and that the arrest warrant violated international law pertaining to diplomatic immunity. In addition, the DRC filed a request for the indication of a provisional measure to withdraw the arrest warrant.

On 14 February 2002, the Court *held* (a) (15 to1) that Belgium's objections to jurisdiction, mootness, and admissibility be rejected; (b) (15 to1) that it had jurisdiction to adjudicate the DRC's application; (c) (15 to1) that the DRC's application was not without object and the case was not moot; (d) (15 to1) that the DRC's application was admissible; (e) (13 to 3) that international arrest warrant violated the diplomatic immunity of Abdoulaye Yerodia Ndombasi; and (f) (10 to 6) that Belgium must withdraw the arrest warrant and accordingly notify the States that received the warrant.

arret de prince "Another kind of *embargo* is the so-called *arret de prince*—that is, detention of foreign ships to prevent the spread of news of political importance": *II Oppenheim 142.*

artificial islands, installations and structures Art. 60 of the UN Convention on the Law of the Sea 1982 (*1833 U.N.T.S. 3*) provides that "[i]n the **exclusive economic zone**, the coastal State shall have the exclusive right to construct and to authorize and regulate the construction, operation and use of: (a) artificial islands; (b) installations and structures for the purposes provided for in article 56 [viz. "exploring and exploiting, conserving and managing the natural resources, whether living or non-living, of the waters superjacent to the sea-bed and of the sea-bed and its subsoil, and . . . other activities for the economic exploitation and exploration of the zone, such as the production of energy from the water, currents and winds"]; (c) installations and structures which may interfere with the exercise of the rights of the coastal State in the zone." While the coastal State must not establish artificial islands, installations, and structures, so as to cause interference with recognized sea lanes essential to international navigation (art. 60(7)), and must give due notice of their construction and maintain a permanent means for giving warning of their presence (art. 60(3)), the coastal State has exclusive jurisdiction over such artificial islands, installations and structures (art. 60(2)), and may establish "reasonable" **safety zones** around them (art. 60(4)). Artificial islands, installations and structures do not have the status as **islands** and do not generate a territorial sea or affect the baselines for measuring maritime zones (art. 60(8)). Abandoned or disused artificial islands, installations and structures must be removed to ensure safety of navigation in light of generally accepted international standards (art. 60(3)). Artificial islands, not being functionally qualified like installations and structures, could be established as, *e.g.*, deep-water ports or offshore airports. See Churchill and Lowe, *The Law of the Sea* (3rd ed.), 167-8; Brown, *International Law of the Sea* (1994), Vol. 1, 259-61.

ASEAN An acronym for the Association of South-East Asian Nations, ASEAN was established from earlier associations in the region by the Bangkok Declaration of 8 August 1967, subscribed to by Indonesia, Malaysia, the Philippines, Singapore and Thailand (*6 I.L.M. 1233 (1967)*). Subsequent members are Brunei, Cambodia, Myanmar, Laos and Vietnam. The aims of ASEAN are to accelerate the economic growth, social progress and cultural development in the region through joint endeavors in the spirit of equality and partnership in order to strengthen the foundation for a prosperous and peaceful community of Southeast Asian nations, and to promote regional peace and stability through abiding respect for justice and the rule of law in the relationship among countries in the region and adherence to the principles of the United Nations Charter. Additional substance was given to these objectives by the Treaty of Amity and Cooperation in South-East Asia of 24 February 1976 (*1025 U.N.T.S. 297*). Since 1996, ASEAN has operated through 6 Plans of Action, on Social Development, on Culture and Information, on Science and Technology, on the Environment, on Drug Abuse Control, and on Combating Transnational Crime.

The ASEAN machinery is constituted by an annual meetings of Heads of State and Government, referred to as summits, annual meetings of Foreign Ministers, and sectoral ministerial meetings. Decisions are made on the basis of unanimity and consensus. Supporting these ministerial bodies are 29 committees of senior officials and 122 technical working groups. A full-time Secretary-General was provided for by the Agreement of Establishment of the Permanent Secretary of ASEAN 1976 *(1331 U.N.T.S. 243)* and this official's functions have been extended to all summits and ministerial meetings, replacing the role formerly undertaken by national secretariats. *See* Jorgensen-Dahl, *Regional Organisation and Order in SE Asia* (1982); Broinswski, *Understanding ASEAN* (1982). *See* <www.aseansec.org>.

ASIL *See* **American Society of International Law**.

Asphyxiating Gases, Declaration respecting the Prohibition of the Use of Projectiles diffusing The second declaration adopted by the Hague Peace Conference of 1899 *(187 C.T.S. 45)*, and still in force, prohibits the use of "projectiles the sole object of which is the diffusion of asphyxiating or deleterious gases" in any "war" between the parties.

Asphyxiating, Poisonous or other Gases, etc., Protocol Prohibiting the Use in War of This instrument, the so-called Geneva Gas Protocol of 15 June 1925 *(94 L.N.T.S. 65)*, adding to the **Asphyxiating Gases, Declaration** etc. and other conventional provisions on the employment of gases to which the majority of Powers were party, declared that the parties "so far as they are not already Parties to Treaties prohibiting such use, accept this prohibition, agree to extend this prohibition to the use of bacteriological methods of warfare and agree to be bound as between themselves according to the terms of this declaration." The principal earlier treaty provisions would seem to be those of the Treaty of Versailles, art. 171 *(225 C.T.S. 188)*, and the corresponding articles of the other Peace Treaties of 1919. *See also* **bacteriological methods of warfare**; **chemical weapons**; **disarmament**; **poison**; **prohibited weapons**.

assessors Art. 30(2) of the ICJ Statute states that "[t]he Rules of Court may provide for assessors to sit with the Court, or with any of the Chambers, without the right to vote." Rule 9(1) of the Rules of Court 1978 provides that the Court may "either *proprio motu* or upon a request made not later than the closure of the written proceedings, decide, for the purpose of a contentious case or request for advisory opinion, to appoint assessors to sit with it without the right to vote." Assessors are to be appointed by a majority of the votes of the Court's, or Chamber's, judges: Rule 9(3) and (4). The last time an assessor was appointed was in 1922 before the Permanent Court of International Justice.

associate member(s), membership A number of international organizations provide in their constitutions for a form of membership by entities which do not meet the conditions of full membership, referred to as associate membership. "An alternative to full membership [of an international organization] is provided for in some organisations, which permit certain entities not meeting the conditions for membership to become associate members. In several specialised agencies, 'territories or groups of territories which are not responsible for the conduct of their international relations' may be admitted as associate members upon application by the state or other authority having responsibility for these relations. . . . Not unnaturally, such associate membership does not confer quite the same rights as full membership": Sands and Klein, *Bowett's Law of International Institutions* (5th ed), 536-7. For example, art. 8 of the **WHO** Constitution *(14 U.N.T.S. 186)* provides: "Territories or groups of territories which are not responsible for the conduct of their international relations may be admitted as Associate Members by the Health Assembly upon application made on behalf of such territory or group of territories by the Member or other authority having responsibility for their international relations. . . . The nature and extent of the rights and obligations of Associate Members shall be determined by the Health Assembly." The rights accorded associate members are usually specified in the organization's constitution, but they may be set out in a separate resolution. Typically, associate members are permitted to vote in the plenary organ, but cannot stand for, or vote in, the executive organ. The UN Charter makes no provision for associate membership, but the General Assembly does grant **observer status**.

associated instruments In treaty law, it is not uncommon for agreements to be made at the time, or soon after, the conclusion of the principal agreement, referred to as associated instruments. In terms of the Vienna Convention on the Law of Treaties 1969, such instruments, referred to in that article as "relating to" (art. 32(2)(a)) or "made . . . in connection with" (art. 31(2)(b)), the term "associated" not being employed, are part of the "context" within which the treaty is to be interpreted (art. 32(1)). *See* the *Ambatielos Case (Preliminary Objections) 1952 I.C.J. Rep. 28. See also* Aust, *Modern Treaty Law and Practice* (2000), 189-91.

associated State(s) Free association with an existing State being one of the possible outcomes of the exercise by **non-self-governing territories** of the right of **self-determination** (*see* Principle 7 of the **Friendly Relations Declaration** of 24 October 1970 (Res. 2625 (XXV)), there has been some question of the international status of territories in free association. Crawford, *The Creation of States in International Law* (1979), 376, postulates five criteria for associated State if it is to be recognized by the UN: free choice by the inhabitants; clear and in legally-binding terms of association; substantial internal self-government for the associated territory; limited reserved powers for the State accepting the association; a procedure for terminating the association. Crawford concludes that associated territories "are clearly not independent States, but equally they are not for international purposes merely part of the metropolitan State."

astronauts Without defining the term, art. 5 of the Treaty on Principles Governing the Activities of States in the Exploration and Use of **Outer Space** 1967 *(610 U.N.T.S. 205)* provides that the parties shall "regard astronauts as envoys of mankind in outer space and shall render to them all possible assistance in the event of accident, distress, or emergency landing on the territory of another State Party or on the high seas. When astronauts make such a landing, they shall be safely and promptly returned to the State of registry of their space vehicle." The Agreement on the **Rescue and Return** of Astronauts, etc. 1968 *(672 U.N.T.S. 119)* expands upon these provisions.

Asylum Cases (Colombia/Peru) 1950 I.C.J. Rep. 266. In the *Asylum Case,* in which the ICJ acquired jurisdiction by the so-called Act of Lima of 31 August 1949 between the parties, the claimant state, in whose embassy at Lima Sr. Haya de la Torre, one of the leaders of an unsuccessful rebellion in Peru, had been granted asylum when sought on a criminal charge, asked the Court to rule that it, as the State granting asylum, was competent to qualify the offence charged for this purpose by virtue both of treaty and of "American international law in general," or "regional or local custom peculiar to Latin-American states." Finding the relevant treaties (the Bolivian Convention on Extradition of 18 July 1911 (*214 C.T.S. 129*) and the Havana Convention on Asylum of 20 February 1928 *(22 A.J.I.L. Supp. 158 (1928))*, in effect simply to refer to or re-state customary law, and laying it down that "the Party which relies on a custom of this kind must prove that [it] is established in such a manner that it has become binding on the other Party . . . [i.e.] that the rule evoked . . . is in accordance with a constant and uniform usage practiced by the States in question" and accepted as law, the Court *held* (9 to 6) that this burden of proof had not been discharged, the evidence adduced disclosing uncertainty and confusion in the matter. The Court's description of custom quoted above, though given in relation to local custom, has been accepted by many writers as applicable to general custom also: *I Oppenheim 30. See also **US Nationals in Morocco Case** 1952 I.C.J. Rep. 176* at 200.

Immediately upon the delivery of the judgment, the Government of Colombia requested an interpretation of it on the ground that it was impossible to execute the judgment because of gaps in it. This request was *declared* (12 to 0) to be inadmissible: *1950 I.C.J. Rep. 399*. In the *Haya de la Torre Case 1951 I.C.J. Rep. 82*, the Court *held* (14 to 0) that it could not accede to the request of the parties that it should determine how effect was to be given to the earlier judgment; that (13 to 1) Colombia was under no obligation to surrender Sr. Haya de la Torre; but that (14 to 0) his asylum ought to have ceased after the delivery of the earlier judgment and should terminate.

asylum seekers A term in popular parlance, usually used pejoratively, to denote those seeking status as **refugees**.

asylum, diplomatic "A right to give asylum in diplomatic missions to refugees from the authorities of the receiving State has often been claimed, but it has not always been accepted and there is as yet no universal agreement among [S]tates on the circumstances in which the right may be exercised. . . . Among Latin-American countries, a right of diplomatic asylum has as a matter of local usage been very generally accepted. [see *Asylum Cases*]. . . . In general, however, diplomatic asylum is regarded as a matter of humanitarian practice rather than a legal right . . .": *Satow's Diplomatic Practice* (5th ed.), 274.

asylum, so-called right of "The fact that every State exercises territorial supremacy over all persons on its territory, whether they are its nationals or aliens, excludes the exercise of the power of foreign States over [their] nationals in the territory of another State. Thus a foreign State is, provisionally at least, an asylum for every individual who, being prosecuted at home, crosses its frontier. In the absence of treaties stipulating to the contrary, no State is by International Law obliged to refuse admission into its territory to such a fugitive or, in case he has been admitted, to expel him or deliver him up to the prosecuting State. On the contrary, States have always upheld their competence to grant asylum, if they choose to do so. Since there is now an extensive network of extradition treaties, which generally allow for extradition to be refused where a fugitive's return is sought for an offence of a political character, the effectiveness in practice of a grant of political asylum is closely related to the principle of non-extradition of political offenders The so-called right of asylum is not a right possessed by the alien to demand that the State into whose territory he has entered should grant protection and asylum. For such State need not grant such demands. The Constitutions of a number of countries expressly grant the right of asylum to persons prosecuted for political reasons, but it cannot yet be said that such a right has become a 'general principle of law' recognized by civilized States and as such forming part of International Law. Neither is any such right conferred by Article 14 of the Universal Declaration of Human Rights, which lays down that 'everyone has the right to *seek* and to *enjoy* in other countries asylum from persecution.' The Declaration, which in any case is not a legally binding instrument, does not confer a right to *receive* asylum. . . . At present it is probable that the so-called right of asylum is nothing but the competence of every State to allow a prosecuted alien to enter, and to remain on, its territory under its protection Such fugitive alien enjoys the hospitality of the state which grants him asylum; but it might be necessary to make his entry subject to conditions, to place him under surveillance, or even to intern him at some place. For it is the duty of every State to prevent individuals living on its territory from endangering the safety of another State by organising a hostile expeditions or by preparing common crimes against its Head, members of its government or its property": *I Oppenheim 901-3.*

Art. 3(1) of the Declaration on Territorial Asylum of 14 December 1967 (G.A. Res. 2312 (XXII)) provides that no person entitled to invoke art. 14 of the Universal Declaration "shall be subjected to measures such as rejection at the frontier or, if he has already entered the territory in which he seeks asylum, expulsion or compulsory return to any State where he may be subjected to persecution." However, the provisions of the UN Convention relating to the Status of Refugees 1951 *(189 U.N.T.S. 137)* that unauthorized entry of refugees shall not be penalized by States (art. 31) and that in general refugees shall not be expelled or returned if their lives or freedom would thereby be threatened (art. 33), made prospective as well as retrospective by the Additional Protocol of 1967 *(606 U.N.T.S. 267),* go some way towards securing a true individual right of asylum, but establish no right of entry.

Atlantic Charter   A joint declaration of the President of the United States of America and Prime Minister Churchill, dated 14 August 1941, "mak[ing] known certain common principles in the national policies of their respective countries on which they based their hopes for a better future for the world": text in *35 A.J.I.L. Supp. 191 (1941).* This short and elegant instrument declared that the parties sought no territorial aggrandizement and asserted the **self-determination** of peoples, free trade and economic co-operation, freedom of navigation on the high seas, the renunciation of the **use of force** and future assurances against force. While included in the League of Nations Treaty Series (as *204 L.N.T.S. 381),* the Charter is generally accepted as having established political and moral, rather than legal, principles: *I Oppenheim* 1190 and associated footnote; *see also* Stone, *The Atlantic Charter* (1943), 144-8. In the **Declaration by United Nations** of 1 January 1942, 26 States formally endorsed the purposes and principles of the Atlantic Charter.

Atomic Energy Agency, International   *See* **International Atomic Energy Agency.**

Atomic Energy Commission (UN)   A Commission consisting of the States represented on the Security Council and Canada (when not so represented) set up by the General Assembly on 24 January 1946 (GA Res. 1(I)) "to deal with the problems raised by the discovery of atomic energy and other related matters." The Commission, along with a related Commission on Conventional Armaments, was merged into the Disarmament Commission by SC Res. 502 (VI) of 11 January 1952. *See* **disarmament.**

attaché   An *attaché* is a person attached to a diplomatic mission in a subordinate capacity, being commonly, though not invariably, not a member of the diplomatic service of the sending State, but, *e.g.,* a military, naval or air force officer or a home civil servant appointed as military, etc. or commercial *attaché.* An *attaché* is a member of the diplomatic staff of a mission within the sense of the Vienna Convention on Diplomatic Relations 1961 *(500 U.N.T.S. 95),* art. 7 whereof providing that "[i]n the case of military, naval or air attachés, the receiving State may require their names to be submitted beforehand, for its approval."

attentat **clause**   "The first attempt [to limit the **political offence** exception to extradition] was the enactment of the so-called *attentat* clause, to the effect that murder of the Head of a foreign Government or of a member of his family, should not be considered as a political crime. Although the *attentat* clause originated in Belgium in 1856, it has since been widely adopted": *I Oppenheim 969.* The clause, the name of which is derived from the French word *attentat,* meaning criminal attempt or outrage, is to be found in many extradition treaties as well as laws; *see, e.g.,* the European Convention on Extradition 1957 *(359 U.N.T.S. 273),* art. 3(3). *See* Harvard Research, Draft Convention on Extradition *(29 A.J.I.L. Supp. 114-7 (1935)).* The Convention on the Prevention and Punishment of Crimes against Internationally Protected Persons, including Diplomatic Agents of 14 December 1973 *(1035 U.N.T.S. 167),* designed to protect, *inter alios,* heads of government and their families, does not contain an *attentat* clause, thereby permitting the political offence exception to apply to any request for extradition.

attribution Attribution, or as it was more frequently referred to in the past imputation, is a term of art in the law of **State responsibility**, denoting "an intellectual operation necessary to bridge the gap between the individual or a group of individuals [who perpetrated an unlawful act under international law] and the attribution of the breach of an obligation and responsibility to the State": Amerasinghe, *State Responsibility for Injuries to Aliens* (1967), 49. While there is no difficulty in attributing an unlawful act to a State where that act is perpetrated by the organs of the State (executive, legislative and judicial central authorities, and local authorities), problems may arise where the act is perpetrated by State officials acting *ultra vires* or by private individuals. The decided case law appears to establish that the State is liable for the unlawful acts of its officials who exceed their competence where they act with apparent or manifest authority *(**Youmans Claim** (1926) 4 R.I.A.A. 110; **Mallen Claim** (1927) 4 R.I.A.A. 173; **Caire Claim** (1929) 5 R.I.A.A. 516; **Zafiro Claim** (1925) 6 R.I.A.A. 160).* The State is not liable for the unlawful acts of private individuals unless it encourages, connives in, or benefits from, the act, or fails to take reasonable measures to protect aliens, or clearly fails to punish the wrongdoers. *(**U.S. Diplomatic and Consular Staff Case** 1979 I.C.J. Rep. 21, 1980 I.C.J. Rep. 3 ("students"); **Massey Claim** (1927) 4 R.I.A.A. 155; **Neer Claim** (1926) 4 R.I.A.A. 60; **Janes' Claim** (1926) 4 R.I.A.A. 82; **Home Missionary Society Claim** (1920) 6 R.I.A.A. 42; Mazzei Claim (1903) 10 R.I.A.A. 525).*

The ILC's Draft Articles on State Responsibility 2001 *(UN Doc. A/56/10 Chap. IV.E.1)* make a State liable for the conduct of any State organ, "whether the organ exercises legislative, executive, judicial or any other functions, whatever position it hold in the organization of the State, and whatever its character as an organ of the central government or of a territorial unit of the State": art. 4(1). Liability also attaches to the State for the conduct of a person or entity empowered by internal law to exercise governmental authority: art. 5. It does not matter that a State organ or an empowered person or authority acts *ultra vires*: art. 7. Liability is attributed to the State for acts of individuals "acting on the instructions of, or under the direction or control of, that State" (art. 8); and for individuals "in fact exercising elements of governmental authority in the absence or default of the official authorities and in circumstances such as to call for the exercise of those elements of authority" (art. 9).

See generally Borchard, *The Diplomatic Protection of Citizens Abroad* (1927); Eagleton, *The Responsibility of States in International Law* (1928); Spinedi and Simma, *United Nations Codification and State Responsibility* (1987); Brownlie, *System of the Law of Nations: State Responsibility* (Part 1, 1983); Crawford, *The International Law Commission's Articles on State Responsibility* (2002), Chap. 2.

Austro-German Customs Union Case *(1931) P.C.I.J. Ser. A/B, No. 41.* The Treaty of Peace with Austria signed at St. Germain on 10 September 1919 *(226 C.T.S. 8),* art. 88, contained an undertaking by Austria "to abstain from any act which might . . . compromise her independence"; and Austria further undertook by Protocol No. 1 for the Restoration of

Austria of 4 October 1922 *(12 L.N.T.S. 386)* "in accordance with the terms of Article 88 of the Treaty of St. Germain . . . to . . . abstain from any negotiations or from any economic or financial engagement calculated directly or indirectly to compromise [her] independence." Upon the conclusion of a Protocol between Austria and Germany providing for negotiations "for a treaty to assimilate the tariff and economic policies" of the two countries, the Council of the League of Nations requested of the PCIJ an advisory opinion on the question: "Would a régime established between Germany and Austria on the basis and within the limits of the principles laid down in [this] Protocol . . . be compatible with Article 88 of the Treaty . . . and with . . . Protocol No.1 . . .?" The Court on 5 September 1931 *advised* (8 to 7) that the régime contemplated would not be compatible with Protocol No. 1 of 1922 because "considered as a whole from the economic standpoint adopted by the . . . Protocol of 1922, it is difficult to maintain that this régime is not calculated to threaten the economic independence of Austria." Six of the judges concurring in this opinion declared further that the projected régime, "since it would be calculated to threaten the independence of Austria in the economic sphere, would constitute an act capable of endangering the independence of that country and would, accordingly, be . . . also and in itself incompatible with Article 88 of the Treaty of St. Germain." Judge Anzilotti, while agreeing with the majority, delivered a powerful individual opinion in which he stated: "It also follows that the restrictions upon a State's liberty, whether arising out of ordinary international law or contractual engagements, do not as such in the least affect its independence. As long as these restrictions do not place the State under the legal authority of another State, the former remains an independent State however extensive and burdensome those obligations may be." The dissenters perceived the proposed customs union as an "assimilation" rather than a "fusion," and therefore not incompatible with Austria's conventional obligation of independence.

aut dedere aut judicare "Several multilateral treaties dealing with offences evoking the general condemnation of the international community have adopted the practice of obliging parties either to extradite persons found on their territory but wanted for trial by another party, or to try such persons themselves": *1 Oppenheim 953.* This conventional principle, which cannot yet be said to be part of customary law, is found in a number of international conventions: for example, the **Genocide Convention** 1948, art. 7 *(78 U.N.T.S. 277)*; the 4 Geneva Conventions on international humanitarian law 1949 (Convention for the Amelioration of the Condition of Wounded and Sick in Armed Forces in the Field, art. 49 *(75 U.N.T.S. 31)*; Convention for the Amelioration of the Wounded, Sick and Shipwrecked Members of the Armed Forces at Sea, art. 50 *(75 U.N.T.S. 85)*; Convention Relative to the Treatment of Prisoners of War, art. 129 *(75 U.N.T.S. 135)*; Convention Relative to the Protection of Civilian Persons in Time of War, art. 146 *(75 U.N.T.S. 287)*) and the 1977 Protocol Relating to the Protection of Victims of International Armed Conflict, art. 88 *(1125 U.N.T.S. 30)*; **Torture Convention** 1984, art. 7 *(1465 U.N.T.S. 85)*; Single Convention on Narcotic Drugs 1961, art. 36 *(520 U.N.T.S. 521, 976 U.N.T.S. 3)*; Convention on Psychotropic Substances 1971, art. 22 *(1019 U.N.T.S. 175)*. The principle is central to international **terrorism** conventions, where its classic formulation appears. Thus, the Montreal Convention for the Suppression of Unlawful Acts Against the Safety of Civil Aviation 1971 *(974 U.N.T.S.177)* states, in art. 7: "The Contracting State in the territory of which the alleged offender is found shall, if it doers not extradite him, be obliged, without exception whatsoever and whether or not the offence was committed in its territory, to submit the case to its competent authorities for the purpose of prosecution." *See* Bassiouni and Wise, *Aut Dedere Aut Judicare* (1995).

authentication Art. 10 of the Vienna Convention on the Law of Treaties 1969 provides: "The text of a treaty is established as authentic and definitive: (a) by such procedure as may be provided for in the text or agreed upon by the States participating in its drawing up; or (b) failing such procedure, by the signature, signature *ad referendum* or initialing by the representatives of those States of the text of the treaty or of the Final Act of a conference incorporating the text." Art. 79 of the Convention prescribes a detailed procedure to be followed for the correction of any error found "after the authentication of the text of a treaty," and art. 33 a special régime for the "interpretation of treaties authenticated in two or more languages" which includes the rule that "[a] version of the treaty in a language other than one of those in which the text was authenticated shall be considered an authentic text only if the treaty so provides or the parties so agree." Art. 85, titled "Authentic Texts," states the languages whose text of the Vienna Convention is "equally authentic."

automatic reservation The term automatic is applied to a reservation to declarations under the **Optional Clause** of art. 36(2) of the ICJ Statute which purports to exclude acceptance of the jurisdiction of the Court in respect of matters determined solely by the reserving state. The best-known example is the so-called Connally Amendment to the United States Declaration of 14 August 1946 *(1 U.N.T.S. 9)*, withdrawn *in toto* in 1986, providing for its non-application to "[d]isputes with regard to matters which are essentially within the domestic jurisdiction of the United States of America as determined by the United States of America." The invalidity of these self-judging reservations has been argued, especially by Judge Lauterpacht in the ***Norwegian Loans Case** 1957 I.C.J. Rep. 9* at 43-66 and the ***Interhandel Case** 1959 I.C.J. Rep. 6* at 77-8. *See also* the ***Nuclear Tests Case** 1974 I.C.J. Rep. 253*. In practice, the ICJ has tended to circumvent the issue of the validity of an automatic reservation, despite the fact that they appear to contravene art. 36(6) of the Court's Statute empowering it to determine its own jurisdiction. *See* Rosenne, *Law and Practice of the International Court* (1985), Vol. 1, 395-9.

autonomy While "autonomy" is not strictly a term of art under international law, it is widely used in the literature of international law. A typical definition would be that of Crawford, *The Creation of States in International Law* (1979), 211-2: "Autonomous areas are regions of a State, usually possessing some ethnic or cultural distinctiveness, which have been granted separate powers of internal administration, to whatever degree, without being detached from the State of which they are part. For such status to be of present interest, it must be in some way internationally binding upon the central authorities. Given such guarantees, the local entity may have a certain status, although since that does not normally involve any foreign relations capacity, it is necessarily limited. Until a very advanced stage is reached in the progress towards self-government, such areas are not States." The hallmark of autonomous régimes is their "extreme diversity . . . and the wide variations exhibited in the degree of autonomy or internal self-government each one enjoys"; the "growing demands for regional self-government, the proliferation of small, newly independent states, and the increasingly complex interdependence of contemporary world politics no longer correspond to the sovereign nation-state simplicity of the nineteenth century. Autonomy remains a useful, if imprecise, concept within which flexible and unique political structures may be developed to respond to that complexity": Hannum and Lillich, The Concept of Autonomy in International Law, *74 A.J.I.L. 858 at 889 (1980)*.

While the Declaration on the Granting of Independence to Colonial Countries and Peoples of 14 December 1960 (GA Res. 1514 (XV)), para. 2, and common art. 1(1) of the International Covenants on Civil and Political Rights *(999 U.N.T.S. 171)* and on Economic, Social and Cultural Rights *(993 U.N.T.S. 3)* of 1966 affirm the right of **self-determination**, they do not specify the outcome of the exercise of that right; the **Friendly Relations Dec-**

laration of 24 October 1970 (GA Res. 1625 (XXV)) stipulates three possible outcomes, the final being "any . . . political status freely determined by a people," presaging some measure of autonomy. *See* Hannum, *Autonomy, Sovereignty and Self-Determination* (1990).

Avena Case (Provisional Measures) *(Mexico v. USA) 2003 I.C.J. Rep. forthcoming.* On 9 January 2003, Mexico instituted proceedings in the ICJ against the United States in respect of 54 Mexican nationals, among them Avena, all then on death row in the US. Mexico contended that the Court had jurisdiction by virtue of art. 1 of the Court's Statute and art. 1 of Protocol I to the Vienna Convention of Consular Relations 1963 *(596 U.N.T.S. 261)*; and requested a declaration that the named Mexican nationals had not been informed of their right to consular representation under art. 36(1)(b) of the Convention. Mexico having also requested the Court to indicate provisional measures under art. 41(1) of its Statute, on 5 February 2003 the Court, citing the ***LeGrand Case***, *indicated* (unanimously) that, pending the determination of the case, the US should not execute 3 named Mexican nationals, due for early execution. *See* the ***Consular Convention Cases***.

avulsion "A distinction is drawn between accretion and avulsion, the former being the slow and gradual deposit of soil by alluvion so as to modify a river channel imperceptibly, the latter being a sudden and violent shift in the channel so as to leave the old riverbed dry. The public law principles which have been applied distinguish between these two events, allowing the modification of boundary as a result of gradual shift in the *thalweg*, fixing the boundary in the old *thalweg* when the river suddenly alters course. The case of *Louisiana v. Mississippi [282 U.S. 458 (1931)]* illustrates both processes": O'Connell, *International Law* (1965), Vol. 1, 47. *See **Chamizal Arbitration (1911) 11 R.I.A.A. 316**. See also* **accretion**, *thalweg*.

award This term is used to connote the decision of an arbitral tribunal. "An arbitral award is binding, but not necessarily final. For it may be open to the parties to take further proceedings to interpret, revise, rectify, appeal from or nullify the decision. Whether such steps are permissible . . . depends partly on general international law, but mainly on the terms of the arbitration agreement": Merrills, *International Dispute Settlement* (3rd ed.), 105.

axis of evil In his State of the Union address on 29 January 2002, President George W. Bush described Iran, Iraq and North Korea "and their terrorist allies" as an axis of evil which posed a grave and growing danger. He stated that he would "work closely with our coalition allies to deny terrorists and their state sponsors the materials, technology, and expertise to make and deliver weapons of mass destruction." Subsequently, Cuba, Libya and Syria were described as "beyond the axis of evil." The US State Department maintains a list of terror-sponsoring States, which adds Sudan to those States in and beyond the axis of evil. *See also* **Bush doctrine**.

Ayala, Balthasar 1548-1584; Judge-Advocate of the Spanish armies in the Netherlands; one of the early writers on international law, who attacked the doctrine that war knows no law, and argued in favor of *jus naturale* and a *jus gentium* established by common consent. Principal work: *De Jure et officiis Bellicis* (1582; text and translation in *Classics of International Law* No. 2 (1912)).

B

bacteriological methods of warfare This phrase was apparently first used in the Geneva Protocol for the Prohibition of the Use of Asphyxiating, Poisonous or Other Gases, and of Bacteriological Methods of Warfare of 17 June 1925 *(94 L.N.T.S. 65)*, which embodies a declaration extending the prohibition of the uses of gases, etc. in warfare "to the use of bacteriological methods of warfare." The Convention on the Prohibition of the Development, Production, and Stockpiling of Bacteriological (Biological) and Toxin Weapons and their Destruction of 10 April 1972 *(1015 U.N.T.S. 163)* prohibits the development, production and stockpiling of bacteriological weapons. While not explicitly regulating their use in warfare, this Convention obviously impacts on how armed conflicts can be conducted. *See also* **Chemical Weapons Convention**; **weapons of mass destruction**.

Baghdad Pact The Pact of Mutual Cooperation between Iraq and Turkey, concluded on 24 February 1955 *(233 U.N.T.S. 199)*, acceded to by the United Kingdom, Pakistan and Iran on 5 April, 23 September and 3 November 1955 respectively, providing for mutual security and defense consistently with art. 51 of the UN Charter (art. 1), and for the establishment, when there should be at least four parties, of a Permanent Council. By the Declaration of 28 July 1958 *(335 U.N.T.S. 206)*, provision was made for the co-operation of the United States with the Pact Powers, now organized into the Middle East, later the Central Treaty Organization (CENTO), and by the further agreement of 9 November 1960 provision as to the status of the organization, the national representatives thereto and the international staff thereof. The Pact was terminated in 1979 after the denunciation by Iraq in 1959 and the withdrawal of Iran and Pakistan in that year.

Balfour Declaration A statement contained in a letter dated 2 November 1917 from Arthur Balfour, UK Secretary of State for Foreign Affairs, to Lord Rothschild of the World Zionist Organization, expressed to be a declaration of sympathy with Zionist aspirations which had been approved by the British Cabinet. The text reads: "His Majesty's Government view with favour the establishment in Palestine of a national home for the Jewish people, and will use their best endeavours to facilitate the achievement of this object, it being clearly understood that nothing shall be done which may prejudice the civil and religious rights of existing non-Jewish communities in Palestine or the rights and political status enjoyed by the Jews in any other country": Report of the Commission on the Palestine Disturbances of August 1929, etc. *(Cmd. 3530)*. The preamble to the instrument of mandate for Palestine of 24 July 1922 *(Cmd. 1785)* recites that "the Principal Allied Powers . . . have agreed that the Mandatory should be responsible for putting into effect the declaration originally made on November 2nd 1917, by the Government of His Britannic Majesty, and adopted by the said Powers."

Banjul Charter *See* the **African Charter on Human and Peoples' Rights**.

Bank for International Settlements (BIS)   This institution was established by the Convention of 20 January 1930 between Belgium, France, Germany, Great Britain, Italy, Japan and Switzerland *(104 L.N.T.S. 441)*—or rather by the Charter which, by art. 1 of the Convention, Switzerland undertook to enact and which is set out in the Convention, along with the Statutes of the Bank. Under the Charter, the founders of the Bank are the central banks of the parties, together with a group of American banks. Following amendments to the Charter, the Bank has come to comprise as members the central banks of some 30 countries—virtually all European apart from the American group mentioned. From the legal point of view, the Bank represents an organization *sui generis.* Though it was brought into existence by inter-governmental agreement, its real establishment was a matter for Central Banks, most of which were not Government institutions at the time of its foundation and its incorporation under Swiss Law. BIS has legal personality in the municipal laws of member countries, but not in international law. It is endowed with certain privileges and immunities; see the Protocol regarding the Immunities of the Bank for International Settlements of 30 July 1936 *(197 L.N.T.S. 31). See* Baker, *The Bank for International Settlements: Evolution and Evaluation* (2002). *See also* <www.bis.org>.

Barcelona Statute   Convention and Statute on Freedom of Transit and the Régime of Navigable Waterways of International Concern of 20 April 1921 *(7 L.N.T.S. 12,36).* The Statute provided that merchant vessels of all States party have free navigation in the (identified) navigable waterways within the sovereignty or control of each State party: art. 2. While intended ultimately to create a global régime, "the principle of free navigation upon rivers . . . can hardly be described as a recognized rules of customary international law": *I Oppenheim 582.*

Barcelona Traction Co. Case   *(Belgium v Spain) 1964 I.C.J. Rep. 6; 1970 I.C.J. Rep. 3.* The Government of Belgium in 1958 filed an application seeking reparation for damage to the Barcelona Traction, Light and Power Company arising from acts of organs of the Spanish State, but in 1961 gave notice of discontinuance. To a new application made in 1962 following the failure of fresh negotiations between the parties, the respondent raised four preliminary objections. By its judgment of 24 July 1964, the ICJ *rejected* (12 to 4) the first objection to the effect that the discontinuance disabled Belgium from further proceedings, and equally the second objection that the Court lacked jurisdiction, joining the remaining objections to the merits. The basis of the jurisdictional objection advanced was that, although the Belgian-Spanish Treaty of Conciliation of 19 July 1927 *(80 L.N.T.S. 17)* was still in force, the obligation to submit to jurisdiction upon a unilateral application under art. 17(4) thereof had lapsed because the tribunal contemplated, the PCIJ, had ceased to exist, and was not revived by art. 37 of the Statute of the ICJ because Spain had not been a party to the latter on its first entry into force. The Court (10 to 6) *dismissed* this argument as well as the subsidiary contention that, if art. 37 did apply to revive the jurisdictional obligation, it did so with respect only to disputes arising after Spain's admission to the UN. Upon the trial of the merits, the Court proceeded first to examine the third Spanish preliminary objection: that the Government of Belgium had no standing to protect the company, which was incorporated and had its head office in Canada, although a majority (88%) of the shareholders were Belgian nationals. This objection was *upheld* (15 to 1), the view being expressed in the joint judgment of the majority that there existed no grounds for admitting any exception to the normal rule that the right of protection belongs exclusively to the State in which a corporation is incorporated, the circumstance that the company here was in receivership not putting an end to its existence and the right of Canada to protect it being acknowledged and having been actually asserted from time to time to a certain extent.

Barotseland Boundary Case *(Great Britain v. Portugal) (1905) 11 R.I.A.A. 59.* By a Declaration dated 12 August 1903 *(194 C.T.S. 34)*, the parties submitted to the arbitration of the King of Italy the question as to what were the limits of the territory of the Barotse Kingdom within the meaning of art. 4 of the Treaty of 11 June 1891 *(175 C.T.S. 197)*, which provided that that territory should fall within the British, as opposed to the Portuguese, sphere of influence in Central Africa. By an award dated 30 May 1905, the arbitrator *held* that a precise delimitation was not possible, partly because of the absence of distinct geographical divisions and partly because of the notorious instability of the tribes involved and their frequent intermixture, which was conceded by the parties, so that, where natural lines were lacking, it was necessary to resort to conventional geographical lines, which the award proceeded to indicate.

baseline   The term baseline connotes the line from which the breadth of the territorial sea (and other maritime zones) is measured, "the normal baseline," according to the UN Convention on the Law of the Sea 1982 *(1833 U.N.T.S. 3)*, being "the low-water line along the coast as marked on large-scale charts officially recognized by the coastal State": art. 5. "[T]he method of straight baselines joining appropriate points" is permitted in "localities where the coastline is deeply indented and cut into, or if there is a fringe of islands along the coast," such not departing to any appreciable extent from the general direction of the coast, and the sea areas lying within the line being sufficiently closely linked to the land domain to be subject to the regime of internal waters; account may be taken of peculiar economic interests in the determination of particular baselines; but straight baselines may not be drawn to and from **lowtide elevations** unless surmounted by light-houses or similar installations permanently above sea level, nor be drawn so as to cut off from the high seas or an exclusive economic zone the territorial waters of another State: art. 7. The straight baseline across the mouth of a **bay** is referred to as a **closing line**. As to the drawing of base-lines in relation to archipelagic waters and bays, see **archipelagic State**. *See* Brown, *The International Law of the Sea* (1994), Vol. 1, 22-7.

Bassiouni, Cherif   1937- . Professor, DePaul University from 1964. Member and Chairman of the UN Commission to Investigate International Humanitarian Law Violations in the former Yugoslavia (1992). Vice-Chairman of the UN General Assembly's Committee for the Establishment of an International Criminal Court (1995-98). His works include *International Extradition: US Law and Practice* (4th ed. 2002); *The Law of the International Criminal Tribunal for the Former Yugoslavia* (with Manikas, 1996); *The Statute of the International Criminal Court: A Documentary History* (1998); *Crimes Against Humanity in International Criminal Law* (2nd ed, 1999).

Baty, Thomas   1869-1954. Sometime Legal Adviser, Foreign Ministry of Japan. Principal works: *International Law* (1909); *War: Its Conduct and Legal Results* (with Morgan, 1915); *The Canons of International Law* (1930); *International Law in Twilight* (1954).

Baxter, Richard R.   1921-80. American; Professor, Harvard 1959-80; Judge, ICJ 1978-80; Member, PCA 1968-75; Editor in Chief, A.J.I.L. 1970-78. Works include *Documents on the St. Lawrence Seaway* (1960*); The Law of International Waterways* (1964); *The Panama Canal* (with Carroll, 1965); *Recent Codification in the Law of State Responsibility to Aliens* (with Garcia-Amador and Sohn, 1974).

bay   For the purposes of the articles of the UN Convention on the Law of the Sea 1982 *(1833 U.N.T.S. 3)* dealing with the limits of the territorial sea, "a bay is a well-marked indentation whose penetration is in such proportion to the width of its mouth as to contain landlocked waters and constitute more than a mere curvature of the coast" (art. 10(2)). But "[a]n indentation shall not, however, be regarded as a bay unless its area is as large as, or larger than, that of the semi-circle whose diameter is a line drawn across the mouth of that indentation," such area being taken for this purpose to be "that lying between the low-water mark around the shore of the indentation and a line joining the low-water mark of its natural entrance points," or, where there is more than one mouth, "a line as long as the sum total of the lengths of the lines across the different mouths" (art. 10(3)). The Convention permits a 24-mile **closing line** to be employed in relation to bays the coasts of which belong to a single State (art. 10(4)). A longer line is permissible, however, where there is in question an **historic bay** or the straight **baseline** system is generally applicable. *See generally* Bouchez, *The Regime of Bays in International Law* (1964); Westerman, *The Juridical Bay* (1987).

Beagle Channel Arbitration *(Argentina v. Chile) 52 I.L.M. 93 (1977)*. By the *compromis* of 22 July 1971, the parties agreed to submit to the arbitration of the Government of the UK questions arising out of the Argentine-Chile Boundary Treaty of 23 July 1881 *(189 C.T.S. 45)*, and notably the question whether the stipulation of art. 3 that "to Chile shall belong all the islands to the south of the Beagle Channel" invested that State with title to Picton, Nueva and Lennox Islands (the PNL group), which lie to the south of the Channel if its western end is taken to emerge between Isla Grande (Tierra del Fuego) and Picton Island, but one at least of which would be excluded if the southerly limit of the western entrance were taken to be the southerly extremity of the passage between Isla Navarina and Picton Island. *Held* (unanimously) that the negotiators of the Treaty of 1881 must be taken to have understood the western entrance of the Channel to be its northern arm, with the result that the PNL group of islands fell to Chile, principally because the boundary line with respect to more northerly areas laid down in art. 2 proceeded no further than the south shore of Isla Grande, thereby implying that the northern arm of the Channel constituted in principle the southern limit of Argentina's attributions under the Treaty. In a Note dated 25 January 1978, Argentina rejected the award: *17 I.L.M. 738 (1977)*. Ultimately, on 19 October 1984, Argentina and Chile signed an Agreement resolving the matters in dispute: *24 I.L.M. 11 (1985)*. Under the Agreement, title to Picton, Neueva and Lennox Islands is vested in Chile; extensive maritime boundaries are fixed; provision is made regarding navigation rights; and conciliation and arbitration provisions are stipulated.

Behring Sea Arbitration *(Great Britain and United States)* (1893-9) *Moore, Int. Arb., 755*. By the Treaty of 29 February 1892 *(176 C.T.S. 447)*, art. VI, the parties referred to a Tribunal of seven persons the questions: "1. What exclusive jurisdiction in . . . the Behring Sea, and what exclusive rights in the seal fisheries therein, did Russia assert and exercise prior . . . to . . . the cession of Alaska? . . . 2. How far were these claims of jurisdiction as to the seal fisheries recognized and conceded by Great Britain? 3. Was the . . . Behring Sea included in the phrase 'Pacific Ocean' as used in the Treaty of 1825 between Great Britain and Russia *[75 C.T.S. 95]*; and what rights, if any, in the Behring Sea were held and exclusively exercised by Russia after said Treaty? 4. Did not all the rights of Russia as to jurisdiction and as to the seal fisheries in Behring Sea east of the water boundary in the Treaty between the United States and Russia of the 30th March, 1867 *[134 C.T.S. 331]* pass unimpaired to the United States? . . . 5. Has the United States any right, and if so, what right, of protection or property in the fur-seals frequenting the islands of the United States in Behring Sea when such seals are found outside the ordinary 3-mile limit?" The Treaty provided further (art. VII) that if the determination of these questions should leave the subject in such a position that the concurrence of Great Britain was necessary to the establishment of regulations for the proper protection of the fur-seal, the arbitrators should determine what regulations were necessary. By its award of 15 August 1893 (printed also *179 C.T.S.*

97), the tribunal *held* (1) that Russia had never asserted or exercised exclusive jurisdiction in Behring Sea; (2) that Great Britain had not recognized or conceded any exclusive jurisdiction outside territorial waters to Russia; (3) that the Behring Sea was within the meaning of the phrase "Pacific Ocean" in the Treaty of 1825; and that no rights were held and exclusively exercised by Russia after that Treaty; (4) that all Russia's rights passed unimpaired under the Treaty of 1867; and (5) that the United States had no rights of protection or property in seals found outside the 3-mile limit. The Tribunal further formulated in nine articles concurrent regulations applicable outside the exclusive jurisdictional limits of the parties.

Beijing Rules Properly styled the UN Standard Minimum Rules for the Administration of Juvenile Justice, the Rules were adopted on 29 November 1985 as GA Res. 40/33 and aim towards "the full mobilization of all possible resources . . . for the purpose of promoting the well-being of the juvenile, with a view to reducing the need for intervention under the law, and of effectively, fairly and humanely dealing with the juvenile in conflict with the law" (Rule 1(3)). For the purposes of the Rules, a juvenile is a child or young person who "under the respective legal systems, may be dealt with for an offence in a manner which is different from an adult" (Rule 2(2)(a)). While the Rules, being part of a General Assembly resolution, are not legally binding, some of them have become of legal effect through their repetition in art. 40 of the Convention on the Rights of the Child (*see* **Child, Convention on the Rights of the**; *1577 U.N.T.S. 3*). *See also* the **Riyadh Guidelines**; **JDL Rules**.

Belli, Pierino 1502-1575. Italian lawyer and statesman, adviser to the Duke of Savoy; author of *Re Militari et Bello Tractatus (A Treatise on Military Matters and War)* (1558).

belligerency, belligerent The term "belligerency" in classical international law connotes primarily engagement in a war on the part of a State or other entity possessed of the *jus belli*, or right of war, and a "belligerent" is a State or other entity which is at war. *See* **recognition of belligerency**. However, the titles to Sect. 1 and Chap. 1 of the Regulations respecting the Laws and Customs of War on Land annexed to Hague Convention IV of 1907 *(206 C.T.S. 277)* employ the expressions "On Belligerents" and "The Qualifications of Belligerents" respectively in reference to individual members of the armed forces of belligerent States. The more modern term for belligerent is **combatant**.

belligerent occupation There exists a considerable body of conventional law on belligerent occupation, more commonly referred to as military occupation, which term may be taken to mean the control by a belligerent State over the territory and inhabitants of another State. "Since . . . the ousted sovereign still retains all the residue of legal authority not attributed to the occupant, it is apparent that belligerent occupation involves at its core a complicated trilateral set of legal relations between the Occupant, the temporarily ousted sovereign and the inhabitants": Stone, *Legal Controls of International Conflict* (2nd imp. revised 1954), 694. In terms of art. 42 of the Hague Convention (IV) respecting the Laws and Customs of War on Land of 18 October 1907 *(205 C.T.S. 277)* a territory is considered occupied when it is "actually placed under the authority of the hostile army," the occupation extending only over territory where such authority has been established and can be exercised. The basic duty on the occupying State is to "take all the measures in his power to restore, and ensure, as far as possible, public order and safety, while respecting, unless absolutely prevented, the laws in force in the country" (art. 43). The occupying State is prohibited from compelling information on the army of the other belligerent, or about its means of defense (art. 44); from insisting on inhabitants swearing allegiance (art. 45); from interfering with personal and property rights (art. 46); from pillaging (art. 47); from exacting additional taxes, except those necessary for administration (arts. 48 and 49; *see also* arts. 50 and 51); from requisitions in kind or services from inhabitants or communes, except for the necessities of the occupying army (art. 52): Requisition of State property is permissible (art. 53) though the occupying State is regarded as administrator and usufructuary of public buildings, real property, forests and agricultural works (art. 55). (In similar terms are arts. 42 to 56 of The Hague Convention (II) with Respect to the Laws and Customs of War on Land of 29 July 1899 *(187 C.T.S. 429))*. These provisions are developed in the Geneva Convention (IV) Relative to the Protection of Civilian Persons in Time of War of 12 August 1949 *(75 U.N.T.S. 287)*. Among the additional prohibitions are those on deportations and forcible transfers (art. 49); and on the destruction of private or State property, except where rendered absolutely necessary by military operations (art. 53). Additionally, the occupying power is required to fulfil certain obligations in relation to the care and education of children (art. 50); in relation to judges and public officials (art. 54); in relation to food, medical supplies, hygiene and public health (arts. 55 and 56); in relation to relief schemes (arts. 59 to 63); and in relation to penal laws and their enforcement (arts. 64 to 78). *See also* the Geneva Convention relative to the Treatment of Civilian Persons in Time of War of 12 August 1949 *(75 U.N.T.S. 287)* and Protocol 1 to the Geneva Convention of 8 June 1977 *(1125 U.N.T.S. 3)*. *See* McNair and Watts, *The Legal Effects of War* (4th ed.), Chaps.17-18; von Glahn, *The Occupation of Enemy Territory* (1957); Feilchenfeld, *The International Economic Law of Belligerent Occupation* (2000); US Department of Defense *Law of Land Warfare, Field Manual* (2003), Chap. 6. *See also* **protected persons**.

bellum injustum *See **bellum justum***.

bellum justum The concept of *bellum justum* or *bellum justum et pium* originated in the Roman *jus fetiale*, it being the function of the *fetiales* "to certify to the senate the existence of a just cause of war. . . . The proceeding gave assurance to the Romans that in the contest the gods would side with them. . . . Theoretically, the *jus fetiale* was Roman municipal law, . . . but in the hypothesis of an offence committed against the Roman by the foreign nation, it contained a crude international notion. . . . [I]n fact, the invention of the 'just war' doctrine constitutes the foremost Roman contribution to the history of international law. . . . The outstanding contribution of the Middle Ages, . . . consists of the theological revival of the . . . doctrine. [It] was resuscitated and altered in the Christian spirit by St. Augustine (354-430) in connection with the objections on the basis of the Scriptures which Tertullian (160-230) and other early Church Fathers had raised against Christian participation in war and military service. In this situation St. Augustine opened a middle road by requiring that the war be just. . . . Thomas Aquinas (1225-1274) [i]n the Second Part of his *Summa Theologica* . . . answers the question 'whether it is always a sin to wage a war' in the negative provided (1) that the prince has authorized the war (that there is *auctoritas principis*); (2) that there is a *justa causa*—to wit, that the adverse party deserved to be fought against because of some guilt of his own *(propter aliquam culpam);* and (3) that the belligerent is possessed of *a recta intentio*. . . . In substance this does not go much beyond the tenets of St. Augustine; but it is primarily through Thomas Aquinas' immense authority that the just war doctrine became the cornerstone of the Roman Catholic doctrine on war": Nussbaum, *A Concise History of the Law of Nations* (Revised ed 1954), 10-11, 36-37. *See also* **just war**. *See* Johnson, *Just War Tradition and the Restraint of War: A Moral and Historical Inquiry* (1981).

Benelux Benelux, the oldest of the post-1945 arrangement for economic integration in Europe, with cooperation beginning as early as 1943, whose members are now members of **the European Economic Community**, is a **customs union** established between Belgium, the Netherlands and Luxembourg by the Treaty Establishing the Benelux Economic Union of 3 February 1958 *(381 U.N.T.S. 165)*. The Union entails free movement of persons, goods, capital and services, and includes also both the co-ordination of economic, financial and social policies and the pursuit of a joint economic policy towards third countries: art. 1. Executive power resides in the Committee of Ministers; by unanimous vote it may take binding decisions on the manner in which the Treaty is to be given effect; it may draft conventions for submission to the three member States; it may make non-binding recommendations on the functioning of the Union; and it may issue directives to the other institutions. The Interparliamentary Consultative Council of 49 members was established in 1955 *(250 U.N.T.S. 201)* and a Court of Justice in 1965.

Bentham, Jeremy   1748-1832. Utilitarian philosopher, jurist, political, legal and social reformer, who first coined the term "international law" in his *Introduction to the Principles of Morals and Legislation* (1789). *See* Bowring & Burton, *The Works of Jeremy Bentham* (2002).

Bentwich, Norman   1883-1971. British; Attorney General of British Mandate Administration of Palestine 1920-31; Professor, Hebrew University of Jerusalem 1932-51. Works include *The Law of Private Property in War (*1907); *The Declaration of London* (1911); *The Mandate System* (1930); *The Religious Foundations of Internationalism; From Geneva to San Francisco* (1946); *A Commentary on the Charter of the United Nations* (with Martin, 1950).

Berlin, General Act 1885   *See* **Congo Act.**

Berlin, Treaty of   Treaty between Austria-Hungary, France, Germany, Great Britain, Italy, Russia and Turkey for the Settlement of Affairs in the East, signed 13 July 1878 *(153 C.T.S. 171)*, involving the dismantling of parts of the Ottoman Empire, with guarantees for minorities.

Bermuda I and II   Bermuda I is the Agreement relating to Air Services between the United Kingdom and the United States, signed at Bermuda on 11 February 1946 *(3 U.N.T.S. 253)*, which long served as the model for bilateral agreements of this sort and which provided machinery for future consultation and review. It was replaced by the more liberal Bermuda II, otherwise the Agreement of 23 July 1977 *(28 U.S.T. 5367)*, which in turn also became the template for subsequent bilateral agreements. *See* Havel, *In Search of Open Skies: Law and Policy for a New Era of International Aviation* (1997), 41-8.

Bhopal Case   On 3 December 1984, a tank of methyl isocyanate (MIC) leaked at a Bhopal, India, plant owned and operated by Union Carbide India Limited (UCIL), as a result of which approximately 3,800 persons died and 2,700 were disabled. The victims of the spill brought suit in the U.S. and, on 14 January 1987, the U.S. Second Circuit Court of Appeals upheld a U.S. District Court decision to send the legal case against Union Carbide to India and reaffirmed that UCIL was a separate and independent legal entity that was managed and staffed by Indian citizens. In February 1989, the Supreme Court of India directed the Union Carbide Corporation and UCIL to pay a total of $470 million in full settlement of all claims arising from the incident. This award is the largest in the history of India and is also $120 million more than the settlement accepted by the U.S attorneys representing the Indian victims in the U.S. courts. *See* Janis, The Doctrine of Forum Non Conveniens and the Bhopal Case, *(1987) 34 Netherlands International Law Review 192.*

bilateral Literally, on two sides, parts. In relation to treaties and negotiations, bilateral (or bipartite) therefore connotes only two States involved in the process. Cf. **multilateral**. *See also **traité-lois**; **traité-contrats***.

Bill of Rights, International *See* **International Bill of Rights**.

biological diversity In terms of the Convention on Biological Diversity concluded at Rio de Janeiro on 5 June 1992 (*31 I.L.M. 818 (1992)*), biological diversity is "the variability among living organisms from all sources including, *inter alia*, terrestrial, marine and other aquatic ecosystems and the ecological complexes of which they are part; this includes diversity within species, between species and of ecosystems": art. 2. The Convention aims to conserve diversity thus defined and to ensure the sustainable use of its components and the equitable sharing of its benefits: art. 1. To these ends, a Conference of the Parties oversees the implementation by States of the Convention (art. 23(4)), guided and assisted by a Subsidiary Body on Scientific, Technical and Technological Advice (art. 25) and a permanent Secretariat (art. 24). The Cartagena Protocol on Biosafety to this Convention, adopted on 29 January 2000 *(39 I.L.M. 1027 (2000))* provides procedures for the safe handling, transfer and use of living modified organisms resulting from modern biotechnology. *See* Louka, *Biodiversity and Human Rights* (2002).

biological methods of warfare *See* **bacteriological methods of warfare**.

bipartite *See* **bilateral**.

BIS *See* **Bank for International Settlements**.

blockade "Blockade is the blocking by men-of-war of the approach to the enemy coast, or part of it, for the purpose of preventing ingress and egress of vessels or aircraft of all nations. Blockade must not be confused with siege, although it may take place concurrently with siege. Whereas siege aims at the capture of the besieged place, blockade endeavours merely to intercept all intercourse, and especially commercial intercourse, by sea between the coast and the world at large": *II Oppenheim 768.* By the Declaration of Paris 1856 (*111 C.T.S. 1;* see **Paris, Declaration of**), art. 4, "blockades, in order to be binding, must be effective, that is to say, maintained by a force sufficient to prevent access to the coast of the enemy." This requirement apart, there was no conventional law of the matter, the Declaration of London 1909 (*208 C.T.S. 338)*, arts. 1-21 whereof purported to provide a code of rules, having failed of ratification, although applied provisionally, with some modification, by the Allied Powers during 1914-16. The practice of some States, notably Great Britain, Japan and the United States, differed from that of the Continental States in not requiring public notification as an invariable pre-requisite to the validity of a blockade. On the other hand, actual or constructive knowledge in the blockade-breaker, arising from notoriety, was a universal prerequisite to liability to condemnation for breach, which, in Anglo-American practice, might persist until the completion of the round voyage. During the American Civil War, the American prize court enforced penalties upon vessels knowingly carrying cargo to neutral countries in ignorance of its ultimate destination to a blockaded port: *The Springbok 5 Wall. 1 (1866); The Peterhoff 5 Wall. 28 (1866).* With the advent of the submarine and of aircraft, the maintenance of blockades *stricto sensu*, or close blockades, became impracticable. The "long-distance blockade" instituted instead during World War I and II has been defended as a logical, and thus lawful, development: Colombos, *The International Law of the Sea* (6th ed.), 841; *II Oppenheim 791-7.* In effect, however, this development, coupled with the adoption of retaliatory measures, wholly obscured the traditional distinction between capture for carriage of contraband and capture for breach of blockade. *See also* **blockade, pacific**; **quarantine**; **war zones**.

blockade, pacific   A form of reprisal or intervention involving the seizure at sea and sequestration by the maritime forces of one State or international person of the vessels of another seeking to enter or leave the latter's ports. "[A]ll writers agree that the blockading State has no right to seize . . . such ships of third States as try to break a pacific blockade": *II Oppenheim 147*. Hogan, *Pacific Blockade* (1908), examines some two dozen instances of pacific blockade during the 19th century, many of them associated with conditions of civil war. Though not *per se* prohibited by the **General Treaty for the Renunciation of War 1928** *(94 L.N.T.S. 57)*, the institution of a pacific blockade today would no doubt be generally inconsistent with art. 2(4) of the Charter of the UN: Colombos, *International Law of the Sea* (6th ed.), 469. *See* **blockade**.

Blue Book   (1) A collection, in readily readable form, of the basic principles of criminal justice, human rights and humanitarian law, for the use of the civilian police components of United Nations **peace-keeping** operations, covering arrest and detention, force and firearms, trials, victims, detainees and prisoners, torture and cruel treatment, illegal executions, genocide, humanitarian rules and refugee protection; available in hard copy or online (at <www.uncjin.org/Documents/BlueBook>).

(2) Also called the Blue Book, though properly styled *Permanent Missions to the United Nations*, is the UN publication setting out the names of members of **permanent missions** and those entities with **observer status**; this identifies those entitled to privileges and immunities under art. 4 of the Convention on Privileges and Immunities of the United Nations of 13 February 1946 *(1 U.N.T.S. 15)*.

blue helmets (or blue berets)   The name given to forces in UN **peacekeeping** operations after the color of the helmets (or berets) worn. *See* UN, *The Blue Helmets* (2nd ed. 1990).

Bodin, Jean   1530-1594. French lawyer, law teacher and political philosopher who formulated the concept of sovereignty, meaning (for him) the absolute and perpetual power within a State, which was subject only to the Laws of God and the Law of Nature. Author of *Six livres de la republique* (1574).

Boffolo Case   *(Italy v. Venezuela) (1903) 10 R.I.A.A. 528.* Boffolo, an Italian subject, was ordered expelled from Venezuela on 4 April 1900, under the constitution of 1893, which permitted the expulsion of foreigners having no local domicile and notoriously prejudicial to the public order. It was suggested that Boffolo, who had settled in Caracas in 1898, had spoken disrespectfully of the President, had criticized a subordinate member of the judiciary and had recommended the reading of a socialist paper. *Held* (by Umpire Ralston) that, while a State possesses a general right of expulsion, expulsion should be resorted to only in extreme circumstances, and must be accomplished in the manner least injurious to the individual affected; that the State exercising the power must, when occasion demands, state the reason for such expulsion before an international tribunal, and accept the consequences of an insufficient reason or no reason; that the reasons advanced by Venezuela were insufficient.

Bogotá Charter   Properly styled the Charter of the Organization of American States of 30 April 1948 *(119 U.N.T.S. 3)*. *See* **Organization of American States**.

Bogotá Declaration   Properly styled the American Declaration of the Rights and Duties of Man, approved in 1948 at the Ninth International Conference of American States at

Bogotá as OAS Res. XXX *(43 A.J.I.L. Supp. 133 (1949))*, this **human rights** declaration is, like the Universal Declaration of Human Rights 1948 upon which it is modeled, intended not to be strictly binding in law. The Declaration is the direct precursor of the **American Convention on Human Rights**.

Bogotá Pact Properly styled the American Treaty on Pacific Settlement *(30 U.N.T.S. 84)*, the Pact was signed at the same time as the **Bogotá Charter** on 30 April 1948, and was intended to replace eight earlier instruments and to establish detailed procedures for the settlement of disputes between the States of the Americas.

Bolivar Railway Company Case (Great Britain v. Venezuela) (1903) 9 R.I.A.A. 445. Held by the Mixed Claims Commission set up by the Protocol of 13 February 1903 *(192 C.T.S. 414)* that the Government of Venezuela was liable for the cost of services furnished by the company to the successful Castro revolutionary régime, as opposed to various unsuccessful revolutionary parties, on the principle that a State is responsible for all the acts of a revolutionary movement which in fact achieves governmental power.

Bombardments by Naval Forces, Convention respecting Otherwise, the Hague Convention IX of 18 October 1907 *(205 C.T.S. 345)* prohibiting the naval bombardment of undefended ports, towns, dwellings and buildings (art. 1) and regulating other naval bombardments (arts. 2-6).

bona fides See **good faith**.

booby-trap "Booby-trap means any device any device or material which is designed, constructed or adapted to kill or injure and which functions unexpectedly when a person disturbs or approaches an apparently harmless object or performs an apparently safe task": art. 2(2) of Protocol II to the Convention on Prohibitions or Restrictions on the Use of Certain Conventional Weapons which may be Deemed to be Excessively Injurious or to have Indiscriminate Effects of 10 April 1981 *(19 I.L.M. 1523 (1980))*. Their use against civilians is prohibited and against combatants restricted: art. 3.

booty "According to a former rule of the Law of Nations, all enemy property, public or private, which a belligerent could get hold of on the battlefield was booty and could be appropriated. . . . [I]t is obvious from Articles 4 and 14 of the Hague Regulations [respecting the Laws and Customs of War on Land annexed to Hague Convention IV, 1907, *205 C.T.S. 277]* as well as from Article [18 of the Prisoners of War Convention of 1949, *75 U.N.T.S. 135]* that it is now obsolete as regards private enemy property, except military papers, arms, horses, and the like. But as regards *public* enemy property this customary rule is still valid. Thus not only weapons . . . may be seized but . . . all other public property. . . . To whom the booty ultimately belongs is not for International Law but for Municipal Law to determine. . .": *II Oppenheim 310-311. See also* Stone, *Legal Controls of International Conflict,* (2nd imp. rev.), 559, n. 72 who provides a bibliography.

Borchard, Edwin M. 1884-1951. American; Professor, Yale 1917-50. Works include *The Declaratory Judgment* (1918, rev. ed. as *Declaratory Judgments* (1941)); *Coastal Waters* (1910); *Diplomatic Protection of Citizens Abroad* (1915).

Borchgrave Case (Belgium v. Spain) (1938) P.C.I.J. Ser. A/B, Nos. 72,73. By a special agreement of 20 February 1937, the Governments of Belgium and Spain submitted to the PCIJ the question of the responsibility of Spain in respect to the death of Baron Jacques de Borchgrave, a Belgian national associated with the Belgian embassy in Madrid, who was found dead in circumstances which remained unexplained. The Belgian memorial having contained a submission that the Spanish Government was responsible *inter alia* for failure to exercise sufficient diligence in the apprehension and prosecution of the murderers, that Government entered a preliminary objection that the special agreement did not refer to facts subsequent to the death. The Court (unanimously) *overruled* the objection because "the history of the controversy between the Parties" left no room for so narrow a construction. A further preliminary objection that the local remedies rule had not been satisfied was withdrawn.

boundary delimitation, demarcation *See* **delimitation**.

boundary river(s) "Boundary rivers are those which separate different States from each other. If such a river is not navigable, the boundary line as a rule follows the mid-line of the river; or of its principal arm if it has more than one. If navigable, the boundary line follows the mid-line of the so-called *thalweg,* of the principal channel of the river. . . . But it is possible for the boundary line to be one bank of the river, so that the whole bed then belongs to one of the riparian states only. This is an exceptional case created by immemorial possession, by treaty, or by the fact that a State has occupied the lands on one side of a river at a time prior to the occupation of the lands on the other side by some other state": *I Oppenheim*, 664-5.

boundary/ies The imaginary lines on the surface of the earth which separate the land territory or maritime zones (**continental shelf** and **EEZ**) of one State from that of another. Ideally, as a matter of common sense but little more, a land boundary should be easy to identify and difficult to cross: ***British-Guiana Boundary Case (1899) 188 C.T.S. 76***; ***Alaska Boundary Arbitration (1903) 15 R.I.A.A. 481***. In relation to land boundaries, there is no corpus of law especially for resolving boundary disputes, and recourse is made to the rules for acquiring title to territory in international law (*see* **territory, acquisition of**). In relation to maritime territory, special rules have emerged from conventions. For the **territorial sea** and **contiguous zone**, in the absence of agreement as to the boundary, a State is not entitled "to extend its territorial sea or contiguous zone beyond the median line every point of which is equidistant from the nearest points on the baselines from which the breadth of the territorial sea . . . is measured": arts. 15 and 33(2) of the UN Convention on the Law of the Sea 1982 (*1833 U.N.T.S. 3*). For the **continental shelf** and the **exclusive economic zone**, the boundary is to be effected by agreement "on the basis of international law . . . in order to achieve an equitable solution": arts. 74 and 83. Failing such an agreement, the States concerned are to utilize the dispute-settlement procedures in Part XV of the Convention. *See* Bernstein, *Delimitation of International Boundaries* (1974); Sharma, *International Boundary Disputes and International Law* (1976); Brownlie, *African Boundaries. A Legal and Diplomatic Encyclopaedia* (1979); Tanja, *The Legal Delimitation of International Maritime Boundaries* (1989); Charney and Alexander, *International Maritime Boundaries* (1993).

Boutros-Ghali, Boutros 1922- . Egyptian scholar (professor of international relations, Cairo 1949-79), journalist, politician (member of Egyptian Parliament 1979-81) and statesman (Minister of State for Foreign Affairs 1977-91). Sixth Secretary-General of the UN for one term, 1992-96. Promoter of reform in the UN, particularly in its peace and security functions. Author of the ***Agenda for Peace (1992) and its 1995 Supplement; Unvanquished: A US-UN Saga* (1997).

Bowett, Derek William 1927- . Law teacher, Professor Cambridge. Long-time editor of the British Yearbook of International Law; sometime member, ILC. Principal works include *Self-Defence in International Law* (1958); *United Nations Forces* (1964); *Law of In-*

ternational Institutions (1964; 5th ed. 2001 by Sands and Klein); *The Law of the Sea* (1967); *The Search for Peace* (1972).

boycott As borrowed by the literature of international law, the notion of boycott "is really a modern form of reprisals whereby a State may institute by itself and through its nationals an interruption of commercial and financial relationships with another State. Opinion is divided as to whether, independently of any illegal acts committed by the State against whom the boycott is directed, it is a breach of public international law. It is at least an unfriendly act, but some writers go further and say that in some circumstances it may amount to an act of economic aggression which should be prohibited by law": Stone, *Legal Controls of International Conflict* (2nd imp. rev.), 291. The most significant boycott in recent times has been that organized, beginning in 1946, by Arab States against Israeli goods and products; *see* Chill, *The Arab Boycott of Israel* (1976).

BP v. Libya, *(1973 and 1974) 53 I.L.R. 297, 375.* BP obtained an interest in a petroleum concession in Libya. In 1971, in retaliation for certain actions by the UK Government in the Persian Gulf, the Libyan Government nationalized these operations of BP, which thereupon began arbitration proceedings under the concession. The Libyan Government did not appear. *Held* by Lagergren, sole arbitrator, sitting in Denmark, that (1) the applicable procedural law was the law of Denmark, and the law governing the merits was (as stipulated in the concession), in the absence of principles common to the law of Libya and international law, the general principles of law, including such as may have been applied by international tribunals; (2) the nationalization law was a fundamental breach of the concession; (3) the taking by Libya of the property, rights and interests of BP violated public international law and was confiscatory; (4) the concession had been effectively terminated, except as the basis for the tribunal's jurisdiction and BP's right to claim damages; (5) BP was not entitled to specific performance of the concession, but could only seek a remedy in damages; (6) BP was not entitled to oil extracted from the concession after the date of nationalization. On BP subsequently seeking to have the award re-opened, *held* that the request must be rejected.

Brazilian Loans Case *(Brazil v France) (1929) P.C.I.J., Ser. A, No. 2.* By the Special Agreement of 27 August 1927 *(75 L.N.T.S. 91)*, the Brazilian and French Governments submitted to the Court the question whether payment of the interest and principal of certain pre-World War I Brazilian loans might continue to be made in paper French francs, which had depreciated greatly, or was required to be made in the equivalent of gold. *Held* (9 to 2) that, the relevant contracts containing a "gold clause" and the law of Brazil, the borrower State, applying rather than French law, according to which the paper franc had been made legal tender, payment was due in the equivalent of gold. *See also* **Serbian Loans Case**.

breach of the peace *See* **peace, breach of**.

Breard Case *(Paraguay v United States of America) 1998 I.C.J. Rep. 248.* By application of 3 April 1998, Paraguay instituted proceedings against the USA alleging violations of the Vienna Convention on Consular Relations 1963 *(596 U.N.T.S. 261)* with respect to the case of Angel Francisco Breard, a Paraguayan national convicted of murder in the State of Virginia and sentenced to be put to death on 14 April 1998. Art. 36(1)(b) of the Vienna Convention requires the competent authorities of a State party to advise "without delay," a national of another State party whom such authorities arrest or detain of the national's right to consular assistance under art. 36. Breard was not informed of his rights and was consequently unaware of those rights under the Vienna Convention. In an order of 9 April 1998, the International Court of Justice *indicated* (unanimously) that the United States should take all measures at its disposal to ensure that Breard was not executed pending the final decision in the proceedings. Breard was nevertheless executed on 14 April 1998. By an order of 10 November 1998, the case was removed from the Court's List at the request of Paraguay: *1998 I.C.J. Rep. 426. See also LeGrand Case. See generally Agora, Breard, 92 A.J.I.L. 666-712 (1998).*

Bretton Woods The location in New Hampshire of the United Nations Monetary and Financial Conference of July 1944. The Conference drew up the Articles of Agreement of the **International Monetary Fund** and the Articles of Agreement of the **International Bank for Reconstruction and Development.** These two organizations, along with the **International Finance Corporation, International Development Association** and the **Multilateral Investment Guarantee Agency** and the International Center for the Settlement of Investment Disputes (**ICSID**), are referred to as the "Bretton Woods Group" (or the "World Bank Group"). *See* Mason, *The World Bank Since Bretton Woods: The Origins, Policies, Operations, and Impact of the International Bank for Reconstruction and Development* (1973); James, *International Monetary Cooperation since Bretton Woods* (1996).

Brewster, Kingman Jr. 1919- . Professor, Harvard 1953-60; Professor and Provost 1961-63, President 1963-77, Yale; US Ambassador to UK 1977-80. Works include *Antitrust and American Business Abroad* (1959, 3rd ed. 1997); *Law of International Transactions and Relations* (with Katz, 1960).

Brezhnev Doctrine Following democratic reforms in Czechoslovakia and the consequent incursion by Soviet and other Eastern European forces to restore the *status quo ante* in 1968, Soviet leader Leonid Brezhnev justified this intervention by the right, and indeed duty, of communist States to act to safeguard communism in other States. Acknowledging that each communist party was free to apply the principles of Marxism-Leninism, none could depart from these principles. Any departure would "conflict with its own vital interests would . . . [be] detrimental to the other socialist states." *See* Valenta, *Soviet Intervention in Czechoslovakia 1968* (rev. ed. 1991).

Briand, Aristide 1862-1932. French statesman; co-sponsor with Kellogg of the **General Treaty for the Renunciation of War** as an Instrument of National Policy of August 27, 1928 (Kellogg-Briand Pact) *(94 L.N.T.S. 57).*

Brierly, James Leslie 1881-1955. Professor, Oxford 1922-47; Member, ILC, rapporteur on the Law of Treaties 1949-50, Chairman 1951. Principal works include *Law of Nations* (1928; 6th ed. (ed. Waldock) 1962); *The Outlook for International Law* (1944); *The Basis of Obligation in International Law* (1958); translator of Zouche's *Juris et Judicii Fecialis Explicatio (Classics of International Law).*

Briggs, Herbert W. 1900-84. Professor Cornell 1937-69; editor-in-chief A.J.I.L. 1955-62; Member ILC 1962-66. Author of *The Doctrine of Continuous Voyage* (1926); *The Law of Nations* (1938, 2nd ed. 1953); *The Progressive Development of International Law* (1947); *The International Law Commission* (1965).

British Guiana Boundary Case *(Great Britain v. Venezuela) (1899) 188 C.T.S. 76.* By the Treaty of 2 February 1897 *(184 C.T.S. 188),* the parties stipulated for the determination of the boundary line between the Colony of British Guiana and Venezuela by a Tribunal of five persons. By their award of 3 October 1899, the arbitrators indicated the precise line of the boundary. The *compromis* is notable for its provision (art. IV) that adverse holding or prescription during a period of fifty years should make a good title, and that exclusive political control, as well as actual settlement, might be deemed sufficient to constitute adverse holding or to make title by prescription. The award is equally notable for its incidental decision that, in times of peace, the rivers Amakuru and Barima should be open to navigation by merchant ships of all nations.

British Institute of International and Comparative Law Established in 1895, the BIICL's mission is to understand and influence the development of law on a global rather than merely national basis, particularly in the international legal order, global business law, protection of human rights and common law in Europe. It publishes the *International and Comparative Law Quarterly* (since 1952); and a bi-monthly *Bulletin of Legal Developments* (since 1966). *See* <www.biicl.org>.

Brown, Robert E., Claim *(U.S. v. Great Britain) (1923) 6 R.I.A.A. 120.* In 1895, Brown, a citizen of the United States, made elaborate preparations in anticipation of the opening of a public gold digging at Witfontein, in the territory of the Republic of South Africa, placing a large number of his agents on the land and arranging for the transmission to these agents by heliograph from Doorknop, the site of the office of the Responsible Clerk, of notice of the actual grant of licenses (before which claims could not be staked). Confronted with these unorthodox methods, the South African authorities first refused to grant the licenses demanded, and then withdrew the proclamation opening the field. Though Brown succeeded in an action in the courts of the Republic in establishing the validity of his claim to no less than 1200 licenses, there ensued a controversy between the executive and the judiciary resulting in the dismissal of the Chief Justice and the virtual reversal of the judgment in Brown's favor. Brown thereupon petitioned the Queen of Great Britain as suzerain of the Republic for redress, and was referred in the first instance to his own government. After the annexation of the Republic by Great Britain in 1901, Brown petitioned the British Governor of Transvaal Colony. But the matter was not taken up by the Government of the United States until 1903, nor submitted to arbitration by the Anglo-American Arbitral Tribunal constituted under the Special Agreement of 18 August 1910 *(211 C.T.S. 408)* until 1923, when it was dismissed on the ground that the "doctrine [that] a State acquiring a territory by conquest without any under-taking to assume such liabilities is bound to take affirmative steps to right the wrongs done by the former State" could not be indorsed; and that the authority over the Republic involved in the British suzerainty "fell far short of what would be required to make [Great Britain] responsible for the wrong. . . ."

Brownlie, Ian 1932- . International law teacher (1956-99; Chichele Professor, Oxford, 1980-99) and practitioner; long-time editor of the British Yearbook of International Law. Principal works include *International Law and the Use of Force by States* (1963); *Principles of Public International Law* (1966, 5th ed. 1998); *African Boundaries: A Legal and Diplomatic Encyclopaedia* (1979); *State Responsibility (Part I)* (1983); *The Rule of Law in International Affairs* (1998). *See* Goodwin-Gill and Talmon, *The Reality of International Law: Essays in Honour of Ian Brownlie* (2000).

Brussels Act, Conference General Act of the Brussels Conference relating to the African Slave Trade, signed on 2 July 1890 *(173 C.T.S. 293)*. Revised by the Convention of St. Germain of 10 September 1919 *(8 L.N.T.S. 26)*. *See* **slavery**.

Brussels Maritime Conventions The principal of these instruments for the unification of maritime law which have come into force are those respecting: (1) Collisions, 23 September 1910 *(212 C.T.S. 178)*; (2) Assistance and Salvage at Sea, 23 September 1910 *(212 C.T.S. 187)*; (3) Bills of Lading, 25 August 1924 *(120 L.N.T.S. 155)*; (4) Limitation of Liability, 25 August 1924 *(120 L.N.T.S. 125)*; (5) Immunity of State-owned Vessels, 10 April

1926 *(176 L.N.T.S. 199)*; (6) Maritime Mortgages, 10 April 1926 *(120 L.N.T.S. 187)*; (7) Civil Jurisdiction in Matters of Collision, 10 May 1952 *(439 U.N.T.S. 217)*; (8) Penal Jurisdiction, etc. *(439 U.N.T.S. 233)*; (9) Arrest of Sea-Going Ships *(439 U.N.T.S. 193)*.

Brussels Treaty Organization The Organization set up by the Treaty of Economic, Social and Cultural Collaboration and Collective Self-Defence of 17 March 1948 between Belgium, France, Luxembourg, the Netherlands and the United Kingdom *(19 U.N.T.S. 51)*. As to the status of this Treaty as an instrument of collective self-defense within the meaning of art. 51 of the UN Charter, see art. IV thereof; and *see* Beckett, *The North Atlantic Treaty, The Brussels Treaty and the Charter of the United Nations* (1950). The Treaty was modified and extended to include the Federal Republic of Germany and Italy by the Protocols of 23 October 1954 *(211 U.N.T.S. 342)* and renamed the **Western European Union**.

Brussels, Declaration of The unratified *Projet de Declaration* in 56 articles drawn up at the conference of 27 July to 27 August 1874 (translation in Higgins, *The Hague Peace Conferences* (1909), 273), which became the basis of the Hague Convention on the Laws and Customs of War on Land 1899 *(187 C.T.S. 429)*, and thus of the Regulations annexed to Hague Convention IV of 1907 *(205 C.T.S. 277)*.

Buergenthal, Thomas 1934- . Professor, State University of New York (Buffalo) 1962-75, University of Texas 1975-80, American University 1980-85 and George Washington University Law 1989-2000. Member of the ICJ, 2000- . His works include *International Protection of Human Rights* (with Sohn, 1973); *Public International Law* (with Maier, 2nd ed. 1990); *International Human Rights* (2nd ed. 1995).

Bulama Island Arbitration *(Great Britain and Portugal) (1870) 139 C.T.S. 21*. By the Protocol of Conference of 13 January 1869 (*ibid.*, 18), the parties referred their respective claims to the island of Bulama on the west coast of Africa to the arbitration of the President of the United States. By his award of 21 April 1870, President Grant *held* the Portuguese claim, based on discovery in 1446 and settlement in 1699, as well as formal claim in 1752 and later settlement, superior to the British, based exclusively on native cessions not acquiesced in by Portugal.

Bunche, Ralph 1904-71. American political scientist, civil rights activist and international civil servant. Credited with securing the armistice between Israel and its four Arab neighbors in 1949, for which he was awarded the Nobel Peace Prize the following year. Publications include *Peace and the United Nations* (1952).

Burkina Faso/Mali Frontier Dispute Case *1986 I.C.J. Rep. 554*. By joint letter of 14 October 1983, the Ministers of Foreign Affairs of the Republic of Mali and the Republic of Upper Volta submitted to the Registrar of the ICJ a Special Agreement of 16 September 1983 by which Mali and Upper Volta (which changed its name to Burkina Faso from 4 August 1984) agreed to submit to a Chamber of the Court a dispute relating to the delimitation of part of their common frontier. In its decision, the Chamber laid down in detail the precise delimitation of the boundary between the States. In their Special Agreement, the Parties specified that the decision should be based on the "intangibility of frontiers inherited from colonisation." Because of this, the Chamber found that it "could not disregard the principle of ***uti possidetis***" (at 565). In applying the principle, the Chamber noted that "[t]he essence of the principle lies in its primary aim of securing respect for the territorial boundaries at the moment when independence is achieved. . . . There is no doubt that the obligation to respect pre-existing international frontiers in the event of a State succession derives from a general rule of international law, whether or not the rule is expressed in the formula *uti possidetis*" (at 566). The Chamber also addressed the apparent conflict between *uti possidetis* and self-determination: "At first sight this principle conflicts outright with another one, the right of peoples to self-determination. In fact, however, the maintenance of the territorial status quo in Africa is often seen as the wisest course, to preserve what has been achieved by peoples who have struggled for their independence, and to avoid a disruption which would deprive the continent of the gains achieved by much sacrifice" (at 567).

Bush doctrine In his National Security Strategy of September 2002, President George W. Bush, citing the ineffectiveness of traditional deterrence against "rogue" States and terrorists and the use of weapons of mass destruction as "weapons of choice," redefined the circumstances justifying the exercise of the right of **self-defense**. He asserted: "For centuries, international law recognized that nations need not suffer an attack before they can lawfully take action to defend themselves against forces that present an imminent danger of attack. . . . We must adapt the concept of imminent threat to the capabilities and objectives of today's adversaries. . . . To forestall or prevent . . . hostile acts by our adversaries, the United States will, if necessary, act preemptively." However, he said that the US would not use force in all cases to preempt emerging threats and States should not use preemption as a pretext for aggression.

Bustamante y Rivero, Jose Luis 1894-1975. Peruvian national; Professor, Arequipa 1930-34; Judge of the ICJ 1961-70. Principal Publications: *El laudo arbitral sobre Tacna y Arica* (1929); *El Tratado de Derecho Civil Internacional de 1940 de Montevideo* (1942); *La ONU en la Palacio de Chaillot* (1952); *Panamericanismo e Ibero-americanismo* (1953); *La sub-estimacon del Derecho en el mundo moderno* (1954); *Las Nuevas Concepciones Juridicas sobre el alcance del mar territorial* (1955).

Bustamante y Sirven, Antonio Sanches de 1865-1951. Cuban. Judge, PCIJ 1921-39. Author of the *Code Bustamante* (of private international law); *Derecho International Publico* (5 vols., 1933-8); *El Mar Territorial* (1930); *The World Court* (trans. Read) (1925).

Butler, Sir (George) Geoffrey (Gilbert) 1887-1929. British scholar; fellow of Corpus Christi College, Cambridge 1910-29. Works include *Handbook to the League of Nations* (1919 and 1925); *Studies in Statecraft* (1920); *The Development of International Law* (with Maccoby, 1928).

Bynkershoek, Cornelius van 1673-1743. A classical Dutch writer on international law of the positivist school. His principal works are: *De Dominio Maris (Sovereignty over the Sea); De Foro Legatorum (Jurisdiction over Ambassadors)* (1721); *and Quaestionum Juris Publici (Questions of Public Law)* (1737).

C

cables and pipelines, submarine   Though the régime of cables under the high seas, the main principles of which are set out in *I Oppenheim 760-762,* continues to depend on the International Convention for the Protection of Submarine Telegraphic Cables of 14 March 1884 *(163 C.T.S. 391),* that instrument is supplemented, particularly in relation to the laying of pipelines, by the provisions of the UN Convention on the Law of the Sea 1982 *(1833 U.N.T.S. 3)*, which provides (1) generally for the freedom of all States to lay cables and pipelines on the bed of the high sea, including the continental shelf (arts. 79 and 112); (2) that each State shall have a duty to constitute willful or negligent injury to such installations criminal offences under its law (arts.113 and 114); and (3) that each State shall similarly provide for indemnification of injury to one cable, etc., occasioned by laying or repairing another, and losses of anchors, nets, etc., incurred in avoiding injury to cables, etc. (art. 115). As to treatment of submarine cables in war, see art. 54 of the Regulations respecting the Laws and Customs of War on Land annexed to Hague Convention IV 1907 *(205 C.T.S. 277)*; and *see also* Colombos, *International Law of the Sea* (6th ed.), 535-9.

cabotage   "The littoral State may, in the absence of special treaties to the contrary, exclude foreign vessels from navigation and trade along the coast, the so-called *cabotage*, and reserve this *cabotage* exclusively for its own vessels. *Cabotage* meant originally navigation and trade along the same stretch of coast between the ports thereof, such coast belonging to one and the same State. However, the term *cabotage* or coasting trade as used in commercial treaties comprises now sea trade between any two ports of the same country, whether on the same coasts or different coasts, provided always that the different coasts are all of them the coasts of one and the same country as a political and geographical unit in contradistinction to the coasts of colonies or dominions of such countries": *I Oppenheim (3rd ed.) 493*. Arts. 2 and 7 of the **Chicago Convention** on International Civil Aviation 1944 *(15 U.N.T.S. 295)* reserve air *cabotage* to the territorial State, and that reservation extends to traffic between the territorial State and its overseas territories.

CACM   *See* **Central American Common Market**.

CADIZ   *See* **air defense identification zones**.

Caire Claim   *(France v. Mexico) (1929) 5 I.L.R. 146*. Upon a claim in respect of the murder of a French national in an attempt at extortion by Mexican military officers, *held* by the Mixed Claims Commissions set up by the Convention of 25 September 1924 *(79 L.N.T.S. 418)* that Mexico was liable irrespective of fault or the exclusion of liability for banditry by the *compromis* on the principle of "objective responsibility," the offenders having acted in and taken advantage of their military capacity. The liability of a State for the actions of its military, even where acting *ultra vires*, is dealt with in art. 7 of the ILC Draft Articles on State Responsibility 2001 *(UN Doc. A/56/10 Chap. IV.E.1)* which provides that "[t]he conduct of an organ of a State or of a person or entity empowered to exercise elements of the governmental authority shall be considered an act of the State under international law if the organ, person or entity acts in that capacity, even if it exceeds its authority or contravenes instructions."

Calvo clause, doctrine   The so-called "Calvo clause," at one time frequently incorporated in contracts between government of Latin American States and nationals of other States and commonly providing that such nationals shall rely exclusively upon local remedies for the solution of any disputes and shall not attempt to invoke diplomatic intervention, derives from the "Calvo doctrine," propounded by the Argentine writer Carlos Calvo (*Le droit international* (5th ed., 1896), vol. 3, § 1276), to the effect that foreign nationals are entitled to no more protection than domestic nationals, which was incorporated into the constitutions of some Latin-American States in the shape of provisions, *e.g.*, implying "Calvo Clauses" in contracts. For a celebrated example of the clause, see *North American Dredging Co. Claim (1926) 4 R.I.A.A. 26*. A Calvo clause, generally speaking, is either unnecessary (in that the exhaustion of **local remedies** is usually a condition precedent of the making of a diplomatic claim) or ineffective (because the right of diplomatic intervention belongs to the State, not the individual, and cannot be renounced by the latter). *See generally* Summers, Recent Aspects of the Calvo Doctrine and the Challenge to International Law, *19 Virg. L. R. 459 (1932-3)*; Lipstein, The Place of the Calvo Clause in International Law, *22 B.Y.I.L. 130 (1945)*; Freeman, The Calvo Clause, *40 A.J.I.L. 121 (1946)*.

Calvo, Carlos   1824-1906. Argentine historian, diplomat and jurist who lived much of his life in diplomatic service abroad, primarily in Europe. Major works include *Derecho internacional teorico y practico de Europa y America* (1863); *Dictionnaire du droit international public et privé* (1885). He is credited with the development of the so-called Calvo doctrine which forms the basis of the **Calvo clause**.

Cameroon-Nigeria Boundary Case (Cameroon v. Nigeria) 2002 I.C.J. Rep. forthcoming. The case was initiated on 29 March 1994 by Cameroon against Nigeria concerning matters relating essentially to the question of sovereignty over the Bakassi Peninsula and to the delimitation of the maritime boundary between the two States. By an additional application of 6 June 1994, the Court was asked to consider a further dispute relating essentially to the question of sovereignty over a part of the territory of Cameroon in the area of Lake Chad. The application founded the jurisdiction of the Court on the basis of the declarations of the two parties under art. 36(2) of the its Statute. Nigeria filed preliminary objections to the jurisdiction of the Court and the admissibility of the application. In its judgment of 11 June 1998, the Court *found* that it had jurisdiction to adjudicate upon the merits and that Cameroon's requests were admissible: *1998 I.C.J. Rep. 275*. On 28 October 1998, Nigeria submitted a request for interpretation of the judgment of 11 June 1998; by its judgment of 25 March 1999, the Court found that Nigeria's request for interpretation was inadmissible: *1999 I.C.J. Rep. 24*. On 30 June 1999, the Republic of Equatorial Guinea filed an application for permission to intervene in the case pursuant to art. 62 of the Court's Statute. By an Order of 21 October 1999, the Court authorized Equatorial Guinea to intervene on the basis that it had sufficiently established that it had an interest of a legal nature which could be affected by any judgment which the Court might hand down for the purpose of determining the maritime boundary between Cameroon and Nigeria: *1999 I.C.J. Rep. 1029*.

In its judgment of 10 October 2002, the Court *held* (14 to 2) that the land boundary between the two countries had been fixed by treaties entered into during the colonial period and upheld the validity of those treaties. In doing so, it rejected the theory of **historic con-**

solidation put forward by Nigeria. The Court proceeded to delimit both the land and maritime boundaries between the two States. As a consequence of its delimitation, the Court called upon Nigeria to withdraw from, *inter alia*, the Bakassi Peninsula. Finally, the Court rejected Cameroon's claims for reparations, holding that any injury to Cameroon sustained as a result of Nigeria's occupation of its land would be sufficiently addressed by the evacuation of those territories.

canals "When canals are confined within the territory of a single state they are integral parts of the territory. Thus, the Corinth Canal, although it is kept open to vessels generally, is exclusively within the control of Greece. Where, however, a canal is so constructed as to affect an international waterway system, or an international drainage area, it may be subject to [other] rules. . . . The great interoceanic canals, such as the Suez and Panama Canals, have been subjected to particular international treaty regimes": *I Oppenheim 591.* Cf *Wimbledon Case P.C.I.J., Ser. A, No. 1. See also* **rivers**.

Canevaro Case *(Italy v. Peru) (1912) 11 R.I.A.A. 405.* By the Protocol of 25 April 1910 *(211 C.T.S. 7)*, there was submitted to arbitration the claim of the three Canevaro brothers arising out of default on payments due to the firm of Jose Canevaro & Sons, including the question whether Don Rafael Canevaro had any right to be considered as an Italian claimant. A tribunal of the PCA (MM. Renault, Fusinato, Calderon) *held* that Peru had the right to deny him that status, he being a double national born in Peru who had accepted election to the Peruvian Senate, for which only citizens were eligible, and had obtained the authorization of both the Peruvian Government and the Peruvian Congress for his acceptance of appointment as the Netherlands' consul-general.

capital punishment *See* **death penalty**.

capitulation Derived from *caput*, a head, the term capitulation has been used in three particular senses in the literature of international law: (1) as denoting an agreement to surrender on certain heads or terms: cf. the several Capitulations *eo nomine* of French fortresses, etc., in the Franco-Prussian War 1870-1 *(142 C.T.S. 287f, 465f.)*; (2) as denoting an agreement for the hire of troops; cf. the General Capitulation of 3 November 1764 between France and the Catholic Swiss Cantons *(43 C.T.S. 89)*; and (3) as designating a treaty regulating, on the basis of extraterritoriality, the status of nationals of Christian or Western States in the territory of Mohammedan or Eastern States; cf. the Capitulations between Great Britain and Turkey of September 1675 *(13 C.T.S. 429)*, renewed *eo nomine* by the Treaty of the Dardanelles of 1809 *(60 C.T.S. 323)*. Cf. also the Treaty of Commerce and Navigation of 29 April 1861 between Great Britain and Turkey *(124 C.T.S. 83)* with its specific reference in the preamble to "existing Capitulations and Treaties." The term "capitulation" was not used in or in relation to treaties establishing extra-territorial régimes in the Far East. The use of the term in the first sense given above is adopted in the title and language of Chapter IV of the Hague Regulations respecting the Laws and Customs of War on Land 1899 and 1907 *(187 C.T.S. 429, 205 C.T.S. 277) (Des Capitulations)*, providing in its single article (art. 35) that "capitulations *(capitulations)*" agreed on between contracting parties must be in accordance with the rules of military honor and must be scrupulously observed.

capture "The general principle governing the capture of a vessel as between the captor and the captured ship appears to be that capture is complete when the vessel submits to the will of the captor, and this may be done without necessarily placing a prize crew on board. The following principles are deemed to represent the English point of view as to the time of capture: (1) as between the capturing vessel and the prize, the capture is complete when the prize is under the control of the captor; (2) as between the owner of the captured ship and the captor, property does not pass to the Crown until it has been condemned by the Prize Court of the captor; (3) condemnation by a Prize Court constitutes a valid and complete title in favour of the Crown and divests the owner of the captured vessel and his cargo as from the date of capture. . . . In the English statutes regulating naval prize, the words employed are 'capture,' 'take a prize' and in judicial decisions, the words 'seize' or 'seizure' or 'seize in prize' or 'capture' are common. All import the same meaning. . . . The French Instructions of 1934 contained detailed definitions of the terms *capture, saisie* and *déroutement.* . . . The latest German Prize Ordinance of 1939 uses the words . . . *beschlagname* (capture of the vessel) and *einziehung* (capture of the cargo)": Colombos, *International Law of the Sea* (6th ed.), 780-2. *See also* the San Remo Declaration on International Law Applicable to Armed Conflicts at Sea of June 1994 (text in Doswald-Beck, *San Remo Manual of International Law Applicable to Armed Conflicts at Sea (1995)*), of which arts. 135-40 deal with capture of enemy vessels and goods, arts. 141-5 with capture of enemy civil aircraft and goods, arts. 146-52 capture of neutral merchant vessels and goods and arts. 153-8 capture of neutral civil aircraft and goods. *See also* **Capture in Maritime War, Convention etc.**

Capture in Maritime War, Convention relative to Restrictions on the Right of The Hague Convention XI 1907 *(205 C.T.S. 367)*, which bears this title, stipulates for the exemption of postal correspondence on board neutral vessels, and of coastal fishing vessels and vessels charged with religious, scientific or philanthropic missions, from capture in maritime warfare, and prescribes a régime for the treatment of crews of captured enemy merchant vessels.

Carnegie Endowment for International Peace This institution, founded by Andrew Carnegie in 1910 "to advance the cause of peace among nations," did much before World War II through its Division of International Law to encourage teaching and publication in international law, being responsible in particular for the establishment of the *Academie de Droit International*, the sponsorship of the **Harvard Research**, and such notable publications as the periodical *International Conciliation, Moore's International Adjudications* and the 22-volume series, **Classics of International Law**. After World War II, the foundation largely turned its attention elsewhere, but in the 1960s organized a "New Program in International Law" of which a notable result was the publication of the internationally-written *Manual of Public International Law* (ed. Sørensen). The Endowment continues to regard its mandate in general terms, with studies and publications relevant to peace broadly defined; it also publishes the bimonthly *Foreign Policy* (since 1970). *See* <www.ceip.org>.

Caroline Incident *(Moore, Digest of International Law, Vol. 2, 25).* On the night of 29 December 1837, the *Caroline*, an American vessel being used in support of the Canadian rebellion, was cut out by a British force from her berth on the American side of the Niagara River and sent adrift over the falls, the incident resulting in the death of two American citizens. Subsequently, in 1841, one Alexander McLeod, a British subject, was arrested in New York on a charge of murder as a result of his having, under the influence of liquor, boasted of having taken part in the destruction of the vessel. He was ultimately acquitted on proof of an alibi. *See **McLeod's Case**.* The two incidents were the subject of prolonged diplomatic exchanges in the course of which "self-defense was changed from a political excuse to a legal doctrine" (Jennings, The Caroline and McLeod Cases, *32 A.J.I.L. 82 (1938)*), it being accepted that urgent necessity, such as had existed here, may justify an incursion into another State's territory in self-defense. "[T]he basic elements of the right of self-defence were aptly set out . . . by the American Secretary of State, Daniel Webster, who considered that there had to be a 'necessity of self-defence, instant, overwhelming, leaving no choice of means and no moment for deliberation' and also that the act should involve 'nothing unreasonable or excessive since the act justified by the necessity of self-defence must be limited by that necessity and kept clearly within it.'": *I Oppenheim 420*. The diplomatic exchanges are to be found in Moore, *Digest of International Law* (1906), Vol. 2, 409. *See* **self-defense**.

cartel (1) "Cartels are conventions between belligerents concluded for the purpose of permitting certain kinds of non-hostile intercourse between them which would otherwise be prevented by war. . . . Thus, communication by post, telegraph, telephone, and railway, which would otherwise not take place, can be arranged by cartels, as can also the exchange of prisoners, . . . Cartel ships are vessels of belligerents which are commissioned for the carriage by sea of exchanged prisoners, . . . or for the carriage of official communications to and from the enemy": *II Oppenheim 542*. (2) "Cartel means in international law, the terms of agreement between belligerents for the exchange or ransom of prisoners. . . . By analogy, the word Kartell is now often used by German economists to denote a Trust, i.e. an agreement between rival merchants to limit production or otherwise temper the extremity of competition": Palgrave, *Dictionary of Political Economy* (1987), 229. In this extended sense, though formerly popular, the term is now more often than not subsumed under the expression restrictive practice.

Carthage Arbitration *(France v. Turkey) (1913) 11 R.I.A.A. 449*. On 16 January 1912, during the war between Turkey and Italy, the French mail steamer Carthage, on a voyage between Marseille and Tunis, was stopped by an Italian torpedo destroyer. An airplane, belonging to a French aviator and being carried to the aviator's address in Tunis, was considered by Italian authorities to be contraband of war. The Carthage was taken to the Italian port of Cagliari where it was detained until 20 January. Being asked whether the capture and temporary seizure of the Carthage was lawful and what, if any, consequences might flow from these acts, the Tribunal (Hammarskjold, Fusinato, Kriege, Renault and de Taube) *held* that the arrest and visit of a neutral vessel on the high seas was lawful; that Italy had insufficient information about the airplane to conclude that it was contraband; and that accordingly the capture and temporary seizure of the Carthage was unlawful. While ordering compensation for the owners of the Carthage, the passengers and shippers and the aircraft owner, the Tribunal declined to award compensation to France, stating that its determination of illegality on the part of Italy was sufficient.

Cassese, Antonio Professor of international law, Florence, 1972- ; judge of the ICTY 1993-2000; one of the drafters of the Rome Statute of the ICC. Principal works include *International Law in a Developing World* (1989); *Human Rights in a Changing World* (1990); *Self-Determination of Peoples: A Legal Reappraisal* (1999); *International Law* (2001); *The Rome Statute of the International Criminal Court: A Commentary* (with others, 2001); *International Criminal Law* (2003).

Cassin, René Samuel 1887-1976. Professor, Lille (1919); Paris (1929—1950); French representative to the League of Nations 1924-38; member and President of the UN Commission on Human Rights; judge (1959-76) and president (1965-68) of the European Court of Human Rights. He has been described as the individual most responsible for the draft of the **Universal Declaration of Human Rights** approved by the UN General Assembly on 10 December 1948. He was awarded the Nobel Prize for Peace in 1968.

casus belli, casus foederis "These terms appear to be sometimes confused. The former signifies an act or proceeding of a provocative nature on the part of one Power which, in the opinion of the offended Power, justifies it in making or declaring war. . . . The latter is an offensive act or proceeding of one state towards another, or any occurrence bringing into existence the condition of things which entitles the latter to call upon its ally to fulfill the undertakings of the alliance existing between them, i.e. a case contemplated by the treaty of alliance": *Satow's Guide to Diplomatic Practice* (5th ed.) 461.

CAT The acronym for the Convention against Torture 1984 *(1465 U.N.T.S. 85)* (*see* **Torture, Convention against**) and for the Committee against Torture established by art 17 of the Convention.

cause of action "In international law, no less than in domestic law, a plaintiff must be able to point to some rule that gives him a cause of action. . . . It is not sufficient merely to show some breach of a legal obligation on the part of the respondent; it must be some obligation that touches a legally protected interest of the applicant": Jennings, General Course on Principles of International Law, *(1967) 121 Hague Recueil 327* at 507. The ICJ has stated that its function "is to state the law, but it may pronounce judgment only in connection with concrete cases where there exists at the time of the adjudication an actual controversy involving a conflict of legal interests between the parties. The Court's judgment must have some practical consequence in the sense that it can affect existing legal rights or obligations of the parties. . . .": *Northern Cameroons Case 1963 I.C.J. Rep. 15* at 33-34. *See also* the *South West Africa Case (Second Phase) 1966 I.C.J. Rep. 6* at 39. *See* Brownlie, *Principles of Public International Law* (5th ed.), 476-8.

Cayuga Indians Case *(Great Britain v. United States) (1926) 6 R.I.A.A. 173*. The Agreement of 18 August 1910 *(211 C.T.S. 408)* provided for the arbitration of, *inter alia*, the claim of the Cayuga Indians settled in Canada to continue to share in annuities provided for in treaties or contracts between New York State and "the Cayuga Nation," as they had up to the War of 1812. The Tribunal (M. Nerincx, Dean Pound, Sir C. Fitzpatrick) *held* that, the Canadian Cayuga being British subjects, the claim lay; and that the responsibility of the US Government was engaged by virtue of art. IX of the **Jay Treaty** 1794 *(52 C.T.S. 243)*. This arbitration is invariably cited as authority for the role of equity in international law, the Tribunal itself saying that, in anomalous situations, "recourse must be had to generally recognized principles of justice and fair dealing." However, this precedential value is diminished by the injunction in the 1910 Agreement that the Tribunal was to apply "international law and equity." US Congress ratified this decision on 22 January 1926. However, the related dispute between the Cayuga Indians and New York State in respect of loss of reservation land continues. In 1980, the Cayuga Indians filed a suit in the Federal District Court claiming $350 million for trespass damages in respect of land. In February 2000, a judge awarded the Cayuga Indians $36.9 million which was later increased to $247.9 million to take account of accrued interest. The case is currently on appeal to the United States District Court.

celestial bodies This term, while not defined, is employed throughout the **Outer Space Treaty** of 27 January 1967 *(610 U.N.T.S. 205)*, and appears to mean all heavenly bodies, apart from the moon. Such celestial bodies are declared to be incapable of national appropriation (art. 2); their exploration and use are to be carried out for the benefit of all mankind (art. 1), exclusively for peaceful purposes (art. 4), and under the rules of international law, including the UN Charter (art. 3).

CENTO The Central Treaty Organization: see **Baghdad Pact**.

Central American Common Market Established by the General Treaty on Central American Economic Integration of 13 December 1960 *(455 U.N.T.S. 3),* CACM consisted originally of three members, Guatemala, El Salvador, and Nicaragua, with Costa Rica and Nicaragua acceding subsequently. The imposition of import duties by Honduras in December 1970 after a dispute with El Salvador amounted, in effect, to its withdrawal although it considered itself a *de jure* member and, in August 1982, resumed trade with El Salvador. "In June 1990 . . . an Economic Action Plan for Central America was approved that envisioned insertion of the region's economy into the global economy. In July 1992 . . . it was agreed to include Panama in certain aspects of the economic community. . . . In 1992 Honduras rejoined the integration process. . . . Although numerous impediments to integration, from military to economic issues, remain in the region, the CACM may nevertheless be revived by the recent surge of interest in economic integration triggered by the **North-American Free Trade Agreement (NAFTA)**": Sands and Klein, *Bowett's Law of International Institutions* (5th ed.), 217-8. CACM's organs comprise a Central American Economic Council, an Executive Council and a Secretariat.

Central American Court of Justice The Court established by the additional Convention to the General Convention of the Central American Peace Conference, Washington, 20 December 1907 *(206 C.T.S. 79);* between the five Central American States of Costa Rica, Guatemala, Honduras, Nicaragua and El Salvador, each party appointing one judge. The Court had jurisdiction over disputes between the contracting States and between individuals and a contracting State, whether or not the individual had the support of his government. The Treaty of Washington, which was of ten years' duration, expired in 1918 and was not renewed. *See* de Bustamente, *The World Court*, Chap. 5; Hudson, The Central American Court of Justice, *26 A.J.I.L. 759 (1932).* A new Central American Court of Justice was established by the Charter of the Organization of Central American States in 1965 but without compulsory jurisdiction and without the right of access for individuals. "In its present incarnation the Central American Court of Justice was established in 1991 and is the judicial branch of the Central American Integration System (SICA) [which replaced the Organization of Central American States] . . . [it] has competence in three types of cases: inter-state disputes, complaints against states and complaints against SICA organs": Sands and Klein, *Bowett's Law of International Institutions* (5th ed.), 412-3.

CERD The acronym for the Committee on the Elimination of All Forms of Racial Discrimination, established by art. 8 of the Convention of the same name of 1965 *(660 U.N.T.S. 195) (see* **racial discrimination**), and sometimes for the Convention itself.

CERN Established by the Convention of 1 July 1953 *(200 U.N.T.S. 149),* subsequently revised) as the Organisation Européenne pour la Recherche Nucléaire (European Organization for Nuclear Research), the organization, whose seat is at Geneva, maintains experimental facilities (including the world's largest accelerator for particle physics research). The 12 founding member States are Belgium, Denmark, France, Germany Greece, Italy, Norway, Sweden, Switzerland, The Netherlands, United Kingdom and Yougoslavia. Yugoslavia left in 1961. The current membership is 20, including Austria (1959), Spain (1961), Portugal (1985) Finland (1991) Poland (1991), Hungary (1992), Czech Republic (1993) Slovak Republic (1993), Bulgaria (1999). The Organization is controlled by a Council, made up of two representatives from each member State, assisted by a Scientific Policy Committee and a Finance Committee. The Organization is managed by a Director-General. Member States are free to opt in or out of programs and the financial contributions are adjusted accordingly. CERN's purpose is to further cooperation by enabling research teams of different nationalities to collaborate. CERN's own staff of about 3500 is complemented by a similar number of visiting scientists, fellows, students and apprentices, involving about 165 universities and institutes. *See* Hermann *et al*, *The History of CERN: I* (1987); Hermann *et al*, *The History of CERN: II* (1990); Krige, *The History of CERN: III* (1996). *See* <http://public.web.cern.ch/public/>.

Cerruti Claim *(Italy v. Colombia) (1911) 11 R.I.A.A. 377*. In 1885, Ernesto Cerruti, an Italian national resident in Colombia, was accused of complicity in a revolutionary movement and his goods confiscated by the local authorities of Cauca, Colombia. By the Protocol of 24 May 1886 *(168 C.T.S. 21)*, various questions concerning him, and principally the question whether he had lost his status as a neutral foreigner, were submitted to the mediation of the King of Spain, whose award of 26 January 1888 *(170 C.T.S. 447)* answered this question in the negative. By the Protocol of 18 August 1894, Cerruti's claims were submitted to the arbitration of the President of the United States, whose award, dated 2 March 1897 *(11 R.I.A.A. 394)*, of £60,000 for loss of property was accepted and duly paid, but whose further award that Colombia should assume responsibility for the liquidation of the debts of Cerruti's firm was rejected by Colombia. Under diplomatic pressure, however, Colombia agreed to implement the whole of the award and, by the *compromis* of 28 October 1909 *(209 C.T.S. 410)*, the parties referred to a mixed commission the computation of the balance due, the commission making its award on 6 July 1911.

Certain Phosphate Lands in Nauru *(Nauru v. Australia) 1993 I.C.J. Rep. 240*. On 19 May 1989, Nauru instituted proceedings before the ICJ against Australia, basing jurisdiction on declarations by the parties under art. 36(2) of the Statute of the ICJ . Nauru alleged that Australia had violated **trusteeship** obligations set forth under art. 76 of the UN Charter and arts. 3 and 5 of the Trusteeship Agreement for Nauru of 1 November 1947. In addition, Nauru alleged that Australia breached international standards regarding the principle of **self-determination** and the **permanent sovereignty** over natural resources. Australia raised objections to the admissibility of the application and the Court's jurisdiction.

On 26 June 1992, the Court *held*: (a) (unanimously) against Australia in its preliminary objection based on the reservation it made when accepting the compulsory jurisdiction of the Court; (b) (12 to1) against the preliminary objection alleging that, prior to independence, Nauru waived all claims regarding the rehabilitation of phosphate lands worked out before 1 July 1967; (c) (12 to 1) against the preliminary objection based on the UN's termination of the trusteeship over Nauru; (d) (12 to 1) against the preliminary objection regarding the effect of timing on Nauru's application; (e) (12 to 1) against the preliminary objection of Nauru's supposed absence of good faith; (f) (9 to 4) against the preliminary objection based on New Zealand and United Kingdom's non-involvement in the proceedings; and (g) (unanimously) in favor of the preliminary objection regarding the claim that the overseas assets of British Phosphate Commissioners were new. On 9 September 1993, both parties jointly informed the Court that they had settled and agreed to end the proceedings; and, by order of the Court on 13 September 1993, the case was removed from Court's list: *1993 I.C.J. Rep. 332*.

Certain Property Case *(Liechtenstein v. Germany)*. On 1 June 2001, Liechtenstein instituted proceedings before the ICJ against Germany, basing jurisdiction on art. 1 of the European Convention for the Peaceful Settlement of Disputes 1957 *(E.T.S. No. 23)*. Liechtenstein alleged that, in 1945, Czechoslovakia had passed the Benes decrees, which allowed the confiscation of property belonging to Hungarian and German nationals who were living in Czechoslovakian territory. Czechoslovakia treated Liechtenstein nationals as Germans, thereby confiscating their property. The seized property was never returned, nor was compensation afforded to the victims. In its application, Liechtenstein claimed that Germany had, in 1952, agreed not to object to the seizure of German property for the purposes of reparations as a result of the war. Liechtenstein asserted that it had subsequently made an agreement with Germany that this agreement did not apply to property of Liechtenstein nationals. However, Liechtenstein contended that Germany changed its position in a 1998 court decision, which applied the original agreement to a painting originally belonging to a Liechtenstein national, and allowed for its return to Czechoslovakia. Liechtenstein claimed that Germany had not respected Liechtenstein property rights in its decision which breached international law by failing to make provision for compensation. Liechtenstein requested the Court to declare Germany legally responsible for this loss and obligated to compensate Liechtenstein. In addition, Liechtenstein requested the Court to assess the nature and amount of reparations in separate proceedings, if necessary. The Court has yet to decide this case.

cession   The term cession, clearly derived from the *cessio* of Roman law, is used in international law to denote any transfer of sovereignty over territory by one State to another, and not merely, as in popular speech, a forced transfer. "The only form in which a cession can be effected is an agreement normally in the form of a treaty between the ceding and the acquiring state. . . . The treaty of cession should be followed by actual tradition of the territory, . . . unless such territory is already occupied by the new owner, as in the case where the cession is the outcome of war and the ceded territory has been during such war in the military occupation of the state to which it is now ceded": *I Oppenheim 680*-3. Previous editions of *Oppenheim* suggested that "the validity of the cession does not depend upon tradition, the cession being completed by ratification of the treaty. . . ." However, the current edition notes that "of course, the new owner-state cannot exercise its territorial supremacy thereon until it has taken possession of the ceded territory": *I Oppenheim 683. See also* Jennings, *The Acquisition of Territory in International Law* (1963), 16-9.

Chamizal Case   *(Mexico v. United States) (1911) 11 R.I.A.A. 316.* The question submitted by the Convention of 24 June 1910 *(211 C.T.S. 259)* for arbitration by the joint Boundary Commission, reinforced by a neutral President, was that of the "difference as to the international title of the Chamizal tract," an area located between the abandoned and the new bed of the Rio Grande near El Paso, Texas. Mexico contended that the Treaty of Guadelupe Hidalgo 1848 *(102 C.T.S. 29)* and the Gadsden Treaty 1853 *(111 C.T.S. 235)* had established a fixed boundary, unaffected by later changes in the course of the river. The United States contended that the intention had been to establish a boundary following the channel in the event of gradual **accretion** (though not in that of a sudden change of bed); alternatively that a title to the tract had been established by prescription. *Held* that (the US commissioner dissenting in some respects) the treaties referred to were ambiguous, but must be construed in the light of the subsequent practice of the parties to have established an arcifinious rather than a fixed boundary; that the possession of the United States, having been constantly protested by Mexico, was not of such a character as to give rise to any title by prescription; and that, applying the Convention of 1884 *(164 C.T.S. 337)* in the light of which the earlier treaties must be interpreted, that part of the tract formed by gradual accretion up to 1864 was to be awarded to the United States, and the remainder, formed by a cutoff in the floods of 1864, was to be awarded to Mexico.

charge d'affaires   Art. 14 of the Vienna Convention on Diplomatic Relations 1961 *(500 U.N.T.S. 95)* states that there are three classes of heads of mission, the third being "that of charge d'affaires accredited to Ministers for Foreign Affairs"—unlike the other two classes of ambassadors and ministers, etc., accredited to Heads of State. The article goes on to provide however, that, "[e]xcept as concerns precedence and etiquette, there shall be no differentiation between heads of mission by reason of their class." With respect to modern practice, it appears that the title of *charge d'affaires*, along with that of all other heads of missions except ambassador has all but disappeared. *See* Denza, *Diplomatic Law*, (2nd ed.), 94. Art. 5(2) of the Vienna Convention provides that, "[i]f the sending State accredits a head of mission to one or more other States it may establish a diplomatic mission headed by a *chargé d'affaires ad interim* in each State where the head of mission has not his permanent seat." However, such individuals are not themselves heads of mission.

Charter on the Rights and Welfare of the African Child *See* **African Charter on the Rights and Welfare of the Child**.

Chemical Weapons Convention Properly styled the Convention on the Prohibition of the Development, Production, Stockpiling and Use of Chemical Weapons and on their Destruction, the convention was adopted on 3 September 1992 *(1974 U.N.T.S. 3)*. Art. 2(1) defines chemical weapons as "(a) Toxic chemicals and their precursors, except where intended for purposes not prohibited under this Convention, as long as the types and quantities are consistent with such purposes; (b) Munitions and devices, specifically designed to cause death or other harm through the toxic properties of those toxic chemicals specified in subparagraph (a), which would be released as a result of the employment of such munitions and devices; (c) Any equipment specifically designed for use directly in connection with the employment of munitions and devices specified in subparagraph (b)."States parties are required "never under any circumstances" to develop, produce, acquire, stockpile, retain or transfer any chemical weapons (art. 1(a)); to use them (art. 1(b)); to engage in any military preparation to use them (art. 1(c)); or to assist, encourage or induce any person to engage in a prohibited act under the convention (art. 1(d)). Additionally, any chemical weapons within a State's jurisdiction or control are to be destroyed (art. 1(2)), as are any production facilities (art. 1(4)). An Organization for the Prohibition of Chemical Weapons was established "to achieve the object and purpose of this Convention, to ensure the implementation of its provisions, including those for international verification of compliance with it, and to provide a forum for consultation and cooperation among States Parties" (art. 8(A)(1)). *See* Bothe, *The New Chemical Weapons Convention: Implementation and Prospects* (1998). *See* <www.opcw.org>.

Cheng, Bin 1921- . Visiting Professor of Law, Detroit Mercy; Professor of Air and Space Law, London 1967-1986, *Officier, Ordre des Palmes Academique*, 1988. Works include: *General Principles of Law as Applied by International Courts and Tribunals* (1953); *The Law of International Air Transport* (1962).

Chevreau Claim *(France v. UK) (1931) 2 R.I.A.A. 1113*. In early 1918, British military personnel on expedition in Persia arrested Julien Chevreau, a French citizen, on suspicion of espionage. Chevreau was detained in Baghdad until, following representations by the French Government, he was transferred to French authorities in Port Said on 7 March 1919, having been deported via India to Egypt. Chevreau, who died in 1925 and whose widow pursued his claims, alleged on his release that he had been given no reason for his arrest and detention and afforded no contact with the French Consul, and had been maltreated during his detention. The matter having been submitted to arbitration by the two governments, the Sole Arbitrator (Beichman) *held* that the allegations against Chevreau were sufficient to justify his arrest (he had been observing British petroleum warehouses and a Russian wireless telegraphy installation; he had in his possession a portrait of the Kaiser and Empress; he had prevaricated under questioning); that his move to, and incarceration at, Baghdad was unlawful, there having been no investigation or adjudication by the UK; and that France had adduced no evidence of maltreatment. Damages for illegal detention were assessed at £2,000.

Chicago Convention The Convention on International Civil Aviation, signed at Chicago on 7 December 1944 *(15 U.N.T.S. 295)*, laying down the general principles of air navigation (Part I), establishing the **International Civil Aviation Organization** (ICAO) (Part II), the contemporary system of international air transport (Part III), and stipulating for the denunciation of the Paris Convention of 1919 (see **air navigation**) and the **Havana Convention** of 1928, and the abrogation of inconsistent arrangements (arts. 80, 82). The Conference which elaborated the Convention also drew up the International Air Services Transit Agreement *(84 U.N.T.S. 389)*, otherwise known as the **Two Freedoms Agreement,** stipulating for reciprocal rights of overflight and non-traffic landing, and the similarly named **Five Freedoms Agreement** *(171 U.N.T.S. 387)*, which proved abortive. *See I Oppenheim 652-8*; Johnson, *Rights in Air Space* (1965), 58-70; Cheng, *The Law of International Air Transport* (1962).

Chief Executives Board Properly styled the United Nations System Chief Executives Board, the CEB is a renamed (in 2000) **Administrative Committee on Co-ordination** with expanded functions and altered operational methods. Composed of the executive heads of the 27 member organizations and chaired by the UN Secretary-General, CEB is assisted by two High-Level Committees, on Management and on Programmes. It has established a series of priorities, including the follow-up to the Millennium Summit, the security and safety of staff and a partnership for African development. *See* <http://ceb.unsystem.org>.

Child, Convention on the Rights of the Thirty years after the adoption of the Declaration on the Rights of the Child by the General Assembly (GA Res. 1386 (XIV) of 20 November 1959), the Assembly adopted the Convention on the Rights of the Child on 20 November 1989 as GA Res. 44/25 *(1577 U.N.T.S. 3)*; the Convention entered into force on 2 September 1990. While a child enjoys the full range of **human rights** guaranteed under the conventional régime, these rights being applicable to "everyone" without limitation as to age, and indeed in some cases the child meriting particular addition rights (*see* art. 24 of the International Covenant on **Civil and Political Rights** 1966; *999 U.N.T.S. 171*), it was nonetheless thought important to promulgate a human rights instrument especially for children on the basis that a child "by reason of his physical and mental immaturity, needs special safeguards and care, including appropriate legal protection" (Convention, Preamble). For the purposes of the Convention, a child is "every human being below the age of 18 years unless, under the law applicable to the child, majority is attained earlier" (art. 1). Two cardinal principles underlie the Convention: that, in all actions concerning the child, "the best interests of the child shall be the primary consideration" (art. 3(1)); and that, in all matters affecting the child, the child has the right to express his or her views, these views "being given due weight in accordance with the age and maturity of the child" (art. 12(1)).

The rights afforded the child are all expressed in terms of obligations upon States parties rather than as rights directly for the child; and are also all expressed in child-specific terms, often involving an intermingling of the civil and political and the economic and social. These rights may be grouped under 4 heads (*per* LeBlanc, *The Convention on the Rights of the Child: UN Lawmaking on Human Rights* (1995), Part 2): (1) Survival rights: to life (art. 6); to an adequate standard of living (art. 27), to social security (art. 26) and to health (arts. 24-5). (2) Membership rights: to non-discrimination on the basis of "race, color, sex, language, religion, political or other opinion, national, ethnic or social origin, property, birth or other status" (art. 2(1)); to a name and nationality (art. 7); to family life, the parents or legal guardians having "the primary responsibility for the upbringing and development of the child" (art. 18(1)); and, if necessary, to alternative care arrangements, including, where permitted, adoption (arts. 20-1). (3) Protection rights: against illicit transfer (art. 11); against "all forms of physical and mental violence, injury or abuse, neglect or negligent treatment, maltreatment or exploitation. . . ." (art. 19(1)); against economic exploitation and harmful work (art. 32; see **child labor**); against narcotic drugs and psychotropic substances (art. 33); against sexual exploitation and abuse (art. 34; *see also* art. 36; see **child exploitation**); against abduction (art. 35); against torture, cruel, inhuman or degrading treatment or punishment (art. 37 (a)); and to due process rights (art. 37(b)-(d)). (4) Empowerment rights: to free expression (arts. 12-3); to information (art. 17); to thought, conscience and religion (art. 14); to association and assembly (art. 15); and to education (arts. 28-9). These right have been supplemented by two Optional Protocols of 25 May 2000, on the Sale of Children, Child Prostitution and Child Pornography (*see* **child exploitation**) and on the Involvement of Children in Armed Conflicts (*see* **child soldiers**).

The Convention established a Committee on the Rights of the Child (CRC) of ten experts (art. 43) to consider and comment upon reports from States as to the measures they have taken to give effect to the Convention (art. 43(1)). States are to report every five years (art. 44(1)(b)). *See generally* Van Bueren, *The International Law on the Rights of the Child* (1995); LeBlanc, *supra*; Dettick, *The United Nations Convention on the Rights of the Child* (1992); Saulle, *The Rights of the Child: International Instruments* (1995).

child exploitation   The Convention on the Rights of the Child 1989 *(1577 U.N.T.S. 3*; see **Child, Convention on the Rights of the**) contains general provisions to protect children from exploitation (*see* particularly arts. 32-36). To supplement these provisions, an Optional Protocol on the Sale of Children, Child Prostitution and Child Pornography was adopted by the General Assembly on 25 May 2000 as Res. 54/263 *((2000) 39 I.L.M. 1290)*; the Protocol entered into force on 18 January 2002. Under art. 1, States parties are to "prohibit the sale of children, child prostitution and child pornography." Sale of children is defined as "any act or transaction whereby a child is transferred by any person or group of persons to another for remuneration or any other consideration (art. 2(a)); child prostitution as "the use of a child in sexual activities for remuneration or other consideration (art. 2(b)); and child pornography as "any representation, by whatever means, of a child engaged in real or simulated sexual activities or any representation of the sexual parts of a child for primarily sexual purposes" (art. 2(c)). These acts are to be criminalized by States (art. 3(1)) and punishable "by appropriate penalties that take into account their grave nature" (art. 3(2)). States are to submit a comprehensive report on their implementation of the Optional Protocol to the Committee on the Rights of the Child within two years of its entry into force (art. 12(1)); thereafter, States are to include implementation information in their periodic, regular reports to the CRC (art. 12(2)). While a child is not defined in the Optional Protocol, the term bears the same meaning as in art. 1 of the Convention on the Rights of the Child: a "human being below the age of 18 years."

child labor   The Convention on the Rights of the Child 1989 *(1577 U.N.T.S. 3*; *see* **Child, Convention on the Rights of the**) contains, in art. 32(1), a general obligation on States parties to protect a child from "economic exploitation and from performing any work that is likely to be hazardous to or to interfere with the child's education, or to be harmful to the child's or physical, mental, spiritual, moral or social development." To these ends, States are, *inter alia*, to set a minimum age for employment and to adopt regulations on the hours and conditions of employment (art. 32(2)). The ILO has been active in the area of child labor with two main conventions. The Minimum Age Convention of 20 June 1973 *(ILO Convention 138)* sets a minimum age of 15 years for admission to employment (art. 2(3)); 14 years for States "whose economy and educational facilities are insufficiently developed (art. 2(4)). The minimum age for admission to employment "which by its nature or the circumstances in which it is carried out is likely to jeopardize the health, safety or morals of young persons" is 18 years (art. 3(1)). "Insufficiently developed" States may limit the application of the Convention (art. 5(1)), though not in respect of "mining and quarrying; manufacturing; construction; electricity, gas and water; sanitary services; transport, storage and communication; and plantation and other agricultural undertakings mainly producing for commercial purposes" (art. 5(3)).

On 17 September 1999, the ILO General Conference adopted the Worst Forms of Child Labor Convention *(ILO Convention 182; 38 I.L.M. 1207 (1999))*, requiring States parties to "take immediate and effective measures to secure the prohibition and elimination of the worst forms of child labor as a matter of urgency" (art. 1). For the purposes of the Convention, a child is ant person under the age of 18 years (art. 2); and the worst forms of child labor include all forms of slavery and kindred practices, such as the sale and trafficking in children, debt bondage, serfdom and forced and compulsory labor; the use or procuring of a child for prostitution or pornographic purposes; the use or procuring of a child for illicit activities, in particular drug trafficking; and any work which, by its nature or the circumstances in which it is carried out, is likely to harm the health, safety or morals of children (art. 3).

child pornography *See* **child exploitation.**

child prostitution *See* **child exploitation**.

child soldiers The Convention on the Rights of the Child 1989 (*1577 U.N.T.S. 3*; see **Child, Convention on the Rights of the**) requires States parties to take "all feasible measures to ensure that persons who have not attained the age of 15 years do not take an direct part in hostilities" (art. 38(2)). States are to "refrain from recruiting any person [under 15] into their armed forces" (art. 38(3)). To supplement these quite vague and unsatisfactory provisions, an Optional Protocol on the Involvement of Children in Armed Conflicts was adopted by the General Assembly on 25 May 2000 as Res. 54/263 *((2000) 39 I.L.M. 1285)*; the Protocol entered into force on 12 February 2002. States parties are to "ensure that persons [under 18] are not compulsorily recruited into their armed forces" (art. 2) and to raise the minimum age for voluntary recruitment beyond that in art. 38(3) of the Convention, without mandating the extent of the raise. However, where States allow voluntary recruitment under 18, they must ensure that the recruitment is genuinely voluntary, accompanied by the informed consent of the child's parents or guardians and by reliable proof of age (art. 3(3)). Art. 4 provides that armed groups distinct from a State's armed forces "should not, under any circumstances, recruit or use in hostilities persons under the age of 18 years" (art. 4). States are to submit a comprehensive report on their implementation of the Optional Protocol to the Committee on the Rights of the Child within two years of its entry into force (art. 8(1)); thereafter, States are to include implementation information in their periodic, regular reports to the CRC (art. 8(2)).

children, sale of *See* **child exploitation.**

Chinn, Oscar, Case *(United Kingdom v. Belgium) (1934) P.C.I.J., Ser. A/B, No. 63.* By the Special Agreement of 13 April 1934 *(154 L.N.T.S. 361)*, the parties referred to the PCIJ the question whether the economic measures of the Belgian Government, taken in circumstances of depression and involving the reduction of the Congo river transport rates and the subsidization of a State-controlled concern to the detriment of the rival business of Oscar Chinn, a British national, were incompatible with obligations towards the United Kingdom. *Held* (6 to 5) that the measures in question did not infringe Belgium's obligations—notably the freedom of trade and equality of treatment provisions of the Convention of St. Germain of 10 September 1919 revising the General Act of Berlin and the Declaration of Brussels respecting the Congo *(8 L.N.T.S 26)*.

Chorzów Factory (Indemnity) (Merits) Case *(Germany v. Poland) (1928) P.C.I.J., Ser. A., No. 17*. By this judgment dated 13 September 1928, the Court *held* (9 to 3) that Poland was under an obligation to pay as reparation to the German Government, not merely the value of the undertakings expropriated at the time of their acquisition, but a compensation corresponding to the damage sustained by their owners, such compensation to be by way of a lump sum payment, the calculation of which was reserved pending the consultation of experts. Experts were appointed by the President's Order *(P.C.I.J., Ser. C, No. 16 at 11)* but, following a settlement of the dispute by agreement between the parties, their inquiry was terminated by a further Presidential order and an order of the Court put an end to the entire proceedings *(P.C.I.J., Ser. A., Nos. 18/19)*.

Chorzów Factory Case (Jurisdiction) *(Germany v. Poland) (1927) P.C.I.J., Ser. A, No. 9*. Germany sought a declaration that the Court, having decided in the **German Interests in Polish Upper Silesia Case** (1926) *P.C.I.J., Ser. A., No. 7*, that the Polish Government's attitude towards certain German companies whose undertakings it took over was not in conformity with arts. 6-22 of the Convention concerning Upper Silesia of 15 May 1922 *(9 L.N.T.S. 466)*, Poland was now under a duty to compensate these companies. The Polish Government raised a preliminary objection to the jurisdiction, art. 23(1) of the Convention, which gave jurisdiction over "differences of opinion resulting from [its] interpretation and application," not contemplating differences in regard to reparation claimed for its violation, and that Convention further providing alternative remedies for the latter. *Held* principally (10 to 3), overruling the objection, that "It is a principle of international law that the breach of an engagement involves an obligation to make reparation. . . . Differences relating to reparations, which may be due by reason of failure to apply a convention, are consequently differences relating to its application." Following this judgment, the German Government requested an interim measure of protection under art. 41 of the PCIJ Statute in the shape of an order for the payment of RM 30m. within one month. This the Court refused as an endeavor in effect "to obtain an interim judgment in favour of a part of the claim": *P.C.I.J., Ser. A., No. 12*. The judgment of the Court of 16 December 1927 upon Germany's application for the interpretation of Judgments Nos. 7 (that in the **German Interests in Polish Upper Silesia Case**) and 8 *(P.C.I.J., Ser. A, No. 13)* does not in fact touch the latter judgment.

cipher Any method of encrypting text (concealing its readability and meaning). It is also sometimes used to refer to the encrypted text message itself. Its origin is in the Arabic *cifr* meaning empty or zero. Art. 27(1) of the Vienna Convention on Diplomatic Relations 1961 *(500 U.N.T.S. 95)* provides that "the mission may employ all appropriate means [of communication] including diplomatic couriers and messages in code or cipher." "Without the right to send messages in code . . . an embassy cannot usefully perform its function of observing and reporting, and it will be seriously hampered in the conduct of negotiations on any matter of importance if it cannot receive confidential instructions. *Satow's Guide to Diplomatic Practice* (5th ed.), 427.

CITES The Convention on International Trade in Endangered Species of Wild Fauna and Flora and Fauna (CITES) was signed on 3 March 1973 *(998 U.N.T.S. 243)* and entered into force on 1 July 1975. The Convention provides for a licensing system for all trade in specimens of selected species. The most stringent safeguards are provided for those species contained in Appendix I to the Convention, which includes species threatened with extinction (art. 3). Less stringent safeguard are provided from species in Appendix II, which includes species not necessarily threatened with extinction, but in which trade must be controlled in order to avoid utilization incompatible with their survival (art. 4). Finally, Appendix III includes all species that are protected in at least one State, which has asked other CITES parties for assistance in controlling the trade (art. 5). This latter group is subject to the least stringent safeguards. There are currently 162 state parties to CITES. The organization holds a biennial Conference of the Parties and the CITES Standing Committee meets twice a year. The management of the Convention is undertaken by the CITES Secretariat based in Geneva. *See* <www.cites.org>.

citizen In strictness a term of municipal rather than international law, connoting membership of a political community with republican forms of government but often employed to describe nationals even of monarchical States—*e.g.*, British Citizen (British Nationality Act 1981). More recently, the concept of European citizenship has been used to define "a demos beyond the nation . . . the debates and politics of European citizenship attempt to create social integration on a transnational and postnational level": Eder and Giesen, *European Citizenship* (2001), 2.

Civil and Political Rights, International Covenant on, Following on the **Universal Declaration of Human Rights** of 10 December 1948 (GA Res. 217(III), the General Assembly adopted two International Covenants on 16 December 1966: on Civil and Political Rights *(999 U.N.T.S. 171)* and on **Economic, Social and Cultural Rights**. The International Covenant on Civil and Political Rights, and its (First) Optional Protocol, came into force on 23 March 1976. The International Covenant guarantees, *inter alia,* the rights of self-determination (art. 1(1)), of free disposition of natural wealth and resources (art. 1(2)), of non-discrimination (arts. 2(1) and 26), of equal rights of men and women (art. 3), of life (art. 6), of freedom from torture, cruel, inhuman or degrading treatment or punishment (art. 7), of freedom from slavery or servitude (art. 8), of freedom from arbitrary arrest or detention (art. 9), of freedom of movement within a State (art. 12), of a fair and public hearing by an impartial tribunal in respect of criminal charges (arts. 14-15), of privacy, family, home or correspondence (arts. 17 and 23), of thought, conscience and religion (art. 18), of opinion (art. 19), of peaceful assembly (art. 21), of association (art. 22) and of participation in public affairs (art. 25). The Second Optional Protocol to the Covenant, annexed to GA Res. 44/128 of 15 December 1989 *((1990) 29 I.L.M. 1464)*, abolishing the **death penalty** (art. 1), save for serious military offences in time of war (art. 2), entered into force on 11 July 1991.

To enforce the International Covenant, a **Human Rights Committee** was established, consisting of eighteen members (art. 28(1)), elected by the States parties (art. 29(1)). The basic method of enforcement is by scrutiny and comment upon reports submitted by the States parties on the domestic implementation of the guaranteed rights (art. 40). Additionally, where a State recognizes the competence of the Committee to receive and consider complaints of violations identified by another State party, the Committee seeks a friendly solution (art. 4; *see also* art. 42 on *ad hoc* conciliation commissions). Under the Optional Protocol to the International Covenant, a State may recognize the competence of the Committee to receive and consider a petition from an individual alleging violations of the guaranteed rights (art. 1). As to the admissibility of such petitions, see arts. 2, 3 and 5. In such cases, the Committee, after investigation, forwards its views to the State party and the individual complainant (art. 5(4)). *See* Henkin, *The International Bill of Rights* (1981); McGoldrick and Brownlie, *The Human Rights Committee: Its Role in the Development of the International Covenant on Civil and Political Rights* (1994); Ghandhi, *The Human Rights Committee and the Right of Individual Communication* (1998); Joseph, *The International Covenant on Civil and Political Rights: Cases, Materials and Commentary* (2001).

civil society "Civil society is not itself a political philosophy but describes the institutions, habits and beliefs—the culture—associated with a particular political philosophy: 'liberty rightly understood.' This latter phrase is not intended to imply that this is the 'correct' liberal view, only that it is an authentic voice within the liberal tradition which can be traced in the mainstream writings of scholars such as Hume, Adam Smith, Montesquieu, Tocqueville, Acton, Popper, Hayek and Oakeshott" Green, *Civil Society* (2000), 1. **Non-governmental organizations** are a core part of civil society. *See* <www.civitas.org>.

civil war *Semble* this is not a term of art in international law and any definition of it is difficult to find in the writings of that discipline. **War**, in terms of international law, is essentially international war—between entities at least one of which is a State (no other being, strictly, required to be such, provided that the State party treats the conflict as governed by the laws of war). By contrast, therefore, a civil war appears to be a conflict, no doubt necessarily of a public character, either between entities none of which are States or which is otherwise not governed by international law (because, as in most cases, it falls within the sphere of intra-State or constitutional rather than inter-State law and relations). But a civil war in this sense of a conflict internal to a State may nevertheless be of concern to international law. Indeed, the majority of conflicts since 1945 have been intra-State: UN Secretary-General Boutros-Ghali, *Agenda for Peace* (1992), paras. 8-19, and its *Supplement* (1995), para. 10. The Geneva Conventions for the Protection of War Victims 1949 *(75 U.N.T.S. 3ff)* each stipulate (art. 3) for the application of certain minimum provisions of these Conventions "in the case of armed conflict not of an international character occurring in the territory of one of the . . . Parties"; Additional Protocol II to the 1949 Geneva Conventions of 8 June 1977 *(1125 U.N.T.S. 609)* specifically addresses, in 18 substantive articles, as its title states, the "Protection of Victims of Non-International Armed Conflicts": the recognition of insurgent or belligerent status of contending factions (*see* **recognition of belligerency**; **recognition of insurgency**), whether by the parent State or by third States, may or must elevate a hitherto internal conflict into an international war for purposes of at least that part of international law which has to do with war and neutrality. *See generally*: Castren, *Civil War* (1966); Falk (ed.), *The International Law of Civil War* (1971); Green, *The Contemporary Law of Armed Conflict* (2000); Moir, *The Law of Internal Armed Conflict* (2002).

civilian, civil population Though the Fourth Geneva Convention of 12 August 1949 is entitled the Convention relative to the Protection of Civilian Persons in Time of War *(75 U.N.T.S. 287)*, neither it nor, *semble*, any earlier instrument defined the term "civilian." *But see* the use of the term in art. 232 of the Treaty of Versailles *(225 C.T.S. 188)* and see thereon the award in the *Damson Claim (U.S. v. Germany) 7 R.I.A.A. 184*. Moreover, Protocol I of 8 June 1977 to the Geneva Conventions *(1125 U.N.T.S. 3)*, Part IV of which bears the cross-title "Civilian Population" and lays down rules for the protection of such population, gives the following definitions in art. 50: "1. A civilian is any person who does not belong to one of the categories of persons referred to in Article 4(A) (1), (2), (3) and (6) and the Third Convention of 1949 [in effect combatants, including *levies en masse*] and in Article 43 of this Protocol [which similarly details categories of combatants]. In case of doubt whether a person is a civilian, that person shall be considered to be a civilian. 2. The civilian population comprises all persons who are civilians. 3. The presence within the civilian population of individuals who do not come within the definition of civilians does not deprive the population of its civilian character."

claim Although the term "claim" is utilized in a number of contexts in international law, its proper meaning (cases involving direct damage to the State apart) is the intimation and possible prosecution of a demand by one State for redress in respect of a breach of international law by another State causing injury to one of the former State's nationals. Only the State of which the injured individual is a national can make an international claim (*see* **nationality of claims**), although it has been decided by the ICJ that the UN can make claims in respect of its agents: ***Reparation for Injuries Case** 1949 I.C.J. Rep. 174*. Before a claim may be taken up and prosecuted by a State at the international level, the injured individual must have endeavored to obtain redress in the courts and tribunals of the offending State (*see* **local remedies, exhaustion of, rule**). A State is not obliged to espouse a claim, and a State has discretion how to proceed to settle a claim. Once a State has espoused a claim, it "is in reality asserting its own right, the right to ensure in the person of its nationals respect for the rules of international law": ***Panevezys-Saldutiskis Railway Co. Case** (1939) P.C.I.J., Ser. A/B, No. 76; see also **Barcelona Traction Co. Case** 1970 I.C.J. Rep. 3*. In certain limited circumstances, States have agreed to allow individuals and corporations to pursue their own claims: *see, e.g.*, the Convention on the Settlement of Investment Disputes between States and the Nationals of other States 1965 *(575 U.N.T.S. 159)* and the **Iran-US Claims Tribunal** which was established in 1981 to deal with private claims in the aftermath of the Tehran Hostage Crisis.

Classics of International Law   A series of 22 volumes, published by the **Carnegie Endowment for International Peace** from 1911 to 1950 under the general editorship of James Brown Scott, of the works of major classical writers on international law in their original language and English, including the works of Ayala (No. 2), Belli (No. 18), Van Bynkershoek (Nos. 11, 14, 17 and 21), Gentili (Nos. 9, 12 and 16), Da Legnano (No. 8), Grotius (Nos. 3 and 22), Von Pufendorf (Nos. 10 and 15), Rachel (No. 5), Suarez (No. 20), Textor (No. 6), Vattel (No. 4), De Victoria (No. 7), Wheaton (No. 19), Wolff (No. 13) and Zouche (No. 1).

clausula rebus sic stantibus   *See **rebus sic stantibus***.

Climate Change Convention   The United Nations Framework Convention on Climate Change was adopted at New York on 9 May 1992 *(31 I.L.M. 848 (1992))*; it entered into force on 21 March 1994. The objective of the Convention is the "stabilization of greenhouse gas concentrations in the atmosphere at a level that would prevent dangerous anthropogenic interference with the climate system" (art. 1). The States parties are committed, *inter alia*, to take "precautionary measures to anticipate, prevent and minimize the causes of climate change and mitigate its adverse effects" (art. 3(3); *see also* art. 4 for the full list of commitments). A Conference of the Parties, the supreme body of the Convention, monitors the implementation of the commitments undertaken by the parties and adopts decisions to promote effective implementation (art. 7(2)). The Kyoto Protocol of 11 December 1997 *(37 I.L.M. 32 (1998))*, not yet in force, seeks to set targets for emissions of greenhouse gasses, as listed in Annex A, for industrialized States, as listed in Annex B, "with a view to reducing their overall emissions . . . by at least 5 per cent below 1990 levels in the commitment period 2008 to 2012 (art. 3(1)); these States are to have made "demonstrable progress" towards these targets by 2005 (art. 3(2)). *See* Faure, *Climate Change and the Kyoto Protocol: The Role of Institutions and Instruments to Control Global Change* (2003). *And see* <http://unfccc.int>.

Clipperton Island Case   *(France v. Mexico) (1931) 2 R.I.A.A. 1105*. The *compromis* of 2 March 1909 *(208 C.T.S. 361)* referred to the arbitration of the King of Italy the question of the whereabouts of sovereignty over the island, which had been the subject of a proclamation of sovereignty by France in 1858 but had remained uninhabited until 1897, when a Mexican gunboat procured the withdrawal of some resident American citizens. *Held* that title was in France, it being unnecessary to reduce an uninhabited place into possession to establish sovereignty and France not having lost her rights by dereliction since she never had the *animus* of abandoning the island.

closing line   The **baseline** for measuring the territorial sea (and other maritime zones) across the mouth of a **bay** is referred to as a closing line. The UN Convention on the Law of the Sea 1982 *(1833 U.N.T.S. 3)* provides that, where the distance between the natural entrance points of a bay does not exceed 24 miles, a closing line may be drawn between them (art. 10(4)); where the distance exceeds 24 miles, a straight baseline (not a closing line) of 24 miles "shall be drawn within the bay in such a manner as to enclose the maximum area of water that is possible with a line of that length" (art. 10(5)). These provisions do not apply to "so-called **historic bays**" where the régime of **straight baselines** is to be employed (art. 10(6)); see the *Land, Island and Maritime Frontier Dispute Case*.

coastal trade   *See cabotage.*

co-belligerent   In strictness, co-belligerents are simply States engaged in a conflict with a common enemy, whether in **alliance** with each other or not. "Allies are not necessarily co-belligerents, for the particular *casus foederis* may not have arisen. . . . [N]or are co-belligerents necessarily allies, for they may merely be associated with one another for the purpose of the war. Thus, in the First World War, the United States of America was an 'Associated,' not an 'Allied' Power. . . . During the Second World War, Norway, Belgium, Holland, Greece, Yugoslavia and other countries, although co-belligerents of Great Britain, were not Allies. The Declaration by the various United Nations of 1 January 1942 *[204 L.N.T.S. 381]* in which they pledged themselves to employ their full resources against Germany, Italy, Japan, and their adherents and not to conclude a separate armistice or peace with them was not probably in the nature of an alliance—although no impropriety attached to [their] describing themselves as 'Allies.' On the other hand, although Egypt, Iraq and Turkey had concluded before the war treaties of alliance with Great Britain, they never become co-belligerents. . . . When in October 1943 Italy, hitherto an ally of Germany, declared war on Germany, she was accepted by Great Britain, the United States and Russia as a co-belligerent, but not as an ally. That co-belligerency did not put an end to the state of war between Italy and the Allies. . . . The Preamble to the Peace Treaty with Italy of 1947 *[49 U.N.T.S. 3]* stated that as a result of her declaration of war on Germany . . . Italy had become 'a co-belligerent against Germany'": *II Oppenheim 253 n.*

"[I]n 1918, during the First World War, Great Britain, France, Italy, and the United States of America recognized the Czecho-Slovaks as co-belligerents. Similar recognition was granted in 1917 to the Polish national army composed to a substantial degree of subjects of the enemy Powers. It has been maintained that, as in the case of insurgents in a civil war, the enemy is entitled to disregard such recognition and to treat the members of the insurgent army, when they fall into his hands, in accordance with the provisions of his criminal law. [see **recognition of belligerency**] The better opinion is probably that when such recognition is granted by the adversary to large bodies of men effectively organized on foreign soil in anticipation of independent statehood, a point is reached at which the belligerent . . . can no longer . . . assert the provisions of his own criminal law as the only legally relevant element in the situation": *ibid., 251-3.*

codification   "The idea of a codification of the Law of Nations in its totality was first suggested by Bentham at the end of the eighteenth century. [But it] was not until 1861 that a real attempt was made. . . . This was done by an Austrian jurist, Alfons von Domin-Petruschévecz, who published in that year at Leipzig a *Précis d'un code de droit interna-*

tional. In 1863 Professor Francis Lieber . . . drafted the Laws of War in a body of rules which the United States published . . . for the guidance of her army. . . . In 1868 Bluntschli, the celebrated Swiss writer, published *Das Moderne Völkerrecht . . . als Rechtsbuch dargestellt.* This draft code has been translated into the French, Greek, Spanish and Russian languages. In 1872 . . . Mancini raised his voice in favour of codification. . . . Likewise in 1872 appeared . . . David Dudley Field's *Draft Outlines of an International Code.* . . . In 1887 Leone Levi published his *International Law with Materials for a Code.* . . . In 1890, the Italian jurist Fiore published his *II diritto internazionale codificato.* . . .": *I Oppenheim 97-98.*

The first official attempt at codification on an international basis was that made in relation to the Declaration of Brussels, see **Brussels, Declaration of**. This was followed by the **Hague Peace Conferences** of 1899 and 1907. *See also* the **Geneva Conventions**. "In the law of peace the [post-World War I] period produced important partial codification through general instruments like the Covenant of the League of Nations, the Statute of the Permanent Court of International Justice, the General Act for the Pacific Settlement of International Disputes of 1928, the General Treaty for the Renunciation of War. Some of the major multilateral treaties of this period concerning air navigation, and inland and maritime navigation, and a great number of conventions of a scientific, economic and humanitarian character, including the imposing series of conventions concluded under the aegis of the International Labour Organisation, contained elements of codification. Although not primarily codification treaties in the usual sense: *ibid., 100.*

The first, and as it happened the only, League of Nations Conference for the Progressive Codification of International Law sat at The Hague during March-April 1930. Despite very comprehensive preparatory work, it achieved formally no more than the four Hague agreements respecting nationality and statelessness: see **nationality**. And see Alvarez, *Les Résultats de la Ière Conférence de codification de droit international.*

A notable unofficial endeavour undertaken in preparation for the 1930 Conference was the so-called **Harvard Research**, organized by the Law School of Harvard University, which produced a draft Convention on each of the topics which had been recommended for codification under League auspices, viz: *Nationality* (R. Flournoy, Reporter); *Responsibility of States for Injuries to Foreigners* (E.M. Borchard); *Territorial Waters* (C.G. Wilson); *Diplomatic Privileges and Immunities* (J.S. Reeves); *Legal Position and Functions of Consuls* (Q. Wright); *Competence of Courts in regard to Foreign States* (P.C. Jessup); *Piracy* (J.W. Bingham); *Extradition* (C.K. Burdick); *Jurisdiction with respect to Crime* (E.D. Dickinson); *Law of Treaties* (J.W. Garner); *Judicial Assistance* (J.G. Rogers and A.H. Feller); *Neutrality* (P.C. Jessup); *Rights and Duties of States in Case of Aggression* (P.C. Jessup). The Harvard Research also published a *Collection of Nationality Laws* (Flournoy and Hudson); a *Collection of Piracy Laws* (S. Morrison); a *Collection of Diplomatic and Consular Laws* (Feller and M.O. Hudson); and a *Collection of Neutrality Laws* (F. Deak and Jessup).

The UN Charter, providing (art. 13)(1)(a) that the General Assembly should "initiate studies and make recommendations for the purpose of . . . encouraging the progressive development of international law and its codification," in 1947 there was established the **International Law Commission**, whose Statute (GA Res 174(II): *42 A.J.I.L. Supp. 2 (1948)*) develops the distinction between "codification" and the "progressive development of international law" drawn in the Charter, defining or describing the latter as "the preparation of draft conventions on subjects which have not yet been regulated by international law or in regard to which the law has not yet been sufficiently developed in the practice of States," in contrast to the former, which is "the more precise formulation and systematisation of rules of international law in fields where there already has been extensive State practice, precedent and doctrine" (art. 15). *See United Nations Documents concerning Development and Codification of International Law, 41 A.J.I.L. Supp. 29 (1947).* For a full summary of the work of the International Law Commission in the codification and progressive development of international law since 1948, see **International Law Commission**.

coercion Arts. 51 and 52 of the Vienna Convention on the Law of Treaties 1969 deal with coercion, the former providing that a treaty is invalid if a State's consent "has been procured by the coercion of its representative through acts or threats directed against him," and the latter that a treaty is void "if its conclusion has been procured by the threat or use of force" in violation of the principles of international law embodied in the Charter of the United Nations." "The traditional opinion accepted by the majority of writers has, at any rate until recently, been that a treaty becomes and remains binding upon a State in spite of the fact that that State was acting under coercion in concluding the treaty, and that the invalidating effect of coercion must be confined to cases where it is applied to the representative of a State engaged in the final act which concludes the treaty. . . .

The last half-century has, however, witnessed a change, if not a transformation, in the attitude of international law . . . towards the use or threat of force for the purpose of attaining national objectives. . . . Accordingly, it would now be the duty of an international tribunal to scrutinize closely the circumstances in which a treaty or other international engagement was concluded and to decline to uphold it in favour of a party which had secured another party's consent by means of the illegal use or threat of force": McNair, *Law of Treaties* (2nd ed.), 207 and 209-10. *But see* Shearer, *Starke's International Law* (11th ed.), 429-30: "Quaere, whether, as claimed by some states, the word 'force' used in the United Nations Charter is capable of denoting economic or political pressure, which was alleged to be characteristic of 'neo-colonialism.' By way of answer to this claim, it has been objected that it would open a wide door for the invalidation of treaties concluded at arms length."

co-existence, doctrine of peaceful A 20th century doctrine, favored by Marxists writers, the essence of which is that States of differing political or economic ideologies have a right to "co-exist." Formulations of the doctrine vary greatly, some deducing from the right to co-existence a duty of disarmament and even of active economic and cultural co-operation. "[The] aggregate of norms which are created by agreement between states of different social systems, reflect the concordant wills of states and have a generally democratic character, regulate relations between them in the process of struggle and co-operation in the direction of ensuring peace and peaceful co-existence and freedom and independence of peoples, and are secured when necessary by coercion effectuated by states individually or collectively." Tunkin, *Theory of International Law* (1970 in Russian, 1974 in English), 251. It would not appear that, in strict law, the doctrine imports anything novel into international law.

co-imperium In contradistinction to *condominium*, where two or more States jointly assume sovereignty over a territory and accept responsibility for its administration, *co-imperium* implies a territorial entity maintaining a distinct international status, while being administered by two or more States. The clearest example appears to be Germany over which, by the Berlin Declaration of 5 June 1945 *(68 U.N.T.S. 189)*, the Four Occupying Powers assumed supreme authority, such authority being expressly declared not to effect the annexation of Germany. *See R.V. Bottrill, ex parte Kuechenmeister [1947] K.B. 41*; *Lüdecke v Watkins 335 U.S. 160 (1948). See also* Mann, Present Legal Status of Germany,

(1947) 1 I.C.L.Q. 314; Kelsen, The Legal Status of Germany according to the Declaration of Berlin, *39 A.J.I.L. 518 (1945)*.

collective measures This expression acquired a semi-technical connotation as a result of the specification in art. 1(1) of the Charter of the first purpose of the UN as being "[t]o maintain international peace and security, and to that end: to take effective collective measures for the prevention and removal of threats to the peace, and for the suppression of acts of aggression or other breaches of the peace, and to bring about by peaceful means, and in conformity with the principles of justice and international law, adjustment or settlement of international disputes or situations which might lead to a breach of the peace." "The words 'effective collective measures' have been interpreted to have a broader connotation than the words describing the action taken by the Security Council under Chapter VII, and to justify the recommendations of collective measures by the General Assembly under its 'residual responsibility' and the existence of an obligation on the part of members to take collective measures to defeat aggression": Goodrich, Hambro and Simons, *Charter of the United Nations* (3rd. ed.), 28. By the first of the **Uniting for Peace Resolutions** of 3 November 1950 (GA Res. 377 (V)), the General Assembly established a Collective Measures Committee to study "methods which might be used to maintain and strengthen international peace and security," as to the reports of which *see* Goodrich, Hambro and Simons, *supra*, 336-342, 615-616 and Bowett, *United Nations Forces* (1964), 21-28.

collective rights Those human rights generally recognized to be exercisable by collectives and not reducible to the individual, including the right to **self-determination**, the right to **development** and **minority rights**, often also referred to as **third generation human rights**.

collective security *Semble*, this expression is not one of art. "A collective security system can be defined in broad terms as a system where a collective measure is taken against a member of a community that has violated certain community defined values. An important feature of collective security is the maintenance of the status quo of the system. This relies, however, on the perception by States that their individual interest is best served by ensuring that the interest of the community of States—in Charter terms, international peace and security—is preserved": Sarooshi, *The United Nations and The Development of Collective Security* (1999), 5-6. However, the expression can be traced back many hundreds of years with elements of collective security apparent in some of the alliances of the ancient Greek states and in the Middle Ages. More recently, 'Collective Security' was the title of Lord McNair's inaugural lecture as Whewell Professor at Cambridge *((1936) 17 B.Y.I.L. 150)*, being there used to describe the League of Nations system.

collective self-defense Art. 51 of the UN Charter provides that nothing therein "shall impair the inherent right of individual or collective self-defense if an armed attack occurs against a Member of the United Nations, until the Security Council has taken measures necessary to maintain international peace and security. Measures taken by Members in the exercise of this right of self-defense shall be immediately reported to the Security Council" This formulation has been the criticized on the ground that it is a contradiction in terms. Kelsen (*Law of the United Nations* (1950),.792, 797) argues that, since self-defense involves action which is by definition unilateral in character, a 'collective' unilateral right is self-contradictory; the right of self-defense "is the right of the attacked or threatened individual or State, and of no other individual or State." For similar reasons, other authors have preferred to call the right "not self-defense, but defense of another State": Kunz, Individual and Collective Self-Defense in Article 51 of the Charter of the United Nations, *41 A.J.I.L. 872 at 875 (1947)*. "Now whatever are the merits of these criticisms, it is clear firstly, that the provision was intended to cover the sort of collective action in self-defence which regional arrangements might wish to take and for which their constitutive treaties make provision, and secondly, that Art. 51 did not import any novel concept into international law and was declaratory of existing rights": Bowett, *Self-Defence in International Law* (1958), 200.

In ***Military and Paramilitary Activities in and against Nicaragua*** *1986 I.C.J. Rep. 14*, the International Court of Justice required that the exercise of the right of collective self-defense depended on a request for assistance by the victim State. Furthermore, the Court stressed that "for one state to use force against another, on the ground that that state has committed a wrongful act of force against a third state, is regarded as lawful, by way of exception, only when the wrongful act provoking the response was an armed attack": *ibid,* 110. Collective self-defense was one of the justifications used after the invasion by Iraq of Kuwait on 2 August 1990 for the actions of the US-led coalition against Iraq. Although the Security Council authorized the coalition to use "all necessary means" to remove Iraq from Kuwait (SC Res. 678 (1990)), the Council had previously affirmed the inherent right of individual and collective self-defense in response to the invasion of Kuwait (SC Res. 661 (1990)). Thus, it is at least arguable that the actions by the coalition forces were undertaken in furtherance of the right of collective self-defense. *See* Greig, Self-Defence and the Security Council: What Does Article 51 Require? *(1991) 40 I.C.L.Q. 366*; Rostow, The Gulf Crisis: Until What? Enforcement Action or Collective Self-Defense, *85 A.J.I.L. 506 (1991)*.

Colombia-Venezuela Boundary Dispute *(1922) 1 R.I.A.A. 223*. The Treaty of 14 September 1881 *(159 C.T.S. 87)*, supplemented by the Protocol of 15 February 1886 *(167 C.T.S. 327)*, referred to the arbitration of Spain the question of the boundary between the parties. The Queen's award of 16 March 1891 *(175 C.T.S. 21)* indicated a line requiring in part demarcation on the ground, and the parties finally agreed by the Convention of 30 December 1898 *(187 C.T.S. 147)* to set up a delimitation commission the work of which, however, was in 1901 suspended. By the *compromis* of 3 November 1916 *(222 C.T.S. 46)*, the parties submitted to the arbitration of the Swiss Federal Council the question whether the Queen's award could be put into effect partially, as Colombia maintained, so that each party could enter into possession of the areas recognized as belonging to it respectively, or whether, as Venezuela contended, only an integral execution of the award was permissible. In the award of 24 March 1922, *held* that each party might proceed to the occupation of territories delimited by natural frontiers which fell to it under the earlier award, for there are no absolute or obligatory rules as to formalities to be observed in the handing over of territories. Further, there is no rule requiring a formal taking of possession. Indeed, if there was, it would not be applicable here, the parties having accepted the principle of *uti possidetis*, each being presumed to have possessed since 1810 the areas awarded to it. *See also* **Guatemala-Honduras Boundary Arbitration**; **Land, Island and Maritime Frontier Dispute Case**.

Colombo Plan The Colombo Plan for Co-operative Economic Development in South and South-East Asia was established by the meeting of the Foreign Ministers of the Commonwealth in Colombo in January 1950: The Colombo Plan 1950 *(Cmd. 8080)*. The Plan embodies the concept of an intergovernmental effort toward the economic and social development of member countries in the Asia-Pacific region. Its present membership consists of 25 countries. The Council for Technical Co-operation in Asia and the Pacific implements and co-ordinates the operation of the Plan under a Consultative Committee of Ministers of the Member States. The purposes of the Plan include the promotion of technical cooperation and assistance in the sharing and transfer of technology among member states as well as to assist the Least Developed Countries of the Colombo Plan region in their effort of economic development through dissemination of technical and industrial know-how by comparatively advanced countries.

Colombos, Constantine John 1886-1968. English lawyer with an interest in international law and diplomacy. Principal work: *International Law of the Sea* (1943; 6th ed., 1967).

colonial clause "When . . . the United Kingdom Government enters into a treaty of general application . . . it usually seeks to include . . . a form of the so-called 'colonial' or 'colonial application' article. This clause takes many forms and there are two distinctive types: one provides that the United Kingdom may, by giving special notice to any other party to the treaty, declare that the treaty shall apply to any of the territories for whose international relations the United Kingdom is responsible, thus indicating that in the absence of such notice the treaty applies only to the metropolitan territory. . . . The other provides that the treaty shall apply both to metropolitan and overseas territories except in so far as the United Kingdom may by declaration or special notice exclude its operation from any or all of them": McNair, *Law of Treaties* (2nd ed.), 118-9. Such clauses are now commonly styled **territorial application clauses**.

colonial protectorate An institution arising from the provisions of art. 34 of the General Act of the Berlin Conference respecting the Congo of 1885 (*see* **Congo Act**: *165 C.T.S. 485*) requiring a Power taking possession of a territory on the coast of Continental Africa or assuming a protectorate in relation thereto to notify the same to the other signatories. "Colonial protectorates were, with two exceptions (Aden Protectorate and the British Solomon Islands) restricted to Africa. . . . Even though many protectorate agreements over what came to be regarded as colonial protectorates are treaties in international form made with recognized African States (for example Swaziland), or tribes with a certain legal status (for example Somaliland), the continuous accretion of powers by usage and acquiescence to the protecting State was—by virtue of the Berlin Act procedure—opposable to the parties to that Act and in practice a matter of the protecting State's discretion. As a result, the protecting State had international full powers: it was competent, for example, to cede protected territory without consent and in breach of the protectorate agreements. But that is not to say that international law was completely irrelevant to the relationship. . . . [I]t is at least arguable that the continued affirmation of the terms of protection agreements constituted an estoppel binding on the protecting State": Crawford, *The Creation of States in International Law* (1979), 200. *See also* Westlake, *International Law, Part I, Peace* (2nd ed.), 120-9.

colony The term "colony" is one of municipal or constitutional rather than international law. As such, its exact signification may vary from municipal system to municipal system. Thus, the British Interpretation Act 1889 excluded from the expression, not only any part of the British Islands (which include the Channel Islands and the Isle of Man), but also British India. For historical reasons, the term has been eschewed in United States' constitutional law and practice. But the word, generally understood as connoting any non-metropolitan territory of a State, is occasionally employed in instruments of international legal import; *e.g.*, the provision of art. 1(2) of the Covenant of the League of Nations for the availability of membership to "any fully self-governing State, Dominion or Colony," and General Assembly Resolution 1514 (XV) of 14 December 1960, styled a Declaration on the Granting of Independence to Colonial Countries and Peoples. *See* **independence**.

combatant The distinction between combatant and non-combatant was first formally drawn in the Hague Regulations respecting the Laws and Customs of Warfare on Land,

1899 and 1907 *(187 C.T.S. 429; 205 C.T.S. 277*: see **Réglement of the Laws of War***)*, art. 3 whereof states: "The armed forces of the belligerent parties may consist of combatants and non-combatants. In the case of capture by the enemy, both have a right to be treated as prisoners of war." Art. 43 of Protocol I of 6 June 1977 to the Geneva Conventions of 1949 *(1125 U.N.T.S. 3)* purports to define "combatants" as those having "the right to participate directly in hostilities," such being members, other than medical personnel and chaplains within Geneva Convention III, art. 33, of any "organized armed forces, groups and units . . . under a command responsible to a belligerent." The distinction belongs more to customary than to treaty law. Cf. **civilian**.

combatants, enemy *See* **unlawful combatants**.

COMECON The Council for Mutual Economic Assistance, established at the Moscow Economic Conference on 27 January 1949 and governed by its Charter, drawn up and signed at its XIIth session on 14 December 1959 *(368 U.N.T.S. 253)*. The Parties were: Albania (until 1961), Bulgaria, Cuba (from 1972), Czechoslovakia, German Democratic Republic, Hungary, Mongolia (from 1962), Poland, Romania, the USSR and Vietnam (from 1978). It was agreed by the State parties in 1987 that official relations should be established with the **European Community**, and a free-market approach to trading was adopted in 1990. COMECON was formally disbanded in 1991.

comity "[T]his word is or has been used from time to time in connection with international law in the following not easily reconcilable senses: (1) . . . the rules of politeness, convenience, and goodwill observed by states in their mutual intercourse without being legally bound by them. *See, e.g.*, the *Parking Privileges for Diplomats* Case (1971), *I.L.R. 70* at 396. It is probably in this connection that some English judges have expressed the view that 'it would be contrary to our obligations of international comity as now understood' to enforce in England a contract made abroad with a view to deriving profit from the commission of a criminal act in a foreign country and that a decision to enforce it would furnish a just cause of complaint on the part of a foreign government: *Foster v. Driscoll [1929] 1 K.B. 470* . . . (2) as equivalent to private international law, eg Phillimore *[Commentaries upon International Law]* iv, § 1 . . . (3) to quote the *New English Dictionary* (Murray): 'Apparently misused for the company of nations mutually practising international comity (in some instances erroneous association with L. *comes* "companion," is to be suspected); (4) as equivalent to international law . . .": *I Oppenheim 50n*, which, clearly preferring the first sense of the term, states that "[i]t is probable that many a present rule of international comity will in future become one of international law": *ibid., 51*.

command responsibility Art. 7(3) of the Statute of the **International Criminal Tribunal for the Former Yugoslavia** (SC Res. 827 (1993)), art. 6(3) of the Statute of the **International Criminal Tribunal for Rwanda** (SC Res. 955 (1994)), and art. 28 of the Statute of the **International Criminal Court** 1998 *(37 I.L.M. 999 (1998))* all provide for the criminal responsibility of a superior for the acts committed by his subordinates if he "knew or had reason to know that the subordinate was about to commit such acts or had done so and the superior failed to take the necessary and reasonable measures to prevent such acts or to punish the perpetrators thereof." This principle is well established in customary international law and is applicable to military and civilian commanders alike. "Therefore, the crucial question is not the civilian or military status of the superior but the degree of authority the superior exercises over his subordinates": Kittichaisaree, *International Criminal Law* (2001), 251-2. *See also* **superior orders**.

Commission on Human Rights Established by Economic and Social Council Res. 1/5 (1946) in satisfaction of the requirement of art. 68 of the UN Charter, this Commission of 53 members fulfills the general mandate of promoting human rights. It is the pivotal global human rights body, being responsible for the **Universal Declaration of Human Rights** 1948 and the **International Bill of Rights**, as well as other global human rights agreements. Despite the recognition in 1947 that the Commission had no competence to hear individual claims of human right violations (ECOSOC Res. 75(V)), it was given the competence in 1970 to examine complaints of "a consistent pattern of gross and reliably attested violations" (ECOSOC Res. 1503(XLVIII)). *See* McGoldrick and Brownlie, *The Human Rights Committee: Its Role in the Development of the International Covenant on Civil and Political Rights* (1994); Ghandhi, *The Human Rights Committee and the Right of Individual Communication* (1998).

Common Foreign and Security Policy (of the European Union) Introduced in 1993 by the Treaty on European Union, the common foreign and security policy is intended to produce common positions of the **European Union** member states on foreign policy issues. Once adopted, Member States are required to adhere to common positions. The policy also produces common actions and common strategies. The CFSP is developing a common European defense and security policy (CESDP) which envisages a rapid reaction military force in cooperation with **NATO** to carry out peacekeeping and other non-combat tasks. *See* <www.europa.eu.int>.

common heritage (of mankind) This term, of relatively recent origin, reflects a belief that the resources of certain areas beyond national sovereignty or jurisdiction should not be exploited by those few States whose commercial enterprises are able to do so, but rather constitute the common heritage of mankind, to be utilized for the benefit of all States. The application of the term to any particular area, and its substantive content in relation thereto, need elaboration by treaty.

As regards the legal status of the **International Sea-bed Area** and its resources: see art. 1 of the Declaration of Principles Governing the Seabed and the Ocean Floor, and the Subsoil Thereof, Beyond the Limits of National Jurisdiction of 17 December, 1970 (GA Res. 2749 (XXV)), and art. 136 of the UN Convention on the Law of the Sea 1982 *(1833 U.N.T.S. 3)*. The elements of this legal status are enumerated in art. 137 of the UN Convention of 1982: "No State shall claim or exercise sovereignty or sovereign rights over any part of the Area or its resources, nor shall any State or natural or juridical person appropriate any part thereof . . . 2. All rights in the resources of the Area are vested in mankind as a whole, on whose behalf the [International Sea-bed] Authority shall act. These resources are not subject to alienation . . . 3. No State or natural or juridical person shall claim, acquire or exercise rights with respect to the minerals recovered from the Area except in accordance with this Part. . . ."

Art. 11 of the **Moon Treaty** 1979 *(18 I.L.M. 1434 (1979))* states the moon and its natural resources also to be the common heritage of mankind. A similar, though not identical, régime, while not employing the term common heritage of mankind, has been established for outer space by the **Outer Space Treaty** 1967 *(610 U.N.T.S. 205)*. The **Antarctic Treaty** 1959 *(402 U.N.T.S. 71)*, while not employing the term, creates a régime for Antartica that has many of the attributes of common heritage of mankind.

common market This designation of a form of economic integration of States which represents a stage beyond the normal **customs union** is employed primarily in the Treaty establishing the **European Coal and Steel Community** of 18 April 1951 (arts. 2, 4) and the Treaty establishing the **European Economic Community** (the Treaty of Rome) of 25

March 1957 (arts. 3(f), 8 and *passim*). "A customs union becomes a common market with the removal of all restrictions on the movement of productive factors—labor, capital, and enterprise": Root, *International Trade and Investment* (5th ed.), 378.

common standard of civilization *See* **international minimum standard**.

compact The term "compact" appears to have no special meaning in international law. However, Article I, Section 10 of the United States Constitution provides that "[n]o State shall, without the Consent of Congress . . . enter into any Agreement or Compact with another State, or with a foreign Power. . . ." For an analysis of the term "compact," which would not appear to be used in relation to persons in international law, and as to the doctrine that Congressional consent to an "interstate compact" is unnecessary if the arrangement does not impinge on federal authority, see *Wharton v. Wise 153 U.S. 155 (1894)*.

compensation While the primary remedy for an act in contravention of international law is **restitution,** monetary compensation is due where restitution in kind is impossible or where the claimant State is prepared to accept it: *Chorzow Factory (Indemnity) Case (1928) P.C.I.J., Ser. A, No. 17* at 47-8. This position has been affirmed in the Draft Articles on State Responsibility 2001 *(UN Doc. A/56/10 Chap.IV.E.1)*, art. 36 of which states that: "(1) The state liable for an internationally wrongful act is under an obligation to compensate for the damage caused thereby, insofar as damage is not made good by restitution. (2) The compensation shall cover any financially assessable damage including loss of profits insofar as it is established." In its commentary on its draft articles, the International Law Commission pointed out: "of the various forms of reparation, compensation is perhaps the most commonly sought in international practice. In the *Gabcikovo-Nagymaros Project* case (Hungary/Slovakia) (1997) ICJ Reports, 7 at 81, the Court declared that '[i]t is a well-established rule of international law that an injured state is entitled to obtain compensation from the state which has committed an internationally wrongful act for the damage caused by it.' It is equally well-established that an international court or tribunal which has jurisdiction with respect to a claim of State responsibility has, as an aspect of that jurisdiction, the power to award compensation for damage suffered . . . the function of Article 36 is purely compensatory. . . . It is not concerned to punish the responsible State nor does compensation have an expressive or exemplary character." In terms of art. 38, interest "shall be payable when necessary in order to ensure full reparation."

Competence of the ILO in regard to Agriculture Cases (1922) P.C.I.J., Ser. B, Nos. 2,3. In response to the League of Nations Council's request of 12 May 1922, on 12 August 1922 the Permanent Court of International Justice *advised* (8 to 2) that the competence of the ILO extended to the international regulation of the conditions of labor of persons employed in agriculture, the terms of Part XIII of the Treaty of Versailles (the constitution of the ILO) containing no counter-indication. On the same basis of treaty interpretation, the Court (unanimously) *advised* simultaneously in the negative on the Council's further request of 18 July 1922 as to whether examination of proposals for the development of methods of agricultural production and like questions was within the ILO's competence, on the ground that the ILO had no constitutional mandate in relation to the improvement of the means of production.

Competence of the ILO to Regulate Work of the Employer Case (1926) P.C.I.J., Ser. B, No. 13. Upon the League of Nations Council's request for an opinion of 17 March 1926, the Court (unanimously) *advised* on 23 July 1926 that the ILO was competent to draft labor legislation incidentally regulating the same work when performed by the employer, since otherwise in a given case projected measures for the protection of employees might be ineffective.

complementarity A term used to describe the relationship between the **International Criminal Court** and national criminal courts. Art. 17(1) of the Rome Statute of the ICC Statute *(37 I.L.M. 999 (1998))*, titled "Issues of Admissibility," denies the Court jurisdiction in cases under investigation or prosecution in a national criminal court unless the State is "unwilling or unable genuinely to carry out the investigation or prosecution," unwillingness being defined in art. 17(2) and inability in art. 17(3). *See* Holmes, The Principle of Complementarity, in Lee, *The International Criminal Court* (1999), 41.

compliance theory According to Abraham and Antonia Chayes, efforts aimed at strengthening the enforcement régimes of international law are "largely a waste of time" and that the threat of sanctions is irrelevant to the conduct of relations between states. They argue that compliance with international agreements is best achieved through "an iterative process of discourse among the parties [to a treaty], the treaty organization and the wider public": Chayes and Chayes, *The New Sovereignty: Compliance with International Regulatory Agreements* (1995), 2. However, it has been argued that "[w]ithout denying the importance of these [compliance] perspectives to our understanding of the theoretical and practical underpinnings of the system as it has existed up to this point . . . the truly misguided attitude would be to conclude that enforcing international law is unnecessary or unrealistic." Damrosch, Enforcing International Law Through Non-Forcible Means (1997) 269 *Hague Recueil* 13 at 23.

Comprehensive Test-Ban Treaty 1996 *See* **Test-Ban Treaties**.

compromis d'arbitrage "This term denotes an agreement to refer to arbitration or to judicial settlement some matter or matters in dispute, these being defined more clearly in the *compromis*. The normal English equivalent of the term is 'special agreement' (though 'Arbitration Agreement' may, depending on the context, be used); and in French or Spanish it is customary to use only the single word *'compromis,'* or *'compromiso'* respectively. Article 40(1) of the Statute of the I[CJ] provides that: 'Cases are brought before the Court, as the case may be, either by the notification of the special agreement *(compromis)* or by a written application. . . .' [T]he I[LC] drew up in 1958 a set of Model Rules on Arbitral Procedure which the General Assembly brought to the attention of Member States for their consideration and use, in such cases and to such extent as they consider appropriate in drawing up treaties of arbitration or *compromis* (GA Resolution 1262 (XIII), 14 November 1958)": *Satow's Guide to Diplomatic Practice* (5th ed.), 287. *See also* Aust, *Modern Treaty Law* (2000), 293-4.

compromissory clause A clause in a treaty providing for the submission of a matter or matters to arbitration—to be distinguished from a general treaty of arbitration or a *compromis d'arbitrage*, which is an instrument, as distinct from a clause in an instrument, wholly concerned with arbitration. "In the past such clauses were usually drawn in general terms and left most of the important details to be worked out only when one of the parties had invoked the clause. . . . It is better, however, to put into the clause as much detail as possible, omitting only those matters which cannot easily be worked out until the dispute has arisen." Aust, *Modern Treaty Law and Practice* (2000), 292-3. See, for example, the difficulties which arose in relation to UK-US Air Services Agreement when invoked by the United States in 1988, *ibid.*, 293.

concert system (or Concert of Europe) "The Congress of Vienna of 1815 initiated the 'concert system' which, for the purposes of any study of international organisation, constituted a significant development. As sponsored by the Czar Alexander I, what was envisaged was an alliance of the victorious powers pledged to conduct diplomacy according to ethical standards, which would convene at congresses held at regular intervals (the 'Holy Alliance'). Four congresses were held between 1818 and 1822—at **Aix-la-Chapelle** (1818), at **Troppau** and **Laibach** (1820, 1821), and at **Verona** (1822)—but the idea of regular congresses was abandoned and meetings took place as occasion required. The attempt to secure meetings was, however, a significant recognition that the 'pace' of international relations demanded some institution for regular multilateral negotiations. The 'Concert of Europe' remained a quasi-institutionalised system even after the Holy Alliance had broken up, until the First World War destroyed the balance on which it rested (or rather confirmed its demise); the London Conferences of 1912-13, at the end of the Balkan Wars, were the last conferences or congresses convened within the framework of the 'concert system.' The conclusion of a conference would normally be accompanied by a formal treaty or convention, or, where no such binding agreement was desired or obtainable, by a memorandum or minutes of the conference": Sands and Klein, *Bowett's Law of International Institutions* (5th ed.), 3. *See* **Vienna, Congress of, 1815**.

concession, concessionary contract The term concession is one rather of municipal administrative than of international law. *See* the remarks of the Arbitrator in *Germany v. Reparation Commission (1924), 1 R.I.A.A. 429; 2 I.L.R. 341*, respecting the use of the word in art. 260 of the Treaty of Versailles. "[T]he Law of Nations does not contain any principle regarding the characterization of this legal institution": *Aramco Arbitration . . . (1958) 27 I.L.R. 117* at 157 *per* the Tribunal. "International law having not as yet developed any distinct concept of the concession, . . . an approach to a workable notion is made by way of comparison of various like institutions in the legal systems of a number of States. . . . On the basis of this comparison . . . the international concession is defined as a 'synallagmatic act by which a State transfers the exercise of rights or functions proper to itself to a foreign private person which, in turn, participates in the performance of public functions *(Verwaltungszwecke)* and thus gains a privileged position vis-a-vis other private law subjects within the jurisdiction of the State concerned'": Fischer, *Die Internationale Konzession, 549 (English Summary). Qua* a contract between a State and a non-State entity of another nationality an international concession is not governed by international law, but normally by some system of municipal law—usually but not always that of the concessionary State: see Fischer, *A Collection of Concessions and Related Instruments (1976-88)*. There is possibly a distinct rule of international law respecting succession to concessionary contracts. "[They] usually have a local character, and there is much to be said in favour of the view that, if before the extinction of the State which granted the concessions every act necessary for vesting them in the holder had been performed, they would survive the extinction and bind the absorbing State.": *1 Oppenheim 217. See also* O'Connell, *State Succession in Municipal Law and International Law* (1967), Chap. 13. As to the expropriation of concessions, see **expropriation**.

conciliation "The term 'conciliation' has both a broad and a narrow meaning. In its more general sense, it covers the great variety of methods whereby a dispute is amicably settled with the aid of other states or of impartial bodies of inquiry or advisory committees. In the narrow sense, 'conciliation' signifies the reference of a dispute to a commission or committee to make a report with proposals to the parties for settlement. Such proposals not being of a binding character." Shearer, *Starke's International Law* (11th ed.), 467. *See also*, Hudson, *International Tribunals* (1944), 223. Conciliation is one of the means whereby parties to a dispute the continuance of which is likely to endanger the maintenance of international peace and security may and must, under art. 33(1) of the UN Charter, seek a solution. *See generally*, Merrills, *International Dispute Settlement* (3rd ed.), Chap. 4.

conclusion of treaty By inference, the process of "Conclusion of Treaties"—the cross-title given to Part II, Section I of the Vienna Convention on the Law of Treaties 1969—comprehends the stages or steps of (1) adoption of the text (art. 9), (2) its authentication (art. 10), and (3) the indication by the parties of their consent to be bound (arts. 11-17).

concordat "A concordat is an agreement between the Pope and the head of a state which has for its purpose to safeguard the interests of the Roman Catholic Church in the state concerned. It would seem that the concordat is gradually becoming obsolete, being replaced by 'agreement' or *modus vivendi* of lesser scope. . . . [Opinions of writers and a consideration of their content would suggest that it was] fair to conclude that concordats are, in point of form, analogous to treaties, and may operate to create reciprocal rights and obligations as between the Contracting Parties; but that they seek to regulate matters governed by the public law of the state rather than by international law proper. In this context it may be relevant that no concordat appears as yet to have been registered . . . under Article 102 of the Charter": *Satow's Guide to Diplomatic Practice* (5th ed.), 255-6. Concordats are printed in Mercati, *Raccolta di Concordati, etc.* (2 vols. 1954).

condominium "A condominium exists when over a particular territory joint dominion is exercised by two or more external Powers" Shearer, *Starke's International Law* (11th ed.), 105. *1* O'Connell, *International Law* (1965), Vol. 1, 350 questions whether all apparent instances of condominium are in reality such, "where, as a result of a peace treaty, territory of the vanquished is ceded to the victors jointly, [for] in every instance there is grave doubt if it was the intention of the victors to do more than act as trustees of the ceded territory for some other State in being or to be brought into being"; and he cites only two instances of *condominium*, that over the Sudan established by the Agreement between Great Britain and Egypt of 19 January 1899 *(187 C.T.S. 155)* and that over the New Hebrides established by the Agreement between Great Britain and France of 6 August 1914 *(220 C.T.S. 219)*. *See 1 Oppenheim 565-7.*

confederation A union of States in which, "though a central government exists and exercises certain powers, it does not control all the external relations of the member states, and therefore for international purposes there exists not one but a number of states . . . the United States from 1778 to 1787, and the German Confederation from 1820 to 1866, were confederations of many states": Brierly, *The Law of Nations* (6th ed.), 128. Cf. **federation**.

Conference on Security and Co-operation in Europe *See* **Organization for Security and Co-operation in Europe**.

conflict of laws *See* **private international law**.

confrontation While not a term of art in international law, "[a] concept of a new kind made its appearance in the period 1963-1966 in the shape of Indonesia's 'confrontation' of Malaysia, after the establishment of that new state in September, 1963. 'Confrontation' involved action and policies to undermine the integrity and position of Malaysia. It was short-lived, being terminated by the signature on August 11, 1966 of an agreement of peace and co-operation (drawn up at Bangkok, signed at Jakarta)": Shearer, *Starke's International Law* (11th ed.), 483.

Congo Act The General Act of the Conference at Berlin of plenipotentiaries of Austria-Hungary, Belgium, Denmark, France, Germany, Great Britain, Italy, the Netherlands, Portugal, Russia, Spain, Sweden-Norway and Turkey (the United States not ratifying), signed on 26 February 1885 *(165 C.T.S. 485)* embodying (1) a Declaration respecting freedom of trade in the Congo basin, (2) a Declaration respecting the slave trade, (3) a Declaration respecting the neutrality of the conventional basin of the Congo, (4) an Act of navigation for the Congo, (5) an Act of navigation for the Niger river, and (6) a Declaration introducing rules respecting future occupation on the coasts of the African continent. The Act was revised by the Convention of St. Germain of 10 September 1919 *(8 L.N.T.S. 26). See* further **colonial protectorate**.

Connally Amendment *See* **automatic reservation**.

conquest "**Subjugation**, that is the acquisition of territory by conquest followed by annexation, and often called title by conquest, had to be accepted into the scheme of modes of acquisition of title to territorial sovereignty in the period when the making of war was recognised as a sovereign right, and war was not illegal. . . . At no period did conquest alone and *ipso facto* make the conquering State the territorial sovereign of the conquered territory, even though such territory came through conquest for the time under the sway of the conqueror. Conquest was a mode of acquisition only if the conqueror, after having firmly established the conquest, and the state of war having come to an end, then formally annexed the territory. If a belligerent conquered part of the enemy territory and afterwards made the vanquished state cede the conquered territory in the treaty of peace the mode of acquisition was not subjugation but cession. Such a treaty of cession, however, would now be qualified by Article 52 of the Vienna Convention on the Law of Treaties, which provides that 'A treaty is void if its conclusion has been procured by the threat or use of force in violation of the principles of international law embodied in the Charter of the United Nations'" *I Oppenheim* 698-99. "[C]onquest as a title to territorial sovereignty has ceased to be part of the law: though . . . the principle of the **intertemporal law** means that this change cannot be regarded as being retroactive to titles made by conquest in an earlier period": Jennings, *The Acquisition of Territory in International Law* (1963), 56.

consent doctrine This expression connotes the traditional thesis, not in fact subscribed to by **Grotius**, as is sometimes said, that the basis of obligation of all international law, and not merely of treaties, is the consent of States. The thesis is open to such obvious objections as that the fact that international law is considered to be generally binding on new States cannot be explained without the importation of some non-consensual factor, *e.g.*, the fiction of implication of consent from recognition of Statehood. *See generally* Brierly, *The Basis of Obligation in International Law* (1958), 9-18.

constituent instrument The meaning of this expression is clear from the provision of art. 5 of the Vienna Convention on the Law of Treaties 1969 that "[t]he present Conven tion applies to any treaty which is the constituent instrument of an international organization. . . ."

constitutionalism This theory, originating within States and demanding the subjection of government to the terms of the constitution, has been extended to international organizations to import very much the same: that international organizations have only such powers as are conferred on them expressly in their constituent instruments and (perhaps) as required by necessary implication.

constitutive doctrine, theory According to this theory of the **recognition of States**, "through recognition only and exclusively a state becomes an international person and a subject of international law": Brierly, *The Law of Nations* (6th ed.), 138. While the constitutive doctrine is superficially attractive, it has a number of drawbacks. Primarily, the question must be asked as to what is the status of an entity which in fact satisfies all the objective criteria of statehood but is not recognized by a sufficient number of states, whatever that number might be. "Constitutivist doctrine creates a great many difficulties ... cogent argument of principle and the preponderance of state practice thus dictates a preference for declaratory doctrine, yet to reduce, or to seem to reduce, the issues to a choice between the two opposing theories is to greatly oversimplify the legal situation." Brownlie, *Principles of Public International Law* (5th ed.) 88-9. *See generally*, Crawford, *The Creation of States in International Law* (1979).

constitutive treaties A description applied by writers to "semi-legislative," as opposed to "purely contractual" treaties. *See* McNair, *Law of Treaties* (2nd ed), 259. The Vienna Convention on the Law of Treaties 1969 does not employ the expression. *But see* **constituent instrument**.

constructivism A theory on international organizations which holds that they "are more than mere clearing houses for the opinions of their member-states: they take on a role and dynamics of their own": Klabbers, *An Introduction to International Institutional Law* (2002), 33, citing as an example the European Community.

consul The Vienna Convention on Consular Relations 1963 *(596 U.N.T.S. 261)* contains no definition of a "consul" but defines a "consular officer" as meaning "any person ... entrusted in that capacity with the exercise of consular functions," providing further that "[c]onsular officers are of two categories, namely career consular officers and honorary consular officers" (art. 1(1), (2)), and giving in art. 5 an exhaustive definition of "consular functions" under thirteen heads. "So various are the functions of a consul that there can be no precise and at the same time acceptable definition of the term. ... The essential difference between diplomatic and consular work is that whereas the diplomat does business with and through the central government of the receiving state, the consul for the most part conducts official business with local or municipal authorities. ... Overall, however, it is the function of protection, in its broadest sense, which is the most important consular function. ... From an examination of a list of traditional consular functions, such as is contained in Art. 5 of the Vienna Convention ... it can be seen that, apart from the assisting of persons in trouble and the promotion of commerical interests, most are basically administrative. Among the more important of these are the issue of passports and visas . . ., the notarising of documents . . ., assistance with succession matters . . ., death . . ., the transmission of . . . legal documents . . ., and the registration of births and marriages. . . .": *Satow's Guide to Diplomatic Practice* (5th ed.), 256. There are four classes of heads of consular posts, namely Consuls General, Consuls, Vice Consuls and Consular Agents (Vienna Convention, art. 9(1)).

Consular Convention Cases See Avena Case; Breard Case; LaGrand Case.

consular privileges and immunities The Vienna Convention on Consular Relations *(596 U.N.T.S. 261)*, adopted on 24 April 1963, has been held by the ICJ to have codified the law on consular relations: *United States Diplomatic and Consular Staff in Tehran Case 1980 I.C.J. Rep. 3* at 24. Essentially, the Vienna Convention seeks to assimilate the privileges and immunities of consuls with those of diplomats (*see* **diplomatic privileges and immunities**), and grants to consular posts the following privileges, immunities and exemptions: the right to use the national flag and arms of the sending State (art. 29); inviolability of the consular premises (art. 31; cf. art. 49); exemption from taxation thereon (arts. 32 and 60); inviolability of archives and documents (arts. 33, 61); freedom of movement and communication (arts. 34-8); exemption from taxation on fees (arts. 39); personal inviolability for consular officers, subject to waiver (art. 45), this privilege involving certain concessions in the event that criminal proceedings are instituted (art. 41; cf. also arts. 42, 63, 64); immunity from jurisdiction of judicial and administrative authorities for consular officers and employees in respect of acts performed in the exercise of consular functions (save in respect of actions *ex contractu* or third-party collision etc., claims) (art. 43); certain concessions in the matter of liability to give evidence (art. 44); exemption from alien registration etc. (art. 46), work permit requirements (art. 47), social security taxes (art. 48), general direct taxation other than on private property or income (art. 50), and customs duties and inspection (art. 51), as well as personal services (art. 52). The Convention makes specific provision in respect also of the duration of privileges etc. (art. 53), and on the status of consular officers in transit through third countries (art. 54). *See* Lee, *Consular Law and Practice* (2nd ed.); Lee, *The Vienna Convention on Consular Relations* (1966).

consultative status Art. 71 of the UN Charter provides that "[t]he Economic and Social Council may make suitable arrangements for consultation with non-governmental organizations which are concerned with matters within its competence. Such arrangements may be made with international organizations and, where appropriate, with national organizations after consultation with the Member of the United Nations concerned." *See* "Arrangements for Consultiion with Non-Governmental Organizations," ECOSOC Res. 1996/31 updating Resolution 1296 (XLIV) which implements this provision.

contemporanea expositio In the interpretation of treaties, the application of the relevant rules of international law as they existed at the time of the conclusion of the treaty, and not as they exist at the time an issue of interpretation falls to be determined. Art. 32 of the Vienna Convention on the Law of Treaties 1969 provides for recourse to be had "to supplementary means of interpretation, including . . . the circumstances of [the treaty's] conclusion. . . ." *See also* **intertemporal law**.

contextual interpretation Art. 31 of the Vienna Convention on the Law of Treaties 1969 lays down as the "general rule of interpretation" that "[a] treaty shall be interpreted in good faith in accordance with the ordinary meaning to be given to the terms of the treaty in their context . . ." and provides that the context for this purpose shall comprise, in addition to the text, including the preamble and annexes, any agreement relating to the treaty made between all the parties in connexion with the conclusion of the treaty, and any instrument made by one or more parties in that connexion and accepted by the other parties as an instrument related to the treaty.

contiguity doctrine A "geographical doctrine" the name of which is self-explanatory (*see also* **continuity doctrine**; **hinterland, doctrine of**; **sector claims**), which has been held not to be "admissible as a legal method of deciding questions of territorial sovereignty; for it is wholly lacking in precision and would in its application lead to arbitrary results": *Island of Palmas Case (1928) 2 R.I.A.A. 829* per Judge Huber, Arbitrator. "Such doctrines were much in vogue in the nineteenth century. They were invoked principally to mark out areas claimed for future occupation. But, by the end of the century, international law had decisively rejected geographical doctrines as distinct legal roots of title and had made effective occupation, the sole test . . . Geographical proximity . . . is certainly relevant, but as a fact assisting the determination of the limits of an effective occupation, not as an independent source of title": Waldock, Disputed Sovereignty in the Falkland

Islands Dependencies, *(1948) 25 B.Y.I.L. 311* at 342. *See also* Jennings, *The Acquisition of Territory in International Law* (1963), 74-6; and Blum, *Historic Titles in International Law* (1965), 176-7 (and 329-31 in relation to the application of the doctrine to the **continental shelf**).

contiguous zone "International law accords States the right to exercise preventive or protective control for certain purposes over a belt of high seas contiguous to their territorial sea": International Law Commission's Commentary on its Draft Articles on the Territorial Sea and Contiguous Zone, *[1956] II I.L.C. Yearbook 294-5.* Art. 33 of the UN Convention on the Law of the Sea 1982 *(1833 U.N.T.S. 3)* provides: "(1) In a zone contiguous to its territorial sea, described as the contiguous zone, the coastal State may exercise the control necessary to: (a) prevent infringement of its customs, fiscal, immigration or sanitary regulations within its territory or territorial sea; (b) punish infringement of the above regulations committed within its territory or territorial sea. (2) The contiguous zone may not extend beyond 24 nautical miles from the baselines from which the breadth of the territorial sea is measured." The ILC pronounced against any special security rights and exclusive fishing rights in the contiguous zone: *[1956] II I.L.C. Yearbook 294-5.* The status of **air defence identification zones**, neutrality zones, and pollution zones is unclear. *See* Churchill & Lowe, *The Law of the Sea* (3rd ed.), Chap. 7; Lowe, The Development of the Concept of the Contiguous Zone (1981) 52 *B.Y.I.L.* 109; Oda, The Concept of the Contiguous Zone, *(1962) 11 I.C.L.Q. 131.*

continental shelf In geological terms, this is "the zone around the continent, extending from the low-water line to the depth at which there is a marked increase of slope to greater depth . . . conventionally [the edge of the continental shelf] is taken at 100 fathoms or 200 meters": International Committee on the Nomenclature of Ocean Bottom Features 1953, quoted by the International Law Commission in *[1956] 1 I.L.C. Yearbook 131.* In legal terms, "[t]he continental shelf of a coastal State comprises the seabed and subsoil of the submarine areas that extend beyond its territorial sea throughout the natural prolongation of its land territory to the outer edge of the continental margin, or to a distance of 200 nautical miles from the baselines [of the territorial sea] where the outer edge of the continental margin does not extend up to that distance": art. 76(1) of the UN Convention on the Law of the Sea 1982 *(1833 U.N.T.S. 3)*. Art. 76 goes on to establish a complicated formula for determining the outer edge of the continental margin (art. 76(2)-(7)), and to establish a Commission on the Limits of the Continental Shelf, on the basis of whose recommendations a coastal State will determine the outer edge of the margin (art. 76(8) and Annex II). Where a State claims beyond 200 miles (i.e. to the outer edge of the continental margin), it must make either payments or contributions in kind in respect of the resources beyond the 200 miles line (art. 82).

Beyond the definition of the continental shelf, the UN Convention of 1982 replicates many of the provisions of the Geneva Convention on the Continental Shelf 1958 *(499 U.N.T.S. 311)* which were held in the ***North Sea Continental Shelf Cases** 1969 I.C.J. Rep. 3* to represent customary law. Within the continental shelf thus defined, the coastal State has "sovereign rights for the purpose of exploring it and exploiting its natural resources" (art. 77(1)), these rights not being of sovereignty, but rather of **jurisdiction and control**. These rights are exclusive to the coastal State (art. 77(2)), and do not depend on any claim or proclamation by the coastal State (art. 77(3)); and they do not affect the status of the superjacent waters (art. 78(1)). The natural resources to which the coastal State is entitled are the "mineral and other non-living of the seabed and subsoil together with living organisms belonging to **sedentary species** . . ." (art. 77(4)). The coastal State is entitled to establish on its continental shelf artificial island, installations and structures (art. 80), with safety zones round them (*see* art. 60(4)-(8)).

The vexed question of **continental shelf boundaries** was first regulated by art. 6 of the Geneva Convention and is now governed by art. 83 of the UN Convention, providing that delimitation of a continental shelf boundary between opposite or adjacent States "shall be effected by agreement on the basis of international law, as referred to in Article 38 of the Statute of the International Court of Justice, in order to achieve an equitable solution." *See* Mouton, *The Continental Shelf* (1952); Brown, *Sea-Bed Energy and Minerals: The International Legal Regime*, Vol. 1, *The Continental Shelf* (1992); Churchill and Lowe, *The Law of the Sea* (3rd ed.), Chap. 8.

continental shelf boundaries Considerable difficulty and controversy has surrounded the legal rules for delimiting the continental shelf between opposite and adjacent States. The formulation in art. 6 of the Geneva Convention on the Continental Shelf 1958 *(499 U.N.T.S. 311)*, the so-called **equidistance-special circumstances rule**, was held in the *North Sea Continental Shelf Cases 1969 I.C.J. Rep. 3* not to represent customary law; and the ICJ laid down that that delimitation was to achieve an equitable solution taking account of all relevant circumstances. While these apparently quite different criteria might well have the same object and effect (*Anglo-French Continental Shelf Case (1978) 18 R.I.A.A. 3* at 271), the customary test has come to prevail (*see Continental Shelf Cases*). Art. 83(1) of the UN Convention on the Law of the Sea 1982 *(1833 U.N.T.S. 3)* promulgates a clumsy and unhelpful compromise between the two tests: "The delimitation of the continental shelf between States with opposite or adjacent coasts shall be effected by agreement on the basis of international law, as referred to in Article 38 [of the ICJ], in order to achieve an equitable solution." *See* Brown, *The International Law of the Sea* (1994), Vol. 1, Chap. 11; Churchill and Lowe, *The Law of the Sea* (3rd ed.), 184-98.

Continental Shelf Cases The **continental shelf**, particularly issues involving **continental shelf boundaries**, has been one of the most litigated areas of international law. *See* **Aegean Sea Continental Shelf Case; Anglo-French Continental Shelf Case; Guinea-Bissau/Senegal Maritime Delimitation Case; Gulf of Maine Case; Jan Mayen Case; Libya-Malta Continental Shelf Case; North Sea Continental Shelf Cases; Tunisia-Libya Continental Shelf Case; Qatar-Bahrain, Maritime Delimitation Case; Nicaragua-Honduras Maritime Delimitation Case.**

continental shelf doctrine While two arbitrations decided that there were no customary rules governing the **continental shelf** in early 1950s (*Abu Dhabi Arbitration (1951) 18 I.L.R. 144*; *Qatar Arbitration(1951) 18 I.L.R. 161*), rules clearly evolved sometime between the adoption of the Geneva Convention on the Continental Shelf 1958 *(499 U.N.T.S. 311)* and the decision in the *North Sea Continental Shelf Cases 1969 I.C.J. Rep. 3*, which held that arts. 1-3 of the Geneva Convention represented customary law (but that art. 6 on delimiting **continental shelf boundaries** did not). It can now safely be contended that most of the contemporary conventional rules, if not their detail, as contained in Part VI of the UN Convention on the Law of the Sea 1982 *(1833 U.N.T.S. 3)*, represent customary law, including the rules on delimiting continental shelf boundaries in art. 83.

continuity doctrine (1) The term "continuity" is sometimes used interchangeably with "contiguity," connoting geographical or topographical proximity. *See* Waldock, Disputed Sovereignty in the Falkland Islands Dependencies, *(1948) 25 B.Y.I.L. 311* esp. at 343; and Jennings, *The Acquisition of Territory in International Law* (1963), 74. *See* **contiguity doctrine**. (2) A "notion not far removed from contiguity, which has sometimes been made the basis of claims for a change of title . . . may perhaps be called the principle of historical continuity. . . . The argument is that what has at some time in the past been a territorial unit of nationhood, or even a territorial unit of administration by a colonial power, should persist under a new sovereignty—such being an essentially political argument" to be differentiated from "strictly legal arguments touching title": Jennings, *The Acquisition of Territory in International Law* (1963), 76-7.

continuous voyage, transportation, doctrine of   "The so-called doctrine of continuous voyage dates from the time of the Anglo-French wars at the end of the eighteenth century, and is generally regarded as connected with the application of the so-called 'rule of the war of 1756.' Neutral vessels engaged in French and Spanish colonial trade, which had been thrown open to them during the war, sought to evade seizure by British cruisers and condemnation by British Prize Courts according to the 'rule of 1756,' by taking their cargo to a neutral port, landing it and paying import duties there, and then re-loading it and carrying it to the mother-country of the particular colony." *II Oppenheim 675n*. The doctrine, which permitted capture on the first leg of the voyage, was extended to carriage of contraband by the American courts during the Civil War and equally to the case where the onward journey was by land rather than sea and thus a case of continuous transportation rather than continuous voyage. These innovations attracted some approval and some disapproval. "The Declaration of London offered a compromise which, if it had been accepted, would have settled the controversy by applying the doctrine . . . to *absolute* contraband, but not, except in cases where the enemy country had no seaboard, to *conditional* contraband. However, the compromise . . . was not accepted by the Allies during the World War, and the doctrine . . . was applied to the circuitous and indirect carriage of conditional as well as absolute contraband": *II Oppenheim 679-80*. "By the Order in Council of March 30, 1916, it was enacted that 'neither a vessel nor her cargo shall be immune from capture for breach of blockade upon the sole ground that she is on her way to a non-blockaded port.' Similarly, the Maritime Rights Order in Council of July 7, 1916, provided that 'the principle of continuous voyage or ultimate destination shall be applicable both in cases of contraband and of blockade.' France adopted an identical rule. . . . A similar rule was enacted by Italy. . . .": Colombos, *International Law of the Sea* (6th ed.), 732.

contra proferentem   "[T]here is a familiar rule for the construction of instruments that, where they are found to be ambiguous, they should be taken *contra proferentem*" [in a sense against the interest of the party on whose initiative the provisions were included]: **Brazilian Loans Case** *(1929) P.C.I.J., Ser. A., Nos. 20/21, 93* at 114. For other instances, see McNair, *Law of Treaties* (2nd ed.), 464-5. There is no reference to the rule in the Vienna Convention on the Law of Treaties 1969.

contraband   Contraband of war consists in goods the carriage of which in neutral vessels, a belligerent is considered, in classical international law, to be entitled to penalize on grounds either of their intrinsic utility to an enemy (*e.g.*, arms and ammunition, sometimes denominated absolute contraband) or of the presumption of their utility which is to be derived from the fact of their hostile destination (*e.g.*, means of transport, fuel or foodstuffs consigned to the enemy government or forces, styled conditional contraband). What in fact has been considered contraband in any particular war from the point of view of any belligerent has depended on its designation as such by that belligerent—classically in a published contraband list. The penalty exacted for carriage of contraband has, equally, varied—from confiscation of the whole adventure, non-contraband as well as contraband, in case of absolute contraband, to no more than a species of compulsory purchase of conditional contraband, with or without forfeiture of freight. The attempt made in the Declaration of London 1909 *(208 C.T.S. 338*: see **London, Declaration of, 1909)**, Chap. II, to achieve an international agreement failed of ratification. Though the United Kingdom published a contraband list on the outbreak of the Second World War, it was expressed in the most general terms and included only one category of conditional contraband—food and clothing. *See generally* Colombos, *International Law of the Sea* (6th ed.), Chap. 17; Shearer, *Starke's International Law* (11th ed.), 532-536.

contracting State   A "State which has consented to be bound by the treaty, whether or not the treaty has entered into force": Vienna Convention on the Law of Treaties 1969, art. 2(1)(f).

contributions   (1) In the law of war, "Contribution is a payment in ready money demanded either from municipalities or from inhabitants [of occupied territory]. Arts. 49 and 51 of the Hague Regulations [respecting the Laws and Customs of Warfare on Land, annexed to Hague Convention IV, 1907 *(205 C.T.S. 277)*] enacted that contributions might not be demanded extortionately, but exclusively for the needs of the army. . . . They may be imposed by written order of a commander-in-chief only, in contradistinction to requisitions which may be imposed by a mere commander in a locality. They may not be imposed indiscriminately . . . but must so far as possible be assessed . . . in compliance with the rules . . . regarding the assessment of taxes. Finally . . . a receipt must be given": *II Oppenheim 412.* The Hague Convention IX of 1907 respecting Bombardments by Naval Forces *(205 C.T.S. 345)* provides that the bombardment of undefended places for the non-payment of money contributions is forbidden (art. 4).

(2) Many international organizations levy contributions from their member States as the method of funding their budgets. Thus, art. 17(2) of the UN Charter refers to the expenses of the UN being apportioned among the members by the General Assembly, these apportionments being referred to as "contributions" in art. 19 (concerning the suspension of voting rights for States in arrears on their contributions). *See* Sands and Klein, *Bowett's Law of International Institutions* (5th ed.), Chap. 17.

convention   "The designation 'convention' tends to be utilized for multilateral treaties of a law-making type. Illustrative of this tendency are the various Hague . . . Geneva . . . Vienna Conventions. . . . However, . . . [t]he designation is also used for a wide range of bilateral treaties—for example, consular conventions, [and] double taxation conventions. . . .": S*atow's Guide to Diplomatic Practice* (5th ed.), 241-242. That said, art. 38(1)(a) of the Statute of the International Court of Justice refers to **treaties**, the normal term used, as "international conventions, whether general or particular. . . ."

Corfu Channel Case   *(United Kingdom v. Albania) 1948 I.C.J. Rep. 15; 1949 I.C.J. Rep. 4.* The dispute arose out of the mining of two British warships on 22 October 1946 at a point in the Corfu Channel within Albanian territorial waters, resulting in severe damage and loss of life. The UK having purported to initiate proceedings by unilateral application under art. 40(1) of the ICJ Statute, Albania raised as a preliminary objection that, in the absence of any treaty stipulating for compulsory jurisdiction, only both parties could validly do this. *Held* (15 to 1) that the objection failed, the letter in which it was first raised having accepted the jurisdiction in precise terms. *See also forum prorogatum.* The Special Agreement of 25 March 1948 entered into following the decision of the ICJ on the Preliminary Objection confined the issues to: "(1) Is Albania responsible under international law for the explosions . . . and for the damage and loss of human life . . . and is there any duty to pay compensation? (2) Has the United Kingdom . . . violated the sovereignty of . . . Albania . . . by reason of the acts of the Royal Navy in Albanian waters on the 22nd October and on the 12th and 13th November [when the British squadron re-entered the channel to seek evidence of the origin of the minefield] and is there any duty to give satisfaction?" *Held* (1) (11 to 5) that Albania was responsible, since the laying of the minefield (the origins of which were not established in the proceedings) could not have been accomplished without the knowledge of the Albanian Government, which took no steps to warn shipping of its existence, the Court (10 to 6) reserving the assessment of compensation for further consideration; (2) (14 to 2) that the UK did not violate Albanian sovereignty by sending the warships through the channel on 22 October without the prior authorization of Albania, the strait being an international highway through which a right of passage exists; but (3) (unanimously) that the minesweeping operation of 12-13 November was justifiable neither as a permissible form of intervention nor as an act of self-defense and therefore did constitute a violation of Albanian sovereignty, of which, however, "this declaration by the Court constitutes in itself appropriate satisfaction." In a further judgment, dated 15 December 1949 *(1949) I.C.J. Rep. 244* the Court (12 to 2) fixed the compensation at £843,947. *See also* the **Monetary Gold Case** *1954 I.C.J. Rep. 19.*

corporal punishment   The issue of corporal punishment is dealt with in international law primarily in relation to the punishment of children. With regard to adults, the **Universal Declaration of Human Rights** of 10 December 1948 (GA Res. 217(III)) and the two International Covenants of 1966 on **Civil and Political Rights** *(999 U.N.T.S. 171)* and **Social, Economic and Cultural Rights** *(993 U.N.T.S. 3)* enshrine respect for human dignity and the right to physical integrity. However, with regard to children, the position is less clear. Art. 19 of the Convention on the Rights of the Child 1989 *(999 U.N.T.S. 171)* requires States to take "all appropriate legislative, administrative, social and educational measures to protect the child from all forms of physical or mental violence, injury or abuse, neglect or negligent treatment, maltreatment or exploitation, including sexual abuse, while in the care of parent(s), legal guardian(s) or any other person who has the care of the child." Nevertheless, in October 1994, the Committee on the Rights of the Child noted: "As for corporal punishment, few countries have clear laws on this question. Certain States have tried to distinguish between the correction of children and excessive violence. In reality the dividing line between the two is artificial. It is very easy to pass from one stage to the other. It is also a question of principle. If it is not permissible to beat an adult, why should it be permissible to do so to a child? One of the contributions of the Convention [on the rights of the Child] is to call attention to the contradiction in our attitudes and cultures." *(UN Doc. CRC/C/SR 176). See generally* Fottrell, *Revisiting Children's Rights* (2000), Chap. 8.

Costa Rica Packet Arbitration   *(Great Britain v. Netherlands) (1897) 184 C.T.S. 240.* By the Convention of 16 May 1895 *(181 C.T.S. 253)*, the parties referred to arbitration the claim of the owners and crew of a British vessel arising out of the detention of her master on a charge of maliciously appropriating the contents of a derelict native pirogue found at sea. The award of Professor F. de Martens in the name of the Czar of Russia in favor of the claimants was based on the finding of fact that the appropriation took place outside territorial waters and on the conclusion that the abandonment of the prosecution demonstrated its impropriety. The case is commonly cited, however, as an illustration of the proposition that the jurisdiction of the flag State on the high seas is exclusive.

Council for Mutual Economic Assistance *See* **COMECON**.

Council of Europe   The Council of Europe, established by the Statute of 5 May 1949 *(87 U.N.T.S. 103)*, was designed "to achieve a greater unity between its Members for the purpose of safeguarding and realising the ideals and principles which are their common heritage and facilitating their economic and social progress" (art. 1(a)); this aim to be pursued "through the organs of the Council by discussion of questions of common concern and by agreements and common action in economic, social, cultural, scientific, legal and administrative matters and in the maintenance and further realisation of human rights and fundamental freedoms" (art. 1(b)). The Council, which began with ten members, now has 45 with a number of former Communist European States, including Russia, having joined in the 1990's. There are two organs: a Committee of Ministers, representing all the member States and responsible for considering "the action required to further the aim of the Council of Europe, including the conclusion of conventions or agreements and the adoption by Governments of a common policy with regard to particular matters" (art. 15 (a)); and a Parliamentary Assembly, representation on which is weighted (*see* art. 26, as amended), and which is "the deliberative organ of the Council of Europe" (art. 22). There is also an elected Secretary-General and the Congress of Local and regional Authorities of Europe. The Council of Europe is most renowned for its works in human rights: see the **European Convention on Human Rights.** In 1997, the Committee of Ministers adopted a Plan of Action based on four broad themes: democracy and human rights, social cohesion, security of citizens and education for democracy and cultural diversity. *See* <www.coe.org>.

counter-claim Before the International Court of Justice, a cross-claim made by the respondent State in a contentious case instituted by means of an application. It must be "directly connected with the subject-matter of the application and must come within the jurisdiction of the Court": Rules of Court 1978, art. 80(1).

counter-measures Art. 22 of the ILC's Draft Articles on the State Responsibility 2001 *(UN Doc. A/56/10 Chap.IV.E.1)* provides that "[t]he wrongfulness of an act of State not in conformity with an international obligation towards another state is precluded if and to the extent that the act constitutes a countermeasure taken against the latter State in conformity with Chapter II of Part 3." Chapter II of Part 3 is headed "Countermeasures" and comprises arts. 49-54. Lawful countermeasures must only be taken to induce compliance with the earlier wrong (art. 49); they must be proportionate (art. 51); and must be terminated when the responsible State has complied with its obligation (art. 53). Lawful countermeasures cannot involve the threat or use of force (art. 50). Although the Draft Articles have no direct legal force, they are generally considered as being reflective of customary international law. *See* Elagab, *The Legality of Non-Forcible Counter-Measures in International Law* (1988); Damrosch, Enforcing International Law Through Non-Forcible Means *(1997) 269 Hague Recueil 13.*

counter-memorial The second of the written pleadings in a contentious case before the ICJ instituted by means of an application, in which the respondent State replies to the statement of facts and law and the submissions contained in the **memorial** of the applicant State: see the ICJ Statute, art. 43(2) and Rules of Court 1978, arts. 45(1), 49(2). *See also* **reply** and **rejoinder.**

Counter-Terrorism Committee Established by Security Council Res. 1373 (2001), para. 6, the CCT consists of all the members of the Council. Its mission is to monitor, on the basis of reports submitted by States, the implementation of the resolution, particularly the measures taken by States to prevent the financing, planning, preparation and perpetration of terrorist acts.

courbe tangente A "term which is sometimes used to denote the **envelope line**": Shalowitz, *Shore and Sea Boundaries* (1962), Vol. 1, 170. *See also* **arcs-of-circles.**

courier, diplomatic *See* **diplomatic courier.**

covenant "The *Covenant (pacte)* of the League of Nations is believed to be the first use of the term 'Covenant' to describe a treaty, and probably owes its existence to the Presbyterian origin of President Woodrow Wilson. It has also been applied to the draft Covenant of Human Rights": McNair, *Law of Treaties* (2nd ed.), 25. *See also* the International Covenant on **Economic, Social and Cultural Rights** *(993 U.N.T.S. 3)* and the International Covenant on **Civil and Political Rights** *(999 U.N.T.S. 171)* of 16 December 1966.

Crawford, James 1948- . Whewell Professor of International Law, Cambridge, and Director of the Lauterpacht Research Centre for International Law. Member of the International Law Commission (1992-); Special Rapporteur on State Responsibility. His works include *The Creation of States in International Law* (1979); *The Appropriation of Terra Nullius. A Review Symposium* (1989); *The ILC's Articles on State Responsibility. Introduction, Text and Commentaries* (2002).

CRC The acronym used for both the Convention on the Rights of the Child 1989 *(1577 U.N.T.S. 3)* (*see* **Child, Convention on the Rights of the**) and the Committee on the Rights of the Child established by art. 43 of the Convention.

credentials The Vienna Convention on Diplomatic Relations 1961 *(500 U.N.T.S. 95)*, art. 13 provides: "(1) The Head of the [diplomatic] mission is considered as having taken up his functions in the receiving State either when he has presented his credentials or when he has notified his arrival and a true copy of his credentials has been presented to the Ministry of Foreign Affairs of the receiving State, or such other ministry as may be agreed, in accordance with the practice prevailing in the receiving State which shall be applied in a uniform manner. (2) The order of presentation of credential or of a true copy thereof will be determined by the date and time of the arrival of the head of the mission." Art. 16 of the Vienna Convention further provides that Heads of Mission shall take precedence in their respective classes in the order and time of taking up their function in accordance with art. 13. *See* further: *Satow's Guide to Diplomatic Practice* (5th ed.), 55-64 and 96-105; Denza *Diplomatic Law* (2nd ed.), 87-9. International organizations also require a presentation of credentials to verify that a member State's representative is authorized to represent the government of that State. *See* **representation of a member State**.

crime against humanity *See* **humanity, crime against**.

crime against peace *See* **peace, crime against**.

crime, international The notion of criminality was lacking in classical international law. Nevertheless, even that system was so far concerned with crimes as to concede a **universal jurisdiction** to States with respect to at least one class of offender, the pirate, who was described as *hostis humani generis*, and whose offence has often been designated as an international crime or "crime against the Law of Nations." In addition to **piracy**, engaging in the slave trade (*see* **slavery**) has for a substantial period of time been termed an international crime. Though so-called **war crimes**, that is to say offences against the laws and customs of war, have always been punishable by any belligerent into whose hands an offender may fall, they were not commonly styled international crimes before the adoption of the Charter of the International Military Tribunal of 8 August 1945 *(82 U.N.T.S. 279)*. But it is from the Judgment of that Tribunal, though it did not in fact use the expression, that the modern user of the term stems. "When laying down that individuals are liable to be punished for crimes against international law, the Court did not give any precise definition of international crimes. Nor does such a definition appear in the Charter. . . . However, in demonstrating that the crimes listed in article 6 of the Charter [i.e. crimes against peace, war crimes, and crimes against humanity] were crimes against international law already before the [Charter] the Tribunal gave some indication as to what, in its opinion, makes certain acts crimes against international law. . . . An international crime is something more than merely a violation of international law. . . . It must be said, however, that the reasoning of the Court permits more definite conclusions concerning what is not necessary than what is imperative in order to establish the criminality of an illegal act. . . . It need not be doubted that . . . the explicit branding of certain acts as criminal, express provisions for the punishment of perpetrators of such acts or the actual punishing in practice of those who commit them, would . . . be sufficient proof of the criminal character of the acts. But . . . the . . . Court held that the solemn renunciation, through the **Kellogg-Briand Pact**, of war as an instrument of national policy made such a war both illegal and criminal in international law, and reinforced its construction of the pact by citing international documents which it regarded as strong evidence of the intention entertained by the vast majority of . . . States. . . . The existence of such an intention within the international community was . . . the deciding factor making prohibited acts criminal under international law": *The Charter and Judgment of the Nurnberg Tribunal, Memorandum of the Secretary-General, UN Doc. A/CN.4/5*. It is thus to be concluded that the category of international crimes is not a closed one. However, there remains great controversy over what is included in the category of international crimes. Other crimes which undoubtedly fall within this category are the crimes of **genocide** and **crimes against humanity**. The crime of aggression also probably falls within this category in spite of the fact that there is no clearly accepted definition of what constitutes the crimes. However, "customary international law . . . now appears to consider the planning, or organizing or preparing or participating in the first use of armed force by a State against the territorial integrity and political independence of another State in contravention of the UN Charter, provided the acts of aggression concerned have large-scale and serious consequences, to be an international crime": Cassese, International Criminal Law, in Evans (ed.), *International Law* (2003), 747. Other possible inclusions are **torture**, even where it is committed outside the context of a widespread or systematic practice, and **terrorism** (*see* Cassese, *supra*, 748-754). In its Draft Code of Crimes Against the Peace and Security of Mankind 1996 *(UN Doc. A/48/10)*, as well as the crimes of aggression (art. 16), genocide (art. 17) crimes against humanity (art. 18) and war crimes (art. 20), the ILC also included as "crimes under international law and punishable as such, whether or not they are punishable under international law" (art. 1(2)), crimes against United Nations and associated personnel (art. 19). A previous draft in 1991 *(UN Doc. A/46/10)* had also included the crimes of **apartheid** (art. 20), recruitment, use, financing and training of mercenaries (art. 23), international terrorism (art. 34), illicit traffic in narcotic drugs (art. 15) and willful and severe damage to the environment (art. 26). It should be noted that the Draft Code is not a binding legal texts and many of the categories of international crimes suggested, particularly in the 1991 Draft, were controversial and remain so (*but see* relevant treaties referred to below).

In respect of international crimes, not only is there a duty on every State to prosecute or extradite individuals responsible for the commission of those crimes, but, also, individual responsibility for those crimes is enforceable at the international level. Until recently, an unresolved problem with the concept of international crime was the absence of any international tribunal with appropriate criminal jurisdiction. This problem has been partially addressed by the creation of the **International Criminal Tribunal for the Former Yugoslavia**, the **International Criminal Tribunal for Rwanda**, and the **International Criminal Court** all of which have jurisdiction over the "core" international crimes: war crimes, crimes against humanity, genocide and aggression. More recently, internationalized or mixed criminal courts or tribunals have been set up in the **Special Court for Sierra Leone** (by SC Res. 1315 (2000)) and East Timor Special Panel for the Trials of Serious Crimes *(UNTAET Regulations 2000/11 and 2000/15)* exhibiting features of both national and international jurisdiction.

A distinction may be drawn between international crimes properly so-called and offences which attract multi-State jurisdiction on the basis of international treaty law. For example, the **hijacking** of aircraft is constituted an offence within multi-State jurisdiction by art. 7 of the Hague Convention for the Suppression of Unlawful Seizure of Aircraft of 16 December 1970 *(860 U.N.T.S. 105)*; and see **terrorism**. The 4 **Geneva Conventions** on the Laws of War of 12 August 1949 *(75 U.N.T.S. 35ff.)* likewise provide for the sanctioning of "grave breaches" of their provisions on a multi-State basis. *See* similarly, Convention of 14 December 1973 on the Prevention and Punishment of Crimes against **Internationally Protected Persons**, including Diplomatic Agents of 14 December 1973 *(1035 U.N.T.S. 167)*; the International Convention Against the Taking of **Hostages** of 18 December 1979 *(1316 U.N.T.S. 205)*; The Convention on the Safety of United Nations and Associated Personnel of 9 December 1994 *(2051 U.N.T.S. 363)*; and the International Convention for the Suppression of Terrorist Bombings of 15 December 1997 *(37 I.L.M. 249 (1998))*. *See also* the Convention on the Non-Applicability of Statutory Limitations to War Crimes, etc., of 26 November 1968 *(8 I.L.M. 68 (1969))*. *And see generally* Cassese, *International Criminal Law* (2003); Kittichaisaree, *International Criminal Law* (2001).

crime, war *See* **war crimes**.

critical date This term, though the concept it connotes has always been implicit in territorial disputes, if not in all litigated matters, appears to have been derived from the terminology employed by the arbitrator in the ***Island of Palmas Case (1928) 2 R.I.A.A. 829*** at 845. As there used and in the ***Eastern Greenland Case (1933) P.C.I.J., Ser A/B, No. 53*** at 45, the term indicates the date as at which the rights of the parties are to be determined and actions subsequent to which are, for the purposes of the proceedings, irrelevant. For an analysis of possible criteria for the determination of the critical date see Fitzmaurice, The Law and Procedure of the ICJ, etc., Part II, *(1955-6) 32 B.Y.I.L. 20* at 23-4. *See also* the ***Minquiers and Ecrehos Case 1953 I.C.J. Rep. 47*** at 59-60. And see Jennings, *The Acquisition of Territory in International Law* (1963), 31-5; Blum, *Historic Titles in International Law* (1958), 208-22.

cruel, inhuman and degrading "Any act of torture or other cruel, inhuman or degrading treatment or punishment is an offence to human dignity and shall be condemned as a denial of the purposes of the Charter of the United Nations and as a violation of the human rights and fundamental freedoms proclaimed in the Universal Declaration of Human Rights." Declaration on the Protection of All Persons from Being Subjected to Torture and Other Cruel, Inhuman or Degrading Treatment or Punishment (GA Res. 3452 (XXX)), art. 2. The Convention Against Torture and other Cruel, Inhuman or Degrading Treatment adopted on 10 December 1984 (*see* **Torture Convention**; *1465 U.N.T.S. 85*) does not define the phrase "cruel, inhuman or degrading treatment" and excludes from the definition of torture "pain or suffering arising only from, inherent in or incidental to lawful sanctions." (art. 1). However, art. 16 of the Convention provides that "[e]ach State Party shall undertake to prevent in any territory under its jurisdiction other acts of cruel, inhuman or degrading treatment or punishment which do not amount to torture as defined in article 1, when such acts are committed by or at the instigation of or with the consent or acquiescence of a public official or other person acting in an official capacity."

Many have argued that the **death penalty** is a cruel, inhuman and degrading: "Precisely because the basic international human rights instruments appear to authorize the death penalty, some have turned to the prohibition of cruel and unusual punishment in order to attack capital punishment indirectly. Challenges have addressed such issues as the method of execution, delay in informing offenders of reprieves and the 'death row' phenomenon": Schabas, *The Abolition of the Death Penalty in International Law* (3rd ed.), 19. See, for example, *Pratt et al v Attorney-General for Jamaica* [1993] 4 All E.R. 769; *Soering v United Kingdom et al.* 11 EHRR 439. *See also* Schabas, *The Death Penalty as Cruel and Unusual Punishment: Capital Punishment Challenged in the World's Courts* (1996).

CSCE *See* **Organization for Security and Co-operation in Europe**.

CTC *See* **Counter-Terrorism Committee**.

CTT Comprehensive Test-Ban Treaty: *see* **Test-Ban Treaties**.

Cultural Property, Convention for Protection of The Hague Convention for the Protection of Cultural Property in the Event of Armed Conflict *(249 U.N.T.S. 215)* was opened for signature on 14 May 1954, art. 1 containing a definition of such property for its purposes: "(a) movable or immovable property of great importance to the cultural heritage of every people, such as monuments of architecture, art or history, whether religious or secular; archaeological sites; groups of buildings which, as a whole, are of historical or artistic interest; works of art; manuscripts, books and other objects of artistic, historical or archaeological interest; as well as scientific collections and important collections of books or archives or of reproductions of the property defined above; (b) buildings whose main and effective purpose is to preserve or exhibit the movable cultural property defined in sub-paragraph (*a*) such as museums, large libraries and depositories of archives, and refuges intended to shelter, in the event of armed conflict, the movable cultural property defined in sub-paragraph (*a*); (c) centres containing a large amount of cultural property as defined in sub-paragraphs (*a*) and (*b*), to be known as 'centres containing monuments.'"

cultural relativism Cultural relativism is not a term of art, being borrowed from social anthropology and moral philosophy and applied to **human rights** to mean "the position according to which local cultural traditions (including religious, political, and legal practices) properly determine the existence and scope of civil and political rights enjoyed by individuals in a given society. The central tenet of relativism is that no transboundary legal or moral standards exist against which human rights practices may be judged acceptable or unacceptable": Tesón, International Human Rights and Cultural Relativism, *25 Va. J. Int'l L. 869* at 870 *(1984-85)*. While attractive as a recognition of cultural **self-determination**, cultural relativism detracts from the prevailing belief in the universality of human rights norms, expressed somewhat ambiguously in the Vienna Declaration of the UN World Conference on Human Rights 1993 *(32 I.L.M. 1661 (1993))*, Section I, para. 5, thus: "all human rights are universal, indivisible, and interdependent and interrelated. . . . While the significance of national and regional particularities and various historical, cultural and religious backgrounds must be borne in mind, it is the duty of States, regardless of their political, economic and cultural systems, to promote and protect all human rights and fundamental freedoms." *See* McWhinney, *United Nations Law Making: Cultural and Ideological Relativism and International Law for an Era of Transition* (1984).

custom Art. 38(1) of the ICJ Statute directs the Court to apply, *inter alia*, "international custom, as evidence of a general practice accepted as law" although "it is generally accepted that it custom that is the source to be applied, and that it is practice which evidences the custom. . . . Thus Article 38 could more correctly have been phrased to read 'international custom as evidenced by a general practice accepted as law.' In fact this is the way in which the clause is interpreted in practice": Higgins, *Problems and Process: International Law and How We Use It* (1994), 18. However one chooses to read this definition, it is clear that customary international law envisages two principal elements: a concordant practice of a number of States acquiesced in by others; and a conception that the practice is required by or consistent with the prevailing law (*opinio juris*). As to the fact that, if the practice be uniform, the period during which it has been followed need not necessarily be very long, and as to the nature of the subjective element of *opinio juris,* see the judgment of the ICJ in the *North Sea Continental Shelf Cases*. As to regional or **local custom** in international law, see the *Asylum Cases*. Other World Court cases in which significant discussions of custom are to be found include the *Lotus Case, Anglo-Norwegian Fisheries Case, Fisheries Jurisdiction Case, Rights of US Nationals in Morocco Case* and *Military and Paramilitary Activities in and Against Nicaragua Case. And see generally* Akehurst, Custom as a Source of International Law *(1974-5) 47 B.Y.I.L. 1*; Parry, *The Sources and Evidences of International Law* (1965), 56-82; D'Amato, *The Concept of Custom in International Law* (1971); Thirlway, *International Customary Law and Codification* (1972); Byers *Custom Power and the Power of Rules* (1999).

customary law, international *See* **custom.**

customs union "[T]he requirements of a customs union [are]: uniformity of customs law and customs tariff, unity of the customs frontiers and of the customs territory vis-à-vis third States; freedom from import and export duties in the exchange of goods between partner States; apportionment of the duties collected according to a fixed quota": Austrian Memorial, p. 4 in the *Austro-German Customs Union Case (1931) P.C.I.J., Ser. A/B, No. 41.* "A customs union becomes a common market with the removal of all restrictions on the movement of productive factors—labor, capital and enterprise": Root, *International Trade and Investment: Theory, Policy, Enterprise,* 378. *See also* **free trade area**; **common market**; **economic union.**

customs zone "Many States have adopted the principle that in the contiguous zone the coastal State may exercise customs control in order to prevent attempted infringements of its customs and fiscal regulations within its territory or territorial sea, and to punish infringements of those regulations committed within its territory or territorial sea. The [International Law] Commission considered that it would be impossible to deny to States the exercise of such rights": ILC's Commentary on its Draft Articles on the Territorial Sea and Contiguous Zone, *[1956] II I.L.C. Yearbook 294.* Art. 33 of the UN Convention on the Law of the Sea 1982 *(1833 U.N.T.S. 3)* includes infringement of "customs and fiscal" regulations as one example of the preventative jurisdiction which the coastal State may exercise in its **contiguous zone.** *See* Jessup, *The Law of Territorial Waters and Maritime Jurisdiction* (1927), Chap. II; Dickinson, Jurisdiction at the Maritime Frontier, *40 Harv. L. Rev. 1 (1926).*

Cutting Incident *(U.S. v. Mexico)* (1886) Moore, *Digest of International Law*, Vol. 2, 228. Cutting, a United States national resident in Mexico, having been proceeded against for the publication of defamatory statements appearing in a Mexican newspaper of which he was editor, consented to a "judgment of conciliation" requiring the publication of a retraction. But, instead of complying, he repeated the defamatory statements in a Texas newspaper. Having returned to Mexico, he was thereupon sentenced by a Mexican court to imprisonment and the payment of a civil indemnity on the ground of the original libel and also under art. 186 of the Penal Code, which provided for the punishment of offences committed abroad. The legitimacy of this basis of jurisdiction (styled the principle of **passive personality**) was strongly contested by the United States in diplomatic exchanges following the incident. Ultimately, Cutting was released by order of a superior court, the complainant having withdrawn from the proceedings. *See generally* Moore, *Report on Extraterritorial Crime and the Cutting Case* (1887).

Cysnes, The *See* ***Portugal v. Germany (1928, 1930)***.

D

damage, indirect   *See* **indirect damage**.

damages, penal   *See* **damages, punitive**.

damages, punitive   "It is sometimes maintained that, having regard to the sovereignty of states, their responsibility for international wrongs is limited to such reparation . . . as does not exceed the limits of restitution, and that damages in excess of those limits (often referred to as penal or punitive damages) are excluded. This view hardly accords either with principle or practice": *I Oppenheim 533*. In some instances where the power to award punitive damages was denied (***Lusitania Cases (1923) 7 R.I.A.A. 32***; ***Naulilaa Incident Case (1928) 2 R.I.A.A. 1013***), the award of punitive damages was held to be *ultra vires* the tribunal. There are some cases in which the principle seems to have been admitted though on the facts no award was made: *Metzger's Case (Germany v. Venezuela)(1904) 10 R.I.A.A. 417*; *Torrey's Case (U.S. v. Venezuela) (1903) 9 R.I.A.A. 225*; ***I'm Alone Case (1935) 3 R.I.A.A. 1609***. There are some instances of punitive damages in diplomatic practice: Whiteman, *Damages in International Law* (1937), 716. "The practice of states and tribunals shows other instances of reparation, indistinguishable from punishment, in the form of pecuniary redress unrelated to the damage actually inflicted": *I Oppenheim 533*.

D'Amato, Anthony   1937- . Professor of Law at Northwestern University 1974- . His works include *The Concept of Custom in International Law* (1971); *International Law and World Order* (with Weston and Falk, 2nd ed. 1990); *International Law: Process and Prospect* (2nd ed.1995); *International Law Anthology* (1997).

damnum emergens   *See* ***lucrum cessans***.

Danzig and the ILO Case   *(1930) P.C.I.J., Ser. B, No. 18.* By resolution dated 15 May 1930, the League of Nations Council requested an advisory opinion as to whether the special legal status of the Free City of Danzig was such as to enable it to become a member of the ILO. On 26 August 1930, the Court *advised* (6 to 4) in the negative on the ground that, though the right of Poland to control the foreign relations of the Free City was not absolute, the latter could not participate in the work of the ILO until some arrangement had been made ensuring in advance that no objection could be made by the Polish government to any action which the Free City might desire to take as a member of the ILO.

Danzig, Jurisdiction of the Courts of, Case   *(1928) P.C.I.J., Ser. B, No. 15.* By resolution dated 22 September 1927, the League of Nations Council requested of the PCIJ an advisory opinion as to whether the League High Commissioner's decision of 8 April 1927 as to the jurisdiction of the Danzig courts in respect of actions by Danzig railway employees passing into the service of the Polish railways administration was legally well founded. The jurisdiction of the League Council and the High Commissioner in the matter arose out of the Convention of 9 November 1920 between the Free City and Poland *(6 L.N.T.S. 189),* providing, *inter alia,* for the administration of the railways within the area of the Free City and (art. 39) for the resolution of differences by the decision of the High Commissioner subject to a right of appeal to the Council. The decision appealed against was to the effect that, though the Danzig courts had jurisdiction in claims arising out of contracts of service, they had no such jurisdiction in actions based exclusively on the Agreement of 22 October 1921 respecting the transfer of employees to the Polish service (the *Beamtenabkommen*) because that instrument did not form part of any individual's contract of service. On 3 March 1928, the Court *advised* (unanimously) that the decision was not well founded, saying: "It may be readily admitted that, according to a well-established principle of international law, the *Beamtenabkommen,* being an international agreement, cannot, as such, create direct rights and obligations for private individuals. But it cannot be disputed that the very object of an international agreement, according to the intention of the contracting parties, may be the adoption by the Parties of some definite rules creating individual rights and obligations and enforceable by the national courts. That there is such an intention in the present case can be established by reference to the terms of the *Beamtenabkommen*."

Danzig, Polish Postal Service in, Case *(1925) P.C.I.J., Ser. B, No. 11.* The matter referred to the PCIJ in this case by the League of Nations Council resolution of 13 March 1925 involved, first, a procedural question whether there had been a prior decision in the merits by the League High Commissioner for Danzig pursuant to art. 39 of the Danzig-Polish Convention of 9 March 1920 (*see* the ***Danzig, Jurisdiction of Courts of, Case***); and, secondly, the question whether, under art. 29 of the Convention, Poland was entitled to institute in the port of Danzig a general postal service, not confined to officials nor to the Polish postal premises. Art. 29 provided indeed that "Poland shall have the right to establish in the port of Danzig a post, etc., service communicating directly with Poland" but, art. 30 stipulating for the lease of a building for this service by Danzig and art. 31 for the reservation of all other postal matters to Danzig, a restrictive interpretation was contended for. Having answered the procedural question negatively, the Court *advised* (unanimously) on 16 May 1925 in the positive on the merits, saying: "It is a cardinal principle of interpretation that words must be interpreted in the sense they would normally have in their context, unless such interpretation would lead to something unreasonable or absurd."

David, Claim respecting The *(Panama v. U.S.A.) (1933) 6 R.I.A.A. 38.* Upon a claim for damages by the owners of a vessel arrested in admiralty proceedings at the entrance to the Panama Canal based on the contention that the arrest took place outside the jurisdiction of the US District Court, *held* by the US-Panama General Claims Commission that there was no clear authority that vessels in passage through territorial waters were immune from civil arrest. The very broad principle on which the decision is expressed to be based is no longer regarded as good law and has to be read in the light of the stipulation of art. 27 of the UN Convention on the Law of the Sea 1982 *(1833 U.N.T.S. 3)* to the effect that the coastal State may not arrest a ship passing through territorial waters otherwise than in respect of obligations or liabilities incurred in the course or for the purpose of the passage or in the case that the vessel is leaving internal waters.

"days of grace" The period during which in customary international law enemy ships in port at the outbreak of war, or entering in ignorance of the outbreak of war, or neutral ships in port at the commencement of a blockade were permitted freely to depart. Art. 1 of Hague Convention VI of 1907 relative to the Status of Enemy Merchant Ships at the Outbreak of Hostilities *(205 C.T.S. 305)* declared the granting of such a period of grace as desirable, but still left the matter to negotiation in any particular instance. *See* Colombos, *International Law of the Sea* (6th ed.) 615-21, 722-4.

Dayton Peace Agreement   Properly styled the General Framework Agreement for Peace in Bosnia and Herzegovina *(35 I.L.M. 89, 172 (1996))* was concluded between the Bosnia and Herzegovina, and Bosnia and the Federal Republic of Yugoslavia, in November 1995, and witnessed by the so-called Contact Group (France, Germany, Russia, UK and USA) and the EU Special Negotiator. It provided for the mutual recognition of the Parties and the mutual acceptance of the their sovereign equality (art. 1); the peaceful settlement of disputes (art. 1); respect for human rights and the rights of refugees and displaced persons (art. 7); full cooperation with investigation and prosecution of violations of international humanitarian law (art. 2); and full implementation of the peace settlement, including the 11 Annexes to the Agreement (art. 9). These Annexes dealt with Military Aspects, including the cease-fire and the withdrawal of forces (Annex 1-A); Regional Stabilization, including confidence-building measures and arms limitations (1-B); the Inter-Entity Boundary, including the reunification of Sarajevo within the FRY (2); Elections (3); Constitution for Bosnia Herzegovina (4); Arbitration obligations on the FRY and the Bosnian Serb Republic (5); Human Rights, including machinery for their enforcement (6); Refugees and Displaced Persons (7); Commission to Preserve National Monuments (8); Bosnia and Herzegovina Public Corporations (9); Civilian Implementation, including humanitarian aid, economic reconstruction and human rights promotion (10); and the International Police Task Force to train and advise local law enforcement personnel (11).

de facto   Existing as a matter of fact. Cf. ***de jure*** and see **recognition**.

de jure   Existing as a matter of law. Cf. ***de facto*** and see **recognition**.

De Sabla Claim   *(USA v. Panama) (1933) 6 R.I.A.A. 358*. Mrs. de Sabla inherited a tract of land known as Bernardino from her husband on his death in 1914: both were US nationals. Between 1910 and 1928 the Panamanian authorities adjudicated to third parties 40 plots comprised in Bernardino as public land, and issued over 100 licenses to cultivate parts of the estate. Under the law of Panama, it had been open to Mrs. de Sabla to oppose each separate grant of the land; she had not done so. Mrs. de Sabla's claim arising out of the adjudications and licenses relating to the land of which she was the private owner was referred to the USA-Panama Claims Commission established by the USA-Panama Claims Convention 1931 *(138 L.N.T.S. 120)*, which *held* that the claim must be allowed: the Panamanian authorities knew of the extent of the Bernardino land and that it was private property, and their actions in relation to it were wrongful acts for which the Government of Panama was responsible internationally, it being axiomatic that acts of a government in depriving an alien of his property without compensation imposed international responsibility; the procedures available to the claimant to oppose the adjudications, as actually administered, did not constitute an adequate remedy to the claimant for the protection of her property; the claimant could properly present a claim for acts committed before her husband's death.

De Visscher, Charles   1884-1972. Belgian law teacher and scholar. Member, PCA 1923; Judge, PCIJ 1937 and ICJ 1946-1952. Principal publication: *Theorie et réalites en droit international public* (1953, 4th ed. 1970), translated as *Theory and Reality in Public International Law* (Corbet, 1957).

death penalty   There are conventional prohibitions on the death penalty in some **human rights** instruments; the Second Optional Protocol to the International Covenant on Civil and Political Rights 1989 *(29 I.L.M. 164 (1990))*, the Protocol to the American Convention on Human Rights of 8 June1990 *(29 I.L.M. 1447 (1990))* and Protocols 6 and 13 to the European Convention on Human Rights (*E.T.S. No. 114* and *E.T.S. No. 187*), which abolish the death penalty (art. 1 of all four), though the Optional Protocol, the American Convention Protocol and Protocol 6 allow its retention for serious military crimes committed in time of war (art. 2 of all three). These limited instances apart, human rights instruments have sought mainly to regulate its use. In the International Covenant on Civil and Political Rights 1966 *(999 U.N.T.S. 171)*, it is provided that, "in countries which have not abolished the death penalty" (art. 6(2)), the death penalty may be carried out in respect of "the most serious crimes" and after the final decision of a competent court (*id.*), with amnesty, pardon or commutation available (art. 6(4)); and no death sentence may be imposed on anyone under 18 years at the time of the offence, nor carried out on a pregnant woman (art. 6(5)). There being no substantial majority of States that have abandoned the death penalty, it is not possible to state that the death penalty is prohibited under customary law.

In its nature, international humanitarian law is more tolerant of the death penalty, such being permitted in Geneva Convention III relative to the Treatment of Prisoners of War 1949 *(75 U.N.T.S. 135)*, arts 100, 101 and 107, and Geneva Convention IV Relative to the Protection of Civilian Persons in Time of War 1949 *(75 U.N.T.S. 187)*, arts. 68, 71 and 74-5. Protocol I to the Geneva Conventions 1977 *(1125 U.N.T.S. 3)*, prohibits the death penalty for pregnant women and mothers having dependent children (art. 76(3)) and for children under 18 at the time of the offence (art. 77(5)). Protocol II 1977 *(1125 U.N.T.S. 609)*, art. 6(4), similarly and shortly provides: "The death penalty shall not be pronounced on persons who were under the age of eighteen years at the time of offence and shall not be carried out on pregnant women or mothers of young children." *See* Schabas, *The Abolition of the Death Penalty in International Law* (2nd ed.); Hood, *The Death Penalty: A World-Wide Perspective* (2nd ed.); Rodley, *The Treatment of Prisoners under International Law* (2nd ed.).

debellatio "The term *debellatio* is used to indicate a conquest of a foreign State which is so total that it includes a devolution of sovereignty. In practice within the past three centuries, conquest has been followed by change of sovereignty in a treaty of cession. *Debellatio* as the informal extinction of sovereignty remains, therefore, a theoretical possibility. Its essential characteristic is that one State expires and another acquires sovereignty over it; and since there must be the *animus* of sovereignty before the devolution is complete mere conquest and elimination of the conquered State's government does not destroy that State's identity in international law": O'Connell, *International Law* (1965), Vol. 1, 441. It is doubtful that there is any room for *debellatio* today as it essentially runs counter to the prohibition on the use of force.

Decade for Human Rights Education By Res. 49/184 of 23 December 1994, the General Assembly proclaimed 1995-2004 the Decade of Human Rights Education, essentially to implement the Plan of Action on Education for Human Rights and Democracy *(UN Doc. A/51/506)* through "national focal points" surveying the current provision and reporting to the UN High Commissioner for Human Rights who will suggest strategies and modalities for addressing educational needs.

Decade of International Law By Res. 44/23 of 17 November 1989, the General Assembly proclaimed 1990-99 to be the Decade of International Law, whose main goals were promoting acceptance of and respect for international law, promoting the peaceful settlement of disputes, encouraging the progressive development of international law and its codification and encouraging the teaching, dissemination and study of international law (para. 1). In pronouncing the Decade a success, Res. 54/28 of 21 January 2000 called for more publications and scholarly meetings in the area of international law (para. 18), more courses in international law (para. 19) and more progressive development and codification (para. 17); and called on the Secretary-General to eliminate the backlog in the **United Nations Treaty Series** (para. 7) and to progress the electronic version of U.N.T.S. (para. 6).

Decade of the World's Indigenous Peoples By Res. 48/163 of 21 December 1993, the General Assembly proclaimed 1995-2004 to be the World's Indigenous Peoples, whose main object was to be the strengthening of international cooperation in solving problems in areas such as human rights, the environment, development, education and health. The goals of the decade were set out in more detail in the Annex to GA Res. 50/157 of 29 February 1996. *See* **indigenous peoples**.

declaration A treaty designated a declaration is usually one that "declares existing law, with or without modification, or creates new law, such as the Declaration of Paris [see **Paris, Declaration of**]; . . . or which affirms some common principle of policy, such as non-aggression or mutual assistance. (There is a type of document which has become increasingly common during and since the Second World War, namely a Declaration published after a conference of . . . heads of State such as those that took place at Yalta . . . and Potsdam in 1945. The contents of these documents are partly agreements to do or not to do something, and partly records of agreement upon a common policy; the method of their conclusion is unorthodox, they differ in their purpose, and it is unsafe to generalize upon them, but there is no reason in principle why binding obligations should not be created in this way . . .)": McNair, *Law of Treaties* (2nd ed.), 23.

Chapter XI of the UN Charter is given the title of a Declaration (regarding Non-Self-Governing Territories). No other Chapter is similarly designated. Instruments of acceptance of the compulsory jurisdiction of the ICJ under art. 36(2) of the Statute are designated "declarations" both in that article and in general usage. Some General Assembly resolutions, intended to have general, normative effect, are designated as declarations; *e.g.*, the **Universal Declaration of Human Rights** 1948 (GA Res. 217(III)), Declaration on Principles of International Law Concerning Friendly Relations and Cooperation Among Nations in Accordance with the Charter of the United Nations 1971 (the **Friendly Relations Declaration**, GA Res. 2625 (XXXV)). Unilateral statements, whether written or oral, creative of obligations, are commonly referred to as declarations: cf. the declaration of M. Ihlen considered by the PCIJ in the *Eastern Greenland Case (1933) P.C.I.J., Ser. A/B, No. 53.*

declaratory judgment In international litigation or arbitration, the court or tribunal may declare that the act or omission of a respondent State was illegal. A declaratory judgment is to be distinguished from an advisory opinion, in that the former emerges from a contentious case involving a respondent State, while the latter arises from a request for a legal opinion of the ICJ. While the Statute of the ICJ is silent on the issue of declaratory judgments, the ICJ has on occasion given such judgments: *German Interests in Polish Upper Silesia (1926) P.C.I.J., Ser. A, No. 7*; and see Lauterpacht, *The Development of International Law by the International Court* (1958), 205-6, 250-2; Rosenne, *The Law and Practice of the International Court* (1965), 125-6, 619-21.

declaratory theory According to this theory of the **recognition of States**, "[a] state may exist without being recognised, and if it does exist in fact, then, whether or not it has been formally recognised by other states, it has a right to be treated by them as a state": Brierly, *The Law of Nations* (6th ed.), 139. "Practice over the last century or so is not unambiguous but does point to the declaratory approach as the better of the two theories": Shaw, *International Law* (4th ed.), 298. Cf. **constitutive theory**.

decolonization This term, while not one of art in international law, is frequently employed in.UN practice to connote the process whereby territories evolve from colonial status to full sovereign statehood. Thus, the landmark Declaration on the Granting of Independence to Colonial Countries and Peoples (General Assembly Res. 1514 (XV) of 14 December 1960) is often referred to as the Declaration on Decolonization, and the Special Committee on the Situation with Regard to the Implementation of the Declaration on the Granting of Independence to Colonial Countries and Peoples (established by GA Res. 1654 (XVI) of 27 November 1961) is often referred to as the Special Committee on Decolonization. *See* **self-determination**.

deep-sea mining International concern over the exploitation of the hard minerals, in particular manganese nodules, on the sea-bed and ocean floor beyond the limits of national jurisdiction (i.e. beyond the **continental shelf**) was articulated first by Ambassador Arvid Pardo of Malta in his proposed agenda item for the General Assembly on 18 August, 1967: *U.N. Doc. A/66.5*. After the establishment of an *ad hoc* committee (by G.A. Res. 2340 (XXII) of 18 December 1967), the General Assembly subsequently adopted the Declaration of Principles governing the Sea-bed and Ocean Floor, and the Subsoil thereof, beyond the Limits of National Jurisdiction of 17 December 1970 (Res. 2749 (XXV)) and a resolution placing a moratorium on deep-sea mining of 15 December 1969 (Res. 2574D (XXIV)).

Deep-sea mining was one of the central, and most controversial, issues of the Third UN Conference on the Law of the Sea (1974-82). Despite the international attempts to declare the area beyond national jurisdiction, and its minerals, to be the **common heritage of mankind** and not subject to national appropriation or exploitation, and to devise an international régime to exploit the resources (*see* the Declaration of Principles of 1970 and Part XI of the UN Convention on the Law of the Sea 1982 *(1833 U.N.T.S. 3)*), some States declined to ratify the UN Convention because of the provisions on deep-sea mining and some few enacted legislation providing for the licensing and control of deep-sea mining by their nationals (*see* the (US) Deep Sea-bed Hard Minerals Resources Act 1980 and the (UK) Deep Sea Mining (Temporary Provisions) Act 1981).

Part XI of the UN Convention (on the régime for seep-sea mining) was subsequently amended by the Agreement Relating to the Implementation of Part XI of the UN Convention on the Law of the Sea of July 1994 (GA Res. 48/263 *(33 I.L.M. 1309 (1994))*). This agreement, which substantially recast some of the provisions of Part XI, was to be read as part of the UN Convention for the parties to it (art. 1(2)) and, indeed, was to prevail over inconsistencies with the UN Convention (art. 2(1)). *See* Luard, *The Control of the Seabed* (1975); Kronmiller, *The Lawfulness of Deep Seabed Mining* (2 vols., 1980); O'Connell, *The International Law of the Sea* (1982), Vol. 1, Chap. 12; Brown, *Sea-Bed Energy and Mineral Resources and the Law of the Sea* (3 vols., 1986); Brown, *The International Law of the Sea* (1994), Vol. 1, Chap. 17. *See* **International Seabed Area**; **International Seabed Authority**.

default (of appearance) A phrase used by, *e.g.*, Rosenne, *The Law and Practice of the International Court of Justice* (1985), and the I.C.J. *Yearbook*, but not the ICJ Statute or the Rules of Court 1978, for what is expressed in art. 53(1) of the Statute thus: "Whenever one of the parties does not appear before the Court, or fails to defend its case, the other party may call upon the Court to decide in favour of its claim." Before deciding, the Court must be satisfied that it has jurisdiction and that the claim is well founded in fact and law: art. 53(2) of the ICJ Statute.

Delagoa Bay Arbitration *(Great Britain v. Portugal)* (1875) *149 C.T.S. 363*; *Moore, Int. Arb., 4984.* By the Protocol of 25 September 1872 *(145 C.T.S. 115)*, the parties submitted to the arbitration of the President of the French Republic their respective claims to certain East African coastal regions, Portugal relying on discoveries by her navigators in the 16th century, followed up by occupations which had been defended in arms against the Netherlands in 1732 and Austria in 1781; and Great Britain on treaties made with native potentates in 1822. The arbitrator *held* wholly in favor of Portugal, pointing out that the British hydrographic expedition which had concluded the treaties had been commended by the British Government to the good offices of the Portuguese Government; that, as soon as the British vessels had left, the chieftains renewed their acknowledgments of dependence on Portugal; and that the treaties themselves had ceased to have effect through lapse.

Delagoa Bay Railway Arbitration *(Great Britain and U.S.A. v. Portugal) (1898) Moore, Int. Arb., 1865.* By the Protocol of 13 June 1891 *(175 C.T.S. 217)*, the parties referred to the arbitration of the Swiss Federal Council the determination of the amount of compensation due in consequence of the recision of the concession of the Lourenco Marques Railway and the taking possession of the railway by the Portuguese Government. A tribunal consisting of three experts, rather than lawyers, made on 29 March 1900 an award of 15,314,000 Swiss francs in addition to the sum of £28,000 paid in advance. It is to be doubted whether the arbitration is to be considered an inter-State proceeding or whether it is any authority for the proposition that a State may be entitled to protect a corporation in liquidation against the State in which it is incorporated (as to which see Jones, Claims on behalf of Nationals who are Shareholders in Foreign Companies, *(1949) 26 B.Y.I.L. 225*).

delict, international As late as 1996, the International Law Commission, in its Draft Articles on State Responsibility 1978 *([1978] 2 I.L.C. Yearbook 78)*, categorized an "internationally wrongful act" (art. 19(1)) as either an international crime or an international delict, an international delict being defined as "any internationally wrongful act which is not an international crime," without further specification: art. 19(4). An international crime was a breach of an international obligation "so essential for the protection of fundamental interests of the international community that its breach is recognized as a crime by that community as a whole": art. 19(2). This distinction and the terms international crime and international delict have been abandoned in the ILC's latest Draft Articles of 2001 *(UN Doc. A/56/10 Chap. IV.E.1)*, replacing the old art. 19 by a much simpler provision: "There is a breach of an international obligation by a State when an act of that State is not in conformity with what is required of it by that obligation, regardless of its origin or character": art. 12. The 1996 text "may have suggested that the distinction between delicts and crimes was misleading or even that it was not taken seriously": Crawford, *The International Law Commission's Articles on State Responsibility* (2002), 12.

delimitation "It is common practice to distinguish delimitation and demarcation of a boundary. The former denotes description of the alignment in a treaty or other written source, or by means of a line marked on a map or chart. Demarcation denotes the means by which the described alignment is noted, or evidenced, on the ground, by means of cairns of stones, concrete pillars, beacons of various kinds, cleared roads in scrub, and so on. The principle of the distinction is clear enough, but the usage of the draftsman of the particular international agreement or political spokesman may not be consistent. In fact the terms are sometimes used to mean the same thing": Brownlie, *African Boundaries. A Legal and Diplomatic Encyclopaedia* (1979), 4.

demarcation *See* **delimitation**.

demilitarization This term "denotes the agreement of two or more States by treaty not to fortify, or station troops upon, a particular zone of territory; the purpose usually being to prevent war by removing the opportunities of conflict as the result of frontier incidents, or to gain security by prohibiting the concentration of troops on a frontier": *II Oppenheim 244n*. Demilitarization constitutes a **servitude** of a military nature. Under Protocol I to the Geneva Conventions Relating to the Protection of Victims of International Armed Conflict 1977 *(1125 U.N.T.S. 3)*, weight is put on the terms of the agreement establishing the demilitarized zone, which agreement would normally include provisions for the evacuation of all combatants, weapons and equipment, the non-use of military establishments, the non-involvement of the authorities or the population in the hostilities and the cessation of all military efforts: art. 60(3). Material breach of these conditions releases the innocent party from the agreement: art. 60(7). Making a demilitarized zone the object of attack is a grave breach of the Protocol: art. 85(3)(d).

democratic governance, so-called right to It is asserted that there is a (human) right to democratic governance, derived from three sources: the established rights of self-determination, of freedom of expression and trend towards defining and monitoring free elections: Franck, The Emerging Right to Democratic Governance, *86 A.J.I.L. 46 (1992)*. Certainly, art. 21 of the Universal Declaration of Human Rights 1948 (GA Res. 217(III)) and art. 25 of the International Covenant on Civil and Political Rights 1966 *(999 U.N.T.S. 171)*, with their emphasis on the rights to participate in the conduct of public affairs and to vote in genuinely free elections, imply such a right, though it is not unequivocally part of contemporary human rights law. *See* Fox and Roth, *Democratic Governance and International Law* (2000).

denial of justice "An examination of the literature . . . reveals that no less than six distinguishable categories of meanings have been applied to the term by the text writers: (1) For one school of thought it is considered as the equivalent of every international wrong committed to the prejudice of foreigners by any organ of the State. This is what is frequently referred to as the 'broad' view. (2) According to a second, more usual definition of the term, it is limited to certain unlawful acts or omissions on the part of *judicial* authorities. Here, however, we encounter a variety of different conceptions as to the extent of the State's responsibility for judicial organs: (3) A minority group—composed, principally of publicists in Latin America—maintain that denial of justice must be understood in the procedural sense of a refusal of access to court, and that only in the contingency of such a refusal (or its equivalent) can a diplomatic claim arise. (4) Still another group of writers . . . retain the meaning of denial of justice in municipal law, [i.e., refusal or failure on the part of judicial officers to perform their legal functions] but admit that international responsibility is engaged by various other acts of judicial misconduct, including wrongful judgments. . . . (5) A few authorities contend that the proper sense of the term according to international practice is that of a failure on the part of an alien plaintiff to obtain redress for an earlier wrongful act committed either by a private person or by a State agent. (6) But the view which has come more and more into favor within recent years is that under which a denial of justice includes any failure on the part of organs charged with administering justice to aliens to conform to their international duties": Freeman, *The International Responsibility to States for Denial of Justice* (1939), 96-7.

"[T]he question is how far the responsibility of a state for the acts of its judicial personnel can reasonably be extended given that, although often entirely independent of the government, they are nevertheless organs of the State and their acts accordingly attributable to the state": *I Oppenheim 543*, which gives as examples of a refusal "to entertain proceedings for the redress of injury suffered by an alien, or if the proceedings are subject to undue delay, or if there are serious inadequacies in the administration of justice, or if there occurs an obvious and malicious act of misapplication of the law by the courts which is injurious to a foreign state or its nations": *ibid.*, 543-4. A denial of justice is both a substantive ground of **State responsibility** and a circumstance relevant to the requirement in making an international **claim** that **local remedies** be exhausted. *See also* **international minimum standard.** *See* Eagleton, Denial of Justice in International Law, *22 A.J.I.L. 538 (1928)*; Fitzmaurice, The Meaning of the Term "Denial of Justice," *(1932) 13 B.Y.I.L. 93*; Spiegel, Origin and Development of Denial of Justice, *32 A.J.I.L. 63 (1938)*; Harvard Research Draft Convention on The Law of Responsibility of States for Damage done in their Territory to the Person or Property of Foreigners, *23 A.J.I.L. Supp. 173-8 (1929)*.

denization "Not to be confused with naturalisation proper is naturalisation through *denization* by means of letters patent under the Great Seal. . . . This way of making an alien a British subject is based on a very ancient practice . . . which has not been used for many years and seems not likely to be resorted to": *I Oppenheim 875n.*

denunciation The Vienna Convention on the Law of Treaties 1969 employs the term denunciation, the meaning of which is perhaps obvious enough, without in fact defining it, art. 56 bearing the cross-title "Denunciation of . . . a treaty containing no provision regarding termination, denunciation or withdrawal" and providing that such a treaty is not subject to denunciation or withdrawal unless it is established that the parties intended to admit the possibility thereof or a right thereto may be implied by the nature of the treaty, in which case a party shall give not less than twelve months notice of its intention to denounce. The term connotes a process of termination of a treaty, or of a State's continuance as a party, at the will of the State concerned in accordance with the terms of the treaty, express or implied. It does not refer to **repudiation** of a treaty. *See* Aust, *Modern Treaty Law and Practice* (2000), Chap. 16.

dependent territories *See* **non-self-governing territories.**

deportation "One of the rights possessed by the supreme power in every State is the right to refuse to permit an alien to enter that State, to annex what conditions it pleases to the permission to enter it, and to expel or deport from the State, at pleasure, even a friendly alien, especially if it considers his presence in the State opposed to its peace, order, and good government, or to its social or material interests": *A. G. for Canada v. Cain [1906] A.C. 542* at 546. During a state of belligerency, a State may expel all enemy subjects: *II Oppenheim 693.* While the right of a State to deport friendly aliens is well-established *(I Oppenheim 940)*, it appears that this right must not be abused by the State proceeding in an arbitrary manner *(id.; **Boffolo Claim** (1903) 10 R.I.A.A. 528; Maal Case (1903) 10 R.I.A.A. 730)*. Mass deportations are *prima facie* unlawful. As an alien has a duty to abide by the laws of a State, violation of these laws, at least for all but the most trivial offences, constitutes a legitimate ground for deportation. It is not clear whether, as a matter of customary law, a State must give reasons for the deportation of an alien. Certainly, art. 13 of the International Covenant on **Civil and Political Rights** 1966 *(999 U.N.T.S. 171)* permits expulsion of an alien "only in pursuance of a decision reached in accordance with law [and the alien] shall, except where compelling reasons of national security otherwise require, be allowed to submit the reasons against his expulsion and to have his case reviewed by, and be represented for the purpose before, the competent authority. . . ."

Deportation has on occasions been used as a disguised form of extradition, thereby circumventing the procedures established to protect aliens in extradition treaties and legislation: *see e.g., R. v. Governor of Brixton Prison, ex parte Soblen [1963] 2 Q.B. 243.* It appears that a State cannot deport its own nationals: see art. 12 of the International Covenant on Civil and Political Rights 1966, *supra*; art. 3 of the **European Convention on Human Rights** 1950 *(213 U.N.T.S. 221)*; art. 22 of the **American Convention on Human Rights** 1969 *(9 I.L.M. 99 (1970))*.

depositary Art. 76 of the Vienna Convention on the Law of Treaties 1969 provides that the depositary of a treaty may be designated by the negotiating States either in the treaty itself or in some other manner and may be one or more States, an international organization or the chief administrative officer of such an organization, that the functions of the depositary are international in character and that the depositary is under an obligation to act impartially in their performance. In particular, the fact that the treaty has not entered into force between certain of the parties or that a difference has arisen between a State and the depositary with regard to the latter's functions is not to affect that obligation. Art. 77 goes on to define the depositary's functions as comprising, in particular, in the absence of contrary provision, the keeping custody of the text and of any full powers delivered to the depositary, preparing certified copies and copies in additional languages and transmitting them, receiving signatures and the like, and ensuring that such are in due form, notifying the achievement of numbers of signatures or ratifications requisite to entry into force, and registering the treaty with the UN Secretariat. Arts. 78-80 deal further with the functions of depositaries in various detailed matters. *See* UN Treaty Section, *Treaty Handbook* (2002), Section 2; *and see* Aust, *Modern Treaty Law and Practice* (2000), Chap. 18.

***derelictio* (dereliction)** A mode of loss of title to territorial sovereignty corresponding to **occupation** as a mode of acquiring it, effected by actual abandonment coupled with the intention of giving up sovereignty. Dereliction is not to be presumed from mere withdrawal alone. As to possible historical instances, see *I Oppenheim 717-8. See also* the **Eastern Greenland Case *(1933) P.C.I.J., Ser. A/B, No. 53*; *Clipperton Island Case (1931) 2 R.I.A.A., 1105*; *Delagoa Bay Case (1875), Moore, Int. Arb. 4984*;** and ***Rann of Kutch Case (1968) 17 R.I.A.A. 1*.**

derivative personality *See* **personality, derivative**.

derogation A contracting out by a State of one or more provisions of a treaty under the terms of that treaty or by a separate agreement. Thus, *e.g.*, art. 4 of the International Covenant on **Civil and Political Rights** 1966 *(999 U.N.T.S. 171)* permits a State to derogate from its obligations under the Covenant (except arts. 6, 7, 8(1) and (2), 11, 15, 16 and 18), "in time of public emergency which threatens the life of the nation." The Vienna Convention on the Law of Treaties 1969 does not use the term in this sense, and refers to derogation only in art. 53 in the definition of a peremptory norm of general international law (***jus cogens***) as "a norm accepted and recognized by the international community of States as a whole as a norm from which no derogation is permitted."

Deserters at Casablanca Arbitration *(Germany v. France) (1909) 11 R.I.A.A. 119*. In September 1908, six deserters from the French Foreign Legion, three of German nationality, sought the protection of the German Consulate at Casablanca, then under French military occupation. The consul granted safe-passage to the deserters; but, while they were being conducted to the port of Casablanca by German consular agents to board a German vessel, they were forcibly taken by French forces. *Held* by the *ad hoc* tribunal established by the agreement of 24 November 1908 that, despite the **capitulations** rule, the German deserters were subject to French military jurisdiction; but that, the German deserters being under *de facto* consular protection, they should not have been forcibly interfered with beyond preventing their departure until the question of competent jurisdiction could be resolved.

desuetude The termination of a treaty through desuetude, non-use over time or disuse, is not expressly recognized by the Vienna Convention on the Law of Treaties 1969, and the ILC, in drafting the Convention, regarded it, along with obsolescence, as part of the consent of the parties to abandon a treaty: *[1966] II I.L.C. Yearbook 237. See* McNair, *The Law of Treaties* (2nd ed.), 516-8 and 681-91. For desuetude, or obsolescence, to terminate a treaty (through fundamental change of circumstances: art. 61(1)), more would be needed than the antiquity of the instrument: "only the most conclusive evidence of the intention of the parties . . . to regard it as terminated could warrant . . . treating it as obsolete and inapplicable": *Anglo-French Continental Shelf Case (1977) 54 I.L.R. 64* at 47. *See* **rebus sic stantibus**.

détente The term used to describe the process of improvement in the relationship between the United States and the Soviet Union during the Cold War. "Literally, 'détente' means a relaxation of tensions. But it is frequently used as shorthand for a complex process of adjustment. It is not a static condition or a simple standard of conduct. It does not imply 'entente,' or an understanding or alliance": (US) Assistant Secretary for European Affairs Arthur A. Hartman, US-Soviet Détente: Perceptions and Purposes, *(1974) 120 Dept. of State Bulletin 597.* The process of détente has resulted in a number of agreements between the US and USSR: see Timberlake, *Détente, A Documentary Record* (1978). Détente is also used to refer to the process initiated by the **Helsinki Agreement** (1975).

Deutsche Continental Gas-Gesellschaft v Polish State *(1929) 5 I.L.R. 11.* Upon an objection to the Polish liquidation of the plaintiff's property in former Russian territory as not in conformity with art. 297 of the Treaty of Versailles *(225 C.T.S. 188)* which provided a régime for liquidations in Polish territory, because the territory in question was not yet territory of Poland, *held*, by the German-Polish Mixed Arbitral Tribunal, that the theoretical non-recognition of Poland at the date of the treaty was irrelevant, the State existing irrespective of recognition, the effect of which was merely declaratory; and that the signing of a treaty of this kind with parties including Poland implied full recognition.

developed countries Not a term of art or a precise description, but a convenient term of reference for States with relatively high *per capita* incomes and higher standards of living. While international organizations differ in their classification of countries as developed or **developing**, in general the **First World** and **Second World** (insofar as it still exists) are considered developed.

developing countries Though not a term or art, but rather a useful descriptor, this term is used synonymously with **Third World** or less developed countries or underdeveloped countries or the South, for States with low (but not appallingly so) *per capita* incomes and with low standards of living. *See also* **Fourth World**.

development law, international "One of the most significant developments in contemporary international economic relations has been the proliferation of a complex network of arrangements and undertakings for the benefit of the lesser developed countries. These arrangements range from declarations and final acts adopted at international conferences to more solemn obligations binding on various combinations of states or other international legal persons": Mutharika, *International Law of Development* (1978), Vol. 1, ix, which contains the text of the principal instruments of international development law. While most of these instruments embody economic and social policy concerns, they are, by and large, not creative of legal rules, though they may, if elaborated in binding instruments, result in a new a new branch of international law. Cf. **economic law, international**.

development, so-called right of The "right to development" has been asserted as a collective **human right**; the Declaration on the Right to Development of 4 December 1986 (GA Res. 41/128), asserting that development was an "inalienable human right" (art. 1(1)). The content and compass of the right is vague: "to participate in, contribute to, and enjoy economic, social, cultural and political development" (*id.*) which implies "the full realization of the right of peoples to self-determination, which includes . . . the exercise of their inalienable right to full sovereignty over all their natural wealth and resources" (art. 1(2)). States are to ensure equal opportunity of access to education, health services, food, housing and employment (art. 8). Despite claims that the right to development is part of human rights law, indeed *jus cogens* (Bedjaoui, The Right to Development, in Bedjaoui, *International Law: Achievements and Prospects* (1991), 1182), it is better regarded as a political or moral, rather than a legal, imperative, absent incorporation of its content in human rights instruments, particularly the International Covenant on Economic, Social and Cultural Rights 1966 (*993 U.N.T.S. 3*).

devolution A term used, colloquially in municipal law rather than technically in international law, to connote the transfer of certain governmental powers by the central government of a unitary State to some part of that State. The term was used, *e.g.*, in the Report of the (UK) Royal Commission on the Constitution 1969-73 *(Cmnd. 5460)*, though it did not appear in any of the (largely unenacted) legislative proposals in 1976 and 1978 that followed it. The Scotland Act 1998 and the Government of Wales Act 1998 accorded each of these parts of the UK different measures of devolution in accordance with the expressed wishes of the electorates of each, Scotland having legislative and taxing competence, Wales having only deliberative and supervisory competence. *See* **federalism**.

devolution agreement The name "devolution" or "inheritance" agreement has been given to an agreement between a parent State and a new State, set up by the grant of independence to a portion of the territory of the former, providing for the devolution or inheritance of treaties of the parent affecting the territory in question. Such a purported novation is obviously not binding on a third party unless expressly or impliedly assented to, but it may be noted that devolution agreements have influenced the practice of the Secretary-General of the UN in the matter of determination as to who are parties to treaties. *See generally* O'Connell, State *Succession in Municipal Law and International Law* (1967), Vol. 2, 352-73. Art. 8 of the Vienna Convention on Succession of States in respect of Treaties 1978 *(1946 U.N.T.S. 3)* would, for States parties to it, subordinate devolution agreements to the provisions of the Convention. *See* **State succession**.

Dickinson, Edwin de Witt 1887-1961. Professor, Michigan 1919-33, California 1933-48, Pennsylvania 1948-52. Principal works include *Equality of States in International Law* (1920); *A Selection of Cases and Other Readings on the Law of Nations Chiefly as it is Interpreted and Applied by British and American Courts* (1929); *Cases and Materials on International Law* (1950); *Law and Peace* (1951).

Dickson Car Wheel Co. Case *(U.S.A. v. Mexico) (1931) 4 R.I.A.A. 669.* Upon the contention that the Government of Mexico was responsible upon a contract for the purchase of car wheels by the National Railways Company because the company's inability to pay arose from the seizure of its undertaking by the Government, *held* by the United States-Mexican Special Claims Commission that the claim failed, there being no succession by the Government to the obligations of the extinct company, any doctrine of unjust enrichment being as yet not accepted in international law, international responsibility not being engaged merely as a result of pecuniary loss arising out of injury to a person in contractual relationship only with the claimant, and the seizure of the railways being in the event an act done in an emergency threatening the social order and independence of Mexico. *See* **unjust (or unjustified) enrichment**.

Difference Relating to Immunity from Legal Process of a Special Rapporteur of the Commission on Human Rights *1999 I.C.J. Rep. 62.* By resolution dated 5 August 1998, the Economic and Social Council (ECOSOC) requested of the ICJ an advisory opinion "on the legal question of the applicability of Article VI, section 22, of the Convention on the Privileges and Immunities of the United Nations *[1 U.N.T.S. 15]* in the case of Dato' Param Cumaraswamy as Special Rapporteur of the Commission on Human Rights on the independence of judges and lawyers . . . and on the legal obligations of Malaysia in this case." Plaintiffs in Malaysian courts sued Cumaraswamy for allegedly using defamatory words in an interview, seeking damages of US \$112 million. However, UN Secretary-General Kofi Annan claimed that Cumaraswamy was acting in his official capacity during the interview and consequently was immune from legal process.

On 29 April 1999, the Court *advised*: (a) (14 to1) that art. VI, section 22, was applicable to Cumaraswamy as a special rapporteur; (b) (14 to1) that Cumaraswamy was entitled to immunity from legal process of every kind for the words spoken by him during an interview as published in an article in the November 1995 issue of *International Commercial Litigation*; and (c) (13 to 2) that the Malaysian government had a duty to notify the Malaysian courts of the Secretary-General's determination that Cumaraswamy was entitled to immunity from legal process; (d) (14 to1) that the Malaysian courts had a duty to deal with the issue of legal immunity as a preliminary issue to be expeditiously decided *in limine litis*; (e) (unanimously) that Cumaraswamy would not be financially responsible for costs imposed by the Malaysian courts, specifically taxed costs; and (f) (13 to 2) that the Malaysian government had the duty to inform the Malaysian courts of this advisory opinion so that Cumaraswamy's immunity would be implemented.

digest of international law "[A] compilation of materials, some official and others not, which by their presentation may serve to indicate in some measure the direction of prevailing currents in the development of international law, or at least supply a certain amount of background on that subject": Whiteman, *Digest of International Law* (1963), Vol. 1, iv-v. The principal Anglophone digests are (USA) Cadwalader (1877), Wheaton (1886), Moore (1906), Hackworth (1940), and Whiteman (1963-73); *see also* the *Digest of US Practice in International Law* (1973-80) and the *Cumulative Digest of US Practice in International Law* (1980-); (UK) Parry, *British Digest of International Law* (1860-1914; incomplete).

dignity (1) "Traditional international law has ascribed certain legal consequences to the dignity of states as inherent in their international personality": *I Oppenheim 379.* Among these consequences are the right to demand that heads of State are not defamed, heads of State and diplomatic envoys are afforded special treatment abroad, warships are granted special privileges in foreign waters and State flags and coats of arms are not disrespected abroad. However, absent specific national legislation, "it is doubtful whether, apart from obligations in such matters as the protection of diplomatic and consular property, a state is bound to prevent its subjects from committing acts which violate the dignity of foreign states, and to punish them for acts of that kind which it was unable to prevent": *id.*

(2) International human rights are premised, to a large extent, on the dignity of the human person. The Preamble to the UN Charter "reaffirm[ed] faith in fundamental human rights, in the dignity and worth of the human person, in the equal rights of men and women. . . ."

The Preambles to both the International Covenant on **Civil and Political Rights** 1966 *(999 U.N.T.S. 171)* and the International Covenant on **Economic, Social and Cultural Rights** 1966 *(993 U.N.T.S. 3)* expressly recognize that the rights set out therein "derive from the inherent dignity of the human person."

Dikko Incident Alhaji Umaru Dikko came to international notice in 1984 after a failed kidnap attempt in which he was found drugged in a crate labeled with a Nigerian diplomatic seal at London's Stanstead Airport. Following the incident, British immigration granted Dikko political asylum for five years and he was placed under protection by the British government. The resultant diplomatic crisis cooled relations between Britain and Nigeria for two years despite Nigeria's position as Britain's most significant African trading partner. A former Nigerian cabinet minister and politician, Dikko became notorious for his corruption and, during a 1993 military coup, he escaped to England to avoid corruption charges; the British government refused to extradite him.

Dillard, Hardy C. 1902-82. Professor, Virginia 1938-70, Dean 1963-68. Judge, ICJ 1970-79. Editor of *Proceedings of the Institute of Public Affairs* (8 vols.). Author of *Some Aspects of Law and Diplomacy* (1957).

diplomacy "[T]he application of intelligence and tact to the conduct of official relations between the governments of independent states, . . . or, more briefly still, the conduct of business between states by peaceful means": *Satow's Guide to Diplomatic Practice* (5th ed.), 3.

diplomatic agent, mission The Vienna Convention on Diplomatic Relations 1961 *(500 U.N.T.S. 95)* defines a "diplomatic agent" as either "the head of the mission or a member of the diplomatic staff of the mission" and the "head of the mission" as "the person charged by the sending State with the duty of acting in that capacity": art. 1(e), (a). "The function of a diplomatic mission is to represent the sending state, to protect its interests and those of its nationals, to negotiate with the government to which it is accredited, to report to the sending government on all matters of importance to it, and to promote friendly relations in general between the two countries. It must also endeavour to develop, in accordance with the instructions it receives, cooperation useful to its government in matters of commerce, finance, economics, labour, scientific research and defense. For such purposes the head of mission will be assisted either by permanent members of the diplomatic service specially trained under the auspices of the ministry of foreign affairs, or by officers belonging to the army, navy, or air force, or to other ministries of the government specially selected for appointment as attachés to the mission": *Satow's Guide to Diplomatic Practice* (5th ed.), 69.

diplomatic bag The Vienna Convention on Diplomatic Relations 1961 *(500 U.N.T.S. 95)* provides that "[t]he diplomatic bag shall not be opened or detained" (art. 27(3)); and that "packages constituting the diplomatic bag must bear visible external marks of their character and may contain only diplomatic documents or articles intended for official use" (art. 27(4)). *See also* art. 27(7) on carriage of the diplomatic bag by commercial aircraft; and **diplomatic courier**. The Convention offers no definition of permissible contents of a diplomatic bag, which has led to abuses and to ILC work in the area. *See* Barker, *The Abuse of Diplomatic Privileges and Immunities* (1996), 162-88; Denza, *Diplomatic Law* (2nd ed.), 185-203.

diplomatic corps "The diplomatic body (*corps diplomatique*) comprises the heads and the diplomatic staff of all the missions accredited to a government. At most capitals a list of the diplomatic body, compiled from lists furnished by each mission is furnished, is published and distributed to missions from time to time": *Satow's Guide to Diplomatic Practice* (5th ed.), 161. *See also* **Doyen of the diplomatic corps**.

diplomatic courier   The Vienna Convention on Diplomatic Relations 1961 *(500 U.N.T.S. 95)* provides (art. 27(5)) that "[t]he diplomatic courier, who shall be provided with an official document indicating his status and the number of packages constituting the diplomatic bag, shall be protected by the receiving State in the performance of his functions. He shall enjoy personal inviolability and shall not be liable to any form of arrest or detention." These provisions are expressed also to apply to any courier designated ad hoc "except that the immunities . . . mentioned shall cease to apply when such a courier has delivered to the consignee the diplomatic bag in his charge": art. 27(6). Art. 40(3) provides further that "[t]hird States . . . shall accord to diplomatic couriers, who have been granted a passport visa if such visa was necessary, and diplomatic bags in transit the same inviolability and protection as the receiving State is bound to accord." The ILC has undertaken further work on the topic of the status of diplomatic couriers and the diplomatic bag not accompanied by diplomatic couriers. *See* Denza, *Diplomatic Law* (2nd ed.), 204-8.

diplomatic list   It had long been practice in most States to maintain a list or register of the personnel of foreign diplomatic missions. The obligation on notification of personnel appointments and movements contained in art. 10 of the Vienna Convention on Diplomatic Relations 1961 *(500 U.N.T.S. 95)* gave the diplomatic list more significance, not least in indicating those entitled to diplomatic privileges and immunities. *See* Denza, *Diplomatic Law* (2nd ed.), 72-6.

diplomatic privileges and immunities   The Vienna Convention on Diplomatic Relations 1961 *(500 U.N.T.S. 95)*, adopted on 18 April 1961 and in force from 24 April 1964, has been held by the ICJ to "codify the law of diplomatic relations, state principles and rules essential for the maintenance of peaceful relations between States and accepted through the world by nations of all creeds, cultures and political complexions": *United States Diplomatic and Consular Staff in Tehran Case 1980 I.C.J. Rep. 3* at 24. The ICJ also stated, and upheld in its unanimous judgment, that the obligation on States to respect the rules of diplomatic law is absolute and must be fulfilled in all circumstances: *ibid,* at 38-41. A **diplomatic agent** (defined as the head of the mission or a member of the diplomatic staff (art. 1(e)) enjoys complete immunity from criminal, civil and administrative jurisdiction (except in relation to actions involving private immovable property, succession and private professional or commercial activity) (art. 31). Lesser personnel in a mission do not enjoy the same extent of immunity: administrative and technical staff (and their families) enjoy complete immunity from criminal jurisdiction, but their immunity from civil and administrative jurisdiction does not extend to acts performed outside the course of their duties (art. 37(2)); and service staff enjoy immunity from criminal, civil and administrative jurisdiction only in respect of acts performed in the course of their duties (art. 37(3)). Immunity may be waived: see **waiver**. The premises of a mission, the person of a diplomatic agent and the agent's private residence are inviolable (arts. 22, 29 and 30). The Convention on the Prevention and Punishment of Crimes against Internationally Protected Persons, including Diplomatic Agents of 14 December 1973 *((1035 U.N.T.S. 167)* requires parties to make crimes, *inter alia*, against diplomats "punishable by appropriate penalties which take into account their grave nature" (art. 2(2)). The Convention provides for multi-State jurisdiction and establishes a "prosecute or extradite" rule (*see **aut dedere aut judicare**).

The archives and documents of the mission are inviolable (Vienna Convention, art. 24), and members of the mission are, subject to national security restrictions, to enjoy

---

freedom of movement and travel (art. 26). Freedom of communication (including the use of a diplomatic courier and diplomatic bag) are guaranteed (art. 27). The mission is exempt from all dues and taxes (art. 23), and diplomatic agents are exempt from social security payments (art. 33) and all dues and taxes (art. 34), including customs duties and taxes (art. 36). Diplomatic agents are exempt from all public service, including military service (art. 35). Nonetheless, all persons enjoying privileges and immunities are obliged to respect the laws and regulations of the receiving State (art. 41(1)), and the mission is not to be used in a manner incompatible with its functions (art. 41(3)). The Convention also contains provisions on establishing and accrediting of diplomatic missions, on rejecting diplomatic agents, or appointing and ranking of heads of mission (arts. 2-19), and on ending the appointment of diplomatic agents and diplomatic relations (arts. 43-45). *See* Denza, *Diplomatic Law* (2nd ed.); Hardy, *Modern Diplomatic Law* (1967); Wilson, *Diplomatic Privileges and Immunities* (1967); Frey and Frey, *The History of Diplomatic Immunity* (1999).

diplomatic protection "It is an elementary principle of international law that a State is entitled to protect its subjects, when injured by acts contrary to international law committed by another State, from whom they have been unable to obtain satisfaction through the ordinary channels. By taking up the case of one of its subjects and by resorting to diplomatic action or international judicial proceedings on his behalf, a State is in reality asserting its own rights—its right to ensure, in the person of its subjects, respect for the rules of international law": ***Mavrommatis Palestine Concessions Case (Jurisdiction) (1924) P.C.I.J., Ser. A, No. 2*** at 12; *see also* ***Serbian Loans Case (1929) P.C.I.J., Ser. A, Nos. 20, 21***; ***Panevezys-Saldutiskis Railway Case (1939) P.C.I.J., Ser. A/B, No. 76***; ***Nottebohm Case (Second Phase) 1955 I.C.J. Rep. 4***; ***Barcelona Traction Case** (Preliminary Objections) and (Second Phase) 1964 I.C.J. Rep. 44 and 1970 I.C.J. Rep. 32*. "To exercise protection . . . is to place oneself on the plane of international law. It is international law which determines whether a State is entitled to exercise protection and to seize the Court": ***Nottebohm Case (Second Phase) 1955 I.C.J. Rep. 4*** at 20-1. International law lays down two conditions for the exercise of the right of protection: "The first is that the defendant State has broken an obligation towards the national State in respect of its nationals. The second is that only the party to whom an international obligation is due can bring a claim in respect of its breach": ***Reparation for Injuries Case** 1949 I.C.J. Rep. 174* at 181-182; *see also* ***Barcelona Traction Case** (Second Phase) 1970 I.C.J. Rep. 3* at 32. However, "within the limits prescribed by international law, a State may exercise diplomatic protection by whatever means and to whatever extent it thinks fit, for it is its own right that the State is asserting. Should the natural or legal persons on whose behalf it is acting consider that their rights are not adequately protected, they have no remedy in international law. . . . The State must be viewed as the sole judge to decide whether its protection will be granted, to what extent it is granted, and when it will cease": ***Barcelona Traction Case** (Second Phase) 1970 I.C.J. Rep. 3* at 44; *see also* ***Administrative Decision No. V** (1924) 7 R.I.A.A. 119*. *See* **Calvo clause**. *See* Borchard, *Diplomatic Protection of Citizens Abroad* (1915).

diplomatic relations Diplomatic relations between two States exist when they have so agreed, usually involving the establishment in each other's country of, and the conduct of their bilateral international relations through, resident diplomatic missions. Diplomatic missions may be temporarily withdrawn without necessarily terminating or suspending diplomatic relations, although that will often be the consequence. Non-existence of diplomatic relations must be distinguished from non-recognition, although the existence of diplomatic relations necessarily implies mutual recognition. The Vienna Convention on Diplomatic Relations 1961 *(500 U.N.T.S. 95)* does not define "diplomatic relations" as such, but states that "[t]he functions of a diplomatic mission consist *inter alia* in: (a) representing the sending State in the receiving State; (b) protecting in the receiving State the interests of the sending State and of its nationals, within the limits permitted by international law; (c) negotiating with the Government of the receiving State; (d) ascertaining by all lawful means conditions and developments in the receiving State, and reporting thereon to the Government of the sending State; (e) promoting friendly relations between the sending State and the receiving State, and developing their economic, cultural and scientific relations": art. 3(1). Cf. **diplomatic agent, mission**.

direct applicability, effect   A term used in the **European Community** to describe provisions in the relevant treaties and subordinate legislation that apply directly within the legal systems of the member States, without any national legislative intervention, and accord right to individuals enforceable in national courts. *See also* **self-executing treaty**.

disabilities, rights of persons with   The Vienna Declaration and Program of Action on Human Rights 1993 *(UN Doc. A/CONF.157/23)* Part II(B), recognizing a paucity of international instruments affording protection to persons with disabilities, called for "[s]pecial attention . . . to be made to ensuring non-discrimination, and the equal enjoyment of all human rights and fundamental freedoms by disabled persons, including their active participation in all aspects of society": para. 22. The General Assembly has called for the drafting of a convention on the rights of disabled persons (GA Res. 56/168 of 26 February 2002). The extant norms, in the form of recommendations for government action, are contained in the Standard Rules on the Equalization of Opportunities for Persons with Disabilities, annexed to GA Res. 48/96 of 20 December 1993. The 22 rules deal with such matters as accessibility (Rule 5), education (Rule 6), employment (Rule 7), income maintenance and social security (Rule 8), family life and personal integrity (Rule (9) and religion (Rule 10). Disability is defined (in para. 17 of the Standard Rules) as a term that "summarizes a great number of different functional limitations occurring in any population in any country of the world. People may be disabled by physical, intellectual or sensory impairment, medical conditions or mental illness. Such impairments, conditions or illnesses may be permanent or transitory in nature." *See* the Bangkok Recommendations on the Elaboration of a Comprehensive and Integral International Convention to Promote and Protect the Rights and Dignity of Persons with Disabilities of 27 June 2003 *(UN Doc. A/AC.265/2003/CRP.10) See Degener and Koster-Dreese, Human Rights and Disabled Persons* (1995).

disappearances   Disappearances, or rather enforced or involuntary disappearances, occur when "persons are arrested, detained or abducted against their will or otherwise deprived of their liberty by officials of different branches or levels of Government, or by organized groups or private individuals acting on behalf of, or with the support, direct or indirect, consent or acquiescence of the Government, followed by a refusal to disclose the fate or whereabouts of the persons concerned or a refusal to acknowledge the deprivation of their liberty": Declaration on the Protection of All Persons from Enforced Disappearances of 18 December 1992 (GA Res. 47/133), Preamble. Declaring such acts in violation of, *inter alia*, the rights to recognition as a person before the law, to liberty and security of the person and not to be subjected to torture and other cruel, inhuman or degrading treatment or punishment; and as a grave threat to the right to life: art. 1. Enforced disappearances are prohibited (art. 2), and are to be criminalized and subject to "appropriate penalties which . . . take into account their extreme seriousness" (art. 4). States are under an obligation to investigate any allegations of enforced disappearances (art. 13). The UN Commission on Human Rights established, by Res. 20 (XXXVI) of 29 February 1980, a Working Group on Enforced and Voluntary Disappearances which has investigated in excess of 50,000 individual cases. *See* Amnesty International, *Getting Away with Murder: Political Killings and "Disappearances" in the 1990s* (1993).

disarmament Disarmament, hardly a term of art in international law, is both an end and a process, involving, in modern parlance, the interrelated concepts of arms limitation (or reduction) and disarmament; the former implies a quantitative process, the latter a process with quantitative and qualitative features. The first essay in qualitative arms limitation by treaty, which is what is generally understood by disarmament, was, *semble*, the Declaration of St. Petersburg of 11 December 1868 *(138 C.T.S. 297)* for the renunciation of the use of explosive projectiles under 400 gr. weight, which was followed by the Hague Declarations of 1899 respecting projectiles diffusing gases, projectiles discharged from balloons and expanding bullets *(187 C.T.S. 453f.)*. An interesting but isolated instance of a general agreement between two States for quantitative arms limitation is provided by the Convention between the Argentine Republic and Chile of 28 May 1902 *(191 C.T.S. 214)*. The first instance of a regional arrangement for disarmament is no doubt the Rush-Bagot Agreement of 28-9 April 1817 between Great Britain and the United States restricting the size, number and armament of vessels on the Great Lakes *(67 C.T.S. 153)*. But there is no clear line between regional disarmament and neutralizations of which instances are to be found as far back as the Peace of Westphalia of 1648 and the Treaties of Utrecht of 1713. *See* **neutralization**. The Hague Peace Conference of 1899 adopted a Resolution affirming that the restriction of military budgets was extremely desirable for the increase of the material and moral welfare of mankind: Final Act. But the first attempt at a general control of the arms trade may be said to have been the provision in the **Brussels Act** of 2 July 1890 *(173 C.T.S. 299)* of a restrictive régime in respect of Africa (arts. 8-14). Efforts in this direction reached their culmination with the Convention between the preponderance of the Allied States signed at St. Germain on 10 September 1919 for the Control of the Trade in Arms and Ammunition *(225 C.T.S. 482)*. This, however, was not of course the only part of the general peace settlement concerned with arms control or limitation, the Treaty of Versailles with Germany *(225 C.T.S. 188)* in especial providing for severe restrictions on German armaments (Part V) and the League of Nations Covenant, which formed part of the Peace Treaties, reciting the recognition of the member States that the maintenance of peace requires the reduction of national armaments to the lowest point consistent with national safety and the enforcement by common action of international obligations, as well as their agreement that the private manufacture of arms was open to grave objections, instructed the Council to formulate detailed disarmament plans to be reconsidered every ten years (art. 8). The same article envisaged the adoption of national arms limits not to be exceeded without the Council's concurrence, the exchange of information as to the scale of their armaments between members and the Council's giving attention to the private trade in arms. Art. 9 provided, moreover, for a permanent Commission to advise the Council on the execution of these provisions and other military, etc., questions. Art. 23(d) further provided for the entrusting of the Council with the general supervision of the arms trade "with the countries in which the control of this traffic is necessary in the common interest." The League Assembly at its first session in 1920 set up a Temporary Mixed Commission to deal with disarmament questions, which sat until 1924. In 1925, preparatory studies for a disarmament conference were inaugurated and in 1932 the Conference met. In parallel with these steps, naval armaments were regulated by the successive treaties of Washington of 6 February 1922 *(25 L.N.T.S. 202)* and London of 22 April 1930 *(112 L.N.T.S. 65)* and 25 March 1936 *(184 L.N.T.S. 115)*. During the League period, too, the Hague Declaration respecting projectiles diffusing gases was replaced by the Geneva Gas Protocol of 17 June 1925 *(94 L.N.T.S. 65*; see **Asphyxiating, Poisonous or other Gases, etc., Protocol Prohibiting the Use in War of**).

The UN Charter states with respect to disarmament that the General Assembly may consider the principles governing this matter and the regulation of armaments and make recommendations in relation thereto (art. 11(1)); and that the Security Council shall be responsible, with the assistance of the Military Staff Committee referred to in art. 47, for the formulation of plans of a system for the regulation of armaments (art. 26). The Moscow Conference of Foreign Ministers agreed in December 1945 to recommend the establishment by the General Assembly of a commission for the control of atomic energy. By a resolution dated 24 January 1946, the General Assembly established such a Commission consisting of the members of the Security Council and also Canada. By resolutions of 14 December 1946, the General Assembly called for speedy action by the Security Council in relation to disarmament. Thereunder, the Commission on Conventional Armaments was established on 13 February 1947 by the Security Council *(UN Doc. S/268/Rev 1)*. By a resolution dated 5 December 1949 (Res. 300 (IV)), the General Assembly recommended that this body continue its studies despite the lack of unanimity in the Security Council. By GA Res. 502(VI) of 11 January 1952, the Atomic Energy and Conventional Armaments Commissions were combined into a single Disarmament Commission. Meanwhile a partial disarmament had been in effect imposed on the States defeated in World War II by the insertion in the Constitution of Japan of a prohibition upon the maintenance of any land, sea, or air forces whatsoever (art. 9), and in Protocols III and IV to the Paris Agreements of 23 October 1954 respecting the admission of Germany and Italy to the **Western European Union** *(211 U.N.T.S. 342)* of a prohibition on the manufacture of atomic, chemical, and biological weapons, as well as certain other categories of war material. By its Statute of 26 October 1956 *(276 U.N.T.S. 3)*, the **International Atomic Energy Agency** was established, being subsequently assigned some role in relation to disarmament. By Resolution 1252 (XIII) of 4 November 1958, the General Assembly extended membership of the Disarmament Commission *ad hoc* to all UN members and urged the continuance of negotiations for the cessation of nuclear tests. In its latest incarnation, the Disarmament Commission was established by GA Res. S-10/2 of 30 June 1978.

Progress in arms limitation and disarmament was steady if slow in the years since the inception of the UN. Among the notable international instruments of the period are the Non-Proliferation Treaty of 1 July 1968 *(729 U.N.T.S. 161)*; the **Test-Ban Treaties**: the Treaty Banning Nuclear Weapons Tests in the Atmosphere, in Outer Space and under Water of 5 August 1963 *(480 U.N.T.S. 43)*, the Treaty on the Limitation of Underground Nuclear Weapon Tests of 3 July 1974 *(13 I.L.M. 906 (1974))* and the Comprehensive Nuclear Test-Ban Treaty of 10 September 1996 *(36 I.L.M. 230 (1997))*; the Convention on the Prohibition of the Development, Production, and Stockpiling of Bacteriological (Biological) and Toxin Weapons and their Destruction of 10 April 1972 *(1015 U.N.T.S. 163)*; the Convention on the Prohibition of Military or any other Hostile Use of Environmental Modification Techniques of 10 December 1976 *(1108 U.N.T.S 151)*; the Convention on Prohibitions or Restrictions on the Use of Certain Conventional Weapons which may be deemed to be Excessively Injurious or to have Indiscriminate Effects of 10 October 1980 *(1342 U.N.T.S. 137)*; the Convention on the Prohibition of the Development, Production, Stockpiling and Use of Chemical Weapons and on their Destruction of 3 September 1992 *(1974 U.N.T.S. 45)*; and the Convention on the Prohibition of the Use, Stockpiling, Production and Transfer of Anti-personnel Mines and on their Destruction (the **Land Mines Convention**) of 18 September 1997 *(36 I.L.M. 1509 (1997))*. *See also* the (now superfluous) Treaty on the Limitation of Anti-Ballistic Missile Systems (SALT I) between the United States and the USSR of 29 May 1972 *(11 I.L.M. 784 (1972))* and Treaty on the Limitation of Strategic Offensive Arms (SALT II) between the same parties of 18 June 1979 *(18 I.L.M. 1112 (1979))*. *See* Dupuy and Hammerman, *A Documentary History of Arms Control and Disarmament* (1974); UN, *United Nations Disarmament Yearbook. See* <http://disarmament.un.org>.

---

discontinuance   Art. 88 of the Rules of Court of the ICJ of 1978 (as amended in 2000) which, together with art. 89, bears the cross-title "Discontinuance," provides that, if at any time before judgment has been delivered, the parties conclude an agreement for the discontinuance of the case and so inform the Court in writing, the Court, or the President if the Court is not sitting, shall make an order officially recording the discontinuance and remove the case from the list. Art. 89 makes provision in relation to proceedings instituted by application (as distinct from special agreement), permitting the applicant State have the case removed from the list by the Court where the respondent State "has not yet taken any step in the proceedings" (art. 89(1)). However, where the respondent State "has already taken some step in the proceedings," it must be given an opportunity to oppose the continuance; if it does not oppose the discontinuance, the case is removed from the list; if it objects, the proceedings must continue (art. 89(2)). As to instances of discontinuance, see *Protection of French Nationals and Protected Persons in Egypt Case 1950 I.C.J. Rep. 59*; **Electricite de Beyrouth Co. Case** *1954 I.C.J. Rep. 107*; **Aerial Incident of July 27 1955 Case** *1959 I.C.J. Rep. 264*; **Barcelona Traction Case** *1961 I.C.J. Rep. 9*; *Compagnie du Port, etc., de Beyrouth and Societe Radio Orient Case 1960 I.C.J. Rep. 186*; **Pakistani Prisoners of War Case** *1973 I.C.J. Rep. 347*.

discovery   Mere discovery of a territory does not of itself give a good title to that territory in contemporary international law. It creates merely an "inchoate title" which "must be completed within a reasonable period by the effective occupation of the region claimed to be discovered": **Island of Palmas Case** *(1928) 2 R.I.A.A. 829* at 838. *See* the **Clipperton Island Case** *(1931) 2 R.I.A.A. 1105*. At one time, discovery coupled with some symbolic act of asserting sovereignty gave title to **terra nullius**: Keller, Lissitzyn and Mann, *Creation of Rights of Sovereignty Through Symbolic Acts 1400-1800* (1938), 148. *See also* Jennings, *The Acquisition of Territory in International Law* (1963).

discrimination   The prohibition against discrimination, be it in respect of "race, sex, language or religion" (art. 1(3) of the UN Charter) or "of any kind, such as race, color, sex, language, religion, political or other opinion, national or social origin, property, birth or other status" (art. 2 of the Universal Declaration of Human Rights 1948 (GA Res. 217(III); art. 2(1) of the International Covenant on Civil and Political Rights 1966 *(999 U.N.T.S. 171)*; art. 2(2) of the International Covenant on Economic, Social and Cultural Rights 1966 *(993 U.N.T.S. 3)*), having been the subject of specific conventions in respect of **racial discrimination** and discrimination against women (*see* **Women, Convention on the Elimination of All Forms of Discrimination against**), is so central to the law relating to international **human rights** that it has arguably become **jus cogens**. *See generally* Vierdag, *The Concept of Discrimination in International Law* (1973).

discrimination, racial   *See* **racial discrimination**.

discrimination against women   *See* **Women, Convention on the Elimination of All Forms of Discrimination against**.

dismemberment of State   *See* **dissolution of State**.

dispositif   This term of French law is employed in the ICJ Rules of Court of 1978 (rule 95(1)) as the equivalent of "the operative provisions of the judgment."

dispositive treaty   "There is a class of treaties called 'transitory' (unfortunately, as Westlake points out, because their characteristic is the permanence of their effect), or 'dispositive;' these are treaties whereby one state creates in favour of another, or transfers to another, or recognizes another's ownership of, real rights, rights *in rem*, for instance, in particular, treaties of cession including exchange": McNair, *Law of Treaties* (2nd ed.), 740.

dispute "A dispute is a disagreement on a point of law or fact, a conflict of legal views or of interests between two persons": ***Mavrommatis Palestine Concessions Case (Jurisdiction) (1924) P.C.I.J., Ser. A, No. 2*** at 11, quoted with approval in ***South West Africa Case (Preliminary Objections) 1962 I.C.J. Rep. 318*** at 328. The existence or otherwise of a dispute, and in particular the relevance to the determination of that question of prior negotiations or diplomatic exchanges, have been important questions in a number of ICJ cases. The distinction between a dispute and a **situation** is important in the UN in that the obligation to submit to various specified settlement procedures applies only to disputes, and the provisions on "situations which might lead to international friction or give rise to a dispute" are merely permissive: Chapter VI of the UN Charter.

There exist a number of general conventional obligations to settle disputes by peaceful means: *e.g.*, arts. 2, 9 and 37 of the Hague Convention on the Pacific Settlement of Disputes 1907 *(205 C.T.S. 233)*; arts. 12, 13, 15 and 17 of the Covenant of the League of Nations; art. 2 of the General Treaty for the Renunciation of War as an Instrument of National Policy 1928 *(94 L.N.T.S. 57)*; and art. 2(2) and Chapter VI of the UN Charter. The Friendly Relations Declaration 1970 (GA Res. 2625 (XXV)) promulgates a general and non-conventional principle on the pacific settlement of disputes.

It is often said that some disputes are justiciable and others are non-justiciable, but "probably today most writers would regard it as depending upon the attitude of the parties: if, whatever the subject matter of the dispute may be, what the parties seek is their legal rights, the dispute is justiciable: if, on the other hand, one of them at least is not content to demand its legal rights, but demands the satisfaction of some interest of its own even though this may require a change in the existing legal situation, the dispute is non-justiciable": Brierly, *The Law of Nations* (6th ed.), 367. *See also* Merrills, *International Dispute Settlement* (3rd ed.), 155-9 and 233-8.

Dispute Settlement Understanding Annexed to the Agreement Establishing the **World Trade Organization** of 1994 is the Understanding on Rules and Procedures Governing the Settlement of Disputes (DSU)*(33 I.L.M. 1226 (1994))*, providing a mechanism for the settlement of disputes over multilateral trade agreements (identified in Appendix 1) under the overarching control of the Dispute Settlement Board (DSB)(art. 2). The initial obligation is for the parties to seek a solution through consultation (art. 4); if unsuccessful, the complaining party may require the creation of an expert panel (arts. 6-8). The function of a panel is to make an objective assessment of the facts and a finding as to the merits of the complaining party's claims in order to assist the DSB (art. 11) in making recommendations and rulings in conformity with the relevant trade agreement (art. 3(4)). Appeals from panels go to the Appellate Body (art. 17(1)), which also reports to the DSB (art. 17(14)). *See* Merrills, *International Dispute Settlement* (3rd ed.), Chap. 9.

dissent (1) This denotes a separate and disagreeing judicial or arbitral opinion. Since the ***Alabama Claims*** (1872) Moore, *Int. Arb. 653*, it has been the practice to allow dissents. Art. 57 of the Statute of the ICJ permits a judge to deliver a separate and dissenting opinion to any judgment or order of the Court, which provision is amplified by art. 95(2) of the Rules of Court 1978 (as amended in 2000): "Any judge may, if he so desires, attach his individual opinion to the judgment, whether he dissents from the majority or not; a judge who wishes to record his concurrence or dissent without stating his reasons may do so in a declaration." (2) The term is sometimes used synonymously with **protest** (use of which is more common) to indicate the opposition by a State to an emerging factual or legal situation whose outcome, without express negative indication, might be prejudicial to the State, e.g., an emerging customary rule of international law. *See Asylum Case 1950 I.C.J. Rep. 266*; *Anglo-Norwegian Fisheries Case 1951 I.C.J. Rep. 116*; *North Sea Continental Shelf Case 1969 I.C.J. Rep. 3*.

dissolution of State The establishment of one or more new States on territory formerly belonging to the predecessor State, usually in the form of a union or federation of States and bringing about the complete disappearance of the predecessor State, *e.g.*, the dissolution of the Austro-Hungarian Empire in 1919; termination of the United Arab Republic between Syria and Egypt in 1960; dissolution of the USSR in 1991 and of Yugoslavia in 1991-2. *See also* **merger of States**; **redistribution of territory**; **secession of territory**.

distinct will It has been asserted that one of the essential characteristics of an international organization is that "at least one organ should have a will of its own": Schermers and Blokker, *International Institutional Law* (3rd ed.), 29. "As long as an organization is not empowered to take decisions binding its membership by a mere majority of its members, one can hardly speak, in a literal sense, of the organization having a 'distinct will'": Klabbers, *Introduction to International Institutional Law* (2002), 55, who questions whether the concept of distinct will "is more than a useful legal fiction."

distress, entry in "A foreign vessel which takes refuge in port by reason of stress of weather or other disaster endangering its safety is exempt from the local jurisdiction": O'Connell, *International Law of the Sea* (2nd ed), 627. The distress must be urgent and of grave necessity: *The Eleanor Edw. 135 (1809)*; *The New York 3 Wheat 59 (1818)*; *Kate A. Hoff Claim (1929) 4 R.I.A.A. 444*. The immunity is not absolute; while it is an immunity from arrest and from paying local duties, it cannot be an immunity from every local law: O'Connell, *supra*, 629; *Cushin and Lewis v. R. [1935] L.R. Ex. C.R. 103*.

For the purpose of the right of **innocent passage** through the territorial sea, passage "includes stopping and anchoring, but only insofar as the same are incidental to ordinary navigation or are rendered necessary by *force majeure* or distress or for the purpose of rendering assistance to persons, ships or aircraft in danger or distress": art. 18(2) of the UN Convention on the Law of the Sea 1982 *(1833 U.N.T.S. 3)*.

Diversion of Water from the Meuse Case *(Netherlands v. Belgium) (1937) P.C.I.J., Ser. A/B, No. 70.* The Netherlands sought a declaration that the construction by Belgium of works rendering it possible for a canal below Maastricht to be supplied with water taken from the Meuse elsewhere than at that town was contrary to the Treaty of 12 May 1863 *(127 C.T.S. 435)*. A counterclaim was advanced that the Netherlands had violated the treaty by raising the level of the river at Maastricht. *Held* (10 to 3) that both claim and counterclaim failed. The Dutch contention that the treaty gave the Netherlands a general right of control to which Belgium could not lay claim involved a construction that would be contrary to the principle of equality between the parties. But the Belgian complaint was unjustified, the raising of the level in itself, not involving the discharge of any volume of water greater than the permitted maximum, not being contrary to the treaty. Judge Hudson's Separate Opinion is notable for the statement that "under Article 38 of the Statute, if not independently of that Article, the Court has some freedom to consider principles of equity as part of the international law which it must apply."

divided States "It might seem that on one and the same territory there could exist only one full sovereign state; and that for there to be two or more full sovereign states on one and the same territory is not possible. But in practice sovereignty is sometimes divided. . . ." *1 Oppenheim 565*. While the author goes on to list five exceptions to this rule (**condominium;** the exercise of sovereignty by a foreign power with the consent of the owner-State; a **lease** or **pledge**; a conventional grant in perpetuity; a federal State; a mandated (*see* **Mandates System**) or trusteeship territory (*see* **trust territory**)), no mention is made of the division of China, Germany, Korea and Vietnam. In each of the last three cases, two States became established on the territory of the former State, each acting in respect of distinct portions of its territory, and each being recognized by certain other States, so that eventually North and South Vietnam and the Federal Republic of Germany and the German Democratic Republic, both now unified, became and are now members of the UN, while North nor South Korea each became members in 1991 in acknowledgement of their enduring division. China is somewhat different, the situation for many years essentially involving which of two competing régimes represented the State of China. Since 1971, the Government of the People's Republic of China has represented China at the UN and in most other international *fora*, the former nationalist government now exercising control only over Taiwan, which, while satisfying the *indicia* of Statehood, is not universally regarded as a separate State and is not a UN member.

Dix Claim *(U.S.A. v. Venezuela) (1903), 9 R.I.A.A. 119. Held* by the American-Venezuelan Commission that the Government of Venezuela was responsible for the loss sustained as a result of the confiscation of the cattle of Ford Dix, a United States citizen engaged in the cattle business in Venezuela, by the revolutionary forces of General Cipriano Castro, the revolution having been successful and the acts of the revolutionaries falling in consequence to be considered as acts of a *de facto* government; items in the claim in respect of alleged losses through forced sales and damages paid for non-fulfillment of contracts were dismissed, however, as too remote.

Dogger Bank Incident *(Great Britain v Russia)* Brown, *The Hague Court Reports*, 403. During the Russo-Japanese War in 1904, the Russian Baltic fleet, which was on its way to the Far East, fired on the Hull fishing fleet off the Dogger Bank in the North Sea, whereby two fishermen were killed and considerable damage was done to several trawlers. Great Britain demanded from Russia an apology and ample damages, and also severe punishment of the officer responsible. As Russia contended that, as the firing was caused by the approach of Japanese torpedo-boats, she could therefore not punish the officer in command. The parties agreed upon the establishment of an International Commission of Inquiry pursuant to Title III of the Hague Convention for the Pacific Settlement of International Disputes of 1899 *(187 C.T.S. 410)* by means of the Declaration signed at St. Petersburg on 25 November 1904 *(197 C.T.S. 232)*. This Commission, consisting of five naval officers of high rank (one British, one Russian, one American, one French and one Austrian) was charged, not only to ascertain the facts of the incident, but also to pronounce an opinion concerning the responsibility for the incident, and the degree of blame attaching to the responsible persons.

The Report of the Commission of 26 February 1905 stated that no torpedo-boats had been present, that the opening of fire on the part of the Baltic fleet was not justifiable, that Admiral Rojdestvensky, the commander of the Baltic fleet, was responsible for the incident, but that these facts were "not of a nature to cast any discredit upon the military qualities or the humanity of Admiral Rojdestvensky or of the personnel of his squadron." In consequence of the last part of this Report, Great Britain could not insist upon punishment of the responsible Russian admiral, but Russia paid a sum of $3000,000 to indemnify the victims of the incident and the families of the two dead fishermen.

domaine reservé *See* **domestic jurisdiction**.

domestic court (or tribunal) *See* **municipal court (or tribunal)**.

domestic jurisdiction Art. 2(7) of the UN Charter provides that "[n]othing contained in the present Charter shall authorize the United Nations to intervene in matters which are essentially within the domestic jurisdiction of any State or shall require the Members to submit such matters to settlement under the present Charter; but this principle shall not prejudice the application of enforcement measures under Chapter VII." Art. 2(7), the successor to art. 15(8) of the Covenant of the League of Nations, has been restrictively interpreted in the practice of the UN. Thus, the term "intervene" has been interpreted to connote "dictatorial interference" in the affairs of a State "amounting to denial of the independence of the State": Lauterpacht, The International Protection of Human Rights, *(1947) 70 Hague Rec. 19*; Kelsen, *Law of the United Nations* (1950), 770; *see also* Goodrich, Hambro and Simons, *The Charter of the UN* (3rd ed), 67-8. Matters are essentially within the domestic jurisdiction of a State if they are not regulated by international law: ***Interpretation of the Peace Treaties Case** 1950 I.C.J. Rep. 65*. As international relations and law develop, matters which were previously within domestic jurisdiction may cease to remain there: ***Nationality Decrees Case** (1923) P.C.I.J., Ser. B, No. 4*; ***Nottebohm Case** 1955 I.C.J. Rep. 4*. The following can be asserted as not within the domestic jurisdiction of a State: obligations of an international character; actions, originally within domestic jurisdiction, the implementation of which constitute a threat to the peace; issues of human rights: Lauterpacht, *International Law and Human Rights* (1950), 176-80. *See also **Norwegian Loans Case** 1957 I.C.J. Rep. 9*; ***Interhandel Case** 1959 I.C.J. Rep. 6. And see* Rajan, *The United Nations and Domestic Jurisdiction* (2nd ed.); Higgins, *The Development of International Law through the Political Organs of the United Nations* (1963), 58-130.

domestic law *See* **municipal law**.

domicile This familiar term of private international law or the conflict of laws connotes the place, in the sense of a civil jurisdiction in which a person has his or her permanent home, or, in virtue of the rule that in law no person can be without domicile, is construed to have his or her permanent home. *See generally Dicey and Morris on the Conflict of Laws* (13th ed.), Chap.7. The term is applied by extension or analogy to corporations. *See* Farnsworth, *The Residence and Domicile of Corporations* (1982).

"Quite independently of the ordinary or civil domicile in time of war, there is another domicile which is acquired by trading with an enemy country. The only requirement necessary for the acquisition of such a 'commercial domicile' . . . is that a person should be in a country for the purpose of trade or otherwise as makes a person's trade or estate form part of its resources. . . . According to the English Prize law and practice the commercial domicile of a merchant determines his hostile or neutral character independently of his origin, descent, place of birth or nationality": Colombos, *International Law of the Sea* (6th ed.), 556.

dominium As an aspect of **sovereignty**, the other being *imperium*, *dominium* (sometimes referred to as territorial sovereignty or territorial authority), is generally accepted as a State's ultimate title to all the territory on which it is located, consequently implying "the power of a State to exercise supreme authority over all persons and things within its territory": *I Oppenheim 382. See Tietz v. People's Republic of Bulgaria (1959) 28 I.L.R. 368* at 376.

DOMREP The Mission of the Special Representative of the Secretary-General in the Dominican Republic (acronym DOMREP) was mandated by Security Council Res. 205

(1965) to monitor the cease-fire between the two *de facto* authorities within the territory between May 1965 and October 1966.

double criminality In relation to **extradition**, most States follow the rule of double criminality, i.e. that it is a condition of extradition that the crime of which the fugitive is accused is punishable according to the law of both the extraditing State and the State to which the fugitive is being extradited (*see*, for example, s. 2 of the Extradition Act 1989 (UK)). This rule was central to the decision of the British House of Lords in the third ***Pinochet Case (R v Bow Street Metropolitian Stipendiary Magistrate, Ex p. Pinochet Ugarte (No. 3) [1999] 2 All ER 97)*** in which Pinochet was found to be extraditable to Spain only in respect of those crimes of torture which constituted a crime under United Kingdom law. Because the crimes of which he was accused were committed in Chile, the UK had to constitute the offence of torture carried out in a foreign State as an offence under UK law, something which they did not do until 29 September 1988 by virtue of the coming into force of s. 134 of the Criminal Justice Act 1988. Thus, although Pinochet was alleged to have been committing crimes of torture since 1973, he could only be prosecuted for those offences which had occurred at a time when they constituted crimes under both UK and Spanish law. *See* further Barker, *International Law and International Relations* (2000), Chap. 6. *See* **extraditable offence**.

double veto The device by which a permanent member of the Security Council may, by deploying two successive vetoes, prevent any substantive decision being taken. Art. 27 of the UN Charter draws a distinction between "procedural matters," for decisions on which the affirmative vote of any nine members is required (para. 2), and "all other matters," for decisions on which the affirmative vote of nine members, including the concurring votes of the permanent members, is required (para. 3) and thus open to **veto**. A vote on whether a matter comes under para. 2 or 3 is itself a non-procedural matter coming under para. 3 and thus open to veto. A permanent member can therefore exercise the veto, first, on a vote on the procedural issue and again if a vote is taken on the substance under para. 3. The Yalta voting formula (Statement of the Four Sponsoring Powers on Voting Procedure in the Security Council; see **Yalta formula**), while considering this type of situation "unlikely," recognized the legitimacy of deciding the preliminary question as to whether or not the issue was procedural in accordance with the non-procedural vote. *See* Rudzinski, The So-called Double Veto, *45 A.J.I.L. 443 (1951)*; Gross, The Double Veto and the Four-Power Statement on Voting in the Security Council, *67 Harv. L.R. 67 (1953)*; Bailey, *Voting in the Security Council* (1970), Chap. 2.

***Doyen* of the diplomatic corps** The *Doyen* (or Dean) of the **diplomatic corps** in a State is the senior diplomatic representative appointed to that State, reflecting, though long preceding, the statement in art. 16(1) of the Vienna Convention on Diplomatic Relations 1961 *(500 U.N.T.S. 95)* that heads of mission take precedence in accordance with the date and time of taking up their functions. The *Doyen* has responsibilities in respect of protocol and ceremony and is the defender of the privileges and immunities of the diplomatic corps as a whole. *See Satow's Guide to Diplomatic Practice* (5th ed.), 161-2.

Drago Doctrine This doctrine, which was expounded in an instruction dated 29 December 1902 from Dr. Luis M. Drago, Argentine Minister of Foreign Affairs, to the Argentine Minister in Washington, is to the effect that the public debt of a State cannot justify armed intervention nor even the actual occupation of the territory of American nations by a European power. *See* Drago, State Loans in their Relation to International Policy, *1 A.J.I.L. 695 (1907)*, in which he explained that the doctrine did not apply to ordinary contracts between an alien and a foreign government. Art. 1 of the Hague Convention on the Limitation of Employment of Force for Recovery of Contract Debts of 18 October 1907 *(205 C.T.S.*

250) goes further in providing that the Contracting Powers "agree not to have recourse to armed force for the recovery of contract debts claimed from the Government of one country by the Government of another country as being due to its nationals. This undertaking is, however, not applicable when the debtor State refuses or neglects to reply to an offer of arbitration, or after accepting the offer, prevents any 'compromis' from being agreed upon, or after the arbitration, fails to submit to the award."

Draper, G.I.A.D. 1914-86. Military Prosecutor (Nuremberg) 1945-49; lecturer, then Reader, London 1956-76; Professor, Sussex 1976-79. Publications include *The Red Cross Conventions* (1958): *Civilians and the NATO Status of Forces Agreement* (1966); *Implementation of the Modern Law of Armed Conflict* (1974). *See* Meyer, *Reflections on Law and Armed Conflict: The Selected Works on the Laws of War by the Late Professor Colonel G.I.A.D. Draper* (1998).

Dreyfus Case *(France v. Chile) (1901) 15 R.I.A.A. 77.* In 1869, Dreyfus Frères et Cie, a French company, made a loan to the Government of Peru secured by certain rights for Dreyfus in connection with the exploitation of Peruvian guano deposits. In 1879, war broke out between Chile and Peru during which Chile occupied those parts of Peru containing guano deposits. In December 1879, the constitutional authorities in Peru being incapable of acting, Nicholas de Pierola assumed dictatorial powers in Peru. In November 1880, Dreyfus and the Pierola Government agreed upon the payment to Dreyfus of a sum of money in settlement of certain outstanding accounts. However, also in 1880, Chile authorized foreign holders of Peruvian bonds to exploit the guano deposits in the area occupied by Chile in order to satisfy the debts owing to them and later provided, by a decree of 9 February 1882, for the sale of a large quantity of the guano and for the net proceeds of the sale to be distributed in equal shares between the Government of Chile and those creditors of Peru whose investments were guaranteed by Peruvian guano. This decree was confirmed by the Peace Treaty of 20 October 1883 between Chile and Peru. In 1886, the Pierola régime having ended, Peru passed a law annulling all acts of internal administration performed by the Pierola régime. Dreyfus asserted rights over the guano sold by Chile which were prejudiced by the Chilean provisions in favor only of bondholders, and claimed payment of the sums agreed with the Pierola Government in 1880. In 1892 Chile and France concluded a protocol providing for the establishment of an arbitral tribunal to determine disputes arising out of the application of the Chilean Decree of 1882. *Held* that the capacity of a government to represent the State in international relations did not depend on the legitimacy of its origin, and foreign States could not refuse recognition to governments *de facto*, while the new government, which in fact wielded power with the express or tacit consent of the nation, acted and validly concluded in the name of the State treaties which the subsequently restored legitimate government had to respect; that this rule applied equally in the public internal law of the State as regards contractual relations between government *de facto* and an individual; that, although this doctrine did not apply to agreements concluded by insurgents, it applied fully to the acts of a provisional government which exercised power in fact without being in conflict with a competing regular government; that the principle of general public law which established the validity of the acts of a government, even a revolutionary government, when that government had become established and in fact exercised power to the exclusion of any other government meant that the recognition of the debt in 1880 by the Pierola Government must be considered as validly given by the then legal representative of Peru and thus gave rise to an obligation for Peru, notwithstanding the Peruvian law of 1886; that the debt acknowledged by the 1880 decision was, pursuant to the 1869 contract, guaranteed by the guano as envisaged in the

Chilean Decree of 1882; and that therefore Dreyfus was entitled to benefit from the payment provisions of the 1882 Decree. Cf. *French Claims against Peru Case*.

droit de chapelle The right of chapel, one the outdated privileges enjoyed by diplomatic envoys. "This is the privilege of having a private chapel of his own religion, which must be granted to an envoy by the law of the receiving State": *I Oppenheim 1103*.

droit de renvoi *See* **reconduction**.

droit d'enquête "[A] universally recognised customary rule of international law that warships of all nations, in order to maintain the safety of the high seas, have the power to require suspicious private vessels on the high seas to show their flag. . . .": *I Oppenheim 737*. *See* **ships, right of visit**.

drugs Upon the establishment of the UN, a Commission on Narcotic Drugs was set up in 1947 by ECOSOC Resolution I/9. Under the auspices of this body the Single Convention on Narcotic Drugs of 30 March 1961 *(520 U.N.T.S. 204)* was elaborated, replacing earlier international agreements in the matter and establishing the International Narcotics Control Board (INCB). This Convention was amended by the Protocol of 25 March 1972 *(976 U.N.T.S. 3)*. A Convention on Psychotropic Substances of 21 February 1971 *((1971) 10 I.L.M. 261)* completes the basic drugs régime under the direction and supervision of the INCB. As to the history of international drug control before the Single Convention see Rendborg, *International Drug Control*. *See* **narcotic drugs**. *See* <www.unodc.org>.

drying rocks, shoals These terms were used by the International Law Commission in its draft articles and commentary on the **baselines** of the territorial sea *([1956] 1 I.L.C. Yearbook 195 and 283)*, but were substituted in art. 11 of the Geneva Convention on the Territorial Sea etc. 1958 *(516 U.N.T.S. 205)* and later in art. 13 of the UN Convention on the Law of the Sea 1982 *(1833 U.N.T.S. 3)* by the term **low-tide elevations**.

DSU *See* **Dispute Settlement Understanding**.

dual (or plural) nationality This phenomenon arises from the circumstance that nationality is primarily a concept of municipal rather than international law, so that a person may be invested with the nationality of more than one State under the several laws of the States concerned. Though the legal systems of some States discourage plural nationality and sometimes visit the retention of a foreign nationality with the loss of domestic status when the former is capable of divestment, the occurrence of cases of plural nationality at birth (*e.g.*, by reason of birth in the territory of one State of a parent—if not of both parents—having the nationality of another State or of other States) is accepted as inevitable and is to some extent provided for by treaty. *See* the Hague Convention on Certain Questions relating to the Conflict of Nationality Laws and the International Protocol relating to Military Obligations in Certain Cases of Double Nationality 1930 *(178 L.N.T.S. 237)*, essentially promulgating the effective nationality principle. "Where an individual possesses dual nationality, either state of which he is a national may adopt a claim of his against a third state, and it may be that the state with which he has the more effective connection may be able to espouse his claim as against the other state: Shaw, *International Law* (4th ed.), 565. *See* the *Mergé Claim (1955) 14 R.I.A.A. 236*; *Canevaro Case (1912) 11 R.I.A.A. 405*; *Nottebohm Case 1955 I.C.J. Rep. 1*.

dualism The theory according to which "international law and the internal law of states are totally separate legal systems. Being separate systems international law would not *as such* form part of the internal law of a state: to the extent that in particular instances rules of international law may apply within a state they do so virtue of their adoption by the internal law of the state, and apply as part of that internal law and not as international law. Such a view avoids any question of the supremacy of the one system over the other since they share no common field of application: each is supreme in its own sphere": *I Oppenheim 53.* Cf. **monism**.

due diligence (1) The degree of care in the prevention of the organization of hostile expeditions in the territory of a neutral State required by the "Three Rules of Washington" laid down by the Treaty of 1871 *(143 C.T.S. 145)* for the arbitration of the *Alabama Case.* The Tribunal held the requisite degree of care to be proportionate to the risks to which a belligerent might be exposed through a failure by the neutral State in its duty. The Second Hague Peace Conference, however, regarded this standard as too high. Accordingly, Hague Convention XIII of 1907 respecting the Rights and Duties of Neutral Powers in Maritime Law, art. 8, *(205 C.T.S. 395)* provides merely that a neutral government is obliged in this context to use the means at its disposal—*d'user des moyens don't il dispose.*

(2) Due diligence is also often stated to represent the standard which, if not observed by a State in preventing the occurrence of injury or damage to aliens (*e.g.*, in cases of mob violence) or in prosecuting those who have injured an alien, engages the State's international responsibility. *See, e.g. Janes Claim (1926) 4 R.I.A.A. 82*; and **international minimum standard**.

Dumbarton Oaks Conference The meetings between 21 August and 28 September 1944 of the USSR, UK and USA, and between 29 September and 7 October 1944 of China, the UK and USA at a mansion in Washington, DC, that laid the foundations of the United Nations. The proposals agreed at this conference concerned the purposes and principles of the organization, its membership and organs, and arrangements to maintain international peace and security and to promote international economic and social co-operation. After the **Yalta Conference** of February 1945, and meetings of various regional groups, the Charter was drawn up and signed at the **San Francisco Conference** in June 1945. *See* Goodrich, Hambro and Simons, *Charter of the United Nations* (3rd ed.), 3-4.

dumdum bullets "[B]ullets which expand or flatten easily in the human body, such as bullets with a hard envelope which does not entirely cover the core or is pierced with incisions": Hague Declaration 3 of 29 November 1868 (*187 C.T.S. 459*). Named after the Dum-Dum arsenal near Calcutta where they were first manufactured, and otherwise know as "expanding bullets," their use was prohibited among the parties to the Declaration.

dumping at sea According to the principal global instrument on the matter, the International Convention on the Prevention of Marine Pollution by Dumping of Wastes and Other Matter, adopted on 29 December 1992 following a conference at London the previous month *(11 I.L.M. 1294 (1992))*, art. 1 (a), "Dumping" means: (i) any deliberate disposal at sea of wastes or other matter from vessels, aircraft, platforms or other man-made structures at sea; (ii) any deliberate disposal at sea of vessels, aircraft, platforms or other man-made structures at sea." Dumping does not include disposal at sea of waste incidental to the normal operations of vessels, aircraft or fixed platforms, nor from mineral extractive activities (art. 1(b)). All dumping, thus defined, is prohibited, except as regulated under three categories (art. 4(1)). Dumping of waste and other matter listed in Annex I (the "black list," including mercury, persistent plastics, oils, and high-level radio-active material) is at all times and places prohibited (art. 4(1)(a)); dumping of waste and other matter listed in Annex II (the grey list," including arsenic, lead, copper and cyanides) requires a prior special licence (art. 4(1)(b)); dumping of all other waste and matter requires a prior general licence (art. 4(1)(c)). Each party is to designate an appropriate authority to issue licences and keep records of dumping (art. 6) from vessels flying its flag, loading waste and other matter from its territory or territorial sea or from fixed platforms under its jurisdiction (art. 7). The London Convention has been amended in 1978 (twice, incineration and disputes), 1980 (list of substances), 1989 (licences), and 1993 (banning dumping of low-level radio-active waste, phasing out dumping of industrial waste, banning of incineration of waste at sea); and a Revised Convention, to replace the London Convention, was agreed in a 1996 Protocol *(36 I.L.M. 7(1997))* which is not yet in force. Art. 210 of the UN Convention on the Law of the Sea 1982 *(1833 U.N.T.S. 3)* to adopt and enforce regulations to "prevent, reduce and control pollution of the marine environment by dumping," dumping being defined (in art. 1(1)(5)) as "any deliberate disposal of wastes or other matter from vessels, aircraft, platforms or other man-made structures at sea; [and] any deliberate disposal of vessels, aircraft, platforms or other man-made structures at sea."

Dupuis, Charles Alfred Marie 1863-1938. French law teacher and scholar. Publications include *Le droit de la guerre maritime d'apres doctrines anglaises contemporaines* (1898). *Le principe d'equilibre et le concert europeen* (1909). *Le droit de la guerre maritime d'apres les conferences de la Haye et de Londres* (1911). *Le droit des gens et les rapports entre les grandes Puissances et les autres Etats* (1921).

duress *See* **coercion**.

E

Eagleton, Clyde 1891-1958. Professor, New York 1923-56. Principal works include *The Responsibility of States in International Law* (1928); *International Government* (1932; 3rd ed., 1957); *Analysis of the Problem of War* (1937); *The Forces that Shape our Future* (1945).

East Timor Case *(Portugal v. Australia) 1995 I.C.J. Rep. 89.* By application of 22 February 1991, Portugal instituted proceedings against Australia concerning "certain activities of Australia with respect to East Timor." According to Portugal, the fact that Australia had negotiated and concluded a treaty with Indonesia on 11 December 1989 whereby a "Zone of Cooperation" was created in "an area between the Indonesian Province of East Timor and Northern Australia" amounted to a failure by Australia to observe its obligations to respect the duties and powers of Portugal as the administering power, constituted an infringement of the right of the people of East Timor to self-determination and contravened Security Council Res. 384 and 389 concerning the status of East Timor. Australia objected to the jurisdiction of the Court, arguing that no dispute existed between it and Portugal; that the application would require the Court to rule on the rights an obligations of a State which was not party to the proceedings, namely Indonesia; and that Portugal lacked standing to bring the case, not having sufficient interest in the situation. *Held* (14 to 2) that the Court did not have jurisdiction to hear the case. The Court found that "it is clear that the Parties are in disagreement, both on the law and on the fact, on the question whether the conduct of Australia in negotiating, concluding and initiating performance of the 1989 Treaty was in breach of an obligation due by Australia to Portugal"(at 100); and that "Portugal's assertion that the rights of peoples to **self-determination** as it evolved from the Charter and from UN practice had an *erga omnes* character is irreproachable"(at 102). It noted, nevertheless, "that the *erga omnes* character of a norm and the rule of consent to jurisdiction are two different things. Whatever the nature of the obligations invoked, the Court could not rule on the lawfulness of the conduct of a State when its judgment would imply an evaluation of the lawfulness of the conduct of another State which is not a party to the case" (at 102).

Eastern Carelia Case *(1923) P.C.I.J., Ser. B., No. 5.* Upon the complaint of Finland that the Government of the USSR (not then a member of the League) was in breach of its engagements under the Treaty of Peace of Dorpat of 14 October 1920 between the two States *(3 L.N.T.S. 6)* respecting the autonomy of Eastern Carelia, the League of Nations' Council requested an advisory opinion of the PCIJ on the question whether that Treaty and the annexed Declaration "constitute engagements of an international character which place Russia under an obligation to Finland as to the carrying out of the provisions contained therein." The USSR having refused to appear, the Court (7 to 4) *declined* to give an opinion, the question bearing on an actual dispute, it being a fundamental principle of international law that no State can be compelled to submit its disputes to settlement without its consent, and the non-appearing State having information essential to the determination of an opinion.

Eastern Greenland, Legal Status of, Case (*Denmark v. Norway*) (*1933*) *P.C.I.J., Ser. A/B, No. 53.* The Government of Norway having by proclamation declared part of Eastern Greenland to be under Norwegian sovereignty, the Government of Denmark sought a decision that this proceeding was invalid, the whole of Greenland being already under Danish sovereignty, as Norway had herself recognized, notably in an oral statement by the Minister of Foreign Affairs, Hr. Ihlen, to the Danish Minister to the effect "that the Norwegian Government would not make any difficulties in the settlement of th[e] question" of the extension of Danish political and economic interests over all Greenland. The Court, which assumed jurisdiction under the **Optional Clause**, *held* (12 to 2) that it was "beyond all dispute that a reply of this nature given by the Minister of Foreign Affairs on behalf of his Government in response to a request by the diplomatic representative of a foreign Power, in regard to a question falling within his province, is binding upon the country to which the Minister belongs," and in consequence that Norway was "under an obligation to refrain from contesting Danish sovereignty over Greenland as a whole and, *a fortiori* to refrain from occupying a part of Greenland" (at 71 and 73). The Court also stressed the relative nature of the test of establishing title to territory by means of occupation, noting that "in many cases the tribunal [deciding the question of territorial sovereignty] has been satisfied with very little in the way of the actual exercise of sovereign rights, provided that the other State could not make out a superior claim. This is particularly true in the case of claims to sovereignty over areas in thinly populated or unsettled countries" (at 46).

ECB *See* **European Central Bank.**

Eclectics The name given to juridical writers of a particular school, sometimes also called "Grotians," who stood somewhere between the **Naturalists** and the **Positivists**. They espoused a dualistic character of the law building upon Grotius's distinction between the law of nature and the law of nations. The foremost proponents of this approach to international law are Christian Wolff and Emerich de Vattel.

The term "eclecticism" has also been used in a prejorative sense to describe the approach of writers who "pick and choose from natural and positive law exactly as they think fit": Schwarzenberger, *The Inductive Approach to International Law* (1965), 13.

Economic and Social Council (ECOSOC) An organ designated as a principal organ of the UN under art. 7 (1) of the Charter, Chapter X of which makes provision as to its constitution, functions and powers, voting rules and procedure. Art. 61 originally provided that ECOSOC should be made up of 18 members, but this number was increased to 27 as from 31 August 1965 in virtue of GA Res.1991 (XVIII), and to 54 by GA Res. 2847 (XXVI), which also provided for specific numbers of representatives from each of Africa, Asia, Latin America, Western Europe and other States, and Eastern Europe, and which entered into force on 24 September 1973. Members are elected by the General Assembly for a term of three years and, though there is no provision as to permanent membership, a consistent pattern of election has emerged: *see* Goodrich, Hambro and Simons, *Charter of the United Nations* (3rd ed.), 409-10. In terms of art. 62, the Council may make or initiate studies and may make recommendations with respect to international economic, social cultural, educational, health and related matters. It may also make recommendations for the purposes of promoting respect for, and observance of human rights and fundamental freedoms for all. The Council at its first establishment inaugurated a number of standing Commissions respecting Human Rights, Narcotic Drugs, Transport and Communications etc. Pursuant to art. 63, it has entered into agreement with the **Specialized Agencies,** bringing them into relationship with the UN. It has further established regional economic commissions for Africa, Asia and the Pacific, Europe, Latin America and Western Asia. *See generally* Sharp, *The U.N. Economic and Social Council* (1969); Sands and Klein, *Bowett's Law of International Institutions* (5th ed.) 55-63; Simma, *The Charter of the United Nations: A Commentary* (1994), 827-921.

economic interests In the *Anglo-Norwegian Fisheries Case 1951 I.C.J. Rep. 115* at 133, the ICJ said, in relation to the drawing of **straight baselines** to the territorial sea along coasts which are deeply indented or fringed with islands: "[T]here is one consideration not to be overlooked . . . : that of certain economic interests peculiar to a region, the reality and importance of which are clearly evidenced by a long usage." This criterion of economic interests is included as art. 4(4) of the Geneva Convention on the Territorial Sea, etc. 1958 *(516 U.N.T.S. 205)* and art. 7(5) of the UN Convention on the Law of the Sea 1982 *(1833 U.N.T.S. 3)*, both without further definition or explanation. The precise import of the criterion is unclear, but the ILC has said: "The application of the straight baseline system should be justified in principle on other grounds before purely economic considerations could justify a particular way of drawing the lines": *[1956] 2 I.L.C. Yearbook 268.*

economic law, international "If international economic law is not necessarily congruent with the laws of international economics, it is nevertheless true that economics has a strong influence on the shape and evolution of the international law of international trade, investment, and financial transactions": Lowenfeld, *International Economic Law* (2002), 3. Cf. van Themaat, *The Changing Structure of International Economic Law* (1981), 9: "[I]nternational economic law can be described in overall terms as the total range of norms (directly or indirectly based on treaties) of public international law with regard to transnational economic relations."

Economic Rights and Duties of States, Charter of Following a number of earlier resolutions, including in particular the Declaration and Programme of Action on the Establishment of a New International Economic Order of 1 May 1974 (GA Res. 3201 and 3202 (S-VI)), the General Assembly adopted this Charter in a resolution dated 12 December 1974 (GA Res. 3281 (XXIX)). The Charter contains 34 substantive articles which, *inter alia,* provide that every State has the right to choose its economic system without outside interference (art. 1); to exercise full permanent sovereignty over all its wealth, natural resources and economic activities (art. 2(1)); to regulate foreign investment, transnational corporations and to expropriate property (art. 2(2)); to engage in international trade (art. 4); to benefit from developments in science and technology (art. 13); to benefit from world trade (art. 27); among the duties placed upon every State include the duty to co-operate in promoting world trade (art. 14); to promote disarmament (art. 15); to eliminate colonialism, *apartheid* and racial discrimination (art. 16); to respond to the needs of developing States (art. 22); and to refrain from coercing other States (art. 32). *See also* **New International Economic Order**.

economic sanctions This is not a term of art but was widely used during the time of the League of Nations to describe those non-military measures which the Covenant required to be imposed automatically on any member resorting to war in disregard of its obligations under arts. 12, 13, 14, 15, namely "the severance of all trade or financial relations, the prohibition of all intercourse between . . . nationals, . . . and the prevention of all financial, commercial or personal intercourse [with] the nationals of any other State. . . ." (art. 16(1)). The expression is used, equally, to describe certain of those "measures not involving the use of armed force" which may at discretion be employed by the Security Council to give effect to its decisions under Chapter VII of the UN Charter and which "may include complete or partial interruption of economic relations and of rail, sea, air, postal, telegraphic, radio, and other means of communication, and the severance of diplomatic relations" (art. 41). While there are some, and increasing, examples of selective economic sanctions being applied by the Security Council, there are only two instances of situations where the Council has imposed a complete economic boycott on a state, specifically against Rhodesia (Res. 232 (1966)) and against Iraq (Res. 661 (1990) and 687(1991)).

economic union "The completion of the final stage of economic union involves a full integration of the member economies with supranational authorities responsible for economic policy making. In particular, an economic union requires a single monetary system and central bank, a unified fiscal system, and a common foreign economic policy. The task of creating an economic union differs significantly from the steps necessary to establish the less ambitious forms of economic integration. A **free trade area**, a **customs union**, or a **common market** mainly result from the abolition of restrictions, whereas an economic union demands a positive agreement to transfer economic sovereignty to new supranational institutions": Root, *International Trade and Investment—Theory, Politics, Enterprise,* (4th ed.) 379. Cf. the definition of Trebilcock and Howse, *The Regulation of International Trade* (2nd ed.), 28: "In considering institutional arrangements to promote regional economic integration, it is useful to think of an integration continuum. First there are **free trade areas** (like **NAFTA**). . . . Second there are **customs unions**. . . . Third there are **common markets** or economic unions (like the **European Union**), where in addition to removing border restrictions on trade in good amongst member countries and harmonizing external trade policy, free trade in or free movement of services, capital and people, as well as perhaps a common monetary policy might be contemplated."

Economic, Social and Cultural Rights, International Covenant on Following the Universal Declaration on Human Rights of 10 December 1948, the General Assembly adopted two International Covenants on 16 December 1966: on Economic, Social and Cultural Rights *(993 U.N.T.S. 3)* and on **Civil and Political Rights**. The International Covenant on Economic, Social and Cultural Rights came into force on 3 January 1976. The International Covenant guarantees, *inter alia*, the rights of self-determination (art. 1(1)), of free disposition of natural wealth and resources (art. 1(2)), of non discrimination (art. 2), of equal rights of men and women (art. 3), to work (art. 6), to just and favorable conditions of work (art. 7), to form and join free trade unions (art. 8), to social security (art. 9), to family life, with special measures of protection and assistance to children (art. 10), to an adequate standard of living (art. 11), to the highest attainable standard of physical and mental health (art. 12), to education (art. 13), and to participate in cultural life (art. 15). To enforce the International Covenant, States Parties are obliged to submit reports on the domestic implementation of the guaranteed rights (arts. 16 and 17). These reports may be transmitted by ECOSOC to the Commission on Human Rights for study and recommendation (art. 19). *See* Alston, *Economic and Social Rights: A Bibliography* (2000); Craven, *The International Covenant on Economic, Social and Cultural Rights* (1995); Krause and Rosas, *Economic, Social and Cultural Rights: A Textbook* (1994).

ECOSOC *See* **Economic and Social Council**.

ECSC *See* **European Coal and Steel Community**.

EEA *See* **European Economic Area**.

EEC *See* **European Economic Community**.

*Effect of Awards Case See **Administrative Tribunal of the UN, Effect of Awards Case***.

effective nationality, principle of The principle of effective (or active or master) nationality is to the effect that "in cases of plural nationality a person is to be considered as having the nationality which in fact he exercises": Weis, *Nationality and Statelessness in International Law* (2nd ed.), 170. The leading case thereon is the **Mergé Claim** in which the Italian-United States Conciliation Commission held that, in dual nationality cases, it is the effective nationality to which priority should be given, was a principle of international law. (*See* also the **Canevaro Case**, but cf. the **Salem Case** in which the alleged principle was disapproved). More recently in *Islamic Republic of Iran v USA (Case No. A/18, 5 Iran-US CTR 251(1986))* the US-Iran Claims Tribunal held that "it had jurisdiction over claims against Iran by a dual national when the 'dominant and effective nationality' at the relevant time was American": Shaw, *International Law* (4th ed.), 565. In relation to third States, the principle is reflected in the Convention on Certain Questions relating to the Conflict of Nationality Laws of 1930 *(179 L.N.T.S. 89)* in the stipulation in art. 5 that a third State shall "recognize exclusively . . . either the nationality of the country in which a plural national is habitually and principally resident, or the nationality of the country with which in the circumstances he appears to be in fact most closely connected." However, see the *Salem Case*, in which the tribunal held that "the rule of international law [is] that in the case of dual nationality, a third power is not entitled to contest the claim of one of the two powers whose national is interested in the case by referring to the nationality of the other power": *(1932) 2 RIAA 1161* at 1188*). See* also Martin and Hailbronner, *Rights and Duties of Dual Nationals: Evolution and Prospects* (2002).

effectiveness, principle of The principle that law in general, and rights and obligations thereunder, should be effective rather than not, expressed sometimes in the maxim *ut res magis valeat quam pereat*. As to its operation, often at the expense of abstract or historic right or legitimacy, in relation, in particular, to acquisition of territorial title, recognition, and the process of change and adaptation of the law, see De Visscher, *Theory and Reality in Public International Law* (rev. ed.), Book III, Chap. IV (where the original French is infelicitously translated as "effectivity"). *And see* Stone, *Legal Controls of International Conflict* (rev. ed.), Chap. XXXIII. As to the principle as a rule of treaty interpretation, see the **Interpretation of the Peace Treaties Opinion (Second Phase) (1950 I.C.J. Rep. 65** at 229.

effects doctrine A concept relating to the exercise of jurisdiction developed first in US antitrust law whereby a State exercises jurisdiction over a non-national for activities outside its territory simply on the basis of the international production of economic effects within that State. See, for example, *US v Aluminium Co. of America 148 F.2d 416* (1945); *Timberlane Lumber Co. v Bank of America 549 F.2d 597* (1976); *Hartford Fire Insurance Co v California 113 S. Ct. 2891* (1993). The assertion of extraterritorial jurisdiction by the US in this way has been met with strong protests from many other States, including the United Kingdom (*see Rio Tinto Zinc Corp. v Westinghouse Electric Corp [1978] 1 All ER 434*, the Protection of Trading Interests Act 1980) and the EC more generally.

effet utile A form of interpretation of treaties and other instruments derived from French administrative law which looks to the objects and purpose of a treaty, as well as the context, to make the treaty more effective. Use of the concept has been most apparent in the interpretation of European Community law by the European Court of Justice: "A concept also frequently used . . . is that of *effet utile*, whereby the [European] Court [of Justice] has held that the efficacy of Community law would be weakened if it did not interpret EC law in such a way as to fulfil the treaty's objectives": Douglas-Scott, *Constitutional Law of the*

European Union (2002), 210. It is at least arguable that the International Court of Justice used the concept in its decision in the ***Reparation for Injuries Case*** *1949 I.C.J. Rep. 174.*

EFTA *See* **European Free Trade Association**.

EIB *See* **European Investment Bank**.

Eichmann Incident, Case On 10 May 1960, a group of Israeli citizens seized Adolf Eichmann in Buenos Aires and, some days later, took him by air to Israel, where he was charged under an Israeli statute, the Nazis and Nazi Collaborators (Punishment) Law 1950, on fifteen counts of "crimes against the Jewish people," **crimes against humanity**, **war crimes** and membership of an hostile (i.e. Nazi) organization. By Res. 138 (1960) of 23 June 1960, the Security Council declared that such acts, "which affect the sovereignty of a Member State and therefore cause international friction, may if repeated endanger international peace and security," and requested the Government of Israel "to make appropriate reparation in accordance with the Charter . . . and the rules of international law." A joint statement of the Government of Israel and Argentina of 3 August 1960 announced their resolve "to view as settled the incident which was caused in consequence of the action of the citizens of Israel, which violated the basic rights of the State of Argentina." *See* Fawcett, The Eichmann Case, *(1962) 38 B.Y.I.L. 181.*

As to the proceedings in Israel, in *A-G of the Government of Israel v Adolf Eichmann (36 I.L.R. 5)*, the accused was on 12 December 1961 convicted on all the counts charged, the Supreme Court on 29 May 1962 dismissing his appeal against both conviction and sentence. The lower court held, in particular, and the appellate tribunal confirmed, that it was of course bound to apply Israeli law and could not entertain the contention that that law conflicted with international law; but that there was no rule of international law precluding a State from assuming jurisdiction over acts done in the territory of another State, nor any rule of that system prohibiting retrospective legislation. Looking at the matter positively, moreover, the crimes which were constituted offences by the law of Israel—the crimes charged, were to be deemed always to have borne the stamp of international crimes, the peculiar international character of which vested in every State authority to try and to punish them. Thus, the crimes against the Jewish people charged were nothing but the most heinous instances of crimes against humanity; war crimes were a well-known category; and the conviction of Eichmann for membership of a hostile organization had not rested on his membership of Nazi organizations alone, but was grounded on the additional fact of his participation in the extermination of Jews. The jurisdiction assumed could further be upheld on the "protective" and "passive personality" principles by reason of the connecting link between the State of Israel and the Jewish people. That the accused had been brought to Israel against his will was no obstacle to the taking of jurisdiction. In particular, any objection there might be existed on the international plane exclusively and was cured by the waiver on the part of Argentina. Nor could any plea that his acts were **acts of State** avail the accused. Even before the Charter of the International Military Tribunal, which excluded it, it was agreed that such a defense was not open to a person charged with a war crime. Nor was the somewhat different defense of superior orders admissible in the absence of any duress upon the accused, compelling him to act as he had acted.

Eisenhower doctrine In response to a request from President Eisenhower dated 5 January 1957, Congress on 7 March 1957 enacted Public Law 85-7, subsequently amended by Public Law 87-195, entitled "Resolution to Promote Peace and Stability in the Middle East." Under this measure, the President "is authorized to undertake, in the general area of the Middle East, military assistance programs with any nation or group of nations of that area desiring such assistance. . . . To this end, if the President determines the necessity thereof, the United States is prepared to use armed forces to assist any nation or group of such nations requesting assistance against armed aggression from any country controlled by international communism" (sec. 2). Action taken under the Eisenhower doctrine is to be reported to Congress (sec. 5). Cf. **War Powers Resolution**.

Eisler Incident *(1949)* The *de cujus*, a German Communist, was arrested on board the Polish vessel *Batory*, then lying in Cowes roads and thus in British territorial waters, on an extradition warrant issued at the request of the United States Government on a charge of perjury. The Chief Metropolitan Magistrate found that the facts of the offence charged (the making of false statements in a sworn application for a visa to enter the United States) did not constitute the offence of perjury within the Extradition Act 1870 and the treaty with the United States, and Eisler was accordingly released. Meanwhile the Government of Poland protested against the arrest on the ground that he was a political refugee, entitled under international law to asylum and protection under the Polish flag, and that a State is not entitled to arrest persons on foreign vessels in territorial waters for purposes of extradition to third States. The United Kingdom Government replied that it was "quite contrary to the practice of States to recognize any principle of asylum in connexion with merchant ships." See notes by Jennings in *(1949) 26 B.Y.I.L. 468* and Dayton in *35 Cor. L.Q. 424 (1950)*.

El Triunfo Co. Arbitration *(United States v. Salvador) (1902) 15 R.I.A.A. 467*. To the claim of American nationals who were shareholders in a Salvador corporation formed to exploit a concession for the construction and operation of a port in El Salvador, submitted to arbitration under the Protocol of 19 December 1901 between the parties *(190 C.T.S. 311)*, in respect of the loss of their investment following an attempt by Salvadorian shareholders to have the company declared bankrupt and executive governmental measures closing the port and granting an incompatible concession to others, it was objected by way of defense that local remedies had not been exhausted. *Held* by the Tribunal set up by the Protocol (2 to 1) that the defense failed because "an appeal to the courts for relief from the bankruptcy would have been in vain after the acts of the executive had destroyed the franchise." The decision is also notable for the exclusion from the award, in accordance with the *compromis* "and by the accepted rules of international courts in such cases" of any element in respect of expected future profits.

Electricity Company of Sofia Case *(1939) P.C.I.J., Ser. A/B, No. 77*. On 26 July 1938, the Government of Belgium instituted proceedings in respect of a failure by Bulgaria in its international obligations by reason of its actions in relation to the company, which was a Belgian concern, relying alternatively on the two States' acceptance of the **Optional Clause** and on the Treaty of Conciliation, Arbitration and Judicial Settlement between them of 23 June 1931 *(137 L.N.T.S. 191)*. The respondent entered a preliminary objection on the grounds that the conditions laid down in the Treaty with respect to the exhaustion of **local remedies** had not been complied with, and further that the dispute arose before the date of the Belgian acceptance, which was restricted to disputes arising after that date "with regard to situations or facts subsequent" thereto, so limiting the area common to both declarations. While finding that the objection based on the Treaty had substance, the Court *held* (9 to 5) that the objection with respect to the declarations of acceptance failed because it was common ground between the parties that the dispute arose only in 1937, well after the dates of the two declarations. It was true that in some sense it arose out of earlier events but it could not be said that it arose "with regard to" any such prior event so that the latter might be said to be its real cause. Following this decision, the Court made an order indicating an interim measure of protection at the suit of Belgium: *P.C.I.J., Ser. A/B, No. 79*. The

German invasion of the Netherlands precluded the trial of the merits and, in 1945, Belgium agreed to the discontinuance of the proceedings: *P.C.I.J., Ser. E, No. 16, 153.*

El-Erian, Abdullah 1920-1982. Egyptian national. Professor, Cairo 1943-61; member, ILC 1957-8 and 1961-78; judge, ICJ 1979-1982. Principal works include *Condominium and'Related Situations in International Law* (1951); co-editor of *International Documents* (in Arabic, 1956).

Elias, Taslim Olawale 1914-1991. Nigerian Attorney-General 1960-72; Minister of Justice 1960-66; Chief Justice 1972-75; professor, Lagos 1966-72; member, ILC 1961-75; judge, ICJ 1976-85; Vice-President, 1979-82; President 1982-85. Major works include *Africa and the Development of International Law* (1972); *Law in a Developing Society* (1973); *The Modern Law of Treaties* (1974).

ELSI Case *(USA v. Italy) 1989 I.C.J. Rep. 15.* By application of 6 February 1987, the United States of America instituted proceeding against Italy in a dispute arising out of the requisition by the Government of Italy of the plant and related assets of *Elettronnica Sicula S.p.A.* (ELSI), an Italian company wholly owned by two American corporations. *Held* by the Chamber of the Court formed to deal with the case, (1) (unanimously) that, in the circumstances, all local remedies had been exhausted and it was for Italy to show that further remedies existed which it had failed to do; (2) (4 to 1) that Italy had not committed any of the breaches, alleged in the application, of the Treaty of Friendship, Commerce and Navigation between the parties signed at Rome on 2 February 1948, or of the Agreement supplementing that Treaty signed by the parties at Washington on 26 September 1951; (3) (4 to 1) that no reparation was payable by Italy to the United States of America.

embargo "This term of Spanish origin (from Spanish *embargar*, Late Latin *imbarricare. . .*) means detention, but in International Law it has the technical meaning of detention of ships in port. Now, as by way of reprisal all acts, otherwise illegal, may be performed, there is no doubt that ships of the delinquent State may be prevented from leaving the ports of the injured State, for the purpose of compelling the delinquent State to make reparation for the wrong done. But the important point is to distinguish *embargo* by way of reprisal from detention of ships for other reasons. (i) It was formerly the practice, when war seemed imminent, for each conflicting State to lay an *embargo* upon the merchant ships of the other in its ports, by way of anticipation and with a view to facilitating capture and condemnation in the event of war breaking out; but this practice is believed to be obsolete, even when the conflicting States are not parties to Hague Convention VI [of 1907 relative to the Status of Enemy Merchant Ships at the Outbreak of Hostilities *(205 C.T.S. 305)*]. (ii) Another kind of *embargo* is the so-called **arrèt de prince**. And (iii) there is *embargo* arising out of the *jus angariae* [see **angary**]": *II Oppenheim 141-2.* Art. 41 of the UN Charter provides for the possibility of arms embargoes (*see,* for example, SC Res. 918 (1994) against Rwanda) and embargoes on international air flights (*see,* for example, SC Res. 748 (1992) against Libya) to be imposed by the UN Security Council as forms of non-military sanctions.

emergency, state of A term of art used by many States to signify a situation of national emergency or civil disorder, whether in the form of a natural disaster or, as has occurred in many States since the terrorist attacks of September 11, 2001 in the US, a threat to national security. When used in relation to civil disorder, real or anticipated, certain **human rights** treaties reserve to States parties the right to derogate from certain human rights. For example, the International Covenant on Civil and Political Rights 1966 *(993 U.N.T.S. 3)* provides that "[i]n time of public emergency which threatens the life of the nation. . . . [States parties] . . . may take measures derogating from their obligations under the present Convention to the extent strictly required by the exigencies of the situation, provided that such measures are not inconsistent with their other obligations under international law and do not involve discrimination solely on the ground of race, colour, sex, language, religion or social origin" (art. 4(1)). However, even when such a derogation is made, certain provisions of the Convention continue to apply (art. 4(2)): the inherent right to life (art. 6), the prohibition on torture (art. 7), on slavery and forced labour (art. 8(1)-(2)), on imprisonment for debt (art. 11), on retrospective criminal laws (art. 15), the right to recognition as a person (art. 16) and to freedom of thought, conscience and religion (art. 18).

enclosed seas   An enclosed, or semi-enclosed, sea is "a gulf, basin or sea surrounded by two or more States and connected to another sea or the ocean by a narrow outlet or consisting entirely or primarily of the territorial seas and exclusive economic zones of two or more coastal States": UN Convention on the Law of the Sea 1982 *(1833 U.N.T.S. 3)*, art. 122. Without altering the rights of coastal States in their **territorial seas** and **exclusive economic zones**, the Convention provides that States bordering such seas "should" cooperate and seek to coordinate their management and exploitation of the living resources, their responsibilities in respect of the marine environment and their scientific research policies (art. 123).

endangered species   *See* **CITES**.

enemy combatants   *See* **unlawful combatants**.

enemy, enemy character   The term "enemy," connoting an adversary in war, is so far a term of international law that it is employed incidentally in the UN Charter (arts. 77, 107). It applies principally to a State. But in prize law, and equally in municipal law in regard to deprivation of liberty on grounds of public safety and to the repression of trade or intercourse with the enemy State, as well as in the context of such rules as that of English common law that an individual alien enemy cannot sue, enemy character is ascribed also to individuals, to bodies corporate and unincorporate, and to vessels and cargoes or goods. There are, however, no generally agreed rules of international law as to what constitutes enemy character in these extended senses.

Individuals. Continental legal systems and notably that of France have for a great while applied nationality as in principle the test of enmity. This approach may be said to be agreeable to the rule that "nationals of a State which is not taking part in the war are considered to be neutrals" recited in art. 16 of Hague Convention V of 1907 with respect to the Rights and Duties of Neutral Powers and Persons in War on Land *(205 C.T.S. 299)*, this neutral or non-belligerent or non-enemy character being lost by active participation in the war through the commission of hostile acts or other conduct favouring one of the belligerents such as voluntary enlistment in his forces (art. 17), though not by the mere furnishing of supplies to, or subscription to loans of, a belligerent by persons resident neither in enemy nor in enemy-occupied territory (art. 18). These sketchy treaty provisions were presumably not intended to involve that a belligerent might not treat as enemies nationals of neutral States resident in enemy territory. For the common law States have traditionally applied as the test of enemy status that of **domicile,** or rather commercial domicile—voluntary residence or carrying on business in enemy territory, irrespective of nationality; and have held, equally, that an enemy national resident in friendly territory is *amy* rather than enemy for purposes of the rule that an enemy cannot sue: *McConnell v. Hector [1803] 3 Bos. & Pul. 113*; *Porter v. Freudenberg [1915] 1 K.B. 857*; *Princess Thurn and Taxis v. Moffit [1915] 1 Ch. 58*. But the resort during World War I to statutory powers to enable the internment of persons "of hostile origin or associations" (cf. Defence of the Realm (Consolidation) Regulations, 1914, reg. 14B, considered in *R. v. Halliday [1917] A.C. 260))* involved a departure from the domicile test and at least a partial adoption of the nationality test. During World War II, equally, a "personal" rather than a "territorial" test was applied in relation to liability to internment in United Kingdom law: Defence Regulations, 1939, reg. 18B, considered in *Liversidge v. Anderson [1942] A.C. 206*. During both wars, moreover, power was taken to designate *inter alios* any person of enemy nationality as an enemy for purposes of the trading with the enemy legislation by inclusion of his name in the "statutory list," sometimes called the "black list": *Trading with the Enemy (Extension of Powers) Act, 1915, s. 1*; *Trading with the Enemy Act, 1939, s. 2 (2)*. At the same time "French legislation departed from the exclusive test of nationality": *II Oppenheim 275*.

Bodies corporate and unincorporated. Civil law countries tended to look to the place of incorporation to determine the character of a corporation. In the first instance the same test was applied by common law courts: *Janson v. Driefontein Consolidated Mines [1902] A.C. 484*. But during World War I this approach was departed from to the extent that the "control test" was so far accepted as to permit the corporate veil to be pierced and the prima facie friendly character of a corporation incorporated in friendly territory to be displaced where it could be shown to be under the direction of individual enemies: *Daimler Co. Ltd. v. Continental Tyre and Rubber Co. (Great Britain) Ltd. [1916] A.C. 207*; *see also Sovfracht (V/O) v. Van Udens Scheepvaart etc. [1943] A.C. 203*. The Trading with the Enemy Act 1939 *(s. 2(1)c)* extended the "control test" to unincorporated bodies. "The French Decree of September 1, 1939, expressly adopted the tests both of registration and control": *II Oppenheim 277*.

Vessels. The fact that a vessel sails under the flag of an enemy State entitles a belligerent to capture and appropriate her *jure belli*. Subjection or submission on the part of a neutral vessel to enemy government control, the taking of a direct part in the war, or resistance to visit or search similarly attracts enemy character: Declaration of London 1909 *(208 C.T.S. 338*; see **London, Declaration of, 1909**), arts. 46, 53 (here declaratory of customary law). This unratified code left open the question whether participation in a trade closed in time of peace had the same effect: art. 57. *See* **rule of war of 1756.** But that article purported to declare the general rule that, save where a transfer of flag was involved, the character of a vessel as either neutral or enemy was determined by the flag it was entitled to fly. Owing to large-scale enemy operations under neutral flags the application of this rule was abandoned by Allied prize courts during World War I in favor of the earlier practice according to which captors might investigate the realities behind ostensible friendly character: *The Hamborn [1919] A.C. 993*. The Declaration of London contained also (arts. 55, 56) rules as to the effect of transfer before or during war to a neutral flag which, however, were not wholly accepted during World War I: *II Oppenheim 284-7*.

Goods. According to customary law, reflected in the Declaration of Paris, 1856, (*see* **Paris, Declaration of**) there was a presumption that all goods on board a vessel fastened with enemy character also had that character. This apart, it was generally recognized that the character of goods depended on the character of their owner. But as there were no generally recognized rules as to the character of individuals (*see* above) there were no such rules as to the character of goods. With respect to goods *in transitu* there has not, again, been any universal understanding as to their treatment and the courts of, notably, the common law countries have been unwilling to apply normal municipal rules as to the time at which the property passes and to substitute such precepts as that "capture is considered as delivery": *The Sally (1795) 3 C.Rob. 300, 302*.

See in general *II Oppenheim 268-89*; McNair & Watts, *The Legal Effects of War* (4th ed.), *passim*; Stone, *Legal Controls of International Conflict* (2nd. Imp. revised), 417f., 451f;

Colombos, *The International Law of the Sea* (6th ed.), 555-70. *See also* **trading with the enemy**.

enforced disappearances *See* **disappearances**.

enforcement The perceived lack of enforcement mechanisms in international law have caused many to argue that international law cannot truly be called law. "[W]ithout mechanisms to bring transgressors into line, international law will be 'law' in name only. . . . This state of affairs, when it occurs, is ignored by too many lawyers who delight in large bodies of rules but often discount patterns of non-compliance." Ratner, "International Law: The Trials of Global Norms," 110 *Foreign Affairs* 65 at 69-70 (1998). Others have argued, on the contrary, that international law is a specific form of law in which "there is neither a similar necessity for sanctions (desirable though it may be that international law should be supported by them) nor a similar prospect of their safe and efficacious use": Hart, *The Concept of Law* (1961), 214. Adherents of so-called **compliance theories** have argued that "enforcement regimes are largely a waste of time" Chayes & Chayes, *The New Sovereignty: Compliance With International Regulatory Agreements* (1995), 2. Nevertheless, it is possible to identify various enforcement mechanisms at work in international law. For example, the UN Charter envisages a system of **collective security** which allows the Security Council to "determine the existence of a threat to the peace, a breach of the peace or an act of aggression" (art. 39); to provide for measures to be taken not involving the use of force (art. 41); and ultimately to authorise the use of force against an offending state (art 42). *See also* **collective measures** and **peace-keeping**. International organizations and multilateral treaties are increasingly resorting to optional and, in some cases, compulsory dispute settlement mechanisms (*see*, for example, the WTO's **Dispute Settlement Understanding**). Individual states have the opportunity to enforce their legal rights in a variety of ways, for example, through the use of peaceful **counter-measures** and, where necessary, by way of forcible **self-defense** measures. However, to a certain extent, international law, as a system of law based upon consent rather than command, is enforced by considerations outside the law itself. "In domestic society individuals observe law principally from fear of consequences, and there are extra-legal consequences that are often enough to deter violation, even where punishment is lacking. . . . In international society, law observance must depend more heavily on these extra-legal sanctions, which means that law observance will depend more closely on the law's current acceptability and on the community's . . . current interest in vindicating it." Henkin, *How Nations Behave* (2nd ed.), 97. Thus, for example, the "broad social concept of **reciprocity**, which States apply on the basis of either short- or long-term considerations of self-interest, may be responsible for a great deal of inter-State cooperation or exchange, outside or in addition to any international legal obligations." Byers, *Custom, Power and the Power of Rules* (1999), 89. *See* further Barker, *International Law and International Relations* (2000), 21-36.

Enterprise The Enterprise is the operating arm of the **International Seabed Authority**.

entry in distress *See* **distress, entry in**.

entry into force According to the Vienna Convention on the Law of Treaties 1969, art. 24, the entry into force of a treaty, which is to be distinguished from the entry of any or all of its stipulations into operation, takes place in such manner and on such date as the treaty may provide or the negotiating States agree, or, failing any such provision or agreement, as soon as all the negotiating States have consented to be bound. Where a State joins the circle of parties after a treaty has already come into force, unless the treaty otherwise provides, it enters into force for that State on that date. Provisions respecting the authentication of the text, the establishment of consent to be bound, the manner or date of entry into force, reservations, depositary functions and other matters necessarily arising before entry into force apply, however, from the time of the adoption of the text of a treaty. *See* Aust, *Modern Treaty Law and Practice* (2000), Chap. 9.

envelope line "Geometrically, the envelope line is the locus of the center of a circle the circumference of which is always in contact with the coastline, that is, with the low-water line or the seaward limits of inland waters. Although often referred to as the 'arcs-of-circles' method, because of the manner in which the line can be drawn (by swinging arcs from points along the coastline), it will occasion less confusion if thought of in its geometric sense, that is, as a derivative of the coastline": Shalowitz, *Shore and Sea Boundaries* (1962), Vol. 1, 171. *See also* **arcs-of-circles**.

environmental law, international "International environmental law, a new branch of international law, is already complex and vast, comprising hundreds of international norms the purpose of which is to protect the earth's living and non-living elements and ecological processes": Kiss and Shelton, *International Environmental Law* (2nd ed.), 1.

environmental modification "As used in Article I, the term 'environmental modification techniques' refers to any technique for changing—through the deliberate manipulation of natural processes—the dynamics, composition or structure of the Earth, including its biota, lithosphere, hydrosphere and atmosphere, or of outer space": art. II, UN Convention on the Prohibition of Military or any Other Hostile Use of Environmental Modification Techniques 1976 *(1108 U.N.T.S. 151)*. *See* **Hostile Environmental Modification Convention**.

Environmental Modification Convention *See* **Hostile Environmental Modification Convention**.

epicontinental sea This is a term employed in some Latin American States to denote an area of sea, co-existensive with the **continental shelf**, over which the coastal State claimed exclusive rights to the area and its mineral and living resources. Such claims provided for freedom of navigation in the area. Claims to an epicontinental sea were made by Argentina from 1946 to 1966, Panama (1946-1967), Costa Rica (1948-1949), Brazil (which claimed only the resources, 1950-1970), Nicaragua (1961-1965) and Uruguay (1969-1970). *See* Szekely, *Latin America and the Development of the Law of the Sea* (1976), Vol. 1, 89-102. *See also* **patrimonial sea**.

equality of States, doctrine of The doctrine that States are equal in law or legal rights, associated often with Vattel but in fact antedating that writer. The doctrine is said to follow from the sovereignty or independence of States and is affirmed in art. 2(1) of the UN Charter: "The Organization is based on the principle of the sovereign equality of all its Members" and in the Declaration of International Law concerning **Friendly Relations** and Cooperation among States in accordance with the Charter of the United Nations of 24 October 1970 (G.A. Res. 2625 (XXV)): "All States enjoy sovereign equality. They have equal rights and duties and are equal members of the international community, notwithstanding differences of an economic, social, political or other nature. In particular sovereign equality includes the following elements: (a) States are juridically equal; (b) each State enjoys the rights inherent in full sovereignty; (c) each State has the duty to respect the personality of other States; (d) the territorial integrity and political independence of the State are inviolable; (e) each State has the right freely to choose and develop its political, social, economic and cultural systems; (f) each State has the duty to comply fully and in good faith with its international obligations and to live in peace with other States." The doctrine is further said to involve, for instance, that the courts of one State have no jurisdiction over another. "Although the abstract principle of state equality is open to certain objections when pressed to extremes, and although it is sometimes departed from in circumstances which require account to be taken of undeniable inequalities in political and economic power . . . the principle of juridical equality is firmly established as one of the basic principles of international law": *I Oppenheim 340*. Cf. **quality of States.**

equidistance/special circumstances rule This is the criterion for delimiting **continental shelf boundaries** promulgated by art. 6(2) of the Geneva Convention on the Continental Shelf 1958 *(499 U.N.T.S. 311)*, whereby, "[i]n the absence of agreement, unless another boundary line is justified by special circumstances, the boundary shall be determined by application of the principle of equidistance from the nearest points of the baselines from which the breadth of the territorial sea of each State is measured." This criterion did not become customary law *(North Sea Continental Shelf Cases 1969 I.C.J. Rep. 3)*; and did not survive as a matter of conventional law into the UN Convention on the Law of the Sea 1982 *(1833 U.N.T.S. 3)*. See **continental shelf boundaries.**

equitable geographical representation *See* **geographical representation.**

equity Judge Hudson said in his separate opinion in the ***Diversion of Waters from the Meuse Case (1937) P.C.I.J., Ser. A/B, No. 70*** at 76: "What are widely known as principles of equity have long been considered to constitute a part of international law, and as such have often been applied by international tribunals. . . . It must be concluded, therefore, that under Article 38 of the [PCIJ] Statute, if not independently of that Article, the Court has some freedom to consider principles of equity as part of the international law which it must apply." There remains uncertainty as to the status and role of equity in international law, largely as to whether it is subsumed within the **general principles of law recognized by civilized nationals** under art. 38(1)(2) of the ICJ Statute, or is a source in its own right, or is an inherent part of the judicial function. In part, this uncertainty arises from the powers, sometimes expressly granted to tribunals, to decide *ex aequo et bono*: see art. 38(3) of the ICJ Statute. The International Court in the ***North Sea Continental Shelf Cases 1969 I.C.J. Rep. 3*** at 48 saw a clear distinction between a decision *ex aequo et bono* and one in which equity played a part: "Whatever the legal reasoning of a court of justice, its decisions must by definition be just, and therefore in that sense equitable. Nevertheless, when mention is made of a court dispensing justice or declaring the law, what is meant is that the decision finds its objective justification in considerations lying not outside but within the rules, and in this field it is precisely a rule of law that calls for the application of equitable principles. There is consequently no question in this case of any decision *ex aequo et bono*." "Considerations of equity form part of the underlying moral basis for rules of law. In this sense equity may be regarded as a material source of law, but not as a formal source, nor in itself constituting a legal rule. It is perhaps in this sense that equity has its widest significance for international law": *1 Oppenheim 43-4*. See the ***Barcelona Traction Case 1970 I.C.J. Rep, 3*** at 48; ***Fisheries Jurisdiction Case 1974 I.C.J. Rep. 3*** at 31-2; ***Tunisia-Libya Continental Shelf Case 1982 I.C.J. Rep. 18***; ***Rann of Kutch Case (1968) 17 R.I.A.A. 1***. See Lauterpacht (E.), *Aspects of the Administration of International Justice* (1991), Chap. 7; Rossi, *Equity and International Law* (1993).

erga omnes "Opposable to, valid against, 'all the world,' i.e. all other legal persons, irrespective of consent on the part of those thus effected." Brownlie, *Principles of Public International Law* (5th ed. 1998), xlvii. The concept emerged from *dicta* in the ***Barcelona Traction Co. Case 1970 I.C.J. Rep. 6*** at 32: "[A]n essential distinction should be drawn between the obligations of a State towards the international community as a whole, and those arising vis-à-vis another State in the field of diplomatic protection. By their very nature the former are the concern of all States. In view of the importance of the rights involved, all States can be held to have a legal interest in their protection; they are obligations *erga omnes*." Like *jus cogens*, to which it is closely related, the *erga omnes* concept is predicated on certain universal standards of State behavior. "One can also distinguish between those rules of international law which, even though they may be of universal application, do not in any particular situation give rise to rights and obligations *erga omnes*. Thus, although all states are under certain obligations as regards the treatment of aliens, those obligations (generally speaking) con only be invoked by the state whose nationality the alien possesses; on the other hand, obligations deriving from the outlawing of acts of aggression, and of genocide, and from the principles and rules concerning the basic rights of the human person, including protection from slavery and racial discrimination, are such that all states have an interest in the protection of the rights involved. . . . There is, however, no generally agreed enumeration of rights and obligations *erga omnes,* and the law in this area is still developing." *I Oppenheim 5*. The *Barcelona Traction* Court provided four examples of obligations to which the concept applied: "the outlawing of acts of aggression, and of genocide, [and] the principles and rules concerning the basic rights of the human person, including protection from slavery and racial discrimination." *See* Ragazzi, *The Concept of International Obligations* Erga Omnes (1997); de Hoogh, *Obligations* Erga Omnes *and International Crimes* (1996).

error   Art. 48 of the Vienna Convention on the Law of Treaties 1969 so far imports the notion of error or mistake in relation to the validity of contracts into international law as to provide that an error relating "to a fact or situation which was assumed by that State to exist at the time when the treaty was concluded and formed an essential basis of its consent to be bound" may be invoked by a State as invalidating such consent provided that the State concerned did not contribute to the error by its conduct or was not in the circumstances on notice of the possibility of error. This rule does not apply to a mere error in wording, which (art. 48(3)) does not affect the validity of a treaty and for the correction of which detailed provision is made by art. 79. As to the very few and dubious cases in which error or mistake has been of any significance, see McNair, *Law of Treaties* (2nd ed.), 211-3. *See* further **treaties, validity**.

espionage   "In the early years of the operation of the Vienna Convention [on Diplomatic Relations 1961], suspicion of spying was the most common reason for declaring a diplomatic agent *persona non grata* or 'requesting his recall.' . . . The end of the Cold War diminished the number of diplomats declared *persona non grata* 'for activities incompatible with their status'—the standard euphemism for espionage. . . . Requests for withdrawals of diplomats from friendly countries on grounds of espionage are extremely rare": Denza, *Diplomatic Law* (2nd ed.), 63-4.

estoppel   (in international law) The principle, alternatively called preclusion in civil law systems, well-known in municipal law that a party which has acquiesced in a particular situation or has taken a particular position with respect thereto cannot later act inconsistently. It has often been referred to in disputes respecting the nationality of claims. *See* the ***Canevaro Case, (1912) 11 R.I.A.A. 397.*** It may be said to have been applied in relation to the acquisition of territorial sovereignty in the ***Eastern Greenland Case, (1933) P.C.I.J., Ser. A/B, No. 53,*** and to have been invoked by the ICJ in the ***Temple Case, (1962) I.C.J., 6, the North Sea Continental Shelf Case (1969), I.C.J. Rep., 3, 26,*** and in the ***I.C.A.O. Council Case, (1972) I.C.J. Rep., 46. See*** Greig, *International Law* (2nd ed.), 34-6, where, however, it is suggested that "estoppel in international law probably has more in common with recognition than it has with municipal notions of estoppel based upon detriment [to another party]." And *see* Bowett, Estoppel before International Tribunals and its Relation to Acquiescence *(1957) 33 B.Y.I.L., 176.*

Estrada Doctrine A doctrine of recognition of governments declared by Don Genaro Estrada, Secretary of Foreign Affairs of Mexico, and published on 27 September 1930. According to the doctrine, recognition "which allows foreign governments to pass upon the legitimacy or illegitimacy of the régime existing in another country . . . is an insulting practice and . . . offends the sovereignty of other nations. . . ." Estrada instructed Mexican diplomats to issue "no declarations in the sense of grants of recognition. . . ." For text of the Estrada Doctrine in English, see *25 A.J.I.L. Supp. 203 (1931)* . In 1969, a U.S. State Department survey found 31 States which indicated that they had abandoned traditional recognition policies and substituted the Estrada Doctrine or some variant thereof: see Galloway, *Recognizing Foreign Governments. The Practice of the United States (1978), App. A.* On 28 April 1980, Lord Carrington, UK Secretary of State for Foreign and Commonwealth Affairs, announced that "we have decided we shall no longer accord recognition to Governments. [W]e shall continue to decide the nature of our dealings with regimes which come to power unconstitutionally in the light of our assessment of whether they are able of themselves to exercise effective control of the territory of the state concerned, and seem likely to continue to do so": *Hansard, Lords,* cols. 1121-2. "In recent years, US practice has been to deemphasize and avoid the use of recognition in cases of changes of governments and to concern ourselves with the question of whether we wish to have diplomatic relations with the new governments": *77 State Dept. Bull. 462 (1977). See also* **recognition, modes of**.

ethnic minorities *See* **minorities**.

eugenics Concerned with improving the quality of human stock, eugenics can be traced back to the work of Francis Galton in late 19th century Britain. It became popular in the UK and US at the turn of the 20th century but its use by the Nazis through compulsory sterilisation and a policy of genetic cleansing of certain ethnic groups led to it being discredited and satirised in Huxley's *Brave New World* (1932). The science of genetics is advancing steadily and a New Eugenics movement has begun. Although not directly outlawed by international law, the Statute of the **International Criminal Court** 1998 *(37 I.L.M. 999)* includes within the definition of **crimes against humanity** forced pregnancy and enforced sterilization as well as "persecutions against any identifiable group or collectivity on political, racial, national, ethnic, cultural, religious gender . . . or other grounds that are universally recognized as impermissible under international law." (art. 7). *See also* Statute of the **ICTY** 1993 *(SC Res. 827 (1993)),* art. 5 and the ICTY case of *Kupreskic and Others*, (2000), paras. 749-54, 761-3.

Euratom *See* **European Atomic Energy Community**.

Euro Officially launched on 1 January 1999 in 11 member States of the European Union (Austria, Belgium, Finland, France, Germany, Ireland, Italy, Luxembourg, Netherlands, Portugal and Spain), the single European currency came into circulation on 1 January 2002 in 12 EU countries, Greece having joined the other 11. All national notes and coins ceased to be legal tender on 28 February 2002. Denmark and Sweden have voted against joining the Euro, while the UK is still considering whether or not to join. The Euro is set to become the world's second biggest global currency behind the dollar. The **European Central Bank**, based in Frankfurt, is charged with governing the currency and setting interest rates. *See* <www.euro.ecb.int>.

EUROCONTROL   The International Convention relating to Cooperation for the Safety of Air Navigation of 13 December 1960 *(523 U.N.T.S. 117)* provided for the establishment of a European system organized jointly by the member States for the control of general air traffic in the upper airspace of which the European Organisation for the Safety of Air Navigation (EUROCONTROL) is the institutional arm. A control center was established at Maastricht in 1972, but coverage was limited to North Germany, Belgium and Luxembourg (and excluding the Netherlands). The Maastricht center in the event proved unpopular with the member States and an attempt was made by the Protocol of 12 February 1981 amending the EUROCONTROL Convention to coordinate Maastricht with the Karlsruhe (Germany) and Shannon Control Centers as well as certain other facilities in Ireland within a looser EUROCONTROL framework. In the 1980s, an amended Convention led to the abandonment of a common air traffic control system and the emphasis was switched to European cooperation instead. This signaled the accession of many new States, including many in Eastern Europe and the creation of the Central Flow Management Unit (CFMU) to make best possible use of the airspace being made available by air traffic control centers throughout Europe. The CFMU became fully responsible for air traffic flow management in relation to all 36 member States in March 1996. A further revision to the EUROCONTROL Convention allowed for the expansion of EUROCONTROL's authority to include airport taxiways and runways, giving rise to the so-called gate-to-gate system. At the same time, the Central European Air Traffic Services Agreement was signed providing for the management of the combined management of the airspace of 8 Central European countries, to be operational by 2007. EUROCONTROL currently has 31 member States. *See* <www.eurocontrol.be>.

European Atomic Energy Community   A further Treaty of Rome of 25 March 1957 *(298 U.N.T.S. 3)*, signed with the **European Economic Community** Treaty, established an Atomic Energy Community. The Treaty establishes a common market in nuclear materials and equipment (arts. 92-95). To ensure supplies and control, the Treaty sets up a system of nuclear safeguards (arts. 77-85) and the Euratom Supply Agency (arts. 53-76) which has a right of option on all ores, source and fissile materials produced in the Community and an exclusive right to conclude supply contracts for materials wherever originating. Special fissile materials are the property of the Community (art. 86). The Community has major research, information and health and safety programmes (Title Two, Chapters I, II and III). On institutional aspects of Euratom, see **European Economic Community** and **European Union**.

European Central Bank   Established on 1 June 1998 and responsible for governing the **Euro** currency and setting interest rates, the European Central Bank is part of the European System of Central Banks (ESCB) which itself is made up of the European Central Bank and the Central Banks of all 15 member States of the European Union. Based in Frankfurt, the Bank is governed by a Governing Council which is made up of 6 members of the Executive Board and the 12 governors of the national central banks in the Euro area. A third body, the General Council comprises the President and Vice-President of the Bank and the governors of the national central banks of all 15 EU member States. *See* <www.ecb.int>.

European Coal and Steel Community   The central creation of the Treaty of Paris of 18 April 1951 *(261 U.N.T.S. 140)*, instituting the Community, is a **common market** (art. 1), introduced for coal, iron and steel in 1953 and for special steels in 1954. The common market entails the abolition of tariffs between member States and the erection of an external tariff towards third countries—both achieved by the end of the transitional period on 8 February 1958. The purpose of the common market was to bring about a fusion of national markets and thereby to contribute to economic expansion, growth of employment and a rising standard of living (art. 2). Based on a liberal free trade economic philosophy aimed at rational distribution of production (art. 2(3)), the common market was bolstered by detailed prohibitions on anti-competitive practices and State subsidies (art. 4), coupled with powers to ensure orderly supply, fair and non-discriminatory prices and equal access to the market, while promoting improved production, trade and working conditions (art. 3).

The Treaty Establishing the European Coal and Steel Community was concluded for a period of 50 year and, having entered into force on 23 July 1952, it expired on 23 July 2002. The net assets and liabilities of the ECSC were handed over to the overall EU budget and a new "Research Fund for Coal and Steel" was established. "It was the ECSC which first established shared, supranational institutions—the basis of the EU as we know it today and a milestone in political history. . . . History will record the founding of the ECSC as a defining moment in the story of mankind's struggle to manage our affairs more effectively, more fairly and more democratically." EU Commission President, Romano Prodi, *Doc. IP/02/898* (19 June 2002). On membership, see **European Union**. On institutions and structure, see **European Community**. *See generally* Reuter, *La Communauté Européenne du Charbon et de l'Acier* (1953); Spierenburg, *The History of the High Authority of the European Coal and Steel Community: Supranationality in Operation* (1994); and works on the EEC and EU. *See* <www.europa.eu.int/ecsc/index.htm>.

European Commission of Human Rights Established by the **European Convention on Human Rights** signed at Rome, 4 November 1950 *(213 U.N.T.S. 221; E.T.S. No.5)*, arts. 19(1), 20-37, 44-47, 58-59. The Commission consisted of a number of members equal to that of the parties to the Convention. The function of the Commission was to "ensure the observance of the engagements" contained in the Convention by receiving complaints alleging breaches from any Party and, where the State against which the complaint was made recognized its competence to receive individual petitions, from "any person, non-governmental organization or group of individuals claiming to be the victim of a violation." The Commission had the power to attempt to secure a friendly settlement and thereafter to draw up a report, containing its opinion, for transmission to the Committee of Ministers of the **Council of Europe**. The Commission was then, within three months of its report, entitled to refer the case to the **European Court of Human Rights**, provided the State against which the complaint was made recognized the jurisdiction of the Court. This two-tier system of referral of breaches of the Convention first to the Commission and then to the Court proved to be very cumbersome and the Commission was abolished by Protocol 11 to the Convention *(E.T.S. 155)* which came into force on 1 October 1998.

European Communities Following the establishment of the **European Coal and Steel Community** (ECSC) by the Treaty of Paris of 18 April 1951, consideration was given successively to the creation of a European Defence Community and of a European Political Community among the six original member States of the ECSC (France, Germany, Italy, Belgium, the Netherlands and Luxembourg). Each of these projects failed upon rejection of the draft treaties by the French National Assembly in 1954. On the defence side, it was instead agreed to extend membership of the **Brussels Treaty Organization** (which already consisted of the UK, France and the Benelux countries) to Germany and Italy, the remodelled organization being restyled **Western European Union**.

On the economic side, the Foreign Ministers of the Six meeting at Messina in June 1955 proposed the establishment of a common market and nuclear materials pool. Following negotiations based on detailed suggestions of the Spaak Committee reporting in 1956, treaties establishing a **European Economic Community** (EEC) and a **European Atomic**

Energy Community (Euratom) were signed in Rome on 25 March 1957. The Treaties came into force, and the Communities into being, on 1 January 1958.

The term European Communities was commonly applied to three organizations: ECSC, EEC and Euratom. But the two remaining institutions, the ECSC having been disestablished in 2002, are now jointly referred to as the **European Community** which constitutes the first Pillar of the **European Union**. On membership, see **European Union**. On institutions and structure, see **European Community**. *See generally*, Craig and De Búrca, *EU Law* (3rd ed.), Chap.1. *See* <www.europa.eu.int>.

European Community The European Community came formally into existence with the creation of the **European Union**. Until then, common reference had been made to the existence of the European Community, either in reference to the European Communities constituted by the **European Economic Community**, **Euratom** and the **European Coal and Steel Community**, or simply in reference to the most important of these institutions, the European Economic Community.

According to the Consolidated Version of the Treaty Establishing the European Community, "The Community shall have as its task, by establishing a **common market** and an economic and monetary union and by implementing common policies or activities referred to in Articles 3 and 4, to promote throughout the Community a harmonious, balanced and sustainable development of economic activities, a high level of employment and of social protection, equality between men and women, sustainable and non-inflationary growth, a high degree of competitiveness and convergence of economic performance, a high level of protection and improvement of the quality of the environment, the raising of the standard of living and quality of life, and economic and social cohesion and solidarity among Member States" (art. 2).

Alongside the free movement of goods (Title I, arts. 25-31), there exists four further freedoms (Title III): freedom for nationals of member States to find work in other member States (arts. 39-42) and for businesses to establish themselves (arts. 43-48) or to provide services in other m ember States (arts. 49-55), as well as free movement of capital and payments (arts. 56-60).

Besides the four freedoms, the Community has a number of general policies transcending specific sectors of economic and social activity: agriculture (arts.32-38); immigration and asylum (arts. 61-69); transport (arts. 69-80); common rules on competition (arts. 81-86); State aids (arts. 87-89); taxation (arts. 90-93); and approximation of laws (arts. 94-97); economic policy (arts. 98-104); monetary policy (arts. 105-110), including the setting up of institutional arrangements including the European System of Central Banks and the **European Central Bank** (arts. 111-115); employment (arts. 125-130); social policy, (arts. 136-145), including the creating of a European Social Fund (arts. 146-148); vocational training, education and youth (arts. 149-150); culture (art. 151); public health (art. 152); consumer protection (art. 153); trans-European networks (arts. 154-156); industry (art. 157); economic and social cohesion (arts. 158-162); research and technological development (arts. 163-173); the environment (arts. 174-176); development cooperation (arts. 177-181); and economic, financial and technical cooperation with third countries (art. 181(a)). The Community has also developed a number of sectoral policies on the basis of general powers in the treaty.

The Community enjoys legal personality (art. 281). It has power to enter into commercial relations (arts. 131-134: Common commercial policy) and to conclude treaties (art. 300). Specific powers are conferred to enter into relations with international organizations (arts. 302-304). The European Court of Justice has held that the Community also enjoys implied powers in external relations by virtue of its responsibilities under the treaties or derived policies *(Case 22/70 ETRA [1971] E.C.R. 263* and *Opinion 1/76, Laying-up Fund, [1977] E.C.R. 741)*. Where the subject-matter of international negotiation or a treaty is shared between the Community and its member States, they are conducted or concluded by the Community and by the member States as separate entities *(Ruling 1/78 Physical Protection [1978] E.C.R. 2871)*.

The Community has bilateral trade agreements with many States. Relations with other trading partners are regulated by tariff concessions negotiated in GATT, by the Community's Generalized System of Preferences or, particularly in relation to State trading countries, by rules adopted unilaterally. By virtue of agreements with the **European Free Trade Agreement** countries, there is tariff-free trade in industrial goods throughout the Community and EFTA. The Community participates in most international trade and commodity organizations. It has observer status in the UN (GA Res. 3208 (XXIX)), ECOSOC and in Specialized Agencies.

The principal institutions of the Community are (art. 7) a European Parliament, a Council, a Commission and a Court of Justice. The Convention on Certain Institutions Common to the European Communities of 25 March 1957 and signed with the Treaties establishing the **European Economic Community** and the **European Atomic Energy Community** provided that the Assembly, Court of Justice and Economic and Social Committee established by each of these Treaties should be constituted in each instance by a body common to both organizations. In the case of the Assembly and the Court of Justice, moreover, the common institution was to supplant the institution established for the **European Coal and Steel Community**. But each organization retained a separate Commission (High Authority in the case of the ECSC) and Council. The latter institutions were in their turn converted into institutions common to the three Communities by the so-called Merger Treaty (Treaty Establishing a Single Council and a Single Commission of the European Communities of 8 April 1967: *O.J. 1967 152/2*).

The Community has legislative power but this is complex and essentially envisages six procedures: Commission acting alone; Council and Commission acting together; Council and Commission in consultation with Parliament; Council and Commission and the cooperation of the Parliament (art. 252); Council, Commission and Parliament acting together (the co-decision procedure)(art. 251); assent procedure.

The principal legislative instruments are regulations which are directly applicable and take effect as laws in the Member States; directives, essentially setting binding goals but leaving it to member States to take legislative action to implement them; and decisions, which are binding on the addressees, but are not normally used as legislative instruments of general character (art. 249). "The Community constitutes a new legal order of international law for the benefit of which the states have limited their sovereign rights . . . and the subjects of which comprise not only Member States but also their nationals": *(Case 26/62 van Gend en Loos, [1963] E.C.R. 1)*. This doctrine implies the supremacy of Community over national law, so that Community law prevails in case of conflict and direct applicability or direct effect in the sense that directly applicable Community rules (principally Treaty articles and regulations) apply without further enactment at national level. Moreover, it creates "individual rights which national courts must protect" *(ibid.)*.

The Court of Justice ensures the observance of the rule of law with powers to oversee the interpretation and application of Community law (art. 220). Direct actions can be brought before the Court by member States, the Council, the Commission and, under certain conditions, interested natural or legal persons. Actions can be brought before the Court by way

of what is in effect an interlocutory reference from a national court for a so-called preliminary ruling on a point of Community law (art. 234). Judgments of the ECJ can be enforced
against the member State concerned by way of pecuniary penalty (art. 228). In the case of
preliminary references, enforcement is as through national enforcement machinery. *See
generally*, Craig and De Búrca, *EU Law* (3rd ed.); Weatherill and Beaumont, *EU Law*
(1999); Hartley, *The Foundations of European Community Law* (7th ed.). On membership, see **European Union**. *See* <www.europa.eu.int>.

European Convention on Human Rights The Convention for the Protection of Human
Rights and Fundamental Freedoms, opened for signature at Rome on 4 November 1950
(213 U.N.T.S. 221; E.T.S. No 5) and has been ratified or acceded to by 45 European States.
The Convention lays down a code of human rights, being mainly civil and political rights,
including the right to life (art. 2), prohibition of torture (art. 3), prohibition of slavery and
forced labor (art. 4), right to liberty and security (art. 5), right to a fair trial (art. 6), no punishment without law (art. 7), right to respect for private and family life (art. 8), freedom of
thought, conscience and religion (art. 9), freedom of expression (art. 10), freedom of assembly and association (art. 11), right to marry (art. 12), right to an effective remedy
(art. 13) and prohibition of discrimination (art. 14). Art. 15 of the Convention provides that
States may derogate from the provisions of the Convention, except arts. 2, 3, 4 and 7, in
times of emergency. The Convention further establishes machinery for the enforcement of
these rights by individuals in the shape of a **European Commission on Human Rights**
(abolished by Protocol No. 11 *(E.T.S.155)* on 1 November 1998) and a **European Court
of Human Rights**.

To date, there have been 13 Protocols to the European Convention, the most recent of
which, Protocol No. 13 *(E.T.S. 187)* of 3 May 2002, seeks to abolish the death penalty in
member States in all circumstances. This Protocol has been acceded to by 41 of the 45
member States. The text of the Convention itself has been amended by the provisions of
Protocol No. 3 *(E.T.S. 45)*, amending arts. 29, 30 and 34 of the Convention, which entered
into force on 21 September 1970, of Protocol No.5 *(E.T.S. 55)*, amending arts. 22 and 34 of
the Convention, which entered into force on 20 December 1970 and of Protocol No. 8
(E.T.S. 118) amending arts. 20, 21, 23, 28, 29, 30, 31, 34, 40, 41 and 43 of the Convention,
which entered into force on 1 January 1990 and comprised also the text of Protocol No. 2
(E.T.S. 44) on the competence to give advisory opinions, which, in accordance with
art. 5(3) thereof had been an integral part of the Convention since its entry into force on 21
September 1970. All provisions which had been amended or added to by these Protocols
were replaced by Protocol No. 11 *(E.T.S. 155)* restructuring the control machinery of the
Convention, as from the date of its entry into force on 1 November 1998. As from that date,
Protocol No. 9 *(E.T.S 140)* amending arts. 31, 44, 45 and 48 of the Convention, which entered into force on 1 October 1994, was repealed and Protocol No. 10 *(E.T.S. 146)*, amending art. 32 of the Convention, has lost its purpose. The remaining Protocols are Protocol
No. 1 *(E.T.S. 9)* which introduced new rights relating to the protection of property,
education, and free elections; Protocol No. 4 *(E.T.S. 46)* which introduced new rights relating to prohibition of imprisonment for debt, freedom of movement, prohibition of expulsion of nationals, and prohibition of collective expulsion of aliens; Protocol No. 6 *(E.T.S.
114)* concerning the abolition of the death penalty; Protocol No. 7 *E.T.S. 117)* which introduced new rights relating to procedural safeguards on the expulsion of aliens, the right of
appeal in criminal matters, compensation for wrongful conviction, the right not to be tried
or punished twice, and equality between spouses; and Protocol No 12 *(E.T.S. 177)*
introducing a general prohibition on discrimination. For a detailed commentary on the
Convention and the Protocols, see Jacobs and White, *The European Convention on*

Human Rights (3rd ed.); Harris, O'Boyle and Warbrick, *Law of the European Convention on Human Rights* (2nd ed.). *See also* <www.coe.int/T/E/Human_rights>.

European Court of Human Rights A tribunal established by the **European Convention on Human Rights** *(213 U.N.T.S. 221; E.T.S. No. 5)*, art. 19. The Court has its seat in Strasbourg and comprises one judge for each member State of the **Council of Europe**. The jurisdiction extends "to all cases concerning the interpretation and application of the Convention which are referred to it as provided in articles 33, 34 and 47." (art. 32); i.e. in matters "specifically referred to it by a High Contracting Party" (art. 33) or "from any person, non-governmental institution or group of individuals claiming to be the victim of a violation by one of the High Contracting Parties of one of the rights set forth in the Convention and the Protocols thereto" (art. 34). The Court also has competence "at the request of the Committee of Ministers [of the **Council of Europe**], [to] give advisory opinions on legal questions concerning the interpretation of the convention and the Protocols thereto": (art. 47). Reports of cases before the Court are to be found in *European Court of Human Rights [Reports]*. *See generally* Jacobs and White, *The European Convention on Human Rights* (3rd ed.); Harris, O'Boyle and Warbrick, *Law of the European Convention on Human Rights* (2nd ed.). The Court's official website is to be found at <www.echr.coe.int> and contains information on pending cases and full text of all its judgments and decisions.

European Economic Area By the Agreement on the European Economic Area signed at Oporto, Portugal, on 2 May 1992 *(O.J. L 1, 3)*, the members of the **European Free Trade Association** and the **European Community** and its member States agreed to strengthen their economic relations in order to establish "a homogeneous European Economic Area" (art. 1). The agreement is concerned primarily with the freedom movement of goods, persons, services and capital (Part III). Equal conditions of competition are assured, essentially by incorporating the European Community's rules (Part IV). The principal organs for the EEA are a Council, "responsible for giving the political impetus in the implementation of this Agreement and laying down the general guidelines for the EEA Joint Committee" (art. 89), and a Joint Committee "to ensure the effective implementation and operation of this Agreement" (art. 92). See Blanchet, Piipponen and Westman-Clement, *The Agreement on the European Economic Area* (1997).

European Economic Community The European Economic Community (EEC) was established in the Treaty of Rome 1957 *(298 U.N.T.S. 3)*. Along with **Euratom** and the **European Coal and Steel Community**, the EEC made up the **European Communities** which in turn became the **European Community** in 1992 at which time it was subsumed within the broader framework of the **European Union**.

European Free Trade Association EFTA was established by the Convention of 4 January 1960 *(370 U.N.T.S. 3)*, as amended. The original members were Austria, Denmark, Norway, Portugal, Sweden, Switzerland and the UK. Austria, Denmark, Portugal, Sweden and the UK subsequently left to join the **European Union**. Iceland joined in 1970 and Liechtenstein in 1991. EFTA's objectives are "to promote continuous and balanced strengthening of trade and economic relations between the Member States with fair conditions of competition, and the respect of equivalent rules within the area of the Association; the free trade in goods; to progressively liberalise the free movement of persons, the progressive liberation of trade in services and of investment; to provide fair conditions of competition affecting trade between the Member States; to open the public procurement markets of the Member States; to provide appropriate protection of intellectual property rights, in accordance with the highest international standards" (art. 2). A free trade area between the members was achieved by 1966 and the EFTA States have jointly concluded free trade agreements with a number of countries worldwide. In 1992, Iceland, Liechtenstein and Norway (but not Switzerland) entered into an Agreement on the **European Economic Area** (EEA) with the **European Community** and each of the EC member States, as well as Finland. The principal organs of EFTA are a Council, consisting of representatives of all members, and adopting measures involving new obligations by unanimous vote, a Secretariat, a Surveillance Authority and a Court. *See* <www.efta.int>.

European integration   There was some public discussion of ideas for the unification of Europe before World War II. The responses to the situation in the post-war world—the **Brussels Treaty Organization** and **NATO** to the Soviet threat; the **Organization for European Economic Co-operation** to the Marshall Plan—were sectoral responses involving intergovernmental co-operation along traditional lines. The **Council of Europe**, a child of the **Brussels Treaty** powers, developed along the same lines. None of them had the effect of integrating the economies of the former Axis powers with the rest of Western Europe. A new "Community approach" was proposed by Robert Schuman, the French Foreign Minister, and Jean Monnet, French *Commissaire au Plan*. The Schuman Plan of 9 May 1950 proposed the placing of the French and German coal and steel industries under the authority of a European organization so that "the solidarity in production thus established will make it plain that any war between France and Germany becomes not merely unthinkable but materially impossible." On the basis of the Schuman Plan, the **European Coal and Steel Community** was established by the Treaty of Paris of 18 April 1951. The common market in coal and steel was to be followed by the establishment of the common market in all other sectors of activity and in atomic energy by the Treaties of Rome of 25 Rome 1957 setting up the **European Economic Community** and the **European Atomic Energy Community**. The three **European Communities** have subsequently been subsumed within the **European Union**, although the ECSC was officially disestablished on 23 July 2002. European integration is evident now in the moves to establish, in the words of art. 1 of the Treaty of European Union, "an ever closer union" within the framework and mechanisms of the European Union. See generally Holland, *European Integration from Community to Union* (1993); Urwin, *The Community of Europe: A History of European Integration* (2nd ed.).

European Investment Bank   Established by art. 266 of the Treaty Establishing the European Community of 25 March 1957, as amended *(298 U.N.T.S. 3)* among the member States of the EC, the Bank has the general purpose of contributing, "by having recourse to the capital market and utilising its own resources, to the balanced and steady development of the common market in the interest of the Community. . . ." (art. 267). Operating on a non-profit-making basis, the Bank gives loans and guarantees to help finance projects in less developed regions, to modernize or convert undertakings or develop fresh activities, to assist in projects of common interest to the States. The Statute of the Bank is a Protocol to the EC Treaty. *See* Bourin, *The European Investment Bank* (2002). *See* <www.eib.eu.int>.

European Laboratory for Particle Research   *See* **CERN**.

European Law of Nations   *See* **Family of Nations**.

European Organization for Nuclear Research   *See* **CERN**.

European Parliament   The Treaty establishing the European Community, as amended (art. 189) provides for a European Parliament (Changed from Assembly by Resolution of

30 March 1962), consisting of representatives of the peoples of the States brought together in the Community, to exercise advisory and supervisory powers. Initially the Parliament consisted of delegates designated by national Parliaments. It is now directly elected by constituencies in the Member States (Decision and Act concerning the Election of the Representatives of the Assembly by Direct Universal Suffrage of 20 September 1976). The Budget Treaty of 22 July 1975 conferred a first real legislative power by giving the Parliament the last and decisive word in the budgetary procedure. However, subsequent amendments to the Treaty, primarily in the form of the Treaty on European Union (the Maastricht Treaty) have given increased legislative powers to the Parliament in the form of the cooperation procedure (art. 252) and the co-decision procedure (art. 251). *See* **European Community**. For membership, *see* **European Union**.

European Payments Union   The EPU, established by agreement of 19 September 1950, provides an automatic mechanism for the multilateral settlement of the accounts of its members. The **Bank for International Settlements** acts as clearing agent for the EPU, the clearing process leaving a single claim or debt towards the EPU for each member (principally **OECD** countries).

European Social Charter   The Charter signed at Turin of 18 October 1961 (in force 26 February 1965) *(529 U.N.T.S. 89)*, is intended to supplement the **European Convention on Human Rights** signed at Rome on 4 November 1950 *(213 U.N.T.S. 221)* by guaranteeing social and economic rights to the peoples of the Contracting Parties: see arts. 1-19 for an enumeration of the rights. Enforcement of its undertakings is secured by the submission of reports to an independent Committee of Experts (art. 25), whose conclusions are transmitted to the Consultative Assembly of the Council of Europe (art. 28) and to a Sub-Committee of the Governmental Social Committee (art. 27), both of whom communicate their views to the Committee of Ministers of the **Council of Europe**, which may make any necessary recommendations (art. 29). An Additional Protocol providing for a System of Collective Complaints *(E.T.S. 158)* was agreed in November 1995. The original Social Charter is being gradually replaced by a much more detailed Revised Social Charter *(E.T.S. 163)* which was opened for signature on 3 May 1996 and which entered into force on 1 July 1999. The Revised Charter is intended to take account of the fundamental social changes which have occurred since the original text was adopted. However, the Charter's enforcement procedures remain the same (Revised Charter, art. C). *See* Harris and Darcy, *The European Social Charter* (2001).

European Space Agency   The Convention of 30 May 1975 *(14 I.L.M. 855 (1975))* which entered into force on 30 October 1980 provides for the establishment of a European Space Agency to be formed out of the European Space Research Organization (ESRO) and the European Organization for the Development and Construction of Space Vehicle Launchers (ELDO). The purpose of the new Agency is "to provide for and to promote, for exclusively peaceful purposes, co-operation among European States in space research and technology and their space applications, with a view to this being used for scientific purposes and for operational space applications systems": art. II. The organs of the Agency are the Council composed of representatives of the 15 Member States (Austria, Belgium, Denmark, Finland, France, Germany, Ireland, Italy, the Netherlands, Norway, Portugal, Spain, Sweden, Switzerland and the United Kingdom) and a Director General assisted by a staff (art. X). The Agency (headquartered in "the Paris area" (art. I (4)) has legal personality (art. XV). It has concluded cooperative arrangements with a number of third countries and has a substantial record of launches to its credit. *See* <www.esa.int>.

European Union The **European Coal and Steel Community** was established in 1951 with six original members: Belgium, France, Germany, Italy, Luxembourg and the Netherlands. 1957 saw the establishment of **Euratom** and the **European Economic Community**. The three institutions came to be collectively known as the **European Communities**. The United Kingdom, Denmark and Ireland acceded to the European Communities on 1 January 1973 and Greece on 1 January 1981, by Treaties of Accession of 22 January 1972 and 28 May 1979 respectively. Norway signed the 1972 Accession Treaty but did not ratify following rejection of membership by a national referendum. Spain and Portugal became members in 1986. In 1992, the Treaty on European Union (TEU) established the European Union. Austria, Sweden, Finland and Norway applied for membership in 1992 with Austria, Sweden and Finland joining in 1995 but again, a national referendum in Norway voted against membership.

The Treaty on European Union envisaged three main Pillars of the European Union: the **European Community** pillar which contained the common institutional framework of the European Communities; the Justice and Home Affairs Pillar; and the **Common Foreign and Security Policy** Pillar. The latter two Pillars existed as intergovernmental aspects of the European Union and did not fall within the institutional framework of the European Community. "Undoubtedly the popular profile of the Community was raised more by the 'Maastricht' debate than by any previous development in the Community's history. Apart from the detailed commitment to full economic and monetary union, the most striking feature of the TEU was the institutional change it brought about, establishing the 'three-pillar' structure for what was henceforth to be the European Union, with the Communities as the first of these pillars and the EEC Treaty being officially renamed the European Community (EC) Treaty." Craig and De Búrca, *EU Law* (3rd ed.), 22. Apart from the establishment of the Union, one of the other main features of the TEU was the introduction of the concept of European citizenship "Every person holding the nationality of a Member State shall be a citizen of the Union." (EC Treaty, art. 17).

A further amendment to the European Union came in the form of the Treaty of Amsterdam (ToA): "The two major features of the ToA . . . were the integration of parts of the former third pillar on Justice and Home Affairs [renamed Police and Judicial Cooperation in Criminal Matter] into the EC Treaty, and the introduction of the provisions on 'closer cooperation.' The ToA known as a 'vanishing Treaty' since its provisions existed only to make amendments to the other existing Treaties and disappeared in effect once these changes were made, was signed in 1997 and came into effect on 1 May 1999." Craig and De Búrca, *supra,* 29-30. Most recently, the Treaty of Nice (TN) was concluded in December 2000, the primary purpose of which was to look towards enlargement and the future of the Union. With regard to enlargement, the European Union is currently negotiating with 12 countries: Cyprus, Czech Republic, Estonia, Hungary, Latvia, Lithuania, Malta, Poland, Slovakia, Slovenia are expected to join in May 2004 and Bulgaria and Romania hope to join by 2007. Turkey has applied for membership but is not currently negotiating accession.

Further future changes are already planned for the European Union. The Laeken summit in 2001 agreed a Declaration on the Future of the Union calling for "deeper and wider debate about the future of the Union." To that end, an Intergovernmental conference is planned for 2004, along with the introduction of a new Constitutional Treaty. *See generally*, Craig & De Búrca, *EU Law* (3rd ed.); Weatherill & Beaumont, *EU* Law (1999); Hartley, *The Foundations of European Community Law* (7th ed.). *See* <www.europa.eu/int>.

EUTELSAT The Agreement on the constitution of a provisional telecommunications satellite organization "Interim Eutelsat" (text *in 11 Annals of Air and Space Law 416*

(1986)) provides for the establishment between European telecommunications administrations, members of the Conférence européenne des postes et telecommunications (CEPT), of a provisional organization, pending the working out of the final organization, for operating commercial satellite telecommunications systems. The Interim Eutelsat was to ensure the establishment, operation and maintenance of the space segments of satellite telecommunications systems and to conclude the necessary agreements to that end, notably with ESA. The organization was composed of an assembly of signatory parties (art. 5) and Councils responsible for the space segment concerned (ECS and MAROTS) (arts. 7 and 8) and a permanent general secretariat (art. 9). The organization was headquartered in Paris (art. 11). EUTELSAT was restructured as a company registered under French Law in 2001. *See* <www.eutelsat.org>.

evacuation Under art. 15 of the Geneva Convention for the Amelioration of the Condition of the Wounded and Sick in Armed Forces in the Field 1949 *(75 U.N.T.S. 31)*, in respect of land forces, and under art. 18 of the Geneva Convention for the Amelioration of the Condition of the Wounded, Sick and Shipwrecked Members of Armed Forces at Sea 1949 *(75 U.N.T.S. 85)*, in respect of armed forces at sea, the parties to a conflict are obliged to search for, and collect, incapacitated members of the armed forces, and to remove them from the area of battle. Under art. 19 of the Geneva Convention relative to the Treatment of Prisoners of War 1949 *(75 U.N.T.S. 135)*, prisoners of war are to be evacuated, as soon as possible after capture, to camps away from the combat zone; such evacuation is to be effected humanely (art. 20).

evidences of international law An ambiguous term, "sometimes referring to the substantive rules set forth in treaties, judicial decisions and State papers, and sometimes being confined to 'documentary sources' in which the substantive rules of international law find expression. *See* Rousseau, I *[Principes Généraux du Droit International Public]*, 109ff. In the first sense 'evidences of international law' is identical with international law and in the second meaning it may be taken literally as indicating where documentary evidence of international law may be found": Briggs, *The Law of Nations*, (2nd ed.), 44. Though the Committee on the Progressive Development of International Law and its Codification, which drew up the plans for the International Law Commission, employed the term (Report, *U.N. Doc. A/AC. 10/51*, para. 18), the Commission's Statute speaks rather of "evidence" of customary law in the context of making such more readily available (art. 24). See Briggs, *The International Law Commission* (1975), 203-4.

ex aequo et bono The International Court of Justice has the power under art. 38(2) of its Statute, if the parties to a contentious case agree, to take a decision, not on the basis of the sources listed in art. 38(1), but *ex aequo et bono*, denoting what is fair, right, reasonable or appropriate. However, while the World Court has not yet been requested to take a decision on this basis, it appears that the Court would not have complete discretion as to the rules to be applied: ***Free Zones Case** (1930) P.C.I.J., Ser. A., No. 24. See also* **equity**. It would, of course, be perfectly possible for an arbitration to be determined on the basis of *ex aequo et bono*. See the ***Heathrow Airport User Charges Arbitration** 1994 Y.B. Com. Arb. 33*, where the tribunal was instructed to decide on the basis of whether airport charges were "just and reasonable" and "equitably apportioned among categories of users."

exchange control, restrictions "It follows . . . that the International Monetary Fund Agreement *[2 U.N.T.S. 40]* draws a distinction between exchange controls and exchange restrictions and seeks to prohibit only the latter—that is, it prohibits only those aspects of domestic exchange control systems which constitute a real interference rather than a mere nuisance to the making of financial settlements. Under the fund regime, therefore, the requirements that a resident trader surrender all foreign exchange proceeds to the official monetary agency or that a resident comply with certain licensing requirements as a prerequisite to the allocation of foreign exchange will not in themselves constitute restrictions. Such requirements may create additional complications for the resident trader, but they do not negate his ability to consummate international transactions owing to the unavailability of exchange": Shuster, *The Public International Law of Money* (1973), 142-3. The IMF publishes an *Annual Report of Exchange Restrictions.*

Exchange of Greek and Turkish Populations Case *(1925) P.C.I.J., Ser. B, No. 10.* By resolution dated 13 December 1924, the League of Nations' Council requested of the PCIJ an advisory opinion as to the meaning of the word "established" in art. 2 of the Lausanne Convention of 1923 respecting the exchange of Greek and Turkish populations *(32 L.N.T.S. 75)*, providing for the exception from the general exchange stipulated for of Greeks "already established before 30 October 1918" in Constantinople and Moslems "established in the region to the east of the frontier line laid down in 1913 [by the Treaty of Bucharest *(218 C.T.S. 322)*]." The Court was further asked what conditions the Greeks referred to were required to fulfil in order to be considered as "established" in this sense. On 21 February 1925, the Court *advised* (unanimously) that the word "established" was to be taken to refer to a situation of fact constituted by residence of a lasting nature, and that residence with the intention of an extended stay at some date previous to 30 October 1918 constituted "establishment," whatever the state of affairs at the date of the Convention.

exchange of notes "The treaty concluded in the form of an exchange of notes or letters is, in modern times, the most frequently used device for formally recording the agreement of two governments upon all kinds of transactions. It takes the form not of a single instrument but of an ordinary exchange of correspondence between the ambassador of one state and the minister for foreign affairs of the state to which he is accredited. The content of the agreement to be recorded . . . will of course have been agreed in advance. The initiating Note sets out the provisions of the proposed agreement and goes on to suggest that if the proposals are acceptable . . . the initiating Note and the . . . reply to that effect should constitute an Agreement. . . . It is not customary to exhibit full powers for an exchange of Notes . . . [n]or are [they] normally subject to ratification. . . . Exceptionally, there may be more than two states concerned in an exchange of notes or letters. Thus the agreement between the Bank for International Settlements, on the one hand, and the United Kingdom, United States and French governments, on the other hand, for the return . . . of gold looted by Germany was constituted by [such an exchange: *140 U.N.T.S. 187*]": *Satow's Guide to Diplomatic Practice* (5th ed.) 247-9. Though the term "exchange of notes" is not employed in the Vienna Convention on the Law of Treaties 1969, such is within the provisions of that Convention by virtue of the definition therein (art. 2(1)(a)) of a "treaty" as meaning "an international agreement concluded between States in written form and governed by international law, whether embodied in a single instrument or in two or more related instruments and whatever its particular designation." *See also* Aust, *Modern Treaty Law and Practice* (2000), 21-2, 355-8.

exclusive economic zone The exclusive economic zone (EEZ) is a concept developed at the Third UN Conference on the Law of the Sea 1974-82, and was intended to accord to every coastal State exclusive jurisdiction and control over the natural resources of the sea-bed, sub-soil and superjacent waters adjacent to its coast to a maximum of 200 miles from the baselines from which the breadth of the territorial sea is measured. *See* arts. 55-75 of the UN Convention on the Law of the Sea 1982 *(1833 U.N.T.S. 3)*. In relation to the **continental shelf**, the zone may extend beyond 200 miles to the outer edge of the continental margin, and a complicated set of formulae has been devised in art. 76 to determine the outer edge of the continental margin. The coastal State's rights in the EEZ are: "(a) sovereign rights for the purpose of exploring and exploiting, conserving and managing the natural resources, whether living or non-living, of the waters superjacent to the sea-bed and of the sea-bed and its sub-soil, and with regard to other activities for the economic exploitation and exploration of the zone, such as the production of energy from the water, currents and winds; (b) jurisdiction as provided for in the relevant provisions of this Contention with regard to: (i) the establishment and use of artificial islands, installations and structures; (ii) marine scientific research; (iii) the protection and preservation of the marine environment; (c) other rights and duties provided for in this Convention": art. 56(1). Other States are to enjoy within the EEZ freedom of navigation, overflight and the laying of submarine cables and pipelines (art. 58). The coastal State alone can establish artificial islands, installations and structures in the EEZ (art. 60). In relation to fish, the coastal State is to determine the maximum sustainable yield (art. 61(3)), to identify its capacity to harvest the entire allowable catch (art. 62(2)) and to afford other States access to any surplus fish stocks (art. 62(2)); *and see* arts. 62 and 69-70 on the States entitled to the surplus stocks, and their obligations). Special provision is made for highly migratory species (art. 64 and Annex I), marine mammals (art. 65), anadromous stocks (art. 66), catadromous species (art. 67), sedentary species (art. 68), the rights of land-locked States (art. 69) and of geographically disadvantaged States (art. 70). *See* O'Connell, *The International Law of the Sea* (1983), Vol. 1, Chaps. 14 and 15; Attard, *The Exclusive Economic Zone in International Law* (1987); Churchill and Lowe, *The Law of the Sea* (3rd ed.), Chaps. 9 and 10.

exclusive fisheries (fishery) zone *See* **fisheries zone**.

executive agreement "While Article II, Section 2, of the Constitution authorizes the President by and with the advice and consent of the Senate to make treaties with foreign nations, it does not say that no other form of international agreement shall be concluded by the President. . . . Agreements concluded by the President which fall short of treaties are commonly referred to as executive agreements. . . . Hundreds of executive agreements . . . have been negotiated. . . . Some of them were concluded under authority of acts of Congress; others were concluded not by specific congressional authorization but in conformity with policies declared in acts of Congress with respect to the general subject matter, such as tariff acts; while still others, particularly with respect to the settlement of claims against foreign governments, were concluded independently of any legislation": Statement by the Legal Adviser, Department of State, before the House Ways and Means Committee, 1 February 1940: Hackworth, *Digest of International Law* (1940), Vol. 5, 397. *Semble*, the expression is confined to United States constitutional practice.

executive certificate "At common law it is the practice of English courts to accept as conclusive statements by or on behalf of the Secretary of State for Foreign and Commonwealth Affairs relating to certain categories of questions of fact in the field of international affairs": *I Oppenheim 1046-7*. But such statement need not originate with the Foreign (and Commonwealth) Office and has on occasion come from other Departments such as the former Colonial, India, Commonwealth Relations and War Offices. Nor is the term "certificate" exact, oral testimony having sometimes been tendered. But the "certificate" as thus broadly understood has been employed with reference to the following types of questions: (1) whether a foreign State has been recognized by the Crown or a foreign government recognized either *de jure* or *de facto* (but cf. now **Estrada Doctrine**); (2) whether a particular territory is under the sovereignty of one foreign State or another; (3) as to the status of a foreign government or State as sovereign or otherwise; (4) as to the status of property the subject-matter of claims by foreign States or sovereigns to immunity from suit; (5) as to whether a state of war exists between the Crown and a foreign State; (6) as to whether a person is or has ceased to be entitled to diplomatic status; (7) as to the existence or extent of British jurisdiction in any foreign place; (8) as to the extent of territory or territorial waters claimed by the Crown; and (9) as to the status of British or allied armed forces. On certain matters, the conclusiveness of such certificates is established by statute: State Immunity Act 1978, s. 21; Diplomatic Privileges Act 1964, s. 4. As to the comparable practice of other States, see **suggestion of State Department**; and see Lyons, Conclusiveness of the Statements of the Executive: Continental and Latin-American Practice, *(1948) 25 B.Y.I.L. 180*; Lyons, The Conclusiveness of the "Suggestion" and Certificate of the American State Department, *(1947) 24 B.Y.I.L. 116*; Vallat, *International Law and the Practitioner* (1966), 51-64. On executive certificates in UK practice, see Warbrick, Executive Certificates in Foreign Affairs: Prospects for Review and Control, *(1986) 35 I.C.L.Q. 138*; Wilmshurst, Executive Certificates in Foreign Affairs: The United Kingdom, *(1986) 35 I.C.L.Q. 157*; *Republic of Somalia v. Woodhouse, Drake and Carey (Suisse) SA (1993) 94 I.L.R. 608*.

exequatur Derived from *exequor* and meaning "let him perform," this term, which originally denoted a temporal sovereign's authorization of a bishop or the publication of a Papal bull, is employed in the context of international law in two different senses: (1) It is the "authorization from the receiving State, whatever the form of this authorization," whereby "the head of a consular post is admitted to the exercise of his functions": Vienna Convention on Consular Relations 1963, art. 12(1). (*See Satow's Guide to Diplomatic Practice* (5th ed.), 213-5); (2) It is equally the designation given in some systems of Continental law to the executive judgment or order whereby a foreign judgment or an arbitral award is rendered locally enforceable. Cf. Wolff, *Private International Law*, 275.

exhaustion of local remedies *See* **local remedies, exhaustion of, rule**.

exile governments For various reasons, a government may not be able to operate from the territory over which it asserts authority (*e.g.*, in cases of belligerent occupation, or where it is in the process of seeking to establish or retain power in a State engaged in civil war), and, with the consent of another State, operates instead from the latter's territory. International law lays down no privileges and immunities for governments in exile, it being for each State to determine the nature and extent of the privileges and immunities of such an entity. "[T]he legal status of an 'exile government' is consequential on the legal condition of the community it claims to represent, which may be a state, belligerent community, or non-self-governing people. *Prima facie* its legal status will be established the more readily when its exclusion from the community of which it is an agency results from acts contrary to the *jus cogens,* for example, an unlawful resort to force": Brownlie, *Principles of Public International Law* (5th ed.), 65. *See also* Talmon, *Recognition of Governments in International Law: With Particular Reference to Exile Governments* (1999).

Expenses of the United Nations Case *1962 I.C.J. Rep. 151*. By Resolution dated 20 December 1961, the UN General Assembly requested of the ICJ an advisory opinion as to whether expenditures authorized by General Assembly resolutions relating to operations in the Congo (ONUC) and to the UN Emergency Force employed in the Middle East (UNEF) constituted "expenses of the Organization" within art. 17(2) of the Charter, objection having been made to the apportionment of these expenditures among all the member States on the ground that the operations to which they related were *ultra vires* the General Assembly and not strictly authorized by the Security Council. On 20 July 1962, the Court *advised* (9 to 5) in a positive sense. The term "expenses of the Organization" in art. 17 meant all the expenses and not just certain types which might be considered "regular expenses." There was no limitation on the budgetary authority of the General Assembly, and in particular no limitation in respect of the maintenance of international peace and security, a matter in relation to which that body, no less than the Security Council, had powers and functions. The argument *contra* relied principally on the reference to "action" in art. 11(2) of the Charter. But this was to be construed as a reference merely to "enforcement action," which was indeed within the exclusive competence of the Security Council under chapter VII, and art. 11(2) had no application when other action of the General Assembly came in question, notably action under arts. 10 or 14. The argument that art. 43, providing for agreements between the Security Council and individual Member States respecting armed assistance, constituted a *lex specialis* derogating from the general rule of art. 17, could not, either, be accepted. It was not to be assumed that all such agreements would necessarily provide that the States concerned would bear the entire cost of the assistance provided for. Further, the resolutions in relation to ONUC clearly authorized the Secretary-General to incur obligations on behalf of the Organization and, following the reasoning in the *Administrative Tribunal of the UN, Effect of Awards Case*, the General Assembly had no alternative but to honor such obligations, which constituted expenses of the Organization within art. 17(2). Equally, the operations of UNEF were manifestly undertaken to fulfill a prime purpose of the UN—the promotion and maintenance of a peaceful international settlement. Hence the expenses thereof were proper expenses of the Organization and had in practice been treated as such from year to year. Nor was there any merit in the argument that the implementation of the Security Council's resolution authorizing ONUC otherwise than by itself determining which States should act was in any way *ultra vires*. The Security Council was not forbidden to act through any instruments it might choose, and both that body and the General Assembly had ratified the action the Secretary-General had, in consultation with the Republic of the Congo, been authorized to take. The fact that the General Assembly had classified the expenses involved as "extraordinary" or "*ad hoc*" did not make them any less expenses of the Organization. The majority opinion, which was "accepted" by the General Assembly by GA Res. 1854A (XVII) of 19 December 1962, is less explicit than the extensive concurring separate opinions of Judges Fitzmaurice, Spender and Spiropoulos.

Expropriated Religious Property Arbitration *(Spain/France/Great Britain/Portugal) (1920) 1 R.I.A.A. 7*. After the proclamation of the Portuguese Republic in October 1910, certain church property belonging to Spanish, French and British nationals was seized by the Portuguese Government. By an agreement of 31 July 1913, supplemented by a further agreement of 13 August 1920, it was agreed to submit claims in respect of the seized property to an arbitral tribunal, the tribunal having complete freedom in settling these claims according to equity and by a single judgment or several judgment. On 2 and 4 September 1920, the Tribunal (Root, Jonkheer, de Savornin, Lohman and Lardy), in a single judgment, *determined* a number of awards which it described as "just and equitable and of a nature to satisfy the respective legitimate expectations of the parties, such that all claims . . . are declared definitively settled and in future extinguished." The Tribunal declared one French claim and 17 Spanish claims inadmissible as the States had not been able to produce satisfactory evidence of the nationality of the claimants.

expropriation   The notion of expropriation, that is, the compulsory divestment of ownership of property for public purposes, is familiar in municipal law. but neither the concept nor the terminology associated with it is precise. "Nationalization" and "socialization" are preferred alternative terms in some circumstances. The process such terms connote is of significance in international law when it is carried out by a State in relation to the property of another or the latter's nationals. The view is tenable that, as respects anything within the territory of a particular State, expropriation is always within the competence of that State as an aspect or incident of its sovereignty, though in some cases it may have an obligation to compensate the dispossessed owner. But it is contended at least sometimes that in certain cases expropriation is *per se* contrary to international law. Among these exceptional cases contended for are: where the property affected is that of a foreign State itself and is used for public purposes; where the taking is effected in breach of an international agreement; where it is effected by way of a measure of reprisal which is excessive; or where the expropriation is discriminatory against particular racial or national groups. Though there is some at least persuasive authority in relation to some of these exceptions they do not all have much coherence. Moreover, the practical distinction between expropriation said to be unlawful *per se* and expropriation which is simply unlawful *sub modo* in the absence of whatever compensation may be due would seem to amount only to this: that the former may involve liability for consequential, in addition to direct loss, unlike the latter; and that a title purporting to be acquired as a result of expropriation which is *per se* unlawful may possibly be denied recognition. *See* in especial Brownlie, *Principles of Public International Law* (5th ed.), 541-2 and the authorities there listed. As to what compensation is due when expropriation is not unlawful *per se,* the case to some extent varies. In some instances, it is argued, no compensation at all is payable. These would include the case where it is otherwise stipulated by treaty, and probably the case where the so-called expropriation involves no more than confiscation of property as a criminal penalty. The case where the taking constitutes a legitimate exercise of the police power of the State, including a measure taken for defense purposes, might also qualify in this regard. Where property is taken under health or planning legislation the case is more doubtful. In any event some measure of compensation is more often than not provided in such cases. And it has been strongly argued by some writers and even held by some tribunals (*see*, for instance the **Canevaro Case**) that the foreign owner of property cannot complain if he is accorded "national treatment" or compensation on the same scale as prescribed for nationals of the expropriating State. A larger body of opinion contends for an "international minimum standard"; see the **Neer Claim** *(1926) 4 R.I.A.A. 60; and see* the Declaration on **Permanent Sovereignty** over Natural Resources, 1962, GA Res. 1803 XVII, (*see also* **Economic Rights and Duties of States, Charter of,** art. 2, GA Res. 3281 (XXIX) of 12 December 1974) which (art. 4) speaks of "appropriate compensation" and contemplates its computation in the last resort by international processes. A considerable number of States, especially "western" States, takes the view that compensation is insufficient unless, in the phrase employed in a well-known exchange between the Governments of the United States and of Mexico in 1938 (Hackworth, *Digest of International Law* (1940), Vol. 3, 655), it be "prompt, adequate and effective." In practice, however, deferred compensation is held not to be unacceptable. Equally, it would appear to be generally recognized that the measure of compensation payable in respect of major measures of expropriation of natural resources is less than in other cases. *See* Brownlie, *op. cit.,* 533-47; White, *Nationalisation of Foreign Property* (1962); Foighel, *Naturalization* (1982); Wortley, *Expropriation in Public International Law* (1958).

expulsion (of aliens) *See* **deportation**.

extensive interpretation "[A] common and not very helpful statement is to the effect that treaties should receive a liberal or extensive rather than a strict construction. It is difficult to assign any precise meaning to this statement, which seems to be little more than an exhortation to the contracting parties to show good faith in the application of the treaty. Like so many of the supposed rules of interpretation, the doctrine of liberal construction seems to overlook the fact that a construction which is liberal as regards one party can easily be illiberal or restrictive as regards the other, with the result that we are no further forward in our attempt to do justice": McNair, *Law of Treaties* (2nd ed.), 385. Though the

Vienna Convention on the Law of Treaties 1969 calls for the interpretation of a treaty "in good faith in accordance with the ordinary meaning to be given to the terms of the treaty in their context and in the light of its object and purpose" (art. 31(1)), it makes no mention of extensive interpretation as such.

extinctive prescription *See* **prescription, extinctive**.

extraditable offence It may be doubted whether this expression (though employed by writers: see *Restatement, Third, of the Foreign Relations Law of the United States*, § 475), descriptive of an offence in respect of which **extradition** may be provided for in legislation or in treaties, is one of art. It is not, for example, employed in British extradition treaties nor in the British Extradition Act 1989, the latter speaking rather of an "extradition crime," defined as a crime "which, if committed in the United Kingdom would constitute an offence punishable with imprisonment for a term of 12 months, or any greater punishment and which, however described in the law of the foreign state, Commonwealth country or colony is so punishable under that law" (s. 2). *See also* **double criminality**.

extradition "The term 'extradition' denotes the process whereby under treaty or upon a basis of reciprocity on state surrenders to another state at its request a person accused or convicted of a criminal offence committed against the laws of the requesting state, such requesting state being competent to try the offender. Normally the alleged offence has been committed within the territory of aboard a ship flying the flag of the requested state, and normally it is within the territory of the surrendering state that the alleged offender has taken refuge. . . . Before an application is made through the diplomatic channel, two conditions are as a rule required to be satisfied: (a) there must be an extraditable person; (b) there must be an extradition crime [see **extraditable offence**]." Shearer, *Starke's International Law* (11th ed.), 317-9. With regard to the extradition crime, the rules of **double criminality** and speciality apply. The latter rules requires that "the requesting state is under a duty not, without the consent of the state of refuge, to try or punish the offender for any other offence that that for which he was extradited." Shearer, *ibid*, 321.

extradition crime *See* **extraditable offence**.

extradition of nationals, principle of non- "Many States, . . . such as France and Germany, never extradite one of their own nationals to a foreign State, but themselves have the power to punish them for grave crimes committed abroad. Other states, including the United Kingdom, have not adopted this principle . . . and . . . make no distinction between their own nationals and other persons whose extradition from their territory is requested.": *I Oppenheim, 955-6*. As to nationality exclusion clauses which, because of the attitude of other States, appear in British extradition treaties reserving a discretion in the matter, *see* Hartley Booth, *British Extradition Law and Procedure* (1981), Vol. 1, 69-73.

Extradition, European Convention on There is no duty in customary international law on States to extradite individuals to strand trial in another State except, perhaps, in relation to crimes of **universal jurisdiction**. "As a result, numerous [bilateral] treaties have been concluded stipulating the cases in which extradition shall take place. . . . There also gradually developed a tendency towards the conclusion of multilateral treaties in certain parts of the world": *I Oppenheim 950*. One of the earliest of such treaties is the European Convention on Extradition 1957 *(359 U.N.T.S. 273)*. Concluded under the auspices of the **Council of Europe**, the Convention obliges the Contracting Parties "to surrender to each other, subject to the provisions and conditions laid down in [the] Convention, all persons against whom the competent authorities of the requesting Party are proceeding for an offence or who are wanted by the said authorities for the carrying out of a sentence or detention order" (art. 1). The Convention defines an **extraditable offence** as an offence "punishable under the laws of the requesting Party and of the requested Party by deprivation of liberty or under a detention order for a maximum period of at least one year or by a more severe penalty (art. 2). The Convention allows for the refusal of extradition if "the offence in respect of which [extradition] is requested is regarded by the requested Party as a **political offence** or as an offence connected with a political offence (art. 3). The taking or attempted taking of the life of a Head of State or member of his family is excluded from the definition of a political offence (art. 3(3)). Furthermore, art. 1 of the Additional Protocol to the European Convention on Extradition 1975 *(E.T.S. No. 86)* specifically excludes from the definition of a political offence, crimes against humanity specified in the Genocide Convention, violations of the Geneva Conventions and comparable violations of the laws of war. There are 45 Contracting Parties to the Convention and 33 States have ratified or acceded to the 1975 Protocol.

Extra-judicial executions   The right to life is enshrined in international law as the most basic and fundamental of human rights (**Universal Declaration on Human Rights** 1948, art. 3; International Covenant on **Civil and Political Rights**, art. 6). In Res. 2393 (XXIII) of 26 November 1968, the UN General Assembly invited governments to ensure that in countries where the death penalty could be imposed, persons accused of capital crimes were given the benefit of the most careful legal procedures and the greatest possible safeguards. In Res. 35/172 of 15 December 1980, on "Arbitrary and Summary Executions", the General Assembly urged member States "to respect as a minimum standard the content of Articles 6, 14 and 15 of the International Covenant on Civil and Political Rights" (para. 1). In Res.1982/35 of 7 May 1982, ECOSOC established the mandate of the Special Rapporteur on extra judicial-summary or arbitrary executions. The role of the Special Rapporteur is detailed in ECOSOC Res. 1997/61 and requires the Special Rapporteur to "continue to examine cases of extra-judicial, summary or arbitrary executions; to respond effectively to information which comes before him . . . ; to enhance further his dialogue with governments; to continue to pay special attention to the extra-judicial, summary or arbitrary executions of women and children . . . and minorities; and . . . where the victims are individuals who are carrying out peaceful activities in defence of human rights and fundamental freedoms; to continue monitoring the implementation of existing international standards on safeguards and restrictions relating to the imposition of capital punishment; to apply a gender perspective in his work." *See also* **capital punishment**.

extra-territorial jurisdiction   *See* **jurisdiction**.

extraterritoriality   "The so-called fiction of 'extra-terrioriality' is an effort to describe diplomatic immunity in terms of a territorial concept of jurisdiction. It is an expression of the doctrine that an ambassador while residing in the State to which he is accredited should be treated, with respect to matters of jurisdiction, as if he were actually residing within the territory of his own State. This theory followed in the wake of the sixteenth century ideas on territorial sovereignty and exaggerated diplomatic privileges." Ogdon, *Bases of Diplomatic Immunity*, 63. While many of the classical writers used the theory in an essentially descriptive manner (*see*, for example, **Grotius**, *De Jure Belli ac Pacis* (1625)), the theory was seized upon in the practice of States which apparently had little difficulty in accepting the residence of the ambassador as foreign soil. However, this willingness to cede control over territory quickly gave rise to the so-called *franchise du quartier* according to which not only the residence of the ambassador but also vast areas of the surrounding city were considered to be foreign territory. These areas often became dens for outlaws and criminals. *See* Adair, *The Exterritoriality of Ambassadors in the Sixteenth and Seventeenth Cen-*

turies (1929). The practical excesses and the reliance by theorists on other bases of diplomatic privileges and immunities such as representative character and functional necessity ultimately led to the abandonment of the theory as a justification for the granting of immunities. "It is perfectly clear that exterritoriality is a fiction which has no foundation either in law or in fact, and no effort of legal construction will ever succeed in proving that the person and the legation buildings of a diplomatic agent situated in the capital of State X are on territory which is foreign from the point of view of the State in question. There are sound practical as well as theoretical reasons for abandoning the term 'exterritoriality'": Report of Special Rapporteur to the Sub-Committee on Diplomatic Immunities of the Committee of Experts for the Progressive Development of International Law, League of Nations Document C.45M.22.1926, *20 A.J.I.L. Supp. 153 (1926)*. The theory was not considered during the drafting of the Vienna Convention on **Diplomatic Relations** 1961 *(500 U.N.T.S. 95)*. *See generally* Denza, *Diplomatic Law*, (2nd ed.); Wilson, *Diplomatic Privileges and Immunities* (1967; *The Abuse of Diplomatic Privileges and Immunities: A Necessary Evil?* (1996).

F

fact-finding Of the role of fact-finding in the process whereby international disputes are settled, Sir Francis Vallat has said (The Peaceful Settlement of Disputes, in *Cambridge Essays in International Law* (1965), 155 at 161): "The exposure and investigation of the facts is also important. In some cases, there may be a genuine lack of understanding of the truth even between the parties themselves which may be dissipated by debate, a detailed report or the dispatch of observers to the spot. Investigation of the facts may be especially valuable where the dispute hovers on the edge of becoming a threat to the peace." In this context, fact-finding is not in itself a method of settling a dispute, but rather a preliminary to settlement by other means. Fact-finding is also used as a component of the procedure whereby supervision is exercised over a State's adherence to international standards. Thus, for example, the European Court of Human Rights is enjoined, if it decides that a petition from an individual is admissible, to ascertain the facts before placing itself at the disposal of the parties with a view to securing a friendly settlement: art. 38 of the European Convention on Human Rights 1950 *((606 U.N.T.S. 267; E.T.S. Nos. 5 and 155))*. The term fact-finding is often used synonymously with inquiry: Merrills, *International Dispute Settlement* (3rd ed.), 44-5. *See* Shore, *Fact-Finding in the Maintenance of International Peace* (1970); Ramcharan, *International Law and Fact-Finding in the Field of Human Rights* (1982).

Falk, Richard A. 1930- . American professor and peace activist. Major works include *Law, War and Morality in the Contemporary World* (1963)*; Legal Order in a Violent World* (1968); *The Status of Law in International Society* (1970); *The Strategy of World Order* (with Mendlovitz, 1966); *The Vietnam War and International Law* (4 vols., 1968-76); *International Law and Organization* (with Black 1968); *The Future of the International Legal Order* (4 vols. 1970-2); *Crimes of War* (with Mendlovitz 1971); *Human Rights and State Sovereignty* (1981); *International Law: A Contemporary Perspective* (with Kratochwil and Mendlovitz, 1985); *Human Rights Horizons: The Pursuit of Justice in a Globalizing World* (2000).

Family of Nations An expression, now obsolete, used to describe the community of sovereign States between which the rules of international law applied. *I Oppenheim 87-8,* eschewing the term in favor of "community" of States (Cf. *I Oppenheim (8th ed.) 48-9*), states the origins of modern international law to be "largely a product of Western European Christian civilization during the 16th and 17th centuries. . . . Whenever a new Christian state made its appearance in Europe, it was received into the existing community of states. But, during its formative period, this international law was confined to those states. In former times European states had only very limited intercourse with states outside Europe, and even that was not always regarded as being governed by the same rules of international conduct as prevailed between European states. But gradually the international community expanded by the inclusion of Christian states outside Europe (such as various

---

former colonies of European states in America as they became independent, foremost of which in the development of international law has been the United States of America) and, during the 19th century at the latest, by the inclusion of non-Christian states."

FAO *See* **Food and Agriculture Organization**.

Fauchille, Paul Auguste Josephe 1858-1926. French lawyer and scholar. Founder (with Pillet) of *Revue generale de droit international public* in 1894. Editor of *La Guerre de 1914—recueil de documents interessant le droit international* (1916 *et seq.*); and *La Guerre de 1914* (1916 *et seq.*). Publications include *Etude de droit international de droit compare* (1882); *La diplomatie francaise et la ligue des neutres de 1780* (1893); *Traitee de droit international public:* vol. I, *La Paix* (1922, 1924 and 1926), vol. II, *Guerre et neutralite* (1921).

Faulkner Claim *(United States v. Mexico) (1926) 4 R.I.A.A. 67*. The individual claimant averred that he had been imprisoned in poor conditions without being informed of the charge against him and denied access to his consul. *Held*, by the Mexican-US General Claims Commission sitting under the Convention of 8 September 1923, that compensation was due in respect of the insufficiency in prison standards which had been proved, the remaining averments not being supported by evidence.

fault *See* **State responsibility**.

Fawcett, Sir James E.S. 1913- . British law professor and sometime member of the European Commission on Human Rights. Principal works include *The British Commonwealth in International Law* (1960)*; International Law and the Uses of Outer Space* (1968); *The Law of Nations* (2nd ed. 1971); *The Application of the European Convention on Human Rights* (1969); *International Economic Conflicts* (1977); *Law and Power in International Relations* (1982).

FCTC *See* **Tobacco Control Convention**.

federal State clause The name given to the provision inserted into the Constitution of the International Labour Organization (art. 19(9); see now art. 19(7): *15 U.N.T.S. 35*) for the treatment in effect of International Labour Conventions as Recommendations in federal States for purposes of legislative implementation. A comparable clause, stipulating that "[w]ith respect to those articles of this Convention that come within the legislative jurisdiction of the federal legislative authority, the obligations of the Federal Government shall to this extent be the same as those of Parties which are not Federal States," but that "[w]ith respect to those articles . . . that come within the legislative jurisdiction of constituent states, provinces or cantons which are not, under the constitutional system of the federation, bound to take legislative action, the Federal Government shall bring such articles with a favourable recommendation to the notice of appropriate authorities of states [etc.]" was adopted as art. 41 of the Convention relating to the Status of Refugees, 1951 *(189 U.N.T.S. 137)*. *See* Looper, 'Federal State' Clauses in Multilateral Instruments, *(1955-6) 32 B.Y.I.L. 162;* Liang, Colonial Clauses and Federal Clauses in United Nations Multilateral Instruments, *45 A.J.I.L. 108 (1951)*; Sörensen, Federal States and the International Protection of Human Rights, *46 A.J.I.L. 195 (1952)*.

federation "[A] union of states in which the control of the external relations of all the member states has been permanently surrendered to a central government so that the only state which exists for international purposes is the state formed by the union. . . .": Brierly, *The Law of Nations* (6th ed.), 128. Cf. **confederation**.

female circumcision *See* **female genital mutilation**.

female genital mutilation (FGM) FGM is a term used to refer to any practice which includes the removal or the alteration of the female genitalia, and is generally of three types: Sunni circumcision, excision (or cliterodectomy) or infibulation (or Pharaonic circumcision). It has been estimated that some 135 million women and girls have been subjected to this practice, mainly in parts of Africa, the Arabian peninsula and Asia. Having no religious basis or other benefit, apart from acceptance into the practising society, and having many and serious health, sexual and psychological consequences, it has been condemned by a number of **NGOs**, particularly **Amnesty International**. The practice contravenes, *inter alia*, (i) the Universal Declaration of Human Rights of 10 December 1948 (GA Res. 217 (III)) as discriminatory against women and girls (art. 2) and as inimical to security of the person (art. 3); (ii) the Convention on the Elimination on all forms of Discrimination against Women 1979 *(1249 U.N.T.S. 13)* as discriminatory (art. 2) and as inimical to the dignity (art. 5(a)) and health rights (art. 11(1)(g)) of women; and (iii) in respect of the girl child, the UN Convention on the Rights of the Child 1989 *(1577 U.N.T.S. 3)* as discriminatory (art. 2), as abusive, neglectful or negligent (art. 19(1) and as a proscribed "traditional practice prejudicial to the health of children" (art. 24(3)). The General Assembly Declaration on the Elimination of Violence against Women of 20 December 1993 (GA Res. 48/104*)*, in condemning violence against women (art. 4), defined such violence as including female genital mutilation (art. 2(a)), and provided that violence against women could not be justified by "any custom, tradition or religious consideration" (art. 4). *See* Rahman and Toubia, *Female Genital Mutilation: A Guide to Laws and Policies Worldwide* (2000).

feminist analysis The feminist analysis of international law has as its central tenet "that the absence of women in the development of international law has produced a narrow and inadequate jurisprudence that has, among other things, legitimized the unequal position of women around the world rather than challenged it": Charlesworth and Chinkin, *The Boundaries of International Law. A Feminist Analysis* (2000), 1. The primary focus of feminist analysis of international law has been the so-called public/private divide. Feminist scholars argue that the focus of international law on the "public" relations of nation-States ignores the private or domestic concerns of women and, consequently banishes women's voices.

Fenwick, Charles G. 1880-1973. American national, professor and scholar. Principal works include *Neutrality Law of the United States* (1913); *Wardship in International Law* (1919); *Types of Restricted Sovereignty* (1919); *Political Systems in Transition* (1920); *Foreign Policy and International Law* (1968).

FGM *See* **female genital mutilation**.

Field, David Dudley 1805-1894. American lawyer, known as "the Father of United States legal reform": Sprague, *Speeches of David Dudley Field,* 3 vols. (1884-90). Major international law works include *Amelioration of the Laws of War Required by Modern Civilization* (1887); *Outlines of an International Code* (1872; 2nd ed., 1876).

filing and recording The Executive Committee to the Preparatory Commission of the UN having recommended that the General Assembly consider the invitation of the sending to the Secretariat for registration and publication of treaties not strictly registrable under art. 102 of the Charter, the Regulations for registration etc. adopted by the General Assembly provided not only (art. 1) for the registration of treaties of members, but also (art. 10) that the Secretariat should further "file and record . . . (a) Treaties or international agreements entered into by the United Nations or by one or more of the specialized agencies; (b) Treaties or international agreements transmitted by a Member . . . which were entered into before the coming into force of the Charter, but which were not included in the treaty series of the League of Nations; (c) Treaties or international agreements transmitted by a party not a member of the United Nations which were entered into before or after the coming into force of the Charter which were [similarly] not [so] included. . . .": GA Res. 97 (I) of 14 December 1946. *See I Oppenheim 1315-7.*

Final Act "The term 'Final Act' (*Acte Final*) is normally used to designate a document which constitutes a formal statement or summary of the proceedings of an international conference, enumerating treaties or related treaty instruments drawn up as a result of its deliberations, together with any resolutions or *voeux* adopted by the conference. The signature of an instrument of this nature does not in itself entail any expression of consent to be bound by the treaties or related treaty instruments so enumerated, which require separate signature and, to the extent necessary, ratification. . . . Exceptionally a treaty instrument designated as a Final Act may constitute a treaty *stricto sensu*": *Satow's Guide to Diplomatic Practice* (5th ed.), 260-2. The term is only mentioned once in the Vienna Convention, in art. 10(b), providing that one of the ways in which the text of a treaty may be established as authentic and definitive is through the incorporation of the text in the Final Act of a conference. The Vienna Convention itself is a good example, being the Final Act of the UN Conference on the Law of Treaties which convened in Vienna in 1968 and 1969.

Finnish Ships Case *(Finland v. United Kingdom) (1934) 3 R.I.A.A. 1479.* By the *compromis* of 30 September 1932, the parties submitted to the arbitration of Judge Bagge the question whether the owners of ships requisitioned for the Allied service and operated by the British Government in 1916-7, who had failed in their endeavors to recover the hire of the vessels and the value of those which had been sunk, "had exhausted the means of recourse placed at their disposal by British law." *Held* that they had done so, notwithstanding that they had not appealed from the finding of the Admiralty Transport Arbitration Board that the vessels had been requisitioned by the Russian rather than the British Government since no appeal lay from that finding of fact and such appealable points of law as there were would obviously have been insufficient to procure a reversal of the decision.

First Generation (human rights) A descriptor for civil and political rights, being the oldest, most widely acknowledged and accepted and least controversial of the three "generations" of human rights. Archetypically, these rights are enumerated in the International Covenant on **Civil and Political Rights** 1966 *(999 U.N.T.S. 171)* and in the European Convention on Human Rights 1950 *(606 U.N.T.S. 267; E.T.S. Nos. 5 and 155).* See also **Second Generation** and **Third Generation** human rights.

First World The rich industrialized States; "the North"; the **developed countries**, *e.g.*, USA, Canada, the States of Western Europe, Australia, New Zealand and Japan. *See also* **Second World, Third World, Fourth World**.

Fischer Williams, Sir John 1870-1947. British writer and practitioner. Principal works include *Chapters on Current International Law and the League of Nations* (1929); *International Change and International Peace* (1932); *Some Aspects of the Covenant of the League of Nations* (1934); *Aspects of Modern International Law* (1939). *See* Jenks, Fischer Williams—The Practitioner as Reformer *(1964) 40 B.Y.I.L. 233.*

fisheries (fishery) zone A zone adjacent to its coast in which a coastal State claims the exclusive right to control the activities of its own, and of foreign, fishing vessels. Until the middle of the 20th century such a zone was thought not to be capable of extension beyond the territorial sea. The Geneva Convention on Fishing and Conservation of the Living Resources of the High Seas, 1958 *(559 U.N.T.S. 285)* conceded, however, the "special interest" of a coastal State in the maintenance of the productivity of the living resources in "any area of the high seas adjacent to its territorial sea" (art. 6(1)) and empowered such a State to adopt unilateral measures of conservation with respect to any such area failing agreement with other interested States (art. 7), besides imposing a duty of appropriate regulation in the case where the coastal State's nationals alone are engaged in fishing the available stocks (art. 3). Neither this nor any other contemporary convention set any limit to the extent of fishery zones, but the decision of the ICJ in the *Fisheries Jurisdiction Cases 1974 I.C.J. Rep. 3* at 175 suggested that a 50-mile zone in which the coastal State claims no more than a preferential right, conceding any historic rights of other States, was not be unacceptable at the date thereof. The specific terms of the UN Convention on the Law of the Sea 1982 *(1833 U.N.T.S)*, art. 57, and the subsequent practice of States, established the acceptance of a 200-mile fisheries zone, subsumed within the exclusive economic zone of the same breadth; *see also* arts. 55-75. *See also* **exclusive economic zone**. *And see generally* Brown, *The International Law of the Sea* (1994), Chap. 10; Churchill and Lowe, *The Law of the Sea* (3rd ed.), Chap. 14.

Fisheries Jurisdiction (Spain v Canada) Case *(Spain v. Canada) 1998 I.C.J. Rep. 58*. Spain filed an application against Canada in respect of the Canadian boarding of a Spanish fishing boat, the *Estai*, in 1995. Canada claimed that the patrol boat was acting under applicable Canadian legislation. Spain claimed that the boarding, and the legislation that Canada invoked to justify it, was an unlawful infringement of the freedom of navigation and fishing on the high seas and of Spain's exclusive jurisdiction on the high seas over vessels flying its flag. Spain's application was based on the Court having jurisdiction under art. 36(2) of its Statute. Canada contested jurisdiction through the reservation in its art. 36(2) declaration in respect of "disputes arising out of or concerning conservation and management measures taken by Canada with respect to vessels fishing in [Northwest Atlantic Fisheries Organization's] Regulatory Area . . . and the enforcement of such measures. *Held* (12 to 5) that, the dispute coming within the terms of the Canadian reservation, the Court lacked jurisdiction to consider the merits.

Fisheries Jurisdiction Cases *(United Kingdom v. Iceland; Federal Republic of Germany v. Iceland)(1972-4)*. The United Kingdom invoked the jurisdiction of the ICJ pursuant to art. 36(1) of the ICJ Statute in reliance upon an Exchange of Notes of 11 March 1961 with the respondent State, resolving a dispute arising out of the latter's assertion in 1958 of a 12-mile exclusive fishing zone upon terms, *inter alia,* that the United Kingdom would no longer object to such a zone in principle and that Iceland should give six months' notice of any further extension of her fisheries jurisdiction, "and, in case of a dispute in relation to such an extension, the matter sh[ould], at the request of either party, be referred to the [ICJ]." The application arose out of a resolution of the Icelandic legislature of 15 February 1972 envisaging the extension of the exclusive zone to 50 miles. Iceland failed to appear in the proceedings. Examining the matter of jurisdiction *ex proprio motu* in accordance with its practice, on 2 February 1972 the Court *held* (14 to 1) that it had jurisdiction. On the face of it, the dispute was exactly within the compromissory clause and this was borne out completely by the negotiations leading up to the Exchange of Notes, which in the circumstances of the case it was desirable to explore. Further, the thesis understood to be entertained by Iceland that a fundamental change of circumstances had rendered earlier agreements on fishery limits no longer applicable could not affect the obligation to submit to the Court's jurisdiction: *1973 I.C.J. Rep. 3*. In response to the parallel application of the

Federal Republic of Germany on the basis of an Exchange of Notes of 19 July 1961 containing an identical jurisdictional clause, Iceland similarly failed to appear and the Court similarly *held* (14 to 1) that it had jurisdiction on the same grounds: *1973 I.C.J. Rep. 49.*

The applicants, the UK and the FRG, having on 19 July and 5 June 1972 respectively, requested the indication of interim measures of protection, the Court, on 17 August 1972 *indicated* (14 to 1) that each of the parties should refrain from any action which might aggravate the disputes and should ensure that no action was taken which might prejudice the rights of its opponent; that Iceland should refrain from enforcing its regulations beyond the 12-mile exclusive zone earlier agreed upon; and that the UK and Germany should limit their annual catches in the disputed areas to specified totals pending final judgment. By further orders of 12 July 1973, following its findings that it had jurisdiction, the Court confirmed these measures: *1973 I.C.J. Rep. 12, 30*; *1973 302, 320.*

In its judgments of 25 July 1974, the Court *found* (10 to 4) (1) that the Regulations of 1972, constituting a unilateral extension of the exclusive fishing rights of Iceland to 50 nautical miles from the baselines specified, were not opposable to the applicant Governments; (2) that in consequence Iceland was not entitled unilaterally to exclude British or German fishing vessels from the areas between the 12-mile and 50-mile limits or to impose restrictions on their activities; and *held* (10-4) (3) that the parties were under mutual obligations to undertake negotiations in good faith for the equitable settlement of their differences concerning their respective rights in the areas in question; and (4) that in these negotiations the parties were to take into account *inter alia* (a) that in the distribution of the fishing resources of these areas Iceland was entitled to a preferential share to the extent of the special dependence of her people on the fisheries; (b) that by reason of its fishing activities there the United Kingdom also had established rights in those resources; (c) the obligation to pay due regard to the interests of other States in the conservation and equitable exploitation thereof; (d) that the rights of the several parties should each be given effect to the extent compatible with the conservation and development of such resources in the areas concerned and with the interests of other States in their conservation and equitable exploitation; (e) their obligation to keep under review such resources and to examine together, in the light of scientific and other available information, such measures as might be required for conservation etc., making use of the machinery established by the North-East Atlantic Fisheries Convention or other agreed means. The Court observed that State practice revealed an increasing and widespread acceptance of the concept of preferential fishing rights for coastal States, although that concept was not compatible with the exclusion of all fishing activity of other States. The Exchange of Notes as a whole, and in particular its final provision as to advance notice of any further extension of regulation, impliedly acknowledged the existence of United Kingdom fishing rights: *1974 I.C.J. Rep. 3.*

The Court was moved by similar considerations in the parallel proceedings at the instance of the German Federal Republic. But its simultaneous judgment in those proceedings is distinguished by the specific negation of the applicant's submission that the respondent was in principle responsible for damage to German fishing vessels interfered with and under an obligation to pay full compensation as being too abstract in the absence of any request that the Court should receive evidence and determine the amount of damages due: *1974 I.C.J. Rep. 175.*

Fitzmaurice, Sir Gerald Gray 1901-1982. Legal Adviser, UK Foreign Office, 1953-60. Member ILC, 1955-60; Rapporteur on Law of Treaties; Chairman, 1959-60. Judge, ICJ, 1960-73. Judge, European Court of Human Rights, 1974-82. Principal work: *The Law and Procedure of the International Court of Justice* (2 vols., 1986). *See* Merrills, *Judge Sir Gerald Fitzmaurice and the Discipline of International Law* (1998).

Five Freedoms Agreement   The International Air Transport Agreement of 1944 *(171 U.N.T.S. 387)* adopted by the Chicago Conference 1944, art. 1, was to have afforded to parties the first five freedoms of the air: the first two being the freedoms of overflight and of landing for non-traffic purposes; the third freedom of putting down passengers and cargo from the flag-State of the carrier; the fourth of taking on board passengers and cargo for carriage back to the flag-State of the carrier; and the fifth freedom of carriage to and from any other contracting State in any of its three forms (*see* **freedoms of the air**). Many countries did not wish to see such broad commercial rights given on a multilateral basis. The Conference therefore also adopted the **Two Freedoms Agreement** embodying the first two freedoms only. The Five Freedoms Agreement failed by virtue of withdrawal by the US in 1946 and more generally for want of ratification. *See* **Chicago Convention**.

flag of convenience   "The flag of any country allowing the registration of foreign-owned and foreign-controlled vessels under conditions which, for whatever reason, are convenient and opportune for the persons who are registering the vessels": Boczek, *Flags of Convenience: An International Legal Study* (1962), 2. States that grant flags of convenience to foreign vessels are referred to as open registry States. As far as international law is concerned, a flag of convenience can be identified as any flag granted in breach of art. 5 of the Geneva Convention on the High Seas 1958 *(450 U.N.T.S. 82)*, which requires "a genuine link between the State and the ship; in particular, the State must effectively exercise its jurisdiction and control in administrative, technical and social matters over ships flying its flag" (cf. **flag State**). The failure of the Geneva Convention to suppress flags of convenience has led to a tightening of the **genuine link** test. While art. 91 of the UN Convention on the Law of the Sea 1982 *(1833 U.N.T.S.)* maintains that there must exist a genuine link between the State and the ships flying its flag, art. 94 specifies in some detail the duties incumbent on a flag State in order for it to exercise effectively its jurisdiction and control in administrative, technical and social matters. These duties include the maintenance of a register (art. 94(2)(a)), the assumption of jurisdiction over the ship, officers and crew (art. 94(2)(b)), the adoption of measures to ensure safety at sea (art. 94(3)), the surveying, equipping, and crewing of ships (art. 94(4)), and the convening of inquiries into marine casualties and incidents of navigation (art. 84(7)). *See* Meijers, *The Nationality of Ships* (1967); Osieke, Flags of Convenience Vessels: Recent Developments, *73 A.J.I.L. 604 (1979)*; Metaxas, *Flags of Convenience* (1985).

flag of truce   Chapter III of the Regulations annexed to the Hague Convention No. IV of 1907 *(205 C.T.S. 277)*, entitled (in translation) "Flags of Truce," provides for the inviolability of any person bearing a white flag and possessing the authority of one of the belligerents to enter into communication with the other: art. 32. A commander is not obliged to receive a flag of truce, and may take all the necessary steps to prevent the envoy taking advantage of his mission to obtain information; in case of abuse, he may detain the envoy temporarily: art. 33. "The parlementaire [envoy] loses his rights of inviolability if it is proved in a clear and incontestable manner that he has taken advantage of his privileged position to provoke or commit an act of treachery": art. 34.

flag State   The State of registration of a ship. The UN Convention of the Law of the Sea 1982 *(1833 U.N.T.S. 3)*, repeating provisions found in virtually identical terms in arts. 4-6 of the Geneva Convention on the High Seas 1958 *(450 U.N.T.S. 82)*, provides that "[e]very State, whether coastal or not, has the right to sail ships under its flag on the high seas" (art. 90); that "[e]ach State shall fix the conditions for the grant of its nationality to ships, for the registration of ships in its territory, and for the right to fly its flag. Ships have the nationality of the State whose flag they are entitled to fly. There must exist a genuine link between the State and the ship; in particular, the State must effectively exercise its jurisdiction and control in administrative, technical and social matters over ships flying its flag" (art. 91(1)); and that "[s]hips shall sail under the flag of one State only and, save in exceptional cases provided for in international treaties or in this Convention, shall be subject to its exclusive jurisdiction on the high seas." (art. 92(1)). The UN Convention on the Law of the Sea 1982 adds more detailed duties on the flag State in order to satisfy the genuine link test (art. 94). *See also* **flag of convenience**. The term flag State is used in reference to the State of registration of aircraft by analogy only; see **aircraft, nationality**.

flag, abuse of "It is [a] universally recognised rule [of customary international law] that warships of every State may seize, and bring to a port of their own for punishment, any foreign vessel sailing under a flag of such state without authority": *I Oppenheim 605*. Art. 110(1) of the UN Convention on the Law of the Sea 1982 *(1833 U.N.T.S. 3)* provides that a warship which encounters a foreign merchant ship on the high seas is not justified in boarding her "unless there is reasonable ground for suspecting: . . . (c) That, though flying a foreign flag or refusing to show its flag, the ship is, in reality, of the same nationality as the warship."

flag, right to fly (1) "Every State shall fix the conditions . . . for the right to fly its flag": UN Convention on the Law of the Sea 1982 *(1833 U.N.T.S. 3)*, art. 91(1). (2) "The mission and its head shall have the right to use the flag and emblem of the sending State on the premises of the mission, including the residence of the head of mission, and on his means of transport": Vienna Convention on Diplomatic Relations 1961 *(500 U.N.T.S. 95)*, art. 20. (3) "The sending State shall have the right to the use of its national flag and coat-of-arms in the receiving State in accordance with the provisions of this Article. The national flag of the sending State may be flown . . . on the building occupied by the consular post and at the entrance door thereof, on the residence of the head of the consular post and on his means of transport when used on official business. In the exercise of the rights accorded by this article regard shall be had to the laws regulations and usages of the receiving State": Vienna Convention on Consular Relations 1963 *(596 U.N.T.S. 261)* art. 29(1)-(3).

Flag, UN The UN Flag was authorized by General Assembly Res. 167(II) of 20 October 1947, which empowered the Secretary-General to draw up regulations for "the regulated use of the flag and the protection of its dignity." *See The United Nations Flag Code and Regulations* (1967).

Flegenheimer Claim *(United States v. Italy) (1958) 25 I.L.R. 9*. On the question whether a claim was that of a "United Nations national" and thus admissible under the compensation and restitution provisions of art. 78 of the Peace Treaty with Italy of 10 February 1947 *(49 U.N.T.S. 3), held,* by the Italy-United States Conciliation Commission, that, being the claim of a person who had lost his original United States nationality through his father's naturalization in Germany and had not regained it upon deprivation of German nationality, it was not admissible. The decision is principally interesting for the remarks of the tribunal upon the argument that, even if the claimant had nominally recovered his American nationality, such would not constitute, in relation to Italy, an effective nationality in the light of the decision of the ICJ in the ***Nottebohm Case*** *1955 I.C.J. Rep. 4*. "The Commission is of the opinion that it is doubtful that the International Court of Justice intended to establish a rule of general international law in requiring, in t[hat] case, that there must exist an effective link between the person and the State in order that the latter may exercise its right of diplomatic protection. . . . The theory of effective or active nationality [is inapplicable] when a person is vested with only one nationality. . . ."

Fletcher incident   On 17 April 1984, WPC Yvonne Fletcher of the Metropolitan Police Force was killed in St James' Square, London. The bullets which killed WPC Fletcher and injured 11 others were fired from the premises of the Libyan People's Bureau, the Libyan diplomatic mission in London. The British Government chose to observe the terms of the Vienna Convention on Diplomatic Relations 1961 *(500 U.N.T.S. 95)* and allowed those present on the premises of the mission to leave the United Kingdom without charge. The incident led to a Parliamentary Review of the United Kingdom's obligations under the Vienna Convention which concluded that "[g]iven the difficulties in the way of achieving any restrictive amendment of the Vienna Convention, and the doubtful net benefit of so doing, it would be wrong to regard amendment of the Vienna Convention as the solution to the problem of abuse of diplomatic immunities": House of Commons Foreign Affairs Committee, First Report, "The Abuse of Diplomatic Immunities and Privileges," *H.C. Paper 127 (1984-85)*, para. 11. *See also* Barker, *The Abuse of Diplomatic Privileges and Immunities: A Necessary Evil* (1996); Higgins, The Abuse of Diplomatic Privileges and Immunities: Recent United Kingdom Experience, *79 A.J.I.L. 641 (1985).*

floating island (territory) theory   A theory, now discredited, that public vessels of any State were to be assimilated with the territory of that State while on the high seas. "[M]en-of-war and other public vessels on the high seas as well as in foreign territorial waters are essentially in every point treated as though they were floating parts of their home State. . . . Again, merchantmen on the high seas are in certain respects treated as though they were floating parts of the territory of the State under whose flag they legitimately sail": *I Oppenheim (8th ed.) 461*. Though this passage was expressly disapproved by the Privy Council in *Chung Chi Cheung v. The King [1939] A.C. 160, 174*, the theory of **exterritoriality** it reflects was accorded some semblance of credence as late as 1927 when, in the ***Lotus Case***, the majority of the PCIJ conceded that "by virtue of the principle of the freedom of the seas, a ship is placed in the same position as national territory," rejecting, however, any rule establishing the exclusive jurisdiction of the flag State: *P.C.I.J., Ser. A, No. 10 at 25.*

Flutie Cases   *(United States v. Venezuela) (1903) 9 R.I.A.A. 148.* In these cases the US-Venezuelan Claims Commission, sitting under the Protocol of 17 February 1903 *(193 C.T.S. 1)*, *held* the claims advanced not to be admissible because, though the claimants or one of them appeared to be the possessor of a certificate of naturalization in due form, this was obtained by fraud, he not having satisfied the statutory requirement as to residence prior to naturalization.

Food and Agriculture Organization (FAO)   This body, the full title of which is Food and Agriculture Organization of the United Nations, was set up as a Specialized Agency of the UN by its Constitution, opened for signature at Ottawa on 19 October 1945 *(12 U.N.T.S. 980)*. The functions of the organization are outlined in art. 1(1) are to "collect, analyse, interpret and disseminate information relating to agriculture and food," agriculture including "fisheries, marine products, forestry and primary forest products." Beyond the original signatories (art. 1(1); see **original member(s)**), the FAO is open to membership by "any nation" that has accepted the obligations of the Constitution (art. 2(2)) and any regional economic integration organization" (art. 2(3)) to associate membership by any territory not responsible for the conduct of its international relations (art. 2(11)), all to be effected by a two-thirds majority in the Conference. The FAO presently has 183 members; and is the first Specialized Agency to admit another international organization, the European Community, as a member. A member can withdraw on one year's notice (art. 19).

The FAO operates through a plenary Conference which determines policy and approves the budget (art. 4(1)) and which has the power, by two-thirds majority, to make recommendations to member States with a view to implementation by national action (art. 4(4)); it also has the power to conclude conventions and agreements (art. 15). The Council, of 49 members elected by the Conference (art. 5(1)), executes the policy determined in the Conference and performs such other functions as are delegated to it. It operates through 8 committees, including committees on commodity problems, fisheries, forestry, agriculture and world food security. A small secretariat supports the activities of these organs (arts. 7 and 8). *See* Marchisio and Di Blasé, *The Food and Agriculture Organization* (1991). *And see* <www.fao.org>.

force   Art. 2(4) of the UN Charter establishes as one of the Principles of the UN the following: "All Members shall refrain in their international relations from the threat or use of force against the territorial integrity or political independence of any State, or in any other manner inconsistent with the purposes of the United Nations." The ambit of the term "force" has been open to almost continual debate since 1945, the point at issue being whether the term was restricted to the use or threat of armed or military force or embraced also political and economic pressure. The **Friendly Relations Declaration** (GA Res. 2625 (XXV) of 24 October 1970), intended as an expansion on art. 2 of the Charter, offers no clear guidance. While not without controversy, it appears that "while various forms of economic and political coercion may be treated as threats to the peace . . . they are not to be treated as coming necessarily under the prohibition in Article 2(4), which is to be understood as directed against the use of armed force": Goodrich, Hambro and Simons, *Charter of the U.N.* (3rd ed.), 49. The prohibition on the use of force should not be confused with the competence of the Security Council to act under Chapter VII of the UN Charter in respect of "threats to the peace, breaches of the peace or acts of aggression" (art. 39), which encompass more than merely the prohibition contained in art. 2(4).

force majeure   Higher force; an occurrence which is beyond human control. Art. 18(2) of the UN Convention on the Law of the Sea 1982 *(1833 U.N.T.S. 3))* permits stopping and anchoring by a foreign vessel exercising the right of **innocent passage** through a State's territorial sea only, *inter alia*, in so far as these "are rendered necessary by force majeure." No liability arises for the owner of a vessel where oil pollution occurs as a result of "a natural phenomenon of an exceptional, inevitable and irresistible character": art. III(2)—of the International Convention on Civil Liability for Oil Pollution 1969 *(973 U.N.T.S. 3)*. Diplomatic and consular personnel, official communications and diplomat bags present in third States due to force majeure are entitled to certain inviolabilities, immunities and protection: Vienna Convention on Diplomatic Relations 1961 *(500 U.N.T.S. 95)*, art. 40(4); Vienna Convention on Consular Relations 1964 *(596 U.N.T.S. 261)*, art. 54(4).

forced labor   Under art. 2(1) of the Convention concerning Forced or Compulsory Labour, adopted at Geneva on 28 June 1930, as amended by the Final Articles Revision Convention 1946 *(39 U.N.T.S. 55)*, forced or compulsory labor "shall mean all work or service which is exacted from any person under the menace of any penalty and for which the said person has not offered himself voluntarily." Excluded from this definition is compulsory military service (art. 2(2)(a)), normal civil obligations (art. 2(2)(b)), penalties imposed by a court (art. 2(2)(c)), action taken in an emergency (art. 2(2)(d)), and minor communal services (art. 2(2)(e)). Forced and compulsory labor was to be suppressed in each member of the ILO within the shortest possible period (art. 1(1)). Art. 5 of the **Slavery** Convention of 25 September 1926 *(60 L.N.T.S. 253)* called on parties to take all necessary measures to prevent forced or compulsory labor from developing into conditions analogous to slavery; and the Supplementary Convention on the Abolition of Slavery, the Slave Trade and Institutions and Practices Similar to Slavery of 7 September 1956 *(266 U.N.T.S. 3)* provided for the complete abolition of, *inter alia*, debt bondage and serfdom. The Convention concerning the Abolition of Forced Labour, adopted at Geneva on 25 June 1957 *(320 U.N.T.S. 291)*, without altering the definition contained in art. 2 of the 1930 Convention, provided that every ratifying member of the ILO is bound "to suppress and not to make use of any form of forced or compulsory labor (a) as a means of political coercion or education or as a punishment for holding or expressing political views or views idealogically opposed to the established political, social or economic system; (b) as a method of mobilizing and using labor for purposes of economic development; (c) as a means of labor discipline; (d) as a punishment for having participated in strikes; (e) as a means of racial, social, national or religious discrimination." Cf. also, International Covenant on Civil and Political Rights 1966 *(999 U.N.T.S. 171)*, art.8(3)(a): "No one shall be required to perform forced or compulsory labour," certain forms of labor being exempted: paras. (b) and (c). Similarly, European Convention on Human Rights 1950 *(606 U.N.T.S. 267; E.T.S. 5 and 55)*, art. 4; American Convention on Human Rights 1969 *(1144 U.N.T.S. 123)*, art. 6. *See* **slavery**. *See* Kloosterboer, *Involuntary Labour Since the Abolition of Slavery* (1960); Jenks, *Human Rights and International Labour Standards* (1960).

forcible transfers The deportation or forcible transfer of civilians was first recognised as a crime against humanity by art. 6 of the Charter of the (Nuremberg) International Military Tribunal 1945 *(82 U.N.T.S. 279)*. The Genocide Convention 1948 *(78 U.N.T.S. 277)*, art. 2(e) established as genocide "forcibly transferring children of [a] group to another group" where the intent was to destroy, in whole or part, that national, ethnic, racial or religious group. The Statute of the International Criminal Court 1998 *(37 I.L.M. 999 (1998))* repeats the Genocide Convention's criminalization of forcible transfers of children as genocide (art. 6(e)); and makes the "deportation or forcible transfer of population" a crime against humanity where committed as part of a widespread or systematic attack against civilians (art. 7(1)d)). For these purposes, forcible transfer is defined as "forced displacement of the persons concerned by expulsion or other coercive acts from the area in which they were lawfully present, without grounds permitted under international law" (art. 7(2)(d)). In modern practice and parlance, forcible transfers are often euphemised as ethnic cleansing.

Foreign Office certificate *See* **executive certificate**.

foreign relations law "Foreign relations law consists of rules of public international law which are binding upon [a State], and such parts of [a State's] law as are concerned with the means by which effect is given to the rules of public international law or which involve matters of concern to [a State] in the conduct of its relations with foreign states and governments or their nationals": Parry and Collier, *Foreign Relations Law*, in 18 *Halsbury's Laws of England* (4th ed.), 717. *See also Restatement, Third, of the Foreign Relations Law of the United States*, § 1.

formal source (of international law) A source "imparting to a given rule the force of law" (such as **treaties**, **custom** or **general principles of law recognized by civilized nations**); to be distinguished from **material sources** which are those from which "the substance [of a rule] is drawn": Parry, *The Sources and Evidences of International Law* (1965), 1. This distinction was drawn in English legal theory on the nature of the sources of law in general and, despite difficulties of application in practice, is still followed in traditional enquiry in international law. For a discussion of the problems involved in categorizing sources of international law and suggestions as to a new direction of enquiry into sources and evidences, *see* Parry, *supra,* 1-27.

forum prorogatum   Originally a term of Roman and Romanesque law descriptive of the case in which a matter is, by agreement of the parties, submitted to a judge other than the judge ordinarily competent in the matter. The term has been adopted into international law to connote the rather different case in which, in the absence of any express agreement between the parties to submit to the jurisdiction of a tribunal, "one of them . . . actually makes an application to the Court, or takes some other step implying consent to, or recognition of, the Court's jurisdiction in the case, and the other party thereupon decides to accept or submit to the jurisdiction, or can be held to have done so, either by signifying acceptance—whether to the first party or to the Court—or by taking some step in the proceedings": Fitzmaurice, *The Law and Procedure of the International Court of Justice* (1986), 506-7. The expression appears to have been first used in relation to the World Court in 1934 in the course of the discussion of revision of the Rules of Court of the PCIJ. As to cases before the PCIJ in which the principle of *forum prorogatum* is said to have been applied, see in particular the ***Mavrommatis Jerusalem Concessions Case (1925) P.C.I.J. Ser. A, No.5***; *and see* Lauterpacht, *The Development of International Law by the International Court* (1982), 104f. The principle is similarly said to have been invoked in the ***Corfu Channel Case (Preliminary Objection) 1948 I.C.J. Rep. 15*** and the ***Asylum (Interpretation of Judgment) Case 1950 I.C.J. Rep. 395***. But *semble* the only case in which the principle is referred to *eo nomine* is the ***Anglo-Iranian Oil Co. Case (Preliminary Objection) 1952 I.C.J. Rep. 93 at 113-4***. *See* Rosenne, *The Law and Practice of the International Court of Justice 1920-96* (1997), 695-725.

Four Freedoms   In an address to Congress on 6 January 1941, President Franklin D. Roosevelt proposed four freedoms for the post-WWII world: "The first is freedom of speech and expression. . . . The second is freedom of every person to worship God in his own way. . . . The third is freedom from want . . . The fourth is freedom from fear. . . ." These freedoms found some expression in 1948 in the **Universal Declaration on Human Rights**. *See* Hargrove, *Franklin D. Roosevelt's Four Freedoms Speech* (2000).

Fourteen Points   In a message to Congress on 4 July 1918, President Woodrow Wilson enumerated fourteen points designed to achieve "the reign of law, based upon the consent of the governed, and sustained by the organized opinion of mankind." In addition to territorial issues, Wilson called for "open covenants of peace" (Point 1), absolute freedom of navigation on the high seas (Point 2), the removal of barriers to trade (Point 3), guarantees to reduce armaments (Point 4), the adjustment of colonial claims (Point 5), and "a general association of nations . . . formed under specific covenants for the purpose of affording mutual guarantees of political independence and territorial integrity to great and small states alike" (Point 14).

Fourth World   The **developing countries** with extremely low *per capita* incomes, little economic growth and few natural resources. This term is frequently used as synonymous with the term least developed countries. *See also* **First World**, **Second World**, **Third World**.

framework treaty   A term used to describe a multilateral treaty which provides a framework for later, more detailed instruments, frequently called protocols, utilized particularly in the environmental area. *See* Aust, *Modern Treaty Law and Practice* (2000), 97.

France-United States Air Transport Arbitration   *See* ***Air Transport Services Agreement Arbitration***.

franchise du quartier Obsolete from the 18th century, *franchise du quartier* inferred a "so-called right of asylum, whereby [diplomatic] envoys claimed the right to grant asylum, within the boundaries of their residential quarters, to any individual who took refuge there": *I Oppenheim* 1076.

Franck, Thomas M. 1931- . Professor, New York 1960-2000. Director of International Legal Program, Carnegie Endowment 1973-79. Principal works include *Verbal Strategy Among the Superpowers* (with Weisband, 1971); *Foreign Policy in Congress* (with Weisband, 1979); *New International Economic Order: International Law in the Making* (1982); *The Power of Legitimacy Among Nations* (1990); *Fairness in International Law and Institutions* (1998); *The Empowered Self: Law and Society in the Age of Individualism* (2000).

Francois, Jean Pierre 1889-1960. Law professor at Rotterdam; sometime Secretary-General of the PCA; member, ILC 1948-1960. Principal works include *Nederland's aandeel in de ontwikkeling van het Volkenrecht* (1920); *Grondlijnen van het Volkenrecht* (1950).

fraud Art. 49 of the Vienna Convention on the Law of Treaties 1969 provides that "[i]f a State has been induced to conclude a treaty by the fraudulent conduct of another negotiating State, the State may invoke the fraud as invalidating its consent to be found by the treaty." *See* McNair, *Law of Treaties* (2nd ed.), 211-3.

free association *See* **associated State(s), self-determination**.

free trade area This term connotes an arrangement whereby a group of States abolishes barriers and restrictions on mutual trade, but each member retains its own tariff and quota system on trade with third countries. Such an arrangement may be for industrial products only or for all products. Examples are, as their names suggest, the **European Free Trade Area** (EFTA) and the **North American Free Trade Area** (NAFTA). Cf. **common market**; **customs union**; **economic union**.

Free Zones of Upper Savoy and District of Gex Case *(France v. Switzerland) (1932) P.C.I.J., Ser. A/B, No. 46.* This case arose out of the arrangements made at the Peace of Vienna for the benefit of the Canton of Geneva, involving the neutralization of a part of Savoy and the withdrawal of both the Sardinian and French customs barriers a certain distance from the political frontiers. These arrangements were to a degree compromised by subsequent events and notably the substitution in 1849 of a Swiss Federal customs regime for the earlier Cantonal system and the transfer of Savoy from Sardinian to French sovereignty pursuant to the Treaty of Turin of 24 March 1860 *(122 C.T.S. 23)*. Accordingly, at the time of the Peace Conference of Paris, France sought their abolition and procured the inclusion in the Treaty of Versailles *(225 C.T.S. 188)* of a provision (art. 435) declaring both the earlier treaty stipulations for the neutralization of Savoy and those concerning the "free zones" to be "no longer consistent with present conditions," taking note of the agreement reached between France and Switzerland for the abrogation of the former and declaring that it was for the same parties to come to an agreement together with a view to settling between themselves the future status of the free zones. The Exchange of Notes between France and Switzerland in the matter was incorporated as an Annex to this article. Switzerland being unable to ratify a further agreement in relation to the free zones owing to its disapprobation by a plebiscite, the parties sought the opinion of the Court as to whether art. 435 and its Annex had in fact, as between them, abrogated, or had had for their object the abrogation of, the original treaty provisions respecting those zones. By its Judgment of

7 June 1932, the Court *held* (6 to 5) in the negative. The article in question said no more than that the parties were to settle the matter by agreement and, in particular, did not lay it down that the abrogation of the old stipulations was a necessary consequence of their inconsistency with present conditions. Even if it were otherwise, the article was not binding on Switzerland, which was not a party to the Treaty, save to the extent that she had accepted it. And that was determined by the annexed Exchange of Notes, whereby she had neither agreed nor yet undertaken to come to a subsequent agreement. The decision is notable for two celebrated observations of the Court. On the question as to whether Switzerland had a contractual right to the benefit of the treaty stipulations of 1815-6, having found that in fact these had "the character of a contract to which Switzerland is a Party" irrespective of formal accession, the Court said further: "It cannot lightly be presumed that stipulations favourable to a third State have been adopted with the object of creating an actual right in its favour. There is however nothing to prevent the will of sovereign States from having this object and effect. The question . . . is one to be decided in each particular case; it must be ascertained whether the States which have stipulated in favour of a third State meant to create for that State an actual right which the latter has accepted as such" (at 147-8). Then, upon the French argument that the institution of Federal customs in 1849 constituted a change of the circumstances on the basis of which the original treaty stipulations were entered into so as to cause their lapse, having found this to fail for lack of proof that the free zones had been established in view of the existence of circumstances which had ceased in 1849 to exist, the Court held it to be "unnecessary . . . to consider any of the questions of principle which arise in connection with the theory of the lapse of treaties by reason of change of circumstances, such as the extent to which the theory can be regarded as constituting a rule of international law, the occasions on which and the method by which effect can be given to the theory if recognized, and the question whether it would apply to treaties establishing rights such as that which Switzerland derived from the treaties of 1815 and 1816" (at 158).

freedoms of the air   The freedoms of the air commonly referred to are: First. Freedom of overflight; Second. Freedom to land for non-traffic and non-commercial purposes (*e.g.*, to refuel); Third. Freedom to discharge passengers and cargo from the **flag State** of the aircraft; Fourth. Freedom to take on board passengers and cargo for carriage to the flag State of the aircraft; Fifth. Freedom of carriage of passengers and cargo between any two contracting States, being one of (i) anterior-point: traffic from a third State through the carrier flag-State to the State granting this freedom, or (ii) intermediate-point: traffic from the carrier flag-State, through a third State to the granting State, or (iii) posterior-point: traffic from the carrier State, through the granting State to a third State; Sixth. Third and fourth freedoms combined, resulting in the carriage of persons or goods between two States *via* the carrier flag-State. This can be an effect of two unrelated bilateral agreements, and can result in traffic between the two non-carrier States; Seventh. Freedom of carriage directly between two foreign States; Eighth. *cabotage*: art. 7 of the **Chicago Convention** on International Civil Aviation 1944 *(15 U.N.T.S. 295)* prohibits an exclusive grant of *cabotage* to another State, though *cabotage* resulting through Sixth Freedom traffic (i.e. via the carrier State) is permitted. This list is, in effect, an amalgamation of the freedoms in the International Air Transport Agreement 1944 *(171 U.N.T.S. 387)*, the "**Five Freedoms Agreement**," and the "**Two Freedoms Agreement**," otherwise the International Air Services Transit Agreement 1944 *(84 U.N.T.S. 389)*. *See* **air navigation**.

freedoms of the sea   A basic freedom of navigation on the high seas, first argued for by **Grotius** in *Mare Liberum* (1609) in opposition to the prevalence of the *mare causum* (closed sea) doctrine prevalent at the time, was established by the end of the 18th century.

The UN Convention on the Law of the Sea 1982 *(1833 U.N.T.S. 32)*, which in its Preamble is declared, at least in part, to codify existing international law, provides in art. 87(1): "Freedom of the high seas is exercised under the conditions laid down by this Convention and by other rules of international law. It comprises, *inter alia*, both for coastal and land-locked States: (a) freedom of navigation; (b) freedom of overflight; (c) freedom to lay submarine cables and pipelines, subject to Part VI [concerning **continental shelf** rights]; (d) freedom to construct artificial islands and other installations permitted under international law, subject to Part VI; (e) freedom of fishing, subject to the conditions laid down in Section 2 [concerning the conservation and management of the living resources]; (f) freedom to conduct scientific research, subject to Parts Vi and XIII [concerning marine scientific research]." Art. 87(1) of the UN Convention on the Law of the Sea 1982 slightly recasts and augments the freedoms established by the Geneva Convention on the High Seas 1958 *(450 U.N.T.S. 82)*, art. 2 of which does not mention (d) or (f) and expresses (c) and (e) differently. *See* Fulton, *The Sovereignty of the Sea* (1911); O'Connell, *The International Law of the Sea* (1984), Vol. II, 792-830; Brown, *The International Law of the Sea* (1994), Chap. 14.

French Claims against Peru Case *(1920) 1 R.I.A.A. 215; 1 I.L.R. 182.* By the *compromis* of 2 February 1914 *(219 C.T.S. 266)*, the parties agreed to submit to the arbitration of a tribunal of the PCA. By its award of 11 October 1920, the Tribunal (MM. Ostertag, Sarrut, Elguera) *held* upon the claim of Messrs Dreyfus Freres et Cie arising out of various contracts for the sale of guano that the respondent State was liable in the amount agreed by the former de facto Pierola Government of Peru during its period of power, a later Peruvian law purporting to annul all internal acts of this regime notwithstanding. Cf. ***Dreyfus Case***.

French Company of Venezuela Railroads Case *(France v. Venezuela) (1903) 10 R.I.A.A. 285.* In this claim before the Commission sitting under the Protocol of 27 February 1903 *(193 C.T.S. 40)*, *held* that the claim succeeded insofar as it related to damage to the Company's undertaking resulting from use of its property by the contending parties to a civil war, but failed insofar as it sought to show that the respondent Government was responsible for the "ruin" of the company. Further, a claim for the rescission of the Company's concession was beyond the jurisdiction of the Commission and rescission in any event would be dependent on the assent of the Government, which was not forthcoming.

Friedmann, Wolfgang G. 1907-1972. Lawyer and judge in Germany, 1933-4. Law teacher in UK, Australia and Canada, 1934-55. Professor, Columbia 1955-72. Major international law works include *What's Wrong with International Law?* (1941); *International Law and the Present War* (1941); *The Allied Military Government in Germany* (1947); *An Introduction to World Politics* (1951; 5th ed. 1965); *The Changing Structure of International Law* (1964); *Cases and Materials on International Law* (with Lissitzin and Pugh 1969); *The Future of the Oceans* (1971).

Friendly Relations Declaration On 24 October 1970, the General Assembly adopted a Declaration of Principles of International Law Concerning Friendly Relations and Cooperation among States in Accordance with the Charter of the United Nations (Res. 2625 (XXV)), setting out, and expanding upon, seven principles in Section 1: 1. "The principle that States shall refrain in their international relations from the threat or use of force against the territorial integrity or political independence of any State, or in any other manner inconsistent with the purposes of the United Nations"; 2. "The principle that States shall settle their international disputes by peaceful means in such a manner that international peace and security and justice are not endangered"; 3. "The principle concerning the duty not to intervene in matters within the domestic jurisdiction of any State, in accordance with the Charter"; 4. "The duty of States to co-operate with one another in accordance with the Charter"; 5. "The principle of equal rights and self-determination of peoples"; 6. "The principle of sovereign equality of States"; 7. "The principle that States shall fulfill in good faith the obligations assumed by them in accordance with the Charter."

Res. 2625 (XXV) expressly provides in Section 3 that "the principles of the Charter which are embodied in this Declaration constitute basic principles of international law," and has been characterized as an authoritative interpretation of the UN Charter: *I Oppenheim 48 and 334*; *Military and Paramilitary Activities in and against Nicarugua Case 1986 I.C.J. Rep. 14* at 89-90; cf. Schwarzenberger, The Principles of the United Nations in International Judicial Perspective, *(1976) 30 Y.B.W.A. 307* at 334-7.

Friends of the Earth International An **NGO**, Friends of the Earth International is a global federation of autonomous environmental organizations campaigning on the most urgent environmental and social issues of our day, while simultaneously promoting a shift toward sustainable development. *See* <www.foei.org>.

frontier Though this term is frequently used interchangeably with the term **boundary**, it perhaps has a less exact significance, connoting a zone with width or depth as well as length.

Frontier Dispute (Benin/Niger) Case *(Benin/Niger) (2002—)*. On 3 May 2002, the parties jointly applied to the ICJ pursuant to the special agreement of 15 June 2001 to have a Chamber of the Court decide a boundary dispute between them. In terms of the special agreement, the Court was requested to determine the course of the boundary between Benin and Niger in the sector of the River Niger; to specify which State owns each of the river's islands, particularly Lété Island; and to determine the course of the boundary in the sector of the River Mekrou. The written pleadings will not be concluded until mid-2004.

Frontier Land Case *(Belgium v. Netherlands) 1959 I.C.J. Rep. 209*. By the Special Agreement of 7 March 1957, the parties submitted to the Court the question of sovereignty over two plots of land on their common frontier which, by a "Communal minute" of delimitation dated 1836, had been declared to belong to the Commune of Baarle-Nassau (an area which remained part of the Netherlands on the separation of the two countries), but which fell to the Belgian Commune of Baerle-Duc under the terms of a descriptive minute drawn up by the boundary commissioners sitting under the Boundary Convention of 8 August 1843 *(95 C.T.S. 223)*. *Held* (10 to 4) that the contention that this result must have been reached by mistake had not been made out; further, that governmental acts done since had not established sovereignty of the Netherlands, being acts of a routine administrative character performed by local officials.

frozen seas "The question has often been raised as to whether, in case the sea is frozen, the sovereignty of the riparian State extends to the limits of the ice forming a continuous pack from the shore, without taking into consideration the normal limits of the territorial sea. . . . From a reasonable point of view, one does not see why a physical accident, often temporary, should be able to produce a change in the legal position of the high seas": Colombos, *International Law of the Sea* (6th ed.), 131. The Antarctic Treaty, 1959 *(402 U.N.T.S. 72)* stipulates that its provisions "shall apply to the area south of 60° South Latitude, including all ice shelves, but nothing [there]in . . . shall prejudice or in any way affect the rights, or the exercise of the rights, of any State under international law with regard to the high seas within the area" (art. 6). The Arctic region, being no more than frozen high seas, is generally regarded as incapable of **occupation** to acquire title; and **sector claims** by adjacent States are not regarded as sound bases for title: *I Oppenheim 692-3.*

full powers The authority of an individual to adopt or authenticate the text of a treaty, or to indicate consent to be bound by a treaty, on behalf of a State. In terms of art. 2(1)(c)(c) of the Vienna Convention on the Law of Treaties 1969, full powers "means a document emanating from the competent authority of a State designating a person or persons to represent the State for negotiating, adopting or authenticating the text of a treaty, for expressing the consent of the State to be bound by a treaty, or for accomplishing any other act with respect to a treaty." *See also* arts. 7 and 8. For examples of full powers, see *Satow's Guide to Diplomatic Practice* (5th ed.), 58-64. *See also* Aust, *Modern Treaty Law and Practice* (2000), Chap. 5.

functional immunity While *stricto sensu* the privileges and immunities of diplomats are functional in that their extent and content are limited to what is necessary to enable diplomats to perform their tasks with the minimum of hindrance, the term functional immunity is usually employed to connote the immunity of international organizations. Art. 105 of the UN Charter provides that the UN is to enjoy in the territory of its members "such privileges and immunities as are necessary for the fulfilment of its purposes." In commenting on what became art. 105, a Committee of the San Francisco Conference indicated that the UN must have "all that could be considered necessary to the realization of the purposes of the Organization, to the free functioning of its organs and to the independent exercise of the functions and duties of their officials": *13 U.N.C.I.O. Docs. 704.* The privileges and immunities of the UN are spelled out in the Convention on Privileges and Immunities of the UN 1946 *(1 U.N.T.S. 15). See also* the Convention on the Privileges and Immunities of the Specialized Agencies of the UN 1947 *(33 U.N.T.S. 261). See* Jenks *International Immunities* (1961); Ahluwalia, *The Legal Status, Privileges and Immunities of the Specialized Agencies and Certain Other International Organizations* (1965).

functional protection Protection afforded by an international organization to its agents to ensure the efficient and independent performance of their duties. Such protection includes the right of the organization to bring an international claim on behalf of its agents for reparation for injuries suffered by them in the performance of their duties in circumstances involving the responsibility of a State. In such a case, "the organization does not represent the agent, but is asserting its own right, the right to secure respect for undertakings entered into towards the organization": ***Reparations for Injuries Case 1949 I.C.J. Rep. 174*** at185. One of the differences between functional protection and **diplomatic protection** is that the latter is based on the nationality of the victim in accordance with the **nationality of claims rule,** while the former is based upon the victim's status as agent of the organization. "Therefore it does not matter whether or not the State to which the claim is addressed regards [the agent] as its own national, because the question of nationality is not pertinent to the admissibility of the claim": *ibid,* 186. Where the injury suffered by the agent engages the interests both of his national State and of the organization, competition between the State's right of diplomatic protection and the organization's right of functional protection might arise. "In such a case, there is no rule of law which assigns priority to the one or to the other, or which compels either the State or the Organization to refrain from bringing an international claim": *ibid,* 185. In such a situation, "although the bases of the two claims are different, that does not mean that the defendant State can be compelled to pay the reparation due in respect of the damage twice over": *ibid,* 186. *See also **Barcelona Traction Case** (Second Phase) 1970 I.C.J. Rep. 38. See also* **State responsibility; reparation.**

functional theory A modern theory of international law which attempts to "correlate the development and study of international law with the satisfaction of certain social functions in the international system," and separates interests seen by States as vital from non-vital interests, with non-vital interests, such as communications, health, safety, being entrusted to international rules": Falk, *The Status of Law in International Society* (1970), 463. One of the chief exponents of this theory is **Friedmann**; see his *The Changing Structure of International Law* (1964).

fundamental (human) rights Within the large and expanding scope of human rights, some rights are claimed to be of particular significance. Support for this view comes from the non-derogability of some rights. Thus, the International Covenant on Civil and Political Rights 1966 *(999 U.N.T.S. 171)*, art. 4(1), permits derogation "in time of public emergency threatening the life of the nation," but proceeds (art. 4(2)) to prohibit any derogation from arts. 6 (right to life), 7 (torture), 8(1) and (2) (slavery and servitude), 11 (imprisonment for breach of contractual obligation), 15 (retroactive criminal liability), 16 (recognition as a person in law) and 18 (freedom of thought, conscience and religion). Likewise, the 4 Geneva Conventions on the Laws of War 1949 *(75 U.N.T.S. 3, 85, 135 and 287)*, by common art. 3, prohibit "at any time and in any place whatsoever" violence to life and person, including murder, mutilation and torture, hostage taking, outrages on personal dignity and executions without proper judicial determination in non-international conflicts. From these instruments, it is argued that there exist some fundamental human rights: van Boven, Distinguishing Criteria of Human Rights, in Vasak and Alston, *The International Dimension of Human Rights* (1982), Vol. 1, 43. However, the trend, particularly among human rights NGOs, is to regard all human rights as "universal, indivisible and interdependent and interrelated" to be treated "in a fair and equal manner, on the same footing and with the same emphasis" Vienna Declaration and Programme of Action on Human Rights 1993 *(UN Doc. A/CONF.157/23,* Part I, para. 5).

fundamental change of circumstances *See **rebus sic stantibus**.*

fundamental freedoms *See **human rights**.*

fundamental guarantees Art. 75 of the Protocol to the 1949 Geneva Convention IV Relating to the Protection of Victims of International Armed Conflict of 12 December 1977 *(1125 U.N.T.S. 3)*, titled "Fundamental guarantees" sets out the basic rights to be accorded to persons in the power of a party to a conflict who does not benefit from other provisions of the 1949 Convention or 1977 Protocol. Such persons "shall be treated humanely in all circumstances and shall enjoy, as a minimum, the protection provided by this Article without any adverse distinction based upon race, colour, sex, language, religion or belief, political or other opinion, national or social origin, wealth, birth or other status, or on any other similar criteria. Each Party shall respect the person, honour, convictions and religious practices of all such persons." The guarantees are against violence, including murder, torture, corporal punishment and mutilation, outrages upon personal dignity, hostage-taking and collective punishments, whether committed by military or civilian personnel (art. 75(2)). There are further fundamental guarantees in respect of arrest and detention, prosecution, sentencing, women's detention accommodation.

Fundamental Principles and Rights at Work In June 1998, the International Labour Conference adopted a Declaration on Fundamental Principles and Rights at Work *(37 I.L.M. 1233 (1998))*, applicable to all members of the ILO whether or not they have ratified the relevant conventions, setting out four fundamental principles: "(a) freedom of association and the effective recognition of the right of collective bargaining; (b) the elimination of all forms of forced or compulsory labour; (c) the effective abolition of child labour; (d) the elimination of discrimination in respect of employment and occupation" (art. 2). These obligations are subject to follow-up procedures (art. 4).

Fundamental Rules of International Humanitarian Law in Armed Conflicts Because of the complexity of the laws of war, the Red Cross published seven Fundamental Rules of International Humanitarian Law in Armed Conflicts in 1978 *(1978 I.R.R.C. 248)*. These Rules have no official or legal status, and were not intended so to have; they are distillations of principles in the four 1949 Geneva Conventions, the two 1977 Protocols and the relevant customary law. They are nonetheless instructive as a comprehensive and intelligible articulation of international humanitarian law:

1. Persons *hors de combat* and those who do not take a direct part in hostilities are entitled to respect for their lives and physical and moral integrity. They shall is all circumstances be protected and treated humanely without any adverse distinction.

2. It is forbidden to kill or injure an enemy who surrenders or who is *hors de combat*.

3. The wounded and sick shall be collected and cared for by the party to the conflict which has them in its power. Protection also covers medical personnel, establishments, transports and *materiel*. The emblem of the red cross (red crescent, red lion and sun) is the sign of such protection and must be respected.

4. Captured combatants and civilians under the authority of an adverse party are entitled to respect for their lives, dignity, personal rights and convictions. They shall be protected against all acts of violence and reprisals. They shall have the right to correspond with their families and to receive relief.

5. Everyone shall be entitled to benefit from fundamental judicial guarantees. No one shall be responsible for an act he has not committed. No one shall be subjected to physical or mental torture, corporal punishment or cruel or degrading treatment.

6. Parties to a conflict and members of their armed forces do not have an unlimited choice of methods and means of warfare. It is prohibited to employ weapons or methods of warfare of a nature to cause unnecessary losses or excessive suffering.

7. Parties to a conflict shall at all times distinguish between the civilian population and combatants in order to spare civilian population and property. Neither the civilian population nor civilian persons shall be the object of attack. Attacks shall be directed solely against military objectives."

Fundamental Rights of the European Union, Charter on Signed at Nice on 7 December 2000 *(O.J. C 64/1; 40 I.L.M. 266 (2001))*, this Charter is divided into chapters promulgating rights in the areas of Dignity (Chapter I), Freedoms (II), Equality (III), Solidarity (IV), Citizens' Rights (V), Justice (VI) and General Provisions (VII). Described as reaffirming rights already existing in the constitutional traditions and international obligations of the member States, including the **European Convention on Human Rights** and the **European Social Charter**, and being necessary "to strengthen the protection of fundamental rights in the light of changes in society, social progress and scientific and technological developments by making those rights more visible" (Preamble), the Charter reiterates rights already contained in other instruments, while carefully keeping within the delegated competence of the **European Union** (art. 51). The Charter is addressed to the institutions of the EU and to the member States, which are to "respect the rights, observe the principles and promote the application thereof in accordance with their respective powers" (art. 51(1)).

G

Gabcikovo-Nagymaros Case *(Hungary v. Slovakia) 1997 I.C.J. Rep. 68.* Instituted on 2 July 1993 by Special Agreement signed at Brussels on 7 April 1993, the case arose out of the signature, on 16 September 1977, by Hungary and Czechoslovakia of a treaty concerning the construction and operation of the Gabcikov-Nagymaros system of locks on a 200 kilometre stretch of the Danube between Bratislava and Budapest. The joint investment envisaged by the Treaty was essentially aimed at the production of hydroelectricity, the improvement of navigation and protection from flooding along the banks. As a result of intense criticism the project had generated in Hungary, the Hungarian Government initiated a process of suspensions of work on 13 May 1989, which eventually led to their abandonment at Nagymaros on 27 October 1989. During this period, negotiations continued between the parties and Czechoslovakia put forward an alternative plan (Variant C) which included the construction of an overflow dam. In November 1991, the Czechoslovak Government began work on Variant C and on 19 May 1992, the Hungarian Government transmitted to the Czechoslovak Government a *note verbale* terminating the 1977 Treaty with effect from 25 May 1992. On 15 October 1992, Czechoslovakia began work to enable the Danube to be closed and, starting on 23 October, proceeded to dam the river. On 1 January 1993, Slovakia became an independent State.

Held 1(A) (14 to 2) that Hungary was not entitled to suspend, and subsequently abandon, in 1989, the works on the Nagymaros Project and on the part of the Gabcikovo Project for which the Treaty of 16 September 1977 and related instruments allocated responsibility to it; (B) (9 to 6) that Czechoslovakia was entitled to proceed, in November 1991, to the "provisional solution" as described in terms of the Special Agreement; (C) (10 to 5) that the Czechoslovakia was not entitled to put into operation, from October 1992, this "provisional solution"; (D) (11 to 4) that the notification on 11 May 1992, of the termination of the Treaty of 16 September 1977 and related instruments by Hungary did not have the legal effect of terminating them; 2(A) (12 to 3) that Slovakia, as successor to Czechoslovakia, became a party to the Treaty of 16 September 1977 as from 1 January 1993; (B) (13 to 2) that Hungary and Slovakia must negotiate in good faith in the light of the prevailing situation, and must take all necessary measures to ensure the achievements of the Treaty of 16 September 1977, in accordance with such modalities as they may agree upon; (C) (13 to 2) that, unless the Parties otherwise agree, a joint operation régime must be established in accordance with the Treaty of 16 September 1977; (D) (12 to 3) that, unless the parties otherwise agree, Hungary shall compensate Slovakia for the damage sustained by Czechoslovakia and Slovakia on account of its suspension and abandonment of works for which it was responsible; and Slovakia shall compensate Hungary for the damage it has sustained on account of the putting into operation of the "provisional solution" by Czechoslovakia and its maintenance in service by Slovakia; (E) (13 to 2) that the settlement of accounts for the construction and operation of the works must be effected in accordance with the relevant provisions of the Treaty of 16 September 1977 and related instruments, taking due account of such measures as will have been taken by the parties in application of Points 2(B) and (C) of the present operative paragraph.

Vice-President Weeramantry appended a separate opinion addressing certain questions of environmental law including sustainable development and the principle of continuing environmental impact assessment. On 3 September 1998, Slovakia filed a request for an additional judgment in the case because of the unwillingness of Hungary to implement the judgment of the Court. The request for an additional judgment has been transmitted to Hungary and remains outstanding.

García-Amador, Francisco V. 1917-93. Cuban national and law professor, teaching at Panama, Havana and Miami; member, ILC 1954-61, president 1956, special *rapporteur* on State Responsibility 1955-61; Legal Counsel, OAS, 1962-77. Principal works include *The Exploitation and Conservation of the Resources of the Sea* (2nd ed. 1958); *Principios de Derecho Internacional que rigen la Responsibilidad* (1963); Draft Articles on the Responsibility of States for Injuries to . . . Aliens, in Garcia-Amador, Sohn and Baxter, *Recent Codification of the Law of State Responsibility for Injuries to Aliens* (1974); *The Andean Legal Order, a New Community Law* (1978); *The Changing Law of International Claims* (1984).

Garner, James Wilford 1871-1938. US national. Professor, Illinois 1904-38. Principal international law works include *International Law and the World War* (1920); *Recent Developments in International Law* (1925); *American Foreign Policies* (1928).

gas *See* **Asphyxiating, Poisonous or other Gases, etc., Protocol Prohibiting the Use in War of.**

Gelbtrunk Claim *See **Rosa Gelbtrunk Claim**.*

General Act "A General Act became familiar in the later nineteenth century and early twentieth century as the name of a treaty of general import negotiated at an international conference. The Berlin Conference of 1885 drew up a series of detailed provisions . . . united in a single General Act, itself clearly constituting a treaty. . . . Further instances of the use of the term are the General Act of the Brussels Conference of 1890 relative to the African Slave Trade; the General Act of the Algeciras Conference of 1906 relative to the Affairs of Morocco; . . . the General Act for the Pacific Settlement of International Disputes of 28 April 1949 *[71 U.N.T.S. 101]* . . .": Satow, *Guide to Diplomatic Practice* (5th ed.), 259-260.

General Act of Geneva, 1928 Properly styled the General Act for the Pacific Settlement of International Disputes, this instrument *(93 L.N.T.S. 343)* instituting methods of conciliation for political disputes and providing for the ultimate submission to arbitration of disputes not settled by such methods has been revised pursuant to General Assembly Res. 268 (III) of 28 April 1949 to take account of the disappearance of the League of Nations and the PCIJ. The revised text *(71 U.N.T.S. 101)* entered into force on 20 September 1950 but applies only as between six States. In the ***Nuclear Tests Cases** 1974 I.C.J. Rep. 253, 457*, Australia and New Zealand invoked art. 17 of the original text, read with arts. 36(1) and 37 of the ICJ Statute as founding the jurisdiction of the Court. *See also* the ***Aegean Sea Continental Shelf Case** 1978 I.C.J. Rep. 3. See generally* Brierly, The General Act of Geneva, 1928, *(1930) 11 B.Y.I.L. 119*; Merrills, The International Court of Justice and the General Act of 1928, *[1980] C.L.J. 137*.

General Agreement on Tariffs and Trade This institution, most commonly known by its acronym GATT, originated as a contractual arrangement, signed at Geneva on 30 October 1947, and put into force by the simultaneous Protocol of Provisional Application *(55 U.N.T.S. 194, 308)*, wherein the parties recited (art. XXIX) their recognition of the need for an International Trade Organization and their undertaking to observe the principles of the Draft Charter of that body, then under consideration. That organization, however, never came into existence. *See* **Havana Charter**. In consequence, "it was left to the trade negotiations (or 'rounds') held under the auspices of the GATT to devise a *de facto* institutional machinery of a GATT Council of Ministers, as well as various committees, sub-committees and working groups. . . . The last round of negotiations, the Uruguay Round (1986-93) saw the creation in 1994 of the **World Trade Organization** (WTO) as the new principal institution of the multilateral trading system": Sands and Klein *Bowett's Law of International Institutions* (5th ed.), 116. The GATT remains the foundation of the WTO framework and is the pre-eminent agreement in the international trade arena.

Key provisions of the GATT (as amended) include the **most-favored-nation clause** (art. I) and the **national treatment** provision (art. III), which together amplify the fundamental principle of non-discrimination. "Article VI of the GATT recognizes the right of Members to take unilateral action under domestic trade laws where domestic industries are being materially injured because of unfair foreign trading practices, specifically wither dumping or subsidization." Trebilcock and Howse, *The Regulation of International Trade* (2nd ed.), 31. Other provisions provide for general elimination of quantitative restrictions (art. XI); non-discriminatory administration of quantitative restrictions (art. XIII); exceptions to the rule of non-discrimination (art. XIV); subsidies (art. XVI); State-trading enterprises (art. XVII); general exceptions (art. XX); security exceptions (art. XXI); as well as trade and development (Part IV).

The original treaty has been considerably amended and supplemented, notably by the introduction of a Part IV on trade and development in 1965. On the original agreement (GATT 47), see Jackson, *The Law of G.A.T.T.* (1969); Flory, *Le GATT: Droit International et Commerce Mondial*; Fawcett, Trade and Finance in International Law *(1968) 123 Hague Rec. 260*. On the WTO and the 1994 amendments to the GATT (GATT 94), see Sands and Klein *Bowett's Law of International Institutions* (5th ed.); Trebilcock and Howse, *The Regulation of International Trade* (2nd ed.); Das, *The World Trade Organization: A Guide to the Framework for International Trade* (1999); Cameron and Campbell, *Dispute Resolution in the World Trade Organization* (1998). *See also* <www.wto.org>.

General Assembly The plenary organ of the United Nations, whose composition, functions and powers, voting rules and procedure are specified in Chapter IV of the Charter. It consists of representatives of all the member States (art. 9(1)), of which there are currently 191. "The General Assembly may discuss any questions or any matters within the scope of the . . . Charter or relating to the powers and functions of any organs provided for in the . . . Charter, and except as provided in Article 12, may make recommendations to the Members of the United Nations or to the Security Council or to both on any such questions or matters" (art. 10). Specifically, "the General Assembly may consider the general principles of co-operation in the maintenance of international peace and security, including principles governing disarmament and the regulation of armaments" (art. 11(1)); it may also "initiate studies and make recommendations for the purposes of promoting international cooperation in the political field and encouraging the progressive development of international law and its codification" (art. 13(1)(a)); and "promoting international cooperation in the economic, social cultural, educational and health fields, and assisting in the realization of human rights and fundamental freedoms for all without distinction as to race, sex, language or religion" (art. 13(1)(b)).

Art. 11 provides that "the General Assembly may discuss any questions relating to the maintenance of international peace and security." Similarly, art. 14 provides that "subject to the provisions of Article 12, the General Assembly may recommend measures for the peaceful adjustment of any situation, regardless of origin, which it deems likely to impair the general welfare or friendly relations among nations." However, art. 12 precludes the General Assembly from making recommendation on any matter in respect of which the Security Council is exercising its functions. This division of functions was rendered unworkable at an early stage by the lack of unanimity in the Security Council. Accordingly, by the **Uniting for Peace Resolution** of 3 November 1950 (377(V)) the General Assembly assumed for itself a "residual responsibility" for the maintenance of international peace and security where the Security Council fails to act because of the exercise of the veto by a permanent member. The resolution envisaged that the General Assembly could make recommendations to members for **collective measures** that could involve the use of force when necessary. In furtherance of the resolution, the General Assembly created the United Nations Emergency Force (**UNEF I**) in 1956 and the United Nations Force in the Congo (**ONUC**) in 1960. The constitutionality of forces created by the General Assembly was challenged by a number of States and the matter was referred to the ICJ for an advisory opinion. In the **Certain Expenses of the United Nations Case** *1962 I.C.J. Rep 151*, the ICJ held that the General Assembly could authorize **peace-keeping** forces as long as such forces were not concerned with enforcement action, which remained within the exclusive remit of the Security Council, the organ which had been charged by the Charter with primary responsibility for the maintenance of international peace and security.

Art. 18 governs voting in the General Assembly. Each member of the Assembly has one vote (art. 18(1)). Decisions on important questions, including, *inter alia*, recommendations on the maintenance of international peace and security, the election of non-permanent members of the Security Council and the suspension of rights and privileges of membership, require a two-thirds majority of members present and voting (art. 18(2)). Decisions on all other questions are by a majority of members present and voting (art. 18(3)). The General Assembly has responsibility for the budget of the United Nations and can issue binding resolutions in respect thereof (art. 17). Otherwise, General Assembly resolutions normally only have the force of recommendations for member States and are therefore not legally binding. However, certain resolutions may acquire binding effect indirectly by virtue of their evolution into or crystalization as **customary international law**. The International Court of Justice in the **Military and Paramilitary Activities in and Against Nicaragua Case** *1984 I.C.J. Rep. 392* noted that "***opinio juris*** may, though with all due caution, be deduced from, *inter alia*, the attitude of the Parties [i.e. Nicaragua and the US] and the attitude of States towards certain General Assembly resolutions, and particularly resolution 2625 (XXV) entitled 'Declaration on Principles of International Law concerning Friendly Relations and Co-operation among States in accordance with the Charter of the United Nations.'" Alternatively, the way States vote in relation to certain General Assembly resolutions may provide evidence of State practice on that issue: "Where the vast majority of states consistently vote for resolutions and declarations on a topic, that amounts to state practice and a binding rule may very well emerge provided that the requisite *opinio juris* can be proved." Shaw *International Law* (4th ed.), 91.

general participation clause This phrase is used to describe the stipulation in some of the Hague Conventions (*e.g.*, Conventions IV, art. 2; V, art. 20; VI, art. 6; VII, art. 7 *(205 C.T.S. 277, 299, 305, 319)*) that their provisions are applicable only to the contracting parties and only in conflicts in which all the belligerents are such parties. Though strictly the effect of this was to deprive the Conventions of application in both World Wars (*see The Möwe [1915] P. 1; The Blonde [1922] 1 A.C. 313*), their substance was generally invoked as "being declaratory of the laws and customs of war": *Judgment of the International Military Tribunal for the Trial of German Major War Criminals* (Nuremberg), *(1946, Cmnd. 6964),* 64-5, 125. As to the attitude of the Tokyo Tribunal, see Schwarzenberger, *International Law* (1968), vol. 2, 20-1.

general principles of law recognized by civilized nations Art. 38(1)(c) of the Statute of the International Court of Justice lists general principles of law recognized by civilized nations as one of the **formal sources** of international law along with **treaties** and **custom** (art. 38(1)(a) and (b)). "The legal principles which find a place in all or most of the various national systems of law naturally commend themselves to states for application in the international legal system, as being necessarily inherent in any legal system within the experience of states. . . . The intention [of art. 38(1)(c)] is to authorize the Court to apply the general principles of municipal jurisprudence, insofar as they are applicable to relations of states. . . . The Court has seldom found occasion to apply 'general principles of law,' since as a rule conventional and customary international law have been sufficient to supply the necessary basis of decision": *1 Oppenheim 36-8. See Chorzów Factory (Indemnity) (Merits) Case (1928) P.C.I.J., Ser. A., No. 17; German Minorities in Upper Silesia Case (1928) P.C.I.J., Ser. A., No. 15; Chorzów Factory Case (Jurisdiction) (1927) P.C.I.J., Ser. A, No. 9; Danzig, Jurisdiction of the Courts of, Case (1928) P.C.I.J., Ser. B, No. 15; Corfu Channel Case 1949 I.C.J. Rep. 4.* The principle of **good faith** is a general principle derived, in part at least, from national systems of law. Cf. **principles of international law**. *See* Cheng, *General Principle of Law as Applied by International Courts and Tribunals* (1953).

General Treaty for the Renunciation of War, 1928 Otherwise known as the Pact of Paris or Kellogg-Briand Pact, this instrument contains two operative articles: "1. The High Contracting Parties solemnly declare in the names of their respective peoples that they condemn recourse to war for the solution of international controversies, and renounce it as an instrument of national policy in their relations with one another. 2. The High Contracting Parties agree that the settlement or solution of disputes or conflicts of whatever nature or of whatever origin they may be, which may arise among them, shall never be sought except by pacific means": *94 L.N.T.S. 57.* Generally regarded as a failure, although still in force today, the Pact has, nevertheless, an importance in marking a stage in the legal and intellectual process that led to the prohibition on the use of force in art. 2(4) of the UN Charter.

Geneva Conventions The first Geneva Convention for the Amelioration of the Condition of the Wounded in Armies in the Field was signed on 22 August 1864 *(129 C.T.S. 361)*. This was supplemented by the Additional Articles of 20 October 1868 *(138 C.T.S. 189)* and replaced by the Convention of 6 July 1906 bearing the same title *(202 C.T.S. 144)*, which was itself supplemented by Hague Convention X of 1907 for the Adaptation of the Principles of the Geneva Convention to Maritime War *(205 C.T.S. 359)*. The 1906 Convention was replaced by that of 27 July 1929 *(118 L.N.T.S. 303)*, to which there was a companion Convention of the same date relative to the Treatment of Prisoners of War *(118 L.N.T.S. 343)* elaborating the provisions of Chapter II of the Réglement relative to the Laws and Customs of War on Land annexed to Hague Convention IV of 1907 *(205 C.T.S. 277)*. The two Conventions of 1929 were expanded into the four opened for signature on 12 August 1949, viz.: I Convention for the Amelioration of the Condition of the Wounded and Sick in Armed Forces in the Field; II Convention for the Amelioration of the Condition of Wounded, Sick and Shipwrecked Members of Armed Forces at Sea; III Convention relative to the Treatment of Prisoners of War; IV Convention relative to the Protection of Civilian Persons in Time of War *(75 U.N.T.S. 3f.)*. *See* Draper, *The Red Cross Conventions*. The Diplomatic Conference on Reaffirmation and Development of International Humanitarian Law on 8 June 1977 adopted by consensus two Protocols additional to the 1949 Conventions which were opened for signature on 12 December 1977: texts in *16 I.L.M. 1391 (1977)*. According to the International Court of Justice in its Advisory Opinion on the ***Legality of the Threat or Use of Nuclear Weapons*** [1996] *I.C.J. Rep* 66: the rules contained in the Geneva Conventions constitute "intransgressible principles of customary international law" (para.95). The UN Conference on Prohibitions or Restrictions of Use of Certain Conventional Weapons which may be deemed to be excessively injurious or to have Indiscriminate Effects on 10 October 1980 adopted a Convention on Prohibitions or Restrictions on the use of such weapons together with Protocols on Non-Detectable Fragments; Mines and Booby Traps; and Incendiary Weapons together with a Resolution on Small-Calibre Weapon Systems *((1980) 19 I.L.M. 1523)*. *See* generally, Green, *The Contemporary Law of Armed Conflict* (1993); De Lupis, *The Law of War* (1987). *See also* <www.icrc.org>.

Geneva Conventions on the Law of the Sea   The designation given to the four Conventions elaborated at the First United Nations Conference on the Law of the Sea and opened for signature on 29 April 1958, viz: the Convention on the Territorial Sea and the Contiguous Zone, in force 10 September 1964 *(516 U.N.T.S. 205)*; the Convention on the High Seas, in force 30 September 1962 *(450 U.N.T.S. 82)*; the Convention on the Continental Shelf, in force 10 June 1964 *(499 U.N.T.S. 311)*; and the Convention on Fishing and Conservation of the Living Resources of the High Seas, in force 20 March 1966 *(559 U.N.T.S. 285)*. The UN Convention on the Law of the Sea 1982 is, by art. 311(1) and as between States Parties, to prevail over the Geneva Conventions.

Geneva Gas Protocol   *See* **Asphyxiating, Poisonous or other Gases, etc., Protocol Prohibiting the Use in War of**

Geneva Protocol on the Pacific Settlement of Disputes   *(1924) League of Nations Doc. C. 606.M.211.1924 IX.* This draft instrument, purporting to prohibit recourse to war in any circumstances, establishing a method of determining the aggressor by presuming a State refusing to resort to or accept the results of methods of peaceful settlement to be an aggressor, and making the application of sanctions against an aggressor compulsory, though adopted by the League of Nations Assembly and signed by fourteen States, failed to secure general acceptance.

genocide   In terms of the Convention on the Prevention and Punishment of Genocide, adopted by the General Assembly on 9 December 1948 *(78 U.N.T.S. 277)*, which entered into force on 12 January 1951, "genocide means any of the following acts committed with intent to destroy, in whole or in part, a national, ethnical, racial or religious group, such as (a) Killing members of the group; (b) Causing serious bodily or mental harm to members of the group; (c) Deliberately inflicting on the group conditions of life calculated to bring about its physical destruction in whole or in part; (d) Imposing measures intended to prevent births within the group; (e) Forcibly transferring children of the group to another group" (art. 2). Genocide, "whether committed in time of peace or in time of war, is a crime under international law which [the Contracting Parties] undertake to prevent and punish" (art. 1), and is subject to prosecution in "a competent tribunal of the State in the territory of which the act was committed, or by such international penal tribunal as may have jurisdiction. . . ." (art. 6). The Contracting Parties are obliged to enact legislation making genocide a crime within their territories and to provide "effective penalties for persons guilty of genocide" or of associated acts (art. 5); such associated acts being conspiracy, direct and public incitement, attempt and complicity (art. 3). Punishment for genocide and associated acts applies to "[c]onstitutionally responsible rulers, public officials or private individuals" (art. 4). Art. 2 of the Genocide Convention is replicated in art. 4(2) of the Statute of the **International Criminal Tribunal for the Former Yugoslavia** (ICTY) *(32 I.L.M. 1203 (1993))*, art. 2(2) of the Statute of the **International Criminal Tribunal for Rwanda** (ICTR) *(33 I.L.M. 1598 (1994))* and art. 6 of the Statute of the **International Criminal Court** (ICC) *(37 I.L.M. 999 (1998))*. Accordingly, those accused of genocide may now be prosecuted before a relevant international tribunal. Genocide is regarded as part of **jus cogens**: Whiteman, Jus Cogens in International Law, with a Projected List, *7 Ga. J. Int. & Com. L. 609 (1977)*. *See generally* Lemkin, *Axis Rule in Occupied Europe* (1944), where the term "genocide" is first used; Robinson, *The Genocide Convention* (1960); Schabas, *Genocide in International Law: The Crime of Crimes* (2000); Kittichasaree, *International Criminal Law* (2001), Chap. 4. *And see **Reservations to the Genocide Convention Case** 1951 I.C.J. Rep. 15*; **Genocide Convention Cases**.

Genocide Convention Cases *(Bosnia and Herzegovina v. Yugoslavia)*. On 20 March 1993, the Republic of Bosnia-Herzegovina instituted proceedings against the Federal Republic of Yugoslavia in respect of a dispute concerning alleged violations of the Convention on the Prevention and Punishment of Crimes of Genocide 1948 *(78 U.N.T.S. 277)*, to which both Bosnia-Herzegovina and Yugoslavia are parties, including, *inter alia*, executing a policy of ethnic cleansing, property damage, murder, rape, disappearances and damage and destruction of religious and cultural property. The application invoked art. 11 of the Convention as the basis of jurisdiction. By order of 8 April 1993, the Court indicated certain provisional measures with a view to the protection of rights under the Genocide Convention *(1993 I.C.J. Rep. 3)*; and by a further order of 13 September 1993, the Court reaffirmed the measures indicated in its order of 8 April and declared that those measures should be immediately and effectively implemented *(1993 I.C.J. Rep. 325)*. Yugoslavia then proceeded to raise certain preliminary objections relating to the admissibility of the application and the jurisdiction of the Court to entertain the case. On 11 July 1996, the Court *held* (1) (13 to 2) that, on the basis of art. 11 of the Genocide Convention, it had jurisdiction to adjudicate the dispute; (2) (13 to 2) that the application filed by Bosnia-Herzegovina on 20 March 1993 was admissible *(1996 I.C.J. Rep. 595)*.

On 22 July 1997, Yugoslavia filed a counter-claim requesting the Court to adjudge and declare that "Bosnia-Herzegovina [was] responsible for the acts of genocide committed against the Serbs in Bosnia and Herzegovina" and that it "ha[d] the obligation to punish the persons held responsible" for these acts. By order of 17 December 1997, the Court *held* Yugoslavia's counter-claims were admissible *(2001 I.C.J. Rep. forthcoming)*. By letter of 20 April 2001, Yugoslavia informed the Court that it intended to withdraw its counter-claims as stated in its counter-memorial. The withdrawal was accepted by Bosnia-Herzegovina by letter dated 12 July 2001 and placed on record by order of 10 September 2001.

In the meantime, on 24 April 2001, Yugoslavia filed an application requesting revision of the judgment of 11 July 1996, arguing that the admission of Yugoslavia to United Nations constituted a new fact which, when the judgment was given, was unknown and that the FRY at the time had been party to neither the ICJ Statute nor the Genocide Convention. The UN General Assembly in Res. 47/1 of 22 September 1992 had considered that the Federal Republic of Yugoslavia (Serbia and Montenegro) could not automatically continue in nor succeed to the membership in the UN of the former Socialist Federal Republic of Yugoslavia. In its decision of 3 February 2003, the Court *held* (10 to 3) that Res. 47/1 did not affect the Federal Republic of Yugoslavia's right to appear before the Court or be a party to a case before the Court. Nor did it affect the position of the Federal Republic of Yugoslavia in relation to the Genocide Convention. Accordingly, the admission of the Federal Republic of Yugoslavia to the United Nations on 1 November 2001 made no difference to the case and the application for revision was accordingly rejected. The case relating to the original application by Bosnia Herzegovina on 20 March 1993 is continuing.

On 2 July 1999, the Republic of Croatia instituted proceedings against the Federal Republic of Yugoslavia, basing jurisdiction on Article 11 of the Genocide Convention, to which both Croatia and Yugoslavia are parties. Croatia contended that, between 1991 and 1995, Yugoslavia committed violations of the 1948 Convention, including ethnic cleansing against Croatian citizens and of property damage; Croatia asserted that Yugoslavian aggression resulted in 20,000 deaths, 55,000 injuries, and the 3,000 disappearances. In addition, Croatia alleged that the violence resulted in destruction of homes, churches, cultural monuments and government infrastructure; the planting of explosive equipment had also rendered useless Croatian land. Croatia requested the ICJ to adjudge and declare that Yugoslavia had breached its legal obligations under the Genocide Convention and that Yugoslavia make reparations for the casualties and for damage to property, as well as to the Croatian economy and environment. The Court has yet to make a final decision.

Gentili (Gentilis), Alberico 1552-1608. Italian jurist who emigrated to England and in 1587 became Regius Professor of Roman Law at Oxford; said to be the first great writer on international law as distinct from theology and ethics. His available writings include: *De jure belli libri tres (Three Books on the Law of War); De legationibus libri tres (Three Books on Embassies); Hispanicae Advocationis libri duo (Two Books of Pleas of a Spanish Advocate.) (Classics of International Law). See* Nussbaum, *Concise History of the Law of Nations* (revised ed.) 94-101.

genuine link "A State cannot claim that the rules [pertaining to the acquisition of nationality] which it has [laid down by virtue of its internal laws] are entitled to recognition by another State unless it has acted in conformity with this general aim of making the legal bond of nationality accord with the individual's genuine connection (link) with the State which assumes the defence of its citizens by means of protection against other States. . . . According to the practice of States, to arbitral and judicial decisions and to the opinions of writers, nationality is a legal bond having as its basis a social fact of attachment, a genuine connection of existence, interests and sentiments, together with the existence of reciprocal rights and duties." ***Nottebohm Case 1955 I.C.J. Rep. 4*** at p. 23-24. "In the ***Flegenheimer Claim*** . . . it was considered that a person who had only one nationality was not to be regarded as disentitled to rely on it against another state because he had no effective link with the state of nationality but only with a third state." *I Oppenheim 854 n. 12. See also* Donner *The Regulation of Nationality in International Law* (2nd ed., 1995) and Weiss *Nationality and Statelessness* (1956).

With regard to ships, art. 5 of the Geneva Convention on the High Seas 1958 (450 U.N.T.S. 82) requires that "[e]ach state shall fix the conditions for the grant of its nationality to ships, for the registration of ships in its territory, and for the right to fly its flag. Ships have the nationality of the state whose flag they are entitled to fly. There must exist a genuine link between the State and the ship; in particular, the state must effectively exercise its jurisdiction and control in administrative, technical and social matters over ships flying its flag." This position has been the subject of considerable criticism: "the assumption that the 'genuine link' formula, invented for dealing with people, is capable of immediate application to ships and aircraft, smacks of a disappointing naiveté. . . . A provision which might seem to encourage governments to make subjective decisions whether or not to recognize the nationality of this aircraft or that vessel is clearly open for abuse and for that reason to grave criticism." (Jennings, The General Course on Principles of International Law, (1967) 121 *Hague Recueil* 327 at 463). Nevertheless, the provisions of art. 5 are replicated in art. 91 of the UN Convention on the Law of the Sea 1982 (1833 U.N.T.S. 3), albeit, accompanied by an enumeration of the duties of the flag state in art. 94. *See* further **flag of convenience**.

Arts. 17-21 of the Chicago Convention on International Civil Aviation 1944 (15 U.N.T.S. 295) provide that the nationality of aircraft is governed by the state of registration. There does not appear to be a general requirement of a genuine link. However, "[i]n the absence of substantial connections the state of registry will not be in a position to ensure that the aircraft is operated in accordance with the Chicago Convention." Brownlie, *Principles of Public International Law*, (5th ed. 1998), 431, *See* further **aircraft, nationality**.

geographical representation   The Charter of the UN recognizes that in relation to those of its Organs which are not open to universal membership, one of the factors to be taken into account in the election of States to those organs is the need to ensure adequate geographical representation. "The Security Council shall consist of fifteen Members of the United Nations. . . . The General Assembly shall elect ten other Members . . . due regard being specially paid, in the first instance to the contribution . . . to the maintenance of international peace and security . . . and also to equitable geographical distribution." (art. 23.). Although no reference is made in the Charter to geographical representation, "[i]n elections **[to ECOSOC]** an attempt is always made to represent a variety of social, economic cultural and geographical interests": Sands and Klein, *Bowett's Law of International Institutions* (5th ed.), 57. In relation to the **International Court of Justice**, one of the primary criteria for the election of judges is that the body of judges as a whole should represent "the main forms of civilization and . . . the principal legal systems of the world" (Statute of the ICJ, art. 9). "In practice election of the judges is based upon a degree of 'equitable geographical distribution' which characterizes the composition of most UN organs or bodies of limited composition." Sands and Klein, *supra*, 353. Other international organizations include provisions on ensuring equitable geographical representation. *See* for example, UN Convention on the Law of the Sea *(1833 U.N.T.S. 3)*, art. 161 (composition of the Council of the International Seabed Authority).

geostationary orbital position   A narrow volume or *torus* of space, approximately 22,300 miles (35,800 km) above the Equator. Satellites orbiting within the *torus* have an orbital period of 24 hours, i.e. they remain virtually fixed relative to points on the surface of the earth. For this reason, and because such an orbital position is "visible" between 81.5° N and 81.5° S, such positions are in demand for military and communications satellites. Three satellites spaced 120° apart afford a total coverage of the bulk of the centers of population. The geostationary orbital position is a limited natural resource, as are space radio frequencies, and members of the **International Telecommunication Union** are bound by art. 33(2) of the ITU Convention 1982 to make efficient and economic use of it. The Bogotá Declaration of 3 December 1976 *(ITU Doc. WARC-BS (1977) 81-E)* and the claims of equatorial countries to exercise sovereign rights over segments of the geostationary satellite orbit are not generally accepted.

German External Debts Case *(Swiss Confederation v. Federal Republic of Germany) (1958) 25 I.L.R. 33*. This decision of the Arbitral Tribunal established by the German External Debt Agreement of 27 February 1953 *(333 U.N.T.S. 4)* is relevant to international law insofar as that Tribunal, upon a reference by Switzerland concerning the interpretation of a provision of the Agreement, *held* (unanimously) that an objection based on failure to exhaust local remedies must be overruled. It was true that the Tribunal's Charter did not specifically require the application of the local remedies rule, but that rule had nevertheless to be applied *qua* a generally accepted rule of international law which the Tribunal was required to apply. But the rule related only to cases where there was a claim against a State based on injury to an individual and here there was no such specific claim and merely a request for the interpretation of a treaty. The award of the Tribunal contains an exhaustive survey of the authorities and literature respecting the local remedies rule.

German Interests in Polish Upper Silesia Case *(1925-26)*. On 15 May 1925, the German government filed an application under art. 23 of the German-Polish Convention of 15 May 1922, providing for jurisdiction in disputes concerning the interpretation and application of arts. 6-22, alleging the expropriation by Poland of the properties of certain nitrate undertakings at Chorzów, and that such expropriation was in violation both of art. 8 of the Convention and of arts. 92 and 297 of the Treaty of Versailles of 1919 *(225 C.T.S. 188)* governing the disposition of German property in territory assigned to Poland; and further averring that the Polish government had announced its intention to expropriate certain rural estates in violation of the Convention. The application asked for a declaration that the violations alleged had occurred, for an indication as to what attitude the Polish government should have adopted towards the factories, and for a declaration that the projected rural expropriations would not be in conformity with the Convention. By way of preliminary objection, the Polish government submitted principally that there was no difference at the date of the application within the meaning of art. 23, that the dispute was not within that provision in any event, that the relief claimed amounted virtually to an advisory opinion such as the Court was not competent to give at the request of a single State, and that, alternatively, the application could not be entertained until the German-Polish Mixed Arbitral Tribunal had given judgment in the same matter. By its judgment of 25 August 1925 the Court *held* (12 to 1) that there was no substance in this preliminary objection, which related to the form rather than the merits of the application. On the same day as this judgment, the German government filed a further application requesting that it might be joined to the earlier application and asking for judgment that two additional cases of liquidation of rural estates would constitute a violation of the Convention. *German Interests in Polish Upper Silesia Case (Jurisdiction) (1925) P.C.I.J., Ser. A, No. 6.*

On 25 May 1926, in the *German Interests in Polish Silesia (Merits) Case (1926) P.C.I.J., Ser. A, No. 7* the Court *held* (9 to 1) that Polish legislation complained of was contrary to art. 6 and, following of the Convention; that the attitude of the Polish government towards the nitrate companies was not in conformity with those provisions; but that it was not called on to say what attitude would have been in conformity therewith; and that various of the notices of intention to liquidate rural estates were also not in conformity with the provisions referred to. These conclusions were reached by means of an interpretation of the relevant treaty provisions in the course of which the Court said with respect to art. 23 of the Convention of 1922 that that provision, in common with other provisions respecting interpretation, appeared "also to cover interpretations unconnected with concrete cases of application . . . There seems to be no reason why States should not be able to ask the Court to give an abstract interpretation . . . Article 59 of the Statute . . . does not exclude purely declaratory judgments. . . It should also be noted that the possibility of a judgment having a purely declaratory effect has been foreseen by Article 63 of the Statute, as well as by Article 36 [paragraph (2)(a)]." The Court said further with respect to the possible difficulty that it was apparently called on to interpret Polish legislation: "From the standpoint of International Law and of the Court which is its organ, municipal laws are merely facts which express the will and constitute the activities of States, in the same manner as do legal decisions or administrative measures. The Court is certainly not called upon to interpret the Polish law as such; but there is nothing to prevent the Court's giving judgment on the question whether or not, in applying that law, Poland is acting in conformity with its obligations towards Germany under the . . . Convention" (at 18-19). With respect to Poland's argument that she was entitled to rely incidentally on the Armistice Convention of 11 November 1918 *(224 C.T.S. 286)* and the Protocol of Spa of 1 December 1918 *(ibid, 319)* the Court said: "A treaty only creates law as between the States which are parties to it; in case of doubt, no rights can be deduced from it in favour of third States" (at 29).

German Minorities in Upper Silesia, Rights of, Case *(1928) P.C.I.J., Ser. A., No. 15.* In this case instituted by Germany under art. 72 of the German-Polish Convention of 15 May 1922 respecting Upper Silesia *(9 L.N.T.S. 466)*, conferring on any member of the League of Nations Council the right to bring before the Court any dispute arising out of the preceding articles of the Convention, the Court *held* (8 to 4) that the objection of Poland to the jurisdiction on the ground that the precise dispute arose out of other and later articles was to be overruled. That State had implicitly accepted the jurisdiction with respect to the entire merits and had raised its objection only in its rejoinder. Upon the interpretation of the Convention, the Court further *held* that that instrument bestowed on every national the right freely to declare that he did or did not belong to a racial, religious of linguistic minority and to declare what was the language of any pupil or child for whom he was legally responsible, such declarations being subject to no verification.

German Minority Schools In Upper Silesia, Access, Case *(1931) P.C.I.J., Ser. A/B, No. 40.* Upon the refusal of the Polish authorities to admit certain children to the German minority schools in Upper Silesia pursuant to declarations of membership of the minority (as to which see the ***German Minorities in Upper Silesia, Rights of, Case***), an appeal was taken to the League of Nations Council, which body, on 24 January 1931, requested of the Court an advisory opinion as to whether children excluded from the schools on the basis of language tests instituted under the Council's auspices as a practical solution of the matter could in law be refused access. On 15 May 1931, the Court *advised* (11 to 1) in the negative, the German Polish Convention of 1922 still controlling and the Council not having intended to modify it.

German Settlers in Poland Case *(1923) P.C.I.J., Ser. B., No. 6.* On 3 February 1923, the League of Nations Council requested an advisory opinion as to (1) whether measures directed to the dispossession and non-recognition of the leases of colonists settled by Germany in what had become territory of Poland on the re-establishment of that State involved international obligations of the kind contemplated by the Minorities Treaty with Poland of 28 June 1919 *(225 C.T.S. 412)* so as to fall within the competence of the League under that treaty and, if so, (2) whether such measures were in conformity with the international obligations of Poland. The Court *advised* as to (1) affirmatively and as to (2) negatively. The treaty stipulated, *inter alia*, for the equality before the law of all persons becoming Polish nationals and for the placing of such stipulations under the guarantee of the League. Though the principle that upon a change of sovereignty private rights are to be respected was not formally expressed in the treaty, it was nevertheless clearly recognized thereby.

Gidel, (Alphonse) Gilbert Charles 1880-1958. Professor, Montpellier 1908-20, Paris 1920-46. Author of *Les aspects juridiques de la lutte pour l'antarctique* (1946); *Droit International de la Mer,* of which only three volumes were published, *La haute mer* (1932), *Les eaux intérieures* (1932), and *La mer territoriale* (1934).

good faith Good faith (*bona fides*) is one of the fundamental principles of international law. "One of the basic principles governing the creation and performance of legal obligations, whatever their source, is the principle of good faith": ***Nuclear Tests Cases** 1974 I.C.J. Rep. 254* at 267. Good faith "touches every aspect of international law": *1 Oppenheim 38*. It is without question one of the general principles of law as specified in art. 38(1) of the Statute of the ICJ: see Cheng, *General Principles of Law as Applied by International Courts and Tribunals* (1953), Chaps. 4-5. It may be more. The UN Charter, art. 2(2), requires States to fulfill all obligations arising under it in good faith. The **Friendly Relations Declaration** 1970 (GA Res. 2625 (XXV)) extends that duty to "obligations under the generally recognized principles and rules of international law."

In the law of treaties, treaties must be observed in good faith: art. 26 of the Vienna Convention on the Law of Treaties 1969. Likewise, treaties must be interpreted in good faith: art. 31(1). Good faith in relation to the formation of treaties is stipulated for by implication by art. 18 which recites that a State is "obliged to refrain from acts which would defeat [its] object and purpose" when it has signed or expressed its consent to be bound by the text of a treaty.

good offices "A theoretical distinction exists between good offices and mediation. The difference between them is that, whereas *good offices* consist in various kinds of action tending to call negotiations between the conflicting States into existence, *mediation* consists in direct conduct of negotiations between the parties at issue on the basis of proposals made by the mediator. However, diplomatic practice and treaties do not always distinguish between [them]": *II Oppenheim 10*; see to the same effect, *Satow's Guide to Diplomatic Practice* (5th ed.), 351. Hague Convention I of 1907 for the Pacific Settlement of International Disputes *(205 C.T.S. 233)* provides (art. 2) that, in case of serious disagreement or dispute, the parties shall, before an appeal to arms, agree to have recourse so far as circumstances allow "to the good offices or mediation" of one or more friendly States and (art. 3) that, independently of this recourse, the parties to the Convention deem it expedient that States strangers to a dispute should on their own initiative offer good offices or mediation, and that such States have the right to do so. It is also stipulated (art. 6) that good offices and mediation have exclusively the character of advice and never have binding force.

government A term used primarily to connote the organization of public power within any given territory. In this sense, it is said that a government is an essential element of the **State**. The term is further used to connote the executive organs of States in their relations with one another. Cf. the Preamble to the Charter of the United Nations: "We the Peoples of the United Nations, Determined . . . Accordingly our respective Governments, through representatives . . . have agreed to the present Charter. . . ." "The Court considers it beyond all dispute that a reply of this nature given by the Minister for Foreign Affairs on behalf of his Government . . . is binding upon the country to which the Minister belongs": *Legal Status of **Eastern Greenland Case**, (1933) P.C.I.J., Ser. A/B, No. 53*, at 71. It is in this sense that **recognition of governments** is spoken of. But the term may be applied to any political authority, whether the central authority of a State or not, *e.g., de facto* government, local government.

governments in exile *See* **exile governments**.

***Greco-Bulgarian Communities Case** (1930) P.C.I.J., Ser. B., No. 17*. In its advisory opinion of 31 July 1930, the PCIJ furnished answers to a series of questions put to it by the League of Nations' Council at the instance of the Greco-Bulgarian Commission and by the Bulgarian and Greek Governments with respect to the interpretation of the Convention of

27 November 1919 respecting Reciprocal Emigration of Minorities *(226 C.T.S. 435)*. The questions related primarily to the meaning of the expression "communities" in arts. 6 and 7 of the Convention.

Greenpeace   Established in 1971, Greenpeace is an NGO committed to non-violent, creative confrontation to expose global environmental problems, campaigning for the oceans, ancient forests and sustainable development and against climate change, toxic chemicals, the "nuclear threat" and genetically modified organisms. *See* <www.greenpeace.org>.

Grisbådarna Arbitration   *(Norway v. Sweden) (1909) 11 R.I.A.A. 147*. By the Convention of 14 March 1908 *(206 C.T.S. 280)*, the parties requested a tribunal of the Permanent Court of Arbitration (Messrs. Beichmann, Hammarskjöld, Loeff) to determine the sea boundary between the two countries insofar as it had been left undetermined on their separation, taking into account the stipulations of the Boundary Treaty of 1661 *(6 C.T.S. 297)*. By its award dated 23 October 1909 the Tribunal *held* that the contention advanced by Norway and not contested by Sweden that territorial waters are appurtenant was correct, so that when, by the Peace of Roskild of 1658 *(5 C.T.S. 1)* the fief of Bahus was ceded to Sweden, its cession carried territorial waters with it. In order to determine what this involved, however, it was necessary to apply contemporary rules as to boundary delimitation and not rules developed in later times such as the median line rule. The applicable rule was in fact that of the line perpendicular to the coast. This would assign the Grisbådarna banks to Sweden—a solution to which support was given by the circumstance that the Swedish lobster fishery there was more extensive and of older establishment than the Norwegian and that Sweden had made herself responsible for the lighting and buoying of the area.

Grotian Society   A society for the study of the history of international law founded in the United Kingdom *circa* 1965 by C.H. Alexandrowicz and others. The Society has published two volumes of *Papers* (1968, 1972).

Grotius   The Latin version of the name of Hugo de Groot, 1583-1645. Dutch jurist, historian, theologian and diplomat, often described as the "Father of International Law," largely for his systematic exposition of its rules. His philosophy of international law combined natural law doctrines with positivistic regard for the practice of States. Those who adhered to this philosophy are known as *Grotians*. Principal works include *De Jure Praedae* (published only in 1868); *Mare liberum* (1609); *The Jurisprudence of Holland* (in Dutch) (1624); *De jure belli ac pacis* (1624). *See* Nussbaum, *A Concise History of the Law of Nations* (rev. ed.), 102-114.

Grotius Society   Founded in 1915, originally "to afford facilities for discussion of the laws of War and Peace, . . . and to make suggestions for their reform, and generally to advance the study of International Law," these objects being later amended to those of affording "facilities for the study, discussion and advancement of public and private international law and to make suggestions for their reform." The Society published 44 volumes of *Transactions* to 1958. The Society was wound up on the foundation of the **British Institute of International and Comparative Law**.

Group of 77   A grouping, originally of 75, later 77 and now some 133 States originally organized in the preparatory stages of the First United Nations Conference on Trade and Development (UNCTAD I) and maintained in existence as a caucus for the developing States in most organizations and conferences in the UN System. The Group maintains a permanent institutional structure consisting primarily of the Ministerial Meeting and the Intergovernmental Follow-up and Coordination Committee on Economic Cooperation among Developing Countries. "As the largest Third World coalition in the United Nations, the Group of 77 provides the means for the developing world to articulate and promote its collective economic interests and enhance its joint negotiating capacity on all major international economic issues in the United Nations system and promote economic and technical cooperation among developing countries": *see* <www.g77.org>. *See* Sauvant, *The Group of 77, Evolution, Structure, Organisation; The Collected Documents of the Group of 77*; Williams, *Third World Cooperation: The Group of 77 in UNCTAD. And see* **non-aligned countries**.

group rights *See* **collective rights**.

Guadalajara Convention 1961 Properly, the Convention Supplementary to the **Warsaw Convention** of 12 October 1929 for the Unification of Certain Rules relating to International Carriage by Air Performed by a Person other than the Contracting Carrier, opened for signature 18 September 1961 *(500 U.N.T.S. 31)*.

Guardianship of Infants Convention Case (Netherlands v. Sweden) 1958 I.C.J. Rep. 55. This case, instituted under the parties' declarations of acceptance of the **Optional Clause** of art. 36(2) of the ICJ Statute, raised the question of the compatibility of a régime of protective upbringing imposed by the Swedish authorities in relation to a minor of Netherlands' nationality. The Court (12 to 4) *held* that the régime complained of, though placing obstacles in the way of the full exercise of the right of custody of the Dutch guardian, was not incompatible, as had been averred by the applicant State, with the Hague Convention on the Guardianship of Infants of 12 June 1902 *(191 C.T.S. 264)*.

Guatemala-Honduras Boundary Arbitration (1933) 2 R.I.A.A. 1322. By the Treaty of 16 July 1930 *(137 L.N.T.S. 232)*, the parties referred to a Special Arbitral Tribunal the question whether the boundary issue pending between them was within the competence of the International Central American Tribunal established by the Convention of 7 February 1923, requiring the Special Tribunal to proceed to a determination of that matter in the event of a negative decision on the preliminary question. Having decided the preliminary question in the negative on 8 January 1932 *(2 R.I.A.A. 1316)*, the Special Tribunal (Hughes, President, Castro-Urena, Bello Codesido) dealt with the substance in accordance with art. 5 of the Treaty, providing: "The . . . Parties are in agreement that the only juridical line which can be established between the[m] is that of the 'Uti Possidetis of 1821.' Consequently . . . the Tribunal shall determine this line. If the Tribunal finds that one or both parties, in their subsequent development, have established, beyond that line, interests which should be taken into account in establishing the definitive boundary, the Tribunal shall modify, as it may see fit, the line of the Uti Possidetis of 1821, and shall fix the territorial or other compensation which it may deem just that either party should pay to the other." Disregarding earlier mediation proceedings as having no controlling effect on the initial question of interpretation, the Tribunal *held* the expression "Uti Possidetis of 1821" to refer to possession in the sense of administrative control at the will of the Crown of Spain at the relevant date, the extent of which was in general to be deduced from the limits asserted by the States concerned upon the establishment of their independence. In relation to a section of the disputed boundary in the district of Chiquimula, the Tribunal further *held* the evidence furnished by acts of legislative and administrative sovereignty by Guatemala, found not to have led to any opposition by Honduras, to be decisive. But in relation to the Omoa district and Motagua Valley sections, the Tribunal found that the evidence did not justify a decision in favor of either party. Though this meant that the establishment here of the line of *uti possidetis* was impossible the Tribunal was not relieved of its duty to determine the definitive boundary to its full extent. And this it must do having regard (1) to the facts of actual possession; (2) to the question whether possession by one party had been acquired in good faith and without invading the rights of the other party; and (3) to the relation of territory actually occupied to that as yet unoccupied. On the basis of these considerations the Tribunal proceeded to lay down in detail a definitive frontier. *See **uti possidetis***; *Colombia-Venezuela Boundary Dispute;. Land, Island and Maritime Frontier Dispute Case*.

Guggenheim, Paul 1899-1978. Associate and Professor, Geneva, 1931-78. Adviser to Swiss Government and international bodies. Member, PCA. Principal Works: *Traité de droit international public, avec mention de la pratique internationale et suisse*, vol. I (1953), vol. II (1954); *Emer de Vattel et l'etude des relations internationales en Suisse* (1956); *Die Schweiz in der Völkergemeinschaft* (1957).

Guinea-Bissau/Senegal Maritime Delimitation Case *(Guinea-Bissau v. Senegal) 1995 I.C.J. Rep. 423*. An application of 12 March 1991, Guinea-Bissau instituted proceedings against Senegal in a dispute concerning the maritime delimitation between the two States. A number of meetings took place between the parties and the President of the Court at which time the parties reported on the progress they had made towards settlement of the dispute, culminating in the signing of an Agreement between the Parties at Dakar on 14 October 1993, as well as a Protocol to the Agreement at Bissau on 12 June 1995. Guinea-Bissau, by letter of 2 November 1995 indicated its intention to discontinue the proceedings. By letter of 6 November 1995 Senegal agreed to the discontinuance and, on 8 November 1995, the Court placed on record the discontinuance of the proceedings by Guinea-Bissau.

Gulf of Maine, Case concerning the Delimitation of the Maritime Boundary of the *(Canada/USA) 1984 I.C.J. Rep. 246*. On 25 November 1981, Canada and the United States submitted, by special agreement dated 29 March 1979, to a Chamber of the ICJ the question as to the course of the maritime boundary dividing the continental shelves and fisheries zones of the parties in the Gulf of Maine area. On 12 October 1984, the Chamber of the Court *decided* (4 to 1) on a single maritime boundary defined by geodetic lines connecting specific co-ordinates. The Chamber, as required by the special agreement, drew the actual line of delimitation, and not, as in previous cases, merely indicated the criteria and factors for that delimitation. The Chamber stated the general principle to be applied in such delimitations: "delimitation is to be effected by the application of equitable criteria and by the use of practical methods capable of ensuring, with regard to the geographic configuration of the area and other relevant circumstances, an equitable result."

H

Hackworth, Green Heywood 1883-1973. US national, official of US State Department 1916-46. Member, PCA, 1937-60. Judge, ICJ 1946-1960, President 1955-8. Principal work: *Digest of International Law,* 8 vols. (1940-4).

Hague Academy of International Law Established in 1923 with the support of the Carnegie Endowment for International Peace, the Hague Academy (or *Academie de Droit International*) offers annual courses in English and French in Public and Private International Law, published as the *Recueil des Cours*. The Academy offers a diploma and a number of residential scholarships for doctoral candidates. It has a Centre for Studies attracting up to 24 participants researching within an annual thematic framework and an external program, which consists in sending a team of professors to Africa, Latin America and Asia to provide instruction on a specific topic of interest to the region concerned. Its overall mission is to teach international law as a way to improve the possibilities for peace and international cooperation, providing high-level education to individuals who are particularly sensitive to the development and use of international law, such as future law professors, diplomats and practitioners. *See* <www.hagueacademy.nl/eng-home.html>.

Hague Hijacking Convention 1970 *See* **hijacking (of aircraft)**.

Hague Peace Conferences, Conventions The first Hague Peace Conference of 26 States, convened upon the initiative of Russia, sat from 20 May to 31 July 1899 and adopted three Conventions: for the Pacific Settlement of International Disputes; with respect to the Laws and Customs of War on Land; and for adapting to Maritime Warfare the Principles of the Geneva Convention of 1864; as well as three Declarations: respecting the Prohibition of the Use of Projectiles diffusing Asphyxiating Gases; respecting the Prohibition of the Discharge of Projectiles from Balloons; and respecting the Prohibition of the Use of Expanding Bullets: texts in *187 C.T.S. 410f.* The Conference also adopted a Resolution respecting the restriction of military budgets and a number of *voeux* respecting the continuation of its work.

The second Conference, first proposed by the United States, was attended by nearly double the number of delegates accredited in 1899 and sat from June until October 1907. It adopted thirteen Conventions as follows: I. Convention for the Pacific Settlement of International Disputes (elaborating that of 1899); II. Convention respecting the Limitation of the Employment of Force for the Recovery of Contract Debts; III. Convention relative to the Opening of Hostilities; IV. Convention respecting the Laws and Customs of War on Land (again elaborating that of 1899); V. Convention respecting the Rights and Duties of Neutral Powers and Persons in Case of War on Land; VI. Convention relative to the Status of Enemy Merchant-Ships at the Outbreak of Hostilities; VII. Convention relative to the Conversion of Merchant-Ships into Warships; VIII. Convention relative to the Laying of Automatic Submarine Contact Mines; IX. Convention respecting Bombardment by Naval Forces in Time of War; X. Convention for the Adaptation to Maritime War of the Principles of the Geneva Convention (elaborating that of 1899); XI. Convention relative to Certain Restrictions with regard to the Exercise of the Right of Capture in Naval War; XII. Convention relative to the Creation of an International Prize Court; XIII. Convention concerning the Rights and Duties of Neutral Powers in Naval War. Further the Declaration Prohibiting the Discharge of Projectiles from Balloons was renewed: texts in *205 C.T.S. 216f.* The Conference also recorded a number of *voeux,* as had its predecessor. Apart from Convention XII, which failed of general ratification, the Hague Conventions and Declarations largely remain as an operative codification of the law of war in most of its aspects. There is no doubt that some of this code is declaratory of customary law. And *see generally* Scott, *The Hague Peace Conferences* (1915); Pearce Higgins, *The Hague Peace Conferences* (1921); Rosenne, *The Hague Peace Conferences of 1989 and 1907 and International Arbitration* (2001).

Hall, William Edward 1835-94. British writer. Principal publications: *The Rights and Duties of Neutrals* (1874); *International Law* (1880; 8th ed. by Pearce Higgins 1924); *A Treatise on the Foreign Powers and Jurisdiction of the British Crown* (1894).

Hambro, Edvard 1911-77. Norwegian. Director of International Relations Department, Bergen 1937-40. Chief of UN Legal Department, 1945-6. Registrar of ICJ, 1946-53. Professor, Norwegian School of Economics and Business Law 1957-66. Principal works include *L'Execution des Sentences Internationales* (1936); *Charter of the United Nations* (with Goodrich 1946; 3rd ed. with Goodrich and Hambro 1969); *The Case Law of the International Court* (2 vols.1952-58).

Hammarskjold, Dag 1905-61. Swedish national. Second Secretary-General of the UN 1953-61, generally credited with reforming the UN Secretariat and seeking to apply the full range of the powers of the office. Author of *The International Civil Servant in Law and in Fact* (1961). *See* Zacher, *Dag Hammarskjold's United Nations* (1970).

Hanseatic League "The most celebrated of [the numerous leagues of trading towns for the protection of their trade and trading citizens] was the Hanseatic, formed in the thirteenth century. These leagues stipulated for arbitration on controversies between their member-towns. They acquired trading privileges in foreign States. They even waged war, when necessary, for the protection of their interests": *I Oppenheim (8th ed.) 80-1.* At its peak in the 14th century, the League claimed a membership of about 100 towns, mostly German, including Bremen, Hamburg and Lubeck, as well as commercial enclaves *(Kontore),* in foreign towns, *e.g.*, Bergen (Norway), Bruges (modern Belgium), Novgorod (Russia) and London. The League published a code to regulate its affairs in 1614 under the title *Jus Maritimium Hanseaticum.*

Harcourt, Sir William Vernon 1827-1904. British statesman. Professor, Cambridge, 1869-87. Principal publication: *Letters by Historicus on Some Questions of International Law* (1863).

Harley, J. Eugene 1892-1964. US national. Professor, Lafayette 1919-20, Southern California 1920-64. Principal works include *Documentary Textbook of the United Nations: Humanity's Struggle for Peace.*

Harris, David J. 1938- . Law teacher and professor, Nottingham, 1964- . Principal works include *Cases and Materials on International Law* (1973; 5th ed. 1998); *The Euro-*

pean Social Charter (1988); *An Index to British Treaties 1969-88* (1992); *Law of the European Convention on Human Rights* (with O'Boyle and Warbrick, 1995; 2nd ed. 2000).

Harvard Research This term is used to denote the research projects, initiated by Harvard Law School under the directorship of **Manley O. Hudson**, in anticipation of the First League of Nations Conference on the Codification of International Law and continued until 1939. The projects, all of which resulted in the preparation of draft conventions, fell into four phases. The first phase (1927-9) dealt with nationality *((1929) 23 A.J.I.L. Supp. 13-79)*, the responsibility of States for injuries to foreigners *(ibid., 133-218)* and territorial waters *(ibid., 243-365)*. The second phase (1929-32) dealt with diplomatic privileges and immunities *((1932) 26 A.J.I.L. Supp. 19-143)*, the legal position and functions of consuls *(ibid., 193-375)*, the competence of courts in regard to foreign States *(ibid., 455-736)*, and piracy *(ibid., 743-872)*. The third phase (1932-5) dealt with extradition *((1935) 29 A.J.I.L. Supp. 21-240)*, jurisdiction with respect to crime *(ibid., 439-635)* and treaties *(ibid., 657-1204)*. The fourth and final phase (1935-9) dealt with judicial assistance *((1939) 33 A.J.I.L. Supp. 15-118)*, neutrality *(ibid., 175-817)* and the rights and duties of States in case of aggression *(ibid., 827-909)*. The Harvard Research has been described "as the most important contribution to the systematization of international law while at the same time indicating the desirable law in certain areas": Dhokalia, *The Codification of Public International Law* (1970), 71. *See* **codification**.

Havana Convention 1928 Otherwise the Pan-American Convention on Air Navigation *(129 L.N.T.S. 223)*, superseded by the **Chicago Convention** 1944.

Hawaiian Claims *(UK v. US) (1925) 6 R.I.A.A. 157*. The UK presented claims against the US in respect of wrongful imprisonment, detention in prison, enforced departure from the country, and other indignities, claimed to have been inflicted upon British subjects by the authorities of the Hawaiian Republic prior to its annexation by the US. *Held*, by the UK-US Arbitral Tribunal constituted under the Special Agreement of 18 August 1910, that the claims must be rejected because, on annexation, the legal unit that did the wrong no longer existed and legal liability for the wrong had been extinguished with it.

Haya de La Torre Case *See* ***Asylum Cases***.

Hay-Pauncefote Treaty Treaty between Great Britain and the United States relative to the Establishment of a Communication by Ship Canal between the Atlantic and Pacific Oceans, Washington, 18 November 1901 *(190 C.T.S. 215)*. *See* **Panama Canal**.

Hay-Varilla Treaty Convention between Panama and the United States for the Construction of a Ship Canal, Washington, 18 November 1903 *(194 C.T.S. 263)*. *See* **Panama Canal**.

head of state immunity "The Court would observe at the outset that in international law it is firmly established that, as also diplomatic and consular agents, certain holders of high-ranking office in a State, such as the Head of State, Head of Government and Minister for Foreign Affairs, enjoy immunities from jurisdiction in other States, both civil and criminal" *Arrest Warrant Case 2002 I.C.J. Rep. 3* at para. 51. There are two aspects to the immunity of a head of State. First, there is immunity *rationae personae* which attaches to the person of the serving head of State and is analogous to diplomatic immunity (*see* **diplomatic privileges and immunities**). "A head of state's immunity is enjoyed in recognition of his very special status as holder of his state's highest office . . . his position is one which he has *erga omnes*, at all times wherever he is": Watts, The Legal Position in International Law of

Heads of State, Heads of Government and Foreign Ministers, *(1994) 247 Hague Recueil 9* at 40. Immunity *rationae personae* exists only as long as the recipient remains in office.

Secondly, on leaving office, a head of State is entitled to a residual immunity *rationae materiae* which attaches to the official acts of the head of State or other top-ranking official. This is more akin to **sovereign** (or State) **immunity**. Crucially, the acts in question are deemed not to be the personal acts of the head of State. Rather they are acts of the State for which an individual is not held personally responsible. However, there is considerable dispute as to whether this principle would apply in the case of criminal acts by a former head of State (*see* the **Pinochet Case**). For the equivalent immunity of Ministers of Foreign Affairs, see the ***Arrest Warrant Case***. On 9 December 2002, the Republic of the Congo filed an application before the ICJ challenging the legality of investigations and prosecution measures taken in France against the President of the Republic of the Congo and the Congolese Minister of the Interior. On 17 June 2003, the Court rejected a request for indication of provisional measures, but a decision on the merits of the case is awaited: *Certain Criminal Proceedings in France, (Republic of the Congo v. France)* as yet unreported. *See* Watts, *supra*; Barker, The Future of Former Head of State Immunity After *ex parte Pinochet (1999) 48 I.C.L.Q. 937*.

Headquarters Agreements Agreements between international organizations and the host State have been concluded to regulate the headquarters of those organizations with fixed residences. Thus, the Headquarters Agreement between the UN and the USA of 26 June 1947 *(11 U.N.T.S. 12)* provides that the headquarters district "shall be under the control and authority of the United Nations as provided in this agreement" (art. 3(7)); in particular, US law which is inconsistent with a regulation of the UN is inapplicable within the headquarters district (art. 3(8)), and the headquarters district is declared to be "inviolable" (art. 3(9)(a)). Many headquarters agreements and municipal legislation relating to them, or abstracts therefrom, have been published by the UN as *Legislative Text and Treaty Provisions concerning the Legal Status, Privileges and Immunities of International Organizations (UN Doc. ST/LEG/SER.B/10 and ST/LEG/SER.B/11)*. See also **WHO-Egypt Agreement Case**.

Heathrow Airport User Charges Arbitration *(USA v. UK) 1994 Y.B. Com. Arb. 33*. The Air Services Agreement between the UK and USA of 23 July 1977 (Bermuda II; *28 U.S.T. 5367*) required that airport charges be "just and reasonable" and "equitably apportioned among categories of users" (art. 10(1)), not discriminatory against foreign airlines (art. 10(2)) and reflective of, but not exceeding, the full cost of the facilities and services (art. 10(3)). It also provided for arbitration (art. 17), a provision invoked by the United States in 1988 to challenge a new pricing régime instituted by the British Airports Authority, the owner of Heathrow Airport, in 1984. It was *held* by the Tribunal (Foighel, Fielding and Lever) that the new user charges were not just and reasonable insofar as they reflected the cost of providing domestic services, thereby involving an inequitable apportionment among categories of users; and that, for some years of the arbitration period, the UK had breached art. 10 of Bermuda II, there being no rational or consistent relationship between the economic cost of facilities and services and the charges imposed by the BAA. The Tribunal rejected a subsequent US request to revise its award; and the parties agreed to a settlement on the quantum of damages in March 1994.

Helsinki Agreement This name is given to the Final Act of the Conference on Security and Co-operation in Europe, opened at Helsinki in July 1973, continued at Geneva in September 1973 to July 1975 and concluded at Helsinki on 1 August 1975 between virtually all European States, Canada, the United States and the USSR. The Final Act *(14 I.L.M. 1293 (1975))* contains (1) a Declaration on Principles guiding Relations between Participating States; (2) a "Document" on confidence-building measures and certain aspects of security and disarmament; and declarations on; (3) co-operation in the fields of economics, science and the environment; (4) questions relating to security and co-operation in the Mediterranean; and (5) in humanitarian and other fields; as well as (6) a resolution respecting "follow-up" to the Conference. The Helsinki Agreement is remarkable in a number of respects; while, its substantive provisions were in the form of a declaration and were not intended to be legally binding, they nonetheless were of normative effect; it resulted ultimately (in 1990) in the emergence of the Organization for Economic Cooperation and Development (OECD); and its confidence-building measures, in particular relating to opening contact with Eastern bloc States, are credited with being important in the eventual collapse of communism in Eastern Europe.

Henkin, Louis 1917- . Consultant to the UN Legal Department; served with the Department of State in the UN Bureau. Professor of law at Pennsylvania (1957-62) and Columbia (1962-). US member of the Permanent Court of Arbitration (1963-69). Coeditor-in-chief of the AJIL (1976-84). His works include *How Nations Behave: Law and Foreign Policy* (1979); *The Age of Rights* (1989); *International Law: Politics and Values* (1995); *Foreign Affairs and the U.S. Constitution* (1996).

Heritage Convention *See* **World Heritage Convention**.

Hertslet, Godfrey 1870-1947. British diplomat. Assistant editor *Hertslet's Commercial Treaties*, 1905. Joint editor of *Hertslet's China Treaties* (3rd ed. 1900). Editor, *Foreign Office List*, 1902-1914.

Hertslet, Lewis 1787-1870. English civil servant and author. Works: *A Complete Collection of the Treaties and Conventions at present subsisting between Great Britain and Foreign Powers, so far as they relate to Commerce and Navigation, to the Repression and Abolition of the Slave Trade, and to the Privileges and Interests of the Subjects of the high contracting Powers* (2 vols., 1820); *A Complete Collection of the Treaties and Conventions and reciprocal Relations subsisting between Great Britain and Foreign Powers, and of the Laws, Decrees, and Orders in Council Concerning the same* (16 vols., of which the last five were completed by his son, **Sir Edward Hertslet**, 1827-85); *Treaties etc. between Turkey and Foreign Powers 1835-55* (1855).

Hertslet, Sir Edward 1824-1902. Son of Lewis Hertslet and librarian of the Foreign Office. Joint, then sole, editor of the *Foreign Office List* (1855-1902). Works: vols. 12-16 and (with eldest son, Sir Cecil Hertslet) 17-19 of *Hertslet's Commercial Treaties* (1871-1895); *The Map of Europe by Treaty* (vols. 1-3 1875, vol. 4 1896); *The Map of Africa by Treaty* (2 vols. 1894).

Hickenlooper amendment *See* **act of State, doctrine of; Sabbatino Amendment**.

Higgins, Alexander Pearce 1865-1933. British. Professor, Cambridge 1891-33. Member, PCA 1907-33, President 1929-31. Principal works include *The Hague Peace Conferences* (1909); *War and the Private Citizen* (1912); *Armed Merchant Ships* (1914); *Defensively-Armed Merchant Ships and Submarines* (1917); *Studies in International Law and Relations* (1928).

Higgins, Rosalyn 1937- . Professor of international law at the Universities of Kent (1978-81) and London (1981-95). Member of the Human Rights Committee, 1984-95. First woman judge appointed to the International Court of Justice, 1995- . Principal works include *The Development of International Law through the Political Organs of the United*

Nations (1963); *UN Peacekeeping: Documents and Commentary* (4 vols. 1969-81); *Problems and Process: International Law and How We Can Use It* (1994).

High Commission/Commissioner The usual style of a diplomatic mission, and its head, of one British Commonwealth country in another. *See* **ambassador**; **diplomatic privileges and immunities**. Cf. United Nations High Commissioner for Refugees (UNHCR), United Nations High Commissioner for Human Rights (UNHCHR).

high sea(s) The traditional definition of the term is reflected in art. 1 of the Geneva Convention on the High Seas, 1958 *(450 U.N.T.S. 82)* as being "all parts of the sea that are not included in the territorial sea or the internal waters of a State." Art. 86 of the UN Convention on the Law of the Sea 1982 *(1833 U.N.T.S. 3)* redefines the high seas as "all parts of the sea that are not included in the exclusive economic zone, in the territorial sea or in the internal waters of a State, or in the archipelagic waters of an archipelagic State," while maintaining the freedoms for all States of navigation, overflight and laying of submarine cables and pipelines in the **exclusive economic zone** (art. 58(1)). As to legal rights on the high seas generally, see **freedoms of the sea**. *See* Colombos, *The International Law of the Sea* (6th ed.), Chap. 2; Brown, *The International Law of the Sea* (1994), Chap. 14. *And see* **artificial islands**; **contiguous zone**; **territorial sea**; **archipelagic waters**.

hijacking (of aircraft) In terms of art. 1 of the Hague Convention for the Suppression of Unlawful Seizure of Aircraft 1970 *(860 U.N.T.S. 105),* it is an offence for "any person who on board an aircraft in flight: (a) unlawfully, by force or threat thereof, or by any other form of intimidation, seizes, or exercises control of, that aircraft, or attempts to perform any such act, or (b) is an accomplice of a person who performs or attempts to perform any such act." The convention excludes State aircraft (art. 3(2)), and applies only if the place of take-off or the place of actual landing is situated outside the State of registration of the affected aircraft (art. 3(3)), thereby excluding wholly domestic "hijackings."

The State of registration of an aircraft on board which an offence has been committed, the State where the aircraft lands with the offender still on board, the State in which a lessee of an aircraft has his principal place of business or his permanent residence, and the State in which the alleged offender is found to be present, are bound by the Convention to take measures to establish their jurisdiction in these circumstances (art. 4). A Contracting State may extradite an offender but, if it does not, it is obliged "without exception and whether or not the offence was committed within its territory," to try the case itself (art. 7). The offence is deemed to be an extraditable offence in extradition treaties already existing between Contracting States and must be included in future extradition treaties (art. 8(1)); if there is no extradition treaty in force between two Contracting States, the Convention itself can be used as such in respect of the offence (art. 8(2)). The extradition provisions apply to offenders found in any Contracting State notwithstanding the limitation in art. 3(3). Abramovsky, Multilateral Conventions for the Suppression of Unlawful Seizures and Interference with Aircraft. Part I: The Hague Convention, *13 Colum. J. Transnat'l L. 381 (1974)*.

The Tokyo Convention on Offences and Certain other Acts Committed on Board Aircraft 1963 *(704 U.N.T.S. 219)* deals with offences and other "acts, whether or not they are offences, [which] may or do jeopardize the safety of the aircraft or of persons or property therein or which jeopardize good order and discipline on board" (art. 1(1)(b)); and the Montreal Convention for the Suppression of Unlawful Acts against the Safety of Civil Aviation 1971 *(974 U.N.T.S. 177)* (the **Montreal (Sabotage) Convention**) creates offences for acts against persons or property likely to destroy or incapacitate an aircraft or to endanger its safety in flight (art. 1).

hinterland, doctrine of "Since an occupation is valid only if effective, it is obvious that the extent of an occupation ought only to cover so much territory as is effectively occupied. . . . [However, States] have always tried to attribute to their occupation a much wider area. . . . The uncertainty of the extent of an occupation, and the tendency of every colonising State to extend its occupation constantly and gradually into the interior, or 'hinterland,' of an occupied territory, led several States with colonies in Africa to secure for themselves 'spheres of influence' by international treaties with other interested Powers. . . . In this way disputes could be avoided for the future, and the interested Powers could gradually extend their sovereignty over vast territories without coming into conflict with other Powers. Thus, to give some examples, Great Britain concluded treaties regarding spheres of influence with Portugal in 1890 *[174 C.T.S. 91]*, with Italy in 1891 *[175 C.T.S. 67]*, with Germany in 1886 and 1890 *[167 C.T.S. 397; 173 C.T.S. 271]*, and with France in 1898 *[186 C.T.S. 313]*. But the establishment of a sphere of influence did not in itself vest territorial rights of a legal nature in the State exercising the influence": *I Oppenheim (8th ed.), 559-62. See also* **continuity**; **contiguity**; **sector claims**; **spheres of influence**.

historic bay(s) Art. 10(6) of the UN Convention on the Law of the Sea 1982 *(1833 U.N.T.S. 3)*, repeating, in identical terms, art. 7(6) of the Geneva Convention on the Territorial Sea etc. 1958 *(516 U.N.T.S. 205)*, states that the provisions of art. 7 relative to the delimitation of baselines for the territorial sea in bays do "not apply to so-called 'historic bays.'" While the Convention offers no definition of or criteria for an historic bay, it is generally accepted that "the criteria for the establishment of title to a historic bay are similar to those for the establishment of any other historic title to territory. The claimant State must produce evidence of a long-standing intention to claim sovereignty over the bay in question and of effective, peaceful and unopposed exercise of authority over the waters of the bay. A record of historical consolidation would be expected in the form of evidence of recognition or at least acquiescence on the part of other States": Brown, *The International Law of the Sea* (1994), Vol. 1, 31, who suggests that, on these criteria, "Libya's claim to the Bay of Sirte almost certainly fails these tests. Hudson Bay in Canada and the Sea of Azov in the Soviet Union do appear to satisfy the criteria and like the Bay of Fonesca, have attracted general recognition as historic bays." As to the status of the Gulf of Fonseca, see the *Land, Island and Maritime Frontier Dispute Case. See also* UN Secretariat study, *Juridical Regime of Historic Waters, including Historic Bays* in *[1962] II I.L.C. Yearbook*, 1-26.

historic consolidation Territory or rights of a territorial nature acquired through consolidation by historical titles have been explained thus: "Proven long use, which is its foundation, merely represents a complex of interests and relations which in themselves have the effect of attaching a territory or an expanse of sea to a given State. It is these interests and relations, varying from one case to another, and not the passage of a fixed term, unknown in any event to international law, that are taken into direct account by the judge *in concreto* on the existence or non-existence of a consolidation by historic titles": de Visscher, *Theory and Reality in Public International Law* (1968), 209. *See* **historic rights (or title)**. *See I Oppenheim 709-10.*

historic rights (or title) "The term 'historic rights' is used here to mean title created in derogation of international law through historical processes by which one State has asserted a jurisdiction originally illegal, and this has been acquiesced in by the community of nations. . . . One may point out that no real distinction exists or has been judicially recognised between the processes of proof of title in derogation from international law and title through adverse possession and it may well be enquired if the category of historic right is anything but abstract": O'Connell, *International Law* (1965), Vol. 1, 496-7. In the ***Anglo***

Norwegian Fisheries Case 1951 I.C.J. Rep. 116 at130, 142, Norway asserted and the United Kingdom in some measure conceded an historic title to waters. In the *Fisheries Jurisdiction Case (Merits) 1974 I.C.J. Rep. 3* at 28, the Court took note of Iceland's "historic and special interests in the fishing in the disputed waters." *See* **prescription, acquisitive**; **historic consolidation**. *See* also Blum, *Historic Titles in International Law* (1965).

historic waters "By 'historic waters' are usually meant waters which are treated as internal waters but which would not have that character were it not for the existence of an historic title": *Anglo-Norwegian Fisheries Case 1951 I.C.J. Rep. 116 at 130*. Blum, *Historic Titles in International Law* (1965), 248-9, identifies three requirements for historic waters: "the State whose rights have been incroached upon or are likely to be infringed, by an historic claim, has by its conduct, acquiesced in such an exceptional claim"; the manifestations of State authority over the waters (in the form of effectiveness, continuity and notoriety) differ from those required for land territory; "historic rights can never be acquired merely by means of occupation of an hitherto ownerless territory . . . [and] . . . must be based on adverse holding by the claimant." *See also* UN Secretariat study, *Juridical Regime of Historic Waters, Including Historic Bays* in *[1962] II I.L.C. Yearbook,* 1-26.

historical interpretation Hardly a term of art, using historical data to interpret a treaty is no more than applying the cannons of the Vienna Convention on the Law of Treaties 1969 that a treaty be interpreted in its "context" (art. 31(1)), having resort, in certain circumstances, to supplementary means, "including the preparatory work of the treaty and the circumstances of its conclusion" (art. 32). *See travaux préparatoires.*

Historicus The pseudonym under which **Sir W. Vernon Harcourt** published his *Letters on Some Questions of International Law* (1863) concerning the obligations of neutrality, originally appearing in *The Times* during the American Civil War.

Holland, Sir Thomas Erskine 1835-1926. Professor, Oxford, 1874-1910. Editor of *Gentilis' De Jure Belli* (1877). Other publications: *The Brussels Conference of 1874* (1876); *Manual of Naval Prize Law* (1888); *Manual of the Laws and Customs of War on Land* (1904); *Neutral Duties in Maritime War* (1905); *The Law of War on Land* (1908); ed. of Zouche, *Juris et Judicii Fecialis Explicatio* (1911); ed. of Legnano, *De Bello* (1917); *Lectures on International Law* (1933).

Holy See "The Holy *See* is . . . a *permanent* subject of *general* customary international law *vis-à-vis* all States, Catholic or not. That does not mean that the Holy *See* has the same international status as a sovereign State. But the Holy *See* has, under general international law, the capacity to conclude agreements with States (**concordats**). The Holy *See* can also conclude normal international treaties, formerly on behalf of the Papal State, now on behalf of the State of the City of the Vatican, but also in its own capacity. . . . The Holy *See* has the active and passive right of legation under general international law, not restricted to Catholic states": Kunz, The Status of the Holy *See* in International Law, *46 A.J.I.L. 308* at 310 *(1952). See I Oppenheim 325-9*; Cardinale, *The Holy See and the International Order* (1976). *See also* **Lateran Treaty**.

Home Missionary Society Case (United States v. Great Britain) (1920) 6 R.I.A.A. 42. Upon a claim on behalf of an American religious body in respect of losses in the course of a rebellion in the Colony of Sierra Leone in 1898, allegedly provoked by the imposition of a "hut tax," *held,* by the British-American Claims Tribunal established under the Special Agreement of 18 August 1910 *(211 C.T.S. 408),* that the claim failed. "It is a well-established principle of international law that no government can be held responsible for the act of rebellious bodies of men committed in violation of its authority, where it is itself guilty of no breach of good faith, or of no negligence in suppressing insurrection."

***hors de combat*, person** "A person is *hors de combat* if: (a) he is in the power of an adverse Party; (b) he clearly expresses an intention to surrender; or (c) he has been rendered unconscious or is otherwise incapacitated by wounds or sickness, and therefore is incapable of defending himself, provided that in any of these cases he abstains from any hostile acts and does not attempt to escape": art. 41(2), Protocol 1 to the Geneva Conventions relating to the Protection of Victims of International Armed Conflicts 1977 *(1125 U.N.T.S. 3)*. Such a person must not be made the object of attack: art 41(1).

hostage(s) "For the purpose of this opinion the term 'hostages' will be considered as [connoting] those persons of the civilian population who are taken into custody for the purpose of guaranteeing with their lives the good conduct of the population of the community from which they were taken": *In re List 15 I.L.R. 632* (Decision of the US Military Tribunal at Nuremberg). According to art. 34 of the Geneva Convention IV relative to the Protection of Civilian Persons in Time of War 1949 *(75 U.N.T.S. 287)*, the taking of hostages is "prohibited" in war. In terms of the International Convention against the Taking of Hostages 1979 *(1316 U.N.T.S. 205)*, each State Party must make it an offence, "punishable by appropriate penalties which take into account the grave nature of [the offence]" (art. 2), for "any person who seizes or detains and threatens to kill, to injure or to continue to detain another person . . . in order to compel a third party, namely a State, an international organization, a natural or juridical person, or a group of persons, to do or abstain from doing any act as an explicit or implicit condition for the release of the hostage," this offence extending to those who attempt the offence and who act as accomplices (art. 1). Each State party must assume jurisdiction over the offence of "hostage-taking" committed in its territory or on board its ships and aircraft; by its nationals or habitually-resident stateless persons; done in order to compel that State to do or abstain from doing any act; and with respect to a hostage who is a national of that State, if considered appropriate (art. 5). Any State party may take into custody an alleged offender present in its territory and, if it does, it must investigate the facts and notify the Secretary-General of the UN and a representative of the State of which the alleged offender is a national (art. 6); and thereafter "if it does not extradite him, [is] obliged, without exception whatsoever and whether or not the offence was committed in its territory, to submit the case to its competent authorities for the purpose of prosecution. . . ." (art. 8). Hostage-taking is to be deemed to be an extraditable offence under existing extradition treaties, and is to be included in future extradition treaties; the Convention itself, in the absence of an extradition treaty, may be considered as the legal basis for extradition (art. 10). The States Parties are to cooperate to prevent hostage-taking, in particular by adopting measures to prohibit in their territories illegal activities that "encourage, instigate, organize or engage in" hostage-taking and by exchanging information (art. 4). As to the taking hostage of diplomatic and consular officials, see the Convention on the Prevention and Punishment of Crimes against Internationally Protected Persons, including Diplomatic Agents 1973 *(1035 U.N.T.S. 167)*, the Vienna Convention on Diplomatic Relations 1961 *(500 U.N.T.S. 95)* and the Vienna Convention on Consular Relations 1963 *(596 U.N.T.S. 261)*; *and see also **United States Diplomatic and Consular Staff in Tehran Case** 1980 I.C.J. Rep. 3.*

Hostages Case *See **United States Diplomatic and Consular Staff in Tehran Case**.*

hostage-taking *See* **hostage(s)**.

Hostile Environmental Modification Convention   The Convention on the Prohibition of Military or other Hostile Use of Environmental Modification Techniques was opened for signature at Geneva on 18 May 1977 *(1108 U.N.T.S. 151)*. States parties to the Convention undertake "not to engage in military or other hostile use of environmental modification techniques having widespread, long-lasting or severe effects as a means of destruction, damage or injure any other State Party" (art. I(1)). Art. II defines the term "environmental modification techniques" as any technique "for changing—through the deliberate manipulation of any natural processes—the dynamics, composition or structure of the Earth, including its biota, lithosphere, hydrosphere and atmosphere, or of outer space." The peaceful use of such techniques, subject to generally recognized principles of international law, is permitted by art. III(1), with undertakings for the exchange of data in art. V(2). Consultation is provided for under art. IV(1), using, if necessary, an *ad hoc* Committee of Experts constituted under art. V(2). Any report of the Committee is circulated to the parties. Parties may lodge a complaint of breach of obligation with the Security Council (art. V(3)), and each Party is bound to assist a party on its request if the Security Council finds that it is or may be harmed by a breach of the treaty obligations (art. V(5)). The Convention is of unlimited duration (art. VII), but may be amended (art. VI), and is subject to periodic review (art. VIII).

Hostilities, Hague Convention relative to the Opening of   Hague Convention III of 1907 *(205 C.T.S. 263)*, which bears this title, recites that the parties recognize that hostilities between them must not commence without a previous and unequivocal warning in the form either of a reasoned declaration of war or of an ultimatum with a conditional declaration of war (art. 1). "The indictment of the major German war criminals before the International Military Tribunal at Nuremberg included this provision . . . among the Treaties violated by Germany, and the Tribunal duly took note of that aspect. . . ." *II Oppenheim 293*. In modern practice, while declarations of war may be important under States' constitutions, they have fallen, along with "war" in the legal sense, into desuetude.

hostis humani generis   "A pirate has always been considered outlaw, a *hostis humani generis*. According to international law the act of piracy makes the pirate lose the protection of his home state and thereby his national character; and his vessel, or aircraft, although it may formerly have possessed a claim to sail under a certain state's flag, loses such claim": *I Oppenheim 746. See* arts. 100-7 of the UN Convention on the Law of the Sea 1982 *(1833 U.N.T.S. 3)*. Thus, **piracy**, as an **international crime**, renders its perpetrators *hostes humani generis*. The question arises as to what other international crimes so render their perpetrators; and, there being no other international crimes to which **universal jurisdiction** on the lines of that for piracy applies, it is tempting to conclude that pirates alone are *hostes humani generis*.

hot pursuit, doctrine of   (1) At sea, the doctrine posits that "subject to certain conditions, a government enforcement vessel (not necessarily, or even usually, a warship) of a coastal state may pursue onto the high seas a foreign merchant ship, where the competent authorities of the coastal state have good reason to believe that the ship has violated that state's laws and regulations, whilst in waters within the state's jurisdiction, and has escaped from those waters. Since the right is essentially a temporary extension onto the high seas of the coastal state's jurisdiction, the pursuit must commence within the jurisdiction. . . .": *I Oppenheim 739*. The right of hot pursuit is stipulated for in art. 111 of the UN Convention on the Law of the Sea 1982 *(1833 U.N.T.S. 3)* substantially on the basis indicated in the passage quoted. *See also* Colombos, *The International Law of the Sea* (6th ed.) 168-75. *And see **The I'm Alone** (1933-5) 3 R.I.A.A. 1609*.

(2) On land, the so-called doctrine, based on the maritime doctrine, is more controversial, and posits the right of a State's military forces to pursue fugitives across a frontier into a neighboring State. While such pursuit provided for by treaty raises no problems (*Santa Isabel Claims (1926) 4 R.I.A.A. 787*), absent consent any incursion in pursuit of fugitives violates the territorial sovereignty of the neighboring State. *See I Oppenheim 387 n. 13.*

"Hot-Line" Agreements The popular name of the Memorandum of Understanding between the United States and the USSR regarding the Establishment of a Direct Communications Link signed 20 June 1963 "for use in time of emergency," modified by a further agreement of 30 September 1971 and expanded by yet another agreement of 17 July 1984. Similar agreements were concluded between the USSR and France in 1976 and the USSR and the UK in 1977.

hovering laws This term connotes municipal legislation that purports to subject vessels in a specified area of water adjacent to the State's territory, but outside its **territorial sea**, to some aspect of its jurisdiction. "Following in part the pattern of British legislation, the laws of the United States have since 1790 prohibited various acts within 12 miles, or 4 leagues, of the shore, as a means to enforce compliance with the customs laws. These provisions have varied from time to time, and for many years have been specifically made applicable to foreign vessels as well as to American. . . . Penalties, often forfeiture, are provided for failure to produce the manifest or carrying unmanifested goods, unlading merchandise after arrival within four leagues and before coming to a proper place for unloading, and attempting to depart from a collection district without making a report": Bishop, *International Law* (3rd ed.), 521-522. These laws become important, and controversial, during the eras of prohibition in the United States (1919-33) and of "**radio pirates**" in European waters (approximately 1960-70). The UN Convention on the Law of the Sea 1982 *(1833 U.N.T.S. 3)*, in art. 33, titled "**contiguous zone**," provides for a coastal State to exercise the control necessary to prevent, and punish infringement "of its customs, fiscal, immigration and sanitary laws and regulations within its territory or territorial sea" in a zone extending to 24 miles from the baselines of the territorial sea. *See Masterton, Jurisdiction in Marginal Seas* (1929), 1-162; Colombos, *The International Law of the Sea* (6th ed.), 135-46.

HRC *See* **Human Rights Committee**.

Hudson, Manley Ottmer 1886-1960. US national. Professor, Harvard University 1918-1953. Judge, PCIJ 1936-46. Chairman, ILC 1948-51. Principal publications: *International Legislation* (9 vols. 1931-50); *World Court Reports* (4 vols. 1934-48); *The Permanent Court of International Justice* (1934-1943); *Cases and Other Materials on International Law* (1929, 1936, 1951). Hudson played a principal part in the organization and conduct of the **Harvard Research** project.

human rights This expression does not appear at all in the proposals discussed at the **Dumbarton Oaks Conference** which constituted the principal basis for the UN Charter and appears to have been coined at the **San Francisco Conference** by Field Marshal Smuts. The expression is employed six times in the text of the Charter: in the Preamble, reciting the determination of the peoples of the United Nations "to reaffirm faith in fundamental human rights"; art. 1(3), declaring as a Purpose of the UN to "achieve international cooperation in . . . promoting and encouraging respect for human rights and for fundamental freedoms"; art. 13(1)(b), mandating the General Assembly to initiate studies and make recommendations for the purpose of "assisting in the realization of human rights and fundamental freedoms for all"; art. 55, requiring the UN to promote universal respect for such rights and freedoms in the area of economic and social co-operation; art. 62(2), empowering the Economic and Social Council to make recommendations for the purpose of promoting respect for and observance of them; art. 68, requiring that organ to establish commissions for special purposes including "the promotion of human rights"; and art. 76(c), encouraging of respect for human rights as one of the "basic objectives" of the trusteeship system.

Pursuant to these stipulations, the UN has established the **Commission on Human Rights**, which sponsored the **International Bill of Rights**, comprising the **Universal Declaration of Human Rights** 1948 and the International Covenants on **Economic Social and Cultural Rights** and on **Civil and Political Rights** 1966. In addition, the Commission has been instrumental in the adoption of the International Convention on the Elimination of All Forms of Racial Discrimination 1965 (*see* **racial discrimination**); Convention on the Elimination of All Forms of Discrimination against Women 1979 (*see* **Women, Convention on the Elimination of All Forms of Discrimination against**); Convention against Torture 1984 (*see* **Torture, Convention against**); Convention on the Rights of the Child 1989 (*see* **Child, Convention on the Rights of**); and International Convention on the Protection of the Rights of All Migrant Workers and Members of Their Families 1990 (*see* **Migrant Workers' Convention**). Alongside this global activity through the United Nations, there are a number of regional human rights agreements: *see* the **African Charter on Human and Peoples' Rights** 1981; **American Convention on Human Rights** 1969; **European Convention on Human Rights** 1950.

In classifying human rights, it is common to refer to them as belonging to generations, **First Generation** human rights being civil and political rights, **Second Generation** being economic and social rights and **Third Generation** being group rights.

Given that human rights are the creation of conventional law, the question arises as to how many of these rights are customary law. It is commonly accepted that some of the provisions of the Universal Declaration of Human Rights were, or have subsequently become, part of customary law. The *Restatement (Third) of the Foreign Relations of the United States*, § 702, identifies as customary law: "(a) genocide; (b) slavery or slave trade; (c) the murder or causing the disappearance of individuals; (d) torture or other cruel, inhuman, or degrading treatment or punishment; (e) prolonged arbitrary detention; (f) systematic racial discrimination; (g) a consistent pattern of gross violations of internationally recognized human rights." While common sense may indicate that human rights constitute a hierarchy, the trend, particularly among human rights **NGO**s, is to regard all human rights as "universal, indivisible and interdependent and interrelated" to be treated "in a fair and equal manner, on the same footing and with the same emphasis": Vienna Declaration and Programme of Action on Human Rights 1993 (*UN Doc. A/CONF.157/23*, Part I, para. 5). *See* Henkin, *The International Bill of Rights* (1981); Meron, *Human Rights in International Law* (1984); Robertson and Merrills, *Human Rights in the World* (4th ed.).

Human Rights Commission   *See* **Commission on Human Rights**.

Human Rights Committee   This body was established by art. 28(1) of the International Covenant on **Civil and Political Rights** 1966 *(999 U.N.T.S. 171)* to perform monitoring and enforcement functions under the Covenant and its Optional Protocol 1966 *(id.)*. It consists of 18 members (art. 18(1)), elected from persons of high moral character, recognized competence in human rights and with at least some with legal experience (art. 28(2)) by the States parties to the Covenant (art. 29(1)), who serve a four-year term (art. 32(1)). It receives reports submitted by States on measures taken to give effect to the Covenant and progress made in the enjoyment of these rights (art. 40(1)), studies these reports (art. 40(4)) and transmits its observations and any general comments to the reporting State (art. 40(4)). Provided that a State has recognized the right of the Committee to receive "communications" from other States, the Committee may receive and consider communications alleging a violation of the Covenant (art. 41(1)); in these circumstances, the Committee attempts a friendly settlement (art. 41(1)(e)). Under the Optional Protocol, provided that the State has recognized the right of the Committee to receive "communications" from individuals, the Committee may receive communications from individuals alleging that they are victims of violations of the Covenant (art. 1)); in these circumstances, the Committee transmits its views to the individual and the State (art. 4(4)). For both types of communications, local remedies must be exhausted (art. 41(1)(c), art. 5(2)((b)). *See* McGoldrick, *The Human Rights Committee: Its Role in the Development of the International Covenant on Civil and Political Rights* (1994); Ghandhi, *The Human Rights Committee and the Right of Individual Petition* (1998).

human rights defenders The Declaration on the Right and Responsibility of Individuals, Groups and Organs of Society to Promote and Protect Internationally Recognized Human Rights and Fundamental Freedoms, annexed to General Assembly Res. 53/144 of 8 March 1999, while recognizing that each State has the primary responsibility to protect and promote human rights (art. 2), acknowledges the role of individuals and groups (invariably **NGO**s). The right of everyone, individually or in association with others, to promote human rights is asserted (art. 1), that right entailing, *inter alia*, the obtaining, holding and imparting of information on human rights (art. 6) and the participation in, and meeting of, human rights groups (art. 5). States are to ensure that those promoting human rights are not subject to harassment (art. 12(2)) or any adverse reaction by the State (art. 12(3)), provided that they conform to "the just requirements of morality, public order and the general welfare in a democratic society" (art. 17).

human rights movement A term in general usage denoting the international instruments adopted and agreed by the international community from about the middle of the 20th century to protect and promote **human rights**, including particularly the role of **non-governmental organizations** in that process.

Human Rights Watch The successor to Helsinki Watch, established after the **Helsinki Agreements** on Security and Co-operation in Europe, this **NGO**'s activities support victims and activists to prevent discrimination, upholds political freedom, protects people from inhumane conduct in wartime, and seeks to bring offenders to justice. As well as thematic and other investigations, HRW produces an authoritative *World Report* on the human rights situation in a large number of States. *See* <www.hrw.org>.

humanitarian intervention One of the vexed issues in contemporary international law is the legality of a State or a collectivity of States intervening militarily in another State in the face of egregious human rights abuses perpetrated by the target State against its own population. Historically, when "the treatment meted out by a State to its own population, particularly to minorities, was so arbitrary, persistently abusive, and cruel that it shocked the conscience of mankind, other States, usually the great powers of the period, took it upon themselves to threaten or even to use force in order to come to the rescue of the oppressed minority": Schwelb, *Human Rights and the International Community* (1964), 13-14. The present position is succinctly stated by *I Oppenheim 442-4* thus: "[A] substantial body of opinion and of practice has supported the view that there are limits to [the] discretion [of a State as to how it treats its own nationals] and that when a state commits cruelties against and persecution of its nationals in such a way as to deny their fundamental human rights and to shock the conscience of mankind, the matter ceases to be of sole concern to that state and even intervention in the interests of humanity might be legally permissible. However, the fact that, when resorted to by individuals states, it may be—and has been—abused for selfish purposes tended to weaken its standing as a legal practice. That objection does not apply to collective intervention, and the growing involvement of the international community on both a global and regional basis with the protection of human rights diminishes any need for states to retain or exercise an individual right of humanitarian intervention." In relation of the NATO bombings of Serbia and Serb targets in Kosovo in 1999, the independent international Kosovo Commission concluded in the *Kosovo Report* (2000) that the bombings were "illegal but legitimate . . . because it did not receive prior approval from the United Nations Security Council. However, the Commission considers that the intervention was justified because all diplomatic avenues had been exhausted and because the intervention had the effect of liberating the majority population of Kosovo from a long period of oppression under Serbian rule." Critical of several aspects of the intervention, the Commission recognized the urgent need to clarify the "conditions under which justifiable humanitarian intervention in UN member states can be undertaken in the future." *See* Lillich, *Humanitarian Intervention and the United Nations* (1973); Tesón, *Humanitarian Intervention: An Inquiry into Law and Morality* (2nd ed.); Murphy, *Humanitarian Intervention: The United Nations in an Evolving World Order* (1996); Chesterton, *Just War or Just Peace: Humanitarian Intervention and International Law* (2001).

humanitarian law, international *See* **international humanitarian law**.

humanity, crime against The first articulation as to what constitutes a crime against humanity appears in art. 6 of the Charter of the Nuremberg International Military Tribunal 1945 *(82 U.N.T.S. 279)*: "murder, extermination, enslavement, deportation, and other inhumane acts committed against any civilian population . . . or persecutions on political, racial or religious grounds in execution of or in connection with any crime within the jurisdiction of the Tribunal. . . ." Thus defined, this category was intended to fill any gaps in the Tribunal's jurisdiction for egregious acts not covered by the other limbs of art. 6, viz. crimes against peace and war crimes. Since the judgment of the Nuremberg Tribunal *((1947) 41 A.J.I.L. 172)* and the adoption of the **Nuremberg Principles** by the International Law Commission on 2 August 1950, crimes against humanity have become a recognized part of international criminal law, being within the jurisdiction of the **International Criminal Tribunal for the Former Yugoslavia** and the **International Criminal Tribunal for Rwanda**. The Rome Statute of the **International Criminal Court** 1998 *(37 I.L.M. 999 (1998))* defines a crime against humanity, in art. 7(1)), as "any of the following acts when committed as part of a widespread or systematic attack directed against any civilian population, with knowledge of the attack: (a) Murder; (b) Extermination; (c) Enslavement; (d) Deportation or forcible transfer of population; (e) Imprisonment or other severe deprivation of physical liberty in violation of fundamental rules of international law; (f) Torture; (g) Rape, sexual slavery, enforced prostitution, forced pregnancy, enforced sterilization, or any other form of sexual violence of comparable gravity; (h) Persecution against any identifiable group or collectivity on political, racial, national, ethnic, cultural, religious, gender . . ., or other grounds that are universally recognized as impermissible under international law, in connection with any act referred to in this paragraph or any crime within the jurisdiction of the Court; (i) Enforced disappearance of persons; (j) The crime of apartheid; (k) Other inhumane acts of a similar character intentionally causing great suffering, or serious injury to body or to mental or physical health." *See **Eichmann Case**. See* Bassiouni, *Crimes Against Humanity in International Criminal Law* (2nd ed.); Lattimer and Sands, *Justice for Crimes Against Humanity* (2003).

Hurst, Sir Cecil James Barrington 1870-1963. Legal Adviser, Foreign Office 1918-29; Judge, PCIJ 1929-46; President 1934-6; founder of the *British Yearbook of Interna-*

tional Law, (B.Y.I.L.) Principal publication: *International Law, The Collected Papers of Sir Cecil J. B. Hurst* (1950).

Hyde, Charles Cheney 1873-1952. Professor, Northwestern 1899-1923; Solicitor to State Department 1923-5; Professor, Harvard, 1925-41. Principal publication: *International Law, Chiefly as Interpreted and Applied by the United States* (3 vols. 1922-1945).

I

IADB *See* **Inter-American Development Bank.**

IAEA *See* **International Atomic Energy Agency.**

IAFD *See* **International Fund for Agricultural Development.**

IATA *See* **International Air Transport Association.**

IBRD *See* **International Bank for Reconstruction and Development.**

ICAO *See* **International Civil Aviation Organization.**

ICAO Council Case, Appeal Relating to the Jurisdiction of (India v. Pakistan) 1972 I.C.J. Rep. 46. The proceedings in this case were instituted by an application in reliance upon art. 84 of the Chicago Convention on International Civil Aviation 1944 *(15 U.N.T.S. 295)* and art. II(2) of the International Air Services Transit Agreement 1944 *(84 U.N.T.S. 387)*, providing for the settlement of disagreements relating to the interpretation or application of those instruments on application to the Council of ICAO, subject to appeal either to an agreed *ad hoc* tribunal or to the ICJ. The application averred that the Council had no jurisdiction in regard to the particular matter in relation to which it had purported to act: a complaint by Pakistan respecting the suspension by India of overflights of Indian territory by Pakistani civil aircraft as from 4 February 1971 arising out of a hijacking incident involving the diversion of an Indian aircraft to Pakistan. In the view of India, the instruments of 1944 had not, since the hostilities of August-September 1965 between the parties, been in force, or at least in operation, between them. In response, Pakistan contended principally that the jurisdictional clauses in question provided only for an appeal from a decision on the merits of a disagreement and not from a decision simply concerning that body's jurisdiction to entertain a matter. Upon this preliminary issue, in its judgment of 18 August 1972, the Court *held* (13 to 3) that the objection failed. A jurisdictional decision, though it does not determine the ultimate merits, is still a decision of a substantive character, a constituent part of the case, often involving important questions of law. Proceeding then to the question whether the ICAO Council had jurisdiction to entertain the merits, the Court further *held* (14 to 2) in the affirmative, dismissing the appeal, on the basis that the question whether the relevant treaties were or were not suspended or terminated between the parties was one as to their interpretation or application.

ICC *See* **International Criminal Court.**

ICES *See* **International Council for the Exploration of the Sea.**

ICJ *See* entries under **International Court of Justice**; *see also* **International Commission of Jurists**.

ICRC *See* **International Committee of the Red Cross**.

ICSID *See* **International Centre for the Settlement of Investment Disputes**.

ICTR *See* **International Criminal Tribunal for the Rwanda**.

ICTY *See* **International Criminal Tribunal for the Former Yugoslavia**.

IDA *See* **International Development Association**.

IFC *See* **International Finance Corporation**.

IFRC *See* **International Federation of Red Cross and Red Crescent Societies**.

IHL *See* **international humanitarian law**.

Ihlen declaration The term commonly given to the oral statement of the Norwegian Minister for Foreign Affairs, Hr. Ihlen, recorded in a minute made by the Minister himself, to the Danish Minister to Norway on 22 July 1919 to the effect "that the Norwegian Government would not make any difficulties in the settlement of th[e] question" of the recognition of Danish sovereignty over Eastern Greenland. The Declaration, *qua* a communication of an official character on a matter within the Minister's province, was regarded by the PCIJ in its advisory opinion in the ***Eastern Greenland, Legal Status of, Case*** as "beyond all dispute . . . binding upon the country to which the Minister belongs": *(1933) P.C.I.J., Ser. A/B, No. 53* at 36 and 71.

ILA *See* **International Law Association**.

ILO *See* **International Labor Organization**.

ILO Administrative Tribunal, Advisory Opinion respecting Judgments of *1956 I.C.J. Rep. 77.* By resolution dated 18 November 1955, the Executive Board of UNESCO requested of the ICJ, pursuant to Art. XII of the Statute of the Administrative Tribunal of the ILO (text in Amerasinghe, *Documents on International Administrative Tribunals* (1989), 31), an opinion as to: I, whether the Tribunal was competent to hear complaints introduced against UNESCO by certain individuals (the ground of whose complaints had been the non-renewal of fixed-term contracts of service); II, if the answer here was affirmative, then whether the Tribunal was competent (a) to determine whether the power of the Director-General not to renew such appointments had been exercised for the good of the service and in the interest of the Organization (as the Staff Regulations permitted); and (b) to pronounce on the attitude which the Director-General should maintain in his relations with a member State; and III, in any case, what was the validity of the decisions in point.

On 23 October 1956, the Court *decided* (9 to 4) that it would comply with the request notwithstanding that the Statute of the Tribunal afforded the right to challenge its judgments only to the Executive Board and not to individual claimants, this apparent inequality not being an inequality before the Court, but antecedent to its examination of the question and no more than nominal in the light of the individual claimants' success before the Tribunal. The obstacle of inequality in proceedings before the Court had, furthermore, been surmounted by the transmission to it of the observations of the individual claimants via the intermediary of UNESCO. Proceeding then to Question I, the Court *advised* (10 to 3) affirmatively, for the complaints were within the Tribunal's competence under art. II(5) of its Statute as "complaints alleging non-observance in substance or in form of the terms of appointment of officials and of provisions of the Staff Regulations," the holders of fixed-term contracts in the practice of international organizations being often treated as entitled to be considered for continued employment. But the Court *advised* (9 to 4) that Question II did not call for an answer, the Tribunal's Statute providing for a request for an advisory opinion only where the Executive Board challenged a decision of the Tribunal confirming its jurisdiction or where it considered that such a decision was vitiated by a fundamental fault in procedure, and not by way of appeal on the merits such as was in effect involved in this question. The Court further *advised* (10 to 4) upon Question III that the validity of the decisions referred to was no longer open to challenge, having been impugned without result on the sole ground of lack of competence of the Tribunal.

Iloilo Claims *(Great Britain v. United States) (1925) 6 R.I.A.A. 158.* These were claims in respect of the destruction of the property of British subjects at Iloilo, Philippines, during the period of confusion between the signature of the Treaty of Peace of 10 December 1898 *(187 C.T.S. 100)* stipulating for the cession of the islands by Spain and the landing of United States forces at the instance of the commercial community to restore order, upon which the British-American Arbitral Tribunal constituted under the Special Agreement of 18 August 1910 *(211 C.T.S. 408) held* that the United States had no responsibility, having had neither sovereignty nor *de facto* control at the relevant time.

I'm Alone Case *(Canada v. United States) (1933-5) 3 R.I.A.A. 1609.* This was a claim referred to the Commission established under the Pecuniary Claims Agreement between Great Britain and the United States of 18 August 1910 pursuant to art. 4 of the Anglo-American Liquor Treaty of 23 January 1924 *(27 L.N.T.S. 182).* It arose out of the sinking of the *I'm Alone,* a British vessel of Canadian registry, summoned to stop while engaged in smuggling liquor into the United States at a point outside US territorial waters but apparently within the one-hour steaming zone designated by art. 2 of the 1924 Convention as one within which Great Britain would raise no objection to examination of vessels on suspicion of violation of the US liquor laws. Having refused to stop, the vessel was eventually sunk upon the high seas by a sister vessel of the coastguard cutter which originally hailed her. *Held* that the sinking was not justified either by the terms of the Convention or by general international law. Even assuming that the United States was entitled to exercise the right of **hot pursuit** (upon which question the Commissioners did not, apparently, declare themselves), the intentional sinking of the vessel went beyond the exercise of necessary and reasonable force for the purpose of her apprehension. In consequence, the Commission recommended that the US should formally acknowledge the illegality of the sinking and pay the Government of Canada $25,000 "as a material amend in respect of the wrong"; further, that the US should pay certain sums for the benefit of the captain and crew, who were not implicated in the conspiracy to smuggle liquor into the US; but that no compensation ought to be paid in respect of the loss of the ship or cargo because, although a British ship, she was *de facto* owned, controlled and at the critical time managed and her movements directed and her cargo dealt with and disposed of "by a group of persons acting in concert who were entirely, or nearly so, citizens of the United States."

IMCO *See* **International Maritime Organization**.

IMCO Maritime Safety Committee, Constitution of, Advisory Opinion *1960 I.C.J. Rep. 150.* By resolution dated 19 January 1959, the IMCO Assembly requested of the ICJ an advisory opinion as to whether the Maritime Safety Committee of the Organization was duly constituted in accordance with the Convention of 6 March 1948 for the establishment of

IMCO *(89 U.N.T.S. 48)*, art. 28(a) of which provided that that body should consist of 14 members elected by the Assembly, not less that 8 being "the largest ship owning nations." The request arose from the non-election of Liberia and Panama, despite the fact that the merchant fleets under their flags were, among the members, respectively the third and the eighth largest. On 8 June 1960, the Court *advised* (9 to 5) that the Committee was not regularly constituted. In the context of the Convention, the phrase "ship-owning nations" was to be interpreted as referring to registered tonnage under the flag of a State, and could not be taken to permit the Assembly to make its own judgment as to what it might regard as the realities of the matter in relation to the whereabouts of beneficial ownership in shipping. This being the case, it was irrelevant to examine further the contention that there might be taken into consideration the notion of a **genuine link** between the State of registry and the shipping it might register, required by art. 5 of the (then unratified) Geneva Convention on the High Seas of 1958 *(450 U.N.T.S. 82)*.

IMF *See* **International Monetary Fund.**

immigration zone The zone of the high seas, identical with the **contiguous zone**, within which a coastal State may, pursuant to art. 33 of the UN Convention on the Law of the Sea 1982 *(1833 U.N.T.S. 3)*, prevent and punish infringement of, *inter alia*, its immigration laws and regulations.

immunities, immunity The term immunity is employed primarily to denote exemption from legal process. As such, an immunity does not imply or involve non-amenability to law or non-liability *ratione materiae*, as must be clear when it is appreciated that an immunity may invariably be waived. Possibly, indeed probably, the term should not be used in relation to anything other than curial jurisdiction. Cf. the Vienna Convention on Diplomatic Relations 1961 *(500 U.N.T.S. 95)*, arts. 31 and 32. *But see* the Vienna Convention on Consular Relations 1963 *(596 U.N.T.S. 261)*, art. 43, which speaks of non-amenability to "jurisdiction of the judicial or administrative authorities of the receiving State" under the cross-title "Immunity from Jurisdiction." *And see* the General Convention on the Privileges and Immunities of the United Nations of 13 February 1946 *(1 U.N.T.S. 13)* which, though its language is generally consistent with the usage suggested above, purports to provide that UN officials shall be "immune" from national service obligations and immigration restrictions: art. V(18). *See also* **consular privileges and immunities**; **diplomatic privileges and immunities**; **privileges and immunities of international organizations**.

IMO *See* **International Maritime Organization.**

imperium As an aspect of **sovereignty**, the other being *dominium*, *imperium* (sometimes referred to as personal authority or political sovereignty), is "the power of a state to exercise supreme authority over its citizens at home and abroad": *I Oppenheim 382*. Cf. Westlake, *International Law, Part 1 (Peace) (1904)*, 86-7. *See Tietz v. People's Republic of Bulgaria (1959) 28 I.L.R. 368* at 376.

implied powers In the law of international organizations, this term connotes competences conferred by implication, and not expressly conferred in constituent documents. In the *Reparations Case 1949 I.C.J. Rep. 174* at 182 the ICJ stated: "Under international law, [the United Nations] must be deemed to have those powers which, though not expressly provided in the Charter, are conferred upon it by necessary implication as being essential to the performance of its duties . . ."; quoted with approval in the *Administrative Tribunal of the UN Case 1954 I.C.J. Rep. 47* at 56. For a competence to be implied, it appears that it must be necessary to fulfill the objects and purposes of the organization (*South West Af-*

rica Case 1950 I.C.J. Rep. 128; ***Reparations Case***, *supra*; ***Expenses Case** 1962 I.C.J. Rep. 151*) and must not go beyond those objects and purposes *(**Competence of the I.L.O in regard to Agriculture Cases** (1922) P.C.I.J. Ser. B, Nos. 2 and 3*; ***Competence of the ILO to Regulate Work of the Employer** (1926) P.C.I.J., Ser. B, No. 13*). Cf. **inherent powers**. *See* Amerasinghe, *Principles of the Institutional Law of International Organizations* (1996), Chap. 7: White, *The Law of International Organisations* (1996), 128-31.

imputation *See* **attribution**.

inchoate title This expression derives its currency in the literature of international law from the following passage in the award of the Arbitrator, M. Max Huber, in the ***Island of Palmas Case***: "If . . . we consider as positive law at the period in question the rule that discovery as such, i.e. the mere fact of seeing land, without any act, even symbolical, of taking possession, involved *ipso jure* territorial sovereignty and not merely an 'inchoate title,' a *jus ad rem,* to be completed eventually by an actual and durable taking of possession within a reasonable time, the question arises whether sovereignty yet existed at the critical date, i.e. the moment of conclusion and coming into force of the Treaty of Paris": *(1928) 2 R.I.A.A. 829* at 845.

incorporation, doctrine of The school of thought which, in opposition to the doctrine of **transformation**, "says that the rules of international law are incorporated into English law automatically and are considered to be part of English law unless they are in conflict with an Act of Parliament. . . . The difference is vital when you are faced with a change in the rules of international law. Under the doctrine of incorporation, when the rules of international law change, our English law changes with them. . . . The doctrine of incorporation goes back to 1737. . . . As between those two schools of thought, I now believe that the doctrine of incorporation is correct. Otherwise I do not see that our courts could ever recognize a change in the rules of international law. It is certain that international law does change": *Trendtex Trading Corporation v. Central Bank of Nigeria [1977] 1 Q.B. 529* at 553-4 *per* Lord Denning M.R.

independence "Inasmuch as it excludes subjection to any other authority, and in particular the authority of another State, sovereignty is *independence.* It is *external* independence with regard to the liberty of action outside its borders. It is *internal* independence with regard to the liberty of action within its boundaries": *I Oppenheim 382.* In interpreting the term "independence" as used in art. 88 of the Treaty of Saint-Germain of 10 September 1919 *(226 C.T.S. 8)* and Protocol No. 1 of 4 October 1922 *(12 L.N.T.S. 386),* the PCIJ defined the term as meaning "the continued existence of Austria within her present frontiers as a separate State with sole right of decision in all matters economic, political, financial or other with the result that that independence is violated, as soon as there is any violation thereof, either in the economic, political or any other field, these different aspects of independence being in practice one and indivisible": ***Austro-German Customs Union Case** (1931) P.C.I.J., Ser. A /B, No. 41* at 45. In an authoritative separate opinion, Judge Anzilotti defined independence as "the normal condition of States according to international law; it may also be described as *sovereignty (suprema potestas),* or *external sovereignty,* by which is meant that the State has over it no other authority than that of international law": *id* at 57. *See generally* DeLupis, *International Law and the Independent State* (2nd ed.), 3-138.

Independence to Colonial Countries and Peoples, Declaration on the Granting of General Assembly Res. 1514(XV) of 14 December 1960, titled a "Declaration," condemning alien subjugation, domination and exploitation of peoples to be contrary to the

UN Charter, proclaimed the right of **self-determination** of "all peoples" (para. 2), without explicitly providing what should be the outcome of the exercise of the right. This resolution was reinforced by further resolutions of the General Assembly. The principle of self-determination was further elaborated in the **Friendly Relations Declaration** (GA Res. 2625 (XXV)), the 5th Principle of which provided that the outcome, as had been acknowledged since 1960, should be "establishment as a sovereign and independent State, . . . free association or integration with an independent State or . . . emergence into any other political status freely determined. . . ."

indigenous peoples The UN Draft Declaration on the Rights of Indigenous Peoples of 20 April 1994 *(34 I.L.M. 546 (1995))* accords rights to indigenous peoples, without defining the term. These rights include self-determination (art. 3; *see also* art. 31); the maintenance and strengthening of their distinct political, economic, social and cultural characteristics, as well as their legal systems, while retaining their right to full participation in the political, economic, social and cultural life of the State (art. 40); freedom from discrimination (art. 16); the ownership and control over their own lands and territories (art. 26); and the restitution of traditional lands that have been taken from them (art. 27). Among the estimated 300 million indigenous peoples are the Indians of the Americas (*e.g.*, the Mayas of Guatemala or the Aymaras of Bolivia), the Inuit and Aleutians of the circumpolar region, the Saami of northern Europe, the Aborigines and Torres Strait Islanders of Australia, and the Maori of New Zealand; these and other indigenous peoples have retained social, cultural, economic and political characteristics which are clearly distinct from those of the national population at large. Two ILO Conventions on Indigenous and Tribal Peoples of 26 June 1957 *(ILO Doc C.107)* and 27 June 1989 *(ILO Doc. C.169; 28 I.L.M. 1384 (1989))* both define the term indigenous peoples, at least for their own purposes, the latter providing the following (in art. 1(1)): "(a) tribal peoples in independent countries whose social, cultural and economic conditions distinguish them from other sections of the national community, and whose status is regulated wholly or partially by their own customs or traditions or by special laws or regulations; (b) peoples in independent countries who are regarded as indigenous on account of their descent from the populations which inhabited the country, or a geographical region to which the country belongs, at the time of conquest or colonisation or the establishment of present state boundaries and who, irrespective of their legal status, retain some or all of their own social, economic, cultural and political institutions"; art. 2(1) declares "self-identification as indigenous or tribal shall be regarded as a fundamental criterion. . . ." *See* **minorities**. *See* Anaya, *Indigenous Peoples in International Law* (2000); Thornberry, *Indigenous Peoples and Human Rights* (2002).

indirect damage (1) In the law of **State responsibility**, a distinction is sometimes drawn between direct and indirect damage, between proximate and remote damage. *See lucrum cessans*. (2) Again in the law of State responsibility, a distinction is sometimes drawn between an internationally wrongful act against a State and its personnel, assets and interests and such an act against individuals, the latter being referred to as indirect damage and raising the possibility of **diplomatic protection**.

individual opinion *See* **separate opinion**.

individuals While international law was traditionally, and largely still is, the law governing the relations between States and created by States, it has increasingly been accepted that individuals have some status under international law. It has been said that "transformation of the position of the individual is one of the most remarkable developments in contemporary international law": Oda, The Individual in International Law, in Sørensen, *Manual of Public International Law* (1968), 471. The status of individuals is derivate, in the sense that the *indicia* of status emanate from the willingness of States to confer them on individuals. The debate as to whether individuals are subjects of international law (with the same, or similar, rights, duties and capacities as States) or merely objects of international law (with the possibility of their indirectly acquiring some rights and duties, much in the same way as territory, fish or aircraft) is sterile and unhelpful in practice. Thus, *I Oppenheim 848-9* concludes: "It is no longer possible, as a matter of positive law, to regard states as the only subjects of international law, and there is an increasing disposition to treat individuals, within a limited sphere, as subjects of international law." As to rights, alien individuals have for a long time been accorded by customary international law the right to a minimum standard of treatment by host States: *see* **international minimum standard**; **State responsibility**. After World War I, minority groups in certain European States were guaranteed some basic rights in Minorities Treaties (*see* **minorities**). Today, individuals, national or alien, are accorded a wide range of human rights and fundamental freedoms through international agreements: see **Universal Declaration of Human Rights** 1948; **Civil and Political Rights, International Covenant on**, 1966; **Economic, Social and Cultural Rights, International Covenant on**, 1966; **European Convention on Human Rights** 1950; **American Convention on Human Rights** 1969; **human rights**. As to duties, individuals engaged in **piracy** are subject to the jurisdiction of any State: art. 105 of the UN Convention on the Law of the Sea 1982 *(1833 U.N.T.S. 3)*, representing a long-established rule of customary law. The crime of **genocide** is punishable whether the persons committing it are "constitutionally responsible rulers, public officials or private individuals": art. 4 of the Genocide Convention 1948 *(78 U.N.T.S. 277)*. According to the Charter of the **International Military Tribunal** (annexed to the Agreement for the Prosecution and Punishment of the Major War Criminals of the European Axis Powers of 8 August 1945 *(82 U.N.T.S. 279))* the Tribunal had jurisdiction over individuals responsible for crimes against peace (*see* **peace, crimes against**), **war crimes** and crimes against humanity (*see* **humanity, crimes against**). The International Criminal Court, through its Rome Statute of 1998 *(37 I.L.M. 999 (1998))*, applies to all "natural" persons (art. 25(1)). The conventional régime on **terrorism** creates offences for acts by individuals.

Individuals have very limited procedural capacity—power to enforce their rights under international law. Individuals injured in their person and property as a result of an act by a State in breach of international law may only seek redress at the international level through their national State (*see* **diplomatic protection**); and the ICJ is not open to individuals (art. 34(1) of the ICJ Statute). Some human rights agreements accord individuals the right to complain to an international body about violations, but only where that right is recognized by the State complained against; *see, e.g.*, the Optional Protocol to the International Covenant on Civil and Political Rights 1966; cf. arts. 34-39 of the **European Convention on Human Rights** 1950 where no express prior State recognition is required. The possibility exists of individuals enforcing their rights under international law before municipal tribunals, but only where such was clearly intended in an international agreement. Thus, in a dispute involving whether individuals could enforce the terms of a treaty between Danzig and Poland before the courts of Danzig, despite the fact that the treaty was not incorporated into Danzig law, the PCIJ said: "it cannot be disputed that the very object of an international agreement, according to the intention of the contracting Parties, may be the adoption by the Parties of some definite rules creating individual rights and obligations and enforceable by the national courts": *Danzig Railway Officials Case (1928) P.C.I.J., Ser. B., No. 15* at 17-18. *See generally* Corbett, *The Individual and World Society* (1958); Gormley, *The Procedural Status of the Individual before International Tribunals* (1966); Norgaard, *The Position of the Individual in International Law* (1962); Lauterpacht, Subjects of the Law of Nations, *(1947) 63 L.Q.R. 438* and *(1948) 64 L.Q.R. 97*.

inductive approach A method of arriving at the rules of international law by inference from particular facts or evidence, whose principal exponent, Schwarzenberger, described it as an approach whereby "alleged rules and principles of international law arrived at by means of deduction, speculation, or intuition, are treated as hypotheses until they have been inductively verified, that is by reference to the rules governing the law-creating processes and law-determining agencies enumerated or implied in Article 38 of the Statute of the World Court": Schwarzenberger, *The Inductive Approach to International Law* (1965), 129. The inductive approach is said to have four distinctive features: (i) emphasis on the exclusive character of the three formal sources mentioned in art. 38 of the ICJ Statute (treaty, custom and general principles recognized by civilized nations), accepting natural law only if authenticated by one of these three sources; (ii) the establishment of law-determining agencies "in accordance with rationally verifiable criteria," (iii) the characterization of the rules of international law as the only binding norms unless a principle abstracted from such rules has acquired the character of overriding rule; and (iv) the realization of the differences in applying international law in the varying degrees of organization in international society: Schwarzenberger, *supra*, 5-6.

INF Following proposals made by President Ronald Reagan in November 1981, negotiations between the US and the USSR on Intermediate-Range Nuclear Forces (INF) (formerly known as theater nuclear forces: TNF) began on 30 November 1981. The USSR discontinued the INF negotiations on 23 November 1983.

inherent powers In the law of international organizations, and allied to the doctrine of **implied powers**, there is a view that international organizations have powers beyond those expressed in their constituent instruments, and beyond those necessarily implied, to a range of inherent powers. In essence, this amounts to a claim that international organizations have competences absent any prohibition. *See* Seyersted, *United Nations Forces* (1966), 133-4.

initialing (1) A commonly used technique whereby the negotiators of a text indicate, usually by placing their initials at the bottom of each page, that the text is that on which they have settled, thereby fixing it so that their governments can consider it and then proceed to the preparation of a text for formal signature. (2) Art. 12 of the Vienna Convention on the Law of Treaties 1969 provides that "the initialling of a text constitutes a signature of the treaty when it is established that the negotiating States so agreed" for purposes of the provisions of that article respecting the expression of consent to be bound by a treaty by the signature of representatives of States. *See* Aust, *Modern Treaty Law and Practice* (2000), 78-9.

INMARSAT *See* **International Maritime Satellite Organization**.

innocent passage "A State's control over foreign merchant vessels [in the territorial sea] is, however, subject to their right of innocent passage which was upheld by several international jurists in the past and remains equally valid to-day": Colombos, *International Law of the Sea* (6th ed.), 132. Part II, Section 3, of the UN Convention on the Law of the Sea 1982 *(1833 U.N.T.S. 3)*, entitled "Innocent Passage in the Territorial Sea," sets down detailed rules on innocent passage, commencing with the general principles that "ships of all States, whether coastal or land-locked, shall enjoy the right of innocent passage through the territorial sea" (art. 17) and that "[t]he coastal State must not hamper innocent passage through the territorial sea" (art. 24(1)). For the purposes of this right, "[p]assage means navigation through the territorial sea for the purpose of: (a) traversing that sea without entering internal waters or calling at a roadstead or port facility outside internal waters; or

(b) proceeding to or from internal waters or a call at such roadstead or port facility" (art. 18(1)); and must be "continuous and expeditious" though can include "stopping and anchoring, but only in so far as the same are incidental to ordinary navigation or are rendered necessary by *force majeure* or by distress or for the purpose of rendering assistance to persons, ships or aircraft in danger or distress" (art. 18(2)). "Passage is innocent so long as it is not prejudicial to the peace, good order or security of the coastal State. Such passage shall take place in conformity with this Convention and with other rules of international law". (art. 19(1)); there then follows (in art. 19(2)(a)-(l)) a list of 12 categories of activity that are not to be considered as innocent, including any exercise or practice of weapons, any act of propaganda or information collection, any act of willful and serious pollution. All foreign vessels exercising the right of innocent passage must observe the laws and regulations and in particular those relating to transport and navigation (art. 21), and must observe sea lanes and traffic separation schemes adopted by the coastal State (art. 22). "[S]ubmarines and other underwater vehicles are required to navigate on the surface and to show their flag" (art. 20). The coastal State is entitled "to take the necessary steps to prevent any breach of the conditions to which admission of those ships to [internal] waters is subject" (art. 25(2)); and to suspend innocent passage, provided that this is done to protect its security, temporarily and on a non-discriminatory basis, although no suspension is permissible for **international straits** (art. 25(3)).

The UN Convention, like its predecessor the Geneva Convention on the Territorial Sea etc. 1958 *(516 U.N.T.S. 205)*, is not wholly clear as to whether **warships** enjoy the right of innocent passage. "The better view appears to be that such user should not be denied in time of peace where the territorial waters are so placed that passage through them is necessary for international traffic": Colombos, *supra*, 133; *see also* art. 30 of the UN Convention and the *Corfu Channel Case 1949 I.C.J. Rep. 4*. It appears that some 40 States allow the entry of warships into the territorial sea only with prior permission or after notification: UK Hydrographic Office, *Annual Notice to Mariners No. 12* (2003). *See generally*, O'Connell, *The International Law of the Sea* (1982), Vol. 1, Chap. 7; Brown, *The International Law of the Sea* (1994), 52-62.

installations   The Geneva Convention on the Continental Shelf 1958 *(499 U.N.T.S. 311)* empowered a coastal State to construct and maintain or operate on its **continental shelf** "installations and other devices necessary for its exploration and the exploitation of its natural resources. . . ." (art. 5(2)). While the term installations was not defined, it is clear that a State may establish on its continental shelf any structure that is required for the purposes of exploration and exploitation. Around installations, a coastal State was entitled to establish **safety zones** of 500 meters for their protection (art. 5(2) and (3)). Installations are under the jurisdiction of the coastal State, but do not have the status of islands; and they have no territorial sea of their own, their presence does not affect the territorial sea of the coast State (art. 5(4)) and they must not be established where interference may be caused to the use of recognized sea lanes essential to international navigation (art. 5(6)). Due notice must be given of installations and they must have a permanent means of warning (art. 5(5)); abandoned or disused installations must be entirely removed (*id.*). The UN Convention on the Law of the Sea 1982 *(1833 U.N.T.S. 3)* essentially replicates these provisions (in art. 80, incorporating for the continental shelf the terms of art. 60), though calling them "**artificial islands**, installations and structures." Additionally, the coastal State's jurisdiction over installations and structures is expressly stated to include jurisdiction with regard to customs, fiscal, health, safety and immigration laws and regulations (art. 60(2)); the 500-meter breadth of a safety zone may be exceeded if authorized by generally accepted international standards or recommended by the competent international organization (art. 60(5)); abandoned or disused installations and structures are to be removed "to ensure safety of navigation," taking account of generally accepted international standards, fishing, the protection of the marine environment and the rights and duties of other States (art. 60(3)); and where any installations or structures are not entirely removed, appropriate publicity must be given as to their depth, position and dimensions (*id.*).

Institut de Droit International This body was established in 1873 and has remained a strictly scientific body, its *Associes* being elected from among persons who have rendered service to the discipline of international law in either the theoretical or the practical sphere. Promotion to *Membre* now depends on diligent attendance at the biennial sessions, held in different places and reported in the *Annuaires*. The method of work follows a pattern of drafting of resolutions on selected topics. The continued utility of this method now that such institutions as the **International Law Commission** have come into existence, with greater resources and staff, is under examination.

instrument The Vienna Convention on the Law of Treaties 1969 employs the term "instrument" to denote a State act in writing. Thus, a treaty may be embodied "in a single instrument or in two or more related instruments" (art. 1(a)). In the case of an exchange of notes etc. this may be one of the documents forming the text of a treaty (art. 13: ". . . a treaty constituted by instruments exchanged between [States] . . ."). In the case of ratification, acceptance, approval or accession, it is the document which establishes the consent of the State to be bound by a treaty (art. 16).

insurgency, insurgent, insurrection. These terms, descriptive of some sort of rising or rebellion within a State and the rebellious party thereto, have no precise meaning in the sense that any distinction can be drawn between a mere revolt or rising and an insurrection. Thus, the use of the expression **recognition of insurgency** is misconceived insofar as it implies any such formal distinction, although it has sometimes served a useful purpose in indicating a stage in a civil war when foreign States need to have some regard to its existence, but where full **recognition of belligerency** is not appropriate. Equally, although responsibility of States for insurgents (but also for rioters) is sometimes spoken of as a distinct category of vicarious responsibility, it is maintained by others that such responsibility "is the same as for acts of other private individuals": *I Oppenheim 550*. The conduct of an insurrection movement which succeeds in establishing a new government are acts of State for the purpose of State responsibility: *see* Crawford, *The International Law Commission's Articles on State Responsibility* (2002), 116-20.

***inter se* doctrine** In its extreme form, this doctrine is or was to the effect that international law did not apply as between the constituent members of the (British) Commonwealth because of their constitutional ties. Though no longer tenable in this form, the doctrine is still acceptable to the extent that some aspects of *inter se* relations are governed by the conventions (in the sense of accepted practices) of the Commonwealth rather than international law. *See* Jennings, The Commonwealth and International Law, *(1953) 30 B.Y.I.L. 320*; Fawcett, *The British Commonwealth in International Law* (1963), Chap. 4.

Inter-American Development Bank (IADB) Established by the Agreement Establishing the Inter-American Development Bank of 8 April 1959 *(389 U.N.T.S. 69)*, the IADB was set up to "contribute to the acceleration of the process of economic development of the member countries, individually and collectively" (art. I(1)). To that end, the Bank promotes developmental investment of public and private capital, utilizes its own capital for financing development, giving priority to loans and guarantees that will contribute most effectively to economic growth, encourages and supplements private investment and cooperates with member countries to coordinate their policies towards the better utilization of resources and provides technical assistance (art. I(2)(b)). Membership is open to any member of the Organization of American States (art. II(1)(b)) and presently stands at 46, 26 of whom are designated as borrowing members. A Social Progress Fund was established in 1961 *(410 U.N.T.S. 33)* and has become an increasingly important part of the Bank's activities. *See* Dell, *Inter-American Development Bank: A Study in De-*·*velopment Financing* (1971); Tussie, *Inter American Development Bank* (1995). *See* <www.iadb.org>.

Intercosmos   The name given to the program of cooperation among Soviet bloc States in the exploration of outer space, inaugurated in 1967, and set forth in the Agreement on Cooperation in the Exploration and Use of Outer Space for Peaceful Purposes of 13 July 1976 *(16 I.L.M. 1 (1977))*. The contracting parties were Bulgaria, Hungary, the German Democratic Republic, Cuba, Mongolia, Poland, Romania, the USSR and Czechoslovakia.

Inter-Governmental Maritime Consultative Organization   *See* **International Maritime Organization**.

intergovernmental organizations   *See* **organizations, international, intergovernmental**.

Interhandel Case   *(Switzerland v. USA) (1967, 1959)*. By an application dated 2 October 1957, Switzerland sought a declaration that the United States was under an obligation to restore the assets of Interhandel, a Swiss corporation, seized during World War II as enemy property, or alternatively that the dispute was fit for submission to judicial settlement under conditions the Court should determine, pursuant to agreements in force between the parties. The following day, the applicant requested the ICJ to indicate interim measures of protection under art. 41 of its Statute in the shape of a request to the US Government to take no steps to part with the company's property or to prejudice any right to the execution of any judgment of the Court in the applicant's favor. By order of 24 October 1957 the Court *held* (14 to 1) that there was no need in the circumstances to indicate interim measures of protection since it appeared that any disposal of the assets in question could be effected only after the termination of judicial proceedings still pending in the United States and unlikely to be speedily concluded: *Interhandel Case (Switzerland v. USA) (Interim Measures of Protection) 1957 I.C.J. Rep. 105.*

The United States entered a plea to the jurisdiction on the grounds: (1) that the dispute arose before 26 August 1946, the date on which the US Declaration of Acceptance of the **Optional Clause** under art. 36(2) of the Court's Statute became effective; (2) that it arose before 28 July 1948, the date of the Swiss Declaration; (3) that Interhandel had not exhausted its local remedies; and (4) that the issues raised concerning the sale or disposition of the shares of the General Aniline and Film Corporation (part of the assets of Interhandel) had been determined by the US pursuant to para. (b) of the conditions attached to its Declaration of Acceptance to be a matter essentially within the jurisdiction of that State (the "automatic reservation") and further that any issues respecting the seizure and retention of the shares in question were according to international law within the domestic jurisdiction of the US. By its Judgment of 21 March 1959, the Court: *rejected* (10 to 5) the first preliminary objection on the ground that the dispute clearly originated with the US State Department's final and considered refusal in regard to the return of the company's assets, which was dated 26 July 1948; similarly *rejected* (unanimously) the second objection because the Swiss Declaration contained no limitation as to disputes arising before a certain date and such a limitation in the US Declaration could not be read into it; *upheld* (9 to 6) the third objection because proceedings by the company were still pending in the US. As to the fourth objection, the majority of the Court did not find it necessary to pronounce on the validity of the "automatic reservation" in the US Declaration. However the Court *rejected* (14 to 1) the remaining part of this objection—principally on the ground that the questions involved were ones of international law and as such open to challenge. *Interhandel Case (Switzerland v. USA) (Jurisdiction) 1959 I.C.J. Rep. 6.*

interim measures of protection Art. 41 of the Statute of the ICJ, following that of the PCIJ, provides that "[t]he Court shall have the power to indicate, if it considers that circumstances so require, any provisional measures which ought to be taken to preserve the respective rights of either party" and that, pending the final decision, notice of any such measures shall forthwith be given to the parties and to the Security Council. Subs. I of Section D (Incidental Proceedings) of the Rules of Court adopted in 1978, which bears the cross-title "Interim Protection," provides that a written request for the indication of provisional measures may be made by a party at any stage of the proceedings (art. 73); that such a request shall have priority over all other business and shall be treated as a matter of urgency (art. 74); that the Court may at any time decide to examine *ex proprio motu* whether such measures are required and may, in the event of a request, indicate measures other than those requested (art. 75); that provisional measures indicated may at any time be revoked or modified at the request of a party if such appears justified (art. 76); and that the Court may request information from the parties on any matter connected with the implementation of provisional measures which have been indicated (art. 78). An instance of the indication of interim measures is provided by the ***Electricity Company of Sofia Case***. In relation to the ICJ, see in particular the ***Fisheries Jurisdiction Cases***, ***Nuclear Tests Case*** and the ***Anglo-Iranian Oil Co. Case***. *See also* the ***Interhandel Case***, ***Aegean Sea Continental Shelf Case*** and the ***Pakistani Prisoners of War Case***. The most controversial aspect of the Court's power to indicate provisional measures relates to whether the Court can so indicate even where there is doubt about its jurisdiction to determine the merits of a claim. The Court has decided that, provided it has jurisdiction *prima facie*, it can utilize its powers under art. 41. *See* the ***Lockerbie Cases***. The Court has resolved the question of the nature of an indication of provisional measures in favor of their legally-binding effect: ***LaGrand Case***. *See* Dumbauld, *Interim Measures of Protection in International Controversies* (1932); Elkind, *Interim Measures: A Functional Approach* (1981); Sztucki, *Interim Measures in the Hague Court* (1983).

interior waters This expression is used by some writers as equivalent to **national waters**, "consist[ing] of a State's harbours, ports and roadsteads and of its internal gulfs and bays, straits, lakes and rivers. In these waters, apart from special conventions, foreign States cannot, as a matter of strict law, demand any rights for their vessels or subjects although for reasons based on the interests of international commerce and navigation, it may be asserted that an international custom has grown in modern times that the access of foreign vessels to these waters should not be refused except on compelling national grounds": Colombos, *The International Law of the Sea* (6th ed.), 87-8. *See also* **internal waters**.

internal waters This expression is a term of art to the extent that art. 8 of the UN Convention on the Law of the Sea 1982 *(1833 U.N.T.S. 3)*, titled "Internal waters," provides that "waters on the land-ward side of the baseline of the territorial sea form part of the internal waters of the State" (art. 8(1)). Art. 8(2) goes on to provide that, "where the establishment of a straight baseline in accordance with article 7 has the effect of enclosing as internal waters areas which had not previously been considered as such, a right of innocent passage . . . shall exist in those waters." Special arrangements are in place for the internal waters of archipelagic States (Part IV of the UN Convention). Internal waters "consist of a State's harbours, ports and roadsteads and of its internal gulfs and bays, straits, lakes and rivers. In these waters, apart from special conventions, foreign States cannot, as a matter of strict law, demand any rights for their vessels or subjects although for reasons based on the interests of international commerce and navigation, it may be asserted that an international custom has grown in modern times that the access of foreign vessels to these waters should not be refused except on compelling national grounds": Colombos, *The International Law of the Sea* (6th ed.), 87-8. *See* also **national waters**.

International Air Transport Association A **non-governmental organization** having the status of a company limited by guarantee under the I.A.T.A. Incorporation Act 1945 of the Canadian Parliament established following a meeting of operators on 6 December 1944 at Chicago in succession to the International Air Traffic Association set up in 1919. Membership is open to airlines of the nationality of any State eligible for membership of the **International Civil Aviation Organization** operating scheduled air services between two or more States, domestic operators being eligible for associate membership without voting rights. There are currently approximately 280 airline members, comprising 95% of all international scheduled air traffic. The objects of the Association are the promotion of safe, regular and economical air transport, the fostering of air commerce and the study of problems connected therewith, the provision of means of collaboration among international airlines and co-operation with ICAO and other international organizations. The head office of the Association is at Montreal. It functions through an annual General Meeting of all its members, which is its governing body, an Executive Committee, a permanent secretariat and five standing committees (Financial, Legal, Technical, Traffic Advisory, Medical). *See* <www.iata.org>.

International Atomic Energy Agency This institution was established as an autonomous body under the aegis of the UN (rather than as a Specialized Agency) by its Statute, opened for signature at New York on 26 October 1956 *(276 U.N.T.S. 3)*. The Agency, which has its seat in Vienna, has for its purposes the acceleration and enlargement of the contribution of atomic energy to peace, health and prosperity throughout the world, ensuring insofar as it is able that nothing done under its auspices is used for the furtherance of any military purpose (art. 2). It thus both promotes and regulates atomic energy. It comprises a plenary General Conference meeting annually (art. 5), and a Board of Governors (art. 6). It presently has 132 members. It conducts substantial research and publication activities. *See* Szasz, *The Law and Practice of the International Atomic Energy Agency* (1970); Scheinman, *The International Atomic Energy Agency and World Nuclear Order* (1988). *See* <www.iaea.org>.

International Bank for Reconstruction and Development This institution was established by Articles of Association drawn up at the **Bretton Woods Conference** along with those of the IMF and signed at Washington on 27 December 1945 *(2 U.N.T.S. 134)*. The IBRD, or World Bank, is in reality not a bank, even less a central bank, but rather a Specialized Agency of the UN with specific functions relating to developing the economies of its 184 member States. The aims of the Bank were expressed to be to assist in post-war reconstruction and generally to promote the development of the member States (art. I) by making loans to governments or with government guarantees in cases where capital might not otherwise be easily available. Upon the promulgation of the Marshall Plan in 1948, the Bank largely turned to development projects, particularly in connection with power-generation and communications, and has made thousands of loans to wealthier countries at advantageous interest rates (in fiscal year 2002, it loaned some $11 billion), as well as financial assistance to poorer countries (in fiscal 2002, $8.1 billion). The IBRD is endowed with a structure very similar to that of the International Monetary Fund, there being a Board of Governors, in which voting is linked to a State's subscriptions to fund its activities (art. V(3)), a number of Executive Directors and a President (art. V of the Articles of

Association, which provides also for an Advisory Council and for Loan Committees). The Articles of Association have been amended on a number of occasions, most significantly in 1965 when art. VIII was amended by resolution of the Board of Governors so as to introduce an additional section 6 to art. III, governing the use of the resources of the Bank, so as to permit loans to the **International Finance Corporation**.

See also **International Development Agency, International Development Association, Multilateral Investment Guarantee Agency** and **International Centre for the Settlement of Investment Disputes**. *See* Shihata, *The World Bank in a Changing World* (2 vols. 1991-1995); Salda, *World Bank* (1995). *See* <www.worldbank.org>.

International Bill of Rights   The term is used to denote three core **human rights** instruments: the **Universal Declaration of Human Rights** of 10 December 1948 (GA Res. 217(III)); the International Covenant on **Civil and Political Rights** of 16 December 1966 *(999 U.N.T.S. 171)*; and the International Covenant on **Economic, Social and Cultural Rights** of the same date *(993 U.N.T.S. 3)*. *See* Henkin, *The International Bill of Rights* (1981); Williams, *The International Bill of Human Rights* (1999).

International Center for the Settlement of Investment Disputes   ICSID was established, as part of the World Bank Group, by the Convention for the Settlement of Investment Disputes between States and the Nationals of Other States of 18 March 1965 *(575 U.N.T.S. 159)*. The purpose of the ICSID is "to provide facilities for conciliation and arbitration of investment disputes between Contracting States and nationals of other Contracting States. . . ." (art. 1(2)). ICSID does not itself settle investment disputes, but rather provides parties with Panels of Conciliators and of Arbitrators (arts. 12-16) from which they may establish Conciliation Commissions (arts. 29-33) and (arbitral) Tribunals (arts. 37-40). The Center's jurisdiction extends to "any legal dispute arising directly out of an investment, between a Contracting State (or any constituent subdivision or agency of a Contracting State designated to the Center by that State) and a national of another Contracting State" (art. 25(1)). The parties to the dispute must consent in writing to submit to the Center (art. 25 (1)), whereupon the State of the national involved may not give **diplomatic protection** in respect of the dispute (art. 27). Settlement may be by either conciliation under the provisions of Chapter III or arbitration under the provisions of Chapter IV, at the instance of either party. With some 134 States parties to the Convention, ICSID has become a major force in the settlement of investment disputes. *See* Shihata, *Towards the Depolitization of Investment Disputes: The Roles of ICSID and MIGA* (1992); Shreurer, *The ICSID Convention: A Commentary* (2001). *See* <www.icsid.org>.

International Civil Aviation Organization   This organization was brought into being on 4 April 1947 by Part II of the **Chicago Convention** on Civil Aviation of 7 December 1944 *(15 U.N.T.S. 295)* as the definitive successor to the Provisional Civil Aviation Organization (PICAO) provided for in the Interim Agreement of the same date *(171 U.N.T.S. 345)*. The Organization, membership of which is co-extensive with the circle of parties to the Chicago Convention (cf. art. 48 (b)) now has more than 188 members. Its aims and objects are "to develop the principles and techniques of international air navigation and to foster the planning and development of international air transport" (art. 44). The seat of the Organization has been fixed at Montreal pursuant to art. 45. The organs of ICAO consist in a plenary Assembly (arts. 48-9), a Council (arts. 50-55) of 33 members with "adequate representation" being stipulated for, in respect of States of chief importance in relation to air transport and the provision of facilities for international air navigation, and an Air Navigation Commission (arts. 56-7). There is also an important Legal Committee (not provided for in the Convention). The primary organ is the Council and its chief function is the adoption and amendment of the Annexes to the Convention, laying down "international standards and recommended practices and procedures" as respects "matters concerned with the safety, regularity and efficiency of air navigation" (arts. 54(1), 37). *See* Buergenthal, *Law-Making in ICAO* (1969). *See* <www.icao.org>.

international claim *See* **claim.**

International Commission of Jurists Founded in 1952, the International Commission (confusingly using the acronym ICJ) is an **non-governmental organization** dedicated to an impartial, objective and authoritative legal approach to the protection and promotion of **human rights** through the rule of law. It researches and publishes reports on such matters as judicial independence, disappearances, military tribunals, terrorism and human rights and torture. *See* <www.icj.org>.

International Committee of the Red Cross This institution came into existence at Geneva in 1873 under the name of the International Standing Committee for Aid to Wounded Soldiers, assuming its present title in 1880 and being incorporated and invested with legal personality under Swiss law. Under its 1998 Statutes (*(1998) Int. Rev. Red Cross, No. 324*, 537), ICRC is "an independent humanitarian organization having a status of its own . . . [and] one of the components of the International Red Cross and Red Crescent Movement" (art. 1). Its functions are set out in art. 2 of these Statutes. The Committee is accorded a degree of official recognition in the **Geneva Conventions** of 1949 *(75 U.N.T.S. 35 ff))*, Conventions I and II thus providing that "[a]n impartial humanitarian body such as the" ICRC may offer its services to the Parties to a conflict (art. 3), and Convention III alluding to its services to prisoners of war (arts. 72,73,75), besides investing its delegates with the same prerogatives as delegates of **Protecting Powers** (art. 126). *See also* Convention IV, arts. 109,143. Protocol I to the Geneva Conventions of 1949 relating to the Protection of Victims of International Armed Conflict of 12 December 1977 *(1125 U.N.T.S. 3)*, apart from giving the ICRC a role as a Protecting Power (art. 5), in relation to missing persons (art. 33), to the evacuation of children (art. 78) and to revision of the Protocol (art. 98), conferred on the ICRC substantial general powers: "The Parties to the conflict shall grant to the [ICRC] all facilities within their power so as to enable it to carry out the humanitarian functions assigned to it by the Conventions and this Protocol in order to ensure protection and assistance to the victims of conflicts; the [ICRC] may also carry out any other humanitarian activities in favour of these victims, subject to the consent of the Parties to the conflict concerned" (art. 81(1)). *See* Forsythe, *Humanitarian Politics: The International Committee of the Red Cross* (1977). *See* <www.icrc.org>.

International Council for the Exploration of the Sea This body, established at Copenhagen in 1902 to carry out research programs in the North Atlantic formulated at conferences held in Stockholm in 1899 and Christiania in 1901, was endowed with a new constitution by the Convention for the International Council for the Exploration of the Sea, entered into at Copenhagen on 12 September 1964 *(652 U.N.T.S. 237)*. Nineteen States are members of the Council, which publishes a *Journal du Conseil* three times yearly and numerous technical papers. *See* <www.ices.org>.

International Court of Justice The International Court of Justice was established as a principal organ of the UN by art. 7 of the UN Charter and constituted the principal judicial organ of the organization by art. 92, which provides further that the Court shall function in accordance with its Statute, annexed to the Charter and stated expressly both to be based on the Statute of the **Permanent Court of International Justice** and to form an integral part of the Charter. Art. 93 provides that all members of the UN are *ipso facto* parties to the

Statute, and also for non-member States to become parties on conditions to be determined by the General Assembly on the recommendation of the Security Council. Art. 94 contains an undertaking by every member to comply with the decision of the Court in any case in which it is party and for the Security Council, in case of need, to make recommendations or decide upon measures to give effect to a judgment. Art. 96 empowers the General Assembly or Security Council, as well as any other organ of the UN or a Specialized Agency at any time authorized by the General Assembly, to request an **advisory opinion** of the Court on any legal question. The Court's decisions and opinions are published in the *International Court of Justice Reports (I.C.J. Rep.)*. The Court also publishes the *Pleadings, Oral Arguments and Documents* in any proceedings before it; its Rules of Court in a series entitled *Acts and Documents concerning the Organisation of the Court*, as well as successive numbers of the *International Court of Justice Yearbook*, containing incidentally an exhaustive bibliography of the Court. Links to, and information about, all contentious decisions and advisory opinions are available online: <www.icj-cij.org>.

International Court of Justice, advisory jurisdiction *See* **advisory opinion**.

International Court of Justice, competence in contentious cases Chapter II of the Statute of the I C J, which bears the title "Competence of the Court," deals only with its competence or jurisdiction in contentious cases, and not with its capacity to give **advisory opinions**, the subject-matter of Chapter IV. The jurisdiction in contentious cases is expressed to be restricted to cases to which the parties are States (art. 34(1)), the Court being open to those States which are party to the Statute (art. 35(1)) and, on conditions laid down by the Security Council, to other States also (art. 35(2)-(3)). Such jurisdiction is further expressed to "comprise . . . all cases which the parties refer to it and all matters specially provided for in the Charter of the United Nations or in treaties or conventions in force" (art. 36(1)). The basis of the contentious jurisdiction is thus in all cases the consent of the parties, whether given *ad hoc* by special agreement or *compromis*, or in some treaty or other instrument anterior to the particular proceedings. The Optional Clause so-called (*infra*), otherwise art. 36(2) of the Statute, providing for the acceptance of the jurisdiction as compulsory "ipso facto and without special agreement, in relation to any other State accepting the same obligation," constitutes a particular instance of consent anterior to the particular proceedings. "The consent of States, parties to a dispute, is the basis of the Court's jurisdiction in contentious cases": *Interpretation of the Peace Treaties Opinion 1950 I.C.J. Rep. 65* at 71; *see also* **Monetary Gold Removed from Rome Case** *1954 I.C.J. Rep. 19* at 32. "In the event of a dispute as to whether the Court has jurisdiction, the matter shall be settled by the decision of the Court:" ICJ Statute, art. 36(6).

Art. 36(1) of the ICJ Statute provides that the Court has jurisdiction in three situations. (1) In all cases which the parties refer to it by special agreement. An example of a case reaching the Court under special agreement is provided by the **Minquiers and Ecrehos Case** *1953 I.C.J. Rep. 47* submitted under the Agreement of 29 December 1950 between the parties, the United Kingdom and France *(118 U.N.T.S. 149)*. A more recent example can be found in relation to the case concerning the **Gabcíkovo-Nagymaros Project** *1997 I.C.J. Rep 7* which was submitted under the Agreement of 7 April 1993 between Slovakia and Hungary *((1993) 32 I.L.M. 1294)*. But an agreement relating to a particular dispute may stipulate not so much for its actual submission, defining the issue to be tried, but so as to enable the parties to institute proceedings by application under the normal procedural rules. *See, e.g.*, the **Asylum Case** *1950 I.C.J. Rep. 266,* where the proceedings were begun by an application filed by the Colombian Government pursuant to art. 40 of the Statute. In strictness, such a case is simply another example of jurisdiction on the basis of anterior conventional stipulation. On the other hand, the case of *forum prorogatum* so-called, or tacit consent of one party to unilateral institution of proceedings by another, provides a further, though highly exceptional instance of submission by special agreement. See the *Corfu Channel Case 1949 I.C.J. Rep. 4. See also Frontier Land Case 1959 I.C.J. Rep 209; North Sea Continental Shelf Cases 1969 I.C.J. Rep. 32; Tunisia/Libya Continental Shelf Case 1979 I.C.J. Rep. 3*, and arts. 35(2) and 40(1) of the ICJ Statute and art. 39 of the Rules of Court 1978.

(2) In all matters specially provided for in the Charter of the United Nations. This part of art. 36(1) is misleading and almost certainly a drafting error in that the Charter contains no provisions requiring the submission of disputes to the ICJ. The only Charter provision of even peripheral relevance is art. 36(3), under which the Security Council may recommend to the parties to a dispute before it that they refer the case to the ICJ; this does not create a new limb of compulsory jurisdiction: *Anglo-Iranian Oil Co. Case 1952 I.C.J. Rep. 93*.

(3) In all matters specially provided for in treaties or conventions in force. The Optional Clause apart *(infra)*, these are of two sorts: (i) provisions of treaties for the general settlement of disputes, *e.g.*, the **General Act of Geneva 1928** unsuccessfully adduced as a basis of jurisdiction in the *Nuclear Tests Case 1974 I.C.J. Rep. 253*; (ii) provisions with respect to jurisdiction contained in treaties of a general sort, *e.g.*, art. 19 of the Trusteeship Agreement approved on 13 December 1947, relied on in the *Northern Cameroons Case 1963 I.C.J. Rep. 15. See* **compromissory clause**. Such a stipulation must be in force, as art. 36(1) of the Statute expressly states, art. 37 providing, however, that provisions in treaties for the reference of disputes to a tribunal to have been instituted by the League of Nations, or to the PCIJ, are to be treated, as between the parties to the Statute, as conferring jurisdiction on the ICJ. Pursuant to this provision jurisdiction was established in the *Ambatielos Case 1952 I.C.J. Rep. 28* at 43, on the basis of the Anglo-Greek Treaty of Commerce of 16 July 1916 providing for the reference of disputes to the PCIJ. *See also* the *Haya de la Torre Case 1951 I.C.J. Rep. 71*, where jurisdiction was established on the basis of the Protocol of Friendship and Co-operation between Colombia and Peru of 1934. Similarly in the (first) *South-West Africa Case 1950 I.C.J. Rep. 128* at 138, the Court held that South Africa was under an obligation to accept the compulsory jurisdiction of the ICJ under the Instrument of Mandate with respect to disputes relating to its interpretation or application. In the *Barcelona Traction Case 1964 I.C.J. Rep. 6*, the Court held that the jurisdiction conferred on the PCIJ by the Belgo-Spanish Treaty of Conciliation of 1927 had not lapsed on the dissolution of the PCIJ, and had been reactivated in virtue of art. 37 of the Statute upon Spain's becoming a party to that instrument upon her admission to the UN after a period of some nine years during which the jurisdictional clause had not operated. The position with respect to declarations of acceptance of the Optional Clause is to be contrasted with this. *See* the *Aerial Incident Case 1959 I.C.J. Rep. 127. See also* art. 40(1) of the ICJ Statute and art. 38(1) and (2) of the Rules of Court 1978. For a list of treaties and conventions providing for submission of disputes to the ICJ, see current *I.C.J. Yearbook*, and *Collection of Texts Governing the Jurisdiction of the Court (P.C.I.J., Ser. D, No. 6)* and Chapter X of the P.C.I.J. *Annual Reports (P.C.I.J., Ser. E, Nos. 8-16)*.

Art. 36(2) is the so-called **Optional Clause**. It provides that a State may recognize as compulsory, in relation to any other State accepting the same obligation, the jurisdiction of the Court in legal disputes. For a list of declarations under the Optional Clause, and their terms, see current *I.C.J. Yearbook*. Declarations under art. 36(2) "may be made unconditionally or on condition of reciprocity . . . or for a certain time" (art. 36(3) of the ICJ Statute). They must be deposited with the UN Secretary-General (art. 36(4) of the ICJ Statute). "Jurisdiction is conferred on the Court only to the extent to which the two declarations coincide in conferring it": *Phosphates in Morocco Case (1938) P.C.I.J. Rep., Ser. A/B, No.*

74; **Electricity Company of Sofia and Bulgaria Case** *(1939) P.C.I.J. Rep., Ser. A/B, No. 77*; **Anglo-Iranian Oil Co. Case** *1952 I.C.J. Rep. 93*; **Norwegian Loans Case** *(1957) I.C.J. Rep. 9*; **Right of Passage over Indian Territory Case** *1957 I.C.J. Rep. 6*; **Temple Case** *1961 I.C.J. Rep. 17*. With regard to time limits, the Court held in its preliminary objection judgment in **Military and Paramilitary Activities In and Against Nicaragua** *1984 I.C.J. Rep. 392* that once a declaration is made for a fixed time limit or made terminable by a stated notice period (in this case the USA declaration of 1964 contained a six-month notice period) the declaration cannot be unilaterally terminated prior to the end of the fixed period or the period of notice. Declarations made under art. 36 of the Statute of the PCIJ and which are still in force are deemed to be acceptances of the compulsory jurisdiction of the ICJ for the period they still have to run (art. 36(5)). See **Military and Paramilitary Activities in and against Nicaragua** *1984 I.C.J. Rep. 392* in which the Court accepted that a declaration made by Nicaragua in 1929 fell within art. 36(5). *See generally* Shihata, *The Power of the International Court to Determine its Own Jurisdiction* (1965); Rosenne, *The Law and Practice of the International Court* (2nd ed.); McWhinney, *Judicial Settlements of International Disputes* (1991); Rosenne, *The World Court: What it is and How it Works* (1995).

International Court of Justice, incidental jurisdiction What is termed (Sands and Klein, *Bowett's Law of International Institutions* (5th ed.), 359) the incidental jurisdiction of the ICJ includes (1) the power of the Court to indicate **interim measures of protection** under art. 41 of its Statute; (2) its capacity under art. 36(6) by its decision to settle any dispute as to whether it has competence or jurisdiction in a contentious case; (3) its jurisdiction in relation to **intervention (in ICJ proceedings)**, in virtue of arts. 62-3 of the Statute; and (4) its power under art. 60 to construe a judgment in the event of a dispute as to its meaning or scope. *See* **International Court of Justice, construction or interpretation of judgment**.

International Court of Justice, judges of The ICJ has fifteen judges: ICJ Statute, art. 3(1). Judges are elected for a term of nine years, and may be re-elected: Statute, art. 13(1). Five judges complete their terms every three years: Statute, art. 13(1). "The Court shall be composed of a body of independent judges, elected regardless of their nationality from among persons of high moral character, who possess the qualifications required in their respective countries for appointment to the highest judicial offices, or are jurisconsults of recognized competence in international law": Statute, art. 2. No two judges shall be nationals of the same State: Statute, art. 3. Candidates for the Court are nominated, after consultations with the highest Court of Justice, law faculties and schools of law, and national academies and national sections of international academies devoted to the study of law in the State, by national groups in the Permanent Court of Arbitration or *ad hoc* national groups: Statute, arts. 4-6. The General Assembly and Security Council, acting independently of one another, elect candidates to membership of the Court by an absolute majority of votes in each organ: Statute, art. 10; *and see* arts. 11-12 on procedure where elections are inconclusive. The names and biographies of the judges appear in Chap. II of the *I.C.J. Yearbook*. Any party to a dispute which does not have a national as a member of the Court may appoint an *ad hoc* judge; see *ad hoc* **judges**. "No member of the Court can be dismissed unless, in the unanimous opinion of the other members, he has ceased to fulfil the required conditions": Statute, art. 18(1).

The independence of the members of the Court is secured in a member of ways. "No member of the Court may exercise any political or administrative function, or engage in any other occupation of a professional nature": Statute, art. 16(1). "No member of the Court may act as agent, counsel, or advocate in any case": Statute, art. 17(1). "The members of the Court, when engaged on the business of the Court, shall enjoy diplomatic privileges and immunities": Statute, art. 19. "Every member of the Court shall, before taking up his duties, make a solemn declaration in open court that he will exercise his powers impartially and conscientiously": Statute, art. 20. The remuneration of judges of the Court "shall be free of all taxation": Statute, art. 32(8). The quorum of the Court is nine judges: Statute, art. 25(3). The Court may form one or more chambers, composed of three or more judges, for dealing with particular categories of cases (*e.g.*, labor cases and cases relating to transit and communications); and the Court may at any time form a chamber for dealing with a particular case, the number of judges being determined by the Court with approval of the parties: Statute, art. 26(1)-(2). *See also* arts. 26(3), 27-28 and the Rules of Court, arts. 15-18 and 90-93.

International Court of Justice, judgment, construction or interpretation of   While a judgment of the International Court of Justice in a contentious case is "final and without appeal" (art. 60 of the ICJ Statute), a request may be made to the Court to construe the judgment in the event of a dispute as to its meaning: art. 60 of the ICJ Statute. The request may be made either by a special agreement between the parties or by an application by one or more of the parties: art. 98(2)-(3) of the Rules of Court 1978, as amended 5 December 2000. *See also* arts. 98 and 100 of the Rules of Court; *Asylum Case 1950 I.C.J. Rep. 395*; *Tunisia/Libya Continental Shelf Case 1985 I.C.J. Rep. 191*. Cf. **International Court of Justice, judgment, revision of**.

International Court of Justice, judgment, execution of   Art. 94 of the UN Charter provides that each member of the UN undertakes to comply with the decision of the ICJ in any case to which it is a party, and that, if any party fails to perform its obligations under a judgment, the other party may have recourse to the Security Council, which may, if it deems necessary, make recommendations or decide upon measures to be taken to give effect to the judgment. Accordingly, it is not the within the role of the Court to enforce its own judgments: "Once the Court has found that a state has entered into a commitment concerning its future conduct it is not the Court's function to contemplate that it will not comply with it." *Nuclear Test Case 1974 I.C.J Rep. 253* at 477.

International Court of Justice, judgment, revision of   While a decision of the ICJ is final and without appeal (ICJ Statute, art. 60), a very limited right to request revision is afforded by the Statute. Art. 61 provides that an application for the revision of a judgment may be made only when it is based on the discovery of some fact constituting a decisive factor, unknown both to the Court and to the party claiming revision, the ignorance of such party not being due to negligence. An application for revision must be made within six months of the discovery of the new fact and will not lie more than ten years after the judgment. *See* also the Rules of Court, 1978, arts. 99-100. See, for example, *Application for Revision of the Judgment of 11 September 1992 in the Case Concerning the Application of the Convention on the Prevention and Punishment of the Crime of Genocide (Bosnia-Herzegovina v Yugoslavia) 2003 I.C.J. Rep. forthcoming* in which the Court held that the admission of the Federal Republic of Yugoslavia to membership of the United Nations on 1 November 2001 was not a new fact within the terms of art. 61.

International Court of Justice, procedure   The procedure of the ICJ is governed primarily by Chap. III of its Statute (arts. 39 to 64). This deals with the languages in which the proceedings are conducted and the judgments delivered (art. 39), the manner in which proceedings are instituted (art. 40), the power of the Court to indicate provisional or **interim measures** of protection pending the decision of a case (art. 41), the representation of the parties before the Court and the privileges and immunities of their representatives (art. 42), the manner of conduct of the proceedings, written and oral (art. 43), service of notices (art. 44), the control, conduct and recording of the proceedings generally (arts. 45-52), the effect of non-appearance of a party (art. 53), the manner of formulation and the form and effect of the judgment (arts. 54-60), the questions of revision of judgments and **intervention** of third parties **in ICJ proceedings** (arts. 61, 62-63), and costs (art. 64). The provisions of the Statute itself are supplemented in considerable detail by the **Rules of Court** made under art. 30 and adopted in their latest revised version on 14 April 1978, as amended on 5 December 2000: text in *I.C.J. Acts and Documents, Nos. 4 and 5*; *17 I.L.M. 1286 (1978)*.

international crime *See* **crime, international**.

International Criminal Court Created by the Rome Statute of the International Criminal Court 1998 *(UN Doc. A/CONF.183/9; 37 I.L.M. 999 (1998))*, the Court, which has its seat at The Hague in the Netherlands (art. 3), came into existence on 1 July 2002, sixty days after the ratification of the Statute by the sixtieth State. Its establishment by art. 1 of the Statute represents the culmination of efforts since the end of the Second World War to create such a permanent body. Although it is formally in existence, the Court will not begin functioning for some time yet as there is considerable work to be done on setting up the required infrastructure. Nevertheless, the entry into force of the Statute has ensured that anyone who commits a crime subject to the jurisdiction of the Court after 1 July 2002 will be liable for prosecution by the Court (art. 11; *see also* art. 24).

"The jurisdiction of the Court shall be limited to the most serious of crimes of concern to the international community as a whole" (art. 5(1)). These include, specifically, the crime of **genocide** (art. 6); **crimes against humanity** (art. 7); **war crimes** (art. 8); and the crime of **aggression**. However, with respect to aggression, "[t]he court shall have jurisdiction over the crime of aggression once a provision is adopted in accordance with Articles 121 and 123 defining the crime and setting out the conditions under which the Court shall exercise jurisdiction with respect to this crime" (art. 5(2)). The Court may exercise jurisdiction where the State on the territory of which the alleged offence has been committed, or the State of which the person accused of the crime is a national, is a party to the Statute (art. 17(2)). Alternatively, if the relevant State is not a party to the Statute, it may accept the jurisdiction of the Court by declaration lodged with the Registrar (art. 17(3)). Art. 13 provides that a matter may be referred to the Court by a State Party (*see also* art. 14); the Security Council acting under Chapter VII of the UN Charter; or the prosecutor may initiate an investigation in accordance with art. 15. An investigation or prosecution may be deferred for a renewable period of 12 months by the Security Council acting under Chapter VII of the UN Charter (art. 16).

The jurisdiction of the Court "shall be complementary to national criminal jurisdictions" (art. 1). Accordingly, a case will be inadmissible where the case is being investigated or prosecuted, or where a decision not to prosecute has been made, by a State with jurisdiction, unless that State is unwilling or unable to carry out the investigation or prosecution, or is unwilling or unable genuinely to prosecute (art. 17(1)(a)-(b)). A case will be inadmissible also where the accused has already been tried and convicted or acquitted, insofar as the proceedings were not for the purposes of shielding the accused from prosecution or were not otherwise conducted impartially or independently (art. 17(1)(c) and art. 20), and where the case is not of sufficient gravity (art. 17(1)(d)). The Court itself is required to determine the question of unwillingness or inability to prosecute. In making this determination, the Court shall consider whether national proceedings were undertaken for the purposes of shielding the accused from criminal responsibility, whether there has been an unjustified delay in the proceedings, as well as the independence and impartiality of the proceedings (art. 17(2)). Part 3 (arts. 22-33) of the Statute deals with the general principles of criminal law and includes provisions dealing with, *inter alia*, non-retroactivity (art. 24); individual criminal responsibility (art. 25); irrelevance of official capacity (art. 27, *but see also* art. 98 dealing with the need for waiver of immunity); responsibility of commanders and other superiors (art. 28); and ground for excluding liability (arts. 31-33).

The Court is composed of the Presidency, an Appeals Division, a Trial Division and a Pre-Trial Division, the Office of the Prosecutor, and the Registry (art. 34). The Court will comprise 18 judges (art. 36(1)) who shall be elected for a term of nine years and will not be eligible for re-election. (Special arrangements apply in respect of the first election of judges to ensure staggered appointments in subsequent three-yearly periods (art. 36(9)). "The judges shall be chosen from among persons of high moral character, impartiality and integrity who possess qualifications required in their respective States for appointment to the highest judicial offices" and they shall have "established competence in criminal law and procedure" or "in relevant areas of international law"(art. 36(3)). They "shall be independent in the performance of their functions" (art. 40). "The Appeal Division shall be comprised of the President and four other judges, the Trial Division of not less than six judges and the Pre-Trial Division of not less than six judges"(art. 39(1)). The Office of the Prosecutor is to be an independent, separate organ of the Court, headed by the Prosecutor and one or more Deputy Prosecutors, elected for a term of nine years (art. 42).

The Statute contains extensive provisions dealing with matters such as Investigation and Prosecution (arts. 53-61); The Trial (arts. 62-76); Penalties (arts. 77-80); Appeal and Revision (arts. 81-85); International Cooperation and Judicial Assistance (arts. 86-102); Enforcement (arts. 103-111); and Financing (arts. 113-118). The Statute provides for the establishment of an Assembly of State Parties (art. 112) comprising one representative from each State Party to supervise the work of the Court. On the negotiation of the Rome Statute, see Sunga, *The Emerging System of International Criminal Law* (1997); Lee, *The International Criminal Court: The Making of the Rome Statute* (1999). On the ICC generally, see Cassese, Gaeta and Jones, *The Rome Statute of the International Criminal Court* (2002); Bassiouni, *Introduction to International Criminal Law* (2003); Kittichaisaree, *International Criminal Law* (2001). *See* <www.un.org/law/icc>.

international criminal law "International criminal law is reflected in the convergence of two disciples: the penal aspects of international law and the international aspects of national criminal law": Paust *et al*, *International Criminal Law* (2nd ed.), 3. The distinguishing feature of international criminal law is that it attaches criminal liability to individuals, normally though the medium of national courts, but increasingly through international criminal tribunals (*see* the Nuremberg Tribunal, ICTY, ICTR, ICC). The earliest international crime was piracy, to which may now be added **genocide**, crimes against **peace** and **humanity**, **war crimes**, **slave trading** and **terrorism**. *See* Cassese, *International Criminal Law* (2003); Kittichaisaree, *International Criminal Law* (2001).

International Criminal Tribunal for Rwanda The *ad hoc* International Criminal Tribunal for the Prosecution of Persons Responsible for Genocide and Other Serious Violations of International Humanitarian Law Committed in the Territory of Rwanda and Rwandan Citizens responsible for Genocide and Other Such Violations Committed in the Territory of Neighboring States, between 1 January 1994 and 31 January 1994 (in short, the International Criminal Tribunal for Rwanda or ICTR) was established by the United Nations Security Council acting under Chapter VII of the UN Charter in SC Res. 955 of 8 November 1994 *(33 I.L.M. 1598 (1994))*. The ICTR is the first international tribunal having competence over crimes committed in an internal armed conflict. In terms of its Statute, adopted as part of Res. 955, the ICTR has jurisdiction natural persons (art. 5) accused of committing the crime of **genocide** (art. 2), **crimes against humanity** (art. 3) and violations of Common Article 3 of the **Geneva Conventions** and of Additional Protocol II (art. 4) on the territory of Rwanda or by Rwandan citizens on the territory of neighboring states between 1 January 1994 and 31 December 1994 (arts. 1 and 7). The jurisdiction of the Tribunal is concurrent with that of national courts (art. 8(1)), but it has primacy over those courts: "At any stage of the procedure the International Tribunal for Rwanda may formally request national courts to defer to its competence . . ." (art. 8(2)) (cf. the complementarity principle which operates in relation to the **International Criminal Court**).

The International Tribunal has its seat at Arusha, Tanzania and consists of three Trial Chambers and an Appeals Chamber, together with the Prosecutor and a Registry (art. 11). There are 16 permanent judges elected by the General Assembly for a renewable four-year term. Each Trial Chamber consists of three permanent judges. The Appeal Chamber, which is shared with the **International Criminal Tribunal for the Former Yugoslavia (ICTY),** consists of seven permanent judges. Each appeal is heard and decided by five judges. Sixty-six arrests have been made in connection with the proceedings of the Tribunal. Three detainees have been released and one has died. A further six are serving prison sentences imposed by the tribunal. As of 1 September 2003, there are 20 detainees on trial and 30 awaiting trial. The remainder are awaiting transfer or have an appeal pending. *See* Morris and Scharf, *The International Criminal Tribunal for Rwanda* (1998); Cassese, *International Criminal Law* (2003); Kittichaisaree, *International Criminal Law* (2001). *See* <www.ictr.org>.

International Criminal Tribunal for the Former Yugoslavia The *ad hoc* International Tribunal for the Prosecution of Persons Responsible for Serious Violations of International Humanitarian Law Committed in the Territory of the Former Yugoslavia since 1991 was established by the United Nations Security Council acting under Chapter VII of the UN Charter in SC Res. 827 of 25 May 1993 *(32 I.L.M. 1203 (1993))*. Its Statute was adopted by the Security Council in Res. 827 and has been subsequently amended by SC Res. 1166 (1998), 1329 (2000) and 1411 (2002). The Tribunal has jurisdiction over natural persons (art. 6) accused of committing acts constituting grave breaches of the **Geneva Conventions of 1949** (art. 2), violations of the laws and customs of war (art. 3), **genocide (**art. 4) and **crimes against humanity** (art. 5) on the territory of the former Socialist Republic of Yugoslavia after 1 January 1991 (art. 8). The jurisdiction of the Tribunal is concurrent with that of national courts (art. 9(1)), but it has primacy over those courts: "At any stage of the procedure the International Tribunal may formally request national courts to defer to the competence of the International Tribunal . . ." (art. 9(2)) (cf. the complementarity principle which operates in relation to the **International Criminal Court**).

The International Tribunal has its seat at The Hague in the Netherlands and consists of three Trial Chambers and an Appeals Chamber, together with the Prosecutor and a Registry (art. 11). There are 16 permanent judges elected by the General Assembly for a renewable four-year term, as well as a maximum at any time of nine *ad litem* judges drawn from a pool of 27 judges who are also elected by the General Assembly for a period of four-years on a non-renewable basis (arts. 12-13). Each Trial Chamber consists of three permanent judges and a maximum, at any one time, of six *ad litem* judges. The Appeal Chamber, which is shared with the **International Criminal Tribunal for Rwanda**, consists of seven permanent judges. Each appeal is heard and decided by five judges. The ICTY has indicted 75 individuals of whom 56 are currently in proceedings before the tribunal. Thirteen individuals are serving prison sentences imposed by the Tribunal. Eighteen indictees remain at large. *See* Morris and Scharf, *An Insider's Guide to the International Criminal Tribunal for the Former Yugoslavia: A Documentary History and Analysis* (1995); Jones, *The Practice of the International Criminal Tribunals for the Former Yugoslavia and Rwanda* (2nd ed. 1999); Ackerman and O'Sullivan, *Practice and Procedure of the International Criminal Tribunal for the Former Yugoslavia* (2000). *See* <www.un.org/icty>.

international custom (or customary law) *See* **custom**.

International Development Association Established by the Articles of Agreement of the International Development Association of 26 January 1960 *(439 U.N.T.S. 249)*, the IDA's purposes are "to promote economic development, increase productivity and thus raise standards of living in the less-developed areas of the world included within the Association's membership, in particular by providing finance to meet their important developmental requirements on terms which are more flexible and bear less heavily on the balance of payments than those of conventional loans, thereby furthering the developmental objectives of the International Bank for Reconstruction and Development . . . and supplementing its activities": (art. I). With 163 members, and 81 members eligible for support, the IDA is effectively the soft loans arm of the IBRD; it works to reduce poverty by providing "credits" towards development projects, which are loans at zero interest with a 10-year grace period and long maturities. Its structure of Board of Governors, with voting linked to subscriptions towards its activities (art. VI(3)), Executive Directors and President replicates that of the IBRD (art. VI). *See* Weaver, *The International Development Association: A New Approach to Foreign Aid* (1965). *See* <www.worldbank.org>.

international economic law *See* **economic law, international**.

international environmental law *See* **environmental law, international**.

International Federation of Red Cross and Red Crescent Societies The Federation, prior to 1991 called the League of Red Cross Societies, was established to coordinate the work of national Red Cross and Red Crescent societies in providing assistance to any national society affected by natural disasters and epidemics. *See* <www.ifrc.org>.

International Finance Corporation This organization was established by the Articles of Agreement of the International Finance Corporation of 25 May 1955 *(264 U.N.T.S. 117)* "to further economic development by encouraging the growth of productive private enterprise in member countries [of the **International Bank for Reconstruction and Development**], particularly the less developed areas, thus supplementing the activities of the . . . Bank" (art. I). With 175 member States, the IFC invests directly in profit-making projects to which local investors contribute and provides technical assistance to local development finance companies. While the IBRD is limited in its capacity to lend directly, the IFC actively participates in private investments, being rather an investing organization than a lending institution. The IFC's structure of Board of Governors, with voting linked to a member State's stock holding (art. IV(3)), Board of Directors and President replicates that of the IBRD (art. IV). *See* Baker, *The International Finance Corporation* (1968). *See* <www.ifc.org>.

International Fisheries Co. Case *(United States v. Mexico) (1931) 4 R.I.A.A. 691.* Upon a claim on behalf of an American company for loss resulting from the cancellation of a Mexican concession of which the grantee was a Mexican company in which the American company had a preponderant interest, *held* by the US-Mexico Special Claims Commission that the claim was to be rejected following the same tribunal's decision in the *North American Dredging Co. Case (1926) 4 R.I.A.A. 26* to the effect that a **Calvo clause** in a concession contract excluded jurisdiction pending the exhaustion of local remedies. The claimant company, as a shareholder in the Mexican company, had the same rights and obligations as the latter, but no more. The mere cancellation of the concession was not *prima facie* a violation of international law and in consequence within the exceptions laid down in the *North American Dredging Co. Case.*

International Frequency Registration Board *See* **International Telecommunication Union**.

International Fund for Agricultural Development The objective of the Fund, set up as a Specialized Agency by the Agreement of 10 June 1976 *(1059 U.N.T.S. 19)*, is to mobilize additional resources to be made available on concessional terms for agricultural development in developing member States (art. 2), membership being open to any State member of the UN System (art. 3). Entry into force was made dependent on the deposit of initial contributions of at least $750 million (art. 7); and IFAD's activities are funded by contributions (periodically replenished) by member States (art. 4), these activities involving grants, loans and co-financing (art. 7). IFAD has a plenary Governing Council of general competence (art. 6(2)-(4)), an Executive Board, of 18 members, to oversee operations, including the approval of loans and grants, and with a elaborate system of weighted voting (art. 6(5)-(7)), and a President and staff (art. 6(8)). The Fund currently has 163 member States and has financed 633 projects in 115 countries since its creation, committing $7.7 billion in loans and $35.4 million in grants. *See* <www.ifad.org>.

international humanitarian law An expression employed to describe the rules of international law especially designed for the protection of the individual in time of war or armed conflict; cf. the designation of the Diplomatic Conference for the Reaffirmation and Development of International Humanitarian Law applicable in Armed Conflicts (1974-7), and the title to Part III, Sect. III of the *International Red Cross Handbook* (13th ed.): "International Humanitarian Law." International humanitarian law is a major part of the laws of war (*jus in bello*), the rules governing the conduct of armed conflict; cf. *jus ad bellum*, the rules governing the circumstances in which resort to armed conflict is legal. IHL is largely a product of conventional law, through treaties and other instruments adopted at The Hague in 1899 and 1907 and at Geneva in 1949 and in 1977, along with surrounding and relevant case law and customary law. For a comprehensive and intelligible account of the fundamental principles of IHR, see the **Fundamental Rules of International Humanitarian Law in Armed Conflicts**. *See* Cassese, *The New Humanitarian Law of Armed Conflict* (2 vols., 1979-80); Fleck, *The Handbook of Humanitarian Law in Armed Conflict* (2000).

International Labour Office The Constitution of the **International Labour Organization** *(15 U.N.T.S. 40)* provides (art. 2) that the permanent organization shall consist, in addition to the General Conference of representatives of member States, of "a Governing Body . . . and an International Labour Office controlled by the Governing Body," the seat of such Office, which is at Geneva, to be changed only by a two-thirds vote of the Conference (art. 6), and the Office to have a Director-General appointed by the Governing Body to be responsible under that organ for its efficient conduct and for the appointment of its subordinate staff (arts. 8-9). The functions of the Office are expressed to include "the collection and distribution of information on all subjects relating to the international adjustment of conditions of industrial life and labor and particularly the examination of subjects which it is proposed to bring before the Conference with a view to the conclusion of international Conventions, and the conduct of such special investigations as may be ordered by the Conference or the Governing Body." It is also specified, in the general statement of the Office's duties (art. 10), that if shall "carry out the duties required of it by the provisions of this Constitution in connection with the efficient observance of the Conventions"—a reference in particular to the provisions of arts. 24-9 respecting the handling of complaints of failure to observe any international labor convention.

International Labour Organization (ILO) This organization was established by the Peace Treaties of 1919, its original Constitution forming Part XIII of the Treaty of Versailles *(225 C.T.S. 188)* and a corresponding part of the other Peace Treaties. As successively amended the Constitution provides, first, for a General Conference of 4 representatives of each member State, two being government delegates, one representing employers and one "the working people" (art. 3). As to the designation of workers' delegates, see *Nomination of the Workers' Delegate for the Netherlands to the International Labour Conference Opinion (1922) P.C.I.J., Ser. B, No. 1.* There is further a Governing Body of 56 persons, 28 representing governments (10 appointed by the members of chief industrial importance), 14 employers, and 14 workpeople (art. 7, as amended by the Instrument of Amendment of the Constitution of 22 January 1972; *(1975) T.S. No. 110.)* The Governing Body, which is elected for a three-year term, commonly meets three or four times a year, settles the agenda for the Conference, which is convened at least once annually (art. 14(1), 3(1)), appoints the Director-General and the third organ of the Organization, the **International Labour Office,** and lays down regulations for the recruitment of its subordinate staff (arts. 8,9).

The objects of the ILO are laid down in the Preamble to the Constitution and the Declaration of aims and purposes adopted by the General Conference at Philadelphia on 10 May 1944 and annexed to the Constitution and has been further amended (*see 1 Oppenheim 986-7*). They are, broadly, the furtherance of programs to achieve full employment and enhanced standards of living and the employment of individuals in satisfying and satisfactory conditions, with adequate security, adequate wage levels and adequate social protection, by the international adjustment of conditions of industrial life and labor. For these ends, a specific procedure is prescribed in the shape of a virtually continuous process of consultation through the meeting of the General Conference which adopts and sends forward to governments proposals in the form of draft International Labor conventions and recommendations (arts. 14-19). The Constitution imposes on members in relation to conventions a duty of reporting annually on measures taken for their implementation (art. 22). It further prescribes means for the representation to governments concerned of complaints of non-observance of conventions put forward by associations of employers or workers (art. 24-5). And it provides also an elaborate procedure for the investigation by commissions of enquiry of such complaints made by one member State against another, this procedure providing an ultimate right of reference to the ICJ (arts. 26-34). The ILO publishes the *International Labour Review* in four yearly issues. *See* Johnston, *The International Labour Organization* (1970); Ghebali, *The International Labour Organization* (1988). *See also* <www.ilo.org>.

international law   "Bentham invented the term 'International law' in one of his happiest linguistic innovations, in his *Introduction to the Principles of Morals and Legislation* (1789). It is especially felicitous because it leads itself easily to derivatives. Perhaps something like 'interstatal' would have been more exact. . . .": Nussbaum, *A Concise History of the Law of Nations* (Revised ed.), 136. International law may be defined as "[T]he standard of conduct, at a given time for states and other entities subject thereto": Whiteman, *Digest* *of International Law*, Vol. 1 (1963), 1. It includes "(a) the rules of law relating to the functioning of international institutions or organizations, their relations with each other, and their relations with states and individuals; and (b) certain rules of law relating to individuals and non-state entities so far as the rights or duties of such individuals and non-state entities are the concern of the international community": Shearer, *Starke's International Law* (11th ed.), 3.

International Law Association The Association for the Reform and Codification of the Law of Nations, as this body was originally called, was founded at Brussels in 1873 largely through the interest and efforts of American publicists. Unlike the ***Institut de Droit International***, established in the same year, it has not been a purely scientific body but includes in its membership not only lawyers, whether or not specialists in international law, but others involved in international trade and business and delegates from affiliated bodies, such as chambers of commerce and shipping, and arbitration or peace societies. Its stated aims are the study, clarification and development of both public and private international law; and it pursues these aims through various international committees and a biennial conference, whose proceedings are published as *Reports*. *See* <www.ila-hq.org>.

International Law Commission Art. 13(1) of the UN Charter, having directed the General Assembly to "initiate studies and make recommendations for the purpose of . . . encouraging the progressive development of international law and its codification," by Res. 94(I) of 31 January 1947, that body established a Committee on the Progressive Development of International Law and its Codification which recommended the establishment of an International Law Commission. The ILC established by GA Res. 174(II), to which was annexed its Statute (*see also 42 A.J.I.L. Supp. 2 (1948)*), providing for a body of 15 (expanded to 25 in 1961, 34 in 1981) persons of differing nationalities "of recognized competence in international law" (art. 2), to be elected by the General Assembly from a list of candidates nominated by member States of the UN (art. 3) for periods of three years, renewable (art. 10) to sit normally at the European Office of the UN in Geneva in annual session (art. 12, as amended in 1955), receiving traveling expenses and an allowance (art. 13), the UN Secretary-General providing them with staff facilities (art. 14). Members of the Commission sit in their personal capacity as experts rather than as representatives of their respective governments. The Statute preserves the distinction drawn in art. 13 of the Charter between "progressive development" and "codification," the former embracing the preparation of drafts on the basis of questionnaires to governments and the consideration of proposals and draft conventions submitted by UN members and other UN organs and Specialized Agencies etc. (arts. 16-7), and the latter the formulation by the Commission itself of draft articles in relation to topics selected as appropriate and their submission to the General Assembly for appropriate action—mere noting, adoption by resolution, recommendation to members with a view to a convention, or convocation of a conference to conclude a convention (arts. 18-24). Since its first session in 1949, the Commission has prepared upwards of 17 substantive drafts, including those resulting in the elaboration and adoption of the four Geneva Conventions on the Law of the Sea of 1958, the Vienna Conventions on Diplomatic Relations (1961), Consular Relations (1963), and the Law of Treaties (1969), the Convention on Special Missions (1969), the Convention on the Prevention and Punishment of Crimes against Internationally Projected Persons, including Diplomatic Agents (1973), the Vienna Convention on the Representation of States in their relations with International Organizations of a Universal Character (1975); the Vienna Convention on the Succession of States in Respect of Treaties (1978) and in respect of matters other than Treaties (1983), the Vienna Convention on the Law of Treaties between States and International Organizations or Between International Organizations (1986), the

Convention on the Law of the Non-Navigational Uses of International Watercourses (1997), and the Rome Statute of the International Criminal Court (1998). It finally adopted its Draft articles on the Responsibility of States for Internationally Wrongful Acts, one of its longest running projects, in 2001. "[O]ne can see that the International Law Commission is involved in at least two of the major sources of international law. Its drafts may form the bases of international treaties which bind those states which have signed and ratified them and which may continue to form part of general international law, and its work is part of the whole range of state practice which can lead to new rules of international law." Shaw, *International Law* (4th ed.), 94. The Commission produces an annual *Yearbook* which includes reports on its activities. *See* United Nations, *The International Law Commission. Fifty Years After* (1998); Briggs, *The International Law Commission* (1965); Morton, *The International Law Commission of the United Nations* (2000). *See also* <www.un.org/law/ilc>.

international legislation "The term *international legislation* would seem to describe quite usefully both the process and the product of the conscious effort to make additions to, and changes in, the law of nations. While it is a term of some apparent novelty, it has come into such common use that it may now be employed with little hesitation. Almost a quarter of a century ago, Professor John Basset Moore listed among the methods for the development of international law, 'the specific adoption of a rule of action by an act in its nature legislative' [International Law, Its Present and Future, *(1907) 1 A.J.I.L. 11*]; and shortly afterward, Professor Oppenheim devoted a part of his monograph *Die Zukunft des Völkerrechts* [1911] to the process of international legislation. The term has come to be used in various doctrinal writing. . . . The term 'international legislation' seems to describe, more accurately than any other, the contributions of international conferences at which states enact a law which is to govern their relations. Nor should it be limited in application to those instances in which states may make it possible for other states to accept the same Law": Hudson, *International Legislation,* Vol. 1 (1931), xiii-xiv. *See* also McNair, International Legislation, *19 Iowa L. Rev. 177 (1934)*. Cf. **law-making treaties**.

International Maritime Organization The Intergovernmental Maritime Consultative Organization was established by the agreement of 6 March 1948 *(289 U.N.T.S. 48)*; in 1982, its name was changed to the International Maritime Organization *(1276 U.N.T.S. 468)*. The objectives of the IMO are "to provide machinery for cooperation among Governments in the field of governmental regulation and practices relating to technical matters of all kinds affecting shipping engaged in international trade; to encourage and facilitate the general adoption of the highest practicable standards in matters concerning maritime safety, efficiency of navigation and prevention and control of marine pollution from ships" (art. 1(a)). The plenary Assembly of 162 member States is, to all intents and purposes, not in the dominant position of the equivalent bodies in other Specialized Agencies (*see* art. 15). The Council is composed on 32 members, elected by the Assembly according to a formula that accords 8 seats to the States with "the largest interest in providing international shipping," 8 to those with "the largest interest in international seaborne trade" and 16 with "special interests" in maritime transport and navigation and whose election will ensure equitable geographic representation (art. 17). The IMO has established four important and plenary Committees: the Maritime Safety Committee, Legal Committee, Marine Environment Protection Committee and Technical Cooperation Committee. *See* Mankabady, *The International Maritime Organisation* (1984); Simmonds, *The International Maritime Organisation* (1994). *See* <www.imo.org>.

International Maritime Satellite Organization This organization was established by the Convention on the International Maritime Satellite Organization signed at London on

3 September 1976 *(15 I.L.M. 1051 (1976))* "to make provision for the space segment necessary for improving maritime communications" (art. 3), being endowed with an Assembly made up of all the parties generally to consider and review the activities and objectives of the Organization (arts. 10-12), a Council of 22 representatives of signatories primarily representing the largest investment shares and having responsibility for the provision of the requisite space segment (arts. 13-15), and a Directorate made up of a Director-General and subordinate staff (art. 16). INMARSAT has legal personality (art. 25) and is established in London. Since 1999, INMARSAT has been a limited company. *See* <www.inmarsat.com>.

International Military Tribunals There were two International Military Tribunals established in the immediate post-World War II period. The Nuremberg Tribunal was set up by the Agreement for the Prosecution and Punishment of the Major War Criminals of the European Axis Powers signed in the first instance by the Government of the USA, the USSR and the United Kingdom and the Provisional Government of France at London on 8 August 1945 *(82 U.N.T.S. 279)*. The Charter of the Tribunal, annexed to the Agreement and expressed by art. 2 to be an integral part of it, set up a Tribunal of four members, each with an alternate, appointed by the four signatories (art. 1). It was empowered to try and to punish the major European Axis war criminals as designated by the prosecution, three categories of crimes being specified as coming within the jurisdiction: crimes against peace (*see* **peace, crimes against**), **war crimes** and crimes against humanity (*see* **humanity, crimes against**) (art. 6). In addition, the Tribunal was given jurisdiction to declare organizations criminal (art. 9). The Charter laid it down that the official position of a defendant should neither free him from responsibility nor mitigate his punishment (art. 7), and that the plea of superior orders should be acceptable only in mitigation of punishment (art. 8). The Tribunal sat from 20 November 1945 until 31 August 1946 for the trial of 24 individuals (including Goering, Hess, Ribbentrop, and also Borman, who was tried *in absentia*) and eight organizations (including the SS and the German General Staff) on a first count of a common plan or conspiracy and upon three further counts comprehending the categories of crimes mentioned above. Twelve individuals were sentenced to death on one or more counts, one (Ley) committed suicide during the trial, three (Schacht, Papen, Firtzsche) were acquitted and the remainder sentenced to imprisonment for life or a term of years. The judgement of the Nuremberg Tribunal is reported in *21 A.J.I.L. 172 (1947)*. *See The Charter and Judgment of the Nurnberg Tribunal, History and Analysis (UN Doc. 1949 V. 7)*, Taylor, *Nuremberg Trials: War Crimes and International Law* (1949); Woetzel, *The Nuremberg Trials in International Law* (1962).

The Charter of the Tokyo International Military Tribunal, which was embodied in a Special Proclamation of the Allied Supreme Commander *(14 State Dept. Bull. 391, 890; T.I.A.S. No. 1589)* differs marginally from that of the Nuremberg Tribunal, not conferring any jurisdiction in respect of organizations, nor specifically excluding appeal. The Tokyo Tribunal tried 28 individuals between June 1946 and April 1948. *See Trial of the Japanese Major War Criminals (1948) 15 I.L.R. 356.*

Cf. the **International Criminal Tribunal for the Former Yugoslavia** and the **International Criminal Tribunal for Rwanda** which, although set up to deal with war crimes, crimes against humanity and **genocide**, were established by the UN Security Council and are not military tribunals, though their roots lie in the two international military tribunals, not least in the crimes subject to their jurisdiction, their reach to individuals irrespective of status and their rejection of superior orders as a defense. *See also* the **International Criminal Court**. *See generally* Appleman, *Military Tribunals and International Crimes* (1954).

international minimum standard   In its treatment of an alien present within its territory (or the property of an alien located within its territory), a State is required to observe a minimum standard set by international law. This international minimum standard is not susceptible to precise formulation in the abstract, but only in concrete cases: see O'Connell, *International Law* (2nd ed), Vol. I, 943. However, it is possible to identify broad guide-lines for the major causes of injuries to aliens.

In relation to **denial of justice**, the test for responsibility appears to be that of "a denial, unwarranted delay or obstruction of access to the courts, gross deficiency in the administration of judicial or remedial process, failure to provide those guarantees which are generally considered indispensable to the proper administration of justice, or a manifestly unjust judgment": art. 9 of the Harvard Research Draft Convention on the Responsibility of States for Damage Done in their Territory to the Person or Property of Foreigners 1929 *((1929) 23 A.J.I.L. Supp. 131)*. In relation to injuries to aliens, or failure to punish those who injure aliens, the test appears to be that of "due diligence to prevent the injury, if local remedies have been exhausted without adequate redress for such failure" (*ibid.*, art. 10); or that amounting "to an outrage, to bad faith, to wilful neglect of duty, or to an insufficiency of governmental action so far short of international standards that every reasonable and impartial man would readily recognise its insufficiency": (*Neer Claim (1926) 4 R.I.A.A. 60). See also **Faulkner Claim** (1926) 4 R.I.A.A. 67; **Roberts Claim** (1926) 4 R.I.A.A. 77; **Swinney Claim** (1926) 4 R.I.A.A. 98.* If the international minimum standard is not met, it will often be a defense that aliens are treated in the same way as nationals (the **national treatment** standard): *Roberts Claim*, *supra*. The increasing insistence that aliens voluntarily residing within a State should be entitled to no better treatment than that State's own nationals has reinforced the rule that the degree of grossness and culpability on the part of the State must be high before the State can be responsible internationally. In relation to expropriation, that trend is continued in art. 2(2)(c) of the Charter of **Economic Rights and Duties of States** 1974 (GA Res. 3281(XXIX)), which provides that, while on the compulsory taking of an alien's property, compensation should (not must) be paid, "taking into account its relevant laws and regulations and all circumstances that the State considers pertinent . . . [disputes] shall be settled under the domestic law of the nationalizing State and by its tribunals." On the other hand, the development of international human rights law has resulted in a more positive spin being placed on the efforts to assimilate the two standards of international and national treatment by referring to all individuals present within the particular territory who are to be treated without discrimination. *See* Jessup, *A Modern Law of Nations* (1958), 94-122; Roth, *The Minimum Standard of International Law applied to Aliens* (1949). *See also* **State responsibility**.

International Monetary Fund   The original Articles of Agreement drafted at the United Nations Monetary and Financial Conference (the **Bretton Woods** Conference) were signed on 27 December 1945 *(2 U.N.T.S. 39)* and entered into force immediately. The fund currently has 184 member states. The purposes of the Fund are to promote international monetary cooperation and the expansion and balanced growth of international trade; to promote exchange stability and generally to assist in the smoothing of the international payments system and the elimination of restrictions (art. I). The member States are assigned quotas, expressed in **special drawing rights** and subject to review (art. III) (the Eleventh General Review was completed in 2003, increasing the total quotas to SDR 213 billion). The quotas determine a member's maximum financial commitment to the IMF, its voting power and is the basis for determining access to IMF financing. The member States undertake notification obligations regarding their exchange rates and confer on the IMF a power of surveillance (art. IV). Its transactions consist primarily in sales and loans of currencies required by member States to meet balance of payments problems and also sales and purchases of gold (art. V). IMF loans are usually provided under an "arrangement" which stipulates the conditions the country must meet in order to gain access to the loan. The IMF also provides a number of loan facilities including the Poverty Reduction and Growth Facility at concessional rates of interest for low income countries, which was introduced in 1999 to replace the Enhanced Structural Adjustment Facility. It also provides non-concessional facilities in the form of Stand-By Arrangements, the Extended Fund Facility, the Supplemental Reserve Facility, the Contingent Credit Lines and the Compensatory Financing Facility. IMF resources come from subscriptions under quota and from borrowings, notably under the general arrangements to borrow which began in 1962 and by which ten of the IMF's wealthiest members agreed to allow direct loans of their currency to the IMF whenever supplementary resources are needed by it "to forestall or cope with an impairment of the international monetary system." Transactions are largely restricted to current as opposed to capital transfers (art. VI). The prime obligations of members include the avoidance of restrictions on current payments and of discriminatory currency practices and the maintenance of convertibility of foreign-held balances (art. VIII).

All powers of the Fund are vested in a Board of Governors upon which each member has one governor and one alternate. Voting power of members is proportionate to their several quotas (art. XII). The conduct of the business of the Fund is delegated to the Board of Executive Directors which meets several times each week. Five of the 24 members of the Executive Board are appointed by the five members having the largest quotas (France, Germany, Japan, United Kingdom and United States). The Managing Director, who is the Chairman of the Executive Directors and chief of the operating staff, conducts the ordinary business of the Fund under the direction of the Board. *See* Aufricht, *The IMF: Legal Basis, Structure, Functions* (1964); Salda, *The International Monetary Fund* (1992); Vreeland, *The IMF and Economic Development* (2003). For a critique of the role of the IMF see Stigliz, *Globalization and Its Discontents* (2002). *See also* <www.imf.org>.

international organization *See* **organization, international, intergovernmental**.

international person, personality *See* **person**; **personality, international**.

international private law *See* **private international law**.

international responsibility *See* **State responsibility**.

international river *See* **river, international**.

International Seabed Area This is defined in art. 1(1) of the UN Convention on the Law of the Sea 1982 *(1833 U.N.T.S. 3)* as "the seabed and ocean floor and subsoil thereof, beyond the limits of national jurisdiction." The limits of national jurisdiction are set by art. 76 (1) at "the outer edge of the continental margin, or to a distance of 200 nautical miles from the baselines" of the territorial sea. The Area and its resources (i.e. mineral resources *in situ*) are expressed to be "the common heritage of mankind" (art. 136), and activities in the Area are to be "carried out for the benefit of mankind as a whole" (art. 140 (1)). The Area and its resources are not subject to appropriation (art. 137(1)), and the Area is open to use exclusively for peaceful purposes (art. 141). Conduct of activities in the area is controlled by the **International Seabed Authority** under arts. 143-155 (art. 137 (2)). *See also* **deep-sea mining**. *See* Brown, *The International Law of the Sea* (1994), Vol. 1, Chap. 17; Churchill and Lowe, *The Law of the Sea* (3rd ed.), Chap. 12.

International Seabed Authority The International Seabed Authority (the Authority) "is the organization through which States Parties shall . . . organize and control activities in the **[International Seabed] Area**, particularly with a view to administering the resources of the Area": art. 157(1) of the UN Convention on the Law of the Sea 1982 *(1833 U.N.T.S. 3)*. The powers and functions of the Authority are stated to be those expressly conferred upon it by the Convention, and "such incidental powers, consistent with this Convention, as are implicit in and necessary for the exercise of those powers and functions with respect to activities in the Area" (art. 157(2)). The Authority has three principal organs: an Assembly, a Council and a Secretariat; and, in addition, the Enterprise (art. 158). The Assembly, comprising all the member States (art. 159(1)), is declared to be "the supreme organ of the Authority to which the other principal organs shall be accountable," with "the power to establish general policies. . . ." (art. 160(1)). Decisions of the Assembly on questions of substance are taken by a two-thirds majority of members present and voting (art. 159 (8)). The Council is to consist of 36 members, elected by the Assembly under formulae that seek to ensure representation of the major interests in sea-bed mining (art. 161(1) and (2)). The Council is the "the executive organ of the Authority" (art. 162(1)), with specific powers, *inter alia*, to supervise and co-ordinate the implementation of Part XI of the Convention (art. 162 (2)(a)), to approve plans of work for the exploitation of the Area (art. 162(2)(j)), and to exercise control over activities in the Area (art. 162(2)(1)). Decisions on questions of substance are to be taken by majorities of two-thirds, three-fourths or consensus, depending upon the subject matter (art. 161(6)-(8)). Operating under the Council, and reporting to it, are an Economic Planning Commission and a Legal and Technical Commission, both of 15 members elected by the Council (arts. 163-5). The Secretariat comprises the Secretary-General and such staff as the Authority may require (art. 166(1)). The independence and international character of the Secretariat is provided for in art. 168. The Enterprise, the operating arm of the ISA is to "carry out activities in the Area directly . . ., as well as the transporting, processing and marketing of minerals recovered from the Area" (art. 170(1); *see also* the Statute of the Enterprise in Annex IV). *See* Brown, *The International Law of the Sea* (1994), Vol. 1, Chap. 17; Churchill and Lowe, *The Law of the Sea* (3rd ed.), 239-48.

international straits *See* **straits**.

International Telecommunication Union The first general International Telegraph Convention was signed at Paris on 17 May 1865 *(130 C.T.S. 123, 198)*. Upon its revision at St. Petersburg on 22 July 1875, an article was introduced (art. XIV) providing for a central organ to collect and publish relevant information and undertake studies in relation to telegraph services *(148 C.T.S. 416)*. Following the revision of the Service Regulations annexed to the Convention at Lisbon on 11 June 1908 *(207 C.T.S. 89)*, the designation International Telegraph Union was given to the skeleton organization that had thus grown up. This institution was replaced by the International Telecommunication Union (ITU) in virtue of art. 1(1) of the Telecommunication Convention signed at Madrid on 9 December 1932 *(151 L.N.T.S. 5)*, which instrument replaced both the Telegraph Convention and the Radiotelegraph Convention originally signed at Berlin on 3 November 1906 and revised at London on 5 July 1912 and at Washington on 25 November 1927 *(84 L.N.T.S. 97)*. After a number of amendments up to 1996, the Union, made up of the States named in the Annex which sign or ratify or accede to the Convention, of such other States becoming members of the UN as may accede to it and of such States, not being members of the UN, as are admitted by a two-thirds majority of the membership (art. 1), is expressed to have as its purposes: (a) to maintain and extend international cooperation between all Members of the Union for the improvement and rational use of telecommunications of all kinds, as well as to promote and to offer technical assistance to developing countries in the field of telecommunications; (b) to promote the development of technical facilities and their most efficient operation with a view to improving the efficiency of telecommunication services, increasing their usefulness and making them, so far as possible, generally available to the public; (c) to harmonize the actions of nations in the attainment of those ends. To this end, the Union shall in particular: (a) effect allocation of the radio frequency spectrum and registration of radio frequency assignments in order to avoid harmful interference between radio stations of different countries; (b) coordinate efforts to eliminate harmful interference between radio stations of different countries and to improve the use made of the radio frequency spectrum; (c) foster international cooperation in the delivery of technical assistance to the developing countries and the creation, development and improvement of telecommunication equipment and networks in developing countries by every means at its disposal, including through its participation in the relevant programs of the United Nations and the use of its own resources, as appropriate; (d) coordinate efforts with a view to harmonizing the development of telecommunication facilities, notably those using space techniques, with a view to full advantage being taken of their possibilities; (e) foster collaboration among its Members with a view to the establishment of rates at levels as low as possible consistent with an efficient service and taking into account the necessity for maintaining independent financial administration of telecommunication on a sound basis; (f) promote the adoption of measures for ensuring the safety of life through the cooperation of telecommunication services; (g) undertake studies, make regulations, adopt resolutions, formulate recommendations and opinions, and collect and publish information concerning telecommunication matters (art. 4).

The organs of ITU comprise the Plenipotentiary Conference of representatives of member States, having power to determine the general policies for fulfilling the purposes of the Union and to revise the Convention if it considers this necessary (art. 6(2)(a), (j)); Administrative Conferences, both world and regional (art. 7); the Administrative Council of 41 elected members which acts on behalf of the Conference in the intervals between the latter's meetings and within the limits of the powers delegated to it, being responsible for taking steps to facilitate implementation of the convention, regulations etc., for determining the technical assistance policy, coordination of the work of the Union and generally for promoting technical cooperation (art. 8); the General Secretariat, directed by a Secretary-General (art. 9); the International Frequency Registration Board of 5 persons elected by the Conference, having as its essential duties the recording and registration of frequency assignments in accordance with the Radio Regulations, the recording of positions of geo-stationary satellites, and generally the provision of advice and technical assistance (art. 10); International Radio (CCIR) and Telegraph and Telephone (CCITT) Consultative Committees of the whole membership of the Union plus recognized private operating agencies (art. 11); and a Coordination Committee (art. 12). The former associate membership available to dependent territories has been abolished, the ITU, whose seat is the Geneva, now having a membership some 158 independent States. *See* Leive, *International Telecommunications and International Law: The Regulation of the Radio Spectrum (1970);* Ratkowski and Codding, *The International Telecommunications Union in a Changing World* (1998).

international terrorism *See* **terrorism**.

International Trade Organization At the instigation of the USA, discussions were held from 1946 to 1948 in London, Lake Success (New York), Geneva and Havana to draft a charter for an international trade organization (*see* **Havana Charter**). The **General Agreement on Tariffs and Trade** was to have been a subsidiary agreement under the ITO

Charter, and to depend upon the ITO Charter and secretariat for servicing and enforcement. The failure of the US Congress to approve the Havana Charter effectively aborted the ITO. However, the provisional GATT came to provide a permanent institutional structure for the world trading system until the establishment of the **World Trade Organisation** in 1994. *See* Diebold, *The End of the I.T.O.* (1952); Wilcox, *A Charter for World Trade* (1949).

internationally protected persons Defined in the Convention on the Prevention and Punishment of Crimes against Internationally Protected Persons, including Diplomatic Agents of 14 December 1973 *(1035 U.N.T.S. 167)* as "(a) a Head of State, including any member of a collegial body performing the functions of a Head of State under the constitution of the State concerned, a Head of Government or a Minister of Foreign Affairs, whenever such person is in a foreign State, as well as members of his family who accompany him; (b) any representative or official of a State or any official or other agent of an international organization of an intergovernmental character who, at the time when and in the place where a crime against him, his official premises, his private accommodation or his means of transport is committed, is entitled pursuant to international law to special protection from any attack on his person, freedom or dignity, as well as members of his family forming part of his household" (art. 1(1)). The Convention builds upon the **inviolability** of Heads of State, Ministers of Foreign Affairs, diplomatic agents (*see* Vienna Convention on Diplomatic Relations 1961 *(500 U.N.T.S. 95)*, art. 29), consular officials (Vienna Convention on Consular Relations 1963 *(596 U.N.T.S. 261)*, art. 41), as well as other governmental officials serving abroad, by providing not simply for their protection, but also by requiring State parties to make the intentional commission of a murder, kidnapping, or an other attack on the person or liberty of the internationally protected person or a violent attack on the official premises, private accommodation or means of transport of an internationally protected person, or a threat or attempt to do so, punishable by appropriate penalties, taking into account their grave nature (art. 2). Each State party is required to take such measures as may be necessary to establish its jurisdiction over such crimes (art. 3), as well as to take all practicable measures to prevent the commission of such crimes (art. 4). *See* Bloomfield, *Crimes Against Internationally Protected Persons, Prevention and Punishment: An Analysis of the UN Convention* (1975).

internationally wrongful act *See* **wrongful act, internationally**.

internment This term, connoting deprivation of liberty in virtue of the laws and customs of war, in its French variety of *internement,* appears to have been imported into international law by the Draft Convention considered at the Brussels Conference on the Laws and Customs of War of 1874, the articles respecting prisoners of war in which were reproduced with relatively little alteration in the *Règlement* concerning the Laws and Customs of War on Land annexed to Hague Convention II of 1899 and Hague Convention IV of 1907, art. 5 of the latter thus coming to provide: "Prisoners of war may be interned . . . but they can only be confined as an indispensable measure of safety" *(205 C.T.S. 290)*. The 1899 *Règlement (187 C.T.S. 436)* provides (arts. 57-60) as to the "internment" of belligerent forces in neutral territory, as does Hague Convention V 1907 respecting the Right and Duties of Neutral Powers and Persons in War on Land (arts. 11-15; *205 C.T.S. 301)*. In the expanded version of the provisions of the Hague *Règlement* respecting prisoners of war in the Geneva Conventions of 1949 the same terminology is used: Convention III (Prisoners of War), Part III; Captivity, Section II, Internment of Prisoners of War; Convention IV (Civilians), Part III Status and Treatment of Protected Persons, Section IV, Regulations for the Treatment of Internees *(75 U.N.T.S. 3ff)*.

internuncio *Internuncios* are included within the second class of Heads of Mission as defined in art. 14(1) of the Vienna Convention on Diplomatic Relations 1961 *(500 U.N.T.S. 95)*. "The title of nuncio denoted a permanent diplomatic representative of the Holy *See . . .* Internuncios were originally papal representatives who might not be permanent, but by the time of the 1815 Vienna Regulation were permanent representatives within the second class": Denza, *Diplomatic Law* (2nd ed.), 91.

interpretation *See* **treaties, interpretation of**.

Interpretation of Article 3(2) of the Treaty of Lausanne Case *See Mosul Boundary Case*.

Interpretation of Peace Treaties with Bulgaria, Hungary and Romania, Advisory Opinions *1950 I.C.J. Rep. 65, 221*. By resolution dated 22 October 1949, the General Assembly of the UN requested of the ICJ an advisory opinion on the questions "I. Do the diplomatic exchanges between Bulgaria, Hungary and Romania, on the one hand, and certain Allied and Associated Powers signatories to the Treaties of Peace, on the other, concerning the implementation of Article 2 of the Treaties with Bulgaria and Hungary and Article 3 of the Treaty with Romania, disclose disputes subject to the provisions for the settlement of disputes contained in Article 36 of the Treaty of Peace with Bulgaria, Article 40 of the Treaty of Peace with Hungary, and Article 38 of the Treaty of Peace with Romania? In the event of an affirmative reply to Question I: II. Are the Governments of Bulgaria, Hungary and Romania obligated to carry out the provisions of the articles referred to in Question I, including the provisions for the appointment of their representatives to the Treaty Commissions? In the event of an affirmative reply to Question II and if within thirty days from the date when the Court delivers its opinion, the Governments concerned have not notified the Secretary-General that they have appointed their representatives to the Treaty Commissions, and the Secretary-General has so advised the International Court of Justice: III. If one party fails to appoint a representative to a Treaty Commission . . . where that party is [so] obligated . . ., is the Secretary-General . . . authorized to appoint the third member of the Commission upon the request of the other party to a dispute . . .? In the event of an affirmative reply to Question III: IV Would a Treaty Commission composed of one party and a third member appointed by the Secretary-General . . . constitute a Commission, within the meaning of the relevant Treaty articles, competent to make a definitive and binding decision in settlement of a dispute?" The treaty provisions referred to (other than the provisions for the settlement of disputes) were stipulations for the securing of human rights within the territories of the States concerned and the diplomatic exchanges mentioned consisted in charges by the United Kingdom and US Governments of violations of these stipulations and denials on the part of Bulgaria, Hungary and Romania. The provisions for the settlement of disputes provided for Treaty Commissions made up of one representative of each party to a dispute and a third person selected by mutual agreement or, failing agreement within one month, appointed by the UN Secretary-General.

In its opinion of 30 March 1950, in which it *advised* affirmatively (11 to 3) upon Questions I and II, the Court initially dealt with an objection to its entertaining the matter on the ground, first, that the request for an opinion was *ultra vires* the General Assembly having regard to art. 2(7) of the UN Charter as an intervention in matters essentially within the domestic jurisdiction of the States concerned; and, secondly, that no opinion could be given "without violating the well-established principle of international law according to which no judicial proceedings relating to a legal question pending between States can take place without their consent." The Court regarded these arguments as misconceived: it was not called upon to deal with the charges of alleged violation of treaty provisions but simply to furnish "certain clarifications of a legal nature regarding the applicability of the procedure for the settlement of disputes . . . provided for in . . . the Treat[ies]"—indisputably a question of international law. Equally, though the Court's duty to reply to a request for an opinion was not absolute, and though art. 68 of its Statute further provided that in the exercise of its advisory functions it should be guided by the rules applicable in contentious cases, "[i]n the present case the Court is dealing with a request for an opinion, the sole object of which is to enlighten the General Assembly as to the opportunities which the procedure contained in the Peace Treaties may afford for putting an end to a situation which has been presented to it. That being the object of the request, the Court finds in the opposition made to it by Bulgaria, Hungary, and Romania no reason why it should abstain from replying. . . ."

Then as to Question I: whether there exists an international dispute is a matter for objective determination. Where the one side had made charges and the other denials, the mere denial of the existence of a dispute did not prove its non-existence. The two sides held clearly opposite views concerning the performance of certain treaty obligations and the Court must conclude that a dispute had arisen. And upon Question II: The expression "the provisions of the Articles referred to in Question I" must relate exclusively to the articles providing for the settlement of disputes, and not to the human rights articles. The question thus asked whether, in view of the disputes which had arisen, Bulgaria etc. was obligated to carry out the disputes settlement provisions. And as to this the Court found that "all the conditions required for the commencement of the stage of settlement of disputes by the Commissions have been fulfilled."

The UN Secretary-General having on 1 May 1950 notified the Court that none of the Governments of Bulgaria, Hungary and Romania had appointed its representative to the Treaty Commissions, in a further Opinion of 18 July 1950 the Court *advised* (11 to 2) negatively in relation to Question III and that it was not in consequence necessary to consider Question IV. The case envisaged in the Treaties was exclusively that of the failure of the parties, having appointed their own members to the Commissions, to agree upon the selection of the third member, "and by no means the much more serious case of a complete refusal of co-operation by one of them, taking the form of refusing to appoint its own Commissioner"—such as had in fact arisen.

Interpretation of the Greco-Turkish Agreement of 1 December 1928 Advisory Opinion *(1928) P.C.I.J., Ser. B, No. 16.* By a resolution dated 5 June 1928, the Council of the League of Nations requested of the PCIJ an advisory opinion as to the interpretation of art. IV of the Final Protocol to the Agreement of 1 December 1926 between Greece and Turkey for the facilitation of the application of certain provisions of the Treaty of Peace of Lausanne of 24 July 1923 *(28 L.N.T.S. 11)*. This Article provided that "Any questions of principle of importance which may arise in the mixed Commission [for the Exchange of Populations] in connection with the new duties entrusted to it by the Agreement signed this day . . . shall be submitted to the President of the Greco-Turkish Arbitral Tribunal . . . for arbitration. The arbitrator's awards shall be binding." In the contention of Greece, this provision constituted an arbitration clause, with the implication that no matter could be referred for decision thereunder save by the two States concerned, or failing agreement, one of them, and that they alone might appear as parties. In its opinion of 28 August 1928, the Court *advised* (unanimously) that it was for the Mixed Commission alone to decide whether the conditions enumerated in art. IV for arbitration were or were not fulfilled and that, their having been fulfilled, the right to refer a question to the arbitrator contemplated belonged to the Commission alone. The Commission was made up of individuals, not State delegates, so that there were no "parties" able to present a dispute for "arbitration" in the strictest sense. Further, art. IV provided for the reference of "questions of principle" with respect to which there might be doubt but no disagreement among members of the Commission.

Intersputnik The name given to the international system of communications via satellites established in the Soviet bloc by the Agreement on the Establishment of the "Intersputnik" International System and Organization of Space Communications of 15 November 1971 *(862 U.N.T.S. 3)* which entered into force 12 July 1972. The basic function of Intersputnik was to "ensure cooperation and coordination of efforts in the design, establishment, operation and development of the communications system": art. 1(2). It coordinates its activities with the International Telecommunication Union: art. 7. The Organization is now open to membership by any State which wishes to join and currently has 24 member States, the majority of whom are States situated in the former Soviet bloc and States created after the break-up of the former Soviet Union. *See* Queeney, *Direct Broadcast Satellites and the United Nations* (1978). *See* <www.intersputnik.com>.

inter-temporal law The doctrine of international law whereby "a juridical fact must be appreciated in the light of the law contemporary with it, and not of the law in force at the time when the dispute in regard to it arises or falls to be settled": *Island of Palmas Case (1928) 2 R.I.A.A. 831.* The Arbitrator in this case, Max Huber, further extended the doctrine thus: "As regards the question which of different legal systems prevailing at successive periods is to be applied in a particular case (the so-called inter-temporal law), a distinction must be made between the creation of rights and the existence of rights. The same principle which subjects the acts creative of a right to the law in force at the time the right arises, demands that the existence of the right, in other words its continued manifestation, shall follow the conditions required by the evolution of law." The extension of the doctrine, which is applicable to acquisitions of territory (*see **Grisbadarna Case (1909) 11 R.I.A.A. 155; Minquiers and Ecrehos Case 1953 I.C.J. Rep. 47***) and to the interpretation of treaties *(**Rights of U.S. Nationals in Morocco Case (1952) I.C.J. Rep. 176; Right of Passage over Indian Territory Case** 1960 I.C.J. Rep. 6)*, has been criticized "on the ground that logically the notion that title has to be maintained at every moment of time would threaten many titles and lead to instability [citing Jessup, The Palmas Island Case, *22 A.J.I.L. 725* at 739-40 *(1982)*; Jennings, *The Acquisition of Territory in International Law* (1963), 28-31; and Jennings, The General Course in Public International Law, *(1967) Hague Recueil 323* at 422]. It would seem that the principle represented by extension of the doctrine is logically inevitable, but that the criticism is in point in so far as it emphasizes the need for care in applying the rule": Brownlie *Principles of Public International Law* (5th ed.), 127.

intervention (in ICJ proceedings) Art. 62 of the Statute of the ICJ, following that of the PCIJ, provides "1. Should a State consider that it has an interest of a legal nature which may be affected by the decision in the case, it may submit a request to the Court to be permitted to intervene. 2. It shall be for the Court to decide upon this request." Art. 63 provides: "1. Whenever the construction of a convention to which States other than those concerned in the case are parties is in question, the Registrar shall notify all such States forthwith. 2. Every State so notified has the right to intervene in the proceedings; but if it uses this right, the construction given by the judgment will be equally binding upon it." The Rules of Court 1978 amplify these provisions somewhat, laying it down in particular that an application under art. 62 of the Statute "shall set out: (a) the interest of a legal nature which the State applying to intervene considers may be affected by the decision in th[e] case; (b) the precise object of the intervention; (c) any basis of jurisdiction which is claimed to exist as between the State applying to intervene and the parties . . .": art. 81; *see also* arts. 82-6. In *The Wimbledon (1923) P.C.I.J. Rep., Ser. A, No. 1*, the Government of

Poland based its initial application to intervene in the proceedings instituted by Great Britain, France, Italy and Japan against Germany on art. 62 of the PCIJ Statute (virtually identical in terms with art. 62 of the ICJ Statute) but in a further communication changed its ground, invoking instead art. 63 (identical to art. 63 of the ICJ Statute), so that, in its judgment of 28 June 1923 accepting the intervention, the Court found it "unnecessary . . . to consider and satisfy itself whether [the] intervention . . . is justified by an interest of a legal nature, within the meaning of article 62. . . ." (at 11, 13). The Government of Cuba filed a declaration of intervention under art. 63 of the Statute in the **Haya de la Torre Case 1951 I.C.J. Rep. 71** between Colombia and Peru anent the interpretation of the Havana Convention on Asylum of 1927, the intervention being admitted when stated to be confined to an interpretation of an aspect of the Convention which was not *res judicata*. In the **Monetary Gold Case 1954 I.C.J. Rep. 19** between Italy on the one hand and France, the UK and the US, in which the Court found that the jurisdiction conferred on it by the agreement of the parties (to the effect that Italy should apply to the Court for the determination of the question whether a certain quantity of gold taken from Albania by Italy and removed from Rome by the Germans in 1943, should be delivered to Italy rather than Albania) did not, in the absence of consent by Albania, authorize it to adjudicate, it was suggested that Albania might have intervened under art. 62 of the Court's Statute and that the fact that she had not chosen to do so should not make it impossible for the Court to proceed. The Court, however, observed that "[i]n such a case the Statute cannot be regarded, by implication, as authorizing proceedings to be continued in the absence of Albania" 9 (at 32). In the **Nuclear Tests Cases *(Australia v. France) 1974 I.C.J. Rep. 553***, the Court found the application of the Government of Fiji to intervene under art. 62 to have lapsed in view of its judgment that the claim no longer had any object, so that it was not called on to give a decision, a number of the judges, however, making observations on the merits of the applications In the **Tunisia/Libya Continental Shelf Case 1981 I.C.J. Rep. 3**, the Government of Malta applied to intervene, adducing as its interest of a legal nature capable of being affected by the decision its own continental shelf boundaries with either or both of the parties but expressly making reservation of any intention to put its own rights or claims in issue, thus, in the view of the Court" seek[ing] permission to enter into the proceedings in the case but to do so without assuming the obligations of a party to the case." The application was denied unanimously. In the **Libya-Malta Continental Shelf Case 1984 I.C.J. Rep. 3**, Italy's application to intervene on the ground that the claims of Libya and Malta extended to areas of the continental shelf over which Italy had sovereign rights, was rejected by the Court as involving the introduction of a fresh dispute between Italy and each of the other two States without their consent.

More recently, for the first time in the history of the Court, the ICJ granted permission for a third State to intervene in proceedings under art. 62. in the case concerning the **Land, Island and Maritime Frontier Dispute *(El Salvador v. Honduras), 1990 I.C.J. Rep. 92***. A Chamber of the Court allowed Nicaragua to intervene in the proceedings, holding unanimously that "Nicaragua has shown that it has an interest of a legal nature which may be affected by part of the Judgment of the Chamber on the merits in the present case"(at 137). In making this decision, the Chamber pointed out "first, that it is for a State seeking to intervene to demonstrate convincingly what it asserts and thus to bear the burden of proof; and, second, that it has only to show that its interest "may" be affected, not that it will or must be affected" (at 117). *See also* unanimous decision of the full court to allow Equatorial Guinea to intervene in the case concerning the **Land and Maritime Boundary between Cameroon and Nigeria 1999 I.C.J. Rep. 1029**. *See* Rosenne, *Intervention in the International Court of Justice* (1993).

Investment Disputes between States and Nationals of Other States, Convention on the Settlement of This Convention was adopted under the auspices of the **World Bank** on 18 March 1965 *(575 U.N.T.S. 159)* and entered into force on 14 October 1966. It established the **International Center for the Settlement of Investment Disputes** (ICSID) "to provide facilities for conciliation and arbitration of investment disputes between Contracting States and nationals of other Contracting States. . . ." (art. 1(2)). The parties to the dispute must consent in writing to submit to the Center (art. 25 (1)), whereupon the State of the national involved may not give diplomatic protection in respect of the dispute (art. 27). Settlement may be by either conciliation (Chap. III) or arbitration (Chap. IV), at the instance of either party. Some 139 states have ratified the Convention. *See* Nathan, *The ICSID Convention: The Law of the International Centre for the Settlement of Investment Disputes* (2000); Schreuer, *The ICSID Convention: A Commentary* (2001); *ICSID Reports: Volumes 1-6* (1993-2003). *See* <www.icsid.org>.

investment law, international Laws relating to investment fall within the province of municipal law, except in those situations in which they are governed by a treaty régime, such as economic unions. The Convention on the Settlement of Investment Disputes between States and Nationals of other States of 18 March 1965 *(575 U.N.T.S. 159)* is the most important international instrument relative to investment law. Many bilateral treaties have been concluded for the promotion and protection of investments by nationals of the one party in the territory of the other. *See* **International Center for the Settlement of Investment Disputes**.

inviolability "Personal inviolability is of all the privileges and immunities of missions and diplomats the oldest established and the most universally recognised. . . . Personal inviolability of a diplomatic agent is now guaranteed under Article 29 of the Vienna Convention [on Diplomatic Relations, 1961 *[500 U.N.T.S. 95]*, the opening words of which are: 'The person of a diplomatic agent shall be inviolable']. Like the inviolability of mission premises [see further below], this has two aspects. There is first the immunity from any action by law enforcement officers of the receiving state. . . . The second aspect, which raises more problems of interpretation, is the special duty of protection: 'The receiving State shall treat him with due respect, and shall take all appropriate steps to prevent any attack on his person, freedom or dignity.' Many states, in fulfillment of their duty to prevent any attack on the person, freedom or dignity of a diplomatic agent, have created special offences in regard to attacks on diplomats, or punish offences against diplomats with especially severe penalties. . . . The Vienna Convention, however, does not make [this] compulsory; nor does the Convention on the Prevention and Punishment of Crimes against Internationally Protected Persons, including Diplomatic Agents *[1035 U.N.T.S. 167]*, which however obliges State Parties to 'make [relevant] crimes punishable by appropriate penalties which take into account their grave nature'. . . . What are the 'appropriate steps' the receiving state must take to protect diplomats and other inviolable persons must be determined in the light of . . . relevant circumstances. . . . Major capitals will have several thousand diplomats . . . all entitled to inviolability, and clearly it would be an impossible burden for each . . . to have special police protection. . . . But where there is evidence of a threat to the safety of a diplomat, such as a likely mob attack or indications that a kidnapping is being planned, then the sending state can demand . . . special protection. . . . It seems now to be clearly established that the 'appropriate steps' . . . do not include surrendering to demands made by kidnappers when a diplomatic kidnapping has taken place. . . .": *Satow's Guide to Diplomatic Practice* (5th ed.), 120-122.

The Vienna Convention on Diplomatic Relations, 1961 stipulates for the inviolability of mission premises, archives and documents, official correspondence, the person of a diplomatic agent, his private residence, papers and correspondence, the members of his household (other than local nationals) and members of the administrative and technical staff of a diplomatic mission, together with their respective households: arts. 22, 24, 27, 29, 30, 37 (1), (2). The Vienna Convention on Consular Relations 1963 *(596 U.N.T.S. 261)* similarly stipulates for the inviolability of consular premises, consular archives and documents (including those of a post headed by an honorary officer) and the persons of consular officers: arts. 31, 33, 61, 41. *See also* the Convention on the Prevention and Punishment of Crimes against International, Protected Persons, including Diplomatic Agents, 1973, and the Vienna Convention on the Representation of States in their Relations with International Organizations of a Universal Character, 1975 *(69 A.J.I.L. 730 (1975))*. In the **United States Diplomatic and Consular Staff in Tehran Case** *1980 I.C.J. Rep. 3*, the ICJ found various of these treaty stipulations, besides others, to have been the subject of successive and continuous breaches by the respondent State, with the result that it had incurred responsibility towards the United States, the Court considering it to be its duty in consequence to draw to the attention of the entire international community the irreparable harm which such events might cause. *See generally* Denza, *Diplomatic Law* (2nd ed.).

ISA An acronym for the **International Seabed Authority**, sometimes also for the **International Seabed Area**.

ISAF The International Security Assistance Force was established by Security Council Res. 1386 (2001) to work with the UN and the Afghan government in developing national security structures and the training of Afghan security forces in the post-Taliban era. Intended to be of short duration, ISAF's initial mission was limited to Kabul and its environs.

island In terms of art. 121(1) of the UN Convention on the Law of the Sea 1982 *(1833 U.N.T.S. 3)*, "an island is a naturally formed area of land, surrounded by water, which is above water at high tide." Thus defined, an island is a high-tide elevation (i.e. not submerged at high tide) as opposed to a **low-tide elevation**. An island a **territorial sea**, **contiguous zone**, **exclusive economic zone** and **continental shelf** (art. 121(2)); however, "[r]ocks which cannot sustain human habitation or economic life of their own shall have no exclusive economic zone or continental shelf" (art. 121(2)). In situations in which "there is a fringe of islands along the coast in its immediate vicinity, the method of straight baselines joining appropriate points may be employed in drawing the baseline from which the breadth of the territorial sea is measured" (art. 7(1)). *See* Bowett, *The International Legal Regime of Islands* (1981); Jayewardene, *The Regime of Islands in International Law* (1990).

Island of Palmas Case *(U.S. v. Netherlands) (1928) 2 R.I.A.A. 829.* By the Special Agreement of 23 January 1925, the parties submitted to the arbitration of a tribunal of the Permanent Court of Arbitration, consisting in a single arbitrator, the question of the whereabouts of sovereignty over the island of Palmas (or Miangas), an island situated within the Philippines, and therefore ostensibly within the terms of the cession by Spain to the United States effected by art. III of the Treaty of Paris of 10 December 1898 *(187 C.T.S. 100)* terminating the Spanish-American War, but claimed by the Netherlands as having come under the suzerainty of the Dutch East India Company as early as 1677, if not 1648, and as having remained under Netherlands sovereignty ever since. By his award, celebrated for its lucidity, M. Max Huber *held* in favor of the Netherlands.

The decision begins by pointing out that, when territorial sovereignty is disputed, "it cannot be sufficient to establish the title by which [it] was validly acquired at a certain moment; it must also be shown that the territorial sovereignty has continued to exist and did exist at the moment which for the decision of the dispute must be considered as critical. This demonstration consists in the actual display of State activities such as belongs only to the territorial sovereign." Here, since the US relied for its claim on the cession by Spain, and since, if Spain had no valid title she could convey none, the essential point was the status of the island at the moment of the conclusion and coming into force of the Treaty of Paris—"the critical moment." The US, it was true, based its claim as successor to Spain in the first place on discovery, and it did appear that the island was discovered by Spain in the sense that it was probably sighted by a Spanish navigator in 1526. The effect of that event was to be judged according to the notions of international law then entertained notwithstanding that they were later profoundly modified. But upon the view most favorable to the claimant State, discovery gave no more than an **inchoate title**, a *jus ad rem* to be completed by actual and durable taking of possession within a reasonable time. In the application of the principle of the so-called **inter-temporal law**, moreover, a distinction was to be drawn between the creation of rights and their existence. "The same principle which subjects the act creative of a right to the law in force at the time the right arises, demands that the existence of the right, in other words its continued manifestation, shall follow the conditions required by the evolution of law." Since the middle of the 18th century it had come to be accepted that occupation, to constitute a claim to territorial sovereignty, must be effective. Thus discovery could not now suffice to establish sovereignty, even if it ever did so. If it merely created an inchoate title, such had never been completed by any act of occupation on the part of Spain. Further, even if an inchoate Spanish title had still persisted in 1898, it could not prevail over "the continuous and peaceful display of authority by another State." The award contains further significant statements respecting the value to be placed on maps in territorial disputes and as to the application of the principle of **contiguity** in relation to islands.

Italian Subjects Resident in Peru Claims *(Italy v. Peru) (1901) 15 R.I.A.A. 389.* In this series of claims arising out of damage sustained by Italian nationals resident in Peru during the civil war of 1894-5, the Sole Arbitrator (Sr. Uríbarri) sitting in virtue of the Arbitration Agreement of 25 September 1899 *held* the respondent State liable in the amounts specified in the individual awards though not liable upon other claims advanced in reliance upon the rule that a State is responsible for the acts of the contending parties in a civil conflict; that it must exercise due diligence to safeguard the interests of non-nationals; but that it is not responsible for acts not imputable to troops or specified persons, nor in respect of indirect damage.

J

Jan Mayen, Maritime Delimitation in the Area between Greenland and, Case *(Denmark v. Norway) 1993 I.C.J. Rep. 38.* On 16 August 1988, Denmark instituted proceedings against Norway based on a dispute regarding the delimitation of Denmark's and Norway's continental shelf and fishing zones. Denmark wanted the Court to draw a line of delimitation of those areas at a distance of 200 nautical miles measured from Greenland's baseline; alternatively, Denmark argued that, if the Court could not draw such a line, then a line should be drawn in adherence to international law. Norway's primary contention was that the delimitation had already been decided between Jan Mayen and Greenland by two agreements requiring the delimitation in accordance with the median line: a bilateral Agreement of 1965 and the 1958 Geneva Convention on the Continental Shelf 1958 *(499 U.N.T.S. 311)*. On 14 June 1993, the Court *held* (14 to 1) that "to the north by the intersection of the line of equidistance between the coasts of Eastern Greenland and the western coasts of Jan Mayen with the 200-mile limit calculated as from the said coasts of Greenland . . . to the south, by the 200-mile limit around Iceland, as claimed by Iceland, between the points of intersection of that limit with the said lines . . . [and] the delimitation line dividing the continental shelf and the fishery zones of Denmark and Norway is to be drawn as specified in . . . the present Judgment." Concluding that a definitive maritime boundary had not been determined by the two treaties invoked by Norway, nor by the practice of the parties, the Court concluded that the boundary must lie somewhere between the median line and the 200-mile line. The Court drew a provisional median line and then considered whether there were special circumstances requiring an adjustment of that line to ensure an equitable delimitation. Opining that special circumstances under art. 6 of the Geneva Convention and relevant circumstances under customary law tend to be assimilated, as having the same broad purport, the Court examined the disparity in the length of the parties' coasts, access to resources, population and economy and security before determining the delimitation.

Janes Claim *(United States v. Mexico) (1926) 4 R.I.A.A. 82.* The United States claimed $25,000 for losses and damages "suffered on account of the murder on or about July 10 1918, at . . . Sonora, Mexico" of Byron Everett Janes, an American citizen, the claim being expressed to be presented on behalf of the victim's widow individually and as guardian of her children and its basis being that the Government of Mexico "did not take proper steps to apprehend the slayer of Janes," who was well-known but nevertheless remained at liberty after 8 years. *Held*, by the US-Mexican General Claims Commission, that though the theory that lack of diligence in apprehending and/or punishing culprits imposed a species of derivative liability on the State concerned "assuming the character of some kind of complicity with the perpetrator himself and rendering [it] responsible for the very consequences of the individual's misdemeanor" was not applicable in a case where, as here, such State could not have prevented the crime, there was still responsibility: "The international delinquency in this case is one of its own specific type, separate from the private de-

---

linquency of the culprit. The culprit is liable for having killed . . . an American national; the Government is liable for not having measured up to its duty of diligently prosecuting and properly punishing the offender." Further, the State's responsibility was not simply to the claimant State. "The indignity done the relatives of Janes by non-punishment in the present case is [equally] a damage directly caused to an individual by a Government. If this damage is different from the damage caused by the killing, it is quite as different from the wounding of the national honor and national feeling of the State of which the victim was a national. . . ."

Jaworzina Question *See Polish Czechoslovak Frontier Delimitation Opinion.*

Jay Treaty The Treaty of Amity, Commerce and Navigation between Great Britain and the United States, signed at London, on 19 November 1794 *(52 C.T.S. 243)*, the US plenipotentiary for the conclusion of which was John Jay, Chief Justice of the US. The Treaty is noteworthy for its provisions for the reference of outstanding questions between the parties for settlement by commissioners or arbitration. *See* Bemis, *Jay's Treaty. A Study in Commerce and Diplomacy* (2nd. ed. 1928).

JDL Rules Properly styled the UN Rules for the Protection of Juveniles Deprived of their Liberty, these Rules were adopted by the General Assembly on 14 December 1990 as GA Res. 45/113 and are based on two cardinal principles: that the deprivation of liberty should be the disposition of last resort (Rule 1(2)); and that any deprivation of liberty should be "consistent with human rights and fundamental freedoms . . . with a view to counteracting the detrimental effects of all types of detention and to fostering integration into society (Rule 1(3)). Being part of a General Assembly resolution, the Rules are not legally binding. *See also* the **Beijing Rules**; **Riyadh Guidelines**.

Jellinek, Georg 1851-1911. Professor, Vienna 1883-9, Basel 1889-91, Heidelberg 1891-1911. Principal works: *Die sozialethische Bedeutung von Recht, Unrecht und Strafe* (1878); *Die rechtliche Natur der Staatenvertrage* (1880); *Die Lehre von den Staatenverbindungen* (1882); *Gesetz und Verordnung* (1887); *Die Erklärung der Menschen und Büurgerrechte* (1895); *Das Recht der Minoritäten* (1898); *Das Recht des modernen Staates* (1900; 2nd ed. 1905).

Jenkins, Sir Leoline 1625-85. English lawyer, who was Judge of the Admiralty from 1665-1680, in which capacity be contributed greatly to the development of Prize Law, particularly during the Anglo-Dutch Wars of 1664-7 and 1672-4. *See* Wynne, *the Life of Sir Leoline Jenkins* (1924).

Jenkinson, Charles 1727-1808. British politician and statesman. First Earl of Liverpool and first Baron Hawkesbury. Principal work: *Collection of Treaties between Great Britain and the Powers from 1648 to 1783* (1785).

Jenks, Clarence Wilfred 1909-1973. An eminent international civil servant of British nationality whose career with the ILO culminated in his becoming Director-General in 1970. Author of *The International Labour Code* (1951,1971). His numerous works include: *The Head-quarters of International Institutions* (1945); *The International Protection of Trade Union Freedom* (1957); *The Common Law of Mankind* (1958); *Human Rights and International Labour Standards* (1960); *International Immunities* (1961); *The Proper Law of International Organisations* (1962); *Law, Freedom and Welfare* (1963); *The Prospects of International Adjudication* (1964); *Space Law* (1965); *Law in the World*

Community (1967); *The World beyond the Charter* (1968); *Social Justice in the Law of Nations* (1970).

Jennings, Sir Robert Yewdall 1913- . UK national. Whewell Professor, Cambridge 1955-81, international practitioner and international judge. Joint editor, *I.C.L.Q.* 1956-61; *B.Y.I.L.* 1960-82. Publications: *The Acquisition of Territory in International Law* (1963); editor of *Oppenheim's International Law. Vol. 1. Peace* (9th ed. 1992 with Watts).

Jessup, Philip C. 1897-1986. Professor, Columbia Univ., 1925-61. Asst. Secretary-General of first Council Session of UNRRA, 1943, Bretton Woods Conference, 1944. US representative at various sessions of the UN Security Council and General Assembly, 1948-53. Judge of the ICJ 1961-70. Works include *The Law of Territorial Waters and Maritime Jurisdiction* (1927); *American Security and International Police* (1928); *The United States and the World Court* (1929); *International Security* (1935); *Neutrality, Its History, Economics and Law,* Vol. I, *The Origins* (with F. Deak) (1935); Vol. IV, *Today and Tomorrow* (1936); *International Problem of Governing Mankind* (1947); *A Modern Law of Nations* (1948); *Transnational Law* (1956); *The Use of International Law: Controls for Outer Space and the Antarctic Analogy* (with H.J. Taubenfeld, 1959); *The United States and the World Court* (1972); *The Birth of Nations* (1974).

joinder (of ICJ proceedings) Art. 47 of the ICJ Rules of Court 1978 provides that the Court "may at any time direct that the proceedings in two or more cases be joined," also that the written or oral proceedings be in common, or may direct common action in any of these respects without effecting formal joinder. So, in the ***South West Africa Cases*** *1961 I.C.J. Rep. 13* the proceedings instituted against the Union of South Africa by the applications of the Governments of Ethiopia and of Liberia were joined by Order dated 20 May 1961. The proceedings of the Federal Republic of Germany against Denmark and against the Netherlands were similarly joined in the ***North Sea Continental Shelf Cases*** *1968 I.C.J. Rep. 9.*

judicial decisions Art. 38(1) of the Statute of the ICJ stipulates that the Court, "whose function it is to decide in accordance with international law such disputes as are submitted to it, shall apply . . . (d) subject to the provisions of Article 59, judicial decisions . . .," art. 59 providing that the decision of the Court itself has no binding force except between the parties and in respect of the particular case. It would seem that art. 38 has in contemplation as judicial decisions primarily, if not exclusively, those of the Court itself. The terms of art. 59 would seem in some sense to negate the applicability of any principle of *stare decisis* (binding precedent). In practice, the Court refers frequently to its own previous decisions and to those of its predecessor, the PCIJ. It refers also, though in somewhat generalized fashion, to arbitral decisions. It is not believed that the majority of the Court, as distinct from individual judges, has as yet had occasion to refer explicitly to any decision of a municipal court. *See* Lauterpacht, *The Development of International Law by the International Court* (1958), 8-22; Parry *The Sources and Evidences of International Law* (1965), 91-103.

judicial law-making (or legislation) "Where-ever there are courts, the law grows in the hands of the judges. Yet, as a rule, courts are shy of saying so openly. They prefer to 'find' the law and maintain the pious fiction that they have merely applied the law as it stands. . . . Apart from fictions and equity, analogies are one of the means by which courts develop the law with less than their usual reticence. . . . That so much scope for the exercise of judicial discretion exists is not the fault of international courts or tribunals. It is the inevitable concomitant of the pliable state of the rules of international law which courts and tribunals are charged to apply. Yet, while between the parties, every judgment or award is binding as *res judicata,* other subjects of international law remain free to accept or reject any particular judicial pronouncement as a true exposition of *lex lata*. If an international court or tribunal should acquire the reputation of an inclination to depart too far from the generally recognized rules of international law, it would soon find that its list of pending cases suffered from a mysterious process of shrinkage. Thus, in a legal system in which international adjudication is largely optional, the tempo of judicial development of international law must necessarily be slow": Schwarzenberger, *International Law: International Courts* (3rd ed.), 62, 63, 65. *See also* McWhinney, *The World Court and the Contemporary International Law-Making Process* (1979), 59-68.

jure gestionis In relation to **sovereign immunity**, the term acts *jure gestionis* connotes acts performed in a commercial or private capacity, as distinguished from acts *jure imperii,* acts performed in a governmental or public capacity. This distinction is by no means clear-cut, and it is often a matter of judgment for a municipal tribunal whether a particular act is *jure gestionis* or *jure imperii*. The trend has been away from the absolute doctrine of sovereign immunity, conferring immunity for acts both *jure gestionis* and *jure imperii,* to the restrictive doctrine, conferring immunity only for acts *jure imperii*; see the European Convention on State Immunity 1972 *(E.T.S. No. 74)*; the (US) Foreign Sovereign Immunities Act 1976 and the (UK) State Immunity Act 1978.

jure imperii *See **jure gestionis**.*

jurisdiction In international law, the term has two related meanings: (1) "When public international lawyers pose the problem of jurisdiction, they have in mind the State's right under international law to regulate conduct in matters not exclusively of domestic concern. . . . Jurisdiction involves a State's *right* to exercise certain of its powers. It is a problem, accordingly, that is entirely distinct from that of internal power or constitutional capacity or, indeed, sovereignty. . . . The existence of the State's right to exercise jurisdiction is exclusively determined by *public international law*. . . . [R]egulation may occur either by prescribing or enforcing legal rules and one thus speaks of prescriptive or, more attractively, of legislative jurisdiction which designates a State's international right to make legal rules, and of enforcement or prerogative jurisdiction involving the right of a State to give effect to its legal rules in a given case": Mann, The Doctrine of Jurisdiction in International Law, *(1964) 111 Hague Recueil 1* at 9-13. *See also* Harvard Research in International Law, *Jurisdiction with Respect to Crime (29 A.J.I.L. Supp. 435 (1935))*. It is generally accepted that in international law a State is entitled to exercise jurisdiction in respect of persons and events within its territory, and in respect of its nationals (including corporations) even when they are outside its territory (cf. **nationality** and **territoriality**), although in that case enforcement may not be possible so long as they remain abroad. Controversy has arisen over the degree to which States may exercise jurisdiction in respect of things done in another State. There are two main problem areas: where a State requires its nationals abroad to act in a way which may be contrary to the law of the country in which they reside; and where, by an extension of the accepted territorial basis for jurisdiction, a State purports to enforce its laws in respect of conduct outside its territory by non-nationals, on the basis that their conduct, although taking place abroad, has effects within the State. Cf. also **passive personality principle**. Such problems have arisen almost entirely in the context of the application of US laws by US courts and certain federal agencies.

(2) In relation to international organizations, and especially international courts and tribunals, jurisdiction means competence. Thus, Chapter II of the Statute of the International Court of Justice, titled "Competence of the Court," contains art. 36(1) providing that [t]he

jurisdiction of the Court comprises all cases which the parties refer to it and all matters specially provided for in the Charter of the United Nations or in treaties and conventions in force." Art. 36(2), the **Optional Clause**, sets out the conditions under which the Court can have "compulsory" jurisdiction.

jurisdiction and control   This term (or sometimes "control and jurisdiction") is sometimes used to describe the rights of a coastal State in its **continental shelf** and **exclusive economic zone**. Stated to be "sovereign rights" in arts. 77(1) and 56(1)(a) respectively of the UN Convention on the Law of the Sea 1982 *(1833 U.N.T.S. 3)*, these rights are functionally qualified and therefore not equivalent to full sovereignty. They are, consequently, better described as rights of exclusive jurisdiction and control over the resources of the two maritime zones.

jurisdiction follows the flag   A maxim connoting the principle that, on the high seas, vessels are subject to the exclusive jurisdiction of the **flag State**, reflected in art. 92(1) of the UN Convention on the Law of the Sea 1982 *(1833 U.N.T.S. 3)*.

jurisprudence   A term in general legal usage, denoting the case-law of a court (as in the jurisprudence of the International Court of Justice) or the theory of law or a branch thereof (as in the jurisprudence of international law).

juristic writings   *See* **publicists**.

jus ad bellum   Literally, the right to resort to war, considered in mediaeval and later law to be confined to sovereigns or princes, not to be confused with the *jus in bello*, or laws and customs of war. Later usage of the term emphasized the criteria for a legal or **just war**. The prohibition on the use of force in art. 2(4) of the UN Charter, with limited exceptions for self-defense (art. 51) and Security Council action or authorization (Chapter VII), necessarily reduces to the point of extinction any general right to resort to war.

jus aequum   This expression, with which he contrasts *jus strictum*, is employed by Schwarzenberger, to connote a "legal system in which rights are relative and must be exercised reasonably and in good faith," the *"jus aequum* rule" thus being that resorted to by an international court or tribunal when in "the exercise of judicially tempered discretion . . . it is necessarily inspired by considerations of common sense, reasonableness and good fai.., or, in short, equitable considerations." *See* Schwarzenberger, *International Law and Order* (1971), 5; and *International Law, Vol. I, International Courts* (3rd. ed.), esp. 52-5.

jus cogens   This term, connoting a rule of law which is peremptory in the sense that it is binding irrespective of the will of individual parties, in contrast to *jus dispositivum*, a rule capable of being modified by contrary contractual engagements, is not one of classical Roman Law, though it was employed by the Pandectists. Though occasionally employed at an earlier date by international law writers, the term gained general currency only with its employment in the Vienna Convention on the Law of Treaties 1969 in the cross-titles to arts. 53 and 64 respecting the avoidance of treaties conflicting with peremptory norms of international law. The cross-title to art. 53 reads "Treaties conflicting with a peremptory norm of general international law (*jus cogens*)," that article defining such a norm as one "accepted and recognized by the international community of States as a whole as a norm from which no derogation is permitted and which can be modified only by a subsequent norm of general international law having the same character." Art. 64, bearing the cross-title "Emergence of a new peremptory norm of general international law (*jus cogens*)," similarly stipulates that, should such a new peremptory norm emerge, any treaty in conflict with it becomes void and terminates. It is not, however, wholly undisputed that these provisions of the Vienna Convention reflect customary international law or that the notion of *jus cogens* is reconcilable with the general theory of international law. Equally, it cannot be claimed that there is any general agreement as to what, if any, are the rules of international law at present having a peremptory character in the sense described. Nonetheless, there is judicial recognition that some norms of international law have a peremptory status: *Reservations to the Genocide Convention Case 1951 I.C.J. Rep. 15* (the crime of genocide); *Barcelona Traction Co. Case 1970 I.C.J. Rep. 3* (international wrongs and the right of diplomatic protection); *Western Sahara Case 1975 I.C.J. Rep.* 12 (the right of self-determination); *United States Diplomatic and Consular Staff in Tehran Case 1980 I.C.J. Rep. 3* (the inviolability of diplomatic missions and personnel); *Military and Paramilitary Activities in and against Nicaragua* Case *1986 I.C.J. Rep. 14* (the prohibition on the use of force). *See* Rozakis, *The Concept of Jus Cogens in the Law of Treaties* (1976); Sinclair, *The Vienna Convention on the Law of Treaties* (2nd ed.), Chap. V; Ragazzi, *The Concept of International Obligations Erga Omnes* (1997), 43-73.

jus dispositivum   A law or rule "capable of being modified by contrary consensual engagements" (Schwarzenberger, *International Law and Order* (1971), 5), thus to be contrasted with *jus cogens*.

jus gentium   Originally, the body of law governing the status of foreigners in ancient Rome and their relations with Roman citizens (cf. *jus civile*, which applied to Roman citizens only); from the time of **Grotius** onwards, the customary law of nations. *See* Brierly, *The Law of Nations* (6th ed.), 17-18.

jus in bello   This term is habitually used by early writers to denote the corpus of the laws and customs of war, to be distinguished from the *jus ad bellum*, or right to resort to war—and is now referred to as the laws of war or international humanitarian law.

jus inter gentes   "Quoting the passage in Justinian's Institutes regarding those bound by the *jus gentium [I. II. 2: Jus autem gentium omni humano generi commune est]*, [Fancisco Vitoria] replaced the *inter homines* (among men) of the original text by *inter gentes*. This has quite erroneously been taken as a reference to a law among 'states,' hence to international law. However, *gens* (pl. *gentes*) does not mean 'state.' It is a vague term approximately equivalent to 'people'. . . . Zouche . . . was not quite satisfied with his choice [of title of his work on international law, *Juris et judicii fecialis*]: he added as a second title *jus inter gentes*, leaning on the phraseology of the Spaniards—namely, the law prevailing among princes or commonwealths of the various nations *(inter principes vel populus diversarum gentium)*. Neither term has won favor in later literature": Nussbaum, *A Concise History of the Law of Nations* (Revised ed.), 80-1, 165.

jus naturale   This term, meaning **natural law** or the law of nature, was employed by Roman jurists to connote the philosophical conception "which, as developed by the Stoics in Greece and borrowed from them by the Romans, meant, in effect, the sum of those principles which ought to control human conduct, because founded in the very nature of man as a rational and social being. In the course of time *jus gentium,* the new progressive element which the practical genius of the Romans had imported into their actual law, and the *jus naturale,* the ideal law conforming to reason, came to be regarded as generally synonymous. . . . Mediaeval writers later developed this conception of a law of nature . . ., and St. Thomas Acquinas, for example, taught that the law of nature was that part of the law of God which was discoverable by human reason. . . . The effect of such a conception as this, when applied to the theory of the relations of the new national states to one another, . . .

meant that it was not in the nature of things that those relations should be merely anarchical . . . 'The grandest function of the law of nature,' Sir Henry Maine has written, 'was discharged in giving birth to modern international law': and even if such a foundation had not been a sound one, no other would have been possible in the sixteenth century. Afterwards, . . . the mediaeval tradition of a law to which man's rational nature bids him everywhere and always to conform became obscure, and later writers returned to another meaning of the term, traces of which are also to be found in Stoic and early Christian writers. They used it to denote a law under which men are supposed to have lived in a state of nature, that is to say, in an imaginary pre-political condition of human society which they are supposed to have left behind when they formed themselves into political societies. This development had unfortunate effects on international law. . . .": Brierly, *Law of Nations* (6th ed.), 17-25. *See also* as to the origins of the notion of *jus naturale*, Bryce, *Studies in History and Jurisprudence* (1901), Vol. II, Essay XI.

jus paciarri   This term, literally the law of peacekeepers, connotes the emerging body of legal rules governing the activities of UN **peacekeeping** operations. *See* Sharp, *Jus Paciarri* (2001).

jus sanguinis   In relation to the acquisition of nationality, "[s]ome states make parentage alone the decisive factor (*jus sanguinis*), so that a child born of their nationals becomes *ipso facto* by birth their national likewise, be the child born at home or abroad. . . . Other states make the territory on which the birth occurs the decisive factor (*jus soli*). According to this rule, every child born on the territory of such a state, whether the parents be citizens or aliens, becomes a national of that state, whereas a child born abroad if foreign although the parents may be nationals": *I Oppenheim 870.* "From an examination of the nationality laws of the various states it appears that seventeen are based solely on *jus sanguinis,* two equally upon *jus soli* and *jus sanguinis,* twenty-five principally upon *jus sanguinis* but partly upon *jus soli,* and twenty-six principally upon *jus sanguinis.* The nationality law of no country is based solely upon *jus soli*": Harvard Research on International Law, *Draft Convention on Nationality (23 A.J.I.L. Supp. 24 (1929)),* art. 3, Comment. In modern times, many States adopt a mixed system.

jus soli   *See jus sanguinis.*

jus strictum   A term of general usage, employed in international law to connote a "legal system in which rights are absolute and may be exercised irrespective of equitable considerations": Schwarzenberger, *International Law and Order* (1971), 6. Cf. ***jus aequum.***

jus voluntarium   This term meaning "volitional" rather than "voluntary" law or rules, in contrast to *jus necessarium* or "necessary" law or rules is employed by Wolff, particularly in his *Jus gentium methodo scientifica perpetratum* (1749), to denote a law derived from the nature of a hypothetical organization of nations, the *civitas maxima.* "Regarding its content we are left pretty much in the dark. Confusion is increased by the fact that in the accepted Grotian terminology the term *jus voluntarium* is reserved for customary and treaty law": Nussbaum, *A Concise History of the Law of Nations* (Revised ed.), 154.

just war   The distinction between a just and an unjust war, so much part of early legal analysis of war (*see **bellum justum, injustum***) and abandoned in the positivist era of the 19th and early 20th centuries (*see II Oppenheim 174-8*), ceased to have significance after the adoption of the UN Charter and the prohibition, with limited and specific exceptions, of the use of force in art. 2(4). The distinction to be drawn now is between a use of force that is in self-defense (art. 51) or authorized by the Security Council (Chapter VII) and thereby lawful on the one hand and one that is not so justified and thereby unlawful on the other, rather than the legitimacy or otherwise of the causes of the use of force, integral to the just/unjust war distinction.

justiciability This term "has acquired popularity with politicians as well as with lawyers. It is, however, used ambiguously to designate the suitability of a dispute for settlement, both as to law and fact, by legal process and on the basis of the application of rules of law, and to characterize a dispute where the risk of an adverse decision is greater than the risk of political tension resulting from the continuance of the dispute": O'Connell *International Law* (2nd. ed.), Vol. 2, 1182. It is sometimes maintained that political disputes are not suitable for settlement by adjudication. The distinction between "legal" and "political" disputes, or "justiciable" and "non-justiciable" disputes, finds recognition and application in a number of treaties. Thus for example the arbitration treaty between the United Kingdom and France of 1903, renewed in 1923 *(20 L.N.T.S. 185)*, excluded disputes which affect "the vital interests, the independence, or the honour of the two contracting parties." Art. 36(2) of the ICJ Statute restricts the application of declarations under the **Optional Clause** to specified categories of "legal disputes." There is a body of opinion that the distinction is unsustainable and that, provided the parties are willing to abide by a judicial determination, any dispute is justiciable. *See* Lauterpacht, *The Function of Law in the International Community* (1933), Part 3; Kelsen, *Peace through Law* (1944), 23-32. *See* the **United States Diplomatic and Consular Staff in Tehran Case** *1980 I.C.J. Rep. 3*; **Military and Paramilitary Activities in and against Nicaragua Cas**e *(Jurisdiction and Admissibility) and (Merits) 1984 I.C.J. Rep. 551 and 1986 I.C.J. Rep. 14. See also* **legal disputes**.

K

Kaeckenbeeck, Georges 1892-1973. Belgian national. President, Upper Silesian Arbitral Tribunal 1922-37. Secretary-General, International Authority of the Ruhr 1954. Principal publications: *International Rivers* (1920); *The International Experiment of Upper Silesia* (1942); The Protection of Vested Rights in International Law, *(1936) 17 B.Y.I.L. 1*; *(1937) 59 Hague Recueil 316.*

Katz, Milton US national. Government official, professor at Harvard Law School from 1940. Principal publications *The Law of International Transactions and Relations* (with Brewster,1960); *The Relevance of International Adjudication* (1968).

Kellogg, Frank B. 1856-1937. US national. Secretary of State 1925-9 and, in that capacity, co-sponsor of the **General Treaty for the Renunciation of War 1928**, or Kellogg-Briand Pact. Judge of the PCIJ 1930-5.

Kellogg-Briand Pact *See* **General Treaty for the Renunciation of War 1928**.

Kelsen, Hans 1881-1973. Austrian, subsequently US national. Professor, Vienna 1911-30, Cologne 1930-3, Geneva 1933-9, Harvard 1940-2, Berkeley 1942-52. The principal contributions to international law of this great jurist are: *Peace through Law* (1944); *The Law of the United Nations* (1950), with supplement *Recent Trends in the United Nations* (1951); *Principles of International Law* (1952); *Collective Security under International Law* (1957).

Kiel Canal This artificial waterway, connecting the Baltic and North Seas and lying wholly within the territory of Germany, was, by art. 380 of the Treaty of Versailles of 1919 *(225 C.T.S. 188)*, together with its approaches, stipulated to be maintained "free and open to the vessels of commerce and of war of all nations at peace with Germany on terms of entire equality." In its judgment of 17 August 1923 in the *Wimbledon (Merits) P.C.I.J., Ser. A, No. 1*, the PCIJ *held* that the German authorities had been wrong in refusing access to the canal to the *S.S. Wimbledon*, a British merchant vessel under charter to a French armament firm engaged in the carriage of war material to Poland, then in a state of war with the USSR, Germany's obligation under the treaty being paramount over any domestic neutrality regulations. On 14 November 1936, Germany purported to repudiate arts. 380-6, there being "no express protest on the part of the majority of the interested signatories": *I Oppenheim 483*. In the *Kiel Canal Collision Case (1950) 17 I.L.R. 133*, the Supreme Court of the British Occupation Zone of Germany held that a collision within the waters of the canal was governed by German law since the provisions of the Treaty of Versailles did not exclude the competence of the German courts and related only to freedom of transit. "The other important aspect of th[is] case is its calling in question the continuing force of the provisions of the Treaty of Versailles regarding the Kiel Canal, by reason of the German denunciation in 1936. . . .": Baxter, *The Law of International Waterways (1969) 89n.*

King's (Queen's) Advocate-General This office, that of the principal English or British Law Officer for ecclesiastical, admiralty and international matters originated about 1600, but remained unfilled after the resignation of Sir Travers Twiss, the last holder, in 1872. The Advocate-General was the principal legal adviser to the Foreign Office for the first century of its existence. *See* McNair, The Debt of International Law in Britain to the Civil Law and the Civilians, *(1954) 39 T.G.S. 183.*

King's Chambers, the "Formerly, the English Kings claimed jurisdiction over the sea areas between lines drawn from headland to headland round the British coasts such as from Orfordness to the Foreland and from Beachy Head to Dunnose Point, and James I instructed Commissioners to prepare maps showing these areas which were called The King's Chambers. This method of drawing a line connecting headlands on a coast and claiming the waters on the landward side of that line as territorial waters is very often referred to as 'the headland theory'": Colombos, *The International Law of the Sea* (6th ed.), 182. "It is unlikely that Great Britain would still . . . claim the territorial character of the . . . King's Chambers": *I Oppenheim (8th ed.) 508.*

Kiss, Alexandre-Charles 1925- . French national. Professor, Strasbourg, 1953- . Principal publications: *Répertoire de la pratique francaise en matiére de droit international public* (6 vols., 1962-9).; *L'abus de droit en droit international* (1953).

Knight, Gary 1939- . Professor, Louisiana 1968- . Principal works include *The International Law of the Sea: Cases, Documents and Readings* (1975; 1991 edition, with Chiu); *The Future of International Fisheries Management* (1975); *Ocean Thermal Conversion* (with Nyhart and Stein, 1977); *Evidence: The Case against Milosovic* (with Loyd, 2002).

Korowicz, Manek Stanislaw 1903-64. Polish teacher and diplomat who settled in USA. Professor, Fletcher School of Law and Diplomacy 1954-64. Principal works include *Disputes over Implementation of Geneva Convention* (1931, in Polish); *German-Polish Upper Silesian Convention* (1937, in Polish); *Individuals as Subjects of International Law* (1938, in Polish); *La Souverainete des Etats et l'avenir du droit international* (1945); *Introduction to International Law* (1959).

Koskenniemi, Martti Professor, University of Helsinki, Global Professor of Law, New York University School of Law; sometime Counsellor for Legal Affairs, at the Finnish Ministry for Foreign Affairs; member, International Law Commission 2002- . Principal publications include *From Apology to Utopia: The Structure of International Legal Argument* (1989); *State Succession: Codification Tested Against the Facts* (with Eismann, 1999); *The Gentle Civilizer of Nation: The Rise and Fall of International Law 1870-1960* (2002).

Kosovo Commission Properly styled the Independent International Commission for Kosovo, an initiative of the Swedish government, the Commission examined the origins of the Kosovo crisis, the diplomatic efforts to end the conflict, the role of the United Nations and NATO's decision to intervene militarily. Its report, published in October 2000, concluded that the NATO military intervention was illegal but legitimate. It proposed that the rules governing **humanitarian intervention** be clarified. A follow-up report was published in 2001. *See* <www.kosovocommission.org>.

Krstic Case *ICTY, Case #IT-98-33.* General Radislav Krstic, a Bosnian Serb and deputy commander of the Drina Corps, was the first person convicted of genocide before the International Criminal Tribunal for the Former Yugoslavia in respect of the attack on the town of Srebrenica between July and November 1995. He was sentenced to 45 years imprisonment.

Kunz, Josef L. 1890-1970. Born in Vienna, he settled in USA, where he taught at Toledo from 1934 until retirement. Some forty of his selected essays are reprinted in *The Changing Law of Nations—Essays on International Law* (1968).

Kyoto Protocol *See* **Climate Change Convention**.

L

La Pradelle, Albert de Geouffre de 1871-1955. French Professor, Grenoble and Paris, and Director of the Institut d'Etudes et de Recherches Diplomatiques. Founder and director of the *Revue de droit international*. Principal works include *Les Principes Generaux du Droit des Gens* (1928); *La Justice Internationale* (1936); *La Mer* (1937); *Les Grands Cas de la Jurisprudence Internationale* (1938); *Maitres et Doctrines du droit des gens* (1939; 2nd ed. 1950); *Recueil des arbitrages internationaux* (with Politis, 2nd ed. 1957).

Lachs, Manfred 1914-93. Polish law professor, international law commissioner and arbiter; Judge ICJ 1967-93, President 1973-76. Major works include *War Crimes, An Attempt to Define the Issues* (1945); *The Geneva Agreements on Indochina* (in Polish, 1955); *Multilateral Treaties* (in Polish, 1958); *The Polish German Frontier* (2nd ed., 1965); *The Law of Outer Space* (1972). *See* McWhinney and Lachs, *Judge Manfred Lachs and Judicial Law-Making: Opinions on the International Court of Justice, 1967-1993* (1995).

lacuna/ae This term, which is in general usage, connotes, in relation to international law, the situation in which there is a gap or gaps in international law due to the absence of express rules governing a situation. *See **non-liquet**.*

LaGrand Case *(Germany v United States) 1999 I.C.J. Rep. 9; 2001 I.C.J. Rep. forthcoming.* Brothers Karl and Walter LaGrand, German nationals who had been permanently residing in the United States since childhood, were arrested Arizona in 1982 and convicted in 1984 of murder in the first degree and sentenced to death. The Vienna Convention on Consular Relations 1963 *(596 U.N.T.S. 261)* required the competent authorities of the US to inform them without delay of their right to communicate with the consulate of Germany. The US acknowledged that this did not occur. Karl LaGrand was executed on 24 February 1999. On 2 March 1999, the day before the scheduled execution of Walter LaGrand, Germany brought the case to the International Court of Justice. On 3 March 1999, the Court made an order *indicating* provisional measures stating, *inter alia*, that the United States should take all measures at its disposal to ensure that Walter LaGrand was not executed pending a final decision of the Court. On that same day, Walter LaGrand was executed. On the merits, the Court *held* (14 to 1) that, by not informing the brothers without delay of their rights under art. 36(1)(b) of the Vienna Convention, the US had breached its obligations to Germany and to the LaGrand brothers; (14 to 1) that, by not permitting a review and reconsideration of the convictions and sentences after the violations of the Convention had been established, the US had breached its obligations to Germany and to the LaGrand brothers under art. 36(2) of the Convention; and (13 to 2) that, by failing to take all measures at its disposal to ensure Walter LaGrand was not executed pending its final decision, the US breached the obligation incumbent upon it under the order indicating provisional measures. The Court held thereby for the first time that indications of provisional measures under art. 41 of its Statute are binding on States.

Laibach, Congress of (1821)   This, the third of the four Congresses of the **Concert of Europe**, was concerned with Austrian intervention in Italy, in accordance with the principles agreed at the **Troppau Congress** in 1820 (Hertslet, *Map of Europe by Treaty* (1875), No. 105). Russia, Austria and Prussia issued a declaration at the close, on 12 May 1821 (Hertslet, No. 108), affirming the principles agreed at the Troppau Conference, but France did not sign and Great Britain had dissociated itself from the principles originally agreed.

laissez-passer   Art. VII (Section 24) of the General Convention on the Privileges and Immunities of the United Nations 1946 *(1 U.N.T.S. 16)* provides that the UN "may issue United Nations laissez-passer to its officials. These laissez-passer shall be recognized and accepted as valid travel documents by the authorities of Members, taking into account the provisions of Section 25 [relating to visas]." While a number of **headquarters agreements** require a laissez-passer issued by the UN to be treated as equivalent to a passport, some member States in practice do not permit travel without a national passport and an appropriate visa. The UN/US Headquarters Agreement 1946 *(11 U.N.T.S. 11)* makes no mention of laissez-passer, though it guarantees an absence of impediments to transit to the Headquarters District (art. IV (Section 11)).

lake   A lake located "entirely enclosed by the land of one and the same state [is] part of the territory of that State": *I Oppenheim 589.* Where a lake is surrounded by more than one State, general international law prescribes no specific rules as to boundaries, the allocation of resources and navigation, etc., and particular conventional regimes have been established for particular lakes: *ibid., 590. See, e.g.*, Piper, *The International Law of the Great Lakes* (1967).

Lake Lanoux Arbitration   *(France v. Spain) (1957) 12 R.I.A.A. 281.* By the *compromis* of 19 November 1956, the parties referred to a tribunal of five persons the question whether the French Government was justified in its contention that the execution, without prior agreement with Spain, of certain works in connection with the utilization of the waters of Lac Lanoux did not contravene the Treaty and Additional Act of Bayonne of 26 May 1866 *(133 C.T.S. 359)* defining the frontier and making provision for joint use of the frontier waters. *Held,* the French contention was correct. The question was divisible into two parts: A., whether the works in question infringed Spain's rights; and, B., if not, whether their execution without prior agreement with Spain nevertheless constituted an infringement of the treaty stipulations referred to. As to A: It appearing that no guaranteed user of water would, having regard to the compensatory devices employed, suffer any deprivation or diminution of his rights, Spain could have no complaint. As to B: The fact that art. XI of the Additional Act explicitly called only for notification to the other party of any proposed works involving the alteration of the course or volume of any watercourse made it clear that the parties had no intention of imposing any obligation of prior agreement since any such requirement would have obviated any necessity for notification.

Lakhtine doctrine   This is the proposal by the Soviet jurist that **sector claims** should include the intermediate ice: Lakhtine, Rights over the Arctic, *24 A.J.I.L. 703 (1930).*

Land and Maritime Boundary between Cameroon and Nigeria Case   *See* **Cameroon-Nigeria Boundary Case**.

Land Mines Convention   Properly styled the Convention on the Prohibition of the Use, Stockpiling, Production and Transfer of Anti-personnel Mines and on their Destruction, adopted at Ottawa on 18 September 1997 *(36 I.L.M. 1509 (1997)),* the LMC required its parties "never under any circumstances" to use anti-personnel mines (art. 1(1)(a); not to develop, produce, acquire, stockpile, retain or transfer anti-personnel mines, or assist or induce others to perform these prohibited acts (art. 1(1)(b) and (c)). Existing land mines are to be destroyed (art. 1(2); *see also* arts. 4 and 5) and States are to cooperate towards that end, particularly in mine-clearance (art. 6). For the purposes of the Convention a mine is "a munition designed to be placed under, on or near the ground or other surface area and to be exploded by the presence, proximity or contact of a person or vehicle" (art. 2(2), while an anti-personnel mine is a mine, so defined, "that will incapacitate, injure or kill one or more persons" (art. 2(1). *See* <www.icbl.org>.

Land, Hague Convention concerning the Laws and Customs of War on This Convention, to which is annexed the Réglement or Regulations respecting the Laws and Customs of War on Land, was adopted as Convention II of the Hague Peace Conference of 1899 *(187 C.T.S. 429)* and in its revised form constitutes Convention IV of the Conference of 1907 *(205 C.T.S. 277)*. *See* Holland, *The Laws of War on Land* (1908).

Land, Island and Maritime Frontier Dispute Case *(El Salvador/Honduras) 1992 I.C.J. Rep. 351.* By a special agreement of 24 May 1986, El Salvador and Honduras submitted to a Chamber of the ICJ a long-standing dispute concerning (1) the delimitation of six sectors of the land frontier between them; (2) the juridical status of the islands in the Gulf of Fonseca; and (3) the juridical status of the waters of the Gulf and related maritime spaces. Nicaragua, located on the east side of the Gulf, applied to intervene under art. 62 of the ICJ Statute as having an interest of a legal nature that may be affected by the outcome of the case. On 13 September 1990, the Chamber *held* (unanimously) that Nicaragua's legal interest extended to the legal régime of the waters of the Gulf and that it could intervene only with respect to that issue: *1990 I.C.J. Rep. 92.*

On 11 September 1992, the Chamber *held* (2) (unanimously) that the island of El Tigre was part of Honduras; (unanimously) that the island of Meanguera was part of El Salvador; (4 to 1) that the island of Meanguerita was part of El Salvador; (3) (4 to 1) that the Gulf of Fonseca, as an **historic bay**, was to continue to be held in sovereignty jointly by the parties, with the exception of the littoral belt of 3 miles accruing to each, and with the central portion of the **closing line** across the mouth of the bay being subject to the joint entitlement of El Salvador, Honduras and Nicaragua; (4 to 1) that the waters outside the Gulf of Fonseca from the closing line across its mouth were to be delimited in respect of their relevant **maritime zones** by agreement among the parties on the basis of international law. As to (1), the delimitation of the land frontier, the Chamber applied, as required by the parties, the ***uti possidetis*** principle, including "colonial *effectivités,*" as well as "post-colonial *effectivités*"; and, on the basis of that substantial and compelling analysis, drew a land boundary for each of the six sectors, unanimously for all but one sector.

land-locked States The UN Convention on the Law of the Sea 1982 *(1833 U.N.T.S. 3)* defines a land-locked State as "a State which has no sea-coast" (art. 124(1)(a)). In all there are 31 land-locked States: 14 in Africa, 6 in Asia, 9 in Europe and 2 in South America. Such States are accorded the right of access to the sea to enable them to exercise their rights under the freedom of the high seas and the common heritage of mankind, the terms and modalities to be agreed with the transit State(s) (art. 125). The Convention on Transit Trade of Land-Locked States adopted at New York on 8 July 1965 *(597 U.N.T.S. 42)* establishes, as between the parties, the principle of freedom of transit between land-locked States and the sea, and sets conditions for the exercise of the freedom. One authority has opined that a general right of transit, apart from contractual obligations, "is difficult to sustain": Brownlie, *Principles of Public International Law* (5th ed.), 284. Further, in addition to the full freedoms of the sea (art. 87 of the UN Convention on the Law of the Sea), land-locked States are accorded the right to participate, on an equitable basis, in the exploitation of part of the living resources of the **exclusive economic zone,** the terms and modalities to be agreed with coastal States (art. 69). *See* Glassner, *Access to the Sea for Developing Land-locked States* (1974).

languages, authentic, official, working (of the UN)   Art. 111 of the UN Charter stipulates that "the Chinese, French, Russian, English, and Spanish texts [thereof] are equally authentic." Art. 39 of the ICJ Statute provides: "1. The official languages of the Court shall be French and English. If the parties agree that the case shall be conducted in French, the judgment shall be delivered in French *[and vice versa].* 2. In the absence of . . . agreement . . . each party may, in the pleadings, use the language which it prefers; the decision of the Court shall be given in French and English. In this case the Court shall at the same time determine which of the two texts shall be considered as authoritative. 3. The Court shall, at the request of any party, authorize a language other than French or English to be used by that party." By Resolution dated 1 February 1946, the General Assembly adopted the rule that "[i]n all organs of the United Nations, other than the International Court of Justice, Chinese, French, English, Russian and Spanish shall be the official languages, and English and French the working languages." This rule is reproduced as Rule 44 of the Rules of Procedure of the General Assembly, but in 1948 Spanish was added to the number of working languages, in 1968 Russian, and in 1973 Chinese for all purposes and Arabic for the General Assembly and its Committees (Resolutions 3189 (XXVIII), 3190 (XXVIII)) so that Rule 51 now reads: "Chinese, English, French, Russian and Spanish shall be both the official and the working languages of the General Assembly, its Committees and subcommittees. Arabic shall be both an official and a working language of the General Assembly and the main Committees."

Lateran Treaty   The term generally given to the Treaty and Concordat concluded between Italy and the **Holy** *See* on 11 February 1929 *((1929) 23 A.J.I.L. Supp. 187).* Italy recognized "the sovereignty of the Holy *See* in the international domain as an attribute inherent in its nature" (art. 2), and the "full ownership, exclusive and absolute power, and sovereign jurisdiction [of the Holy See] over the Vatican" (art. 3); and Italy undertook not to interfere in the City of the Vatican (art. 4). *See* Sereni, *The Italian Conception of International Law* (1943), 292-3; Kunz, The Status of the Holy *See* in International Law, *46 A.J.I.L. 308 (1952).*

Latin American Integration Association   Founded by the Montevideo Treaty establishing the Latin American Integration Association of 12 August 1980 *(20 I.L.M. 672 (1981)),* this Association replaced, from 1981, the Latin American Free Trade Association with "the long range objective [of] the gradual and progressive formation of a Latin American Common Market" (art. 1). The Association comprises a Conference of Evaluation and Convergence, consisting of all the members and responsible for general overview of the Association's work (arts. 34-5); a Council of Foreign Ministers, described as "the highest body of the Association [which] shall adopt the decisions relating to the broad policy orientation of the economic integration process" (art. 30); and a Committee of Representatives, consisting of all members and described as "the permanent body of the Association" (art. 35). The Contracting Parties are Argentina, Bolivia, Brazil, Chile, Colombia, Ecuador, Mexico, Paraguay, Peru, Uruguay and Venezuela. *See* <www.aladi.org>.

Latin-American Nuclear-Free Zone   *See* **Tlatelolco, Treaty of.**

Latin-American Economic System   This organization, established by the Convention of Panama of 17 October 1975 *(15 I.L.M. 1081 (1976) (1976))* and comprising 28 Latin

American and Caribbean States, seeks to coordination joint positions and common strategies for its members on economic issues vis-à-vis third States and international organizations. *See* <www.sela.org>.

Lausanne, Treaty of On 24 July 1923, two major agreements were concluded at Lausanne. (1) The Treaty of Peace between the British Empire, France, Italy, Japan, Greece, Romania, and the Serb-Croat-Slovene State on the one hand and Turkey on the other *(28 L.N.T.S. 11)* ended the war with Turkey. This Treaty effected certain territorial changes (arts. 2-22), contained provisions for the protection of minorities within Turkey (arts. 37-45), the Ottoman Public Debt (arts. 46-57) and the regulation and settlement of property, rights and interests (arts. 64-98). (2) The Convention relating to the Régime of Straits was concluded on the same day and between the same parties *(28 L.N.T.S. 115)*, establishing "the principle of freedom of transit and of navigation by sea and by air in the strait of the Dardanelles, the Sea of Marmara and the Bosphorus. . . ." (art. 1). Merchant vessels were guaranteed free passage in times of peace and war (Regulation 1(a)-(c), annexed to the Convention); a limit was placed on the number of warships entitled to pass through the Straits in time of war (Regulation 2). A Straits Commission was established to supervise the régime (Regulations 10-16). The Convention regarding the Régime of the Straits, signed at Montreux, 20 July 1936 *(173 L.N.T.S. 213)* reaffirmed the principle of freedom of transit and navigation through the straits (art. 1), but transferred to Turkey the functions of the Straits Commission (art. 24). On the Straits Commission, see Baxter, *The Law of International Waterways* (1964), 159-68.

Lauterpacht, Elihu, Sir 1928- . Son of Hersch Lauterpacht, scholar (reader and, since 1994, honorary professor, Cambridge; Director of the Research Centre for International Law 1983-95) and practitioner of international law. Editor *I.L.R.* 1960- . Principal publications: *Collected Papers of Sir Hersch Lauterpacht* (4 vols.1970-78); *Aspects of the Administration of International Justice* (1991).

Lauterpacht, Hersch, Sir 1897-1960. Professor, Cambridge 1937-65. Consultant to UN on codification. Member, ILC 1951-55. Judge, ICJ 1955-60. Co-founder (with McNair) of *A.D.*, and sole editor 1935-60; editor, *B.Y.I.L.* 1944-54. Principal works include *Private Law Sources and Analogies of International Law* (1927); *Development of International Law by the Permanent Court of International Justice* (1933); *The Function of Law in the International Community* (1934); *An International Bill of the Rights of Man* (1945); *Recognition in International Law* (1948); *International Law* (1948); *International Law and Human Rights* (1950); *The Development of International Law by the International Court* (1958); editor of Oppenheim's *International Law,* successive editions 1935-55. His son, **Lauterpacht, Sir Elihu** has edited *Hersch Lauterpacht. International Law. Collected Papers (*4 vols. 1974-8).

law of nations This somewhat obsolete term is synonymous with international law: Brierly, *Law of Nations* (6th ed.), 1. The first two chapters of *I Oppenheim (8th ed.)* refer to the law of nations (Chap.1: Foundation of the Law of Nations; Chap. 2: The Subjects of the Law of Nations), while the 9th edition eschews reference to the term, using instead "international law." Most writers and practitioners have for the last century preferred the term "international law."

law of nature *See jus naturale*; **natural law**.

law of the sea A term used to describe the rules of international law applicable to the sea, now substantially codified in the UN Convention on the Law of the Sea 1982 *(1833*

U.N.T.S. 3), as distinct from maritime law, which deals with the sea in its commercial aspects, mainly from a domestic vantage; shipping law, which deals with vessels and trade by sea, again mainly from a domestic vantage; and admiralty law, which deals with the domestic exercise of jurisdiction over ships and shipping.

Law of the Sea, codification of The first significant attempt to codify the customary rules of international law on the sea occurred at the League of Nations Conference for the Codification of International Law, whose second Committee considered the question of the territorial sea. While no definitive agreement was reached, State practice and attitudes concerning the territorial sea were explored. *See* Rosenne, *League of Nations Conference for the Codification of International Law* (1974). The First United Nations Conference on the Law of the Sea (UNCLOS I) met in Geneva from 24 February 1958 to 28 April 1958 and, basing its work on drafts submitted by the International Law Commission, adopted four Conventions, on the Territorial Sea and the Contiguous Zone *(516 U.N.T.S. 205)* on the High Seas *(450 U.N.T.S. 82),* on Fishing and the Conservation of the Living Resources of the High Seas *(559 U.N.T.S. 285)* and on the Continental Shelf *(499 U.N.T.S. 311).* For the reports and commentary of the ILC, *see [1950] I.L.C. Yearbook,* vols. 1 and 2; *see also Official Records of the United Nations Conference on the Law of the Sea of 1958,* UN Doc. A/Conf. 13. The Second United Nations Conference on the Law of the Sea (UNCLOS II) met in Geneva from 17 March to 27 April 1960, but could reach no agreement on the issues before it: the breadth of the territorial sea and fishing limits. *See* the *Official Records of the United Nations Conference on the Law of the Sea 1960,* UN Doc. A/Conf. 19. General Assembly Res. 2750 (XXV) of 17 December 1970 instructed the convening of a further conference on the law of the sea. The Third United Nations Conference on the Law of the Sea (UNCLOS III) met first, for an organizational session, in New York, on 3 December 1973, thereafter in substantive sessions in Caracas, Venezuela; Geneva and New York from 20 June 1974. The Conference based its deliberations on a number of negotiating texts and drafts: The Single Negotiating Text of 7 May 1975, UN Doc. A/CONF 62/WP 8, *14 I.L.M. 682 (1975)*; the Revised Single Negotiating Text of 6 May 1976, U.N. Doc. A/CONF 62/WP 8/Rev. 1; the Informal Composite Negotiating Text of 15 July 1977, UN Doc. A/CONF 62/WP 10, *16 I.L.M. 1108 (1977)*; Revised Informal Negotiating Text of 28 April 1979, UN Doc. A/CONF 62/WP 10/Rev. 2, *18 I.L.M. 686 (1979)*; the Draft Convention on the Law of the Sea of 27 August 1980, UN Docs. A/CONF 62/WP 10/Rev. 3 and A/CONF 62/122, *19 I.L.M. 1129 (1980).*

On 30 April 1882, the UN Convention on the Law of the Sea was signed at Montego Bay, Jamaica, the Convention being opened for signature on 10 December 1982 *(1833 U.N.T.S. 3).* Part XI (on the regime for seep-sea mining) was subsequently amended by the Agreement Relating to the Implementation of Part XI of the UN Convention on the Law of the Sea of July 1994 (GA Res. 48/263; *33 I.L.M. 1309 (1994)*). *See Third UN Conference on the Law of the Sea: Official Records* (27 vols. 1975-84). *See also* Stevenson and Oxman, *The Preparations for the Law of the Sea Conference, 68 A.J.I.L. 1 (1974)*; Stevenson and Oxman, UNCLOS III: The 1975 Geneva Session, *69 A.J.I.L. 763 (1975)*; Oxman, UNCLOS III: The 1976 New York Session, *71 A.J.I.L. 247 (1977)*; Oxman, UNCLOS III: The 1977 New York Sessions, *72 A.J.I.L. 57 (1978)*; Oxman, UNCLOS III: The Seventh Session, *73 A.J.I.L. 1 (1979)*; Oxman, UNCLOS III: The Eighth Session, *74 A.J.I.L. 1 (1980)*; Oxman, UNCLOS III: The Ninth Session, *75 A.J.I.L. 211 (1981)*; Oxman, UNCLOS III: The Tenth Session, *76 A.J.I.L 1 (1982)*; Platzoder, *Third United Nations Convention on the Law of the Sea: Documents* (15 vols., 1982-94).

Law Officers Opinions These are the opinions of British Law Officers of the Crown (principally the Attorney- and Solicitor-General, and formerly the Advocate-General) delivered in relation to questions of international law chiefly to the Foreign Office (but also to other Departments) and forming a notable reservoir of international legal learning. Law officers opinions "have a greater value, even, than opinions of jurisconsults or private practitioners, however learned, furnished to private persons. For they partake of a quality which . . . belongs also to the pronouncements of courts on questions of international law. They are produced, usually with reference to a precise factual situation, in the full knowledge on the part of their authors that the State may, and probably will, act on them. And they are produced by persons who are, normally, officers of State, and thus participate in the process whereby States act in law. If their opinions do not represent the actual practice of states, which is a source of the law, they are thus nevertheless an element, or an element in the expression, of that practice": Parry, *British Digest of International Law*, Vol. 7 (1965), 243. Such opinions have been relied upon by British writers. General selections of the opinions have been published in Smith, *Great Britain and the Law of Nations* (1932, 1935), and McNair, *International Law Opinions* (1956).

law-making treaties "[T]reaties concluded for the purpose of laying down general rules of conduct among a considerable number of States . . . may be termed 'law-making' treaties. . . . In a sense the distinction between law-making and other treaties is merely one of convenience. In principle, all treaties are law-making inasmuch as they lay down rules of conduct which the parties are bound to observe as law. However, relatively extensive participation in a treaty, coupled with a subject matter of general significance and stipulations which accord with the general sense of the international community, do establish for some treaties an influence far beyond the limits of formal participation in them. These factors give such a treaty something of the complexion of a legislative instrument, and assist the acceptance of the treaty's provisions as customary international law in addition to their contractual value for the parties": *I Oppenheim 1204. See* the *Reparation for Injuries Case 1949 I.C.J. Rep. 174*; Status of *South-West Africa 1950 I.C.J. Rep. 128. See also* **international legislation**.

Lawrence, Thomas Joseph 1849-1919. Priest and law teacher, who taught at Cambridge, England and Chicago. Principal works include *Essays on Disputed Points of International Law* (1884); *The Handbook of International Law* (10th ed. 1918); *The Principles of International Law* (6th ed. 1913); *International Problems and Hague Conferences* (1908); *Documents Illustrative of International Law* (1914).

League of Arab States *See* **Arab League**.

League of Nations The first global international organization, forerunner of the United Nations, whose constituent document, the Covenant, formed Part I of the Peace Treaty of Versailles with Germany of 28 June 1919 *(225 C.T.S. 188)* and equally of the Peace Treaties of St Germain-en-Laye of 10 September 1919 with Austria *(226 C.T.S. 8)* and of Neuilly of 27 November 1919 with Bulgaria *(226 C.T.S. 332)*. At its zenith the League had 58 members, but the United States, not having ratified the Treaty of Versailles, never joined; and Japan, Germany and Italy withdrew to pursue expansionist policies unembarrassed by membership, and the USSR was somewhat spuriously expelled. The principal apparent contrast between the structure of the League and that of the UN was that the former had but a single Council and the latter three (the Security, Economic and Social and Trusteeship Councils), but the difference here is more apparent than real. As respects function, the League Assembly and Council were equally omnicompetent, there being no provision in the Covenant comparable to arts. 12 and 24 of the Charter, according the Security Council a primacy in relation to matters of peace and security. Under art. 5(1) of the Covenant, moreover, the unanimity rule applied in general in relation to voting in both Council and Assembly, in contrast to the majority rule prescribed by arts. 18 and 27 of the Charter. The League's method of decentralized guarantees against aggression under art. 16 having notoriously failed, the UN Charter is Chapter VII established a centralized system of keeping international peace and security. The League was dissolved by resolution of the Assembly on 18 April 1946. As to the history of the organization, see Walters, *A History of the League of Nations* (2 vols. 1952); Northedge, *The League of Nations* (1988). As to the Covenant in its legal aspects, see Fischer Williams, *Some Aspects of the Covenant of the League of Nations* (1934); Zimmern, *The League of Nations and the Rule of Law* (1939).

League of Red Cross Societies *See* **International Federation of Red Cross and Red Crescent Societies**.

lease, international It seems that the term "international lease" is used in two sense. (1) The term is employed to describe an arrangement entered into between States, or between a national of one State and another State, whereby property is made available by the lessor State, or national, to the lessee State, *e.g.*, for use as diplomatic premises. This type of arrangement, being expressly governed by municipal law, is not an international lease properly so called, though it may have international law implications, *e.g.*, in the status of the leased building under the law relating to **diplomatic privileges and immunities**. *See* Lauterpacht, *Private Law Sources and Analogies of International Law* (1927), 183. Lauterpacht's first category is rather of quasi-international leases such as those of a site for a bonded warehouse at Kismayu, British East Africa, effected by the exchange of notes between Great Britain and Italy of 13 January 1905 *(197 C.T.S. 403)*, or of sites for landing and transshipment on the Niger stipulated for in art. VIII and Annex 4 of the Delimitation Convention of 14 June 1898 between Great Britain and France *(186 C.T.S. 313)* and effected by the Agreements of 20 May 1903 *(193 C.T.S. 193)* (both referred to by Lauterpacht). (2) The term is employed to describe an arrangement whereby territory is leased or pledged by the owner-State to another State. In such cases, sovereignty is, for the term of the lease, transferred to the lessee State. "Perhaps the best-know historical examples were the 'Chinese' leases. In 1898 China leased the district of Kiaochow to Germany, Wei-Hai-Wei and the land opposite Hong Kong to Great Britain, Kuang-chou to France, and Port Arthur to Russia. . . . Some of these transactions may have comprised, for most practical purposes, cessions of territory; nevertheless, in strict law these remained the territory of the leasing state": *I Oppenheim 568-9*. An excellent example is the lease of the so-called Hong Kong New Territories effected by the Convention of 9 June 1898 *(186 C.T.S. 310)*; this lease is expressed to be for a term of 99 years and was thus due to expire in 1997; by the UK/China Hong Kong Agreement of 26 September 1984 *(1984) 23 I.L.M. 1366)*, whereby Hong Kong Island, Kowloon and the New Territories were "restored" to China. . . . Apart from the question of whether these type of international lease are in fact terminable, which seems now to be fully accepted, the "political" lease differs from the "quasi-international" in that the former conveys full rights of sovereignty to the lessee State for the period of the lease; cf. the terms of the Hong Kong New Territories lease. *See* Verzijl, *International Law in Historical Perspective*, Vol. 3 (1970), 397-408.

least developed countries This term refers to those **developing countries** with very low *per capita* incomes, little economic growth and few natural resources, sometimes also referred to as the **Fourth World**.

legal disputes The precise dichotomy between legal and *(semble)* political disputes, though it of course is no more than a particular formulation of the doctrine of the inherent limitations of the judicial process in international law which dates at least from Vattel *(see* Lauterpacht, *The Function of Law in the International Community* (1933), Part 3), would appear to stem from the specification in the **Optional Clause** in the PCIJ Statute (art. 36(2)), repeated exactly in the ICJ Statute (art. 36(2)), of the category of controversies potentially within the compulsory jurisdiction of the Court as "all legal disputes." As to "the question whether the term 'legal' is in this context descriptive or qualifying," see Lauterpacht, *supra*, Part 18 and the works there cited. *See* **justiciability**.

Legality of the Threat or Use of Nuclear Weapons *1996 I.C.J. Rep. 226.* By Resolution 49/75 dated 15 December 1994, the UN General Assembly requested the ICJ for an advisory opinion on the following question: "Is the threat or use of nuclear weapons in any circumstance permitted under international law?" After determining that a legal question was involved, the Court concluded that the most relevant applicable laws were the UN Charter's provisions on the use of force and the law applicable in armed conflict, as well as any particular treaties on nuclear weapons that the Court deemed pertinent.

On 8 July 1996, the Court *decided* (13 to 1) that it had jurisdiction to give an advisory opinion. The Court *advised*: (a) (unanimously) that neither customary nor conventional international law specifically authorized the threat or use of nuclear weapons; (b) (11 to 3) neither customary nor conventional international law comprehensively and universally prohibited the threat or use of nuclear weapons; (c) (unanimously) that a threat or use of force by nuclear weapons that was contrary to art. 2(4) of the UN Charter, the prohibition on the use or threat of force, and that did not meet the requirements of art. 51, concerning **self-defense**, was unlawful; (d) (unanimously) that a threat or use of nuclear weapons should coincide with the requirements of international law applicable in armed conflict, especially the rules and principles of international humanitarian law, as well as treaty provisions and other rules involving nuclear weapons; and (e) (7 to 7) that the threat or use of nuclear weapons would generally contradict the rules of international law applicable to armed conflict, especially the principles and rules of humanitarian law. However, the Court could not reach a definitive conclusion as to whether the threat or use of nuclear weapons would be lawful or unlawful in an extreme case of self-defense, where a State's survival was at issue.

Legality of the Use by a State of Nuclear Weapons in Armed Conflict *1996 I.C.J. Rep. 66.* By resolution dated 14 May 1993, the World Health Assembly requested the ICJ for an advisory opinion on the following question: "In view of the health and environmental effects, would the use of nuclear weapons by a State in war or other armed conflict be a breach of its obligations under international law including the WHO Constitution?" On 8 July 1996, the Court *advised*: (11 to 3) that it was unable to give the advisory opinion requested by the WHO. The Court noted that, in order to have jurisdiction under art. 65(1) of the ICJ Statute and art. 96(2) of the UN Charter, three conditions must be met: the Charter must authorize the agency to request opinions from the Court; the requested opinion must be a legal question; and the question must arise within the scope of the activities of the requesting agency. Finding the first two conditions to be satisfied, the Court determined that WHO's request for an advisory opinion did not involve a question that arose within its scope of activities; the Court noted that, while the WHO Constitution authorized it to deal with the effects of the use of nuclear weapons on health, the question presented concerned only the legality of the use of nuclear weapons in light of their health and environmental effects.

Legality of Use of Force Case *(Yugoslavia v. United States of America, United Kingdom, France, Germany, Italy, the Netherlands, Belgium, Canada, Portugal, and Spain).* On 29 April 1999, the Federal Republic of Yugoslavia instituted separate proceedings before the ICJ against 10 States allegedly involved in the NATO aerial action in protection of

Kosovo. Yugoslavia based its claims on the obligations not to use force against another State and not to intervene in its internal affairs, the provisions of the Geneva Convention of 1949 and of the Additional Protocol No. 1 of 1977 on the Protection of Civilians and Civilian Objects in Time of War, the Convention on Free Navigation on the Danube, the International Covenants on Civil and Political Rights and on Economic, Social and Cultural Rights of 1966, and the Convention on the Prevention and Punishment of the Crime of Genocide of 1948. In addition, Yugoslavia asserted that these States' operations breach art. 53(1) of the Charter of the United Nations. Yugoslavia alleged that the NATO bombings resulted in both military and civilians casualties; that infrastructure, schools, cultural landmarks, hospitals and other properties were damaged; and that there were serious environmental and health consequences. Yugoslavia requested the ICJ to adjudge that these States had violated international law and were liable to make reparations; and to indicate provisional measures of protection, ordering the immediate cessation of military operations.

On 2 June 1999, in *Yugoslavia v USA*, the Court *held* (a) (12 to 3) that Yugoslavia's request for the indication of provisional measures submitted on 29 April 1999 be denied; (b) (12 to 3) that the case against the USA be removed from the Court's list on the basis of lack of jurisdiction: *1999 I.C.J. Rep. 916*. On 2 June 1999, in *Yugoslavia v. Spain*, the Court *held*: (a) (14 to 2) that Yugoslavia's request for the indication of provisional measures submitted on 29 April 1999 be denied; and (b) (13 to 3) that the case be removed from the Court's list: *1999 I.C.J. Rep. 761*.

In the other eight cases, (*Yugoslavia v. Belgium; Yugoslavia v. Canada; Yugoslavia v. France; Yugoslavia v. Germany; Yugoslavia v. Italy; Yugoslavia v. Netherlands; Yugoslavia v. Portugal; Yugoslavia v. United Kingdom*), the Court *found* that it lacked *prima facie* jurisdiction under art. 41 of the Statute to indicate provisional measures, and that it therefore no provisional measures could be indicated; the Court, however, decided to remain seized of those cases and emphasized that its findings, at that point, "in no way prejudge[d] the question of the jurisdiction of the Court to deal with the merits" of the cases and left "unaffected the right of the Governments of Yugoslavia and [of the respondent States] to submit arguments in respect of those questions": *1999 I.C.J. Rep. 99, 124, 259, 363, 422, 481, 542, 656, 826, 916*.

"Leonine" treaties "So-called 'unequal' or 'Leonine' treaties are those which are said to have been forced upon a weaker state by a stronger one. However, the concept has never been accepted in international law. No two states are ever equal, and to allow a state to avoid its treaty obligations on this ground could undermine the stability of treaty relations": Aust, *Modern Treaty Law and Practice* (2000), 257.

less developed countries *See* **developing countries**.

Leticia Incident (1932-34) Hackworth, *Digest of International Law* (1940), Vol. 1, 752-4. In accordance with a Treaty concluded in 1922 between Colombia and Peru, territory formerly claimed by Peru, and including the town of Leticia, was transferred to Colombia on 17 August 1930. On 1 September 1932, an armed band of Peruvians took possession of the town, claiming that the 1922 Treaty had been approved under a dictatorial regime. Peru at once informed Colombia that it had nothing to do with the planning or execution of these acts. Colombia regarded the question of sovereignty over Leticia as strictly and exclusively of an internal nature; Colombia accordingly rejected a Peruvian suggestion that the matter be submitted to the Permanent Commission of Inter-American Conciliation, and sent an expeditionary force to restore law and order. In January 1933, the Council of the League of Nations transmitted to Peru a Colombian communication expressing those views, and expressed confidence that Peru would refrain from acting contrary to the Covenant; Peru replied to the effect that the 1922 Treaty contained imperfections and that there should be a re-examination of the question in dispute. An attempt at mediation by Brazil in early 1933 was unsuccessful. Peru refused to desist from protecting her citizens who seized Leticia. On 17 February 1933 Colombia referred the matter to the Council of the League of Nations under art. 15 of the Covenant. On 18 March 1933, the Council adopted a report recommending the complete evacuation of the area by Peruvian forces and the withdrawal of all support from the Peruvians who had occupied that area. On 10 May 1933, the Advisory Committee of the Council proposed that Leticia be evacuated by Peru and that a Commission of the League in the name of Colombia and at her expense should take over the area and enforce law and supervise negotiations for settlement of the territorial question. Colombia and Peru accepted the proposals and on 23 June 1933 the Commission took over Leticia. On 24 May 1934, Colombia and Peru signed a Protocol of Peace, Friendship and Co-operation in which Peru deplored events subsequent to 1 September 1932, and the two States agreed to various measures to facilitate the restoration and subsequent maintenance of peaceful relations between them. The League Commission transferred Leticia to Colombia on 19 June 1934, and ratifications of the 1934 Protocol were exchanged on 27 September 1935.

levy en masse "[I]t may happen during the War that on the approach of the enemy a belligerent calls the whole population to arms, and so makes them all, more or less, irregulars of the armed forces. Those who take part in such an organized levy *en masse* also enjoy the privilege that is due to members of the armed forces, provided they carry arms openly and respect the laws of war, and receive some organisation. Again, a levy *en masse* may take place spontaneously without organization by the belligerent . . . [and] such inhabitants taking part in a levy *en masse* are entitled to the rights and status of a belligerent," provided that they carry arms openly and respect the laws and customs of war; this latter provision "attaches only to the population of a territory not under occupation, and who take up arms on the approach of the enemy": *In re von Manstein* (1949) *16 A.D. 509* at 515. Art. 13(6) of the Geneva Convention for the Amelioration of the Condition of the Wounded and Sick in Armed Forces in the Field 1949 *(75 U.N.T.S. 31)*, art. 13(6) of the Geneva Convention for the Amelioration of the Condition of Wounded, Sick and Shipwrecked Members of Armed Forces at Sea 1949 *(75 U.N.T.S. 85)* and art. 4 of the Geneva Convention relative to the Treatment of Prisoners of War 1949 *(75 U.N.T.S. 135)* afford protection to "inhabitants of non-occupied territory, who on the approach of the enemy, spontaneously take up arms to resist the invading force, without having had time to form themselves into regular armed units, provided they carry arms openly and respect the laws and customs of war."

lex ferenda *Lex ferenda* imports the law which is being sought to establish; the law as it "ought" to be. *Lex lata* imports the law which is presently in force: the law as it "is." The terms are used, derogatively, by some writers in international law, especially those who subscribe to the **inductive approach**, to warn against an unscientific and eclectic approach to the sources of international law, whereby the distinction between *lex lata* and *lex ferenda* becomes blurred: see Schwarzenberger, *The Inductive Approach to International Law* (1965). Cf. O'Connell, *International Law* (1965), Vol. 1, 20: "[Customary law's] lack of fixation and its plasticity, while they render it difficult to decide at what moment a practice *de lege ferenda* has become a custom *de lege lata*, permit the adaptation of behaviour pasterns to altered situations, thereby reflecting the strains and tendencies of international intercourse . . . [and] has the distinct advantage of retaining a dynamic element in the law."

lex lata *See lex ferenda.*

liberation movements Movements of liberation attempting to seize control of particular territory have no inherent status in international law. However, they may be, and have been, accorded aspects of status. Thus, it is said that there has evolved in practice recognition of liberation movements other than recognition of them as a government: "The status accorded such entities by third-State recognition is probably non-opposable; recognition would appear to be constitutive of such consequences, if any, as the recognizing State wishes to attach to it": Crawford, *The Creation of States in International Law* (1979), 269 n. 106. By General Assembly Res. 3280 (XXIX) the Assembly decided to invite national liberation movements recognized by the Organisation of African Unity to participate as observers and on a regular basis in Assembly debates and in all other UN activities relating to their countries. Particular invitations have been made to the South West Africa Peoples Organization and the Palestine Liberation Organization to participate as observers in all UN efforts over Namibia and Palestine respectively: General Assembly Res. 3430 (XXXI) and 3237 (XXIX). On the basis of the UN resolutions, African liberation movements have participated in UN bodies, in the Specialized Agencies and in international conferences convened by the UN; they also participated in the Diplomatic Conference on Humanitarian Law in Armed Conflicts 1974-77, attended by 11 liberation movements. See Ronzitti, *Le guerre de liberazione nazionale e il diritto internazionale* (1974). A number of international acts dealing with the use of force purport to exclude the actions of liberation movements from their scope. Thus, under Principle 1 of the **Friendly Relations Declaration** 1970 every State has the duty to refrain from any forcible action which might deprive peoples of their "right" to self-determination and freedom and independence. Principle 5 recognizes that liberation movements are entitled to use "forcible action in pursuit of the exercise of the . . . right of self-determination." Taken literally, States are thereby debarred from opposing liberation movements' actions, even forcible actions. *See also* **aggression**.

Libya/Chad Territorial Dispute Case *1994 I.C.J. Rep. 6*. By letter dated 31 August 1990, the Government of Libya submitted to the ICJ a notification of an agreement entitled "Framework Agreement on the Peaceful Settlement of the Territorial Dispute Between the Great Socialist People's Libyan Arab Jamahiriya and the Republic of Chad" of 31 August 1989. On 3 September 1990, Chad filed an application instituting proceedings against Libya by reference to the Framework Agreement and art. 8 of the Franco-Libyan Treaty of Friendship and Good Neighbourliness of 10 August 1955; and asking the Court "to determine the course of the frontier between the Republic of Chad and the Libyan Arab Jamahiriya, in accordance with the principles and rules of international law applicable in the matter as between the Parties." On 24 October 1990, the parties agreed with the President of the Court that the proceedings had in effect been instituted by two successive notifications of the special agreement. Despite the existence of an agreement between Libya and Chad on 12 August 1974, art. 2 of which stated that "frontiers between the two countries are a colonial conception in which the two peoples and nations had not hand, and this matter should not obstruct their co-operation and fraternal relations," the ICJ *held* (16 to 1) that the boundary between Libya and Chad was defined by the Treaty of Friendship and Good Neighbourliness of 10 August 1955, thereby confirming the application of the principle of *uti possidetis* to the delimitation of boundaries derived from the process of decolonisation. *See also* **Burkina Faso/Mali Frontier Dispute Case**.

Libya-Malta Continental Shelf Case, *(Libya v. Malta) 1985 I.C.J. Rep. 13*. By a Special Agreement of 23 May 1976, Libya and Malta provided for the submission to the ICJ of a dispute concerning the delimitation of the continental shelf between those two States. In 1983 Italy, considering that the claims of Libya and Malta extended to areas of continental shelf over which Italy could have sovereign rights, sought to intervene under art. 62 of the

Statute of the Court. On 21 March 1984, the Court *held* (11 votes to 5) that permission to intervene could not be granted, since to permit the intervention would in the circumstances involve the introduction of a fresh dispute between Italy and Libya/Malta without the consent of the latter: *1984 I.C.J. Rep. 3.* In its judgment of 3 June 1985, the Court *held* (14 to 3) (1) that the delimitation had to be effected in accordance with equitable principles and taking account of all relevant circumstances in order to reach an equitable result and that, in the present case, the principle of natural prolongation offered no assistance in this task; and (2) that the relevant circumstances were the general configuration of the coastlines of the two States and their relationship to each other, the disparity in length of the coastlines and the necessity of avoiding any excessive disproportion between the areas of continental shelf allocated to each State and the length of their respective coastlines. The Court then suggested a boundary line, having declared that there was nothing in the *compromis*, as Libya contended, to prevent it from doing so.

Lie, Trygve Halvdan   1896-1968. Norwegian parliamentarian and statesman. First Secretary-General of the UN, 1945-53. Author of *The International Secretariat of the Future* (1944) and *In the Cause of Peace* (1954).

Lieber Code   A code on the law and usages of war intended for military commanders during the Civil War prepared by **Francis Lieber** in 1863. The code was promulgated as (US) General Orders No. 100, entitled "Instructions for the Government of Armies of the United States in the Field." The Lieber Code became of intense interest in Europe, was adopted by many European States and furnished much of the basis of the Hague Conventions of 1899 and 1907 *(187* and *205 C.T.S.).* For the text of the Lieber Code, see Friedman, *The Law of War. A Documentary History* (1972), Vol. 1, 158-186.

Lieber, Francis   1800-72. German-American philosopher and teacher; Professor, Columbia 1857-72. Principal architect of the "Instructions for the Government of the Armies of the United States in the Field." This code, commonly referred to as the **Lieber Code**, became the basis of subsequent American and European codifications of the rules of the warfare on land.

lighthouses   "Since the most important lighthouses are built outside the territorial sea of the coastal states, the question has arisen whether a State can claim a territorial sea around its lighthouses constructed on low tide elevations on the open sea. . . . It is tempting to compare such lighthouses with islands, and argue in favour of a territorial sea around them; but such an identification is misleading. Lighthouses should be treated on the same lines as anchored lightships. Just as a state may not claim sovereignty over a territorial sea belt around an anchored lightship, so it may not make such a claim for a lighthouse outside the territorial sea": *I Oppenheim 611.* Art. 7(4) of the UN Convention on the Law of the Sea 1982 *(1833 U.N.T.S. 3)* provides that straight **baselines** of the territorial sea shall not be drawn to and from low-tide elevations "unless lighthouses or similar installations which are permanently above sea level have been built on them." *See also* **island**.

Lighthouses in Crete and Samos Case   *(France v. Greece) (1937) P.C.I.J., Ser. A/B, No. 71.* In the *Lighthouses Case between France and Greece* (1934) *P.C.I.J., Ser. A/B, No. 62,* the parties had, by the Special Agreement of 15 July 1931, referred the question whether the concession for the maintenance of lighthouses agreed between the Ottoman Government and the French firm of Collas & Michel in April 1913 was "operative as regards the Greek Government in so far as concerns lighthouses situated in territories assigned to it after the Balkan Wars or subsequently." On 17 March 1934, the Court *held* (10 to 2) affirmatively, the fact that negotiations for the concession had begun before the war making it clear that there had been no intention to exclude from its scope territories which by 1913 were occupied by adversaries of Turkey, and that the terms of art. 9 of Protocol XII of Lausanne of 24 July 1923 *(28 L.N.T.S. 204)* stipulated for the subrogation of successor States to Turkish concessionary contracts. The Court left open, however, the question which in fact were the territories detached from Turkey and assigned to Greece. By the further Special Agreement of 28 August 1937, there was referred the question of the applicability of the principles of the earlier judgment as regards lighthouses in Crete and Samos, which were already autonomous in 1913 and therefore, in the contention of Greece, not in contemplation in the Protocol referred to above. *Held* (10 to 3) that the contention failed, Turkish sovereignty over Crete and Samos having persisted up to the time of its formal renunciation in treaties following the end of the First World War.

Lillich, Richard B. 1933-96. Professor, Syracuse 1960-3, Virginia 1963-96. Principal works include: *International Claims: Their Adjudication by National Commissions* (1962); *The Protection of Foreign Investment: Six Procedural Studies* (1965); *International Claims: Their Settlement by Lump Sum Agreements* (with Weston, 1975); *International Human Rights: Problems of Law and Policy* (with Newman, 1979).

Lissitzyn, Oliver James 1912-94. Professor, Columbia 1946-94. Major works include *Creation of Rights of Sovereignty Through Symbolic Acts 1400-1800* (with Keller, 1967); *International Air Transport and National Policy* (1942); *The I.C.J. Its Role in the Maintenance of International Peace and Security* (1951); *International Law Today and Tomorrow* (1965).

Litvinov Agreement The **executive agreement** concluded by an exchange of notes on 16 November 1933 between Maxim M. Litvinov, Soviet Commissar for Foreign Affairs, and President Franklin D. Roosevelt, whereby US recognition was extended to the USSR in consideration of certain pledges relating to the tranquility, prosperity, order or security of the US and the settlement of claims. *See 11 Bevans 1248. See U.S. v. Belmont 301 U.S. 324* (1937) and *U.S. v. Pink 315 U.S. 203* (1942) as to the validity of the Agreement in US law.

Litvinov Doctrine In a note addressed to the French Ambassador in Moscow, dated 31 August 1928, the Soviet Commissar for Foreign Affairs said: "The Soviet government believes that there should also be put among the non-pacific means that are forbidden by the Covenant [of the League of Nations] such means as a refusal to resume normal pacific relations between nations and breaking such relations, for acts of that character, by setting aside the pacific means which might decide differences, aggravate relations and contribute in creating an atmosphere that is conducive to the unleashing of wars." *See* Buehler *et. al., Recognition of Soviet Russia* (1931), 160.

LMC *See* **Land Mines Convention.**

local custom A local rule or rules of customary law, as opposed to general, universal **custom,** is international customary law confined to, and valid among, a particular group of States, whether as a geographical unit or a political or other unit. On local (or regional or special) custom, the ICJ said in the ***Asylum Case** 1950 I.C.J. Rep. 266* at 276: "The Party which relies on a custom of this kind must prove that this custom is established in such a manner that it has become binding on the other Party . . . that the rule invoked by it is in accordance with a constant and uniform usage practiced by the States in question, and that this usage is the expression of a right appertaining to the [one State] . . . and a duty incumbent on the [other]." *See **Rights of U.S. Nationals in Morocco Case** 1952 I.C.J. Rep. 176;*

Right of Passage over Indian Territory Case 1960 I.C.J. Rep. 6. Because local custom is in the nature of a departure from generally accepted law, its existence is subject to "strict proof . . . [involving] clear assent to the practice as law" by the State against which the custom is invoked: *I Oppenheim 30. See* D'Amato, *The Concept of Custom in International Law* (1971), Chap. 8; Parry, *The Sources and Evidences of International Law* (1965), 58-61.

local remedies, exhaustion of, rule "The rule that local remedies must be exhausted before international proceedings may be instituted is a well-established rule of customary international law; the rule has been generally observed in cases in which a State has adopted the cause of its national whose rights are claimed to have been disregarded in another State in violation of international law. Before resort may be had to an international court in such a situation, it has been considered necessary that the State where the violation occurred should have an opportunity to redress it by its own means, within the framework of its own domestic legal system": *Interhandel Case (Preliminary Objections) 1959 I.C.J. Rep. 6* at 27. It is "an important principle of customary international law": *ELSI Case 1989 I.C.J. Rep. 15* at 42. The principle is reiterated in art. 44(b) of the International Law Commission's Draft Articles on State Responsibility of 2001 *(UN Doc. A/56/10 Chap. IV.E.1)*, which provides that the responsibility of a State may not be invoked if "the claim is one to which the rule of exhaustion of local remedies applies and any available and effective remedy has not been exhausted."

Local remedies include all effective remedies available to natural or legal persons under the domestic law of the State concerned and capable of redressing the situation complained of, whether judicial or administrative, ordinary or extraordinary, of the first, second or third instance, including procedural means and other formal remedies. In general, the injured person must advance all legal grounds and arguments calculated to achieve a favorable decision. Ineffective remedies, i.e. those which hold out no real prospects of obtaining the redress sought, need not be used. "There can be no need to resort to the municipal courts if those courts have no jurisdiction to afford relief; nor is it necessary again to resort to those courts if the result must be a repetition of a decision already given": *Panevezys-Saldutiskis Railway Case* (1939) *P.C.I.J., Ser. A/B, No. 76* at 18; art. 44(b) of the ILC's Draft Articles on State Responsibility, which refers to the exhaustion of any "available and effective remedy"; *Mavrommatis Jerusalem Concessions Case* (Jurisdiction) (1924) *P.C.I.J., Ser. A. No. 2* at 12; *Electricity Company of Sofia Case (Preliminary Objection)* (1939) *P.C.I.J., Ser. A/B, No. 77* at 79; *Brown Claim (1923) 6 R.I.A.A. 120*; *Spanish Zones of Morocco Claims (1925) 2 R.I.A.A. 731*; *Mexican Union Railway Case (1930) 5 R.I.A.A. 122*; *Finnish Ships Case (1934) 3 R.I.A.A. 1502*; *Ambatielos Case (1956) 12 R.I.A.A. 118-119, 122*; *German External Debts Case (1958) 25 I.L.R. 42*.

The requirement to exhaust local remedies has been incorporated into a number of human rights agreements that allow individual petition. "The [Human Rights] Committee shall not consider any communication from an individual unless it has ascertained: . . . (b) The individual has exhausted all available domestic remedies": art. 5(2) of the Optional Protocol to the International Covenant on Civil and Political Rights 1966 *(999 U.N.T.S. 171)*. *See* art. 14(2) of the International Convention on the Elimination of All Forms of Racial Discrimination 1965 *(660 U.N.T.S. 195)*; art. 21(1)(c) of the Convention Against Torture 1984 *(1465 U.N.T.S. 85)*; art. 35(1) of the European Convention on Human Rights 1950 *(E.T.S. No. 5 as amended by E.T.S. 155)*; art. 46(1)(a) of the American Convention on Human Rights 1970 *(1144 U.N.T.S. 123)*.

See generally, Borchard, *The Diplomatic Protection of Citizens Abroad* (1916); Law, *The Local Remedies Rule in International Law* (1961); Haesler, *The Exhaustion of Local Rem-*

edies Rule in the Case Law of International Courts and Tribunals (1968); Amerasinghe, *Local Remedies in International Law* (1995).

Locarno Pact 1925 Properly styled the Locarno Treaties of Mutual Guarantee *(54 L.N.T.S 305)*, this is a series of bipartite agreements concluded between Germany on the one hand and Belgium, Czechoslovakia, France and Poland on the other, requiring the submission of "any question with regard to which the parties are in conflict as to their respective rights" to arbitration or to judicial settlement.

Lockerbie Cases *(Libya v. UK) 1992 I.C.J. Rep. 14; 1998 I.C.J. Rep. 9; (Libya v. USA) 1992 I.C.J. 115; 1998 I.C.J. Rep. 114*. Immediately prior to the Security Council adopting Res. 748 (1992) requiring the surrender of the two Libyan suspects in the Pan Am 103 bombing of December 1988 for trial in either Scotland or the US, Libya raised a case in the ICJ against both the UK and USA, basing jurisdiction on art 14(1) of the Montreal Convention 1971. It sought a declaration that, while it had fulfilled all its obligations under the Montreal Convention (*see* **aircraft sabotage**), the UK and US had not; and asked that the Court order these two States to cease and desist from such breaches and from the use of any and all force or threats against Libya and from all violations of the sovereignty, territorial integrity, and the political independence of Libya. Libya also requested provisional measures of protection under art 41 of the Court's Statute. The UK and US arguments ran along similar lines—that the Court had no jurisdiction, either to indicate provisional measures or to adjudicate on the merits, because Security Council Res. 748 (1992) and 883 (1993) were being binding under art. 25 of the UN Charter and prevailed over other treaty arrangements, including the Montreal Convention, under art. 103 of the Charter.

On 14 April 1992, without determining definitively whether the Security Council resolutions prevailed over the Montreal Convention, the Court (11 to 5, in the *Libya v. USA Case* 13 to 2) *declined* to indicate provisional measures. On 27 February 1998, the Court *held* (13 to 3) that it had jurisdiction to hear the dispute. Without ruling on the effect of the Security Council resolutions, the majority noted that they were adopted after the Libyan application; and, in accordance with its established jurisprudence, the Court had jurisdiction if it had jurisdiction on the date of the application. The Court also *held* (12 to 4, in the *Libya v USA Case* 12 to 3) that Libya's application was admissible. The Court rejected the contention that the issues in dispute were now regulated by binding Security Council resolutions. The relevant date for judging the admissibility of Libya's application was the date it was made, 3 March 1992, and the only Security Council resolution preceding that date was non-binding resolution 731 (1992), both the binding resolutions being adopted after that date. It was for the merits phase to determine the precise effect of the Security Council resolutions on Libya's claims. By two letters of 9 September 2003, the Governments of Libya and the United Kingdom on the one hand, and of Libya and the United States on the other, notified the Court that they had agreed to "discontinue with prejudice the proceedings." By order of 10 September 2003, the President of the Court directed the removal of the case from the Court's list. *See also* **Lockerbie Trial**.

Lockerbie Trial The bombing of Pan Am Flight 103 on 21 December 1988 over the Scottish town of Lockerbie, resulting in the loss of 270 lives, led to indictments being issued in November 1991, in both Scotland and the US, against two Libyans, Abdelbaset Ali Mohmed Al Meghrahi and Al Amin Khalifa Fhimah. The Libyan government having refused to surrender or allow the surrender of its two nationals, the UK and US governments induced the Security Council to adopt resolutions, first to request their surrender for trial (SC Res. 731 (1992)), then, under Chapter VII of the Charter, to require their surrender and to impose sanctions on Libya for its failure to comply (SC Res. 748 (1992) and 883

(1993)). Libya and the UK and USA reached an agreement in 1998 and the Security Council endorsed and mandated the arrangements for the trial (SC Res. 1192 (1998)). The unique arrangements called for trial in a neutral venue (the Netherlands), before a panel of three Scottish judges (and no jury as would be normal in such a trial in Scotland), applying Scots law, procedure and evidence in return for the surrender of the two Libyans. Megrahi and Fhimah surrendered for trial in April 1999, which began the following year and concluded in 2001. Initially charged with murder, conspiracy to murder and breaches of the (UK) Aviation Security Act 1982, the last two being later abandoned, Al Megrahi was found guilty of murder (and sentenced to life imprisonment with a minimum of 20 years), while Fhimah was found not guilty: *H. M. Advocate v. Megrahi and Fhimah 40 I.L.M. 582 (2000)*. Megrahi's appeal was unsuccessful: *Megrahi v H. M. Advocate 2002 J.C. 99; 2002 S.L.T. 1433*. The importance of these proceedings lies in that, while the Montreal Convention 1971 on **aircraft sabotage** was clearly applicable, it was not utilized, the case being founded on Security Council Res. 1192 (1998); for the first time, the Security Council imposed sanctions on a State to compel it to surrender its nationals for trial abroad; and the flexibility of the aggrieved States ensured that a trial was held, albeit in unique circumstances, against persons accused of international terrorism. The sanctions on Libya, which had been suspended by SC Res. 1192 (1998) on the surrender of the two indictees for trial, were formally revoked by SC Res. 1506 (2003) of 12 September 2003 on the Libyan government's acceptance of responsibility for the Pan Am 103 bombing, its renunciation of terrorism and the payment of appropriate compensation to the victims' families. *See also* the *Lockerbie Cases*. *See* <www.ltb.org.uk>.

London Agreement for the Prosecution and Punishment of the Major War Criminals of the European Axis *See* **Nuremberg Charter**.

London Declaration of 1909 Ten States participated in the conferences in London in 1908-9, which adopted the Declaration concerning the Laws of Naval War of 26 February 1909 *(208 C.T.S. 338)*. While the Declaration was not ratified, its provisions were regarded at the time as corresponding to established practice and decisions of municipal prize courts. The provisions of the Declarations were recognized by several belligerents during the First World War, but were abandoned by the UK, and others, in July 1916. The Declaration represented a code comprising rules on blockade (art. 1-21), contraband (arts. 22-44), unneutral service (arts. 45-47), destruction of neutral prizes (arts. 48-54), transfer to neutral flag (arts. 55-56), enemy character (arts 57-60), convoy (arts. 61-62), resistance to search (art. 63) and compensation (art. 64). *See II Oppenheim 633-644*; Bentwich, *The Declaration of London* (1911).

London Dumping Convention *See* **dumping at sea**.

London Naval Construction Treaties (1930, 1936) The Treaties referred to in this way are the International Treaty for the Reduction and Limitation of Naval Armament of 22 April 1930 between Australia, Canada, India, Japan, New Zealand, Union of South Africa, United Kingdom, United States, Irish Free State, France and Italy *(112 L.N.T.S. 65)*, and the Treaty for the Limitation of Naval Armament of 25 March 1936 between the same parties other than the Union of South Africa and the Irish Free State *(184 L.N.T.S. 115)*, both seeking, *inter alia*, to limit the size and weaponry of warships of the contracting parties.

London *Proces-Verbal* on the Rules of Submarine Warfare To augment the provisions of the **London Naval Construction Treaty** 1930, this agreement was adopted on 6 November 1936 *(173 L.N.T.S. 353)* to protect merchant ships to be protected from unrestricted submarine attack. Germany, one of the 39 parties, justified its unrestricted submarine attacks during World War II on the basis that they were legitimate reprisals and that the British merchant fleet was integrated into its military establishment.

Loreburn, Robert Threshie Reid, 1st. Earl of 1846-1923. British Solicitor-General 1894, Attorney-General 1894-5, Lord Chancellor 1906-12. Counsel for Great Britain in the *British Guiana Boundary* (1897-9) and *Alaska Boundary* (1903). Principal publication: *Capture at Sea* (1913).

Lorimer, James 1818-90. Professor, Edinburgh, 1865-90. Co-founder of the *Institut de Droit International*. Principal works: *Institutes of Law* (1872; 2nd. ed. 1888); *Institutes of the Law of Nations* (1883-4); *Studies, National and International* (1890).

LOS Somewhat confusingly, this acronym, for law of the sea, is sometimes used to connote the international **law of the sea** in general, the UN Conferences on the Law of the Sea 1958, 1960 and 1973-82 (also referred to as UNCLOS, *see* **Law of the Sea, codification**) and the UN Convention on the Law of the Sea 1982 *(1833 U.N.T.S. 3)* (also sometimes referred to as UNCLOS).

Lotus Case *(France v. Turkey) (1927) P.C.I.J, Ser. A, No. 10.* By the special agreement of 12 October 1926, the parties requested a decision as to (1) whether Turkey had, contrary to art. 15 of the Convention of Lausanne of 24 July 1923 *(28 L.N.T.S. 152)* "respecting conditions of residence and jurisdiction, acted in conflict with the principles of international law—and if so what principles—by instituting, following the collision . . . on the high seas between the French steamer *Lotus* and the Turkish steamer *Boz-Kourt* and upon the arrival of the French steamer at Constantinople—as well as against the captain of the Turkish steamship—joint criminal proceedings against M. Demons, officer of the watch on board the *Lotus* [and (2), if yes] what pecuniary reparation is due to M. Demons, provided, according to the principles of international law, reparation should be made in similar cases?"

Held (6 to 6, by the President's casting vote), as to (1), in the negative ((2) in consequence not arising): "there is no rule of international law in regard to collision cases to the effect that criminal proceedings are exclusively within the jurisdiction of the State whose flag is flown. . . . On the contrary, there is concurrent jurisdiction where, as here, the offence consists in an act originating on board a vessel under one flag and whose effects make themselves felt on another vessel under another flag." The decision has been much criticized and a contrary rule was adopted in the Brussels Convention relating to Penal Jurisdiction in Matters of Collision or other Accidents of Navigation of 10 May 1952 *(439 U.N.T.S. 234)*; and in art. 11 of The Geneva Convention on the High Seas 1958 *(450 U.N.T.S 82)*; and art. 97(1) of the UN Convention on the Law of the Sea 1982 *(1833 U.N.T.S. 3)*.

low-tide elevations In terms of art. 13(1) of the UN Convention on the Law of the Sea 1982 *(1833 U.N.T.S. 3)*, a low-tide elevation is "a naturally formed area of land which is surrounded by and above water at low-tide but submerged at high tide." Cf. **island**, a high-tide elevation. "Where a low-tide elevation is situated wholly or partly at a distance not exceeding the breadth of the territorial sea from the mainland or an island, the low-water line on that elevation may be used as a baseline for measuring the breadth of the territorial sea" (art. 13(1)). "Where a low-tide elevation is wholly situated at a distance exceeding the breadth of the territorial sea from the mainland or an island, it has no territorial sea of its own." (art. 13(2)). *See* Brown, *The International Law of the Sea* (1996), Vol. 1, 34-6.

Lowenfeld, Andreas 1930- . Senior State Department official, scholar and law professor. (1961-63). Principal works include *International Legal Process* (with Chayes and Ehrlich) (1968-69); *Conflict of Laws, Federal, State and International Perspectives* (1986, 2nd ed., 1998); *International Litigation and Arbitration* (1993); *International Litigation: The Quest for Reasonableness* (1996).

low-water line Art. 5 of the UN Convention on the Law of the Sea 1982 *(1833 U.N.T.S. 3)* provides that "the normal baseline for measuring the breadth of the territorial sea is the low-water line along the coast as marked on large-scale charts officially recognized by the coastal State." *See* **baseline**. *See* Brown, *The International Law of the Sea* (1996), Vol. 1, 35-6.

lucrum cessans "Although pronouncements can be found both in textbooks and [arbitral] awards to the effect that international law, while requiring compensation to be paid for actual losses suffered (*damnum emergens*), does not sanction the award of 'consequential damages' such as loss of possible business profits (*lucrum cessans*), a formidable array of awards is in existence which give damages of this nature": *I Oppenheim 530 n. 10*. For an analysis of cases on the measure of damages, see Lauterpacht, *Private Law Sources and Analogies of International Law* (1927), Parts 65, 66; Whitemen, *Damages in International Law* (3 vols. 1937-43).

lump-sum agreement "Much of [the] development [of the law relating to the responsibility of States for wrongs to aliens] from the beginning of the nineteenth century to the Second World War has been through the decisions of international arbitral tribunals, or mixed claims commissions, established to deal with disputes in this area. But in the years since 1945 there has been relatively little use of such international adjudicative machinery in this type of controversy. . . . Instead, we find that nations have tried to adjust those disputes . . . by making lump sum Settlement Agreements, usually followed by the allocation to individual claimants by a domestic claims authority of a share of the funds made available. The use of such lump sum agreements and domestic commissions goes back at least as far as 1802 as a parallel method for dealing with international claims, but it has become paramount only in the last three decades": Foreword by Bishop to Lillich and Weston, *International Claims: Their Settlement by Lump Sum Agreements* (1975). *See also* the Sixth Report of Garcia Amador to the I.L.C. *[1961] 2 I.L.C. Yearbook, 42-3 sub nom.* "en bloc reparation"; Lillich, *International Claims: Their Adjudication by National Commissions* (1962); Weston, Lillich and Bederman, *International Claims: Their Settlement by Lump Sum Agreements, 1975-95* (1999).

Lushington Dr. Stephen 1782-1873. Civilian. Member of Parliament 1806 to 1841. Judge of the High Court of Admiralty 1838-1867 in which capacity he was influential in the development of maritime law.

Lusitania Cases (United States v. Germany) (1923) 7 R.I.A.A. 32. The award of the United States-German Mixed Claims Commission upon these claims arising out of the sinking of the British vessel *Lusitania* by a German submarine in 1915 dealt (issues of nationality apart) only with the measure of damages, Germany having accepted liability for losses sustained by United States nationals by a note dated 4 February 1916. Parker, Umpire, laid it down that "[i]n death cases the . . . basis of damages is not the physical or mental suffering of deceased or his loss or the loss to his estate, but the losses resulting to claimants from his death. . . . Bearing [this] in mind . . . our formula expressed in general terms . . . is: Estimate the amounts (a) which the decedent, had he not been killed, would probably have contributed to the claimant, add thereto (b) the pecuniary value to such claimant of the deceased's personal service in claimant's care, education, or supervision, and also add (c) reasonable compensation for such mental suffering or shock, if any, caused by the violent severing of family ties, as claimant may actually have sustained. . . . No exemplary, punitive or vindictive damages can be assessed. . . . But it is not necessary for this Commission to go to the length of holding that exemplary damages cannot be awarded in any case by any international arbitral tribunal. [T]his Commission is . . . without the power to make such awards under the terms of its Charter—the Treaty of Berlin [of 25 August 1921, *7 R.I.A.A. 9*]." *See* **damages, punitive**.

M

mailcert system "A further innovation was inaugurated in June 1941, when the Ministry of Economic Warfare announced the introduction from July 1 of a system of 'mailcerts' intended to be complementary to the 'navicert' method. Its object was to enable senders of parcels, small packets or letters containing merchandise to certain neutral countries, to ascertain in advance of posting whether facilities could be given for their passage through the British contraband control": Colombos, *International Law of the Sea* (6th ed.), 692.

majority vote "Most international organizations take at least some of their decisions by a majority vote and base their decision-making process on equality of the voting power of all Members. . . . The terminology used for different kinds of majorities is not entirely consistent. Four kinds of majorities will be distinguished: (a) the smallest possible majority is a *simple majority* which is more than half of the voters who actually vote (i.e. disregarding abstention). (b) When *qualified majority* is required, a proposal can only be adopted by a given percentage of the votes, which is higher than for a simple majority. . . . The most common qualified majority is two-thirds but other qualified majorities (*e.g.*, three-quarters or three-fifths) are also used. (c) A *relative majority* is larger by a number of votes than the number which is obtained for any other solution. In a case where the voters have a choice between two alternatives, relative majority is the same as a simple majority. However, if there is a choice between more than two alternatives it may be considerably less than the number of votes required for a simple majority. . . . (d) An *absolute majority* is a number of votes greater than the number which possibly can be obtained at the same time for any other solution. . . . However, definitions of absolute majority vary greatly. . . . Majorities may be calculated on the basis of the total membership, from the members present, or from the members expressly taking part in the voting": Schermers and Blokker, *International Institutional Law* (3rd revised ed.) 518, 529-532. *See also* **qualified majority**; **unanimity**; and **voting**.

Makarov, Alexander N 1888-1973. Professor, Petrograd 1919-23; Kaiser Wilhelm Institute Berlin 1928-45 and subsequently Max Planck Institute Heidelberg; Professor, Tübingen and Heidelberg. Principal works: *Algemeine Lehren des Staatsangehörigkeitsrechts* (1947); *Internationales Privatrecht und Rechtsvergleichung* (1949).

Mallén Claim (Mexico v. US) (1927) 4 R.I.A.A. 173. Mallén, a Mexican national and Mexican Consul in El Paso Texas, was on two occasions in 1907 assaulted by Franco, a Deputy Constable in Texas. On the first occasion, Franco struck Mallén while in the street; he was prosecuted and fined, although Mallén abstained from submitting any complaint. On the second occasion Franco violently struck Mallén in the course of arresting him and taking him to the county jail for (allegedly) illegally carrying a gun; Franco was prosecuted and fined 100 dollars, but the fine was not paid, and although his appointment as Deputy Constable was cancelled he was re-appointed shortly afterwards as a Deputy Sheriff. *Held* by the Mexico-US General Claims Commission established by the General Claims Convention of 28 September, 1923, that: (1) as the first assault was a private act (although committed by a person who happened to be an official) the US was not directly responsible for the assault, although in not disciplining Franco and maintaining him in office the authorities bore full responsibility for the consequences; (2) governments should exercise greater vigilance in respect of the security and safety of foreign consuls than in respect of ordinary residents; (3) the US was liable for the second assault since taken as a whole the acts in question could only be considered as those of an official, for denial of justice because of the non-execution of the penalty imposed, and for the lack of protection of a foreign consul arising from the re-appointment of Franco to an official position; (4) while punitive damages should not be awarded on account of the claimant's consular status, the damages, in addition to covering material losses and damages directly suffered by the claimant, should also include an amount for the indignity suffered, for lack of protection, and for denial of justice.

Malta, Sovereign Order of   Properly styled the Sovereign Military Order of St. John of Jerusalem (of Malta), the Order is a charitable organization dating back a thousand years, having its seat in Rome and maintaining close links with the **Holy See**. "Certain states at least regard the Order as an international person and have exchanged diplomatic representatives with it": *I Oppenheim 329 n. 7*. "After the loss of its territories [in Rhodes, Malta and elsewhere], the Order of St. John continued to enjoy its status in international law independently from its territorial rights; the activities of the Order were centered on assistance to the sick of all nations; the organization of the Order was supra-national in character; it was federal in structure, since the Priories were distributed among different countries, as are the various national associations of the Order today": Breycha-Vauthier, The Order of St. John in International Law, *48 A.J.I.L. 544* at 559-60 *(1954)*. *See also* De Fischer, L'Ordre Souverain de Malte, *(1979) 163 Hague Recueil 1*; *Sovereign Order of Malta v. Brunelli (1931-2) 3 A.D. 46*; **Nanni v. Pace and Sovereign Order of Malta** *(1935-7) 8 A.D. 2.*

mandated territories, nationality of inhabitants   No special provision was made respecting the nationality of the inhabitants of what were to become the mandated territories on the divestment of German and Turkish sovereignty. The nationality of the white inhabitants of South-West Africa was the subject of special agreement between Germany and South Africa and of special legislation by the latter. *See* Parry, *Nationality and Citizenship Laws of the Commonwealth* (1957), Vol. 1, 666. A distinct citizenship was created for each of the "A" mandates. As to Palestinian citizenship, see *R. v. Ketter [1940] 1. K.B. 787*. By Resolution dated 23 April 1923 the Council of the League of Nations laid it down that the native inhabitants of a mandated territory had a status distinct from that of the nationality of the mandatory power: *1923 L.N.O.J. 604*. *See also R. v. Jacobus Christian (1924) A.D. 101* and *Westphal & Westphal v. Conducting Officer (1948) (2) S.A. 18 (C)*, which are South African decisions to the effect that inhabitants of South-West Africa were not as such British subjects. *See* **mandates system**; **mandates system, sovereignty and.**

Mandates System   The system of administration and supervision for "those colonies and territories which as a consequence of [World W]ar [1] ceased to be under the sovereignty of [Turkey or Germany] inhabited by peoples not yet able to stand by themselves" conformably to "the principle that the well being and development of such peoples form a sacred trust of civilisation," given effect to by the entrusting of their "tutelage to advanced nations . . . as Mandatories on behalf of the League": art. 22 of the Covenant of the League of Nations. That Article envisaged three classes of "mandate" (which term, adopted from Roman-Dutch law by General **Smuts,** one of the originators of the system, properly denotes the legal transaction or relationship between a Mandatory Power and the League, embodied in the relevant "instrument of mandate" but which is loosely used to connote, in addition or alternatively, either such instrument or the territory (mandated territory) to which it relates), referred to commonly as "A," "B" and "C" mandates. These applied respectively to "[c]ertain communities formerly belonging to the Turkish Empire [which] have reached a stage of development where their existence as independent nations can be provisionally recognized subject to the rendering of administrative advice and assistance by a Mandatory. . . .; Other peoples, especially those of Central Africa, [which] are at such a stage that the Mandatory must be responsible for the administration of the territory under conditions which will guarantee freedom of conscience and religion" . . . this is made subject only to the maintenance of public order, the prohibition of abuses such as the slave trade, demilitarization and the securing of equal opportunities for all Members of the League; "[and] territories, such as South West Africa and certain of the South Pacific islands, which . . . can best be administered under the laws of the Mandatory as integral portions of its territory, subject to . . . safeguards in the interests of the indigenous population. . . ."

The system provided for the submission of annual reports by the Mandatories to a League organ, the **Permanent Mandates Commission**. The mandates were assigned by the Supreme Council of the Peace Conference of Versailles as follows: "A" mandates: to Great Britain, Iraq, Palestine and Transjordan; to France, Syria and Lebanon. Projected "A" mandates in respect of Constantinople, the Straits and Armenia were not proceeded with. "B" mandates: to Great Britain, Tanganyika, "British" Togoland, "British" Cameroons; to France, "French" Togoland, "French" Cameroons; to Belgium, Ruanda-Urundi. "C" Mandates: to Australia, New Guinea; to New Zealand, Western Samoa; to the British Empire (Great Britain, Australia and New Zealand), Nauru; to Japan, the former German Pacific Islands; to South Africa, South-West Africa. The instruments of mandate were drawn up in somewhat vague treaty form, omitting any precise indication of parties thereto and were approved by the League Council in 1920-22. The mandate for Iraq took the unusual form of a Treaty of Alliance between Great Britain and Iraq, dated 1 October 1922 *(35 L.N.T.S. 14)*. It was a feature of the instruments of mandate (other than that for Iraq) that they provided for the compulsory jurisdiction of the PCIJ in disputes between the Mandatory and any other member of the League. Pursuant to these stipulations the *Mavrommatis Palestine Concessions Case (1924) P.C.I.J., Ser. A, Nos. 2, 5 and 11* and *Oscar Chinn Case, (1934) P.C.I.J., Ser. A/B, No. 63* were taken to the Court. *See also* the *Northern Cameroons Case 1963 I.C.J. Rep. 15*, the *South-West Africa Case 1950 I.C.J. Rep. 128* and the *South-West Africa Cases 1962 I.C.J. Rep. 319, 335,* and *1966 I.C.J. Rep. 6*. The mandate for Iraq terminated with the admission of that State to the League in 1932. A portion of the mandated territory of Syria and the Lebanon, the Sanjak of Alexandretta, was returned to Turkey in 1939.

The mandate for Palestine was unilaterally abandoned by Great Britain on 14 May 1948, the *de facto* independence of Transjordan having been earlier recognized by Great Britain (Agreement of 20 February 1928 *(1930 T.S. 79))*. The mandate for Syria and the Lebanon may be said to have lapsed on the admission of those States as original members of the United Nations. The "B" and also the "C" mandates other than that for South-West Africa lapsed when the territories concerned were brought under the **Trusteeship System.** The mandate for South-West Africa was declared to be revoked for fundamental breach: by Res. 264 and 269 (1969); the Security Council thereupon called on South Africa to withdraw from the territory, now re-designated Namibia, and by Res. 276 (1970) declared the continued presence there of South Africa to be "illegal." In its Advisory Opinion on *Legal Consequences for States of the Continued Presence of South Africa in Namibia* (the

Namibia Advisory Opinion) *1971 I.C.J. Rep. 16*, the ICJ endorsed the termination of the mandate by the General Assembly as being "not a finding on facts, but the formulation of a legal situation." The Security Council approved the opinion in Res. 301(1971) which reaffirmed the national unity and territorial integrity of Namibia. South Africa finally agreed to Namibian independence in 1978 but problems continued and Namibia did not actually gain its independence until 23 April 1990 *(I Oppenheim 295-307)*. As to the mandates system generally, see Bentwich, *The Mandate System* (1930); Wright, *Mandates under the League of Nations* (1930); Hall *Mandates, Dependencies and Trusteeship* (1948). As to specific legal problems arising out of the mandates régime see **mandated territories, nationality of inhabitants**; **Mandates System, sovereignty and**.

Mandates System, sovereignty and The whereabouts of sovereignty in relation to the mandated system was formerly much discussed, the alternatives canvasses being: (1) In the mandatory powers. *See R. v. Jacobus Christian (1924) A.D. 101*; Lindley, *The Acquisition and Government of Backward Territory* (1931), 263, 267. (2) In the mandatory power, acting with the consent of the League of Nations Council. *See* Wright, *Mandates under the League of Nations* (1930). (3) In the Principal Allied Powers. (4) In the League. *See* Bentwich, *The Mandate System* (1930). (5) In the inhabitants. *See* Stovanovsky, *La Théorie générale des mandats internationaux* (1930).

Manila Pact *See* **SEATO**.

Mann, Frederick (Francis) Alexander 1897-91. Born Germany, taught Berlin 1929-33. Practised law in England from 1933. Principle works include *The Legal Aspect of Money: With Special Reference to the Comparative Private and Public International Law* (1938; 5th ed. 1993); *Studies in International Law* (1973).

Manouba Case *(France v. Italy) (1913) 11 R.I.A.A. 463.* In 1912, during the war between Turkey and Italy over Tripoli and Cyrenaica, France agreed to provide facilities for a Turkish Red Crescent Mission to reach the war zone via Tunis. France gave assurances in Paris to the Italian Ambassador about the status of the members of the Mission but before the Ambassador's message conveying the assurances reached his Government the *Manouba*, a French vessel on which the Turks were being transported, was captured by an Italian warship and taken to Cagliari. Italy, claiming that the Turks were carrying arms and money for the use of the Ottoman Forces in Tripoli, demanded their surrender and, on the refusal of the *Manouba's* Captain to comply, seized the vessel. The French Embassy was informed, and in view of assurances from the Italians that the Turks were belligerents, agreed to their removal from the vessel which then proceeded on her voyage. France disputed the legality of the Italian actions, and the matter was referred under a compromis of 6 March 1912 to an Arbitral Tribunal selected from the members of the PCA, which *held* that (1) as the Italian naval authorities had sufficient reason to believe that some of the passengers were enemy soldiers, they had the right to demand that the Captain surrender them and to compel him to do so if he refused; (2) however, no demand having been made to the Captain to surrender the passengers, the capture of the vessel and its diversion to Cagliari were not legal; and (3) once the vessel was at Cagliari, the Italian naval authorities had the right to compel the surrender of the Turkish passengers and to detain the vessel until they were surrendered.

marauders "Marauders are individuals moving, either singly or collectively in bands, over battlefields, or following advancing or retreating forces, in quest of booty. They have nothing to do with warfare in the strict sense of the term; but they are an unavoidable accessory to warfare, and frequently consist of soldiers who have left their corps. Their acts are considered to be acts of illegitimate warfare, and they are punished in the interest of the safety of either belligerent": *II Oppenheim (6th ed.) 458.*

margin of appreciation A concept developed in the jurisprudence of the **European Court of Human Rights** dealing with the problem of balancing the discretion of Contracting Parties with the requirement that the Court and other institutions exercise a degree of control through their decisions. "To assist it in resolving this problem, which is present in all human rights adjudication, the Court has developed a concept known as the 'margin of appreciation.' The underlying idea is a simple one: that in respect of many matters the [**European Convention of Human Rights** (the Convention)] leaves the Contracting Parties an area of discretion. However easy this is to state, its application in practice in concrete situations is fraught with difficulty": Merrills, *The Development of International Law by the European Court of Human Rights* (2nd ed.), 151. The margin of appreciation concept, which is nowhere mentioned in the Convention itself, has been applied in areas relating to emergency powers, restrictions "in the public interest," restrictions "necessary in a democratic society," the scope of the rights guaranteed in the Convention itself, and the principle of non-discrimination (*see* Merrills, *supra*, 151-76 and the cases referred to therein).

The impact of the concept on international law more generally, has been limited even in the field of human rights. Thus, for example, "any reference to the concept [in the jurisprudence of the **Human Rights Committee**] where one would expect to find it most—namely in the derogation jurisprudence; similarly in the area of public morality, the Committee [has] refrained expressly from having recourse to any margin of appreciation doctrine *[Toonen v Australia, 1994 Report of the Human Rights Committee, Vol II, 226].*" Ghandhi, *The Human Rights Committee and the Right of Individual Communication* (1998), 314. However, in relation to human rights more generally, it has been suggested that "the margin of appreciation is a way of recognising that the international protection of human rights and sovereign freedom of action are not contradictory but complementary. Where the one ends, the other begins. In helping the international judge to decide how and where the boundary is to be located, the concept of margin of appreciation has a vital part to play": Merrills, *supra*, 174-5.

marginal belt, seas A term used, especially in older treatises, to connote a zone of water beyond the territorial sea over which States have claimed jurisdiction to protect their fiscal interests. The **hovering laws** are an example of this type of claim of jurisdiction. The concept of the **contiguous zone**, established by art. 24 of the Geneva Convention on the Territorial Sea etc. 1958 *(516 U.N.T.S. 205)* and continued in art. 33 of the UN Convention on the Law of the Sea 1982 *(1833 U.N.T.S. 3),* has subsumed what used to be marginal seas jurisdiction. *See generally,* Masterton, *Jurisdiction in Marginal Seas* (1929).

marine pollution Within the UN system, marine pollution is defined as "[t]he introduction by man, directly or indirectly, of substances or energy into the marine environment, including estuaries, which results or is likely to result in such deleterious effects as harm to living resources and marine life, hazards to human health, hindrance to marine activities, including fishing and other legitimate uses of the sea, impairment of quality for use of sea water and reduction of amenities": UN Convention on the Law of the Sea 1982 *(1833 U.N.T.S. 3),* art. 1(1)(4). The UN Convention places a general obligation on States to protect and preserve the marine environment (art. 129); and in Part XI (arts. 192-237) details the obligations on States and establishes an enforcement mechanism. Among the principle obligations are those requiring national and international measures to control pollution from land-based sources (art. 207); pollution from sea-bed activities (art. 208); pollution from activities in the Sea-Bed Area (art. 209), pollution by dumping (art. 210); pollution from vessels (art. 211) and pollution from or through the atmosphere (art. 212).

The main thrust of activity, through the **International Maritime Organization** and its predecessor, IMCO, has been against oil pollution from ships. Originally the principal convention is the International Convention for the Prevention of Pollution of the Sea by Oil, concluded at London on 12 May 1954 (OILPOL) *(327 U.N.T.S. 3)*, as amended in 1962, in 1969 and in 1971. All the Amendments are now in force (OILPOL as amended to 1969 can be found in *9 I.L.M. 1 (1970))*; the 1971 Amendments are in *11 I.L.M. 267 (1972)*. Operational discharges (through cargo tank cleaning procedures) are dealt with by the 1969 Amendments, which give legal force to the practice introduced by the oil companies in 1964 of Load-on-Top. All discharges of oil and oily mixtures from a tanker are prohibited unless the ship is proceeding en route, the instantaneous rate of discharge is at a certain rate per mile, the total quantity of oil discharged does not exceed a certain proportion the ship's cargo-carrying capacity, and the ship is more than 50 miles from land (art. III(b)). These standards could not be met without operating Load-on-Top. To deal with oil pollution as a result of maritime accidents (collisions, strandings and groundings) the 1971 Amendments require that new tankers have their cargo tanks constructed and aligned in such a way as to minimize the amount of oil entering the sea in the event of an accident (art. 6 *bis* and Annex C). These standards have been reenacted, replace and tightened in the International Convention for the Prevention of Pollution from Ships concluded in London on 2 November 1973 *(12 I.L.M. 1319 (1973))*, as amended by the Protocol of 17 February 1978 *(17 I.L.M. 546 (1978))*. These instruments, which have themselves been subject to 3 further protocols and 5 annexes (including 9 appendices), are known by the acronym MARPLOL 73/78; and have as their objective the complete elimination of international pollution of the marine environment by oil and other harmful substances and the minimization of accidental discharge of such substances" (art. 1).

Liability for oil pollution damage and compensation are provided for in the International Convention on Civil Liability for Oil Pollution Damage of 29 November 1969 *(973 U.N.T.S. 3)* as amended on 19 November 1976 *(16 I.L.M. 617 (1977))* and the International Convention on the Establishment of an International Fund for Compensation for Oil Pollution Damage of 18 December 1971 *(11 I.L.M. 284 (1972))*. The **dumping at sea** of wastes is (principally) regulated by the (global) London Convention on the Prevention of Marine Pollution by Dumping of Wastes and Other Matter of 29 December 1972 *(11 I.L.M. 1294 (1972))* and the (European regional) Oslo Convention for the Prevention of Marine Pollution by Dumping from Ships and Aircraft of 15 February 1972 *(11 I.L.M. 262 (1972))*.

See Abecassis, *The Law and Practice Relating to Oil Pollution from Ships* (1978); Brubaker, *Marine Pollution and International Law: Principles and Practice* (1993); Brown, *The International Law of the Sea* (1994), Vol. 1, Chap. 15, Kindt, *Marine Pollution and the Law of the Sea* (1986-).

marine resources The resources of the sea are to a large extent regulated by international law. Despite failure to reach agreement on the extent of an exclusive fishery zone at the UN Conferences on the Law of the Sea at Geneva in 1958 and 1960, State practice now points to the legitimacy of an exclusive **fishery zone** extending to 200 miles from the baselines of the territorial sea. Cf. *Fisheries Jurisdiction Cases, (1974) I.C.J. Rep. 3,* where a majority of the Court were unable to agree on the validity *erga omnes* of Iceland's claim to a 50-mile exclusive fishing zone. Arts. 56, 61 and 62 of the UN Convention on the Law of the Sea 1982 *(1833 U.N.T.S. 3)* confer on coastal States the exclusive management rights in respect of fish in a zone extending to 200 miles from their coastlines, referred to as the **exclusive economic zone.** Beyond what are the legitimate exclusive fishery zones of

States, fishing is one of the freedoms of the high seas: art. 2(2) of the Geneva Convention on the High Seas 1958 *(450 U.N.T.S. 82);* art. 87 and 116-120 of the UN Convention on the Law of the Sea 1982, *supra*. Fisheries on the high seas may be regulated by agreement between States whose vessels fish in areas of the high seas where, for conservation or other reasons, some regulation is called for: *e.g.*, North Atlantic Fisheries Convention of 1 June 1967, *(1967) 6 I.L.M. 760;* Convention on the Conservation of Antarctic Marine Living Resources of 20 May 1980, *(1980) 19 I.L.M. 837.* The right to explore for, and exploit, the mineral resources, together with the living resources of a **sedentary species,** of the **continental shelf,** is conferred upon the coastal State: art. 2 of the Geneva Convention on the Continental Shelf 1958 *(499 U.N.T.S. 311);* **North Sea Continental Shelf Cases (1969)** *I.C.J. Rep. 4;* art 77 of the UN Convention on the Law of the Sea 1982 *supra*. The outer limit of the continental shelf is the edge of the continental margin: *[1956] II I.L.C. Yearbook 296;* **North Sea Continental Shelf Cases,** *supra;* art. 76 of the UN Convention on the Law of the Sea, *supra*; cf. art. 1 of the Geneva Convention on the Continental Shelf 1958, *supra*. The mineral resources beyond the outer edge of the continental shelf have been declared to be the **common heritage of mankind:** art. 1 of the Declaration of Principles governing the Sea-bed and the Ocean Floor, and the Subsoil thereof, beyond the Limits of National Jurisdiction of 17 December 1970 (G.A. Res. 2749 (XXV)); art. 136 of the UN Convention on the Law of the Sea 1982. Part XI (arts. 133-191) of the UN Convention on the Law of the Sea 1982, *supra* as amended by the Agreement relating to the Implementation of Part XI of the United Nations Convention on the Law of the Sea 1994 (GA Res. 48/263; *(1994) 33 I.L.M. 1309*) establishes a regime for the exploration for, and exploitation, of these resources. *See also* **deep-sea mining.** *See* O'Connell, *The International Law of the Sea,* vol. 1, (1982); Churchhill and Lowe, *The Law of the Sea,* (3rd ed. 1999) chaps. 8, 9, 11 and 13.

maritime belt *See* **marginal belt.**

maritime boundaries Maritime boundaries are the boundaries between the **maritime** zones of States whose coasts are opposite or adjacent to each other. In relation to the **territorial sea**, the boundary is to be fixed, failing agreement to the contrary, and where another frontier is not made "necessary by reason of historic title or other special circumstances," at "the median line every point of which is equidistant from the nearest points on the baselines" of the territorial sea: art. 15 of the UN Convention on the Law of the Sea 1982 *(1833 U.N.T.S. 3)*. In relation to the **continental shelf**, art. 6 of the Geneva Convention on the Continental Shelf 1958 *(499 U.N.T.S. 311)* provided that the boundary was to be fixed, failing agreement to the contrary and in the absence of special circumstances justifying another boundary line, at the median line (as defined above) for opposite States and, for adjacent States, "by the application of the principle of equidistance from the nearest point of the baselines" of the territorial sea. Art. 6 of the Geneva Convention was held by the ICJ not to represent customary law, and the Court set out factors to be applied in fixing a continental shelf boundary where one, or both, of the States was not a party to the Geneva Convention: **North Sea Continental Shelf Case** *1969 I.C.J. Rep. 3. See also* the **Anglo-French Continental Shelf Case** *(1977) 18 R.I.A.A. 3;* **Tunisia/Libya Continental Shelf Case** *(1982) I.C.J. Rep. 3;* **Libya-Malta Continental Shelf Case** *1984 I.C.J. Rep. 3; Gulf of Maine Area Case 1984 I.C.J. Rep 246;* and the decisions of arbitration tribunals in *Guinea/Guinea Bissau Maritime Delimitation Case (1983) 77 I.L.R. 636* and *Canada/France Maritime Delimitation Arbitration 31 I.L.M. 1145 (1992).* Art. 83(1) of the UN Convention on the Law of the Sea 1982, *supra*, provides that a continental shelf boundary "shall be effected by agreement on the basis of international law, as referred to in Article 38 of the Statute of the International Court of Justice, in order to achieve an equitable solution." Failure to reach such an agreement within a reasonable time requires the States concerned to resort to the disputes settlement procedures in Part XV of the UN Convention (art. 83(2)). In relation to the **exclusive economic zone**, the boundary is to be fixed in the same way as for continental shelf boundaries under art. 83 of the UN Convention: art. 74 of the UN Convention.

maritime ceremonials "At the present time, the right to a salute on the high seas is not treated as a matter of strict law, but merely as an act of courtesy, due to the mutual acknowledgment by sovereign States of the rank and dignity appertaining to each other. It is normally carried out by 'dipping' the flag, or firing a fixed number of guns. As between warships belonging to different nations, the order of salutes is settled on the principle of reciprocity": Colombos, *International Law of the Sea* (6th ed.), 50. *See* Irving, *The Manual of Flag Etiquette* (1934); *Satow's Guide to Diplomatic Practice* (5th ed.), Chap. 6.

maritime claims As much of the pre-conventional law of the sea was customary law, claims made by States to **maritime zones** were an important part in its evolution and development; and such claims still constitute an important element for the law governing States or zones not regulated by the UN Convention on the Law of the Sea 1982 *(1833 U.N.T.S. 3)*. The UK Hydrographic Office, *Annual Notice to Mariners No. 12* (2003), reporting on States (and their dependent territories) with coastlines, provides data on current claims. As to the **territorial sea**, there are 151 claims to a zone of 12 miles; 11 of 3 miles, 3 of 4 miles. 1 of 6 miles, 1 of 30 miles, 1 of 35 miles and 9 at 200 miles (Benin, Congo, Ecuador, El Salvador, Liberia, Nicaragua, Peru, Sierra Leone and Somalia), these against a 12-mile territorial sea recognized by the UN Convention on the Law of the Sea 1982 *(1833 U.N.T.S. 3)*, art. 3. As to those States making claims to a **contiguous zone**, all apply to a zone of 24 miles or less, except one (Sweden) claiming 41 miles; the UN Convention, art. 33, recognizes 24 miles. As to an **exclusive economic zone**, all claims are to 200 miles, the limit recognized by the UN Convention, art. 57. As to an exclusive **fisheries zone**, the vast majority of claims (27) relate to 200 miles, a breadth recognized by customary law. The *Annual Notice* does not record claims made to a **continental shelf**, such claims being invariably expressed in terms of geological features rather than in miles (*see* UN Convention, art. 76).

maritime codes "From the eighth century world trade . . . began slowly to develop again. The sea trade specially flourished, and fostered the growth of rules and customs of maritime law, which were collected into codes, and gained some kind of international recognition. The most important of these collections are the following: *The Consolato del Mare,* a private collection made at Barcelona in Spain in the middle of the fourteenth century; the *Laws of Oléron,* a collection, made in the twelfth century, of decisions given by the maritime court of Oléron in France; the *Rhodian Laws,* a very old collection of maritime laws which probably was compiled between the seventh and the ninth centuries; the *Tabula Amalfitana* the maritime laws of the town of Amalfi in Italy, which date at latest from the tenth century; the *Leges Wisbuenses,* a collection of maritime laws of **Wisby** on the island of Gothland, in Sweden, dating from the fourteenth century": *I Oppenheim 80 (8th ed.*; passage removed from 9th ed.). *See* Colombos, *International Law of the Sea* (6th ed.), Chap. 1.

Maritime Delimitation and Territorial Questions between Qatar and Bahrain *See **Qatar-Bahrain, Maritime Delimitation and Territorial Questions between, Case***.

maritime flag *See* **flag, right to fly**; **nationality of ships**.

maritime frontiers *See* **maritime boundaries**.

maritime law Strictly, this term refers to the rules of municipal legal systems as they relate to ships, shipping and transport by sea. Maritime law is sometimes referred to as shipping law or admiralty law. The international legal rules relating to the sea and its resources are referred to as the (international) law of the sea. Thus, as foreign maritime law is not part of international law, its rules must be proved in court as foreign law: *In re Piracy Jure Gentium [1934] A.C. 586*.

Maritime Ports, Convention on the International Régime of The Convention was signed at Geneva on 9 December 1923 *(58 L.N.T.S. 287)* and came into force on 26 July 1926. The Statute annexed to the Convention establishes the régime for maritime ports, which are defined as "all ports which are normally frequented by sea-going vessels and used for foreign trade" (art. 1). Each Contracting State is obliged, subject to the principle of reciprocity, "to grant the vessels of every other Contracting State equality of treatment with its own vessels" in all aspects of access to and use of maritime ports (art. 2). The régime does not apply to the maritime coasting trade (**cabotage**) (art. 9), and States are free to determine towage and pilotage arrangements provided they are non-discriminatory (art. 10-11). *See* Laun, Le régime international des ports, (1926) *15 Hague Recueil 1*.

maritime State A maritime State is a State with a coastline, irrespective of its length, and falls to be contrasted with a **land-locked State** which is "a State which has no sea-coast" (art. 124(1)(a) of the UN Convention on the Law of the Sea 1982 *(1833 U.N.T.S. 3)*. *See also* **maritime claims**.

maritime territory This term appears to have acquired two meanings. Some writers (*e.g.*, Greig, *International Law* (2nd ed.), 149 and Shearer, *Starke's International Law* (11th ed.), 220, the latter referring to "Maritime Areas") for convenience treat the term as referring to those areas of sea, and subsoil, within which a coastal State may exercise rights of sovereignty and other rights to the exclusion of, or additionally to, the rights of other States. Thus expressed, a State's maritime territory extends over **internal waters**, the **territorial sea**, the **contiguous zone**, the **continental shelf**, the **fishery zone** and the **exclusive economic zone**. While for internal waters and the territorial sea, the rights of a coastal State are identical or akin to those of territorial sovereignty, the same is not the case for the other areas, where the rights do not approximate to those of territorial sovereignty. A more appropriate usage of maritime territory appears to be that of Brownlie, *Principles of Public International Law* (5th ed.), 163-6, who restricts the term to internal waters and the territorial sea, classifying as maritime territory such things as **historic bays** in internal waters, **historic waters** in the territorial sea, sedentary fisheries, **boundary rivers** and boundary lakes. *See* Blum, *Historic Titles in International Law* (1965), 241-334; McDougal and Burke, *The Public Order of the Oceans* (1962), 357-68.

maritime zones There are five maritime zones, if **internal waters** (UN Convention on the Law of the Sea 1982 *(1833 U.N.T.S. 3)*, art. 8) and the **high seas** (Part VII) are excluded as being régimes and not zones: the **territorial sea** (Part II); **contiguous zone** (art. 33); **exclusive economic zone** (Part V); **continental shelf** (Part VI); and exclusive **fisheries zone**, a variant of the exclusive economic zone established under and regulated by customary law and not the UN Convention. *See* **maritime claims**; **maritime territory**.

market value While a number of General Assembly resolutions have called for the payment of "appropriate compensation" as a condition of a legitimate expropriation of the property of aliens, no unequivocal definition is offered as to what constitutes appropriate

compensation. *See* art. 4 of the Declaration on Permanent Sovereignty over Natural Resources of 14 December 1962 (GA Res. 1803) and art. 2(c) of the Charter of Economic Rights and Duties of States of 12 December 1974 (GA Res. 3281). *See* **permanent sovereignty** and **Economic Rights and Duties of States, Charter of**. It is generally accepted, at least in capital-exporting countries, that compensation must be full, prompt and effective. "According to international judicial practice, *full* compensation is the market value of the expropriated property. Yet, anybody who has any practical experience with the valuation of any property knows how widely even experts may differ on the market value of any such property. If the property involved is complex and liable to suffer in value through technological changes, or because of the absence of other comparable properties, the market value of a property is rather hypothetical, the subjective factors involved in any such valuation multiply": Schwarzenberger, *Foreign Investments and International Law* (1969), 11. For further problems associated with market value, see Weigel and Weston in Lillich, *The Valuation of Nationalized Property in International Law* (1972), 3.

MARPOL 73/78 *See* **marine pollution**.

Married Women, Convention on the Nationality of The Convention on the Nationality of Married Women was concluded on 20 February 1957 *(309 U.N.T.S. 65)*, and came into force on 11 August 1958. Each contracting State undertook that "neither the celebration nor the dissolution of a marriage between one of its nationals and an alien, nor the change of nationality by the husband during marriage, shall automatically affect the nationality of the wife" (art. 1); that "neither the voluntary acquisition of the nationality of another State nor the renunciation of its nationality by one of its nationals shall prevent the retention of its nationality by the wife of such national" (art. 2); that "the alien wife of one of its nationals may, at her request, acquire the nationality of her husband through specially privileged naturalization procedures" subject to limitations based on national security and public policy (art. 3 (1)); and that the "Convention shall not be construed as affecting any legislation or judicial practice by which the alien wife of one of its nationals may, at her request, acquire her husband's nationality as a matter of right:" (art. 3 (2)). Cf. also entries under **women**.

Martens, Frederic de 1845-1909. Legal advisor to Russian Department of Foreign Affairs 1869-1909. Principal works include *Consuls and Consular Jurisdiction in the Orient* (1873); *Collection of Treaties and Conventions concluded by Russia with Foreign Powers* (15 vols. 1874-1909); *Treatise on International Law* (1883-7); *The Peace Conference at the Hague* (1901); *Through Justice to Peace* (1907).

Martini Case (Italy v Venezuela) (1930) 2 R.I.A.A. 975. In 1898, Venezuela granted Lanzoni, Martini et Cie a railroad and mining contract for 15 years. After revolutionary disturbances in 1902, the Italian-Venezuelan Mixed Claims Commission in 1904 made an award in favor of the Company. In 1903, Venezuela made a contract with one Feo which overlapped in some degree the contract granted to the Company, although by a treaty of 1861 between Italy and Venezuela the latter was obliged not to grant any monopoly, exemption or privilege to the detriment of the commerce, flag or citizens of Italy. In 1904 the Venezuelan Government instituted proceedings against the company alleging non-fulfillment of certain obligations. In 1905, the Venezuelan Federal Court of Cassation found against the company, in particular rejecting the Company's argument that the Feo contract affected the company's rights under its own contract. On 21 December 1920, Italy and Venezuela concluded a Special Arbitration Agreement requesting the tribunal to determine whether the court's decision involved a denial of justice or a manifest injustice, or a breach of the 1861 treaty. *Held* that the decision of the court did not involve a breach of the

1861 treaty; that Italy and Venezuela intended the reference to "a denial of justice or a manifest injustice" to require a determination whether the decision of the court was manifestly incompatible with Venezuela's international obligations; and that while there was no such incompatibility in parts of the decision, other parts were contrary to the findings of the Mixed Claims Commission, which constituted an international obligation for Venezuela and thus involved "a denial of justice or a manifest injustice," with the consequence that Venezuela had to annul the obligations arising for the company from those parts of the decision.

Massey Claim *(USA v Mexico) (1927) 4 R.I.A.A. 155*. In October 1924, Massey, a US national, was killed by a Mexican national named Saenz. Saenz was captured and confined in prison, but escaped with the help of the assistant jail-keeper and was not apprehended. The jail-keeper was then arrested and action taken against him. *Held*, by the USA-Mexico General Claims Commission, that Mexico was liable for allowing Saenz to escape and failing to take adequate measures to punish him, it being immaterial that the gaol-keeper was subsequently punished. The rule of international law which requires a government to take proper measures to apprehend and punish nationals who have committed wrongs against aliens applies irrespective of the character or conduct of the alien; Mexico was responsible for the acts of the assistant jail-keeper as an official or other person acting for the government, both under the Convention establishing the Commission and in accordance with the general principle that whenever misconduct on the part of any such person, whatever their particular status or rank under domestic law, results in the failure of a State to perform its international obligations, the State must bear the responsibility for the wrongful acts of its servants; there was no evidence to show that any effective action had been taken by the appropriate Mexican authorities to apprehend Saenz. On the responsibility of a State for the conduct of its organs, *see* ILC Articles on State Responsibility, 2001 *(UN Doc. A/56/10 Chap.IV.E.1)*, art. 4.

material source The means by which the substance of a rule of international law is derived, *e.g.*, State practice, the material source of custom, to be distinguished from a formal source, which imparts to a given rule the force of law (such as treaty, custom, acceptance as a general principle of law recognized by civilized nations). This distinction was set forth in English jurisprudence and, and despite difficulties of application in practice, is still followed in traditional enquiry in international law. For a discussion of the problems involved in categorizing sources of international law and suggestions as to a new direction of enquiry into **sources** and **evidences of international law**, *see* Parry, *The Sources and Evidences of International Law* (1965), 1-27.

Mavrommatis Jerusalem Concessions Case *(Greece v UK) (1924), (1925), (1927) P.C.I.J., Ser. A, Nos. 2, 5 and 11*. Mavrommatis, a Greek national, was in 1914 granted concessions by the Ottoman authorities for certain public works in what later became Palestine: after the 1914-18 war Great Britain was granted a mandate for Palestine. Greece alleged that Great Britain, through the Palestine Government, had refused fully to recognize the concessions in Jerusalem and Jaffa, principally by having granted to a Mr Rutenberg concessions partially overlapping those enjoyed by Mr Mavrommatis, and accordingly sought compensation. Art. 26 of the mandate, conferring jurisdiction on the Court, applied to disputes relating to the interpretation or application of the provisions of the mandate between Great Britain and another member of the League of Nations which could not be settled by negotiation. On a preliminary objection by Great Britain to the Court's jurisdiction, *held* (7 to 5) that the Court had jurisdiction in respect of the Jerusalem concessions, but not the Jaffa concessions. The dispute was between Great Britain and another member of the League of Nations. "It is an elementary principle of international law that a State is entitled to protect its subjects, when injured by acts contrary to international law committed by another State, from whom they have been unable to obtain satisfaction through the ordinary channels. By taking up the case of one of its subjects and by resorting to diplomatic action or international judicial proceedings on his behalf, a State is in reality asserting its own rights—its right to ensure, in the person of its subjects, respect for the rules of international law. The question, therefore, whether the present dispute originates in an injury to a private interest, which in point of fact is the case in many international disputes, is irrelevant from this standpoint. Once a State has taken up a case on behalf of one of its subjects before an international tribunal, in the eyes of the latter the State is sole claimant." The dispute could not in the circumstances of the case be settled by negotiation; and (so far as concerned the Jerusalem concession, but not the Jaffa concession) related to a relevant provision of the mandate. Although Protocol XII of the Treaty of **Lausanne** 1923, which formed the Peace Treaty with Turkey, contained provisions expressly relating to the recognition of concessions in Palestine but without recognizing the Court's jurisdiction in cases of dispute, it complemented the Mandate and did not render inoperative its jurisdictional clauses.

In its judgment on the merits the Court *held* (unanimously) that, the Jerusalem concession being valid, Protocol XII required the maintenance of concessions such as those granted to Mavrommatis, and accordingly a grant to Rutenberg of a concession allowing him for a time to request the annulment of Mavrommatis' concession was contrary to Great Britain's obligations under the Protocol; but (11 to 1) that Greece's claim for an indemnity must be dismissed since the Mavrommatis concession was not in fact annulled nor was there any proof of other loss he may have suffered; and (unanimously) that, under the Protocol, Mavrommatis was entitled to have his concessions adapted so as to be brought into conformity with the new economic conditions in Palestine.

Greece subsequently claimed that Great Britain had so delayed the negotiations for the adaptation of the concessions as to amount to a breach of its international obligations under the Mandate and had thereby caused injury to Mavrommatis for which Great Britain should make adequate reparation. On a preliminary objection by Great Britain to the Court's jurisdiction, *held* (7 to 4) that the alleged breach by Great Britain of its international obligations did not in the circumstances come within the jurisdiction conferred on the Court by the terms of the Mandate.

MBFR An acronym for mutual and balanced force reductions. Properly styled the Mutual Reduction of Forces and Armaments and Associated Measures in Central Europe, this acronym refers to the negotiation begun in 1973 in Vienna between member States of **NATO** and the **Warsaw Pact** on the reduction of forces in Central Europe, defined as Belgium, the Netherlands, Luxembourg, East and West Germany, Poland and Czechoslovakia. The negotiations encountered difficulties over whether air forces and nuclear weapons should be included as well as ground forces; over whether the reductions should be equal or directed towards a common ceiling; and over whether the reductions should apply to each alliance as a whole or to separate contingents. The negotiations ultimately failed in 1989 with the ending of the Cold War and were replaced by the Conventional Forces in Europe negotiations under the auspices of the OSCE which succeeded in introducing confidence building measures focusing on the exchange of military information.

McDougal, Myers Smith 1906-1998. *(1992)* Professor, Illinois 1931-4, Yale 1934-77. Principal works include *Law and Minimum World Public Order* (with Feliciano) (1961); *The Public Order of the Oceans* (with Burke) (1962); *Law and Public Order in Space* (with Lasswell and Miller) (1967); *Human Rights and World Public Order* (with Lasswell and Chen) (1980). "McDougal's written work will surely establish him as one of the seminal figures of modern international law. The vocabulary he assembled, which was initially resisted, has proved to be indispensable for describing the contemporary international legal process and distinctive objectives of modern international law": Falk, Higgins, Reisman and Weston, Myers Smith McDougal, 92 *A.J.I.L. 729-33 (1998).*

***McLeod's Case** (1841) Moore, Digest of International Law, Vol. 2, 25*. In 1840, McLeod, a British national, was arrested by the authorities of the State of New York and held for trial on a charge of murder committed in the course of the attack on the *Caroline* (*see* **Caroline Incident**). Britain requested McLeod's release on the ground that the destruction of the *Caroline* by British forces was a "public act of persons in Her Majesty's service" and, as such, could "not justly be made the ground of legal proceedings in the United States against the persons concerned." On 15 March 1841, US Secretary of State Daniel Webster stated: "That an individual, forming part of a public force, and acting under the authority of his Government, is not to be held answerable as a private trespasser or malefactor, is a principle of public law sanctioned by the usages of all civilized nations, and which the Government of the United States has no inclination to dispute." He said, however, that the US Government was unable to comply with the demand for McLeod's release, which was a matter for the courts before which he had been charged. McLeod was denied habeas corpus, but was eventually acquitted on proof of an alibi: *People v. McLeod 25 Wend. 483 (1841), 26 Wend. 664 (1841)*. As a result of this case, in 1842 the Congress adopted an Act to provide for the removal of cases involving international relations from State to Federal Courts. *See also* **act of State, doctrine of**.

McNair, Arnold Duncan (Lord) 1885-1973. Lawyer and law teacher, and Professor, Cambridge 1919-26, 1929-39, London School of Economics 1926-29. Vice-Chancellor, Liverpool 1937-45. Member, ICJ 1946-55. Member, European Court of Human Rights 1959-65. Principal works include *Legal Effects of War* (1920; 4th ed. with A.D. Watts 1966); editor of 4th ed. of Oppenheim's *International Law* (1928); *Law of the Air* (1932); later editions by other authors); *Law of Treaties* (1938; 2nd ed. 1961); *International Law Opinions,* 3 vols. (1956).

mediation "Mediation, as a method of peaceful settlement of international disputes, means the participation of a third State or a disinterested individual in negotiations between States in dispute. The role of the mediator is well expressed in Article 4 of the Hague Convention on the Pacific Settlement of Disputes of 1899 *[187 C.T.S. 410]* as 'reconciling the opposing claims and appeasing the feelings of resentment which have arisen between the States at variance'": David Davies Memorial Institute of International Studies, *International Disputes. The Legal Aspects* (1972), 83. *See* Merrills, *International Dispute Settlement* (3rd ed.), Chap. 2. Cf. **conciliation**.

medical personnel In terms of art. 24 of the Geneva Convention for the Amelioration of the Condition of the Wounded and Sick in Armed Forces in the Field of 12 August 1949 *(75 U.N.T.S. 31),* medical personnel (defined as those "exclusively engaged in the search for, or the collection, transport or treatment of the wounded or sick, or in the prevention of disease, staff exclusively engaged in the administration of medical units and establishment") are to "be respected and protected in all circumstances." This extends to members of armed forces specially trained for medical duties and carrying out medical functions (art. 25), and to staff of national Red Cross Societies and other Voluntary Aid Societies (art. 26). Medical personnel, if captured, are not to be prisoners of war (art. 28), and are to be returned to their own party to the conflict (art. 30). *See* Pictet, *Commentary on the Geneva Conventions of 12 August 1949*, Vol. 1 (1952), Chaps. III and IV.

members of the United Nations   Art. 3 of the UN Charter states that the original members of the United Nations "shall be the States which, having participated in the United Nations Conference on International Organization at San Francisco, or having previously signed the Declaration by United Nations of January 1, 1942, sign the present Charter and ratify it in accordance with Article 110." The UN had 51 original members. Fifty States participated in the San Francisco Conference, 46 of whom had signed the Declaration by United Nations: Australia, Belgium, Bolivia, Brazil, Canada, Chile, China, Colombia, Costa Rica, Cuba, Czechoslovakia, Dominican Republic, Ecuador, Egypt, El Salvador, Ethiopia, France, Greece, Guatemala, Haiti, Honduras, India, Iran, Iraq, Lebanon, Liberia, Luxembourg, Mexico, Netherlands, New Zealand, Nicaragua, Norway, Panama, Paraguay, Peru, Philippines, Russian Federation, Saudi Arabia, South Africa, Turkey, UK, Uruguay, USA, Venezuela and Yugoslavia. Four States were invited to participate in the Conference: Argentina, the Byelorussian SSR, the Ukrainian SSR and, after its liberation 5 June 1945, Denmark. Poland with no generally-recognized government at the time, could not participate, but a place was reserved for Poland as an original member. Art. 4 of the UN Charter provides for subsequent (or admitted) members. Membership is open "to all other [i.e., other than original members] peace-loving States which accept the obligations contained in the present Charter and, in the judgment of the Organization, are able and willing to carry out these obligations" (art. 4(1)), admission to "be effected by a decision of the General Assembly upon a recommendation of the Security Council" (art. 4(2)). As to the criteria which may be taken into account in voting on the admission of a State under art. 4, see the ***Admission of a State to Membership in the U.N., Conditions for, Opinion 1948 I.C.J. Rep. 57***; and as to whether the General Assembly may admit a member in the absence of a favorable recommendation from the Security Council, see the ***Admission of a State to the U.N., Competence of the General Assembly for the, Opinion 1950 I.C.J. Rep. 4***.

The UN presently has 191 members, of which 145 (including those States emerging from the break-up of Czechoslovakia, the USSR and Yugoslavia, which were all original members of the UN) were admitted under art. 4: Afghanistan, Albania, Algeria, Andorra, Angola, Antigua and Barbuda, Armenia, Austria, Azerbaijan, Bahamas, Bahrain, Bangladesh, Barbados, Belize, Benin, Bhutan, Bosnia and Herzegovina, Botswana, Brunei Darussalam, Bulgaria, Burma, Burkina Faso, Burundi, Cameroon, Cape Verde, Central African Republic, Chad, Comoros, Congo, Croatia, Cuba, Cyprus, Czech Republic, Democratic Kampuchea, Democratic People's Republic of Korea, Democratic Republic of the Congo, Djibouti, Dominica, Equatorial Guinea, Eritrea, Estonia, Federated States of Micronesia, Fiji, Finland, Gabon, Gambia, Georgia, Germany, Ghana, Grenada, Guinea, Guinea-Bissau, Guyana, Hungary, Iceland, Indonesia, Ireland, Israel, Italy, Ivory Coast, Jamaica, Japan, Jordan, Kazakhstan, Kenya, Kiribati, Kuwait, Kyrgyzstan, Lao People's Democratic Republic, Latvia, Lesotho, Libyan Arab Jamahiriya, Liechtenstein, Lithuania, Madagascar, Malawi, Malaysia, Maldives, Mali, Malta, Marshall Islands, Mauritania, Mauritius, Moldova, Monaco, Mongolia, Morocco, Mozambique, Myanmar, Namibia, Nauru, Nepal, Niger, Nigeria, Oman, Pakistan, Palau, Papua New Guinea, Portugal, Qatar, Republic of Korea, Romania, Rwanda, Saint Kitts and Nevis, Saint Lucia, Saint Vincent and the Grenadines, Samoa, San Marino, Sao Tome and Principe, Senegal, Serbia and Montenegro, Seychelles, Sierra Leone, Singapore, Slovak Republic, Slovenia, Solomon Islands, Somalia, Spain, Sri Lanka, Sudan, Suriname, Swaziland, Sweden, Switzerland, Tajikistan, Thailand, The former Yugoslav Republic of Macedonia, Timor-Leste, Togo, Tonga, Trinidad and Tobago, Tunisia, Turkmenistan, Tuvalu, Uganda, United Arab Emirates, United Republic of Tanzania, Uzbekistan, Vanuatu, Viet Nam, Yemen, Zambia,

Zimbabwe. *See* Goodrich, Hambro and Simons, *Charter of the United Nations* (3rd ed. rev.), Chap. 2. *See also* **representation of a member State**; **suspension**; and **withdrawal**.

membership of international organizations Membership of international organizations is generally of two types: original and admitted (or subsequent). The original members are those who subscribed to and ratified the basic constituent instrument. Subsequent members are generally admitted by a decision of the plenary organ of the organization, as in the case of the UN, followed, in some instances, by deposit of an instrument of accession. Cf. **members of the United Nations**. Some international organizations allow (usually) non-autonomous territories to join with limited rights, as **associate members.** Other organisations allow for partial members, those States being members of certain organs but not full members of the organization as such while the **World Tourism Organization** has a special category of membership known as **affiliate membership**. Most international organizations also grant some form of **observer status** to non-member States and other entities. *See* Schermers & Blokker, *International Institutional Law* (3rd ed.), 45-137; Sands & Klein, *Bowett's Law of International Institutions* (5th ed.), 533-564.

Memel Territory Statute, Interpretation of *(UK, France, Italy and Japan v. Lithuania) (1932) P.C.I.J., Ser. A/B, Nos. 47, 49.* By art. 99 of the Treaty of Versailles 1919 *(225 C.T.S. 188)*, Germany renounced in favor of Great Britain, France, Italy and Japan (the Four Powers) all rights and title to, *inter alia*, the Memel Territory. By a Convention concluded with Lithuania on 8 May 1924 *(29 L.N.T.S. 87)*, the Four Powers transferred to Lithuania sovereignty over the Memel Territory which was, however, to be autonomous in accordance with a Statute annexed to the Convention. Under the Statute, the Lithuanian Government was represented in Memel by a Governor, and Memel was governed by a Directorate under a President appointed by the Governor, and by a Chamber of Representatives. In 1932, the Governor dismissed the President and took certain other acts, the consistency of which with the Statute was questioned. The Four Powers, acting under art. 17 of the 1924 Convention, referred a series of questions to the PCIJ. After *dismissing* (13 to 3) preliminary objections by Lithuania to two of the questions, the Court *held* (10 to 5) that: (1) while the Statute might for internal purposes form part of the local law it was also part of a treaty and must be interpreted as such; (2) the autonomy of Memel in accordance with the Statute operated within the framework of Lithuania's full sovereignty which was subject to the limitations on its exercise laid down by the Statute; (3) the Statute must be interpreted as allowing the Governor to dismiss the President where he commits serious acts calculated to breach the sovereign rights of Lithuania and violates the Statute, no other means of redress being available; (4) the Statute vested foreign relations exclusively in the Lithuanian Government and the President's conduct in having talks in Germany with the German government, without consulting the Lithuanian Government justified his dismissal; (5) dismissal of the President did not itself involve the termination of the appointments of other members of the Directorate; (6) the appointment by the Governor of a new President conformed with the Statute; (7) the subsequent dissolution of the Chamber of Representatives by the Governor was not in order under the Statute in its treaty aspect, but this did not mean that it was of no effect in municipal law.

mémoire *See* **memorandum**.

memorandum *"Memorandum* (sometimes called *mémoire,* or, especially when it embodies a summary of a conversation, *pro-memoria,* or *aide-mémoire*). This is often a detailed statement of facts, and of arguments based thereon, not differing essentially from a Note, except that it does not begin and end with a formula of courtesy and need not be signed, since it is usually delivered either personally, following an interview, or by means of a short covering Note. An important example is the memorandum communicated by the German Government to the French Government 9 February 1925, initiating the correspondence which led to the Locarno Conference of that year": *Satow's Guide to Diplomatic Practice* (5th ed.), 451.

memorandum of agreement While similar in purpose and form to a **memorandum of understanding**, a memorandum of agreement is more likely to show an intention on the part of the participating governments to enter into an informal but nevertheless legally binding agreement giving rise to legal rights and obligations. The expression "memorandum of agreement" is referred to in the Commentary on the ILC draft articles on the Law of Treaties as one of the titles commonly used for the less formal types of international agreement: *[1966] II ILC Yearbook 188*, para. (3).

memorandum of understanding A memorandum of understanding is an international instrument of a less formal kind, often setting out operational arrangements under a framework international agreement or otherwise dealing with technical or detailed matters. It will typically be in the form of a single instrument signed by the governments concerned, recording their understandings as to matters of fact or their future conduct, but in such a way as to reflect an intention on their part not to enter into a legally binding agreement upon the matters covered or otherwise to create legal rights and obligations for themselves. Understandings of this kind may also be recorded in an exchange of notes. A memorandum of understanding has political or moral force, but is not legally binding (although it may not be without legal effects, *e.g.*, it may operate as an estoppel or preclusion). The Commentary on the ILC draft articles on the Law of Treaties refers to a memorandum of understanding as being within that category of instruments which, while not formal, "are undoubtedly international agreements subject to the law of treaties": *[1966] II ILC Yearbook 188*, para. (2). Strictly, this is probably only true to the extent that the participating governments' intention was to enter into an agreement, in which case the designation of the instrument as a memorandum of understanding would not of itself deprive the instrument of its character as an international agreement. Where a memorandum of understanding does not constitute an international agreement it will not be subject to the obligations of registration under Article 102 of the Charter, and may accordingly remain confidential to the participating governments. For an example of a memorandum of understanding subsequently published as a treaty, see Memorandum of Understanding of 5 October 1954 between Italy, UK, USA and Yugoslavia regarding the Free Territory of Trieste *(235 U.N.T.S. 99)*. See Aust, *Modern Treaty Law and Practice* (2000), 20-1.

memorial The first of the written pleadings in a contentious case before the ICJ, in which the applicant States sets out the relevant facts, law and the submissions in relation to its claim: art. 43 of the ICJ Statute and arts. 45(1) and 49(1) of the Rules of Court 1978. *See* **counter-memorial, reply** and **rejoinder**.

men of war *See* **warships**.

Mendlovitz, Saul Howard 1925- . Professor, Rutgers-Newark 1961- . Principal works include *Strategy of World Order* (with Falk) (1966); *Regional Politics and World Order* (with Falk, 1973); *On the Creation of a Just World Order*) (1975); *Preferred Futures for the United Nations* (with Weston, 1995).

mercenaries While mercenaries have been used in war from Roman times, the laws of war have contained no explicit references to them. The appearance, and role, of mercenaries in recent international and internal conflicts has caused concern, and resulted in provisions on mercenaries in art. 47 of Protocol I Additional to the Geneva Conventions of 12 August 1949, relating to the Protection of Victims of International Armed Conflicts, adopted at the Diplomatic Conference on the Reaffirmation and Development of International Humanitarian Law Applicable in Armed Conflicts of 8 June 1977 *(1125 U.N.T.S. 3)*. A mercenary is defined as any person who is specially recruited locally or abroad to fight in a conflict, has a direct part in hostilities, is motivated by the desire for private gain and is promised compensation greater than equivalently ranked combatants, is neither a national nor a resident of a Party to the conflict, is not a member of the armed forces of a Party, and has not been sent by a State which is not a Party to the conflict on official duty as a member of the armed forces (art. 47(2)). A mercenary, so defined, "shall not have the right to be a combatant or a prisoner of war" (art. 47(1)). *See* Burmester, The Recruitment and Use of Mercenaries in Armed Conflicts, *72 A.J.I.L. 37 (1978)*. A number of unsuccessful attempts to outlaw the use of mercenaries have been attempted most recently by the United Nations during the 1980s. On the contrary, many States are now actively promoting the use of mercenaries through private companies in peacekeeping roles.

Mergé Claim *(United States v. Italy) (1955) 14 R.I.A.A. 236.* The United States presented a claim for compensation under art. 78 of the Treaty of Peace with Italy of 10 February 1947 *(49 U.N.T.S. 3)* for the loss of personal property owned by Mrs. Mergé, who was both a United States and an Italian national. *Held*, by the Italian-United States Conciliation Commission, that art. 78 of the Treaty of Peace, in defining those on whose behalf claims could be presented, did not refer to cases of dual nationality; that the principle that a State may not afford diplomatic protection to one of its nationals against a State whose nationality such person also possesses, and the principle that, in dual nationality cases, it is the effective nationality to which priority should be given, were principles of international law; that a claimant State whose effective nationality an individual possesses was entitled to present a claim under the Peace Treaty even though the individual also possessed Italian nationality; that the criterion of effective nationality involved consideration of an individual's habitual residence, his conduct in economic, social, political, civic and family life, and the extent of his bond with one or other of the States in question; that on the facts of the case Mrs. Mergé was not dominantly a United States national for purposes of art. 78 of the Treaty of Peace because the family did not have its habitual residence in the United States and the interests and permanent professional life of the head of the family were not established there; and that therefore the United States was not entitled to present a claim against Italy in her behalf.

merger of States "A State ceases to be an international person when it ceases to exist. In practice this may happen when one state merges into another and becomes merely part of it . . . or when two or more states merge to form a single new state.": *I Oppenheim 206-7*. The new State may be a federal State (*e.g.*, the formation of the United States of America, Switzerland, the German Federation of 1871) or a non-federal State (*e.g.*, the merger of Egypt and Syria in 1958 under the name of United Arab Republic, (from which Syria withdrew in 1961 and which Egypt renamed the Arab Republic of Egypt in 1971), and the merger of Tanganyika and Zanzibar in 1964 into the United Republic of Tanzania).

Meron, Theodor 1930- . Sometime member of Israeli Foreign Service. Law professor at New York University and at the Graduate Institute of International Studies, Geneva. President, **International Criminal Tribunal for the Former Yugoslavia** 2003- . Principal works include *Human Rights Law-Making in the United Nations* (1987); *Human Rights in Internal Strife: Their International Protection* (1987); *Human Rights in International* Law (1991); *Henry's Wars and Shakespeare's Laws* (1994); *Bloody Constraints: War and Chivalry in Shakespeare* (1998); *War Crimes Law Comes of Age: Essays* (1999).

Mervyn Jones, John 1912-57. Law teacher (UK). Foreign Office official and member of UN Secretariat. Principal works include *Full Powers and Ratification* (1946); *British Nationality Law and Practice* (1947).

metropolitan territory This term refers to the territory of a parent State of a colony (*OED, passim*) or any other type of dependent territory in respect of which the metropolitan State exercises international functions. "Unless a different intention appears from the treaty or it is otherwise established, a treaty is binding upon each party in respect of its entire territory [i.e. whether metropolitan or non-metropolitan]": Vienna Convention on the Law of Treaties art. 29 (the Vienna Convention is indeed itself an illustration of the general rule stated). At least until the 1914-18 War it was the general practice of colonial powers to conclude international agreements without differentiating between the metropolitan and non-metropolitan territories. After 1945 it became usual to include a **territorial application clause** in multilateral treaties so as to enable relations with dependent territories to be regulated separately. This was done chiefly for two reasons: (1) because the instrument might not be relevant to all dependent territories (*e.g.*, commodity agreements regulating tropical products might not be relevant to territories in the temperate zone); (2) because ratification might predicate legislation by the local legislature in each territorial unit or after consultation with the territory (*e.g.*, conventions on matters of status or criminal law). For examples, *see* Blix, *The Treaty Maker's Handbook* (1973), Section 12. More recently, requests for the inclusion of territorial application clauses have encountered resistance and there has been a reversion to an earlier practice of declaring upon ratification to which territories the treaty is to apply. *See* Aust, *Modern Treaty Law and Practice* (2000), Chap. 11.

Mexican Eagle Oil Company Case *(1938).* The Mexican Eagle Oil Company, incorporated in Mexico but with a majority British shareholding, had an award made against it by the Mexican Labor Board and confirmed by the Supreme Court. In response to the company's non-compliance with the award, the Mexican Government in 1938 expropriated the company's assets on grounds of public interest. In an exchange of diplomatic correspondence in 1938, the British Government, while not questioning the general right of a government to expropriate in the public interest and on payment of adequate compensation, maintained that the expropriation was arbitrary, disproportionate and tantamount to confiscation, and asserted the right to protect the interests of the British shareholders since the company had been rendered virtually incapable of doing so by the Mexican Government's actions; the British Government further maintained that the judicial proceedings were in certain respects erroneous and constituted a denial of justice, and that, although a challenge to the validity of the expropriation decree was still *sub judice*, it was likely to last a considerable time, and as the British shareholders had already suffered great damage the British Government was entitled to make representations. For its part, Mexico asserted the right of any State on payment of adequate compensation to expropriate property in the public interest, the assessment of which was a matter for its own discretion (and it denied in any event that the expropriation in the present case was disproportionate or arbitrary or not in the public interest); Mexico also rejected the UK's right to defend the Mexican company's interests on the basis of its British shareholding and denied the UK's right to intervene on behalf of the shareholders in the Mexican company, which had not ceased its separate legal existence and the payment to which of compensation for the expropriated properties would adequately safeguard the shareholders' interests; furthermore, the shares themselves contained a renunciation of the alien owner's right to seek the protection of his government; and, finally, as the legal recourse open to the company in the Mexican courts had not been exhausted there could not be any denial of justice. After further prolonged diplomatic exchanges, an agreement was reached in 1947 between Mexico and the company whereby Mexico agreed to pay compensation of $81,250,000; the British Government noted with satisfaction that this agreement would ensure that the British shareholders would receive just and equitable compensation. *See* Wortley, The Mexican Oil Dispute 1938-46, *(1957) 43 T.G.S. 15.*

Mexican Union Railway Company Claim *(UK v. Mexico) (1930) 5 R.I.A.A. 115* The Mexican Union Railway Company, a British company operating in Mexico under a concession granted by the Mexican Government, suffered losses in the course of revolutionary disturbances in Mexico between 1919 and 1920. The concession contained a "**Calvo clause**" providing for the company to be always a Mexican corporation irrespective of its members being aliens, for the company to be exclusively subject to the Mexican courts, and for the company and all having an interest in it to forego foreign diplomatic protection. The company did not seek redress in the Mexican courts for the losses suffered by it. In agreeing to submit various claims to a Claims Commission, Great Britain and Mexico agreed in the Convention 19 November 1926 *(85 L.N.T.S. 51)* that claims should not be rejected on the grounds that legal remedies had not been exhausted prior to the presentation of the claim. On a claim being made by Great Britain on behalf of the company, the Great Britain-Mexico Claims Commission *held* that the Commission had no jurisdiction. Although a Calvo clause could not deprive a government of its right to invoke its international legal rights or deprive the company of its British nationality to the extent of waiving its right to appeal to the British Government in cases of violation of international law, the clause was in this case an integral part of the concession, requiring the company to seek redress for any complaints through Mexican tribunals, and as the company had not attempted to do so there could be no question of any denial or delay of justice, as there could have been if the company had, as agreed, resorted to Mexican tribunals and had nevertheless failed thereby to obtain justice. The provision in the 1926 Convention waiving the requirement for exhausting all legal remedies had to be read subject to particular obligation in the concession requiring recourse to Mexican tribunals. *See generally* Amerasinghe *Local Remedies in International Law* (1990), 255.

MFN *See* **most-favored-nation clause/treatment**.

Micronesia Micronesia (the Caroline and Marshall Islands archipelagos) was originally a German Colony, placed into the **Mandates System** of the League of Nations on 17 December 1920 (League of Nations, *Official Journal*, Vol. 2, 87) to be administered by Japan. Following the Second World War, Micronesia was transferred into the **Trusteeship System** to be administered by the United States: Trusteeship Agreement for the Former Japanese Mandated Islands, approved by the Security Council on 2 April 1947 *(8 U.N.T.S. 189)*. This was designated as a "strategic" trust under arts. 82-3 of the UN Charter. Micronesia, properly called the Trust Territory of the Pacific Islands, was administered as four districts: the Northern Marina Islands, the Federated States of Micronesia, the Marshall Islands and Palau. The Northern Marina Islands entered into a Covenant with the United States of America whereby they became a self-governing commonwealth in political union with and under the sovereignty of the United States *(15 I.L.M. 651 (1976)*. The United States also entered into Compacts of Free Association with the Federated States of Micronesia, the Marshall Islands and Palau. Security Council Agreement to end the trusteeships of the Northern Marina Islands, the Federated States of Micronesia and the Marshall Islands was provided in Res. 683 (1990) and in respect of Palau (the population of which had initially rejected but later accepted the Compact of Free Association with the United States) by Res. 956 (1994). The Federated States of Micronesia and the Marshall Islands both became members of the United Nations in 1991; Palau became a member of the United Nations in 1994.

micro-States *See* **mini-States**.

MIGA *See* **Multilateral Investment Guarantee Agency**.

migration of workers "By customary international law no state can claim the right for its nationals to enter into, and reside on, the territory of a foreign state. The reception of aliens is a matter of discretion, and every state is, by reason of its territorial supremacy, competent to exclude aliens from the whole, or any part of its territory. States may, however, by treaty confer on each other's nationals a right to enter their territories, especially in treaties of commerce and friendship, which often entitle the foreign nationals concerned not merely to enter the state but to establish themselves in business there": *I Oppenheim, 897-8. But see Establishment of Foreign Workers Case (1969) 38 I.L.R. 261* in which a distinction was drawn between the right of residence and the right of establishment.

The free movement of workers and the right of establishment for all citizens of the European Union within other Member States of the Union are fundamental elements of the single market established within the Union. *See* art. 39 (free movement of workers) and art. 43 (freedom of establishment) of the Consolidated Text of the Treaty Establishing the European Community *(Official Journal C 325 of 24 December 2002)*.

The International Convention on the Protection of the Rights of All Migrant Workers and Members of Their Families of 18 December 1990 *(30 I.L.M. 1517 (1991))* seeks to provide for the prevention and elimination of the exploitation of migrant workers (defined as a person who is to be engaged, is engaged or has been engaged in remunerated activity in a State of which he or she is not a national (art. 2(1))), in particular by ending the illegal recruitment or trafficking of migrant workers and also provides standards for the treatment, welfare and human rights of registered and unregistered migrant workers and their families. The Convention entered into force on 1 July 2003, but currently has only 20 States Parties.

Military and Paramilitary Activities in and against Nicaragua (Jurisdiction) *(Nicaragua v. USA) 1984 I.C.J. Rep. 169.* On 9 April 1984, Nicaragua instituted proceedings before the ICJ against the USA, alleging violations by the latter of its international obligations arising out of its alleged involvement in military and paramilitary actions in and against Nicaragua; Nicaragua also asked the Court to indicate provisional measures of protection. Nicaragua had accepted the compulsory jurisdiction of the PCIJ in 1929, although Nicaragua's instrument of ratification of the Protocol of Signature of the Statute of the PCIJ did not appear to have been received by the League of Nations. The USA had accepted the compulsory jurisdiction of the ICJ under the **Optional Clause** in 1946, subject to a proviso that its declaration of acceptance would remain in force for 5 years and thereafter until the expiry of 6 months notice of termination; and on 6 April 1984 the USA deposited a further declaration which, notwithstanding the terms of the 1946 declaration, was to take effect immediately and which excluded from the scope of that declaration disputes with any Central American State or arising out of or related to events in Central America. The Court *held* that (1) without finally deciding that it had jurisdiction on the merits, the provisions invoked by Nicaragua appeared *prima facie* to afford a basis on which the jurisdiction of the Court might be founded; (2) it should indicate as provisional measures that (a) (unanimously) the USA should immediately cease any action restricting, blocking or endangering access to or from Nicaraguan ports, and, in particular, the laying of mines; (b) (14 to 1) Nicaragua's right to sovereignty and political independence should be fully respected and should not in any way be jeopardized by any military and paramilitary activities prohibited by the principles of international law, in particular the principle that States should refrain in their international relations from the threat or use of force against the territorial integrity or the political independence of any State, and the principle concerning the duty not to intervene in matters within the domestic jurisdiction of a State; (c) (unanimously) the two Parties should each of them ensure that no action was taken which might aggravate or extend the dispute submitted to the Court, or which might prejudice the rights of the other Party in respect of the carrying out of whatever decision the Court may render in the case.

On 26 November 1984, the Court *held* (1) (11 to 5) that it had jurisdiction on the basis of Nicaragua's 1929 declaration accepting the compulsory jurisdiction of the Court; (2) (14 to 2) that it had jurisdiction in so far as Nicaragua's application related to a dispute concerning the US-Nicaragua Treaty of Friendship, Commerce and Navigation of 21 January 1956; (3) (15 to 1) that it had jurisdiction to entertain the case; (4) (unanimously) that Nicaragua's application was admissible. *See* Leigh, Judicial Decisions, *79 A.J.I.L. 442 (1985).* *See also **Military and Paramilitary Activities in and against Nicaragua (Merits)**.*

Military and Paramilitary Activities in and against Nicaragua (Merits) *(Nicaragua v. USA) 1986 I.C.J. Rep. 14.* On 9 April 1984, Nicaragua instituted proceedings before the ICJ against the USA, alleging violations by the latter of its international obligations arising out of its alleged involvement in military and paramilitary actions in and against Nicaragua. Having found that the application was admissible (*see **Military and Paramilitary Activities in and against Nicaragua (Jurisdiction)***), the ICJ turned to consider the merits. In its decision of 27 June 1986, the Court *held* (1) (11 to 4) that it was required to apply the "multilateral treaty reservation" contained in the USA's 1946 declaration Accepting the compulsory jurisdiction of the Court; (2) (12 to 3) that the justification of collective self-defense maintained by the USA was rejected; (3) (12 to 3) that the USA, by training, arming, equipping, financing and supplying the *contra* forces or otherwise encouraging, supporting and aiding military and paramilitary activities in and against Nicaragua, had acted, against the Republic of Nicaragua, in breach of its obligation under customary international law not to intervene in the affairs of another State; (4) (12 to 3) that the USA had, by certain attacks on Nicaraguan territory in 1983-84 acted, against the Republic of Nicaragua, in breach of its obligation under customary international law not to use force against another State; (5) (12 to 3) that the USA had, by the same and other acts, acted, against the Republic of Nicaragua in breach of its obligation under customary international law not to violate the sovereignty of another State; (6) (12 to 3) that by laying mines in the internal or territorial waters of the Republic of Nicaragua during the first months of 1984, the USA had acted, against the Republic of Nicaragua, in breach of its obligations under customary international law not to use force against another State, not to intervene in its affairs, not to violate its sovereignty and not to interrupt peaceful maritime commerce; (7) (14 to 1) that by the same acts, the USA had acted, against the Republic of Nicaragua, in breach of its obligations under Article XIX of the Treaty of Friendship, Commerce and Navigation of 21 January 1956; (8) (14 to 1) that the USA, by failing to make known the existence and location of the mines laid by it had acted in breach of its obligations under customary international law in this respect; (9) (14 to 1) that the USA, by producing and distributing to the *contras* a manual on guerrilla warfare, had encouraged the commission by them of acts contrary to the general principles of international humanitarian law, but did not find that any such acts that may have been committed were imputable to the USA; (10) (12 to 3) that the USA had committed various acts calculated to deprive of its objects and purpose the Treaty of Friendship, Commerce and Navigation of 21 January 1956; (11) (12 to 3) that the USA by the same acts had acted in breach of its obligations under Article XIX of the Treaty of Friendship, Commerce and Navigation of 21 January 1956; (12) (12 to 3) that the USA was under a duty immediately to cease and to refrain from all such acts as may have constituted breaches of the foregoing legal obligations; (13) (12 to 3) that the USA was under an obligation to make reparation to the Republic of Nicaragua for all injury caused to

Nicaragua by the breaches of obligations under customary international law; (14) (14 to 1) that the USA was under an obligation to make reparation to the Republic of Nicaragua for all injury caused to Nicaragua by the breaches of the Treaty of Friendship Commerce and Navigation of 21 January 1956; (15) (14 to 1) that the form and amount of reparation, failing agreement between the parties was to be settled by the Court; (16) (unanimously) that both parties were under an obligation to seek a solution to their dispute by peaceful means in accordance with international law. By order of 26 September 1991, the Court ordered that the case be removed from the list at the request of the Republic of Nicaragua: *1991 I.C.J. Rep. 47. See generally*, Miller (ed.), Appraisals of the ICJ's Decision: Nicaragua v. United States (Merits), *81 A.J.I.L. 1-173 (1987)*.

military necessity   Art. 23(g) of the Hague Convention on the Laws and Customs of War on Land of 18 October 1907 *(205 C.T.S. 293)* prohibits the destruction or seizure of enemy property "unless such destruction or seizure be imperatively demanded by the necessities of war"; and art. 53 of the Geneva Convention relative to the Protection of Civilian Persons in Time of War of 12 August 1949 *(75 U.N.T.S. 287)* prohibits the destruction by an occupying power of any property "except where such destruction is rendered absolutely necessary by military operations." In *In re von Manstein (1949) 16 A.D. 509* the Judge Advocate stated (the British Military Court not delivering a reasoned judgment): "Once the usages of war have assumed the status of laws they cannot be overriden by necessity, except in those special cases where the law itself makes provision for the eventuality. Reference to the preamble to the 4th Hague Convention makes this abundantly clear. . . . In other words, the rules themselves have already made allowance for military necessity." "**[H]umanitarian law** in armed conflicts is a compromise between military and humanitarian requirements. Its rules comply with both military necessity and the dictate of humanity. Considerations of military necessity cannot, therefore, justify departing from the rules of humanitarian law in armed conflict to seek a military advantage using forbidden means." Greenwood, *The Handbook of Humanitarian Law in Armed Conflict* (ed. Fleck, 1995), 32. Cf. **necessity**.

military objectives   This term is defined in art. 52(2) of Protocol 1 Additional to the Geneva Conventions of 12 August 1949, and Relating to the Protection of Victims of International Armed Conflicts, of 10 June 1977 *(1125 U.N.T.S. 3)* as "limited to those objects which by their nature, location, purpose or use make an effective contribution to military action and whose total or partial destruction, capture or neutralization, in the circumstances ruling at the time, offers a definite military advantage." If an object "normally dedicated to civilian purposes . . . is being used to make an effective contribution to military action, it shall be presumed not to be so used" (art. 52(3)). In terms of art. 52(2) attacks are "limited strictly to military objectives." It is specifically provided that civilian objects, i.e. "all objects that are not military objectives," shall not be "the object of attack or reprisals" (art. 52(1)). The Protocol contains provisions protecting cultural objects and places of worship (art. 53), objects indispensable to the survival of the civilian population (art. 54), the natural environment (art. 55), and works and installations containing dangerous forces (art. 56). "Much controversy has arisen concerning attacks on 'dual use' objects used by both civilians and the military . Whether a dual use object is a military objective depends upon whether its military use is sufficient to bring it within the test laid down in Article 52(2)": Greenwood, The Law of War (International Humanitarian Law), in *International Law* (ed. Evans, 2003), 798.

military occupation   *See* **belligerent occupation**.

Military Staff Committee Art. 47 of the UN Charter required the establishment of a Military Staff Committee, consisting of the Chiefs of Staff of the permanent members of the Security Council, "to advise and assist the Security Council on all questions relating to [its] military requirements for the maintenance of international peace and security, the employment and command of forces placed at its disposal, the regulation of armament and possible disarmament" (art. 47(1)). The Committee was also responsible "under the Security Council for the strategic direction of any armed forces placed at the disposal of the Security Council" (art. 47(3)). "The only task the Military Staff Committee has undertaken has been the preparation for the Security Council of a report on the 'General Principles Governing the Organization of the Armed Forces Made Available to the Security Council by Member Nations of the United Nations.' . . . [T]his report revealed a fundamental disagreement among the members of the Committee. Following the failure to break this deadlock, the Military Staff Committee, for all practical purposes ceased to function": Goodrich, Hambro and Simons, *Charter of the United Nations* (3rd ed.) 332; *see also* 319-24.

Millennium Declaration The United Nations Millennium Declaration was adopted by the General Assembly on 18 September 2000 as GA Res. 55/2. Part I (arts. 1-7) enunciated Values and Principles, among which are six fundamental values for the 21st century: freedom, equality, solidarity, tolerance, respect for nature and shared responsibility (art. 6). Thereafter, Part II (arts. 8-10) deals with peace, security and disarmament, Part III (arts. 11-20) with development and poverty eradication, Part IV (arts. 21-3) with protecting our common environment, Part V (arts. 24-5), Part VI (art. 26) with protecting the vulnerable, Part VI (arts. 27-8) with meeting the special needs of Africa and Part VII (arts. 29-32) with strengthening the UN. Progress towards the goals set out in the Declaration are to be regularly reported to the General Assembly (art. 31); see the Secretary-General's Report on the Implementation of the United Nations Millennium Declaration of 2 September 2003 *(UN Doc. A/58/323)*. The Declaration concludes (in art. 32) with a reaffirmation that "the United Nations is indispensable common house of the entire human family, through which we will seek to realize our universal aspirations for peace, cooperation and development." *See also* **Multilateral Treaty Framework**.

Miller, David Hunter 1875-1961. American lawyer and civil servant. Principal works include *Drafting of the Covenant* (1921); *Treaties and other International Acts of the United States of America* (8 vols. 1934-47).

mines (in naval warfare) Because of the wide-scale use of contact mines by the belligerents in the Russo-Japanese war of 1904, the Second Hague Peace Conference sought to regulate such use in the Hague Convention Relative to the Laying of Automatic Submarine Contact Mines 1907 (Convention VIII: *205 C.T.S. 331*). The Convention reflected a compromise between the British demands for a prohibition on the use of unanchored mines and of mines except in the territorial waters of a belligerent or of his enemy within ten miles of a military port, and the German insistence for a greater latitude in mine-laying (discussed, *II Oppenheim 471-493*; Colombos, *International Law of the Sea* (6th ed.), 531-3); and the resultant Convention has been described as "emasculated" (Westlake, *International Law,* vol. II, (1913), 314). It prohibited the laying of anchored contact mines which do not become harmless (a) one hour after those who laid them have lost control over them, and (b) as soon as they have broken free from their moorings (art. 1); and further prohibited the placing of such mines "before the coasts and ports of the enemy with the sole object of intercepting commercial navigation" (art. 2). The major weakness of the Convention is contained in art. 3 which permitted belligerents discretion in safeguarding peaceful shipping and in rendering mines harmless. The Convention's provisions were disregarded by Germany in both World Wars, countered by the establishment of **war zones** and permanent mine-fields. However, in relation to the duty to take "every possible precaution . . . for the security of peaceful shipping" and "to notify danger zones as soon as military exigencies permit," Judge Schwebel in his dissenting opinion in *Military and Paramilitary Activities in and against Nicaragua 1986 I.C.J. Rep. 14* at 379 noted: "If the United States were to be justified in taking blockade-like measures against Nicaraguan ports, as by mining, it could only be so if its mining of Nicaraguan ports were publicly and officially announced by it and if international shipping were duly warned by it about the fact that mines would be or had been laid in specified waters; international shipping was not duly warned by it in a timely official manner." Art. 4 of Convention VIII permits neutral states to lay mines off their coasts, subject to the same duties placed upon belligerents and, in addition, a duty to give warning of the location of such mines. The 1980 Geneva Protocol on Prohibitions or Restrictions on the use of Mines, Booby-Traps and other Devices (*see* **Geneva Conventions**; **booby-traps**) does not apply to the use of anti-ship mines at sea or in inland waterways.

minimum standard *See* **international minimum standard**.

mining (under the high seas) While the Geneva Convention on the Continental Shelf 1958 *(499 U.N.T.S. 311)* recognizes the sovereign rights of a coastal State over its **continental shelf** and the resources thereof (art. 2), the continental shelf being defined as the "seabed and subsoil of the submarine areas . . ., to a depth of 200 metres or" to the limits of the capacity to exploit (art. 1(a)), these rights are not to "prejudice the right of the coastal State to exploit the subsoil by means of tunnelling irrespective of the depth of the water above the subsoil" (art. 7). Although the continental shelf is defined differently in art. 76 of the UN Convention on the Law of the Sea 1982 *(1833 U.N.T.S. 3)*, the provision on tunnelling remains unchanged in art. 85. For a discussion of the legal basis upon which a coastal State is entitled to mine from its land territory under the high seas, *see I Oppenheim 629-31. See also* **deep-sea mining**.

mining, deep sea-bed *See* **deep-sea mining**.

mini-States Mini-States are entities of such small size that membership in international organizations does not seem appropriate, even though they qualify as States under international law. UN Secretary-General U Thant considered that "it appears desirable that a distinction be made between the right of mini-State independence and the question of full membership in the United Nations" and he advocated "a thorough and comprehensive study": *Introduction to the Annual Report of the Secretary-General on the Work of the Organization, 22 U.N. GAOR, Supp. (No. 1A) 20*. A Committee of Experts was established by the Security Council on 29 August 1969. The Committee was unable to reach any conclusions. For an account of its work, see Gunter, The Problem of Mini-state Membership in the United Nations System, *12 Colum. J. Transnat'l L. 468 (1973)*; Gunter, What Happened to the United Nations Mini-state Problem, *71 A.J.I.L. 110 (1977)*. For an analysis of the problem of mini-States, see UNITAR, *Status and Problems of Very Small States and Territories* (1969); and UNITAR, *Small States and Territories: Status and Problems* (1971).

minorities While treaty stipulations guaranteeing certain rights to minorities date back to the time of the Reformation, the movement to protect the rights of minorities emerged as a consequence of the territorial readjustments that followed the 1914-18 War. "The Principal Allied and Associated Powers were able to stipulate by treaty with Poland, Czecho-Slovakia, the Serb-Croat-Slovene State, Romania, Greece, Austria, Bulgaria, Hungary, and Turkey, for the just and equal treatment of their racial, religious, and linguistic minorities. Subsequently, as a condition of their admission to the League of Nations, similar obligations were undertaken by Albania, Estonia, Latvia, Lithuania, and Iraq, in the form of unilateral declarations accepted and rendered obligatory by various resolutions of the Council of the League": *I Oppenheim 973*. These stipulations were to constitute fundamental law; and those stipulations in favor of minorities were to constitute obligations of international concern and could not be modified except with the assent of the Council of the League of Nations. The Council exercised a supervisory role by dealing with alleged infractions brought to its attention. See ***German Settlers in Poland Opinion (1923)*** *P.C.I.J., Ser. B, No. 6*; ***Polish Nationals in Danzig Opinion (1932)*** *P.C.I.J., Ser. A/B, No. 44*; ***Minority Schools in Albania Opinion*** *(1935) P.C.I.J., Ser A/B, No. 64*. See Macartney, *National States and National Minorities* (1933); Mair, *The Protection of Minorities* (1928); Stone, *International Guarantees of Minority Rights* (1932).

"After the Second World War the interest in the protection of particular minorities was subsumed in the increasing international concern with the protection of fundamental human rights in general." *I Oppenheim 976*. The Declaration on the Rights of Persons Belonging to National or Ethnic, Religious or Linguistic Minorities, adopted by the General Assembly on 18 December 1992 as Res. 47/135, defined minorities by implication as groups identified by their distinctive nationality, ethnicity, religion or language from the population of a State at large. While minorities so defined enjoy all universally recognized human rights (arts. 4(1) and 8), their existence and their distinctiveness are to be protected by States (art. 1(2)). Minorities have the right "to enjoy their own culture, to profess and practise their own religion, and to use their own language, in private and in public" (art. 2(1)); they have the right to participate effectively in all aspects of national and public life (art. 2(2)), including political life (art. 2(3)). Minorities are not to be discriminated against (art. 3). States are to take measures to "create favourable conditions" for minorities to express and develop their distinctive characteristics (art. 4(2)), particularly in relation to their mother tongue (art. 4(3)) and to education on their history, traditions, language and culture (art. 4(4)). *See also* the European Framework Convention for the Protection of National Minorities of 1 February 1995 *(34 I.L.M. 353 (1995))*. *See* Thornberry, *International Law and the Rights of Minorities* (1991); Dinstein and Tabory, *The Protection of Minorities and Human Rights* (1992). *See also* **indigenous peoples**.

Minorities in Upper Silesia Case See ***German Minorities in Upper Silesia, Rights of, Case***.

Minority Schools in Albania Opinion *(1935) P.C.I.J., Ser A/B, No. 64*. On 2 October 1921, Albania pursuant to a resolution of the Assembly of the League of Nations signed a declaration relating to the position of minorities in Albania. This declaration included provisions granting Albanian nationals belonging to racial, religious or linguistic minorities "the same treatment and security in law and in fact as other Albanian nationals" and in particular an equal right to maintain or establish religious and social institutions and schools. In 1933, Albania amended the Albanian constitution so as to close all private schools. Albania maintained that, as the abolition of private schools was a general measure applying to the majority as well as the minority, it was in conformity with the declaration. In response to a request from the Council of the League of Nations in January 1935 concerning the conformity of this Albanian measure with the letter and spirit of the declaration, the PCIJ in an advisory opinion expressed the view (by 8 to 3) that the Albanian argument was not well founded: to satisfy the requirement of equality in fact as well as in law minorities must be on a footing of perfect equality with other nationals and they must have available to them suitable means, which included their separate institutions, for the preservation of the traditions and characteristics of their minority group; Albanian nationals belonging to the minority groups in question thus had the right under the declaration to maintain, manage and establish their own charitable, religious, social and educational institutions, and therein freely to use their own language and exercise their religion.

Minquiers and Ecrehos Case *(France v. UK) 1953 I.C.J. Rep. 47.* The Minquiers and Ecrehos groups of islets and rocks lie between the British Channel Island of Jersey and the coast of France. Both the UK and France claimed sovereignty over the two groups, on the basis of original title going back to the 11th century and an effective display of sovereignty subsequently. By a Special Agreement in 1950 *(118 U.N.T.S. 149)* the UK and France submitted to the ICJ the question whether the sovereignty over the islets and rocks (insofar as they were capable of appropriation) of the Minquiers and Ecrehos groups respectively belonged to the UK or to France. *Held* (unanimously) that the evidence prior to the 19th century was for the most part inconclusive or ambiguous as regards sovereignty, but particular probative value attached to the acts which related to the exercise of jurisdiction and local administration and to legislation; that as regards the Ecrehos group, it was at the beginning of the 13th century considered and treated as an integral part of the fief of the Channel Islands which were held by the King of England, and continued to be under the dominion of that King, who in the beginning of the 14th century exercised jurisdiction in respect thereto, while during the 19th century and in the 20th century the British authorities had exercised State functions in respect of the group; France, on the other hand, had not produced evidence showing that it had any valid title to the group; that as regards the Minquiers group, it was in the beginning of the 17th century treated as a part of the fief of Normont in Jersey and the British authorities during a considerable part of the 19th century and in the 20th century had exercised State functions in respect of the group, whereas France had not established any valid title to the group; and that accordingly the sovereignty over the Minquiers and Ecrehos groups belonged to the UK.

mistake *See* **error**.

mob violence "The principles governing the responsibility of the State for injuries sustained by aliens as a result of mob violence are closely related to those governing its responsibility for injuries committed by individuals. In all parts of the world it occasionally happens that mobs in sudden outbursts of passion sweep away all restraint and vent their fury upon aliens. . . . In such cases, if the authorities have used some diligence to prevent or repress the riot and punish those who may be concerned in it, the government is relieved from legal liability, unless it is under special obligations to render protection, either by virtue of a treaty or of the official character of the person asailed": Borchard, *The Diplomatic Protection of Citizens Abroad or the Law of International Claims* (1915), 220-1. *See also* the **United States Diplomatic and Consular Staff in Tehran Case** *1980 I.C.J. Rep. 3* in which the International Court of Justice found that "no suggestion has been made that the militants, when they executed their attack on the [U.S.] Embassy, had any form of official status as recognized 'agents' or organs of the Iranian State. Their conduct in mounting the attack, overrunning the Embassy and seizing its inmates as hostages cannot, therefore, be regarded as imputable to that State on that basis" (para. 58). However, Iran was found to be responsible for failing to take appropriate steps to protect the **inviolability** of the premises, staff and archives of the US mission as required in terms of both the Vienna Convention on Diplomatic Relations 1961 *(500 U.N.T.S. 95)* and the Vienna Convention on Consular Relations 1963 *(596 U.N.T.S. 261)*.

Mob violence must be distinguished from organized **insurgency**; the ILC's Draft Articles on the Responsibility of States for Internationally Wrongful Acts 2001 *(UN Doc. A/56/10 Chap.IV.E.1)* provide that the conduct of an organ of an insurrectional movement will be considered as an act of that State under international law where the movement becomes the new government of that State (art. 10(1)), or where the movement succeeds in establishing a new State in part of the territory of an existing State in which case it will be considered as an act of that new State (art. 10(2)).

modern international law   This term is often used to describe the change in international law from a system of rules governing relationships between States (sometimes called classical or traditional international law) to one concerned also and increasingly with rules relating to, and guidelines or recommendations emanating from, international organizations, and also concerned with the protection of human rights, social development, and other matters of concern to the international community. In his separate opinion in the *Anglo-Norwegian Fisheries Case 1951 I.C.J. Rep. 116* at 148-9, Judge Alvarez considered that the traditional means by which the "juridical conscience of peoples" could be reflected in international law (treaties, custom and writings) were too slow in rapidly-changing times, and said: "The further means by which the juridical conscience of peoples may be expressed at the present time are the resolutions of diplomatic assemblies, particularly those of the United Nations and especially the decisions of the International Court of Justice. Reference must also be made to the recent legislation of certain countries, the resolutions of the great associations devoted to the study of the law of nations, the work of the Codification Commission set up by the United Nations, and finally, the opinions of qualified jurists. These are the new elements on which the new international law, still in the process of formation, will be founded. This law will, consequently, have a character entirely different from that of traditional or classical international law, which has prevailed to the present time." *See* Friedmann, *The Changing Structure of International Law* (1964).

modification (of treaty)   While it is a cardinal principal of the law of treaties that the terms of a treaty must be performed by the parties (*pacta sunt servanda*: art. 26 of the Vienna Convention on the Law of Treaties 1969), the terms of a multilateral treaty may be modified by agreement of two or more of the parties provided that such a possibility is contemplated in the treaty or the modification is not prohibited and neither affects the enjoyment of treaty rights by other States parties nor relates to a provision, derogation from which is incompatible with the effective execution of the object and purpose of the treaty (art. 41(1)). See, for example, the Agreement Relating to the Implementation of Part XI of the United Nations Convention on the Law of the Sea 1994 *(33 I.L.M. 1309 (1994)*. "[A]lthough the Agreement is not cast formally as an amending instrument, in practice that is exactly what it has achieved. The entry into force of the 1994 Agreement has modified substantially the provisions of Part XI of the [1982 UN] Convention [on the Law of the Sea]. The Agreement is to be regarded as an integral part of the Convention and the two instruments are to be interpreted and applied as one, the Agreement prevailing in cases of conflict." Dixon, *Textbook on International Law* (4th ed.) 218. A bilateral treaty may be modified by agreement between the parties at any time (cf. art. 39 of the Vienna Convention).

modus vivendi   "This is the title given to a temporary or provisional agreement, usually intended to be replaced later on, if circumstances permit, by one of a more permanent and detailed character. It may not, however, always be designated as such: more often than not, what is in substance a *modus vivendi* may be designated as a 'temporary agreement' or an 'interim agreement.' An example of a treaty which is in fact formally designated as a *modus vivendi* is the Modus Vivendi between the Belgo-Luxemburg Economic Union and

Turkey relating to the application of Most-Favoured National Treatment, signed at Ankara on 12 March 1947 *[37 U.N.T.S. 223]*. . . . Another example is the Temporary Commercial Agreement between the United Kingdom Government and the Government of the Union of Soviet Socialist Republics signed at London on 16 April 1930 *[101 L.N.T.S. 409]*. . . . A more recent example of what is in substance a *modus vivendi* (although not so designated) is the Exchange of Notes of 13 November 1973, constituting an Interim Agreement in the Fisheries Dispute between the United Kingdom and the Icelandic Government. . . . The agreement was to run for two years from the date of the Exchange of Notes, and it is specifically provided (in paragraph 3) that 'its termination will not affect the legal position of either Government with respect to the substantive dispute.' . . . In its judgment on the merits of the **Fisheries Jurisdiction Case**, the [International] Court [of Justice] states the following: 'The interim agreement of 1973 . . . does not describe itself as a "settlement" of the dispute and, apart from being of limited duration, clearly possesses the character of a provisional arrangement. . . .' *[1974 I.C.J. Rep. 3 at 18]*": *Satow's Guide to Diplomatic Practice* (5th ed.), 262-3.

Monaco Describing Monaco as a former European **protectorate**, *I Oppenheim 271n* states: "The Principality of Monaco, which was under the protectorate of Spain from 1523 to 1641, afterwards of France until 1814, and then of Sardinia, became through **desuetude** a full sovereign State, since Italy never exercised the protectorate. The present status of Monaco is not easy to classify. By a treaty of July 17, 1918, between France and Monaco, France, 'assure à la principauté de Monaco la défense de son indépendence et de sa souveraineté, et garantit l'intégrité de son territoire' *[111 B.F.S.P. 727]*. . . . Monaco agreed that her international relations should always be the object 'd'une entente préalable' between the two Governments, and that in the event of a vacancy in the Crown of Monaco 'notamment faute d'héritier direct ou adoptif' the territory of Monaco would form, under the protectorate of France, an autonomous State. (This treaty is recognized by the parties to the Treaty of Peace with Germany of 1919: see Article 436). Until that event happens, it seems preferable to regard Monaco as an independent State in close alliance with France."

As a consequence of Monaco not possessing full capacity to enter into foreign relations, another commentator has opined that it cannot be regarded as a fully sovereign independent State: Mugerwa, Subjects of International Law, in Sørensen, *Manual of Public International Law* (1968), 247 at 262. Prior to becoming a member of the United Nations, Monaco maintained a permanent observer to the Organization, and was a member of a number of **Specialized Agencies**, including UNESCO, the World Health Organization, the Universal Postal Union and the International Telecommunication Union. Monaco was admitted to full membership of the United Nations in 1993.

Monetary Gold Case *(Italy v. France, UK and USA) 1954 I.C.J. Rep. 19.* Part III of the Agreement on Reparation from Germany, on the Establishment of an Inter-Allied Reparation Agency and on the Restitution of Monetary Gold, signed on 14 January 1946, made provision for the restitution of monetary gold found in Germany or other countries. Implementation of Part III was entrusted to France, UK and USA. Albania, on the basis of Part III, claimed certain gold of the National Bank of Albania: Italy also laid claim to the gold. France, UK and USA by an Agreement signed at Washington on 25 April 1951 *(91 U.N.T.S. 21)* referred the question of the ownership of the gold to an arbitrator, who found that, within the meaning of Part III, it belonged to Albania. The three governments had, at the time of the Washington Agreement, issued a Statement recording their decision that if the arbitrator reached that conclusion, the gold would be delivered to the UK in partial satisfaction of the Judgment of the ICJ in the ***Corfu Channel Case*** unless within 90 days either Albania or Italy made an application to the Court for determinations as to the appropriate destination of the gold. Italy (but not Albania) made an application to the Court, formulating two claims to the gold: but Italy then raised as a preliminary objection the question whether the Court had jurisdiction to deal with the first of those claims in the absence of Albania. *Held* (unanimously) that the Court was validly seized of the Italian application since, notwithstanding that Italy had accepted the jurisdiction of the Court and had filed an application, in the circumstances of the case Italy was not prevented from raising a preliminary objection as to the Court's jurisdiction, and had not thereby ceased to act in conformity with the terms of the Washington Statement or in effect withdraw its application; that, since Italy's first claim to the gold depended on Albania being found to have committed an international wrong against Italy, the Court could not decide the matter in the absence of Albania; and (13 to 1) that, since Italy's second claim to the gold concerned the question of priority between the claims of Italy and the UK, it was dependent upon the outcome of the first claim and the Court must therefore refrain from examining it.

monetary unit of account *See* **unit of account**.

monism "The opposing school of legal thought [to the **dualists**], commonly referred to as the 'monists,' affirm . . . that there is no real difference between international and domestic law, that they really represent two manifestations of one and the same conception of law. It maintains that there exists a single legal order in which all norms (principles, rules) exist in the form of a hierarchy in which, according to such writers as Max Wenzel and Albert Lorn, domestic law occupies the higher rank. **Kelsen** and his followers, on the other hand, have asserted with much vigour that international law merited the higher position and thus could be held to limit national authority from international law": von Glahn, *Law Among Nations* (2nd ed.), 6. "Since international law can thus be seen as essentially part of the same legal order as municipal law, and as superior to it, it can be regarded as incorporated in municipal law, giving rise to no difficulty in principle in its application as international law within states." *I Oppenheim, 54.*

Monroe Doctrine This doctrine was contained in President James Monroe's Message to Congress on 2 December 1823 *(Foreign Relations, Vol. V, 246)*: "We owe it, therefore, to candor, and to the amicable relations existing between the United States and those European, former colonial powers, to declare that we should consider any attempt on their part to extend their system to any portion of this hemisphere as dangerous to our peace and safety." The Doctrine was recognized by art. 21 of the Covenant of the League of Nations, which provides that "[n]othing in this Covenant shall be deemed to affect the validity of international engagements, such as . . . regional understandings like the Monroe Doctrine, for securing the maintenance of peace." *See* Moore, *The Monroe Doctrine* (1895); Hart, *The Monroe Doctrine* (1915); Perkins, *The Monroe Doctrine 1823-1907* (3 vols. 1927-37). "The so-called Roosevelt Corollary, enunciated by President Theodore Roosevelt in 1904, seemed to be an extension of the doctrine presaging claims by the USA to the right of intervention in the affairs of Latin American states. In 1923 Secretary of State Hughes formally stated that the US had no such intention, and in 1930 was published a memorandum previously prepared by Under-Secretary J. Reuben Clark, stating that the Corollary was not justified by the terms of the Monroe Doctrine": *Satow's Guide to Diplomatic Practice* (5th ed.) 519 n. 57. The relevance of the Monroe Doctrine to modern American practice is open to question, given that it was not invoked to justify the US intervention in Grenada in 1983. Cf. **Brezhnev Doctrine**.

Montevideo Convention 1933 The most famous Montevideo Convention is the Convention on the Rights and Duties of States, adopted by the Seventh International Conference of American States at Montevideo on 26 December 1933 *(165 L.N.T.S. 19)*. The Convention provides what is generally regarded as the standard definition of a **State** (art. 1); and declares that the "political existence of the State is independent of recognition by other States" (art. 3; on recognition, *see also* arts. 6-7). All States are declared juridically equal (art. 4), and no State may intervene in the internal or external affairs of another (art. 8). The jurisdiction of States within their territorial limits applies to all the inhabitants, national and alien (art. 9). The contracting States established an obligation "not to recognize territorial acquisitions or special advantages which have been made by force," and the territory of a State is expressed to be "inviolable" (art. 11). Other Montevideo Conventions, of more regional interest, are the Convention on Extradition 1933 *(181 L.N.T.S. 444)* and the Convention on Political Asylum and Refuge 1939 *(*Hudson, *8 Int. Leg., 404)*.

Montevideo Declaration on the Law of the Sea 1970   This declaration, signed by Argentina, Brazil, Chile, Ecuador, El Salvador, Panama, Peru, Nicaragua and Uruguay on 8 May 1970 *((1970) 9 I.L.M. 1081)*, and adhered to by Columbia, the Dominican Republic, Guatemala, Honduras and Mexico on 8 August 1970, stated the principles recognized by those States in the emerging law of the sea, and constituted mutual recognition of the resource zones of 200 miles claimed by all of them. This declaration is based on the "ties of geographic, economic and social nature . . . from which there arises a legitimate priority in favor of littoral peoples to benefit from the natural resources" and "the geographic realities of coastal States and . . . the special economic and social requirements of the less developed States." *See* Szekely, *Latin America and the Development of the Law of the Sea* (1977), vol. 1. The Declaration formed the basis of claims by Latin-American and other states to a 200-mile resources jurisdiction for all sea and seabed resources which led ultimately to the development of the Exclusive Economic Zone at the Third United Nations Conference on the Law of the Sea. *See* United Nations Convention on the Law of the Sea 1982 *(1833 U.N.T.S. 3)*, Part V.

Montreal Convention 1971   The Convention for the Suppression of Unlawful Acts Against the Safety of Civil Aviation (the Sabotage Convention) was signed at Montreal on 23 September 1971 *(974 U.N.T.S. 177)* and came into force on 26 January 1973. It is the third Convention, after the **Tokyo Convention** on Offences and Certain Other Acts Committed on Board Aircraft of 14 September 1963 *(704 U.N.T.S. 219)* and the Hague Convention for the Suppression of Unlawful Seizure of Aircraft of 16 December 1970 *(869 U.N.T.S. 105)*, to address the issue of aircraft **hijacking** and other illegal acts concerning air transport. The Convention is directed against the sabotage of aircraft, and requires the Contracting States to make specified offences "punishable by severe penalties" (art. 3; the offences are in art. 1). Each Contracting State has jurisdiction when one of the offences is committed in its territory, against or on board an aircraft registered in that State, when the aircraft lands in its territory, or against an aircraft the lessee of which has his principal place of business or permanent residence in the State (art. 5). Each Contracting State is required to prosecute an offender, or to extradite him (art. 7). The Convention declares the specified offences to be extraditable offences under existing extradition treaties (art. 8(1)); if there is no extradition treaty, the Convention itself may be treated as such (art. 8(2)). *See* Abramovsky, Multilateral Conventions for the Suppression of Unlawful Seizures and Interference with Aircraft. Part II: The Montreal Convention, *14 Colum. J. Transnat'l L. 298 (1975)*.

On 3 March 1992, Libya initiated proceedings against the United Kingdom and the United States of America in respect of disputes concerning the interpretation and application of the 1971 Convention arising from the aerial incident at Lockerbie. After the United Kingdom and United States raised preliminary objections to the jurisdiction of the Court and the admissibility of the applications, the Court, in two separate judgements of 27 February 1998, found that there existed a dispute between the parties, that the Court had jurisdiction to hear the case and that the Libyan application was admissible: see *Lockerbie Cases*. By two letters of 9 September 2003, the Governments of Libya and the United Kingdom on the one hand, and of Libya and the United States on the other, notified the Court that they had agreed to "discontinue with prejudice the proceedings." By order of 10 September 2003, the President of the Court directed the removal of the case from the Court's list.

Montreux Convention *See* **Lausanne, Treaty of.**

Moon Treaty Property styled the Agreement Governing the Activities of States on the Moon and other Celestial Bodies, this treaty was adopted on 18 December 1979 *(18 I.L.M. 1434 (1979))*. The Moon Treaty applies to celestial bodies, other than the Earth, and to Moon orbits and trajectories (art. 1). To be used only for peaceful purposes (art. 3), exploration and use of the Moon is to be the province of all mankind and is to be carried out for the benefit and in the interests of all countries (art. 4). The moon and its natural resources are the common heritage of mankind (art. 11). Freedom of scientific investigation is specifically guaranteed in art. 6(1). Art. 5 imposes a duty to report to the UN Secretary-General activities and discoveries to the "greatest extent feasible and practicable." The Moon is not open to national appropriation in whole or in part (art. 11(2)(3)), though samples may be taken (art. 6(2)), landings made, bases constructed and movement of equipment occur (arts. 8 and 9), subject to a duty not to disrupt the Moon environment (art. 7). Parties retain jurisdiction over facilities and personnel (art. 12), with a duty to comply with international law (art. 2) and to accept international responsibility for their actions (art. 14). As in the **Antarctic Treaty**, inspection of the installations of other Parties may occur (art. 15). There is a duty to assist others (art. 10), and to inform the launch State and the Secretary-General of any crash or otherwise unintended landing of a vehicle belonging to another party (art. 13). "Several points are worth noting. First, the proposed international regime is only to be established when exploitation becomes feasible. Second, it appears that until the regime is set up, there is a moratorium on exploitation, although not on 'exploration and use'. . . . Thirdly it is to be noted that private ownership rights of minerals in natural resources not in place are permissible under the Treaty": Shaw, *International* Law (4th ed. 1997), 386. *See* **Outer Space Treaty**. *See also* Jasentulajana and Lee, *Manual on Space Law* (4 vols., 1979); Christol, *Space Law* (1991).

Moore, John Bassett 1860-1947. US State Department official, law professor (Columbia) and judge, PCIJ 1921-1927. The major works of this prodigious scholar include: *History and Digest of the International Adjudications to which the Unites States has been a Party* (6 vols. 1898); *Digest of International Law* (8 vols. 1906); *International Adjudications, Ancient and Modern* (8 vols. 1937); *The Permanent Court of International Justice* (1924); *The Collected Papers of John Bassett Moore* (7 vols. 1945).

Moore, John Norton 1937- . Professor, Virginia 1969- . Principal works include *Law and the Indo-China Conflict* (1972); *Law and Civil War in the Modern World* (1975); *The Arab-Israeli Conflict Vols. I-III* (1975) *Vol. IV* (1991); *The Secret War in Central America* (1986); *National Security Law* (with others) (1990); *Crisis in the Gulf* (1992); *Treaty Interpretation, The Constitution and The Rule of Law* (2001); *The National Law of Treaty Implementation* (2001); *Current Marine Environmental Issues and the International Tribunal for the Law of the Sea* (with Nordquist 2001); *The Real Lessons of the Vietnam War: Reflections Twenty-Five Years After the Fall of Saigon* (2002).

Morelli, Gaetano 1900-89. Professor of law at Modena, Padua, Naples and Rome. Sometime member, PCA; Member, ICJ 1961-70. Principal works include *La sentenza internazionale* (1931); *Nozioni di diritto internazionale* (5th ed. 1958); *Lezioni di diritto privato* (2nd ed. 1943); *Elementi di diritto internazionale privato italiano* (6th ed. 1959); *Studi di diritto processuale civile internazionale* (1961).

Moreno Quintana, Lucio Manuel University teacher in Argentina, and diplomat. Member, PCA 1945-55; judge, ICJ 1955-64. Principal works include *Immigration* (1920); *The American International System* (1925-7); *Public International Law* (with Bollini Shaw 1950); *Right of Asylum* (1952); *Preliminaries of International Law* (1954); *Elements of International Policy* (1955); *Treatise on International Law* (1963).

Morgenthau, Hans J. 1904-1980. German lawyer and teacher 1927-33, who taught in Geneva and Madrid before emigrating to the US in 1937 and becoming a leading proponent of the realist school of international relations theory. Principal works include *Politics Among Nations* (1948; 5th ed. 1973); *In Defense of National Interest* (1951); *A New Foreign Policy for the United States* (1969); *Truth and Power* (1970). *See also* Frei, *Hans J. Morgenthau. An Intellectual Biography* (2001).

Morocco, Rights of US Nationals in, Case *See* **Rights of US Nationals in Morocco Case**.

Mosler, Hermann Professor, Bonn 1946-9. Frankfurt-am-Main 1949-51. Head, Legal Department, Ministry of Foreign Affairs 1951-3. Professor, Heidelberg; Director, Max Planck Institute 1954-76. Member, PCA and ICJ. Editor (with Bernhardt) of *Judicial Settlement of International Disputes: International Court, Other Courts and Tribunals, Arbitration and Conciliation* (1974).

most-favored-nation clause/treatment "An embryonic version of the MFN clause has been traced as far back as 1417, but the origins of the Most-Favored-Nation commitment in international commercial matters are generally considered to stem mainly from the Seventeenth and Eighteenth Centuries. Prior to that time, special trade concessions and monopolies seemed to be the general order of the day but, as states negotiated for protection abroad for their traders, MFN became a convenient shorthand to incorporate by reference the advantages previously granted in other treaties": Jackson, *World Trade and the Law of GATT* (1969), 250-1. A general MFN clause is the basis of the General Agreement on Tariffs and Trade, art. I of which provides that in all restrictions and procedures on international trade "any advantage, favor, privilege or immunity granted by any contracting party to any product originating in or destined for any other country shall be accorded immediately and unconditionally to the like product originating in or destined for the territories of all other contracting parties" *(55 U.N.T.S. 187)*. MFN is also a priority in the General Agreement on Trade in Services 1994 (GATS) (art. 2), and the Agreement on Trade-Related Aspects of Intellectual Property Rights 1994 (TRIPS) which since 1994, together with the GATT (as amended by GATT 1994), combine to form the core legal framework of the **World Trade Organization**. MFN treatment is also commonly stipulated for in bilateral commercial agreements. See the ILC draft articles on the MFN Clause *([1976] II (2) I.L.C. Yearbook 11)* and the commentary thereon by special *rapporteur* Ushakov *([1978] II (1) I.L.C. Yearbook 1)*. However, no substantive action has yet been taken on these Draft Articles: "The General Assembly has in effect repeatedly deferred action [on the Draft Articles] while making a series of requests for comments on the Commission's draft. See GA Res 33/139 (1978), 35/161 (1980), 36/111 (1981) and 40/65 (1985) and Decision 43/429 (1988) [as well as GA Res 46/416 (1991)]" *I Oppenheim 108 n 43*. Cf. **pref-**

erential treatment. See Trebilcock and Howse, *The Regulation of International Trade* (2nd ed.).

Mosul Boundary Case *(Interpretation of Article 3(2) of the Treaty of Lausanne) (1923) (1925) P.C.I.J., Ser. B, No. 12*. At the end of the 1914-18 war, Great Britain was allotted a mandate for what became Iraq and it was necessary, in the peace treaty with Turkey, to establish the frontier between Turkey and Iraq. This proved difficult, particularly as regards the Mosul area, and as a result art. 3(2) of the Treaty of Lausanne 1923 *(28 L.N.T.S. 13)* provided that the frontier would be laid down by Turkey and Great Britain within nine months of its entry into force, and that, in the absence of agreement, the dispute would be referred to the Council of the League of Nations. In the event, no agreement could be reached and Great Britain referred the question to the Council which, in 1925, sought an advisory opinion from the PCIJ on the nature of the Council's role in the matter and the procedure to be followed. The Court *advised* that, by art. 3(2) of the Treaty of Lausanne, the parties intended to provide for a definitive settlement of the frontier by way of a decision of the Council which, while not constituting a tribunal of arbitrators, was capable by the mutual consent of the parties of giving a decision binding on them; and that, consistently with the Covenant, the Council's decision required unanimity, although the votes of the parties should not be counted in ascertaining whether there was unanimity.

Mouton, Martinus Willem 1901-1968. Dutch legal adviser and teacher. Titular naval rank of Rear Admiral (Schout bij nacht). Principal works include *Oorlogsmisdrijven en het Internationale Recht* (1947); *The Continental Shelf* (1952).

multilateral Literally, on many sides, parts. In relation to treaties and negotiations, multilateral (or multipartite) therefore connotes the involvement of many States in the process. Cf. **bilateral**. *See also* ***traité-lois***; ***traité-contrat***.

Multilateral Investment Guarantee Agency (MIGA) Created within the World Bank Group by the Convention Establishing the Multilateral Investment Guarantee Agency of 11 October 1985 *(24 I.L.M. 270 (1985))*, MIGA's purpose is "to promote economic development, increase productivity and thus raise standards of living in the less-developed areas of the world included within the Association's membership, in particular by providing finance to meet their important developmental requirements on terms which are more flexible and bear less heavily on the balance of payments than those of conventional loans, thereby furthering the developmental objectives of the International Bank for Reconstruction and Development . . . and supplementing its activities" (art. 2). With 161 member States, MIGA, as its name suggests, guarantees investments through the conclusion of contracts of reinsurance in respect of specific investments (Chap. 111). Its structure consists of a Council of Governors, a Board of Directors and a President (Chap. V). *See* Shihata, *MIGA and Foreign Investment—The Origins, Operations, Policies and Basic Documents of the Multilateral Investment Guarantee Agency* (1988). *See* <www.miga.org>.

Multilateral Treaty Framework As an emanation from art. 9 of the **Millennium Declaration** of 18 September 2000 (GA Res. 55/2; *see also* GA Res. 67/175), the UN has instituted an annual emphasis (or focus) on specific areas covered by treaties, inviting States to sign, ratify or acceded to the relevant instruments and to implement those instruments to which they are parties, and involving also major UN activity, particularly a debate in the General Assembly and conferences, in these areas (referred to as treaty events). Focus 2001 concerned the Rights of Women and Children; Focus 2002, Sustainable Development; Focus 2003, Treaties Against Transnational Organized Crime and Terrorism.

multinational corporations "The multinational enterprise or corporation (sometimes referred to as a transnational or global corporation) is an established feature of international economic life, but it has not yet achieved special status in international law or in national legal systems. A multinational corporation generally consists of a group of corporations, each established under the law of some state, linked by common managerial and financial control and pursuing integrated policies": *Restatement, Third, of the Foreign Relations Law of the United States*, 126. While this statement remains generally true today, multinational corporations are increasingly being considered as potential subjects of international law, or at least as participants in the international legal system (*see* Higgins, *Problems and Process: International Law and How We Use It* (1994), Chap. 3). Nevertheless, corporations, like individuals, lack procedural capacity in international law. See, for example, the **Barcelona Traction Case** in which the ICJ held that it was the State of incorporation which could bring a claim and not the State of residence of the majority of the shareholders. This may well prove problematic for multinational corporations established in a number of jurisdictions. *See* Charney, Transnational Corporations and Developing Public International Law, *Duke L. J. 748 (1983).*

multipartite *See* **multilateral**.

municipal law The law applying within States, as opposed to international law, the law applying between States and other subjects of international law. As to the differences between municipal law (sometimes called domestic law) and international law, *see I Oppenheim 53-4*.

municipal court (or tribunal) A State or national or domestic court or tribunal, whose decisions may be a subsidiary means of determining rules of international law under art. 38(1)(d) of the ICJ Statute, as a statement of what a rule is considered to be; or as evidence of State practice or *opinio juris*; or as a **general principle of law** recognized by States under art. 38(1)(c) of the ICJ Statute. *See* Parry, *The Sources and Evidences of International Law* (1965), 10-13, 94-103.

Muscat Dhows Arbitration *(UK v France) (1905) 6 R.I.A.A. 92.* France and Britain having in 1862 undertaken to respect the independence of the Sultan of Muscat, differences arose between them over the bearing of this undertaking on the authorization given by France to certain Muscat subjects to fly the French flag on their vessels (dhows) and on the privileges and immunities enjoyed by owners, captains and crews, and their families, of such vessels. Britain and France agreed in 1904 to refer the matter to arbitration. *Held* that (1) although it was in general for France to decide who should be allowed to fly the French flag, and to lay down the rules therefor, so that for France to allow Muscat subjects to fly the French flag did not infringe the Sultan's independence, this right was limited by the Brussels General Act for the Suppression of the Slave Trade 1890, after which France, in accordance with its obligations under the General Act, could only grant Muscat subjects the right to fly the French flag in the case of owners who had been "protégés" of France; and (2) Muscat dhows authorized to fly the French flag were, in Muscat territorial waters, inviolable under the France-Muscat Treaty of Friendship and Commerce 1844, but their owners, captains, crews, and their families, did not thereby enjoy any extra-territoriality exempting them from the sovereignty or jurisdiction of the Sultan.

Mutual and Balanced Force Reductions *See* **MBFR**.

N

NAFTA *See* **North American Free Trade Area.**

Namibia Advisory Opinion *1971 I.C.J. Rep. 16.* South Africa had been granted a Mandate for South West Africa (re-named Namibia in 1968). In Res. 2145 (XXI) (1966), the UN General Assembly decided that the Mandate was terminated and that South Africa had no other right to administer the territory; subsequently the Security Council adopted various resolutions, including in particular Res. 276 (1970) declaring the continued presence of South Africa in Namibia illegal. On 29 July 1970, the Security Council, in Res. 284, requested an advisory opinion on "the legal consequences for States of the continued presence of South Africa in Namibia, notwithstanding Security Council resolution 276 (1970)." The Court *advised* (13 to 2) that South Africa was obliged to withdraw its administration from Namibia immediately and put an end to its occupation of the territory, and (11 to 4) that members of the UN were obliged to recognize the illegality of South Africa's presence in Namibia and the invalidity of its acts on behalf of or concerning Namibia and to refrain from any acts and dealings with South Africa implying recognition of the legality of, or lending support or assistance to, such presence and administration, and that it was incumbent on non-members of the UN to assist in the action which had been taken by the UN with regard to Namibia.

In the course of formulating its opinion, the Court found that (i) despite the abstention of two permanent members of the Security Council during the vote on Res. 284 (1970), for a long time the voluntary abstention of a permanent member had consistently been interpreted as not preventing the adoption of resolutions by the Security Council; (ii) as the question of Namibia had been placed on the Council's agenda as a "situation" and not a "dispute," non-observance of Charter provisions relating to participation in Security Council discussions in cases involving disputes did not invalidate Res. 276 (1970); (iii) as the Court had been asked to deal with a request put forward by a UN organ seeking legal advice on the consequences of its own decision, and as the request did not relate to a legal dispute actually pending between States nor a dispute between South Africa and the UN, it was not one on which the Court should decline to give an opinion; (iv) in view of South Africa's material breach of its international obligations under the Mandate, General Assembly Res. 2145 (XXI) and Security Council Res. 276 (1970) had been validly adopted by the UN organs having competence in the matter as successor to the League of Nations in exercise of its supervisory role in relation to Mandates; (v) under art. 25 of the Charter, member States were obliged to comply with Security Council decisions even if they had voted against them in the Council or were not members of the Council; (vi) a binding determination made by a competent organ of the UN to the effect that a situation was illegal could not remain without consequences; (vii) accordingly, South Africa, being responsible for having created and maintained that situation, was obliged to put an end to it and withdraw its administration from the territory and, by occupying the territory without title, incurred international responsibilities arising from a continuing violation of an international obligation, and furthermore remained accountable for any violations of the rights of the people of Namibia or of its obligations under international law towards other States in respect of the exercise of its powers in relation to the territory; (viii) members of the UN were obliged to recognize the illegality and invalidity of South Africa's continued presence in Namibia and to refrain from lending any support or assistance to South Africa with reference to its occupation of Namibia; (ix) while the precise determination of the acts permitted was a matter which lay within the competence of the appropriate political organs of the UN, the Court indicated certain dealings with South Africa which, under the Charter and general international law, should be considered as inconsistent with Res. 276 (1970) in such fields as treaty relations, diplomatic or consular relations and economic and other relations with South Africa on behalf of or concerning Namibia; (x) as to non-members of the UN, the termination of the Mandate and the declaration of the illegality of South Africa's presence in Namibia were opposable to all States in the sense of barring *erga omnes* the legality of the situation which was maintained in violation of international law. *See also **South West Africa Cases**.*

Nanni v. Pace and the Sovereign Order of Malta *(1935) 8 I.L.R. 2.* In 1863, a church was endowed for the maintenance of an incumbency to descend, eventually, to the Sovereign Order of Malta; the Order was to approve each candidate for the incumbency. In granting investiture of the benefice to Giuseppe Pace in 1923, the Order required him to recover part of the church's land which had previously been sold by his father. In the ensuing litigation, it was argued that, as the Order was a religious institution, the original gift or endowment in favor of the Order required State authorization, in the absence of which the endowment was invalid so that the Order could not therefore now seek restitution of the land. The Italian Court of Cassation *held* that the restitution must be granted since the Order, as an international person existing apart from the national sovereignty of Italy, was by virtue of a customary norm of international law exempt from the need to obtain the permission of the Government for the acquisition of immovable property for its own institutional purposes.

narcotic drugs   The Convention relating to the Suppression of the Abuse of Opium and Other Drugs of 23 January 1912 *(8 L.N.T.S. 187)*, the Convention of Limiting the Manufacture and Regulating the Distribution of Narcotic Drugs of 13 July 1931 *(139 L.N.T.S. 301)*, the Protocol Bringing under International Control Drugs outside the Scope of the Convention of 13 July 1931, of 19 November 1948 *(44 U.N.T.S. 277)*, and the Protocol for Limiting and Regulating the Cultivation of the Poppy Plant, the Production of, International and Wholesale Trade in, and Use of Opium of 23 June 1953 *(456 U.N.T.S. 3)*, have been replaced, as between the contracting parties, by the Single Convention on Narcotic Drugs of 30 March 1961 *(520 U.N.T.S. 521)*, which in turn has been amended by the Protocol of 25 March 1972 *(976 U.N.T.S. 3)*. For the purpose of the Single Convention, drugs are listed in four categories annexed to the Convention in Schedules, and the measures of control vary to some extent as between the categories (art. 2). Special measures were adopted for opium (arts. 23-4), the poppy straw (art. 25), coca bush and leaves (arts. 26-7) and cannabis (art. 28). The Commission on Narcotic Drugs of ECOSOC was entrusted with considering all matters relating to the Convention; in particular, it was authorized to amend the Schedules, to call any matter to the attention of the International Narcotics Control Board, of 11 Members (art. 9(1)), administer the drug estimates system (art. 12) and the statistical returns system (art. 13), and has the power to identify defaulting States and to call the attention of ECOSOC or the Commission to such defaults (art. 14). *See* <www.unodc.org>.

Narrow Seas ". . . Great Britain used formerly to claim the Narrow Seas—namely, the St. George's Channel, the Bristol Channel, the Irish Sea, and the North Channel—as territorial; and Phillimore [*Commentaries upon International Law* (3rd ed., 1879), i, § 189] asserts that the exclusive right of Great Britain over these Narrow Seas is uncontested. But it must be emphasised that this right is contested, and . . . it is doubtful how far Great Britain would now persist in upholding her former claim": *I Oppenheim (8th ed.) 511.* In *Attorney-General for British Columbia v. Attorney-General for Canada [1914] A.C. 153* at 174 the Privy Council pointed out that "the three-mile limit is something very different from the 'narrow seas' limit discussed by the older authorities, such as Selden and Hale, a principle which may safely be said to be now obsolete."

national A person enjoying the **nationality** of a given State. "[A]s stated in Article 1 of the Hague Convention of 1930 on Certain Questions Relating to the Conflict of Nationality Laws *[179 L.N.T.S. 89],* while it is for each State to determine under its own law who are its nationals, such law must be recognised by other States only 'in so far as it is consistent with international conventions, international custom, and the principles of law generally recognised with regard to nationality'": *I Oppenheim 852-3.* In certain municipal systems, notably that of the United States, the term "nationals" has been used to designate persons enjoying narrower rights than those described as citizens: *I Oppenheim 856-7.*

national court (or tribunal) *See* **municipal court (or tribunal).**

national treatment The **international minimum standard** "is to be distinguished from the 'national treatment' standard, not infrequently relied upon by respondent States, according to which the alien can expect no better legal protection than that accorded by a respondent State to its own nationals. The acceptance of the view that international responsibility should be governed by the 'national treatment' standard would entail as a necessary consequence that a violation of international law as regards the treatment of an alien could be established only if the alien was in fact discriminated against in the application of national law": Sohn and Baxter, Draft Convention on the International Responsibilities for Injuries to Aliens, 15 April 1961 *55 A.J.I.L. 545* at 547 *(1961).* "The national standard cannot be used as a means of evading international obligations under the minimum standard of international law": Schwarzenberger, *International Law: International Courts* (3rd ed.), 248. These views are representative of the traditional and capital-exporting approach, and they have been argued as being inapplicable to Third World and Soviet States: Guha Roy, Is the Law of Responsibility of States for Injuries to Aliens a Part of Universal International Law? *55 A.J.I.L. 863 (1961).* For an evaluation of the various criteria that may be applied for aliens, see Fatouros, International Law and the Third World, *50 Virg. L. Rev. 783 (1964).* Certainly, the trend in the UN resolutions (albeit not supported by all States) in respect of **expropriation** has been from an international minimum standard (art. 4 of the Declaration on **Permanent Sovereignty** over Natural Resources of 14 December 1962: GA Res. 1803 (XVII)) to a national treatment standard (art. 3 of the Declaration of Permanent Sovereignty over Natural Resources of 17 December 1973: GA Res. 3171 (XXVIII); art. 4(d) of the Declaration on the Establishment of a **New International Economic Order** of 1 May 1974: GA Res. 3201 (S-VI); and art. 2(c) of the Charter of Economic Rights and Duties of States of 12 December 1974: GA Res. 3281 (XXIX)). This particular development has been traced in Lillich, *The Valuation of Nationalized Property in International Law* (1976), Vol. 3, 191-5. Likewise, international **human rights** instruments tend to assimilate the two standards, by conferring rights, invariably to be applied on the basis of non-discrimination, on all persons, nationals or aliens, within the jurisdiction of a State.

national waters   "The territory of a State consists in the first place of the land, including its subsoil, within its boundaries. To this must be added, if the state has a sea coast, certain waters which are within or adjacent to its land boundaries. These waters are of two kinds—national, or internal, waters; and territorial sea. . . . National or internal waters consist of lakes, canals, rivers and their mouths, and harbours, and sometimes waters landward of fringing islands, and some of its gulfs and bays. . . . Internal waters are legally equivalent to a state's land, and are entirely subject to its territorial sovereignty": *I Oppenheim 572.* Art. 8(1) of the UN Convention on the Law of the Sea 1982 *(1833 U.N.T.S. 3)* provides that "waters on the landward side of the baseline of the territorial sea form part of the **internal waters** of the State."

nationality   This is a term of art denoting the legal connection between an individual and a State. "[N]ationality is a legal bond having as its basis a social fact of attachment, a genuine connection of existence, interests and sentiments, together with the existence of reciprocal rights and duties. It may be said to constitute the juridical expression of the fact that the individual upon whom it is conferred, either directly by law or as a result of the act of the authorities, is in fact more closely connected with the population of the State conferring nationality than with that of any other State": ***Nottebohm Case (Second Phase) 1955 I.C.J. Rep. 4*** at 23. However, it has to be admitted that the term is used inconsistently as between international law and municipal law, and even within each legal system. Thus, while a State may diplomatically protect its nationals, there are occasions in which international law will not allow a State to protect individuals who, under the State's law, are regarded as its nationals: *Nottebohm Case, supra.* And, while the English and Scots would regard themselves as of different nationality in the sense of different race, both are of UK nationality under international law: see *I Oppenheim 857.* The main purpose for which nationality is relevant in international law is as the basis for the international protection of the individual. "It is an elementary principle of international law that a State is entitled to protect its subjects, when injured by acts contrary to international law committed by another State, from whom they have been unable to obtain satisfaction through ordinary channels": ***Mavrommatis Palestine Concessions Case (1924) P.C.I.J., Ser. A, No. 2*** at 12; *see also* references under **nationality of claims**. Another purpose for which nationality is relevant is as a basis for a State claiming **jurisdiction** over an individual. Art. 5 of the Harvard Research in International Law, Jurisdiction with Respect to Crime, *29 A.J.I.L. Supp. 519 (1935)* provides: "A State has jurisdiction with respect to any crime committed outside its territory, (a) by a natural person who was a national of that State when the crime was committed or who is a national of that State when prosecuted or punished; or (b) by a corporation or other juristic person which had the national character of that State when the crime was committed." *See* Weis, *Nationality and Statelessness in International Law* (2nd ed.); van Panhuys, *The Role of Nationality in International Law* (1959); Donner, *The Regulation of Nationality in International Law* (1983). "The five most common modes of acquiring nationality, are birth, **naturalisation**, **redintegration**, **annexation**, and **cession**": *I Oppenheim 869.*

Nationality Decrees (of Tunis and Morocco) Case *(1923) P.C.I.J., Ser. B, No. 4.* In 1921, Decrees were made by France, and by Tunis and the French Zone of Morocco (both being then French Protectorates), imposing French and (respectively) Tunisian and Moroccan nationality on certain persons born in Tunis and Morocco. The Decrees affected certain British subjects. The UK protested against the Decrees on the ground that they were inconsistent with international law and treaty obligations. The matter was brought before the Council of the League of Nations under art. 15 of the Covenant, paragraph 8 of which excluded from the Council's power to make recommendations disputes which "arise out of a matter which by international law is solely within the domestic jurisdiction" of the party in question. In October 1922, the Council requested an advisory opinion whether the dispute over the application of the Decrees to British subjects was by international law solely a matter of domestic jurisdiction. In the Court's *opinion* the dispute was not by international law solely a matter of domestic jurisdiction. Matters "solely within the domestic jurisdiction" were those which, though they might closely concern the interests of more than one State, were not in principle regulated by international law, and as regards such matters each State was the sole judge. Whether a matter was solely within the jurisdiction of a State depended on the development of international relations, and at that time questions of nationality were in principle in that reserved domain. The mere fact of recourse to the Council, or that a party invoked international engagements, was not enough to exclude a dispute from the scope of art. 15(8); but, if the legal grounds relied on justified the provisional conclusion that they were of juridical importance and required consideration of their validity and construction, the matter ceased to be one solely of domestic jurisdiction and entered the domain governed by international law. In these proceedings, the questions raised as to a State's jurisdiction in matters of nationality in respect of its protectorates, the application of the principle *rebus sic stantibus* to certain 19th century treaties, and the interpretation of treaties and instruments invoked by the parties, were matters calling for examination of the position under international law, and therefore were not matters exclusively of domestic jurisdiction.

nationality of aircraft   Art. 17 of the **Chicago Convention** on International Civil Aviation of 7 December 1944 *(15 U.N.T.S. 225)* provides that "[a]ircraft have the nationality of the State in which they are registered." "The nationality of the aircraft finds expression in its registration on the national register of aircraft. Such registration does not create a nationality but is evidence of nationality. Originally the Paris Convention [relating to the Regulation of Aerial Navigation of 13 October 1919 *(11 L.N.T.S. 174)*] stipulated that only aircraft belonging to nationals of a certain State could be entered on the aircraft register of that State. This was altered in 1929 and it was left to the various States to determine the conditions on which they would enter aircraft on their national register. The Chicago Convention adopted this same principle. However, most States do not allow registration of aircraft owned wholly or partly by aliens": Honig, *The Legal Status of Aircraft* (1956), 56-7. *See* Bin Cheng, *The Law of International Air Transport* (1962), 128-32.

nationality of claims, rule of   This is a rule of international law according to which the right of a State to afford **diplomatic protection** "is necessarily limited to intervention on behalf of its own nationals because, in the absence of a special agreement, it is the bond of nationality between the State and the individual which alone confers upon the State the right of diplomatic protection, and it is as a part of the function of diplomatic protection that the right to take up a claim and to ensure respect for the rules of international law must be envisaged": *Panevezys-Saldutiskis Railway Case (1939) P.C.I.J., Ser. A/B, No. 76* at 16; *Nottebohm Case (Second Phase) 1955 I.C.J. Rep. 4*; *Barcelona Traction Co. Case (Second Phase) 1970 I.C.J. Rep. 4* at 33; *Dickson Car Wheel Co. Case (1931) 4 R.I.A.A. 660*. Generally, international law leaves it to each State to determine who are its nationals; but where nationality is invoked as a title to the exercise of diplomatic protection, it must satisfy certain requirements laid down by international law. *See Nationality Decrees (of Tunis and Morocco) Case (1923) P.C.I.J., Ser. B, No.4*; *Nottebohm Case, supra*. In the case of both natural and legal persons, the claim must be national not only at the time of its presentation, but also continuously during the whole time since the injury occurred: *Panevezys-Saldutiskis Railway Case, supra*; cf., however, *Administrative Decision No.*

V *(1924) 7 R.I.A.A. 119. See I Oppenheim 511-22*; Joseph, *Nationality and Diplomatic Protection* (1969).

nationality of company/corporation   According to the traditional rule, the nationality of a company/corporation is the State under whose laws it is incorporated and in whose ter-,ritory it has its registered office. This rule was upheld in the **Barcelona Traction Co. Case** *(Second Phase) 1970 I.C.J. Rep. 4* at 46. However, from time to time further or different tests have been applied. Some States afford diplomatic protection to a company only if, in addition to incorporation under their law, it has its seat *(siége social)* or management or center of control in their territory, or if a majority or a substantial proportion of the shares is owned by their nationals. The ICJ, preferring the traditional rule, rejected the *siége social* test, though in the circumstances of the case the *siége social* of the company was also the State of incorporation. The ICJ also rejected the protection of shareholders in the *Barcelona Traction Co. Case, supra,* because such an approach "by opening the door to competing diplomatic claims, could create an atmosphere of confusion and insecurity in international economic relations," though the Court did acknowledge that the State of the shareholders might exceptionally have a right of diplomatic protection "when the State whose responsibility is invoked is the national State of the company," or possibly where the original right of diplomatic protection of the national State of the company has for some reason ceased to exist or was otherwise not available. *See* Al-Shawi, *The Role of Corporate Entity in International Law* (1957); Seidl-Hohenveldern, *Corporations in and under International Law* (1987).

nationality of ships   Art. 91(1) of the UN Convention on the Law of the Sea 1982 *(1833 U.N.T.S. 3)*, titled "Nationality of ships," provides that "[s]hips have the nationality of a State whose flag they are entitled to fly. . . . Every State shall fix the conditions for the grant of its nationality to ships, for the registration of ships in its territory, and for the right to fly its flag. . . . There must exist a genuine link between the State and the ship." To bolster the genuine link requirement, art. 94(1) requires that "[e]very State shall exercise its jurisdiction and control in administrative, technical and social matters over ships flying its flag"; and then proceeds (in art. 94(2)-(7)) to set out a number of specific duties in satisfaction of this effective jurisdiction and control. These involve the maintenance of a register of ships, assumption of jurisdiction over the officers and crew, and adoption of measures to ensure safety of life at sea, including standards as to construction and seaworthiness, manning, labor conditions and training, and the use of signals and communications; there are requirements as to inspections of vessels, qualifications of officers and crew, and inquiries in respect of marine casualties or any incident of navigation on the high seas. On the high seas, except as otherwise provided in the 1982 Convention or other treaties, ships are subject to the exclusive jurisdiction of the **flag State** (art. 92(1)). *See* Rienow, *The Test of the Nationality of a Merchant Vessel* (1937); Meyers, *The Nationality of Ships* (1967).

nationality, conditions for the grant of   Under international law, the basic principle was stated thus: "in the present state of international law, questions of nationality are, in the opinion of the Court, in principle within [the] domain [reserved to States]": **Nationality Decrees Case** *(1923) P.C.I.J., Ser. B, No. 4* at 24. However, this does not mean that a State is free to grant internationally effective nationality to whomsoever it pleases completely free of international law. This is confirmed in art. 1 of the Hague Convention on Conflict of Nationality Law 1930 *(179 L.N.T.S. 89)*: "It is for each State to determine under its own law who are its nationals. The law shall be recognised by other States in so far as it is consistent with international conventions, international custom, and the principles of law generally recognised with regard to nationality." And in relation to the claim by Lichtenstein to protect one of its nationals under Lichtenstein law, the International Court of Justice said that the issue "does not depend on the law or on the decision of Liechtenstein whether that State is entitled to exercise its protection, in the case under consideration. To exercise protection, to apply to the Court, is to place oneself on the plane of international law. It is international law which determines whether a State is entitled to exercise protection and to seise the Court": *Nottebohm Case (Second Phase) 1955 I.C.J. Rep. 4* at 20-21. While it is true "that the diversity of demographic conditions has thus far made it impossible for any general agreement to be reached on the [municipal] rules relating to nationality" (*Nottebohm Case, supra,* at 23), certain general principles have emerged; as to which, see **jus sanguinis; jus soli; married women, nationality of; naturalization; dual nationality; stateless person**. *See* Weis, *Nationality and Statelessness in International Law* (2nd ed.); Donner, *The Regulation of Nationality in International Law* (1983).

nationalization *See* **expropriation**.

native communities "It appears that at least some communities were generally regarded not only as legal occupants of their territory but as fully sovereign States in international law. Although some writers required a certain degree of civilization as a prerequisite for statehood, it had long been established that the only necessary precondition was a degree of governmental authority sufficient for the general maintenance of order, and subsequent practice was not sufficiently consistent or coherent to change that position. This did not of course mean that identical rules were applied to such States as were by European *inter se*, but that is to be explained not by any distinction between 'civilized' and 'barbarous' States but because many of those rules were what would now be called regional customs rather than general international law": Crawford, *The Creation of States in International Law* (1979), 176. *See* the **Western Sahara Case** *1975 I.C.J. Rep. 12. See also* Sinla, *New Nations and the Law of Nations* (1967), 12-27.

NATO *See* **North Atlantic Treaty Organization**.

natural justice The term "natural justice" is common to most municipal legal systems, denoting the minimum standards of fair and impartial decision-making imposed (usually by the common law) on bodies charged with acting judicially or quasi-judicially. While of varying content in municipal legal systems, natural justice commonly comprises at least two rules: that there should be an absence of bias in the decision-making body (commonly expressed *nemo judex in sua causa*) and that both sides should be heard fairly (*audi alteram partem*). In relation to **denial of justice**, it appears that a State eludes responsibility if, in its judicial or administrative dealings with aliens, it ensures a fair and impartial hearing and affords the opportunity of rebuttal: **Faulkner's Claim** *(1926) 4 R.I.A.A. 67*; **Janes' Claim** *(1925) 4 R.I.A.A. 82*; **Stetson's Claim,** *Moore, Int. Arb., 3131*; **Chattin's Claim** *(1927) 4 R.I.A.A. 282*. In relation to the United Nations, there exist in the procedure of its organs elements designed to attain natural justice. Thus, when the Security Council is discussing any question which it considers specially affects the interests of a UN member which is not a member of the Council, that member may participate without a vote (art. 31); and when the Security Council is considering a dispute, any UN member which is not a member of the Council (or any State which is not a member of the UN) must be invited to participate without a vote (art. 32). Likewise, in a contentious case before the ICJ, a State which considers that it has "an interest of a legal nature which may be affected by the decision" may submit a request to intervene, the determination of whether the requesting State may intervene being left to the Court (art. 62). A right to intervene exists for parties to a convention whose construction is in question in a case in which they are not involved (art. 63). *See* also arts. 81-86 of the Rules of Court 1978.

natural law This is a theory, applied alike to international and municipal law, which holds that the rules of international law are drawn from the moral law of nature "which had its roots in human reason, and which could therefore be discerned without any knowledge of positive law. . . . It is now generally admitted that, in the absence of rules of law based on the practice of States, International Law may be fittingly supplemented and fertilized by recourse to rules of justice and to general principles of law, it being immaterial whether these rules are defined as the Law of Nature in the sense used by Grotius, or a modern Law of Nature with a variable content . . . or, in short, from reason": *I Oppenheim (8th ed.)* 92 and107. While Grotius, often described as the first promoter of natural law as applied to the relations of States, saw a role for positive law, some subsequent 17th and 18th century writers went as far as to deny the existence of anything other than natural law. Foremost in this movement were Samuel Pufendorf and Christian Thomasius. The "naturalists" gave place to those who subscribed to **positive law** theories, the **"positivists."** *See also* **jus naturale**.

natural resources, permanent sovereignty over The Declaration on Permanent Sovereignty over Natural Resources of 14 December 1962 (GA Res.1803 (XVII)) asserted "[t]he right of peoples and nations to permanent sovereignty over their natural wealth and resources [to] be exercised in the interest of their national development and of the well-being of the people. . ." (para. 1). Violation of the rights to natural wealth and resources was declared to be "contrary to the spirit and principles of the Charter of the United Nations" (para. 7). The Declaration of the same name of 17 December 1973 (GA Res. 3171 (XXVIII)) referred to "the inalienable rights of States to permanent sovereignty over all their natural resources, on land within their international boundaries as well as those in the sea-bed and subsoil thereof within their national jurisdiction and in the superjacent waters" (art. 1). The Charter of **Economic Rights and Duties of States** of December 1974 (GA Res. 3281 (XXIX)) reaffirmed the right of every State freely to "exercise full permanent sovereignty, including possession, use and disposal, over all its wealth, natural resources and economic activities" (art. 2(1); *see also* arts. 2(2) and 3). Permanent sovereignty is essentially an extrapolation of the right of **self-determination.** Cf. **mining, deep sea-bed.**

naturalists *See* **natural law.**

naturalization "Naturalisation . . . can be defined as reception of an alien into the citizenship of a State through a formal act on the application of the individual concerned. International law does not provide detailed rules for such reception, but it recognizes the competence of every state to naturalise those who are not its nationals and who apply to become its nationals": *I Oppenheim 875.* Absent a **genuine link** between the naturalized individual and the State, a grant of naturalization need not be recognized by other States: *Nottebohm Case (Second Phase) 1955 I.C.J. Rep. 4. See* Weis, *Nationality and Statelessness in International Law* (2nd ed.), 96-102.

Naulilaa incident *See* **Portugal v. Germany** (1928, 1930).

navicerts "The difficulties which arose out of the practice of diverting neutral vessels for search in belligerent ports led to the adoption at the beginning of 1916 of the system of so-called navicerts. Navicerts were certificates issued by the diplomatic or consular representative of the belligerent in a neutral country and testifying that the cargo on a vessel proceeding to a neutral port was not such as to be liable to seizure. The effect of the issue of the navicert was that, in the absence of supervening suspicious circumstances, the vessel when encountered by the naval forces of the belligerent was allowed to proceed on her voyage without being conducted to port for search. The system of navicerts was adopted two months after the outbreak of the war in 1939 and used on a wide scale": *II Oppenheim 855*. *See* Ritchie, *The "Navicert" System During the World War* (1938); Moos, The Navicert in World War II, *38 A.J.I.L. 115 (1944)*.

navigation, freedom of *See* **freedoms of the sea**.

ne varietur **initialling**   Initialling by the negotiators of a treaty, or parts thereof, indicating that the text is authentic, but that their governments are not to be considered bound, thereby allowing further time for governments to satisfy themselves that the instrument is acceptable as a whole before committing themselves to signature. *See* art. 10(b) of the Vienna Convention on the Law of Treaties 1969.

necessity   "The chief difficulty in making an analysis of the development of the doctrine of necessity has been the problem of endeavoring to determine the extent to which the pleas of necessity should be given consideration for the purpose of furnishing a legal excuse for a departure from a normal rule of law. An examination of the authorities tends to indicate that the doctrine of necessity as a legal principle should be subject to the following limitations:—(a) It should be confined with all possible strictness to those circumstances in which the law has in advance given an express sanction for its use; (b) it should be confined with all possible strictness to the defense of acknowledged rights, so that, other things being equal, a decision should be rendered in favor of that side which has employed the doctrine in the defense of the more clearly acknowledged rights; (c) it should be confined to cases in which the necessity of defending the state actually exists in point of fact; and in which it can be demonstrated that the action taken is essential to the preservation and continuity of the state and its ability to continue in the full and free exercise of its rights and duties; (d) the means employed should be characterized by no greater amount of extra-legal force than is rendered obligatory by the particular circumstances of the case and the need of defending the particular rights involved; (e) the danger must be so imminent and overwhelming that time and opportunity are lacking in which to provide other and adequate means of defense; (f) other things being equal, the equities of the situation must always be considered; the principles of equity do not permit a nation, because it has gone to war, to consider the rights of other nations as having become generally subordinate to its own, or justify it either in employing the doctrine of necessity in defense of its less important rights, or in sacrificing the more important rights and the safety of an unoffending state to its exigencies; (g) the fact that a state has acted in lawful self-defense does not necessarily relieve it from financial responsibility for any excessive damage that its action has produced; and if the two states immediately concerned are unable to agree upon the measure of this damage, the matter had best be left to the equitable determination of an international tribunal": Rodick, *The Doctrine of Necessity In International Law* (1928), 119-20. "More generally . . . and not only in connection with violations of territory, the necessity of safeguarding the integrity and inviolability of the territory of the state may in strictly limited circumstances justify acts which would otherwise be internationally wrongful": *I Oppenheim 416*. In this regard, the same authority mentions the intervention to protect a State's own nationals, intervention to protect the target's State's nationals (**humanitarian intervention**) and **self-defense** (in which, according to the criteria of the *Caroline incident*, the necessity to act must be "instant, overwhelming, and leaving no choice of means, and no moment for deliberation"). *See* the references to self-preservation and necessity in the *Legality of the Threat or Use of Nuclear Weapons Case 1996 I.C.J. Rep. 226. See* also **military necessity**.

Neer Claim *(US v. Mexico) (1926) 4 R.I.A.A. 60.* In 1924, Neer, an American national, was killed in Mexico by a group of armed men. A claim was presented to the US-Mexico General Claims Commission alleging that the Mexican authorities had shown lack of diligence in prosecuting the culprits. *Held* that the claim must be disallowed, since there was no evidence of such lack of diligence as to constitute an international delinquency: the propriety of governmental acts was decided according to international standards, and the treatment of an alien, in order to constitute an international delinquency, should amount to an outrage, to bad faith, to willful neglect of duty or to an insufficiency of governmental action so far short of international standards that every reasonable and impartial man would readily recognize its insufficiency, it being immaterial whether the insufficiency proceeded from deficient execution of an intelligent law or from the laws of the country not empowering the authorities to measure up to international standards.

negative succession theory In the law of **State succession**, this theory emerged in the latter part of the 19th Century. "It was contended that the sovereignty of the predecessor State over the absorbed territory is abandoned. A hiatus is thus created between the expulsion of the sovereignty and the extension of the other. The successor State does not exercise its jurisdiction over the territory in virtue of a transfer of power from its predecessor, but solely because it has acquired the possibility of expanding its own sovereignty in the manner dictated by its own will. None of the incidences of sovereignty passes to the successor State. The latter seizes what it can and repudiates what it will": O'Connell, *State Succession in Municipal and International Law* (1967), Vol. I, 14-5. This theory, often referred to as the *tabula rasa* (or "clean slate") doctrine, became increasingly popular with emerging States. A compromise was reached between this theory and the universal succession theory in the Vienna Convention on Succession of States in Respect of Treaties of 23 August 1978 *(1946 U.N.T.S. 3)* by establishing the general rule that a **newly independent State** "is not bound to maintain in force, or to become a party to, any treaty by reason only of the fact that at the date of the succession of States the treaty was in force in respect of the territory to which the succession of States relates" (art. 16), while at the same time excluding this "clean slate" doctrine from boundary and territorial régimes established by treaty (arts. 11 and 12).

negotiation(s) "Negotiations are the simplest method of peaceful settlement of disputes, in the sense that in negotiations the parties to the dispute alone are involved in the procedure. These negotiations may be bilateral or multilateral according to the number of parties to the dispute. By contrast, all the other methods [of international disputes' settlement], namely, good offices, mediation, conciliation, arbitration or judicial settlement, bring into the procedure other States or individuals who are not themselves parties to the dispute. . . . Negotiations will continue to have in the future a vital role to play as a method of settlement of disputes; in addition to the independent role, negotiations can be useful both before and in conjunction with other methods": David Davies Memorial Institute of International Studies, *International Disputes: The Legal Aspects*, (1972), 77 and 82. "[N]egotiation is employed more frequently than all the other methods [of disputes' settlement] put together. Often, indeed, negotiation is the only means employed, not just because it is always the first to be tried and is frequently successful, but also because states may believe its advantages to be so great as to rule out the use of other methods. . .": Merrills, *International Dispute Settlement* (3rd ed.), 2. *See also* Iklé, *How Nations Negotiate* (1964); De Waart, *The Element of Negotiation in the Pacific Settlement of Disputes between States* (1973).

Neo-Kantian theory This is an aspect of **neopositivist** juristic theory, seen in the writings of Hans Kelsen (*Pure Theory of Law*) and based on the philosophy of Kant and the

Marburg school of neo-Kantian philosophy, which favors a unitary conception of law, contending that international law can "be regarded in the same sense as national law," with its rules conceived as "hypothetical judgments," and which attempts to meet the question of sanctions in international law by the principle of "coercive norms" grounded in a basic norm, such as that States ought to behave according to custom, or that treaties should be observed. See Stone, *Legal Controls of International Conflict* (2nd Imp. revised), xlv-xlvi, '32-35; O'Connell, *International Law* (2nd ed.), 39-42.

neo-naturalism This is a modern theory of international law which tends to revive natural law theories through reliance on "an inborn sense of justice" (Whiteman, *Digest of International Law*, Vol. 1 (1963), 21) and on "ethical standards," particularly in matters such as **self-determination**, **human rights**, and the condemnation of aggression.

neo-positivism This is a 20th century legal theory which questioned the traditional positivist or voluntarist concepts, while still having objectivist tendencies, seen mainly in the sociological positivism of Leon Duguit, which sought to base law on "men's direct perception of social necessities," implemented by States, and in the pure science of law of Hans Kelsen, under which law consists of rules or norms for behavior, which depend on prior norms, in turn dependent on a "basic norm" for validity. De Visscher, *Theory and Reality in Public International Law,* (Rev. ed. Corbett translation, 1957) 64-68; Stone, *Legal Controls of International Conflict* (2nd Imp. revised), xlvi.

neutrality While the concept of neutrality has ancient lineage, first appearing as early as the 14th Century *(II Oppenheim 624-42)*, the scope of its application in contemporary conditions is uncertain. During the Second World War, the attitude of the Axis Powers to neutral States, and indeed the non-observance of the perceived canons of neutrality by these States themselves, undermined the very basis of the laws of neutrality (*see* Orvik, *The Decline of Neutrality* (1953)). States seeking to avoid the horrendous consequences of any nuclear war are as likely to be protected by their geographical or political irrelevance to the belligerents as by any declarations of neutrality. Further, the scheme of **collective security** established by Chapter VII of the UN Charter runs counter to the idea that some States should remain neutral in a conflict: thus art. 48(1) of the Charter provides that the "action required to carry out the decisions of the Security Council for the maintenance of international peace and security [including, of course, the imposition of sanctions and the severance of diplomatic relations under art. 41, and the use of armed force under art. 42] shall be taken by all the Members of the United Nations or by some of them, as the Security Council may determine." It is probably the case that the laws "of neutrality can be expected to be operative in the future only in secondary wars, fought by licence of the major Powers": Schwarzenberger, *International Law and Order* (1971), 178-9.

Traditionally, the rules on neutrality have attempted an accommodation between the interests of the belligerents and of the neutral State. Neutrality applies only to war, and not to the use of force short of war. In so far as neutrality has any continuing reality in international law, its rules derive from both customary and conventional sources. Under customary law, the principal obligations on neutral States are those of impartiality and abstention, i.e. duties to neither assist nor hinder either side in a war. In relation to land warfare, the principal conventional instrument is the Hague Convention (V) concerning the Rights and Duties of Neutral Powers and Persons in Case of War on Land of 18 October 1907 *(205 C.T.S. 299)*. In relation to naval warfare, the principal instruments are the Hague Convention XIII concerning the Rights and Duties of Neutral Powers in Naval War of 18 October 1907 *(205 C.T.S. 395)* and the Havana Convention on Maritime Neutrality of 20 February 1928 *(35 L.N.T.S. 187)*. While there are no ratified instruments in relation to air warfare,

Chapters V and VI of the Hague Rules of Air Warfare 1922-3 *(17 A.J.I.L. Supp. 245 (1923))* are generally accepted by commentators as authoritative (*e.g., II Oppenheim 519*). *See, generally,* Castren, *The Present Law of War and Neutrality* (1954); Ogley, *The Theory and Practice of Neutrality in the Twentieth Century* (1970); Neff, *The Rights and Duties of Neutrals: A General History* (2000).

neutralized States "A neutralised state is a state whose independence and integrity are for all future time guaranteed by treaty, on condition that such state binds itself not to enter into military alliances (except for defence against attack) and not to enter into such international obligations as could indirectly involve it in war": *I Oppenheim 319*. The current examples are Switzerland and Austria.

New International Economic Order (NIEO) On 1 May 1974, the UN General Assembly, by Res. 3201 (S-VI) entitled the Declaration on the Establishment of a New International Economic Order, called for the establishment of a new international economic order based on "equity, sovereign equality, interdependence, common interest and cooperation among all States, irrespective of their economic and social systems which shall correct inequalities and redress existing injustices, make it possible to eliminate the widening gap between developed and the developing countries and ensure steadily accelerated economic and social development and peace and justice for present and future generations. . . ." (Preamble). At the same time, the General Assembly adopted, in Res. 3202 (S-VI) a Program of Action. Subsequently, the General Assembly adopted on 12 December 1974 the Charter of Economic Rights and Duties of States (Res. 3281 (XXIX) (*See* **Economic Rights and Duties of States, Charter of**)) by 120 votes to 6 against (Belgium, Denmark, Luxembourg, United Kingdom, United States and West Germany), with 10 abstentions (Austria, Canada, France, Ireland, Israel, Italy, Japan, the Netherlands, Norway and Spain). The Charter is expressed in art. 1 as being based on 15 principles, which are explained and amplified in 29 substantive articles: (a) sovereignty, territorial integrity and political independence of States; (b) sovereign equality of all States; (c) non-aggression; (d) non-intervention; (e) mutual and equitable benefit; (f) peaceful coexistence; (g) equal rights and self-determination of peoples; (h) peaceful settlement of disputes; (i) remedying of injustices which have been brought about by force and which deprive a nation of the natural means necessary for its normal development; (j) fulfillment in good faith of international obligations; (k) respect for human rights and fundamental freedoms; (l) no attempt to seek hegemony and spheres of influence; (m) promotion of international social justice; (n) international co-operation for development; (o) free access to and from the sea by land-locked countries within the framework of the above principles. The concept of a new international economic order, while receiving further promotion in the General Assembly, the UN Industrial Development Organization (UNIDO) and the UN Conference on Trade and Development (UNCTAD), remains opposed by the bulk of the developed States. One authority states that "[i]t seems probable that at the present the three instruments represent (save insofar as they restate existing rules of international law) formally expressed aspirations of the international community rather than legally binding rights and obligations": *I Oppenheim 338*. Many of the goals of the NIEO have been further promoted through the assertion of a right to **development**. *See* Bergsten, *Towards a New International Economic Order* (1975); Hossain, *Legal Aspects of the New International Economic Order* (1980); Makarczyk, *Principles of the New International Economic Order* (1988).

Newchwang (1921) 6 R.I.A.A. 64. This case concerned the collision on 11 May 1902 between the *Newchwang*, owned by the China Navigation, Co., a British company, and the United States Government collier *Saturn. Held* by the Arbitral Tribunal established pursuant to the Special Agreement of 18 August 1910 for the submission to Arbitration of Pecuniary Claims outstanding between the United States and Great Britain *(6 R.I.A.A. 9)*, excluding a claim for legal expenses arising from proceedings brought in the Supreme Court of China and Corea in Admiralty, a British Court sitting in Shanghai: "It may be that the item for legal expenses might have been claimed in an appeal from the Shanghai decision. But this Tribunal has not to deal with such appeal, and has no authority either to reverse or affirm that decision or to deal with damages arising out of the action brought by the United States. It is true that such expenses are damages indirectly consequent to the collision; but it is a well known principle of the law of damages that *causa proxima non remota inspicitur*."

newly independent State For the purposes of the Vienna Convention on Succession of States in respect of Treaties 1978 *(1946 U.N.T.S. 3)*, a newly independent State is "a successor State the territory of which immediately before the date of the succession of States was a dependent territory for the international relations of which the predecessor State was responsible" (art. 2(1)(f)). Such a State "is not bound to maintain in force, or to become a party to, any treaty by reason only of the fact that at the date of the succession of States the treaty was in force in respect of the territory to which the succession of States relates" (art. 16). This "clean slate" doctrine for newly independent States does not apply to boundary and territorial regimes established by treaty (arts. 11 and 12), because it was thought to be too disruptive *([1972] II I.L.C. Yearbook 48)*. In relation to existing multilateral treaties, a newly-independent State may establish its status as a party by a notification of succession, unless that would be incompatible with the object and purpose of the treaty or would radically change the conditions for its operation; and the consent of the other parties is required when the terms of the treaty or the limited number of negotiating States and the object and purpose of the treaty so indicate (art. 17). In relation to an existing bilateral treaty, the newly independent State is only considered bound when the two parties expressly agree or when, by reason of their conduct, they can be considered as having agreed (art. 24).

The Vienna Convention on Succession of States in Respect of State Property, Archives and Debts 1983 *(22 I.L.M. 298 (1983))*, which uses the same definition of newly independent State (art. 2(1)(e)), provides for more or less automatic passing of State **archives** relating to and property situated in the territory to which the succession relates (arts. 28, 15), but applies a more restrictive régime in relation to debts: *see* **odious debts**. *See* further **State succession**; **negative succession theory**.

NGO(s) *See* **non-governmental organization(s)**.

Nicaragua Case *See* ***Military and Paramilitary Activities in and against Nicaragua Case (Jurisdiction)*** and ***(Merits)***.

Nicaragua-Honduras, Maritime Delimitation in the Caribbean Sea, Case between *(Nicaragua v. Honduras)*. On 8 December 1999, Nicaragua instituted proceedings before the ICJ against Honduras, regarding legal issues arising out of the maritime delimitation in the Caribbean Sea. Nicaragua based jurisdiction on Art. XXXI of the American Treaty on Pacific Settlement of 30 April 1948 (officially known as the Pact of Bogotá: *30 U.N.T.S. 84*). In addition, Nicaragua invoked declarations under art. 36(2) of the ICJ Statute, by which both States had accepted the compulsory jurisdiction of the Court. Nicaragua asserted that it had historically adopted the position that the maritime delimitation with Honduras had been undetermined, whereas Honduras accepted that a delimitation existed, which "runs straight easterly on the parallel of latitude from the point fixed [in an Arbitral Award of 23 December 1906 made by the King of Spain concerning the land boundary between Nicaragua and Honduras, which was found valid and binding by the International Court of Justice on 18 November 1960; see *1960 I.C.J. Rep. 192*] on the mouth of the Coco river." Nicaragua claimed that Honduras' position had led to recurring confrontations between both States and that diplomatic negotiations had been unsuccessful. Nicaragua requested the Court to determine the delimitation boundary between the territorial seas, continental shelf, exclusive continental shelf belonging to it and Honduras. In addition, Nicaragua reserved the right to "compensation for interference with fishing vessels of Nicaraguan nationality or vessels licensed by Nicaragua, found to the north of the parallel of latitude 14°59' 08" claimed by Honduras to be the course of the delimitation line." The Court has yet to make a decision in this case.

Niemeyer, Theodor 1857-1939. German public servant and professor at Kiel from 1894 until his retirement. Founder of the Institut für internationales Recht at Kiel. Principal works include *Prinzipien des Seekriegsrechts* (1912); *Handbuch des Abrüstungsproblems* (1927).

NIEO *See* **New International Economic Order**.

Nomination of the Workers' Delegate for the Netherlands to the International Labor Conference Opinion *(1922) P.C.I.J., Ser. B, No. 1*. The Council of the League of Nations on 12 May 1922 requested an advisory opinion on "whether the Workers' Delegate for the Netherlands at the Third Session of the International Labor Conference was nominated in accordance with the provisions of paragraph 3 of Article 389 of the Treaty of Versailles." That paragraph required the nomination of employers' and workers' delegates to be made "in agreement with the industrial organizations, if such organizations exist, which are most representative of employers or work-people, as the case may be." The Netherlands Government had nominated the Workers' Delegate with the agreement of three of the principal confederations of trade unions but without the agreement of the fourth. The PCIJ *delivered the opinion* that, as the "most representative" organizations were those which, in the particular circumstances of each country and in the judgment of its government, best represented the workers, and as art. 389(3) obliged governments to take into consideration all relevant organizations but did not require unanimous agreement where that was unattainable, the Netherlands Government, having done its best to secure an agreement to ensure the best representation of Netherlands workers, had acted in accordance with art. 389(3). "Even admitting that [an interpretation requiring agreement with all the most representative organizations] is reconcilable with the letter of paragraph 3 of Article 389 it is clearly inadmissible . . . the construction in question would make it possible for one single organization, in opposition to the wishes of the great majority of workers, to prevent the reaching of an agreement. A construction which would have this result must be rejected."

non-aligned countries/movement This is a grouping of States which initially asserted political and military independence from both the Western and the Soviet blocs and now asserts independence from any alignment of States. Growing out of informal meetings, the movement was formally established at the first summit in Belgrade in 1961, which was attended by 25 States. The Seventh Summit of the non-aligned movement, held in New Delhi in 1983, brought together 98 States, including virtually all States which have attained independence since 1945. While the early emphasis within this grouping was political, since the mid-1970s emphasis has been increasingly on economic issues, particularly the **New International Economic Order**, subsequently recast as the right to **development**. Within the UN and Specialized Agencies, the members of the non-aligned movement caucus and frequently negotiate as the **Group of 77**.

non-appearance The non-appearance before the ICJ of a party to a case being not infrequent, the Court has had to have recourse to art. 53 of its Statute, requiring it, before deciding the case in favor of the applicant State, "to satisfy itself, not only that it has jurisdiction . . ., but also that the claim is well founded in fact and law." *See* the *Fisheries Jurisdiction Cases 1974 I.C.J. Rep. 3, 175*; *United States Diplomatic and Consular Staff in Tehran Case 1980 I.C.J. Rep. 3*; *Military and Paramilitary Activities in and against Nicaragua Case 1986 I.C.J. Rep. 14.*

non-governmental organization(s) While there is no clear and unambiguous definition of non-governmental organizations (Schermers and Blokker, *International Institutional Law* (3rd ed.), 52), the same authors state that is it not "usually difficult to distinguish between (public) international organizations and international non-governmental organizations (ngo's). The notion 'non-governmental organization refers to the function of the organizations: they are not endowed with governmental tasks. Ngo's are not created by treaty; nor are they established under international law. Apart from these characteristics, ngo's share little. . . . They vary from large and influential organizations such as Amnesty International, the International Chamber of Commerce, the International Committee of the Red Cross and the Roman Catholic Church to smaller organizations like the Commonwealth Legal Education Association, the International Diabetes Federation, the International Federation of Bodybuilders, the International Skeletal Society and the United Elvis Presley Society." Art. 71 of the UN Charter empowers ECOSOC to "make suitable arrangements for consultation with non-governmental organizations which are concerned with matters within its competence." Such arrangements have been made with a large number of NGOs under ECOSOC Res. 1996/31, whereby NGOs are ranked in three categories according to their contribution to the work of the UN and are granted consultation rights commensurate with that contribution: NGOs in Category I, of which there are over 100, have a basic interest in most of the activities of ECOSOC; those in Category II, of which there are in excess of 750, have a special interest in some of the activities of ECOSC; and those on the **Roster**, of which there are over 750, have an interest in some activities of ECOSOC. NGOs play an increasingly important role in international law and politics, particularly in areas such as **human rights**, and are the main component of **civil society**. NGOs derive their legitimacy and credibility from the justice of their cause and the methods by which they promote that cause; they certainly have no democratic mandate. Cf. **organizations, inter-governmental**. *See* **human rights defenders**. *See generally* Weiss and Gordenker, *NGOs, The UN, and Global Governance* (1996); Mendelson and Glenn, *The Power and Limits of NGOs* (2002).

non-intervention Often described as a fundamental principle of international law, non-intervention is enshrined in art. 2(4) of the UN Charter: "All Members shall refrain in their international relations from the threat or use of force against the territorial integrity or political independence of any State, or in any other manner inconsistent with the Purposes of the United Nations." This provision is spelt out in more detail in Principles 1 and 2 of the **Friendly Relations Declaration** of 24 October 1970 (GA Res. 2625 (XXV)); the 1970 Declaration prohibits, in addition to the threat or use of force forbidden in art. 2(4) of the Charter, any interference by a State against the "political, economic, social and cultural elements" of another State (Principle 2). *See also* the Declarations on the Inadmissibility of Intervention of 21 December 1965 (GA Res. 2131 (XX)) and of 9 December 1981 (GA Res. 36/103). *See* Romas and Romas, *Non-Intervention* (1956). Cf. also the **domestic jurisdiction** reservation of art. 2(7) of the Charter: "Nothing contained in the present Charter shall authorize the United Nations to intervene in matters which are essentially within the domestic jurisdiction of any state or shall require the Members to submit such matters to settlement under the present Charter; but this principle shall not prejudice the application of enforcement measures under Chapter VII."

***non-liquet*, doctrine of** This is a juristic doctrine, now believed to be obsolete, that an international tribunal should decline to decide a case where rules are not available for its determination because of gaps or *lacunae* in international law. The justification for the doctrine has been stated as "a safeguard against tribunals, faced with the absence of necessary evidence or of an applicable rule of law, deciding according to their personal whim or arbitrary decision and thus discrediting the idea of settlement of disputes on the basis of law. . . . Others have referred with some impatience, as savouring of dogmatic formalism, to the insistence on the completeness of international law. . . . Others still, in addition to denying to international law the character of a rule of universal validity, have questioned its claim to be a positive factor in the administration of international justice and the preservation of peace": Lauterpacht, *International Law* (1948), Vol. 2, 214. "The constancy of international judicial and arbitral practice on the subject has made the rejection of *non liquet* appear as self-evident": *ibid,* 223. "It is . . . not permissible for an international tribunal to pronounce a *non-liquet*": *I Oppenheim 13*.

non-member States States which are not members of an international organization acquire none of the rights or duties of members (*but see* **non-member States, obligations on**). Their only access to the rights and duties, benefits and costs, of an international organization is through membership, which is available to them only as admitted members (*see* **admission**). On rare occasions, this may be difficult. For example, admission to the League of Nations being open to States not named in the Annex of original members (art. 1 of the Covenant), the USA being named in the Annex but not, through Senate refusal to ratify the Covenant, an original member, the USA could not, in strict law, have become a member by admission.

non-national *See* **alien**.

Non-Proliferation Treaty The Treaty on the Non-Proliferation of Nuclear Weapons *(729 U.N.T.S.)* was opened for signature on 1 July 1968 and came into force on 5 March 1970. Nuclear-weapons States are not to transfer, directly or indirectly, nuclear weapons or devices, nor to assist, encourage or induce non-nuclear weapons States to acquire them (art. I). Non-nuclear-weapons States are not to seek to acquire nuclear weapons or devices or to do anything to assist in their manufacture (art. II). The peaceful use of nuclear energy is safeguarded (art. IV) through agreements with the **International Atomic Energy Agency** (art. III). The NPT regime is subject to regular review, the seventh review to be held in 2005. With 188 States parties, including the five major nuclear powers, it has more ratifications than any other arms limitation and disarmament agreement, though 3 States with some nuclear weapons capacity (India, Israel and Pakistan) are not parties.

non-recognition A distinction is to be drawn between the circumstance that a particular State or government has not as yet been recognized by the government of another particular State and the case where the latter withholds recognition from the former as a matter of deliberate policy. Such a policy was proclaimed by the United States Secretary of State, Stimson in 1932 in a note to Japan and China intimating that the United States "cannot admit the legality of any situation de facto nor does it intend to recognize any treaty or agreement entered into between those Governments which may impair the treaty rights of the United States . . . [or] any situation, treaty or agreement which may be brought about by means contrary to the Pact of Paris": Hackworth, *Digest of International Law,* Vol. 1 (1940), 334.

Various attempts were made to induce members of the League of Nations to adopt a similar policy in relation to the affairs of China and Japan, and indeed to deduce a legal duty of non-recognition from the Pact of Paris and from art. 10 of the Covenant of the League. No such duty, however, is explicitly to be discerned in either of those instruments, or even in the Charter of the United Nations. However, the International Court of Justice expressed in the *Namibia Opinion 1971 I.C.J. Rep. 16* the view that a "duty of non-recognition" of South Africa's continued presence in Namibia was imposed on Members of the United Nations pursuant to art. 25 of the Charter and Security Council Res. 276 (XXXV), and that it was equally for non-member States to act in accordance with the Security Council's decisions. There is an increasing trend towards seeking to establish a duty of non-recognition in respect of new States (or expanded States) and governments established in breach of international law, but these are not universally supported by State practice. *See I Oppenheim 183-203. See also* **recognition**; **Tobar doctrine**.

non-scheduled flight Under art. 5 of the **Chicago Convention** on International Civil Aviation 1944 *(15 U.N.T.S. 295)*, the aircraft of contracting States "being aircraft not engaged in scheduled international air services" have the right, subject to the Convention, to overfly other contracting States and make stops for non-traffic purposes without prior permission, but subject to the right of the State to require landing, and to control as to route over certain areas. Further, "traffic purpose" landing is permitted, but may be subject to control. There is, however, no definition of non-scheduled flight in the Convention other than the negative definition implicit in the reference to scheduled flight.

non-self-governing territories Chapter XI of the UN Charter, entitled Declaration Regarding Non-Self-Governing Territories and comprising arts. 73 and 74, is stated to apply to "territories whose peoples have not yet attained a full measure of self-government" (art. 73). The UN Members responsible for the administration of such territories are obliged to recognize that "the interests of the inhabitants . . . are paramount" and that the promotion of the well-being of the inhabitants constitutes a "sacred trust" (art. 73). In addition to other general obligations, including the development of self-government (art. 73(b)), UN Members responsible for administration of such territories are specifically required to transmit regularly to the Secretary-General "for information purposes . . . statistical and other information of a technical nature relating to economic, social and educational conditions. . . ." (art. 73(e)). The General Assembly has asserted its competence to determine whether an obligation existed to transmit information on a particular territory, and when it ceased, and to examine transmitted information and make recommendations (this latter scrutiny role now being performed by the "Committee of 24"—the Special Committee on the Situation with regard to the implementation of the Declaration on the Granting of Independence to Colonial Countries and Peoples—established by GA Res. 1654 (XVI), amended by GA Res. 1810 (XVII), adopted in consequence of the principal Declaration of 14 December 1960 (GA Res. 1514 (XV): see **Independence to Colonial Countries and Peoples, Declaration on the Granting of**. The criterion of non-self-governing status would appear to be largely non-representation in the legislature of the administering States—though not exclusively, since neither Puerto Rico nor the United Kingdom dependencies of the Channel Islands and the Isle of Man are treated as non-self-governing territories.

non-traffic purposes For the purposes of the **Chicago Convention** on International Civil Aviation 1944 *(15 U.N.T.S. 295)*, "'[s]top for non-traffic purposes' means a landing for any purpose other than taking on or discharging passengers, cargo or mail": art. 96(d). *See also* **non-scheduled flight**.

normative theory This theory, primarily associated with Hans **Kelsen**, considers international law as being made up of a series of norms, ultimately deriving their validity from a basic norm (or *Grund-norm*). In relation to customary law, this basic norm is that States should behave as they have customarily behaved; and in relation to treaty law, the related principle **pacta sunt servanda**. *See* Kelsen, *General Theory of Law and State* (1946), 328-88; Kelsen *Principles of International Law* (1952), *passim. See also* Engel, *Law, State and International Legal Order. Essays in Honor of Hans Kelsen* (1964).

North American Dredging Company v. Mexico *(1926) 4 R.I.A.A. 26.* The North American Dredging Company, an American corporation, concluded a contract in Mexico City with the Government of Mexico in 1912. Its subject matter concerned dredging services to be rendered in Mexico by the company, payment to be made in Mexico. The contract contained a so-called **Calvo clause** which provided that the company was to be considered as Mexican in all matters within Mexico concerning the fulfillment of the contract; was to have in that connection the same rights as those granted by Mexican law to Mexicans, and was consequently deprived of any rights as an alien and was not permitted foreign diplomatic intervention in any matter related to the contract. The company claimed to have suffered loss and damage as a result of breaches of the contract, and the US presented a claim on behalf of the company to the Mexico-US General Claims Commission established by the Mexico-US General Claims Convention 1923. *Held* that the Commission was without jurisdiction. An international tribunal must seek a proper and adequate balance between the sovereign right of national jurisdiction and the sovereign right of national protection of citizens. Although an individual cannot by contract deprive his government of its right to apply international remedies to violations of international law committed to his damage, he can (and in the circumstances of the case the claimant company did) by a Calvo clause in a contract agree to forego the right to invoke or accept the assistance of his government in matters arising out of the contract, and thus by such a clause precluded the US Government from espousing a case before the Commission. Each case involving a clause of the nature of a Calvo clause must be considered on its merits: if a Calvo clause purported to preclude a government from protecting its nationals if any of their rights had been infringed by another government in violation of international law, or if the effect of a Calvo clause was secured otherwise than by express contractual provisions signed by the claimant (or a predecessor in title) or in any constitution or law to which the claimant had not in some form expressly subscribed in writing, it would not necessarily be given effect so as to prevent him presenting his claim to his government or the government from espousing it.

North American Free Trade Area This **free trade area** was established by art. 101 of the North American Free Trade Agreement, concluded in 1993 between Canada, Mexico and the United States *(32 I.L.M. 189 (1993))*. Its objectives are to: "(a) eliminate barriers to trade in, and facilitate the cross-border movement of, goods and services between the territories of the Parties; (b) promote conditions of fair competition in the free trade area; (c) increase substantially investment opportunities in the territories of the Parties; (d) provide adequate and effective protection and enforcement of intellectual property rights in each Party's territory; (e) create effective procedures for the implementation and application of this Agreement, for its joint administration and for the resolution of disputes; and (f) establish a framework for further trilateral, regional and multilateral cooperation to expand and enhance the benefits of this Agreement" (art. 102(1)). In addition, the parties have adopted Supplementary Agreements on Labor Cooperation *(32 I.L.M. 1499 (1993))* and on Environmental Cooperation *(32 I.L.M. 1480 (1993))*. NAFTA has a Free Trade Commission, whose tasks are to supervise the implementation of the Agreement and to oversee its further elaboration (art. 2001(2)); and a Secretariat, whose principal function is to administer the dispute settlement provisions of Chapter 20(b) of the Agreement (art. 2002(3)). *See* Mayer, *Interpreting NAFTA* (1998); Chambers, Smith and Perley, *NAFTA in the New Millenium* (2002).

North Atlantic Fisheries Case *(1910) 11 R.I.A.A. 167*. In 1818, Great Britain and the US concluded a treaty defining the rights of inhabitants of the US to take fish in certain waters off the North Atlantic Coast of what is now Canada ("the treaty coast") and to enter bays or harbors for the purpose of repairs, shelter and obtaining wood and water. Differences arose as to the scope and meaning of these provisions and of the rights and liberties of US inhabitants. In 1909, the two States agreed to submit the dispute to a tribunal of the Permanent Court of Arbitration, which *held,* (a) that, as an attribute of its territorial sovereignty, Great Britain was entitled, without the consent of the United States, to make regulations applicable to American fishermen in treaty waters, but such regulations must be made in good faith and not be in violation of the treaty; (b) that regulations which were appropriate or necessary on grounds of public order and morals without unnecessarily interfering with the fishery itself, and which were fair as between local and American fishermen, were not inconsistent with the obligation to execute the treaty in good faith, and were therefore not in violation of the treaty; (c) that the reasonableness of a regulation was to be decided not by either of the parties but by an impartial authority, to which end the tribunal recommended certain rules and methods of procedure to be followed in such cases; (d) that US inhabitants, while exercising their rights under the treaty, were entitled to employ as members of the crews of their fishing vessels persons who were not inhabitants of the US, although such non-inhabitants derived no rights from the treaty but only from their employer; (e) that vessels of US inhabitants could reasonably be required to report at Customs if this could be done conveniently either in person or by telegraph, but the exercise of fishing rights by US inhabitants should not be subject to the purely commercial formalities of report, entry and clearance at Customs, nor to light, harbor or other dues not imposed upon local fishermen; (f) that the treaty provisions allowing fishermen to enter bays or harbors on the non-treaty coast for the purpose of repairs, shelter, etc, were an exercise of the duties of hospitality and humanity which all civilized nations imposed upon themselves, and were not dependent upon the payment of dues or other similar requirements, although the privilege should not be abused; (g) that, for purposes of the treaty provision excluding the US from taking fish on or within 3 marine miles of any of the coasts, bays, creeks or harbors on the non-treaty coast, the word "bays" must be interpreted as applying to geographical bays; (h) that for bays the 3 marine miles were to be measured from a straight line drawn across the body of water at the place where it ceased to have the configuration and characteristics of a bay, and elsewhere the 3 marine miles were to be measured following the sinuosities of the coast: the tribunal recommended a procedure to determine the limits of specified bays, and provided that for other bays the limits of exclusion should be 3 miles seaward from a straight line across the bay at the part nearest the entrance at the first point where the width did not exceed ten miles; (i) that US inhabitants had the liberty of taking fish in the bays, harbors and creeks on the treaty coast; and (j) that nothing in the treaty disentitled US vessels which resorted to the treaty coasts to exercise their fishing rights from also having such commercial privileges as were accorded to US trading vessels generally, provided the treaty liberty of fishing and the commercial privileges were not exercised concurrently.

North Atlantic Treaty Organization The North Atlantic Treaty Organization (NATO) was established by the North Atlantic Treaty, adopted in Washington on 4 April 1949 *(34 U.N.T.S. 243)*. The original parties were Belgium, Canada, Denmark, France, Iceland, Italy, Luxembourg, Netherlands, Norway, Portugal, UK and USA. The membership has since risen to 19, with a further seven States from the former USSR and Eastern Europe due to become members in 2004. In 1966, France unilaterally withdrew from its NATO commitments, but not from the treaty itself. The core of the treaty regime is contained in art. 5: "The Parties agree that an armed attack against one or more of them in Europe or North America shall be considered an attack against them all; and consequently they agree that, if such an armed attack occurs, each of them, in exercise of the right of the individual or collective self-defense recognized by Article 51 of the Charter of the United Nations, will assist the Party or Parties so attacked by taking forthwith, individually and in concert with the other Parties, such action as it deems necessary, including the use of armed force, to restore and maintain the security of the North Atlantic area." The North Atlantic Treaty mentions only two organs, a Council and a Defense Committee (art. 9). The Council is the supreme organ, representing all the parties, and, as a matter of practice, seeks unanimity in its deliberations. The Defense Committee was absorbed into the Council in 1951, and the civil functions mentioned in the Treaty are performed by the Council operating through committees. A Military Committee has been established under the Council to provide strategic guidance. Ironically, NATO, being unneeded during the Cold War, for which it was created, has, after the Kosovo bombings in 1999, become increasingly concerned to address conflicts beyond its territorial boundaries. *See NATO Handbook 2001* (2001); NATO, *NATO in the 21st Century* (2002). *See* <www.nato.int>.

North Pole *See* **polar regions sovereignty over**.

North Sea Continental Shelf Cases *(Denmark v. FRG; (Netherlands v. FRG) 1969 I.C.J. Rep. 3.* Agreements concluded by the Federal Republic of Germany with the Netherlands in 1964 and with Denmark in 1965 established partial maritime boundaries in the immediate vicinity of their North Sea coasts. By special agreements concluded in February 1967 *(606 U.N.T.S. 97, 105)* by Germany with Denmark and with the Netherlands, the ICJ was asked to declare the principles and rules of international law applicable to the delimitation as between the parties of the areas of the North Sea continental shelf appertaining to each of them beyond the previously agreed partial boundaries. The Court joined the proceedings in the two cases. Denmark and the Netherlands contended that the boundary line should be based on the equidistance principle whereas Germany maintained that the line should be such as to give it a just and equitable share of continental shelf area on the basis of proportionality to the length of its North Sea coastline. *Held* (11 to 6) that, as the use of the equidistance method of delimitation was not obligatory as between the parties and no other single method of delimitation was in all circumstances obligatory, delimitation was to be effected by agreement in accordance with equitable principles and taking account of all relevant circumstances, in such a way as to leave as much as possible to each party all those parts of the continental shelf that constituted a natural prolongation of its land territory, without encroachment on the natural prolongation of the land territory of the other; and, if such delimitation produced overlapping areas, they were to be divided between the parties in agreed proportions, or, failing agreement, equally, unless they decided on a régime of joint jurisdiction, user, or exploitation: the Court indicated various factors to be taken into account in the course of negotiations. In reaching this conclusion the Court found that (i) inherent rights of the coastal State in respect of the area of continental shelf constituting a natural prolongation of its land territory existed *ipso facto* and *ab initio,* by virtue of its sovereignty over the land; (ii) although Denmark and the Netherlands were parties to the Continental Shelf Convention 1958 *(499 U.N.T.S. 311),* art. 6 of which incorporated the equidistance principle, Germany, although having signed the Convention, was not a party to it and it was not, as such, binding on Germany, (iii) Germany had not assumed the obligations of the Convention by its conduct (for which a very definite and consistent course of conduct would be necessary), nor was it by estoppel precluded from denying the applicability of the Conventional régime; (iv) the equidistance principle was not inherent in the basic doctrine of the continental shelf; (v) although a conventional rule might become a new rule of customary international law if it was of a potentially norm-creating character, if participation by States in the Convention was sufficiently representative and widespread, or if (even after only a short period of time) State practice, including that of States whose interests were specially affected, had during the period been extensive and virtually uniform in the sense of the provision invoked and had occurred in such a way as to show a general recognition that a rule of law was involved, in the present case the equidistance principle, as in art. 6 of the Convention, did not reflect or crystallize a mandatory rule of customary international law, and neither its subsequent effect nor State practice had been sufficient to constitute such a rule; (vi) the parties were under obligation to enter into meaningful negotiations with a view to arriving at an agreement, and to act in such a way that in the particular case, and taking all the circumstances into account, equitable principles would be applied.

Northern Cameroons Case *(Republic of Cameroons v. UK) 1963 I.C.J. Rep. 15*. The Trust Territory of the Cameroons under British Administration, the Trusteeship Agreement for which entered into force on 31 December 1946, was administratively divided into Northern and Southern Regions. On 1 June 1961, consequent upon a plebiscite conducted under the auspices of the UN, the Northern Cameroons joined the Federation of Nigeria: a similar plebiscite resulted in the Southern Cameroons joining the Republic of Cameroon on 1 October 1961. The result of these plebiscites was endorsed in April 1961 by the UN General Assembly in Res. 1608 (XV), which terminated the Trusteeship Agreement with effect from 1 June 1961 (Northern Cameroons) and 1 October 1961 (Southern Cameroons). On 30 May 1961, the Republic of Cameroons instituted proceedings against the UK as Administering Authority alleging, in respect of the Northern Cameroons, various violations of the Trusteeship Agreement. *Held* by the ICJ (9 to 5) that any adjudication by the Court would be devoid of purpose, and the proper limits of the judicial function did not permit it to entertain the claims submitted to it.

Norwegian Loans Case *(France v. Norway) 1957 I.C.J. Rep. 9*. Certain Norwegian loans were floated between 1885 and 1909 and a proportion of the bonds was held by French nationals. France contended that the bonds contained a gold clause. The convertibility into gold of notes of the Bank of Norway was suspended at various dates from 1914, being finally suspended in 1931; and in 1923 a Norwegian law provided that, where a debtor had agreed to pay in gold a pecuniary debt in Kroner and the creditor refused to accept payment in Bank of Norway notes according to their nominal gold value, payment could be postponed in a prescribed manner. There was protracted diplomatic correspondence between 1925 and 1955: the French bond-holders did not meanwhile submit their case to the Norwegian courts. France objected to a unilateral decision being relied upon as against foreign creditors and requested the recognition of the rights claimed by the French bond-holders. Norway maintained that the claims of the bond-holders were within the jurisdiction of the Norwegian courts and involved solely the interpretation and application of Norwegian law. In 1955, France referred the matter to the ICJ on the basis of declarations made by France and Norway accepting the compulsory jurisdiction of the Court. *Held* (12-3), upholding a preliminary objection filed by Norway, that the Court had no jurisdiction to decide the dispute since France's declaration contained a reservation (the validity of which had not been questioned by the parties) excluding differences relating to matters which were essentially within national jurisdiction as understood by France and, in accordance with the condition of reciprocity embodied in Article 36(2) of the Statute of the

Court, Norway was entitled to except from the compulsory jurisdiction of the Court disputes understood by Norway to be essentially within its national jurisdiction. The existence between France and Norway of the Second Hague Convention of 1907 on the Limitation of the Employment of Force for the Recovery of Contract Debts did not make the question of payment of such debts a matter of international law so as to prevent Norway invoking the reservation in the French Declaration; nor did the Franco-Norwegian Arbitration Convention 1904 or the **General Act for the Pacific Settlement of International Disputes 1928** (to which France and Norway were parties) justify the Court in seeking a basis for its jurisdiction different from that which France had set out in its application and by reference to which both Parties had presented the case to the Court.

Norwegian Ship-owners' Claim *(Norway v. USA) (1921) 1 R.I.A.A. 307.* Fifteen Norwegian ship-owners placed contracts for the building of ships in US shipyards. After the US declared war on Germany on 6 April 1917, the US requisitioned the Norwegian ship-owners' property. Negotiations between the US and Norway failed to lead to a settlement of the claims for compensation presented by Norway on behalf of the ship-owners, and by an Agreement signed on 13 June 1921 *(14 L.N.T.S. 20)* they referred the dispute to a tribunal of the Permanent Court of Arbitration for decision in accordance with the principles of law and equity. *Held* that the US must pay compensation to Norway. The claimants were deprived of their property by a requisition in exercise of the power of eminent domain (the power of the State to take property within its jurisdiction which may be required for the public good); while the tribunal could not disregard the municipal law of the parties (unless it was contrary to the equality of the parties or to principles of justice common to all civilized nations) which had been accepted by foreign nationals in their private dealings, the tribunal was not governed by that law but could examine it for consistency with the equality of the parties, treaties binding the party in question, well established principles of international law, including customary law and the practice of judges of international courts; under US law, as well as under international law, just compensation was due to the claimants based upon respect for private property, and providing such compensation was paid without undue delay the US was entitled to take the claimants' property for the duration of the special war emergency; just compensation implied a complete restitution of the *status quo ante* based upon loss of profits of the Norwegian owners as compared with other owners of similar property and compensation was accordingly awarded on the basis of the fair market value of the claimants' property.

note A note may be any type of written diplomatic communication between States. As one of the two constituents of an **exchange of notes**, a note may indeed contain the text of a treaty. In some circumstances, a unilateral declaration contained in a note may have the effect of binding the State originating it: **Ihlen declaration**; *Nuclear Tests Cases*.

note verbal "A *note verbal* is an unsigned document containing a summary of conversations or of events, and the like": *I Oppenheim (8th ed.) 878.* A *note verbal* is not a treaty. Cf. **note**.

notification "By notification, states communicate to other states certain facts and events of legal importance. In some circumstances notifications are obligatory; but they are often made voluntarily in order to ensure that other states cannot, on grounds of lack of knowledge, avoid the legal consequences which flow from the facts and events in question": *I Oppenheim 1193.*

Nottebohm Case *(Liechtenstein v. Guatemala) 1953 I.C.J. Rep. 111; 1955 I.C.J. Rep. 12.* Nottebohm, a naturalized national of Liechtenstein but resident in Guatemala, had in 1943 been detained, interned and expelled, and his property sequestered and confiscated by the Guatemalan authorities. In 1951, Liechtenstein instituted proceedings before the ICJ seeking the restoration of Nottebohm's property and the payment to him of compensation. Both Guatemala and Liechtenstein had accepted the compulsory jurisdiction of the ICJ in accordance with art. 36 of the Statute of the Court, the Guatemalan acceptance being made in 1947 for a period of 5 years. On a preliminary objection raised by Guatemala, *held* (unanimously), in exercise of the Court's competence to decide its own jurisdiction, that the expiry of Guatemala's acceptance of the Court's jurisdiction after the Court had been regularly seised of the dispute did not deprive the Court of jurisdiction to deal with the claim presented to it.

At a later stage in the proceedings Guatemala objected to the admissibility of the claim on grounds related to Nottebohm's nationality; he had had German nationality by birth in 1881, had generally resided in Guatemala from 1905 until 1943 and established a business there, and had been granted naturalization by Liechtenstein in 1939. *Held* (11-3) that (a) although it was for every sovereign State to settle by its own legislation the rules relating to the acquisition of its nationality and to confer that nationality in accordance with that legislation, that internal act did not automatically have the international effect of entitling the State to exercise protection, which was a matter to be determined by international law; (b) "nationality is a legal bond having as its basis a social fact of attachment, a genuine connection of existence, interests and sentiments, together with the existence of reciprocal rights and duties. It may be said to constitute the juridical expression of the fact that the individual upon whom it is conferred, either directly by the law or as the result of an act of the authorities, is in fact more closely connected with the population of the State conferring nationality than with that of any other State. Conferred by a State, it only entitles that State to exercise protection vis-à-vis another State, if it constitutes a translation into juridical terms of the individual's connection with the State which has made him its national"; (c) the facts disclosed the absence of any bond of attachment between Nottebohm and Liechtenstein and, on the other hand, the existence of a longstanding and close connection between him and Guatemala, and accordingly Liechtenstein was not entitled to extend its protection to Nottebohm vis-à-vis Guatemala.

novation "This title of acquisition [to territory] is very rare. It consists in the gradual transformation of a right *in territorio alieno*, for example a lease, or a pledge, or certain concessions of a territorial nature, into full sovereignty without any formal and unequivocal instrument to that effect intervening. The Orkney and Shetland Islands, Corsica, Nijmegen, originally only given in pledge, may serve as historical examples": Verzijl, *International Law in Historical Perspective* (1970), Vol. 3, 384-5. Verzijl goes on to discuss two cases of considerable political controversy: Belize and certain Portuguese enclaves in India; *see **Right of Passage over Indian Territory Case**.*

noxious fumes *See **air pollution**.*

Noyes Claim *(USA v. Panama) (1933) 6 R.I.A.A. 308.* Noyes, a US national, while travelling through a village near Panama City in June 1927 was subjected to acts of violence at the hands of a crowd attending a meeting in the village. The Panamanian authorities knew that the meeting would take place, but had not strengthened the local police force in advance, though later sending reinforcements. The police who were present took active steps to protect Noyes. No assailants were prosecuted. A claim was presented under the US-Panama Claims Convention signed on 28 July 1926, which was ratified on 3 October 1931. *Held* by the US-Panama General Claims Commission, that (i) the Convention gave the Commission jurisdiction over claims arising after signature but before ratification of the

Convention; (ii) the mere fact that an alien suffered at the hands of private persons an injury which could have been avoided by the presence of sufficient police did not make the Government liable for damages under international law, which required special circumstances (not present in the instant case) from which responsibility might arise; and (iii) in the circumstances the failure to prosecute the assailants did not give rise to any liability on the part of the Panamanian Government.

NPT *See* **Non-Proliferation Treaty**.

nuclear cargoes The Convention Relating to Civil Liability in the Field of Maritime Carriage of Nuclear Material of 17 December 1971 *(974 U.N.T.S. 255)* extends the provisions of the Paris Convention on Third Party Liability in the Field of Nuclear Energy of 29 July 1960 *(956 U.N.T.S. 251)* and the Vienna Convention on Civil Liability for Nuclear Damage of 21 May 1963 *(1063 U.N.T.S. 265)* to the maritime carriage of nuclear materials. Any person who might be held liable for a nuclear incident is exonerated from liability if the operator of a nuclear installation is liable for the damage under the Paris and Vienna Conventions or under national law no less favorable to victims (art. 1). *See* **nuclear damage**. Under the UN Convention on the Law of the Sea 1982 *(1833 U.N.T.S. 3)*, nuclear ships and ships carrying nuclear or other inherently dangerous or noxious substances or materials may be required to confine their exercise of the right of **innocent passage** to designated or prescribed sea lanes (art. 22) and must in any event carry documents and observe special precautionary measures established for such ships by international agreements (art. 23).

nuclear damage The Vienna Convention on Civil Liability for Nuclear Damage of 21 May 1963 *(1063 U.N.T.S. 265)* makes the operator of a nuclear installation liable for nuclear damage (art. II). This liability is absolute (art. IV), subject only to the defenses of fault or gross negligence of the person suffering the damage and of damage caused by armed conflict etc. *(ibid.)*. Liability may be limited to not less than US $5 million per incident (art. V). Rights of compensation are extinguished if an action is not brought within 10 years (art. VI). The operator is obliged to maintain insurance (art. VII). The Vienna Convention is open to all States. The Paris Convention on Third Party Liability in the Field of Nuclear Energy of 29 July 1960 *(956 U.N.T.S. 251)* was concluded between the members of the European Nuclear Energy Agency (Statute of 20 December 1957, in force 1 February 1958: *53 A.J.I.L. 1012 (1959)*), established within the framework of the OECD and charged with encouraging the elaboration and harmonization of legislation relating to nuclear energy in participating countries, in particular with regard to third party liability and insurance against atomic risks. The principles of liability and the obligations of the operator are similar in all essentials to those under the Vienna Convention. *See also* **nuclear cargoes; nuclear ships**.

nuclear energy *See* **International Atomic Energy Agency**.

nuclear safeguards *See* **Test-Ban Treaties**.

nuclear ships In terms of art. I (1) of the Convention of the Liability of Operators of Nuclear Ships, signed at Brussels on 25 May 1962 and not in force *(57 A.J.I.L. 268 (1963))*, nuclear ship "means any ship equipped with a nuclear power plant"; a "nuclear power plant" is "any power plant in which a nuclear reactor is, or is to be used as, the source of power, whether for propulsion of the ship or for any other purpose" (art. I (9)). The operator of a nuclear ship is absolutely liable, with a limited range of defenses (arts. II (4) and VIII), for any nuclear incident (art. II (1)), up to a maximum of 1500 million francs (art. III (1)), provided the action is brought within 10 years (art. V (1)). The operator is required to maintain insurance or other financial security to cover this liability (art. III (2)). Warships and other State-owned or operated ships on non-commercial service are included in the substantive provisions of the Convention (although they are not thereby subject to arrest, attachment or seizure or jurisdiction: art. X (3)). *See* **nuclear damage**. Under the UN Convention on the Law of the Sea 1982 *(1833 U.N.T.S. 3)*, nuclear ships and ships carrying nuclear or other inherently dangerous or noxious substances or materials may be required to confine their exercise of the right of **innocent passage** to designated or prescribed sea lanes (art. 22) and must in any event carry documents and observe special precautionary measures established for such ships by international agreements (art. 23).

Nuclear Tests Cases *(Australia v. France; New Zealand v. France) 1973 I.C.J. Rep. 99, 1974 I.C.J. Rep. 253, 457.* In 1972 (and in earlier years) France conducted atmospheric nuclear tests in the South Pacific. Australia and New Zealand (in separate but essentially identical proceedings which were dealt with by the ICJ in the same terms) claimed that the tests were inconsistent with international law and had caused radioactive fall-out damage in their countries. They instituted proceedings against France, founding the jurisdiction of the Court on the **General Act for the Pacific Settlement of International Disputes 1928** and arts. 36 and 37 of the Statute of the Court. By a letter of 16 May 1973, France stated that it considered the Court manifestly not competent in the case and that it did not accept its jurisdiction. On the request of Australia and New Zealand for interim measures of protection, the Court, in June 1973, *indicated* (8 to 6) that the non-appearance of France could not by itself preclude the Court from indicating interim measures and that, as there was a *prima facie* basis for the Court's jurisdiction and the possibility of irreparable damage to Australia and New Zealand by radioactive fall-out could not be excluded, France should, pending a final decision, avoid nuclear tests causing the deposit of radioactive fall-out on Australian territory. In July-August 1973 and June-September 1974, a further series of atmospheric tests took place. Australia and New Zealand presented written and oral arguments to the Court on the question of jurisdiction; France did not do so, resting on the letter of 16 May 1973. *Held* (9 to 6) that the claims of Australia and New Zealand no longer had any object and that the Court was therefore not called upon to give a decision. As the applicants' objective was to obtain a termination of French atmospheric nuclear tests in the Pacific, and France by a series of unilateral statements had made public its intention to cease the conduct of atmospheric nuclear tests following the conclusion of the 1974 series, and as, having regard to the intention behind those statements and to the circumstances in which they were made, they constituted an engagement of the French State, the applicants' objective had in effect been accomplished inasmuch as France had undertaken the obligation to hold no further nuclear tests in the atmosphere in the South Pacific; the dispute had accordingly disappeared and the claim no longer had any object.

nuclear waste *See* **radioactive products and waste**.

nuclear weapons *See Legality of the Threat or Use of Nuclear Weapons*.

nullum crimen sine lege The principle *nullum crimen sine lege*, denoting that no-one should be subject to prosecution for a crime unless pursuant to a previous law establishing that crime, has wide currency in municipal legal systems, and finds limited expression in international law. Thus, while the defense invoked the principle in relation to those arraigned before the Nuremberg International Military Tribunal, the Tribunal, holding that the principle was a general principle of justice, nonetheless regarded itself as bound by its Charter, irrespective of any retroactivity. The Statute of the International Criminal Court 1998 *(37 I.L.M. 999 (1998))* specifically requires for criminal responsibility that "the conduct in question constitute, at the time it takes place, a crime within the jurisdiction of the

Court" (art. 22(1)), further providing that the definition of a crime is to be strictly construed and, in cases of ambiguity, in favor of the individual (art. 22(2)). Art. 11(2) of the Universal Declaration of Human Rights of 10 December 1948 (GA Res. 217 (III)) provides that "[n]o one shall be held guilty of any penal offence on account of any act or omission which did not constitute a penal offence, under national or international law, at the time when it was committed." *Accord* art. 15(1) of the International Covenant on Civil and Political Rights 1966 *(999 U.N.T.S. 171)*; art. 7(1) of the European Convention on Human Rights 1950 *(E.T.S. No. 5, as amended by No. 155)*; art. 9 of the American Convention on Human Rights of 22 November 1969 *(1144 U.N.T.S. 123)*. For the distinction between this principle and that of *nullum crimen sine poena,* see the ***Danzig Legislative Decrees Case (1935) P.C.I.J., Ser. A/B, No.65*** at 54-8: Statute of the ICC 1998 *(supra)*, art. 23.

nuncios   Art. 14 of the Vienna Convention on Diplomatic Relations 1961 *(500 U.N.T.S. 95)* includes in the first of three classes of heads of diplomatic mission "ambassadors or nuncios accredited to Heads of State." Envoys of the Holy *See* are termed *nuncios* or *legati missi* and *legati a latere* or *de latere*. "There is no difference in rank between *Nuncios* and *Legati a latere* or *de latere*. A *legatus a latere* or *de latere* is a Papal envoy who is a Cardinal, whereas a *Nuncio* is not a Cardinal": *I Oppenheim 1060n.* While *nuncios* obviously enjoy privileges and immunities set out in the Vienna Convention, there is only one other specific reference to them: in relation to precedence of heads of missions, the receiving State may maintain any practice "regarding the precedence of the representative of the Holy See" (art. 16(3)). *See Satow's Guide to Diplomatic Practice* (5th ed.), 86-7.

Nuremberg Charter   Properly styled the Agreement for the Prosecution and Punishment of the Major War Criminals of the European Axis Powers, the Charter was signed at London on 8 August 1945 *(82 U.N.T.S. 279)*. It established an International Military Tribunal (art. 1) with jurisdiction over the major war criminals of the European Axis countries in respect of crimes against peace, war crimes and crimes against humanity (art. 6). This jurisdiction extended to political and military leaders, organizers, instigators and accomplices (*id.*). Superior orders was explicitly excluded as a defense, though could be considered in mitigation of sentence (art. 8). Provision was made for the defendants to receive a fair trial (art. 16).

Nuremberg Military Tribunal   *See* **International Military Tribunals**.

Nuremberg Principles   The UN General Assembly having "affirm[ed] the principles of international law recognized by the Charter of the Nuremberg Tribunal and the judgment of the Tribunal" in Res. 91(I) of 11 December 1946, then asked "the Committee on the codification of international law" (the International Law Commission when later established) what these principles were. On 2 August 1950, the ILC adopted seven principles, styled "The Principles of International Law Recognized by the Charter of the Nuremberg Tribunal and in the Judgment of the Tribunal" *((1950) II ILC Yearbook 374)*:

> I. Any person who commits an act which constitutes a crime under international law is responsible therefore and liable to punishment.

> II. The fact that internal law does not impose a penalty for an act which constitutes a crime under international law does not relieve the person who committed the act from responsibility under international law.

> III. The fact that a person who committed an act which constitutes a crime under international law acted as Head of State or responsible government official does not relieve him from responsibility under international law.

IV. The fact that a person acted pursuant to order of his Government or of a superior does not relieve him from responsibility under international law, provided a moral choice was in fact possible to him.

V. Any person charged with a crime under international law has the right to a fair trial on the facts and law.

VI. The crimes hereinafter set out are punishable as crimes under international law: (a) Crimes against peace: (i) Planning, preparation, initiation or waging of a war of aggression or a war in violation of international treaties, agreements or assurances; (ii) Participation in a common plan or conspiracy for the accomplishment of any of the acts mentioned under (i). (b) War Crimes: Violations of the laws or customs of war which include, but are not limited to, murder, ill-treatment or deportation of slave-labour or for any other purpose of the civilian population of or in occupied territory, murder or ill-treatment of prisoners of war or persons on the seas, killing of hostages, plunder of public or private property, wanton destruction of cities, towns, or villages, or devastation not justified by military necessity. (c) Crimes against humanity: Murder, extermination, enslavement, deportation and other inhumane acts done against any civilian population, or persecutions on political, racial, or religious grounds, when such acts are done or such persecutions are carried on in execution of or in connection with any crime against peace or any war crime.

VII. Complicity in the commission of a crime against peace, a war crime, or a crime against humanity as set forth in Principle 6 is a crime under international law.

Nussbaum, Arthur 1877-1964. German lawyer. Professor, Berlin 1914-33, Columbia 1934-50. Principal works include *Money and the Law, National and International* (1939; 2nd ed. 1950); *A Concise History of the Law of Nations* (1947; 2nd ed. 1954).

Nyon Agreements 1937 *See* **piracy**.

O

OAPEC *See* **Organization of Arab Oil Exporting Countries**.

OAS *See* **Organization of American States**.

OAU *See* **Organization of African Unity**.

objective (treaty) régimes "The [International Law] Commission considered whether treaties creating so-called 'objective régimes,' that is, obligations and rights valid *erga omnes,* should be dealt with separately as a special case. . . . It considered that the position in article [36 of the Vienna Convention on the Law of Treaties 1969], regarding treaties intended to create rights in favour of States generally, together with the process mentioned in [art. 38] furnish a legal basis for the establishment of treaty obligations and rights valid *erga omnes,* which goes as far as is at present possible. Accordingly, it decided not to propose any special provision on treaties creating so called 'objective régimes'": *[1966] II I.L.C. Yearbook 231. See Aaland Islands Case (1920) L.N.O.J. Spec. Supp. No. 3*; **Antarctic Treaty**; *erga omnes* **obligations**.

objective responsibility *See* **responsibility, objective**.

objects of international law "In order to draw a clear distinction between the personality of a state or of an international institution on the one hand, and the position of the individual on the other, some elaboration is required of the ways in which international law does apply to individuals. Historically, those rules which first developed imposed duties designed to prevent piracy and the slave-trade, and to protect the persons and status of foreign sovereigns and their diplomatic representatives. It was from the existence of rules of this type that certain writers at the end of the nineteenth century classified states as the "subjects," and individuals as the "objects," of international law. Whatever the merits of the 'objects' theory in its historical context, it was certainly inadequate to explain situations, such as under a number of minority and other treaties after the First World War, where individuals were granted rights directly or indirectly enforceable against foreign states": Greig, *International Law* (2nd ed.), 116. The subject/object dichotomy has been described as "an intellectual prison of our own choosing." Many writers now argue that international law is a decision-making process in which individuals, as well as other entities such as multilateral corporations and non-governmental organizations, participate along with States and international organizations. *See,* for example, Higgins, *Problems and Process: International Law and How We Use It* (1994), 49.

Obligation to Arbitrate Opinion *1992 I.C.J. Rep. 62.* By a resolution of 2 March 1988, the UN General Assembly referred to the International Court of Justice the following question: "In the light of facts reported in the reports of the Secretary General [A/42/915 and Add. 1], is the United States of America, as a party to the Agreement between the United

Nations and the United States of America regarding the Headquarters of the United Nations [see resolution 169 (II)], under an obligation to enter into arbitration in accordance with section 21 of the Agreement?" The request for an **advisory opinion** had arisen in consequence of the enacting of by the United States Congress of the Anti-Terrorism Act in December 1987 which, *inter alia*, declared illegal the establishment or maintenance of an office of the Palestine Liberation Organization within the jurisdiction of the United States. The coverage of the Act, by necessity, included the office of the PLO observer mission to the United Nations which had been established in New York in 1974. The maintenance of the Office had been held by the UN Secretary-General to fall within the ambit of the Headquarters Agreement concluded with the United States on 26 June 1947. The Court *advised* (unanimously) that the US was bound to respect the obligation to enter into arbitration, noting that it was sufficient to recall the fundamental principle of international law that international law prevailed over domestic law.

observer status "[O]bserver status is a means whereby a government which is not a Member of the United Nations can have its representatives on the scene where international affairs are being discussed and where decisions are being made and have them there as accepted members of a community of diplomats, free to mingle and do everything a representative of a Member can do except speak and vote in official sessions. . . . Observer status cannot be defined in formal terms because the United Nations has never taken any action which would explicitly create or describe this relationship. Since the role is based on usage, not legal prescription, its meaning must be found in the behavior, privileges, and liabilities of observer countries as they actually function at United Nations Headquarters": Mower, Observer Countries: Quasi Members of the United Nations, *20 Int. Org. 266* at *267 (1966)*. Those countries with observer status are listed in *Permanent Missions to the United Nations* (commonly called the **Blue Book**) and on the United Nations' official website under the heading "Non-Member States Maintaining Permanent Observers' Offices at UN Headquarters." The number of States having observer status has decreased in recent years with States which have previously maintained observer status, including the Democratic Peoples' Republic of Korea, Monaco, Republic of Korea and Switzerland, all having recently joined the United Nations. The only "State" remaining on the list of Non-Member States Maintaining Permanent Observers' Offices at UN Headquarters is the Holy See. The constituent acts of Specialized Agencies in many instances also provide for the admission of observers. Cf. **associate membership**. Certain inter-governmental organizations (*see* **organizations, inter-governmental**) and **liberation movements** also enjoy observer status in the UN and in Specialized Agencies. **Non-Governmental Organizations** have **consultative status**. *See also* the *Obligation to Arbitrate Opinion 1988 I.C.J. Rep. 12* concerning the observer status of the PLO at the United Nations. *See* Sybesma-Knol, *The Status of Observers in the United Nations* (1981).

occupation This is a method of acquiring title to territory, derived from *occupatio* in Roman Law. Only territory that is subject to no State's sovereignty (*terra nullius)* may be acquired by occupation: *Western Sahara Case 1975 I.C.J. Rep. 12*. Occupation, "based . . . merely upon continued display of authority, involves two elements each of which must be shown to exist: the intention and will to act as sovereign, and some actual exercise or display of such authority": *Eastern Greenland Case 1933 P.C.I.J., Ser. A/B, No. 53* at 45-46. When the territory is uninhabited or uninhabitable, less is needed by way of the display of authority: *Clipperton Island Case (1931) 2 R.I.A.A. 1105*. The *locus classicus* on title to territory by occupation is the *Island of Palmas Case (1928) 2 R.I.A.A. 829; see also British Guiana Boundary Case (1904) 11 R.I.A.A. 21; Grisbadarna Arbitration (1909) 11 R.I.A.A. 155; Minquiers and Ecrehos Case 1953 I.C.J. Rep. 47; Frontier Land Case 1959*

I.C.J. Rep. 209; *Temple of Preah Vihear Case 1962 I.C.J. Rep. 6*. It has been suggested that occupation is now obsolescent as most of the temperate territory on the earth is subject to some State's sovereignty: Jennings, *The Acquisition of Territory in International Law* (1963), 20.

occupation, belligerent *See* **belligerent occupation**.

O'Connell, Daniel P. 1924-1979. Professor, Adelaide 1962-72, Oxford 1972-1979. Principal works include *The Law of State Succession* (1956); *International Law* (1965; 2nd ed. 1970); *International Law in Australia* (1966); *State Succession in Municipal Law and International Law* (1967); *The Influence of Law in Seapower* (1975); *The International Law of the Sea* (vol. I, 1982; vol. II, 1984). *See* Crawford, The Contribution of Professor D.P. O'Connell to the Discipline of International Law *(1980) 51 B.Y.I.L. 1*.

Oda, Shigeru 1924- . Professor, Tokyo 1953-59, Tôhoku 1959-76; member, ICJ 1976-92. Editor, *Japanese Annual of International Law* (1973-77). Principal works in English include: *International Control of Sea Resources* (1962); *International Law of Ocean Development* (4 vols. 1972-79); *The Law of the Sea in Our Time* (2 vols.1977); *International Law of the Resources of the Sea* (reprinted 1979); *The Practice of Japan in International Law* (with Owada, 1982). *See* McWhinney, *Judge Sigeru Oda and the Progressive Development of International Law* (1993).

Oder Commission, Territorial Jurisdiction of, Case *(Great Britain, Czechoslovakia, Denmark, France, Germany and Sweden v. Poland) (1929) P.C.I.J., Ser. A, No. 23*. Art. 341 of the Treaty of Versailles 1919 *(225 C.T.S. 188)* established an international régime for the River Oder under the administration of an International Commission comprising representatives of Poland, Prussia, Czechoslovakia, Great Britain, France, Denmark and Sweden. The River Oder and its tributaries flowed in part through Germany, in part through Poland, and in part formed the German-Polish frontier. Differences arose over the sections of the river to which the regime was to apply, and in particular whether it excluded navigable sections of tributaries of the Oder which were situated exclusively in Polish territory (as was maintained by Poland, and denied by the other six States who relied on the Barcelona Convention on the Régime of Navigable Waterways of International Concern 1921 *(7 L.N.T.S. 12)* and certain Articles of the Treaty of Versailles). By a special agreement of 30 October 1928 *(87 L.N.T.S. 103)*, the seven States submitted the issue to the PCIJ which *held* that the régime applied to the navigable sections of the Oder situated in Polish territory. The Barcelona Convention could not be relied on against Poland which had not ratified it. However, since the competence of a river commission charged with the practical application of an international régime was, failing indications to the contrary, territorially coincident with the internationalized sections of the river system, and since the Treaty of Versailles adopted the principles governing international fluvial law (according to which a waterway traversing the territory of more than one State was dealt with by reference to the riparian States' community of interest which in a navigable river became the basis of a common legal right involving the equality of all riparian States in the user of the whole navigable course of the river), the Treaty of Versailles must be interpreted as providing that the internationalization of such a river extended to the whole of its navigable course.

odious debts In the law of **State succession** it is often contended that certain public debts incurred by a predecessor State do not pass to the successor State. Odious debts have been defined as "such debts which for ethical, moral or political reasons are disapproved by the successor": Cahn, The Responsibility of the Successor State for War Debts, *44 A.J.I.L.*

480 (1950). Such a broad definition could obviously be used as a pretext by successor States to avoid debt obligations. Accordingly, one authority has sought to restrict odious debts to "those imposed on a community without its consent and contrary to its true interests, and those intended to finance the preparation and prosecution of a war against the successor State, and possibly against other States": O'Connell, *State Succession in Municipal and International Law* (1967), Vol. I. 459. *See also [1979] II I.L.C. Yearbook 46*. The Vienna Convention of 7 April 1983 on Succession of States in Respect of State Property, Archives and Debts *(22 I.L.M. 298 (1983))* envisages "equitable proportion" in relation to partial succession (arts. 37-41). In relation to a **newly independent State**, State debts are to pass only by agreement and "in view of the link with its activity in the territory to which the succession of States relates and the property, rights and interests which pass to the newly independent State." Moreover, any such agreement "shall not infringe the principle of the permanent sovereignty of every people over its wealth and natural resources, nor shall its implementation endanger the fundamental economic equilibria of the newly independent State": art. 38.

OECD *See* **Organization for Economic Co-operation and Development**.

OEEC *See* **Organization for Economic Co-operation and Development**.

OHCHR *See* **United Nations High Commissioner for Human Rights**.

Oil Platforms Case *(Islamic Republic of Iran v. United States of America)*. On 2 November 1992, the Islamic Republic of Iran instituted proceedings against the United States in respect of a dispute arising out of the attacks on and destruction of three offshore oil production complexes owned and operated by the National Iranian Oil Company, by several United States warships on 19 October 1987 and 18 April 1988. Iran alleged a breach of various provisions of the Treaty of Amity, Economic Relations and Consular Rights of 15 August 1955 between the United States and Iran, art. XXI (2) of which reads: "Any dispute between the High Contracting Parties as to the interpretation or application of the present treaty, not satisfactorily adjusted by diplomacy shall be referred to the International Court of Justice, unless the High Contracting Parties agree to settlement by some other pacific means." The US challenged the admissibility of the case on the basis that the lawfulness of the actions of its naval forces did not fall within the ambit of the Treaty, which concerned commercial, economic and consular relations between the two States. In its judgment on the US preliminary objections, the Court *held* (1) (14 to 2) that the preliminary objections of the United States should be rejected; (2) (14 to 2) that the Court had jurisdiction in the case on the basis of Article XXI (2) of the Treaty of 1955: *1996 I.C.J. Rep. 803*. On 2 March 2003, the public hearings in the case were concluded. No decision has yet been made on the merits of the case.

Oil-for-Food program To ameliorate the humanitarian conditions in Iraq consequent upon the extensive sanctions régime imposed by Security Council Res. 661 (1990), and maintained by Res. 687 (1991), the Council, by Res. 986 (1995) of 14 April 1995, authorized the sale of controlled amounts of Iraqi oil (art. 1), the proceeds to be placed in an escrow account (art. 7) and applied "to meet the humanitarian needs of the Iraqi population" (art. 8)—hence the term "oil-for-food." While sanctions were abandoned by Res. 1483 (2003) of 22 May 2003 (art. 10), the program was to be phased out over 6 months (art. 16).

Oliver, Covey T. 1913- . Professor at Berkeley and Pennsylvania; U.S. Ambassador to Colombia, 1964-66; Assistant Secretary of State for Inter-American Affairs 1967-68. Principal works include *Restatement of the Law II: Foreign Relations Law of U.S.* (with co-reporters) (1965); *The Inter-American Security System and the Cuban Crises* (1964); *Cases and Materials on International Law* (with others 1973; 4th ed. 1995), 5th ed. with Firmage, Blakesley, Scott and Williams *sub nom. The International Legal System* (2001).

ONUC Established by Security Council Res. 143 (1960), the United Nations Operation in the Congo was mandated to oversee the withdrawal of Belgian forces from the region, while aiding the government in ensuring law and order. ONUC operated from July 1960 to June 1964. ONUC's expenses were the subject of the *Expenses of the United Nations Case 1962 I.C.J. Rep. 151.*

ONUCA An acronym for the United Nations Observer Group in Central America, ONUCA was established by Security Council Res. 644 (1989). Headquartered in Teguci-galpa, Honduras, the mission was established to confirm compliance by the governments of Costa Rica, El Salvador, Guatemala, Honduras and Nicaragua with their agreement to terminate assistance to irregular forces and insurrectionist movements in the region. The mission was operational from November 1989 through January 1992.

ONUMOZ Established by Security Council Res. 797 (1992), the United Nations Opera-tion in Mozambique assisted in implementing the 1992 General Peace Agreement between the President of the Republic of Mozambique and the President of the Resistencia Nacional Mocambicana (RENAMO). ONUMOZ operated from December 1992 to December 1994.

ONUSAL An acronym for the United Nations Observer Mission in El Salvador. ONUSAL was established by Security Council Res. 693 (1991). ONUSAL was authorized to ensure implementation of each agreement between the El Salvadorean government and Frente Farabundo Marti para la Liberacion Nacional and operated between July 1991 and April 1995.

OPEC *See* **Organization of Petroleum Exporting Countries.**

open diplomacy "The contemporary 'open,' as distinguished from the 'secret' diplo-macy before the First World War, has been greatly facilitated by technological advances in the communications media which, in turn, have aided the development of propaganda techniques. The vast opportunities for public debate of delicate issues led to a discernible change in tone in dealings among certain governments. But the difference between 'clas-sic' and modern diplomacy should not be exaggerated. A number of years of experience with 'open' and 'conference'diplomacy have shown that traditional methods of unpubli-cized negotiations—or to use Mr. Hammerskjöld's term, 'quiet' diplomacy—still have a useful part to play in furthering the success of 'conference' diplomacy": Déak, Organs of States in their External Relations, in Sörensen, *Manual of Public International Law* (1968), 381 at 395.

open door This term, now generally considered to be obsolete, has been used to describe those provisions of commercial and other treaties which are designed to allow access to States for trade and commerce. Open door provisions are exemplified in art. 22(5) of the Covenant of the League of Nations *(225 C.T.S. 188)*, requiring Mandatory Powers in B mandates to "secure equal opportunities for the trade and commerce of other Members of the League"; art. 23(e) of the Covenant, requiring Mandatory Powers in all mandates to make provision for "equitable treatment for the commerce of all Members of the League"; and art. 76(e) of the UN Charter, requiring all Administering Authorities in trust territories "to ensure equal treatment in . . . economic, and commercial matters for all Members of the United Nations and their nationals." *See also* **Mandates System**; **Trusteeship System**.

open registry States *See* **flag of convenience**.

open sea This term, little used in modern literature, is synonymous with the **high seas**. *See I Oppenheim 722.*

opinio juris This phrase (in full, *opinio juris sive necessitates*) connotes an element in the formation of customary rules of international law, expressed in art. 38(1)(b) of the ICJ Statute as "a general practice accepted as law." "It is not sufficient to show that States follow habitually a certain course of conduct, either doing or not doing something. To prove the existence of a rule of international customary law, it is necessary to establish that States act in this way because they recognize a *legal* obligation to this effect": Schwarzenberger and Brown, *A Manual of International Law* (6th ed.), 26. *See **Lotus Case (1927) P.C.I.J., Ser. A, No. 10**; **Asylum Case 1950 I.C.J. Rep. 266**; **North Sea Continental Shelf Cases 1969 I.C.J. Rep. 3**.* As a concept, *opinio juris* is the subject of great controversy: "*opinio juris* is far more difficult to identify and define than general, framework principles of international law. Although most international lawyers agree that *opinio juris* plays a role in transforming state practice into rules of customary international law, they have not been able to agree on its character nor to resolve many theoretical problems associated with it": Byers, *Custom, Power and the Power of Rules* (1999), 18. Thus, one can contrast the rather extreme position of Bin Cheng who argued that there need be "no usage at all in the sense of repeated practice" provided that *opinio juris* can be "clearly established" (Cheng, United Nations Resolutions on Outer Space: Instant Customary International Law? *5 Indian J. Int. L. 23* at 35-6 *(1965)*) with that of Kelsen who argued that it was "almost impossible" to discover the sentiments or thoughts of States as to why they were engaging in a particular practice (Kelsen, *Principles of Public International Law* (1966), 450-54). Certainly, it is the case that in practice the difficulty lies in proving that a line of conduct is followed because of a conviction of legal obligation. In the absence of express statements declaring this obligation, it would seem that *opinio juris* is to be presumed from repetition of the line of conduct: "if a course of conduct is repeatedly followed, the only presumption, or at least a fair presumption, is that it was so followed, and another course not followed, because of the existence of a conviction of obligation": Parry, *The Sources and Evidences of International Law* (1965), 62. Nevertheless, particularly in relation to the emergence of a new rule of customary international law, there remains what one writer has described as a "chronological paradox [which requires that] states creating new customary rules must believe that those rules already exist, and that their practice, accordingly, is in accordance with the law": Byers, *supra*, 131. However, "any assertion of *opinio juris* in such circumstances cannot be an assertion of what the law is but what the state making the claim wishes the law to be . . . whether or not the state is successful in its desire to change the law will depend upon the reaction of other states . . . if states acquiesce in a practice, they are effectively asserting, along with the acting state, the belief in a developing rule of customary international law": Barker, *International Law and International Relations* (2000), 63. *See* **custom**.

opinion (1) The opinion of a law officer may be important evidence of a State's attitude to a particular practice and hence its adherence, or non-adherence, to a rule of customary law. *See, e.g.*, the (UK) ***Law Officers' Opinions***. (2) Art. 95(2) of the ICJ Rules of Court permits any judge to attach to a judgment an individual opinion, either in concurrence with, or in dissent from, the judgment. (3) Opinion, advisory. *See* **advisory opinion**.

Oppenheim, Lassa Francis Lawrence 1858-1919. Professor, Freiburg-in-Breisgau 1885-92, Basle 1892-95, LSE 1895-1908, Cambridge 1908-1919. The principal works of this exceptional scholar include *International Law*, Vol. I *(Peace)* (1905; 2nd ed. 1912; subsequent editions by others, though retaining Oppenheim's name), Vol. II *(War and Neutrality)* (1906; 2nd ed. 1912; subsequent editions by others); *International Incidents for Discussion in Conversation Classes* (1909; 2nd ed. 1911); editor, *Contributions to International Law and Diplomacy* (1911); *The Panama Canal Conflict* (1919); *The League of Nations and its Problems* (1919).

Optional Clause This is the name commonly given to art. 36(2) of the ICJ Statute: "The States parties to the present Statute may at any time declare that they recognize as compulsory *ipso facto* and without special agreement, in relation to any other state accepting the same obligation, the jurisdiction of the Court in all legal disputes concerning: (a) the interpretation of a treaty; (b) any question of international law; (c) the existence of any fact which, if established, would constitute a breach of an international obligation; (d) the nature or extent of the reparation to be made for the breach of an international obligation." Declarations under the Optional Clause "may be made unconditionally or on condition of reciprocity on the part of several or certain states, or for a certain time" (art. 36(3)); and they must be deposited with the Secretary-General of the United Nations (art. 36(4)). For a list of those States that have made Declarations under the Optional Clause, and the terms of these Declarations, see current *I.C.J. Yearbook*. See Damrosch (ed.), *The International Court of Justice at a Crossroads* (1987), especially Gross, Compulsory Jurisdiction Under the Optional Protocol: History and Practice, at 19, and Gordon, "Legal Disputes" under Article 36(2) of the Statute, at 183; Lowe and Fitzmaurice, *Fifty Years of the International Court of Justice* (1996); Rosenne, *The Law and Practice of the International Court* (3rd ed.); Waldock, Decline of the Optional Clause, *(1955-56) 32 B.Y.I.L. 244*; Merrills, The Optional Clause Today, *(1979) 50 B.Y.I.L. 87*; Merrills, The Optional Clause Revisited, *(1993) 64 B.Y.I.L. 197*. *See also* **automatic reservation**; **compromissory clause**; *Norwegian Loans Case*; *Military and Paramilitary Activities in and against Nicaragua (Jurisdiction)*.

Organization for Economic Cooperation and Development (OECD) The OECD is the successor to the Organization for European Economic Cooperation (OEEC), which had been established by the Convention for European Economic Cooperation, signed at Paris on 16 April 1948. OEEC was set up primarily to administer the Marshall Plan of U.S. aid, but the Convention included provisions designed to promote economic cooperation among its European members. On OEEC, see Price, *The Marshall Plan and its Meaning* (1955). The OECD was established by the Convention on the Organization for Economic Cooperation and Development, signed at Paris on 14 December 1960 *(888 U.N.T.S. 179)*. The purposes of OECD are to promote policies to achieve the highest sustainable economic growth while maintaining financial stability and thus to contribute to the development of the world economy, to contribute to sound economic expansion, to contribute to the expansion of world trade on a multilateral, non-discriminatory basis (art. 1). Eighteen Western European and other developed States (Canada and the USA) are parties to the 1960 Convention. Any government prepared to assume the obligations of membership may be invited to accede to the Convention: Australia, the Czech Republic, Finland, Hungary, Japan, Korea, Mexico, New Zealand, Poland, and the Slovak Republic have become members of OECD in this way. OECD operates through a Council, composed of all members and the "body from which all acts of the Organization derive" (art. 7); and an Executive Committee, established by the Council to carry out the routine functions of the Organization. *See* Sands and Klein, *Bowett's Law of International Institutions* (5th.ed.), 167-171. *See also* <www.oecd.org>.

Organization for European Economic Cooperation *See* **Organization for Economic Cooperation and Development**.

Organization for Security and Co-operation in Europe The OSCE emerged out of the Conference on Security and Co-operation in Europe (CSCE) discussions for which were started in 1973 with the aim of providing a forum for discussion between Eastern and Western Europe and led to the adoption of the Final Act of Helsinki in 1975 *(14 I.L.M. 1292 (1975))*. This document was not a legally binding treaty but rather a set of political objectives. The Final Act produced a series of principles in three principal areas (baskets): "Questions relating to security in Europe"; "Co-operation in the field of economics, of science and technology and of the environment"; and "Co-operation in Humanitarian and Other Fields." The CSCE was not endowed with a permanent intuitional structure, but instead progressed through a series of follow-up meetings provided for in the Final Act, as well as specialized conferences and experts meetings which have been organised since 1978. In 1990, the Charter of Paris for a New Europe *(30 I.L.M. 190 (1991))* provided for a system of consultation and decision-making bodies consisting of regular summit meetings of Heads of State or Government, the Council of Ministers (now Ministerial Council) consisting of Ministers for Foreign Affairs of participating States, the Committee of Senior Officials (now the Senior Council) which was to deal with day to day affairs. A Parliamentary Assembly was established in 1991, consisting of representatives of national parliaments of each of the participating States. The CSCE was renamed the Organization for Security and Co-operation in Europe (OSCE) in the Budapest Declaration in 1994 with effect from 1 January 1995. "Even though the Budapest Declaration makes it clear that the change in name from CSCE to OSCE alters neither the character of the participating states' CSCE commitments nor the status of the CSCE and its institutions, one may take the view that the OSCE now qualifies as a full-fledged international organization" Sands and Klein, *Bowett's Law of International Institutions* (5th ed.), 201. The OSCE currently has 55 participating States from Europe, Central Asia and North America and is headquartered in Vienna. The OSCE approach to security is comprehensive, dealing with a wide range of security-related issues including arms control, **preventive diplomacy**, confidence- and security-building measures, **human rights**, democratization, election monitoring and environmental security; all OSCE participating States have equal status and decisions are based on consensus. *See* <www.osce.org>.

Organization of African Unity The OAU was established by the Charter of the Organization of African Unity, concluded at Addis Ababa on 25 May 1963 *(479 U.N.T.S. 39)* and in force on 13 September 1963. It was replaced by the **African Union** on 9 July 2002. The purposes of the OAU were to promote unity among African States, to achieve a better life for African peoples, to defend sovereignty, territorial integrity and independence, to eradicate all forms of colonialism and to promote international cooperation (art. II(1)). Membership was open to all independent African States (art. IV). There were ultimately 53 members, including the whole of the African continent. The OAU acted through an Assembly of Heads of State and Government, described as "the Supreme Organ" and empowered to establish the general policy (art. VIII); a Council of Ministers, operating under the Assembly and implementing inter-African cooperation and decisions of the Assembly (art. XIII); and a number of Specialized Commissions, Economic and Social; Educational and Cultural; Health, Sanitation and Nutrition; Defence; Scientific, Technical and Research; Jurists; Communications (art. XX). "There is wide agreement that the Organization's record in the field of decolonisation is by far its most impressive contribution. It has legitimised the action of national liberation movements and been successful in maintaining the question on the international agenda for long periods of time": Sands and Klein,

Bowett's Law of International Institutions (5th ed.), 248. *See* Cervenka, *The Organization of African Unity and its Charter* (2nd ed.). *See* <www.oau-oua.org>.

Organization of American States (OAS) The origin of the OAS was the International Union of American Republics, founded in 1890; this Union was nothing more than a series of conferences on matters of mutual concern. The constituent document of the OAS is the Charter of the Organization of American States, concluded at Bogotá on 30 April 1948 *(119 U.N.T.S. 3)*, and in force on 13 December 1951. The purposes of the OAS are to strengthen the peace and security of the continent, to promote and consolidate representative democracy, with due respect to the principle of non-intervention, to prevent possible causes of difficulty and ensure pacific settlement of disputes, to provide common action against aggression, to settle political, juridical and economic problems, to promote economic, social and cultural development, to eradicate extreme poverty, and to achieve an effective limitation of conventional weapons (art. 2). Membership is open to all American States (art. 4), and there are at present 35 members. Cuba is a member, but has since January 1962 been excluded from participation in OAS affairs. The OAS operates through a General Assembly of all members, known as the Inter-American Conference, and described as "the supreme organ" (art. 54) and laying down "the general action and policy . . . [and] . . . the structure and function of its organs"; a Meeting of Consultation of Ministers of Foreign Affairs, convening "to consider problems of an urgent nature and of common interest" (art. 61); a Permanent Council to "keep vigilance over the friendly relation among the member states" (art. 84); and a number of autonomous Councils, the Inter-American Council for Integral Development, the Inter-American Juridical Committee and the Inter-American Commission on Human Rights, as well as a General Secretariat (art. 107) having its seat in Washington (art. 121). The OAS Charter reaffirmed (in arts. 28 and 29) the commitment to mutual defense set out in the Inter-American Treaty of Reciprocal Assistance, concluded at Rio de Janeiro on 2 September 1947 *(21 U.N.T.S. 93)*; Protocol of Amendment signed at San José 29 July 1975: *14 I.L.M. 1122 (1975)*. *See* Thomas and Thomas, *The Organization of American States* (1963); Leblanc, *OAS and the Promotion and Protection of Human Rights* (1977); Morse, *The OAS: The Next Fifty Years* (1999); Sands and Klein, *Bowett's Law of International Institutions* (5th. ed.), 205-214.

Organization of Arab Oil Exporting Countries The Organization of Arab Petroleum Exporting Countries (OAPEC in acronym) is an offshoot of the Organization of Petroleum Exporting Countries (OPEC). It was established by the Agreement concluded at Beirut on 9 January 1968 *(7 I.L.M. 759 (1968))*. Its aims are cooperation in economic activity in the oil industry and realization of "equitable and reasonable terms" for oil sales (art. 2). Membership consists of three founding members (Kuwait, Libya, and Saudi Arabia) and any other Arab State which has oil as a principal source of national income. Membership is approved by three-quarters of the existing members, including the three founding members (art. 7). There are currently eleven member states: the three original members together with Algeria, Bahrain, Egypt, Iraq, Qatar, Syria, Tunisia and United Arab Emirates. Tunisia's membership has been suspended since 1986 at her own request. OAPEC operates through a Council of all members, this Council being "the supreme authority" (art. 10); a Bureau of all members, operating under the Council (art. 15); a General Secretariat; and a Judicial Commission to deal with disputes relating to the interpretation and application of the Agreement or relating to oil operations (art. 23). *See* <www.oapecorg.org>.

Organization of Petroleum Exporting Countries The Agreement Concerning the Creation of the Organization of Petroleum Exporting Countries was concluded at Baghdad on 14 September 1960 *(443 U.N.T.S. 247)*, and came into force on 1 October 1960. OPEC is based upon the premise that the Members "can no longer remain indifferent to the attitude heretofore adopted by the Oil Companies in effecting price modifications" (Res. 1(1)(1)). OPEC is conceived as a forum for regular consultation with a view to coordinating and unifying policies (Res. 1(2)(1)), especially in the area of stabilizing prices "by, among other means, the regulation of production, with due regard to the interests of the producing and of the consuming nations, and to the necessity of securing a steady income to the producing countries, an efficient and regular supply of this source of energy to consuming nations, and a fair return on their capital to those investing in the petroleum industry" (Res. 1(1)(3)). The original members are Iran, Iraq, Kuwait, Saudi Arabia and Venezuela; membership is open to any State with "a substantial net export of Crude Petroleum . . . if unanimously accepted by all five original Members. . . ." (Res. 1(2)(3)). Membership has been extended to Algeria (1969), Ecuador (1973), Indonesia (1962), Nigeria (1971), Qatar (1961), and the United Arab Emirates (1967). The Statute of OPEC, originally adopted in 1961 and now of 2000, establish a Conference of all members, having power to lay down policy and set rules; a Board of Governors originally consisting of representatives of the five original members and one other collectively representing those States subsequently admitted, but now consisting of one representative for each member state. The Board directs the management of the Organization, implements Conference decisions and draws up the budget. The organization also has a Secretariat based at its headquarters in Vienna, Austria. *See* Amuzegar, *Managing the Oil Wealth: OPEC's Windfalls and Pitfalls* (1999). *See* <www.opec.org>.

Organization of the Islamic Conference The Organization of Islamic the Conference was established in 1969 in Rabat, Morocco and is governed by the Charter of the Islamic Conference adopted in 1972. The aims of the Organization are to promote Islamic solidarity; to consolidate co-operation in the political, economic, social, cultural, and scientific fields; to endeavour to eliminate racial segregation, discrimination and to eradicate colonialism in all its forms; to take necessary measures to support international peace and security founded on justice; to coordinate efforts for the safeguarding of Holy Places and support of the struggle of the people of Palestine, to help them regain their rights and liberate their land; to support the struggle of all Muslim people with a view to preserving their dignity, independence and national rights; to create a suitable atmosphere for the promotion of co-operation and understanding between member States and other countries (art. II(A)). The Organization is composed of the Conference of Kings and Heads of State and Government (art. IV); the Conference of Foreign Ministers (art. V); and the General Secretariat headed by the Secretary-General (art. VI). Membership is made up of the States which took part in the original Conference of Kings and Heads of State and Government held in Rabat and signed the Charter, as well as States which have subsequently joined in accordance with the provisions of art. VIII of the Charter. Membership is open to every Muslim State and there are currently 56 member States. The Organization has its headquarters in Jeddah, Saudi Arabia. *See* <www.oic-oci.org>.

organizations, international, intergovernmental These are not terms of art. In its widest sense, the expression "international organization" is capable of embracing not only organizations composed of governments, but **non-governmental organizations** and even industrial and commercial organizations. It is nevertheless in the sense of "intergovernmental organization" that the expression "international organization" is commonly understood. Cf. ECOSOC Res. 288(X) of 27 February 1950: "Any international organization which is not established by inter-governmental agreement shall be considered as a non-governmental organization for the purpose of" the arrangements governing **consultative status** for NGOs. It is in this sense that some of the older specialized agencies use the term. More recent practice has favored the expression "intergovernmental organization" to describe the same type of organization (*e.g.*, UNEP: GA Res. 2997 (XXVII) of 15 December 1972, para. IV(5): "Also invites other intergovernmental and . . . non-governmental organizations . . . to lend their full support . . ."). The UN Convention on the Law of the Sea 1982 *(1833 U.N.T.S. 3)* applies to intergovernmental organizations: "For the purposes of [signature and participation by international organizations], 'international organization' means an intergovernmental organization constituted by States. . . ." (Annex IX, art. 1).

The European Community has sought to distinguish itself from traditional organizations, which normally lack the direct legislative powers or "competence" with which it is endowed. Thus, Annex IX, art. 1 of the UN Convention on the Law of the Sea 1982 embraces the Community in the phrase "intergovernmental organization constituted by States to which its Member States have transferred competence over matters governed by this Convention, including the competence to enter into treaties in respect of those matters." In some contexts, "grouping of States" (IFAD) or "regional economic integration organizations" (ECE Conventions; *e.g.*, Convention on Long-Range Transboundary Air Pollution 1979 *(1302 U.N.T.S. 217)* has been used instead. *See* Commission of the European Communities, *The European Community, International Organizations and Multilateral Agreements* (1983); *and see* **supranational organizations**.

It will be apparent that the open or closed, general or technical, universal or regional character of the organization is of no consequence to its status as an international organization, but there are perhaps a minimum of criteria to confer an organizational character, namely separate international personality (usually to be conferred by treaty or less formal international accord), membership and representation at the level of central government or organs of central government and, if it is to be distinguished from a standing conference or an appendage of another organization or of a national government, a separate support structure or secretariat.

The last twenty years has seen considerable growth in the number and coverage of international organizations: "[I]n recent years international organizations have played an ever more active role in international affairs, with implications at the international and national levels. Their activities address subjects previously not addressed by international co-operation—for example, the exploitation of the deep-sea bed, regional monetary union, international trade in services at the global level (as opposed to goods), and a wide range of environmental issues from climate change to biotechnology. Within the more traditional fields of activity, the involvement of international organizations is increasingly significant": Sands and Klein, *Bowett's Law of International Institutions,* (5th ed.), 14. *See also* Schermers and Blokker, *International Institutional Law*, (3rd ed.), Chap. 1.

organizations, non-governmental *See* **non-governmental organization(s)**.

original member(s) Within international organizations, there are invariable two classes of members, original members and **admitted members**. Thus, in art 3 of the UN Charter, the original members of the Organization were "those States which, having participated in the United Nations Conference on International Organization at San Francisco, or having previously signed the Declaration of United Nations of 1 January 1942, sign the present Charter and ratify it. . . ." There were 51 original members of the UN, 50 having satisfied the conditions of art. 3, plus Poland which, while not satisfying either condition, was permitted to sign and ratify the Charter as an original member.

original responsibility *See* **responsibility, original**.

Orinoco Steamship Company Case *(USA v. Venezuela) (1904), (1910) 9 R.I.A.A. 180, 11 R.I.A.A. 227.* The Orinoco Shipping and Trading Company Limited, an English company, transferred with effect from 1 April 1902 to the Orinoco Steamship Company, a US company, all its claims against the Venezuelan Government. These claims included claims in respect of the cancellation by Government Decree of a contract concluded in 1894, a debt arising under a contract concluded in 1900 and losses sustained in the context of a revolution in Venezuela. Art. 14 of the 1894 contract and art. 4 of the 1900 contract contained so-called **Calvo clauses** requiring the concessionary under the contract to submit disputes regarding its interpretation or execution only to Venezuelan tribunals and not to refer such disputes for an international claim; and art. 13 of the 1894 contract required prior notice to the Government of Venezuela of any transfer of the contract to another person, while Venezuelan law imposed a similar requirement to notify a debtor of a transfer of the debt. The USA presented a claim on behalf of the Orinoco Steamship Company to the USA-Venezuela Mixed Claims Commission established by a Protocol of 17 February 1903. *Held* (by Barge, umpire, deciding "on a basis of absolute equity" as stipulated in the Protocol), in partially allowing the claim, that: (1) the Protocol covered claims owned by US companies on the date of its signature even if at the time of their origin they were owned by a national of another State; (2) the claims in respect of the cancellation of the 1894 contract and the debt under the 1900 contract had to be disallowed because, *inter alia*, the concessionary had to comply with the Calvo clauses in arts. 14 and 4 of the respective contracts but had failed to do so, and furthermore the absence of prior notification to Venezuela of the transfer to the claimant of the contract and the debt made the transfers ineffective; (3) while for the same reason claims for losses connected with the revolution must be disallowed so far as they relied on a transfer of claims on 1 April 1902, claims for subsequent losses were directly vested in the claimant and Venezuela must pay damages for its forced detention and use of the claimant's vessels and for goods and services rendered to Venezuela, but was not obliged to pay compensation in respect of losses suffered as a result of the stoppage of one of the claimant's vessels by Venezuela in the course of resisting the revolution or as a result of Venezuela having closed the Orinoco River to navigation, which was not a blockade in the international legal sense (the rebels not having been recognized as belligerents) but a legitimate measure taken by Venezuela as sovereign in its own territory.

Although, under art. 1 of the 1903 Protocol, the decision of the umpire was to be final and conclusive, the USA contended that the award was based on excessive exercise of jurisdiction and contained essential errors of law and fact. By a further Protocol signed on 13 February 1909, the USA and Venezuela agreed to submit the matter to arbitration by a tribunal of the Permanent Court of Arbitration which *held* that, since it followed from the 1903 and 1909 Protocols that Venezuela had renounced invoking the Calvo clause in the 1900 contract (as also that in the 1894 contract) and prior notice to a debtor of a transfer of a debt could not be considered to be required by absolute equity, the umpire's rejection of the claims in regard to the debt under the 1900 contract and the losses connected with the revolution arising before 1 April 1902 was void and those claims should be allowed.

Oscar Chinn Case *See* ***Chinn, Oscar, Case***.

OSCE *See* **Organization for Security and Co-operation in Europe**.

Ottoman Debt Arbitration *(1925) 1 R.I.A.A. 529.* Certain territories formerly belonging to the Ottoman Empire were detached from it and either attributed to other States or became newly created States. After World War I, the public debt of the Ottoman Empire and the annual charges for the servicing of the debt were, on terms laid down in arts. 46-57 of the Treaty of Lausanne 1923 *(28 L.N.T.S. 13)* distributed between Turkey and those other States. Questions arose as to the application of those terms in respect of various parts of the Ottoman public debt and as to the apportionment of responsibility for the Ottoman public debt, and were referred to arbitration under art. 47 of the Treaty of Lausanne. Bulgaria, Greece, Italy, Turkey, Iraq, Palestine, Transjordan and territories under French mandate participated in the arbitration. Borel (sole Arbitrator), in the course of disposing of the various questions referred to him, *held* that: where Bulgaria had by the Treaty of Neuilly, which entered into force on 9 August 1920, ceded certain former Ottoman territories to the Allied and Associated Powers who had in turn, by a separate Treaty signed in 1920 but which did not enter into force until 1924, ceded the territory to Greece, (a) Bulgaria's loss of sovereignty dated from 9 August 1920 and not from the time in 1919 when the territories were occupied by the Allied and Associated Powers, since mere military occupation did not operate as a transfer of territory, and (b) the common intention of the parties was that Greece's share in responsibility for the Ottoman public debt in respect of those territories dated from 1920; a State which acquired territory by cession was not in strict law bound to take over a corresponding part of the public debt of the ceding State; in international law the Turkish Republic continued the international personality of the Ottoman Empire; the revival by art. 99 of the Treaty of Lausanne of certain economic or technical treaties concluded with the Ottoman Empire was necessary because otherwise, as treaties between former belligerents, they would have been terminated by the War, and their revival did not therefore indicate that the Turkish Republic was a new State; the principle of equality of States required the costs of the Arbitration, which was conducted in the common interest of the participating States, to be borne in equal shares, for which purpose Iraq, Palestine, Transjordan, Syria and Lebanon, although subject to Mandates, were to be regarded as separate States.

Ottoz Claim *(France v. Italy) (1950) 18 I.L.R. 435.* The claimants, French nationals, owned in Italy a villa and an adjacent house under construction. They were sequestered by Italy in 1943, during World War II, and in 1944 the sequestrator entered into a new lease of the villa with the previous tenant and also granted him a lease of the house under construction. In 1946, the sequestration was annulled by Italian legislation and remedies against acts of sequestrators were provided. In 1947, the claimants sought possession of their properties; in 1949, an Italian Court made an order for possession of the house under construction, but not of the villa; an appeal was pending while the present claim was before the Franco-Italian Conciliation Commission, to which it had been submitted by France under art. 78 of the Treaty of Peace with Italy. The Conciliation Commission *held* that Italy must ensure, by such means as it deemed fit, the restoration to the claimants of their property, and insofar as the lease granted by the sequestrator stood in the way of such restoration Italy must nullify it. Italian laws relating to tenancies granted by sequestrators passed during the armistice period only partially satisfied the international obligation of *restitutio in integrum* imposed by the Peace Treaty: those laws could not limit the right of UN nationals to obtain the restitution of their property, which flowed directly from the Peace Treaty, and accordingly acts by the claimants, including the institution of legal proceedings still in progress, based on those laws could not prejudice the right to full restitution flowing from the Peace Treaty.

Outer Space Treaty The Treaty on Principles Governing the Activities of States in the Exploration and Use of Outer Space, including the Moon and other Celestial Bodies, of 27 January 1967 *(610 U.N.T.S. 206)* builds on many discussions and statements, notably General Assembly Resolutions 1721 (XVI) of 20 December 1961, 1884 (XVIII) Of 17 October 1963 and 1962 (XVIII) of 13 December 1963. It has been supplemented by later treaties. The exploration and use of outer space (which term is undefined), the moon and celestial bodies are to be carried out for the benefit and in the interests of all countries and shall be the province of all mankind (art. I). Access to space and such bodies is free, in accordance with international law, as is scientific investigation, which States are to facilitate (art. I.). Outer space, including the moon and celestial bodies, is not subject to national appropriation (art. II). All activities are to be carried out in accordance with international law and the UN Charter (art. III). Each party has a right to access to the installations and vehicles of other parties on the moon or celestial bodies on a basis of reciprocity (art. XII). Space is for peaceful purposes only, and States undertake not to place nuclear weapons in orbit (art. IV); cf. Nuclear Test Ban Treaty. Astronauts are to be regarded as "envoys of mankind" to be aided and assisted (art. V; cf. **Rescue and Return** of Astronauts **Agreement** 1968 *(672 U.N.T.S. 1218))*, and parties are to notify dangerous phenomena encountered in outer space (art. V). Contamination and harmful interference with other activities are to be avoided, though there is provision for consultation on such matters (art. IX). States bear international responsibility for their national activities in outer space, and must authorize and supervise their non-governmental entities (art. VI). States are liable for damage caused by launches (art. VII). The State of registry of a space object retains jurisdiction over the object and personnel (art. VIII). *See also* **Moon Treaty** and **space objects**. *See* Lachs, *The Law of Outer Space* (1972); Jasentulajana and Lee, *Manual on Space Law* (4 vols., 1979); Christol, *Space Law*, (1991); Wassenbergh, *Principles of Outer Space Law in Hindsight* (1991); Forkosch, *Outer Space and Legal Liability* (2002).

outlawry (of war)   In the attempts by the international community to prevent war, two instruments stand out. **The General Treaty for the Renunciation of War** (the Kellogg-Briand Pact) of 27 August 1928 *(94 L.N.T.S. 57)* condemned "recourse to war for the solution of international controversies and renounc[ed] it as an instrument of national policy. . ." (art. I); and the Parties undertook to settle all disputes or conflicts by peaceful means (art. II). The UN Charter, in art. 2(4), requires all members to refrain from the threat or use of force; and art. 2(3) requires all members to settle disputes by peaceful means "in such a manner that international peace and security, and justice, are not endangered." The fact that war is, under contemporary international law, outlawed and therefore illegal does not mean that the conduct of any war is outwith the accepted rules on warfare: see *II Oppenheim 154*; *See* Wehberg, *The Outlawry of War* (1931); Stone, *Legal Controls of International Conflict* (2nd Imp. Revised, 1959); Green, *The Contemporary Law of Armed Conflict* (2000); Gray, *International Law and the Use of Force* (2001).

overflight   Flight over national territory is not free and open to the aircraft of all States. By the **Chicago Convention** on International Civil Aviation 1944 *(15 U.N.T.S. 295)* **scheduled air services** are subject to permission (art. 6): granted automatically among parties to the **"two freedoms"** agreement (International Air Services Transit Agreement 7 December 1944, *84 U.N.T.S. 389)* and **non-scheduled flight** is subject to controls (art. 5). The UN Convention on the Law of the Sea *(1833 U.N.T.S. 3)*, art. 87 (1), describes "freedom of overflight" as a component of freedom of the high seas. In practice, the manner in which scheduled services may be operated is closely regulated under ICAO rules, particularly in the congested North Atlantic and northern European areas. *See* Kailbronner, Freedom of the Air and the Convention on the Law of the Sea, *77 A.J.I.L. 490 (1983)*.

Oxford Manual   This Manual on the Laws of War on Land, adopted by the *Institut de Droit International* at Oxford on 9 September 1880 *((1881-82) 5 Annuaire de l'Institut de Droit International 156)*, was intended, not as the basis of a treaty, but rather as the basis of national legislation (Preface). It contains 86 articles, commencing with a number of general principles (arts. 1-6), continuing with provisions applying these general principles (arts. 7-83) and concluding with penal sanctions for breaches of the laws of war (arts. 84-6). This Manual, along with the **Brussels Declaration** Concerning the Laws and Customs of War of 27 August 1874, constituted the foundations upon which the **Hague Conventions**, and Regulations, on land warfare of 1899 and 1907 were drafted.

P

pacific blockade A pacific **blockade** is a blockade in time of peace. "All cases of pacific blockade are cases either of intervention or of **reprisals**": *II Oppenheim 145*. 19th century practice implied acceptance of pacific blockade as compatible with international law, although practice varied as to whether it could be enforced against third States. The ships of a State under pacific blockade could be seized and sequestrated until its termination, but not condemned and confiscated. Any remaining right to conduct a pacific blockade is subject to the obligations under the UN Charter to refrain from the threat or use of force (art. 2(4)) and to seek peaceful settlement of disputes (art. 2(3) and Chapter VI). *See also* **quarantine**.

Pacific Charter By the Pacific Charter, signed at the same time as the Manila Pact (*see* **SEATO**) on 8 September 1954 *(209 U.N.T.S. 23)*, the parties affirmed the principle of equal rights and **self-determination** of peoples and their readiness to assist in the process of "orderly achievement" of self-government and independence; their readiness to continue to cooperate in the economic, social and cultural fields; and their determination to prevent or counter any attempt to subvert their freedom or to destroy their sovereignty or territorial integrity.

Pacific Islands, Trust Territory of the *See* **Micronesia**.

pacific settlement of disputes International law abounds with instruments requiring States to submit disputes to some means of peaceful settlement. The first major multilateral instrument was the Hague Convention for the Pacific Settlement of Disputes of 29 July 1899 *(187 C.T.S. 410)*, followed by the Hague Convention of the same name of 18 October 1907 *(205 C.T.S. 233)*, both of which obliged the parties "to use their best efforts to insure the pacific settlement of international disputes" (art. 1 in each); both then laid out appropriate settlement procedures—good offices and mediation (Title II and Part II), international commissions of inquiry (Title III and Part III) and international arbitration (Title IV and Part IV; *see also* **Arbitration, Permanent Court of**). Arts. 12-15 of the Covenant of the League of Nations contained obligations on members to seek peaceful settlement of disputes. The **General Treaty for the Renunciation of War** of 27 August 1928 *(94 L.N.T.S. 57,* the Kellogg-Briand Pact) provided, in art. 2, that the settlement of all disputes "shall never be sought except by peaceful means." The **General Act for the Pacific Settlement of International Disputes** of 26 September 1928 *(93 L.N.T.S. 343)* provided for the submission of disputes which could not be settled by diplomacy to conciliation (arts. 1-16), and of disputes relating to legal rights to the PCIJ or to arbitration (arts. 17-28). One of the Principles of the UN Charter, as expressed in art. 2(3), is the obligation on all members to "settle their international disputes by peaceful means and in such a manner that international peace and security, and justice, are not endangered." Chapter VI of the Charter, entitled "Pacific Settlement of Disputes," sets out the settlement procedures to be adopted:

these include "negotiation, enquiry, mediation, conciliation, arbitration, judicial settle-, ment, resort to regional agencies or arrangements, or other peaceful means of their own choice" (art. 33(1)); the Security Council is empowered to recommend a settlement procedure (art. 36(1)), to consider disputes itself (art. 37(1)), and to make recommendations as to their settlement (art. 38). The necessity for pacific settlement of disputes is reiterated in the Declaration on Principles of International Law Concerning **Friendly Relations** and Cooperation Among States in Accordance with the Charter of the United Nations of 24 October 1970 (G.A. Res. 2625 (XXV)). As to the various mechanisms for settling international disputes, *see* Merrills, *International Dispute Settlement* (3rd ed.).

package deal(s) In negotiations, the linking of two or more disputes or issues together "so that a negotiated settlement can balance gains and losses overall and be capable of acceptance by both [or all] sides. Such 'package deals' are particularly common in multilateral negotiations such as the Third United Nations Conference on the Law of the Sea, where the large number of states involved and the broad agenda made the trading of issues a conspicuous feature of the proceedings": Merrills, *International Dispute Settlement* (3rd ed.), 15.

pacta sunt servanda "In every uncodified legal system there are certain elementary and universally agreed principles for which it is almost impossible to find authority. In the common law of England and the United States of America, where can you find specific authority for the principle that a man must perform his contracts? Yet almost every decision on a contract presupposes the existence of that principle. The same is true of international law. No Government would decline to accept the principle *pacta sunt servanda*. . . .": McNair, *Law of Treaties* (2nd ed.), 493. Art. 26 of the Vienna Convention on the Law of Treaties 1969, entitled "*Pacta sunt servanda*," provides that "[e]very treaty in force is binding upon the parties and must be performed by them in good faith." The Preamble to the Vienna Convention notes that "the principles of free consent and of good faith and the *pacta sunt servanda* rule are universally recognized." *See also* the Preamble and art. 2(2) of the UN Charter. *See* the **Rights of US Nationals in Morocco Case** *1952 I.C.J. Rep. 176;* **North Atlantic Fisheries Arbitration** *(1910) 10 R.I.A.A. 188.*

pacta tertiis nec nocent nec prosunt This term, which means that third parties receive neither rights nor duties from contracts, is common to municipal legal systems, and finds expression in international law in art. 34 of the Vienna Convention on the Law of Treaties 1969: "A treaty does not create either obligations or rights for a third State without its consent"; *see also* arts. 35-38. For examples of rights and duties which may nevertheless be created for third States, see *I Oppenheim 1261-3. See* **Kiel Canal**; **Panama Canal**; **third State**. *And see* Aust, *Modern Treaty Law and Practice* (2000), Chap. 14.

pactum de contrahendo A term "the exact meaning of which is uncertain . . . [and] . . . fortunately . . . rarely employed. It has been used to refer to an agreement to conclude a treaty; an agreement to include certain clauses in future agreements between the same parties; and an agreement to become a party to a treaty which has already been concluded. . . . The term should probably not be used to describe an agreement to negotiate a treaty, even though such an agreement must be carried out in good faith": Aust, *Modern Treaty Law and Practice* (2000), 25. *See also* McNair, *Law of Treaties* (2nd ed.), 27, 29. *See* the *Tacna-Arica Arbitration (1925) 2 R.I.A.A. 92.*

Pakistani Prisoners of War, Case Concerning Trial of *(Pakistan v. India) 1973 I.C.J. Rep. 328.* In 1971, a rebellion in East Bengal, then part of Pakistan, was suppressed by Pakistan armed forces. Shortly afterwards, hostilities broke out between India and Pakistan, and Indian forces took control of East Bengal (which later declared itself independent as the State of Bangladesh). During the fighting Indian forces took a number of Pakistani prisoners of war. In May 1973, Pakistan, believing that India was proposing to transfer some of these prisoners of war to Bangladesh for trial for acts of genocide and crimes against humanity, sought to prevent this transfer by instituting proceedings against India on the basis of certain provisions of the Convention on the Prevention and Punishment of the Crime of **Genocide** 1948 *(78 U.N.T.S. 277)*. At the same time, Pakistan sought interim measures of protection to prevent the transfer of the prisoners of war. India rejected the Court's jurisdiction. In July 1973, Pakistan notified the Court that negotiations with India were expected to take place soon and asked the Court to postpone further consideration of its request for interim measures. The Court *held* that, since urgency was of the essence of a request for interim measures, Pakistan, by asking for postponement, had indicated that its request no longer concerned a matter of urgency and the Court was therefore not called upon to pronounce on that request. Subsequently, the proceedings were discontinued at the request of Pakistan *(1973 I.C.J. Rep. 347)*.

Palmas, Island of See **Island of Palmas Case**.

Pan Am 103 incident *See* the **Lockerbie Cases**; **Lockerbie Trial**.

Panama Canal Art. 3 of the Ship Canal Treaty (referred to as the Hay-Pauncefote Treaty) between the UK and USA of 18 November 1901 *(190 C.T.S. 215)* incorporated into the régime for what became the Panama Canal the principles on freedom of navigation embodied in the Convention of Constantinople of 29 October 1888 *(171 C.T.S. 241)* regarding free navigation on the **Suez Canal**. By art. 2 of the Convention for the Construction of a Ship Canal (the **Hay-Varilla Treaty**) between Panama and the USA of 18 November 1903 *(194 C.T.S. 263)* the US was granted "in perpetuity the use, occupation and control of a zone of land and land under water for the construction, maintenance, operation, sanitation and protection" of a canal; and art. 18 incorporated into the régime the provisions of art. 3 of the **Hay-Pauncefote Treaty**. The Canal was opened in 1914. The Panama Canal Treaty of 7 September 1977 *(16 I.L.M. 1022 (1977))* acknowledged Panama's sovereignty over the entire Canal Zone (Preamble and art. III(1)); abrogated a number of earlier treaties between Panama and the US, including the Hay-Varilla Treaty (art. II); and, until the Treaty terminated on 31 December 1999 (art. II(2)), the USA was granted "the rights to manage, operate and maintain the Panama Canal" (art. III(1)), thereafter these rights devolving to Panama. The Treaty Concerning the Permanent Neutrality and Operation of the Panama Canal of the same date *(16 I.L.M. 1040 (1977))* established a régime for the Canal substantially the same as that operating under the Hay-Pauncefote Treaty; the Treaty has appended to it a Protocol open to accession by all States.

Panevezys-Saldutiskis Railway Case *(1939) P.C.I.J., Ser. A/B, No. 76*. A company known as the Esimene Juurdeveo Rand-teede Selts Venemaal was owner and concessionaire of certain rights in respect of the Panevezys-Saldutiskis Railway. Estonia alleged that Lithuania had wrongfully refused to recognize the company's rights or to compensate the company, and instituted proceedings against Lithuania in the PCIJ on the basis of the acceptance by both States of the compulsory jurisdiction of the Court. Lithuania submitted two preliminary objections. The Court, having by its order of 30 June 1938 joined them to the merits *(P.C.I.J. Ser. A/B, No. 75)*, *held* (10 to 4) that the objection regarding the non-exhaustion of the remedies offered by municipal law was well founded and that the claim presented by Estonia could not be entertained. Although "there can be no need to resort to the municipal courts if those courts have no jurisdiction to afford relief; nor is it necessary again to resort to those courts if the result must be a repetition of a decision already given," Estonia had failed to establish that those propositions applied in the circumstances of the case. The other Lithuanian objection, that Estonia had not observed the rule of international law that a claimant must be a national not only at the time of its presentation but also at the time of the injury, could not be decided without passing on the merits. "In the opinion of the Court, the rule of international law on which the first Lithuanian objection is based is that in taking up the case of one of its nationals, by resorting to diplomatic action or international judicial proceedings on his behalf, a State is in reality asserting its own right, the right to ensure in the person of its nationals respect for the rules of international law. This right is necessarily limited to intervention on behalf of its own nationals because, in the absence of a special agreement, it is the bond of nationality between the State and the individual which alone confers upon the State the right of diplomatic protection, and it is as a part of the function of diplomatic protection that the right to take up a claim and to ensure respect for the rules of international law must be envisaged. Where the injury was done to the national of some other State, no claim to which such injury may give rise falls within the scope of the diplomatic protection which a State is entitled to afford nor can it give rise to a claim which that State is entitled to espouse."

Papal grants Declarations made by the Pope from the 11th to the 15th Centuries authorizing or recognizing territorial acquisitions by European Powers. *See* Verzijl, *International Law in Historical Perspective* (1969), Vol. 3, 326-27.

Papal States "When the Law of Nations began to grow among the states of Christendom, the Pope was the monarch of one of those states—namely, the so-called Papal States. Throughout the existence of the Papal States, until their annexation by the Kingdom of Italy in 1870, the Pope was a monarch and, as such, the equal of all other monarchs": *I Oppenheim 325. See also* **Holy See**; **Lateran Treaty**.

par in parem non habet imperium The principle that, as a consequence of the equality of States in international law, no State can claim jurisdiction over another, manifest in, *e.g.*, the rules on **sovereign immunity**.

Paris, Declaration of The Declaration respecting Maritime Law signed on 16 April 1856 *(115 C.T.S. 1)* by the parties to the Peace Conference following the Crimea War and subsequently acceded to by the bulk of maritime States (though not, formally, the United States) laying down the rules that (1) privateering is abolished; (2) free ship, free goods except contraband; (3) neutral goods are free on enemy ships; (4) blockades to be binding must be effective: *see* **blockade**. The significance of these rules has declined consequent upon the practice of States during the two World Wars.

Parry, Clive 1917-82. Lecturer, Ankara, 1944; London School of Economics, 1945. Successively lecturer, reader and (1969) professor, Cambridge, England, 1945-82. Principal works include *Nationality and Citizenship Laws of the Commonwealth and Republic of Ireland,* (2 vols., 1957, 1960); *The Sources and Evidences of International Law* (1965); Editor: *British Digest of International Law* (5 vols.,1965); *British International Law Cases* (9 vols.,1964-73); *Consolidated Treaty Series* (243 vols., 1969-80); *Encyclopaedic Dictionary of International Law* (with Grant, 1983).

Partial Test-Ban Treaty 1963 *See* **Test-Ban Treaties**.

Passage through the Great Belt Case *(Finland v. Denmark) 1992 I.C.J. Rep. 12.* On 17 May 1991, Finland initiated proceedings before the ICJ against Denmark based on a dispute regarding passage through the Great Belt (*Storebælt*), and Denmark's project to build a fixed connection for road and rail traffic across the East and West Channels of the Great Belt. As a result of this project, the Baltic would be permanently closed to deep-draught ships over 65 meters in height and suspending passage of Finnish drill-ships and oil rigs that did not meet the height requirements. Finland asked the Court to declare that: (a) there was free passage through the Great Belt; (b) this right included drill-ships and oil rigs and reasonably foreseeable ships; (c) Denmark's plans to construct the bridge would interfere with this right of passage; and (d) Denmark and Finland should negotiate how the right of free passage should be maintained. On 29 July 1991, the Court (16 to 0) *dismissed* the request for an indication of provisional measures under art. 41 of its Statute on the basis of a lack of urgency, the East Channel Bridge not being due for construction until 1994; the Court proposed instead that the parties attempt to negotiate an amicable settlement. On 3 September 1992, a representative of Finland notified the Court in writing that the dispute had been settled and requested the discontinuance of the case, which was subsequently endorsed by the Court *(1992 I.C.J. Rep. 348)*.

passage, innocent *See* **innocent passage**.

passage, right of *See* ***Right of Passage Case***; **right of access and freedom of transit**.

passage, transit *See* **transit passage**.

passive personality principle The Research in International Law of the Harvard Law School describes this principle of jurisdiction with respect to crime as "jurisdiction over offences committed against [a State's] nationals by whomsoever committed. An important group of States asserts such jurisdiction; others would contest it. Many writers favor it, while others oppose it. . . . Jurisdiction asserted upon the principle of passive personality without qualifications has been more hotly contested than any other type of competence. It has been vigorously opposed in Anglo-American countries. . . . Of all principles of jurisdiction having some substantial support in contemporary national legislation, it is the most difficult to justify in theory": Commentary on the Draft Convention with Respect to Crime *(29 A.J.I.L. Supp. 578-9 (1935))*. The principle has seen some general revival in the law relating to international **terrorism**. Thus, art. 6(2)(a) of the International Convention for the Suppression of Terrorist Bombing 1997 *(37 I.L.M. 249 (1998))* permits parties to exercise criminal jurisdiction where "the offence is committed against a national of that State." *See also* **Cutting Incident** (1886) Moore, *Digest of International Law*, Vol. 2, 228; ***The Lotus Case (1927) P.C.I.J., Ser. A, No. 10***.

passport(s) "The issuing of passports is a convenient system adopted by states to secure for their citizens a right of transit through foreign countries, which permission might in international legal theory be withheld. Technically, the *foreign* country grants the citizen the passport, and accepts his certificate of citizenship as a title to the right, accorded by all civilized states, of unobjectionable foreigners to pass through. In those countries which even in time of peace exercise strict supervision over aliens entering and residing, the local or national visé on the certificate corresponds to the technical passport. In practice, the certificate itself has received the name passport and actually serves that purpose, being often, if not unregulated by foreign officials, at least only inspected, the visé, where it is affixed, serving merely as evidence of inspection. The passport is the accepted international certificate or evidence of citizenship, although its evidentiary value is *prima facie* only": Borchard, *The Diplomatic Protection of Citizens Abroad* (1915), 493. *See* Turack, *The Passport in International Law* (1972). *See also* **laissez passer**; **visa**.

patrimonial sea This is the term employed in some Latin American States to denote an area of sea, extending from the outer limit of the **territorial sea** to a distance of 200 miles from the baselines of the territorial sea, over which the coastal State claimed exclusive right to the mineral and living resources, such right not interfering with freedom of navigation in the area. *See* Szekely, *Latin America and the Development of the Law of the Sea* (1976), Vol. 1, 89-102. *See also* **epicontinental sea**.

Paust, Jordan 1943- . Professor, Houston College of Law 1975- . Principal works include *War Crimes Jurisdiction and Due Process: A Case Study of Bangladesh* (with Blaustein 1974); *The Military in American Society: Cases and Materials* (with Zillman, Blaustein, Sherman *et al.* 1978); *International Criminal Law* (with Sadat and Bassiouni 2000); *International Law and Litigation in the United States* (2000); *International Law as Law in the United States* (1996, 2nd ed. 2003).

PCIJ *See* **Permanent Court of International Justice**.

peace, breach of Under art. 39 of the UN Charter, the Security Council has exclusive power "to determine the existence of any threat to the peace, breach of the peace, or act of aggression," and power in accordance with arts. 41 and 42 to make recommendations or to take decisions on measures to maintain or restore international peace and security. What constitutes a threat to the peace or breach of the peace depends on the facts and circumstances of each dispute presented to the Security Council; and the determination is as much political as legal, though legal consequences flow from that determination. *See* White, *Keeping the Peace* (2nd ed.), Chap 2. Given that Security Council action can be "triggered" by any of the circumstances set out in art. 39, the definition remains difficult, the term clearly signifying something of less gravity than a breach of the peace or an act of aggression. There are few instances of the Security Council determining a situation as a breach of the peace; *see, e.g.*, SC Res. 82 (1950) in relation to the armed attack upon the Republic of Korea by forces from North Korea; and SC Res. 660 (1990) in relation to the Iraqi invasion of Kuwait (although the reference here is to a "breach of international peace and security"). *See* White, *Keeping the Peace* (2nd ed.), 47-50. *See* **peace, threat to**.

peace, crime against The concept of a crime against peace, for which individuals bear responsibility, first appears in the Report of the Commission on the Responsibility of the Authors of the War and the Enforcement of Penalties of 29 March 1919 *(14 A.J.I.L. 95 (1920))*. Art. 6 of the Charter of the Nuremberg **International Military Tribunal** 1945 *(82 U.N.T.S. 279)* defines crimes against peace as "planning, preparation, initiating or waging a war of aggression, or a war in violation of international treaties, agreements or assurances, or participating in a common plan or conspiracy for the accomplishment of any of the foregoing." The term "crime against peace," having some resonance in the context of criminal responsibility for World Wars, has been replaced by the term "crime of aggression" in art. 5(1)(d) of the Rome Statute of the **International Criminal Court** 1998 *(37 I.L.M. 999 (1998))*, reflecting better the nature of contemporary conflicts. However, that term is undefined in the Rome Statute and, indeed, may not be invoked before the ICC until such time as the Rome Statute is amended to define the crime and set out the conditions under which the Court may exercise jurisdiction over it (art. 5(2)). *See* Cassese, *International Criminal Law* (2003), Part II, Sec. 1.

peace, threat to Under art. 39 of the UN Charter, the Security Council has exclusive power "to determine the existence of any threat to the peace, breach of the peace, or act of aggression," and power in accordance with arts. 41 and 42 to make recommendations or to take decisions on measures to maintain or restore international peace and security. What constitutes a threat to the peace or breach of the peace depends on the facts and circumstances of each dispute presented to the Security Council; and the determination is as much political as legal, though legal consequences flow from that determination. *See* White, *Keeping the Peace* (2nd ed.), Chap 2. Given that Security Council action can be "triggered" by any of the circumstances set out in art. 39, the definition remains difficult, the term clearly signifying something of less gravity than a breach of the peace or an act of aggression. A threat to the peace, sometimes termed a threat to international peace, is the most common basis invoked by the Security Council for enforcement action under Chapter VII of the Charter

Unlike other acts of the UN, the decisions of the Security Council pursuant to art. 39 are binding on the Members (art. 25). In order to prevent an aggravation of the situation, the Security Council can first call upon the parties to comply with provisional measures which it deems necessary or desirable (art. 40). Under art. 41, the Council has power to decide on measures not involving the use of armed force and it may call upon the Members of the UN to apply such measures. These may include complete or partial interruption of economic relations and of rail, sea, air, postal, telegraphic, radio and other means of communication and the severance of diplomatic relations. If the measures under art. 41 are considered inadequate or prove inadequate, the Security Council may take such action by air, sea or land forces as may be necessary to maintain or restore international peace and security (art. 42). Members of the UN undertake a reciprocal obligation to make available armed forces, assistance and facilities including rights of passage (art. 43, 48, 49). A mechanism was envisaged under which forces would be available on a permanent basis for taking urgent military measures (arts. 45-47) but these foundered on the deadlock reached in the **Military Staff Committee.**

peaceful co-existence, doctrine of *See* **co-existence, doctrine of peaceful**.

peaceful settlement of disputes *See* **pacific settlement of disputes**.

peace-keeping Stated to be an "invention of the United Nations" (Boutros-Ghali, *An Agenda for Peace* (1992), *UN Doc. A/47/277—S/24111*, para. 46), UN peace-keeping has been described thus: "As the United Nations practice has evolved over the years, a peace-keeping operation has come to be defined as an operation involving military personnel, but without enforcement powers, undertaken by the United Nations to help maintain or restore international peace and security in areas of conflict. These operations are voluntary and based on consent and cooperation. While they involve the use of military personnel, they achieve their objectives not by force of arms, thus contrasting them with 'enforcement action' of the United Nations under Article 42": *The Blue Helmets: A Review of United Nations Peacekeeping* (2nd ed.), 4. While not explicitly presaged by the UN Charter, peace-keeping operations are legally justified, in respect of the Security Council which mandates the vast majority of them, by the overall tenor of Chapter VII, and by art. 39 in particular; and in respect of the General Assembly, by the general powers conferred by arts. 10 and 14. The essential *indicia* and principles of peace-keeping are "the consent of the parties, impartiality and the non-use of force except in self-defense": Boutros-Ghali, *Supplement to an Agenda for Peace* (1995) *(UN Doc. A/50/60—S/1995/1*, para. 33). Further, peace-keeping operations are mandated by a recommendation, and not any binding decision, and the forces provided for the operation are volunteered by member States. Past and extant peace-keeping operations appear in this *Encyclopaedic Dictionary* under their acronym. *See* Higgins, *United Nations Peacekeeping 1946-67,* Vol. I, *The Middle East* (1969); Vol. II, *Asia* (1970); Vol. III, *Africa* (1980); Wiseman, *Peacekeeping: Appraisals* and Proposals (1984); Diehl, *International Peacekeeping* (1994); White, *Keeping the Peace* (2nd ed.), Chaps. 7-9.

peacemaking   Insofar as it is a term of art, peacemaking is "action to bring hostile parties to agreement, essentially through such peaceful means as those foreseen in Chapter VI of the Charter of the United Nations": *Agenda for Peace* (1992) *(UN Doc. A/47/277-S/24111)*, para. 20. The author of this document, Secretary-General Boutros-Ghali, saw this as an essential part of the UN's role in maintaining and securing international peace and security. The Charter contains a general principle, common to a number of other instruments, that requires States to settle their international disputes by peaceful means; and, indeed, Chapter VI enumerates the means by which this obligation is to be satisfied. *See* peaceful **settlement of disputes**.

Pellat Claim   *(France v. Mexico) (1929) 5 R.I.A.A. 534*. Pellat, a French national living in Mexico, suffered damage between 1913 and 1916 as a result of forced loans exacted by the State of Sonora (a member State of the federal United States of Mexico) for the benefit of revolutionary forces supported by the State of Sonora, the sacking of his commercial establishment and requisitions by revolutionary forces. By the France-Mexico Claims Convention 1924 *(79 L.N.T.S. 418)*, Mexico undertook, *ex gratia*, to indemnify French nationals against acts committed by, *inter alia*, revolutionary forces. *Held* by the France-Mexico Claims Commission, in awarding damages, that the forced loan was to be considered to have been exacted by the revolutionary forces, and Mexico was responsible for the acts of its constituent member States causing damage to foreigners even if the federal Constitution did not give the central Government the right to control the member States or to require them to conform to the prescriptions of international law, and even if the member State had acknowledged, without paying, the debt; the sacking of Pellat's commercial establishment and the requisitions were also acts for which Mexico was liable.

peremptory norm of international law   *See* **jus cogens**.

Peréz de Cuéllar, Javier   1920- . Peruvian lawyer, diplomat and international civil servant. Fifth Secretary-General of the United Nations, 1982-91. Publications: *Manual de Derecho Diplomatico* (1964); *Conference Diplomacy* (with Kaufmann 1996); *Pilgrimage for Peace: A Secretary-General's Memoir* (1997).

perfidy   Art. 37(1) of Protocol I Additional to the Geneva Conventions of 12 August 1949 of 8 June 1977 *(1125 U.N.T.S. 3)* declares that it is prohibited "to kill, injure or capture an adversary by resort to perfidy," and goes on to define perfidy as "[a]cts inviting the confidence of an adversary to lead him to believe that he is entitled to, or is obliged to accord, protection under the rules of international law applicable in armed conflict, with intent to betray that confidence. . . ." Examples of perfidy are given: feigning an intent to negotiate under a flag of truce or of a surrender, feigning an incapacitation by wounds or sickness, feigning civilian, non-combatant status and feigning protected status by the use of signs, emblems or uniforms of the UN or of neutral and other States not parties to the conflict. It is expressly stated that **ruses of war** are not prohibited (art. 37(2)).

Permanent Court of Arbitration   This institution was created by Chapter II of the Hague Convention for the Pacific Settlement of International Disputes 1899 *(187 C.T.S. 410)*, revised by the Convention of 1907 *(205 C.T.S. 277)*. The Court is not an actual tribunal, but consists in an International Bureau at The Hague serving as registry (art. 43), and a panel made up by the appointment by each contracting State of four suitably-qualified persons for six-year terms (art. 44), from which States wishing to have recourse to the Court may each choose two arbitrators, who in turn shall select an umpire (art. 45). Further Chapters of the Convention provide (III) for the procedure to be followed, failing other provision agreed by the parties, by a tribunal appointed under its provisions, as well as (IV) a summary procedure. Despite having 101 parties to one or both of the Hague Conventions, the PCA has been little utilized, particularly since 1945, though **arbitration** as a means of settling international disputes has not. Its primary significance now is its role in the appointment of judges to the International Court of Justice, nominations going to the General Assembly from the national groups on the PCA (or *ad hoc* national groups for non-PCA States): see arts. 4-6 of the ICJ Statute. *See* PCA, *International Alternative Dispute Resolution: Past, Present and Future—The Permanent Court of Arbitration Centennial Papers* (2000). *See* <www.pca-cpa.org>.

Permanent Court of International Justice (PCIJ)   This is the name of the first World Court, established pursuant to art. 14 of the Covenant of the League of Nations. The Council of the League appointed a Committee of Jurists to draft a Statute, and that Statute was approved by the Assembly on 13 December 1920: *Records of First Assembly*, Plenary Meeting, 500; *P.C.I.J., Ser. D, No. 3*, 3. The Court formally opened on 15 February 1922, and closed, with the resignation of the judges, on 31 January 1946. The PCIJ is the direct predecessor of the **International Court of Justice**. Decisions of the PCIJ are collected in *P.C.I.J., Ser. A, P.C.I.J., Ser. B*, and *P.C.I.J., Ser. A/B*; and the major decisions are gathered in Hudson, *World Court Reports*, 4 Vols. (1934-38). *See* Hudson, *The Permanent Court of International Justice 1920-1942* (1943); Fachiri, *The Permanent Court of International Justice* (1932).

Permanent Mandates Commission   Art. 22(9) of the Covenant of the League of Nations provided that "[a] permanent Commission shall be constituted to receive and examine the annual reports of the mandatories and to advise the Council on all matters relating to the observance of the mandates." The Commission was formally constituted in February 1921. The members were not State appointees, but were instead nominated by the Council, with a majority drawn from States which did not hold mandates. The Commission "left behind it a record as satisfactory as that of any of the institutions created by the League. It was a hard-worked body, holding two long sessions every year and having many reports to study between sessions. The Governors or other high officials of the various territories came before it, and supplemented their annual reports by answering the questions put by individual members. The Commission devised a skillful method of publicity: its actual proceedings took place in private, but the full text of question and answer was immediately published": Walters, *A History of the League of Nations* (1952), 173. *See* **mandates system**.

permanent members   Art. 23 of the UN Charter, in establishing a Security Council of fifteen members, provides that "the Republic of China, France, the Union of Soviet Socialist Republics, the United Kingdom of Great Britain and Northern Ireland, and the United States of America shall be permanent members of the Security Council." The Republic of China is represented as a permanent member of the Security Council by the People's Republic of China; and the USSR permanent seat is now held by Russia. The permanent members are given a **veto** on all non-procedural matters (art. 27(3); *see also* **double veto**); no amendment of the Charter can be effective without their ratifications (art. 108); and they alone are the members of the **Military Staff Committee** (art. 47).

permanent missions   Since the establishment of the UN, member States have developed the practice of setting up permanent missions at the seat of the organization. In GA Res. 257 (III) of 3 December 1948 the General Assembly regulated the submission of credentials of permanent representatives and the provision of information on the members of permanent missions. The UN publishes the names of members of permanent missions in *Permanent Missions to the United Nations* (commonly called the ***Blue Book***); this identifies those entitled to privileges and immunities under art. 4 of the Convention on Privileges and Immunities of the United Nations of 13 February 1946 *(1 U.N.T.S. 15)*. It is common now for each permanent mission to maintain a web site: <www.un.int/index-en/webs.html>.

permanent neutrality *See* **neutralized States**.

permanent representative In UN parlance, the head of a **permanent mission** to the UN is called the permanent representative. The submission of permanent representatives' credentials is regulated by GA Res. 257 (III) of 3 December 1948. Their names can be obtained from *Permanent Missions to the United Nations* (the ***Blue Book***). Their privileges and immunities are set out in art. 4 of the Convention on Privileges and Immunities of the United Nations of 13 February 1946 *(1 U.N.T.S. 15)*. The same terminology is used in other organizations, notably NATO; OECD; Council of Europe; European Union; UN Center for Human Settlements (Habitat); and United Nations Environment Program.

permanent sovereignty The term permanent sovereignty is invariably used in the context of natural resources (*see* **natural resources, permanent sovereignty over**) and has no distinct meaning beyond that context.

persistent objector rule This rule postulates that a State, which has persistently objected to the status as custom of a particular practice in the process of evolving into a custom, is not bound by that customary rule. "Evidence of objection must be clear and there is probably a presumption of acceptance [of the status of the practice as custom] which is to be rebutted. Whatever the theoretical underpinnings of the principle, it is well recognized by international tribunals, and in the practice of states": Brownlie, *Principles of Public International Law* (5th ed.), 10. *See* the ***Anglo-Norwegian Fisheries Case** 1951 I.C.J. Rep. 116*; ***North Sea Continental Shelf Cases** 1969 I.C.J. Rep. 3*.

person An entity capable of rights and duties under a given legal system. Thus, in international law, States are the prime persons (subjects) with the totality of rights and duties *(**Reparations for Injuries Case** 1949 I.C.J. Rep. 174)*, while international organizations have personality derived from and defined by their constituent instruments and individuals and groups have such rights and procedural capacities as States confer on them.

persona non grata "The process by which an ambassador or other diplomatic agent who is personally unacceptable to the receiving government is removed has been known under varying descriptions at different periods. . . . There remains, however, a tendency to use the somewhat more polite expression 'request the recall of a diplomat' rather than the blunter 'declare *persona non grata.*' Whatever terminology is employed, the characteristic feature of the *persona non grata* procedure is that it is the diplomat personally who has offended the receiving government. Where the displeasure is not with the diplomat personally but the policies or conduct of the sending state, the correct course is to break diplomatic relations, or in a less serious case recall the ambassador for consultations": *Satow's Guide to Diplomatic Practice* (5th ed.), 178-9. Article 9 of the Vienna Convention on Diplomatic Relations *(500 U.N.T.S. 95)* provides: "1. The receiving State may at any time and without having to explain its decision, notify the sending State that the head of the mission or any member of the diplomatic staff of the mission is *persona non grata* or that any other member of the staff of the mission is not acceptable. In any such case, the sending State shall, as appropriate, either recall the person concerned or terminate his functions with the mission. A person may be declared *non grata* or not acceptable before arriving in the territory of the receiving State. 2. If the sending State refuses or fails within a reasonable period to carry out its obligations under paragraph 1 of this Article, the receiving State may refuse to recognize the person concerned as a member of the mission." The Vienna Convention rules are intended to ensure that, where a diplomat becomes personally unacceptable to the receiving State, the matter is handled with as little personal embarrassment to him as possible and in the way least likely to lead to protracted and unprofitable dispute between sending and receiving State. *See* Satow, *supra*, 178-86.

personal law   In civil law systems, the law of the nationality of the individual; in common law systems, the law of the domicile of the individual.

personal union   *See* **union, personal**.

personality, derivative   International personality derived from States. All entities, other than States, with international personality have only such personality as States have accorded them. Cf. **personality, original**.

personality, international   The ICJ has said that a subject of international law, or an international person, is an entity "capable of possessing international rights and duties, and [which] has the capacity to maintain its rights by bringing international claims": *Reparations for Injuries Case 1949 I.C.J. Rep. 174* at 178. All States have international personality *ab initio* and *ipso jure*: States are the original and principal subjects of international law. Any other entities with international personality have that personality in derivation from States. Thus, State-like entities (or quasi-States, *e.g.*, Danzig, **Holy See**), international organizations (*e.g.*, the UN: *Reparations Case*) and, to a very limited extent, **individuals**, only have such personality as States have accorded them.

personality, objective international   International personality of an international organization effective vis-à-vis all States, and not simply member States. The United Nations is the only international organization with objective international personality: "fifty States, representing the vast majority of the members of the international community [in 1945], had the power, in conformity with international law, to bring into being an entity possessing objective international personality, and not merely personality recognized by them alone. . . .": *Reparations for Injuries Case 1949 I.C.J. Rep. 174* at 178.

personality, original   International personality arising *ab initio* and *ipso jure*; only the personality of States can be termed original, other entities with international personality having that personality derivatively from States. *See* **personality, derivative**.

Peruvian Guano Case   *See* ***Dreyfus Case***.

petition   This is the term universally used to connote the document through which an individual may bring to the notice of some organ of an international organization an alleged breach by a State of some conventional obligation. Thus, *e.g.*, art. 87(b) of the UN Charter empowered the (now defunct) **Trusteeship Council** to accept and examine petitions from the inhabitants of any **trust territory**. While the term "petition" is widely used in to describe the document used by individuals to initiate proceedings relating to an allegation that a State has violated a human rights agreement (*see* Tardu, *Human Rights. The International Petition System* (2 vols., 1979-80)), the term itself is employed in only one instrument—the **American Convention on Human Rights** 1969 *(1144 U.N.T.S. 123)*, art. 44. Within the UN **human rights** system, those instruments which permit individual "petition" do so by means of a "communication" (Optional Protocol to the **Civil and Political Rights, International Covenant on** 1966 *(999 U.N.T.S. 171)*, art. 1; International Convention on the Elimination of All Forms of Racial Discrimination 1965 *(660 U.N.T.S. 195)*, art. 14 (*see* **racial discrimination**); Optional Protocol of 1999 to the **Women, Convention on the Elimination of All Forms of Discrimination against** 1979 *(39 I.L.M. 281 (2000))*, art. 1; **Torture, Convention against** 1984 *(1465 U.N.T.S. 85)*, art. 22; and under the **European Convention on Human Rights** 1950 *(E.T.S. No. 5*, as amended by *E.T.S. No. 155))*, art. 34, the term "application" is used.

phenomenological approach This is a modern approach to international law which is interested in the "contents rather than the form of knowledge; in the meaning of concrete phenomena as objects of interpretation through psychic acts," and which stresses the "psychological experience of phenomena, rather than their supposed independent existence": Stone, *Legal Controls of International Conflict* (2nd Imp. revised), xlix. This approach emphasizes in-depth analyses of cases (not only judicial decisions, but also case studies of wars and debates and votes in international organizations) to clarify issues and shed light on the legal order: Falk, *The Status of Law in International Society* (1970), 468-9.

Phillimore, Sir Robert Joseph 1810-1885. Civilian scholar and judge. Author of *Commentaries on International Law* (4 vols. 1854-61, 2nd ed. 1871, third ed. (completed by Sir Walter Phillimore) 1889).

Phillimore, Sir Walter George Frank 1845-1929. English lawyer and judge. Chairman Naval Prize Tribunal 1918. One of the drafters of the Covenant of the League of Nations and the Statute of the PCIJ. Principal work: *Three Centuries of Treaties of Peace and Their Teaching* (1917).

Phosphates in Morocco Case *(Italy v. France) (1938) P.C.I.J., Ser. A/B, No. 74*. In 1918-19, Morocco issued licenses to certain French nationals to prospect for phosphates; they transferred the licenses to an Italian national. In 1920, a monopoly for phosphates was introduced by law in Morocco, and consequently, in 1925, the Moroccan authorities refused to recognize the rights of the Italian national under the licenses. In 1936, after lengthy negotiations, Italy instituted proceedings against France before the PCIJ on the basis of the acceptance by both States of the compulsory jurisdiction of the Court. France objected to the Court's jurisdiction on the ground, *inter alia*, that France's declaration accepting the Court's jurisdiction, which was ratified in April 1931, only related to disputes arising subsequently to the ratification with regard to situations or facts which were also subsequent to the ratification. The Court *held* (11 to 1) that it did not have jurisdiction since the dispute submitted to it by Italy did not arise with regard to situations or facts subsequent to April 1931.

Physical Protection Convention The Convention on the Physical Protection of Nuclear Materials of 26 October 1979 *(1456 U.N.T.S. 246)* requires States parties not to export or import or authorize the export or import of nuclear material used for peaceful purposes unless assurances have been received that such material will be protected during international nuclear transport at levels prescribed in the annexes to the Convention (art. 4). Each party undertakes to take appropriate steps to ensure that nuclear material in international transport is protected when such material is within its territory, or is on board a ship or aircraft under its jurisdiction and engaged in transport to or from that State (*ibid.*). The Convention also provides a framework for international cooperation in the recovery and protection of stolen nuclear material; in the case of theft, robbery, or other unlawful taking of nuclear material or of credible threat thereof, parties undertake to provide cooperation and assistance "to the maximum feasible extent" to any State that so requests (art. 5). Finally, the Convention defines certain serious offences involving nuclear material that parties are to make punishable under a "prosecute or extradite" system (arts. 7-14). The listed offences (art. 7) are deemed included in existing extradition treaties as extraditable offences (art. 11).

Pig War Arbitration *(U.S./U.K.)* (1872) *Moore, Int. Arb., 196-235*. Art. 1 of the Oregon Treaty of 15 June 1846 *(12 Bevans 95)* having set the western boundary between the US and Canada at the 49th Parallel, then westward of the mainland "to the middle of the channel which separates the continent from Vancouver's Island, and thence southerly through the middle of the said channel, and of [Juan de] Fuca's Straits, to the Pacific . . .," and protracted negotiations having failed to agree a boundary (and hence title to the strategic islands in the San Juan archipelago), an incident occurred on 15 June 1859 which almost propelled the parties to war. Moore *(supra*, 222-3) prosaically describes the incident thus: "A pig belonging to the [Hudson's Bay] company having been killed, one of the American citizens [on San Juan Island] was charged with having shot it; and a threat was made by an officer of the company to arrest him and take him to Victoria for trial under British law." American settlers sought military assistance and both parties garrisoned the island, agreeing on joint occupancy pending the resolution of the boundary issue. Art. 34 of the Treaty of Washington of 8 May 1871 *(12 Bevans 170)* referred the issue to the German Kaiser to determine "finally and without appeal, which of the claims is most in accord with the true interpretation of the [Oregon] treaty." While there were three channels that possibly qualified as the boundary under the Oregon Treaty, the parties sought a ruling on only the most easterly and most westerly, eliminating from the arbitration the middle channel which would have split the islands between them (and place San Juan Island on the Canadian side of the boundary). The experts appointed by Kaiser Wilhelm I advised (by 2 to 1), and the Kaiser on 21 October 1972 *determined* that the Haro Strait represented the true interpretation of the treaty, thus placing the entire San Juan Islands within US territory. This boundary was confirmed by the parties in a Protocol of 10 March 1973 *(12 Bevans 188)*. "Some war. Some pig": Vouri, *The Pig War* (1999), 211.

Pinochet Case Senator Augusto Pinochet, the former President of Chile, was arrested in a London hospital on 17 October 1998 in pursuance of a request for his extradition to Spain to face charges there of torture, hostage-taking and murder. At issue in the ensuing court proceedings were questions of, *inter alia*, the jurisdiction of the United Kingdom in respect of acts allegedly committed on foreign soil by a non-national, and whether Pinochet was entitled to immunity from the criminal jurisdiction of the UK by virtue of his position as a former head of state. The House of Lords held on 23 March 1999 (*R v. Bow Street Metropolitan Stipendiary Magistrate Ex p. Pinochet Ugarte [1999] 2 All ER 97*) that Pinochet could be extradited to Spain but only in respect of those charges which were also crimes under UK law at the time of their commission. This severely limited the number of charges for which Pinochet could be extradited to only those charges of torture which had occurred after the enactment of the UN Convention Against Torture and Other Cruel, Inhumane or Degrading Treatment or Punishment 1984 *(1465 U.N.T.S.85)* into UK law, the Convention having provided for the obligation to punish or extradite those accused of the crime of torture. The House of Lords further held that Pinochet had no immunity *rationae materiae* as a former head of state either because the acts complained of were not committed in his official capacity or because the crime of torture as defined in the 1984 Convention was only a crime under international law where it was committed by an official and, as a consequence, immunity from jurisdiction was impliedly removed. *See* **head of state immunity**. *See also* Barker, The Future of Former Head of State Immunity After *ex parte* Pinochet *(1999) 48 I.C.L.Q. 937*; Ghandhi and Barker, The Pinochet Judgment: Analysis and Implications, *(2000) 40 Indian Journal of International Law 657.*

Pinson Case *(France v. Mexico) (1928) 5 R.I.A.A. 327.* Georges Pinson was born in Mexico in 1875, the son of a French citizen born in France but established in Mexico. In 1915, Pinson suffered loss and damage during the course of revolutionary disturbances. By the French-Mexican Claims Convention of 25 September 1924 *(79 L.N.T.S. 418)*, a Mixed Claims Commission was established to examine claims of French citizens and protected persons for loss and damage arising as a consequence of the revolutions and disturbed conditions in Mexico from 1910 to 1920, due to the acts of, *inter alia*, (1) forces of a government *de jure* or *de facto*, (2) revolutionary forces which had established governments *de jure* or *de facto*, or revolutionary forces opposed to them, and (3) forces arising from the disbanding of those mentioned under (2) up to the time when a government *de jure* established itself as a result of a particular revolution. The Commission was to decide claims in accordance with principles of equity, Mexico undertaking *ex gratia* to make any indemnification called for. The Commission (Verzijl, President) *held* that Mexico was liable to indemnify Pinson for damage he had suffered. As this case was the Commission's first award, it formulated certain general interpretative decisions for guidance in dealing with other claims, and in the course of a lengthy judgment decided that: (1) although the possession by an individual of the nationality of both the claimant and respondent States would preclude a claim, it had not been established that Pinson had such dual nationality since, *inter alia*, a provision in the Mexican Constitution of 1857 conferring Mexican nationality on a foreign purchaser of land in Mexico (i.e. Pinson's father) was to be regarded as permissive and not mandatory, in conformity with the principle that municipal law must in doubtful cases be interpreted so as to conform with international law, and Mexico's contention that the Constitution prevailed over international law had to be rejected; (2) a consular certificate of registration was *prima facie* proof of Pinson's French nationality, but Mexico could adduce evidence to the contrary: an international tribunal could determine for itself what documents or other means of proof were sufficient to establish nationality, independently of national rules of evidence; (3) the *de jure* character of a government depended exclusively on the constitutional law of the State concerned at the time of the change of government, and irrespective of its recognition as *de jure* government by foreign governments, or the refusal for political reasons of a subsequent government to recognize its predecessor as a regular government; (4) the existence of a government *de facto* was exclusively a question of fact, and was not dependent on the constitutional law of the country or recognition (or otherwise) by subsequent governments or by foreign States; (5) for purposes of the reference in the 1924 Claims Convention to "revolutionary forces" for whose acts Mexico was, under the *compromis* although not necessarily under general international law, responsible, "revolution" had no precisely defined meaning in international law and in particular was not dependent upon the ultimate success of the revolt, its political or social ideals, its territorial extent, or its recognition as a belligerent: "revolutionary forces" were all forces which had cooperated in a military movement, i.e. every armed and more or less organized movement which, inspired by a social and political program, or under the influence of prominent leaders, or under the impulse of general discontent with the principal political regime of the State, strives for the overthrow of a particular government or for a fundamental change in the system of government; (6) the fact that the Convention required the question of responsibility to be determined in accordance with principles of equity and not by general principles of international law rendered inapplicable the ordinary rules of international law governing responsibility of States for acts of forces and substituted the rules set out in the *compromis*, but did not exclude the application of general international law in other respects in the application and interpretation of the Convention;

(7) although under international law there was no general obligation on a State to indemnify foreigners in respect of damage suffered in consequence of insurrections, a State could be held responsible in respect of damage incidental to an insurrection in cases involving, for example, pillage by its military forces or by successful revolutionary parties, wrongful acts of the government itself or of regular government forces exceeding the limits of military necessity, wrongful acts committed during a civil war by an eventually successful revolutionary party, or the failure of the authorities to take reasonable measures to suppress mutinies or mob violence; (8) a State was not responsible for the acts of revolutionaries unless the revolution had ended in their ultimate victory, in which case the State was, under international law, responsible for their wrongful acts from the time the revolution broke out until its ultimate success; (9) a State may make military requisitions from foreign nationals in times of revolution, on the same footing as from its own nationals, on condition that full compensation was paid; (10) the Commission was not bound by decisions of a domestic claims commission and the Commission's consideration of a claim which had been decided by a domestic claims commission was not in the nature of an appeal: nor did domestic legislation governing claims have any force before the Commission, which was governed in this respect by the *compromis*; (11) where a treaty was clear there was no need to consider the alleged contrary intentions of its authors (unless the parties were agreed that the text differed from their common intention), but if the text was not clear recourse might be had to their intentions, which should prevail if they were clear and unanimous, but otherwise that meaning must be sought which either best gives a reasonable solution or corresponds best with the impression which the offer of the party which took the initiative must reasonably and in good faith have made on the mind of the other party; every treaty was deemed to refer tacitly to general principles of international law for all questions which it did not itself resolve expressly and in a different way; and where there was doubt as to the scope of a treaty provision it should be interpreted in a sense that assures the possibility of its application, and if it was impossible to ascertain the exact meaning it should be interpreted in favor of the party which had thereby undertaken commitments; (12) in respect of indemnities called for by general principles of international law, payment of interest was not yet clearly required by customary international law either from the date of the injury or from the date of presentation of the claim, and would accordingly in such cases be awarded only from the date of award.

piracy   Piracy is the first **international crime**, its prohibition under international law dating from, at least, the 17th century. It is the first, and to some the only true, crime subject to **universal jurisdiction**, in that those responsible may be seized on the high seas, brought to shore, prosecuted and punished, if found guilty, by any State. In early times, piracy was so disruptive of safety at sea and international trade that universal jurisdiction over the perpetrators was justified as they were enemies of all humankind, *hostes humani generis*. Art. 101 of the UN Convention on the Law of the Sea 1982 *(1833 U.N.T.S.3)* defines piracy as consisting of any of the following acts: "(a) any illegal acts of violence, detention or any act of depradation, committed for private ends by the crew or passengers of a private ship or a private aircraft, and directed: (i) on the high seas, against another ship or aircraft, or against persons or property on board such ship or aircraft; (ii) against a ship, aircraft, persons or property in a place outside the jurisdiction of any State; (b) any act of voluntary participation in the operation of a ship or of an aircraft with knowledge of facts making it a pirate ship or aircraft; (c) any act of inciting or of intentionally facilitating an act described in subparagraph (a) or (b)." As to jurisdiction over pirates, art. 105 of the UN Convention provides: "On the high seas, or in any other place outside the jurisdiction of any State, every State may seize a pirate ship or aircraft, or a ship taken by piracy and under the control of pirates, and arrest the persons and seize the property on board. The courts of the State which carried out the seizure may decide upon the penalties to be imposed, and may also determine the action to be taken with regard to the ships, aircraft or property, subject to the rights of third parties acting in good faith." The same definition of piracy and the same **universal jurisdiction** over **pirate ships and aircraft** were contained in arts. 15 and 19 of the Geneva Convention on the High Seas 1958 *(450 U.N.T.S. 82)*. *See The Lotus Case* (1927) *P.C.I.J., Ser. A, No. 10* at 70 per Judge Moore; *In re Piracy Jure Gentium [1934] A.C. 586. See I Oppenheim 746-55*; Dubner, *The Law of International Sea Piracy* (1980); Rubin, *The Law of Piracy* (1988).

pirate radio *See* **radio pirates**.

pirate ship or aircraft In the law relating to **piracy**, a pirate ship or aircraft is defined by art. 103 of the UN Convention on the Law of the Sea 1982 *(1833 U.N.T.S. 3)* as one "intended by the persons in dominant control to be used for the purpose of committing as one of the acts referred to in article 101 [acts of piracy]. The same applies if the ship or aircraft has been used to commit any such act, so long as it remains under the control of the persons guilty of that act." Warships, government ships and government aircraft become pirate ships and aircraft if the crew "has mutinied and taken control" of the vessel or craft (art. 101(2)).

plant varieties, protection of *See* **World Intellectual Property Organization**.

plebiscite While "[s]everal treaties of cession concluded in the nineteenth century stipulated that the cession should only be valid provided that the inhabitants consented to it through a plebiscite . . ., [i]t cannot be said that international law makes it a condition of every cession that it should be ratified by a plebiscite": *I Oppenheim 684*. However, the contemporary law on **self-determination** would appear to point in quite the opposite direction. Art. 2 of the Declaration on the Granting of Independence to Colonial Countries and Peoples 1960 (GA Res. 1514 (XV)) states that, by virtue of the right of self-determination, all peoples "freely determine their political status and freely pursue their economic, social and cultural development"; and in the *Western Sahara Case 1975 I.C.J. Rep. 12* the ICJ held that "the free and genuine expression of the will of the peoples" of Western Sahara prevailed over legal ties between the territory and Morocco and Mauritania, albeit that the Court did not consider those ties to be ties of territorial sovereignty.

pledge For most purposes, a pledge of territory implies a **lease** (*e.g.*, the leases of the Hong Kong New Territories and Wei-Hei-Wei) which may come to an end by effluxion of time or rescission. True examples of a pledge were those of Corsica to France by the Republic of Genoa and of the town of Wismar by Sweden to the Grand Duchy of Mechlenburg-Schwerin as security for a loan of 1,250,000 thaler against the right to recover the town on repayment of the money with 5% interest after a period of 100 years *(I Oppenheim 568n)*. The practice of seeking pledges as a means of enforcing treaty obligations is obsolete and there is no trace of it in the Vienna Convention on the Law of Treaties 1969 which provides under the heading of observance of treaties (art. 26: *pacta sunt servanda)* that "[e]very treaty in force is binding upon the partners to it and must be performed by them in good faith." *See* Verzijl, *International Law in Historical Perspective,* (1970), Vol. 3, 387-397.

plural nationality *See* **dual (or plural) nationality**.

pluralistic (treaties) "The term 'pluralistic' is probably only used in international law, and then mainly in respect of reservations to treaties. It describes a treaty negotiated between a limited number of states with a particular interest in the subject matter": Aust, *Modern Treaty Law and Practice* (2000), 112. Aust cites as examples the Constantinople Convention concerning the Suez Canal 1988 *(171 C.T.S. 241)* and the Antarctic Treaty 1959 *(402 U.N.T.S. 71)*. Art. 20(2) of the Vienna Convention on the Law of Treaties 1969 requires all the parties to a treaty to consent to any reservation "[w]hen it appears from the limited number of the negotiating States and the object and purpose of the treaty that the application of the treaty in its entirety between all the parties is an essential condition to the consent of each one. . . ."

poison   Art. 23(a) of the Hague Regulations 1899 and 1907 *(187 C.T.S. 436* and *205 C.T.S. 289)* expressly prohibited the use of poison and poisoned weapons. This prohibition extends also, for instance, to poisoning water or wells, probably even if a notice is posted: *II Oppenheim 340 n.* A number of other weapons, and notably **asphyxiating gas, chemical weapons**, and **bacteriological weapons** have poisonous effects and are themselves prohibited: *see also* **prohibited weapons**.

polar regions, sovereignty over   Both the North and the South Pole has been the subject of territorial claims by States, based on the **sector** principle. As there is no land at the North Pole, merely frozen high seas, and as art. 89 as the UN Convention on the Law of the Sea 1982 *(1833 U.N.T.S. 3)* confirms that the high seas are not susceptible to State sovereignty, it appears that no territorial claim may validly be made. Art. 4 of the **Antarctic Treaty** 1959 *(402 U.N.T.S. 71)* has the effect, for the duration of the treaty, of safeguarding the parties' positions regarding existing territorial claims around the South Pole (south of 60° Latitude: art. 6) and of preventing State activities under the treaty from being the basis of territorial claims. *See I Oppenheim 692-6*; Rothwell, *The Polar Regions and the Development of International Law* (1996).

policy oriented theory   This theory, principally associated with the writings of Professor Myers **McDougal** and related to the **phenomenological approach**, views international law as a comprehensive and complex process of decision-making rather than an established body of rules. The focus of the proponents of this theory is on the almost unlimited range of factors utilized by decision-makers, and the emphasis is on the dynamic nature of international law. *See* McDougal and Feliciano, *Law and Minimum World Public Order* (1961). *See also* Falk, *The Status of Law in International Society* (1970), 642-59.

Polish Nationals in Danzig Case *(1932) P.C.I.J., Ser. A/B, No. 44.* Art. 103 of the Treaty of Versailles 1919 *(225 C.T.S. 188)* provided for a constitution for the Free City of Danzig to be drawn up and placed under a guarantee of the League of Nations. Art. 104 provided for the conclusion of a treaty between Poland and Danzig with, by virtue of para. 5, the object, *inter alia*, of prohibiting discrimination within Danzig to the detriment of Polish citizens or other persons of Polish origin or speech: the Convention of Paris was accordingly concluded in 1920, art. 33 of which gave effect to the prohibition of discrimination. A High Commissioner for Danzig was appointed by the Council of the League of Nations. In 1930 Poland sought from the High Commissioner a decision regarding unfavorable treatment of Polish nationals in Danzig. The matter was referred to the Council of the League of Nations which, on 22 May 1931, adopted a resolution asking the PCIJ for an advisory opinion on whether the treatment of Polish nationals in Danzig was to be decided solely by reference to the relevant treaties or also by reference to the Constitution of Danzig, and accordingly whether Poland was entitled to submit to organs of the League (i.e. the High Commissioner) disputes concerning the application to Polish nationals of the Danzig Constitution and Danzig laws; the request also sought the opinion of the PCIJ on the interpretation of art. 104(5) of the Treaty of Versailles, art. 33(1) of the Convention of

Paris and, if appropriate, the relevant provisions of the Danzig Constitution. The Court *advised* that the treatment of Polish nationals in Danzig must be decided solely by reference to art. 104(5) of the Treaty of Versailles and art. 33(1) of the Convention of Paris (and also if necessary, by reference to other treaties or rules of ordinary international law) but not by reference to the Constitution of Danzig, and that consequently Poland could not submit to organs of the League disputes concerning the application to Polish nationals of the Danzig Constitution and other Danzig laws, unless such disputes concerned the violation of Danzig's international obligations towards Poland arising either from treaty provisions in force between them or from ordinary international law. In the course of this part of its opinion the Court said: "It should however be observed that, while on the one hand, according to generally accepted principles, a State cannot rely, as against another State, on the provisions of the latter's Constitution, but only on international law and international obligations duly accepted, on the other hand and conversely, a State cannot adduce as against another State its own Constitution with a view to evading obligations incumbent upon it under international law or treaties in force." The Court went on to give its opinion on the extent of the prohibition of discrimination against Polish nationals on the basis of the interpretation of art. 104(5) of the Treaty of Versailles and art. 33(1) of the Convention of Paris. In this connection the Court said "that the prohibition against discrimination, in order to be effective, must ensure the absence of discrimination in fact as well as in law. A measure which in terms is of general application, but in fact is directed against Polish nationals and other persons of Polish origin or speech, constitutes a violation of the prohibition. . . . Whether a measure is or is not in fact directed against these persons is a question to be decided on the merits of each particular case."

Polish-Czechoslovak Frontier Delimitation Opinion *(Question of Jaworzina) (1923) P.C.I.J., Ser. B, No. 8.* The task of settling frontier disputes between Poland and Czechoslovakia after the 1914-1918 war was under the Peace Treaties assumed by the Principal Allied and Associated Powers. A dispute arose over, *inter alia*, the boundary in the district of Spisz, concerning in particular the commune of Jaworzina. The Delegates of the Allied Powers in the Ambassadors Conference adopted a decision on 28 July 1920 dividing the territory in question. Poland was dissatisfied with the decision, and the matter was further considered by the Conference of Ambassadors which, in July 1923, laid the matter before the Council of the League of Nations. On 27 September 1923, the Council requested from the PCIJ an advisory opinion on whether the question of the delimitation of the frontier between Poland and Czechoslovakia was still open and, if so, to what extent; or whether it should be considered as already settled by a definitive decision. The PCIJ *advised* that the decision of 28 July 1920 definitively settled the question of the delimitation of the frontier, although that portion remained subject (apart from the modifications of detail which the customary procedure of marking boundaries locally may entail) to the possibility of modification, as provided for in that decision, where justified by reason of the interests of individuals or of communities in the neighborhood of the frontier line and having regard to the special local circumstances.

political independence This term appears in art. 2(4) of the Charter as a Principle of the UN: "All Members shall refrain in their international relations from the threat or use of force against the territorial integrity or political independence of any state. . . ." The terms political independence and **territorial integrity** are obviously closely linked. The Declaration on Principles of International Law Concerning **Friendly Relations** and Cooperation Among States in Accordance with the Charter of the United Nations of 24 October 1970 (GA Res. 2625 (XXV)) asserts duties on all States relating to political independence: to refrain from any forcible action that deprives peoples of "their right to self-determination and freedom and independence"; to refrain from organizing, encouraging or assisting irregular forces or armed bands, including mercenaries, and those promoting civil strife or terrorist acts. *See also* **independence**.

political offence This concept, denoting the denial of **asylum** or **extradition** in respect of species of offences, is of relatively recent origin. The concept was unheard of prior to the 19th century; indeed, prior to then, it was "political offenders" rather than "common criminals" that States considered worth the effort of a request for surrender (*see I Oppenheim 962-3*). *See* **attentat clause**. The concept of a political offence derives from treaties on extradition or diplomatic asylum, and accordingly its precise import depends upon the terms of particular treaties. Thus, the Havana Convention on Asylum of 20 February 1928 *(132 L.N.T.S. 323)* defines political crimes negatively, thereby applying diplomatic asylum only "to persons accused or condemned for common crimes" (art. 1). *See* the **Asylum Case** *1950 I.C.J. Rep. 266* at 298, where Judge Alvarez, dissenting, understood the term to mean "any act which purports to overthrow the democratic political order of a country . . .; in that sense even murder may sometimes be termed a political offence." The European Convention on Extradition of 13 December 1957 *(359 U.N.T.S. 273)*, in art. 3, excludes the obligation of extradition among the parties where the requested surrender is "regarded by the requested Party as a political offence or as an offence connected with a political offence," thus leaving it to the Parties to determine, according to their own interpretation of the term, what constitutes a political offence. Extradition treaties between individual States invariably exclude extradition for a political offence, yet here again the definitions differ widely.

Some treaties, because of their object and purpose, specifically declare that crimes specified in them are not to be considered as political crimes for the purpose of extradition: *see, e.g.*, art. 7 of the Genocide Convention 1948 *(78 U.N.T.S. 277)*; art. 3(e) of the Montevideo Convention on Extradition of 26 December 1933 *(162 L.N.T.S. 45)*; art. 3 of the European Convention on Extradition of 13 December 1957 *(supra)* as amended by Additional Protocol No. 1 of 15 October 1975 *(E.T.S. No. 86)*; and the Inter-American Convention on Extradition of 25 May 1981, art. 4(4) *(20 I.L.M. 723 (1981))*. The conventions on **terrorism** exclude political offences from the exceptions to the obligation to extradite.

Politis, Nicolas Socrate 1872-1942. Greek statesman and diplomat who had a hand in drafting the Covenant of the League of Nations, and was active in League affairs, particularly attempts to limit arms. Principal works: *La Justice Internationale* (1924); *Les Nouvelles Tendences de Droit International* (1927).

polluter pays doctrine This doctrine postulates that the goal of the law on environmental protection is that the polluter should bear the costs of remedial measures and compensate for pollution damage. It is not a principle of law, as indicated by the qualified expression of the doctrine in Principle 16 of the Rio Declaration on Environment and Development 1992 *(31 I.L.M. 874 (1992))*: "National authorities should endeavour to promote the internalization of environmental costs and the use of economic instruments, taking into account the approach that the polluter should, in principle, bear the cost of pollution, with due regard to the public interest and without distorting international trade and investment." "Whatever its legal status, . . . the 'polluter pays' principle cannot supply guidance on the content of national or international environmental law without further definition": Birnie and Boyle, *International Law and the Environment* (2nd ed.), 95. *See also* **sustainable development**.

pollution *See* **air pollution**, **marine pollution**.

Ponsonby Rule A British constitutional practice initiated in 1924 by the government of the day *(H.C. Deb. Vol. 171, col. 2007 (1924))* whereby every treaty requiring ratification by the Crown is, when signed, laid on the Tables of both Houses of Parliament for twenty-one days prior to being ratified. The purpose is to secure publicity for treaties, and to give the Houses an opportunity for discussion. *See* McNair, *Law of Treaties* (2nd ed.), 99 and 190.

port-State jurisdiction Art. 218 of the UN Convention on the Law of the Sea 1982 *(1833 U.N.T.S. 3)* allows a State to investigate and prosecute a vessel within one of its ports in respect of any discharge in violation of the applicable international rules and standards on the high seas. *See* Memorandum of Understanding of 26 January 1982 on Port State Control in Implementing Agreements on Maritime Safety and Protection of the Marine Environment *(21 I.L.M. 1 (1982))*.

Portugal v. Germany *(1928, 1930) 2 R.I.A.A. 1013, 1037*. Portugal made claims against Germany in respect of various matters arising when Portugal was still a neutral State in the First World War. These claims concerned: (a) attacks on Portuguese posts at Naulilaa (as **reprisals**) and Maziua (in the mistaken belief that war had broken out); (b) property owned by Portuguese nationals which, during the German occupation of Belgium, had been requisitioned or had disappeared; and (c) the condemnation in prize, and destruction, of the Portuguese vessel *The Cysnes* and the loss of certain other Portuguese vessels and goods. These claims were referred to an Arbitral Tribunal constituted by para. 4 of the Annex to arts. 297 and 298 of the Treaty of Versailles, which *held:* (a) As to the Naulilaa and Maziua incidents *(2 R.I.A.A. 1013* and *1068)*: (1) that Germany was responsible for the direct consequences of the attack on Maziua post; (2) that Germany was responsible for the attacks on Portuguese territory at Naulilaa and other places since those attacks were not justified as reprisals in international law, for which there had to have been a prior violation of a rule of international law by the State against which the reprisals were directed, a prior request to remedy the alleged wrong and proportionality between the reprisals and the act which provoked them; and (3) that Germany was not solely responsible for the indirect damage resulting from the extension of a revolt among the native population and the inter-tribal strife.

In later proceedings, the same Tribunal assessed the damages payable by Germany for losses directly arising from the Naulilaa and Maziua incidents; assessed, *ex aequo et bono*, limited damages in respect of the losses suffered in consequence of the rising of the native population following upon the withdrawal of the Portuguese forces; but declined to award penal damages. The execution of this Award was the subject of a further arbitration Award in 1933: *3 R.I.A.A. 1373*; (b) As to property in Belgium *(2 R.I.A.A. 1037)*: that Germany's responsibility was engaged by specific acts contrary to international law which were ordered or tolerated by the military or civil authorities in occupied territory, and that requisitions, which in time of war were permitted as an exception to the general rule of international law requiring respect for private property, became contrary to international law if not compensated within a reasonable time; (c) As to *The Cysnes* and other vessels *(2 R.I.A.A. 1047)*: that (1) the condemnation by a prize court of *The Cysnes* and its cargo was an act contrary to international law for which Germany was responsible, the cargo not being absolute contraband and treating it as such as reprisals not being justifiable since reprisals were not admissible against neutral States, and as conditional contraband its destination was innocent; and (2) all save one of the other claims did not disclose an act contrary to international law by German authorities or tribunals.

positive law *See* **positivism**.

positivism According to positivist theory developed in the eighteenth century by Bynkershoek, Moser and Martens on foundations laid in the previous century notably by Rachel and Textor, the principal components of international law ("positive international law") are custom and treaties. Taken to its extreme, positivism postulates that the will of States alone constitutes a valid source of international law. "It is now generally admitted that in the absence of rules based on the practice of States, International Law may be fittingly supplemented and fertilized by recourse to rules of justice and to general principles of law. . . . In adopting art. 38 of the [PCIJ Statute] the signatory States sanctioned that practice": *I Oppenheim (8th ed.) 107.* The debate concerning the relationship of positivist doctrine to possible higher rules of international law (**jus cogens**) found a new focus in the preparatory work on art. 50 of the Vienna Convention on the Law of Treaties 1969, according to which "a treaty is void if it conflicts with a peremptory norm of international law. . . ." *See* Sinclair, *The Vienna Convention on the Law of Treaties* (2nd ed.), Chap. V.

postal communications *See* **Universal Postal Union**.

post-conflict peace-building Less a term of art than a descriptor for two broad activities: post-conflict peace-building is the international verification of settlements following a conflict and measures short of **peace-keeping** undertaken in relation to a potential or past conflict: *Supplement to an Agenda for Peace* (1995) *(UN Doc. A/50/60—S/1995/1)*, para. 49. *See also* **preventive diplomacy**.

postliminium "The term 'postliminium' is originally one of Roman Law, derived from *post* and *limen* (i.e. boundary). . . . Modern International Law and Municipal Law have adopted the term to indicate the fact that territory, individuals, and property, after having come in time of war under the authority of the enemy, return, either during the war or at its end, under the sway of the original sovereign. . . . Cases of postliminium occur only [in case of reverter to] the legitimate sovereign": *II Oppenheim 616-619.*

post-modernism This is a school of thought that views contemporary international law essentially in terms of the management of a régime, wherein minor violations of the legal rules may be discounted as long as the régime endures. *See* Chayes and Chayes, *The New Sovereignty: Compliance with International Regulatory Agreements* (1995).

practice (international) of States In setting down the sources of international law, art. 38(1)(b) of the ICJ Statute refers to "international custom, as evidence of a general practice accepted as law." While it has been contended that this formulation is in fact expressed the wrong way round and that a general practice accepted as law is evidence of custom (Schwarzenberger, *International Law* (3rd ed.), 39), it is generally accepted that international custom has two elements: a general practice and a belief that the practice is followed because it conforms to the law (*opinio juris sive necessitatis*). The emergence of a principle or rule of customary international law would seem to require the presence of the following elements: (a) concordant practice by a number of States with reference to a type of situation falling within the domain of international relations; (b) continuation or repetition of the practice over a considerable period of time; (c) conception that the practice is required by, or consistent with, prevailing international law; and (d) general acquiescence in the practice by other States. *See* Judge Hudson, *rapporteur, [1950] II I.L.C. Yearbook 26*, cited with approval in Parry, *Sources and Evidences of International Law* (1965), 62. "The practice of states . . . embraces not only their external conduct with each other, but is also evidenced by such internal matters as their domestic legislation, judicial decisions, diplomatic dispatches, internal government memoranda, and ministerial statements in Parliament and elsewhere": *I Oppenheim 26.* On the history and importance of **digests** of State practice, see Parry, *supra*; *I Oppenheim 27*. On methodology and sources, see Snyder and Schaffer, *Contemporary Practice of Public International* (1997).

preamble The first part of a treaty, the preamble "comprises the names of the contracting parties (and sometimes their duly authorized representatives), and the motives for the conclusion of the treaty": *I Oppenheim 1210*. It may also set out the principal object of the treaty. While international tribunals have resorted to the preamble in order to discover that object, the preamble of itself has no binding force: ***Rights of U.S. Nationals in Morocco Case 1952 I.C.J. Rep. 176***. The preamble is, however, part of the context of a treaty, which must be taken into account in its interpretation: Vienna Convention on the Law of Treaties 1969, art. 31. In relation of a resolution of an international organization, the preamble (sometimes referred to as the "preambular paragraphs") generally set out circumstances of, and authority for, its adoption and the object sought to be attained.

precedent While art. 38(1)(d) of the ICJ Statute provides that judicial decisions are "subsidiary means for the determination of rules of law," that sub-paragraph is expressly subjected to art. 59, which provides: "The decision of the Court has no binding force except between the parties and in respect of that particular case." In the ***German Interests in Polish Upper Silesia Case (1926) P.C.I.J., Ser. A, No. 7*** at 19, the PCIJ stated that the object of art. 59 "is simply to prevent legal principles accepted by the Court in a particular case from being binding on other States or in other disputes." *See* ***res judicata***. "In the absence of anything approaching the common law doctrine of judicial precedent, decisions of international tribunals are not a direct source of law in international adjudication. In fact, however, they exercise considerable influence as an impartial and well-considered statement of the law by jurists of authority made in the light of actual problems which arise before them. They are often relied upon in argument and decision. The [ICJ] . . . has, in the interests of judicial consistency, referred to them with increasing frequency": *I Oppenheim 41*.

preclusion *See* **estoppel**.

pre-emption "[A] State can be fettered in its freedom of action [in alienating its territory] by the less far-reaching international commitment not to proceed to the alienation of a specified part of its territory without having first offered it either to its former sovereign who has reserved the 'right of re-emption,' or to another State which has stipulated for itself a 'right of pre-emption,' preferential to possible offers by other interested States. These latter types of international commitment belong almost completely to the feudal-patrimonial or to the colonial past": Verzijl, *International Law in Historical Perspective*, Vol. 3, (1970), 479.

preferential treatment **Most favored nation treatment** is the lowest level of contractual preference (whether obtained through membership of GATT or under bilateral commercial treaties). More favorable tariff treatment (or "preferential" treatment) is in practice made available by industrialized countries to developing countries, both under the exception in favor of relations with dependent territories in art. I of GATT itself and now principally by virtue of measures (including bilateral preferential agreements) adopted in accordance with Part IV (Trade and Development) of GATT or under the Generalized System of Preferences. Preferential treatment (in the form of elimination of duties and other restrictive regulations of commerce on substantially all the trade between the constituent territories in products originating in such territories) is also permissible within **customs unions** and **free trade areas** in accordance with art. XXIV of GATT: the principal examples here are the **European Community**, **European Free Trade Association** and **North**

American Free Trade Area. *See* Trebilcock and Howse, *The Regulation of International Trade* (2nd ed.).

preliminary objection "Any objection by the respondent to the jurisdiction of the [International] Court [of Justice] or to the admissibility of the application, or other objection the decision upon which is requested before any further proceedings on the merits, shall be made in writing within the time-limit fixed for the delivery of the Counter-Memorial": art. 79(1) of the Rules of the Court 1978. The preliminary objection must "set out the facts and the law on which the objection is based": art. 79(2). The preliminary objection suspends the proceedings on the merits, and the other party to the case may present in writing its observations and submissions: art. 79(3). After hearing the parties the Court gives its decision. Art. 79 of the Rules of Court 1978 was designed to avoid the practice of reserving preliminary questions to the merits stage, much criticized in the *South West Africa Cases 1962 I.C.J. Rep. 319* and *Barcelona Traction Case 1964 I.C.J. Rep. 6*, by promoting early consideration of any preliminary questions. As to the distinction between a preliminary objection to jurisdiction and one to admissibility, "[n]either jurisprudence nor doctrine displays any certainty or unanimity over the categorization of preliminary objections, which have become characterized by ever increasing sophistication and subtlety. All that can be deduced from experience, including some diplomatic experience, is that this is an individual matter to be appreciated in the light of each case": Rosenne, *Procedure in the International Court: A Commentary on the 1978 Rules of the International Court of Justice* (1983), 162.

preneutrality This term is used by some writers (*e.g.*, de Visscher, *Theory and Reality in Public International Law* (Rev. ed., 1968), 315-7) to connote the practice of small States seeking security in a policy of complete impartiality towards potential protagonists. As neutrality properly so-called is only operative in time of war, this practice has been called preneutrality. Preneutrality may have reemerged in the 1960s in the **non-aligned movement**.

prescription, acquisitive This is "the acquisition of sovereignty over a territory through continuous and undisturbed exercise of sovereignty over it during such a period as is necessary to create under the influence of historical development the general conviction that the present condition of things is in conformity with international order": *I Oppenheim 706*, explicitly endorsing the identical statement made in *I Oppenheim (8th ed.) 576*. Jennings, *The Acquisition of Territory in International Law* (1963), 21-2, distinguished two concepts of acquisitive prescription: possession which is so long established that its origins are not only undoubted, but also unknown; possession over a period of time so as to cure a defect in title, the latter being referred to as "prescription strictly so-called." While the exercise of sovereignty necessary to establish a title to territory by prescription is identical to that required for **occupation,** and hence it is often difficult to ascertain whether a case is decided on the basis of prescription or occupation, the essential difference between the two lies in the requirement that for occupation the territory must be *terra nullius. See Island of Palmas Case (1928) 2 R.I.A.A. 829*; *Chamizal Arbitration (1911) 9 R.I.A.A. 316*; *Minquiers and Ecrehos Case 1953 I.C.J. Rep. 47*; *Grisbadarna Arbitration (1909) 11 R.I.A.A. 155*; *Western Sahara Case 1975 I.C.J. Rep. 12. See* Johnson, Acquisitive Prescription in International Law, *(1950) 27 B.Y.I.L. 332.*

prescription, extinctive "The principle of extinctive prescription, that is, the bar of claims by lapse of time, is recognized by international law. It has been applied by arbitration tribunals in a number of cases. The application of the principle is flexible and there are no fixed time limits. . . . Undue delay in presenting a claim, which may lead to it being barred, is to distinguished from effects of the passage of time on the merits of the claim in cases where the claimant state has, by failing to protest or otherwise, given evidence of acquiescence": *I Oppenheim 526-7. See* King, Prescription of Claims in International Law, *(1934) 15 B.Y.I.L. 82.*

preventive diplomacy "[A]ction to prevent disputes from arising between parties, to prevent existing disputes from escalating into conflicts and to limit the spread of the latter when they occur": *An Agenda for Peace* (1992) *(UN Doc. A/47/277—S/24111)*, para. 20. The author of this document, Secretary-General Boutros-Ghali, saw this as an essential part of the UN's role in maintaining and securing international peace and security, while recognizing (*Supplement to an Agenda for Peace* (1995) *(UN Doc. A/50/60—S1995/1)* paras. 29-31) that there were difficulties recruiting suitably experienced personnel and establishing and financing field missions.

Prince von Pless Administration Case, *(1933) P.C.I.J., Ser. A/B, Nos. 52, 54.* By the Geneva Convention of 15 May 1922 concerning Upper Silesia, certain obligations were assumed by Poland which extended, *inter alia*, to the Administration of the Prince von Pless, a Polish national belonging to the German minority in Upper Silesia. Germany alleged that Poland had, in relation to the taxation of the Administration of the Prince von Pless, acted in violation of the Geneva Convention, and in May 1932 instituted proceedings before the PCIJ against Poland under art. 72 of that Convention. Poland raised preliminary objections that there was no "difference of opinion" between the parties within the meaning of art. 72 and that the Prince von Pless had not exhausted the means of redress open to him under Polish law. The Court *held* that those preliminary objections should be joined to the merits, and raised *proprio motu* (although deferring consideration until the merits) the question whether it had jurisdiction to entertain a claim for an indemnity on behalf of a national of the respondent State who was a member of a minority. In May 1933, Germany sought interim measures of protection to prevent Poland imposing certain measures of constraint in respect of property of the Prince von Pless, but as the Polish Government withdrew the measures of constraint complained of by Germany, the Court *held* that the request for interim measures of protection ceased to have any object. In October 1933, Germany withdrew the case submitted by it in 1932 and the proceedings were terminated *(P.C.I.J., Ser. A/B, No. 59).*

principles of international law "For the purposes of systematic exposition and legal education it is valuable to abstract principles from legal rules. Thus, it is possible to extract a principle from the rules on diplomatic immunity. Principles provide the common denominator for a number of related legal rules. The more fundamental the underlying rules, the more fundamental is the legal principle that is extracted from these rules": Schwarzenberger and Brown, *A Manual of International Law* (6th ed.), 35. The authors identify seven fundamental principles: sovereignty, recognition, consent, good faith, freedom of the seas, international responsibility and self-defense. The Declaration on Principles of International Law Concerning **Friendly Relations** and Cooperation Among States in Accordance with the Charter of the United Nations of 24 October 1970 (GA Res. 2625 (XXV)) proclaims seven principles of international law relating to friendly relations and cooperation among States: the prohibition on the use or threat of force; the settlement of disputes by peaceful means; the duty not to intervene in matters within the domestic jurisdiction of any State; the duty of States to co-operate in accordance with the Charter; the principle of equal rights and self-determination of peoples; the sovereign equality of States; the duty to fulfill in good faith the obligations assumed in the Charter. *See also* **rules of international law**. Cf. **general principles of law recognized by civilized nations**.

prisoners of war   While international concern for the treatment of prisoners of war dates back as far as 1874, the law relating to prisoners of war is now largely codified as a result of the experiences of the two world wars by the Geneva Conventions of 12 August 1949 and notably the Convention relative to the Treatment of Prisoners of War (the Third Convention; *75 U.N.T.S. 135*), supplemented by Protocol No. I of 8 June 1977, Part III, Section II on combatant and prisoner of war status *(1125 U.N.T.S. 3)*. The 1977 Protocol simplifies the 1949 definitions of who shall be a prisoner of war by providing that any combatant who falls into the power of an adverse party shall be a prisoner of war (art. 45). Members of the armed forces of a party to a conflict are combatants (art. 43(2)); medical personal and chaplains are covered by special rules under art. 33 of the Third Convention). Armed forces consist of all organized forces, groups and units under a command responsible to that party and subject to an internal disciplinary system (art. 43(1)). A person not falling within the definition of prisoner of war or who has forfeited the right to that status is in any event entitled to minimum guarantees under art. 75 of the 1977 Protocol. Spies and mercenaries, as defined by the Protocol, are in any event excluded from prisoner of war status (arts. 46 and 47). Any doubt as to whether an individual qualifies as a prisoner of war is entitled to have that issue determined by "a competent tribunal" (art. 5 of the Third Convention).

The minimum guarantees include prohibitions on violence; murder; torture; corporal punishment; outrages upon personal dignity, in particular humiliating and degrading treatment, enforced prostitution and any form of indecent assault; the taking of hostages; collective punishment and threats (art. 75(2)). They also include guarantees in regard to arrest, detention and trial (art. 75(3)-(7)).

"The conviction in time became general that captivity should only be the means of preventing prisoners from returning to their corps and taking up arms again, and should as a matter of principle be distinguished from imprisonment as a punishment for crimes. . . . During the nineteenth century, the principle that prisoners of war should be treated by their captor in a manner analogous to that meted out to his own troops became generally recognized": *II Oppenheim 368.*

Supervision of the operation of the Geneva Conventions, and of the Third Convention in particular, is largely through the **protecting power** system and the **International Committee of the Red Cross.** Under Part II, General Protection of Prisoners of War, prisoners are in the hands of the enemy power as such, and not of the individuals or units who have captured them (art. 12). They must be humanely treated (arts. 13 and 14; and cf. the minimum guarantees of the 1977 Protocol above); and reprisals against prisoners of war are prohibited (*ibid.*). Part III lays down specific rules on captivity. Every prisoner is bound to give only his surname, first names and rank, date of birth and number, or equivalent information (art. 17). A prisoner of war identity card is to be provided. Personal effects, including clothing and "effects and articles used for feeding," not arms and military equipment, are to remain in the possession of prisoners of war (art. 18). Prisoners are to be evacuated from the combat zone (art. 14) and not exposed to fire (art. 23). They may be interned (art. 21), but only in premises located on land and affording every degree of hygiene and healthfulness. Prisoners of war are to be quartered under conditions as favorable as those for the forces of the detaining power which are billeted in the same area (art. 25). Adequate provision is to be made for rations, etc. (art. 26) and for hygiene and medical attention (arts. 29-32). As regards discipline, every prisoner of war camp is to be put under the immediate authority of a responsible commissioned officer belonging to the regular armed forces of the detaining power (art. 39). The wearing of badges of rank and nationality, as well as of decorations, is permitted (art. 40). Fit prisoners of war may be made to work, with a view particularly to maintaining them in a good state of physical and mental health. NCOs may only be required to supervise although, if they are not so required, work should be available to them. Officers may not be compelled to work, but suitable work should again be available (art. 49). A list of classes of work is laid down in art. 50. Provision is made for pay, not only for work (art. 54 and 62), but as ordinary pay, considered as advanced on behalf of the power on which the prisoner depends (arts. 60 and 67). Provision is also made for prisoners to hold sums they had upon capture (art. 58) and for remittances (art. 63) and indeed post and parcels etc. (arts. 71-77).

Prisoners of war are subject to the laws, regulations and orders in force in the armed forces of the detaining power: arts. 82-108 contain detailed provisions on discipline, trial and penalties. Prisoners of war are in any event to be released and repatriated without delay after the cessation of active hostilities (art. 118), but the sick and wounded may be repatriated at once or, if appropriate and practicable, interned in neutral territory (arts. 109-117).

private international law   Private international law, or conflicts of laws as it is perhaps more accurately also known, is not a branch of international law as the term is used (and defined) in this Encyclopedic Dictionary. The expression refers rather to that branch of municipal law which deals with cases having a foreign element, i.e. a contact with some system of law other than the domestic system. The central issues for private international law in the Anglo-American systems are choice of jurisdiction, i.e. whether a court in State A has jurisdiction to deal with a case having a foreign element, and choice of law, i.e. whether the ordinary rules of law of State A shall apply to the case, or whether some other system of law shall apply. The question of enforcement of foreign judgments arises as a subsidiary issue. There are necessarily a number of interfaces between public and private international law. The case of a contract between States is simple enough: "Any contract which is not a contract between States in their capacity as subjects of international law is based on the municipal law of some country. The question as to which this law is forms the subject of [private international law]": *Serbian and Brazilian Loans Cases (1929) P.C.I.J., Ser. A, Nos. 20/21, 4.* The relationship has also been of significance in relation to recognition and the powers of the unrecognized State and to the relative rights and duties of nationals and aliens.

privateers   "Privateers were vessels owned and manned by private persons, but furnished with the authority of their Government to carry on hostilities; they were used to increase the naval force of a State by causing vessels to be equipped from private cupidity, which a minister might not be able to obtain by general taxation without much difficulty": Manning, *Law of Nations* (1875), 175. "In practice any prizes they captured were adjudged to them, subject to the rights of their State": Colombos, *International Law of the Sea* (6th ed.), 471. Art. 1 of the Declaration of Paris of 16 April 1856 *(115 C.T.S. 1)* declared that "[p]rivateering is, and remains, abolished." *See* **Paris, Declaration of.**

privileges and immunities of consuls; diplomats   *See* **consular privileges and immunities; diplomatic privileges and immunities; taxation: diplomatic and consular exemptions; waiver.**

privileges and immunities of international organizations   Because international organizations are by definition the creatures of their member States, the practice has been not to endow them with an intergovernmental form of sovereign immunity, but to confer on them only those privileges and immunities necessary for the fulfillment of their purposes ("functional privileges and immunities"). Thus, art. 105(1) of the UN Charter provides that "[t]he Organization shall enjoy in the territory of each of its Members such privileges and immunities as are necessary for the fulfillment of its purposes." Similarly, the representatives of member States and officials of the Organization are to enjoy only "such privileges and immunities as are necessary for the independent exercise of their functions in connection with the Organization" (art. 105(2)). The constituent acts of the Specialized Agencies and other major international organizations for the most part make provision for privileges and immunities in similar very general terms, the detailed enumeration being left, in the case of the UN, to the Convention on the Privileges and Immunities of the United Nations of 13 February 1946 *(1 U.N.T.S. 15)*; in the case of the Specialized Agencies, to the Convention on the Privileges and Immunities of the Specialized Agencies of 21 November 1947 *(33 U.N.T.S. 261)*; and specific agreements for other international organizations. Particularly in the case of organizations within the UN System, these provisions have been supplemented by headquarters agreements with the host country (*e.g.*, Headquarters Agreement between the UN and the USA of 26 June 1947 *(11 U.N.T.S. 11)*.

The organizations within the UN System are all endowed with immunity from legal process, which is subject to express waiver (*e.g.*, UN Convention, § 2); their premises and archives are inviolable (§ 3 and § 4); they enjoy freedom from exchange and financial controls (§ 5); are exempted from taxation (§ 7) and enjoy freedom of communications (§ 9 and § 10). It will be seen that, subject to the functional limitation, the privileges extended are similar to privileges of diplomatic missions (§ 11 to § 16).

The immunities of representatives of Member States, which within the UN System are in practice largely dependent on the headquarters arrangements, are closely assimilated to ordinary diplomatic privileges and immunities in the case of accredited representatives, an assimilation which is reinforced by the Vienna Convention on the Representation of States in their Relations with International Organizations of a Universal Character of 14 March 1975 which parallels the provisions of the Vienna Convention on Diplomatic Relations 1963. Representatives enjoy, in addition, immunity in respect of their official actions in relation to the organization (cf. § 11 of the UN Convention: this may be the sole protection for representatives not enjoying diplomatic status, *e.g.*, national officials sent out for a conference, although the Vienna Convention on Representation of States would assimilate delegations and missions to organizations and to conferences much more closely to accredited representatives (arts. 42-70)). Officials of the organizations at the higher levels enjoy diplomatic level privileges and immunities, whereas other officials enjoy immunity only in respect of their official acts (§ 17 to § 21 of the UN Convention). *See* Amerasinghe, *Principles of the Institutional Law of International Organizations* (1996), Chap. 12.

prize courts "[T]he capture of a private enemy vessel has to be confirmed by a Prize Court, and . . . it is only through its adjudication that the vessel becomes finally appropriated. The origin of Prize Courts is to be traced back to the end of the Middle Ages. . . . The capture of any private vessel, whether *prima facie* belonging to an enemy or a neutral, must, therefore, be submitted to a Prize Court. Prize Courts are not international courts, but national courts instituted by Municipal Law. Every State is, however, bound by International Law to enact only such statutes and regulations for its Prize Courts as are in conformity with International Law": *II Oppenheim 482-5*. The Hague Convention relative to the Establishment of an International Prize Court of 18 October 1907 *(205 C.T.S. 381)* provided for the establishment of an International Prize Court, but the Convention failed of ratification.

procedural matters In terms of art. 27(2) of the UN Charter, decisions of the Security Council on procedural matters are to be made by an affirmative vote of any nine (out of 15) members. Decisions "on all other matters" are to be made by an affirmative vote of nine members, including the concurring vote of the five permanent members (art. 27(3)). The permanent members prepared a memorandum on the distinction between "procedural" and "other" matters at the time the UN was established (known as the **Yalta Formula**): *11 U.N.C.I.O. 711-4*. The General Assembly has listed which of various categories of possible Security Council decisions should be considered procedural: GA Res. 267 (III) of 14 April 1949. In the General Assembly, the distinction drawn in voting is between "important questions" and "other questions" (art. 18(2) and (3)). There is clearly correspondence between the "procedural" and the "other" on the one hand, and the "important" and the "other" on the other hand. *See* Goodrich, Hambro and Simons, *Charter of the United Nations* (3rd ed.), 222-7. *See* **veto**.

progressive development This is defined in art. 15 of the Statute of the International Law Commission (GA Res. 174 (II) of 21 November 1947; *42 A.J.I.L. Supp. 2 (1948)*) as "the preparation of draft conventions on subjects which have not yet been regulated by international law or in regard to which the law has not yet been sufficiently developed in the practice of States." The functions of the ILC are stated in art. 1 to be "the promotion of the progressive development of international law and its codification." In practice, it is often difficult to distinguish progressive development and **codification**: Dhokalia, *The Codification of Public International Law* (1970), 209-11.

prohibited weapons ". . . apart from those expressly prohibited by treaties or by custom, all means of killing and wounding that exist, or may be invented, are lawful. And it matters not whether the means used are directed against single individuals, as are swords and rifles, or against large bodies of individuals, as are, for instance, shrapnel, machine guns, and mines. On the other hand, all means are unlawful that needlessly aggravate the sufferings of wounded combatants": *II Oppenheim 340*. The use of particular weapons may be limited or controlled, or else prohibited altogether, by international convention. Particular weapons have been prohibited as follows: explosive or incendiary projectiles of less than 400 grammes weight: **St. Petersburg Declaration** of 11 December 1868 *(138 C.T.S. 297)*; poison and poisoned weapons: Hague Regulations 1899 *(187 C.T.S. 436)* and 1907 *(205 C.T.S. 289)*, art. 23(a); projectiles diffusing asphyxiating gases: Hague Declaration 1899 *(187 C.T.S. 456)*; expanding bullets: Hague Declaration 1899 *(187 C.T.S. 459)*; asphyxiating, poisonous or other gases and all analogous liquids, materials or devices: Treaty of Versailles 1919 *(225 C.T.S. 188)*, art. 171, confirmed and extended to bacteriological methods of warfare: Geneva Gas Protocol 1925 *(94 L.N.T.S. 65)*; chemical and biological weapons: Geneva Gas Protocol, *supra*, Convention of 10 April 1972 on the Prohibition of the Development, Production and Stockpiling of Bacteriological (Biological) and Toxin Weapons and their Destruction (*1015 U.N.T.S. 163*: *see* **bacteriological methods of warfare**); weapons the primary effects of which are to injure by non-detectable fragments: Protocol I on Non-Detectable Fragments to the Convention on Prohibitions or Restrictions on the Use of Certain Conventional Weapons which may be Deemed to be Excessively Injurious or to have Indiscriminate Effects *(1342 U.N.T.S. 137)*. As to nuclear weapons, *see* ***Legality of the Threat or Use of Nuclear Weapons Case*** *1996 I.C.J. Rep. 226*.

propaganda Attempts have been made to prohibit the dissemination of propaganda which is prejudicial to the peace and security of States. Thus, under the auspices of the League of Nations, there was concluded the Convention concerning the Use of Broadcasting in the Cause of Peace of 23 September 1936 *(186 L.N.T.S. 301)*, under which the Parties undertook to "prohibit and, if occasion arises, to stop without delay the broadcasting within their respective territories of any transmission which to the detriment of good international understanding is of such a character as to incite the population of any territory to acts incompatible with the internal order or security of [another] Party" (art. 1). The UN

General Assembly has on a number of occasions addressed the issue of propaganda. For example, the Declaration on the Inadmissibility of Intervention in the Domestic Affairs of States and the Protection of their Independence and Sovereignty of 21 December 1965 (GA Res. 2131 (XX)) provides that "direct intervention, subversion and all forms of indirect intervention . . . constitute a violation of the Charter of the United Nations" (Preamble). And the Declaration on Principles of International Law concerning **Friendly Relations** and Cooperation among States in Accordance with the Charter of the United Nations of 24 October 1970 (GA Res. 2625 (XXV)) places a duty on States "to refrain from propaganda for wars of aggression" (Principle 1). *See* Martin, *International Propaganda* (1958); Havinghurst, *International Control of Propaganda* (1967).

protected persons For the purposes of the Geneva Convention (IV) relative to the Protection of Civilian Persons in Time of War of 12 August 1949 *(75 U.N.T.S. 287)* protected persons are persons who "at a given moment and in any manner whatsoever, find themselves, in case of a conflict or occupation, in the hands of a Party to the conflict or Occupying Power of which they are not nationals." (art. 4). The Convention specifies a standard of treatment which must be accorded to protected persons, including prohibitions on coercion, corporal punishment, and the taking of reprisals or hostages (arts. 31-4), and the right to leave the territory unless their departure would be contrary to the national interests of the State (art. 35). The term is not employed in Protocol I to the 1949 Conventions of 12 December 1977 *(1125 U.N.T.S. 3)*, though enhanced protection is afforded through Part IV, Section II of which applies to the "Treatment of Persons in the Power of a Party to the Conflict."

Protecting Power(s) For purposes of the four Geneva Conventions on the Protection of War Victims of 1949 *(75 U.N.T.S. 5ff)* and Protocol I of 12 December 1977 *(1125 U.N.T.S. 3)*, "Protecting Power" means a neutral or other State not a Party to the conflict which has been designated by a Party to the conflict and accepted by the adverse Party and has agreed to carry out the functions assigned to a Protecting Power under the Conventions and Protocol. These functions are of particular importance under the Third Convention, on the Treatment of Prisoners of War *(75 U.N.T.S. 135)*, which is to be applied with the cooperation and under the scrutiny of the Protecting Power(s) whose duty it is to safeguard the interests of the Parties to the conflict (art. 8). The Parties to a conflict may agree to entrust to an organization which offers all guarantees of impartiality and efficacy the duties incumbent on the Protecting Power(s) (art. 10), with an obligation to accept the International Committee of the Red Cross if no other Protecting Power can be agreed upon *(ibid.)*. Representatives or delegates of the Protecting Power(s) have a general right of access to all places and premises occupied by prisoners of war and to the prisoners themselves (art. 126) and generally have responsibility to facilitate application of the specific provisions of the Conventions. As to the not dissimilar institution in diplomatic relations, *see* **protection of interests**.

protection of interests The Vienna Convention on Diplomatic Relations 1961 *(500 U.N.T.S. 95)* establishes rules, based on customary law and practice, on the protection of the interests of the sending State in the event of interruption of diplomatic relations (art. 45). The receiving State must in any event respect and protect the premises of the mission, together with its property and archives, even in the case of armed conflict (art. 45(a)). The sending State has the possibility of entrusting the custody of the mission, property and archives to a third State acceptable to the receiving State (art. 45(b)). The sending State may also entrust the protection of its interests and those of its nationals to a third State acceptable to the receiving State (art. 45(c)). The words "acceptable to" make it clear that the prior approval of the receiving State is not necessary although the receiving State could take exception to a particular protecting State. Prior consent is required for the then novel institution of art. 46 under which a sending State may with prior consent undertake the temporary protection of the interests of a third State and of its nationals, not represented in the receiving State at all. Art. 45 on the face of it envisions that the mission of the protecting State shall substitute itself for that of the sending State. In the event of interruption of diplomatic relations, it has nevertheless become common practice in recent years for the sending State, in agreement with the protecting State and the receiving State, to leave behind in the receiving State, upon occasion indeed in the premises of the sending State's mission, a number of diplomatic and supporting staff constituted, *e.g.*, as the "British Interests Section" of the mission of the protecting State. *See* Denza, *Diplomatic Law* (2nd ed.), 278-282.

protectorate(s) "An arrangement may be entered into whereby one state, while retaining to some extent its separate identity as a state, is subject to a kind of guardianship by another state. The circumstances in which this occurs and the consequences which result vary from case to case, and depend upon the particular provisions of the arrangement between the two states concerned": *I Oppenheim 267*. There are, or have been, four main types of protectorate: (1) European protectorates over small States retaining international personality, notably Swiss protection over Liechtenstein and those of France over Monaco, and Italy over San Marino; (2) Non-European protectorates over like international persons, notably Morocco and Tunis under French protection; (3) Non-European protectorates over lesser polities (protected States) not previously possessing any general measure of international personality, though frequently treated as sovereign by the protecting State and the relation of protection being established by quasi-treaty, *e.g.*, the former Indian Princely States, the Malay States, Brunei, Tonga and Zanzibar (all formerly under British protection), the Western Sahara (under Spain), and the Netherlands Indies; (4) So-called "colonial protectorates" usually over politically unorganized areas, though some protectorates were frequently again established by quasi-treaty (*e.g.*, the British treaties with Baganda Toro and with the protectorate of Uganda). Protectorates of this sort were commonly in Africa (though not exclusively so; *e.g.*, British Solomon Islands Protectorate) as a result of the provision of Article 34 of the Act of Berlin or Congo Act of 26 February 1885 *(165 C.T.S. 485)* that any State taking or about to take possession of any place on the coast of Africa outside its existing borders, or assuming a protectorate there (*qui y assumera un protectorat*) should formally notify the other signatories. *See* Kamanda, *A Study of the Legal Status of Protectorates in Public International Law* (1961); Crawford, *The Creation of States in International Law* (1979), 187-214.

protest "Protest is a formal communication from one state to another that it objects to an act performed, or contemplated, by the latter. . . . A protest principally serves the purpose of preserving rights, or of making it known that the protesting state does not acquiesce in, and does not recognise, certain acts: but it does not nullify the act complained of": *I Oppenheim 1193-4*. It is said by most writers that a valid protest requires a governmental origin and degree of formality: see MacGibbon, Some Observations on the Part of Protest in International Law, *(1953) 30 B.Y.I.L. 293*. *See* the *Asylum Case 1950 I.C.J. Rep. 266*; *Anglo-Norwegian Fisheries Case 1951 I.C.J. Rep. 116*; *North Sea Continental Shelf Cases 1969 I.C.J. Rep. 3*; *Military and Paramilitary Activities in Nicaragua Case 1986 I.C.J. Rep. 14*.

protocol (1) This term in its classic formulation "usually denotes a treaty amending, or supplemental to, another treaty, such as the unratified 'Geneva Protocol' of 1924 for the Pacific Settlement of International Disputes. The term 'protocol' is also constantly used, in the expression 'Protocol of Signature,' of a treaty or statute or régime to which it is appended, such as the Protocol of Signature of the Statute of the Permanent Court of International Justice of 16 December 1920. Sometimes it is used in the same sense as *procés-verbal* or the minutes of a conference. . .": McNair, *Law of Treaties* (2nd ed.), 23. Increasingly, the term is employed to connote an agreement supplementary to a principal treaty, adopted at the same time or subsequently, e.g. the Optional Protocol to the International Covenant on **Civil and Political Rights**1966 *(999 U.N.T.S. 171)*. (2) In diplomatic practice, protocol is the term given to the rules and principles governing titles, courtesies, precedence and procedures employed in relations between States. *See Satow's Guide to Diplomatic Practice* (5th ed.), Chaps. 4-6.

provisional application (of a treaty) *See* **application of treaty, provisional**.

provisional measures of protection *See* **interim measures of protection**.

public debt "The history of the effect of change of sovereignty on the public debt is confused and complicated. Hackworth is of the opinion that no definite conclusions can be arrived at 'except that no universal rule of international law on the subject can be said to exist'": O'Connell, *Law of State Succession* (1956), 145. Where a successor State entirely absorbs the debtor State, the latter's rights and obligations are extinguished. The degree to which the successor State may consider itself bound to service the debt will depend, *inter alia*, on whether the debt is secured and on whether acquired rights are involved. *See generally* O'Connell, *op. cit.*, Chap. IX; Verzijl, *International Law in Historical Perspective* (1974), Vol. 7, 39, 110, 156 ff. Cf. ***Ottoman Debt Arbitration (1925) 1 R.I.A.A. 529.*** In the case of a separation of part or parts of the territory of a State, or the dissolution of a State into two or more successor States, and in the absence of agreement, the Vienna Convention on Succession of States in Respect of State Property, Archives and Debts 1983 *((1983) 22 I.L.M. 298)* envisages that the debt shall pass in "equitable proportions, taking into account, in particular, the property, rights and interests which pass to the successor States in relation to that State debt (arts. 37, 40-41). The Convention provides exceptionally that no State debt shall pass to a **newly independent State** in the absence of agreement (art. 38: see further **odious debts**). The Convention states that a succession of States does not as such affect the rights and obligations of creditors (art. 36).

public order *See **jus cogens***.

publicists Art. 38(1)(d) of the ICJ Statute provides that "the teachings of the most highly qualified publicists of the various nations [are a] subsidiary means for the determination of rules of [international] law." The writings of publicists are material, and not formal, sources of law, i.e. they provide evidence of the existence and content of rules of international law, these rules being treaties, custom or general principles (under art. 38(1)(a)-(c) of the Statute): O'Connell, *International Law* (2nd ed.), Vol. 1, 36. For an evaluation of the role of publicists, see Parry, *The Sources and Evidences of International Law* (1965), 103-8.

Pufendorf, Samuel 1632-94. German diplomat in the service of Sweden. Professor, Heidelburg, 1661-70, Lund (Sweden), 1670-77. Subsequently government historiographer. One of the originators of the naturalist school. Principal works include *Elementorum Juris prudentiae universalis libri duo* (on the Elements of Universal Jurisprudence) (1660); *De jure naturae et gentium libri octo* (on the Law of Nature and of Nations) (1672); *De officiis nominis et civis libri duo* (on the Duties of Man and Citizens) (1673).

Pugh Case *(Great Britain (on behalf of the Irish Free State) v. Panama) (1933) 3 R.I.A.A. 1439.* Pugh, an Irishman, was arrested in 1929 in a restaurant in Colón, Panama, after having created a disturbance. He resisted arrest and the two policemen who arrested him had to use their batons. Pugh died shortly afterwards as a result of his injuries. Panama and Great Britain, by an agreement concluded on 15 October 1932, submitted the question of the liability of Panama to a sole arbitrator (Lenihan), who *held* that Panama was not liable. The policemen had not exceeded the powers reasonably vested in them, but had rather acted in legitimate defense while compelling Pugh's submission to the lawful authority of the local law; Pugh's death was due to his own fault in resisting arrest by policemen in the lawful discharge of their duties.

Q

Qatar Arbitration Properly styled *Petroleum Development (Qatar) Ltd. v. Ruler of Qatar (1951) 18 I.L.R. 161*, this arbitration arose out of a dispute between the company and the Sheikh of Qatar over the extent of a concession, dated 17 May 1935, granting the company the sole right to explore for and exploit oil resources "throughout the territory of the Principality." As to whether the concession extended to the resources of the **continental shelf** of Qatar, the Arbitrator (Lord Radcliffe) *held* that it did not. *See also* the ***Abu Dhabi Arbitration***.

Qatar-Bahrain, Maritime Delimitation and Territorial Questions between, Case *(Qatar v. Bahrain) 1994 I.C.J. Rep. 112, 1995 I.C.J. Rep. 6, 2001 I.C.J. Rep. 40*. On 8 July 1991, Qatar filed an application with the ICJ instituting proceedings against Bahrain in respect of disputes between the two States relating to sovereignty over the Hawar Islands, sovereign rights over the shoals of Dibal and Qit'at Jaradah, and delimitation of their maritime areas. Qatar based jurisdiction on two agreements between the parties concluded in December 1987 and December 1990, the subject and scope of the submission to jurisdiction being determined by the "Bahraini formula" of October 1988, accepted by Qatar in December 1990. On 1 July 1994, the Court *held* : (1) (15 to 1) that the exchanges of letters between Saudi Arabia and respectively Qatar of 19 and 21 December 1987 and Bahrain of 19 and 26 December 1987, and the "Minutes" signed at Doha on 25 December 1990 by the foreign ministers of Saudi Arabia, Qatar and Bahrain, were binding international agreements; (2) (15 to 1) that these agreements bound the parties to submit to the Court the dispute between them, as set out in the "Bahraini formula"; and (15 to 1) that the parties must submit the dispute in its entirety: *1994 I.C.J. Rep. 112*. Upon further aspects of the dispute being submitted for adjudication (including archipelagic baselines and fishing zones connected with the maritime boundary), Bahrain challenged the jurisdiction of the Court and the admissibility of the application. On 15 February 1995, the Court *held* (10 to 5) that it had jurisdiction and that the application was admissible: *1995 I.C.J. Rep. 6*.

On 16 March 2001, in the longest judgment to date, the Court *held*: (1) (unanimously) that Qatar had sovereignty over Zubarah, title being gradually consolidated after 1868 and definitively established in 1937; (2) (12 to 5) that Bahrain had sovereignty over the Hawar Islands, the British Government's determination that they belonged to Bahrain having been consented to by Qatar; (3) (unanimously) that Qatari vessels enjoyed the right of innocent passage in the territorial sea of Bahrain located between the Hawar Islands and other Bahraini islands; (4) (13 to 4) that Qatar had sovereignty over Janan Island as part of the Hawar Islands group; (5) (12 to 5) that Bahrain had sovereignty over the island of Qit'at Jaradah; (6) (unanimously) that the low tide elevation of Fasht ad Dibal fell under the sovereignty of Qatar; (7) (13 to 4) that a single maritime boundary should be drawn, the Court listing the co-ordinates of the points to be joined, in a specified order, by geodetic lines. In relation to (7), the Court had to draw a boundary between the territorial seas of the parties

---

in the southern part of the area under scrutiny, while in the northern part it had to draw a boundary between the continental shelves and exclusive fisheries zones of the parties. For the territorial sea boundary delimitation, the Court drew an equidistance line and then considered whether that line must be adjusted in the light of special circumstances. For the continental shelf/EEZ boundary delimitation, the Court drew a provisional equidistance line and then considered whether there were circumstances requiring an adjustment of that line: *2001 I.C.J. Rep. 40.*

qualified majority This term relates to the voting in organs of international organizations. "When a *qualified majority* is required, a proposal can only be adopted by a percentage of the votes, always higher than a simple majority. . . . The most common qualified majority is two-thirds but other qualified majorities (*e.g.*, three-quarters or three-fifths) are also used": Schermers and Blokker, *International Institutional Law,* (3rd ed.), 530. *See* **voting; majority vote**.

quality of States It is one of the fundamental principles of international law that, however unequal States may be in size, population, influence and wealth, they are equal before the law *(I Oppenheim 339)*. With the emergence of international organizations from the middle of 19th century, it became clear that practical reality required that some States be accorded a priority of action. This priority of action was always explained on the basis of according no concomitant superiority of right *(I Oppenheim 340)*, but it is somewhat naive to assume that, with international affairs increasingly regulated through international organizations, priority of action did not, in and of itself, imply a superiority of right. *See* Brierly, *The Law of Nations* (6th ed.) 130-3. This inequality was deliberately recognized in art. 27(3) of the UN Charter, conferring the **veto** power on the permanent members over decisions of the Security Council. Conversely and accidentally, the voting provisions for the General Assembly in art. 18 of the Charter have, since the vast increase in UN membership over the past forty years, guaranteed a decisive majority to the **non-aligned countries**. Cf. **equality of States, doctrine of**.

quantitative empiricism This term describes a method of study of international law though "quantitative methods and canons of behavioralism" using techniques of computerized data collection and analysis, such as study of voting in international organizations and conferences. *See* Falk, *The Status of Law in International Society* (1967), 465.

quantum meruit While the standard rule is that compensation for injuries to an alien in breach of international law is based on the loss caused to the alien claimant, other rules have on occasions been employed by tribunals: *see, e.g.,* **damages, punitive**. It appears that some tribunals have applied to breaches by States of State contracts the principle of *quantum meruit* (as much as is deserved). Thus, in the ***Delagoa Bay Railway Arbitration (1898) Moore, Int. Arb., 1865***, the repudiation of a contract by Portugal was held by the arbitrators to entitle the claimant English company to an amount equivalent to the value of the seized railway, and also to a sum in lieu of expected profits. *See also* the *Landreau Claim (1922) 1 R.I.A.A. 347*; ***Martini Case (1903) 10 R.I.A.A. 644***; *Rudloff Case (1903) 9 R.I.A.A. 244*. *See* **lucrum cessans**.

quarter Art. 40 of Protocol I to the Geneva Conventions (of 1949) of 12 December 1977 *(1125 U.N.T.S. 3)*, titled "Quarter," provides that it is "prohibited to order that there shall be no survivors, to threaten an adversary therewith or to conduct hostilities on this basis." The obligation on belligerents to give quarter appears in other instruments: see arts. 60-68 of the **Lieber Code** of 24 April 1863; art. 13(d) of the **Brussels** Project of an International **Declaration** Concerning the Laws and Customs of War of 27 August 1874; art. 9(b) of the

Oxford Manual on the Laws of War on Land of 9 September 1880; art. 17(3) of the Oxford Manual of Naval War of 9 August 1913; and art. 23(d) of the Hague Convention (II) with respect to the Laws and Customs of War on Land of 29 July 1899 *(187 C.T.S. 429)* and of the Hague Convention (IV) respecting the Laws and Customs of War on Land of 18 October 1907 *(205 C.T.S. 277)*.

quasi-international law This term is used by one authority to connote "the law governing relations on a footing of relative equality and, therefore, akin in substance to those under international law, but outside the realm of international law because one, at least, of the parties is not a subject of international law. This type of legal relations is illustrated by a loan contract between an international banking consortium and a sovereign State. Ultimately, such relations are governed by municipal law": Schwarzenberger and Brown, *A Manual of International Law* (6th ed.), 3. Cf. **transnational law**.

quasi-territorial jurisdiction "The flag State does not, however, exercise jurisdiction merely over the ship or aeroplane [of its nationality], its own nationals and their property on board, but also over foreigners and their property aboard a ship or aircraft. Thus, a probably even stronger analogy to territorial jurisdiction can be invoked and this type of jurisdiction can be described as quasi-territorial": Schwarzenberger and Brown, *A Manual of International Law* (6th ed.), 75.

quasi-universal jurisdiction *See* **universal jurisdiction**.

Quintanilla Claim *(Mexico v. USA) (1926) 4 R.I.A.A. 101*. Quintanilla, a Mexican national, after attacking a person in Texas, USA, was taken into custody by a deputy sheriff, and driven off in a car by the deputy sheriff and another man to the gaol in a nearby town. He never reached the gaol, and his body was later discovered by the roadside. The US Government did not account for the circumstances leading to Quintanilla's death. The deputy sheriff and the other man were arrested, but released on bail; investigations were made but no indictment followed; the deputy sheriff's appointment was cancelled. *Held* by the Mexico-US General Claims Commission, in awarding damages, that a State was liable where a foreigner had been taken into custody by a State official, was subsequently found dead, and the State had failed to account for what had happened.

quorum "Not all members of an organ need to be present for it to be formed. Most international organs can be formed by a certain percentage of their membership: the quorum. Often the quorum is a simple majority of the members, sometimes it is a qualified majority [see, for example, art. 25(3) of the Statute of the International Court of Justice which requires 9 of the 15 judges of the Court to be present], but it may also be a minority [for example, Rule 67 of the UN General Assembly's Rules of Procedure provides that a majority of the members constitute a quorum for the taking of decisions but for meeting and debating, one third of the members is sufficient]": Schermers and Blokker, *International Institutional Law* (3rd ed.) 219. *See* **voting**.

R

Rachel, Samuel 1628-1691. German jurisconsult, diplomat and professor who, in opposition to Grotius, distinguished the Law of Nations from natural law, and set forth a theory of international law based on agreements or custom. Principal work: *De Jure Naturae et Gentium Dissertationes* (1676) (Dissertations on the Law of Nature and of Nations).

racial discrimination The present international law on racial discrimination derives from the UN Charter, which in art. 1(3) states that one of the Organization's purposes is "promoting and encouraging respect for human rights and for fundamental freedoms for all without distinction as to race, sex, language, or religion." The Universal Declaration of Human Rights of 1948 (GA Res. 217(III)) stipulates, in art. 2, that its protection is to apply "without distinction of any kind, such as race, color, sex, language, religion, political or other opinion, national or social origin, property, birth or other status." Provisions with similar effect appear in art. 2(1) of the International Covenant on **Civil and Political Rights** 1966 *(999 U.N.T.S. 171)* and in art. 2(2) of the International Covenant on **Economic, Social and Cultural Rights** 1966 *(993 U.N.T.S. 3)*. The International Convention on the Elimination of All Forms of Racial Discrimination of 21 December 1965 *(660 U.N.T.S. 195)*, based on the General Assembly Declaration of the same name of 20 November 1963 (Res. 1904 (XVIII)), obliges the States parties "to pursue by all appropriate means and without delay a policy of eliminating racial discrimination in all its forms" (art. 2(1)). For the purposes of the Convention, racial discrimination is "any distinction, exclusion, restriction or preference based on race, color, descent, or national or ethnic origin which has the purpose or effect of nullifying or impairing the recognition, enjoyment or exercise, on an equal footing, of human rights and fundamental freedoms in the political, economic, social, cultural or any other field of public life" (art. 1(1)). The Convention specifies the rights to be enjoyed without any racial discrimination (art. 5), and establishes a Committee on the Elimination of Racial Discrimination of eighteen experts (art. 8(1)) to consider and comment upon reports from States as to the measures they have taken to give effect to the Convention (art. 9) and to receive complaints by a State (and, exceptionally, an individual) alleging breaches of the Convention (art. 11(1) and 14(1)), such complaints if they cannot be adjusted to the satisfaction of the parties (art. 11(2)), being referred to an *ad hoc* Conciliation Commission (arts. 12-13).

racist régimes The frequent references in UN resolutions to racist régimes in Southern Africa are to the White minority government of South Africa and its satellites prior to 1990. *See* **apartheid**. The status of those fighting against racist régimes was assimilated to that of other **liberation movements**. *See also* **self-determination**.

Radio Corporation of America v. Government of China *(1935) 3 R.I.A.A. 1621*. In 1928, the Chinese National Council of Reconstruction, representing the Chinese Government, concluded an agreement with the Radio Corporation of America (RCA) to provide a radio service between the USA and China. In 1932, the Chinese Government concluded a radio traffic agreement with the Mackay Radio and Telegraph Company in order to establish public service radio circuits between China and the Pacific Coast of the USA. RCA claimed that the conclusion by the Chinese Government of the 1932 agreement was contrary to the 1928 agreement between RCA and China, by virtue of which the Chinese Government was by necessary implication not entitled to conclude with another party a contract in competition with RCA's contract. Under a provision of the 1928 contract, the dispute was submitted to arbitration, which *held* that the Chinese Government was under no obligation not to conclude the second contract since, although the Chinese Government could either expressly or implicitly restrict its freedom of action so as to prevent it concluding a subsequent contract, as a sovereign government it could not be presumed to have done so unless its acceptance of such a restriction could be ascertained distinctly and beyond reasonable doubt, which in the present circumstances had not been established.

radio pirates This term was popularly coined to describe privately-owned commercial radio stations, sited on vessels or artificial islands outside territorial waters, which broadcast radio programs, without license or authority, into the territory of various European States from 1958. Under the applicable regulations of the ITU, commercial broadcasting from the high seas was prohibited, the duty of enforcement resting on the State in which the vessel was registered. Many of the "pirate" vessels were registered in open registry States (*see* **flags of convenience**), or in a State other than that into which the broadcasts were made, and little action was, or could be, expected of them. Accordingly, the Members of the Council of Europe adopted the European Agreement for the Prevention of Broadcasts Transmitted from Stations outside National Territories of 22 January 1965 *(634 U.N.T.S. 239),* under which each party was obliged to take action to suppress such broadcasting (art. 2(1)). Each party was required to make acts involving such broadcasting punishable as offences (art. 2), and apply its jurisdiction to its nationals, whether on its territory, ships or aircraft, and outside its territory on any ships or aircraft (art. 3(a)); and to non-nationals on its territory, ships or aircraft (art. 3(b)). The Agreement could also be applied to broadcasting stations on artificial islands (art. 4(b)).

While the European Agreement of 1965 is clearly in conformity with the established principles governing criminal jurisdiction, the UN Convention on the Law of the Sea 1982 *(1833 U.N.T.S. 3)* goes further by conferring jurisdiction in respect of unauthorized broadcasting from the high seas on the flag State of the ship, the State of registration of the installation, the State of which any person involved in the proscribed activities is a national, any State where the transmission can be received or any State which suffers interference to authorized radio communication (art. 109(3)). A State with jurisdiction may, on the high seas, arrest any person or ship engaged in unauthorized broadcasting and seize the broadcasting apparatus (art. 109(4)).

radioactive products and waste Radioactive products or waste are defined in the Paris Convention on Third Party Liability in the Field of Nuclear Energy of 29 July 1960 *(1961) 55 A.J.I.L. 1082)*, art. 1(a)(iv). Similar definitions of the expression appear in the Vienna Convention on Civil Liability for Nuclear Damage Convention 1963 *((1963) 2 I.L.M. 727)* and in the Brussels Convention Relating to Civil Liability in the Field of Maritime Carriage of Nuclear Material 1971 *((1972) 11 I.L.M. 277)*: see **nuclear cargoes; nuclear damage.** For the purposes of the Paris Convention as amended, the expression "means any radioactive material produced in or made radioactive by exposure to the radiation incidental to the process of producing or utilizing nuclear fuel, but does not include (1) nuclear fuel, or (2) radioisotopes outside a nuclear installation which are used or intended to be used for any industrial, commercial, agricultural, medical or scientific purpose." Effectively, radioactive waste is assimilated to the other materials which may give rise to liability under the conventions. The physical security aspects are covered by the **Physical Protection of Nuclear Materials, Convention on** 1979 *(1456 U.N.T.S. 246)*. The London Convention on the Prevention of Marine Pollution by Dumping of Wastes and other Matter of 13 November 1972 *((1972) 11 I.L.M. 1294)*, prohibits the deliberate disposal at sea of, *inter alia,* "high-level radioactive wastes or other high-level radioactive matter, defined on public health, biological or other grounds, by the competent international body in this field, at present the International Atomic Energy Agency, as unsuitable for dumping at sea" (para. 6 of Annex I, read with art. IV).

Railway Traffic Between Lithuania and Poland Case *(1931) P.C.I.J., Ser. A/B, No. 42.* During World War I, a sector of the railway line between Poland and Lithuania was destroyed. Negotiations between Lithuania and Poland concerning railway communications were fruitless, and on 24 January 1931 the Council of the League of Nations sought an advisory opinion from the PCIJ on the question whether the international engagements in force obliged Lithuania to take the necessary measures to open the relevant railway sector. After considering possible obligations arising under a resolution of the Council of the League of Nations of 10 December 1927 (which recommended the two Governments to enter into direct negotiations to establish good neighborly relations), art. 23(e) of the Covenant of the League of Nations (which provided for members of the League to make provision to secure and maintain freedom of communication and transit) and the Convention of Paris 1924 (establishing a régime for the Memel Territory, which included a commitment to facilitate rail traffic on routes in use convenient for international transit to or from Memel), the Court *advised* that international engagements in force did not oblige Lithuania to open for traffic the railway sector in question: an obligation to negotiate did not imply an obligation to reach agreement, especially with a predetermined outcome; the general stipulation in art. 23(e) of the Covenant did not give rise to an obligation to open any specific sector, which could only result from a special agreement; and the Convention of Paris was inapplicable because the sector in question was neither in use nor convenient for international traffic to or from Memel.

Rainbow Warrior Case *(New Zealand v. France) (1990) 82 I.L.R. 500.* In July 1985, French secret service agents affixed mines that sank the *Rainbow Warrior*, a ship belonging to the international non-governmental organization Greenpeace International, while it was in harbor in Aukland, New Zealand. A crew member of the vessel, Fernando Pereira, died as a result. Two French agents, Major Mafart and Captain Prieur, were arrested in New Zealand, pled guilty to a number of charges, and were each sentenced to ten years in jail. France demanded the release of its agents; in turn, New Zealand sought compensation for the incident. France and New Zealand asked the Secretary-General of the UN to mediate the dispute and, in 1986, the Secretary-General's ruling was implemented by agreement, requiring agents Mafart and Prieur to be transferred to Hao, a French military base in the Pacific. The agents were to remain on the island for a period of no less than three years and were prohibited from leaving without the mutual consent of both governments. Before expiration of the three-year period, Mafart left Hao on health grounds, with New Zealand doctors refused permission to land there to verify his condition, and Prieur left on grounds of her pregnancy and father's terminal illness before New Zealand doctors could examine her; neither returned to Hao. The Tribunal, appointed under the 1986 agreement, *found* no violation of the agreement in respect of Mafart's departure but a violation in respect of his non-return; and a violation in respect of both the departure and non-return of Prieur. Monetary compensation not having been requested by New Zealand and *restitutio in integrum* not being possible because the three-year period had expired, the Tribunal decided that its determination constituted just satisfaction for New Zealand. However, the Tribunal recommended that France make a $2 million contribution to a fund promoting close and friendly relations between the two countries.

Ralston, Jackson H. 1857-1945. American lawyer and teacher of international law. Principal works include *International Arbitral Law and Procedure* (1909); *Democracy's International Law* (1922); *Law and Procedure of International Tribunals* (1926); *International Arbitration from Athens to Locarno* (1929); *A Quest for International Order* (1941).

rank of States An outdated term described in *I Oppenheim (8th ed.) 28* thus: "Although the States are equals as International Persons, they are nevertheless not equals as regards rank. . . . The difference in rank nowadays no longer plays such an important part as in the past, when questions of etiquette gave occasion for much dispute." *See also* **alternat**. *See* Satow, *Guide to Diplomatic Practice* (5th ed.), Chap. 4.

Rann of Kutch Case *(India v. Pakistan) (1968) 17 R.I.A.A. 1*. The Rann of Kutch was an extensive area on the boundaries of India and Pakistan, incapable of sustaining a permanent population. India and Pakistan disagreed where the boundary ran. Pakistan claimed that the northern part of the Rann had been part of the Province of Sind, which had become part of Pakistan in 1947 and to whose rights as well as to the rights of Great Britain as the territorial sovereign of Sind, Pakistan had succeeded; India asserted that the whole of the Rann had been subject to the sovereignty of Kutch, which became part of India in 1947 and in relation to which Great Britain had previously been the Paramount Power. India and Pakistan, by an agreement concluded on 30 June 1965, established a tribunal (Lagergren, Chairman), to determine the line of the boundary, which *held* in favor of Indian sovereignty over the Rann save in respect of those areas (about 10% of the disputed territory) awarded to Pakistan, where there was evidence of continuous and (for the region) intensive activity by Sind meeting with no effective Kutch opposition. The tribunal found that (i) there was no historically accepted boundary for the whole region; (ii) official acts of the British authorities in India tending to show that potential British territorial rights in respect of Sind had been relinquished did not conclusively preclude Pakistan, as successor to Sind, from successfully claiming the disputed territory; (iii) the evaluation of evidence of acts of sovereignty depended on the circumstances of time, place and political system; (iv) evidence of the exercise of customs functions, police surveillance and jurisdiction, of the attitude of the British authorities and of maps published from 1907 onwards were sufficiently persuasive (although not conclusive) of Kutch sovereignty over the Rann to justify a presumption in favor of India's present sovereignty over the Rann, but was rebutted in certain areas by evidence of a consistent exercise of sovereign rights and duties by Sind authorities, including their presence in circumstances which, in view of the nature of the region, came as close to peaceful occupation and display of government authority as may reasonably be expected.

rapporteur This term refers to a person appointed by a committee of an international conference or organ of an international organization to present the discussions and conclusions on an issue in the form of a report. The term is used in the International Law Commission, art. 16 of the Statute (GA Res. 174(II)) of which calls for the appointment of an ILC member as *rapporteur* when working on the **progressive development** of international law. The *rapporteur* considers replies by States to the questionnaire prepared by the ILC, prepares a draft, considers States' responses to the draft and prepares a final draft and explanatory report. While there is no similar provision concerning the **codification** of international law, the ILC has always appointed a *rapporteur* for all its projects, whether progressive development or codification. In ILC parlance, this is a special *rapporteur*, as opposed to a general *rapporteur* elected to prepare the report on the work of a session. *See* Briggs, *The International Law Commission* (1965), 240-50.

ratification It appears that this term has two related meanings. (1) Ratification in a domestic context denotes the process whereby a State puts itself in a position to indicate its acceptance of the obligations contained in a treaty. Brownlie, *Principles of Public International Law* (5th ed.), 611, describes this as "ratification in the constitutional sense." A number of States have in their constitutions procedures which have to be followed before the government can accept a treaty as binding. For example, Article II Section 2 of the US Constitution confers on the President the "power by and with the advice and consent of the Senate to make treaties, provided two-thirds of the Senators present concur. . . ." While in the US this is frequently referred to as ratification by the Senate, this is probably a misnomer: "the Senate does not *ratify* treaties but, instead, advises and consents to their ratification by the President": Hackworth, *Digest of International Law*, Vol. 5, (1944), 48. *See also* **executive agreements.** In the United Kingdom, ratification is an act of the Executive which will normally follow a period of Laying before Parliament under the **Ponsonby Rule** and possibly also following the enactment of appropriate legislation; but Parliament plays no part in the process of ratification itself. In some continental systems, the legislature may be the body which ratifies.

(2) Ratification in an international context "is the international act so named whereby a State establishes on the international plane its consent to be bound by a treaty" (Vienna Convention on the Law of Treaties 1969, art. 2(1)(b)). There is no obligation to ratify within a particular time or indeed at all, but "[a] State is obliged to refrain from acts which would defeat the object and purpose of a treaty when . . . it has signed the treaty or has exchanged instruments constituting the treaty subject to ratification . . . until it shall have made its intention clear not to become a party to the treaty" (art. 18(a)). A treaty expressed to be subject to ratification is nevertheless concluded upon signature and the fact of **signature**, for instance, gives the signatory the locus to object to **reservations** (art. 20). Instruments of ratification establishing the consent of a State to be bound by a treaty take effect when exchanged between the contracting States, deposited with a depositary or notified to the contracting States or to the depositary, if so agreed (art. 16). "[R]atification must, in principle, be unconditional. Its operative effect cannot, unless the treaty itself specifically so provides, be made dependent on the receipt or deposit of ratifications by other states. . . . [R]atification, being in part a confirmation of a signature already given, must relate to what the signature relates to, and must therefore relate to the treaty in its entirety, and as such, and not merely to a part of it, unless the treaty itself provides that states may elect to become bound by a certain part or parts only; this is of course without prejudice to the possibility of attaching **reservations** to the instrument of ratification. . . .": Satow, *Guide to Diplomatic Practice* (5th ed.), 273. In its deliberations on treaties, the ILC initially considered that, where a treaty is silent as to whether ratification is needed, all treaties in principle require ratification; subsequently, in view of State opposition to this principle, the ILC altered its view (*see [1962] II I.L.C. Yearbook 171; [1966] II I.L.C. Yearbook 197-8*). The Vienna Convention on the Law of Treaties 1969 raises a presumption neither in favor nor against requiring ratification (*see* art. 14). Since about the mid-1940s it has been increasingly popular to refer to acceptance. The terms **acceptance** or **approval** are mentioned in art. 14 of the Vienna Convention along with ratification and now regarded as broadly synonymous. "[A]cceptance has become established as a name given to two new procedures, one analagous to ratification and the other to accession. . . . If a treaty provides that it shall be open to signature 'subject to acceptance,' the process on the international plane is like 'signature subject to ratification.' Similarly, if a treaty is made open to 'acceptance' without prior signature, the process is like accession:" *[1966] II I.L.C. Yearbook 198. See*

Camara, *The Ratification of International Treaties* (1949); Aust, *Modern Treaty Law and Practice* (2000), Chap. 7.

"Ratification is not (or, at any rate, since the days of absolute monarchs it has not been) a mere formality, like the use of a seal, or parchment, or tape. Ratification has a value which should not be minimized. The interval between the signature and the ratification of a treaty gives the appropriate departments of the Governments that have negotiated the treaty an opportunity of studying the advantages and disadvantages involved in the proposed treaty as a whole, and of doing so in a manner more detached, more leisurely, and more comprehensive than is usually open to their representatives while negotiating the treaty. However careful may have been the preparation of their instructions, it rarely happens that the representatives of both parties can succeed in producing a draft which embodies the whole of their respective instructions; some concession on one side and some element of compromise are present in practically every negotiation. It is therefore useful that in the case of important treaties Governments should have the opportunity of reflection afforded by the requirement of ratification. Moreover, the more careful the preparation of the treaty and the more deliberate the decision to accept it, the more likely is the treaty to be founded upon the interests of the parties and to be observed by them": McNair, *Law of Treaties* (2nd ed.), 133-4.

ratio decidendi The term is in widespread use in municipal legal systems, denoting the general reasons or grounds given for a judicial or arbitral decision. The importance of the *ratio,* especially in Anglo-American jurisdictions, lies in identifying what should constitute the precedent for future cases containing similar facts and circumstances. In its practice, the ICJ does not adopt a rigid system of precedent (indeed, in terms of art. 59 of its Statute, is precluded from doing so), and hence the distinction between the *ratio decidendi* of a case and *obiter dicta* (statements made by the judges not contributing to the *ratio*) is of considerably less importance than in many municipal systems. *See* Shahabuddeen, *Precedent in the World Court* (1996), Chap. 11.

real union *See* **union, real**.

rebellion *See* **insurgency, insurgent, insurrection**; and **State responsibility**.

rebus sic stantibus "Almost all writers, however reluctantly, admit the existence in international law of . . . the doctrine of *rebus sic stantibus.* Just as many systems of municipal law recognize that, quite apart from any actual *impossibility* of performance, contracts may become inapplicable through a fundamental change of circumstances, so also, it is held, international law recognizes that treaties may cease to be binding upon the parties for the same reason. Most writers, however, at the same time enter a strong *caveat* as to the need to . . . regulate strictly the conditions under which it may be invoked. . . . The circumstances of international life are always changing, and it is all too easy to find some basis for alleging that the changes have rendered the treaty inapplicable": *[1963] II I.L.C. Yearbook 207.* The *clausula rebus sic stantibus* is, then, a tacit condition attached to treaties, the justification for which has been succinctly explained thus: treaties "were concluded in and by reason of special circumstances, and when those circumstances disappear there arises a right to have them rescinded": Westlake, *International Law, Part 1, Peace* (1910), 295. The PCIJ did not have occasion to address the doctrine directly: see *Free Zones Case (1932) P.C.I.J., Ser. A/B, No. 46;* **Nationality Decrees Case** *(1923) P.C.I.J., Ser. B, No. 4; Denunciation of the Sino-Belgian Treaty of 1865 Case (1927) P.C.I.J., Ser. C, No. 2.* However, the ICJ has addressed the doctrine in two cases. In the **Fisheries Jurisdiction Case** *(Jurisdiction) 1973 I.C.J. Rep. 3,* at 21 the Court said: "In order that a change of circumstances may give rise to a ground for invoking the termination of a treaty it is also necessary that it should have resulted in a radical transformation of the extent of the obligations still to be performed. The change must have increased the burden of the obligations to be executed to the extent of rendering the performance something essentially different from that originally undertaken." The Court considered that art. 62 of the Vienna Convention on the Law of Treaties 1969 represented a codification of existing customary law "in many respects" (p.18). Art. 62(1) provides that a fundamental change of circumstances may only be invoked as a ground for terminating or withdrawing from a treaty where "(a) the existence of those circumstances constituted an essential basis of the consent of the parties to be bound by the treaty; and (b) the effect of the change is radically to transform the extent of obligations still to be performed under a treaty." Fundamental change of circumstances may not be invoked in relation to a treaty establishing a boundary, or where the change is the result of a breach of the treaty or of another international obligation owed to a party to the treaty by the State party invoking it (art. 62(2)). *See also* the **Gabcikovo-Nagymaros Project Case** *1997 I.C.J. Rep. 319.* See Harvard Research in International Law, Draft Convention on the Law of Treaties *(1935) 29 A.J.I.L. (Supp.) 1096*; Chesney Hill, *The Doctrine of Rebus Sic Stantibus* (1934); McNair *Law of Treaties* (2nd ed.), Chap. 42; Elias, *The Modern Law of Treaties* (1974) 119-28; Aust. *Modern Treaty Law and Practice* (2000), 240-2.

reception of international law This term refers to the effect of rules of international law within municipal legal systems. The extent of the reception (i.e. the degree to which international legal rules will form part of municipal law) is not a matter regulated by international law, but instead by the constitution of each State. *See also* **monism, dualism**.

reciprocity "States quite often do not pursue one particular course of action which might bring them short-term gains, because it could disrupt the mesh of reciprocal tolerance which could very well bring long-term disadvantages. For example, states everywhere protect the immunity of foreign diplomats for not to do so would place their own officials abroad at risk. [Reciprocity] is . . . an inducement to act reasonably and moderate demands in the expectation that this will similarly encourage other states to act reasonably and so avoid confrontations": Shaw, *International Law* (4th ed.), 7. *See also* **comity**.

recognition The term recognition in international law is employed primarily to connote the acknowledgment by the government of a State of the existence of a newly emergent State, or of a new government emerging irregularly within an existing State, or of the existence of an insurgent party within a State exercising belligerent rights. In all these cases, what is involved is the acknowledgment of international personality and of rights and duties under international law. But neither the regular nor constitutional succession of governments within States, nor more commonly the constitutional evolution of new States by the division or dismemberment of old States, are considered to call for any specific act of recognition. Nor, usually, do States purport to recognize international organizations.

The term recognition is also used in a secondary sense to denote the acknowledgment of one State or its organs of any specific right or sovereign quality of another State. Thus, the expression "recognition of territorial title" is commonly used. Cf. the reference to "a definitive recognition of Danish Sovereignty" in the judgment of the PCIJ in the *Legal Status of Eastern Greenland Case P.C.I.J., Ser. A/B, No. 53.* Equally "recognition of legislative, judicial and administrative acts of (foreign) States" is spoken of. As to the validity of the latter usage (and as to the "recognition" of private rights grounded in acts of foreign States), see Survey of International Law (1949) *UN Doc. A/CN 4/Rev. 1, 29.*

Modes of Recognition. Recognition, in its primary sense, may be *express*. Alternatively, it may be implied from any act (*e.g.*, conclusion of a treaty or accreditation of a diplomatic envoy) which indicates unequivocally an intention to recognize. The maintenance of informal relations does not necessarily imply recognition. Current British and American practice has moved away from express recognition of governments as opposed to States: see **recognition, modes of**.

recognition as nation The description given to the countenance afforded by the Allied Powers to the Polish and Czechoslovak national movements during the First World War. *See* Smith, *Great Britain and the Law of Nations* (1932), Vol. 1, 234, 236.

recognition of belligerency The recognition that the parties in a civil war are entitled to exercise belligerent rights, thus involving recognition that the rebellious party possesses sufficient international personality to support the possession of belligerent rights and duties. There appears to be no instance of explicit recognition of **belligerency,** but it is said to be implicit in, *e.g.*, the imposition of a blockade by the standing or legitimate government or the formal declaration of neutrality by third States (cf. the Union declaration of a blockade of the Southern States and the British proclamation of neutrality in the American Civil War), as well as less formal indications of an attitude of impartiality: *see* the instances collected by Lauterpacht, *Recognition in International Law* (1947), 180 ff. Recognition of belligerency does not *per se* involve recognition of the rebellious party as a government. But since, in a civil war, the standing government is already recognized as such and since a rebellious party considerable enough to attract belligerent rights and duties must clearly display a substantial measure of general governmental activity—must constitute, that is to say, a *de facto* régime—recognition of belligerency may not in practice, as regards the governmental status of the rebellious party, involve a wholly distinct category. For the most comprehensive discussion, see Lauterpacht, *op. cit.,* Part III. *And see* Chen, *The International Law of Recognition* (1951), Part 6; Smith, *Great Britain and the Law of Nations* (1932), Vol. 1, Chap. IV; Whiteman, *Digest of International Law,* Vol. 2, (1963), 486-523. Cf. **recognition of insurgency**.

recognition of governments The acknowledgment by the government of one State of that of another or others. The process may be express or implied: *see* **recognition, modes of**. It may further be **de facto** or **de jure**. As to the criteria or conditions for recognition of governments, as to whether it may be conditional, or be withdrawn, or the subject of any right or duty, *see* **recognition, conditions for**; **recognition, conditional or qualified**; **recognition, withdrawal**; **recognition, alleged right or duty of**. A specific act, be it express or implied, of recognition of a government is called for only when such government is a new régime which has come into existence irregularly, no such act being called for in relation to regular governmental succession. As to the legal consequences of recognition of governments, *see* **recognition, legal effects**. *And see generally* Lauterpacht, *Recognition in International Law* (1947), Part II; Chen, *The International Law of Recognition* (1951), Part II and *passim;* Smith, *Great Britain and the Law of Nations* (1932), Vol. 1, Chap. III; Whiteman, *Digest of International Law,* Vol. 2, (1963), 242-486.

recognition of insurgency A limited and imprecise form of recognition of a rebellious party, not involving **recognition of belligerency** or recognition of that party as a government, but nevertheless involving on the part of the recognizing State some acknowledgment that the rebels possess a degree of *de facto* authority, and a willingness to treat with them in relation to some limited matters of local concern, *e.g.*, the protection of nationals of the recognizing State. The principal instances are said to be the United States' recognition of the Cuban insurgents in 1869 (*see* Moore, *Digest of International Law* (1908), Vol.

1, 196; *The Three Friends 166 U.S. 63 (1897)*) and the British recognition of the Spanish "Nationalist" authorities in 1938 (Cf. *The Arantzazu Mendi [1939] A.C. 256*). But "[a]ctually, international law knows of no 'recognition of insurgency' as an act conferring upon insurgents international rights flowing from a well-defined status": Lauterpacht, *Recognition in International Law* (1947), 270, in which *see also* Chaps. XVI-XVIII; *and see* Chen, *The International Law of Recognition* (1951), Chap. 26; Whiteman, *Digest of International Law,* Vol. 2, (1963), 486-523. *See also* **insurgency, insurgent, insurrection**.

recognition of States   The acknowledgment by the government of an existing State, whether individually or in conjunction with other existing States, of the international personality of a new State. As to the controversy whether such recognition is constitutive or declaratory in effect or whether it is ever a matter of right or duty *see* **recognition, constitutive and declaratory theories of**; **recognition, alleged right or duty of**. Recognition of a new State may be express (cf. the Treaty of Paris of 3 September 1783 *(48 C.T.S. 487)*, art. 1, whereby Great Britain "acknowledged the . . . United States . . . to be Free, Sovereign and Independent . . .") or implied from conduct; *see* **recognition, modes of**. Where the process of emergence of a new State is one of constitutional evolution or devolution, as in the case of most members of the British Commonwealth (*e.g.*, Canada, India), express recognition is not in practice called for and will be taken to be implied. As to the criteria or conditions for recognition, and as to whether it may be made conditional, *see* **recognition, conditions for** and **recognition, conditional or qualified**. The distinction between **recognition de facto** and **de jure** seldom arises in connection with the recognition of States, but has been exceptionally applied. As to the legal effects of recognition of States, *see* **recognition, legal effects**. *And see generally* Lauterpacht, *Recognition in International Law* (1947), Part I; Chen, *The International Law of Recognition* (1951), Part. 1; Smith, *Great Britain and the Law of Nations* (1932), Vol. 1, Chap III; Whiteman, *Digest of International Law,* Vol. 2, (1963), 133-242.

recognition, alleged right or duty   Lauterpacht advanced the thesis that "[t]o recognize a community as a State is to declare that it fulfils the conditions of statehood as required by international law. If these conditions are present, existing States are under the duty to grant recognition. When [a] government enjoys, with a reasonable prospect of permanency, the habitual obedience of the bulk of the population, outside States are under a legal duty to recognize it in that capacity": *Recognition in International Law* (1947), 6. Under the influence of this teaching, the British Government in effect declared itself without any alternative to recognition of the Communist Government in China in 1949. The doctrine was not wholly new. Thus, Hall, *A Treatise on International Law* (8th ed.), 37-9, declared that belligerents within a State had a right to recognition, this right being based, not on international law, but on a "normal duty of human conduct." But the doctrine runs counter to general opinion and practice; and the present position is that "the recognising state exercises a discretion which, although necessarily wide, is not arbitrary": *I Oppenheim 148*.

recognition, conditional or qualified   Recognition of a new State or government is occasionally purported to be granted *sub modo,* that is to say subject to the concurrent acceptance by the recognized entity of some obligation (*e.g.*, to observe permanent neutrality, to abstain from the slave trade, to adopt democratic forms of government, to respect human rights). Such recognition is not, strictly, conditional, and non-fulfillment of the 'condition' does not vitiate it and is in no way different from non-fulfillment of any obligation undertaken independently of recognition. Recognition accorded subject to a condition precedent (*e.g.*, that some other State shall first recognize the new entity) is similarly not in reality conditional. *See* Lauterpacht, *Recognition in International Law* (1947), 357-64; Chen, *The International Law of Recognition* (1951), Chap. 17.

recognition, conditions for   Though any duty to recognize or right to recognition is generally disclaimed, in practice broad conditions for or criteria of recognition are required or followed in order that it may not be deemed premature. As respects recognition of States, these are approximately the criteria of Statehood—the existence of a population settled upon a defined or definable territory under an independent government: *see* **State**. In regard to recognition of governments, the test has largely been *de facto* establishment, which has frequently been construed to imply a call for a certain degree of permanence and also "effectiveness"—this last requirement being sometimes subject to a further "democratic" interpretation and being considered to involve an expression of electoral or other tangible support for the new régime. *See* the EC criteria for the recognition of the emergent States of former Communist Eastern Europe emphasizing democracy and human rights: EC Guidelines on the Recognition of New States in Eastern Europe and in the Former Soviet Union 1991 *((1992) 31 I.L.M. 1485)*. *See* Chen, *The International Law of Recognition* (1951), 54-62, 105-130; Lauterpacht, *Recognition in International Law* (1947), 98-140, where other suggested conditions for recognition, such as willingness to observe international law, are also discussed.

recognition, constitutive and declaratory theories of   "The principal tenet of the . . . constitutive school is that . . . a State is, and becomes, an International Person through recognition only and exclusively. . . . The opposing theory is, whenever a State in fact exists, it is at once subject to international law, independently of the wills or actions of other States. The act of recognition declares the existence of that fact and does not constitute the legal personality of the State. . . . In the last analysis the question . . . is a reflection of the . . . cleavage between those who regard the State as the ultimate source of international rights and duties and those who regard it as being under a system of law which determines its rights and duties under that law. According to the former view, as a State cannot be bound by any obligation except with its own consent, a new State or Government or insurgent body cannot be allowed to exercise rights against existing States unless it has been recognized by them": Chen, *The International Law of Recognition* (1951), 14-15, 3. To the extent that recognition is widely held to be a matter of political discretion, with the result that existing States may accord recognition to a new entity at widely varying times, the practice of States favors the declaratory theory, which, however, is open to the logical objection that a State is a legal, not a physical, phenomenon, and that personality is likewise a legal and not a natural quality. On the other hand, the constitutive view is open to the ethical objection that it would appear to suggest that nascent entities are outside the law before recognition and liable to be treated at discretion. One of several intermediate hypotheses urges, therefore, that it should be accepted that, once the "factual" characteristics of statehood—an established government, etc.—exist, there is a legal duty to grant recognition. "Although recognition is thus declaratory of an existing fact, such declaration, made in the impartial fulfilment of a legal duty, is constitutive, as between the recognizing State and the community so recognized, of international rights and duties associated with full statehood": Lauterpacht, *Recognition in International Law* (1947), 6. This ingenious compromise is not, however, generally accepted.

recognition, *de facto* and *de jure*   The question whether a government is a government *de jure* or merely *de facto* is in the first instance one of constitutional law. Thus, the relevant *jus* is constitutional or municipal law, and thereunder a *de jure* government is one which is legitimate or constitutional, as opposed to a rebellious or usurping *de facto* régime. So long as doctrines of dynastic legitimacy prevailed, the distinction between a *de* *jure* and a *de facto* government made in municipal law had some international impact also; but, with their abandonment and the firm establishment of the rule that international law has nothing to do with the forms of government of States, the distinction assumed a different significance. What was regarded as a *de jure* government and recognized as such was one which was or had been at some time the uncontested government of a State (notwithstanding that its authority might later have been contested either generally or in some particular locality); and what was regarded or recognized as a government *de facto* only was one which was successful in displacing the actual authority of a *de jure* government as so defined. In relation to the distinction as thus developed, the relevant *jus* was not municipal but international law, according to which its actual establishment without rivals justified the recognition of one government by others irrespective of constitutional legitimacy. But a distinction is further sought to be drawn between recognition *de facto* and recognition *de jure* as opposed to that between *de facto* or *de jure* governments or States. In this usage, there are, as it were, gradations or grades of recognition. Many writers, however, ignore that there are different categories of ideas involved here and use the expressions *de facto (jure)* recognition and recognition as a *de facto (jure)* government (State) interchangeably. The distinction in some form is in fact observed in the practice of many States, at least in relation to the recognition of governments—the question of *de facto* recognition of a State (or recognition of an entity as a *de facto* State) seldom arising because, until an entity is sufficiently established to justify *de jure* recognition, it is customary to accord it recognition *de facto* as an "authority" or by some other designation than that of "State," if at all. Relatively permanent establishment of the government is the common requirement, too, in relation to *de jure* recognition of governments, *de facto* recognition being alone accorded where there is any doubt as to the prospects of survival of a régime. But other considerations may dictate the refusal, at least for a time, of *de jure* recognition to an insurgent régime, such as the continuance in actual authority elsewhere than in the area held by the insurgents of a *de jure* recognized government, or, in the event that the former *de jure* recognized government has been entirely displaced, the persistence of a degree of international disapproval of the insurgent régime. It is sometimes said that States will not maintain full diplomatic relations with régimes recognized merely *de facto,* but only more informal relations. It is equally said that a government recognized merely *de facto* as opposed to *de jure* has no title to the properly abroad of the State wherein it is established, nor to the recognition of its laws as having any extraterritorial effect. But these are results following from the practice and municipal law of individual States which are not necessarily uniform. Current British and American practice has moved away from recognition of governments as opposed to States, which in part avoids these difficulties: see **recognition, modes of**.

recognition, international organizations and   International organizations do not, as a matter of practice, accord formal recognition to new States and governments. However, it is clear that admission to membership carries with it the recognition of the new member as satisfying the criteria for membership of, and for the purposes of, the organization: see Schwarzenberger *International Constitutional Law* (1976), 267. Such minimal recognition may affect the attitude of a State as to whether it will itself accord recognition to the new member, but does not of or in itself imply recognition: see **recognition, modes of**. Cf. *U.S.S.R. v. Luxembourg and Saar Co., (1935) 8 I.L.R. 14*, where a Luxembourg Court held that "the admission of the Union of Soviet Socialist Republics into the League of Nations implies the recognition by Luxembourg of the Soviet Government," even in a situation in which Luxembourg had refrained from voting on Soviet admission. It is generally accepted that the UN has the capacity to accord limited recognition to a State "at all events if it is necessary for it to do so for the performance of the functions for which the Organization was created": Rosenne, *Recognition of States by the United Nations (1949) 26 B.Y.I.L. 437* at 439. *See also* Aufricht, Principles and Practices of Recognition by International Organizations, *(1949) 43 A.J.I.L. 679.* For an example of collective non-recognition, *see* art. 2 of Security Council Res. 283 (1970) on Namibia, and the *Namibia Opinion 1971 I.C.J. Rep. 16*; and **Tobar Doctrine**.

recognition, legal effects (1) International Law. It may appear that there are few rights or capacities in international law that are possessed by a recognized State but denied to an unrecognized State. Thus, a treaty may be made or diplomatic representatives exchanged with a hitherto unrecognized entity as principal modes of implied recognition: see **recognition, modes of**. The situation with respect to recognition of governments may in some respects appear similar: *see* the *Tinoco Claims Arbitration (1923) 1 R.I.A.A. 369. See also United States (Hopkins) v. Mexico (1926) 4 R.I.A.A. 41.* But though to assert this is in effect to deny the constitutive theory (*see* **recognition, constitutive and declaratory theories**), it is not necessarily to deny all international legal character to recognition, which may still, for instance, be claimed possibly to be the subject of a right or duty: *see* **recognition, alleged right or duty of**. Nevertheless, except when States are willing to move towards recognition of a new entity, they in practice usually distinguish between recognized and unrecognized States (and governments), denying to the latter rights and capacities which in international law are enjoyed by "States" and "governments."

(2) Municipal Law. Though it is maintainable that recognition, if it be merely declaratory of fact (*see* **recognition, constitutive and declaratory theories of**), can have no effect even in municipal law, in practice municipal courts tend to attribute to it very considerable effects, a tendency which is reinforced by rules or practices involving judicial deference to the executive branch of government for the ascertainment of whether or not recognition has been effected. What the precise effects of recognition are, however, depends of course on the particular municipal system involved. (a) *English law.* (i) A foreign State or governmental entity acquires capacity to sue as such through recognition alone: *City of Berne v. Bank of England (1804) 9 Ves. Jun. 347.* (ii) Such an entity is entitled to sovereign immunity from impleader only if recognized: *The Arantzazu Mendi [1939] A.C. 256; The Annette, The Dora [1919] P. 105.* (iii) The executive, legislative and judicial acts of such an entity are in principle entitled to credence only if it be recognized: *Luther v. Sagor [1921] 3 K.B. 532; Carl-Zeiss Stiftung v. Rayner & Keeler Ltd. [1967] A.C. 853. Cf. Adams v. Adams [1971] P. 188.* There may be limitations to the attitude of denial of all effect to the laws, etc., of an unrecognized entity (Cf. *Carl-Zeiss Stiftung v. Rayner & Keeler Ltd., supra,* per Lord Reid at 907), but they have not as yet been precisely determined. (b) *United States law.* (i) American courts follow English courts in denying title to sue to unrecognized States or governments: *R.S.F.S.R. v. Cibrario 235 N.Y. 255 (1923); Kunstsammlungen zu Weimar v. Elicofon 478 F. (2d.) 231 (1973); Republic of China v. Merchants' Fire Assur. Corp. of N.Y. 30 F. (2d.) 278 (1929).* (ii) But it has been held that a foreign government is entitled to sovereign immunity from suit notwithstanding non-recognition: *Wulfsohn v. R.S.F.S.R. 234 N.Y. 372 (1923).* (iii) Where there is evidence of a positive executive policy of non-recognition of the laws, etc., of a foreign government, the courts will follow suit: *The Mare 145 F. (2d.) 431 (1944), Latvian State Cargo & Passenger S.S. Line v. McGrath 188 F. (2d.) 1000 (1951).* But where the executive branch has been less adamant, they have been willing to accord a degree of recognition to such laws: *Salimoff v. Standard Oil Co. of New York 262 N.Y. 220 (1933); Sokoloff v. National City Bank 239 N.Y. 158 (1924); Upright v. Mercury Business Machines 213 N.Y. Suppl. (2nd.) 417 (1961).* Current British and American practice has moved away from recognition of governments as opposed to States: see **recognition, modes of**. (c) *Other systems.* Courts of non-common law States appear generally to deny *persona standi* to unrecognized entities,

but at least sometimes to ignore the issues of recognition in relation to the standing of their legislative, etc., acts.

recognition, modes of (1) Express declaration. There are many instances in which a new State or government has been expressly recognized as such in explicit terms, whether in direct communication, public announcement, treaty stipulation or notification to a third State. For examples, see Whiteman, *Digest of International Law*, Vol. 2, (1963), 48-68, *and see* Chen, *The International Law of Recognition* (1951), 191-2, 221-2.

(2) Implied recognition. It is generally agreed that recognition of a new entity may be implied by the conclusion with it of a bilateral treaty—certainly if the treaty be in solemn form or of a political or general character, but less certainly or not at all if of an informal character or dealing with temporary or local matters. The exchange of diplomatic (as distinct from other or non-diplomatic) representatives is regarded as the form of implied recognition least open to dispute. Opinions differ as to whether a request for a grant of a consular *exequatur* implies recognition. The preponderant view is that participation in a multilateral conference by an unrecognized entity does not warrant the implication of its recognition by other participants. It is suggested that simultaneous signature of a multilateral treaty drafted by such a conference gives rise to a stronger presumption of recognition than subsequent adherence to it. It is equally argued that the bare fact of the admission to membership of the United Nations does not imply recognition of a new State by any other member. There is general agreement that recognition by other members is not to be implied from participation in proceedings of organs of the United Nations by representatives of a new government of a member State. The UK Government now "no longer accord[s express] recognition to Governments. . . . [W]e shall continue to decide the nature of our dealings with régimes which come to power unconstitutionally in the light of our assessment of whether they are able of themselves to exercise effective control of the territory of the State concerned, and seem likely to continue to do so": statement of the Foreign Secretary of 28 April 1980 *(Hansard, House of Lords, Vol. 408, Cols. 1121-2). See also* the US State Department statement: "In recent years, US practice has been to de-emphasize and avoid the use of recognition in cases of changes of governments and to concern ourselves with the question of whether we wish to have diplomatic relations with the new governments" *(77 State Dept. Bull. 462 (1977)). See also* **Estrada Doctrine**; **Tobar Doctrine**.

(3) Collective recognition. Though normally recognition of a new State or government is, expressly or by implication, the individual act of the government of another State, instances of collective recognition, by treaty or express declaration, are numerous, as also of individual recognition after multilateral consultation. *See* the EC Guidelines on the Recognition of New States in Eastern Europe and in the Former Soviet Union 1991 *((1992) 31 I.L.M. 1485)*, on which see Müllerson, *International Law, Rights and Politics* (1994), Chap. 4. *And see* Lauterpacht, *Recognition in International Law* (1947), 67-9, 165-74. *See also* **recognition, international organizations and**.

recognition, organs of Recognition, being in principle an act in the sphere of international relations, is primarily a function of the executive governments of States. But having regard to the effects attributed to recognition in international law, it falls to municipal courts very often to decide whether or not the executive government of the State concerned has recognized a new or foreign entity or not. Such is what has been termed a "fact of State," and is to be taken cognizance of in the same manner as any similar fact (*e.g.*, whether a state of war exists), that is to say, in common law countries in the first instance as a matter of judicial notice, or by reference to public documents and archives, or, in case of doubt or difficulty, upon **executive certificate**. Since, however, the executive certificate is sometimes of a temporary or evasive character, the interpretation placed upon it by a court may often be wholly decisive. *See* Chen, *The International Law of Recognition* (1951), Chap. 15; Lauterpacht, *Recognition in International Law* (1947), Chap. VI.

recognition, premature The recognition by a third State or government of an insurgent or secessionist community before it has achieved a measure of permanence and political cohesion is generally characterized as at least an unfriendly act towards the standing government and even as an international delinquency and therefore as 'void.' The better view is perhaps that premature recognition is no recognition at all but should be classified as a form of intervention. *See* Lauterpacht, *Recognition in International Law* (1947), 94-6, 282-4; Chen, *The International Law of Recognition* (1951), 50-1, 85-6. As to the discussion of premature recognition in, and in connection with, the *Alabama Arbitration* (1872), *see* Smith, *Great Britain and the Law of Nations* (1933), Vol. 1, 308, 321.

recognition, retroactivity of The doctrine that recognition is retroactive in effect to the commencement of the existence of the recognized entity was first developed by American courts: *Williams v. Bruffy 96 U.S. 176* (1877); *Oetjen v. Central Leather Co. 246 U.S. 2977* (1918); *Lehigh Valley RR. Co. v. State of Russia 21 F. 2d. 396* (1927); *Salimoff v. Standard Oil Co. of New York 262 N.Y. 220* (1933); *Dougherty v. Equitable Life Assurance Soc. of U.S., 266 N.Y. 261* (1934). In English law, it is so far adopted as to serve to validate the prior acts of a newly recognized régime: *Luther v. Sagor [1921] 3 K.B. 532; Princess Paley Olga v. Weisz [1929] 1 K.B. 718,* though not to invalidate those of a previously recognized government: *Boguslawski v. Gdynia-Ameryka Linie [1951] 1 K.B. 162,* and equally to validate the extraterritorial claims of a government newly recognized *de jure*: *Haile Selassie v. Cable and Wireless Ltd. (No. 2), [1939] 1 Ch. 182.* The date to which retroactivity runs is commonly a matter of executive certification *(Luther v. Sagor, supra; Haile Selassie v. Cable and Wireless Ltd. (No. 2), supra),* but has been determined by the court itself: *The Jupiter (No. 3) [1927] P. 250; Princess Paley Olga v. Weisz, supra; Lazard Bros. v. Midland Bank Ltd. [1933] A.C. 289 at 297.* Whether the principle of retroactivity is inherent in the act of recognition or is a doctrine of international law is, however, disputed despite its wide acceptance in practice. *See generally* Jones. The Retroactive Effect of Recognition of States and Governments, *(1935) 16 B.Y.I.L. 42;* Lauterpacht, *Recognition in International Law* (1947), 59-60; Chen, *The International Law of Recognition* (1951), Chap. 13.

recognition, withdrawal of There are some theoretical objections to the withdrawal of recognition once granted. If recognition be merely declaratory, in effect involving simply the acknowledgment of the existence of a new State or government, then it is not a continuous process but a simple act or unilateral declaration and, as such, incapable of withdrawal. If, on the other hand, recognition has a constitutive effect, to allow it to be withdrawn would seem to put a premium on lawlessness, the victim being first deprived of recognition and then treated at discretion. Again, even if it be conceded that recognition *de facto* as distinct from *de jure* should be capable of withdrawal on the ground that the state of facts on which it has been based may cease to be, it requires to be noted that the distinction between these two sorts of recognition is often simply political. Notwithstanding doubts of this character, in practice recognition is sometimes specifically withdrawn. For instances in which the UK Foreign Office certificate has explicitly stated that upon the recognition of a new government that of a previous government has ceased, *see Haile Selassie v. Cable and Wireless (No. 2) [1939] 1 Ch. 182 at 194*; and *Boguslawski v. Gdynia-Ameryka Linie, [1950] 1 K.B. 162 at 167.* As to the British withdrawal of recognition of the Italian Government in Ethiopia without simultaneous recognition of another succeeding government, *see* Chen, *The International Law of Recognition* (1951), Chap. 16. As to the withdrawal of recognition of belligerency, *see* Smith, *Great Britain and the Law of Nations* (1933), Vol. 1, 322. *See also* Lauterpacht, *Recognition in International Law* (1947), Chap. XIX.

recommendation(s) "The term 'recommendation' is most frequently used to describe non-binding suggestions of international organs. . . . Many organizations use 'resolution' in the same context. . . . 'Recommendation' is used to denote a binding rule of law only in one constitution [that of the European Coal and Steel Community]": Schermers and Blokker, *International Institutional Law* (3rd ed.), 755.

reconduction "The practice of some states . . . whereby destitute aliens, foreign vaga-bonds, suspicious aliens without identity papers, alien criminals who have served their punishment, and the like, are, without any formalities, arrested by the police and reconducted to the frontier. But although such reconduction, often called *droit de renvoi* is materially not much different from expulsion, it nevertheless differs much from it in form, since expulsion is an order to leave the country, whereas reconduction is forcible convey-ing away of foreigners": *I Oppenheim 940n.*

reconfirmation (of treaties) This is the term for "an express statement, often made in a new treaty, that a certain previous treaty whose validity has, or might have, become doubt-ful, is still, and remains, valid. . . . A treaty may be reconfirmed wholly or only in part": *I Oppenheim 1312. See also* **redintegration**.

reconsideration (of treaties) Art. 39 of the Vienna Convention on the Law of Treaties 1969 provides that, as a general rule, any treaty may be amended by agreement between the parties. Some treaties specifically provide for review or reconsideration. While art. 19 of the Covenant of the League of Nations provides that the Assembly may from time to time advise the reconsideration by members of treaties "which have become inapplicable," no equivalent provision appears in the UN Charter. *See also* **desuetude**.

Red Cross *See* **International Committee of the Red Cross.**

Red Sea Islands Arbitration *See* ***Sovereignty over Various Red Sea Islands Arbitration.***

redintegration (of treaties) "Treaties which have lost their binding force may regain it through redintegration. A treaty becomes redintegrated by the mutual consent of the con-tracting parties; this is, as a rule, given in a new treaty": *I Oppenheim 1312. See also* **reconfirmation**.

redistribution of territory This connotes a simple transfer of territory between existing States, altering their geographical dimensions only, and not affecting their legal identity as States. The method of transfer is irrelevant: it may be cession by agreement (*e.g.,* the ces-sion of Alaska by Russia to the USA in 1867), or annexation by force (*e.g.,* the annexation of Alsace-Lorraine by Germany in 1871).

reefs While the term is not defined, reefs receive specific mention in the UN Convention on the Law of the Sea 1982 *(1833 U.N.T.S. 3)*. In the case of islands situated on atolls or of islands having infringed reefs, the seaward low-water line of the reef is the baseline for measuring the breadth of the territorial sea (art. 6). The outermost points of drying reefs may be used for drawing archipelagic baselines (art. 47: see **archipelagic State**).

re-emption *See* **pre-emption**.

reflagging Changing the flag, and thereby the nationality, of a vessel may occur with, *e.g.*, a change of ownership, and provided the **genuine link** requirements of arts. 91(1) and 94 of the UN Convention on the Law of the Sea 1982 *(1833 U.N.T.S. 3)* are met, the vessel is entitled to fly the flag of the new State. Changing the flag of a vessel may occur for other reason, *e.g.*, to avoid fishing quotas applicable to vessels of the original flag State or to exempt the vessel from UN sanctions against the flag State, and such a change will be lawful if it also satisfies the genuine link requirements. In any event, no change of flag can occur "during a voyage or when the vessel is in a port of call, save in the case of a real transfer of ownership or change of registry": art. 92(1) of the UN Convention.

refoulement This is the term given to the expulsion or return of a refugee from one State to another where his life or liberty would be threatened. It is now prohibited by art. 33 of the Convention relating to the Status of Refugees of 28 July 1951 *(189 U.N.T.S. 150)* which bars the expulsion or return of a refugee "in any manner whatsoever to the frontiers of territories where his life or freedom would be b threatened on account of his race, religion, nationality, membership of a particular social group or political opinion."

refugees In terms of art. 1 of the Convention relating to the Status of Refugees of 28 July 1951 *(189 U.N.T.S. 150)*, as amended by the Protocol of 16 December 1966 *(606 U.N.T.S. 267)*, a refugee is any person who: "(1) Has been considered a refugee under the Arrangements of 12 May 1926 *[89 L.N.T.S. 47]* and 30 June 1928 *[89 L.N.T.S. 53 and 63; 93 L.N.T.S. 377; 204 L.N.T.S. 445,* and *205 L.N.T.S. 193]* or under the Conventions of 28 October 1933 *[159 L.N.T.S. 199; 172 L.N.T.S. 432; 181 L.N.T.S. 429; 200 L.N.T.S. 214]* and 10 February 1938 *[192 L.N.T.S. 59; 200 L.N.T.S. 572; 205 L.N.T.S. 218],* the Protocol of 14 September 1939 *[198 L.N.T.S. 141,* and *205 L.N.T.S. 219]* or the Constitution of the International Refugee Organization *[18 U.N.T.S. 3]* . . .; (2) Owing to well-founded fear of being persecuted for reasons of race, religion, nationality, membership of a particular social group or political opinion, is outside the country of his nationality and is unable or, owing to such fear, is unwilling to avail himself of the protection of that country; or who, not having a nationality and being outside the country of his former habitual residence, is unable or, owing to such fear, is unwilling to return to it." The Contracting States undertook a number of obligations in respect of refugees so defined. They are protected from discrimination on grounds of race, religion or country of origin (art. 3) and are to be accorded religious freedom to the same degree as that accorded to nationals (art. 4). For other rights and privileges, see arts. 5-34. The Convention requires States to cooperate with the United Nations High Commissioner for Refugees, who is responsible for supervising the application of the Convention (art. 35(1)). *See* Grahl-Madsen, *The Status of Refugees in International Law,* (2 vols., 1966-72); Goodwin-Gill, *The Refugee in International Law* (1983).

régime theory A theory on international organizations, postulating that "states can and do co-operate on the basis of the realist premise of enlightened self-interest. . . . Thus, in most situations states would actually have an interest in co-operation, since co-operation generally was thought to result in a greater common good": Klabbers, *An Introduction to International Institutional Law* (2002), 32.

regional custom *See* **local custom.**

regional arrangements Regional arrangements are arrangements for the pacific settlement of disputes and the maintenance of peace organized on a regional basis. Art. 21 of the Covenant of the League of Nations provided that the Covenant of the League of Nations is not "to affect the validity of . . . regional understandings like the Monroe doctrine, for securing the maintenance of peace." Chapter VIII of the UN Charter, entitled "Regional Arrangements," makes express provision for the legitimacy of regional arrangements or agencies for the settlement of disputes (art. 52(2)) and the maintenance of international peace and security (art. 52(1)). The Security Council is to encourage settlement of local disputes through such regional arrangements and agencies (art. 52(3)), and may utilize such arrangements and agencies for enforcement action under its authority (art. 53(1)). The Security Council is to be kept informed of all activities undertaken or contemplated by regional arrangements or agencies for the maintenance of international peace and security (art. 54). *See* **NATO, SEATO**.

regional organizations This term is used to describe international organizations established among States in the same region. Two features underlie most regional organizations: in most cases, regional cooperation began as an attempt to counter real or perceived external influence (*e.g.*, Western European cooperation was stimulated by the fear of the USSR); and regional cooperation tends to reflect comparable political, economic, social and cultural standards or aspirations (*e.g.*, OECD among the wealthy industrialized States, originally with a strong European orientation). *See* Schermers and Blokker, *International Institutional Law* (3rd ed.), 37-9; Sands and Klein, *Bowett's Law of International Institutions* (5th ed.), Chaps. 5-10.

regionalism This is the movement and the belief, based upon perceived defects in the global system of dealing with world problems, that international issues may in many issues be more effectively dealt with at the regional level. Cf. **universalism**. *See* White, *The Law of International Institutions* (1996), Chap. 6, esp. 156-65.

registration of treaties In the late 19th century, concern was expressed about "secret" treaties, and proposals were made for treaties to be registered. The first general obligation to register treaties appears in art. 18 of the Covenant of the League of Nations, requiring all treaties concluded by any member of the League to be registered with the Secretariat and published by it; "[n]o such treaty or international engagement shall be binding [i.e. enforceable: *I Oppenheim 1315n*] until so registered." Treaties registered with the League Secretariat were published in the *League of Nations Treaty Series* (*L.N.T.S.*), which began in 1920 and covers treaties registered up to July 1944. Art. 18 of the League Covenant was replaced by art. 102(1) of the Charter which provides that: "[e]very treaty and every international agreement entered into by any Member of the United Nations after the present Charter comes into force shall as soon as possible be registered with the Secretariat and published by it." The sanction for failure to register is that the treaty cannot be invoked before any organs of the United Nations (art. 102(2)). Treaties registered with the Secretariat are published in the *United Nations Treaty Series* (*U.N.T.S.*) which began publication in 1944 and now runs to over 2,000 volumes in hard copy (and available online at <http://untreaty.un.org>), embracing 50,000 multilateral and bilateral treaties. Despite the sanction of art. 102(2), registration has been at best patchy, especially in relation to multilateral instruments. The Secretariat's publication program in any event lags well behind dates of signature with the result that *U.N.T.S.* is now more a publication of record than a current working tool. Texts of current instruments must be sought in national treaty collections *(United States Treaty Series; United Kingdom Treaty Series)* or for instance in *International Legal Materials.* See Hudson, The Legal Effect of Unregistered Treaties in Practice, under Article 18 of the Covenant, *(1934) 28 A.J.I.L. 546,* Brandon, The Validity of Non-Registered Treaties, *(1952) 29 B.Y.I.L. 185;* McNair, *Law of Treaties* (2nd ed.), Chap. 10; Aust, *Modern Treaty Law and Practice* (2000), Chap. 19; UN Treaty Section, *Treaty Handbook* (2002), Sect. 5.

Réglement of the Laws of War Annexed to both the Hague Conventions on Land Warfare of 29 July 1899 *(187 C.T.S. 429)* and 18 October 1907 *(205 C.T.S. 277)* were Regulations respecting the Laws and Customs of War on Land. The parties to the two conventions were required to issue instructions to their armed land forces, which instructions were to be in conformity with the annexed Regulations (art. 1). The 1899 Regulations contain sixty substantive articles, the 1907 Regulations fifty-six articles. "The rules on land warfare expressed in the Convention [of 1907] undoubtedly represented an advance over existing International Law at the time of their adoption . . . but by 1939 these rules . . . were recognized by all civilized nations, and were regarded as being declaratory of the laws and customs of war": Nuremberg International Military Tribunal in its Judgment of 10 October 1946 *((1946) 41 A.J.I.L. 172 at 248)*. *See* Scott, *The Hague Conventions and Declarations of 1899 and 1907* (1915); Scott, *The Proceedings of the Hague Conferences, 1899, 1907* (1921); Higgins, *The Hague Peace Conferences and other International Conferences Concerning the Laws and Usages of War* (1909).

regulation/_réglement_ This is not a term of art in international law. It nevertheless has a fairly well-defined usage in relation to framework international agreements as describing detailed provisions annexed to the main instrument and which may be subject to amendment in a less solemn form (*e.g.*, the Radio Regulations annexed to the International Telecommunication Union Convention). Cf. **Réglement of the Laws of War.**

In the usage of the **European Community,** a regulation is the principal legislative instrument, having general application and being binding in its entirety and directly applicable in all member States (art. 249 of the EEC Treaty).

Reisman, Michael 1939- . American law professor (Yale) and a long-time member of the AJIL editorial board; member (1990-95) and president (1994-95) of the Inter-American Committee on Human Rights. His principal works include *Nullity and Revision* (1970); *International Law in Contemporary Perspective* (with McDougal, 1981); *International Incidents* (with Willard, 1988); *The Laws of War: Basic Documents on International Armed Conflict* (with Christos, 1996); *Jurisdiction in International Law* (editor, 1999).

rejoinder This is the fourth and final of the written pleadings in a contentious case before the ICJ: the rejoinder by the respondent State "shall not merely repeat the parties' contentions, but shall be directed to bringing out the issues that still divide them": art. 49(3) of the Rules of Court 1978. The ICJ decides whether the rejoinder is necessary, either where the parties so agree or where the Court, *ex proprio motu* or at the request of one of the parties, so determines: art. 45(2) of the Rules of Court. *See* **memorial**; **counter-memorial**; and **reply**.

relations agreements This term is used to describe the agreements concluded between the UN and the **Specialized Agencies.** *See* arts. 57 and 63(1) of the UN Charter. These relations agreements, while concluded "in a form and to a degree acceptable to the United Nations and the States involved in any of these optional and, largely, autonomous ventures" (Schwarzenberger, *International Constitutional Law* (1976), 534), tend to have a number of common features. Fairly typical is the Agreement between the United Nations and the World Health Organization of 10 July 1948 *(19 U.N.T.S. 193)*, under which the UN recognizes WHO as the Specialized Agency responsible for attaining the objectives set out in its Constitution (art. I); representatives of the one are to be invited to meetings of the appropriate organs of the other (art. II (1)-(3)), although WHO representatives have no voting rights in UN organs (art. II (3)-(5)); the one can propose agenda items for appropriate organs of the other (art. III); the UN can make recommendations to WHO (art. IV (1)-(2)); WHO submits to cooperate in the coordination by the UN of the activities of Specialized Agencies (art. IV (3)); information and documents are to be exchanged (art. V); WHO is obliged to provide information to the ICJ if requested (art. X(1)), and is also entitled to request advisory opinions (art. X (2)); common personnel arrangements are to be developed (art. XII); and there is to be close cooperation in budgetary and financial arrangement (art. XV). See Sands and Klein, *Bowett's Law of International Institutions* (5th ed.), 79-83.

relative rights This term denotes rights under international law that are not absolute in character. Schwarzenberger, *International Law* (1957), 209-14, 292-3, 457-61, identifies relative rights in relation to title to territory and to aspects of treaties.

remote damages In the law of **State responsibility,** international law generally insists on compensation only for loss or injury that is the proximate result of the wrongful act, and not for remote loss or injury. "Every legal system recognizes that there must be some limit on responsibility for wrongful acts. To disallow remote losses is a method of placing a reasonable limitation upon the amount recoverable": Whiteman, *Damages in International Law,* Vol. 3, (1943), 1801. *See The **Alabama Arbitration** (1872) Moore, Int. Arb. 646; The **Newchwang** (1921) 6 R.I.A.A. 64; Life Insurance Claims (1924) 7 R.I.A.A. 91; Neilson Claim (1926) 7 R.I.A.A. 308; Ousset Claim (1954) 13 R.I.A.A. 252.* Cf. **indirect damage**.

Renaissance *I Oppenheim (8th ed.) 79-83* identifies seven factors of importance which prepared the ground for the growth of the principles of international law from the 15th century, the sixth of which was the Renaissance and Reformation: "The Renaissance of science and art in the fifteenth century, together with the resurrection of the knowledge of antiquity, revived the philosophical and aesthetical ideals of Greek life and transferred them to modern life. Through their influence the spirit of the Christian religion took precedence of its letter. The conviction arose that the principles of Christianity ought to unite the Christian world more than they had done hitherto, and that these principles ought to be observed in matters international as much as in matters national": *ibid.,* 81.

Renault, Louis 1843-1918. French adviser and representative; and law teacher at Dijon (1868-73) and Paris (1873-1918). Nobel Peace Prizewinner 1907. Principal works include *Study of International Law* (1879); *The First Violations of International Law by Germany* (1916); editor, *The Two Peace Conferences—Collection of Texts Adopted by the Conferences of 1899 and 1907* (1909).

rendition *See* **extradition**.

renewal (of treaties) Renewal of treaties denotes "the prolongation, before their expiration, of treaties concluded for a limited period of time. Renewal can take place through a new treaty, and the old treaty may then be renewed as a whole, or only in part. But the renewal can also take, in the absence of notice to the contrary, they are to be considered as renewed for another period": *I Oppenheim 1311-2. See* **reconfirmation**; **redintegration**.

renunciation "Renunciation is the deliberate abandonment of rights. It can be express, or it can be tacit (as when a state fails to protest in circumstances where a protest is necessary to protect its rights). Renunciation may take place by way of the actual admission by a state of the facts underlying the claim of another state": *I Oppenheim 1195*. In relation to treaties, a State may lose its right to invoke a ground for invalidating, terminating, withdrawing from or suspending the operation of a treaty by what amounts to renunciation if it, "after becoming aware of the facts: (a) . . . expressly agreed that the treaty is valid or remains in force or continues in operation, as the case may be; or (b) . . . by reason of its conduct be considered as having acquiesced in the validity of the treaty or in its maintenance in force or operation, as the case may": art. 45 of the Vienna Convention on the Law of Treaties 1969. *See* the *Minquiers and Ecrehos Case 1953 I.C.J. Rep. 47*; *Rights of Passage Case 1960 I.C.J. Rep. 6.* Cf. **protest, waiver of rights**.

Renunciation of War Treaty *See* **General Treaty for the Renunciation of War 1928**.

reparation "It is a principle of international law that the breach of an engagement involves an obligation to make reparation in an adequate form. Reparation therefore is the indispensable complement of a failure to apply a convention and there is no necessity for this to be stated in the convention itself": *Chorzów Factory Case (Jurisdiction) (1927) P.C.I.J., Ser. A, No. 9* at 21; *Chorzów Factory Case (Merits) (1928) P.C.I.J., Ser. A, No. 17* at 43. Art. 31 of the ILC Draft Articles on State Responsibility (2001) *((2001) 40 I.L.M.)* provides that "[t]he responsible State is under an obligation to make full reparation for the injury caused by [an] internationally wrongful act." As a general rule, "reparation must, as far as possible, wipe out all the consequences of the illegal act and re-establish the situation which would, in all probability, have existed if that act had not been committed. Restitution in kind, or, if this is not possible, payment of a sum corresponding to the value which a restitution in kind would bear; the award, if need be, of damages for loss sustained which would not be covered by restitution in kind or payment in place of it—such are the principles which should serve to determine the amount of compensation due for an act contrary to international law": *Chorzów Factory Case (Merits) (1928) P.C.I.J., Ser. A, No. 17* at 43. *See Norwegian Shipowners Case (1922) 1 R.I.A.A. 307; Union Bridge Co. Case (1924) 6 R.I.A.A. 138.* Reparation must thus compensate for both material and moral injury *(Janes Claim (1926) 4 R.I.A.A. 82; Mallén Claim (1927) 4 R.I.A.A. 173)*, and must as a rule cover all losses and expenses actually incurred *(damnum emergens)* as well as loss of expected profits *(lucrum cessans)*. Where reparation is for a wrong done by one State to the nationals of another, the amount of compensation is usually commensurate to the damage which the nationals of the injured State have suffered: *Lusitania Cases (1923) 7 R.I.A.A. 32.* However, this does not alter the character of the reparation itself, which is and remains governed by the rules of international, not domestic, law. "The damage suffered by an individual is never therefore identical in kind with that which will be suffered by a State; it can only afford a convenient scale for the calculation of the reparation due to the State": *Chorzów Factory Case (Merits) ibid.,* 28. Since at the level of international law reparation is always made to the State and not to the individual whose claim it espouses, the recipient State has complete control over any sum received and may freely dispose of it: *Administrative Decision No. V (1924) 7 R.I.A.A. 119; Civilian War Claimants Association v. The King 1931-32 A.D. No. 118. See also* **damages, punitive**; **State responsibility**; **satisfaction**. *See* Whiteman, *Damages in International Law,* (3 vols., 1937-43); Brownlie, *State Responsibility (Part 1)* (1983), 199-240.

Reparation for Injuries Case 1949 I.C.J. Rep. 174. Following the deaths of certain persons while engaged in the service of the UN (principally Count Bernadotte, the UN Mediator in Palestine), the General Assembly of the UN adopted Res. 258 (III) (1948) in which it submitted the following legal questions to the ICJ for an advisory opinion: "I. In the event of an agent of the United Nations in the performance of his duties suffering injury in circumstances involving the responsibility of a State, has the United Nations, as an Organization, the capacity to bring an international claim against the responsible *de jure* or *de facto* government with a view to obtaining the reparation due in respect of the damage caused (a) to the United Nations, (b) to the victim or to persons entitled through him? II. In the event of an affirmative reply on point I (b), how is action by the United Nations to be reconciled with such rights as may be possessed by the State of which the victim is a national?"

The Court *advised* that: (1) on Question I (a) (unanimously) the UN had capacity to bring an international claim against a State which had caused it damage by a breach of its obligations toward the UN. The functions and rights with which the member States had endowed the UN could only be explained on the basis of the possession of a large measure of international personality and the capacity to operate upon an international plane: the members, by entrusting certain functions to the UN, with the attendant duties and responsibilities, had clothed it with the competence required to enable those functions to be effectively discharged. The UN was an international person, i.e. was a subject of international law and capable of possessing international rights and duties, and having the capacity to maintain its rights by bringing international claims; (2) on Question I (b) (11 to 4) the UN had legal capacity to give functional protection to its agents. The powers which were essential to the performance of the duties of the Organization must be considered as resulting necessarily from the Charter, and the provisions of the Charter concerning the functions of the Organization implied for it the power to afford its agents a degree of protection related to the performance of their duties for the Organization; (3) since the members of the UN had created an entity endowed with an objective international capacity, the Court's conclusions on Question I (a) and (b) applied whether or not the defendant State was a member of the UN. "[F]ifty States, representing the vast majority of the members of the international community, had the power, in conformity with international law, to bring into being an entity possessing objective international personality, and not merely personality recognized by them alone, together with capacity to bring international claims"; (4) on Question II (10 to 5), there was no necessary order of priority between the rights of diplomatic protection by the victim's national State and those of functional protection by the UN, although in the case of member States the duty of assistance laid down in art. 2 of the Charter must be stressed; (5) since the UN's claim arising from injury to its agent was not based on the victim's nationality but on his functions as an agent, it was immaterial whether the defendant State was the national State of the victim.

Reparations Commission Case *(Germany v. Reparations Commission) (1924) 1 R.I.A.A. 429.* Art. 260 of the Treaty of Versailles concerned the right of the Reparations Commission to require the German Government to take possession of certain rights of German nationals and to transfer such rights and any similar rights possessed by the German Government itself to the Reparations Commission. The rights in question were rights in "public utility undertakings" or in any "concessions" operating in Russia, China, Turkey, Austria, Hungary, Bulgaria, or in the possessions or dependencies of those States, or in any territory formerly belonging to Germany or her Allies, to be ceded by Germany or her Allies to any Power or to be administered by a Mandatory under the Treaty of Versailles. Certain disputes which arose as to the meaning of art. 260 were referred to a special arbitral tribunal established by a Protocol concluded in 1922, which *held:* (1) art. 260 applied to territories ceded by Germany's Allies under treaties other than the Treaty of Versailles, since that was the clear meaning of the English text of art. 260 and, the French text, being less clear, must be interpreted in the light of, and in conformity with, the English text; (2) although the treaties of St. Germain 1919 and Trianon 1920 with, respectively, Austria and Hungary, referred to Germany's "renunciation" of rights over territories to form part of Czechoslovakia and Serbia, which States were already in existence in fact and in unopposed possession of the territories, the territories were "ceded" for purposes of art. 260, since the term "cession" meant the renunciation by one State in favor of another of the rights and title which the former might have to the territory in question; (3) Upper Silesia, having been transferred to Poland by virtue of a resolution of the Conference of Ambassadors 1921 was not within the scope of art. 260; (4) "public utility undertakings" included railways and tramways, and canals, used by the general public, and water, gas and electricity undertakings supplying the general public, but not mining or petroleum extraction enterprises; (5) "concessions" meant rights to exploit mines or deposits where under the local law the rights had been granted by the State or a State authority; (6) the date for determining which public utility undertakings and concessions were within the scope of art. 260 was the date of entry into force of the Treaty of Versailles, 10 January 1920; (7) as Estonia, Finland, Latvia and Lithuania had been recognized as States separate from Russia at the time of the signature of the Treaty of Versailles, those States were not included within "Russia" for purposes of art. 260.

repatriation   This term is employed in the laws of war to denote the return of some person to his own country. Thus, States are obliged to repatriate seriously wounded or seriously sick prisoners of war during a conflict, and to release and repatriate all prisoners of war after the cessation of hostilities (arts. 109 and 118 of the Geneva Convention (III) Relative to the Treatment of Prisoners of War of 12 August 1949 *(75 U.N.T.S. 135)*). Likewise, **protected persons** are to be repatriated unless their departure would be contrary to the national interests of the State (art. 35 of the Geneva Convention (IV) Relative to the Protection of Civilian Persons in the Time of War of 12 August 1949 *(75 U.N.T.S. 287))*. *See* **prisoners of war**.

reply   This is the third of the written pleadings in a contentious case before the ICJ: the reply by the applicant State "shall not merely repeat the parties' contentions, but shall be directed to bringing out the issues that still divide them": art. 49(3) of the Rules of Court 1978. The ICJ decides whether the reply is necessary, either where the parties so agree or where the Court, *ex proprio motu* or at the request of one of the parties, so determines: art. 45(2) of the Rules of Court. *See* **memorial**, **counter-memorial** and **rejoinder**.

representation of a member State   The question of representation of a member State in an international organization is different from that of **admission**. Admission relates to whether a State should be a member; representation relates to which régime or government should represent a State which is a member. GA Res. 396 (V) of 14 December 1950 asserted that, when one or more authority claims to be the government entitled to represent a UN member, the question "should be considered [by the General Assembly] in the light of the Purposes and Principles of the Charter and the circumstances of each case." The most famous representation problem has concerned China, and whether China as an original member of the UN and a permanent member of the Security Council should be represented by the Communist régime controlling all of mainland China from 1949 or the Nationalist régime banished to Taiwan, but nonetheless holding the Chinese seat until 1971; GA Res. 2758 (XXVI) of 25 October 1971 replaced the Nationalist régime with the Communist régime. *See* Amerasinghe, *Principles of the Institutional Law of International Organizations* (1996), 126-31.

The privileges and immunities governing representation are to be covered, in the absence of a specific agreement relating to the organization in question, by the Vienna Convention on the Representation of States in Relation to International Organizations of a Universal Character of 14 March 1975 *((1975) 69 A.J.I.L. 730),* which takes account of the principles of the Vienna Conventions on **consular** and **diplomatic privileges and immunities** and of the conventions on privileges and immunities of the United Nations and of the Specialized Agencies of 1946 and 1947 respectively. *See* **privileges and immunities of international organizations**.

reprisals "Reprisals are such injurious and otherwise internationally illegal acts of one State against another as are exceptionally permitted for the purpose of compelling the latter to consent to a satisfactory settlement of a difference created by its own international delinquency. Whereas **retorsion** consists in retaliation for discourteous, unfriendly, unfair, and inequitable acts by acts of the same or a similar kind, and has nothing to do with international delinquencies, reprisals are acts, otherwise illegal, performed by a State for the purpose of obtaining justice for an international delinquency by taking the law into its own hands. . . . Reprisals can be positive or negative. Positive reprisals are such acts as would under ordinary circumstances involve an international delinquency. Negative reprisals consist in a refusal to perform such acts as are under ordinary circumstances obligatory, such as the fulfilment of a treaty obligation or the payment of a debt. Reprisals, be they positive or negative, must be in proportion to the wrong done, and to the amount of compulsion necessary to get reparation. . . . Reprisals in time of peace must not be confounded with reprisals between belligerents. Whereas the former are resorted to for the purpose of settling a conflict without going war, the latter are retaliations in order to compel an enemy guilty of a certain illegal act of warfare to comply with the laws of war": *II Oppenheim 136, 140-141, 143*. In international armed conflicts, reprisals are now unconditionally prohibited against all categories of protected persons as enumerated in the four Geneva Conventions on the Laws of War of 12 August 1949 *(75 U.N.T.S. 3 ff.)*. In Geneva Convention IV (relative to the Protection of Civilian Persons in Time of War), this prohibition is extended to the collective punishment of civilians. Reprisals are also prohibited against cultural property by the Hague Convention for the Protection of Cultural Property in the Event of Armed Conflict of 14 May 1954 *(249 U.N.T.S. 240)*. Protocol I Additional to the Geneva Conventions of 12 August 1949 of 8 June 1977 *(1125 U.N.T.S. 3)* prohibits reprisals against the wounded, sick and shipwrecked (art. 51(6)) and against a wide range of civilian objects (art. 52(1). *See* Kalshoven, *Belligerent Reprisals* (1971).

repudiation The Vienna Convention on the Law of Treaties 1969 provides a number of grounds which entitle a party to terminate or suspend the operation of the treaty unilaterally (*see* **treaties, termination or suspension**). One of these is a material breach of the treaty by another party (art. 60). Besides "violation of a provision essential to the accomplishment of the object and purpose of the treaty," material breach may be constituted by "a repudiation of the treaty not sanctioned by the Convention" (art. 60(3). The Convention does not define this concept and the ILC seems to have devoted no detailed consideration to it. According to Judge Fitzmaurice, "[t]o deny the existence of an obligation is *ex hypothesi* not the same as to repudiate it": *Namibia Opinion* (dissent) *1971 I.C.J. Rep. 6* at *300. See also Diversion of Water from the Meuse Case*; *Tacna-Arica Arbitration. See* McNair, Law of Treaties (2nd ed.), Chap. 36; Aust, Modern Treaty Law and Practice (2000), 236-9.

requisition Requisition is the process whereby a State takes possession of, or title to, moveable or immoveable property. Under the traditional view, requisition was accepted as lawful under international law as long as it was occasioned by some exceptional and grave national emergency: O'Connell, *International Law* (1965), Vol. 2, 773. Further, it appears that the return of the property, and compensation for any loss or damage incurred by the original owner, are required on the conclusion of the emergency: *Norwegian Shipowners' Claims (1922) I R.I.A.A. 307*. These rules are of diminishing relevance as international law now recognizes a general right of **expropriation** of the property of aliens. Cf. **angary**.

res communis The concept that certain areas or resources are not subject to appropriation by any State and are vested in the international community as a whole. Thus, outer space, including the moon and celestial bodies, is not subject to national appropriation (Outer

Space Treaty 1967 *(610 U.N.T.S. 205)*, art. 2), the benefits from the exploration of which are to be applied to all countries (art. 1). The high seas likewise are not subject to national appropriation (UN Convention on the Law of the Sea 1982 *(1833 U.N.T.S. 3)*, art. 89) and are available for all States in the exercise of the **freedoms of the sea**. The resources of the deep seabed and ocean floor are not available for appropriation by individual States (UN Convention on the Law of the Sea 1982, art. 137(1)) and are the **common heritage of mankind** (art. 136), whose benefits extend to mankind as a whole (art. 140). *See also* **Antarctic Treaty**.

res judicata Municipal legal systems invariably include a doctrine to the effect that, once a matter is judicially determined, that matter may not be litigated again by the same parties or parties in the same interest. This doctrine, commonly called *res judicata,* applies equally to international arbitral and judicial decisions. Thus, reading together art. 59 ("The decision of the Court has no binding force except between the parties and in respect of that particular case") and art. 60 ("The judgment is final and without appeal") of the ICJ Statute, *res judicata* clearly applies to the International Court of Justice. Further, *res judicata*, deriving as it does from municipal law, is also a "general principle of law recognized by civilized nations" under art. 38(1)(c) of the Statute. The place of the doctrine has been confirmed in a number of decisions of the Court: *Société Commerciale de Belgique (1939) P.C.I.J., Ser. A/B, No. 78; Corfu Channel Case (Compensation) 1949 I.C.J. Rep. 244; Asylum Case 1951 I.C.J. Rep. 71* at 80; *Barcelona Traction Case (Preliminary Objections) 1964 I.C.J. Rep. 6* at 20.

res nullius See **terra nullius**.

Rescue and Return Agreement Properly styled the Agreement on the Rescue and Return of Astronauts and Objects Launched into Space of 19 December 1967 *(672 U.N.T.S. 1218)*, the Agreement was in fact presaged by arts. 5 and 8 of the **Outer Space Treaty** 1967 *(610 U.N.T.S. 206)*. It binds parties to help personnel of space craft landing by reason of "accident, distress, emergency or unintended landing" in their territories (art. 2), or on the high seas (art. 3); to conduct any required search and rescue endeavors, and promptly to return rescued personnel to the launching State's representatives (art. 4); and to recover objects or parts (art. 5). Identifying data must be furnished by the launching State (art. 5(3)), which is also responsible for dealing with dangerous material (art. 5(4)). The expense of recovering objects is borne by the launching authority (art. 5(5)).

reservations The customary rules and case law on reservations to treaties (notably the ***Reservations to the Genocide Convention Case 1951 I.C.J. Rep. 15***) are now reflected in the detailed provisions of Part II, Section 2, of the Vienna Convention on the Law of Treaties 1969. For the purposes of the Convention: "'reservation' means a unilateral statement, however phrased or named, made by a State, when signing, ratifying, accepting, approving or acceding to a treaty, whereby it purports to exclude or to modify the legal effect of certain provisions of the treaty in their application to that State": art. 2(1)(d). Reservations are in principle permitted at the time of signature (in which case they must be confirmed when consent to be bound is expressed (art. 23(2)), at the time of ratification, acceptance or approval, or upon accession, provided the reservation (a) is not prohibited by the treaty or (b) is one of those specified by the treaty as permissible or (c) in other cases is not incompatible with the "object and purpose" of the treaty (art. 19). A reservation expressly authorized by a treaty does not require any subsequent acceptance by the other contracting States unless the treaty so provides (art. 20(1)). But where the application of the treaty in its entirety between all the parties is an essential condition of the consent of each one to be bound, a reservation requires acceptance by all the parties (art. 20(2)). Normally, apart from reservations expressly provided for, a reservation to the constituent instrument of an international organization requires the acceptance of the competent organ of that organization (art. 20(3)).

Acceptance by another contracting State of a reservation constitutes the reserving State a party in relation to that other State if or when the treaty is in force (art. 20(4)(a)). On the other hand, a rejection of a reservation has to be very definitely expressed if it is to prevent the treaty entering into force as between objecting and reserving States (art. 20(4)(b) and *Anglo-French Continental Shelf Case (1978) 18 R.I.A.A. 3*, 271). In the absence of other express provisions, art. 20(5) lays down a period of 12 months in which to object to a reservation. The effect of a reservation which has been established in accordance with the Vienna Convention is to disapply the provisions to which the reservation relates as between the reserving State and the parties against which the reservation has been established, but not as between those other parties inter se (art. 21).

Reservations and objections may be withdrawn unilaterally at any time upon receipt of notice (art. 22). *See* McNair, *Law of Treaties* (2nd ed.), 158-77; Aust, *Modern Treaty Law and Practice* (2000), Chap. 8.

Reservations to the Genocide Convention Case *1951 I.C.J. Rep. 15*. The Convention on the Prevention and Punishment on the Crime of **Genocide** *(78 U.N.T.S. 277)* was approved by the UN General Assembly in 1948. The UN Secretary-General was designated as the depositary. Certain States on ratifying or acceding to the Convention entered reservations; some other States objected to those reservations. By Res. 478 (V) (1950), the General Assembly requested from the ICJ an advisory opinion on (1) whether a reserving State to the Genocide Convention could be regarded as a party to the Convention while still maintaining its reservation if some but not all parties to the Convention objected to the reservation; (2) if so, what was the effect of the reservation as between the reserving State and the parties which objected to the reservation, and between that State and the parties which accepted it; and (3) what would be the legal effect for the answer to (1) if an objection was made by a signatory State which had not yet ratified or by a State entitled to sign or accede but which had not yet done so. The Court *advised* (7 to 5) that in the circumstances of the Genocide Convention: as to (1), the reserving State could be regarded as being a party to the Convention only if the reservation was compatible with the object and purpose of the Convention, it being for each State to make its own appraisal of the admissibility of any reservation; as to (2), an objecting party, which considered the reservation incompatible with the object and purpose of the Convention, could consider the reserving State not to be a party, but if the objecting party accepted the reservation as compatible with the object and purpose of the Convention it could consider the reserving State to be a party; and as to (3), an objection to a reservation made by a signatory State which had not yet ratified the Convention could only have the legal effect indicated in (1) upon ratification, while an objection made by a State which was entitled to sign or accede but had not done so was without legal effect.

resistance movements   This name originates from the groups organized throughout occupied Europe during World War II to resist the occupation (*mouvement de résistance*). The provisions of the Geneva Conventions of 12 August 1949 extend, insofar as they are applicable, to resistance movements, defined thus: "Members of other militias and members of other volunteer corps, including those of organized resistance movements, belonging to a Party to a conflict and operating in or outside their own territory, even if this territory is occupied, provided that such militias or volunteer corps, including such organized resistance movements, fulfil the following conditions: (a) that of being commanded by a person responsible for his subordinates; (b) that of having a fixed distinctive sign recognizable at a distance; (c) that of carrying arms openly; (d) that of conducting their operations in accordance with the laws and customs of war": art. 13(2) of Convention (1) for the Amelioration of the Condition of the Wounded and Sick in Armed Forces in the Field *(75 U.N.T.S. 31). See also* art. 13(2) of Convention (II) for the Amelioration of the Condition of Wounded, Sick and Shipwrecked Members of Armed Forces at Sea *(75 U.N.T.S. 85)* and art. 4(2) of Convention (III) Relative to the Treatment of Prisoners of War *(75 U.N.T.S. 135). See In re Bauer and Others (1946) 13 I.L.R. 305; In re Bruns and Others (1946) 13 I.L.R. 391.* Cf. *levee en masse*.

resolution(s) Many international organizations use this term to describe the non-binding acts of their organs, generally referred to as **recommendations.** The acts of all UN organs are referred to as resolutions, save that, under art. 25 of the Charter, the Security Council may adopt "decisions" notably under Chapter VII of the Charter (action with respect to threats to the peace, breaches of the peace, and acts of aggression) which the Member States "agree to accept and carry out . . . in accordance with the present Charter." These decisions are themselves embodied in resolutions. *See* Amerasinghe, *Principles of Institutional Law of International Organizations* (1996), Chap. 7.

respondent In proceedings in the ICJ in contentious cases, the defendant State is referred to as the respondent. While this term does not appear in the ICJ Statute, it does in art. 38(4) of the Rules of Court of 1978. Cf **applicant**.

responsibility, international *See* **State responsibility**.

responsibility, objective This is the doctrine according to which international responsibility might be incurred by a State notwithstanding the absence of any fault on its part, on the basis that a State is responsible for all acts committed by its officers or organs and constituting delinquencies under international law, regardless of whether the officers or organs in question have acted within the limits of their competence or have exceeded it. However, in order to justify the admission of this objective responsibility of the State for acts committed by its officers outside the limits of their competences, it is necessary either that they should have acted, at least apparently, as authorized officers, or that, in acting, they should have exercised powers or measures connected with their official character: *Caire Claim (1929) 5 R.I.A.A. 516; Janes Claim (1926) 4 R.I.A.A. 82.* The ILC's Draft Articles on State Responsibility of 2001 *(UN Doc. A/56/10 Chap. IV.E.I)* include responsibility for the conduct of its officers (or organs) in excess of authority or incontravention of orders (art. 7), and generally takes an objective approach to State responsibility. *See* **attribution**.

responsibility, original "A distinction is sometimes drawn between the original and so-called vicarious responsibility of a state. 'Original' responsibility is borne by a state for acts which are directly imputable to it, such as acts of its government, or those of its officials or private individuals performed at the government's command or with its authorization. 'Vicarious' responsibility, on the other hand, arises out of certain internationally injurious acts of private individuals (whether nationals, or aliens in the state's territory), and of officials acting without authorization. It is apparent that the essential difference between original and vicarious responsibility in this sense is that whereas the former involves a state being in direct breach of legal obligations binding on it, and is accordingly a particularly serious matter, with the latter the state's responsibility is at one remove from the injurious conduct complained of: in such cases the state's responsibility calls for it to to take certain preventive measures and requires it to secure as far as possible that the wrongdoer makes suitable reparation, and if necessary to punish him: *I Oppenheim 502-3.* The ILC Draft Articles on State Responsibility of 2001 *(UN Doc. A/56/10 Chap. IV.E.I)* are concerned primarily with what Oppenheim describes as original responsibility. *See* **State responsibility**.

responsibility, vicarious *See* **responsibility, original**.

ressortissant "[F]requently in international instruments—as, for example, in the Peace Treaties concluded after the First World War—the term *ressortissant* is used in the French text where the term "national" appears in the English text. Etymologically, the word—derived from *ressortir,* "to spring from, to derive from"—refers particularly to the jurisdiction of origin. A *ressortissant* of a State is a person coming under the sovereign jurisdiction of that State. From the legal point of view this linguistic reference to jurisdiction does not lead very far: both nationals and aliens, the latter while residing on the territory, come under the territorial jurisdiction of the State; only in regard to personal jurisdiction is there a distinction between nationals and aliens. Is, then, the term *ressortissant* wider than the term "national," i.e., a person coming under the personal jurisdiction of a state? The question has been answered in the affirmative by the French Cour de Cassation . . .": Weis *Nationality and Statelessness in International Law* (2nd. ed), 7.

Restatement, Third, of the Foreign Relations Law of the United States Published by the American Law Institute in 1987 and regularly updated, this *Restatement* is an unofficial yet authoritative account of "(a) international law as it applies to the United States; and (b) domestic law that has substantial significance for the foreign relations of the United States or has other substantial international consequences": Introduction, 3; *and see also* § 1.

restitutio in integrum The fundamental principle governing the duty to make reparation for an internationally wrongful act was expressed by the PCIJ in the *Chorzow Factory (Indemnity) Case (1927) P.C.I.J., Ser. A, No. 17* at 47: "reparation must, as far as possible, wipe out all the consequences of the illegal act and reestablish the situation which would, in all probability, have existed if that act had not been committed." Thus, it appears that *restitutio in integrum* is the primary form of reparation, pecuniary reparation only applying where *restitutio* in not possible: art. 35 of the ILC Draft Articles on State Responsibility of 2001 *(UN Doc. A/56/10 Chap. IV.E.I)* that "[a] State responsible for an internationally wrongful act is under an obligation to make restitution, that is, to re-establish the situation which existed before the wrongful act was committed, provided and to the extent that restitution: (a) is not materially impossible; (b)does not involve a burden out of all proportion to the benefit deriving from restitution instead of compensation." However, apart from this theory of primacy, *restitutio* is not now generally applied, injured individuals and their governments preferring pecuniary reparation. *See* the *Spanish Zone in Morocco Claims (1925) 2 R.I.A.A. 617*; *Martini Case (1930) 2 R.I.A.A. 277*; *Russian Indemnity Case (1912) 11 R.I.A.A. 431*; *Temple of Preah Vihear Case 1962 I.C.J. Rep. 6*; *Passage through the Great Belt Case 1992 I.C.J. Rep. 12. And see* Verzijl, *International Law in Historical Perspective*, Vol. VI, (1973), 742-5; Brownlie, *State Responsibility (Part I)* (1980), Chap XIII; Crawford, *The International Law Commission's Articles on State Responsibility* (2002), 213-7.

restitution *See* **restitutio in integrum**.

Restitution of Property (Republic of Italy) Case, (1951) 18 I.L.R. 221. Certain discriminatory laws enacted in Germany between 1933 and 1945 had been such as to make virtually impossible the continued ownership of property by certain categories of people, who had consequently sold it. Some parcels of real property had been purchased in this way by the Republic of Italy. After World War II, a restitution law was enacted enabling people who had sold property in those circumstances to claim its return. The former owners of the real property accordingly instituted proceedings seeking its return. At first instance, it was held that Italy, as a sovereign State, was not subject to the jurisdiction of the German courts. On appeal the Court of Appeal, Hamm, *held* that as the proceedings involved an action *in rem* concerning real property situated in Germany, the general rule conferring upon foreign States exemption from the jurisdiction of German courts did not apply.

restrictive interpretation *See* **treaties, interpretation of**.

resumption of cooperation, membership In a number of instances, a State, having ceased active participation in an international organization for some reason, has subsequently returned to the organization. Thus, after Indonesia's "withdrawal" from the UN for 18 months, it indicated its intention "to resume full cooperation with the UN" on 19 September 1966 and was allowed to retake its seat in the General Assembly. *See* Schermers and Blokker, *International Institutional Law* (3rd ed.), 90-1; Schwelb, Withdrawal from the United Nations: The Indonesian Intermezzo, *(1967) 61 A.J.I.L. 661 See also* **withdrawal, international organizations, from**.

retaliation This term connotes acts taken by a State in direct response to acts of another State which are perceived as injurious to the retaliating State, whether or not these initial acts are in breach of international law. The forms of retaliation may be found under **embargo**; **intervention**; **blockade, pacific**; **reprisals**; and **retorsion**.

retorsion "Retorsion is the technical term for retaliation for discourteous, or unkind, or unfair and inequitable acts by acts of the same or a similar kind. The act which calls for retaliation is not an illegal act; on the contrary, it is an act that is within the competence of its author. . . . The question when retorsion is, and when it is not, justified is not one of law, and is difficult to answer. . . . It depends, therefore, largely upon the circumstances and conditions of each case, whether a State will or will not consider itself justified in making use of retorsion": *II Oppenheim 134*. Cf. **reprisals**.

Reuter, Paul 1911-90. Professor, Nancy, Poitiers, Aix-en-Provence and Paris; Member, PCA and ILC. Principal works include *Droit International public* (5th ed. 1976); *Institutions internationales* (8th ed. 1965); *Institutions et relations internationales* (2nd ed. 1988); *Introduction au droit des traités* (3rd ed. 1990).

revealed tendencies Judge Lauterpacht, in a separate opinion in the ***South West Africa, Voting Procedure Case 1955 I.C.J. Rep. 65*** at 106, said that "[a] proper interpretation of a constitutional instrument must take into account not only the formal letter of the original instrument, but also its operation in actual practice and in the light of the revealed tendencies in the life of the Organization." However, it seems that "revealed tendencies" are not synonymous with the practice of an organization; and that the often conflicting trends within an organization like the UN make it virtually impossible to deduce any principles of legal significance. See Schwarzenberger, *International Constitutional Law* (1976), 27.

reversion, reversibility "Clauses of reversion of feudal tenures and territorial supremacy have played a major role in international relations of the past and continued to do so until as late as the middle of the 19th century. The purpose of the clause was to lay down in advance that in the case, in particular, of the extinction of the male line of succession to the throne of State A, its territory would return to State B. This institution of reversibility has been familiar to different parts of Europe, especially Italy, where it has existed, *inter alia,* in respect of Sardinia and Sicily, of Parma, Piacenza and Guastella, of Modena and of Lucca, and has been the cause of continual complication": Verzijl, *International Law in Historical Perspective,* Vol. 3, (1970), 314.

revision of judgment While a judgment of the ICJ in a contentious case is "final and without appeal" (art. 60 of the ICJ Statute), an application may be made to the Court for revision of the judgment "when it is based upon the discovery of some fact of such a nature as to be a decisive factor, which fact was, when the judgment was given, unknown to the Court and also to the party claiming revision, always provided that such ignorance was not due to negligence" (art. 61(1)). The application must be made within six months of the discovery of the new fact; and no application for revision will be considered after ten years from the date of the judgment (art. 61(4) and (5)). *See also* arts. 99-100 of the Rules of Court 1978. To date, only two such applications have been made: in respect of the ***Tunisia-Libya Continental Shelf Case***, where the Court found no cause to revise the original judgment *(1985 I.C.J. Rep. 192)* and of the ***Genocide Convention Cases***, which is pending before the Court. Cf. **International Court of Justice, judgment, construction or interpretation of**.

revision of treaties "As a question of law, there is not much to be said upon the revision of treaties. . . . [A]s a matter of principle, no State has a legal right to demand the revision of a treaty in the absence of some provision to that effect contained in that treaty or in some other treaty to which it is a party; a revised treaty is a new treaty, and, subject to the same limitation, no State is legally obliged to conclude a treaty": McNair, *Law of Treaties* (2nd ed.), 534. Art. 39 of the Vienna Convention on the Law of Treaties 1969 provides, as a general rule, that any amendment of an international agreement occurs "by agreement between the parties," and that the rules on the conclusion of treaties apply to such amending treaties "except in so far as the treaty may otherwise provide." Art. 19 of the Covenant of the League of Nations empowered the Assembly to "advise the reconsideration by Members . . . of treaties which have become inapplicable. . . ." No equivalent provision appears in the UN Charter.

revolt *See* **insurgency, insurgent, insurrection**; and **State responsibility**.

revolution It is said that the term "revolution" has no precise meaning in international law, but "the rule that revolution *prima facie* does not affect the continuity of the State in which it occurs has been consistently applied to the innumerable revolutions, *coups d'état* and the like in the nineteenth and twentieth centuries. . . . Although it is sometimes argued that 'socialist' revolutions, which result in a changed class-structure of the State, bring about a fundamental discontinuity in relations, it is not at all clear whether this claim is directed to the notion of legal continuity of the State, or is a claim to a more liberal regime of succession": Crawford, *The Creation of States in International Law* (1979), 405-6. *See* **State succession.** International law does not prohibit revolution as a means of effecting a constitutional or governmental change within a State; and, once a revolutionary government is effective and has a reasonable prospect of permanence, it is eligible for **recognition.** *See* Lauterpacht, *Recognition in International Law* (1947), 91-2. A revolutionary change of government accompanied by acts of inhumanity or ruthlessness has been regarded as a legitimate reason for refusing recognition of the new government. *See also* **recognition of insurgency**. It has been asserted that "if international law recognizes the final result of revolution in the form of revolutionary government and State continuity, it must necessarily recognize the means leading to that result": Marek, *Identity and Continuity of States in Public International Law* (2nd ed.), 57. The generally accepted rule that "the government set up by successful revolutionists must accept responsibility for their acts as insurgents"(Eagleton, *Responsibility of States* (1928), 147) appears in some degree to be the reciprocal of eligibility for recognition: see **State responsibility**.

right of access and freedom of transit   Part X of the UN Convention on the Law of the Sea 1982 *(1833 U.N.T.S. 3)* establishes a right of access of **land-locked States** to and from the sea and freedom of transit. Under art. 125(1), land-locked States are given a right of access to and from the sea for the purpose of exercising the rights provided for in the Convention, including those relating to the freedom of the high seas and the common heritage of mankind. The "terms and modalities" for exercising the freedom are nevertheless a matter for agreement with the transit State (art. 125(2)). Transit traffic is, however, exempted from customs duties or taxes (art. 127). The Convention on Transit Trade of Land-Locked States 1965 *(597 U.N.T.S. 42)* establishes, as between the parties, the principle of freedom of transit between land-locked States and the sea, and sets conditions for the exercise of the freedom. One authority has opined that a general right of transit, apart from contractual obligations, "is difficult to sustain": Brownlie, *Principles of Public International Law* (5th ed.), 284. *See* Caflisch, Landlocked States and their Access to and from the Sea, *(1978) 49 B.Y.I.L. 71.*

rights and duties of States   On 23 May 1949 the ILC adopted the Draft Declaration on the Rights and Duties of States *([1949] I.L.C. Yearbook 286)*, based on a draft prepared by Panama and intended for adoption by the General Assembly; the Draft Declaration was not so adopted. The rights vested in States included the right to independence (art. 1), to exercise jurisdiction over its territory and all persons and things therein (art. 2), to equality in law with every other State (art. 5), and to individual or collective self-defense (art. 12). The duties included the duty to refrain from intervention in the affairs of any other State (art. 3), to refrain from fomenting civil strife in another State (art. 4), to treat all persons within its territory with respect for human rights (art. 6), to ensure that conditions in its territory do not menace international peace and security (art. 7), to settle disputes by peaceful means (art. 8), to refrain from the use or threat of force (art. 9), to refrain from assisting those acting contrary to art. 9 (art. 10), to refrain from recognizing territorial acquisitions resulting from force (art. 11), to carry out international obligations in good faith (art. 13), and to conduct relations with other States in accordance with international law (art. 14). Cf. **Economic Rights and Duties of States, Charter of**; **Friendly Relations Declaration**; **permanent sovereignty**.

Rights of Minorities Cases   *See* ***German Minorities in Upper Silesia, Rights of, Case; Minority Schools in Albania Opinion***.

Rights of Passage Case   *(Portugal v. India) 1957 I.C.J. Rep. 125, 1960 I.C.J. Rep. 6.* The Portuguese district of Daman, in India, comprised Daman itself (on the coast) and two inland enclaves of Dadra and Nagar-Aveli. In July and August 1954, Portuguese authority in the two inland enclaves was overthrown: India imposed restrictions upon Portuguese passage to those enclaves, the lawfulness of which Portugal disputed. India having already accepted the compulsory jurisdiction of the ICJ by a declaration under art. 36(2) of the Court's Statute, Portugal made such a declaration on 19 December 1955 and on 22 December 1955 filed an application submitting the dispute to the Court. India raised six preliminary objections to the exercise of jurisdiction by the Court, which, in rejecting four of India's objections and joining two to the merits, *held* that (a) (14 to 3) Portugal's reservation to its declaration permitting it at any time to exclude categories of disputes from the jurisdiction of the Court was not inconsistent with the Court's Statute; (b) (14 to 3) the filing by Portugal of an application three days after filing its declaration under art. 36(2) of the

Statute was not inconsistent with the Statute; (c) (15 to 2) nor did it deprive India of any right of reciprocity under art. 36 so as to constitute an abuse of the **Optional Clause**; and (d) (16-1) in the circumstances of the case, diplomatic negotiations had sufficiently disclosed the legal issue submitted to the Court.

In its judgment on the merits, the Court *held* that (a) (13 to 2) as in the proceedings both parties had invoked arguments of international law, India's preliminary objection that its reservation in its optional clause declaration excluded disputes with regard to questions which by international law fell exclusively within the jurisdiction of India could not be upheld; (b) (11 to 4) as both the dispute and the situation of the enclaves which had given rise to Portugal's claim arose after 5 February 1930, the dispute was not excluded from the Court's jurisdiction by India's acceptance of its jurisdiction only for post-1930 disputes and situations or facts; (c) although, in their origins in the 18th century, Portugal's rights over the territories had been derived from instruments not intended to transfer sovereignty, when Great Britain became sovereign of that part of the country Portuguese sovereignty had been recognized by the British and had subsequently been tacitly recognized by India; also with regard to private persons, civil officials and goods in general, there had existed a constant and uniform practice allowing free passage between Daman and the enclaves, which practice had been accepted as law by the parties; accordingly (11 to 4) Portugal had in 1954 a right of passage over intervening Indian territory between its enclaves to the extent necessary for the exercise of Portuguese sovereignty over the enclaves and subject to the regulation and control of India, in respect of private persons, civil officials and goods in general; (d) but (8 to 7) Portugal did not have in 1954 any such right of passage in respect of armed forces, armed police and arms and ammunition; and (e) India's refusal of passage through Indian territory where there was tension as a result of the events of July and August 1954 was covered by its power of regulation and control of Pakistan's right of passage; and therefore (9 to 6) India had not acted contrary to its obligations resulting from Portugal's right of passage in respect of private persons, civil officials and goods in general.

Rights of US Nationals in Morocco Case *(France v. USA) 1952 I.C.J. Rep. 176.* By the Treaty of Peace and Friendship between the United States and the Shereefian Empire of 16 September 1836 *(9 Bevans 1286)*, the USA was granted the benefit of a most-favored-nation clause and certain rights of consular jurisdiction in respect of US nationals. A Decree of the Resident General in Morocco in 1948 introduced certain measures regarding imports into Morocco. The United States asserted that these measures affected its rights under their Treaties with Morocco, invoking in particular the 1836 Treaty (its most-favored-nation provisions being read with Treaties concluded by Morocco with Great Britain in 1856 and Spain in 1861), and the General Act of Algeciras 1906 *(201 C.T.S. 39)*. The dispute was submitted by France to the ICJ on the basis of the declarations of acceptance by the Parties of the Court's compulsory jurisdiction under art. 36(2) of the Court's Statute. The Court *held* (a) (unanimously) that the 1948 Decree involved a discrimination in favor of France and that, by virtue of the Act of Algeciras and the 1836 Treaty, the US could claim to be treated as favorably as France so far as economic matters in Morocco were concerned; (b) (unanimously) that by virtue of the 1836 Treaty, the US was entitled in the French Zone of Morocco to exercise consular jurisdiction in all cases, civil and criminal, between their citizens or protégés, and (10 to 1) that the US was also entitled by virtue of the General Act of Algeciras to exercise in the French Zone of Morocco consular jurisdiction in all cases, civil or criminal, brought against citizens or protégés of the US to the extent required by the provisions of the Act relating to consular jurisdiction; (c) (6 to 5) that except to that extent US submission as to consular jurisdiction (involving primarily claims to jurisdiction over cases in which only the defendant was a citizen or protégé of the US) had to be rejected, since the treaties with Great Britain and Spain, although providing a more extensive consular jurisdiction, could not be invoked as they had ceased to be operative, while the Convention of Madrid 1880, the Act of Algeciras and custom or usage did not afford a basis for extended consular jurisdiction; (d) (unanimously) that the application to US citizens of all laws and regulations in the French Zone of Morocco did not require the assent of the US Government, but US consular courts might refuse to apply to US citizens laws or regulations which had not been assented to by the US Government; (f) (6 to 5) that no fiscal immunity was conferred by the joint operation of the m.f.n. clause in the 1836 Treaty and Morocco's treaties with Great Britain and Spain, since the US was no longer able to invoke the relevant provisions in those treaties, nor could fiscal immunity be founded upon the Convention of Madrid or the Act of Algeciras; (g) (7 to 4), that the consumption tax provided for by a Moroccan law of 1948 was not in contravention of any treaty rights of the US; and (h) (6 to 5) that, as regards the method of valuation of imports, in applying art. 95 of the Act of Algeciras it was not only the value of merchandise in the country of origin or its value in the local Moroccan market which was decisive, since both were elements in the appraisal of its value.

Rio Declaration 1992   At the conclusion of the UN Conference on Environment and Development, held in Rio de Janeiro in June 1992, a declaration was adopted *(31 I.L.M. 874 (1992))*, enunciating 27 principles, the majority of which are aspirational. Principle 2, however, states a number of principles of law: "States have, in accordance with the Charter of the United Nations and the principles of international law, the sovereign right to exploit their own resources pursuant to their own environmental and developmental policies, and the responsibility to ensure that activities within their jurisdiction or control do not cause damage to the environment of other States or of areas beyond the limits of national jurisdiction." *See also* the **Stockholm Declaration 1972**.

Rio Treaty   *See* **Organization of American States**.

riot   *See* **insurgency, insurgent, insurrection**; and **State responsibility**.

rising   *See* **insurgency, insurgent, insurrection**; and **State responsibility**.

river, boundary   "Boundary rivers are those which separate different states from each other. If such a river is not navigable, the boundary line as a rule follows the mid-line of the river; or of its principal arm if it has more than one. If navigable, the boundary line as a rule follows the mid-line of the so-called *thalweg,* of the principal channel of the river, and this general rule for the two kinds of rivers was adopted by the Treaties of Peace of 1919 except in special cases. But it is possible for the boundary line to be one bank of the river, so that the whole bed then belongs to one of the riparian states only. This is an exceptional case whether created by immemorial possession, by treaty, or by the fact that a state has occupied the lands on one side of a river at a time prior to the occupation of the lands on the other side by some other state:" *I Oppenheim 664-5. See* **thalweg**. Much of the judicial authority on boundary rivers comes from decisions of the US Supreme Court in disputes between the states of the Union: *Nebraska v. Iowa 143 U.S. 359* (1893); *Iowa v. Illinois 147 U.S. 1* (1893); *Louisiana v. Mississippi 202 U.S. 1* (1906); *Washington v. Oregon 211 U.S. 127, 214 U.S. 205; Arkansas v. Tennessee 246 U.S. 158* (1918). *See also* **Grisbadarna Arbitration** *(1909) 11 R.I.A.A. 147;* **British Guiana Boundary Arbitration** *(1904) 11 R.I.A.A. 21;* **Chamizal Arbitration** *(1911) 11 R.I.A.A. 316.* For the effect on boundaries of changes in the course of rivers, see **accretion**; **avulsion**. *See* Boggs, *International Boundaries* (1940); Bouchez, The Fixing of Boundaries in International Boundary Rivers, *(1963) 12 I.C.L.Q. 789.*

river, international A river that forms the boundary between States or traverses the territory of two or more States is referred to as an international river: cf. *I Oppenheim 574-5,* who categorizes all rivers other than national rivers as boundary, pluri-national (or multi-lateral) or international rivers, this last being "navigable from the open sea and which, though belonging to the territories of the different states concerned, are nevertheless named *international rivers,* because freedom of navigation in time of peace is recognized by treaty." More commonly, international rivers are defined as those that form a boundary between States or traverse two or more States, whether navigable or not. In theory, each riparian State has exclusive rights in the river as it passes through its territory, except where the State has conferred or accepted obligations in respect of other States. Particular régimes have been established by treaty for certain rivers, which rivers are sometimes referred to as "internationalized": for example, the Danube, Oder and Rhine. The Barcelona Convention and Statute on the Régime of Navigable Waterways of International Concern 1921 *(7 L.N.T.S. 35)* accorded free navigation, on condition of reciprocity, to the merchant vessels of the parties (art. 2). While intended as a global régime, the Barcelona Convention has not been sufficiently supported for it to be able to contend with any confidence that there exists a general right of free navigation on all international rivers. It is now regarded as appropriate to look to régimes for river basins as a whole and for the multiplicity of uses to which such rivers may be put. The Convention on the Law of Non-Navigable Uses of International Watercourses of 21 May 1997 *((1997) 36 I.L.M. 700)* provided for the equitable and reasonable utilization of, and participation in, international watercourses so as to secure "the optimal and sustainable utilization thereof and benefits therefrom, taking account of the interests of the watercourse States concerned, consistent with adequate protection of the watercourse" (art. 5(1). Cf. **river, national**. *See* Garretson, Hayton and Olmstead, *The Law of International River Drainage Basins* (1967); Vitanyi, *The International Régime of River Navigation* (1979); Chauhan, *The Settlement of International Water Law Disputes in International Drainage Basins* (1981); Zacklin and Caflisch, *The Legal Regime of International Rivers and Lakes* (1981).

river, national A river which flows wholly within the territory of a single State is referred to as a national river. Such a river falls to be considered as part of the territory of that State, subject exclusively to its jurisdiction except where the State may confer or accept obligations in respect of other States.

Riyadh Guidelines Properly styled the UN Guidelines for the Prevention of Juvenile Delinquency, the Guidelines were adopted on 14 December 1990 as GA Res. 45/112 and are predicated on a child-centered approach (Guideline 1(3)) within a total community environment (Guideline 1(2)). Being part of a General Assembly resolution, they are not legally binding. *See also* the **Beijing Rules**; **JDL Rules.**

Roberts Claim *(USA v. Mexico) (1926) 4 R.I.A.A. 77.* After an attack by several men on a private house in May 1922, Mexican police arrested Roberts, a US national. Although Mexican law required that he be brought to trial within a year, this did not happen, and he was eventually released after being detained for 19 months. *Held* by the Mexico-USA General Claims Commission, in awarding damages, that although there were sufficient grounds to warrant the arrest and trial of Roberts, he was held in detention for an unreasonably long period so as to warrant an award of an indemnity under the principles of international law, and was also, while detained, treated in such a way as to warrant an indemnity on the ground of cruel and inhumane treatment. Although he had been treated in jail like all other persons, and "equality of treatment of aliens and nationals may be important in determining the merits of a complaint of mistreatment of an alien ... such equality is not the ultimate test of the propriety of the acts of authorities in the light of international law. That test is, broadly speaking, whether aliens are treated in accordance with ordinary standards of civilization."

Roman law   The contribution of Roman law to international law is substantial in two respects: first, the Romans gave to the future the example of a State with legal (albeit municipal rather than international) rules for its foreign relations *(I Oppenheim 77);* secondly, the substantive provisions of Roman private law, in both terminology and concepts, had a profound influence on the early development of international law (Schwarzenberger and Brown, *A Manual of International Law* (6th ed.), 40).

Romano-Americana Case   *(US v. UK) (1924-28) Hackworth, 5 Digest, 840.* In 1916, when the US was neutral during the First World War, certain property in Romania belonging to Romano-Americana, a Romanian subsidiary of, and wholly owned by, the Standard Oil Company of New Jersey (a US company) was destroyed to prevent it falling into enemy hands by the Romanian authorities with the collaboration of British officers acting under instructions from the British Government. In 1924, the US Government sought compensation from the British Government. The UK denied liability, on the ground that the destruction was the act of the Romanian Government for which it alone was responsible, and contested the right of the US to present a claim in respect of losses suffered by a Romanian Company, Romano-Americana. The US argued that the State whose nationals owned the shares of a foreign corporation could interpose on behalf of the owners where the corporation suffered wrong at the hands of a foreign State when those nationals had no remedy except through the intervention of their own Government.

The UK refused to recognize the right of the US to espouse the claim. No recognized principle of international law supported a claim being made against the UK on behalf of the interests of the American stockholders of the Romanian company, the distinction between the property of the corporation in the corporation's assets and the interest of the stockholders of the corporation was well settled, and the present circumstances did not constitute one of those cases where the right of a government to intervene on behalf of the shareholders of a foreign company, for the purposes of establishing a claim in respect of damage to the corporate property, was admitted. The claim was finally settled through the acceptance by Romano-Americana of compensation paid by Romania in full settlement for the losses suffered by the company.

Rome Statute   *See* **International Criminal Court**.

Roosevelt Corollary   *See* **Monroe Doctrine**.

Rosa Gelbtrunk Claim   *(USA v. El Salvador) (1902) 15 R.I.A.A. 463.* In 1898, a US firm (Maurice Gelbtrunk and Company) suffered loss and destruction of merchandise as a result of acts of lawless violence of revolutionary soldiery in El Salvador; it assigned its claim to Rosa Gelbtrunk, a US national. A claim was referred by agreement of the USA and El Salvador to the arbitrators appointed under the Protocol of 19 December 1901 *(190 C.T.S. 311),* who *held* (unanimously) that, there having been no discrimination in the treatment accorded US nationals in respect of losses incurred in the course of the revolution, the claim should be rejected: an alien carrying on business in a country throws in his lot with nationals of that country and is subject, as they are, to the political vicissitudes of the country, sharing their fortunes in case of loss by military force or by the irregular acts of soldiers in a civil war.

Rosenne, Shabtai   1917- . Israeli lawyer and diplomat. Member, ILC 1962-71. Principal works include *International Court of Justice* (1957); *The Time Factor in the Jurisdiction* *of the International Court of Justice* (1960); *The Law and Practice of the International Court* (2 vols. 1965; 3rd ed. 1997); *The Law of Treaties: A Guide to the Vienna Convention* (1970); *The World Court: What it is and how it Works* (1973; 3rd ed. 2002); *An International Law Miscellany* (1993); *The Hague Peace Conferences of 1899 and 1907 and International Arbitration: Reports and Documents* (2001).

Ross, Alf 1899-1979. Professor, Copenhagen 1938-1969. Judge, European Court of Human Rights 1959-1971. Principal works on international law include *A Textbook of International Law* (1947); *On Law and Justice* (1959); *The United Nations. Peace and Progress* (1966).

Roster Non-Governmental Organizations concerned with most of the activities of ECOSOC or having a special competence in certain activities of ECOSOC are accorded Category I and Category II consultative status respectively under ECOSOC Res. 1996/31. "Organizations which are not admitted into either of these categories may be placed 'on the Roster.' These organizations are not closely related with the work of the ECOSOC but are of sufficient importance to be related in some way to the UN. . . . The organizations on the Roster may have representatives present at such meetings as are concerned with matters within their field of competence. . . . Organizations on the Roster may [submit written statements] at the request of the Secretary General. . . . All organizations in such a consultative relationship may be heard by the commissions and committees of the ECOSOC": Schermers and Blokker, *International Institutional Law* (3rd ed.), 130-1. At present, there are in excess of 750 NGOs on the Roster.

Rule of the War of 1756 This rule, which dates back to the early 17th Century (*see* Schwarzenberger, *International Courts: Armed Conflict* (1968), 399), is to the effect that a neutral merchant ship is equated with a belligerent merchant ship if it is engaged in time of war in a privileged trade closed to her in time of peace, *e.g.*, trade between ports of a belligerent State or between a belligerent's metropolitan and colonial territories. *See* Mootham, The Doctrine of Continuous Voyage, 1756-1815, *(1927) 8 B.Y.I.L. 62. See* **continuous voyage, transportation, doctrine of**.

Rules of Court (of the International Court of Justice) The ICJ is empowered to lay down its own rules of procedure: art. 30(1) of the ICJ Statute. The original Rules, based on the 1936 Rules of the PCIJ, were adopted in May 1946; *I.C.J. Acts and Documents,* No. 1, 2nd ed., 54-83. These Rules were replaced by revised Rules in 1972: *I.C.J. Acts and Documents,* No. 2; *(1972) 11 I.L.M. 899.* The latest rules of procedure were adopted in April 1978: *I.C.J. Acts and Documents,* No. 4; *(1978) 17 I.L.M. 1286.* These Rules were amended in 2000: *I.C.J. Acts and Documents*, No. 5. These Rules govern the constitution and working of the Court (Part I), including Judges and Assessors (Section A), Presidency (Section B), Chambers (Section C), Internal Functioning of the Court (Section D); the Registry (Part II); Proceedings in Contentious Cases (Part III), including Communications to the Court and Consultations (Section A), Composition of the Court for Particular Cases (Section B), Proceedings before the Court (Section C, including the institution of proceedings, written and oral proceedings), Incidental Proceedings (Section D, including interim protection, preliminary objections, counter-claims, intervention, specific reference to the Court and discontinuance), Procedure before the Chambers (Section E), Judgments, Interpretation and Revision (Section F) and Modifications Proposed by the Parties (Section G); and Advisory Opinions (Part IV). The current text is available as one of the Basic Documents at <www.icj-cij.org>.

rules of international law These are norms of conduct which are precise, certain and binding upon subjects of international law. International law has been criticized as lacking rules with these qualities, but it is countered that international law is only in a transient stage in its development: Lauterpacht, *International Law* (1948), Vol. 1, 25-28. Further, while customary law may lack precision and certainty, treaty law, an increasingly important element in the development of international law over the last century and more, does not. *See also* **principles of international law**.

rules of procedure The constituent documents of most international organizations confer on the various organs the power to adopt their own rules of procedure. Thus, within the UN the General Assembly (art. 21 of the Charter), Security Council (art. 30), ECOSOC (art. 72(1)) and the Trusteeship Council (art. 90(1)) have been accorded the power to adopt their own rules of procedure, and all have done so. Rules of procedure are also frequently adopted to regulate the proceedings of international conferences.

ruses of war Ruses of war are considered permissible: art. 24 of the Hague Convention on Land Warfare of 1907 *(205 C.T.S. 277)*. Ruses of war are defined in art. 37(2) of Protocol I Additional to the Geneva Conventions of 12 August 1949 of 8 June 1977 *(1125 U.N.T.S. 3)* as "acts which are intended to mislead an adversary or to induce him to act recklessly but which infringe no rule of international law applicable in armed conflict and which are not perfidious because they do not invite the confidence of an adversary with respect to protection under that law." The same article provides examples of ruses of war: "the use of camouflage, decoys, mock operations and misinformation." Cf. **perfidy**.

Russian Indemnity Case *(Russia v. Turkey) (1911) 11 R.I.A.A. 421*. Art. 5 of the Treaty of Constantinople *(154 C.T.S. 477)* between Russia and Turkey provided for the payment of claims of Russian subjects and institutions in Turkey for indemnity on account of damages sustained during the recent war. Claims were duly examined and presented to the Turkish Government, but payments were delayed; parts of the sums due were paid at intervals over the period 1884 to 1902, leaving a balance outstanding of 1539 Turkish pounds. Russia claimed interest for the delayed payments. By a *compromis* signed in 1910 *(211 C.T.S. 335)*, the controversy over the interest was submitted to an arbitral tribunal (two members of which were selected from the panel of the Permanent Court of Arbitration) which *held* that, as the Treaty of Constantinople was between the two States, Russia was entitled to pursue the matter before the tribunal notwithstanding that the indemnity was to be paid in respect of damages suffered by Russian subjects and institutions; and that, although the general principle of State responsibility implied a special responsibility as regards delay in the payment of a debt, making a debtor State responsible for interest for delayed payments, in the circumstances of this case the actions of the Russian Embassy in referring repeatedly only to the outstanding balance of the principal sum due, implied relinquishment of the right to payment of interest.

Rwanda Tribunal *See* **International Criminal Tribunal for Rwanda**.

S

Saavedra Lamas Pact, 1933   Named after the Minister of Foreign Relations of the Argentine Republic, this refers to the Anti-War Treaty of Non-Aggression and Conciliation of 10 October 1933 *(28 A.J.I.L. Supp. 79 (1934))*. It was ratified or adhered to by each of the 21 American Republics; according to it, the "High Contracting Parties solemnly declare that they condemn wars of aggression in their mutual relations or those with other States, and that settlement of disputes or controversies of any kind that may arise among them shall be effected only by the pacific means which have the sanction of international law" (art. 1).

Sabbatino (or Second Hickenlooper) Amendment   This refers to a provision included in the (US) Foreign Assistance Act of 1964 *(P.L. 88-663; 78 Stat. 1013; 22 U.S.C.A. § 2370(e)(2))* in response to the decision in *Banco Nacional de Cuba v. Sabbatino 376 U.S. 398 (1964)* (in which the Supreme Court held that the **act of State** doctrine precluded the courts from passing upon the legality under international law of acts performed by a foreign State within its territory). In addition to providing for suspension of aid to States illegally expropriating the property of US nationals, the Sabbatino Amendment declares that "no court in the United States shall decline on the ground of the . . . act of State doctrine to make a determination on the merits giving effect to the principles of international law in a case in which a claim of title or other right to property is asserted by any party including a foreign State (or a party claiming through such State) based upon (or traced through) a confiscation or other taking after January 1 1959, by an act of state in violation of the principles of international law. . . ." These principles of international law apply unless the President "determines that application of the act of State doctrine is required in that particular case by the foreign policy interests of the United States and a suggestion to this effect is filed on his behalf." *See* Lillich, *The Protection of Foreign Investment* (1965), 17-111.

sabotage, saboteur   Art. 5 of the Geneva Convention Relative to the Protection of Civilian Persons in Time of War of 12 August 1949 *(75 U.N.T.S. 287)* provides that **protected persons** (i.e. those who find themselves, in case of a conflict or occupation, in the hands of a party to the conflict or an occupying power of which they are not nationals: art. 4) who are detained in respect of, *inter alia*, sabotage, may be denied rights of communication, but must be treated with humanity and given a fair and regular trial. Art. 68 permits an occupying power to impose the death penalty on protected persons in respect of, *inter alia*, "serious acts of sabotage against the military installations of the Occupying Power. . . ." For acts against civil aviation, *see* the so-called Sabotage Convention **(Montreal Convention of 23 September 1971 for the Suppression of Unlawful Acts against the Safety of Civil Aviation** *(974 U.N.T.S. 177)*; and **hijacking (of aircraft)**.

sacred trust   The term "sacred trust of civilization" was first employed in a treaty in the Covenant of the League of Nations *(225 C.T.S. 188)*, art. 22(1) of which proclaimed that the well-being and development of the peoples not yet able to govern themselves formed a sacred trust of civilization; the other paragraphs of art. 22 specified how that sacred trust was to be exercised and scrutinized (*see* **Mandates System**). Chapter XI of the UN Charter, entitled "Declaration Regarding Non-Self-Governing Territories," asserts that the well-being of the inhabitants of such territories is a sacred trust. The **Trusteeship System,** established by Chapter XII of the UN Charter, makes no reference *eo nomine* to sacred trust, but the title of the Chapter and the substance of its provisions, particularly art. 76, clearly import the concept of sacred trust into the system. In the ***South West Africa Case*** *1950 I.C.J. Rep. 128* at 132, the ICJ, in considering the mandate over South West Africa, very largely based its findings on the principle that the mandate "was created, in the interest of the inhabitants of the territory, and of humanity in general, as an international institution with an international object—a sacred trust of civilization." *See also* the ***Namibia Case*** *1971 I.C.J. Rep. 16.*

safe-conduct "A safe-conduct is a written permission given by a belligerent to enemy subjects or others, allowing them to proceed to a particular place for a defined object; for instance, to a besieged town for conducting certain negotiations, or to enable them to return home across the sea. Safe-conducts may also be given for ships and for goods, to allow them to be navigated and carried without molestation to a certain place. . . . [S]afe-conducts make the grantee inviolable so long, and in so far, as he complies with the conditions imposed upon him, or made necessary by the circumstances of the special case": *II Oppenheim 537.* The term "safe-conduct" appears only twice in the Geneva Conventions on the Laws of War of 12 August 1949: States not parties to a conflict are to grant safe-conducts to **Protecting Powers** or relief agencies involved in the transportation of mail and relief supplies: art. 75 of the Convention Relative to the Treatment of Prisoners of War *(75 U.N.T.S. 135)*, and art. 111 of the Convention Relative to the Protection of Civilian Persons in Time of War *(75 U.N.T.S. 287)*.

safety zone The Geneva Convention on the Continental Shelf 1958 *(450 U.N.T.S. 311)* permitted a coastal State to establish safety zones around **installations** and devices on its **continental shelf** (art. 5(2)), but only where no interference would be caused "to the use of recognized sea lanes essential to international navigation" (art. 5(6)). These safety zones may extend to 500 meters from the outer edges of the installations and devices (art. 5(3)). The coastal State is entitled to take in those zones "measures necessary for their protection" (art. 5(2)), but is obliged to take all appropriate measures for the protection of the living resources of the sea from harmful agents (art. 5(7)). These provisions are somewhat recast in art. 60 of the UN Convention on the Law of the Sea 1982 *(1833 U.N.T.S. 3)*. The safety zones are to extend to 500 metres, "except as authorized by generally accepted international standards or as recommended by the competent international organization" (art. 60(5)). In the zones, the coastal State may take measures "to ensure the safety both of navigation and of the artificial islands, installations and structures" (art. 60(4)). All ships are obliged to respect safety zones and to comply with accepted standards regarding navigation (art. 60(6)).

Sakuya, Takahashi 1869-1920. Professor, Tokyo Naval College 1894-1900, Tokyo 1900-20. Principal works include *Cases on International Law during the Chino-Japanese War*; *Le droit international dans l'histoire du Japon*; and in Japanese, *Public International Law in War*; *Treatise on International Law*; *Public International Law in Peace*; *Principles of International Law*; *Digest of International Law in War*.

Salem Case *(USA v. Egypt) (1932) 2 R.I.A.A. 1161.* Salem, whose father had Persian nationality, was born in Egypt and became a US citizen by naturalization. In 1918, he was prosecuted before the Egyptian courts and deposited certain documents with the prosecuting authorities. He secured the discontinuance of the criminal proceedings on the grounds of his US nationality (in view of which he was not subject to the jurisdiction of the local courts), but did not recover the documents. The Mixed Courts established by the capitulatory régime in Egypt having dismissed proceedings brought by Salem for damages arising from the criminal proceedings taken against him and the retention of his documents, in 1931 the USA and Egypt concluded a special agreement *(142 L.N.T.S. 309)* submitting to arbitration the question of Egypt's liability on account of the treatment accorded to Salem. The tribunal *held* Egypt not liable, finding (1) that Salem had not obtained US citizenship by fraud, and the possible continuation of his Persian nationality did not entitle Egypt to oppose the right of the USA to take up his case; (2) although Salem had exhausted local remedies, and the right of diplomatic protection was not wholly excluded in cases within the jurisdiction of the Mixed Courts established by the capitulatory régime in Egypt, Egypt did not incur liability for the continuation of criminal proceedings against Salem after he had acquired US nationality, or for certain errors in the judicial proceedings in the Mixed Courts, which did not amount to a denial of justice in international law (for which there needed to be some exorbitant judicial injustice), particularly since the partially international character of those Courts made Egypt's responsibility for their acts less extensive than for purely Egyptian courts.

SALT *See* **disarmament.**

salvage Art. 2 of the Brussels Convention for the Unification of Certain Rules of Law Relating to Assistance and Salvage at Sea of 23 September 1910 *(212 C.T.S. 187)* provides that "[e]very act of assistance or salvage which has had a useful result gives a right to equitable renumeration." While the Convention does not define salvage, art. 1 declares that "[a]ssistance and salvage of seagoing vessels in danger, of any things on board, of freight and passage money" are to be treated as the same. The amount of remuneration, which must not exceed the value of the property salved (art. 2), is to be fixed by agreement between the parties or, failing agreement, by a court (art. 6). *See* Wildeboer, *The Brussels Salvage Convention* (1965), Kennedy and Rose, *The Law of Salvage* (6th ed.).

Sambiaggio Case *(Italy v. Venezuela) (1903) 10 R.I.A.A. 499.* Sambiaggio, an Italian citizen resident in Venezuela, alleged that he had suffered damage on account of property taken from him, and forced loans exacted on him, by revolutionary forces in Venezuela during a revolution which was ultimately unsuccessful. He presented a claim to the Italy-Venezuela Mixed Claims Commission established under Protocols of 17 February and 7 May 1903, which *held* (Ralston, umpire), in dismissing the claim, that in principle a State was not responsible for the acts of unsuccessful revolutionaries, since they were not agents of the government, were beyond the control of the government, and were dedicated to the destruction of the government; and that, although if the Venezuelan authorities had failed to exercise due diligence to prevent damage being inflicted by revolutionaries Venezuela should be held responsible, no such lack of diligence had been alleged or proved in this case.

San Francisco Conference Following the **Dumbarton Oaks Conference** among China, UK, US and USSR of August to October 1944, invitations were issued to 42 States to join the four Sponsoring Governments at San Francisco to conclude the constituent document of the United Nations. In all, fifty States (Argentina, Byelorussian SSR, Denmark and Ukrainian SSR being subsequently invited) attended the Conference which met from 25 April to 26 June 1945. The official records of the Conference are contained in *United Na-*

tions Conference for International Organization, Documents (U.N.C.I.O.). The UN Charter was signed on 26 June 1945, and entered into force on 24 October 1945.

San Juan Islands Arbitration *See **Pig War Arbitration**.*

San Marino While San Marino (area, 23 sq. miles; population, about 20,000) was described in earlier editions of *I Oppenheim* as a protectorate of Italy, the editor of the 8th edition had doubts, because San Marino had concluded treaties with States. This view was maintained in the 9th edition: *see I Oppenheim 271n*. In describing San Marino as a diminutive State, another authority contends that it "tends to fluctuate in a twilight region between independent and dependent international persons": Schwarzenberger and Brown, *A Manual of International Law* (6th ed.), 61. San Marino was not a member of the League of Nations, nor was it, until recently, a member of the United Nations, although it was a member of some of the Specialized Agencies (*e.g.*, UPU) and a party to the ICJ Statute (*see* GA Res. 806 (VIII) of 9 December 1953 and *186 U.N.T.S. 295*). However, San Marino was admitted to membership of the UN in 1992.

sanctions "Sanctions are measures taken in support of law. It is of the essence of law that sanctions are applied with and by the general authority, not by any individual. With the substitution of the word 'state' for the word 'individual,' this is true in principle, and ought to be true in fact, of the sanctions of international, as well as of national law. . . . Not all sanctions are punitive; some are preventive": Royal Institute of International Affairs, *International Sanctions* (1938), 5. Some authorities have suggested that international law is be a specific form of law in which "there is neither a similar necessity for sanctions (desirable though it may be that international law should be supported by them, nor a similar prospect for their safe and efficacious use" Hart, *The Concept of Law* (2nd ed.), 214. Nevertheless, other writers regard sanction as an essential element in ensuring state compliance with international law. *See*, for example, Damrosch, Enforcing International Law Through Non-Forcible Means, *269 Hague Recueil 13 (1997)*.

In relation to the maintenance of international peace and security, the United Nations Security Council may, pursuant to Chapter VII of the UN Charter, invoke art 41 (measures not involving armed force, including interruption of economic relations and communications and severance of diplomatic relations) and 42 ("such action by air, sea or land forces as may be necessary") against a state guilty of a threat to the peace, breach of the peace or an act of aggression; such are generally referred to as collective sanctions: *see* **peace, threat to**; **peace, breach of**. However, "[i]f the word 'sanctions' be taken in the larger sense of measures, procedures, and expedients for exerting pressure on a state to comply with its international legal obligations, then the above-mentioned provisions of the UN Charter are not exhaustive of the sanctions which may become operative in different areas of international law.": Shearer, *Starke's International Law*, (11th ed.) 25. Thus, "[t]he sanctions of international law appear to be a mixture, in proportions varying according to the circumstances, of the forces of public opinion, habit, good faith, the possibility of self-help, expediency, and the combination of reciprocal advantage when the law is followed and fear of retaliation when it is broken": Bishop, *International Law* (3rd ed.), 10.

Sapphire International Petroleums Limited v. National Iranian Oil Company *(1963) 35 I.L.R. 136*. Sapphire International Petroleums Limited (Sapphire) and the National Iranian Oil Company (NIOC) were parties to an agreement making joint arrangements for the conduct of petroleum operations in Iran. Differences arose between them as to their observance of their contractual obligations. In 1961, NIOC repudiated the agreement, and enforced against Sapphire the penalty provision of $350,000 provided for in the agreement.

Sapphire referred the dispute to arbitration under the agreement. NIOC refused to co-operate in the arbitration procedure. *Held* by Cavin, sole arbitrator, sitting in Lausanne, that (1) the procedural law of the arbitration was that of the seat of the arbitration, and the substantive law applicable to the agreement was the principles of law generally recognized by civilized nations; (2) NIOC had acted in breach of the agreement, which released Sapphire from further obligations under it; and (3) Sapphire was entitled to a refund of the penalty payment and to compensation (including compensation for loss of profit assessed *ex aequo et bono*) for NIOC's failure to perform the agreement.

satellite   Art. 1 (iii) of the Convention Relating to the Distribution of Programme-Carrying Signals Transmitted by Satellite of 21 May 1974 *(13 I.L.M. 1447 (1974))* defines "satellite" for the purposes of that Convention as being any device in extraterrestrial space capable of transmitting signals. This type of satellite may also be referred to as an "active" satellite, as opposed to a "passive" satellite, which merely reflects signals. The notion of satellite being closely connected with telecommunications, it is a narrower concept than **space object**. Satellites may not be used for the positioning of weapons of mass destruction around the earth (art. IV, **Outer Space Treaty**) but there is no direct prohibition on satellites carrying other weapons. Satellites may be used for the purposes of military observation although the UN General Assembly enacted 15 Principles relating to remote sensing of the Earth from Space (Resolution 41/65 of 3 December 1986) which purport to ensure, *inter alia*, that remote sensing is conducted for the benefit of all states (Principle II) and in accordance with international law (Principle III). Satellite broadcasting is subject to some international regulation; **ITU** Regulations governing space telecommunications: Convention of 21 May 1974, *supra*; *Principles on Direct Television Broadcasting* in GA Res. 37/92 of 4 February 1983; and a number of international or regional agencies exist for the provision of satellite communications (**Intersputnik, Intercosmos, European Space Agency, Inmarsat**, Arab-sat). *See* Cristol, *Space Law* (1991).

satisfaction   This is a general term having no precise legal meaning in international law. In its widest sense, it is used to describe any form of redress that is available under international law to make good a wrong done by one State to another: *Maal Claim (1903) 10 R.I.A.A. 730*; *Janes Claim (1926) 4 R.I.A.A. 82*; *Mallén Claim (1927) 4 R.I.A.A. 173*. In a narrower sense, it refers to measures other than **reparation** proper, such as punitive **damages**, apology *(I'm Alone Case (1935) 3 R.I.A.A. 1609*; cf. also the demands of Belgium in the *Borchgrave Case* (Preliminary Objections) *(1937) P.C.I.J., Ser. A / B, No. 72)*, punishment of the guilty persons *(ibid)*, salute to the flag, a declaration made by an international tribunal *(Corfu Channel Case (Merits) 1949 I.C.J. Rep. 45*; *Carthage Case (1913) 11 R.I.A.A. 449*; *Manouba Case (1913) 11 R.I.A.A. 463)* or an acknowledgement given by the guilty party *(I'm Alone Case (1935) 3 R.I.A.A. 1609)* to the effect that a wrongful act has been committed. *See* Brownlie, *State Responsibility: Part I* (1980), 208-209.

Satow, Sir Ernest M.   1843-1929. British diplomat. Member, PCA 1906-12. Principal work: *A Guide to Diplomatic Practice* (1917; 5th ed. 1979).

Savarkar Case   (France v. UK) (1911) Scott, *Hague Court Reports*, 275. Savarkar was being transported on a British merchant vessel from England to India for trial on a criminal charge. Prior to the arrival of the vessel at Marseilles, arrangements had been made between the British and French police to prevent his escape. When the vessel called at Marseilles he escaped to the shore. He was captured by a French police officer who returned him to the vessel which sailed with the fugitive on board the following day. Subsequently, France demanded his return on the grounds that his delivery to the British officers on board the vessel was contrary to international law. Upon the UK's refusal to comply, the matter was, under a *compromis* of 25 October 1910, submitted to the arbitration of a tribunal composed of 5 members of the Permanent Court of Arbitration. *Held* that the UK was not required to restore Savarkar to France. Although the French officer who arrested him may have been ignorant of his identity, there was no recourse to fraud or force to obtain possession of Savarkar, and there was not, in the circumstances of his arrest and delivery to the British authorities and of his removal to India, anything in the nature of a violation of the sovereignty of France. Those who took part in the matter acted in good faith and had not thought of doing anything unlawful. The conduct of the French police officer not having been disclaimed by his superiors before the vessel left Marseilles, the British police might naturally have believed that he had acted in accordance with his instructions or that his conduct had been approved. Although an irregularity had been committed by the arrest of Savarkar and by his being handed over to the British police, no rule of international law imposed, in the circumstances of the case, any obligation on the State which has a prisoner in its custody to restore him because of a mistake committed by the foreign agent who delivered him up to that State.

scales of assessment Scales of assessment are used by most international organizations to determine the percentage of expenditure to be contributed by each Member. The expenses of the UN are broadly apportioned according to capacity to pay: GA Res. 14 (I). GA Res. 2190 (XXI) recommended that the Specialized Agencies harmonize their scales with the UN scale. In practice, the UN system operates minimum and maximum contributions which define the spread of the scale. The minimum is now 0.01% (GA Res. 31/95) and the maximum 25% (GA Res. 2961 B (XXVII)), being also the maximum permitted by the United States Congress (*see 12 I.L.M. 163 (1973)*), the US being the largest single contributor. The UN Scale of Assessment is marked out with the help of the **Committee on Contributions.** *See* Schermers and Blokker, *International Institutional Law* (3rd ed.), 610-620.

Scelle, Georges 1878-1961. French public servant and Professor, Dijon and Geneva (1929-32). Member, PCA (1950-61). Principal works: *Le Pacte des Nations et sa liaison avec les traités de paix* (1919); *Précis de droit des gens* (1932 and 1934); *Théorie et pratique de la fonction executive en droit international* (1936).

Schachter, Oscar 1915- . UN Official 1944-52; Director-General, UN Legal Division 1952-66. Director, UNITAR 1966-75. Professor, Columbia 1975- . Principal works include *The Relations of Law, Politics and Action in the United Nations* (1964); *Towards Wider Acceptance of U.N. Treaties* (with Nawaz, 1971); *Sharing the World's Resources* (1977); *International Law, Cases and Materials* (with Henkin, Pugh and Smit, 1980; 3rd ed., 1993); *International Law in Theory and Practice* (1985, rev. ed. 1991) *United Nations Legal Order* (with Joyner, 1994).

Schücking, Walther 1875-1935. Professor, Marburg (Germany). Member, PCIJ 1930-35. Principal work: *Das Werk vom Haag* (1912).

scheduled (international) air service The **Chicago Convention** on International Civil Aviation 1944 *(15 U.N.T.S. 295)* does not define this term, hence the ICAO Council has put forward for (non-binding) guidance a definition of such a service as being "a series of flights that possess all of the following characteristics: (a) it passes through the airspace of the territory of more than one State; (b) it is performed by aircraft for the transport of passengers, mail or cargo for remuneration in such a manner that each flight is open to . . . members of the public; (c) it is operated so as to serve traffic between the same two or more points, either (i) according to a published timetable, or (ii) with flights so regular and frequent that they constitute a recognizably systematic series": ICAO Council, *Definition of a Scheduled International Air Service,* 10 May 1952 *(ICAO Doc. 7278-C/841).* Under art. 6 of the Chicago Convention, the special permission or other authorization of a State is required before a scheduled air service may be operated over or into its territory. Scheduled international air services are regulated principally by bilateral agreement. The route and airports used by an international air service may be designated by the receiving State (art. 68). Under the International Air Services Transit Agreement, signed concurrently with the Chicago Convention, parties grant each other the right of **overflight** for their scheduled services. Adherence to this latter agreement has always been fairly limited.

Schwarzenberger, Georg 1908-87. Lecturer, Reader and Professor, London 1938-75. Principal works include: *The League of Nations and World Order* (1936); *Power Politics: A Study of World Society* (1940; 3rd ed. 1964); *International Law and Totalitarian Lawlessness* (1943); *International Law as Applied by International Courts and Tribunals,* Vol. 1 (3rd ed. 1957), Vol. II (1968), Vol. III (1976); *A Manual of International Law* (1947; 6th ed. with Brown 1976); *The Legality of Nuclear Weapons* (1958), *The Frontiers of International Law* (1962); *The Inductive Approach to International Law* (1965); *Foreign Investments and International Law* (1969); *International Law and Order* (1971); *The Dynamics of International Law* (1976).

Schwebel, Stephen M. 1929- . Professor, Harvard 1959-61; Johns Hopkins 1967-81. State Department (Assistant Legal Adviser and subsequently Deputy Legal Adviser) 1961-1981. Member, ILC 1977-81; judge, ICJ 1981-2000, vice-president, 1994-97, and president 1997-2000. Principal works: *The Secretary-General of the United Nations: His Political Powers and Practice* (1952); *The Effectiveness of International Decisions* (1971) *Justice in International Law: Selected Writings* (1994).

Scott, James Brown 1866-1943. American lawyer, public servant and law teacher. Professor, Southern California 1896-8, Illinois 1897-1903, Columbia 1903-6, George Washington 1906-11, Johns Hopkins 1908-16, Georgetown 1921-40. Principal works include *Casebook on International Law* (1902; 3rd ed. (with Jaeger) 1937); founder *A.J.I.L.* (1906-); general editor, *Classics of International Law; An International Court of Justice* (1916); *The Status of an International Court of Justice* (1916).

SCSL *See* **Special Court for Sierra Leone**.

SDRs *See* **Special Drawing Rights**.

sea lanes and traffic separation schemes Sea lanes and traffic separation schemes are now imposed on shipping in narrow seas in a number of parts of the world. The power and right to impose such requirements is now sanctioned by the UN Convention on the Law of the Sea 1982 *(1833 U.N.T.S. 3),* arts. 22 (in relation to **innocent passage**), 41 (**transit passage**), 53 (**archipelagic sea lanes passage**).

seabed and subsoil The seabed and subsoil of the **territorial sea** is subject to the sovereignty of the coastal State: art. 2 of the Geneva Convention on the Territorial Sea, etc. 1958 *(516 U.N.T.S. 205).* The seabed and subsoil of the **continental shelf** is subject to the sovereign rights of the coastal State for the purpose of exploration and exploitation: arts. 1 and 2(1) of the Geneva Convention on the Continental Shelf 1958 *(499 U.N.T.S. 311).* These rules are confirmed in the UN Convention on the Law of the Sea 1982 *(1833 U.N.T.S. 3)* (art. 2 and arts. 56(1)(a), 76(1) and 77(1)), which further provides that the **international**

sea-bed area ("the sea-bed and ocean floor and the subsoil thereof, beyond the limits of national jurisdiction": art. 1(1)) is the **common heritage of mankind** (art. 136).

seabed area, international *See* **International Seabed Area**.

Seabed Arms Control Treaty The prohibition of the emplacement of nuclear weapons and other weapons of mass destruction on the seabed and the ocean floor and in the subsoil thereof, contained in article 1 of the Seabed Arms Control Treaty of 11 February *(10 I.L.M. 145 (1971))*, which entered into force on 18 May 1972, covers all implantations, whether or not within the 12 mile zone, save that the undertakings do not extend to the coastal State in respect of its own territorial waters (arts. I and II). Verification procedures are laid down in art. III. Arts V and IX contain the usual provisions regarding continuation of general negotiations on disarmament and the permissibility of nuclear-free zones. Art. VII provides for a review conference to be held five years after the entry into force of the treaty. Review conferences have been held in Geneva in 1977, 1983, 1989, and 1996. All have confirmed that the Treaty continues to be an important and effective arms control measure. *See* **disarmament**.

Seabed Authority, International *See* **International Seabed Authority**.

seal, on diplomatic bag Art. 27(4) of the Vienna Convention on Diplomatic Relations 1961 *(8500 U.N.T.S. 95)* requires that "[t]he packages constituting the **diplomatic bag** must bear visible external marks of their character." In his evidence to the UK's Foreign Affairs Committee in the wake of the **Fletcher** and **Dikko incidents** in 1984, the Secretary of State noted that "under general international practice there are two visible external marks: firstly a seal in lead or wax marked with the official stamp of by the competent authority of the sending state or the diplomatic mission, and secondly, a tag, or stick-on label identifying the contents." *House of Commons Foreign Affairs Committee, First Report: The Abuse of Diplomatic Immunities and Privileges, H.C. Paper 127 (1984-85), p. 50 of Evidence. See also* Denza, *Diplomatic Law* (2nd ed.), 191-2.

seat, of diplomatic mission Art. 12 of the Vienna Convention on Diplomatic Relations 1961 *(500 U.N.T.S. 95)* provides: "The sending state may not, without the prior express consent of the receiving state establish offices forming part of the mission in localities other than those in which the mission itself is established." "Although neither customary international law nor Article 12 requires that diplomatic missions should be established at the seat of government of the receiving state, such a requirement is sometimes imposed by national law or by administrative decree": Denza, *Diplomatic Law* (2nd ed.), 85. US practice, for example, requires foreign missions to reside in Washington (*See* Moore, *Digest of International Law*, Vol . 4, § 645).

SEATO *See* **South-East Asia Treaty Organization**.

secession of territory This connotes the establishment of one or more new States on territory formerly part of a predecessor State without bringing about the complete disappearance thereof (*e.g.*, the separation of Belgium from the Netherlands in 1830, of the Irish Free State from the UK in 1922, of Bangladesh from Pakistan in 1971). One form of secession which has acquired particular importance in the UN era is the attainment of independence by non-self-governing territories as a result of the process of **decolonization**. *See* Crawford, *The Creation of States in International Law* (1979), Chap. 9.

Second Generation (human rights) A descriptor for economic and social rights, being later in time developing, less widely acknowledged and accepted and more controversial than **First Generation** human rights. Archetypically, these rights are enumerated in the **Economic, Social and Cultural Rights, International Covenant on** 1966 *(993 U.N.T.S. 3)*. *See also* **Third Generation** human rights.

Second World A term of no contemporary relevance, connoting the developed Socialist States of Eastern Europe, including the USSR, with centrally-planned economies. *See also* **First World**; **Third World**; **Fourth World**.

Secretariat "Secretariats have become central organs in all international organizations. Loveday [*Reflections on International Administration* (1956), 23-30] compares them with national ministries, a comparison which seems sound, provided it is remembered that international organizations have much less power than national governments": Schermers and Blokker, *International Institutional Law,* (3rd. ed.), 302. The term secretariat, and its present synonymity with an independent international civil service, dates from the League of Nations. "The single most important characteristic of an international civil service is its international character. This constitutes a cornerstone underpinning the impartiality of the activities of international organizations. The Secretariat's international character is safeguarded in the constituent instruments of most international organizations, which enjoin the chief administrative officers and their staff to, in effect, acknowledge this primary allegiance to the organization and generally state the corresponding obligation of all members to respect this international character. These provisions are often supplemented by the staff regulations and by the oath taken by staff members of a number of organizations upon appointment": Sands and Klein *Bowett's Law of International Institutions,* (5th ed.), 309-10.

Within the UN, art. 97 of the Charter states that the Secretariat "shall comprise a Secretary-General and such staff as the Organization may require." Members of the Secretariat are not to seek or receive instructions from any government, and are to "refrain from any action which might reflect on their position as international officials responsible only to the Organization" (art. 100(1)). The member States undertake to respect the exclusively international character of the Secretary-General and staff and not to seek to influence them in the discharge of their responsibilities (art. 100(2)). The General Assembly has drawn up regulations under art. 101(1) governing the Secretariat: see the UN Staff Regulations (Res. 590 (VI), as amended) and the Statute of the Administrative Tribunal of the United Nations (Res. 351A (IV), as amended). *See generally* Schwebel, The International Character of the Secretariat of the United Nations, *(1953) 30 B.Y.I.L. 71*; Langrod, *The International Civil Service* (1963); Amerasinghe, *The Law of the International Civil* Service (2 vols., 2nd ed.); Schermers and Blokker, *supra,* 300-368; Sands and Klein, *supra,* 302-314.

Secretary-General Art. 7 of the Charter establishes the **Secretariat** as a principal organ of the United Nations. However, "[I]t is upon the Secretary-General, not upon the Secretariat, that the Charter confers definite functions. . . . The members of the staff of the Secretariat . . . are organs of the United Nations but subordinate to the Secretary-General, just as the employees of a ministry are organs of the State but subordinate to the Cabinet Minister": Kelsen, *The Law of the United Nations* (1950), 136-137, quoted with approval in Schwebel, *The Secretary-General of the United Nations* (1952), 245n. The Secretary-General is appointed by the General Assembly upon the recommendation of the Security Council (art. 97). In the four decades since it was established, the UN has had 7 Secretaries-General; Trygve Lie; Dag Hammarskjold, U Thant, Kurt Waldheim, Javier Pèrez de Cuèllar, Boutros Boutros-Ghali and, currently, Kofi Annan (*see* individual biographical entries). Perhaps self-evidently, the influence of the Secretariat depends to a considerable extent on the personality of the Secretary-General, but the ability of the Secretary-General to influence events has also been affected by the changing nature of international relationships, notwithstanding the broad power to seize the Security Council of any matters which in his opinion may threaten the maintenance of international peace and security (art. 99).

The Secretary-General is the Chief Administrative Officer of the Organization (art. 97). He acts as Secretary-General in all meetings of the General Assembly, the Security Council, ECOSOC and the Trusteeship Council (art. 98). In language which is common to all international organizations, art. 100 stipulates that the Secretary-General and the staff (who are appointed by him under regulations established by the Assembly: art 101) shall not seek or receive instructions from any government or from any other authority external to the organization. Members of the UN undertake a reciprocal obligation to respect the exclusively international character of the responsibilities of the Secretary-General and staff and not to seek to influence them. "In practice, the role of the Secretary-General has extended beyond the various provisions of the Charter. In particular, the Secretary-General has an important role in exercising good offices in order to resolve or contain international crises. Additionally, the Secretary-General is in an important position to mark or possibly influence developments. [See, for example, Boutros-Ghali, *An Agenda For Peace* (1992)]": Shaw, *International Law* (4th ed.), 834. *See generally* Schwebel, *The Secretary-General of the United Nations* (1952); Bailey, *The Secretariat of the United Nations* (1962); Meron, *The United Nations Secretariat* (1978); Sands and Klein, *Bowett's Law of International Institutions* (5th. ed.), 87-96.

sector claims   These are assertions of territorial sovereignty in **polar regions** by States adjacent to the regions, based on the concept of contiguity and quantified by tracing the meridians of longitude from the extremities of the States' territories to the Poles. It appears that sector claims in themselves give no title to territory: Brownlie, *Principles of Public International Law* (5th ed. 1998), 148-9. In any case, the North Pole is merely frozen high seas, and it is to be doubted, in view of the terms and import of the UN Convention on the Law of the Sea 1982 *(1833 U.N.T.S. 3),* if any State can acquire title to frozen high seas; and while art. 4 of the **Antarctic Treaty** 1959 *(402 U.N.T.S. 71)* safeguards existing positions regarding territorial claims in the South Polar region, that same article precludes the parties making new claims or enlarging existing claims while the Treaty is in force.

Security Council   Established as a principal organ of the UN (art. 7 of the Charter), the Security Council consists of 15 member states, including the five **permanent members** (China, France, Russia (formerly the USSR), the UK and the USA). The non-permanent members are elected by the General Assembly for a term of two years on a rolling basis, "due regard being specially paid in the first instance to the contribution of members of the United Nations to the maintenance of international peace and security and to the other purposes of the Organization and also to equitable geographical distribution (art. 23). The Security Council has primary responsibility for the maintenance of international peace and security (art. 24). Specific powers are granted to the Security Council in Chapters VI, VII, VIII and XII. (*See* **pacific settlement of disputes**; **peace, threat to**; **peace, breach of**; **peacekeeping**; **regional arrangements**; **trusteeship system**). All decisions of the Security Council are binding on the member States of the UN (art. 25). Voting procedure in the Security Council is governed by art. 27. Each member of the Council has one vote. Decisions on procedural matters are passed by the affirmative vote of nine members; decisions on all other matters are passed by the affirmative vote of nine members including the concurring votes of the permanent members. (*See* **veto**; **voting**; **double veto**; and **Yalta Formula**). As to the relationship with the powers of the General Assembly, see **Uniting for Peace Resolutions**.

In terms of the maintenance of international peace and security, the role of the Security Council has been severely limited by (mis)use of the **veto**, particularly during the Cold War period. Thus, between 1945 and 1990, the Security Council authorized the use of force in terms of Chapter VII only twice, in Korea in 1950 (SC Res. 83 and 84) and in Rhodesia in 1965 (SC Res.221). However, since 1990, the Security Council has been considerably more willing and able to invoke Chapter VII, including the authorization of the use of force in relation to Kuwait (SC Res. 678 (1990)); Bosnia (SC Res. 770 (1992)); Somalia (SC Res. 837 (1993)); Rwanda (SC Res. 929(1994)) (For a summary of these and other measures see Shaw, *International Law* (4th ed.), 858-76). The Security Council has also been willing to use its broad powers in a number of different ways, for example by creating the **International Criminal Tribunal for the Former Yugoslavia** (SC Res. 827) and the **International Criminal Tribunal for Rwanda** (SC Res. 955). (The legality of the creation of these tribunals was established in the ***Tadic Case*** ICTY *(Case #IT-94-1-A)*). Nevertheless, the role of the Security Council in the maintenance of international peace and security has more recently been called into question in relation to the **NATO** intervention in Kosovo (1999) which was justified on the grounds of **humanitarian intervention**, and the US-led interventions in Afghanistan (2001) justified on the grounds of **self-defense**; and Iraq (2003) justified on the grounds of pre-emptive self-defense (*see* **Bush Doctrine**)

sedentary species In terms of art. 77(4) of the UN Convention on the Law of the Sea 1982 *(1833 U.N.T.S. 3)*, sedentary species are included in the natural resources which fall to the coastal State as part of its rights to the **continental shelf**, such sedentary species being defined as "organisms which, at the harvestable stage, either are immobile on or under the seabed or are unable to move except in constant physical contact with the seabed or the subsoil."

seisen In the practice of the ICJ a distinction is drawn between jurisdiction and seisen (the state of being seised of a dispute), the latter "depending on the carrying out of the correct procedural steps for bringing the dispute before the Court, as prescribed by the Statute and the Rules of Court. Admittedly, if a tribunal has not been duly seised it is incompetent to hear the case. But it does not follow that because a tribunal is duly seised . . . it possesses on that account substantive jurisdiction and competence to hear and determine [the case] on the merits": Fitzmaurice, *The Law and Procedure of the International Court of Justice* (1985), Vol. 2, 440-1. See ***Nottebohm Case*** *(Preliminary Objection) 1953 I.C.J. Rep. 111.*

SELA *See* **Latin-American Economic System**.

Selden, John 1584-1654. English lawyer, famous for his *Mare Clausum* (1635), a reply to *Mare Liberum* by Grotius. *See* Fletcher, John Selden and his Contribution to International Law, *(1934) 19 T.G.S. 1.*

self-defense (1) Under customary law, it is generally understood that the correspondence between the USA and UK of 24 April 1841, arising out of the ***Caroline Incident***, *(Moore, Digest of International Law, Vol. 2, 25)* expresses the rules on self-defense: self-defense is competent only where the "necessity of that self-defense is instant, overwhelming, and leaving no choice of means, and no moment for deliberation . . . [and] the act, justified by the necessity of self-defense, must be limited by that necessity, and kept clearly within it." These principles were further elucidated in the ***Corfu Channel Case*** *1949 I.C.J. Rep. 4. See* Jennings, The Caroline and McLeod Cases, *32 A.J.I.L. 82 (1938)*; Tucker, Reprisals and Self-Defense: The Customary Law, *66 A.J.I.L. 586 (1972).*

(2) Art. 51 of the UN Charter provides that "[n]othing in the present Charter shall impair the inherent right of individual or collective self-defence if an armed attack occurs against a Member of the United Nations. . . ." The relationship between the right under customary international law and art. 51 of the UN Charter has caused considerable debate. See, for example, Jessup, *A Modern Law of Nations* (1948), 166-7; Stone, *Legal Controls of International Conflicts* (2nd Imp., revised), 245. However, the International Court of Justice in **Military and Paramilitary Activities in and against Nicaragua (Merits)** *1986 I.C.J. Rep. 14*, made it clear that the right of self-defense under international law exists alongside the provision in art. 51 of the Charter: "it cannot be presumed that article 51 is a provision which 'subsumes and supervenes' customary international law." (at 95). It has been argued that customary international law allows for the possibility of anticipatory self-defense (*see*, for example, Franck, *Fairness in International Law and Institutions* (1995), 267) or even pre-emptive self-defense (*see* **Bush Doctrine**). Whether such rights exist appears unsettled; however, it is clear that the legality of a self-defense action, whether in response to an armed attack or in anticipation of it, is dependent upon the key concepts of necessity and proportionality. Thus, in its advisory opinion on the **Legality of the Threat or Use of Nuclear Weapons** *1996 I.C.J. Rep 226* the ICJ made it clear that "[t]he submission of the exercise of the right of self-defense to the conditions of necessity and proportionality is a rule of customary international law." However, "[q]uite what will be necessary and proportionate will depend on the circumstances of the case. It also appears inevitable that it will be the state contemplating such action that will first have to make that determination, although it will be subject to consideration by the international community as a whole and more specifically by the Security Council under the terms of article 51": Shaw, *International Law* (4th ed.), 791.

See generally, Bowett, *Self-Defence in International Law* (1958); Brownlie, *International Law and the Use of Force by States* (1964); Schachter, *International Law in Theory and Practice* (1991), Chap. 8; Gray, *International Law and the Use of Force* (2001), Chaps. 4 and 5. *See also* **collective self-defense**.

self-determination While prior to 1945 the term "self-determination" was employed invariably in a political context (*see* Pomerance, the United States and Self-Determination: Perspectives on the Wilsonian Conception, *70 A.J.I.L. 1 (1976)*), it formed no part of general international law at that time (*see I Oppenheim 282-5*). The principle of self-determination receives only the briefest mention in the UN Charter (*see* arts. 1(2) and 55). On 14 December 1960, the General Assembly adopted the Declaration on the Granting of Independence to Colonial Countries and Peoples (GA Res. 1514(XV)), which declared that "[a]ll peoples have the right to self-determination; by virtue of that right they freely determine their political status and freely pursue their economic, social and cultural development" (art. 2). Similar assertions appeared in other declarations, *e.g.*, Principles of International Law concerning **Friendly Relations** and Cooperation among States in accordance with the Charter of the United Nations of 24 October 1970 (G.A. Res. 2625(XXV)). They likewise appear in a number of international agreements, *e.g.*, common art. 1(1) of the International Covenants on **Civil and Political Rights** and on **Economic, Social and Cultural Rights** of 16 December 1966 *(999 U.N.T.S. 171 and 993 U.N.T.S. 3)*; Principle VIII of the (non-binding) **Helsinki Agreement** of 1 August 1975 *(14 I.L.M. 1293 (1975))*. Self-determination is also referred to in judicial decisions, *e.g.*, **Barcelona Traction Co. Case (Second Phase)** *1970 I.C.J. Rep. 3* at 311-3; **Namibia Opinion** *1971 I.C.J. Rep. 3* at 31. In the **Western Sahara Opinion** *1975 I.C.J. Rep. 12* at 33 the ICJ, citing with approval the Friendly Relations Declaration, Principle IX (b) of which declares that "integration should be the result of the freely expressed wishes of the territory's peoples acting with full knowledge of the change in their status, their wishes having been expressed through informed and democratic processes, impartially conducted and based on universal adult suffrage," assumed the right of the population of Western Sahara to determine their future political status by their own freely expressed will. Previously many Western commentators inclined to the view that self-determination is a political or moral principle rather than a legal right (e.g. Schwarzenberger and Brown, *Manual of International Law* (6th ed.), 59). However, in the **East Timor Case** *1995 I.C.J. Rep. 90* at 102 the Court declared that "Portugal's assertion that the right of peoples to self-determination, as it evolved from the Charter and UN practice, has an *erga omnes* character and is irreproachable ... [It is] one of the essential principles of contemporary international law." In spite of this, an important qualification to the right of self-determination has been established by a Chamber of the International Court of Justice in **Burkino Faso/Mali FrontierDispute Case** *1986 I.C.J. Rep. 554* which held that self-determination was in effect subordinated to the principle of *uti possidetis* in the case of boundaries of former colonial territories. *See* also **self-determination and secession**.

The principle has been extended, beyond this political context, to the economic context, creating an asserted right of economic self-determination. *See* the Declarations on Permanent Sovereignty over Natural Resources of 14 December 1962 and of 17 December 1973 (GA Res. 1803 (XVII) and 3171 (XXVII)), Declaration on the Establishment of a New International Economic Order of 1 May 1974 (GA Res. 3201 S-VI), Charter of Economic Rights and Duties of States of 12 December 1974 (G.A. Res. 3281 (XXIX)). In the economic context, the principle is not accepted as a right under international law by most Western States.

See generally Rigo Suredo, *The Evolution of the Right of Self-Determination,* (1973); Umozuritce, *Self-Determination in International Law* (1972); Higgins, *Problems and Process: International Law and How We Can Use It* (1994), Chap. 7; Cassese, *Self-Determination of Peoples: A LegalReappraisal* (1999); Musgrave, *Self-Determination and National Minorities* (2000); Raic, *Statehood and the Law of Self-Determination* (2003). *See* also **minorities**; **indigenous peoples**.

self-determination and secession   One of the principal difficulties in relation to the exercise o f the right of **self determination** is in the identification of what is a people for the purpose of exercising the right to self determination. The principle clearly applies to colonial peoples, for which it was originally intended. In such cases, the right of self-determination has been used to bring about the independence of colonies and trust territories since the 1960s. However, it would appear that the right of self-determination cannot apply once a colony or trust territory has achieved independence. *See* **Burkino Faso/Mali Frontier Dispute Case** *1986 I.C.J. Rep. 554* in which it was held by a Chamber of the ICJ that self-determination was in effect subordinated to the principle of *uti possidetis* in the case of boundaries of former colonial territories. The question remains, however, as to whether the principle applies to the people of a territory within a State, not ruled colonially from abroad and with a role in their own government (*e.g.*, the people of the Basque region of Spain, Scotland and Quebec)? "The emphasis in all the relevant instruments, and in the state practice . . . on the importance of territorial integrity, means that 'peoples' is to be understood in the sense of *all* the peoples of a given territory . . . minorities *as such* do not have a right of self-determination. That means, in effect, that they have no right to secession, to independence or to join with comparable groups in other states": Higgins, *Problems and Process: International Law and How We Can Use It* (1994), 124. A similar question arises in relation to people implanted on territory outside the State (*e.g.*, the people of the Falklands/Malvinas Islands) where the question of sovereignty over the territory is at issue. However, "until it is determined where territorial sovereignty lies, it is impossible to see if the inhabitants have a right of self-determination." Higgins, *supra*, 127.

self-executing treaty A treaty can be described as self-executing if its provisions are automatically, and without any formal or specific act of incorporation by State authorities, part of the law of the land and enforceable before municipal courts. A number of States recognize this quality in treaties, including Argentina, France, Belgium, Greece, Mexico, Spain, the Netherlands, Russia and USA. Cf. UK, where a treaty can have no internal legal effect without "enabling" legislation: *The Parlement Belge (1880) 5 P.D. 197*; *Walker v. Baird [1892] A.C. 491*; *Republic of Italy v. Hambro's Bank [1950] 1 All E.R. 430*; *I.R.C. v. Collco Dealings Ltd. [1962] A.C. 1*. In the US, in the classic case of *Foster and Elam v. Neilson 27 U.S. (2 Pet.) 253 (1829)*, the position was expressed thus: "A treaty is in its nature a contract between two nations, not a *legislative* act . . . [the US] constitution declares a treaty to be the law of the land. It is, consequently, to be regarded in courts of justice as equivalent to an act of the legislature, wherever it operates of itself without the aid of any legislative provision. But when the terms of the stipulation import a contract, when either of the parties engages to perform a particular act, the treaty addresses itself to the political, not the judicial department; and the legislature must execute the contract before it can become a rule for the Court." *U.S. v. Percheman 32 U.S. (7 Pet.) 51 (1833)*; *See also Adye v. Robertson 112 U.S. 580 (1884)*; *Bacardi Corp. of America v. Domenech 311 U.S. 150 (1940)*; *Clark v. Allen, 331 U.S. 503 (1947)*; *Sei Fujii v. California 217 P. 2d 481 (1950)*.

It appears that the definition of a self-executing treaty "may not be open to generalization for purposes of international law": Evans, Self-Executing Treaties in the United States, *(1953) 30 B.Y.I.L. 178* at 194. Whether a treaty is self-executing "depends on the intent of the treaty maker as expressed in the treaty. To determine this intent we must consider the language of the treaty, looking for words that are legislative in form and meaning. Also, we must look for previous cases involving the same type of treaty, and finally we should investigate the circumstances surrounding the making of the treaty": Henry, When is a Treaty Self-Executing, *27 Mich. L. Rev. 776* at 785 *(1929)*. *See Restatement, Third, Foreign Relations Law of the United States, § 154*.

In the **European Union** there exists a similar concept, described as direct effect, whereby provisions of EU law, be they the treaties themselves or measures taken under the treaties, may automatically be part of the law of the member States and enforceable in the courts of these States. See, in particular, *Van Gend en Loos., Case 26/62, [1963] E.C.R. 1*. See Craig and De Burca, *EU Law* (3rd ed.).

self-help This term relates to measures taken by a State in response to unfriendly and illegal acts by another State. If the initial act is unfriendly and the response not contrary to international law, the response is called **retorsion**; if the initial act is illegal and the response would otherwise be contrary to international law, the response is called **reprisal**. Art. 2(3) and 2(4) of the UN Charter limits self-help measures, by requiring States to settle disputes by peaceful means and to refrain from the threat or use of force against the territorial integrity or political independence of any State, or in any other manner inconsistent with the Purposes of the United Nations (set out in art. 1). Cf. **retaliation**.

self-judging reservation *See* **automatic reservation**.

self-preservation "As a rule, all states are under a mutual duty to respect on another's sovereignty, and are bound not to violate one another's independence. Exceptionally, however, a state may in certain circumstances violate another state's territory. . . . [A] principal exception was formerly regarded as covering violations for the purpose of self-preservation, it being widely maintained that every state had a fundamental right of self-preservation. But this alleged right, if it ever existed, was often a barely colourable excuse for violations of another state's sovereignty. If every state really had a *right* of self-preservation, all the states would have the duty to admit, suffer, and endure every violation done to one another in self-preservation. The inviolability of a state's territory is now so firmly and peremptorily established by Article 2(4) of the Charter of the United Nations, and the prohibition of aggression and other unlawful uses of armed force so fundamental a rule of international law, that self-preservation can no longer be invoked to justify such violations: *I Oppenheim 416*. The use of force by a State is often justified by a plea of **self-help** or **necessity**, and it seems that there is no clear-cut distinction between these three pleas and all would be equally illegal.

semi-sovereign *See* **State**.

separate opinion Art. 95(2) of the Rules of Court of the ICJ permits a judge to attach to the judgment an "individual opinion" (frequently referred to as a separate opinion), whether he dissents from the majority or not. "The generalized responsibility of the Judge . . . puts an emphasis on collegiality. I do not believe that Court Judgments are 'weakened' by separate or dissenting opinions. A Judgement if as good or as bad as the reasoning it relies on. A poor Judgment will be no more persuasive by virtue of unanimity." Higgins, Reflections from the International Court of Justice, in Evans, *International Law* (2003). *See* Anand, *The Role of Individual and Dissenting Opinions in International Adjudication* (1967).

Serbian Loans Case *(France v. Serb-Croat-Slovene State) (1929) P.C.I.J. Ser. A, No. 20*. Between 1895 and 1913, certain Serbian loans were issued in France. French holders of the bonds of these loans claimed a right to payment of interest and redemption in gold currency; the Serb-Croat-Slovene Government claimed only to be bound to make payment in French paper currency. By a special agreement of 19 April 1928, the French and Serbian Governments submitted the dispute to the PCIJ which *held* (9 to 3) that (1) although the strict terms of the special agreement referred to the Court a dispute between the Serbian Government and French bondholders, and although that dispute was exclusively concerned with their relations within the domain of municipal law, the essential international dispute was between the two Governments, the French Government exercising its right to protect its nationals; (2) although under French law stipulations in domestic transactions for payment in gold were null and void, this was not the case as regards international transactions, the loan contracts now in question being governed by the law of the borrowing State; and (3) the loan contracts required payment by reference to a gold standard of value. *See also* ***Brazilian Loans Case***.

servitudes While some doubt exists as to whether servitudes constitute a distinct legal category in international law, or are rather an area of problems (Brownlie, *Principles of Public International Law* (5th ed.), 377), there are examples of situations which would be termed servitudes by a municipal lawyer. *I Oppenheim 670-1* defines servitudes as "[those] exceptional restrictions made by treaty on the territorial supremacy of a state by which a part or the whole of its territory is in a limited way made to serve a certain purpose or interest of another State." According to this definition, a distinction has to be drawn between servitudes *stricto sensu,* i.e. those created by treaty in favor of a particular country, and natural restrictions on territorial supremacy, i.e. those rights conferred by custom on States in general in respect of the territory of another State, *e.g.*, the right of innocent passage of foreign merchant vessels through a State's territorial sea. *See* ***North Atlantic Fisheries Arbitration (1910) 11 R.I.A.A. 167***; ***The Wimbledon Case (1923) P.C.I.J., Ser. A,***

No. 1; ***Right of Passage Case*** *1960 I.C.J. Rep. 6. See* Reid, *International Servitudes* (1932); Vali, *Servitudes in International Law* (2nd ed.).

settlement of disputes *See* **pacific settlement of disputes; peace, threat to; peace, breach of**.

severance of diplomatic relations While it is exceptional for diplomatic relations to be broken off the effect is not to free the receiving State of all obligations, or deprive the sending State of all rights. Thus, under art. 45 of the Vienna Convention on Diplomatic Relations 1961 *(500 U.N.T.S. 95)*, if diplomatic relations are terminated, the receiving State must, even in the case of armed conflict, "respect and protect the premises of the mission, together with its property and archives" (art. 45(a)); and the sending State may nominate a third State *(see* **protecting power**), acceptable to the receiving State, to have custody of the mission, property and archives, and to protect the interests of its nationals (art. 45(b) and (c)). On the termination of diplomatic relations, any person entitled to privileges and immunities normally loses them at the moment of leaving the receiving State, but may continue to enjoy them for a "reasonable period" to enable that person to leave the receiving State (art. 39(2)); *and see In re Suarez [1918] 1 Ch. 176*; and US Secretary of State Root, allowing "a reasonable time for . . . withdrawal" in 1907 (Hackworth, *Digest of International Law* (1940), Vol. 4, 457)). The severance of diplomatic (or consular) relations does not affect treaty relations except in so far as the existence of such relations is indispensable for the application of the treaty (art. 63 of the Vienna Convention on the Law of Treaties 1969). Provision is made in art. 45 for the temporary recall of a diplomatic mission. "[T]his is a more frequent procedure than was formerly the case—perhaps because of the greater ease of travel. It may be used to indicate a sharp cooling off in relations, where neither side wishes to proceed to formal breach of relations and hope that difficulties or displeasure might be short-lived." Denza, *Diplomatic Law* (2nd ed.), 395. The same provisions for protection of the interests of the sending State which apply to the severance of diplomatic relations apply also to temporary recall.

ships, nationality and status of *See* **nationality of ships**.

ships, right of visit Art. 22 of the Geneva Convention on the High Seas 1958 *(450 U.N.T.S. 82)* provided that, subject to any more extensive jurisdiction conferred by treaty, warships are justified in boarding and, if appropriate, proceeding to an examination of a foreign merchant ship on the high seas only if there is reasonable ground for suspecting (a) piracy (b) slave trading (c) that the ship is really of the same nationality. There is a duty of compensation for any loss or damage sustained if the suspicions prove unfounded. Art. 110 of the UN Convention on the Law of the Sea 1982 *(1833 U.N.T.S. 3)* follows the language of the 1958 Convention very closely, but to the classes of case giving rise to the right of visit are now added suspicion that the ship is engaged in unauthorized broadcasting and the flag State of the warship has jurisdiction under art. 109 *(see* **radio piracy**); and that the ship is without nationality. The powers under art. 110 are extended *mutatis mutandis* to military aircraft and to "other duty authorized ships or aircraft clearly marked and identifiable as being on government service." Ships entitled to complete immunity in accordance with arts. 95 and 96 are not subject to the right of visit *(see* **State ships**).

sick and wounded *See* **wounded, sick and shipwrecked**.

siége social *See* **nationality of company/corporation**.

signature The text of a treaty is established as authentic and definitive, in the absence of a different procedure agreed upon by the parties, by "signature . . . by the representatives of those States of the text of the treaty or of the Final Act of a Conference incorporating the text": art 10(b) of the Vienna Convention on the Law of Treaties 1969 *(1155 U.N.T.S. 331)*. It has been stated that "[a]uthentication of the text of a treaty is necessary in order that negotiating States, before they are called upon to decide whether they will become parties to the treaty, may know finally and definitively what is the content of the treaty to which they will be subscribing": *[1966] II I.L.C. Yearbook 195.* All representatives usually sign together, although for some multilateral instruments the treaty remains open for signature for a period of time (*e.g.*, art. 125(1) of the Rome Statute of the International Criminal Court *(37 I.L.M. 999 (1998))*, providing that the Statute was open for signature in Rome from 17 July 1998 to 17 October 1998, and thereafter at New York (UN Headquarters) until 31 December 2000. The United States was one of sixteen states to sign within three days of the expiry of that deadline). Signature can also be a means whereby consent may be expressed to be bound by a treaty if the parties so agree (arts. 11 and 12 of the Vienna Convention on the Law of Treaties 1969).

A State which has signed a treaty subject to **ratification** must refrain from acts which would defeat the object and purpose of the treaty (art. 18(a) of the Vienna Convention; *German Interests in Polish Upper Silesia Case (Merits) (1926) P.C.I.J., Ser. A, No. 7* at 30). Signature in itself creates no obligation to ratify a treaty *([1962] II I.L.C. Yearbook 171). See* McNair, *Law of Treaties* (2nd ed), 120-8, 203-5. With certain types of agreement (notably commodity agreements), it is usual to stipulate for provisional application upon signature but prior to ratification. Where an international organization or régime is to be established, an interim or preparatory organization or committee is sometimes set up upon signature (*e.g.*, Preparatory Commission for the International Criminal Court). *See generally*, Aust, *Modern Treaty Law and Practice* (2000), Chap. 7.

signature *ad referendum* The text of a treaty may be established as authentic and definitive, in the absence of a different procedure agreed upon by the parties, by, *inter alia*, signature *ad referendum* (art. 10(b) of the Vienna Convention on the Law of Treaties 1969. This signifies something less than full **signature**, and has been described as signature "given provisionally and subject to confirmation": *[1966] 2 I.L.C. Yearbook 196.* If signature *ad referendum* is confirmed, this constitutes full signature of the treaty (art. 12(2)(b) of the Vienna Convention). Unlike full signature, signature *ad referendum* does not carry with it an obligation on the State to refrain from acts which would defeat the object and purpose of the treaty (*see* art. 18(a) of the Vienna Convention). *See also* **ratification**.

Simma, Bruno 1941- . Professor of International Law and European Community Law and Director of the Institute of International Law at the University of Munich 1973-2002; member, ILC 1996-2002; judge, ICJ 2002- . Principal publications include: *The Charter of the United Nations: A Commentary* (2nd ed. 2002), together with numerous articles on topics such as State responsibility and human rights.

Sinclair, Sir Ian McT 1926- . A legal adviser to the UK foreign service 1950-1984; Legal Adviser, Foreign and Commonwealth Office 1976-84. Sometime member, ILC. Principal works: *Vienna Convention on the Law of Treaties* (1973; 2nd ed. 1984); contributor to *Satow's Guide to Diplomatic Practice* (5th ed., 1979); The Law of Sovereign Immunity: Recent Developments, *(1980) 167 Hague Recueil 117.*

situation It appears that "situation" is to be distinguished from a dispute. Art. 34 of the UN Charter provides that "[t]he Security Council may investigate any dispute, or any situation which might lead to international friction or give rise to a dispute, in order to determine whether the continuance of the dispute or situation is likely to endanger the maintenance of international peace and security." In this context a situation appears as a lesser form of dispute. The obligation of art. 27(3) to refrain from voting in the Security Council applies only to parties to a dispute. A dispute, "the continuance of which is likely to endanger the maintenance of international peace and security" is, in terms of art. 33(1), to be settled by pacific means. While a UN member may bring a dispute or situation to the Security Council's attention (art. 35(1)), a non-member may only bring a dispute to the Council's attention (art. 35(2)). In practice, the Security Council does not draw a clear distinction between a situation and a dispute and, if it makes such a distinction, only does so at a late stage in its deliberations: Goodrich, Hambro and Simons, *Charter of the United Nations* (3rd ed.), 252. *See* the **Namibia Case** *1971 I.C.J. Rep. 16* at 22-3. *See also* Schwarzenberger, *International Constitutional Law* (1976), 192-6.

slavery Art. 1 of the Slavery Convention of 25 September 1926 *(60 L.N.T.S. 253*; as amended by Protocol of 7 December 1953 *(212 U.N.T.S. 17))* defined slavery as "the status or condition of a person over whom any or all the powers attaching to the right of ownership are exercised." The parties to the Convention undertook "to bring about, progressively and as soon as possible, the complete abolition of slavery in all its forms" (art. 2). Art. 1 of the Supplementary Convention on the Abolition of Slavery, the Slave Trade, and Institutions and Practices Similar to Slavery of 7 September 1956 *(266 U.N.T.S. 3)* extended the ambit of situations to be treated as akin to slavery to include debt bondage, serfdom, any practice whereby a woman is given in marriage without the right to refuse, on payment of consideration or one whereby her husband or a member of his family has the right to transfer her to another person or one whereby a woman on the death or her husband is liable to be inherited by another person, and the exploitation of children or their labour. "A particular slavery-like practice is the traffic in women and children for the purposes of prostitution which has led to the adoption of several treaties": *I Oppenheim, 980*. Enslavement and sexual slavery are both included in the list of crimes against humanity made subject to the jurisdiction of the International Criminal Court in terms of art. 7 of the Rome Statute of the International Criminal Court 1998 *(37 I.L.M. 999 (1998))*. *See generally* Greenidge, *Slavery* (1958).

Smuts, Jan Christian 1870-1950. Born in Cape Colony, and by turns lawyer, soldier, and statesman in South Africa, the United Kingdom and indeed on the world stage, Smuts, with President Woodrow Wilson, was the chief sponsor of the League of Nations *(The League of Nations: A Practical Suggestion* (1918)) and a key figure at the **San Francisco Conference**.

social rights *See* **Economic, Social and Cultural Rights, International Covenant on.**

Société Commerciale de Belgique *(Belgium v. Greece) (1939) P.C.I.J., Ser. A/B, No. 78.* In 1925, the Société Commerciale de Belgique entered into an agreement with the Greek Government for the construction and supply of certain railway equipment, payment by the Greek Government taking the form of Government bonds issued to the Company. In 1932 the Greek Government defaulted on the bonds. The Company resorted to arbitration under the contract and the arbitration awards, in 1936, provided for the cancellation of the contract and the payment by the Greek Government to the Company of a certain sum with interest. The Greek Government did not pay the sum awarded, maintaining that the debt was part of the Greek public debt subject to the same methods of payment as the Greek public external debt. Belgium unilaterally instituted proceedings before the PCIJ against Greece, which did not object and submitted arguments on the merits although in doing so caused

Belgium significantly to amend its initial submissions. The Court, in *holding* that the arbitral awards were definitive and obligatory, held also that (1) although in principle the nature of a dispute brought before the Court could not be transformed by amendments in the submissions into a dispute of another character, in the special circumstances of this case the proceedings should not be regarded as irregular; (2) the actions of Belgium and Greece showed that they agreed to the Court having jurisdiction; and (3) they also agreed that the arbitral awards had the force of *res judicata*, from which it followed that Greece must execute them as they stood and could not claim to subordinate payments under the award to conditions not contained in the award, relating to settlement of the Greek public external debt.

sociological approach This is a modern approach to international law, seen in the works of such writers as Georg **Schwarzenberger**, which emphasizes "the scope and limits of the functional frontiers of international law," and the fact that law is "conditioned by its social environment" and attempts to clarify the characteristics of that environment through inductive research, drawing on the methods of history, law, economics, geography, psychology, anthropology and the natural sciences. Schwarzenberger, *The Inductive Approach to International Law* (1965), 63; Schwarzenberger, *The Frontiers of International Law* (1962), 21-42; Stone, *Legal Controls of International Conflict* (2nd. imp., Rev.), l-li.

Soering Case *(Soering v. UK) (1989) 11 E.H.R.R. 439*. Soering, a German national, was detained in the United Kingdom pending extradition to the US to face two charges of murder in Virginia, having been indicted by a grand jury of the Circuit Court of Bedford County on 13 June 1986. On 29 October 1986, the British Government requested assurances from the UG that the death penalty, if imposed, would not be carried out. Assurances were made by a representative of the US Department of Justice that a representation would be made on behalf of the Government of the UK at the time of sentencing that the death penalty not be imposed. On 16 June 1987, Soering was committed to await the decision of the Secretary of State on his extradition to the US. After unsuccessful appeals to the Divisional Court and the House of Lords, on 3 August 1988, the Secretary of State ordered Soering's surrender to the US authorities. Soering applied to the European Commission alleging that, notwithstanding the assurance given to the UK Government, there was a serious likelihood that he would be sentenced to death if he were extradited to the United States. He argued that the so-called "death row phenomenon" constituted inhuman and degrading treatment and punishment contrary to art 3 of the European Convention on Human Rights (*213 U.N.T.S. 221; E.T.S. No. 5)*; that the absence of legal aid in the State of Virginia to pursue appeals would constitute a violation of art. 6 of the Convention; and that, in breach of art 13 of the Convention, he had not effective remedy against the UK in respect of his complaint under art. 3. The Commission declared the application admissible on 10 November 1988. On 7 July 1989, the European Court of Human Rights *held* that, in the event of the Secretary of State's decision to extradite the applicant to the US being implemented, there would be a violation of art. 3, but that there was no violation of arts. 6 or 13.

soft law A term used to refer to non-binding instruments or documents which have the appearance of law. "This terminology is meant to indicate that the instrument or provision in question if not of itself 'law,' but its importance within the general framework of international legal development is such that particular attention needs to be paid to it.": Shaw, *International Law* (4th ed.), 92. Thus, 'soft law' is not binding, but is can be politically influential in setting down objectives and aspirations. Areas in which soft law has been particularly influential include international economic law and international environmental law. See Chinkin, The Challenge of Soft Law: Development and Change in International Law *(1989) 38 I.C.L.Q. 850.*

Sohn, Louis B. 1914- . Professor, Harvard 1953-81; Professor University of Georgia School of Law 1981-91; Distinguished Research Professor of Law, George Washington School of Law 1991- . Principal works include *Cases on United Nations Law* (1956; 2nd ed., 1967); *World Peace Through World Law* (with Clark; 1958; 3rd ed., 1966); *International Protection of Human Rights* (with Buergenthal, 1973); *African Regional Organizations* (4 vols. 1971-2); *The United Nations Convention on the Law of the Sea* (with Rosenne, 1989); *Rights in Conflict: The United Nations and South Africa* (1994).

Solis Claim *(USA v. Mexico) (1926) 4 R.I.A.A. 358.* A claim was presented to the Mexico-USA General Claims Commission set up by the General Claims Convention of 8 September 1923 *(U.S.T.S. No. 678),* on behalf of Solis, a US national, in respect of the alleged taking of cattle from his ranch by Mexican forces, both governmental and revolutionary. The Commission *held* that, in the light of US law and practice relating to proof of US nationality and of the practice of arbitral tribunals, the claimant's US nationality was adequately established on the basis of affidavits and such other evidence as was available; that, in the absence of convincing evidence of neglect on the part of the Mexican authorities, Mexico was not liable for the taking of cattle by revolutionary forces; and that Mexico was liable for the taking of cattle by government forces, since on the evidence it was to be taken that the soldiers were not stragglers for whom there was no responsibility but were under the command of some officer with responsibility for their acts.

Sörensen, Max 1913-1981. Professor, Aarhus 1947-72. Legal adviser to Danish Ministry of Foreign Affairs 1956-72; Member, European Commission on Human Rights 1955-72; Court of Justice of European Communities 1973-79; European Court of Human Rights 1980-81. Major works: *Les sources du droit international* (1946); *Elements of International Organization* (in Danish; 1962); *Manual of Public International Law* (ed. 1968).

sources While the term "sources" is used in different ways by different commentators *(see* Corbett, The Consent of States and the Sources of Law of Nations, *(1925) 6 B.Y.I.L. 20 at 29-30),* it is generally accepted that the sources of international law "are those things which indicate the actual or concrete content of that system": Parry, *The Sources and Evidences of International Law* (1965), 4. An authoritative enumeration of such sources is contained in art. 38(1) of the ICJ Statute: "The Court, whose function is to decide in accordance with international law such disputes as are submitted to it, shall apply: (a) international conventions, whether general or particular, establishing rules expressly recognized by the contesting states; (b) international custom, as evidence of a general practice accepted as law; (c) the general principles of law recognized by civilized nations; (d) subject to the provision of art. 59, judicial decisions and the teachings of the most highly qualified publicists of the various nations, as subsidiary means for the determination of rules of law." In this enumeration, the first three are formal sources in that they indicate the actual content of the law; the final two sources (grouped under (d)) are expressly stated to be **subsidiary sources,** and are thus **material sources,** i.e. they are evidence of the law, that law having its source in (a) (b) or (c). It has been contended that there are other sources of law beyond these enumerated in art. 38(1), *e.g.,* **equity,** measures adopted by international organizations, but the better view appears to be that these are law only as "the result of the application of legal rules created by operation of sources already recognized": Virally, The Sources of International Law, in Sörensen, *Manual of Public International Law* (1968), 116 at 122. *See* Parry, *op. cit., supra;* Sörensen, *Les sources du droit international* (1946);

Waldock, General Course on Public International Law, *(1962) 106 Hague Rec. 5;* Danilenko, *Law-Making in the International Community* (1993).

South Pole *See* **Antarctic Treaty; polar regions, sovereignty over**.

South West Africa Cases *1950 I.C.J. Rep. 128; 1955 I.C.J. Rep. 68; 1956 I.C.J. Rep. 23; 1962 I.C.J. Rep. 319; 1966 I.C.J. Rep. 6; see also **Namibia Opinion**.*

South West Africa (International Status) Case. By art. 119 of the Treaty of Versailles 1919 *(225 C.T.S. 188),* Germany renounced sovereignty over its Territory of South-West Africa. On 17 December 1920, the Council of the League of Nations, pursuant to art. 22 of the Covenant, confirmed the terms of a Mandate for South-West Africa to be exercised on behalf of Great Britain by the Government of the Union of South Africa. The League of Nations ceased to exist in 1946; but Chapter XII of the UN Charter established a **Trusteeship System** similar to the **Mandates System** operated under the Covenant. Although territories held under a mandate could be placed under the Trusteeship System, South Africa did not take such action with regard to South-West Africa. By Res. 338 (IV) of 6 December 1949, the UN General Assembly sought from the ICJ an advisory opinion on the following questions:

> "What is the international status of the Territory of South-West Africa and what are the international obligations of the Union of South Africa arising therefrom, in particular: (a) Does the Union of South Africa continue to have international obligations under the Mandate for South-West Africa and, if so, what are those obligations? (b) Are the provisions of Chapter XII of the Charter applicable and, if so, in what manner, to the Territory of South-West Africa? (c) Has the Union of South Africa the competence to modify the international status of the Territory of South-West Africa, or, in the event of a negative reply, where does competence rest to determine and modify the international status of the Territory?"

The Court *advised* (unanimously) that South-West Africa is a territory under the international Mandate assumed by the Union of South Africa on 17 December 1920; and that on Questions (a) (12 to 2), the Union of South Africa continues to have the international obligations stated in art. 22 of the Covenant of the League of Nations and in the Mandate for South West Africa as well as the obligation to transmit petitions from the inhabitants of that Territory, the supervisory functions to be exercised by the United Nations, to which the annual reports and the petitions are to be submitted, and the reference to the Permanent Court of International Justice to be replaced by a reference to the International Court of Justice, in accordance with art. 7 of the Mandate and art. 37 of the Statute of the Court; on Question (b) (unanimously), the provisions of Chapter XII of the Charter are applicable to the Territory of South-West Africa in the sense that they provide a means by which the Territory may be brought under the Trusteeship System; and (8 to 6), the provisions of Chapter XII of the Charter do not impose on the Union of South Africa a legal obligation to place the Territory under the Trusteeship System; on Question (c) (unanimously) the Union of South Africa acting alone has not the competence to modify the international status of the Territory of South-West Africa, the competence to determine and modify the international status of the Territory resting with the Union of South Africa acting with the consent of the United Nations. *(1950 I.C.J. Rep. 128).*

South-West Africa (Voting Procedure) Case. In 1954, the General Assembly adopted a special rule on the voting procedure to be followed by the Assembly in taking decisions on questions relating to reports and petitions concerning South-West Africa. By this rule, decisions of the Assembly on the questions referred to were to be regarded as important questions within the meaning of art. 18(2) of the Charter (i.e. as being subject to a requirement for a two thirds majority, whereas for the Mandates régime the Council of the League of Nations was governed by a requirement for unanimity). By resolution 904 (IX) of 23 November 1954, the General Assembly asked the ICJ for an Advisory Opinion on whether the rule corresponded to a correct interpretation of the Advisory Opinion given in 1950. The Court *advised* (unanimously) in the affirmative, since the rule accorded with the Court's statement in the 1950 Opinion that "the degree of supervision to be exercised by the General Assembly should not . . . exceed that which applied under the Mandates system, and should conform as far as possible to the procedure followed in this respect by the Council of the League of Nations." *(1955 I.C.J. Rep. 68).*

South-West Africa (Hearing of Petitioners) Case. The General Assembly, having in 1953 established a Committee on South-West Africa, in 1955 requested from the ICJ an Advisory Opinion on the question whether it was consistent with the Advisory Opinion given by the ICJ in 1950 for the Committee to grant oral hearings to petitioners on matters relating to South-West Africa. The Court *advised* (8 to 5) that it would not be inconsistent with the 1950 Opinion for the General Assembly to authorize a procedure for the grant of oral hearings by the Committee to petitioners who had already submitted written petitions, provided that the Assembly was satisfied that such a course was necessary for the maintenance of effective international supervision of the administration of South-West Africa. Although oral hearings had not in fact been granted to petitioners during the régime of the League of Nations, the Council of the League could have authorized that course had it wished, and the General Assembly in carrying out its supervisory functions in respect of the Mandate had the same authority as the Council. *(1956 I.C.J. Rep. 23).*

Ethiopia and Liberia v. South Africa (First Phase). In 1960, Ethiopia and Liberia instituted proceedings against South Africa contending, in substance, that in a number of enumerated respects South Africa had, in relation to South-West Africa and its inhabitants, acted in its capacity as mandatory in a manner contrary to its obligations under the Mandate for South-West Africa. Ethiopia and Liberia relied on art. 7 of the Mandate, and art. 37 of the Statute of the Court, to found the jurisdiction of the Court. South Africa raised preliminary objections to the Court's jurisdiction. On 21 December 1962, the Court, in *holding* (8 to 7) that it had jurisdiction to adjudicate on the merits, found (a) that the opposing attitudes of the Parties relating to the performance of the obligations of the Mandate by South Africa constituted a "dispute" between the Parties; (b) that the Mandate in fact and in law was an international agreement having the character of a treaty or convention and, notwithstanding the dissolution of the League of Nations, was still in force so that South Africa's acceptance of the compulsory jurisdiction of the PCIJ under art. 7 of the Mandate was by virtue of art. 37 of the Statute of the Court still effective in relation to the ICJ; (c) that, notwithstanding the dissolution of the League of Nations, Ethiopia and Liberia could still be regarded as "another Member of the League of Nations" for the purpose of bringing a dispute before the Court on the basis of art. 7 of the Mandate; (d) that the dispute was within the scope of art. 7 of the Mandate even though it may not affect any material interest of the applicant States or their nationals; and (e) that the dispute could not be settled by negotiation. *(1962 I.C.J. Rep. 319).*

Ethiopia and Liberia v. South Africa (Second Phase). In the subsequent proceedings on the merits, on 18 July 1966 the Court, in *holding* (by the President's casting vote) that the claims of Ethiopia and Liberia had to be rejected as they did not establish any legal right or interest appertaining to them in the subject of the claims, found that, "viewing the matter in the light of the relevant texts and instruments, and having regard to the structure of the League, within the framework of which the Mandates System functioned, . . . even in the time of the League, even as members of the League when that organization still existed, the Applicants did not, in their individual capacity as States, possess any separate self-contained right which they could assert, independently of, or additionally to, the right of the League, in the pursuit of its collective, institutional activity, to require the due performance of the Mandate in the discharge of the 'sacred trust.' This right was vested exclusively in the League, and was exercised through its competent organs. . . . [I]f in the time of the League, if as Members of the League, the Applicant did not possess the rights contended for, evidently they do not possess them now": *(1966) I.C.J. Rep. 6 at 28-31)*.

South-East Asia Treaty Organization The South-East Asia Treaty Organization, established by the South-East Asia Collective Defence Treaty of 8 September 1954 (*209 U.N.T.S. 28*: "the Manila Pact") was conceived as the counterpart of **NATO**, the "treaty area" in the case of SEATO being South-East Asia, including the territories of the Asian parties and the South-West Pacific not including the Pacific area north of 21 degrees 30 minutes north latitude. The direct purpose of SEATO was more specifically to combat communist aggression in Cambodia, Laos and Vietnam, which were all designated by a simultaneous protocol as States or areas attracting a duty to "act to meet the common danger" in the event of "aggression by means of armed attack." The original parties to the Manila Pact were UK, Australia, New Zealand, Pakistan, France, Philippines, Thailand and USA. With the winding up of SEATO in 1977 at the end of the Vietnam war, the remaining defensive alliance in the Pacific Area is **ANZUS**.

sovereign immunity "A study of the law of sovereign immunity reveals the existence of two conflicting concepts of sovereign immunity, each widely held and firmly established. According to the classical or absolute theory of sovereign immunity, a sovereign cannot, without his consent, be made a respondent in the courts of another sovereign. According to the newer or restrictive theory of sovereign immunity, the immunity of the sovereign is recognized with regard to sovereign or public acts (*jure imperii*) of a state, but not with respect to private acts (*jure gestionis*). There is agreement by proponents of both theories, supported by practice, that sovereign immunity should not be claimed or granted in actions with respect to real property (diplomatic and perhaps consular property excepted) or with respect to the disposition of the property of a deceased person even though a foreign sovereign is the beneficiary": **Tate Letter** of 19 May 1952 *((1952) 26 State Dept. Bull. 984)*. Both the US and the UK were traditionally proponents of the absolute theory: see *The Schooner Exchange v. McFaddon 11 U.S. (7 Cranch) 116* (1812); *Berizzi Bros. Co. v. U.S. 271 U.S. 562* (1926); *The Parlement Belge (1880) 5 P.D. 197*; *The Porto Alexandre [1920] P. 30*. These States came to regard the absolute theory as out of step with contemporary conditions and with the attitude of other States. *See The S.S. Cristina [1938] A.C. 485* at 250-1; the Tate Letter; the Brussels Convention on the Unification of Certain Rules Relating to Immunity of State-Owned Vessels of 10 April 1926 *(176 L.N.T.S. 199)*; the European Convention on State Immunity of 16 May 1972 *(11 I.L.M. 470 (1972))*; OAS Draft Convention on Jurisdictional Immunity of States *(20 I.L.M. 287 (1982))*. Following the Tate Letter, US courts began increasingly to recognize immunity only in respect of acts *jure imperii*. *See Alfred Dunhill of London Inc. v. Republic of Cuba 425 U.S. 682* (1976). Similarly, UK courts recognized that the restrictive doctrine was part of customary law, and therefore of the law of England. *See The Philippine Admiral [1976] 2 W.L.R. 214*; *Trendtex Trading Corp. v. Central Bank of Nigeria [1977] 1 Q.B. 529*; *I Congreso del Partido [1983] A.C. 244*. The situation in both States is now regulated by statute, incorporating the restrictive theory so as to limit immunity in relation to commercial transactions: Foreign Sovereign Immunities Act of 1976 (US); State Immunity Act 1978 (UK).

The ILC finally adopted their Draft Articles on the Jurisdiction Immunities of States and Their Property in 1991 (*1991 II(2) ILC Yearbook 142*). The Draft Articles are essentially based on the restrictive theory and follow the same model as the domestic legislation in the US and UK by granting immunity to States from the jurisdiction of the courts of another state (art. 5) but then providing exceptions in respect of, *inter alia*, commercial transactions (art. 10), contracts of employment (art. 11), personal injuries and damage to property (art. 12), ownership, possession and use of property (art. 13), intellectual and industrial property (art. 14) participation in companies and other collective bodies (art. 15), ships owned or operated by a State (art. 16) and in respect of arbitration agreements (art. 17). The difficulty with the Draft Articles is that the primary exception, relating to commercial transactions (art. 10) is limited by reference to art. 2(2) which provides that "in determining whether a contract or transaction is a 'commercial transaction,' reference should be made primarily to the nature of the contract or transaction, but its purpose should also be taken into account if, in the practice of the State which is a party to it, that purpose is relevant to determining the non-commercial character of the contract or transaction." This definition comes close to the re-instatement of the absolute theory and it is primarily for this reason that the Draft Articles have been under consideration by the Sixth Legal Committee of the General Assembly for more than ten years. The prospects for an international treaty providing common standards for the granting of sovereign immunity consequently look bleak.

Attempts to extend the jurisdiction of States so as to cover certain exterritorial acts have, over the years, resulted in conflict between the exercise of jurisdiction and the doctrine of sovereign immunity. Thus, in *Filartiga v Pena-Irala 630 F2d 876* (2d Cir. 1980), the US Court of Appeals for the Second Circuit held that the Alien Tort Claims Act, which provides for the exercise of jurisdiction by the courts of the United States in cases in which an alien sues for a tort "committed in violation of the law of nations or a treaty of the United States," allowed for the exercise of jurisdiction in the US in a case brought by a Paraguayan national against a Paraguayan police official for acts of torture perpetrated in Paraguay. Cf *Al-Adsani v UK 34 E.H.R.R. 12 (2001)* (*see* below). However, in *Siderman v Republic of Argentina 965 F.2d 699* (1992), it was held that the Alien Tort Claims Act does not constitute an exception to the principle of sovereign immunity. Similarly, the extension of national criminal jurisdiction extraterritorially, for example through the doctrine of **universal jurisdiction**, has also led to conflict with the sovereign immunity doctrine and consequently, the immunity of State officials in matters of criminal law has recently come under considerable scrutiny in various domestic and international courts around the world. In the **Pinochet Case**, the residual immunity of a former head of State (immunity *rationae materiae*) which is akin to sovereign immunity and provides for immunity from jurisdiction in respect of the head of State's official acts was held not to apply but only in the case of allegations of official torture contrary to the UN Convention Against **Torture** and Other Cruel, Inhumane or Degrading Treatment or Punishment 1984 (*1465 U.N.T.S.85*) where that Convention had been incorporated into UK law. *See also* the decision of the ICJ in the **Arrest Warrant Case** and *Al-Adsani v UK 34 E.H.R.R. 12 (2001)* (a decision of the **European Court of Human Rights** in a civil case arising out of allegations of torture). In both cases, the claim of immunity was upheld.

See generally Sinclair, The Law of Sovereign Immunity: Recent Developments, *(1980) 167 Hague Recueil 117*; Badr, *State Immunity: An Analytical and Prognostic View* (1984); Schreuer, *State Immunity: Some Recent Developments* (1993); Fox, *The Law of State Immunity* (2002).

sovereignty "Sovereignty as a principle of international law must be sharply distinguished from other related uses of the term: sovereignty in its internal aspects and political sovereignty. Sovereignty in its internal aspects is concerned with the identity of the bearer of supreme authority within a State. This may be an individual or a collective unit. . . . In international relations, the scope of political sovereignty is still less limited [than that within a State]. Political sovereignty is the necessary concomitant of the lack of an effective international order and the constitutional weaknesses of the international superstructures which have so far been grafted on the law of unorganized international society. . . . [D]octrinal attempts at spiriting away sovereignty must remain meaningless. Actually, such efforts appear to minimise unduly the fundamental character of the principle of legal sovereignty within the realm of international law. The rules underlying this principle derive their importance from the basic fact that 'almost all international relations are bound up' with the independence of States. Thus, the principle of sovereignty in general, and that of territorial sovereignty in particular, remains of necessity the 'point of departure in settling most questions that concern international relations' [*Island of Palmas Case (1928) 2 R.I.A.A. 829 at 839*]": Schwarzenberger, *International Law* (3rd ed.), 114-5. Sovereignty is not absolute in the sense of permitting a State to act as it will regardless of international law. "We can no longer regard sovereignty as an absolute and individual right of every State, as used to be the case under the old law founded on the individualist regime, according to which States were only bound by the rules which they had accepted. To-day, owing to social interdependence and to the predominance of general interest, the states are bound by many rules which have not been ordered by their will": Separate Opinion of Judge Alvarez in *Corfu Channel Case 1949 I.C.J. Rep 39 at 43. See also* Barker, *International Law and International Relations* (2000), 44: "The extent to which states can ever be said to have been endowed with an external sovereignty, which placed them above the law, is certainly debatable. However, in modern day international relations where states interact with one another on a daily basis, not only at governmental level but also at all possible levels of interaction, any claim of absolute sovereignty becomes impossible. As regards the impact of international law on the internal sovereignty of states . . . insofar as international law does exist and states accept that it does exist . . . the existence of the internal sovereignty of states stands not as an obstacle to international law but as a mechanism providing for the distribution of power in the international relations of states." *See I Oppenheim, 123-6*; Verzijl, *International Law in Historical Perspective,* Vol. 1, 256-92; Korowicz, *Introduction to International Law* (1959), Chaps. 1-6.

Sovereignty over Various Red Sea Islands Arbitration *(Eritrea v. Yemen) 40 I.L.M. 900 (2001)*. The dispute between Eritrea and Yemen over title to a group of islands in the Red Sea was submitted to arbitration under the Agreement on Principles of 21 May 1996. Eritrea based its claim on a chain of title, beginning with the Italian colonization of territory formerly part of the Ottoman Empire. Eritrea contended that the Treaty of Peace with Italy of 10 February 1947 *(49 U.N.T.S. 3)* transferred this territory to Ethiopia, of which Eritrea was then a part, which exercised sovereignty until Eritrean independence in 1991; Eritrea thereafter patrolled the waters around the islands to regulate fishing. Yemen claimed the islands on "original, historic, or traditional Yemeni title" that preceded its incorporation into the Ottoman Empire in 1538, and on the fact that the Empire had recognized the separate sovereignty of Yemen prior to the Ottoman defeat in 1918. The Turkish renunciation of Ottoman territory in the **Treaty of Lausanne** of 24 July 1923 *(28 L.N.T.S. 11)* did not affect Yemeni title as Yemen was not a party to the treaty. Yemen also contended that third States had recognized Yemeni sovereignty over the islands. On 9 October 1998, the Tribunal (Jennings, Schwebel, El-Kosheri, Highet and Higgins) *held* that the islands fell under the sovereignty of Yemen. The tribunal found that neither party made a significantly more convincing case based on ancient title, as Eritrea argued, or on succession to title, as Yemen argued. Nor was assistance available from the respective exercises of governmental functions over the islands, such exercises being "sparse in useful content . . . owing to the inhospitability of the Islands themselves and the relative meagreness of human history." Finding little to distinguish the parties' claims to consolidation of title, the Tribunal looked to other possible factors; and, to that end, examined the claims to sub-groups of the islands. For one sub-group, the "portico doctrine," involving the attribution of sovereignty over off-shore features which fall within the "attraction" of the mainland, gave Yemen title; for another, the maintenance of lighthouses and two oil production licenses gave Yemen title; for another, a continuous display of sovereignty being absent, "Yemeni happenings and incidents" gave Yemen title; and for yet another, the construction of a lighthouse and an air landing site, a scientific expedition and a joint venture to develop tourism gave Yemen title.

sovereignty, full, permanent *See* **permanent sovereignty**.

sovereignty, territorial This is an aspect of **sovereignty**, connoting the internal, rather than the external, manifestation of the principle of sovereignty. It is the "principle of the exclusive competence of the State in regard to its own territory. . . . Territorial sovereignty is, in general, a situation recognized and delimited in space . . . [and] signifies independence. Independence in regard to a portion of the globe is the right to exercise therein, to the exclusion of any other State, the functions of a State": *Island of Palmas Case (1928) 2 R.I.A.A. 829* at 838.

space law The actual location of the boundary between airspace and outer space remains uncertain. What is clear is that "[b]eyond the point separating air from space, states have agreed to apply the international law principles of *res communis*, so that no portion of outer space may be appropriated to the sovereignty of individual states.": Shaw, *International Law* (4th ed.). Referred to here are some of the most important declarations, treaties and practices that make up the legal rules governing activities in outer space. It thus includes at least General Assembly Resolutions 1721 (XVI) of 20 December 1961, 1884 (XVII) of 17 October 1963 and 1962 (XVIII) of 13 December 1963; the **Outer Space Treaty** 1967 *(610 U.N.T.S. 206);* the **Rescue and Return** of Astronauts **Agreement** 1968 *(672 U.N.T.S. 121; (1968) 7 I.L.M. 149);* Convention on International Liability for Damage Caused by Space Objects 1971 *((1971) 10 I.L.M. 965);* Convention on Registration of Objects Launched into Outer Space 1975; *(1975) 14 I.L.M. 43 (see* **space objects); Moon Treaty** *(1979) 18 I.L.M. 1434);* Principles Relevant to the Use of Nuclear Power Sources in Outer Space, General Assembly Resolution 47/68 of 14 December 1992. Also covered is broadcasting and **satellites** and **remote sensing.** See; Mateesco Matte, *Aerospace Law* (1969) and *Droit aérospatial* (1982); Lachs, *The Law of Outer Space* (1972); Jasentuleyana & Lee, *Manual on Space Law* (1979); Fawcett, *Outer Space* (1984) Christol, *Space Law* (1991).

space object Any object in orbit (art. IV, **Outer Space Treaty**; *610 U.N.T.S. 206*) or indeed any object launched into outer space, including its component parts as well as its launch vehicle and parts thereof (Convention on Registration of Objects Launched into Outer Space of 14 January 1975; *1023 U.N.T.S. 15*, art. 1(b)). *See* **space objects, registration of; damage caused by**.

space objects, registration of; damage caused by Art. II of the Convention on Registration of Objects Launched into Outer Space of 14 January 1975 *(1023 U.N.T.S. 15)*, which entered into force on 15 October 1976, imposes a duty upon launching States to register all **space objects** they launch or whose launching they procure. Data on each entry, including the launching State, an appropriate designator or registration number, date and location of launch, basic orbital parameters and general function of the object are to be transmitted to the UN Secretary-General (art. IV), who is to maintain a register of this information with open access (art. III). States parties are to assist in the identification of objects causing damage (art. VI). The Convention supplements prior registration arrangements, notably those contained in art. VII of the **Outer Space Treaty** 1967 *(610 U.N.T.S. 205)*. The **International Telecommunications Union** also maintains a register of space vehicles for radio purposes (Radio Regulations, art. 9A).

The Convention on International Liability for Damage caused by Space Objects of 29 June 1971 *(10 I.L.M. 965 (1971))* creates an absolute liability in the launching State (or joint and several liability in the case of a joint launch) to pay compensation for damage caused by its space object on the surface of the earth or to aircraft in flight (art. II). Damage elsewhere to other space objects is on the basis of fault (art. III). Claims can only be presented by a State and damage to nationals of the launching State is expressly excluded (arts. VII, XII). Provision is made for arbitration by a Claims Commission of 3 members in the event of failure to settle a claim (arts XIV-XX). The Convention was invoked by Canada in 1979 following the damage allegedly caused by Soviet Cosmos 954 *(18 ILM 899 (1979))*. *See* Forkosch, *Outer Space and Legal Liability* (1982).

Spanish Zone of Morocco Claims *(Great Britain v. Spain) (1924) 2 R.I.A.A. 615*. The Spanish protectorate over Morocco was established by a Spanish-Moroccan treaty of 27 November 1912. By an agreement concluded on 19 May 1923, Great Britain and Spain agreed to submit to arbitration 53 claims of British subjects or British protected persons against the Spanish authorities for damage to life or property in the Spanish zone of Morocco. Before disposing of the various individual claims, the arbitrator (Huber) laid down some general principles in regard to State responsibility, *holding* that (1) the territorial character of sovereignty is so fundamental that the right of diplomatic intervention by a foreign State in the relations between a State and persons in its territory can only be admitted by way of exception in cases where some special element gives rise to international responsibility, as where the general level of security falls below a certain standard, or judicial protection is illusory; (2) while a State is not responsible for the fact that there occurs a war or revolt, it can be held responsible for what its authorities do or omit to do to put a stop to that as far as possible, by exercising appropriate diligence in extending help or taking preventive or protective action; (3) in relation to acts of plunder falling short of a state of rebellion, a State incurs international responsibility if it fails by an appreciable margin to exercise *diligentia quam in suis*; (4) although a State is not internationally responsible for damage caused to aliens by its military operations in suppressing rebellions or waging war against an enemy, a State can be held responsible for acts of its armed forces in such circumstances if there has been a manifest abuse of its right to take necessary military action, and must exercise supervision to prevent members of its armed forces acting in violation of military discipline; (5) a State's international responsibility is engaged when it fails to prosecute wrongdoers who have committed offences against aliens or to apply appropriate civil sanctions, but this is not an absolute requirement, since the circumstances, including the means at the disposal of the State, and the authority it can exert, must be taken into account; (6) as a matter of customary international law, an alien cannot be deprived of his property without just compensation, especially where the free exercise of property rights is interfered with by a measure aimed only at specific persons; and (7) the creation of a protectorate suppresses direct diplomatic relations between the protected State and other States, which must accordingly address any claims in connection with events in the protectorate to the protecting State, which must take upon itself at least a derivative responsibility for the protected State.

Special Committee on Decolonization *See* **decolonization**.

Special Court for Sierra Leone The Special Court for Sierra Leone was established pursuant to SC Res. 1315 (2000) of 14 August 2000 and the Agreement between the UN and the Government of Sierra Leone of 16 January 2002 (appended to the UN Secretary-General's Report on the Establishment of a Special Court for Sierra Leone of 4 October 2000: *UN Doc. S/2000/195*). In terms of the Agreement, this Court's remit is to prosecute "persons who bear the greatest responsibility for serious violations of international humanitarian and Sierra Leonean law" since the beginning of civil unrest in the country in November 1996 (art. 1). From the trial chambers as a whole, with between 8 and 11 independent judges, up to two trial chambers may be constituted, each with 3 judges, one appointed by the Government of Sierra Leone, two by the UN Secretary-General (art. 2(2)(a)); the appeals chamber has 5 judges, two appointed by the Government and three by the Secretary-General (art. 2(2)(b)). The prosecutor was appointed by the UN Secretary-General after consultations with the Government (art. 3). The Statute of the Special Court of 16 January 2002 *(UN Doc. S/2000/195)* confers jurisdiction on the Special Court in respect of specified crimes against humanity (art. 2), violations of common art. 3 of the 4 Geneva Conventions of 1949 *(75 U.N.T.S. 31ff)* and their Protocol II of 1977 *(1125 U.N.T.S. 609)* (art. 3), other serious violations of international humanitarian law (art. 4) and specified crimes under Sierra Leonean law (art. 5). These crimes all carry individual responsibility, regardless of the status of the alleged offender (art. 6). The existence of an amnesty is no bar to prosecution (art. 10). The minimum age of criminal responsibility is 15 years (art. 7). There are due process guarantees in art. 17. The penalties available to the Special Court extend as far as imprisonment (art. 19). This court is a true hybrid, being neither a national court nor an international criminal tribunal on the model of the **International Criminal Court**, the **International Criminal Tribunal for the Former Yugoslavia** or the **International Criminal Tribunal for Rwanda**. *See* <www.scsl.org>.

special custom *See* **local custom**.

Special Drawing Rights The Special Drawing Rights (SDR) is an official international reserve asset created by the **International Monetary Fund** in 1969 to supplement international liquidity in the circumstances of a perceived long-term global liquidity shortage. SDRs were first issued or "allocated" in 1970. Allocation is in proportion to members' quotas. SDRs may be cancelled if long-term global liquidity is deemed to be excessive, although no cancellations have yet been made. SDRs can only be transferred among members of the Fund, some 13 official institutions prescribed by the Fund as other holders (including IBRD, BIS and the Swiss National Bank) and the Fund itself. Members needing to use their holdings of SDRs for wider payments purposes can mobilize them only by encashment for convertible currency with another member or another holder (or, exceptionally, the Fund). The role of SDR's as a reserve currency has become very limited and by, the end of December 2002, accounted for only 1.1 percent of IMF members' non-gold reserves. *See* <www.imf.org>.

special missions A "'special mission' is a temporary mission, representing the State, which is sent by one State to another State with the consent of the latter for the purpose of dealing with it on specific questions or of performing in relation to it a specific task": art. 1(a) of the Convention on Special Missions of 8 December 1969 *(9 I.L.M. 129 (1970))*. For an account of the purposes for which special missions have been employed, see Report to the ILC of Special Rapporteur Sandström, "Ad Hoc Diplomacy," *[1960] II I.L.C. Year-book 108*. The aim of the Convention is to equate the position of special missions, so far as is appropriate, with that of the full diplomatic mission under the Vienna Convention on Diplomatic Relations of 16 April 1961 *(500 U.N.T.S 95)*. While the sending of a special mission is not dependant on diplomatic or consular relations between the States (art. 7), the sending and the functions of such a mission are to be determined by the mutual consent of the States (arts. 2 and 3). The premises of a special mission are inviolable and exempt from taxation (arts. 24 and 25); archives and documents are likewise inviolable (art. 26); freedom of movement and communication is to be accorded to a special mission (arts. 27 and 28); those in the special mission have personal inviolability, and may not be subject to arrest or detention (art. 29); those in the special mission have immunity from criminal jurisdiction (art. 31(1)), and from civil and administrative jurisdiction except in specified situations not relating to the functions of the mission (art. 31 (2)); *see also* the G.A. Resolution concerning the Settlement of Civil Claims Against Members of Special Missions of 8 December 1969 (Res. 2531 (XXIV)). *See also* the Optional Protocol concerning the Compulsory Settlement of Disputes of 8 December 1969 *(9 I.L.M. 149 (1970))*. See *Satow's Guide to Diplomatic Practice* (5th ed.), Chap. 19.

Special Rapporteur Opinion *(1999) I.C.J Rep. 62*. By Decision 1998/297 of 5 August 1998 transmitted to the International Court of Justice by letter dated 7 August 1998, ECSOC requested an advisory opinion from the Court on the legal question of the applicability of art VI sect. 22 of the Convention on the Privileges and Immunities of the United Nations of 13 February 1946 *(1 U.N.T.S. 15)* in the case of Dato' Param Cumaraswamy as Special Rapporteur of the Commission of Human Rights on the Independence of Judges and Lawyers. According to Section 22, "Experts (other than officials coming within the scope of Article V) performing missions for the United Nations shall be accorded such privileges and immunities as are necessary for the independent exercise of their functions during the period of their missions, including time spent on journeys in connection with their missions. In particular they shall be accorded: (b) in respect of words spoken or written and acts done by them in the course of the performance of their mission, immunity from legal process of any kind. . . ."

In November 1995, the Special Rapporteur gave an interview to a British magazine, circulated in Malaysia in which he commented upon certain litigations which had been carried out in the Malaysian courts. As a result of the publication of the interview, two commercial companies in Malaysia filed suit against him in the amount of $US12 million each 'including exemplary damages for slander.' On 7 March, 1997 the UN Secretary-General issued a note confirming Mr Camaraswamy's status and maintaining his immunity from legal process. On 28 June 1997, a judge in the Malaysian High Court for Kuala Lumpur found she was 'unable to hold the Defendant is absolutely protected by the immunity he claims.' New lawsuits were filed on 10 July, 23 October and 21 November 1997 for $US24 million, $US40 million and $US24million respectively. On 19 February 1998, the Federal Court of Malaysia denied Mr Cumaraswamy right to appeal stating that he was neither a sovereign nor a full-fledged diplomat but merely 'an unpaid, part-time provider of information.'

The Court *held* (1)(a) (14-1) that art. VI, sect. 22 of the 1946 Convention applied to Mr Cumaraswamy as Special Rapporteur of the Commission of Human Rights; (b) (14-1) that Mr Cumaraswamy was entitled to immunity from legal process of every kind for the words spoken by him during the interview reported in the British magazine; (2)(a) (13-2) that the Government of Malaysia had a duty to inform the Malaysian courts of the finding of the Secretary-General that Mr Cumaraswamy was entitled to immunity from legal process; (b) (14-1) that the Malaysian courts had the obligation to deal with the question of immunity expeditiously; (3) (Unanimously) the Mr Cumaraswamy should be held financially harmless for any costs imposed upon him by the Malaysian courts (4) (13-2) that the Malaysian Government had aduty to communicate the advisory opinion to the Malaysian courts and that Mr Cumaraswamy's immunity be respected. *See also Applicability of Article VI, section 22 of the Convention on the Privileges and Immunities of the United Nations.*

Specialized Agencies Art. 57 of the UN Charter provides that "[t]he various specialized agencies, established by international agreement and having wide international responsibilities, as defined in their basic instruments, in economic, social, cultural, education, health and related fields, shall be brought into relationship with" the UN in accordance with relationship agreements to be entered into by ECOSOC subject to the approval of the General Assembly (art. 63). An organization established by international agreement and having wide international responsibilities is thus constituted a Specialized Agency by virtue of the relationship agreement.

At present, the following organizations are Specialized Agencies in accordance with this definition (*see* individual entries): the International Telecommunication Union (ITU), the Universal Postal Union (UPU), the International Labour Organization (ILO), the Food and Agriculture Organization (FAO), the International Monetary Fund (IMF) and its affiliate the International Development Association (IDA), the International Bank for Reconstruction and Development (IBRD), the International Finance Corporation (IFC), the Multilateral Guarantee Agency (MIGA), the United Nations Educational, Scientific and Cultural Organization (UNESCO), the International Civil Aviation Organization (ICAO), the World Health Organization (WHO), the World Meteorological Organization (WMO), the International Maritime Organization (IMO), the World Intellectual Property Organization (WIPO) and the International Fund for Agricultural Development (IFAD). A new constitution has been adopted for the United Nations Industrial Development Organization (UNIDO), which will enable it to enter into a relationship agreement, thus becoming the 16th Specialized Agency, once the new constitution is in force.

The International Atomic Energy Agency (IAEA) has a relationship agreement with the UN, the relationship being with the General Assembly and the Security Council rather than ECOSOC *(281 U.N.T.S. 369)*. It is not therefore a Specialized Agency.

The relationship agreements follow a general pattern (for details, see Parry, The Treaty-Making Power of the United Nations, *(1949) 26 B.Y.I.L. 108* at 137-46; Jenks, Coordination in International Organization, *(1951) 28 B.Y.I.L. 28)*. Besides recognizing the organization as a Specialized Agency, the agreements provide (with individual variations) for a degree of linkage of membership; reciprocal representation; reciprocal rights to propose agenda items; and for the UN General Assembly to make recommendations to the Specialized Agency in question. Provision is made for exchange of documentation and cooperation on studies and for regular reports by the agency (in accordance with art. 64 of the Charter) notably so as to enable ECOSOC to fulfill its coordinating role under art. 63. A right is also conferred (except in the case of the UPU) to seek ICJ advisory opinions. *See* Sands and Klein, *Bowett's Law of International Institutions* (5th ed.), 79-83.

The organizations themselves display a number of common features, but these are dictated more by the practical requirements of international organizations (cf. **organizations, international**) and by functional considerations, than by any peculiarity of Specialized Agency status. All Specialized Agencies have a plenary body which meets only periodically, encompassing the entire membership of the organization, and an executive body, which meets regularly, of limited and usually rotating membership. The plenary body may be described as the policy-making body. The organization is supported by a secretariat led by an executive head. Powers of the organization include the power to establish subsidiary bodies, to determine a budget and levy contributions. Institutional clauses provide for reporting; relations with other organizations including the UN; seat, legal capacity and privileges and immunities; dispute settlement; constitutional changes: Sands and Klein, *supra*, 84-114. Certain Specialized Agencies have power to adopt conventions or regulations.

sphere of influence   "The uncertainty of the extent of an occupation, and the tendency of colonising states to extend an occupation constantly and gradually into the interior, or 'hinterland,' of an occupied territory, led several states with colonies in Africa to secure for themselves 'spheres of influence' by treaties with other interested states. 'Sphere of influence' was therefore the description of territory exclusively reserved for future occupation by a state which had effectively occupied adjoining territories . . . but unless and until a title was acquired by effective occupation, a 'sphere of influence' was in essence little more than the area to which particular contractual arrangements extended": *I Oppenheim 691-2*. *See* Lindley, *The Acquisition and Government of Backward Territory in International Law* (1926), 207-36. *See also* **hinterland, doctrine of**.

spies   Spies are secret agents sent abroad for the purpose of obtaining clandestinely information on military, political or, increasingly, industrial and commercial secrets. They have no status in international law save under the laws of war and are subject to the full extent of the jurisdiction of a State in which they may be apprehended, although in a civilian, peacetime context a principle of proportionality may apply: see *I Oppenheim 1176*. Under art. 29 of the Hague Regulations 1907 *(207 C.T.S. 289)*, a spy is a person who clandestinely, or under false pretences, obtains or seeks to obtain information in the zone of operations of one belligerent with the intention of communicating it to the other belligerent. Soldiers not being in disguise and on scouting or despatch-bearing missions are not spies even if they penetrate the enemy zone of operations: the test is the clandestine or false character of the activity *(ibid.)*. Belligerents have a right under international law to use spies but equally belligerents may consider their activities as acts of illegitimate warfare. Under art. 30 of the Hague Regulations, a spy may not be punished without trial before a court martial. The usual penalty is death. Persons suspected of spying may be denied rights of communication but are not otherwise to be denied rights under the Geneva Convention (IV) relating to the Protection of Civilian Persons in Time of War *(75 U.N.T.S. 287*: art. 5). A spy is not, however, entitled to prisoner of war status: Geneva Convention (III) relating to the Treatment of Prisoners of War *(75 U.N.T.S. 135*: art. 4(A)(2)). *See II Oppenheim 421-425, 456, 574-575*.

Spitsbergen (Svalbard)   Generally regarded as *terra nullius* in the early years of this century, the Spitsbergen Archipelago was the subject of the Treaty concerning the Archipelago of Spitsbergen of 9 February 1920 *(2 L.N.T.S. 8)*. Art. 1 recognized the "full and absolute sovereignty of Norway over the Archipelago of Spitsbergen." The nationals of all the parties are given the right to hunt and fish subject to conservation measures taken by Norway (art. 2), free access to waters and ports (art. 3), and the right to own property (art. 7). *See* Nielsen, The Solution to the Spitsbergen Question, *14 A.J.I.L. 232 (1920)*.

sponsio/sponsiones   This term, which is now obsolete, denotes an agreement concluded by representatives of Heads of State rather than the Heads of State themselves. "If they conclude a treaty by exceeding their powers or acting contrary to their instructions, the treaty is not a real treaty, and is not binding upon the State they represent" [unless subsequently approved]: *I Oppenheim (8th ed.) 884*. In later times, in recognition of the fact that treaties were invariably negotiated by representatives, **ratification** became important as a means of enabling a State to avoid being bound by a *sponsio*. The term has no contemporary relevance. *See* art. 47 of the Vienna Convention on the Law of Treaties 1969, whereby a treaty is not invalidated by the fact that the representative of a State has neglected to observe a specific restriction placed on him in relation to expressing the consent of the State to be bound unless the restriction was notified to the other negotiating States.

St. Germain Treaties A number of treaties were concluded at St. Germain-en-Laye on 10 September 1919. (1) Treaty between the Allied and Associated Powers and Czechoslovakia (Protection of Minorities) *(226 C.T.S. 170)*; (2) Treaty between the Allied and Associated Powers and the Serb-Croat-Slovene State (Protection of Minorities) *(226 C.T.S. 182)*. Under these treaties, which were based on the Protection of Minorities Treaty with Poland of 28 June 1919 *(225 C.T.S. 412)*, Czechoslovakia and the Serb-Croat Slovene State undertook "to assure full and complete protection of life and liberty for all inhabitants . . ., without distinction of birth, nationality, language, race or religion" and to respect "the free exercise, whether public or private, of any creed, religion or belief, whose practices are not inconsistent with public order or public morals" (art. 2 of both treaties). In addition to guaranteeing other and specific rights to **minorities**, the treaties provide for supervision of their provisions by the Council of the League of Nations at the instance of any Council member (arts. 14 and 11 respectively). (3) Convention on the Control of Trade in Arms and Ammunition *(225 C.T.S. 482)*. This convention was intended to replace the Brussels Act of 2 July 1890 *(173 C.T.S. 293)*, but, not being ratified by many of these States manufacturing arms and ammunition, was itself replaced in part by the Convention on the Supervision of the International Trade in Arms and Ammunition of 17 June 1925 (Hudson, *Int. Leg.*, Vol. 3, 1634.). (4) Convention on the Revision of the General Act of Berlin of 26 February 1885, and of the General Act and Declaration of Brussels of 2 July 1890 *(225 C.T.S. 500)*. This Convention sought to regulate access to, and trade with, the parties' African colonies. (5) Convention on the Liquor Traffic in Africa *(226 C.T.S. 1)*, by which the parties sought to control the traffic in liquor in much of Africa. 6. Treaty of Peace with Austria *(226 C.T.S. 8: see* Treaty of **Versailles** 1919). Two other treaties were signed among the Allied and Associated Powers, relating to the cost of liberation of Austro-Hungary, and Italian reparation payments *(226 C.T.S. 193; 196)*.

St. Naoum, Monastery of, *(1924) P.C.I.J., Ser. B, No. 9.* After the second Balkan War, the Treaty of London of 1913 reserved to the Great Powers the task of settling Albania's frontiers. The Conference of Ambassadors accordingly met in London, but the First World War prevented the complete fixing of Albania's frontiers. Afterwards, the Conference of Ambassadors continued its consideration of Albania's frontiers, and by its decision of 6 December 1922 allotted to Albania the Monastery of St. Naoum. This decision was contested. The Conference referred to the Council of the League of Nations the question whether the Conference had, by its decision of 6 December 1922, exhausted its role, and by a resolution of 17 June 1924 the Council referred this question to the PCIJ for an advisory opinion. The Court in delivering the *opinion* that the decision of the Conference of Ambassadors exhausted its mission, found that (1) the Albanian frontier at St. Naoum had not been settled in 1913; (2) the decision of 6 December 1922 was an act necessary for the fulfilment of the mission entrusted to the Conference, and was definitive and of legal effect; and (3) there were no grounds for revising that decision.

St. Petersburg, Declaration of By this declaration of 11 December 1868 *(138 C.T.S. 297)* the 18 signatories, and 3 subsequent acceding States, renounced in wars between themselves the use of any explosive or incendiary projectile of less than 400 grammes weight. "The Declaration . . . is the first formal agreement restricting the use of weapons of war. . .": Higgins, *The Hague Peace Conferences* (1909), 7.

Standard Oil Company Tankers Case *(USA v. Reparations Commission) (1926) 2 R.I.A.A. 777.* Under the Treaty of Versailles *(225 C.T.S. 188),* the German Government transferred to the Allied and Associated Governments, represented by the Reparations Commission, all German merchant ships above a specified tonnage, the ships in question being defined as including those flying the German flag or owned by any German national or company. The German Government accordingly delivered to the Reparations Commission certain tankers belonging to a German company. The Standard Oil Company, a US company, protested against this delivery of the vessels, of which it claimed the beneficial ownership, on the basis that it was the owner of all the shares and virtually all the other securities of the German company, The Reparations Commission and the US Government concluded an agreement on 7 June 1920 for the submission of this dispute to arbitration, in which it was *held* that the claim of the Standard Oil Company must be rejected since, given the well-established distinction between the legal personality of a company and the rights of shareholders, the right of ownership of the company's securities did not of itself give rise to any right of "beneficial ownership" of the company's assets.

stand-by credit arrangement "In essence, a stand-by credit arrangement is an agreement entered into between a Fund member on the one hand and the [International Monetary] Fund on the other, whereby the latter, in exchange for assurances from the former (such assurances are normally set out in an unpublished letter of intent), provides the former with an undertaking that it shall be able to draw immediately, without further negotiation, and during a defined period of time (normally twelve months), an agreed amount of currency from the Fund's pool of resources. The arrangement is analogous to a commercial overdraft limit in municipal law": Shuster, *The Public International Law of Money* (1973), 196-7.

stare decisis *See* **precedent**.

Starke, Joseph Gabriel 1911- . International civil servant and Professor. Sometime member, PCA. Principal works include *An Introduction to International Law* (1947; 11th ed. 1994, by Shearer *sub nom. Starke's International Law*); *Studies in International Law* (1965); *The ANZUS Treaty Alliance* (1966).

START *See* **disarmament**.

State The criteria of statehood for purposes of international law are commonly held to be possession of "(a) a permanent population; (b) a defined territory; (c) government; and (d) capacity to enter into relations with the other States": **Montevideo Convention** on the Rights and Duties of States, 1933, art. 1 *(165 L.N.T.S. 19; (1934) 28 A.J.I.L. Supp. 75).* This provision is generally held to have evolved into a rule of customary international law. The requirements of population and territory are relatively uncontroversial. Essentially international law imposes no lower limit on the size of a population and recognizes that a population may be nomadic. (***Western Sahara Case*** *1975 I.C.J. Rep. 12).* The requirement of territory does not require a State to have undisputed borders, simply that it has "a sufficient consistency" (***Deutsche Continental Gas-Gesellschaft v Polish State*** *(1929) 5 I.L.R. 11* at 15*).* The requirement of a government does not specify any particular type of government; it need only exercise effective control over the territory in question. In particular, there is no requirement that a government be democratic. However, "recent practice with regard to the new states of Croatia and Bosnia-Herzegovina emerging out of the former Yugoslavia suggests the modification of the criterion of effective exercise of control by a government by a government throughout its territory. Both Croatia and Bosnia-Herzegovina were recognised as independent states by European Community member states and admitted to membership of the United Nations . . . at a time when both states were faced with a situation where non-governmental forces controlled substantial areas of the territories in question in civil war situations": Shaw, *International Law* (4th ed.), 142.

In relation to the fourth criterion, capacity to enter into international relations with other States, it has been argued that this requires **recognition** of an entity by other states (*see* **constitutive doctrine**). On the contrary, "[a]n entity is not a state unless it has competence, within its own constitutional system, to conduct international relations with other states, as well as the political technical and financial capabilities to do so": *US Restatement of the Law, Third, Foreign Relations Law of the United States*, Vol. 1, § 201. Thus, the essential requirement of capacity is **independence** (*see* **Austro-German Customs Union Case (1931) P.C.I.J., Ser. A/B, No. 41**). Other criteria which have been suggested are a degree of permanence, willingness and ability to observe international law, a degree of civilization, recognition by other States, and the circumstance of constituting a legal order; as well as further the qualities of legality (i.e. of not having been established contrary to international law) and consistency with the principle of self-determination: Crawford, *The Creation of States in International Law* (1979), Chaps. 1-3.

State aircraft The **Chicago Convention** on International Civil Aviation 1944 *(15 U.N.T.S. 295)* is not applicable to State aircraft (art. 1(a)), defined as "[a]ircraft used in military, customs and police service." Moreover, "[n]o state aircraft of a contracting State shall fly over the territory of another State or land thereon without authorization by special agreement or otherwise, and in accordance with the terms thereof" (art. 3(a)). Such an intrusion may allow the State intruded upon to shoot-down the aircraft where such action falls within the criteria of **self-defense**. This would, at the very minimum require a warning to be given to the intruding aircraft. State aircraft, defined as above, are excluded from the application of the **Tokyo Convention** on Offences and Certain Other Acts Committed on Board Aircraft 1963 *(704 U.N.T.S. 219)* (art. 1(4)), the Hague Convention for the Suppression of Unlawful Seizure of Aircraft (*see* **hijacking of aircraft**) 1970 *(860 U.N.T.S. 105)* (art. 3(2)), and the **Montreal Convention** for the Suppression of Unlawful Acts Against the Safety of Civil Aviation 1971 *(974 U.N.T.S. 177)* (art. 4(1)). *See* **hijacking** and **sabotage.**

State immunity *See* **sovereign immunity.**

State practice *See* **practice (international) of States.**

State responsibility Art. 1 of the ILC Draft Articles on State Responsibility 2001 *(UN Doc. A/56/10)* [ILC Draft Articles] provides that: "Every internationally wrongful act of a State entails the international responsibility of that State." Such a responsibility always arises when an act or omission of a State constitutes a breach of an international obligation incumbent upon the State, whether it be customary, conventional or other in origin, and when the act or omission in question is attributable to the State under international law (*see* **attribution**), quite irrespective of whether the same conduct is lawful under domestic law. (*See* **wrongful act, internationally**) While no distinction is made between contractual and non-contractual responsibility, until recently, a distinction was made between two different types of internationally wrongful conduct, i.e. international crimes and international delicts. This distinction was discussed in earlier versions of the Draft Articles on the basis that certain obligations were so essential for the protection of fundamental interests of the international community that its breach should be recognized as a crime. However, many considered the concept to be unjustifiable not least because of the difficulty of imposing penal sanction on States (*See*, for example, Gilbert, The Criminal Responsibility of States, (1990) 39 I.C.L.Q. 345). The distinction was abandoned in 1998.

Conduct is attributable to a State where it is undertaken by a State organ, "whether the organ exercises legislative, executive, judicial or any other functions, whatever position it holds in the organization of the State, and whatever its character as an organ of the central government or as of a territorial unit of the State" (art. 4). The conduct of persons or entities exercising elements of governmental authority are attributable to the State (art. 5), as is the conduct of organs placed at the disposal of a State by another State (art. 6). The State will not escape responsibility "even where the organ or individual exceeds its authority or contravenes instructions" (art. 7).

There is a presumption that a State is not responsible for the acts of private individuals: *Spanish Zone of Morocco Claim (1924) 2 R.I.A.A. 615 at 642*, and *2 R.I.A.A. 730;* cf. *Home Missionary Society Claim (1920) 6 R.I.A.A. 42; Pinson Claim (1928) 5 R.I.A.A. 325*. However, conduct of an individual or group of individuals which is directed or controlled by a State (art. 8), or conduct by an individual or group of individuals which factually amounts to the exercise of governmental authority and which is carried out in the absence or default of the official authorities of a State (art. 9), are attributable to the State.

Special considerations arise regarding responsibility of the State for **insurgency** (a non-technical term which may be said to embrace actions such as rebellion, revolt, riot, rising, and including events during civil wars) in the event of successful **revolution** (art. 10). However unsuccessful uprisings are not attributable to the State: "The principle that as a general rule a government is not responsible for injuries caused to aliens by members of an armed insurrection has been applied with great uniformity by international arbitral jurisprudence" *[1975] II I.L.C. Yearbook 93 ff.* A State is responsible for acts that it adopts as its own (art. 11).

A breach of an international obligation occurs when an act of a State is not in conformity with what is required of it by that obligation, regardless of its origin or character (arts. 12-15). A State can be held responsible for the acts of another State where it aids or assists in the commission of an internationally wrongful act (art. 16), where it directs and controls the commission of an internationally wrongful act by another State (art. 17), or where it coerces another State to commit an internationally wrongful act (art. 18). The wrongfulness of an act of a State is precluded where the wronged State consents to the conduct (art. 20), where the act is taken in self-defense in conformity with the UN Charter (art. 21), where the act is a valid **countermeasure** (art. 22), where the act is caused by *force majeure* (art. 23), where it is carried out in a condition of distress (art. 24), or where it is necessary to safeguard and essential interest of the State and does not impair an essential interest of the wronged State (art. 25). However, acts which are not in compliance with a peremptory norm of international law (*jus cogens*) cannot be excused (art. 26).

The legal consequences of a wrongful act are set out in arts. 28-33 and include the continued duty to perform the obligation breached (art. 29), the duty to cease and not-repeat the wrongful act (art. 30), the duty to pay **reparation** (art. 31) which shall include either singly or in combination (art. 34), restitution (art. 35), compensation (art. 36), satisfaction (art. 37), and shall include interest where necessary (art. 38). In the determination of reparation, account can be taken of contributory negligence by the wronged State (art. 39). Serious breaches of international law invoke the interest of all States in the breach which "shall cooperate through lawful means to end the breach (arts. 40-41). The process of invocation of the responsibility of a State is dealt with in arts. 42-48. Finally, arts 49-54 provide for the possibility of lawful countermeasures to be taken by the wronged State on the basis of proportionality.

The ILC Draft Articles are not legally binding in and of themselves. However, they are generally regarded as being reflective of customary international law. *See* Crawford, *The International Law Commission's Articles on State Responsibility: Introduction, Text and Commentaries* (2002). *See also* <www.un.org/law/ilc>.

State ships   Art. 9 of the Geneva Convention on the High Seas 1958 *(450 U.N.T.S. 82)* provides that "[s]hips owned or operated by a State and used only on government non-commercial service shall, on the high seas, have complete immunity from the jurisdiction of any State other that the flag State." Art. 21 of the Geneva Convention on the Territorial Sea etc. 1958 *(516 U.N.T.S. 205)* extends the provisions on innocent passage (arts. 14-17), on charges levied for passage through the territorial sea (art. 18) and on criminal (art. 19) and civil jurisdiction (art. 20) to "government ships operated for commercial purposes"; and art. 22(1) extends the provisions on innocent passage and charges to "government ships operated for non-commercial purposes." Art. 1 of the Brussels Convention for the Unification of Certain Rules relating to the Immunity of State-Owned Vessels of 10 April 1926 *(120 L.N.T.S. 187)* equates the liability of vessels owned or operated by States with that of private vessels. However, this does not apply to "ships of war, Government yachts, patrol vessels, hospital ships, auxiliary vessels, supply ships, and other craft owned or operated by a State, and used at the time . . . on Governmental and non-commercial service. . . ." (art. 3(1)).

The UN Convention on the Law of the Sea 1982 *(1833 U.N.T.S. 3)* uses a technique which is the converse of that of the 1958 Geneva Convention: the 1982 Convention for most purposes makes no distinction between State ships and other vessels: in principle the Convention applies, subject only to specific exceptions; thus the main body of rules relating to innocent passage in the territorial sea (arts. 17 to 26) apply to all ships. For the purposes of civil and criminal jurisdiction in the territorial sea, State ships operated for commercial purposes are assimilated to merchant ships. Arts. 29 to 32 lay down specific rules for warships and other State ships operated for non-commercial purposes. Warships may be required to leave the territorial sea immediately if they disregard the laws and regulations of the coastal state (art. 30), and the flag State bears responsibility for damage caused by a warship or other government ship operated for non-commercial purposes (art. 31). With these exceptions, nothing affects the immunity of State-owned ships (art. 32). Part III Section 2 on transit passage also applies to all ships (and aircraft). The State responsibility provision is restated for ships and aircraft entitled to sovereign immunity (art. 42(5)).

Warships and ships used only on government non-commercial service enjoy complete immunity on the high seas (arts. 95-96). Moreover, the provisions of the Convention on the protection and preservation of the marine environment do not apply to such vessels or aircraft (art. 236), although States are to ensure that such vessels and aircraft "act in a manner consistent, so far as is reasonable and practicable, with this Convention."

State succession   This term "is used to describe that branch of international law which deals with the legal consequences of a change of sovereignty over territory" (Malanczuk, *Akehurst's Modern Introduction to International Law* (7th ed.), 161), a change which may take place in a number of ways, whether by **cession**, **annexation**, formation of a union or federation, or attainment of independence, the common factor being that one sovereign substitutes itself for another in relation to a given piece of territory. State succession has effects on rights and obligations in three broad areas: treaties, private rights and matters of public administration. For historical survey see Verzijl, *International Law in Historical Perspective*, Part VII (1974).

(1) *Treaties.* The Vienna Convention on Succession of States in Respect of Treaties of 23 August 1978 *(1946 U.N.T.S. 3)*, albeit expressed to apply only in respect of a succession of States which has occurred after the entry into force of the Convention, except as may be otherwise agreed (art. 7), in many respects represents a codification of the customary law, itself profoundly affected by the evolution of State practice in the post-1945 era, with the emergence of so many new States. See Vallat, First Report on Succession of States in Respect of Treaties, in *[1974] II I.L.C. Yearbook 1*. Although a succession of States is stated not to affect boundary régimes (art. 11; *see uti possidetis*), other territorial régimes (art. 12; cf **servitude**), **permanent sovereignty** (art. 13) or questions relating to the validity of a treaty (art. 14), "[t]he main implication of the principle of self-determination has been the clean slate principle for the provisions of the draft articles relating to newly independent States. The clean slate principle did not involve rejection of the continuity of treaties, but did imply that the newly independent State was entitled to choose which treaties concluded by its predecessor would be regarded as continuing and which would be considered as terminated": Vallat, *supra*, 7. Agreements for the devolution of treaty obligations or rights from a predecessor State to a successor State cannot therefore of themselves bind a successor State to accept devolution (art. 8), nor is a newly independent State "bound to maintain in force, or become a party to, any treaty by reason only of the fact that at the date of the succession of States the treaty was in force in respect of the territory to which the succession relates" (art. 16). A newly independent State is therefore free to choose whether or not to become a party to a multilateral treaty (arts. 17 and 19) and may establish its status as a contracting State to a multilateral treaty which is not in force (art. 18), and, if it does exercise those rights, it enjoys all the rights regarding reservations etc. enjoyed by the predecessor State (arts. 20-21). On the other hand, a newly independent State succeeds to a bilateral treaty only with the express or implicit agreement of the other State party (art. 24), the effect being to constitute direct treaty relations that are independent of the fate of treaty relations with the predecessor State (cf. arts. 25-26). Where a succession of States occurs in relation to parts of territory, the guiding principle is that the treaties of the predecessor State cease to apply to that piece of territory and the treaties of the successor State extend to the whole of its territory as newly constituted, unless it appears from the treaty or is otherwise established that this would be incompatible with the object and purpose of the treaty or would radically change a condition for its operation (art. 15; similarly, *mutatis mutandis,* art. 30 in relation to newly independent States formed from two or more territories; arts. 31-33 in relation to a uniting of States and arts. 34-37 in respect of separations). For an account of recent State practice in relation to treaty succession, see Malanczuk, *supra*, 166-8.

(2) *Private Rights.* "It is a fundamental principle of international law that acquired rights of foreign nationals must be respected. In the case of State succession this means that the change of sovereignty works no effect upon such rights": O'Connell, International Law (2nd ed.), Vol. 1, 377; and O'Connell, *The Law of State Succession* (1956); *State Succession in Municipal Law and International Law* (1967), *passim*. "Private rights acquired under existing law do not cease on a change of sovereignty. It can hardly be maintained that, although the law survives, private rights under it have perished": **German Settlers in Poland Case (1923)** P.C.I.J., Ser. B, No. 6; **German Interests in Polish Upper Silesia (1926)** P.C.I.J., Ser. A, No. 7; **Chorzów Factory Case (1927-8)** P.C.I.J., Ser. A, No. 17.

(3) *Matters of Public Administration.* Concessions are subject to particular rules, but administrative contracts (those which provide "only for performance and which lacks the el-

ement of interest in land": O'Connell, *supra*, 383) are generally recognized as surviving if an entity survives capable of executing them (O'Connell, *The Law of State Succession* (1956), 144). Similarly, the national debt, local and localized debts are regarded as normally following the territory the subject of the succession, although changes of government through **revolution** raise special issues (*see also* **odious debts**). Equally, the successor State "in virtue of the extension of its sovereignty becomes possessed of all the property and rights and claims of the predecessor which relate to the acquired territory": O'Connell, *supra*, 380-90. With the exception of State archives (*see* **archives, State**), the Vienna Convention on Succession of States in Respect of State Property, Archives and Debts of 8 April 1983 *(22 I.L.M. 306 (1983))* does not seek to distinguish between classes of State property, laying down that immovable property situated in the territory passes as also do movables "connected with the activity of the predecessor State in respect of the territory" (art. 14). A partial succession or transfer creates particular difficulties, which the Convention is unable to resolve: in the absence of agreement there should be equitable apportionment (arts. 17 and 18 for movables and immovables; arts. 37,40 and 41 for State debt). Newly independent States in principle succeed to no State debt unless agreed that there is a link between the debt and local activity (art. 38; *and see* **odious debts**). The successor State also has complete freedom to maintain or to restructure the national administration, judiciary, armed forces, etc. of the territory, the principal limitations being in relation to acquired private rights. It follows that the nationality of persons in territory which has been the subject of State succession is largely a matter for the municipal law of the predecessor State and of the successor State and automatic acquisition/loss of nationality is not a feature of the common law systems, although the Convention on the Reduction of Statelessness 1961 *(989 U.N.T.S. 175)* requires States, in the event of ceding territory, to make provision that no person shall become stateless as a result (art. 10). As to international claims: "It is usually said that a successor State incurs no responsibility in international law with respect to the torts of its predecessor": O'Connell, *supra*, 386. *See also* ***Robert E. Brown Claim** (1926) 6 R.I.A.A. 120*; ***Hawaiian Claims** (1925) 6 R.I.A.A. 157*; see, however, *Lighthouses Arbitration (1956) 23 I.L.R. 81* at 90. *See generally I Oppenheim 208-44.*

stateless person "A person not having a nationality under the law of any State is called stateless": Weis, *Nationality and Statelessness in International Law* (2nd ed.), 161. "Since stateless individuals do not possess a nationality, the principal link by which they could derive benefits from international law is missing. They may, therefore, lack the possibility of diplomatic protection or of international claims being presented in respect of harm suffered by them at the hands of a state. . . . There has for some time been an effort to reduce by international conventions the possibilities of statelessness or, where that is impossible, to render less difficult the position of stateless persons": *I Oppenheim 886-7*. See, for example Hague Convention of 12 April 1930 on Certain Questions relating to the Conflict of Nationality Laws; the Protocol of the same date Relating to a Certain Case of Statelessness *(179 L.N.T.S. 89)* which sought to reduce the possibility of statelessness by providing, in particular, rules on the position of married women (*see* **women, nationality**) and children as well as providing for the mitigation of the consequences of statelessness. The Convention of 28 September 1954 relating to the Status of Stateless Persons *(360 U.N.T.S. 117)* was modeled on the Convention relating to the Status of Refugees 1951 *(189 U.N.T.S. 150)* "but gave stateless persons slightly less favourable treatment than had been given to refugees": *I Oppenheim 890*. Finally, the 1961 Convention on the Reduction of Statelessness *(989 U.N.T.S. 175)* requires States to grant nationality to persons such as children, foundlings, married persons who might previously have been considered stateless, and not to remove nationality from persons who renounce their nationality, and persons who live abroad for a long period of time. *See generally I Oppenheim 886-90*; Weis, *supra*.

States, economic rights and duties of *See* **Economic Rights and Duties of States, Charter of**.

status of forces agreements In order to regulate the extent to which foreign military personnel have exemption from local jurisdiction, it has become the practice, particularly since the Second World War, to regulate such issues in so-called status of forces agreements between the sending and receiving States. Thus, the Status of Forces Agreement of Parties to the North Atlantic Treaty (NATO) of 19 June 1951 *(199 U.N.T.S. 67)*, which entered into force on 23 August 1953, provides for concurrent jurisdiction vested in the sending and receiving States (art. VII (1)); the sending State has exclusive jurisdiction in respect of offences under its military law, but not under the law of the receiving State (art. VII (2)(a)); the receiving State has exclusive jurisdiction in respect of offences under its law, but not under the law of the sending State (art. VII (2)(b)). Where there is concurrent jurisdiction, the sending State has the primary right to exercise jurisdiction in relation to offences solely against the property or security of that State, solely against the person or property or security of that State, solely against the person or property of another member of the force or done in performance of official duty (art. VII (3)(a)); in all other cases, the receiving State has the primary right to exercise jurisdiction. *See* Rouse and Baldwin, The Exercise of Criminal Jurisdiction under the NATO Status of Forces Agreement, *51 A.J.I.L. 29 (1957)*; Schwartz, International Law and the NATO Status of Forces Agreement, *53 Col. L. Rev. 1091 (1953)*. The 1951 Agreement was extended by the Partnership for Peace Status of Forces Agreement of 19 June 1995 to cover the forces of those States not members NATO which had agreed to participate in NATO's Partnership for Peace Plan.

The **International Criminal Court** will have jurisdiction over the military personnel of any State Party which allegedly commit crimes within the jurisdiction of the court. This aspect of the ICC's jurisdiction has been objected to by the US which, although not party to the Rome Statute of the ICC, has enacted the American Servicemembers' Protection Act on 3 August 2002 in order to guard against the possibility of any member of the US armed forces being tried by the Court.

In relation to **United Nations forces**, such forces, which are composed of national contingents are generally immune from the jurisdiction of the receiving State, but remain subject to the exclusive jurisdiction of their respective sending States. See, for example, Regulation No 2000/47 on the Status, Privileges and Immunities of KFOR and UNMIK and their Personnel in Kosovo *(UN Doc. UNMIK/REG/2000/47)*. *See* Fleck and Addy, *The Handbook of the Law of Visiting Forces* (2001).

Stein, Eric 1913- . In US Government service 1946-55 and subsequently law professor at Michigan. Principal works include *Law and Institutions of the Atlantic Area* (with Hay, 1963); *Impact of New Weapons Technology on International Law* (1971); *Czecho/Slovakia: Ethnic Conflict, Constitutional Fissure, Negotiated Breakup* (with Cutler, 2000); *Thoughts from a Bridge: A Retrospective of Writings on New Europe and American Federalism* (2000).

Steiner and Gross v. Polish State *(1928) 4 I.L.R. 291*. The plaintiffs, one of Czechoslovak nationality and the other of Polish nationality, owned a tobacco factory in what was formerly German territory. Upon the transfer of sovereignty over the area in question from Germany to Poland, the Plaintiffs maintained that the rights they had possessed under German law were injuriously affected by Polish legislation establishing a tobacco monopoly.

They presented a claim against Poland to the arbitral tribunal established under the German-Polish Convention concerning Upper Silesia of 15 May 1922 *(9 L.N.T.S. 466),* which, *inter alia*, made provision for the protection of private rights after the transfer of sovereignty. The tribunal *held* that Poland's objection that as one of the plaintiffs was a Polish national the claim should be disallowed must be rejected: the Convention conferred jurisdiction on the tribunal irrespective of the nationality of the claimants.

Stimson doctrine *See* **non-recognition**.

Stockholm Declaration 1972 It has been said that "the watershed event in the international environmental law was the Stockholm Conference on the Human Environment in 1972 which summed up the awakened conscience and marked the beginning of a truly ecological era": Kiss and Shelton, *Manual of European Environmental Law* (1993), 11. Of the 24 principles enumerated in the Declaration, Principle 1 proclaims: "Man has the fundamental right to freedom, equality and adequate conditions of life, in an environment of a quality that permits a life of dignity and well-being, and he bears a solemn responsibility to protect and improve the environment for present and future generations. . . ." Principle 21 is perhaps its most cited by international lawyers, as an articulation of two emerging, now emergent, rules of customary law as to the rights of States to their resources and their liability for the consequences of activities in relation to these resources: "States have, in accordance with the Charter of the United Nations and the principles of Environmental law, the sovereign right to exploit their own resources pursuant to their own environmental policies, and the responsibility to ensure that activities within their jurisdiction or control do not cause damage to the environment of other states or of areas beyond the limits of national jurisdiction." *See also* the **Rio Declaration 1992**.

Stone, Julius 1907-85. Professor at various law schools in USA, UK, New Zealand and Australia. Principal works include *International Guarantees of Minority Rights* (1932); *Regional Guarantees of Minority Rights* (1933); *The Atlantic Charter—New Worlds for Old* (1943); *Legal Controls of International Conflict* (1954; rev. ed 1958); *Sociological Inquiries Concerning International Law* (1956); *Aggression and World Order* (1958); *Quest for Survival* (1961); *The International Court and World Crisis* (1962); *The Middle East Under Cease-Fire* (1967); *No Peace-No War in the Middle East* (1969); *Approaches to International Justice* (1970); *Towards a Feasible International Criminal Court* (with Woetzel, 1970); *Of Law and Nations* (1974); *Conflict Through Consensus* (1977).

Stowell, William Scott, 1st. Baron 1745-1836. English Admiralty lawyer; Admiralty judge 1788-1828. His decisions on prize law and international law have had a profound influence. *See* Roscoe, *Lord Stowell, His Life and the Development of English Prize Law* (1966).

straight baselines In drawing baselines for the **territorial sea**, art. 7(1) of the UN Convention on the Law of the Sea 1982 *(1833 U.N.T.S. 3)* provides that "[i]n localities were the coastline is deeply indented and cut into, or if there is a fringe of islands along the coast in its immediate vicinity, the method of straight baselines joining appropriate points may be employed. . . ." "The drawing of such baselines must not depart to any appreciable extent from the general direction of the coast, and the sea areas lying within the lines must be sufficiently closely linked to the land domain to be subject to the régime of internal waters" (art. 7(3)); and "account may be taken . . . of economic interests peculiar to the region concerned, the reality and the importance of which are clearly evidenced by a long usage" (art. 7(5)). These rules, and their identical predecessors in art. 4 of the Geneva Convention on the Territorial Sea, etc. 1958 *(516 U.N.T.S. 205),* were derived from the decision in *An-*

glo-Norwegian Fisheries Case 1951 I.C.J. Rep. 116. See Churchill and Lowe, *The Law of the Sea* (3rd ed.), 33-41.

straits, international Few problems arise for the rights of navigation where an international strait is broader than the territorial sea of the littoral States, vessels then exercising the freedom of navigation on the high seas (*see* art. 2(1) of the Geneva Convention on the High Seas 1958 *(450 U.N.T.S. 82)* and art. 87(1)(a) of the UN Convention on the Law of the Sea 1982 *(1833 U.N.T.S. 3)*). Where an international strait is wholly within the territorial sea of one or more States, the right of **innocent passage** permits the navigation of merchant vessels, but not necessarily of warships, subject to the restrictions that may legitimately be placed on such passage by the littoral State(s). Art. 16(4) of the Geneva Convention on the Territorial Sea, etc. 1958 *(516 U.N.T.S. 205)* provides that there must be no suspension of innocent passage "through straits which are used for international navigation between one part of the high seas and another part of the high seas or the territorial sea of a foreign State." This test is broader than that originally proposed by the ILC ("normally used" for international navigation: *[1956] II I.L.C. Yearbook 273*), and more in line with that enunciated in the **Corfu Channel Case** *1949 I.C.J. Rep. 4* at 28-9: "the decisive criterion is rather its geographical situation as connecting two parts of the high seas and the fact of its being used for international navigation. Nor can it be decisive that this Strait is not a necessary route between two parts of the high seas, but only an alternative passage. . . . It has nevertheless been a useful route for international maritime traffic." The UN Convention on the Law of the Sea 1982 has somewhat restricted this term. While defining an international strait as one used for "international navigation between one part of the high seas or an exclusive economic zone and another part of the high seas or an exclusive economic zone" (art. 37), the Convention specifically excludes the situation where "there exists through the strait a route . . . of similar convenience with respect to navigational and hydrographical characteristics" (art. 36). The articulation of right of **transit passage** through international straits was the *quid pro quo* for the increase in the breadth of the territorial sea to 12 miles in art. 3 of the UN Convention. *See* Koh, *Straits in International Navigation* (1982); Jia, *The Regime of Straits in International Law* (1998).

strategic area Within the UN **Trusteeship System**, a **trust territory** containing or consisting in a strategic area differs from other trust territories in only one major particular, viz. that all the functions in respect of it are exercised by the Security Council, rather than the General Assembly (art. 83(1) of the UN Charter). The basic objectives of the Trusteeship System, enumerated in art. 76, apply equally to a strategic area (art. 83(2)). The Security Council may request (art. 83(3)), and has requested (SC Res.of 7 March 1949), the assistance of the Trusteeship Council in performing those functions relating to political, economic, social and educational matters in the strategic areas. Only one territory, the former Japanese Mandated Islands, has been placed under trusteeship as a strategic area pursuant to the Trusteeship Agreement for the Pacific Islands of 2 April 1947 *(8 U.N.T.S. 189)* but that trusteeship has now ended. *See* **Micronesia**. *See* Toussaint, *The Trusteeship System of the United Nations* (1956), 119-124, 155-158.

Strategic Arms Limitation Talks *See* **disarmament**.

Strategic Arms Reduction Talks *See* **disarmament**.

Strupp, Karl 1886-1940. Professor, Frankfurt, 1926-40. Principal works: *Urkunden zur Geschichte des Völkerrechts* (1911); *Wörterbuch des Völkerrechts und der Diplomatik* (1920-27).

Suarez, Francisco 1548-1617. Spanish Jesuit theologian and philospher; exponent of natural law theories. Principal works: *De legibus, ac Deo legislatore* (1621); *Defensio fidei* (1613). (texts of selections of his works and translations in Carnegie Endowment, *Classics of International Law No. 20*).

subjects of international law "States are the principal subjects of international law. This means that international law is primarily a law for the international conduct of states, and not of their citizens. As a rule, the subjects of the rights and duties arising from international law are states solely and exclusively and international law does not normally impose duties or confer rights directly upon an individual human being, such as an alien or an ambassador." *I Oppenheim 16.* According to the conventional definition, "[a] subject of the law is an entity capable of possessing international rights and duties and having the capacity to maintain its rights by bringing international claims": Brownlie, *Principles of International Law* (5th ed.), 57, citing the **Reparation for Injuries Case 1949) I.C.J. Rep. 179.** The proposition established by the *Reparations Case* in relation to international organizations (in that instance, the UN itself) is now well established: cf **personality, international**. In addition to States, and to international organizations which enjoy a derived personality, a large number of entities enjoy a certain more limited status in international law, Brownlie, *supra,* 59 ff. citing the following: among established legal persons; political entities legally proximate to States (*e.g.*, Danzig), condominia (with the ending of the Anglo-French New Hebrides Condominium none at present exists), internationalized territories (*e.g.*, Danzig, Trieste and the Memel Territory); agencies established between States (*e.g.*, an arbitral tribunal); agencies of international organizations (*e.g.*, European Nuclear Energy Agency, an emanation of the OECD): as examples of special types of personality; non-self governing peoples, emergent and defunct States and belligerent and insurgent communities. A number of other entities (*e.g.*, exiled governments) depend for any status they enjoy upon the rights accorded by the host country. For some purposes (notably in relation to international crimes; the right of petition under human rights instruments), the status of the individual is also recognized.

A number of writers have sought to move away from the traditional subject/object dichotomy describing it as "an intellectual prison of our own choosing": Higgins, *Problems and Process: International Law and How We Use It* (1994), 49. These writers argue that international law is a decision-making process in which a wide range of actors participate: "In the way our world is organized, it is states which are most interested in, for example, sea space, or boundaries, or treaties; it is thus states which advance claims and counter-claims about these. Individuals interests lie in other directions: in protection from the physical excesses of others, in their personal treatment abroad, in the protection abroad of their property interests, in fairness and predictability in their international business transactions and in securing some external support for the establishment of a tolerable balance between their rights and duties within the national state. Thus the topics of minimum standards of treatment of aliens, requirements as to the conduct of hostilities and human rights are not simply exceptions conceded by historical chance within a system of rules that operate between states, rather they are part and parcel of the fabric of international law, representing the claims that are naturally made by individual participants in contradistinction to state participants": Higgins, *supra*, 5.

subjugation "Subjugation, that is the acquisition of territory by conquest followed by annexation, and often called title by **conquest,** had to be accepted into the scheme of modes of acquisition to title to territorial sovereignty in the period when the making of war was recognised as a sovereign right, and war was not illegal. . . . At no period did conquest alone and *ipso facto* make the conquering state the territorial sovereign of the conquered territory, even though such territory came through conquest for the time being under the sway of the conqueror. Conquest was a mode of acquisition only if the conqueror, after having firmly established the conquest, and the state of war having come to an end, then formally annexed the territory": *I Oppenheim 698-9.*

submarine cables *See* **cables and pipelines, submarine.**

submarine warfare Art. 1 of the Treaty Relating to the Use of Submarines and Noxious Gases in Warfare of 6 February 1922 *(25 L.N.T.S. 202)*, art. 22 of the Treaty for the Limitation and Reduction of Naval Armaments of 22 April 1930 *(112 L.N.T.S. 65)* and Rules annexed to the *Proces-Verbal* Relating to the Rules of Submarine Warfare of 6 November 1936 *(173 L.N.T.S. 353)* all seek to equate submarines with warships for the purpose of subjecting them to the same rules about action against merchant vessels; in particular, merchant vessels must not be sunk or rendered incapable of navigation without first placing the passengers, crew and ships papers in a place of safety.

submarines Art. 14(6) of the Geneva Convention on the Territorial Sea, etc. 1958 *(516 U.N.T.S. 205)* provided, in relation to the right of **innocent passage** through the territorial sea, that "[s]ubmarines are required to navigate on the surface and to show their flag." The otherwise identical corresponding provision in the UN Convention on the Law of the Sea 1982 *(1833 U.N.T.S. 3)*, art. 20, is extended to "other underwater vehicles."

subrogation This term, in its broadest sense, denotes the substitution of one State for another as regards rights accruing and obligations owed by the first State, and is most commonly encountered in the law of **State succession.**

subsidiary organs Arts. 22 and 29 of the UN Charter permit the General Assembly and Security Council respectively to "establish such subsidiary organs as it deems necessary for the performance of its functions." Subsidiary organs established by the General Assembly include the UN International Children's Emergency Fund (UNICEF) (by Res. 57(I)); the International Law Commission (by Res. 174(II)); the UN Administrative Tribunal (by Res. 351(IV); *Administrative Tribunal of UN, Effect of Awards Case 1954 I.C.J. Rep. 47)* and the UN Emergency Force (UNEF 1956-67) (by Res. 998 (ES-1); *Expenses Case 1962 I.C.J. Rep. 151)*. Most of the subsidiary organs established by the Security Council have been concerned with a particular dispute or situation.

subsidiary sources Art. 38(1) of the ICJ Statute, after enumerating three formal sources of international law, specifies in para. (d) two subsidiary sources, viz. "subject to the provisions of Article 59, judicial decisions and the teachings of the most highly qualified publicists of the various nations. . . ." Art. 59 provides that "[t]he decision of the [International] Court has no binding force except between the parties and in respect of that particular case." Subsidiary sources are intended to be merely material or evidential, and not in themselves establishing a rule of international law. *See* further **sources**; **publicists**; **judicial decisions.**

subsoil *See* **seabed and subsoil.**

succession *See* **State succession.**

Suez Canal The Suez Canal, opened in 1869, was the subject of the Convention of Constantinople of 29 October 1888 *(171 C.T.S. 241)* which provided that the Canal "shall always be free and open, in time of war as in time of peace, to every vessel of commerce or of war, without distinction of flag" (art. 1). In July 1956, Egypt nationalized the (Anglo-French) Suez Canal Company and assumed control of the Canal. However, Egypt has formally declared that it accepts the provisions of the Convention of Constantinople: *265 U.N.T.S. 299*. The status of the Suez Canal was discussed in *The Wimbledon Case (1923) P.C.I.J., Ser. A, No. 1. See* Baxter, *The Law of International Waterways* (1964). *See I Oppenheim 592-5.*

suggestion of State Department "In the twentieth century, foreign states, with increasing frequency, requested the State Department to ask the department of Justice to make a 'suggestion of immunity' [see *The Schooner Exchange v. McFaddon, 11 U.S. (7 Cranch) 116* (1812)] to the court. In 1943, the Supreme Court rules that such a suggestion of immunity by the Executive Branch 'must be accepted by the court as a conclusive determination by the political arm of the Government' that proceeding with the suit 'interferes with the proper conduct of our foreign relations,' and 'it becomes the court's . . . duty to proceed no further in the cause.' [*Ex Parte Peru, 318 U.S. 578, 588-9* (1943). *See also Republic of Mexico v. Hoffman, 324 U.S. 30* (1945)]. . . . In the 1970s both the practicing bar and the Department of State sought to relieve the Department of the task of ruling on claims of sovereign immunity, and to have decisions concerning immunity made by the courts and on the basis of more precise criteria defined by statute. The result . . . was the Foreign Sovereign Immunities Act of 1976": *Restatement, Third, of the Foreign Relations Law of the United States, 392. See* **sovereign immunity**. The practice of the Department of State issuing suggestions still applies in other fields, such as questions of **recognition** or the application of the **act of State** doctrine: *I Oppenheim 1051-2.*

summary procedure "With a view to the speedy dispatch of business, the Court shall form annually a chamber composed of five judges which, at the request of the parties, may hear and determine cases by summary procedure": art. 29 of the ICJ Statute; *see also* arts. 26-28. This summary procedure is set out in art. 92 of the **Rules of Court** 1978. The written proceedings are to consist of a single pleading by either party, with time-limits fixed by the Court, in consultation with the Chamber (if constituted) (art. 92(1)). The Court may authorize or direct that further written pleadings be filed if the parties so agree, or if the Chamber decides, *proprio motu,* or at the request of one of the parties, that such pleadings are necessary (art. 92(2)). If the parties agree, the Court may dispense with oral proceedings, but, even when there are no oral proceedings, the Court may call for further information and oral explanations (art. 92(3)). *See* Rosenne, *The Law and Practice of the International Court* (1965), Vol. I, 200-2. The procedure was first used in the *Gulf of Maine Area Case 1984 I.C.J. Rep. 246.*

superior orders While municipal law frequently recognizes that adherence to orders from a superior constitutes a defense to a criminal charge, art. 8 of the Charter of the International Military Tribunal of 8 August 1945 *(82 U.N.T.S. 280)* expressly provided that the "fact that the Defendant acted pursuant to order of his Government or of a superior shall not free him from responsibility, but may be considered in mitigation of punishment if the Tribunal determines that justice so requires." Art. 6 of the Charter of the Tokyo Military Tribunal is in similar terms. This rule has been accepted by the General Assembly in the Resolution on the Affirmation of the Principles of International Law Recognized by the Charter of the Nuremberg Tribunal, of 11 December 1946 (Res. 95 (I)), and by the ILC in its Principles of International Law Recognized in the Charter of the Nuremberg Tribunal and in the judgment of the Tribunal *([1950] II I.L.C. Yearbook 374)*; see **Nuremberg Principles**.

Art. 17(4) of the Statute of the **International Criminal Tribunal for the Former Yugoslavia** (SC Res. 827 (1993)) provides that "the fact that an accused person acted pursuant to an order of a Government or of a superior shall not relieve him of criminal responsibility, but may be considered in mitigation of punishment in the International Tribunal determines that justice so requires." (*See also* art. 6 of the Statute of the **International Criminal Tribunal for Rwanda** (SC.Res. 955 (1994)) which is framed in identical terms). However, Art. 33 of the Statute of the **International Criminal Court** 1998 *(37 I.L.M. 999 (1998))* provides in rather more equivocal terms that "(1) the fact that a crime within the jurisdiction of the Court has been committed by a person pursuant to an order of a Government or of a superior, whether military or civilian, shall not relieve that person of criminal responsibility unless: (a) the person was under a legal obligation to obey orders of the Government or the superior in question; (b) the person did not know the order was unlawful; and (c) the order was not manifestly unlawful; (2) for the purposes of this Article, orders to commit genocide or crimes against humanity are manifestly unlawful."

super-State   This term has no technical meaning in international law, but has been employed to connote an international organization with powers greater than its member States. Cf. **supranational organization**. In the *Reparations Case 1949 I.C.J. Rep. 174* at 179 the ICJ concluded that the UN had international personality sufficient to bring an international claim, but that was not the same as saying that the UN was a State; "Still less is it the same thing as saying that it is 'a super-State,' whatever that expression may mean."

supranational organization   This term denotes a particular form of international organization, clearly distinguishable from traditional international organizations (which might be referred to as intergovernmental organizations, thereby emphasizing the autonomy left to States) by a number of factors. These have been identified by Schermers and Blokker, *International Institutional Law*, (3rd. ed.), 41-2, thus: "(1) The organization should have the power to take decisions binding on the member states. (2) The organs taking the decisions should not be entirely dependent on the cooperation of all the member states. Some independence may be obtained in two ways. First, by allowing binding decisions to be adopted by majority vote, so that the member states can be bound against their will. Second, by composing the decision-making organ of independent individuals. (3) The organization should be empowered to make rules which directly bind the inhabitants of member states. This power enables the organization to perform government functions without the need or the possibility for national governments to transform the rules of the organization into domestic law. (4) The organization should have the power to enforce its decisions. Enforcement should be possible even without the cooperation of the governments of the states concerned. It may well be possible that other organs of the member states are used to aid the organization in this field. Thus, a national parliament and the national judiciary may coerce their government to fulfil its obligations to the organization. (5) The organization should have some financial autonomy. . . . (6) Unilateral withdrawal should not be possible. . . ." To these it might be added that the decisions taken by the organization should be superior to municipal law, irrespective of whether the municipal law pre-dates or post-dates these decisions. In short and in sum, the organization must be able to take decisions by something less than unanimity, these decisions must be binding on, and in, all member States, creating enforceable rights and duties for natural and juristic persons, and these decisions must be superior to prior and subsequent municipal law. As thus defined, the closest organization to supranational status is the **European Community**.

surrender   *See* **capitulation**.

suspension of membership/voting rights   Suspension of *membership* is sometimes provided for as an alternative to expulsion from an international organization, usually on grounds of persistent violation of the organization's constituent act (WHO, IAEA). In the

UN itself, the penalty for persistent violation is expulsion (UN Charter, art. 6), suspension being provided for in the case of preventive or enforcement action being taken against a member (art. 5). Suspension or expulsion triggers parallel action in a number of other organizations (UNESCO; IMO) or forms the basis for an autonomous decision on similar action (ILO). Suspension of *voting rights* is a common penalty for arrears in payment of financial contributions (UN Charter, art. 19; ILO, FAO, UNESCO, WHO, IBRD, IMO, IAEA, WIPO, IFAO). Voting rights of certain members of the UN were suspended during the 19th Session of the General Assembly following their refusal to meet certain expenses held by the ICJ to be expenses of the organization: ***Expenses of the United Nations, Certain, Case 1962 I.C.J. Rep. 151.*** *See* Schermers and Blokker, *International Institutional Law,* (3rd ed.), 907-918.

suspension of treaty *See* **treaties, termination and suspension**.

sustainable development doctrine Principle 27 of the Rio Declaration on Environment and Development 1992 *(31 I.L.M. 874 (1992))* provides that "States and people shall cooperate in good faith and in a spirit of partnership in the fulfilment of the principles embodied in this Declaration and in the further development of international law in the field of sustainable development." Thus expressed, it is more an aspiration or guideline than legal rule. Birnie and Boyle, *International Law and the Environment* (2nd ed.), 95 state rather optimistically: "It is clear, given the breadth of international endorsement of the concept, that few states would quarrel with the proposition that development in principle should be sustainable and that all natural resources should be managed in this way. What is lacking is any comparative consensus on the meaning of sustainable development, or on how to give it concrete effect in individual cases." *See also* **polluter pays doctrine**.

suzerainty A term of historical interest only as there are no longer any vassal States in existence, explained in *I Oppenheim (8th ed.) 188-9* thus: "Suzerainty is a term which was originally used for the relation between the feudal lord and his vassal; the lord was said to be the suzerain of the vassal, and at that time suzerainty was a term of Constitutional Law only. With the disappearance of the feudal system, suzerainty of this kind likewise disappeared. Modern suzerainty involves only a few rights of the suzerain State over the vassal State which can be called constitutional rights. The rights of the suzerain State over the vassal are principally international rights. Suzerainty is by no means sovereignty. It is a kind of international guardianship, since the vassal State is either absolutely or mainly represented internationally by the suzerain State."

Svalbard *See* **Spitsbergen**.

swap arrangements Dating from the mid-19th century, these are agreements between central banks, invariably acting as agents for States, providing for reciprocal credit, whereby one party agrees to exchange on request its currency for that of the other party up to a maximum amount and for a limited period of time (usually 3 to 6 months). Once a transfer is made both agree to reverse the transaction on a specified date at the same exchange rate. One authority has concluded that swap arrangements may be regarded as international agreements provided the two parties intended to create legally binding obligations in international law: Fawcett, Trade and Finance in International Law, *(1968) 123 Hague Recueil 232-7. See* Shuster, *The Public International Law of Money* (1973), 308-11; Mann, *The Legal Aspects of Money: With Special Reference to Comparative Private and Public International Law* (5th ed.).

Swinney Claim *(USA v. Mexico) (1926) 4 R.I.A.A. 98.* Swinney, a US national, while boating on a river forming part of the US-Mexico frontier, was shot and killed by two Mexican officials who claimed to have thought him engaged in unlawful activities. Both Mexican officials were at first arrested by the Mexican authorities, but were later released without any trial being held. A claim was submitted on behalf of Swinney's parents to the Mexico-US General Claims Commission set up by the General Claims Convention of 8 September 1923, which *held* that, as the killing of Swinney had been an unlawful act of Mexican officials, and Mexico had been dilatory in investigating the matter and had failed to prosecute and punish the offenders, Mexico was liable to pay compensation.

systems theory A modern approach to international law which investigates the extent to which international law is "conditioned by the character of the international system," such investigation being through "historical and analytical models on the way in which power is distributed and conflict conducted. . . .": Falk, *The Status of Law in International Society* (1970), 466-8. *See also* Kaplan and Katzenbach, *The Political Foundations of International Law* (1961).

T

tabula rasa   Literally, clean slate. *See* **negative succession theory**.

tacit consent   *See* **acquiescence; reservations**.

Tacna-Arica Arbitration *(Chile v. Peru) (1925) 2 R.I.A.A. 921*. By art. 3 of the Treaty of Ancon 1883, Chile and Peru agreed that the territory of the provinces of Tacna and Arica should be in the possession of Chile, and subject to Chilean laws and authority, for 10 years, and that there should then be a plebiscite to determine whether the territory should go to Chile or to Peru, the terms of the plebiscite to be prescribed in a special protocol to be negotiated. These negotiations being unsuccessful, the question whether the plebiscite should or should not take place was, by an agreement of 20 July 1922 *(21 L.N.T.S. 142)*, submitted by the parties to the arbitration of the President of the USA who, in *holding* that art. 3 of the Treaty of Ancon was still in effect and that accordingly the plebiscite should be held as stipulated therein, and in accordance with conditions determined by him, found that (1) the undertaking of each party to negotiate in good faith a protocol to fix the terms of the plebiscite did not, so long as it did not act in bad faith, oblige either of them to conclude an agreement it found unsatisfactory, nor did a party's refusal to ratify a particular protocol it considered unsatisfactory demonstrate bad faith; (2) while a party could be discharged from performance of art. 3 if the other party had demonstrated an intent to frustrate the carrying out of the agreement in respect of the plebiscite, such an intent could not be lightly imputed; Chile had not, during its period of administration, acted in the territory in such a way as to frustrate the purpose of the agreement for a plebiscite. (Difficulties arose regarding the execution of the award, and the Tacna-Arica territorial dispute was finally settled by a Treaty of 3 June 1929 between Chile and Peru).

Tadic Case   (ICTY Case # IT-94-1-A). Dusko Tadic, a Bosnian Serb, was brought before the International Criminal Tribunal for the Former Yugoslavia, and charged with crimes against humanity, grave breaches of the 1949 Geneva Conventions and violations of the laws and customs of war. A central part of his defense, at trial and reasserted on appeal against conviction, was the legality of the tribunal, its primacy over national courts and its subject-matter jurisdiction. The trial court held that the constitution of the ICTY, being embodied in Security Council Res. 827 (1993), was not reviewable: *36 I.L.M. 9082 (1997)*. The appellate chamber held that, while the ICTY could review Security Council acts to identify the scope of its jurisdiction, it was for the Tribunal to determine its own jurisdiction: it had inherent *competence de la competence*. The appellate chamber found Tadic guilty of additional crimes against humanity, grave breaches of the Geneva Conventions and violations of the laws and customs of war and increased his sentence from 20 to 25 years imprisonment. The appellate chamber also fined Tadic's former counsel for contempt for presenting false submissions and manipulating two witnesses: *38 I.L.M. 1518 (1999)*.

Tagliaferro Case *(Italy v. Venezuela) (1903) 10 R.I.A.A. 592*. Tagliaferro, an Italian national residing in Venezuela, was in 1872 subjected to an unlawful forced loan by the military authorities in the province where he was residing, for non-payment of which he was imprisoned. He immediately sought his release through judicial processes, but without success. *Held* by the Italian-Venezuelan Mixed Claims Commission set up under a Protocol of 13 February 1903, that since the responsible authorities of the State had full knowlédge of the wrongdoing from the beginning, the claim, although 31 years old, was not barred by prescription; and that the claimant was entitled to compensation for being wrongfully imprisoned for non-payment of an illegal demand, and for the gross denial of justice involved in not granting him redress.

tariff preferences *See* **preferential treatment**.

Tate Letter This is the letter, dated 19 May 1952, from the US State Department's Acting Legal Adviser Jack B. Tate to the Department of Justice *(26 State Dept. Bull. 984 (1952); 47 A.J.I.L. 93 (1953))*, stating the shift in policy of the US Government from support for the absolute theory of **sovereign immunity** to support for the restrictive theory. This theory of restrictive sovereign immunity was given statutory effect in the US by the Foreign Sovereign Immunities Act of 1976.

Tattler *(United States v. Great Britain) (1920) 6 R.I.A.A. 48*. The United States claimed damages respectively for two separate seizures in 1905 of the schooner *Tattler* and its detention for six days on the first occasion and three days on the second by the Canadian authorities, for alleged violations of provisions relating to fishing by foreign vessels. On the first occasion, the owners secured the release of the vessel by paying (under protest) a fine and by guaranteeing the British Crown against all claims arising out of the incident and renouncing all such claims before any courts or tribunals. *Held*, by the GB-US Arbitral Tribunal, that the owners' waiver of any claim or right before any court or tribunal was not subject to any protest or reservation; that the only right the US Government has is that of its national and, consequently, it can rely on no legal grounds other than those which would have been open to its national; that the claim relating to the first seizure and detention should therefore be dismissed; that the second seizure and detention had been the result of an error of judgment by the Canadian authorities; and that, accordingly, the claim relating to the second seizure and detention should be allowed, and an award made in favor of the United States.

Taubenfeld, Howard J. 1924- . Professor, Golden Gate College (1955-61), Southern Methodist Unversity (1964-). Principal works include *Law Relating to Activities of Man in Space* (with Lay, 1970); *Controls for Outer Space* (with Jessup, 1959); *Sex-Based Discrimination—International Law and Organization* (with Taubenfeld, 1978).

taxation: diplomatic and consular exemptions Diplomatic agents and, if they are not nationals of the receiving State, members of their families forming part of the household, are, subject to certain exemptions, exempt from all dues and taxes, personal or real, national, or regional or municipal: Vienna Convention on Diplomatic Relations 1961 *(500 U.N.T.S. 95)*, arts. 34, 37. Members of the administration and technical staff of the mission, together with members of their families forming part of their respective households, enjoy the same exemptions if they are neither nationals nor permanently resident in the receiving State (art. 37(2)). Members of the service staff and private servants enjoy only exemption from dues and taxes on their emoluments if they are neither nationals nor permanently resident in the receiving State (art. 37(3) and (4). Exemptions from tax co-extensive with those available to diplomatic agents and their families apply to consular officers, consular employees and members of their families forming part of their households: Vienna Convention on Consular Relations 1963 *(596 U.N.T.S. 261)*, art. 49(1).

Excepted from the exemptions available to diplomatic agents, consular officers and the subordinate categories are: indirect taxes of a kind which are normally incorporated in the price of goods and services (i.e., not including VAT, sales tax, etc., which are taxes charged on top of the price of goods); dues and taxes on real property unless held for the purposes of the mission or consular post; estate, succession or inheritance taxes except insofar as the property in question was present in the receiving State solely due to the presence there of the deceased in his official capacity or as a member of family; dues and taxes on private income and gains having their source in the receiving State; charges levied for specific services rendered; and, in most instances, registration, court or record fees, mortgage dues and stamp duties: Convention on Diplomatic Relations, art. 34; on Consular Relations, art. 49. *See* Denza, *Diplomatic Law* (2nd ed.), 194-208.

taxation: diplomatic and consular premises The premises of the diplomatic mission and consular premises, the residence of a diplomatic agent and the residence of the career head of consular post, are exempt from all national, regional or municipal dues and taxes, other than such as represent payment for specific services rendered:Vienna Convention on Diplomatic Relations 1961 *(500 U.N.T.S. 95)*, arts. 23, 30; Vienna Convention on Consular Relations 1963 *(596 U.N.T.S. 261)*, art. 32. These exemptions do not extend to taxes and dues which contractors are obliged to pay in their turn, and therefore normally pass on *(ibid.)*.

taxation: enterprise and persons Taxation is for most purposes a matter for municipal law and there are very few limitations on the right of the sovereign to tax those coming within its legislative reach: *M'Cullock v. Maryland, 4 Wheat. 316* (1819). "The right of the State to levy taxes constitutes an inherent part of its sovereignty; it is a function necessary to its very existence and it has often been alleged, not only in Mexico, but in the United States and other countries that legislatures, whether of States or of the Federation cannot legally create exemptions which restrict the free exercise of the sovereign power of the State in this regard": *George W. Cook v. United Mexican States (1930) 4. R.I.A.A. 593* at 595. Taxation becomes a subject for international law in relation to taxation of international persons (*see* **taxation, diplomatic and consular exemptions**; **diplomatic and consular premises**; **taxation and international organizations**) and in relation to conflicts between tax jurisdictions and double taxation. These matters are for the most part regulated by a network of bilateral so-called double taxation agreements. There is no general multilateral instrument on double taxation, but extensive work has been done within the OECD, notably to develop a Model Double Taxation Convention on Income and Capital. A first version was approved in 1963, with regular revisions since (OECD, *Model Tax Convention on Income and Capital* (2003)). The Model Convention uses the criterion of residence as the test of application (art. 1), income arising in any State being available for taxation in most instances in the State of residence. The definition of the term resident (art. 4) also embraces the British concept of domicile, so its application for UK tax purposes is also potentially very wide. So far as concerns business profits, art. 7(1) of the Model Convention stipulates that "the profits of an enterprise of a Contracting State shall be taxable only in that State unless the enterprise carries on business in the other Contracting State through a permanent establishment situated therein. If the enterprise carries on business as aforesaid, the profits of the enterprise may be taxed in the other State but only so much of them as is attributable to that permanent establishment." This approach is widely followed in practice and was widely invoked in representations made against **worldwide unitary taxation**.

taxation: sovereigns and States "It is sometimes said that one state may not levy taxation on another state's property, although it is uncertain whether this is attributable to considerations of the equality and independence of states or to the impropriety of taking any measure of enforcement against a state should it refuse to pay the tax levied": *I Oppenheim 364n.* Certainly, foreign sovereigns and their property and State-owned property (if devoted to public or governmental purposes) are exempt from enforcement of tax laws by the territorial State by virtue of **sovereign immunity**, resting for the most part on customary law. *See also* **taxation: diplomatic and consular premises**.

taxation and international organizations International organizations and their staffs are as a rule exempted from taxation by virtue of their constituent instruments providing for functional immunities; see art. 105(1) of the UN Charter. For the UN, detailed provisions are contained in the Convention on Privileges and Immunities of the United Nations of 13 February 1946 *(1 U.N.T.S. 15)* and, for Specialized Agencies, in the Convention on the Privileges and Immunities of the Specialized Agencies of 21 November 1947 *(33 U.N.T.S. 261)*. Exemption from taxation on salaries paid to officials is a privilege usually to be found, with the notable exception of the UN/US Headquarters Agreement of 26 June 1947 *(11 U.N.T.S. 11)*. The exemption is qualified in the case of some organizations. The purpose of the exemption is to create conditions of equality amongst staff, and in the same spirit a number of organizations (notably the UN, ILO, IMO, the European Community, but not the Council of Europe or OECD) impose an internal income tax or "assessment." In some instances (notably the European Community), there is a bar on taking into account the income exempted from tax for other tax purposes (*e.g.*, to inflate the marginal rate of tax applicable to other sources of income): Plantey, *Droit et Practique de la Fonction Publique International* (1977), 337. *See* Schermers and Blokker, *International Institutional Law* (3rd ed.), 670-8.

Teheran, Proclamation of An international conference on human rights, meeting in Teheran, proclaimed on 13 May 1968 *(UN Doc. A/CONF.34/41)* its faith in the **Universal Declaration on Human Rights** 1948 and other human rights instruments and urged all peoples and States to dedicate themselves to these principles (arts. 1 and 2), declaring the Universal Declaration to be "a common understanding of the peoples of the world concerning the inalienable and inviolable rights of all members of the human family. . . ." (para. 2).

telecommunications *See* **International Telecommunications Union**.

telegraph cables *See* **cables and pipelines, submarine**.

Tellech Case *(US v. Austria and Hungary) (1928) 6 R.I.A.A. 248.* In August 1914, Tellech, while residing in Austria, was arrested as an agitator and interned for 16 months. He was then impressed into service in the Austro-Hungarian Army. The US claimed compensation on his behalf. Tellech had been born in the US of Austrian parents in 1895. Under the constitution and laws of the US, he was by birth an American national. Under the laws of Austria, he also possessed Austrian nationality by parentage. When 5 years old, Tellech accompanied his parents to Austria, where he continued to reside. *Held* by the US-Austria-Hungary Claims Commission established under an Agreement concluded in 1924 *(48 L.N.T.S. 70)* that the claim must be dismissed. The action taken against Tellech by the Austrian civil authorities and by the Austro-Hungarian military authorities was taken in Austria, where he was voluntarily residing, and in his capacity as an Austrian citizen. Citizenship was to be determined by municipal law. Under the law of Austria, to which Tellech had voluntarily subjected himself, he was an Austrian citizen. The Austrian and the Austro-Hungarian authorities were within their rights in dealing with him as such. Although he possessed dual nationality, he voluntarily took the risk incident to residing in Austria and subjecting himself to the duties and obligations of an Austrian citizen under the municipal law of Austria.

Temple of Preah Vihear Case *(Cambodia v. Thailand) 1961 I.C.J. Rep. 17; 1962 I.C.J. Rep. 6.* In the period 1904-1908, France, then conducting the foreign relations of Indo-China, made various boundary settlements with Siam, in particular a treaty of 13 February 1904 which established the general character of the frontier (which in the relevant area was to follow the watershed line), the exact boundary of which was to be delimited by a Franco-Siamese Mixed Commission. The Mixed Commission visited the area of the Temple but there was no record of any decision establishing the boundary line. The Siamese Government later requested that French officers should map the frontier region. These maps were completed in the late 1907, and were communicated to the Siamese Government in 1908. Amongst them was a map showing the Temple on the Cambodian side: the map boundary line departed from the watershed line. The map was never formally approved by the Mixed Commission. The dispute over sovereignty over the Temple was referred by Cambodia and Thailand to the ICJ, which, having first *held* (unanimously) that it had jurisdiction on the basis of acceptances by both parties of the Court's compulsory jurisdiction, then *held* (9 to 3) that the Temple was situated in territory under Cambodian sovereignty, and (7 to 5) that Thailand was under an obligation to restore to Cambodia objects removed from the Temple by Thai authorities. Although the 1907 map had at its inception no binding character, the Siamese authorities had acquiesced in it, and local acts of Siamese/Thai administration to the contrary did not negative the consistent attitude of the central authorities; Thailand was accordingly precluded from denying its earlier acceptance of the map. The acceptance of the map involved its adoption by the parties as an interpretation of the settlement that prevailed over the terms of the Treaty of 1904.

termination *See* **severance of diplomatic relations**; **treaties, termination and suspension**.

terra nullius "The expression *'terra nullius'* was a legal term of art employed in connection with 'occupation' as one of the accepted legal methods of acquiring sovereignty over territory. 'Occupation' being legally an original means of peacefully acquiring sovereignty over territory otherwise than by cession or succession, it was a cardinal condition of a valid 'occupation' that the territory should be *terra nullius*—a territory belonging to no-one—at the time of the act alleged to constitute the 'occupation' . . .": ***Western Sahara Case*** *1975 I.C.J. Rep. 6* at 39. Cf. ***Eastern Greenland Case*** *(1933) P.C.I.J., Ser. A/B, No. 53* at 44 and 63. *See also* ***Clipperton Island Case*** *(1931) 2 R.I.A.A. 1105*; ***Island of Palmas Case*** *(1928) 2 R.I.A.A. 829*; ***Minquiers and Ecrehos Case*** *1953 I.C.J. Rep. 47*; ***Rann of Kutch Case*** *(1968) 17 R.I.A.A. 1*; ***Western Sahara Case*** *1975 I.C.J. Rep. 12.*

territorial application clauses "Unless a different intention appears from the treaty or is otherwise established, a treaty is binding upon each party in respect of its entire territory": Vienna Convention on the Law of Treaties 1969, art. 29. This is so irrespective of the metropolitan or non-metropolitan character of the relevant portion of the State's territory, the test being whether or not there is responsibility for external relations. In practice, States frequently reserve the power by means of a territorial application clause not to apply treaties to non-metropolitan territories, or to extend them at a later date so as to allow time for consultation and local legislation. *See* **colonial clause** as to the two basic types. *See* Aust, *Modern Treaty Law and Practice* (2000), Chap. 11.

territorial integrity While art. 2(4) of the UN Charter proscribed the threat or use of force against, *inter alia,* "the territorial integrity . . . of any State," no definition is provided as to what constitutes territorial integrity. Some commentators have pointed to the consequences of the absence of a definition. Thus, Goodrich, Hambro and Simons, *Charter of the United Nations* (3rd ed.), 51 ask: "Is the prohibition violated if a member sends its armed forces into the territory of another state for 'protective' purposes, with the declared intention of withdrawing them as soon as the threat to the weaker state has been removed? Is the territorial integrity of a state respected so long as none of its territory is taken from it? Or does respect for the territorial integrity of a state require respect for its territorial inviolability?" Some answers to those questions are provided by the **Friendly Relations Declaration** of 24 October 1970 (GA Res. 2625 (XXV)), Principle 1 of which prohibits the military occupation of the territory of a State in contravention of the Charter, and denies any legal effect to territorial acquisitions effected through the threat or use of force. Additionally, the Declaration proscribes any intervention, direct or indirect, in the affairs of a State, especially armed intervention. *See also* **political independence**.

territorial law This term is infrequently used to denote the law of a particular State, the more common term being **municipal law** (or domestic law).

territorial sea It had long been recognized in international law that a coastal State has sovereignty over a belt of water adjacent to its coast, generally termed the territorial sea or territorial waters. From the late 18th century, this belt of water came to be as accepted as extending to three miles. *See* Walter, Territorial Waters: The Cannon Shot Rule, *22 B.Y.I.L. 210 (1945)*; Kent, The Historical Origins of the Three-Mile Limit, *48 A.J.I.L. 537 (1954)*; *and see* **three mile rule**. Attempts to fix a limit failed of agreement at a League of Nations Codification Conference in 1930 *(Conference for the Codification of International Law* (1930), Vol. 3, 210-1); at the First United Nations Conference on the Law of the Sea (UNCLOS I) in 1958, the Geneva Convention on the Territorial Sea etc. 1958 *(516 U.N.T.S. 205)* being silent on the issue of extent; cf. the earlier ILC statement that "international law does not permit an extension of the territorial sea beyond twelve miles": *[1957] II I.L.C. Yearbook 265)*; and again at the Second UN Conference on the Law of the Sea in 1960. The increasing claims to a territorial sea of twelve miles have been recognized in art. 3 of the UN Convention on the Law of the Sea 1982 *(1833 U.N.T.S. 3)*: "Every State has the right to establish the breadth of its territorial sea up to a limit not exceeding 12 nautical miles. . . ." This breadth is to be measured from the **baseline**: art. 4. *See* arts. 3-7 of the 1982 Convention on the identification and drawing of the baseline. *See also* **bays**; **low-tide elevations**. For the rules for delimiting a territorial sea boundary between adjacent or opposite States, see art. 15. The sovereignty of the coastal State extends to its territorial sea, but that sovereignty is exercised subject to conventional and other rules of international law: art. 2. The foremost restriction upon a coastal State's rights in its territorial sea relates to the **innocent passage** of foreign vessels: see arts. 17-26. The sovereignty of the coastal State extends to the airspace above, and the sea-bed below, the territorial sea: art. 2(2). *See* Colombos, *International Law of the Sea* (6th ed.), Chap. 3; O'Connell, *The International Law of the Sea*, Vol. 1, (1982), Chaps. 3-4, Vol. 2 (1984), Chaps. 17 and 19; Brown, *The International Law of the Sea* (1994), Vol. 1, Chaps. 5-6.

territorial sovereignty *See* **sovereignty, territorial**.

territoriality "It is an essential attribute of the sovereignty of this realm, as of all sovereign independent States, that it should possess jurisdiction over all persons and things within its territorial limits and in all causes civil and criminal arising within these limits": *The Cristina [1938] A.C. 485* at 496 *per* Lord Macmillan. This territorial principle of **ju-**

risdiction is the most extensively used in the practice of States; indeed, there exists a presumption that jurisdiction is territorial. In their practice, some States adopt the so-called objective territorial principle of jurisdiction, others the so-called subjective territorial principle. The former asserts the jurisdiction of the State in respect of offences commenced outside the territory of the State but consummated within the territory; the latter asserts the jurisdiction of the State in respect of offences commenced inside the territory of the State but consummated outside the territory. *See* Harvard Research on International Law, Convention on Jurisdiction with Respect to Crime: *29 A.J.I.L. Supp. 491-7 (1935).* "Though it is true that in all systems of law the territorial character of criminal law is fundamental, it is equally true that all or nearly all these systems of law extend their action to offences committed outside the territory of the State which adopts them, and they do so in ways which vary from State to State. The territoriality of criminal law, therefore, is not an absolute principle of international law and by no means coincides with territorial sovereignty": ***The Lotus Case (1927) P.C.I.J., Ser. A, No. 10*** at 20. The other principles of jurisdiction asserted by States are the nationality, the **passive personality,** the **protective** (or security) and the **universal** principles. *See* Mann, Jurisdiction in International Law, *(1964) 111 Hague Rec. 9*; Mann, The Doctrine of Jurisdiction in International Law Revisited after Twenty Years *(1985) 186 Hague Rec. 9*; Akehurst, Jurisdiction in International Law, *(1972-73) 46 B.Y.I.L. 145.*

territory, acquisition of "No unanimity exists with regard to the modes of acquiring territory on the part of members of the international community": *I Oppenheim 678*. However, most commentators have identified five methods by which territory can be acquired under international law: **cession**; **conquest**; **subjugation**; **accretion**; **occupation**; and **prescription**. *See also* **self-determination**. Frequently, but without much practical utility, the methods of acquiring title to territory are classified as either original or derivative, the former applying to territory not subject to prior ownership by a State, the latter to territory subject to prior ownership, the title of the new owning State being derived from the prior owning state. *See* Jennings, *The Acquisition of Territory in International Law* (1963); Crawford, *The Creation of States in International Law* (1979), Part II.

territory, concept of "State territory is that defined portion of the surface of the globe which is subjected to the sovereignty of a state. A state without a territory is not possible, although the necessary territory may be very small. . . . The importance of state territory lies in the fact that it is the space within which the state exercises its supreme, and normally exclusive, authority": *I Oppenheim 563-4*. *See* Crawford, *The Creation of States in International Law* (1979), Chap. 2.

territory, loss of "To the five modes of acquiring sovereignty over territory correspond five modes of losing it—namely, cession, dereliction, operations of nature, subjugation, prescription. But there is a sixth mode of losing territory—namely, revolt": *I Oppenheim 716*. Clearly, just as **cession** gives territory to a State, so another State loses territory; **dereliction** is the obverse of **occupation**; operations of nature both increase and decrease territory (*see* **accretion**); **subjugation** following **conquest** is the loss of territory to a victor State in war; and **prescription** may be both acquisitive and extinctive of territorial rights. While it can be asserted that "[r]evolt followed by secession is a mode of losing territory to which there is no corresponding mode of acquisition" *(I Oppenheim 717)*, this is true only in the sense that the territory lost is not acquired by another pre-existing State. *See* Crawford, *The Creation of States in International Law* (1979), Chap. 9. *See also* **self-determination**.

territory, responsibility for   While it is an incident of sovereignty that a State has exclusive competence in and over its territory, there is a recognized rule of international law that "no State has the right to use or permit the use of its territory in such a manner as to cause injury . . . in or to the territory of another or the properties or persons therein, when the case is of serious consequence and the injury is established by clear and convincing evidence": *Trail Smelter Arbitration (1941) 3 R.I.A.A. 1905* at 1911. *See also* the *Corfu Channel Case 1949 I.C.J. Rep. 4*; and the **Friendly Relations Declaration** of 24 October 1970 (GA Res. 2625(XXV)). *See also* **abuse of rights**; **air pollution**.

terrorism   Terrorism as a phenomenon has a considerable history, but early terrorism was mainly internal and thereby readily subject to national criminal jurisdiction. International terrorism, frequently intended by disaffected groups within States to draw attention to real or perceived grievances, became a matter of international concern with a spate of attacks against aircraft in the late 1950s. As to aircraft, *see* the **Tokyo Convention** on Offences and Certain Other Acts Committed on Board Aircraft 1963 *(704 U.N.T.S. 1971)*, the Hague Convention for the Suppression of Unlawful Seizure of Aircraft 1970 *(806 U.N.T.S. 105*; *see* **hijacking (of aircraft))**, the Montreal Convention for the Suppression of Unlawful Acts against the Safety of Civil Aviation 1971 *(974 U.N.T.S. 177; see* **aircraft sabotage**), extended to airports by a Protocol in 1988 *(27 I.L.M. 672 (1988))*. As to attacks on diplomats and the taking of hostages, *see* the Convention on the Prevention and Punishment of Crimes against Internationally Protected Persons, including Diplomatic Agents 1973 *(1035 U.N.T.S. 167)*, the International Convention against the Taking of Hostages 1979 *(1316 U.N.T.S. 205*; *see* **hostage(s))**. At to protecting the transport of nuclear material, *see* the Convention on the **Physical Protection of Nuclear Materials** 1979 *(1456 U.N.T.S. 246)*. As to terrorist acts at sea, see the Convention for the Suppression of Unlawful Acts against the Safety of Maritime Navigation 1988 *(27 I.L.M. 672 (1988))*, extended to fixed platforms by the Protocol of the same year *(27 I.L.M. 685 (1988))*. As to terrorist bombings, *see* the International Convention for the Suppression of Terrorist Bombings 1997 *(37 I.L.M. 249 (1998))*. As to the Financing of Terrorism, see the International Convention for the Suppression of Financing of Terrorism 1999 *(39 I.L.M. 268 (2000))*. At this time, two further conventions are being elaborated: a Comprehensive Convention against Terrorism and a Convention against Nuclear Terrorism. In addition, there are regional terrorism conventions for the Americas (1971), Europe (1977), South East Asia (1987), Arab States (1998), the CIS (1999), the OIC (1999) and Africa (1999). These global and regional instruments are collected in the UN publication *International Instruments related to the Prevention and Suppression of International Terrorism* (2001); and appear at <http://untreaty.un.org/English/Terrorism.asp>.

The global (UN) conventions share a number of common features: the definition of the proscribed terrorist acts; the obligation to make these acts criminal, subject to each State's jurisdiction and to severe penalties; the obligation of each State to investigate any allegations and to either extradite or prosecute an alleged offender; the facilitation of extradition, with the exclusion of the political offence exception; the obligation to cooperate; and certain human rights guarantees for alleged terrorists. Alongside the convention régime, the Security Council has become increasingly involved in action against terrorism, especially after the 9/11 attacks in the US; *see* SC Res. 1373 (2001).

While terrorism has proved difficult to define, each convention preferring merely to identify specific proscribed acts, the International Convention for the Suppression of Financing of Terrorism 1999 offers (in art. 2(1)(b)) a definition, terrorism being "any . . . act intended to cause death or serious bodily injury to a civilian . . . when the purpose of such act, by its nature and context, is to intimidate a population, or to compel a government or an international organization to do or abstain from doing any act." A better definition is offered in the (as yet un-adopted) Comprehensive Convention against Terrorism, art. 2(1): an act which "by any means, unlawfully and intentionally, causes: (a) Death or serious bodily injury to any person; or (b) Serious damage to public or private property, including a place of public use, a State or government facility, a public transportation system, an infrastructure facility or the environment; or (c) Damage to [such] property, places, facilities, or systems . . ., resulting or likely to result in major economic loss; when the purpose of the conduct, by its nature or context, is to intimidate a population, or to compel a Government or an international organization to do or abstain from doing any act." *See* Walsh, *Terrorism: Documents of International and Local Control* (41 vols. 1979-2003).

terror-sponsoring States *See* **axis of evil**.

Test-Ban Treaties There are three test-ban treaties. The Treaty Banning Nuclear Weapons Tests in the Atmosphere, in Outer Space and under Water (sometimes known as the Partial Test Ban Treaty or the Moscow Treaty) was signed on 5 August 1963 *(480 U.N.T.S. 43)* and came into force on 10 October 1963. The Treaty bans "any nuclear weapon test explosion or any other nuclear explosion" (art. II (1)) in three environments under the jurisdiction and control of a contracting State: "in the atmosphere; beyond its limits, including outer space; or underwater, including territorial waters or high seas" (art. I (1)(a)). Also, a State must not carry out such explosions in any other environment if this causes radioactive debris to be present outside its territory (art. I (1)(b)). The Treaty on the Limitation of Underground Nuclear Weapon Tests of 3 July 1974 *(13 I.L.M. 906 (1974))* bans any underground nuclear weapon test explosion with a yield exceeding 150 kilotons (art. I (1)), and obliges the parties (USA and USSR) to limit the number of other underground nuclear test explosions to a minimum (art. I (2)). The Treaty does not apply to testing for peaceful purposes (art. III). The Comprehensive Nuclear Test-Ban Treaty was signed on 10 September 1996 *(36 I.L.M. 230 (1997))*. It is not yet in force, such depending, according to art. XIV, on ratification by all the States enumerated in Annex I; it has not been ratified by China or the US, nor by the three so-called "threshold States," Israel, India and Pakistan. The Convention contains a blanket prohibition on nuclear testing in art. I: "(1) Each State Party undertakes not to carry out any nuclear weapon test explosion or any other nuclear explosion, and to prohibit and prevent any such nuclear explosion at any place under its jurisdiction or control. (2) Each State Party undertakes, furthermore, to refrain from causing, encouraging, or in any way participating in the carrying out of any nuclear weapon test explosion or any other nuclear explosion." The Convention establishes the Comprehensive Nuclear Test-Ban Treaty Organization (CTBTO) "to achieve the object and purpose of this Treaty, to ensure the implementation of its provisions, including those for international verification of compliance with it, and to provide a forum for consultation and cooperation among States Parties" (art. II (1)). An elaborate verification system is also established (art. IV). *See* <www.ctbto.org>.

Texaco v. Libya *(1975 and 1977) 53 I.L.R. 389, 422.* The two plaintiff companies were parties to 14 Deeds of Concession granting them certain petroleum rights in Libya. In 1973 and 1974, Libya nationalized the properties, rights and assets of the plaintiff companies under these concessions. The nationalization laws provided for the payment of compensation (but none was paid). The companies began arbitration proceedings under the concessions. The Libyan Government did not take part in the proceedings, but it stated certain objections to the arbitration taking place. *Held* by Dupuy, sole arbitrator, that (1) the arbitration was governed by international law, and the concessions (which constituted binding contracts) were within the domain of international law, being governed (in accordance with their terms) by principles of Libyan law so far as they were common to principles of international law, and otherwise by general principles of law including those applied by international tribunals; (2) that Libya had acted in breach of its obligations under the concessions; (3) that a State's sovereignty did not justify disregard of its contractual obligations by an act of nationalization; and (4) that the normal sanction for non-performance of contractual obligations was *restitutio in integrum* which was inapplicable only to the extent that restoration of the *status quo ante* was impossible (of which there was no evidence in this case), and Libya was therefore legally bound to perform and give full effect to the concessions.

text books *See* **publicists.**

Textor, Johann Wolfgang 1638-1701. German jurist and philospher; Professor, Altorf (1666-73), Heidelberg (1673-90). In essence, a positivist. Principal work: *Synopsis juris gentium* (1680; text and translation in *Classics of International Law,* No. 6 (1966)).

thalweg "In the case of rivers separating two States . . . their frontiers are divided by the geographical centre running down the middle, except where the stream in navigable, in which case the centre of the deepest channel, or as it is usually called, the 'thalweg,' is taken as the boundary. The derivation of this word indicates the downward course or the course followed by the vessels of the largest tonnage in descending the river": Colombos, *International Law of the Sea* (6th ed.), 224. The rationale for the thalweg rule was stated by the US Supreme Court in *New Jersey v. Delaware 291 U.S. 361* at 380 (1934) to be based on "equality and justice . . . if the dividing line were to be placed in the center of the stream rather than in the center of the channel, the whole tract of navigation might be thrown within the territory of one state to the exclusion of the other." *See also Louisiana v. Mississippi 282 U.S. 458* (1931); *Arkansas v. Tennessee 310 U.S. 563* (1940); *Chamizal Arbitration (1911) 11 R.I.A.A. 316.*

Thant, U. 1909- . Burmese diplomat and teacher. Third Secretary-General of the UN 1961-71. Publications: *League of Nations* (1933, in Burmese); *Toward World Peace* (1964); *Portfolio for Peace* (1971); *View from the UN* (1978).

Third Generation (human rights) A descriptor for human rights enjoyed by groups rather than individuals, such as the rights to **self-determination** and **development**, being, generally (with the exception of self-determination), the most recent, least widely acknowledged and accepted and most controversial of the three "generations" of human rights. *See also* **First Generation** and **Second Generation** human rights.

third State A third State, sometimes referred to as a third party, is defined in art. 1(h) of the Vienna Convention on the Law of Treaties 1969 as "a State not a party to the treaty." Part II, Section 4 of the Convention, titled "Treaties and Third States," sets out as a general rule: "A treaty does not create either obligations or rights for a third State without its consent" (art. 34), thereafter detailing how a third State may come to acquire duties and rights under a treaty (arts. 35-8). *See pacta tertiis nec nocent nec prosunt. See* Aust, *Modern Treaty Law and Practice* (2000), Chap. 14. *See also* Chinkin, *Third Parties in International Law* (1993) who points out that third parties to disputes have rights to intervene in proceedings before the ICJ under arts. 62-3 of its Statute (in Chap. 6); and that third parties to armed conflicts are subject to both rights and duties (in Chap. 13).

Third World This term, more frequently used in the 1950s and 1960s than today, denotes those States which emerged from colonial status at that time and which saw themselves as constituting a third "bloc," distinct from the Communist and Western blocs, and relatively poor. Broadly synonymous with **non-aligned countries** and **developing countries**. Cf. **First World**; **Fourth World**; **Second World**.

Thomasius, Christian 1655-1728. German jurist and political philosopher. Professor, Halle, 1690-1728. Follower of Grotius and Pufendorf; proponent of natural law doctrine. Principal works: *Institutiones jurisprudentiae divinae* (1688); *Fundementa juris naturae et gentium* (1705).

threat to the peace *See* **peace, threat to**.

three mile rule According to Bynkershoek, a State could claim jurisdiction within the cannon-shot range of its shore batteries *(terrae potestas finitur ubi finitur armorum vis)*. By the end of the 18th century, the range of artillery was about three miles or one marine league and that distance became generally recognized as the breadth of the maritime belt. Due to technical developments, and after World War II in particular, general adherence to the limit of three miles for claims of territorial waters began to break down. The Geneva Convention on the Territorial Sea and the Contiguous Zone 1958 *(516 U.N.T.S. 205)* therefore contained no limit on the breadth of the territorial sea, it being left to the UN Convention on the Law of the Sea 1982 *(1833 U.N.T.S. 3)* to fix a limit of 12 nautical miles (art. 3) and a further 12 miles for the **contiguous zone** (art. 33). *See* Walker, Territorial Waters, the Cannon Shot Rule, *(1945) 22 B.Y.I.L. 210*; Colombos, *International Law of the Sea* (6th ed.), Chap. 3. *See also* **territorial sea**.

tidelands dispute The right to control the sea-bed contiguous to the coasts of the United States has been an issue between the Federal and State Governments since the 1940s. The issues raised are constitutional. In a number of decisions, the Supreme Court held that the US Government had control of the sea-bed throughout the territorial sea *(U.S. v. California 332 U.S. 19* (1947)), and beyond within the scope of US claims to such sea-bed *(U.S. v. Louisiana 339 U.S. 600* (1950); *U.S. v. Texas 339 U.S. 707* (1950)). By the Submerged Lands Act 1953 *(67 Stat. 29)* the US relinquished to the States all its rights in the sea-bed within specified geographical limits (three miles in the Atlantic and Pacific, 9 miles in the Gulf of Mexico), while confirming its rights beyond these limits. The Outer Continental Shelf Lands Act 1953 *(67 Stat. 462)* provided for US jurisdiction (and authority to grant exploitation leases) over the "outer continental shelf," i.e., seaward of the areas relinquished to the States by the earlier Act. Subsequently, the Supreme Court interpreted the Submerged Lands Act as conferring, in the Gulf of Mexico, a nine-mile belt to Florida and Texas, but only a three-mile belt to the other Gulf States: *U.S. v. Louisiana, Texas, Mississippi, Alabama and Florida 363 U.S. 1* (1960). *See* Bartley, *The Tidelands Oil Controversy* (1953).

Tilsit Peace Treaty 1807 This treaty between France and Russia, signed at Tilsit on 25 June (7 July) 1807 *(59 C.T.S. 231)* provides the background for a remarkable example of the exercise of the right of self-preservation. Secret articles of a separate treaty between the parties signed at the same time *(59 C.T.S. 246)*, which became known to Britain, provided that Denmark should, in certain circumstances, be coerced into declaring war against Great Britain, enabling France to seize the Danish fleet so as to make use of it against Great Britain. Britain demanded of Denmark that its fleet be delivered into the custody of Great Britain, to be restored after the war. Denmark refused to comply with the British request, whereupon Britain considered that a case of necessity in self-defense had arisen, and shelled Copenhagen and seized the Danish fleet. Articles of Capitulation were signed at Copenhagen on 7 September 1807 *(59 C.T.S. 315)*. Hall, *A Treatise on International Law* (8th ed.), 326-7, concludes: "The emergency was one which gave good reason for the general line of conduct of the English Government. The specific demands of the latter were also kept within due limits. Unfortunately Denmark, in the exercise of an indubitable right, chose to look upon its action as hostile, and war ensued [resulting in the seizure of the Danish fleet after the shelling of Copenhagen], . . . but offers no justification for the harsh judgments which have been frequently passed upon the measures which led to it." For a contrary view, see Hodges, *The Doctrine of Intervention* (1915), 7.

Tinoco Claims Arbitration *(Great Britain v. Costa Rica) (1923) 1 R.I.A.A. 369.* In January 1917, Frederico Tinoco overthrew the Government of Costa Rica and set up a new Constitution. In August 1919, Tinoco retired, and the next month his Government fell, and the old Constitution was restored. During the Tinoco administration, (a) the Government granted a petroleum concession to a company all the stock of which was owned by a British company; and (b) shortly before the collapse of the Tinoco Government, new arrangements were made for the issue by Costa Rica of currency notes and bonds, on the basis of which the Royal Bank of Canada acquired some of the bonds, and honored checks drawn against them by the Tinoco Government. In 1922, the restored Government of Costa Rica enacted laws invalidating the concession and the Tinoco Government's banking laws and transactions between the State and holders of the bonds issued under those laws. By a special agreement concluded in 1922 *(17 L.N.T.S. 152)*, the resulting claims were referred to the arbitration of Chief Justice Taft, sole arbitrator, who, in rejecting the claims, *held* that (1) a change of government had no effect on the international obligations of the State; (2) notwithstanding that its origins were not in accordance with the former Constitution, the Tinoco Government was an actual sovereign government, in actual and peaceful administration of the country; (3) non-recognition of a government by other States was evidence that it did not have the control and independence entitling it by international law to be regarded as a government where such non-recognition was based on considerations of actual sovereignty and control, and not of constitutional illegitimacy of origin; (4) non-recognition by Great Britain of the Tinoco Government did not estop Great Britain from presenting to the successor Government claims based upon the acts of the Tinoco Government; (5) the provisions in the contract and in Costa Rican banking law committing the claimants not to present their claim through the intervention of their State of nationality did not prevent that State from protecting its nationals by presenting their claims to the tribunal; (6) as the concession was itself invalidly granted by virtue of the terms of the Tinoco Constitution, the cancellation of it did not involve an international wrong; (7) the successor Government was not responsible for the payments made by the Bank of Canada, which were primarily personal to the Tinoco family and not for legitimate governmental use, and accordingly the invalidating of such transactions did not constitute an international wrong.

Tlatelolco, Treaty of By art. 1 of the Treaty for the Prohibition of Nuclear Weapons in Latin America (the Treaty of Tlatelolco, signed on 14 February 1967 *(6 I.L.M. 521 (1967))*, the Contracting Parties undertake to use exclusively for peaceful purposes the nuclear material and facilities under their jurisdiction and to prohibit and prevent in their respective territories the testing, use, manufacture, production or acquisition of nuclear weapons or the receipt, storage, installation or deployment of any such weapons. They further undertake not to participate in any nuclear weapons activities, and not only in Latin America. The agreement is administered by OPANAL (the Organization for the Prohibition of Nuclear Weapons in Latin America and the Caribbean) (art. 7) composed of a General Conference, Council and Secretariat. A control system is established (arts. 12-18). The right to use nuclear energy for peaceful purposes and to carry out explosions for peaceful purposes is safeguarded (arts 17-18). To the Treaty are appended two protocols the first, extending "denuclearization in respect of warlike purposes" to dependent territories, and the second calling on nuclear weapons States to respect "the statute of denuclearization."

Tobacco Control Convention Properly styled the Framework Convention on Tobacco Control, this WHO convention was adopted on 21 May 2003 *(42 I.L.M. 518 (2003))* "to protect present and future generations from the devastating health, social, environmental and economic consequences of tobacco consumption and exposure to tobacco smoke" (art. 3). It does so through 7 guiding principles (in art. 4): information on health consequences; political commitment; international cooperation; multi-sectoral measures; liability; technical and financial assistance; and participation by civil society. Each State party is obliged to develop and implement tobacco control strategies (art. 5(1)); to adopt and implement effective legislative and other measures to prevent or reduce tobacco consumption and exposure to tobacco smoke (art. 5(2)); to prevent commercial interests frustrating its efforts to fulfil its obligations (art. 5(3)); to cooperate with other parties (art. 5(4)), competent international and regional organizations (art. 5(5)) and to raise financial resources (art. 5(6)) to implement the objectives of the Convention.

Tobar doctrine This is a doctrine of non-recognition of governments first enunciated by Dr. Tobar, the then Minister of Foreign Relations of Ecuador in March 1907, and subsequently adopted into two treaties concluded among the Central American Republics: the General Treaty of Peace and Amity between the Central American States of 20 December 1907 *(206 C.T.S. 63)* and Treaty of the same name of 7 February 1923 *(17 A.J.I.L. Supp. 117 (1923))*. According to the doctrine as enunciated in these treaties, the governments of each of the five Republics undertook not to recognize any other government in Central America which had come into power by revolutionary means "so long as the freely elected representatives of the people thereof have not constitutionally reorganized the country" (art. II of the 1923 Treaty). Costa Rica and El Salvador denounced the 1923 Treaty in 1932 and 1933 respectively. The doctrine for a time affected the practice of the five Central American Republics, and the US *(see* McMahon, *Recent Changes in the Recognition Policy of the U.S.* (1933)). *See also* **Estrada doctrine**.

Tokyo Convention 1963 In recognition of the fact that customary international law inadequately coped with the jurisdictional problems arising from crimes on board aircraft in flight, the Tokyo Convention on Offences and Certain other Acts Committed on Board Aircraft was adopted on 14 September 1963 *(704 U.N.T.S. 219)*. The Convention applies to offences against penal law and "acts which, whether or not they are offences, may or do jeopardize the safety of the aircraft or of persons or property therein or which jeopardize good order and discipline on board" (art. 1(1)(b)); to aircraft other than military, customs or police aircraft (art. 1(4)); to aircraft "from the moment when power is applied for the purpose of take-off until the moment when the landing run ends" (art. 1(3)); and to aircraft in flight or on the surface of the high seas or of any other area outside the territory of any State (art. 1(2)). The State of registration has jurisdiction in respect of the proscribed acts (art. 3(1)), as has a State in whose territory the offence has effect, whose nationals and permanent residents are the culprits or victims, against whose security the offence is committed, whose flight rules or regulations are breached, or whose multilateral international obligations require action (art. 4). For the purposes of extradition, the offence is to be treated as if committed, not only where it occurred, but also in the State of registration (art. 16(1)), although the Convention imposes no obligation to extradite (art. 16(2)). *See* Shubber, *Jurisdiction over Crimes on Board Aircraft* (1973). *See also* **hijacking (of aircraft); aircraft sabotage; terrorism**.

Torrey Canyon Incident On 18 March 1967, the Liberian-registered oil tanker *Torrey Canyon* grounded on the Seven Stones Reef between Scilly and Land's End off the South West coast of England, ultimately shedding its entire cargo of 120,000 tons of crude oil. Attempts at salvage having failed, and with the environmental consequences increasingly affecting the coasts of England and France, the UK government ordered the bombing and destruction of the vessel on 28 March. Immediate questions about a State's right to destroy a polluting vessel outside its territorial waters and about civil liability for oil pollution damage were, through the **IMCO**, resolved with the adoption of the International Convention Relating to Intervention on the High Seas in Cases of Oil Pollution Casualties of 29 November 1969 *(970 U.N.T.S. 211)* and the International Convention on Civil Liability for Oil Pollution Damage of the same date *(973 U.N.T.S. 3)*. It was the stimulus for other conventions relating to pollution adopted under the aegis of the IMCO (and IMO). *See* **marine pollution**.

Torture, Convention against The Convention against Torture and Other Cruel, Inhuman or Degrading Treatment or Punishment, adopted by the General Assembly on 19 December 1984 *(1465 U.N.T.S. 85)*, defines torture as "any act by which severe pain or suffering, whether physical or mental, is intentionally inflicted on a person" to obtain information or a confession; to punish, intimidate or coerce; or for any reason based on discrimination of any kind; when such pain or suffering is inflicted by or at the instigation of or with the consent or acquiescence of a person acting in an official capacity; but "[i]t does not include pain or suffering arising only from, inherent in or incidental to lawful sanctions": art. 1(1).

States parties are required to take measures to prevent torture in their jurisdictions and to ensure that acts of torture are legally punishable offences: arts. 2 and 4. No exceptional circumstances, such as war or public emergency, may be invoked to justify torture (art. 2(3)); nor can obeying the orders of a superior officer or other authority be used as justification (art. 2(3)). The Convention requires States with custody of a suspected torturer "if it does not extradite him, [to] submit the case to its competent authorities for the purpose of prosecution": art. 7(1); *see **aut dedere aut judicare***. Provision is made to facilitate extradition of persons believed to have committed acts of torture (art. 8), and for protection and compensation for torture victims (arts. 13-14). It provides for education regarding the prohibition of torture to be included in the training of law enforcement personnel and other persons involved in the custody, interrogation or treatment of prisoners or detainees (arts. 10-11). A Committee against Torture, parallel in its structure to other treaty implementation bodies, such as the **Human Rights Committee**, is provided for consisting of 10 independent experts elected by States parties (art. 17). States parties are required to report regularly to the Committee on measures they had taken to give effect to the Convention, and CAT is empowered to make general comments on the reports of States parties (art. 19). Pursuant to art. 20, CAT, upon receiving "reliable" information that appears to contain "well-founded" indications of the systematic practice of torture in the territory of a State party, may invite that State party "to co-operate in the examination of the information" and to submit observations. States (art. 20) and individuals and groups (art. 22) can make complaints (termed "communications") to CAT alleging violations of the Convention provided the State against which the complaint is made has recognized the right of other States and individuals and groups to do so. An Optional Protocol of 18 December 2002 *(42 I.L.M. 26 (2003))* establishes a system of regular visits by an independent, international body (termed the Sub-Committee on Prevention; see arts. 5-16) and independent national bodies (termed national preventive mechanisms; see arts. 17-23) "to all places where people are deprived of their liberty, in order to prevent torture and other cruel, inhuman or degrading treatment or punishment" (art. 1). *See also* the European Convention for the Prevention of Torture 1987 *(E.T.S. No. 126)*.

Tourism Organization, World *See* **World Tourism Organization**.

tracé parallele A method of determining the outer limit of any area of maritime territory measurable in distance from the baselines of the territorial sea, originally devised as a method of determining the outer limit of the territorial sea itself. "This line . . . results from lifting the low-water line bodily from its existing position, moving it seaward a distance equal to the width of the marginal sea, and laying it down parallel to its former position. Such a line will usually be extremely irregular, following all sinuosities presented by the low-water line. This procedure has never been seriously advocated by geographers and cartographers": Shalowitz, *Shore and Sea Boundaries,* (1962), Vol. 1, 169. Cf. **arcs-of-circles**.

trading with the enemy "Before the First World War . . . most British and American writers and decisions, and also some French and German writers, asserted the existence of a rule of International Law that all intercourse, and especially trade, was *ipso facto* by the outbreak of war prohibited between the subjects of the belligerents, unless it was permitted under the custom of war (as, for instance, ransom bills), or was allowed under special licences, and that all contracts concluded between the subjects of the belligerents before the outbreak of war became extinct or suspended. On the other hand, most German, French, and Italian writers denied the existence of such a rule, but admitted that all belligerents were empowered to prohibit by special orders all trade between their own and enemy subjects. The matter is one essentially of Municipal, as distinct from International, Law": *II Oppenheim 318-9*. In fact, many States specified in legislation the intercourse proscribed during the two World Wars, the UK in the Trading with the Enemy Acts 1914 and 1939, the USA in the Trading with the Enemy Acts of 1917 and 1941. *See also* McNair and Watts, *The Legal Effects of War* (4th ed.), Chap. 16. *See* further **enemy, enemy character**.

tradition of territory *I Oppenheim 682* states: "The treaty of cession should be followed by actual tradition of the territory to the new owner-state, unless such territory is already occupied by the new owner. . . ." As the debate over whether or not actual tradition is required for a valid cession, the same authority concludes: "Perhaps both views go too far. The essence of the question is whether the treaty is in its effects 'personal' or 'real': viz. whether it operates purely as a contract or whether it is also intended to operate as a conveyance of sovereign responsibility. This at least in some measure must depend upon the proper interpretation of the instrument, in the light of the circumstances of the case": *ibid., 683. See* **cession**.

Trail Smelter Arbitration *(USA v. Canada) (1938), (1941) 3 R.I.A.A. 1905*. As a result of smelting operations of a Canadian company at Trail, in Canada, sulfur dioxide fumes were emitted from the company's plant. The USA alleged that these fumes caused damage in the USA to agriculture, livestock, property and businesses. In 1935, Canada and the USA concluded a special agreement *(3 R.I.A.A. 1907)* submitting the dispute to an arbitral tribunal, which *held* that some damage had occurred in the USA as the result of the smelting operations of the Canadian company, and that Canada was responsible in international law for the conduct of the company: under the principles of international law "no State has the right to use or permit the use of its territory in such a manner as to cause injury by fumes in or to the territory of another or the properties or persons therein, when the case is of serious consequence and the injury is established by clear and convincing evidence" (at 1965). In its decision in 1938, the tribunal, in establishing the existence of some damage in the USA due to the fumes traveling down-wind from the smelting plant in Canada, awarded compensation to the USA, and established a temporary régime for the operation of the plant so as to avoid a recurrence of such damage. The USA sought to re-open that part of the decision relating to compensation. In its 1941 award, the tribunal *held* that its earlier decision was *res judicata* and no "manifest error" in the decision had been established justifying its reconsideration; and it established on a permanent basis a régime for operation of the smelting plant.

traité-contrats *See* **traité-lois**.

traité-lois Some writers (*e.g.*, Shearer, *Starke's International Law* (11th ed.), 37-8) have sought to draw a distinction between law-making treaties which lay down rules of universal or general application (*traité-lois*) and 'treaty contracts,' for example, a treaty between two or only a few States, dealing with a special matter concerning these States exclusively (*traité-contrats*) *(ibid.,* 48). This distinction is open to a number of criticisms, not least that to some extent it ignores the essential principle in treaty law that a treaty is contractual and therefore binding only upon those States which have consented to it. Cf. ***jus cogens***; **law-making treaties**.

traitor *See* **treason**.

transboundary air pollution *See* **air pollution**.

transformation, doctrine of The school of thought which, in opposition to the doctrine of **incorporation**, holds that the rules of international law are not part of municipal law without specific legislation. "To be binding, [international] law must have received the assent of the nations who are to be bound by it. This assent may be express, as by treaty or the acknowledged concurrence of governments, or may be implied from established usage. . . . Nor, in my opinion, would the clearest proof of unanimous assent on the part of other nations be sufficient to authorize the tribunals of this country to apply, without an Act of Parliament, what would practically amount to a new law. In so doing we should be unjustifiably usurping the province of the legislature": *The Franconia (R. v. Keyn) (1876) 2 Ex. D. 63* at 203 *per* Cockburn C.J. While some have questioned the precise import and effect of this statement, particularly as to whether it is wholly inconsistent with the doctrine of **incorporation**, British practice in the relationship between customary international law and municipal law clearly favors the doctrine of incorporation. *See* especially *Trendtex Trading Corporation v. Central Bank of Nigeria [1977] 1 Q.B. 529*. *See* **adoption, doctrine of**.

transit passage International law has long recognized an enhanced right of passage through international straits situated wholly within the territorial sea of one or more States (of which there are around 100 used for international navigation). *See* **straits, international** and art. 16(4) of the Geneva Convention on the Territorial Sea etc. 1958 *(516 U.N.T.S. 205)* providing that there shall be no suspension of **innocent passage** through international straits; and the ***Corfu Channel Case** 1949 I.C.J. Rep. 4*. Art. 38 of the UN Convention on the Law of the Sea 1982 *(1833 U.N.T.S. 3)* created, or at least defined, the right of transit passage. The right extends to "all ships and aircraft" (art. 38(1)), including warships and submarines, and military aircraft (*see* art. 39(3): "State aircraft"). It is to be exercised by "continuous and expeditious transit," although entering, leaving or returning from a littoral State is permissible "subject to the conditions of entry to that State" (art. 38(2)). The conditions for the exercise of the right are less restrictive than for **innocent passage**:

vessels and aircraft must merely refrain from the threat or use of force against the territorial integrity or political independence of any littoral State (cf. the detailed enumeration of activities considered not innocent for the purposes of innocent passage in art. 19(2)), and from any activities incidental to normal transit except where rendered necessary by *force majeure* or by distress, and must comply with certain standards relating principally to safety at sea and pollution (art. 39). While a littoral States may designate sea-lanes and ·traffic separation schemes (art. 41), it may not suspend transit passage (art. 44). *See* Brown, *The International Law of the Sea* (1994), Vol. 1, 88-93.

transit, right of, over territory *See* **landlocked States**; **right of access and freedom of transit**.

transnational law This is generally taken "to include all law which regulates actions or events that transcend national frontiers. Both public and private international law are included, as are other rules which do not wholly fit into such standard categories": Jessup, *Transnational Law* (1956), 2. The focus of works on this subject is invariably on the legal relationship between a State and alien individuals or corporations, frequently in commercial, industrial or investment situations.

travaux préparatoires This term refers to the preparatory work (in American parlance, the legislative history) of a treaty, as used as a means of interpretation. Art. 32 of the Vienna Convention on the Law of Treaties 1969 allows recourse to be made "to supplementary means of interpretation, including the preparatory work of the treaty and the circumstances of its conclusion, in order to confirm the meaning resulting from the application of article 31, or to determine the meaning when the interpretation according to article 31: (a) leaves the meaning ambiguous or obscure; or (b) leads to a result which is manifestly absurd or unreasonable." Art. 31(1) requires treaties to be interpreted "in good faith in accordance with the ordinary meaning to be given to the terms of the treaty in their context and in the light of its object and purpose." *See* McNair, *Law of Treaties* (2nd ed.), 411-23; Lauterpacht, *The Development of International Law by the International Court* (1958), 116-41; Aust, *Modern Treaty Law and Practice* (2000), 197-9.

Treadwell and Co. **Case** *(USA v. Mexico)* (1875) *Moore, Int. Arb., 3468.* Claims were presented under the USA-Mexico Claims Convention 1868 by Treadwell and Co., arising out of alleged non-performance by Mexico of a contract for the sale to Mexico of arms and ammunition; the claimants had not formally presented their claims to the Mexican Government. *Held* (by Sir Edward Thornton, umpire), in dismissing the claims, that the Commission should not take cognizance of claims arising out of contracts between US nationals and the Mexican Government unless the validity of the contract was proved by the claimant's evidence and gross injustice had been shown to have been done by the Mexican Government.

treason Treason is an offence essentially defined by municipal law: under English and US law a person commits treason, *inter alia*, if he adheres to the sovereign's enemies, giving them aid and comfort, whether at home or elsewhere: Treason Act 1351 (UK); US Constitution, Article III Section 3(1). The essence of the offence of treason lies in the violation of the duty of allegiance owed to the sovereign. Allegiance is due from the subject wherever he may be. So far as international law is concerned, a traitor is not a protected person for the purposes of Geneva Conventions. III and IV, on Prisoners of War and on Protection of Civilian Persons *(75 U.N.T.S. 135; 287)*. If he has taken part in the hostilities, he will, however, be entitled to the minimum **fundamental guarantees** provided by art. 75

of Geneva Protocol I of 1977 to the Geneva Conventions *(1125 U.N.T.S. 3)*: art. 45 (3). *See* Verzijl, *International law in Historical Perspective*, Vol. IX, (1976), 89-91.

treaties, amendment *See* **amendment**.

treaties, authentication *See* **authentication**.

treaties, change of circumstance *See rebus sic stantibus*.

treaties, conclusion *See* **conclusion of treaty**.

treaties, conventions on the law of The principal instrument on the law of treaties is the **Vienna Convention on the Law of Treaties** 1969 *(1155 U.N.T.S. 331*; text in the **Documents** appended to this *Encyclopaedic Dictionary*). On particular aspects, *see* **agreement, international** and entries under **treaties**. This Convention being applicable to treaties only between States (art. 1), a further convention was adopted to regulate treaties where at least one of the parties was an international organization: the Vienna Convention on Treaties Concluded between States and International Organizations or between Two or More International Organizations of 21 March 1986 *(25 I.L.M. 543 (1986))*. The question of succession to treaty obligations is regulated by the Vienna Convention on Succession of States in Respect of Treaties of 23 August 1978 *(17 I.L.M. 1488 (1978))*; *see* **State succession**.

treaties, correction An error relating to an underlying factor or situation goes to consent and is therefore dealt with in the Vienna Convention on the Law of Treaties 1969 under invalidity (art. 45). Textual errors can be corrected (a) by making and initialing the appropriate correction in the text, (b) by executing an instrument or instruments setting out the agreed correction, or (c) by re-executing the whole treaty (art. 79(1)). Where the treaty is one for which there is a depository, the depository can notify the signatories and parties of the error and of the proposed correction and fix a time-limit for objections. Provided there are no objections the depository can then execute the correction and communicate it to the parties and to States entitled to become parties (art. 79(2)). *See* Aust, *Modern Treaty Law and Practice* (2000), 270-3.

treaties, definition For the purposes of the Vienna Convention on the Law of Treaties 1969, "'treaty' means an international agreement concluded between two or more States in written form and governed by international law, whether embodied in a single instrument or in two or more related instruments and whatever its particular designation": art 2(1)(a). *See* further **agreement, international**. *See* Aust, *Modern Treaty Law and Practice* (2000), Chap. 2.

treaties, denunciation *See* **denunciation**.

treaties, depositories *See* **depository**.

treaties, entry into force *See* **entry into force**.

treaties, error *See* **error**; **treaties, correction**.

treaties, initialing *See* **initialing**.

treaties, interpretation of The Vienna Convention on the Law of Treaties 1969 lays down (art. 31), as the "general rule of interpretation," that a treaty "shall be interpreted in good faith in accordance with the ordinary meaning to be given to the terms of the treaty in their context and in the light of its object and purpose," the context comprising, in addition to the text, any agreement relating to the treaty made between all the parties in connection with its conclusion and any instrument made in that connection by one or more parties and accepted by the others as an instrument related thereto; and there being taken into account, together with the context, (a) any subsequent agreement regarding the interpretation or application of the treaty, (b) any subsequent practice establishing agreement respecting its interpretation, and (c) any relevant rules of international law applicable between the parties. To this, it is added that a special meaning is to be given to a term if the parties so intended and it is further provided (art. 32) that "[r]ecourse may be had to supplementary means of interpretation, including the preparatory work of the treaty and the circumstances of its conclusion, in order to confirm the meaning resulting from the application of" the general rule stated above or to determine the meaning when such application either leaves the meaning ambiguous or obscure or leads to a manifestly absurd or unreasonable result. (*I Oppenheim 1277-82* suggests ten other possible supplementary means of interpretation). There is further laid down (art. 33) a special rule for the interpretation of treaties authenticated in two or more languages: unless otherwise agreed, it is equally authoritative in all versions, and the versions are presumed to have the same meaning in each authentic text (art. 33(1) and (3)). If a discrepancy nevertheless emerges, "the meaning which best reconciles the texts, having regard to the object and purpose of the treaty, shall be adopted." *See also* ***travaux préparatoires***. *See* McNair, *Law of Treaties* (2nd ed.), 345-489; Sinclair, *The Vienna Convention on the Law of Treaties* (2nd ed.), 114-58; Aust, *Modern Treaty Law and Practice* (2000), Chap. 13.

treaties, invalidity *See* **treaties, validity**.

treaties, mistake *See* **error**.

treaties, most ratified/acceded to The most ratified or acceded to treaties, i.e. those with the most State parties, are (1) the Charter of the United Nations (191 parties), (2) the UN Convention on the Rights of the Child 1982 (189 parties; *see* **Child, Convention on the Rights of the**) and (3) the **Non-Proliferation Treaty** 1968 (188 parties). The Statute of the International Court of Justice potentially heads all these treaties, with the full membership of the UN (art. 93(1) of the Charter), plus the possibility of non-UN members becoming parties (art. 93(2) of the Charter, as was the case with Nauru and Switzerland prior to their admission to the UN.

treaties, observance *See pacta sunt servanda*.

treaties, provisional application *See* **application of treaty, provisional**.

treaties, registration of *See* **registration of treaties**; *see also* **filing and recording**.

treaties, repudiation *See* **repudiation**.

treaties, reservations *See* **reservations**.

treaties, revision *See* **revision of treaties**.

treaties, termination and suspension The Vienna Convention on the Law of Treaties 1969 recognizes six means by which a treaty may be terminated: (1) In conformity with its provisions or at any time by consent of all the parties after consultation with the other Contracting States (art. 54(a)). A party may also withdraw under the same conditions *(ibid.)*. In the absence of express provisions on termination, a right to denounce or withdraw is usually to be implied (cf. art. 56(1)), upon not less than 12 months notice (art. 56(2)). *See* **denunciation**. (2) By the conclusion of a later treaty on the same subject matter (art. 59(1)), provided that it can be established that the parties intended the later treaty to prevail, or the provisions of the later treaty are incompatible with the earlier treaty (art. 59(1)(a) and (b)). (3) In consequence of a material breach, thereby entitling the other party to invoke that breach as a ground for termination (or suspension) in whole or in part (art. 60(1)). For these purposes, a material breach is a **repudiation** of a treaty or a violation of a provision essential to the accomplishment of the object or purpose of the treaty (art. 60(3)). *See also [1966] II I.L.C. Yearbook 255*; *Namibia Opinion 1971 I.C.J. Rep. 16.* (4) In the event of supervening impossibility of performance (art. 61). This ground of termination involves "the permanent disappearance or destruction of an object indispensable for the execution of the treaty" (art. 61(1)), provided that the impossibility is not caused by the State invoking it (art. 61(2)). *See [1966] II I.L.C. Yearbook 256.* (5) In the event of a fundamental change of circumstances (art. 62). *See* **rebus sic stantibus**. (6) Where it conflicts with a new peremptory norm of general international law (art. 64). *See* **jus cogens**.

A multilateral treaty does not terminate because the number of parties falls below the minimum necessary to bring it into force, unless it so provides (art. 55). Nor is a treaty terminated by severance of diplomatic or consular relations (art. 63). *See also* **desuetude**. See McNair, *Law of Treaties,* (2nd ed.), Chaps. 30-5; Sinclair, *The Vienna Convention on the Law of Treaties* (2nd ed.), 181-202; Aust, *Modern Treaty Law and Practice* (2000), Chap. 16.

treaties, territorial application   *See* **territorial application clauses**; **colonial clause**.

treaties, third parties and   *See pacta tertiis nec nocent nec prosunt*; **third States**.

treaties, *travaux préparatoires*   *See travaux préparatoires*.

treaties, validity   By art. 42 of the Vienna Convention on the Law of Treaties 1969, "[t]he validity of a treaty or of the consent of a State to be bound by a treaty may be impeached only through application of the present Convention." Arts. 46 to 53 on invalidity draw a number of rather fine distinctions: violation of a provision of internal law regarding competence to conclude treaties (art. 46) and limitations on the authority to express the consent of State (art. 47) may *only* be invoked as invalidating consent if (art. 46) the violation of internal law was manifest and concerned a rule of internal law of fundamental importance (a burden of proof likely to be very difficult to discharge, although the ILC final draft *([1966] II I.L.C. Yearbook 177)* did not specify any examples) and (art. 47) if the restriction on authority had been notified to the other negotiating States (which the ILC considered was already the usual practice).

Error may be invoked as invalidating consent if the error relates to a fact or situation which was assumed to exist at the time when the treaty was concluded and formed an essential basis of consent to be bound (art. 48). In this the draft was based on the *Temple, Eastern Greenland* and *Mavrommatis Cases.* **Fraud** (art. 49: the concept is not defined) and corruption of a representative of a State (art. 50) can be invoked without limitation to invalidate consent to be bound. By contrast, in view of the gravity of the offence, consent to be bound procured by coercion of a representative is without legal effect (art. 51), while a treaty concluded by coercion of a State or by the threat or use of force is void (art. 52). "The traditional doctrine prior to the Covenant of the League of Nations was that the validity of a treaty was not affected by the fact that it had been brought about by the threat or use of force. . . . The Commission considers that these developments [represented by the Covenant, the Pact of Paris, the War Crimes Tribunal Charters, and art. 2(4) of the UN Charter] justify the conclusion that the invalidity of a treaty procured by the illegal threat or use of force is a principle which is *lex lata* in the international law of today": *I.L.C. Final Draft, supra.* A treaty is void if, at the time of its conclusion, it conflicts with a peremptory norm of general international law (*jus cogens*) (art. 53). "The formulation of the article is not free from difficulty, since there is no simple criterion by which to identify a general rule of international law as having the character of *jus cogens.* . . . The emergence of rules having the character of *jus cogens* [e.g., the prohibition on the use of force] is comparatively recent, while international law is in process of rapid development. The Commission considers the right course to be to provide in general terms that a treaty is void if it conflicts with a rule of *jus cogens* and to leave the full content of this rule to be worked out in State practice and in the jurisprudence of international tribunals": *I.L.C. Final Draft, supra.*

Breach, impossibility and fundamental change of circumstances (arts. 60-62) are all matters which may provide grounds for termination or withdrawal, but they do not affect the validity of a treaty. The provisions on invalidity must be read in conjunction with other applicable provisions and notably art. 43 (continuance of obligations imposed by international law independently of their incorporation into a treaty) and art. 44 on separability of treaty provisions. The whole of the treaty is void in the cases falling under arts. 51-53, while the State has the option of avoiding the treaty in the cases falling under arts. 49 and 50. In the cases falling under arts. 46-48, the provisions on separability (art. 44) apply. In the cases where a State has an option as to whether to invoke invalidity (arts. 46-50), the right may be lost if there is an agreement that the treaty is valid or there is **acquiescence** (art. 45). In principle, a treaty which is invalid is void. Except in the cases governed by arts. 49-52, the other party may be required to re-establish the *status quo ante* and, in these cases, acts performed in good faith before the invalidity was invoked are not for that reason unlawful. *See* McNair, *Law of Treaties,* (2nd ed.), 58-77 and 206-13; Sinclair, *The Vienna Convention on the Law of Treaties* (2nd ed.), 159-81 and 196-202; Aust, *Modern Treaty Law and Practice* (2000), Chap. 17.

treatises *See* **publicists**.

treaty collections Most of the major States prepare collections of treaties to which they are parties In addition, there are three global treaty collections: the *Consolidated Treaty Series (C.T.S.)* for treaties concluded between 1645 and 1919; the *League of Nations Treaty Series (L.N.T.S.)* for treaties concluded between 1919 and 1946; and the *United Nations Treaty Series (U.N.T.S.)* for treaties concluded after 1946. These last two series are official, in the sense that **registration of treaties** is compulsory on member States (and their publication automatic), the sanction for non-registration being, in the case of the League, that the treaty was not binding unless registered (art. 19 of the Covenant) and, in the case of the UN, that the treaty may not be invoked before a UN organ unless registered (art. 102(2) of the Charter).

treaty events *See* **Multilateral Treaty Framework**.

Trianon, Treaty of *See* **Versailles, Treaty of, 1919**.

TRIPS Universally known by this acronym, the Agreement on Trade-related Aspects of Intellectual Property Rights *(33 I.L.M. 1197 (1994))* was one of a large number of agreements adopted at Marrakesh, Morocco, on April 1994, TRIPS recognized that widely varying standards for protecting and enforcing intellectual property rights and the absence of a multilateral legal framework, particularly in relation to counterfeit goods, constituted a source of tension in international trade (*see* Preamble). Thus, the agreement provides for the applicability of basic GATT principles and those of relevant international intellectual property agreements to intellectual property rights (Part 1, arts. 1-8); the provision of adequate intellectual property rights, particularly in respect of copyright, trademarks, indus-·trial design and patents (Part II, arts. 9-40); the provision of effective enforcement measures for those rights (Part III, arts. 41-61); and the provision of multilateral dispute settlement arrangements (Parts IV and V, arts. 62-67). The Council for TRIPS was established by art. 68 to "monitor the operation of this Agreement and, in particular, Members' compliance with their obligations hereunder, and shall afford Members of consulting on matters relating to trade-related aspects of intellectual property rights." *See* Blakeney, *Trade Related Aspects of Intellectual Property Rights* (1996). *See also* **World Trade Organization**; **World Intellectual Property Organization**.

Troppau, Congress of (1820)   This was the second of the four congresses of the **Concert of Europe**, largely preliminary to **Laibach Congress** in 1821. At the Troppau Congress, Austria, Prussia and Russia agreed to a Circular Despatch for communication to other States, asserting a right and duty of the powers responsible for peace in Europe to intervene to suppress any revolutionary movement by which they might conceive that peace to be endangered (Hertslet, *Map of Europe by Treaty* (1875) No. 105). Great Britain declined to be associated with these steps (Hertslet, No. 107).

truce   "Armistices or truces, in the wider sense of the term, are all agreements between belligerent forces for a temporary cessation of hostilities. They are in no wise to be compared with peace, and ought not to be called temporary peace, because the condition of war remains between the belligerents themselves, and between the belligerents and neutrals, on all points beyond the mere cessation of hostilities. . . . The Hague Regulations [concerning the Laws and Customs of War on Land 1907, *205 C.T.S. 289*] deal with armistices in Articles 36 to 41, but very incompletely, so that the gaps must be filled from old customary rules": *II Oppenheim* 546-7. *See* **armistice**; also **flag of truce**.

Truman Proclamations   Proclamations 2667 and 2668, issued by US President Harry S. Truman on 28 September 1945 (*10 Fed. Reg. 12303* and *10 Fed. Reg. 12304)* are referred to as the Truman Proclamations. The first proclamation claimed "the natural resources of the subsoil and sea bed of the continental shelf beneath the high seas but contiguous to the coasts of the United States as appertaining to the United States, subject to its jurisdiction and control." The waters above the continental shelf were expressly stated to remain high seas. This proclamation is expressly based on the need for the conservation and prudent utilization of the natural resources, on the fact that the exercise of jurisdiction by the contiguous State is "reasonable and just" and on the continental shelf being regarded as a natural extension of the land-mass of the State. This proclamation formed the inspiration for claims by other States to the resources of the **continental shelf**, and was influential in the preparation of the Geneva Convention on the Continental Shelf 1958 *(450 U.N.T.S. 311)*. *See* the ***North Sea Continental Shelf Case*** *1969 I.C.J. Rep. 3*. The second proclamation claimed the right to establish fishery conservation zones in areas of the high seas contiguous to the US coasts where there is, or will be, substantial fishing activities. While the US claimed the right to regulate fishing activities in these zones fished exclusively by US nationals, it provided for regulation by agreement with other States in those zones fished by US nationals and nationals of other States. This proclamation was based on the inadequacy of the existing conservation arrangements and on the "urgent need to protect coastal fishery resources from destructive exploitation."

trust territory Any territory placed under the **Trusteeship System** of the UN is referred to as a trust territory (UN Charter, art. 75). A total of eleven trusteeship agreements were concluded by 1949 (none since), and all have attained independence. Togoland (administered by the UK) joined with the Gold Coast to form Ghana in 1957; Cameroon (France) and Southern Cameroon (UK) independent in 1960;Togo (France) independent in 1960; Northern Cameroon (UK) became part of Nigeria in 1961; Somaliland (Italy and UK) independent in 1960; Tanganyika (UK) independent in 1961; Western Samoa (New Zealand) independent in 1962; Ruandi Urundi (Belgium) independent as two States, Ruanda and Burundi, in 1962; Nauru (Australia) independent 1968; New Guinea (Australia) independent as part of Papua New Guinea in 1975; the Trust Territory of the Pacific Islands (a strategic trust consisting of 2,125 islands, extending over 3 million square miles in the Western Pacific north of the Equator, with a total land area of 700 square miles, and comprising three island groups, the Marianas, the Carolines and the Marshalls) as the Federated States of Micronesia and as the Republic of the Marshall Islands in 1986 and as Palau in 1994. *See Northern Cameroons Case 1963 I.C.J. Rep. 15. See also* **Micronesia**; **strategic area**.

Trusteeship Council Declared to be one of the principal organs of the United Nations (Charter, art. 7(1)), the Trusteeship Council was charged with the task of assisting the General Assembly in the supervision of territories placed under the **Trusteeship System** (arts. 85(2) and 87). The Council was to consist of each **administering authority**, such other **permanent members** of the Security Council as were not administering trust territories and as many other members (elected by the General Assembly) as were necessary to ensure an equal division in membership between those administering, and those not administering, **trust territories** (art. 86(1)). The Trusteeship Council exercised its functions through annual reports submitted by the administering authority, through petitions submitted by individuals and groups in the trust territory, and through periodic visits to the territory (art. 87). In addition, the Council formulated a questionnaire as a basis for annual reports from the administering authority, requiring responses on the "political, economic, social and educational advancement of the inhabitants of each trust territory" (art. 88). There being no remaining trust territory, the Trusteeship Council is now *functus officio*. *See* Toussaint, *The Trusteeship System of the United Nations* (1956).

Trusteeship System The system established by Chapter XII of the UN Charter, principally for the replacement of the League of Nations **mandate system,** and applicable to: (a) pre-existing mandated territories (to all of which, except **South-West Africa**, it was in fact applied); (b) territories to be detached from the enemy States of World War II (in fact only Italian Somaliland so entered the system); (c) territories voluntarily placed under the system (of which there were none) (art. 77(1)). The territories entered the system by means of trusteeship agreements concluded by the "States directly concerned" (art. 79) and approved by the General Assembly (art. 85), except where a **strategic area** was included, in which case Security Council approval was required (art. 83). The system involves the designation of an **administering authority**, which may be one or more States or the UN itself (art. 81), but which in practice has always been a single State, obliged to administer the territory in accordance with the general aims of the system as set out in art. 76. These aims are broadly comparable with the aims of the mandate system (emphasizing the contribution to international peace and security, the respect for human rights and the equal treatment in social, economic and cultural matters), with the additional emphasis, in art. 76(b), on "progressive development towards self-government or in independence." The administration of each **trust territory** is subject to supervision by the General Assembly (in the case of a strategic trust, the Security Council) through the **Trusteeship Council.** As the last trust territory, Palau, gained independence in 1994, and as no new territories have been placed under the system since 1949, the Trusteeship System has no contemporary application. *See* Hall, *Mandates, Dependencies and Trusteeship* (1948); Toussaint, *The Trusteeship System of the United Nations* (1956).

Tunis and Morocco Nationality Decrees Case *See Nationality Decrees Case.*

Tunisia-Libya Continental Shelf Case, *1981 I.C.J. Rep. 3, 1982 I.C.J. Rep. 18.* Tunisia and Libya (neither being a party to the Geneva Convention on the Continental Shelf 1958: *499 U.N.T.S. 311*) granted oil concessions in respect of submarine areas off their respective (adjacent) coasts, but extending into the continental shelf claimed by the other. In a Special Agreement concluded in 1977, they asked the ICJ to determine the principles and rules of international law to be applied for the delimitation of their respective continental shelves taking account of equitable principles, the relevant circumstances of the area, and recent trends admitted at the Third Conference on the Law of the Sea; they further requested the ICJ to specify how in practice those principles and rules applied in the particular situation. Upon Malta applying to intervene in the proceedings under art. 62 of the ICJ Statute, the Court *held* (unanimously) that the application failed for lack of demonstration of any sufficient legal interest. The litigation indeed related to the principles and rules to be applied in the delimitation of continental shelf boundaries in the central Mediterranean region, in which the interest of Malta could be said to be somewhat more specific and direct than that of States outside that region. But Malta had attached to the request an express reservation against putting in issue its own claims against the parties.

Subsequently, in the main proceedings, it was *held* (10 to 4), that (1) the principles and rules of international law applicable for the delimitation of the areas of continental shelf in the area in dispute were that the delimitation was to be effected in accordance with equitable principles, and taking account of all relevant circumstances; since the area relevant for the delimitation constituted a single continental shelf as the natural prolongation of the land territory of both parties, no criterion for delimitation of shelf areas could be derived from the principle of natural prolongation as such; and the physical structure of the continental shelf areas in question was not such as to determine an equitable line of delimitation; and (2) the relevant circumstances to be taken into account in achieving an equitable delimitation included the area relevant to the delimitation, the general configuration of the coasts of the parties, the existence and position of certain islands, the land frontier between the parties, their conduct prior to 1974 in the grant of petroleum concessions, and a reasonable degree of proportionality between the continental shelf areas appertaining to the coastal State and the length of the relevant part of its coast. The Court went on to indicate the practical method for the application of these principles and rules in the present case.

Tunkin, Grigory I. 1906-93. Distinguished and influential Soviet diplomat and lawyer. Member, ILC 1957-66, Chairman 1961. Principal works: *Fundamentals of Contemporary International Law* (1956, in Russian); *Questions of Theory of International Law* (1962, in Russian); *Ideological Struggle and International Law* (1967, Russian); *Theory of International Law* (1970 in Russian; 1974 in English).

tunneling *See* **mining (under the high seas).**

Turlington, Edgar 1891-1959. American lawyer and public servant. Principal works: *Mexico and her Foreign Creditors* (1930); *Neutrality: The World War Period* (1936).

Turner Claim *(USA v. Mexico) (1927) R.I.A.A. 278.* Turner, a US national, was, as a locomotive engineer, involved in a train collision in Mexico in March 1899. He was arrested shortly afterwards, sent first to a prison hospital and then to the prison, was later freed on bail for a time, but was then in jail again until 28 January 1900 when he died, without having had a trial. The US claimed damages on behalf of his widow (also a US national) alleging direct responsibility by Mexico for an illegal arrest, undue and illegal delay of proceedings, and inhuman treatment in prison, all of which contributed to Turner's death. *Held* by the Mexico-USA General Claims Commission that Turner's arrest was not unjustified and ill-treatment of him in jail had not been established, but, as the latter part of his detention was illegal under Mexican law because of the delay in commencing proceedings, Mexico was responsible for the bad effects of its illegal and careless custody on Turner's health: "having a man in illegal custody . . . renders a government liable for damages and disasters which would not have been his share, or in a lesser degree, if he had been at liberty."

Turri Claim *(USA v. Italy) (1960) 30 I.L.R. 371*. Mrs. Turri sought compensation for damage to her real and personal property in Italy. She was a natural-born US citizen, but had lost that citizenship and had become an Italian citizen on marrying an Italian national, but had in 1938 reacquired US citizenship by naturalization. She and her husband took up permanent residence in the USA: an immigrant visa application was filed on his behalf, but that visa had not been issued by the time of his death in 1945. On a claim being presented under the Italian Peace Treaty 1947 *(49 U.N.T.S. 126)*, the Italian-US Conciliation Commission *held* that, notwithstanding the non-issue to the husband of an immigrant visa, the claimant and her husband had transferred their habitual residence to the USA, which was also the effective center of the family's activities, and that the claimant thus had dominant US nationality during the subsistence of the marriage as well as being solely a US national on the date of entry into force of the Peace Treaty.

Two Freedoms Agreement The International Air Services Transit Agreement signed, with the **Chicago Convention** on International Civil Aviation *(15 U.N.T.S. 295)*, on 7 December 1944 *(84 U.N.T.S. 387)*, affords to parties the first two freedoms of the air for their scheduled air services, viz. the rights of overflight (a privilege of **innocent passage**), and of landing for non-traffic purposes *(e.g.,* to refuel) (art. 1(1)), these rights to be exercised in accordance with the provisions of the Chicago Convention (art. 1(2)). The transit State may designate the route and airport(s) to be used (art. 1(3)). Disputes are referred to the ICAO Council (art. 2). The Two Freedoms Agreement has been ratified by many of the States that are important for international air transit. It is nevertheless usual to stipulate for these two freedoms as well as for traffic rights in bilateral air services agreements. *See* the **Five Freedoms Agreement**.

U

ultimatum This "is the technical term for a written communication by one State to another which ends amicable negotiations respecting a difference, and formulates for the last time and categorically, the demands to be fulfilled if other measures are to be averted. An ultimatum is, theoretically at least, not compulsion, although it may have the same effect. . . .": *II Oppenheim 133*. By art. 1 of the Hague Convention (III) relative to the Opening of Hostilities of 18 October 1907 *(205 C.T.S. 263)*, the Parties recognized that hostilities must not be commenced "without previous and explicit warning, in the form either of a reasoned declaration of war or of an ultimatum with conditional declaration of war." The obligation to give warning of hostilities has not been universally honored in practice. With the clear obligations in the UN Charter (art. 2(4)) not to threaten or use force, it seems that the provisions of the Hague Convention respecting ultimatums are "substantially obsolete": *II Oppenheim 297*.

ultra vires "In the case of acts of international organizations . . . there is nothing comparable to the remedies existing in domestic law in connection with administrative acts. The consequence of this is that there is no possibility of applying the concept of voidability to the acts of the United Nations. If an act of an organ of the United Nations had to be considered as an invalid act, such invalidity could constitute only the *absolute nullity* of the act. In other words, there are only two alternatives for the acts of the Organization: either the act is fully valid, or it is an absolute nullity, because absolute nullity is the only form in which invalidity of an act of the Organization can occur": Judge Morelli in *Expenses of the United Nations Case 1962 I.C.J. Rep. 15*, at 222. Cf. Osieke, The Legal Validity of Ultra Vires Decisions of International Organizations, *77 A.J.I.L. 239 (1983)* who argues that illegal decisions are voidable. It is to be presumed that action by international organizations is not *ultra vires*: *Expenses of the United Nations Case, supra,* at 168; *Namibia Opinion 1971 I.C.J. Rep. 16* at 22. Such issues of *vires* as have arisen for international adjudication reveal that action will be *intra vires* if it falls within the objects or purposes of the organization: *Expenses Case, supra*; *Competence of the ILO in Agriculture Cases (1922) P.C.I.J., Ser. B, Nos. 2 and 3*.

"It must be noted that given the limited opportunities for judicial review, the principle that *ultra vires* acts are void *ab initio* might undermine the certainty of decisions of international organizations and permit States to seek to evade their treaty obligations. However this danger is reduced by the presumption . . . that acts of international organizations directed at the fulfillment of the purposes of the organization are valid, meaning that the burden of proof is on the State arguing otherwise": Akande, International Organizations, in Evans (ed.), *International Law* (2003), 286. *See* Jennings, Nullity and Effectiveness in International Law, *Cambridge Essays in International Law* (1965), 64; Lauterpacht, The Legal Effect of Illegal Acts of International Organizations, *ibid.,* 88; Morgenstern, Legality in International Organizations, *(1976-77) 48 B.Y.I.L. 241*; Osieke, Ultra Vires Acts in International Organizations, *(1976-77) 48 B.Y.I.L. 259. See also* Schwarzenberger, *International Constitutional Law* (1976), 48-63 on implied jurisdiction. As to *ultra vires* acts of officials etc., in relation to States, see **attribution**.

UN Day *See* **United Nations Day**.

UNAMI The United Nations Assistance Mission for Iraq was established by Security Council Res. 1500 (2003) on 14 August 2003 to assist the Secretary-General in the coordination of UN efforts in post-conflict Iraq.

UNAMIC From October 1991 to March 1992, the United Nations Advance Mission in Cambodia served to aid Cambodian parties uphold their ceasefire agreement prior to the deployment of **UNTAC**. UNAMIC was established by Security Council Res. 717 (1991) and its mandate included mine-detection and mine-clearing training for the civilian population.

UNAMIR Established by Security Council Res. 872 (1993), the United Nations Assistance Mission for Rwanda was mandated to aid in the implementation of the Arusha Peace Agreement (1993). UNAMIR operated from October 1993 to March 1996.

UNAMSIL An acronym for United Nations Mission in Sierra Leone, formed to aid in the implementation and assist in the compliance of the Lomé Peace Agreement. UNAMSIL was also mandated to aid the efforts of the Government of Sierra Leone to enlarge its authority as well as restore law and stability in the nation. UNAMSIL was created by Security Council Res. 1270 (1999) as an expansion of a previous mission.

unanimity "Taking decisions by unanimity has both advantages and disadvantages. On the one hand, prolonged negotiations often produce only weak compromises or sometimes culminate in no decision at all. Particularly in large organizations, granting each member a right of veto could in effect paralyze the decision making process. On the other hand, the requirement of unanimity offers two advantages. (1) Many States will participate more readily in an organization if they are sure that they will not be outvoted. . . . (2) The implementation of decisions will be easier when they have been supported by all Members": Schermers and Blokker, *International Institutional Law* (3rd. ed.), 516. While unanimity was required for most decisions of the organs of the League of Nations (*see* Covenant, art. 5), the prevailing voting requirement for the UN and the Specialized Agencies is a majority vote. In actual practice, however, much decision-making is by **consensus**.

UNASOG Operational from May to June of 1994, the United Nations Aouzou Observer Group was mandated to ensure withdrawal of Libyan forces from the Aouzou Strip in accordance with the verdict of the International Court of Justice in *Libya/Chad Territorial Dispute Case 1994 I.C.J. Rep. 6.* UNASOG was established by Security Council Res. 915 (1994).

UNAVEM I Established by Security Council Res. 626 (1988), the first United Nations Angola Verification Mission was mandated to ensure the redeployment and eventual phase-out of Cuban troops from Angola. UNAVEM I operated from December 1988 to June 1991.

UNAVEM II Operational from May 1991 to February 1995, the second United Nations Angola Verification Mission was established by Security Council Res. 696 (1991). UNAVEM II's mission was originally to monitor the ceasefire and observe the police force; it was later expanded to incorporate oversight of elections in Angola.

UNAVEM III An acronym for the third United Nations Angola Verification Mission established by Security Council Res. 976 (1995) as a follow-up to the first two UNAVEM missions. UNAVEM III was established to aid Angola and the Uniao Nacional para a Independencia Total de Angola (UNITA) in reinstating peace in the region as called for in the Peace Accords for Angola (1991) and the Lusaka Protocol (1994). UNAVEM III existed from February 1995 to June 1997.

UNCITRAL *See* **United Nations Commission on International Trade Law**.

unconditional surrender *See* **capitulation**.

UNCRO An acronym for the United Nations Confidence Restoration Operation established in 1995 to replace UNPROFOR in Croatia and mandated to assist as needed in the 1994 ceasefire agreement as well as aid in the restructuring of the area. UNCRO operated between March 1995 and January 1996 and was established by Security Council Res. 981 (1995).

UNCTAD *See* **United Nations Conference on Trade and Development**.

UNDOF An acronym for the United Nations Disengagement Observer Force, established in 1974 by Security Council Res. 350 (1974). The force, whose mandate has been renewed every six months since May 1974, supervised the disengagement of Israeli and Syrian forces.

UNDP *See* **United Nations Development Programme**.

UNEF I The first United Nations Emergency Force, in effect from November 1956 to June 1967. Created by the General Assembly by Res. 997, 998 and 1000 (ES-1) under the procedure established in the Uniting for Peace Resolution (GA Res.377(V)), UNEF I was mandated to supervise the termination of fighting in the Suez Canal sector and the Sinai peninsula, including the withdrawal of troops. The geographic scope of the operation was later expanded to include the Armistice Demarcation Line in Gaza. UNEF's expenses were the subject of the *Expenses of the United Nations Case 1962 I.C.J. Rep. 151*.

UNEF II The second United Nations Emergency Force was formed to oversee the cease-fire between Egyptian and Israeli forces, the redeployment of the same forces and a buffer zone agreed upon by the two nations. Established by Security Council Res. 340 (1973), UNEF II was operational from October 1973 to July 1979.

UNEP *See* **United Nations Environment Programme**.

unequal treaty Treaties entered into under duress are sometimes spoken of as unequal treaties (*see* **treaties, validity**) but the expression is usually applied to treaties concluded between parties whose disparity in power or legal status is such as to negate their sovereign equality, so (it is alleged) rendering them invalid. Similarly, treaties imposed on colonial territories which subsequently attain independence may be so regarded, thus justifying a decision not to succeed to the relevant obligation. *See* **State succession**.

UNESCO *See* **United Nations Educational, Scientific and Cultural Organization**.

UNESCO Constitution Case (1949) 16 I.L.R. 331. Article V of the Constitution of UNESCO, in providing that a member elected to the Executive Board was eligible for re-election, did not expressly provide (as was the case in respect of the initial election of that member) that the person being re-elected must be a member of his country's delegation to the session of the General Conference at which such re-election takes place. The question whether membership of the country's delegation was in such circumstances nevertheless necessary was referred to a special arbitral tribunal (Rolin, Adolfo Du Costa, Lachs) set up by the Executive Board, which *held* that, in the light of the grammatical context of the relevant provisions taken as a whole, their object, the practice of member governments since the Constitution was adopted, analogies with other constitutions and similar instruments, considerations of State sovereignty and (although not strictly relevant because the text of the Constitution was already sufficiently clear) the preparatory work leading to the adoption of the Constitution, membership of a country's delegation at the relevant session of the General Conference was a necessary requirement for re-election to the Executive Board.

UNFCCC An acronym for the United Nations Framework Convention on Climate Control; see **Climate Control Convention**.

UNFICYP United Nations Peacekeeping Force in Cyprus was established in 1964 by Security Council Res. 168 (1964) with a directive to block any further hostilities between Greek and Turkish Cypriots as well as assist in a return to normalcy in the communities. After an outbreak of fighting in 1974, the mandate of UNFICYP was expanded through a number of Security Council resolutions and currently includes the supervision of ceasefire lines and buffer zones. UNFICYP's mandate has been extended numerous times via various Security Council resolutions.

unfriendly act This is not a term of art in international law. In so far as it appears in the international context, its significance is political, denoting that one State considers some act by another State to fall below the accepted canons of behavior, frequently to be countered by a protest or complaint, and some action, by the "aggrieved" State.

UNGOMAP The United Nations Good Offices Mission in Afghanistan and Pakistan was established to aid the Secretary-General in giving his good offices in assisting the two nations implement the Agreements on the Settlement of the Situation Relating to Afghanistan. UNGOMAP was in place from May 1988 to March 1990 and was established by Security Council Res. 622 (1988).

UNHCR *See* **United Nations High Commissioner for Refugees**.

UNICEF *See* **United Nations Children's Fund**.

UNIDIR The United Nations Institute for Disarmament Research. *See* <www.unidir.org>.

UNIDO The United Nations Industrial Development Organization was established to assist developing and transitional countries accelerate their industrial development in a socially and environmentally sustainable fashion. Established in 1966 by General Assembly Res. 2152 (XXI), UNIDO became a specialized agency of the United Nations in 1985. UNIDO has 169 member States and is headquartered in Vienna, Austria. The UNIDO Constitution was adopted in April 1979 *(1401 U.N.T.S. 3)*. The principal organs of

UNIDO are the General Conference (Conference), the Industrial Development Board (Board) and the Secretariat (art. 7). There is also a Program and Budget Committee, which assists the Board in making decisions regarding the work and finances of UNIDO (art. 7). The Conference meets every two years unless it decides otherwise. It determines the guiding principles and policies of UNIDO while taking into account reports of the Board, Director-General and subsidiary organs. The Conference approves UNIDO's work program, as well as the various budgets and adoption of conventions and agreements (art. 8). The Board meets annually and makes reports to the Conference on budgetary and programmatic issues. Additionally, the Board makes requests to members for pertinent information (art. 9). *See* <www.unido.org>.

UNIDROIT The International Institute for the Unification of Private Law, established in 1926, is, as its name suggests, concerned not with international law, but with the modernization, harmonization and coordination of private (particularly commercial) law as between States. *See* <www.unidroit.org>.

UNIFIL Created according to Security Council Res. 425 and 426 in 1978, the United Nations Interim Force in Lebanon was established to reinforce Israel's withdrawal from Lebanon and to aid in the reestablishment of Lebanon's governmental authority. The mandate has been extended by successive Security Council resolutions, most recently SC Res. 1496 (2003) which has extended the mandate until 31 January 2004.

UNIIMOG An acronym for the United Nations Iran-Iraq Military Observer Group, established by SC Res. 619 in August 1988 to monitor the withdrawal of forces from the internationally accepted boundaries agreed to between Iran and Iraq. UNIIMOG's task was completed in February 1992 on the withdrawal of troops from the boundaries.

UNIKOM Acronym for United Nations Iraq-Kuwait Observation Mission established by Security Council Res. 689 in April 1991. UNIKOM was set up to maintain the integrity of the border between the States, supervise a demilitarized zone between Iraq and Kuwait as well as monitor hostilities between the States. UNIKOM marked the first time all permanent members of the Security Council agreed to provide military observers. On 17 March 2003, in advance of the military campaign against Iraq by a US-led coalition, UNIKOM was withdrawn and its mandate suspended.

unilateral declaration "It is well recognized that declarations made by way of unilateral acts, concerning legal or factual situations, may have the effect of creating legal obligations. Declarations of this kind may be, and often are, very specific. When it is the intention of the State making the declaration that it should become bound according to its terms, that intention confers on the declaration the character of a legal undertaking, the State being thenceforth legally required to follow a course of conduct consistent with the declaration. An undertaking of this kind, if given publicly, and with an intent to be bound, even though not made within the context of international negotiations, is binding. In these circumstances, nothing in the nature of a *quid pro quo* nor any subsequent acceptance of the declaration, nor even any reply or reaction from other States, is required for the declaration to take effect, since such a requirement would be inconsistent with the strictly unilateral nature of the juridical act by which the pronouncement by the State was made. . . . One of the basic principles governing the creation and performance of legal obligations, whatever their source, is the principle of good faith. . . . Just as the very rule of *pacta sunt servanda* in the law of treaties is based on good faith, so also is the binding character of an international obligation assumed by unilateral declaration. Thus interested States may take cognizance of unilateral declarations and place confidence in them, and are entitled to require that the obligation thus created be respected": *Nuclear Tests Case 1974 I.C.J. Rep. 253* at 267-8. *See also* the *Eastern Greenland Case (1933) P.C.I.J., Ser. A/B, No. 53.*

Union Bridge Company Claim (US v. UK) (1924) 6 R.I.A.A. 138. The Union Bridge Company, an American Company, in September 1899 shipped certain bridge materials to the Orange Free State Government. By the time it arrived, war had broken out between the UK and the Orange Free State; in May 1900, the UK annexed the Orange Free State. In 1901, an official of the Cape Government Railway at the port of unloading, acting within the scope of his duties but on the basis of certain mistaken beliefs as the character and ownership of the material, forwarded it to Bloemfontein where it was stored until 1908, when it was sold at auction. *Held* by the UK-US Arbitral Tribunal constituted under the Special Agreement of 18 August 1910, that the UK was liable for the wrongful interference with neutral property.

union, personal "A personal union is in existence when two sovereign states and separate international persons are linked together through the accidental fact that they have the same individual as monarch. Thus a personal union existed from 1714 to 1837 between Great Britain and Hanover, from 1815 to 1890 between the Netherlands and Luxembourg, and from 1885 to 1908 between Belgium and the former Congo Free State. A personal union could be said to exist today between the United Kingdom and those other independent members of the Commonwealth, such as Canada and Australia of which Queen Elizabeth II is also Head of State. A personal union is not, and is in no point treated as though it were, an international person, and its two sovereign member states remain separate international persons": *I Oppenheim 245-6. See also* Crawford, *The Creation of States in International Law* (1979) 290. Cf. **union, real**.

union, political "Some organizations may discuss any subject matter they see fit or any topic not belonging to some specifically excluded field. Such organizations are called general or political organizations. . . . The most important general organizations are the United Nations which is concerned with universal co-operation, and a number of organizations dealing with regional cooperation: the **Council of Europe**, the **Organization of American States** and the **Organization of African Unity** [now the **African Union**]. It is not possible to draw a sharp distinction between special and general organizations. If large fields are excluded from the scope of a general organization, it will become more specific. If a special organization is charged with a very important general task (*e.g.*, economic cooperation) it will become more general": Schermers and Blokker, *International Institutional Law* (3rd ed.), 43-4. The most developed political union in existence is the **European Union**, the key features of which include common external tariffs, a single internal market, free movement of capital, goods, persons and freedom of establishment and services and, since 2002, a single European currency, the **Euro**, in 12 of the 15 member States.

union, real "'Where States are not only ruled by the same prince, but are also united for international purposes by an express agreement there is said to exist a real union' [Rivier, *Principes du droit de gens* (1896), I, 97-9; Moore, *Digest of International Law* (1906), Vol. 1, 22]. The phrase 'united for international purposes' is however somewhat of an equivocation. Rather than a general description of 'unitary' States formed by treaty, the term 'real union' has in practice been restricted to those cases where two international units share joint institutions for example for the purposes of foreign affairs, defence or finance. The union of Austria-Hungary from 1867 to 1918 was regarded as a 'real union.'

Nevertheless labels are no substitute for analysis, and in particular the term 'real union' seems to lack precise legal meaning": Crawford, *The Creation of States in International Law* (1979), 290. Cf. **union, personal**.

UNIPOM The United Nations India-Pakistan Observation Mission was established by Security Council Res. 211 of September 1965, and was in existence from September 1965 to March 1966. UNIPOM was mandated to oversee the cease fire along the India-Pakistan border and monitor troop withdrawals.

unit of account "The sovereignty of the State in monetary affairs implies the competence to fix the unit which constitutes the basis of its monetary system—for example, the dollar, mark, franc, pound, peso, rouble etc. This basic unit is commonly referred to as the monetary unit of account and is designated as such either by municipal legislation as with the Canadian dollar . . ., by international law as with the C.F.A. [Communauté française d'Afrique] franc . . ., by custom and usage as with the pound sterling": Shuster, *The Public International Law of Money* (1973), 24. The European Currency Unity (ECU), established by European Community Regulation 3308/80 *(O.J. 1980, L 345/1)* and replacing earlier units (u.a.: EUA) for all accounting purposes by the Community institutions, was regarded by all Community member States except Germany as a foreign currency: *Bull. EC 11-1982 3.1.1.ff*. The ECU has now been replaced by the **Euro** as the common unit of account in 12 of the 15 member States of the European Union. Since the abandonment of the Bretton Woods par-value system, under which gold was the basic numéraire, the **IMF** has used the **Special Drawing Rights** as its unit of account.

UNITAF A multilateral task force in Somalia, led by the United States and comprising troops from over 20 States which was authorized by the Security Council in Res. 794 (1992) to use "all necessary means" to restore, as soon as possible, a suitable setting for humanitarian relief operations in Somalia. The Task Force was expanded and given an enlarged mandate under Chapter VII of the UN Charter becoming **UNOSOM II** in March 1993.

unitary taxation *See* **worldwide unitary taxation**.

United Dredging Company (USA) v. United Mexican States *(1927) 4 R.I.A.A. 263.* The United Dredging Company, a US corporation, entered into an arrangement with the revolutionary "Constitutionalist" forces under the control of General Carranza (which forces were eventually successful and established themselves in power in Mexico) for pumping out and salvaging a sunken gunboat. The claimant company conducted work under this arrangement for a period of 16 days in June and July 1914, but was then informed by General Carranza that the salvage work had to be suspended. *Held* by the USA-Mexico General Claims Commission set up under the USA-Mexico General Claims Convention of 8 September 1923, that Mexico was responsible for the obligations incurred by General Carranza and that an award should be rendered in favor of the claimant.

United International Bureaux for the Protection of Industrial, Literary and Artistic Property/for the Protection of Intellectual Property (BIRPI) *See* **World Intellectual Property Organization**.

United Nations The UN emerged from the Declaration by United Nations of 1 January 1942, the **Dumbarton Oaks Conference** of 21 August to 7 October 1944 and the **San Francisco Conference** (United Nations Conference on International Organization) of 25

April to 26 June 1945. The UN Charter was signed on 26 June 1945, and entered into force on 24 October 1945. To date the Charter has been amended on three occasions: arts. 23, 27 and 61 by GA Res. 1991 A and B (XVIII) of 17 December 1963 *(557 U.N.T.S. 143)*; art. 109 by GA Res. 2101 (XX) of 20 December 1965 *(638 U.N.T.S. 308)*; and art. 61 by GA Res. 2847 (XXVI) of 20 December 1971 *(892 U.N.T.S.119)*. The membership stands at 191 (*see* arts. 3 and 4 of the Charter: see **membership of the UN**). The purposes of the UN are to maintain international peace and security (*see* **peace-keeping**; **collective measures**); to develop friendly relations among nations (*see* **Friendly Relations Declaration; self-determination**); to achieve international cooperation in solving international problems of an economic, social, cultural or humanitarian character (*see* **human rights**); to be a center for harmonizing the action of nations (art. 1). The UN, in pursuit of these purposes, is required to act in accordance with seven principles, enumerated in art. 2: the sovereign **equality** of its members; the duty to fulfill all Charter obligations in good faith; the duty to settle **disputes** by peaceful means (*see* **pacific settlement of disputes**); the duty to refrain from the threat or use of **force**; the duty to assist the UN; the duty to ensure that non-members act in accordance with these principles so far as is necessary to maintain international peace and security; the duty on the UN not to intervene in the domestic affairs of a State (*see* **domestic jurisdiction**). The principal organs of the UN are (art. 7): the **General Assembly**; the **Security Council**; the **Economic and Social Council (ECOSOC)**; the **Trusteeship Council**; the **International Court of Justice** and the **Secretariat**. *See* Bentwich and Martin, *Commentary on the Charter of the United Nations* (1950); Gardner, *In Pursuit of World Peace* (1969); Goodrich, Hambro and Simons, *Charter of the United Nations* (3rd ed.); Higgins, *The Development of International Law by the Political Organs of the United Nations* (1963); Kelsen, *The Law of the United Nations* (1964); Simma, et. al., *The Charter of the United Nations: A Commentary* (2002); Tompkins, *United Nations in Perspective* (1972); Vandenbosch, *United Nations: Background, Organization, Functions, Activities* (1970). *See* <www.un.org>.

United Nations Administrative Tribunal Case *1973 I.C.J. Rep 166*. A dispute having arisen over the non-renewal of a contract made with Mr. Fasla, an official of the United Nations Development Programme, and his complaint having been dismissed by the UN Administrative Tribunal, the Committee on Applications for Review of Administrative Tribunal Judgments, acting under Article 11 of the Statute of the UN Administrative Tribunal, on 20 June 1972 requested on advisory opinion of the ICJ on whether the Tribunal had failed to exercise a jurisdiction vested in it, or had committed a fundamental error in procedure which had occasioned a failure of justice. The Court, holding that the Committee was an organ of the UN, duly authorized to request advisory opinions, so that the Court was competent to entertain the Committee's request for an advisory opinion, *advised* that both questions called for a negative answer (9 votes to 4, and 10 votes to 3 respectively); the first ground of challenge to the Tribunal's decision covered situations where it had either consciously or inadvertently omitted to exercise jurisdictional powers vested in it and relevant for its decision of the case or of a particular material issue in the case, but Mr. Fasla had failed to establish any such omission; an error in procedure was fundamental and constituted a failure of justice when it was of such a kind as to violate a staff member's fundamental right to present his case, either orally or in writing, and to have it considered by the Tribunal before it determined his rights, and in that sense to deprive the staff member of justice, but Mr. Fasla's complaint that the Tribunal's decisions rejecting his claims had been unsupported by adequate reasoning was not such an error in procedure since the reasoning given satisfied the requirement that judgments must state the reasons on which they were based.

United Nations Children's Fund UNICEF was established on 11 December 1946 "by resolution 57(I) of the UN General Assembly as the UN International Children's Emergency Fund (UNICEF), following the decision of the UN Relief and Rehabilitation Agency (UNRRA) on termination of its activities in August 1946 to apply its residual assets to a fund to provide relief for the suffering children in war-devastated Europe. By resolution 417 (V) of 1 December 1950, the UN General Assembly decided to consider the future of the Fund at the end of three years, with the object of continuing it on a permanent basis. By resolution 802(VIII) of 6 October 1953, it unanimously voted to continue the Fund for an indefinite period enabling UNICEF to carry out its programs in Asia, Africa and Latin America as well as in Europe. The official name was shortened to UN Children's Fund, but the well-known acronym UNICEF was retained": *International Organizations Dictionary*. The aim of the organization is to aid governments in their efforts to undertake long-range and far-reaching programs benefiting children and youth. UNICEF, which reports to ECOSOC, has particular responsibility to implement children's rights (*see* **Child, Convention on the Rights of the** 1989). UNICEF has a 36-member Executive Board (GA Res. 36/244 of 29 April 1982), a Programme Committee and a Committee on the Administrative Budget and an Executive Director appointed by the UN Secretary-General in consultation with the Board. In 2002, total income was $1,293 million ($337 million, in 1982) spent on education, childhood disabilities, health services, water supply and sanitation, nutrition and (by far the largest proportion) on emergency relief and rehabilitation. *See* <www.unicef.org>.

United Nations Commission on International Trade Law UNCITRAL was established by the General Assembly on 17 December 1966 for the purpose of promoting "the progressive harmonization and unification of the law of international trade" (GA Res. 2205 (XXI)). "By virtue of the extent of its activities, and broad representation among nations, UNCITRAL is probably the most significant organization working towards the harmonization or unification of laws touching upon international trade": Vishny, *Guide to International Commerce Law* (1981), 2.128. The Commission, which meets annually is presently composed of thirty-six member States (to be increased to sixty-six) elected by the General Assembly for terms of six years. The Commission has established six working groups in relation to privately-financed infrastructure projects, international arbitration and conciliation, transport law, e-commerce, insolvency law, and security interests.

As well as the facilitation of international treaties including the UN Convention on the Carriage of Goods by Sea of 31 March 1978 *(17 I.L.M. 608 (1978))*, the UN Convention on Contracts for International Sale of Goods of 11 April 1980 *(19 I.L.M. 668 (1980))*, the UN Convention on International Bills of Exchange and International Promissory Notes of 9 December 1988 *(UN Doc. A/Res/43/165)*, the UN Convention on the Liability of Operators of Transport Terminals International Trade of 17 April 1991 *(UN Doc. A/CONF/152/13)*, the UN Convention on Independent Guarantees and Stand-By Letters of Credit of 11 December 1995 *(UN Doc. A/50/640)* and the UN Convention on the Assignment of Receivables in International Trade of 12 December 2001 *(UN Doc A/Res/ES56/81)*, the Commission has also produced sets of Rules on Arbitration in 1976 (GA Res. 31/98*)* and Conciliation in 1980 (GA Res. 35/52), and Model Laws on International Commercial Arbitration (1985), International Credit Transfers (1992), Procurement of Goods, Construction and Services (1994), Electronic Commerce (1996), Cross Border Insolvency (1997), Electronic Signatures (2001) and International Commercial Conciliation (2001). *See* Dore, *The UNCITRAL Framework for Arbitration in Contemporary Perspective* (1993); Sanders, *The Work of UNCITRAL on Arbitration and Conciliation* (2001). *See also* <www.uncitral.org>.

United Nations Commission on Trade and Development (UNCTAD) UNCTAD was established in institutional form by the UN General Assembly on 30 December 1964 (Res. 1995 (XIX)), following a conference of the same name (23 March to 16 June 1964) which proposed that it was essential to have "adequate and effective functioning institutional arrangements (Preamble to Annex A of the Final Act of 16 June 1964: *3 I.L.M. 982(1964)*). GA Res. 1995 (XIX) established the Trade and Development Board as the "permanent organ of the Conference" (art. 4), whose functions include the oversight of action by the Conference (art. 15), the initiation of studies and reports (art. 16), and the preparation for future Conference sessions (art. 21). The resolution also specifies the functions of the Conference, which include the promotion of international trade, particularly that involving developing States (art. 3(a) and (b)), the coordination of activities within the UN system relating to trade and development (art. 3(d)), and the harmonization of trade and development policies (art. 3(e)). The Trade and Development Board has three subsidiary bodies: the Commission on Investment, Technology and Related Financial Issues; the Commission in Trade and Goods and Services, and Commodities; the Commission on Enterprise, Business Facilitation and Development. The Conference, which currently has 192 member states, meets every four years (most recently in UNCTAD X in February 2000). *See* Rothstein, *Global Bargaining: UNCTAD and the Quest for a New International Economic Order* (1979). *See also* <www.unctad.org>.

United Nations Day Celebrated on 24 October each year, United Nations Day marks the anniversary of the entry into force of the Charter in 1945 on the deposit of the USSR instrument of ratification (*see* art. 110(3)). On the same day in 1949 the cornerstone of the Headquarters Building in Manhattan, New York, was laid, occupancy by portions of the Secretariat beginning in August 1950 and formal inauguration of the new building occurring on 27 February 1952.

United Nations Development Programme "The UNDP's organizational priority is poverty eradication through sustainable human development. It began operations in 1966 as a result of General Assembly Res. 2029 (XX) which combined the UN Expanded Programme of Technical Assistance (EPTA) with the Special Fund. General Assembly Res. 2688 (XXV), which took effect in 1971, defined the present organizational structure and activities of the UNDP. The UNDP is headed by the Administrator who is the third highest ranking UN official behind the Secretary-General and the Deputy Secretary-General. The primary organ is the Executive Board (formerly the Governing Council (*see* GA Res. 48/162)). The Executive Board includes representatives from 36 States around the world on a rotating basis. It is responsible for providing inter-governmental support to and supervision of the activities of the UNDP. The work of the UNDP is undertaken by 5 Regional Offices covering Africa, Arab States, Asia and the Pacific, Europe and the CIS, Latin America and the Carribean. The Regional Offices are supported by a network of Country Offices of which there are currently 136. Most of the projects funded by the UNDP are executed by agencies and organizations within the UN system, including FAO, ILO, UNIDO, UNESCO, IBRD, WHO, ITU, ICAO, WMO, UNCTAD, IAEA, IMO and UPU.

UNDP is largely funded through voluntary contributions and has an annual budget of close to $1 billion. At the United Nations Millennium Summit in September 2000, a number of Millennium Development Goals were adopted in relation to international development dealing with issues such as the eradication of extreme poverty and hunger; the achievement of universal primary education; promotion of gender equality and the empowerment of women; reduction in children mortality; improvement of maternal health; combating AIDS/HIV, malaria and other diseases; ensuring of environmental sustainability; the development of a global partnership for development. New aid commitments could mean an additional $12 billion per year by 2006. *See* <www.undp.org>.

United Nations Educational, Scientific and Cultural Organization (UNESCO)
UNESCO's primary purpose is "to contribute to peace and security by promoting collaboration among the nations through education, science and culture in order to further universal respect for justice, for the rule of law and for human rights and fundamental freedoms" (art. 1). It currently has 189 member States and 6 associate members and is headquartered in Paris. UNESCO is governed by its Constitution, which was adopted in London on November 16, 1945 *(4 U.N.T.S. 275)*, and which has been subject to 22 amendments, the most recent at the 31st session of UNESCO. The Constitution provides for the basic organs of UNESCO; the decision-making General Conference which is supported by an Executive Board and a Secretariat, which oversees routine administration of policies and programs. The General Conference is empowered to determine the policies of UNESCO (art. 4). It makes determinations on programs submitted to it by the Executive Board. It can also summon international conferences on relevant topical issues. The General Conference will vote on recommendations and conventions submitted to it by lower bodies, as well as advise the United Nations on appropriate educational, scientific and cultural viewpoints. The General Conference typically meets every two years (art. 6).

The duties of the Executive Board include preparation of the agenda for the General Conference as well as working to craft a work program and an accurate budget estimate. The Executive Board is responsible for overseeing the execution of UNESCO programs. It is mandated to meet four times per biennium (art. 5). UNESCO is the only Specialized Agency of the United Nations to provide for the establishment of a National Commission by each of its member States (art. 7). The organization, which is a Specialized Agency (relations agreement of 14 December 1946, as supplemented 11 December 1948) has in the past been the object of considerable controversy owing to the style of management of its former director-general and the politicized nature of some of its work, notably on control of the media. The United States, the largest contributor, withdrew from the organization with effect from 31 December 1984 *(23 I.L.M. 220 (1984))*. *See* Spaulding and Lin, *Historical Dictionary of UNESCO* (1997); Zubov, *UNESCO: A Bibliography With Index* (2002). *See also* <www.unesco.org>.

United Nations Environment Programme   In Res. 1346 (XLV), ECOSOC underlined the urgent need to limit and where possible eliminate the impairment of the human environment. It recommended that the General Assembly consider the desirability of convening a UN conference on the subject. Endorsing this recommendation, the General Assembly in Res. 2398 (XXIII) decided to convene in 1972 a UN Conference on the Human Environment. The conference was held in Stockholm in 1972. Its report included a declaration [*see* **Stockholm Declaration**], an action plan for the human environment, and a resolution concerning future institutional and financial arrangements for international co-operation on environmental questions. In Res. 94 (XXVII) the General Assembly designated 5 June as World Environment Day and urged governments and organizations in the UN system to undertake on that day every year appropriate activities to reaffirm their concern for the preservation and enhancement of the human environment. It also accepted the recommendation of the conference that a UN Environment Programme (UNEP) be established. The Programme is based in Nairobi with a mission to provide leadership and encourage partnership in caring for the environment by inspiring, informing and enabling nations and peoples to improve their quality of life without compromising that of future generations. The structure of UNEP includes the General Council, currently consisting of 58 members elected by the UN General Assembly, which meets annually and reports to the

General Assembly through ECOSOC; a Committee of Permanent Representatives and a High-Level Committee of Ministers and Officials. UNEP recently hosted the 2002 World Summit on Sustainable Development in Johannesburg, South Africa. *See* Petsonk, The Role of the United Nations Environmental Programme (UNEP) in the Development of International Environmental Law, 5 *Am. U. J. Int'l L. & Pol'y 351 (1990). See also* <www.unep.org>.

United Nations Forces *See* **peace-keeping**.

United Nations High Commissioner for Human Rights The High Commissioner (UNHCHR) is the principal UN official with responsibility for human rights and is accountable to the Secretary-General. The post of High Commissioner was created by the General Assembly in 1993 by GA Res. 48/141. The High Commissioner is to be "a person of high moral standing and personal integrity" (para. 2) who shall "function within the framework of the Charter of the United Nations, the Universal Declaration of Human Rights, other international instruments of human rights and international law; Be guided by the recognition that all human rights . . . are universal, indivisible interdependent and interrelated; Recognize the importance of promoting a balance and sustainable development for all people. . . ." (para. 3). The Office of the High Commissioner for Human Rights (OHCHR) is based in Geneva and provides support to the Commission on Human Rights Commission, the Sub-Commission on the Promotion and Protection of Human Rights and the six treaty-monitoring committees. Funding is chiefly by voluntary contributions. The estimated budget in 2002 amounted to $55.8 million. *See* <www.unhchr.ch>.

United Nations High Commissioner for Refugees "After the First World War, machinery was set up in Geneva, under the auspices of the League of Nations, to deal with the problem of refugees. This organization continued in operation after the Second World War under the direction of Sir Herbert Emerson. Since, however, the decision had been taken internationally not to prolong the life of the League of Nations but to replace it by the United Nations, the General Assembly decided on 3 December 1949 [Res. 319 (IV)] to appoint a United Nations High Commissioner for Refugees for a three-year term, which has been renewed at five-yearly intervals": *Satow's Guide to Diplomatic Practice* (5th ed.) 346. The Statute of the Office of the UNHCR is embodied in GA Res. 428(V) of 1950 and the office came into being on 1 January 1951. The UNHCR is assisted by an Executive Committee, presently of 64 members who meet annually in Geneva to review and renew the agency's programme and budgets. Funding is chiefly by voluntary contributions with expenditure in 2002 amounting to just over $1 billion. The UNHCR has a special role in overseeing application of the various international instruments relating to **refugees** including, in particular, the UN Convention on the Status of Refugees 1951 *(189 U.N.T.S. 150)* and the 1967 Protocol thereto *(606 U.N.T.S. 267)*. The office is also concerned with questions of **asylum**, rescue at sea (boat people) and violation of the principle of non-**refoulement** under which no person is to be returned to a territory where he has reason to fear persecution. In addition to its general programs, UNHCR undertakes a number of special programs to assist internees and, in some cases, displaced persons. *See* <www.unhcr.ch>.

United Nations Industrial Development Organization This organization was established in 1961 as an independent organ of the General Assembly. A new constitution was opened for signature on 8 April 1979 *((1979) 18 I.L.M. 667)*, widening its scope so as to make its primary objective the promotion and acceleration of industrial development in the developing countries on global, regional and national as well as sectoral levels, with a view to assisting in the establishment of a new international economic order (art. 1), membership being open to all States (art. 3). With the entry into force of the new constitution upon the 80th ratification, UNIDO became a Specialized Agency in 1985 (art. 18). The principle organs of UNIDO are the General Conference (Conference), the Industrial Development Board (Board) and the Secretariat (Art. 7). There is also a Program and Budget Committee, which assists the Board in making decisions regarding the work and finances of UNIDO (art. 7). The Conference meets every two years unless it decides otherwise. It determines the guiding principles and policies of UNIDO while taking into account reports of the Board, Director-General and subsidiary organs. The Conference approves UNIDO's work program, as well as the various budgets and adoption of conventions and agreements (art. 8). The Board meets annually, making reports to the Conference on budgetary and program issues. Additionally, the Board makes requests to Members for pertinent information (art. 9). The Committee meets annually and is responsible for creation of a program for the upcoming fiscal year as well as work with the Director-General in preparing a budget for the organization (art. 10). During 2002, UNIDO's technical co-operation programs and projects totaled $81.8 million. New project approvals in 2002 amounted to $72.6 million. *See* <www.unido.org>.

United Nations Relief and Works Agency The United Nations Relief and Works Agency for Palestine Refugees in the Near East (UNRWA) was established, as a subsidiary organ of the UN General Assembly under art. 22 of the Charter, on 8 December 1949 (Res. 302(IV)). The original mandate of the Agency was to carry out, in collaboration with local governments, relief and works programmes for Palestine refugees, later extended to the "reintegration of the refugees into the economic life of the Near East, either by repatriation or resettlement" (GA Res. 393 (V)). *See* Dale, UNRWA—A Subsidiary Organ of the United Nations, *(1974) 23 I.C.L.Q. 576.*

United States Diplomatic and Consular Staff in Tehran Case *(USA v. Iran) 1979 I.C.J. Rep. 21, (1980) I.C.J. Rep. 3.* In 1979, militant elements in Iran occupied and seized the US Embassy in Tehran and Consulates at Tabriz and Shiraz, and seized and detained as hostages its diplomatic and consular staff in Tehran as well as two more citizens of the USA. In November 1979, the USA instituted proceedings before the ICJ against Iran, and requested the indication of provisional measures. Iran did not participate in the proceedings, apart from asserting that the Court could not and should not take cognizance of the case. On 15 December 1979, the Court (unanimously) *indicated* provisional measures requiring Iran immediately to ensure the restoration of US diplomatic and consular premises to US possession and control, and their inviolability and effective protection; and to ensure the immediate release of all US nationals held as hostages, and to afford all the US diplomatic and consular personnel the full protection, privileges and immunities to which they were entitled. On the merits the Court, on 24 May 1980, *held* that it had jurisdiction on the basis of the Optional Protocols to the Vienna Conventions of 1961 and 1963 on, respectively, Diplomatic and Consular Relations *(500 U.N.T.S. 95; 596 U.N.T.S. 261)*, and the 1955 Treaty of Amity, Economic Relations, and Consular Rights between the USA and Iran; that as regards the armed attack on and occupation of the Embassy on 4 November 1979 by militants, and their seizure of its inmates as hostages, the failure of the Iranian authorities to protect the US diplomatic and consular premises violated Iran's obligations under the two Vienna Conventions and the 1955 bilateral treaty; that subsequent actions of the Iranian State transformed acts complained of into acts of the Iranian State, the militants becoming agents of the State, which itself became internationally responsible for their acts; that the Iranian authorities' decision to continue the occupation of the Embassy and the detention of its staff as hostages gave rise to repeated and multiple breaches of Iran's treaty obligations under the two Vienna Conventions and the 1955 Treaty; and that accordingly (13 to 2) Iran was in breach of its obligations under international conventions in force between the two countries as well as under long established rules of general international law, which breaches engaged the responsibility of Iran towards the USA under international law; (unanimously) that Iran must immediately take all steps to redress the situation resulting from the events of 4 November 1979, terminate the unlawful detention of the US hostages and ensure that they could leave Iran, and immediately place in the hands of the protecting power the premises and property of the US Embassy and Consulates in Iran; (unanimously) that no member of the US diplomatic or consular staff may be kept in Iran to be subjected to judicial proceedings or to participate in them as a witness; and (12 to 3) that the Government of Iran was under an obligation to make reparation to the USA, although (14 to 1) the form and amount of such reparation, failing agreement between the parties, should be settled later by the Court. On 12 May 1981, the case was discontinued: *1981 I.C.J. Rep. 45.*

Uniting for Peace Resolutions The Uniting for Peace Resolution (GA Res. 377A(V)), adopted by the General Assembly on 3 November 1950, was intended to provide for occasions when disagreement among the Permanent Members of the Security Council prevented the Council fulfilling its "primary responsibility for the maintenance of international peace and security" (art. 24(1) of the Charter). The Resolution is based on two major premises: "that failure of the Security Council to discharge its responsibilities on behalf of all the Member States . . . does not relieve Member States of their obligations or the United Nations of its responsibility under the Charter to maintain international peace and security"; and "that such failure does not deprive the General Assembly of its rights or relieve it of its responsibilities under the Charter in regard to the maintenance of international peace and security" (Preamble). In its main substantive paragraph (1), the Resolution provides that "if the Security Council, because of lack of unanimity of the permanent members, fails to exercise its primary responsibility for the maintenance of international peace and security in any case where there appears to be a threat to the peace, breach of the peace or act of aggression, the General Assembly shall consider the matter immediately with a view to making appropriate recommendations to Members for collective measures, including in the case of a breach of the peace or act of aggression the use of armed force when necessary, to maintain or restore international peace and security." Although the General Assembly did not apparently act under the Resolution in the case of the Korean War, (the occasion of its adoption, because of Soviet vetoes in the Security Council: Petersen, *13 Int. Org, 219 (1959)),* the Uniting for Peace Resolution was used as the constitutional basis for the establishment by the General Assembly of the UN Emergency Force (**UNEF**) on 5 November 1956 (Res. 1000 (ES-I)), and both UNEF and the UN Force in the Congo (**ONUC**) were controlled by the General Assembly (the latter being established by the Security Council in Res. 387 (XV) of 14 July 1960). The legality of General Assembly involvement in **peace-keeping** was accepted by the ICJ in the ***Expenses of the United Nations Case*** *1962 I.C.J. Rep. 151. See* Bowett, *United Nations Forces* (1964); Burns and Hathcote, *Peacekeeping by United Nations Forces* (1963); Rosner, *The United Nations Emergency Force* (1963); Simmonds, *Legal Problems Arising from the United Nations Military Operations in the Congo* (1968); Seyersted, *United Nations Forces in the Law of Peace and War* (1966); Higgins, *United Nations Peacekeeping 1946-1967,* Vol. I, *The Middle East* (1969), Part 2, vol. III, *Africa* (1980), 5; McCoubrey and White, *The Blue Helmets: Legal Regulation of United Nations Military Operations* (1997).

Universal Declaration of Human Rights On 10 December 1948, the UN General Assembly adopted the Universal Declaration of Human Rights (GA Res. 217 (III)) by 48 votes to none with 8 abstentions (Byelorussian SSR, Czechoslovakia, Poland, Saudi Arabia, South Africa, Ukrainian SSR, USSR. and Yugoslavia). The Universal Declaration was adopted under the Charter obligation to promote "universal respect for, and observance of, human rights and fundamental freedoms for all without distinction as to race, sex, language or religion" (art. 55(c); *see also* Preamble; arts. 1(3) and 56). Comprising 30 substantive articles, the Universal Declaration sets out, in fairly skeletal form, the basic rights to be guaranteed to all people, although it is not generally regarded as legally binding. "The Universal Declaration of Human Rights has, since its adoption, exercised a powerful influence throughout the world, both internationally and nationally. Its provisions have been cited as justification for various actions taken by the United Nations, and have inspired a number of international conventions both within and outside the United Nations. They have also exercised a significant influence on national constitutions and on municipal legislation and, in several cases, on court decisions. In some instances, the text of provisions of the Declaration has been used in international instruments or national legislation, and there are many instances of the use of the Declaration as a code of conduct and as a yardstick to measure the degree of respect for and compliance with the international standards of human rights": Sohn and Buergenthal, *International Protection of Human Rights* (1973), 516. From the Universal Declaration came the legally binding International Covenants on **Civil and Political Rights** and on **Economic, Social and Cultural Rights** of 1966. *See* Robinson, *The Universal Declaration of Human Rights: Its Origin, Significance, Application and Interpretation* (1958), Ramcharan, *Human Rights Thirty Years After the Universal Declaration* (1979); Weston and Marks, *The Future of International Human Rights: Commemoration the 50th Anniversary of the Universal Declaration of Human Rights* (2000).

universal human rights "It is sometimes suggested that there can be no fully universal concept of human rights, for it is necessary to take into account the diverse cultures and political systems of the world . . . this is a point advanced mostly by states, and by liberal scholars anxious not to impose the Western view of things on others. It is rarely advanced by the oppressed, who are only too anxious to benefit from perceived universal standards. The non-universal, realist view of human rights, is in fact a very state-centred view and loses sight of the fact that human rights are *human* rights and not dependent on the fact that states, or groupings of states, may behave differently from each other so far as their politics, economic policy, and culture are concerned. Higgins, *Problems & Process: International Law and How We Use It* (1994), 96-76. Cf. **cultural relativism**.

universal international law Jenks, *The Common Law of Mankind* (1958), 29-30 and 62-172, points out that while international law is now universal or global in its application, this has caused some "dilution of the content of [the] law" (at 29) because States are not, as in the 19th Century, basically similar in their ideological stance. After warning of the danger, Jenks perhaps goes too far when he asserts that non-Western legal systems have enough in common with the Western legal system to "give us elements of an effective universal system of international law" (at 169).

universal jurisdiction Universal jurisdiction, or the principle of universality, "provides for jurisdiction over crimes committed by aliens outside the territory . . . on the sole basis of the presence of the alien within the territory of the State assuming jurisdiction": Comment on art. 10 of the Harvard Research in International Law, Draft Convention on Jurisdiction with Respect to Crime, *29 A.J.I.L. Supp. 435* at 573 *(1935)*. The essence of universal jurisdiction is that certain crimes are so heinous that every State is deemed to have an interest in their prosecution. Nevertheless, the concept arose out of attempts to deal with the creams of piracy in the eighteenth century. Accordingly, a second strand to the doctrine of universal jurisdiction is that the crimes are serious and might otherwise go unpunished. *See* Lowe, Jurisdiction, in Evans (ed.) *International Law* (2003), 343. Crimes which properly fall within the principle of universal jurisdiction do so through their acceptance as such in customary international law. As a result, there are probably only two or three categories of crimes that can properly be said to be subject to universal jurisdiction: **piracy** and **war crimes** and probably, **crimes against humanity** (*see* the separate opinion of Judges Higgins, Koolimans and Buergenthal in the ***Arrest Warrant Case 2002 I.C.J. Rep, 3.*** at paras. 60-65*)*. On the other hand, there has been considerable effort in recent years to extend the number of crimes which can be tried even where they are committed by aliens outside the territory of the State assuming jurisdiction. This has been done by international treaty regimes dealing with matters such as **hijacking, internationally protected persons**, the **taking of hostages, torture** (*see also **Pinochet Case***). "The general *aut dedere aut judicare* principle requires the State to prosecute *every* alleged offender found within its territory, if it does not extradite him. The law of States parties must therefore provide for jurisdiction over offenders, whether or not the offence was committed within the State's territory or ships or aircraft, or by or against a national of the State, or in order to compel the State to do something. The broad grounds of treaty jurisdiction are all in effect swallowed up within the quasi-universal jurisdiction that the aut dedere, aut judicare principle requires": Lowe, *supra*, 345. *See* Reydams, *Universal Jurisdiction in International Law* (2003). *See also* **crime, international**; *Eichmann Case*.

Universal Postal Union   Attempts to regulate the movement of mail between states date back to 1863, the name Universal Postal Union appearing in 1878, having been originally established as the General Postal Union. The Union's Constitution was adopted in its present form on 10 July 1964 *(611 U.N.T.S. 63)*, amendments being adopted by the 1969 Tokyo and 1974 Lausanne Congresses. The Constitution is filled out by the General Regulations, last revised at Rio de Janeiro on 26 October 1979. Rules governing postal services as such are contained in the Universal Postal Convention, other Agreements and Detailed Regulations (last revised at the 1979 Rio de Janeiro Congress). Under the Constitution, the Members comprise "a single postal territory for the reciprocal exchange of letter-post items. Freedom of transit is guaranteed throughout the entire territory of the Union" (art. 1(1)). The aim of the Union is to secure the organization and improvement of postal services and to promote in this sphere the development of international collaboration and technical assistance (art. 1(2), (3)). Membership is open to countries having membership status upon entry into force of the 1964 constitution (art. 2) and to countries admitted as members (by accession for UN members; upon application approved by two-thirds of the members for non-members: art. 11). There are currently 189 member states. The jurisdiction of the UPU extends to the territories of member countries, post offices set up by members in territories not included and territories which are postally dependent on member countries (art. 3). There is provision for withdrawal (art. 12), although not expulsion, although South Africa was expelled by resolution at the 1979 Congress but readmitted in 1994. Provision is made for restricted unions (in practice regional postal organizations): art. 8. The Congress, consisting of representatives of member countries, is "the supreme organ of the Union" (art. 14(1)); the Executive Council "ensures the continuity of the work of the Union between Congresses" (art. 17(1)); and the International Bureau, the Union's secretariat, "serves as an organ of liaison, information and consultation for postal administrations" (art. 20). The seat of the Union and of its permanent bodies is Berne, Switzerland. Expenditure is covered by the members, each member choosing the contribution class in which it intends to be included (art. 21). *See* Codding, *The Universal Postal Union* (1964); International Bureau, *Acts of the Universal Postal Union (Anno-*

tated) (4 vols. 2002); Rutkowski and Codding *The International Telecommunications Union in a Changing World* (1988). *See also* <www.upu.int>.

universalism This is the movement and belief that the solutions to the world's problems "are achievable by universal organisations of general competence. In other words those institutions which have general competence over global affairs whether they be economic, social or security": White, *The Law of International Organisations* (1996), 139. Cf. **regionalism**. *See* White, *supra*, Chap. 6.

unjust (or unjustified) enrichment "There is no doubt that at the present time [the] theory [of unjust enrichment] is accepted and applied generally by the countries of the world, even in the absence of a specific law, but the difficulty rests in fixing the limits within which it can and must be applied. In order that an action *in rem verso* may lie in municipal law it is necessary that the following elements coexist: 1. That there be enrichment of the defendant. 2. That this enrichment be the direct consequence of a patrimonial injury suffered by the plaintiff. That is, that the same causative act creates simultaneously the enrichment and the detriment. 3. That the enrichment of the defendant be unjust. 4. That the injured person have in his favour no contractual right which he could exercise to compensate him for the damage": ***Dickson Car Wheel Company Case (1931) 4 R.I.A.A. 669*** at 676. While it is broadly agreed that the doctrine of unjust enrichment "has not yet been transplanted to the field of international law" *(ibid)*, it has been accepted and applied in fields whose structure is not very different from municipal law. Thus, the doctrine has been applied in relation to a concession contract *(Lena Goldfields Company Case (1929-30) 5 A.D. 3)*, and to the relations between international organizations and their employees *(Schumann v. Secretariat of the League of Nations (1933-4) 7 A.D. 461)*. *See* Schwarzenberger, *International Law* (3rd ed.), 577-81.

unjust war *See* **just war**, *bellum justum*; *bellum injustum*.

unlawful combatants This term, used synonymously with enemy combatants, has been applied to the al-Qaeda and Taliban prisoners taken during the conflict in Afghanistan in 2001-2 and held at the US Guantánamo Bay naval base in Cuba. Such a characterization and status are not a generally recognized part of the laws of war. Unlawful combatants, not being accorded the benefits required for **prisoners of war**, nonetheless are entitled (1) to have their status determined by a competent tribunal under art. 5 of the Geneva Convention relative to the Treatment of Prisoners of War of 12 August 1949 *(75 U.N.T.S. 135)*; (2) as protected persons under art. 4 of the Geneva Convention relative to the Protection of Civilian Persons in Time of War of the same date *(75 U.N.T.S. 287)*, to the minimum guarantees set out in Part III of that Convention; and (3) in the event of trial, to the due process protections afforded by art. 14 of the International Covenant on Civil and Political Rights 1966 *(999 U.N.T.S. 171)*.

UNMEE Established by Security Council Res. 1312 (2000) and deployed under the authority of Res. 1320 (2000), the United Nations Mission in Ethiopia and Eritrea was formed to monitor and ensure the termination of hostilities as called for in the Agreement on Cessation of Hostilities between Ethiopia and Eritrea of 18 June 2000 *(40 I.L.M. 260 (2001))*. UNMEE continues to monitor the positions of Ethiopian and Eritrean forces since redeployment.

UNMIBH The United Nations Mission in Bosnia and Herzegovina was created in 1995 as a result of Security Council Res. 1035. The mission has been extended a number of times by various resolutions. UNMIBH is in charge of a wide array of tasks throughout the region. Its primary focus is on law enforcement; other activities UNMIBH coordinates include issues relating to human rights, refugees, elections and the rehabilitation of the region's infrastructure and economy.

UNMIH An acronym for the United Nations Mission in Haiti, established by Security Council Res. 867 (1993). UNMIH was originally mandated to assist in the implementation of the Governors Island Agreement of 3 July 1993 and had its mandate expanded to include stabilization activities in Haiti. UNMIH was operational from September 1993 to June 1996.

UNMIK The United Nations Mission in Kosovo was established by Security Resolution 1244 (1999) in June 1999, after the withdrawal of NATO forces from the region, with the view of establishing an interim civil administration led by the United Nations. UNMIK currently performs the whole spectrum of essential administrative functions and services covering areas such as health, education, banking, finance, telecommunications and law and order.

UNMISET An acronym for the United Nations Mission of Support in East Timor charged with providing transitional assistance until the balance of administrative and operational tasks are assumed by the East Timor government. UNMISET was created by Security Council Res. 1410 (2002).

UNMOGIP The United Nations Military Observer Group in India and Pakistan is charged with monitoring the ceasefire between the two nations in the State of Jammu and Kashmir. UNMOGIP was established by Security Council Res. 47 in April 1948. Since the renewal of hostilities in the region in 1972, UNMIGIP has monitored the ceasefire called for by the UN Secretary-General. There has been disagreement between India and Pakistan as to when the mandate of UNMOGIP lapsed and consequently the Secretary-General maintains that UNMOGIP can only be concluded by a Security Council decision which has not yet been forthcoming and so the mandate continues.

UNMOP Established in 1996 by Security Council Res. 1038, the United Nations Mission of Observers in Prevlaka was charged with monitoring the demilitarization of the Prevlaka peninsula, an important region disputed by the neighboring states of Croatia and the Federal Republic of Yugoslavia. Following successful completion of tits mandate, the Mission was terminated on 15 December 2002.

UNMOT An acronym for the United Nations Mission of Observers to Tajikistan established by Security Council Res. 968 (1994) and was extant from December 1994 to May 2000. UNMOT was charged with oversight of the ceasefire agreed to under the Agreement on a Temporary Ceasefire and the Cessation of Other Hostile Acts on the Tajik-Afghan border. UNMOT's mandate was expanded in 1997 to assist in the execution of the General Agreement on the Establishment of Peace and National Accord in Tajikistan.

UNMOVIC The United Nations Monitoring, Verification and Inspection Commission was established in December 1999 by Security Council Res. 1284 (1999) to replace **UNSCOM** and to act alongside the **International Atomic Energy Agency** in the verification of the destruction, removal or rendering harmless of Iraq's **weapons of mass destruction** and ballistic missiles with a range greater than 150 kilometers, together with related items and production facilities. Headed by its Executive Chairman, Dr Hans Blix, UNMOVIC was not permitted to enter Iraq until 27 November 2002 after the Security Council had given Iraq a "final opportunity" to comply with its resolutions in Security

Council Res. 1441 (2002) of 8 November 2002. On 18 March 2003, UNMOVIC suspended its operations following the decision of the Secretary-General to withdraw all UN staff from Iraq. In Res. 1483 of 22 May 2003, the Security Council reaffirmed its intention to reinstate the disarmament work of UNMOVIC and the IAEA. As of the present date, UNMOVIC remains in a state of readiness to resume its functions.

unneutral service While lack of precision in the past, and recent changes in all the conditions of warfare, especially those relating to **neutrality**, preclude a comprehensive and exact definition, "'unneutral service' seems to comprehend any acts or conduct on the part of the owners or persons in charge of a neutral vessel (or aircraft) whereby the vessel (or aircraft) is employed for objects or purposes which may (to a degree going beyond mere **contraband** or blockade breach) advance the belligerent interests of one State and injure the same interests of an adversary. In face of such activity the injured adversary is empowered (1) to stop the vessel (or aircraft), and remove therefrom certain categories of person; (2) to capture the vessel (or aircraft); and (3) to condemn the vessel (or aircraft) or certain portions of its cargo by proceeding before its prize court": Stone, *Legal Controls of International Conflict* (2nd imp. revised), 511-2. *See also II Oppenheim 831-79*; Neff, *The Rights and Duties of Neutrals* (2000).

UNOGIL The United Nations Observation Group in Lebanon was established in 1958 by Security Council Res. 128 to prevent the illegal introduction of arms and personnel into Lebanon. The Mission was withdrawn the same year as a result of improved and stabilized conditions.

UNOMIG An acronym for United Nations Observer Mission in Georgia established by Security Council Res. 858 (1983) in 1993 to monitor the July 1993 ceasefire agreement between Abkhaz authorities and the Government of Georgia. The mandate was expanded in 1994 when both sides signed the Agreement on a Ceasefire and Separation of the Forces 1994.

UNOMIL Established by Security Council Res. 866 (1993), the United Nations Observer Mission in Liberia was mandated to oversee the ceasefire agreement and monitor compliance with the Cotonou Peace Agreement. Headquartered in Monrovia, UNOMIL operated from September 1993 to September 1997.

UNOMSIL Established by Security Council Res. 1181 (1998), the United Nations Observer Mission in Sierra Leone was mandated to oversee the military and security situation in Sierra Leon as well as aid in the disarmament of former combatants and to secure the observation of international human rights instruments. UNOMSIL operated between July 1998 and October 1999.

UNOMUR The United Nations Observer Mission Uganda-Rwanda was established by Security Council Res. 846 (1993) to monitor the border between the two nations. UNOMUR operated from June 1993 to September 1994.

UNOSOM I An acronym for the first United Nations Operation in Somalia, UNOSOM I oversaw the ceasefire in Mogadishu and guarded humanitarian supplies and convoys. Established by Security Council Res. 751 (1992), UNOSOM I was operational from April 1992 to March 1993.

UNOSOM II An acronym for the second United Nations Operation in Somalia, authorized by Security Council Res. 814 (1993). UNOSOM II took over from the Unified Task Force (**UNITAF**) with a view to completing, through disarmament and reconciliation, the work begun by UNITAF for the restoration of peace, stability, law and order. UNOSOM II was itself authorized to undertake enforcement action and carried out its duties from March 1993 to March 1995.

UNPREDEP An acronym for United Nations Preventative Deployment Force established in March 1995 to replace UNPROFOR in the Former Yugoslav Republic of Macedonia, UNPREDEP's mandate was to monitor the border areas with Albania and the Federal Republic of Yugoslavia (Serbia and Montenegro), as well as give an account on any developments which may endanger that State. UNPREDEP was created by Security Council Res. 983 (1995) and, through successive extensions of its mandate, lasted until February 1999 when a further extension of its mandate was blocked by the veto of China.

UNPROFOR An acronym for United Nations Protection Force, UNPROFOR authorized by Security Council Res. 743 (1992). With an initial mandate to ensure demilitarization in selected areas in Croatia, the mission was later extended to monitor actions in Bosnia and Herzegovina (SC Res. 776 (1992)) and Macedonia (SC Res. 795 (1992)). UNPROFOR's mandate did not provide for the possibility of enforcement action under Chapter VII of the UN Charter, although individual States were given a mandate by a number of resolutions, in particular SC Res. 770 (1992) to take "all necessary measures" to facilitate the delivery of humanitarian assistance in the region. This was to be done in cooperation with UNPROFOR and the Secretary-General. UNPROFOR was operational from February 1992 to March 1995 and was replaced in Croatia by **UNCRO** and in Macedonia by **UNPREDEP** although its mandate continued in Bosnia and Herzegovina until it was replaced, in November 1995, by a multinational implementation force (IFOR) comprised primarily of forces from NATO.

UNPSG Authorized by Security Council Res. 1145 in December 1997, the United Nations Civilian Police Support Group was mandated to watch over actions of Croatian police in the Danube region with a special emphasis on the restoration of displaced persons. The mission was completed in October 1998.

UNRWA *See* **United Nations Relief and Works Agency**.

UNSCOB The United Nations Special Committee in the Balkans, along with **UNTSO**, predate what can properly be called UN **peace-keeping** missions, the origins of which can be traced to these truce supervision missions. UNSCOB was created in 1947 by General Assembly Res. 109 (1947) to monitor a ceasefire in Greece. It operated until 1954.

UNSCOM An acronym for the United Nations Special Commission, established by Security Council Res. 687 in April 1991, the purpose of which was to bring to an end the first Gulf Conflict. Section C of this resolution called for the destruction, removal or rendering harmless, under international supervision, of Iraq's **weapons of mass destruction** and ballistic missiles with a range greater than 150 kilometers, together with related items and production facilities. It also called for measures to ensure that the acquisition and production of prohibited items were not resumed. UNSCOM, in conjunction with the **International Atomic Energy Agency** facilitated the inspection and survey necessary to make an informed assessment of Iraq's capabilities and facilities in the chemical, biological and ballistic missile fields. UNSCOM was also charged with long-term monitoring to ensure ongoing verification of Iraq's compliance with its obligations under para. 10 of Res. 687 (1991), principally not to reacquire banned capabilities, in accordance with the plan prepared by the Special Commission and approved by the Security Council in its Res. 715

(1991). UNSCOM was replaced by the United Nations Monitoring, Verification and Inspection Commission (**UNMOVIC**) in December 1999 (*See* SC Res. 1284 (1999)).

UNSF The United Nations Security Force in West New Guinea (West Irian) was mandated to oversee the ceasefire in the area established under United Nations Temporary Executive Authority, and assist during the period of transfer from rule by the Netherlands to Indonesia. UNSF's duration was from October 1962 to April 1963.

UNSMIH The United Nations Support Mission in Haiti was authorized pursuant to Security Council Res. 1063 (1996). Lasting from July 1996 to July 1997, UNSMIH was established to aid the Haitian government with the creation and maintenance of an effective national police force as well as supporting the UN Special Representative in efforts to stabilize and rehabilitate the nation's infrastructure.

UNTAC The United Nations Transitional Authority in Cambodia was created to guarantee implementation of the Agreements on the Comprehensive Political Settlement of the Cambodia Conflict (October 1991). Established by Security Council Res. 745 (1992), UNTAC's duration was March 1992 to September 1993.

UNTAES Established in 1996 by Security Council Res. 1037, the United Nations Transitional Authority in Eastern Slavonia, Baranja and Western Sirmium was charged with a number of general military and civilian tasks under 1995 Basic Agreement on the Region, which provided for the peaceful integration of the region into Croatia. The mission was completed in January 1998.

UNTAET An acronym for the United Nations Mission in East Timor established by Security Council Res. 1272 (1999) and mandated to assume general administrative responsibility for East Timor, including the exercise of all legislative, executive and judicial authority. UNTAET was operational from October 1999 to May 2002.

UNTAG An acronym for United Nations Transition Assistance Group, UNTAG was established by Security Council Res. 632 (1989) to assist with the early independence of Namibia by supervising its elections as well as guaranteeing that all hostilities in the area were ended. UNTAG operated from April 1989 to March 1990.

UNTSO The United Nations Truce Supervision Organization, along with **UNSCOB**, pre-dates what can properly be called UN **peace-keeping** missions, the origins of which can be traced to these truce supervision missions. UNTSO was established in 1948 under the authority of the Security Council Res. 50 (1948) to assist in the observance of the truce in Palestine. UNTSO military observers remain in the Middle East to monitor ceasefires, supervise armistice agreements and assist the UN in its peace-keeping operations in the region.

UNYOM The United Nations Yemen Observation Mission operated from its base in the Yemen from July 1963 to September 1964. It was established by Security Council Res. 179 (1963) to monitor the disengagement agreement between the United Arab Republic and Saudi Arabia.

Upton Case *(USA v. Venezuela) (1903) 9 R.I.A.A. 234.* Property belonging to Upton, a United States national, was taken by Venezuelan Government authorities for use against revolutionary forces and was damaged, and certain other property of his suffered damage as a result of the civil war which was then taking place. *Held* by the US-Venezuelan Mixed Claims Commission set up under a Protocol of 17 February 1903, in allowing the claim as to the former category of property, that, while a taking by the State of private property for a public purpose was justified by necessity, the taking involved an obligation to pay compensation to the owner; and in disallowing the claim as to the latter category of property, that the loss arose not from Government acts specifically directed against the claimant's property but from the disturbed conditions in Venezuela and a person going to a foreign country voluntarily assumed the risks of residence there as well as the advantages.

UPU *See* **Universal Postal Union**.

Urrutia, Francisco José 1870-1950. Colombian national and diplomat. Sometime member, PCA and judge. Principal publications: *Comentarios de la Declaración del Instituto Americano de Derecho Internacional sobre derechos y deberes de las Naciones* (1915); *Le continent américain et le droit international* (1928).

usage "The terms 'custom' and 'usage' are often used interchangeably. Strictly speaking, there is a clear technical distinction between the two. Usage represents the initial stage of custom. Custom begins where usage becomes general. Usage is an international habit of action that has not yet received full legal attestation. Usages may be conflicting, custom must be unified and self-consistent. . . . A general, though not inflexible, working guide is that before a usage may be considered as amounting to a customary rule of international law, two tests must be satisfied. These tests relate to: (i) the material, and (ii) the psychological aspects involved in the formation of the customary rule": Shearer, *Starke's International Law,* (11th ed.), 31, 33. *See also* **custom**.

uti possidetis "The term is derived from the Roman law, in which it was used to denote an edict of the *praetor,* the purpose of which was to preserve, pending litigation, an existing state of possession of an immovable, *"nec vi, nec clam, nec precario,"* as between opposing individual claimants. . . . [I]n relation to international boundaries in Latin America . . . it is intended . . . to denote permanent instead of temporary possession. When Spanish control over Hispanic America came to an end, each of the new sovereignties which emerged . . . tended to follow the lines of cleavage which in the colonial period had divided Spanish administrative units—vice-royalties, captaincies-general, or provinces. Thus Venezuela, in her Constitution of 1830, declared that the national territory comprised the area which "previously to the political changes of 1810, was denominated the Captaincy-General of Venezuela." When Ecuador separated from Colombia, the boundary between the two countries was declared to be the line which had "separated the provinces of the ancient Department of the Cauca from that of Ecuador." Honduras, in her Constitution of 1839, claimed the territory which had formerly constituted the colonial province of the same name. But it was rarely that the demarcation of the Spanish American administrative units had been clearly defined by the former sovereigns, and the uncertainty resulted in a series of fiercely contested boundary disputes": Fisher, The Arbitration of the Guatemalan-Honduran Boundary Dispute, *27 A.J.I.L. 403* at 415 *(1933). See **Colombia-Venezuela Boundary Dispute**; **Guatemala-Honduras Boundary Arbitration**; **Land, Island and Maritime Frontier Dispute (El Salvador /Honduras)**.

The principle has also been used in the context of the decolonisation process in Africa: "The essence of the principle lies in its primary aim of securing respect for the territorial boundaries at the moment when independence is achieved. Such territorial boundaries might be no more than delimitation between different administrative divisions or colonies all subject to the same sovereign. In that case, the application of the principle of *uti possidetis* resulted in administrative boundaries being transformed into international frontiers in the full sense of the term. . . . It's obvious purpose is to prevent the independence and stability of new states being endangered by fratricidal struggles provoked by the challenging of frontiers following the withdrawal of the administering power: **Burkina Faso v. Republic of Mali** *1986 I.C.J.Rep. 554* at 566. In the *Burkina Faso v Mali Case*, the Chamber of the ICJ considered the potentially conflicting relationship between *uti possidetis* and **self-determination**, concluding that self-determination could exist within the existing boundaries. However, "[t]he principle of *uti possidetis* provides that states accept their inherited colonial boundaries. It places no obligation upon minority groups to stay a part of a unit that maltreats them or in which they feel unrepresented. If they do in fact establish an independent state, or join with an existing state, then that new reality is one which, when its permanence can be shown, will in due course be recognized by the international community": Higgins, *Problems and Process: International Law and How We Use It* (1994), 125.

The principle has an application beyond the purely colonial context and was considered in relation to the break up of the former USSR and the former Yugoslavia. (*see*, for example, Opinion No. 2 and 3 of the Yugoslav Arbitration Commission established by the European Community *(1992) 92 I.L.R. 168 and 172*). *See* LaLonde, *Determining Boundaries in a Conflicted World: The Role of Uti Possidetis* (2003).

Utrecht, Treaty of   This is the general name given to a series of important treaties which concluded the war of the Spanish succession, the principal treaties being concluded on 11 April 1713. By the treaty of peace and friendship between Great Britain and France *(27 C.T.S. 475)*, Louis XIV recognized the Protestant succession in England and undertook to give no further aid to the Stuarts. France ceded to England Newfoundland, Nova Scotia, St. Kitts and the Hudson's Bay Territory, and agreed to destroy the fortifications and fill in the port of Dunkirk. The treaty between France and the United Provinces *(28 C.T.S. 37)* secured to Holland the line of fortresses running from Luxembourg to Nieuport on the coast (near the present Franco/Belgian frontier). Other treaties concluded at the same time were between France and Savoy *(28 C.T.S. 123)*, Prussia *(28 C.T.S. 141)* and Portugal *(28 C.T.S. 169)*. The treaty between England and Spain was concluded on 13 July 1713 *(28 C.T.S. 295)*, ceding to England Gibraltar and Minorca and a monopoly for 30 years of the slave trade with Spanish America (the Asiento). The peace between Spain and the United Provinces was concluded on 26 January 1714 *(29 C.T.S. 97)*, with Portugal on 6 February 1715 *(29 C.T.S. 214)*. Relations between France and the Empire were regulated by treaty of 6 March 1714 concluded at Rastatt *(29 C.T.S. 1)* and a subsequent treaty of 7 September 1714 concluded at Baden *(29 C.T.S. 141)*. The dispositions made by the Treaty of Utrecht were a vital factor in assisting the expansion of Britain's colonial empire.

V

Valentine Petroleum Arbitration *(1967) 44 I.L.R. 79.* Valentine Petroleum and Chemical Corporation, a US company, in 1962 signed a 10 year concession with the Government of Haiti for certain exclusive petroleum rights. Valentine Petroleum was granted a contract of guarantee by the US Agency for International Development, as part of the investment guarantee program under the US Foreign Assistance Act. In October 1964, there were reports that the concession had been annulled and a similar concession granted instead to another person, and in November 1964 personnel of Valentine Petroleum in Haiti were arrested, subsequently released, and returned to the USA. Valentine Petroleum submitted a claim against the Agency under the contract of guarantee and the matter was referred to arbitration in accordance with the contract. *Held,* in allowing Valentine Petroleum's losses to be recovered under the contract of guarantee, that the circumstances involved an expropriation by Haiti, in abrogating, repudiating or impairing the concession and granting substantially the same rights to another person; the unilateral termination of the concession was an arbitrary act of expropriation, there being no evidence of fault by Valentine Petroleum; the **local remedies** rule did not apply to claims under the investment guarantee program, and the contract of guarantee, although requiring Valentine Petroleum to take all reasonable measures to pursue or preserve remedies which might be available against an expropriation, did not require Valentine Petroleum to litigate the legality of measures of a strongly entrenched executive; and the assessment of losses to be recovered depended on the contract of guarantee and was not the same as might apply in relation to a claim against Haiti.

Vallat Sir Francis A. 1912- . A legal adviser to the UK Foreign Service 1945 to 1968, Legal Adviser, FCO, 1960-68. Principal publication: *International Law and the Practitioner* (1966).

Valletta Procedure At Valletta, Malta, in 1991, a committee of experts drew up a system of **conciliation** for the Conference on Security and Cooperation in Europe, subsequently adopted by the organization's Council of Ministers as the CSCE Procedure for Peaceful Settlement of Disputes *(30 I.L.M. 390 (1991); 32 I.L.M. 556 (1993))*. Under this procedure, any party to a dispute which they cannot be resolved by direct negotiations or some other agreed procedure may refer the matter to a Dispute Settlement Mechanism (§ IV). This Mechanism first takes the form of a person or group agreeable to the parties to the dispute (§ V), whose task is to "indicate" an appropriate dispute settlement procedure (§ VIII), then, assuming no settlement, "to provide general or specific comment or advice on the substance of the dispute" so as to enable the parties to resolve their differences (§ XI). *See* Merrills, *International Dispute Settlement* (3rd ed.), 80-2.

vassal State *See* **suzerainty**.

Vattel, Emmerich de 1714-67. Swiss diplomat and international lawyer. In essence an Eclectic, he followed the school of Leibnitz and Wolff. Principal work: *Le droit des gens* (1758; text and translation in *Classics of International Law,* No. 4 (1916)).

VCLT *See* **Vienna Convention on the Law of Treaties**.

Venezuela Boundary Cases *See British Guiana Boundary Case; Colombia-Venezuela Boundary Dispute*.

Venezuelan Preferential Claims Case *(Germany, Italy and UK v. Venezuela) (1904) 9 R.I.A.A. 103*. Upon the failure of attempts to settle by diplomatic negotiations a controversy over certain pecuniary claims of British, German and Italian nationals against Venezuela, the British, German and Italian Governments in 1902 declared a blockade of Venezuelan ports. The US, Mexico, Spain, France, Belgium, the Netherlands, and Sweden and Norway also held claims against Venezuela, but these governments did not resort to forcible measures to secure the settlement of their claims. Venezuela proposed that the claims of all the above-mentioned countries be met from a proportion of the customs receipts of two Venezuelan ports. The three blockading States maintained that their claims should be given priority of payment over the claims of the other, neutral, States. By agreements signed in May 1903, the question was submitted to arbitration. *Held* that, since Venezuela had in various ways acknowledged a distinction between the three blockading States and the neutral States, and since neither Venezuela nor the neutral States had protested against the pretensions of the blockading States to preferential treatment, and since the neutral States could not acquire new rights from the war-like operations in which they had not taken part, although their existing rights remained intact, Germany, Italy and the UK had a right to preferential treatment for the payment of their claims against Venezuela.

Verdross, Alfred 1890-1980. Austrian foreign ministry official 1918-22 and professor of law; member, ILC 1957-66; member, PCA 1958-77; President, International Conference in Vienna for the Codification of the Law of Diplomatic Relations 1961; judge, European Court of Human Rights 1959-77. Principal publications: *Völkerrecht* (1937; 5th ed. with Verosta and Zemanek 1964); *Die Quellen des Universellen Völkerrechts* (1973); *Austria's Permanent Neutrality* (1978).

Verona, Congress of (1822) This was the last of the series of four congresses based on principles enumerated in art. 6 of the Treaty of Paris of 20 November 1815, inaugurating the **Concert System** *(65 C.T.S. 296)*. The principal subject of discussion (issues relating to Turkey and Italy having already been resolved) related to intervention in Spain, to which Great Britain was firmly opposed, thus leading to the open breach of Great Britain with the principles and policy of the Grand Alliance. A declaration on the slave trade was nevertheless adopted on 28 November *(73 C.T.S. 31)*.

Versailles, Treaty of, 1919 The Treaty of Peace of 28 June 1919 between the Allied and Associated Powers (the principal powers being the USA, the British Empire, France, Italy and Japan) and Germany *(225 C.T.S. 188)* is the single most important and enduring instrument concluded at the end of the First World War, peace being accepted on the basis of Woodrow Wilson's **Fourteen Points**. Part I (arts. 1-26) established the **League of Nations**; Part II (arts. 27-30) the Boundaries of Germany; Part III (arts. 31-17), the so-called Political Clauses for Europe, dealt notably with the status of Belgium, Luxembourg, the Saar, Alsace-Lorraine, Austria, the Czecho-Slovak State, Poland, East Prussia, the Memel Territory, Danzig and Russia (abrogation of the Treaty of Brest-Litovsk: art. 116). Under Part IV (arts. 118-158), German Rights and Interests outside Germany, Germany was stripped of her overseas possessions, the **Mandate System** being established under the League Covenant. Parts V and VI (arts. 159-226) regulated military affairs and prisoners of war and graves. Parts VII and VIII (arts. 227-247) imposed penalties (arraignment of the Kaiser, provision for trial of war criminals; express acceptance of responsibility (the war guilt clause: art. 231); establishment of the Reparation Commission and provision for the payment of an initial amount equivalent to 20 billion gold marks and detailed provision for reparations in kind), backed by Part IX, the financial clauses (arts. 248-263). Part X, the economic clauses (arts. 264-312), attempted to regulate trade relations, and in particular made provision for establishment of the mixed Arbitral Tribunal (art. 304). Parts XI and XII (arts. 313 to 386) regulated air and surface transport, notably novating the Act of Mannheim 1868 on the navigation of the Rhine and Moselle. Part XIII (arts. 387-427) is a self-contained part, making provision for the establishment of the **International Labor Organization**. Part XIV attempted to secure guarantees for execution of the Treaty, notably by occupation of German territory to the west of the Rhine (arts. 428-433). Part XV contains miscellaneous provisions and notably recognition of the position of the neutralized zone of Savoy: art. 235; *see Free Zones of Upper Savoy and District of Gex Case*.

Further treaties of peace were concluded as follows: Austria on 10 September 1919 at St. Germain *(226 C.T.S. 8)*; Hungary on 4 June 1920 at Trianon *(6 L.N.T.S. 188)*; Bulgaria on 27 November 1919, at Neuilly-sur-Seine *(226 C.T.S. 332)*; Turkey on 10 August 1920 at Sévres *(28 L.N.T.S. 226)* and on 24 July 1923 at Lausanne *(128 L.N.T.S. 11)*. Although the USA was a signatory to all but the last two of these instruments, it did not ratify any of them. Instead, it concluded separate treaties restoring friendly relations: *2 Bevans 42. See generally The Treaty of Versailles and After: Annotations of the Text of the Treaty* (Department of State, 1947); Grenville, *The Major International Treaties* (1974), 38-57; Carnegie Endowment, *The Treaties of Peace 1919-1923* (1924).

Verzijl, Jan Hendrik Willem 1888-87. Professor Utrecht 1919-38, 1947-58, Amsterdam 1938-45, Leiden 1945-56. Member, PCA. Principal Works: *Jurisprudence of the World Court* (1965-66); and the momumental *International Law in Historical Perspective* (11 vols. 1968-1992, the series completed by Heere and Offerhaus).

vested rights *See* **acquired (or vested) rights**.

veto Art. 27(3) of the UN Charter, providing that "[d]ecisions of the Security Council on [substantive] matters shall be made by an affirmative vote of nine members, including the concurring votes of the permanent member," effectively gives each of the 5 permanent members (China, France, Russia, the UK and USA) a veto on the adoption of decisions. In the practice of the Security Council, and by tacit amendment of the Charter, an **abstention** by a permanent member is no bar to adoption of resolutions; "in order to prevent the adoption of a resolution requiring unanimity of the permanent members, a permanent member has only to cast a negative vote" *(Namibia Opinion 1971 I.C.J. Rep. 22)*. It is argued that the **absence** of a permanent member likewise is no bar to adoption of resolutions: see Kelsen, *Recent Trends in the Law of the UN* (1951), 927-936. The use of the veto, or the threat thereof, has been a principal cause of inertia in the Security Council, particularly in the Cold War era; cf. Bailey, *The Procedure of the UN Security Council* (2nd ed.), 225, arguing that "assertions that the Security Council is impotent because of the veto cannot be substantiated." Any alteration in the present voting arrangements in the Security Council (*e.g.*, by making the veto power applicable only to a more limited range of decisions, by removing the veto power altogether or by adding to the permanent members, with or without the veto) would entail an amendment to the Charter which, in terms of art. 108, requires ratification by all the permanent members. On the demarcation between procedural and non-procedural matters, see **double veto**. As to attempts to circumvent the veto power by giving responsibilities to the General Assembly, *see* **Uniting for Peace Resolutions**. *See* Bailey, *Voting in the Security Council* (1970), Chap. 4; Fassbender, *The UN Security Council and the Right of Veto: A Constitutional Perspective* (1998).

vicarious responsibility "A distinction is sometimes made between the original and the so-called vicarious responsibility of a state. 'Original' responsibility is borne by a state for acts which are directly imputable to it, such as acts of its government, or those of its officials or private individuals performed at the government's command or with its authorisation. 'Vicarious' responsibility, on the other hand, arises out of certain internationally injurious acts of private individuals (whether nationals, or aliens in the state's territory), and of officials acting without authorisation. It is apparent that the essential difference between original and vicarious responsibility in this sense is that whereas the former involves a state being in direct breach of legal obligations binding on it, and is accordingly a particularly serious matter, the with the latter the state's responsibility is at one remove from the injurious conduct complained of: in such cases the state's responsibility calls for it to take certain preventive measures and requires it to secure that as far as possible the wrongdoer makes suitable reparation, and if necessary to punish him. But these preventive and remedial obligations of the state in cases of 'vicarious' responsibility are themselves obligations for the breach of which (as by refusing to take the remedial action which is required) the state bears direct responsibility": *I Oppenheim 501-2*. *See also* **act of State**; **attribution**; **State responsibility**.

Vienna Convention on Consular Relations 1963 *See* **consular privileges and immunities**.

Vienna Convention on Diplomatic Relations 1961 *See* **diplomatic privileges and immunities**.

Vienna Convention on the Representation of States in Relation to International Organizations *See* **representation of a member State**.

Vienna Convention on the Law of Treaties 1969 Described as "one of the prime achievements of the International Law Commission (Aust, *Modern Treaty Law and Practice* (2000), 6), the Convention on the Law of Treaties was adopted by the UN Conference on the Law of Treaties at Vienna on 22 May 1969; and entered into force in accordance with art. 84(1) on 27 January 1980. The text of the Convention appears in the Documents section appended to this *Encyclopaedic Dictionary*. "The Convention is not as a whole declaratory of general international law; it does not express itself so to be (*see* the preamble). Various provisions clearly involve progressive development of the law; and the preamble affirms that questions not regulated by its provisions will continue to be governed by the rules of customary international law. Nonetheless, a good number of articles are essentially declaratory of existing law and certainly those provisions which are not constitute presumptive evidence of emergent rules of international law": Brownlie, *Principles of Public International Law* (5th ed.), 608. *See* entries under **treaties**. *And see generally*, McNair, *Law of Treaties* (2nd ed.); Sinclair, *The Vienna Convention on the Law of Treaties* (2nd ed.); Aust, *Modern Treaty Law and Practice* (2000).

Vienna Convention on the Law of Treaties between States and International Organizations or between International Organizations Signed at Vienna on 21 March 1986 *((1986) 25 I.L.M. 543)* and not in force, this convention sets out the legal rules in respect of treaties in which at least one of the parties is an international organization (art. 1). While it is modeled on the **Vienna Convention on the Law of Treaties 1969** (*see* Preamble), it differs from that convention to the extent mandated by the quite different structure and operation of international organizations from those of States, particularly in relation to the conclusion and entry into force of treaties (Part II) and to the invalidity, termination and suspension of treaties (Part V).

Vienna, Congress of, 1815   The instruments appended to the final act of the Congress of Vienna, signed on 9 June 1815 *(64 C.T.S. 454)* dealt principally with the disposition of all countries which Napoleon's deposition and exile to Elba had freed from French suzerainty. The Congress showed little regard for the emergent forces of nationalism and liberty which had occasioned Napoleon's downfall and failed to institute a lasting system for securing stability in Europe. However, it recognized the integrity of the Swiss Cantons (art. 74) laying the basis for Switzerland's later federalism and established principles governing free navigation of international rivers (arts. 108-117) and of diplomatic law (Declaration of 19 March 1815 on Rank of Diplomatic Agents *(64 C.T.S. 1)* amended by Procés Verbal of Conference, **Aix la Chapelle**, of 9 (21) November 1818 *(69 C.T.S. 385))* and called for the abolition of the slave trade (Declaration of 8 February 1814: *63 C.T.S. 473*). The work of the Congress was interrupted by Napoleon's return from Elba and was concluded in great haste, final settlements being reached in the Paris Treaties of 20 November 1815 *(65 C.T.S. 251ff)* and, as regards Germany, by the Conference of German States held at Vienna in 1820 *(71 C.T.S. 89)*. Art. 6 of the Paris Treaty of 20 November 1815 *(65 C.T.S. 296)* instituted the **Concert System** of European Nations, four conferences of the Concert System being held at **Aix la Chapelle** (1818), at which the withdrawal of the occupying forces from France was agreed; **Troppau** (1820), **Laibach** (1821) and **Verona** in 1822 *(73 C.T.S. 31)*.

Vinogradoff, Sir Paul   1854-1925. Professor, Moscow 1884-1901, Oxford 1903-22. Supporter of theory of law based upon historical types. Principal works: *Roman Law in Mediaeval Europe* (1909; 2nd ed. 1929); *Collected Papers* (1928); *Outlines of Historical Jurisprudence* (1920-2).

Virginius   *(1873)* Moore, *Digest of International Law*, Vol. 2, 895. In 1873, the *Virginius,* a vessel flying the US flag and having a US register, was while on the high seas chased and eventually captured by a Spanish warship, and taken to Santiago de Cuba where 53 of those on board were court-martialed and executed, ostensibly on charges of piracy. Spain asserted that the vessel was engaged in assisting insurgents in Cuba. The US protested, and in November 1873 Spain agreed to return the vessel and the survivors of those on board, to investigate and punish those who might have infringed Spanish laws or treaty obligations, and at a future specified date to salute the US flag unless before that date it was established that the vessel had not been entitled to fly the US flag; for its part the US also agreed to investigate the lawfulness of the vessel's US registry and to institute legal proceedings in respect of any violation of US law that might be revealed. The US Attorney General's investigations revealed that at the time of her capture the *Virginius* was improperly flying the US flag, but that even so Spain had no right to interfere with the vessel on the high seas. The salute to the US flag was accordingly dispensed with. In March 1875, Spain agreed to pay $80,000 for relief of the crew and certain passengers of the *Virginius* and their families.

visa   *See* **passport(s)**.

visit and search   *See* **ships, right of visit**.

visiting forces   *See* **status of forces agreements**.

vital bay(s) *See* **historic bay(s)**.

Vitoria, Francisco de 1480-1546. Spanish Dominican theologian and jurist, one of the founders of modern international law. Professor, Valladolid 1523-6, Salamanca 1526-46. Principal works: *De Indis et de jure belli relectiones* (1532; text and translation in *Classics of International Law,* No. 17, (1917)); *Relectiones theologicae* (1557).

voeu(x) In conference practice, a *voeu* is a resolution or recommendation adopted by a conference, relating to the subject before the conference, in legally non-binding terms, and often included in the Final Act. The Final Act of the Hague Peace Conference 1907 *(205 C.T.S. 216)* lists four *voeux* expressed by the conference: (1) recommendation for the establishment of the Permanent Court of Arbitration and annexed draft convention; (2) *voeu* that special efforts shall be made to ensure continued peaceful relations and in particular commercial and industrial relations between the populations of belligerent States and neutral countries; (3) *voeu* that the right of **requisition** be regulated by bilateral agreement; (4) *voeu* that the Conventions on the Laws and Customs of War be applied as far as possible to maritime warfare pending elaboration of a convention. Nor was this the first occasion on which the use of *voeux* was resorted to, although it was "the first occasion upon which the peculiar character of such a practice became fully understood": Tammes, Decisions of International Organs, *(1958) 94 Hague Recueil 261* at 292 (who cites the *voeu* adopted with the Declaration of Paris 1856, described by Lord Clarendon as "an expression of opinion respecting mediation before war is declared"). The more important types of decision of the League of Nations Assembly required unanimity (art. 5 of the Covenant). "But an important inroad upon the general principle of unanimity was made by the adoption by the Assembly of the rule that a decision which can be described as a *voeu,* however we may translate that word—'recommendation,' 'wish,' 'hope,' 'opinion,' or 'view'—did not require unanimity and that a simple majority would suffice": *I Oppenheim (8th ed.) 388.*

voluntarism This is a form of positivism prevalent in the 19th century, which "made the State sole subject of all norms" and "the will of the State as their exclusive source," and "excluded from the law the higher considerations of reason, justice and common utility": De Visscher, *Theory and Reality in Public International Law* (Rev. ed., 1968), 21.

voluntary abstention In UN parlance, **abstention** in voting is invariable referred to as voluntary abstention, thereby to some extent justifying the abstention of a permanent member of the Security Council as not equivalent to a veto.

voting "Most international organizations take at least some of their decisions by majority vote and base their decision-making process on the principle of equality of voting power of all members states": Schermers and Blokker, *International Institutional Law* (3rd ed.), 518. Majority voting was recognized and accepted with the creation of the earliest of the technical organizations (UPU 1874) but was slower to active acceptance in the general political conferences and organizations. Thus, the plenary decisions of the Hague Conferences of 1899 and 1907 could only be taken by unanimity and the unanimity rule was preserved for many purposes by the Covenant of the League of Nations (art. 5, although **voeux**, as opposed to decisions, could be adopted by majority). "Majorities may vary. They may be simple (more than half the votes counted), qualified (*e.g.,* two-thirds, three-fourths or three-fifths), relative (in the case of alternatives, larger by the number of votes than the number actually obtained for any other solution), or absolute (in the case of alternatives, greater than the number which can be obtained at the same time for any other solution). . . . Further, in general the majority required may in the circumstances be of the membership or of the total voting power or of the members present and voting": Amerasinghe, *Principles of Institutional Law of International Organizations* (1996), 150-1.

Set against the unanimity rule of the League of Nations, majority voting in the UN Charter therefore represented something of a new departure and has not been without its problems. UN General Assembly resolutions, although frequently adopted by large majorities (two-thirds being required for "important questions": Charter, art. 18(2)), only receive general acceptance by States where they enjoy support from all geographical groups within the organization. The experience has been similar in other UN bodies dealing with essentially political matters. Nor is the principle of equality of voting power applied universally without qualification: in the UN itself, decisions of the Security Council on non-procedural matters require nine votes (out of 15), "including the concurring votes of the permanent members": Charter, art. 27(3); *see* **veto.** Within the UN system, voting power in the financial organizations (World Bank family; IMF) is dependent upon the level of contributions. In the commodity organizations, allocation of voting power is dependent upon relative status in the relevant trade. In some of the technical organizations (*e.g.*, UPU, ITU), voting strength is in practice increased because separate administrative units (dependent territories) have their own votes. *See* Schermers and Blokker, *supra,* 516-64; Amerasinghe, *Principles of Institutional Law of International Organizations* (1996), 149-55; White, *The Law of International Institutions* (1996), 72-81; Sands and Klein, *Bowett's Law of International Institutions* (5th ed.), 263-75.

W

waiver of rights "Renunciation is often indistinguishable from waiver, it being largely a matter of usage and convenience which term is customarily employed in particular circumstances. 'Renunciation' may carry with it a flavour of permanence and comprehensiveness (as in the renunciation of all rights to sovereignty over territory), whereas 'waiver' tends to be more specific and related less to the right itself than to its exercise in a particular case (as in the waiver of diplomatic immunity), but no hard and fast distinction on these lines can be maintained": *I Oppenheim 1195n*. Cf. **renunciation**.

waiver, consular and diplomatic immunity The Vienna Convention on Diplomatic Relations 1961 *(500 U.N.T.S. 95)*, codifying customary law in this as in other respects (***United States Diplomatic and Consular Staff in Tehran Case** 1980 I.C.J. Rep. 3* at 24), provides that the immunity from jurisdiction of diplomatic agents and of other persons enjoying immunity under the Convention may be waived (art. 32(1)) by express waiver (art. 32(2)) of the sending State, as in international law the immunity is that of the sending State. Waiver of the immunity of the head of mission will in practice be by an act of the Ministry of Foreign Affairs of the sending State, while waiver of immunity of other diplomatic staff and other persons enjoying immunity will normally be effected by the head of mission. Waiver by contract appears to be ineffective: *Empson v. Smith [1966] 1 Q.B. 426*.

Waiver of immunity with respect to court proceedings does not imply waiver of immunity in respect of execution of the judgment, for which a separate waiver is necessary (art. 32(4)). Although art. 32(4) in terms applies only to civil proceedings, it seems that the principle should apply also to criminal proceedings: Denza, *Diplomatic Law* (2nd. ed.), 284. Art. 32 offers only one case of implied waiver: the initiation of proceedings by a diplomatic agent or person enjoying immunity precludes him from invoking immunity in respect of any directly connected counter-claim (art. 32(3)): Denza, *supra*, 281-4. On the current practice of States in relation to the waiver of immunity, see Denza, *supra*, 286-7. Art. 43 of the Vienna Convention on Consular Relations, 1963 *(596 U.N.T.S. 261)* follows the provisions of art. 32 of the Vienna Convention on Diplomatic Relations in all material respects.

waiver, privileges and immunities of representatives and officials of international organizations Where immunity from jurisdiction is conferred (*see* **privileges and immunities of international organizations**) they are accorded to representatives "not for the personal benefit of the individuals themselves, but in order to safeguard the independent exercise of their functions in connection with the United Nations. Consequently, a Member not only has the right but it is under a duty to waive the immunity of its representative in any case where in the opinion of the Member the immunity would impede the course of justice, and it can be waived without prejudice to the purpose for which immunity is conferred" (Convention on Privileges and Immunities of the United Nations (*1 U.N.T.S. 151)*,

Section 14). Similar provision is made for officials (Section 20), waiver being effected by the Secretary-General or, in the case of the Secretary-General himself, the Security Council. Following *Westchester County v. Ranollo, 67 N.Y.S. 2d 31 (1946)* the UN does not claim immunity for traffic violations. Immunity has been upheld in a suit concerning land grants *(Curran v. City of New York, 77 N.Y.S. 2d 206 (1947)*. Espionage is not covered by immunity: *U.S. v. Coplon and Gubitchev, (1949) 16 I.L.R. 293*.

Waldheim, Kurt 1918- . Austrian diplomat. Fourth Secretary-General of the UN 1972-82, whose repution suffered as a result of subsequent allegations about his wartime activities: see Tittmann and Tittmann, *The Waldheim Affair: Democracy Subverted* (2000); Herzstein, *Waldheim: The Missing Years* (1988). Publications: *The Challenge of Peace* (1980); *Building the Future Order* (1980); *In the Eye of the Storm: A Memoir* (1986).

Waldock, Sir Humphrey 1904-82. Professor, Oxford 1947-72. Member, ILC 1961-81; PCA 1965-82; Judge, European Court of Human Rights 1966-74; ICJ 1973-82, President 1979-82. Principal works: editor of *B.Y.I.L.* (1955-73); editor, Brierly's *Law of Nations* (6th ed., 1963).

Wanderer (Great Britain v. USA) (1921) 6 R.I.A.A. 68. In June 1894, the British vessel, the *Wanderer*, was stopped on the high seas by a US revenue vessel, taken to harbor and there seized for alleged contravention of fur sealing laws. On 2 August 1894, the *Wanderer* was handed over to a British naval vessel, and later that month was released by the British naval authorities. Great Britain's claim for compensation for the unlawful seizure of the vessel was referred to the Great Britain-US Arbitral Tribunal established under the Special Agreement of 18 August 1910 *(21 C.T.S. 408)* which, in awarding compensation to Great Britain, *held* that no State was entitled to visit and search foreign vessels pursuing a lawful vocation on the high seas except in time of war or by special agreement; that although special arrangements were in operation in the North Pacific for the protection of fur seals, whereby, *inter alia*, US naval authorities were entitled to seize British vessels for using arms for fur sealing, in the present case the US vessel, although in good faith, was not acting in exercise of that right since the *Wanderer* was merely in possession of arms and was not shown to have used them; and that the US authorities were liable for the consequences of the wrongful detention of the *Wanderer* until her transference to the British authorities on 2 August 1894.

war crimes The list of crimes coming within the jurisdiction of the International Military Tribunal attracting individual responsibility included "(b) *War crimes:* namely, violations of the laws or customs of war. Such violations shall include, but not be limited to, murder, ill-treatment or deportation to slave labour or for any other purpose of civilian populations of or in occupied territory, murder or ill-treatment of prisoners of war or persons on the seas, killing of hostages, plunder of public or private property, wanton destruction of cities, towns or villages, or devastation not justified by military necessity": Charter of the Tribunal *(82 U.N.T.S. 279)*, art. 6. "The category of war crimes was certainly orthodox law in 1945, and crimes against humanity were to a great extent war crimes writ large": Brownlie, *Principles of Public International Law* (5th ed.), 566. The **Geneva Conventions** 1949 do not in terms refer to the category of war crimes although individual responsibility is attracted for grave breaches and fall squarely within the terms of the Charter of the Nuremberg Tribunal (cf. **crime, international**), and indeed the Tribunal held the earlier Hague Convention on land warfare to be declaratory of customary international law binding on all the belligerents irrespective of the general participation clause: see Wright, The Law of the Nuremberg Tribunal, *41 A.J.I.L. 38* at 60 *(1947)*. The decisions of the Nuremberg Tribunal attracted criticisms for supposedly creating new categories of crime retrospectively (*see* various articles and notably Quincy Wright in *A.J.I.L. 1945-1949*). These criticisms are rejected in *II Oppenheim 579. See generally II Oppenheim 566-588.*

War crimes fall within the jurisdiction of both the **International Criminal Tribunal for the Former Yugoslavia** and the **International Criminal Tribunal for Rwanda**. In the case of the former, art. 3 of its Statute provides that "The international tribunal shall have the power to prosecute persons violating the laws or customs of war. Such violations shall include but not be limited to: (a) employment of poisonous weapons or other weapons calculated to cause unnecessary suffering; (b) wanton destruction of cities, towns or villages or devastation not justified by **military necessity**; (c) attack, or bombardment, by whatever means, of undefended towns, villages, dwellings or buildings; (d) seizure of, destruction or wilful damage done to institutions dedicated to religion, charity and education, the arts and sciences, historic monuments and works of art and science; (e) plunder of public or private property. The Statute of the ICTR in art. 4 is more specific referencing directly "violations of Article 3 common to the **Geneva Conventions** of 1949 and Additional Protocol II of 1977." The Rome Statute of the **International Criminal Court** 1998 contains an extensive definition of war crimes containing a list of 50 crimes arising out of international treaty and customary international law (art. 8). The Elements of Crimes adopted by the Preparatory Commission for the International Criminal Court on 30 June 2000 *(UN Doc. PCNICC/2000/1/Add.2)* which "shall assist the Court in the interpretation and application of Articles 6.7.amd 8 [of the Statute]" (art. 9) lists the crimes which must have taken place "in the context of and [were] associated with an international armed conflict" where "the perpetrator was aware of factual circumstances that established the existence of an armed conflict," *inter alia*, as follows: willful killing; torture; inhuman treatment; biological experiments; willfully causing great suffering; destruction and appropriation of property; compelling service in hostile forces; denying a fair trial; unlawful deportation and transfer; unlawful confinement; taking hostages; attacking civilians; attacking civilian objects; attacking personnel or objects involved in a humanitarian assistance or peace-keeping mission; excessive incidental death, injury or damage; attacking undefended places; killing or wounding a person *hors de combat*; improper use of a flag of truce; improper use of a flag, insignia, or uniform of the hostile party; improper use of a flag, insignia, or uniform of the United Nations; improper use of the distinctive emblems of the Geneva Conventions; transfer directly or indirectly, by the Occupying Power of parts of its own civilian population into the territory it occupies, or the deportation or transfer of all or parts of the population of the occupied territory within or outside the territory; attacking protected objects; mutilations; medical or scientific experiments; treacherously killing or wounding; denying quarter; destroying or seizing the enemy's property; depriving the nationals of the hostile power of rights or actions; compelling participation in military operations; pillaging; employing poison or poisoned weapons; employing prohibited gases, liquids, materials or devices; employing prohibited bullets; employing weapons, projectiles and materials and methods of warfare listed in the annex to the Statute; outrages upon personal dignity; rape; sexual slavery; enforced prostitution; forced pregnancy; enforced sterilization, sexual violence; using protected persons as shields; attacking persons or objects bearing the distinctive emblems of the Geneva Conventions; using starvation as a method of warfare; using, conscripting or enlisting children; murder; sentencing or executing without due process. See Green, *The Contemporary Law of Armed Conflict* (1993); Fleck *The Handbook of Humanitarian Law in Armed Conflict* (1995); Kittichaisaree, *International Criminal Law* (2001).

war crimes tribunals   *See* **International Criminal Tribunal for the Former Yugoslavia**; **International Criminal Tribunal for Rwanda**; **International Military Tribunals**.

war materials *See* **prohibited weapons**.

War Powers Resolution *(50 U.S.C.A. Chap. 33; Pub. L. 93-148; 87 Stat. 55; 68 A.J.I.L. 372 (1976))*. After reciting that the President of the United States enjoys constitutional power to introduce United States Armed Forces into hostilities or situations where hostilities are indicated only "pursuant to (1) a declaration of war, (2) specific statutory authorization, or (3) a national emergency created by an attack upon the United States, its territories or possessions, or its armed forces" (Sec. 1541(c)), this enactment requires the President to consult with Congress "in every possible instance" before the introduction of US forces (Sec. 1542) and while forces are so engaged (*ibid.*). Initial consultation is to take place within 48 hours (Sec. 1543(a)). The President is required to terminate the use of armed forces within 60 days thereafter unless "(1) the Congress has declared war or has enacted a specific authorization for such use of United States Armed Forces, (2) has extended by law such sixty-day period, or (3) is physically unable to meet as a result of an armed attack on the United States" (Sec. 1544(b)). The 60 day period may be extended by a further 30 days if the President certifies "unavoidable military necessity respecting the safety of United States Armed Forces . . . in . . . bringing about a prompt removal of such forces." *(ibid)*. A power or duty of armed intervention laid down by treaty does not of itself displace the War Powers Resolution except insofar as it is implemented by express legislation (Sec. 1547(a)). *See* Turner, *The War Powers Resolution: Its Implementation in Theory and Practice* (1983); Grimmett, *The War Powers Resolution* (2002).

War Risk Insurance Premium Claims 18 A.J.I.L. 580 (1924). The US-Germany Mixed Claims Commission here considered a group of American claims for reimbursement for war-risk insurance premiums although no loss or injury had in the event been sustained. *Held* that although under the terms of the Treaty of Berlin Germany was liable to make full and complete compensation for all losses sustained by American nationals proximately caused by Germany's acts, under the terms of that treaty Germany could not be held liable for all losses incident to the very existence of a state of war. The opinion is chiefly notable for the analysis by Parker, umpire, of the *Alabama Claims* decision, concluding that they hold "(1) that claims for war-risk premiums paid are not recoverable under the applicable principles of international law and (2) that claims . . . for reimbursement of losses . . . of property lost or damaged . . . are direct losses and recoverable as such. The use of the term "indirect" as applied to the "national claims" involved in the Alabama Case is not justified" (at 601).

war treason *See* **treason**.

war zones "A rich variety of terms—war zones, operational zones, barred areas, areas dangerous to shipping, long-distance blockade and total blockade—serve to give a semi-technical character and spurious legality to these additional inroads on the traditional law of sea warfare. . . . [T]heir basic illegality under the traditional law, even in the relations between belligerents, follows from the prohibition of non-differentiation between objects of sea warfare. . . . It is always possible to maintain legal continuity on this issue by explaining the departures from the traditional law by way of reprisals and counter-reprisals. At least in the relations between the belligerents, this type of argument can claim a modicum of formal validity. In substance, however, reasoning on these lines merely hides a breakdown of the law and the resumption by belligerents at sea of an almost complete freedom of action": Schwarzenberger, *Armed Conflict* (1968), 432-3. *See also* Colombos, *International Law of the Sea* (6th ed.), 528-31. In the UK/Argentina conflict over the Falklands/Malvinas Islands, the UK initially, on 12 April 1982, proclaimed a 200-mile maritime exclusion zone around the islands, declaring that "any Argentine warships and

Argentine naval auxiliaries found within this zone will be treated as hostile and are liable to be attacked": *Hansard, HC Deb, 7 April 1982, col. 1045.* This zone was subsequently transformed into a total exclusion zone on 30 April 1982, applying "to all ships and aircraft, whether military or civil, operating in support of the illegal occupation of the Falkland Islands": *Hansard, HC Deb, 29 April 1982, cols. 980-1.* While described as a **blockade** in the statement of 29 April 1982, the UK action clearly was not such. *See* O'Connell, *The International Law of the Sea*, Vol. II (1984), 1111-2 and 1155. The two No-Fly Zones activated by France, the United Kingdom and the United States over Iraq after the Gulf Conflict 1990-91 are of similar legal dubiety. The proponents of these zones argue that they are in conformity with Security Council Res. 687 (1991) which brought the conflict to an end. However, no mention of such zones is made in the resolution which is not overtly based on Chapter VII of the UN Charter which provides for the possibility of enforcement action. France has withdrawn from the enforcement of the no-fly zones and Russia and China, the other two permanent members of the Security Council, have condemned the zones as a breach of Iraqi sovereignty. *See* Gray, After the Ceasefire: Iraq, the Security Forces and the Use of Force, *(1994) 65 B.Y.I.L. 135*; Lobel and Ratner, Bypassing the Security Council: Ambiguous Authorizations to Use Force, Ceasefires and the Iraqi Inspection Regime, *93 A.J.I.L. 124 (1999).*

war, declaration of *See* **Hostilities, Hague Convention relative to the Opening of**.

war, rules on Prior to the 18th century the conduct of war was, in the absence of specific stipulations between States, largely unregulated, as a consequence of which excesses and acts of brutality, directed at combatants and non-combatants, were not uncommon. As a result of the labors of **Francis Lieber**, in 1863 there was issued the first systematic and comprehensive code on the conduct of war: Instructions for the Government of Armies of the United States in the Field, 24 April 1863 (the **Lieber Code**). The Code governed US practice for half a century, was adopted into the practice of a number of other States, and formed the basis of subsequent conventional arrangements. Prior to the turn of the century two significant international instruments were adopted: the Geneva Convention for the Amelioration of the Condition of the Wounded in Armies in the Field of 22 August 1864 *(129 C.T.S. 361)*, and the (unratified) Brussels Declaration concerning the Laws and Customs of War of 27 August 1874 *(148 C.T.S. 133). See also* the **Oxford Manual** 1880. A major international conference at the Hague in 1899 resulted in six instruments on 29 July 1899: I: Convention for Pacific Settlement of International Disputes *(187 C.T.S. 410)*; II: Convention with respect to the Laws and Customs of War by Land, with Annexed Regulations, *(187 C.T.S. 429)*; III: Convention for Adapting to Maritime Warfare the Principles of the Geneva Convention of 1864 *(187 C.T.S. 443)*; IV: Declaration respecting the Prohibition of Discharge of Projectiles from Balloons etc. *(187 C.T.S. 453);* V: Declaration respecting the Prohibition of the Use of Projectiles diffusing Asphyxiating Gases *(187 C.T.S. 456)*; VI: Declaration respecting the Use of Expanding Bullets *(187 C.T.S. 459)*. A second Hague conference resulted in fourteen instruments on 18 October 1907. I: Convention for the Pacific Settlement of International Disputes *(205 C.T.S. 233)*; II: Convention respecting the Limitation of the Employment of Force for Recovery of Contract Debts *(205 C.T.S. 250)*; III: Convention relative to the Opening of Hostilities *(205 C.T.S. 263)*; IV: Convention concerning the Laws and Customs of War on Land, with Annexed Regulations *(205 C.T.S. 277)*; V: Convention respecting the Rights and Duties of Neutral Powers and Persons in War on Land *(205 C.T.S. 299)*; VI: Convention relative to the Status of Enemy Merchant Ships at the Outbreak of Hostilities *(205 C.T.S. 305);* VII: Convention relative to the Conversion of Merchant Ships into Warships *(205 C.T.S. 319)*; VIII: Convention relative to the Laying of Automatic Submarine Contact Mines *(205 C.T.S.*

331); IX: Convention respecting Bombardments by Naval Forces in Time of War *(205 C.T.S. 345)*; X: Convention for the Adaptation of the Principles of the Geneva Convention to Maritime Warfare *(205 C.T.S. 345)*; XI: Convention relative to certain Restrictions on the Right of Capture in Maritime War *(205 C.T.S. 367)*; XII: Convention for the Establishment of an International Prize Court *(205 C.T.S. 381)*; XIII: Convention respecting the Rights and Duties of Neutral Powers in Maritime War *(205 C.T.S. 395)*; XIV: Declaration Prohibiting Discharge of Projectiles and Explosives from Balloons *(205 C.T.S. 403)*. The principal and enduring Hague Conventions on the Laws and Customs of War were generally declaratory of existing customary law: *see II Oppenheim 229.*

Between the two World Wars, four international instruments are worthy of note: the Protocol for the Prohibition of Asphyxiating, Poisonous or other Gases of 17 June 1925 *(94 L.N.T.S. 65)*; the Geneva Convention for the Amelioration of the Condition of the Wounded and Sick in Armies in the Field of 27 July 1929 *(118 L.N.T.S. 303)*; the Geneva Convention relative to the Treatment of Prisoners of War of 27 July 1929 *(118 L.N.T.S. 343)*; the London Procés-Verbal relating to the Rules of Submarine Warfare of 6 November 1936 *(173 L.N.T.S. 353)*.

A further four conventions were adopted at Geneva on 12 August 1949. I: Convention for the Amelioration of the Condition of the Wounded and Sick in Armed Forces in the Field *(75 U.N.T.S. 31)*; II: Convention for the Amelioration of the Condition of Wounded, Sick and Shipwrecked Members of Armed Forces at Sea *(75 U.N.T.S. 85)*; III: Convention relative to the Treatment of Prisoners of War *(75 U.N.T.S. 135)*; IV: Convention relative to the Protection of Civilian Persons in Time of War *(75 U.N.T.S. 287)*. On the 8 June 1977 two protocols to the 1949 Geneva Conventions were adopted: I: Relating to the Protection of Victims of International Armed Conflicts *(1125 U.N.T.S. 3)*; II: Relating to the Protection of Victims of Non-International Armed Conflicts *1125 U.N.T.S. 609)*.

The 1979/80 Conventional Weaponry Conference adopted the following instruments on 10 October 1980: Convention on Prohibitions or Restrictions on the Use of Certain Conventional Weapons Which May be Deemed to be Excessively Injurious or to have Indiscriminate Effects; Protocol on Non-Detectable Fragments (Protocol I); Protocol on Prohibitions or Restrictions on the Use of Mines, Booby-Traps and Other Devices (Protocol II); Protocol on Prohibitions or Restrictions on the Use of Incendiary Weapons (Protocol III). In addition, the Conference at its 1979 session adopted a Resolution on Small-Calibre Weapon Systems. The texts all these instruments are in *19 I.L.M. 1523 (1980)* and of Protocols I-III in *1342 U.N.T.S. 137.*

Other important instruments falling within the general heading of rules on war include: Convention on the Prohibition of the Development, Production of Bacteriological (Biological) and Toxin Weapons and on their Destruction of 10 April 1972 *(1015 U.N.T.S. 163)*; Convention on the Prohibition of Military or any Hostile Use of Environmental Modification Techniques of 10 December 1976 *(1108 U.N.T.S. 151)*; Convention on the Prohibition of the Development, Production, Stockpiling and Use of Chemical Weapons and their Destruction of 3 September 1992 *(1974 U.N.T.S. 3)*; and Convention on the Prohibition of Use, Stockpiling, Production and Transfer of Anti-Personnel Mines and Their Destruction of 18 September 1997 *(36 I.L.M. 1509 (1997))*.

See II Oppenheim 226 et seq; Schwarzenberger, *Armed Conflict* (1968); Miller, *The Law of War* (1975); Green, *The Contemporary Law of Armed Conflict* (1993); Fischer *Yearbook of International Humanitarian Law* (Vol, 1, 1999); Fleck *Handbook of Humanitarian Law in Armed Conflicts* (2000); Carey, *International Humanitarian Law: Origins, Challenges, Prospects* (2003). *See also* entries under **asphyxiating gases**; **bacteriological** methods of warfare; **chemical weapons**; **Chemical Weapons Convention**; **disarmament**; **Geneva Conventions**; **Hague Peace Conferences**; **prisoners of war**; **prohibited weapons**.

Warsaw Convention 1929   Properly styled the International Convention for the Unification of Certain Rules relating to International Carriage by Air of 12 October 1929 *(137 L.N.T.S. 11*; Supplementary Guadalajara Protocol of 18 September 1961: *500 U.N.T.S. 32)*, otherwise known as the Warsaw Convention. Besides laying down certain rules as to the form of documents of carriage, the Convention is concerned principally with rules as to the liability of the carrier for death or injury of passengers and loss or damage of luggage or goods and for delay. The limits of liability have been revised a number of times. The Protocols in effect provide a range of optional levels of liability as between two parties to any given Protocol. *See* Martin and McLean, *Shawcross and Beaumont: Air Law* (1991).

Warsaw Pact   The Treaty of Friendship, Cooperation and Mutual Assistance, signed at Warsaw on 14 May 1955 *(219 U.N.T.S. 24)* and known as the Warsaw Pact, committed the signatories, Albania (withdrew 12 September 1968), Bulgaria, Czechoslovakia, German Democratic Republic, Hungary, Poland, Romania and the USSR, *inter alia*, to providing mutual military assistance. The Warsaw Pact was the Soviet Bloc counterpart to the **NATO** defensive alliance. The Pact was complemented by a series of status of forces agreements between the USSR and its allies. The alliance was officially dissolved on 1 July 1991. Poland, Hungary and the Czech Republic joined NATO in 1999.

warships   Art. 29 of the UN Convention on the Law of the Sea 1982 *(1833 U.N.T.S. 3)* defines a warship as "a ship belonging to the armed forces of a State bearing the external marks distinguishing such ships of its nationality, under the command of an officer duly commissioned by the government of the State and whose name appears in the appropriate service list, and manned by a crew which is under regular armed forces discipline." This definition corresponds with earlier definitions: *O'Connell, The International Law of the Sea*, Vol. II (1984), 1106. It is not clear whether, from the terms of the UN Convention, arts. 17-25, 29-30, whether warships enjoy the right of **innocent passage** through the territorial sea. While there is ample authority for asserting that warships do enjoy such a right at customary international law (*see **Corfu Channel Case** 1949 I.C.J. Rep. 4*; O'Connell, *supra*, Vol. 1, 291), a number of States permit warships to traverse their territorial sea only with authorization or prior notification.

Washington, Three Rules of   As a consequence of US allegations that Great Britain had been in breach of her obligations as a neutral by assisting the Confederate forces during the American Civil War, the Treaty of Washington of 8 May 1871 *(143 C.T.S. 145)* provided for the submission of the controversy to arbitration. Art. VI of the Treaty required the Arbitrators to apply three rules, namely that a neutral Government is bound: "*First*, to use due diligence to prevent the fitting out, arming, or equipping, within its jurisdiction, of any vessel which it has reasonable ground to believe is intended to cruise or to carry on war against a Power with which it is at peace; and also to use like diligence to prevent the departure from its jurisdiction of any vessel intended to cruise or carry on war as above, such vessel having been specially adapted, in whole or in part, within such jurisdiction, to warlike use. *Secondly*, not to permit or suffer either belligerent to make use of its ports or waters as the base of naval operations against the other, or for the purpose of the renewal or augmentation of military supplies or arms, or the recruitment of men. *Thirdly*, to exercise due diligence in its own ports and waters, and as to all persons within its jurisdiction, to prevent any violation of the foregoing obligations and duties." The British Government expressly denied that these rules were principles of international law, but agreed that they should be used in the instant controversy. *See **The Alabama Claims Arbitration*** (1872) *Moore, Int. Arb., 653.* As to the continuing relevance of the three rules, *see* Schwarzenberger, *Armed Conflict* (1968), 564-5; Neff, *The Rights and Duties of Neutrals* (2000).

waste *See* **radioactive products and waste**; **marine pollution**.

watercourses/waterways, international As to the alleged right of freedom of navigation, see arts. 108 and 109 of the Final Act of the Congress of Vienna 1815 *(64 C.T.S. 454).* Art. 1(1) of the Statute on the Régime of Navigable Waterways of International Concern of 20 April 1921 *(7 L.N.T.S. 50)* is declared to apply to "all parts which are naturally navigable to and from the sea of a waterway which in its course, naturally navigable to and from the sea, separates or traverses different States, and also any part of any other waterway navigable to and from the sea, which connects with the sea a waterway naturally navigable which separates or traverses different States." This Convention guaranteed "free exercise of navigation on navigable waterways" (art. 3). *See* Colombos, *International Law of the Sea* (6th ed.), 239. *See also **Oder Commission Case (1929)** P.C.I.J., Ser. A, No. 33 at 27.* For an early attempt at regulating non-navigable use of international waterways, see the Convention Relating to the Development of Hydraulic Power Affecting More than one State of 9 December 1923 *(36 L.N.T.S. 75).* The International Law Association has adopted the Helsinki Rules on the Uses of the Waters of International Rivers (I.L.A., *Report of the Fifty-Second Conference* (1966), 477), which rules are to apply absent agreement or binding custom (art. 1). The key principle is that "[e]ach basin State is entitled, within its territory, to a reasonable and equitable share in the beneficial uses of the waters of an international drainage basin" (art. 4), what is reasonable and equitable being determined in the light of all the relevant factors in each particular case (art. 5(1), art. 5(2) specifying eleven such factors). In relation to pollution, the *Institut de Droit International* has resolved that "States shall be under a duty to ensure that their activities or those conducted within their jurisdiction or under their control cause no pollution in the waters of international rivers and lakes beyond their boundaries (art. 4 of the Resolution on Pollution of Rivers and Lakes, adopted at Athens (1979)). *See* the ***Trail Smelter Arbitration (1941)** 3 R.I.A.A. 1911.* The ILC was charged by the General Assembly in 1970 to examine the question of the codification of the principles of law on non-navigational uses of international water-courses. This work culminated in the adoption by the General Assembly (in GA Res. 51/229) of the Convention on the Law of Non-Navigational Uses of International Watercourses on 21 May 1977 *(36 I.L.M. 700 (1997)).* Part II of the Convention sets out the general principles as follows: equitable and reasonable utilization and participation (art. 5); factors relevant to equitable and reasonable utilization (art. 6); obligation not to cause significant harm (art. 7); general obligation to cooperate (art. 8); regular exchange of data and information (art. 9); relationship between different kinds of uses (art. 10). *See* Baxter, *The Law of International Waterways* (1964); Tanzi and Arcari, *The UN Convention on the Law of International Watercourses* (2001); McCaffrey, *The Law of International Watercourses: Non-Navigational Uses* (2001).

watershed doctrine "It is consistent with the doctrine of international law by which the occupation of a sea-coast carries with it a right to the whole territory drained by the rivers which empty their waters into its line . . . and it is certainly difficult . . . to suggest any point between the seashore and the watershed at which a line could be drawn": *In Re Labrador Boundary (1927) 43 T.L.R. 289* at 294. *See* **continuity**.

weapons *See* **prohibited weapons**.

weapons of mass destruction   While this has not attained the status of a term of art in international law, it is frequently used, particularly in UN disarmament circles, to connote nuclear, chemical and biological weapons. The instruments commonly associated with WMD are the **Non-Proliferation Treaty** of 1 July 1968, the Comprehensive Test-Ban Treaty of 10 September 1996 (*see* **Test-Ban Treaties**), the **Chemical Weapons Convention** of 3 September 1992 and the Biological Weapons Convention of 10 April 1972 (see **bacteriological methods of warfare**). *See* <http://disarmament.un.org>.

weather   *See* **prohibited weapons**; **World Meteorological Organization**.

Western European Union   With the accession of the Federal Republic of Germany and Italy to the **Brussels Treaty Organization** by Protocols of 23 October 1954 *(211 U.N.T.S. 342)*, the organization was renamed Western European Union and the constitution recast so as to remove references to the possibility of German aggression and substitute references to the promotion of European unity. At the same time, a new article was inserted providing for cooperation with NATO. The second, third and fourth protocols made provision for levels of forces; control of armaments and for an Agency for the Control of Armaments. The amended treaty established a new body known as the Council of Western European Union and also a consultative parliamentary assembly (art. 9). In 1984, the French Government proposed resuscitating the WEU so as to provide a specifically European forum for defense discussions. This led to the Rome Declaration which reactivated the WEU as an organization focusing primarily on European security and defense. The membership of the WEU was increased to 10 in the mid-1990s with the accession of Spain, Portugal and Greece (joining the original members: Belgium, France, Luxembourg, the Netherlands and the United Kingdom, as well as Germany and Italy). The Organization was operation in the Gulf Conflict 1990-91 and in the conflict in the Former Yugoslavia and has since been involved in a number of crisis management operations. However, in recent years the WEU has been very much overshadowed by **NATO** and the **European Union**. The WEU now acts at the request of the EU effectively as the operational arm of that organization in area of security and defense. *See* <www.weu.int>.

Western Sahara Case   *1975 I.C.J. Rep. 12.* In connection with the de-colonization of Western Sahara, a controversy arose as to the legal status of the territory. The General Assembly, by Res. 3292 (XXIX) of 13 December 1974, sought from the ICJ an advisory opinion on the questions whether Western Sahara at the time of colonization by Spain was a territory belonging to no one (*terra nullius*); and, if the answer to that question was in the negative, what were the legal ties of the territory with the Kingdom of Morocco and the Mauritanian entity. The Court *advised* (unanimously) that the first question should be answered in the negative, and that there were certain legal ties (not amounting to sovereignty) between Western Sahara and Morocco (14 to 2), and also between it and the Mauritanian entity (15 to 1). In reaching these conclusions, the Court found that, as the questions were in principle of a legal character, even if they also embodied questions of fact, and did not call upon the Court to pronounce on existing rights and obligations, the Court was competent to entertain the request; that neither the existence of a similar dispute over Western Sahara between Spain and Morocco, nor the alleged academic nature of the questions and their lack of practical effect, constituted compelling reasons for refusing to reply to the questions put to the Court; that at the "time of colonization by Spain" (i.e. the period beginning in 1884 when Spain proclaimed its protectorate over the area) Western Sahara was inhabited by peoples which, if nomadic, were socially and politically organized tribes and under chiefs competent to represent them, which according to State practice of the time meant it was not regarded as *terra nullius*; that the evidence indicated neither the existence nor international recognition of legal ties of territorial sovereignty between Western Sahara and Morocco, which had not displayed there any effective and exclusive State activity, although there were indications that a legal tie of allegiance and authority had existed between the Sultan and some of the nomadic peoples of the territory; that the Mauritanian entity did not have separate character distinct from the several emirates or tribes which had comprised it, and thus at the time of colonization by Spain there had not existed between Western Sahara and the Mauritanian entity any tie of sovereignty, or of allegiance, or of simple inclusion in the same legal entity, but the nomadic peoples of the area in question had possessed rights, including some rights relating to the lands through which they migrated, which constituted legal ties between Western Sahara and the Mauritanian entity.

Westlake, John 1828-1913. Professor, Cambridge 1888-1908; member, PCA 1900-6; one of the founders and editors of *Revue de droit international et de législation comparée*. Principal works: *International Law* (1904-7; 2nd ed. 1910-3); *The Collected Papers of John Westlake on Public International Law* (ed. Oppenheim, 1914). *See* Williams, *Memories of John Westlake* (1914).

Weston, Burns H. 1933- . Professor, Iowa 1966- . Principal works include *International Claims: Their Settlement by Lump-Sum Agreements* (with Lillich, 1975); *Towards World Order and Human Dignity: Essays in Honor of Myers S. McDougal* (with Reisman, 1976); *Basic Documents in International Law and World Order* (with Falk and D'Amato, 1980); *Alternative Security: Living Without Nuclear Deterrence* (1990); *Human Rights in the International Community: Issues and Action* (2nd ed.1992); *International Environmental Law and World Order* (1994); *International Law and World Order: Basic Documents* (1994); *Preferred Futures for the United Nations* (1995); *International Law and World Order: A Problem Oriented Coursebook* (with Falk and Charlesworth, 3rd ed. 1998).

Westphalia, Peace of, Treaty of 1648 The Peace of Westphalia, the collective name given to the treaties by which the Thirty Years War was brought to an end, and constituted by the treaty of peace between Spain and the Netherlands of 30 January 1648 *(1 C.T.S. 70)*, the treaty of peace between France and the Empire of 14 (24) October 1648 *(1 C.T.S. 319)*, both signed at Münster, and the treaty of peace between Sweden and the Empire signed on the same day at Osnabröck, *(1 C.T.S. 198)*, is the "foundation of the modern system of States": *(1 C.T.S. vi)*. The territorial sovereignty of the States of the Empire was recognized and the old central authority was almost entirely replaced. The way was opened for the rise of Austria, Bavaria and Brandenburg. France obtained recognition of territorial gains, notably on the Rhine, and Sweden obtained control of the Baltic and a footing on the North Sea.

wetlands The Convention on Wetlands of International Importance of 3 February 1971 *(996 U.N.T.S. 245)* defines wetlands as "areas of marsh, fen, peatland or water, whether natural or artificial, permanent or temporary, with water that is static or flowing, fresh, brackish or salt, including areas of marine water the depth of which at low tide does not exceed six meters" (art. 1(1)). With the aim of conserving wetlands and their flora and fauna (Preamble), the Convention requires each party to designate suitable wetlands within its territory for inclusion in a list of wetlands of international importance (art. 2), and thereafter to take measures to promote the conservation of these listed wetlands (art. 3). The International Union for the Conservation of Nature and Natural Resources performs bureau duties, maintaining the list of Wetlands of International Importance (and amendments to it), and assisting in the convening of subsequent advisory conferences on wetlands and waterfowl (art. 8). *See* <www.wetlands.org>.

whales The first multilateral instrument to regulate the taking of whales was the Convention for the Regulation of Whaling of 24 September 1931 *(155 U.N.T.S. 349)*. *See also* the International Convention for the Regulation of Whaling of 8 June 1937 *(190 L.N.T.S. 79)*, and its Protocols of 24 June 1938 *(196 L.N.T.S. 131)* and 26 November 1945 *(11 U.N.T.S. 43)*. A more systematic régime is established by the International Convention for the Regulation of Whaling on 2 December 1946 *(161 U.N.T.S. 72)*. The Convention set up the International Whaling Commission, consisting of one member from each contracting State (art. 3(1)). The Commission is empowered to initiate research, conduct research and disseminate research findings on whales and whaling (art. 4). More importantly, the Commission is empowered to amend the Schedule annexed to the Convention by regulations which may include "fixing (a) protected and unprotected species; (b) open and closed seasons; (c) open and closed waters . . .; (d) size limits for each species; (e) time, methods, and intensity of whaling (including the maximum catch of whales to be taken in any one season); (f) types and specifications of gear and apparatus and appliances which may be used; (g) methods of measurement; and (h) catch returns and other statistical and biological records" (art. 5(1)). These amending regulations may only be made in conformity with certain criteria: that they are necessary to fulfill the object and purpose of the Convention; that they are based on scientific findings; that they do not discriminate; and that they have regard to the consumers of whale products and the whaling industry (art. 5(2)). These amending regulations are not effective in respect of a State which has objected. *See also* art. 65 of the UN Convention on the Law of the Sea 1982 *(1833 U.N.T.S. 3)* which provides that within the **exclusive economic zone** the coastal State or an international organization may "prohibit, limit or regulate the exploitation of marine mammals more strictly than provided for in [part V of the Convention]." Art. 120 provides that art. 65 "also applies to the conservation and management of marine mammals on the high seas." Despite these provisions and the work of the International Whaling Commission, the number of whales has continued to decline. *See* Friedheim, *Toward a Sustainable Whaling Regime* (2001); International Union for Conservation of Nature, *Legal Measures for the Conservation of Marine Mammals* (1982). *See also* <www.iwcoffice.org>.

Wharton, Francis 1820-1889. American lawyer. Professor Boston 1871-1881. Works on criminal law (*Treatise on the Criminal Law of the United States* 1846, 12th ed. 1932). Chief of Legal Division, State Department, 1885. Editor, *Digest of the International Law of the United States* (3 vols., 1886; 2nd ed. 1887), much of which is incorporated into Moore's *Digest of International Law* (1906). Editor, *Revolutionary Diplomatic Correspondence of the United States* (6 vols. 1889).

Wheaton, Henry 1785-1848. American jurist, diplomat, expounder and historian of international law. Justice, Marine Court New York, 1815-1819. Supreme Court Reporter, 1816-1827. Chargé d'affaires, Denmark 1827-1833, Berlin 1835-1847. Publications: *Elements of International Law* (1836); *History of the Law of Nations in Europe and America* (1842), both works in numerous and varying editions.

white slavery The first convention to use this term was the Convention on the Suppression of White Slave Trade of 18 May 1904 *(195 C.T.S. 326)*, which concerned "the procuration of women or girls with a view to their debauchery in a foreign country" (art. 1). *See also* International Convention for the Suppression of White Slave Traffic of 4 May 1910 *(211 C.T.S. 45)*, amended by Protocol of 4 May 1949 along with the 1904 Convention *(30 U.N.T.S. 23; 92 U.N.T.S. 20 and 98 U.N.T.S. 102)*; the International Convention for the Suppression of the Traffic in Women and Children of 30 September 1921 *(9 L.N.T.S. 415)*; the International Convention for the Suppression of the Traffic in Women of Full Age of 11 October 1933 *(150 L.N.T.S. 431)*, amended by Protocol of 12 November 1947 *(53*

U.N.T.S. 13) along with the 1921 Convention. These measures have been consolidated in the Convention for the Suppression of the Traffic in Persons and of the Exploitation of the Prostitution of Others of 21 March 1950 *(96 U.N.T.S. 271)*. This Convention, which entered into force on 25 July 1951, requires Parties to punish any person who, "to gratify the passions of another," procures, entices or leads away, for purposes of prostitution, or exploits the prostitution of another person, even with the consent of that person (art. 1); or who keeps, manages, knowingly finances or lets or rents a brothel (art. 2). These offences are to be regarded as extraditable offences in any extradition treaties between the Parties (art. 8). The Convention further requires Parties to collect information relating to its objectives (art. 14), to share that information with other Parties (art. 15) and to adopt measures to prevent the traffic in persons of either sex for the purpose of prostitution (art. 17). More recently, at its Millennium Conference, the UN General Assembly adopted on 15 November 2000 (GA Res. 55/25) the Protocol to Prevent, Suppress and Punish Trafficking in Person, Especially Women and Children, attached to the UN Convention against Transnational Organized Crime *(40 I.L.M. 377 (2001))*. The purposes of the Protocol are "to prevent and combat trafficking in persons, paying particular attention to women and children (art. 2). Trafficking in persons is defined as "the recruitment, transportation, transfer, harboring or receipt of persons, by means of the threat or use of force or other forms of coercion, of abduction, of fraud, of deception, of the abuse of power or of a position of vulnerability, or of the giving or receiving of payments or benefits to achieve the consent of a person having control over another person, for the purpose of exploitation. Exploitation shall include, at a minimum, the exploitation of the prostitution of others or other forms of sexual exploitation, forced labor or services, slavery or practices similar to slavery, servitude or the removal of organs" (art. 3). Trafficking, as defined, is to be criminalized in the domestic law of States Parties (art. 5). Part II of the Protocol provides for the protection of victims of trafficking (arts. 6-8), while Part III deals with prevention, cooperation and other measures (arts. 9-13). The Convention against Transnational Organized Crime entered into force on 29 September 2003. However, the Protocol on Trafficking in Person has not yet entered into force, having been signed by 117 States but ratified by only 28.

Whiteman, Marjorie M. 1898-1986. Lifetime career State Department official. Author of *Damages in International Law* (3 vols., 1937-43); *Digest of International Law* (15 vols., 1963-72).

WHO *See* **World Health Organization**.

WHO-Egypt Agreement, Interpretation of, *1980 I.C.J. Rep. 73*. The Eastern Mediterranean Regional Office of the WHO commenced operations on 1 July 1949 at Alexandria, in Egypt. An agreement between WHO and Egypt on the privileges, immunities and facilities to be granted to WHO was concluded in 1951 *(223 U.N.T.S. 87)*. Upon the recommendation by a sub-committee of the Regional Committee for the Eastern Mediterranean that the Regional Office be transferred as soon as possible to Amman (Jordan), the World Health Assembly on 20 May 1980 adopted a resolution by which it sought an advisory opinion on the applicability of the revision clause (art. 37) of the 1951 WHO-Egypt Agreement and, if it was applicable, on the legal responsibilities of WHO and Egypt as regards the Regional Office during the two-year period for notice of termination of the Agreement provided for in art. 37. The Court, *deciding* (12 to 1) to comply with the request notwithstanding its alleged political character, since it fell within the normal exercise of the Court's judicial powers, irrespective of the motives inspiring it, *advised* (12 to 1) that the legal principles and rules applicable in relation to a possible transfer of the Regional Office out of Egypt imposed on WHO and Egypt a duty to consult in good faith as to the conditions and modalities of a transfer, and (if the Regional Office were transferred) a duty to consult and negotiate regarding the various arrangements needed to effect the transfer in an orderly manner and with a minimum of prejudice to the work of WHO and the interests of Egypt; and imposed on the party wishing to effect the transfer a duty to give a reasonable period of notice to the other party for the termination of the existing situation regarding the Regional Office at Alexandria, taking due account of all the practical arrangements needed to effect an orderly and equitable transfer of the Regional Office to its new site; and (11 to 2) if the Regional Office were transferred from Egypt, the legal responsibilities of WHO and Egypt during the transitional period between the notification of the proposed transfer and its accomplishment were to fullfil in good faith the mutual obligations set out above.

Wilson, President Woodrow *See* **Fourteen Points**.

Wimbledon *(France, Great Britain, Italy and Japan v. Germany) (1923) P.C.I.J. Ser. A, No. 1.* In 1921, a British vessel, the *Wimbledon*, chartered to a French company and carrying a cargo of munitions consigned to Poland, was during the Russo-Polish war of 1920-21 refused permission by the German authorities to have access to the Kiel Canal en route from the North Sea to Danzig as it would infringe German neutrality regulations. Art. 380 of the Treaty of Versailles *(225 C.T.S. 188)* provided that the Kiel Canal was to be maintained free and open to the vessels of commerce and war of all nations at peace with Germany on terms of entire equality. On the basis of art. 386(1) of the Treaty of Versailles, France, Great Britain, Italy and Japan instituted proceedings against Germany before the PCIJ, which *held* (9 to 3) that Germany was wrong in refusing access to the Kiel Canal to the *Wimbledon* and was bound to make good the prejudice sustained by the vessel and her charterers; art. 380 of the Treaty of Versailles was clear, and making the Kiel Canal an international waterway in accordance with the terms of that Article did not violate Germany's sovereignty since the restrictions on the exercise of sovereign rights flowing from art. 380 were the result of entering into a treaty which was itself an attribute of State sovereignty; Germany's neutrality regulations could not prevail over the provisions of the Treaty of Versailles.

WIPO *See* **World Intellectual Property Organization**.

Wisby, maritime laws of These laws (the *Leges Wisbuenses*) were a collection of maritime laws adopted by the merchants of Wisby on the island of Gottland in the fourteenth and fifteenth centuries. These laws, along with others, "indirectly influenced the growth of International Law": *I Oppenheim (8th ed.) 80*; reference to the laws was removed in the 9th ed. *See also* Colombos, *International Law of the Sea* (6th ed.), 33.

withdrawal, international organizations from "A specific right of withdrawal is found in the constitution of a large number of international organizations. It is amongst others the case in most the specialized agencies and in most regional organizations. In contrast there is no provision for withdrawal in the UN or WHO, or in the treaties establishing the EU, and the EC, for instance. There is considerable variation in the conditions attached to the right of withdrawal. Whereas the financial organizations allow withdrawal simply upon submission of written notice, and allow this withdrawal to take effect immediately, other organizations impose clear limitations on withdrawal. . . . A . . . condition sometimes attached to withdrawal is that outstanding obligations [usually financial obligations] must be fulfilled before withdrawal is effective. . . . What is certainly clear is that mere silence on the question of withdrawal is not adequate to deprive a member of the right to withdraw." Sands and Klein, *Bowett's Law of International Institutions* (5th ed.), 546-7, 549. *See* **resumption of cooperation, membership**.

withdrawal, treaty from *See* **denunciation**; **treaties, termination and suspension**.

WMD *See* **weapons of mass destruction**.

WMO *See* **World Meteorological Organization**.

Wolff, Christian 1676-1756. Professor, Halle 1706-23; 1740-56. A rigorous and scientific writer, he was more concerned with mathematical constructs than with either the practice of States or legal literature; Wolff was of the naturalist school. Principal works: *Ius naturale methode scientifica perpetratum* (1740-8); *Ius gentium methode scientifica perpetratum* (1749; text and translation in Classics of International Law, No. 13, (1934)); *Institutiones juris naturale et gentium* (1750, in German; translated into Latin 1772).

Women, Convention on the Elimination of All Forms of Discrimination against (CEDAW) Following the Declaration on the Elimination of Discrimination against Women of 7 November 1967 (GA Res. 2263 (XXII)), and prompted by the call for a convention (in GA Res. 33/177 of 20 December 1978), the General Assembly adopted this Convention on 18 December 1979 *(1249 U.N.T.S. 13)*. The Convention came into force on 3 September 1981. The Convention seeks to prohibit all discrimination against women, defined as "any distinction, exclusion or restriction made on the basis of sex which has the effect or purpose of impairing or nullifying the recognition, enjoyment or exercise by women, irrespective of their marital status, on a basis of equality of men and women, of human rights and fundamental freedoms in the political, economic, social, cultural, civil or any other field" (art. 1). States Party are required to take action to prohibit discrimination (art. 2), and to promote the equality of women and men (art. 3 and 5), which may include "temporary special measures aimed at accelerating *de facto* equality" (art. 4(1)). Particular obligations provide for equality in education (art. 10), employment (art. 11), health care (art. 12) and economic and social life (art. 13), particular regard being directed at the problems faced by rural women (art. 14). Equality is provided for before the law (art. 15), and in marriage and family matters (art. 16). A Committee is established to consider the progress made in implementing the Convention (art. 17), which Committee is to examine reports from States Party (art. 18) and to report annually, through ECOSOC, to the UN General Assembly (art. 21). *See* McKean, *Equality and Discrimination under International Law* (1983), 186-92; Halberstan and Defeis, *Women's Legal Rights* (1987); Rehof, *Guide to the Travaux Préparatoires of theUnited Nations Convention on the Elimination of All Forms of Discrimination Against Women* (1993).

Women, Convention on the Political Rights of This Convention was adopted by the UN General Assembly on 20 December 1952 *(193 U.N.T.S. 135)*, and entered into force on 7 July 1954. Based upon "the principle of equality of rights for men and women contained in the Charter of the United Nations" (Preamble), it guarantees for women the following rights on equal terms with men, and without discrimination: to vote in all elections (art. I); to stand for election to all publicly-elected bodies (art. II); and to hold public office and to exercise all public functions (art. III). *See* McKean, *Equality and Discrimination under International Law* (1983), 178-86.

women, nationality *See* **Married Women, Convention on the Nationality of**.

work, fundamental principles and rights *See* **Fundamental Principles and Rights at Work**.

working documents *See travaux préparatoires.*

World Bank *See* **International Bank for Reconstruction and Development.**

World Bank Group The World Bank Group consists of five closely associated financial institutions: the **International Bank for Reconstruction and Development (IBRD)**, the **International Development Association (IDA)**, the **International Finance Corporation (IFC)**, the **Multilateral Investment Guarantee Agency (MIGA)**, and the **International Centre for Settlement of Investment Disputes (ICSID)**. Each institution plays a different role in the Group's goal of combating poverty and improving living standards in the developing world. The term "World Bank Group" encompasses all five institutions. The term "World Bank" refers to two of the five, IBRD and IDA. In September 2000, World Bank Group identified its Millennium Development Goals. They are: to eradicate extreme poverty and hunger, achieve universal primary education, promote gender equality and empower women, reduce child mortality, improve maternal health, combat AIDS/HIV, ensure environmental sustainability and develop a global development partnership. These goals are to be met by a continuation of the World Bank Group's global financing, analytic and advisory services.

World Court A name commonly used to identify the **Permanent Court of International Justice** and the **International Court of Justice.**

World Health Organization (WHO) This organization, dating from 1948 (constitution of 22 July 1946 *(14 U.N.T.S. 185)*, subsequently amended) took over the functions of a variety of international health bodies. The objective of the organization is "the attainment by all peoples of the highest possible level of health" (art. 1), by acting as the directing and coordinating authority on international health work and providing assistance and services and generally promoting activities in the field of health and hygiene (art. 2). A relations agreement establishing WHO as a Specialized Agency was concluded on 10 June 1948.

The primary decision-making body is the World Health Assembly (arts. 10-23). The Assembly meets annually, and is attended by delegations from all 192 Member States. The Assembly determine the policies of the Organization, namely those regarding procedures designed to prevent the international spread of disease, causes of death and public health practices, and biological and pharmaceutical labeling and standards (art. 21). The Executive Board comprises 32 members "technically qualified in the field of health" who are elected for a period of three years. The Executive Board meets at least twice annually and is responsible for giving effect to the decisions and policies of the Health Assembly, to act as the executive organ of the Health Assembly, to prepare the proposals and agenda of meetings of the Health Assembly and to submit to the Health Assembly for consideration and approval a general program of work (arts. 24-29). The Secretariat is headed by a Director-General and is generally charged with maintenance of budgetary and routine administrative matters (arts. 30-37). *See* Beigbeder *et al, The World Health Organization* (1999). *See also* <www.who.int>.

World Heritage Convention Properly styled the Convention for the Protection of the World Cultural and Natural Heritage, this convention was adopted under the aegis of **UNESCO** on 16 November 1972 *(1037 U.N.T.S.)*. It defines cultural heritage (art. 1) as: "monuments: architectural works, works of monumental sculpture and painting, elements or structures of an archeological nature, inscriptions, cave dwellings and combinations of features, which are of outstanding universal value from the point of view of history, art or science; groups of buildings: groups of separate or connected buildings which, because of their architecture, their homogeneity or their place in the landscape, are of outstanding universal value from the point of view of history, art or science; sites: works of man or the combined works of nature and man, and areas including archaeological sites which are of outstanding universal value from the historical, aesthetic, ethnological or anthropological point of view"; and natural heritage (art. 2) as : "natural features consisting of physical and biological formations or groups of such formations, which are of outstanding universal value from the aesthetic or scientific point of view; geological and physiographical formations and precisely delineated areas which constitute the habitat of threatened species of animals and plants of outstanding universal value from the point of view of science or conservation; natural sites or precisely delineated natural areas of outstanding universal value from the point of view of science, conservation or natural beauty."

States parties are to identify qualifying properties (art. 3) and to protect and preserve them for future generations (art. 4). Those properties identified as qualifying, while subject to the sovereignty of the State in which they are located, constitute "a world heritage for whose protection it is the duty of the international community as a whole to co-operate" (art. 6(1)). The World Heritage Committee, established by art. 8, is to draw up a list, from inventories produced by States parties, of properties "having outstanding universal value" (art. 11(2)). The present World Heritage List identifies 754 properties, 582 being cultural, 149 being natural, and 23 being mixed, spread over 128 of the Convention's 175 States parties.

World Intellectual Property Organization   Headquartered in Geneva, Switzerland, the World Intellectual Property Organization is the successor to the United International Bureau for the Protection of Intellectual Property (BIRPI), established in 1893. In 1974, WIPO became a specialized agency of the United Nations (G.A. Res. 3346(XXIX). WIPO operates under the authority of the Convention Establishing the World Intellectual Property Organization, signed at Stockholm on July 14, 1967 *(828 U.N.T.S. 3)*, as amended on September 28, 1979. The term "intellectual property" includes the rights relating to literary, artistic and scientific works, performances of performing artists, phonograms, and broadcasts, inventions in all fields of human endeavor, scientific discoveries, industrial designs, trademarks, service marks, and commercial names and designations, protection against unfair competition, and all other rights resulting from intellectual activity in the industrial, scientific, literary or artistic fields (art. 2). WIPO's goals are to promote the protection of intellectual property throughout the world through cooperation among States and, where appropriate, in collaboration with any other international organization (art. 3). WIPO acknowledges the need to develop new norms and standards to remain current in technology and business practices, as well as to address concerns regarding traditional knowledge, folklore, biodiversity and biotechnology. WIPO also strives to assist in making intellectual property registration systems more accessible by harmonizing and simplifying procedures.

Membership of WIPO is primarily for any State which is a member of one of the unions for which WIPO is responsible or has assumed responsibility but it is also open to any Member of the UN, the Specialized Agencies, the IAEA or any party to the ICJ statute, as well as to any State invited to become a party (art. 5). WIPO's primary governing body is the General Assembly, which meets every other year, and may meet in extraordinary session upon convocation by the Director General either at the request of the Coordination Committee or at the request of one-fourth of the States members of the General Assembly. The General Assembly reviews and approves reports from the Coordination Committee and the Director General and adopts the budget and financial structure for WIPO (art. 6). WIPO's Conference is authorized to discuss matters of general interest in the field of intellectual property and may adopt recommendations relating to such matters, within the limits of the budget of the Conference, establish the biennial program of legal-technical assistance, adopt amendments to this Convention (art. 7). The Coordination Committee gives advice to the governing organs on all administrative, financial and other matters of common interest. The Coordination Committee meets annually and can also meet in extraordinary session, upon convocation by the Director General, either on his own initiative, or at the request of its Chairman or one-fourth of its members (art. 8). The organization is supported by a secretariat called the International Bureau, headed by a Director-General (art. 9). *See* WIPO, *Introduction to Intellectual Property: Theory and Practice*; *WIPO Guide to Intellectual Property Worldwide* (2nd ed.). *See also* <www.wipo.int>.

World Meteorological Organization This organization is the successor to the International Meteorological Organization set up in 1878. The purposes of the organization are to promote worldwide co-operation on the establishment and expansion of meteorological facilities and on the standardization of observations, and to promote exchanges of information. The World Meteorological Congress, consisting of all Members, is the supreme organ of the organization (art. 6(1)); the Executive Committee is responsible for the provision of technical information and the execution of the resolutions of the Congress (art. 14). The Constitution of 11 October 1947 *(77 U.N.T.S. 143)* entered into force on 23 March 1950. A relations agreement establishing the WMO as a Specialized Agency was concluded on 20 December 1951. The World Meteorological Congress is the supreme body of WMO. The Congress meets every four years, determining policy, approving the programs, budgets and regulations. The WMO's Executive Council meets at least every year to coordinate research and prepare recommendations for Congress, to supervise the implementation of Congress directives and to advise members on technical matters. Covering an array of meteorological subjects, the WMO has eight technical commissions: aeronautical meteorology; agricultural meteorology; atmospheric sciences; basic systems; climatology; hydrology; instruments and methods of observation; and marine meteorology. *See also* <www.wmo.ch>.

World Tourism Organization The World Tourism Organization was established from the transformation of the International Union of Official Travel Organizations (IUOTO) by the Statute concluded at Mexico City on 27 September 1970 *(985 U.N.T.S. 339)*. The fundamental aim of the Organization is to promote and develop tourism "with a view to contributing to economic development, international understanding, peace, prosperity, and universal respect for, and observance of, human rights and fundamental freedoms. . . ." (art. 3(1)). The organization is to enter into effective collaboration with the UN and its specialized agencies and in particular UNDP (art. 3(3)). The statute provides for full membership for all sovereign States (existing members of IUOTO, and subsequent applicants: art. 5), associate membership (territories not responsible for their external relations: art. 6), and affiliate membership (international or commercial tourist bodies: art. 7). The Assembly, comprising all full members and meeting in ordinary session every two years, is declared to be the "supreme organ of the organization" (art. 9(1)), its specific competences being set out in art. 12. The Executive Council, comprising one member for every five full members of the Organization (art. 14(1)), is the permanent body providing continuity between ordinary sessions and implementing Assembly decisions (*see* art. 19). The Organization is serviced by a secretariat (arts. 21-24). The budget is funded by contributions from all classes of members in accordance with a scale of assessment (art. 25). *See* <www.world-tourism.org>.

World Trade Organization The General Agreement on Tariffs and Trade 1947 was originally intended as a precursor to the creation of the International Trade Organization

(ITO) which was to provide an institutional structure for international trade matters. The ITO never materialized and the GATT took on rudimentary institutional structures in order to facilitate the development of the international trading system. However, at the conclusion of the Uruguay Round of negotiations in 1994, the World Trade Organization was established (*see* the Marrakesh Agreement Establishing the World Trade Organization *(13 I.L.M. 13 (1994))*. The Organization, which is based in Geneva, came formally into being on 1 January 1995 and currently has 146 member States. The GATT, as amended in 1994 (GATT 1994: *33 I.L.M. 28 (1994)*), together with the General Agreement on Trade in Services (GATS), the Agreement on Trade-Related Aspects of Intellectual Property Rights (TRIPS), the Dispute Settlement Understanding *(33 I.L.M. 112 (1994))* and the Trade Policy Review Mechanism (collectively referred to as the Multilateral Trade Agreements) are integral parts of the Marrakesh Agreement and are binding on all member States (art. II).

The functions of the WTO are to facilitate the implementation, administration and operation of the Marrakesh Agreement and the Multilateral Trade Agreements; to provide the forum for negotiations among its members concerning their multilateral trade relations; to administer the Dispute Settlement Understanding and the Trade Policy Review Mechanism; and to cooperate, as appropriate with the **International Monetary Fund** and the **International Bank for Reconstruction and Development** (art. III). The structure of the WTO includes the Ministerial Council composed of representatives of all the members to meet at least once every two years and the General Council composed of representatives of all the members to meet as appropriate (usually several times a year). The General Council also meets as the Trade Policy Review Body and the Dispute Settlement Body. Reporting to the General Council are the council for Trade in Goods, the Council for Trade in Services and the Council for Trade-Related Aspects of Intellectual Property Rights. Membership of these bodies is open to representatives of all member States. The Councils may further establish subsidiary bodies, as required (art. III). There is also a Secretariat headed by the Director-General (art. V).

The **Dispute Settlement Undertaking** (DSU) established a dispute settlement procedure comprising three bodies: The Dispute Settlement Body (DSB), ad hoc panels, normally comprising three persons approved by the DSB (DSU, arts.6-8) and the Appellate Body, a standing forum comprising seven members elected by the DSB for a once-renewable four-year period (DSU, art. 17). Unlike the previous system of dispute resolution under the GATT, decisions of the panel, as well as those of the Appellate Body, which are adopted by the DSB become legally binding.

See generally Das, *The World Trade Organization: A Guide to the New Framework for International Trade* (1999); Jackson, *The Jurisprudence of GATT and the WTO* (2000). *See also* <www.wto.org>.

worldwide unitary taxation   Under unitary taxation, as operated by certain US States, subsidiaries of multinational companies, having their headquarters outside the US, are taxed not on the normal "arm's length" or "separate" accounting basis which reflects the operating results of the subsidiary in a given jurisdiction, but on a proportion of worldwide group profits. This proportion is worked out through the application of a combination of payroll, property and sales figures in the State to the company's worldwide figures.

Although the principle of unitary taxation was upheld by the Supreme Court in *Franchetti v. Franchise Tax Board, 103 U.S. 1033* (1983) in relation to US-based multinationals, the operation of worldwide unitary taxation by US States is regarded as running counter to the accepted principle of international taxation practice that an enterprise of one country carrying on business in another country should be taxed in the other country only on profits of activities carried on there. Multinational companies centre their criticism on the inequitable and unfair consequences of the unitary system which involves a strong risk of double taxation and high compliance costs besides being a serious impediment to international trade and investment, and disturbing the symmetry of international taxation relationships. The May 1984 Report of the Worldwide Unitary Taxation Working Group established by the President in response to widespread criticism, recommends adoption by states of a "water's edge solution," meaning that multinationals would only declare their activities within the United States and would only be taxable on US earnings. *See* **taxation of enterprise and persons**.

wounded, sick and shipwrecked   Two of the Geneva Red Cross Conventions of 12 August 1949 make provision here: Convention (No. II) for the Amelioration of the Condition of the Wounded, Sick and Shipwrecked Members of Armed Forces at Sea *(75 U.N.T.S. 85)* in respect of forces on board ship and in respect of forces on land (art. 4), Convention (No. I) for the Amelioration of the Condition of the Wounded and Sick in Armed Forces in the Field *(75 U.N.T.S. 31)*. Provision is made in Convention No. I for members of the armed forces and assimilated persons (the definition here parallels that in Convention No. III on prisoners of war) who are wounded or sick, to be respected and protected in all circumstances. They are to be treated humanely and cared for by the Party to the conflict in whose power they may be, without any adverse distinction. Any attempts upon their lives or violence to their persons is strictly prohibited. They are not to be left willfully without medical assistance and care or exposed to contagion or infection (art. 12). If a Party is compelled to abandon wounded or sick to the enemy, medical personnel and material should be left with them "as far as military considerations permit" *(ibid.)*. Art. 15 imposes obligations to search for and collect the sick and wounded and information is to be supplied as to those wounded and sick who are captured (art. 16). The parties are to ensure honorable burial (not normally cremation) (art. 17). Special provisions follow on the immunity from attack on medical units and establishments (arts. 17-23) and respect and protection for medical personnel (arts. 24-32), and on buildings and material and on medical transports (arts. 33-34; 35-37). "As a compliment to Switzerland, the heraldic emblem of the red cross on a white ground, formed by reversing the Federal colours, is retained as the emblem and distinctive sign of the Medical Service of armed forces" (art. 38). Arts. 49 to 54 lay down detailed requirements for the repression of abuses.

Convention No. II, applying to forces on board ship, closely parallels Convention No. I. Both Conventions are to be applied with the cooperation and under the scrutiny of the **Protecting Powers** "whose duty it is to safeguard the interests of the parties to the conflict." Wounded, sick and shipwrecked persons, if they fall into the hands of the opposing Party become prisoners of war (art. 16); if into neutral hands, they become subject to internment so that "they can take no further part in operations of war" (arts. 15 and 17). Detailed provision is made in regard to hospital ships (arts. 22-35) and again in relation to personnel (arts. 36-37) and transports (arts. 38-40).

Wright, Quincy   1890-1970. American lawyer. Taught at Harvard 1916-22, U. Minn. 1922-23, Chicago 1923-31. Professor, Chicago 1931-56; U.Va. 1958-61. Principal publications: *Enforcement of International Law through Municipal Law in the U.S.* (1916); *Mandates under the League of Nations* (1930). *A Study of War* (1942; rev. ed. 1965); *International Law and the United Nations* (1955, 1956); *The Strengthening of International Law* (1959); *The Role of International Law in the Elimination of War* (1961).

writers   *See* **publicists**.

wrongful act, internationally   The ILC's Draft Articles on State Responsibility 2001 *(UN Doc. A/56/10 Chap. IV.E.1)* defines the term "internationally wrongful act," as conduct consisting of an action or omission which is (a) attributable to the State under international law; and (b) constitutes a breach of an international obligation of the State" (art. 2). Every such act entails the international responsibility of that State (art. 1). *See* **state responsibility**.

WTO   *See* **World Trade Organization; World Tourism Organization**.

X

xenophobia The 2001 World Conference on Racism had, as its full title, the World Conference against Racism, Xenophobia and Related Intolerance, and its final Declaration adopted at Durban, South Africa, on September 2001 *(UN Doc. A/CONF. 189/12)* condemned, *inter alia*, xenophobia, without defining it, called for universal adherence to the International Convention on the Elimination of all Forms of Racial Discrimination 1965 *(660 U.N.T.S. 195)* (*see* **racial discrimination**) and established a detailed Program of Action.

Y

Yalta Conference The Yalta (or Crimea) Conference, comprising the Heads of Governments (and their advisers) of the UK, USA and USSR, was held from 4 to 11 February 1945 *(1945 For. Rel. 968)*. Among the matters agreed were: that Germany should, after military defeat, be divided into occupation zones; that German armed forces should be disarmed and disbanded; that all war criminals should be brought to just and swift punishment; that reparation should be exacted from Germany; that a Conference of United Nations should be convened; and that the three Governments should act jointly to liberate the peoples of Nazi-occupied Europe. Further, it called for "a strong, free, independent and democratic Poland," while recognizing the Soviet "liberation" of Poland. The status of the Yalta agreement is unclear. In accordance with the prevailing UK and US view, it has been described as "the personal agreement of the three leaders:" Briggs, The Leaders' Agreement of Yalta, *40 A.J.I.L. 376* at 382 *(1946)*. Cf. *I Oppenheim (7th ed.) 788*: the agreement "incorporated definite rules of conduct which may be regarded as legally binding on the States in question." The same editor is less confident in the subsequent edition: *I Oppenheim (8th ed.) 873*.

Yalta Formula Properly styled the Statement of the Four Sponsoring Governments on Voting Procedure in the Security Council, this formula emerged from the **Yalta Conference** of February 1945 and formed the basis of the provision of the UN Charter relating to voting in the Security Council (art. 27). The Yalta Formula *(11 U.N.C.I.O. Doc. 774)* distinguished between Security Council decisions involving "direct measures," and decisions not involving direct measures. For the former, a "qualified vote" would be required, i.e. the vote of seven (now nine) members, including the concurring votes of the five permanent members; for the latter a "procedural vote" would be sufficient, i.e. the vote of any seven (now nine) members. The distinction drawn in art. 27 of the Charter is between "procedural matters" and "all other matters." *See* Bailey, *Voting in the Security Council* (1969); Goodrich, Hambro and Simons, *Charter of the United Nations* (3rd ed.), 215-31. *And see* **veto** and **voting**.

Yon Claim *(Italy v. Peru) (1901) 15 R.I.A.A. 446*. Italy claimed the sum of Soles 4,000 in respect of the destruction in 1894 of a house and its contents belonging to an Italian national, Don Carlos Yon, who had died prior to the decision on the claim. *Held*, by the Arbitrator of Italian Claims against Peru, that the claim could still be presented by Don Carlos Yon's heirs, in fact his children; that, although it was for each State to apply its own law to decide the attribution of its nationality to a person, in case of conflict between applicable laws an arbitral tribunal must decide according to principles of international law amongst which was one which established that a legitimate child acquired at birth the nationality which his father then possessed; that the children were accordingly Italian nationals, although they could be represented in the proceedings by their mother who had both Peruvian and Italian nationality; that the house was destroyed by forces under the orders of the

Sub-Prefect, and the request for a judicial enquiry had not been met, constituting a denial of justice; and that the claim should accordingly be allowed, and the sum of Soles 2,200 paid by Peru.

Youmans Claim *(United States v. Mexico) (1926) 4 R.I.A.A. 110.* The United States claimed $50,000 for damages arising out of the death of Youmans, an American citizen, who, together with two other Americans, was killed at the hands of a mob on 14 March 1880 in Mexico. The three Americans were in a house which the mob had surrounded. The Mayor was asked for protection for them; he ordered local troops to quell the riot and put an end to the attack on the Americans. Instead the troops, on arriving at the scene, opened fire on the house, and as a result of their action and that of the mob the Americans were killed. Court proceedings were instituted against a few of those responsible, but in the event none was effectively punished. *Held,* by the US/Mexico General Claims Commission, that the Government of Mexico showed a lack of diligence in the punishment of persons implicated in the crime, that adequate protection to foreigners was not afforded where the proper agencies of the law to afford protection participated in murder, and that the participation of the soldiers in the murder could not be regarded as acts committed in their private capacity since at the time of the commission of those acts the men were on duty under the immediate supervision and in the presence of a commanding officer. The Commission awarded damages of $20,000.

Yugoslav Military Mission Case *(1962) 38 I.L.R. 162.* The plaintiff sold some land in Berlin to Yugoslavia, which used it for the Yugoslav Military Mission. The plaintiff subsequently claimed the sale and conveyance invalid, and sought rectification of the land register and an order for possession. The issue of the immunity of foreign States from the jurisdiction of German courts was referred to the Federal German Constitutional Court, which *held* that there was no rule of customary international law precluding local courts in all cases from exercising jurisdiction over actions against a foreign State concerning its embassy premises; that the immunity of mission premises from the jurisdiction of the local courts extended only so far as was necessary to enable the mission to carry out its functions; and that an action for rectification of a land register did not adversely affect a diplomatic mission in the performance of its tasks.

Yugoslav Tribunal *See* **International Criminal Tribunal for the Former Yugoslavia.**

Yukon Lumber Case *(UK v. US) (1913) 6 R.I.A.A. 17.* A quantity of timber was, without the necessary permit, cut in the Yukon by two private persons and sold to the US military authorities without all the Crown dues payable on the timber being paid by them to the Canadian Government. The UK claimed that the US should either pay the dues or the value of the timber in question. *Held* by the UK-US Arbitral Tribunal established by the Agreement of 18 August 1910 *(12 Bevans 344),* that, the Canadian Government and the Crown Agent responsible for timber matters having by their actions treated the timber as no longer in the lawful ownership of the Canadian Government, the claim was solely for the non-payment of Crown dues, and the US military authorities were under no obligation to the Canadian Government to pay those dues.

Z

Ziat Claim *(Great Britain v. Spain) (1924) 2 R.I.A.A. 729.* Great Britain claimed for damage to property arising from a riot which degenerated into pillage of the Moroccan business quarter of the town of Melilla in the Spanish zone of Morocco. The claim was presented on behalf of Mohammed Ziat, a naturalized British subject, who together with a Moroccan had established a business in Melilla, which according to Spanish law had a separate legal personality and, as such, Spanish nationality. *Held*, by Huber, acting as *rapporteur* on the **Spanish Zone of Morocco Claims**, that, for purposes of an international litigation, it is possible to distinguish between participants in a company and the company itself; that it is necessary to consider the merits of each case to determine whether damage has been suffered directly by the person concerned; that a State's r esponsibility is not in general engaged by a riot; that in those circumstances a State is only responsible for negligence in preventing damage or in the repression of wrongful acts, or in its efforts to mitigate their consequences for the victims; that the Spanish authorities had incurred no responsibility on those grounds; and that the claim must therefore be rejected.

zones, exclusion, war *See* **war zones.**

zones, maritime *See* **maritime zones.**

Zouche, Richard 1590-1661. Professor at Oxford, and Admiralty judge. The writer of the first manual of international law, with a strong emphasis on positive law. Principal works: *Juris et iudicii fecialis, sive, juris inter gentes, et questionum de eodem explicatio* (1650; text and translation in *Classics of International Law*, No. 1 (1911)); *Elementa jurisprudentiae* (1629).

DOCUMENTS

Charter of the United Nations

Statute of the International Court of Justice

Vienna Convention on the Law of Treaties

CHARTER OF THE UNITED NATIONS

Adopted at San Francisco on 26 June 1945; in force on 24 October 1945

As amended in 1965 and 1971

Preamble

We the Peoples of the United Nations Determined

to save succeeding generations from the scourge of war, which twice in our lifetime has brought untold sorrow to mankind, and

to reaffirm faith in fundamental human rights, in the dignity and worth of the human person, in the equal rights of men and women and of nations large and small, and

to establish conditions under which justice and respect for the obligations arising from treaties and other sources of international law can be maintained, and

to promote social progress and better standards of life in larger freedom,

And for these Ends

to practice tolerance and live together in peace with one another as good neighbors, and

to unite our strength to maintain international peace and security, and

to ensure by the acceptance of principles and the institution of methods, that armed force shall not be used, save in the common interest, and

to employ international machinery for the promotion of the economic and social advancement of all peoples,

Have Resolved to Combine our Efforts to Accomplish these Aims

Accordingly, our respective Governments, through representatives assembled in the city of San Francisco, who have exhibited their full powers found to be in good and due form, have agreed to the present Charter of the United Nations and do hereby establish an international organization to be known as the United Nations.

CHAPTER I

PURPOSES AND PRINCIPLES

Article 1

The Purposes of the United Nations are:

1. To maintain international peace and security, and to that end: to take effective collective measures for the prevention and removal of threats to the peace, and for the suppression of acts of aggression or other breaches of the peace, and to bring about by peaceful means, and in conformity with the principles of justice and international law, adjustment or settlement of international disputes or situations which might lead to a breach of the peace;

2. To develop friendly relations among nations based on respect for the principle of equal rights and self-determination of peoples, and to take other appropriate measures to strengthen universal peace;

3. To achieve international cooperation in solving international problems of an economic, social, cultural, or humanitarian character, and in promoting and encouraging respect for

human rights and for fundamental freedoms for all without distinction as to race, sex, language, or religion; and

4. To be a center for harmonizing the actions of nations in the attainment of these common ends.

Article 2

The Organization and its Members, in pursuit of the Purposes stated in Article 1, shall act in accordance with the following Principles.

1. The Organization is based on the principle of the sovereign equality of all its Members.

2. All Members, in order to ensure to all of them the rights and benefits resulting from membership, shall fulfill in good faith the obligations assumed by them in accordance with the present Charter.

3. All Members shall settle their international disputes by peaceful means in such a manner that international peace and security, and justice, are not endangered.

4. All Members shall refrain in their international relations from the threat or use of force against the territorial integrity or political independence of any state, or in any other manner inconsistent with the Purposes of the United Nations.

5. All Members shall give the United Nations every assistance in any action it takes in accordance with the present Charter, and shall refrain from giving assistance to any state against which the United Nations is taking preventive or enforcement action.

6. The Organization shall ensure that states which are not Members of the United Nations act in accordance with these Principles so far as may be necessary for the maintenance of international peace and security.

7. Nothing contained in the present Charter shall authorize the United Nations to intervene in matters which are essentially within the domestic jurisdiction of any state or shall require the Members to submit such matters to settlement under the present Charter; but this principle shall not prejudice the application of enforcement measures under Chapter VII.

CHAPTER II

MEMBERSHIP

Article 3

The original Members of the United Nations shall be the states which, having participated in the United Nations Conference on International Organization at San Francisco, or having previously signed the Declaration by United Nations of January 1, 1942, sign the present Charter and ratify it in accordance with Article 110.

Article 4

1. Membership in the United Nations is open to all other peace-loving states which accept the obligations contained in the present Charter and, in the judgment of the Organization, are able and willing to carry out these obligations.

2. The admission of any such state to membership in the United Nations will be effected by a decision of the General Assembly upon the recommendation of the Security Council.

Article 5

A member of the United Nations against which preventive or enforcement action has been taken by the Security Council may be suspended from the exercise of the rights and privileges of membership by the General Assembly upon the recommendation of the Security Council. The exercise of these rights and privileges may be restored by the Security Council.

Article 6

A Member of the United Nations which has persistently violated the Principles contained in the present Charter may be expelled from the Organization by the General Assembly upon the recommendation of the Security Council.

CHAPTER III

ORGANS

Article 7

1. There are established as the principal organs of the United Nations: a General Assembly, a Security Council, an Economic and Social Council, a Trusteeship Council, an International Court of Justice, and a Secretariat.

2. Such subsidiary organs as may be found necessary may be established in accordance with the present Charter.

Article 8

The United Nations shall place no restrictions on the eligibility of men and women to participate in any capacity and under conditions of equality in its principal and subsidiary organs.

CHAPTER IV

THE GENERAL ASSEMBLY

Composition

Article 9

1. The General Assembly shall consist of all the Members of the United Nations.

2. Each member shall have not more than five representatives in the General Assembly.

Functions and Powers

Article 10

The General Assembly may discuss any questions or any matters within the scope of the present Charter or relating to the powers and functions of any organs provided for in the present Charter, and, except as provided in Article 12, may make recommendations to the Members of the United Nations or to the Security Council or to both on any such questions or matters.

Article 11

1. The General Assembly may consider the general principles of cooperation in the maintenance of international peace and security, including the principles governing disarmament and the regulation of armaments, and may make recommendations with regard to such principles to the Members or to the Security Council or to both.

2. The General Assembly may discuss any questions relating to the maintenance of international peace and security brought before it by any Member of the United Nations, or by the Security Council, or by a state which is not a Member of the United Nations in accordance with Article 35, paragraph 2, and, except as provided in Article 12, may make recommendations with regard to any such questions to the state or states concerned or to the Security Council or to both. Any such question on which action is necessary shall be referred to the Security Council by the General Assembly either before or after discussion.

3. The General Assembly may call the attention of the Security Council to situations which are likely to endanger international peace and security.

4. The powers of the General Assembly set forth in this Article shall not limit the general scope of Article 10.

Article 12

1. While the Security Council is exercising in respect of any dispute or situation the functions assigned to it in the present Charter, the General Assembly shall not make any recommendation with regard to that dispute or situation unless the Security Council so requests.

2. The Secretary-General, with the consent of the Security Council, shall notify the General Assembly at each session of any matters relative to the maintenance of international peace and security which are being dealt with by the Security Council and shall similarly notify the General Assembly, or the Members of the United Nations if the General Assembly is not in session, immediately the Security Council ceases to deal with such matters.

Article 13

1. The General Assembly shall initiate studies and make recommendations for the purpose of:

    a. promoting international cooperation in the political field and encouraging the progressive development of international law and its codification;

    b. promoting international cooperation in the economic, social, cultural, educational, and health fields, and assisting in the realization of human rights and fundamental freedoms for all without distinction as to race, sex, language, or religion.

2. The further responsibilities, functions and powers of the General Assembly with respect to matters mentioned in paragraph 1(b) above are set forth in Chapters IX and X.

Article 14

Subject to the provisions of Article 12, the General Assembly may recommend measures for the peaceful adjustment of any situation, regardless of origin, which it deems likely to impair the general welfare or friendly relations among nations, including situations resulting from a violation of the provisions of the present Charter setting forth the Purposes and Principles of the United Nations.

Article 15

1. The General Assembly shall receive and consider annual and special reports from the Security Council; these reports shall include an account of the measures that the Security Council has decided upon or taken to maintain international peace and security.

2. The General Assembly shall receive and consider reports from the other organs of the United Nations.

Article 16

The General Assembly shall perform such functions with respect to the international trusteeship system as are assigned to it under Chapters XII and XIII, including the approval of the trusteeship agreements for areas not designated as strategic.

Article 17

1. The General Assembly shall consider and approve the budget of the Organization.

2. The expenses of the Organization shall be borne by the Members as apportioned by the General Assembly.

3. The General Assembly shall consider and approve any financial and budgetary arrangements with specialized agencies referred to in Article 57 and shall examine the administrative budgets of such specialized agencies with a view to making recommendations to the agencies concerned.

Voting

Article 18

1. Each member of the General Assembly shall have one vote.

2. Decisions of the General Assembly on important questions shall be made by a two-thirds majority of the members present and voting. These questions shall include: recommendations with respect to the maintenance of international peace and security, the election of the non-permanent members of the Security Council, the election of the members of the Economic and Social Council, the election of members of the Trusteeship Council in accordance with paragraph 1(c) of Article 86, the admission of new Members to the United Nations, the suspension of the rights and privileges of membership, the expulsion of Members, questions relating to the operation of the trusteeship system, and budgetary questions.

3. Decisions on other questions, Composition including the determination of additional categories of questions to be decided by a two-thirds majority, shall be made by a majority of the members present and voting.

Article 19

A Member of the United Nations which is in arrears in the payment of its financial contributions to the Organization shall have no vote in the General Assembly if the amount of its arrears equals or exceeds the amount of the contributions due from it for the preceding two full years. The General Assembly may, nevertheless, permit such a Member to vote if it is satisfied that the failure to pay is due to conditions beyond the control of the Member.

Procedure

Article 20

The General Assembly shall meet in regular annual sessions and in such special sessions as occasion may require. Special sessions shall be convoked by the Secretary-General at the request of the Security Council or of a majority of the Members of the United Nations.

Article 21

The General Assembly shall adopt its own rules of procedure. It shall elect its President for each session.

Article 22

The General Assembly may establish such subsidiary organs as it deems necessary for the performance of its functions.

CHAPTER V

THE SECURITY COUNCIL

Article 23

1. The Security Council shall consist of fifteen Members of the United Nations. The Republic of China, France, the Union of Soviet Socialist Republics, the United Kingdom of Great Britain and Northern Ireland, and the United States of America shall be permanent members of the Security Council. The General Assembly shall elect ten other Members of the United Nations to be non-permanent members of the Security Council, due regard being specially paid, in the first instance to the contribution of Members of the United Nations to the maintenance of international peace and security and to the other purposes of the Organization, and also to equitable geographical distribution.

2. The non-permanent members of the Security Council shall be elected for a term of two years. In the first election of the non-permanent members after the increase of the membership of the Security Council from eleven to fifteen, two of the four additional members shall be chosen for a term of one year. A retiring member shall not be eligible for immediate re-election.

3. Each member of the Security Council shall have one representative.

Functions and Powers

Article 24

1. In order to ensure prompt and effective action by the United Nations, its Members confer on the Security Council primary responsibility for the maintenance of international peace and security, and agree that in carrying out its duties under this responsibility the Security Council acts on their behalf.

2. In discharging these duties the Security Council shall act in accordance with the Purposes and Principles of the United Nations. The specific powers granted to the Security Council for the discharge of these duties are laid down in Chapter VI, VII, VIII and XII.

3. The Security Council shall submit annual and, when necessary, special reports to the General Assembly for its consideration.

Article 25

The Members of the United Nations agree to accept and carry out the decisions of the Security Council in accordance with the present Charter.

Article 26

In order to promote the establishment and maintenance of international peace and security with the least diversion for armaments of the world's human and economic resources, the Security Council shall be responsible for formulating, with the assistance of the Military Staff Committee referred to in Article 47, plans to be submitted to the Members of the United Nations for the establishment of a system for the regulation of armaments.

Voting

Article 27

1. Each member of the Security Council shall have one vote.

2. Decisions of the Security Council on procedural matters shall be made by an affirmative vote of nine members.

3. Decisions of the Security Council on all other matters shall be made by an affirmative vote of nine members including the concurring votes of the permanent members; provided that, in decisions under Chapter VI, and under paragraph 3 of Article 52, a party to a dispute shall abstain from voting.

Procedure

Article 28

1. The Security Council shall be so organized as to be able to function continuously. Each member of the Security Council shall for this purpose be represented at all times at the seat of the Organization.

2. The Security Council shall hold periodic meetings at which each of its members may, if it so desires, be represented by a member of the government or by some other specially designated representative.

3. The Security Council may hold meetings at such places other than the seat of the Organization as in its judgment will best facilitate its work.

Article 29

The Security Council may establish such subsidiary organs as it deems necessary for the performance of its functions.

Article 30

The Security Council shall adopt its own rules of procedure, including the method of selecting its President.

Article 31

Any Member of the United Nations which is not a member of the Security Council may participate, without vote, in the discussion of any question brought before the Security Council whenever the latter considers that the interests of that Member are specially affected.

Article 32

Any Member of the United Nations which is not a member of the Security Council or any state which is not a Member of the United Nations, if it is a party to a dispute under consideration by the Security Council, shall be invited to participate, without vote, in the discussion relating to the dispute. The Security Council shall lay down such conditions as it deems just for the participation of a state which is not a Member of the United Nations.

CHAPTER VI

PACIFIC SETTLEMENT OF DISPUTES

Article 33

1. The parties to any dispute, the continuance of which is likely to endanger the maintenance of international peace and security, shall, first of all, seek a solution by negotiation, enquiry, mediation, conciliation, arbitration, judicial settlement, resort to regional agencies or arrangements, or other peaceful means of their own choice.

2. The Security Council shall, when it deems necessary, call upon the parties to settle their dispute by such means.

Article 34

The Security Council may investigate any dispute, or any situation which might lead to international friction or give rise to a dispute, in order to determine whether the continuance of the dispute or situation is likely to endanger the maintenance of international peace and security.

Article 35

1. Any Member of the United Nations may bring any dispute, or any situation of the nature referred to in Article 34, to the attention of the Security Council or of the General Assembly.

2. A state which is not a Member of the United Nations may bring to the attention of the Security Council or of the General Assembly any dispute to which it is a party if it accepts in advance, for the purposes of the dispute, the obligations of pacific settlement provided in the present Charter.

3. The proceedings of the General Assembly in respect of matters brought to its attention under this Article will be subject to the provisions of Articles 11 and 12.

Article 36

1. The Security Council may, at any stage of a dispute of the nature referred to in Article 33 or of a situation of like nature, recommend appropriate procedures or methods of adjustment.

2. The Security Council should take into consideration any procedures for the settlement of the dispute which have already been adopted by the parties.

3. In making recommendations under this Article the Security Council should also take into consideration that legal disputes should as a general rule be referred by the parties to the International Court of Justice in accordance with the provisions of the Statute of the Court.

Article 37

1. Should the parties to a dispute of the nature referred to in Article 33 fail to settle it by the means indicated in that Article, they shall refer it to the Security Council.

2. If the Security Council deems that the continuance of the dispute is in fact likely to endanger the maintenance of international peace and security, it shall decide whether to take action under Article 36 or to recommend such terms of settlement as it may consider appropriate.

Article 38

Without prejudice to the provisions of Articles 33 to 37, the Security Council may, if all the parties to any dispute so request, make recommendations to the parties with a view to a pacific settlement of the dispute.

CHAPTER VII

ACTION WITH RESPECT TO THREATS TO THE PEACE, BREACHES OF THE PEACE, AND ACTS OF AGGRESSION

Article 39

The Security Council shall determine the existence of any threat to the peace, breach of the peace, or act of aggression and shall make recommendations, or decide what measures shall be taken in accordance with Articles 41 and 42, to maintain or restore international peace and security.

Article 40

In order to prevent an aggravation of the situation, the Security Council may, before making the recommendations or deciding upon the measures provided for in Article 39, call upon the parties concerned to comply with such provisional measures as it deems necessary or desirable. Such provisional measures shall be without prejudice to the rights, claims, or position of the parties concerned. The Security Council shall duly take account of failure to comply with such provisional measures.

Article 41

The Security Council may decide what measures not involving the use of armed force are to be employed to give effect to its decisions, and it may call upon the Members of the United Nations to apply such measures. These may include complete or partial interruption of economic relations and of rail, sea, air, postal, telegraphic, radio, and other means of communication, and the severance of diplomatic relations.

Article 42

Should the Security Council consider that measures provided for in Article 41 would be inadequate or have proved to be inadequate, it may take such action by air, sea, or land forces as may be necessary to maintain or restore international peace and security. Such action may include demonstrations, blockade, and other operations by air, sea, or land forces of Members of the United Nations.

Article 43

1. All Members of the United Nations, in order to contribute to the maintenance of international peace and security, undertake to make available to the Security Council, on its call and in accordance with a special agreement or agreements, armed forces, assistance, and facilities, including rights of passage, necessary for the purpose of maintaining international peace and security.

2. Such agreement or agreements shall govern the numbers and types of forces. their degree of readiness and general location, and the nature of the facilities and assistance to be provided.

3. The agreement or agreements shall be negotiated as soon as possible on the initiative of the Security Council. They shall be concluded between the Security Council and Members or between the Security Council and groups of Members and shall be subject to ratification by the signatory states in accordance with their respective constitutional processes.

Article 44

When the Security Council has decided to use force it shall, before calling upon a Member not represented on it to provide armed forces in fulfillment of the obligations assumed under Article 43, invite that Member, if the Member so desires, to participate in the decisions of the Security Council concerning the employment of contingents of that Member's armed forces.

Article 45

In order to enable the United Nations to take urgent military measures Members shall hold immediately available national air-force contingents for combined international enforcement action. The strength and degree of readiness of these contingents and plans for their combined action shall be determined, within the limits laid down in the special agreement or agreements referred to in Article 43, by the Security Council with the assistance of the Military Staff Committee.

Article 46

Plans for the application of armed force shall be made by the Security Council with the assistance of the Military Staff Committee.

Article 47

1. There shall be established a Military Staff Committee to advise and assist the Security Council on all questions relating to the Security Council's military requirements for the maintenance of international peace and security, the employment and command of forces placed at its disposal, the regulation of armaments, and possible disarmament.

2. The Military Staff Committee shall consist of the Chiefs of Staff of the permanent members of the Security Council or their representatives. Any Member of the United Nations not permanently represented on the Committee shall be invited by the Committee to be associated with it when the efficient discharge of the Committee's responsibilities requires the participation of that Member in its work.

3. The Military Staff Committee shall be responsible under the Security Council for the strategic direction of any armed forces placed at the disposal of the Security Council. Questions relating to the command of such forces shall be worked out subsequently.

4. The Military Staff Committee, with the authorization of the Security Council and after consultation with appropriate regional agencies, may establish regional subcommittees.

Article 48

1. The action required to carry out the decisions of the Security Council for the maintenance of international peace and security shall be taken by all the Members of the United Nations or by some of them, as the Security Council may determine.

2. Such decisions shall be carried out by the Members of the United Nations directly and through their action in the appropriate international agencies of which they are members.

Article 49

The Members of the United Nations shall join in affording mutual assistance in carrying out the measures decided upon by the Security Council.

Article 50

If preventive or enforcement measures against any state are taken by the Security Council, any other state, whether a Member of the United Nations or not, which finds itself confronted with special economic problems arising from the carrying out of those measures shall have the right to consult the Security Council with regard to a solution of those problems.

Article 51

Nothing in the present Charter shall impair the inherent right of individual or collective self-defense if an armed attack occurs against a Member of the United Nations, until the Security Council has taken measures necessary to maintain international peace and security. Measures taken by Members in the exercise of this right of self-defense shall be immediately reported to the Security Council and shall not in any way affect the authority and responsibility of the Security Council under the present Charter to take at any time such action as it deems necessary in order to maintain or restore international peace and security.

CHAPTER VIII

REGIONAL ARRANGEMENTS

Article 52

1. Nothing in the present Charter precludes the existence of regional arrangements or agencies for dealing with such matters relating to the maintenance of international peace and security as are appropriate for regional action, provided that such arrangements or agencies and their activities are consistent with the Purposes and Principles of the United Nations.

2. The Members of the United Nations entering into such arrangements or constituting such agencies shall make every effort to achieve pacific settlement of local disputes through such regional arrangements or by such regional agencies before referring them to the Security Council.

3. The Security Council shall encourage the development of pacific settlement of local disputes through such regional arrangements or by such regional agencies either on the initiative of the states concerned or by reference from the Security Council.

4. This Article in no way impairs the application of Articles 34 and 35.

Article 53

1. The Security Council shall, where appropriate, utilize such regional arrangements or agencies for enforcement action under its authority. But no enforcement action shall be taken under regional arrangements or by regional agencies without the authorization of the Security Council, with the exception of measures against any enemy state, as defined in paragraph 2 of this Article, provided for pursuant to Article 107 or in regional arrangements directed against renewal of aggressive policy on the part of any such state, until such time as the Organization may, on request of the Governments concerned, be charged with the responsibility for preventing further aggression by such a state.

2. The term enemy state as used in paragraph 1 of this Article applies to any state which during the Second World War has been an enemy of any signatory of the present Charter.

Article 54

The Security Council shall at all times be kept fully informed of activities undertaken or in contemplation under regional arrangements or by regional agencies for the maintenance of international peace and security.

CHAPTER IX

INTERNATIONAL ECONOMIC AND SOCIAL CO-OPERATION

Article 55

With a view to the creation of conditions of stability and well-being which are necessary for peaceful and friendly relations among nations based on respect for the principle of equal rights and self-determination of peoples, the United Nations shall promote:

a. higher standards of living, full employment, and conditions of economic and social progress and development;

b. solutions of international economic, social, health, and related problems; and international cultural and educational co-operation; and

c. universal respect for, and observance of, human rights and fundamental freedoms for all without distinction as to race, sex, language, or religion.

Article 56

All Members pledge themselves to take joint and separate action in cooperation with the Organization for the achievement of the purposes set forth in Article 55.

Article 57

1. The various specialized agencies, established by intergovernmental agreement and having wide international responsibilities, as defined in their basic instruments, in economic, social, cultural, educational, health, and related fields, shall be brought into relationship with the United Nations in accordance with the provisions of Article 63.

2. Such agencies thus brought into relationship with the United Nations are hereinafter referred to as specialized agencies.

Article 58

The Organization shall make recommendations for the coordination of the policies and activities of the specialized agencies.

Article 59

The Organization shall, where appropriate, initiate negotiations among the states concerned for the creation of any new specialized agencies required for the accomplishment of the purposes set forth in Article 55.

Article 60

Responsibility for the discharge of the functions of the Organization set forth in this Chapter shall be vested in the General Assembly and, under the authority of the General Assembly, in the Economic and Social Council, which shall have for this purpose the powers set forth in Chapter X.

CHAPTER X

THE ECONOMIC AND SOCIAL COUNCIL

Composition

Article 61

1. The Economic and Social Council shall consist of fifty-four Members of the United Nations elected by the General Assembly.

2. Subject to the provisions of paragraph 3, eighteen members of the Economic and Social Council shall be elected each year for a term of three years. A retiring member shall be eligible for immediate re-election.

3. At the first election after the increase in the membership of the Economic and Social Council from twenty-seven to fifty-four members, in addition to the members elected in place of the nine members whose term of office expires at the end of that year, twenty-seven additional members shall be elected. Of these twenty-seven additional members, the term of office of nine members so elected shall expire at the end of one year, and of nine other members at the end of two years, in accordance with arrangements made by the General Assembly.

4. Each member of the Economic and Social Council shall have one representative.

Functions and Powers

Article 62

1. The Economic and Social Council may make or initiate studies and reports with respect to international economic, social, cultural, educational, health, and related matters and may make recommendations with respect to any such matters to the General Assembly, to the Members of the United Nations, and to the specialized agencies concerned.

2. It may make recommendations for the purpose of promoting respect for, and observance of, human rights and fundamental freedoms for all.

3. It may prepare draft conventions for submission to the General Assembly, with respect to matters falling within its competence.

4. It may call, in accordance with the rules prescribed by the United Nations, international conferences on matters falling within its competence.

Article 63

1. The Economic and Social Council may enter into agreements with any of the agencies referred to in Article 57, defining the terms on which the agency concerned shall be brought into relationship with the United Nations. Such agreements shall be subject to approval by the General Assembly.

2. It may coordinate the activities of the specialized agencies through consultation with and recommendations to such agencies and through recommendations to the General Assembly and to the Members of the United Nations.

Article 64

1. The Economic and Social Council may take appropriate steps to obtain regular reports from the specialized agencies. It may make arrangements with the Members of the United Nations and with the specialized agencies to obtain reports on the steps taken to give effect to its own recommendations and to recommendations on matters falling within its competence made by the General Assembly.

2. It may communicate its observations on these reports to the General Assembly.

Article 65

The Economic and Social Council may furnish information to the Security Council and shall assist the Security Council upon its request.

Article 66

1. The Economic and Social Council shall perform such functions as fall within its competence in connection with the carrying out of the recommendations of the General Assembly.

2. It may, with the approval of the General Assembly, perform services at the request of Members of the United Nations and at the request of specialized agencies.

3. It shall perform such other functions as are specified elsewhere in the present Charter or as may be assigned to it by the General Assembly.

Article 67

1. Each member of the Economic and Social Council shall have one vote.

2. Decisions of the Economic and Social Council shall be made by a majority of the members present and voting.

Procedure

Article 68

The Economic and Social Council shall set up commissions in economic and social fields and for the promotion of human rights, and such other commissions as may be required for the performance of its functions.

Article 69

The Economic and Social Council shall invite any Member of the United Nations to participate, without vote, in its deliberations on any matter of particular concern to that Member.

Article 70

The Economic and Social Council may make arrangements for representatives of the specialized agencies to participate, without vote, in its deliberations and in those of the commissions established by it, and for its representatives to participate in the deliberations of the specialized agencies.

Article 71

The Economic and Social Council may make suitable arrangements for consultation with non-governmental organizations which are concerned with matters within its competence. Such arrangements may be made with international organizations and, where appropriate, with national organizations after consultation with the Member of the United Nations concerned.

Article 72

1. The Economic and Social Council shall adopt its own rules of procedure, including the method of selecting its President.

2. The Economic and Social Council shall meet as required in accordance with its rules, which shall include provision for the convening of meetings on the request of a majority of its members.

CHAPTER XI

DECLARATION REGARDING NON-SELF-GOVERNING TERRITORIES

Article 73

Members of the United Nations which have or assume responsibilities for the administration of territories whose peoples have not yet attained a full measure of self-government recognize the principle that the interests of the inhabitants of these territories are paramount, and accept as a sacred trust the obligation to promote to the utmost, within the system of international peace and security established by the present Charter, the well-being of the inhabitants of these territories, and, to this end:

a. to ensure, with due respect for the culture of the peoples concerned, their political, economic, social, and educational advancement, their just treatment, and their protection against abuses;

b. to develop self-government, to take due account of the political aspirations of the peoples, and to assist them in the progressive development of their free political institutions, according to the particular circumstances of each territory and its peoples and their varying stages of advancement;

c. to further international peace and security;

d. to promote constructive measures of development, to encourage research, and to cooperate with one another and, when and where appropriate, with specialized international bodies with a view to the practical achievement of the social, economic, and scientific purposes set forth in this Article; and

e. to transmit regularly to the Secretary-General for information purposes, subject to such limitation as security and constitutional considerations may require, statistical and other information of a technical nature relating to economic, social, and educational conditions in the territories for which they are respectively responsible other than those territories to which Chapters XII and XIII apply.

Article 74

Members of the United Nations also agree that their policy in respect of the territories to which this Chapter applies, no less than in respect of their metropolitan areas, must be based on the general principle of good-neighborliness, due account being taken of the interests and well-being of the rest of the world, in social, economic, and commercial matters.

CHAPTER XII

INTERNATIONAL TRUSTEESHIP SYSTEM

Article 75

The United Nations shall establish under its authority an international trusteeship system for the administration and supervision of such territories as may be placed thereunder by subsequent individual agreements. These territories are hereinafter referred to as trust territories.

Article 76

The basic objectives of the trusteeship system, in accordance with the Purposes of the United Nations laid down in Article 1 of the present Charter, shall be:

a. to further international peace and security;

b. to promote the political, economic, social, and educational advancement of the inhabitants of the trust territories, and their progressive development towards self-government or independence as may be appropriate to the particular circumstances of each territory and its peoples and the freely expressed wishes of the peoples concerned, and as may be provided by the terms of each trusteeship agreement;

c. to encourage respect for human rights and for fundamental freedoms for all without distinction as to race, sex, language, or religion, and to encourage recognition of the interdependence of the peoples of the world; and

d. to ensure equal treatment in social, economic, and commercial matters for all Members of the United Nations and their nationals and also equal treatment for the latter in the administration of justice without prejudice to the attainment of the foregoing objectives and subject to the provisions of Article 80.

Article 77

1. The trusteeship system shall apply to such territories in the following categories as may be placed thereunder by means of trusteeship agreements:

a. territories now held under mandate;

b. territories which may be detached from enemy states as a result of the Second World War, and

c. territories voluntarily placed under the system by states responsible for their administration.

2. It will be a matter for subsequent agreement as to which territories in the foregoing categories will be brought under the trusteeship system and upon what terms.

Article 78

The trusteeship system shall not apply to territories which have become Members of the United Nations, relationship among which shall be based on respect for the principle of sovereign equality.

Article 79

The terms of trusteeship for each territory to be placed under the trusteeship system, including any alteration or amendment, shall be agreed upon by the states directly concerned, including the mandatory power in the case of territories held under mandate by a Member of the United Nations, and shall be approved as provided for in Articles 83 and 85.

Article 80

1. Except as may be agreed upon in individual trusteeship agreements, made under Articles 77, 79, and 81, placing each territory under the trusteeship system, and until such agreements have been concluded, nothing in this Chapter shall be construed in or of itself to alter in any manner the rights whatsoever of any states or any peoples or the terms of existing international instruments to which Members of the United Nations may respectively be parties.

2. Paragraph 1 of this Article shall not be interpreted as giving grounds for delay or postponement of the negotiation and conclusion of agreements for placing mandated and other territories under the trusteeship system as provided for in Article 77.

Article 81

The trusteeship agreement shall in each case include the terms under which the trust territory will be administered and designate the authority which will exercise the administration of the trust territory. Such authority, hereinafter called the administering authority, may be one or more states or the Organization itself.

Article 82

There may be designated, in any trusteeship agreement, a strategic area or areas which may include part or all of the trust territory to which the agreement applies, without prejudice to any special agreement or agreements made under Article 43.

Article 83

1. All functions of the United Nations relating to strategic areas, including the approval of the terms of the trusteeship agreements and of their alteration or amendment, shall be exercised by the Security Council.

2. The basic objectives set forth in Article 76 shall be applicable to the people of each strategic area.

3. The Security Council shall, subject to the provisions of the trusteeship agreements and without prejudice to security considerations, avail itself of the assistance of the Trusteeship Council to perform those functions of the United Nations under the trusteeship system relating to political. economic, social, and educational matters in the strategic areas.

Article 84

It shall be the duty of the administering authority to ensure that the trust territory shall play its part in the maintenance of international peace and security. To this end the administering authority may make use of volunteer forces, facilities, and assistance from the trust territory in carrying out the obligations towards the Security Council undertaken in this regard by the administering authority, as well as for local defense and the maintenance of law and order within the trust territory.

Article 85

1. The functions of the United Nations with regard to trusteeship agreements for all areas not designated as strategic, including the approval of the terms of the trusteeship agreements and of their alteration or amendment, shall be exercised by the General Assembly.

2. The Trusteeship Council, operating under the authority of the General Assembly, shall assist the General Assembly in carrying out these functions.

CHAPTER XIII

THE TRUSTEESHIP COUNCIL

Composition

Article 86

1. The Trusteeship Council shall consist of the following Members of the United Nations:

   a. those Members administering trust territories;

   b. such of those Members mentioned by name in Article 23 as are not administering trust territories; and

c. as many other Members elected for three-year terms by the General Assembly as may be necessary to ensure that the total number of members of the Trusteeship Council is equally divided between those Members of the United Nations which administer trust territories and those which do not.

2. Each member of the Trusteeship Council shall designate one specially qualified person to represent it therein.

Functions and Powers

Article 87

The General Assembly and, under its authority, the Trusteeship Council, in carrying out their functions, may:

a. consider reports submitted by the administering authority;

b. accept petitions and examine them in consultation with the administering authority;

c. provide for periodic visits to the respective trust territories at times agreed upon with the administering authority; and

d. take these and other actions in conformity with the terms of the trusteeship agreements.

Article 88

The Trusteeship Council shall formulate a questionnaire on the political, economic, social, and educational advancement of the inhabitants of each trust territory, and the administering authority for each trust territory within the competence of the General Assembly shall make an annual report to the General Assembly upon the basis of such questionnaire.

Voting

Article 89

1. Each member of the Trusteeship Council shall have one vote.

2. Decisions of the Trusteeship Council shall be made by a majority of the members present and voting.

Procedure

Article 90

1. The Trusteeship Council shall adopt its own rules of procedure, including the method of selecting its President.

2. The Trusteeship Council shall meet as required in accordance with its rules, which shall include provision for the convening of meetings on the request of a majority of its members.

Article 91

The Trusteeship Council shall, when appropriate, avail itself of the assistance of the Economic and Social Council and of the specialized agencies in regard to matters with which they are respectively concerned.

CHAPTER XIV

THE INTERNATIONAL COURT OF JUSTICE

Article 92

The International Court of Justice shall be the principal judicial organ of the United Nations. It shall function in accordance with the annexed Statute which is based upon the Statute of the Permanent Court of International Justice and forms an integral part of the present Charter.

Article 93

1. All Members of the United Nations are ipso facto parties to the Statute of the International Court of Justice.

2. A state which is not a Member of the United Nations may become a party to the Statute of the International Court of Justice on conditions to be determined in each case by the General Assembly upon the recommendation of the Security Council.

Article 94

1. Each Member of the United Nations undertakes to comply with the decision of the International Court of Justice in any case to which it is a party.

2. If any party to a case fails to perform the obligations incumbent upon it under a judgment rendered by the Court, the other party may have recourse to the Security Council, which may, if it deems necessary, make recommendations or decide upon measures to be taken to give effect to the judgment.

Article 95

Nothing in the present Charter shall prevent Members of the United Nations from entrusting the solution of their differences to other tribunals by virtue of agreements already in existence or which may be concluded in the future.

Article 96

1. The General Assembly or the Security Council may request the International Court of Justice to give an advisory opinion on any legal question.

2. Other organs of the United Nations and specialized agencies, which may at any time be so authorized by the General Assembly, may also request advisory opinions of the Court on legal questions arising within the scope of their activities.

CHAPTER XV

THE SECRETARIAT

Article 97

The Secretariat shall comprise a Secretary-General and such staff as the Organization may require. The Secretary-General shall be appointed by the General Assembly upon the recommendation of the Security Council. He shall be the chief administrative officer of the Organization.

Article 98

The Secretary-General shall act in that capacity in all meetings of the General Assembly, of the Security Council, of the Economic and Social Council, and of the Trusteeship Council, and shall perform such other functions as are entrusted to him by these organs. The Secretary-General shall make an annual report to the General Assembly on the work of the Organization.

Article 99

The Secretary-General may bring to the attention of the Security Council any matter which in his opinion may threaten the maintenance of international peace and security.

Article 100

1. In the performance of their duties the Secretary-General and the staff shall not seek or receive instructions from any government or from any other authority external to the Organization. They shall refrain from any action which might reflect on their position as international officials responsible only to the Organization.

2. Each Member of the United Nations undertakes to respect the exclusively international character of the responsibilities of the Secretary-General and the staff and not to seek to influence them in the discharge of their responsibilities.

Article 101

1. The staff shall be appointed by the Secretary-General under regulations established by the General Assembly.

2. Appropriate staffs shall be permanently assigned to the Economic and Social Council, the Trusteeship Council, and, as required, to other organs of the United Nations. These staffs shall form a part of the Secretariat.

3. The paramount consideration in the employment of the staff and in the determination of the conditions of service shall be the necessity of securing the highest standards of efficiency, competence, and integrity. Due regard shall be paid to the importance of recruiting the staff on as wide a geographical basis as possible.

CHAPTER XVI

MISCELLANEOUS PROVISIONS

Article 102

1. Every treaty and every international agreement entered into by any Member of the United Nations after the present Charter comes into force shall as soon as possible be registered with the Secretariat and published by it.

2. No party to any such treaty or international agreement which has not been registered in accordance with the provisions of paragraph I of this Article may invoke that treaty or agreement before any organ of the United Nations.

Article 103

In the event of a conflict between the obligations of the Members of the United Nations under the present Charter and their obligations under any other international agreement, their obligations under the present Charter shall prevail.

Article 104

The Organization shall enjoy in the territory of each of its Members such legal capacity as may be necessary for the exercise of its functions and the fulfillment of its purposes.

Article 105

1. The Organization shall enjoy in the territory of each of its Members such privileges and immunities as are necessary for the fulfillment of its purposes.

2. Representatives of the Members of the United Nations and officials of the Organization shall similarly enjoy such privileges and immunities as are necessary for the independent exercise of their functions in connection with the Organization.

3. The General Assembly may make recommendations with a view to determining the details of the application of paragraphs 1 and 2 of this Article or may propose conventions to the Members of the United Nations for this purpose.

CHAPTER XVII

TRANSITIONAL SECURITY ARRANGEMENTS

Article 106

Pending the coming into force of such special agreements referred to in Article 43 as in the opinion of the Security Council enable it to begin the exercise of its responsibilities under Article 42, the parties to the Four-Nation Declaration, signed at Moscow October 30, 1943, and France, shall, in accordance with the provisions of paragraph 5 of that Declaration, consult with one another and as occasion requires with other Members of the United Nations with a view to such joint action on behalf of the Organization as may be necessary for the purpose of maintaining international peace and security.

Article 107

Nothing in the present Charter shall invalidate or preclude action, in relation to any state which during the Second World War has been an enemy of any signatory to the present Charter, taken or authorized as a result of that war by the Governments having responsibility for such action.

CHAPTER XVIII

AMENDMENTS

Article 108

Amendments to the present Charter shall come into force for all Members of the United Nations when they have been adopted by a vote of two thirds of the members of the General Assembly and ratified in accordance with their respective constitutional processes by two thirds of the Members of the United Nations, including all the permanent members of the Security Council.

Article 109

1. A General Conference of the Members of the United Nations for the purpose of reviewing the present Charter may be held at a date and place to be fixed by a two-thirds vote of

the members of the General Assembly and by a vote of any seven members of the Security Council. Each Member of the United Nations shall have one vote in the conference.

2. Any alteration of the present Charter recommended by a two-thirds vote of the conference shall take effect when ratified in accordance with their respective constitutional processes by two thirds of the Members of the United Nations including all the permanent members of the Security Council.

3. If such a conference has not been held before the tenth annual session of the General Assembly following the coming into force of the present Charter, the proposal to call such a conference shall be placed on the agenda of that session of the General Assembly, and the conference shall be held if so decided by a majority vote of the members of the General Assembly and by a vote of any seven members of the Security Council.

CHAPTER XIX

RATIFICATION AND SIGNATURE

Article 110

1. The present Charter shall be ratified by the signatory states in accordance with their respective constitutional processes.

2. The ratifications shall be deposited with the Government of the United States of America, which shall notify all the signatory states of each deposit as well as the Secretary-General of the Organization when he has been appointed.

3. The present Charter shall come into force upon the deposit of ratifications by the Republic of China, France, the Union of Soviet Socialist Republics, the United Kingdom of Great Britain and Northern Ireland, and the United States of America, and by a majority of the other signatory states. A protocol of the ratifications deposited shall thereupon be drawn up by the Government of the United States of America which shall communicate copies thereof to all the signatory states.

4. The states signatory to the present Charter which ratify it after it has come into force will become original Members of the United Nations on the date of the deposit of their respective ratifications.

Article 111

The present Charter, of which the Chinese, French, Russian, English, and Spanish texts are equally authentic, shall remain deposited in the archives of the Government of the United States of America. Duly certified copies thereof shall be transmitted by that Government to the Governments of the other signatory states.

STATUTE OF THE INTERNATIONAL COURT OF JUSTICE

Adopted in 1945 as an integral part of the UN Charter

Article 1

The International Court of Justice established by the Charter of the United Nations as the principal judicial organ of the United Nations shall be constituted and shall function in accordance with the provisions of the present Statute.

Chapter I. Organization of the Court.

Article 2

The Court shall be composed of a body of independent judges, elected regardless of their nationality from among persons of high moral character, who possess the qualifications required in their respective countries for appointment to the highest judicial offices, or are juris consults of recognized competence in international law.

Article 3

(1) The Court shall consist of fifteen members, no two of whom may be nationals of the same state.

(2) A person who for the purposes of membership in the Court be regarded as a national of more than one state shall be deemed to be a national of the one in which he ordinarily exercises civil and political rights.

Article 4

(1) The members of the Court shall be elected by the General Assembly and by the Security Council from a list of persons nominated by the national groups in the Permanent Court of Arbitration, in accordance with the following provisions.

(2) In the case of Members of the United Nations not represented in the Permanent Court of Arbitration, candidates shall be nominated by national groups appointed for this purpose by their governments under the same conditions as those prescribed for members of the Permanent Court of Arbitration by Article 44 of the Convention of The Hague of 1907 for the pacific settlement of international disputes.

(3) The conditions under which a state which is a party to the present Statute but is not a Member of the United Nations may participate in electing the members of the Court shall, in the absence of a special agreement, be laid down by the General Assembly upon recommendation of the Security Council.

Article 5

(1) At least three months before the date of the election, the Secretary-General of the United Nations shall address a written request to the members of the Permanent Court of Arbitration belonging to the states which are parties to the present Statute, and to the members of the national groups appointed under Article 4, paragraph 2, inviting them to undertake, within a given time, by national groups, the nomination of persons in a position to accept the duties of a member of the Court.

(2) No group may nominate more than four persons, not more than two of whom shall be of their own nationality, In no case may the number of candidates nominated by a group be more than double the number of seats to be filled.

Article 6

Before making these nominations, each national group is recommended to consult its highest court of justice, its legal faculties and schools of law, and its national academies and national sections of international academies devoted to the study of law.

Article 7

(1) The Secretary-General shall prepare a list in alphabetical order of all the persons thus nominated. Save as provided in Article 12, paragraph 2, these shall be the only persons eligible.

(2) The Secretary-General shall submit this list to the General Assembly and to the Security Council.

Article 8

The General Assembly and the Security Council shall proceed independently of one another to elect the members of the Court.

Article 9

At every election, the electors shall bear in mind not only that the person to be elected should individually possess the qualifications required, but also that in the body as a whole the representation of the main forms of civilization and of the principal legal systems of the world should be assured.

Article 10

(1) Those candidates who obtain an absolute majority of votes in the General Assembly and in the Security Council shall be considered as elected.

(2) Any vote of the Security Council, whether for the election of judges or for the appointment of members of the conference envisaged in Article 12, shall be taken without any distinction between permanent and non-permanent members of the Security Council.

(3) In the event of more than one national of the same state obtaining an absolute majority of the votes both of the General Assembly and of the Security Council, the eldest of these only shall be considered as elected.

Article 11

If, after the first meeting held for the purpose of the election, one or more seats remain to be filled, a second and, if necessary, a third meeting shall take place.

Article 12

(1) If, after the third meeting, one or more seats still remain unfilled, a joint conference consisting of six members, three appointed by the General Assembly and three by the Security Council, may be formed at any time at the request of either the General Assembly or the Security Council, for the purpose of choosing by the vote of an absolute majority one

name for each seat still vacant, to submit to the General Assembly and the Security Council for their respective acceptance.

(2) If the joint conference is unanimously agreed upon any person who fulfils the required conditions, he may be included in its list, even though he was not included in the list of nominations referred to in Article 7.

(3) If the joint conference is satisfied that it will not be successful in procuring an election, those members of the Court who have already been elected shall, within a period to be fixed by the Security Council, proceed to fill the vacant seats by selection from among those candidates who have obtained votes either in the General Assembly or in the Security Council.

(4) In the event of an equality of votes among the judges, the eldest judge shall have a casting vote.

Article 13

(1) The members of the Court shall be elected for nine years and may be re-elected; provided, however, that of the judges elected at the first election, the terms of judges shall expire at the end of thee years and the terms of five more judges shall expire at the end of six years.

(2) The judges whose terms are to expire at the end of the above-mentioned initial periods of three and six years shall be chosen by lot to be drawn by the Secretary-General immediately after the first election has been completed.

(3) The members of the Court shall continue to discharge their duties until their places have been filled. Though replaced, they shall finish any cases which they may have begun.

(4) In the case of the resignation of a member of the Court, the resignation shall be addressed to the President of the Court for transmission to the Secretary-General. This last notification makes the place vacant.

Article 14

Vacancies shall be filled by the same method as that laid down for the first election, subject to the following provision: the Secretary-General shall, within one month of the occurrence of the vacancy, proceed to issue the invitations provided for in Article 5, and the date of the election shall be fixed by the Security Council.

Article 15

A member of the Court elected to replace a member whose term of office has not expired shall hold office for the remainder of his predecessor's term.

Article 16

(1) No member of the Court may exercise any political or administrative function, or engage in any other occupation of a professional nature.

(2) Any doubt on this point shall be settled by the decision of the Court.

Article 17

(1) No member of the Court may act as agent, counsel, or advocate in any case.

(2) No member may participate in the decision of any case in which he has previously taken part as agent, counsel or advocate for one of the parties, or as a member of a national or international court, or of a commission of enquiry, or in any other capacity.

(3) Any doubt on this point shall be settled by the decision of the Court.

Article 18

(1) No member of the Court can be dismissed unless, in the unanimous opinion of the other members, be has ceased to fulfil the required conditions.

(2) Formal notification thereof shall be made to the Secretary-General by the Registrar.

(3) This notification makes the place vacant.

Article 19

The members of the Court, when engaged in the business of the Court, shall enjoy diplomatic privileges and immunities.

Article 20

Every member of the Court shall, before taking up his duties, make a solemn declaration in open court that he will exercise his powers impartially and conscientiously.

Article 21

(1) The Court shall elect its President and Vice-President for three years; they may be re-elected.

(2) The Court shall appoint its Registrar and may provide for the appointment of such other officers as may be necessary.

Article 22

(1) The seat of the Court shall be established at The Hague. This, however, shall not prevent the Court from sitting and exercising its functions elsewhere whenever the Court considers it desirable.

(2) The President and the Registrar shall reside at the seat of the Court.

Article 23

(1) The Court shall remain permanently in session, except during the judicial vacations, the dates and duration of which shall be fixed by the Court.

(2) Members of the Court are entitled to periodic leave, the dates and duration of which shall be fixed by the Court, having in mind the distance between The Hague and the home of each judge.

(3) Members of the Court shall be bound, unless they are on leave or prevented from attending by illness or other serious reasons duly explained to the President, to hold themselves permanently at the disposal of the Court.

Article 24

(1) If, for some special reason, a member of the Court considers that he should not take part in the decision of a particular case, he shall so inform the President.

(2) If the President considers that for some special one of the members of the Court should not sit in a particular case, he shall give him notice accordingly.

(3) If in any such case the member of the Court and the President disagree, the matter shall be settled by the decision of the Court.

Article 25

(1) The full Court shall sit except when it is expressly provided otherwise in the present Statute.

(2) Subject to the condition that the number of judges available to constitute the Court is not thereby reduced below eleven, the Rules of the Court may provide for allowing one or more judges, according to circumstances and in rotation, to be dispensed from sitting.

(3) A quorum of nine judges shall suffice to constitute the Court.

Article 26

(1) The Court may from time to time form one or more chambers, composed of three or more judges as the Court may determine, for dealing with particular categories of cases; for example, labour cases and cases relating to transit and communications.

(2) The Court may at any time form a chamber for dealing with a particular case. The number of judges to constitute such a chamber shall be determined by the Court with the approval of the parties.

(3) Cases shall be heard and determined by the chambers provided for in this Article if the parties so request.

Article 27

A judgment given by any of the chambers provided for in Articles 26 and 29 shall be considered as rendered by the Court.

Article 28

The chambers provided for in Articles 26 and 29 may, with the consent of the parties, sit and exercise their functions elsewhere than at The Hague.

Article 29

With a view to the speedy dispatch of business, the Court shall form annually a chamber composed of five judges which, at the request of the parties, may hear and determine cases by summary procedure. In addition, two judges shall be selected for the purpose of replacing judges who find it impossible to sit.

Article 30

(1) The Court shall frame rules for carrying out its functions. In particular, it shall lay down rules of procedure.

(2) The Rules of the Court may provide for assessors to sit with the Court or with any of its chambers, without the right to vote.

Article 31

(1) Judges of the nationality of each of the parties shall retain their right to sit in the case before the Court.

(2) If the Court includes upon the Bench a judge of the nationality of one of the parties, any other party may choose a person to sit as judge. Such person shall be chosen preferably from among those persons who have been nominated as candidates as provided in Articles 4 and 5.

(3) If the Court includes upon the Bench no judge of the nationality of the parties, each of these parties may proceed to choose a judge as provided in paragraph 2 of this Article.

(4) The provisions of this Article shall apply to the case of Article 26 and 29. In such cases, the President shall request one or, if necessary two of the members of the Court forming the chamber to give place to the member of the Court of the nationality of the parties concerned, and, failing such, or if they are unable to be present, to the judges specially chosen by the parties.

(5) Should there be several parties in the same interest, they shall, for the purpose of the preceding provisions, be reckoned as one party only. Any doubt upon this point shall be settled by the decision of the Court.

(6) Judges chosen as laid down in paragraphs 2, 3, and 4 of this Article shall fulfil the conditions required by Articles 2, 17 (paragraph 2), 20, and 24 of the present Statute. They shall take part in the decision on terms of complete equality with their colleagues.

Article 32

(1) Each member of the court shall receive an annual salary.

(2) The President shall receive a special annual allowance.

(3) The Vice-President shall receive a special allowance for every day on which he acts as President.

(4) The judges chosen under Article 31, other than members of the Court, shall receive compensation for each day on which they exercise their functions.

(5) These salaries, allowances. and compensation shall be fixed by the General Assembly. They may not be decreased during the term of office.

(6) The salary of the Registrar shall be fixed by the General Assembly on the proposal of the Court.

(7) Regulations made by the General Assembly shall fix the conditions under which retirement pensions may be given to members of the Court and to the Registrar and the conditions under which members of the Court and the Registrar shall have their travelling expenses refunded.

(8) The above salaries, allowances, and compensation shall be free of all taxation.

Article 33

The expenses of the Court shall be borne by the United Nations in such a manner as shall be decided by the General Assembly.

Chapter II. Competence of the Court.

Article 34

(1) Only states may be parties in cases before the Court.

(2) The Court, subject to and in conformity with its Rules, may request of public international organizations information relevant to cases before it, and shall receive such information presented by such organizations on their own initiative.

(3) Whenever the construction of the constituent instrument of a public international organization or of an international convention adopted thereunder is in question in a case before the Court, the Registrar shall so notify the public international organization concerned and shall communicate to it copies of all the written proceedings.

Article 35

(1) The Court shall be open to the states parties to the present Statute.

(2) The conditions under which the Court shall be open to other states shall, subject to the special provisions contained in treaties in force, be laid down by the Security Council, but in no case shall such conditions place the parties in position of inequality before the Court

(3) When a state which is not a Member of the United Nations is a party to a case, the Court shall fix the amount which the party is to contribute towards the expenses of the Court. This provision shall not apply if such state is bearing a share of the expenses of the Court.

Article 36

(1) The jurisdiction of the Court comprises all cases which the parties refer to it and all matters specially provided for in the Charter of the United Nations or in treaties and conventions in force.

(2) The states parties to the present Statute may at any time declare that they recognize as compulsory ipso facto and without special agreement, in relation to any other state accepting the same obligation, the jurisdiction of the Court in all legal disputes concerning:

(a) the interpretation of a treaty;

(b) any question of international law;

(c) the existence of any fact which, if established, would constitute a breach of an international obligation;

(d) the nature of extent of the reparation to be made for the breach of an international obligation.

(3) The declarations referred to above may be made unconditionally or on condition of reciprocity on the part of several or certain states, or for a certain time

(4) Such declarations shall be deposited with the Secretary-General of the United Nations, who shall transmit copies thereof to the parties to the Statute and to the Registrar of the Court.

(5) Declarations made under Article 36 of the Statute of the Permanent Court of International Justice and which are still in force shall be deemed, as between the parties to the present Statute, to be acceptances of the compulsory jurisdiction of the International Court of Justice for the period which they still have to run and in accordance with their terms.

(6) In the event of a dispute as to whether the Court has jurisdiction, the matter shall be settled by the decision of the Court.

Article 37

Whenever a treaty or convention in force provides for reference of a matter to a tribunal to have been instituted by the League of Nations, or to the Permanent Court of International Justice, the matter shall, as between the parties to the present Statute, be referred to the International Court of Justice.

Article 38

(1) The Court, whose function is to decide in accordance with international law such disputes as are submitted to it, shall apply:

(a) international conventions, whether general or particular, establishing rules expressly recognized by the contesting states;

(b) international custom, as evidence of a general practice accepted as law;

(c) the general principles of law recognized by civilized nations;

(d) subject to the provisions of Article 59, judicial decisions and the teachings of the most highly qualified publicists of the various nations, as subsidiary means for the determination of rules of law.

(2) This provision shall not prejudice the power of the Court to decide a case ex aequo et bono, if the parties agree thereto.

Chapter III. Procedure

Article 39

(1) The official languages of the Court shall be French and English. If the parties agree that the case shall be conducted in French, the judgment shall be delivered in French. If the parties agree that the case shall be conducted in English, the judgment shall be delivered in English.

(2) In the absence of an agreement as to which language shall be employed, each party may, in the pleadings, use the language which it prefers; the decision of the Court shall be given in French and English. In this case the Court shall at the same time determine which of the two texts shall be considered as authoritative.

(3) The Court shall, at the request of any party authorize a language other than French or English to be used by that party.

Article 40

(1) Cases are brought before the Court, as the case may be, either by the notification of the special agreement or by a written application addressed to the Registrar. In either case the subject of the dispute and the parties shall be indicated.

(2) The Registrar shall forthwith communicate the application to all concerned.

(3) He shall also notify the Members of the United Nations through the Secretary-General, and also any other states entitled to appear before the Court.

Article 41

(1) The Court shall have the power to indicate, if it considers that circumstances so require, any provisional measures which ought to be taken to preserve the respective rights of either party.

(2) Pending the final decision, notice of the measures suggested shall forthwith be given to the parties and to the Security Council.

Article 42

(1) The parties shall be represented by agents

(2) They may have the assistance of counsel or advocates before the Court.

(3) The agents, counsel, and advocates of parties before the Court shall enjoy the privileges and immunities necessary to the independent exercise of their duties.

Article 43

(1) The procedure shall consist of two parts: written and oral.

(2) The written proceedings shall consist of the communication to the Court and to the parties of memorials, counter-memorials and, if necessary, replies; also all papers and documents in support.

(3) These communications shall be made through the Registrar, in the order and within the time fixed by the Court.

(4) A certified copy of every document produced by one party shall be communicated to the other party.

(5) The oral proceedings shall consist of the hearing by the Court of witnesses, experts, agents, counsel, and advocates.

Article 44

(1) For the service of all notices upon persons other than the agents, counsel, and advocates, the Court shall apply direct to the government of the state upon whose territory the notice has to be served.

(2) The same provision shall apply whenever steps are to be taken to procure evidence on the spot.

Article 45

The hearing shall be under the control of the President or, if he is unable to preside, of the Vice-President; if neither is able to preside, the senior judge present shall preside.

Article 46

The hearing in Court shall be public, unless the Court shall decide otherwise, or unless the parties demand that the public be not admitted.

Article 47

(1) Minutes shall be made at each hearing and signed by the Registrar and the President

(2) These minutes alone shall be authentic

Article 48

The Court shall make orders for the conduct of the case, shall decide the form and time in which each party must conclude its arguments, and make all arrangements connected with the taking of evidence.

Article 49

The Court may, even before the hearing begins, call upon the agents to produce any document or to supply any explanations. Formal note shall be taken of any refusal.

Article 50

The Court may, at any time, entrust any individual, body, bureau, commission, or other organization that it may select, with the task of carrying out an enquiry or giving an expert opinion.

Article 51

During the hearing any relevant questions are to be put to the witnesses and experts under the conditions laid down by the Court in the rules of procedure referred to in Article 30.

Article 52

After the Court has received the proofs and evidence within the time specified for the purpose, it may refuse to accept any further oral or written evidence that one party may desire to present unless the other side consents.

Article 53

(1) Whenever one of the parties does not appear before the Court, or fails to defend its case, the other party may call upon the Court to decide in favour of its claim.

(2) The Court must, before doing so, satisfy itself, not only that it has jurisdiction in accordance with Article 36 and 37, but also that the claim is well founded in fact and law.

Article 54

(1) When, subject to the control of the Court, the agents, counsel, and advocates have completed their presentation of the case, the President shall declare the hearing closed.

(2) The Court shall withdraw to consider the judgment

(3) The deliberations of the Court shall take place in private and remain secret.

Article 55

(1) All questions shall be decided by a majority of the judges present.

(2) In the event of an equality of votes, the President or the judge who acts in his place shall have a casting vote.

Article 56

(1) The judgment shall state the reasons on which it is based.

(2) It shall contain the names of the judges who have taken part in the decision.

Article 57

If the judgment does not represent in whole or in part the unanimous opinion of the judges, any judge shall be entitled to deliver a separate opinion.

Article 58

The Judgment shall be signed by the President and by the Registrar. It shall be read in open court, due notice having been given to the agents.

Article 59

The decision of the Court has no binding force except between the parties and in respect of that particular case.

Article 60

The judgment is final and without appeal. In the event of dispute as to the meaning or scope of the judgment, the Court shall construe it upon the request of any party.

Article 61

(1) An application for revision of a judgment may be made only when it is based upon the discovery of some fact of such a nature as to be a decisive factor, which fact was, when the judgment was given, unknown to the Court and also to the party claiming revision, always provided that such ignorance was not due to negligence.

(2) The proceedings for revision shall be opened by a judgment of the Court expressly recording the existence of the new fact, recognizing that it has such a character as to lay the case open to revision, and declaring the application admissible on this ground.

(3) The Court may require previous compliance with the terms of the judgment before it admits proceedings in revision.

(4) The application for revision must be made at latest within six months of the discovery of the new fact.

(5) No application for revision may be made after the lapse of ten years from the date of the judgment.

Article 62

(1) Should a state consider that it has an interest of a legal nature which may be affected by the decision in the case, it may submit a request to the Court to be permitted to intervene.

(2) It shall be for the Court to decide upon this request

Article 63

(1) Whenever the construction of a convention to which states other than those concerned in the case are parties is in question, the Registrar shall notify all such states forthwith.

(2) Every state so notified has the right to intervene in the proceedings; but if it uses this right, the construction given by the judgment will be equally binding upon it.

Article 64

Unless otherwise decided by the Court, each party shall bear its own costs.

Chapter IV. Advisory Opinions

Article 65

(1) The Court may give an advisory opinion on any legal question at the request of whatever body may be authorized by or in accordance with the Charter of the United Nations to make such a request.

(2) Questions upon which the advisory opinion of the Court is asked shall be laid before the Court by means of a written request containing an exact statement of the question upon which an opinion is required, and accompanied by all documents likely lo throw light upon the question.

Article 66

(1) The Registrar shall forthwith give notice of the request for an advisory opinion to all states entitled to appear before the Court.

(2) The Registrar shall also, by means of a special and direct communication, notify any state entitled to appear before the Court or international organization considered by the Court, or, should it not be sitting, by the President, as likely to be able to furnish information on the question, that the Court will be prepared to receive, within a time limit to be fixed by the President, written statements, or to hear, at a public sitting to be held for the purpose, oral statements relating to the question.

(3) Should any such state entitled to appear before the Court have failed to receive the special communication referred to in paragraph 2 of this Article, such state may express a desire to submit a written statement or to be heard; and the Court will decide.

(4) States and organizations having presented written or oral statements or both shall be permitted to comment on the statements made by other states or organizations in the form, to the extent, and within the time limits which the Court, or, should it not be sitting, the President, shall decide in each particular case. Accordingly, the Registrar shall in due time communicate any such written statements to states and organizations having submitted similar statements.

Article 67

The Court shall deliver its advisory opinions in open court, notice having been given to the Secretary-General and to the representatives of Members of the United Nations, of other states and of international organizations immediately concerned.

Article 68

In the exercise of its advisory functions the Court shall further be guided by the provisions of the present Statute which apply in contentious cases to the extent to which it recognizes them to be applicable.

Chapter V. Amendment

Article 69

Amendments to the present Statute shall be effected by the same procedure as is provided by the Charter of the United Nations for amendments to that Charter, subject however to any provisions which the General Assembly upon recommendation of the Security Council may adopt concerning the participation of states which are parties to the present Statute but are not Members of the United Nations.

Article 70

The Court shall have power to propose such amendments to the present Statute as it may deem necessary, through written communications to the Secretary-General, for consideration in conformity with the provisions of Article 69.

VIENNA CONVENTION ON THE LAW OF TREATIES

Adopted at Vienna on 23 May 1969; in force on 27 January 1980

1155 U.N.T.S. 331

The States Parties to the present Convention

Considering the fundamental role of treaties in the history of international relations,

Recognizing the ever-increasing importance of treaties as a source of international law and as a means of developing peaceful co-operation among nations, whatever their constitutional and social systems,

Noting that the principles of free consent and of good faith and the *pacta sunt servanda* rule are universally recognized,

Affirming that disputes concerning treaties, like other international disputes, should be settled by peaceful means and in conformity with the principles of justice and international law,

Recalling the determination of the peoples of the United Nations to establish conditions under which justice and respect for the obligations arising from treaties can be maintained,

Having in mind the principles of international law embodied in the Charter of the United Nations, such as the principles of the equal rights and self-determination of peoples, of the sovereign equality and independence of all States, of non-interference in the domestic affairs of States, of the prohibition of the threat or use of force and of universal respect for, and observance of, human rights and fundamental freedoms for all,

Believing that the codification and progressive development of the law of treaties achieved in the present Convention will promote the purposes of the United Nations set forth in the Charter, namely, the maintenance of international peace and security, the development of friendly relations and the achievement of co-operation among nations,

Affirming that the rules of customary international law will continue to govern questions not regulated by the provisions of the present Convention,

Have agreed as follows:

PART I: INTRODUCTION

Article 1. Scope of the present Convention

The present Convention applies to treaties between States.

Article 2. Use of terms

1. For the purposes of the present Convention:

(a) 'treaty' means an international agreement concluded between States in written form and governed by international law, whether embodied in a single instrument or in two or more related instruments and whatever its particular designation;

(b) 'ratification', 'acceptance', 'approval' and 'accession' mean in each case the international act so named whereby a State establishes on the international plane its consent to be bound by a treaty;

(c) 'full powers' means a document emanating from the competent authority of a State designating a person or persons to represent the State for negotiating, adopting or authenticating the text of a treaty, for expressing the consent of the State to be bound by a treaty, or for accomplishing any other act with respect to a treaty;

(d) 'reservation' means a unilateral statement, however phrased or named, made by a State, when signing, ratifying, accepting, approving or acceding to a treaty, whereby it purports to exclude or to modify the legal effect of certain provisions of the treaty in their application to that State;

(e) 'negotiating State' means a State which took part in the drawing up and adoption of the text of the treaty;

(f) 'contracting State' means a State which has consented to be bound by the treaty, whether or not the treaty has entered into force;

(g) 'party' means a State which has consented to be bound by the treaty and for which the treaty is in force;

(h) 'third State' means a State not a party to the treaty;

(i) 'international organization' means an intergovernmental organization.

2. The provisions of paragraph 1 regarding the use of terms in the present Convention are without prejudice to the use of those terms or to the meanings which may be given to them in the internal law of any State.

Article 3. International agreements not within the scope of the present Convention

The fact that the present Convention does not apply to international agreements concluded between States and other subjects of international law or between such other subjects of international law, or to international agreements not in written form, shall not affect:

(a) the legal force of such agreements;

(b) the application to them of any of the rules set forth in the present Convention to which they would be subject under international law independently of the Convention;

(c) the application of the Convention to the relations of States as between themselves under international agreements to which other subjects of international law are also parties.

Article 4. Non-retroactivity of the present Convention

Without prejudice to the application of any rules set forth in the present Convention to which treaties would be subject under international law independently of the Convention, the Convention applies only to treaties which are concluded by States after the entry into force of the present Convention with regard to such States.

Article 5. Treaties constituting international organizations and treaties adopted within an international organization

The present Convention applies to any treaty which is the constituent instrument of an international organization and to any treaty adopted within an international organization without prejudice to any relevant rules of the organization.

PART II: CONCLUSION AND ENTRY INTO FORCE OF TREATIES

SECTION 1. CONCLUSION OF TREATIES

Article 6. Capacity of States to conclude treaties

Every State possesses capacity to conclude treaties.

Article 7. Full powers

1. A person is considered as representing a State for the purpose of adopting or authenticating the text of a treaty or for the purpose of expressing the consent of the State to be bound by a treaty if:

(a) he produces appropriate full powers; or

(b) it appears from the practice of the States concerned or from other circumstances that their intention was to consider that person as representing the State for such purposes and to dispense with full powers.

2. In virtue of their functions and without having to produce full powers, the following are considered as representing their State:

(a) Heads of State, Heads of Government and Ministers for Foreign Affairs, for the purpose of performing all acts relating to the conclusion of a treaty;

(b) heads of diplomatic missions, for the purpose of adopting the text of a treaty between the accrediting State and the State to which they are accredited;

(c) representatives accredited by States to an international conference or to an international organization or one of its organs, for the purpose of adopting the text of a treaty in that conference, organization or organ.

Article 8. Subsequent confirmation of an act performed without authorization

An act relating to the conclusion of a treaty performed by a person who cannot be considered under article 7 as authorized to represent a State for that purpose is without legal effect unless afterwards confirmed by that State.

Article 9. Adoption of the text

1. The adoption of the text of a treaty takes place by the consent of all the States participating in its drawing up except as provided in paragraph 2.

2. The adoption of the text of a treaty at an international conference takes place by the vote of two-thirds of the States present and voting, unless by the same majority they shall decide to apply a different rule.

Article 10. Authentication of the text

The text of a treaty is established as authentic and definitive:

(a) by such procedure as may be provided for in the text or agreed upon by the States participating in its drawing up; or

(b) failing such procedure, by the signature, signature ad referendum or initialling by the representatives of those States of the text of the treaty or of the Final Act of a conference incorporating the text.

Article 11. Means of expressing consent to be bound by a treaty

The consent of a State to be bound by a treaty may be expressed by signature, exchange of instruments constituting a treaty, ratification, acceptance, approval or accession, or by any other means if so agreed.

Article 12. Consent to be bound by a treaty expressed by signature

1. The consent of a State to be bound by a treaty is expressed by the signature of its representative when:

(a) the treaty provides that signature shall have that effect;

(b) it is otherwise established that the negotiating States were agreed that signature should have that effect; or

(c) the intention of the State to give that effect to the signature appears from the full powers of its representative or was expressed during the negotiation.

2. For the purposes of paragraph 1:

(a) the initialling of a text constitutes a signature of the treaty when it is established that the negotiating States so agreed;

(b) the signature ad referendum of a treaty by a representative, if confirmed by his State, constitutes a full signature of the treaty.

Article 13. Consent to be bound by a treaty expressed by an exchange of instruments constituting a treaty

The consent of States to be bound by a treaty constituted by instruments exchanged between them is expressed by that exchange when:

(a) the instruments provide that their exchange shall have that effect; or

(b) it is otherwise established that those States were agreed that the exchange of instruments should have that effect

Article 14. Consent to be bound by a treaty expressed by ratification, acceptance or approval

1. The consent of a State to be bound by a treaty is expressed by ratification when:

(a) the treaty provides for such consent to be expressed by means of ratification;

(b) it is otherwise established that the negotiating States were agreed that ratification should be required;

(c) the representative of the State has signed the treaty subject to ratification; or

(d) the intention of the State to sign the treaty subject to ratification appears from the full powers of its representative or was expressed during the negotiation.

2. The consent of a State to be bound by a treaty is expressed by acceptance or approval under conditions similar to those which apply to ratification.

Article 15. Consent to be bound by a treaty expressed by accession

The consent of a State to be bound by a treaty is expressed by accession when:

(a) the treaty provides that such consent may be expressed by that State by means of accession;

(b) it is otherwise established that the negotiating States were agreed that such consent may be expressed by that State by means of accession; or

(c) all the parties have subsequently agreed that such consent may be expressed by that State by means of accession.

Article 16. Exchange or deposit of instruments of ratification, acceptance, approval or accession

Unless the treaty otherwise provides, instruments of ratification, acceptance, approval or accession establish the consent of a State to be bound by a treaty upon:

(a) their exchange between the contracting States;

(b) their deposit with the depositary; or

(c) their notification to the contracting States or to the depositary, if so agreed.

Article 17. Consent to be bound by part of a treaty and choice of differing provisions

1. Without prejudice to articles 19 to 23, the consent of a State to be bound by part of a treaty is effective only if the treaty so permits or the other contracting States so agree.

2. The consent of a State to be bound by a treaty which permits a choice between differing provisions is effective only if it is made clear to which of the provisions the consent relates.

Article 18. Obligation not to defeat the object and purpose of a treaty prior to its entry into force

A State is obliged to refrain from acts which would defeat the object and purpose of a treaty when:

(a) it has signed the treaty or has exchanged instruments constituting the treaty subject to ratification, acceptance or approval, until it shall have made its intention clear not to become a party to the treaty; or

(b) it has expressed its consent to be bound by the treaty, pending the entry into force of the treaty and provided that such entry into force is not unduly delayed.

SECTION 2. RESERVATIONS

Article 19. Formulation of reservations

A State may, when signing, ratifying, accepting, approving or acceding to a treaty, formulate a reservation unless:

(a) the reservation is prohibited by the treaty;

(b) the treaty provides that only specified reservations, which do not include the reservation in question, may be made; or

(c) in cases not falling under sub-paragraphs (a) and (b), the reservation is incompatible with the object and purpose of the treaty.

Article 20. Acceptance of and objection to reservations

1. A reservation expressly authorized by a treaty does not require any subsequent acceptance by the other contracting States unless the treaty so provides.

2. When it appears from the limited number of the negotiating States and the object and purpose of a treaty that the application of the treaty in its entirety between all the parties is an essential condition of the consent of each one to be bound by the treaty, a reservation requires acceptance by all the parties.

3. When a treaty is a constituent instrument of an international organization and unless it otherwise provides, a reservation requires the acceptance of the competent organ of that organization.

4. In cases not falling under the preceding paragraphs and unless the treaty otherwise provides:

(a) acceptance by another contracting State of a reservation constitutes the reserving State a party to the treaty in relation to that other State if or when the treaty is in force for those States;

(b) an objection by another contracting State to a reservation does not preclude the entry into force of the treaty as between the objecting and reserving States unless a contrary intention is definitely expressed by the objecting State;

(c) an act expressing a State's consent to be bound by the treaty and containing a reservation is effective as soon as at least one other contracting State has accepted the reservation.

5. For the purposes of paragraphs 2 and 4 and unless the treaty otherwise provides, a reservation is considered to have been accepted by a State if it shall have raised no objection to the reservation by the end of a period of twelve months after it was notified of the reservation or by the date on which it expressed its consent to be bound by the treaty, whichever is later.

Article 21. Legal effects of reservations and of objections to reservations

1. A reservation established with regard to another party in accordance with articles 19, 20 and 23:

(a) modifies for the reserving State in its relations with that other party the provisions of the treaty to which the reservation relates to the extent of the reservation; and

(b) modifies those provisions to the same extent for that other party in its relations with the reserving State.

2. The reservation does not modify the provisions of the treaty for the other parties to the treaty inter se.

3. When a State objecting to a reservation has not opposed the entry into force of the treaty between itself and the reserving State, the provisions to which the reservation relates do not apply as between the two States to the extent of the reservation.

Article 22. Withdrawal of reservations and of objections to reservations

1. Unless the treaty otherwise provides, a reservation may be withdrawn at any time and the consent of a State which has accepted the reservation is not required for its withdrawal.

2. Unless the treaty otherwise provides, an objection to a reservation may be withdrawn at any time.

3. Unless the treaty otherwise provides, or it is otherwise agreed:

(a) the withdrawal of a reservation becomes operative in relation to another contracting State only when notice of it has been received by that State;

(b) the withdrawal of an objection to a reservation becomes operative only when notice of it has been received by the State which formulated the reservation.

Article 23. Procedure regarding reservations

1. A reservation, an express acceptance of a reservation and an objection to a reservation must be formulated in writing and communicated to the contracting States and other States entitled to become parties to the treaty.

2. If formulated when signing the treaty subject to ratification, acceptance or approval, a reservation must be formally confirmed by the reserving State when expressing its consent to be bound by the treaty. In such a case the reservation shall be considered as having been made on the date of its confirmation.

3. An express acceptance of, or an objection to, a reservation made previously to confirmation of the reservation does not itself require confirmation.

4. The withdrawal of a reservation or of an objection to a reservation must be formulated in writing.

SECTION 3. ENTRY INTO FORCE AND PROVISIONAL APPLICATION OF TREATIES

Article 24. Entry into force

1. A treaty enters into force in such manner and upon such date as it may provide or as the negotiating States may agree.

2. Failing any such provision or agreement, a treaty enters into force as soon as consent to be bound by the treaty has been established for all the negotiating States.

3. When the consent of a State to be bound by a treaty is established on a date after the treaty has come into force, the treaty enters into force for that State on that date, unless the treaty otherwise provides.

4. The provisions of a treaty regulating the authentication of its text, the establishment of the consent of States to be bound by the treaty, the manner or date of its entry into force, reservations, the functions of the depositary and other matters arising necessarily before the entry into force of the treaty apply from the time of the adoption of its text.

Article 25. Provisional application

1. A treaty or a part of a treaty is applied provisionally pending its entry into force if:

(a) the treaty itself so provides; or

(b) the negotiating States have in some other manner so agreed.

2. Unless the treaty otherwise provides or the negotiating States have otherwise agreed, the provisional application of a treaty or a part of a treaty with respect to a State shall be terminated if that State notifies the other States between which the treaty is being applied provisionally of its intention not to become a party to the treaty.

PART III: OBSERVANCE, APPLICATION AND INTERPRETATION OF TREATIES

SECTION 1. OBSERVANCE OF TREATIES

Article 26. Pacta sunt servanda

Every treaty in force is binding upon the parties to it and must be performed by them in good faith.

Article 27. Internal law and observance of treaties

A party may not invoke the provisions of its internal law as justification for its failure to perform a treaty. This rule is without prejudice to article 46.

SECTION 2. APPLICATION OF TREATIES

Article 28. Non-retroactivity of treaties

Unless a different intention appears from the treaty or is otherwise established, its provisions do not bind a party in relation to any act or fact which took place or any situation which ceased to exist before the date of the entry into force of the treaty with respect to that party.

Article 29. Territorial scope of treaties

Unless a different intention appears from the treaty or is otherwise established, a treaty is binding upon each party in respect of its entire territory.

Article 30. Application of successive treaties relating to the same subject-matter

1. Subject to Article 103 of the Charter of the United Nations, the rights and obligations of States parties to successive treaties relating to the same subject-matter shall be determined in accordance with the following paragraphs.

2. When a treaty specifies that it is subject to, or that it is not to be considered as incompatible with, an earlier or later treaty, the provisions of that other treaty prevail.

3. When all the parties to the earlier treaty are parties also to the later treaty but the earlier treaty is not terminated or suspended in operation under article 59, the earlier treaty applies only to the extent that its provisions are compatible with those of the latter treaty.

4. When the parties to the later treaty do not include all the parties to the earlier one:

(a) as between States parties to both treaties the same rule applies as in paragraph 3;

(b) as between a State party to both treaties and a State party to only one of the treaties, the treaty to which both States are parties governs their mutual rights and obligations.

5. Paragraph 4 is without prejudice to article 41, or to any question of the termination or suspension of the operation of a treaty under article 60 or to any question of responsibility which may arise for a State from the conclusion or application of a treaty, the provisions of which are incompatible with its obligations towards another State under another treaty.

SECTION 3. INTERPRETATION OF TREATIES

Article 31. General rule of interpretation

1. A treaty shall be interpreted in good faith in accordance with the ordinary meaning to be given to the terms of the treaty in their context and in the light of its object and purpose.

2. The context for the purpose of the interpretation of a treaty shall comprise, in addition to the text, including its preamble and annexes:

(a) any agreement relating to the treaty which was made between all the parties in connexion with the conclusion of the treaty;

(b) any instrument which was made by one or more parties in connexion with the conclusion of the treaty and accepted by the other parties as an instrument related to the treaty.

3. There shall be taken into account, together with the context:

(a) any subsequent agreement between the parties regarding the interpretation of the treaty or the application of its provisions;

(b) any subsequent practice in the application of the treaty which establishes the agreement of the parties regarding its interpretation;

(c) any relevant rules of international law applicable in the relations between the parties.

4. A special meaning shall be given to a term if it is established that the parties so intended.

Article 32. Supplementary means of interpretation

Recourse may be had to supplementary means of interpretation, including the preparatory work of the treaty and the circumstances of its conclusion, in order to confirm the meaning resulting from the application of article 31, or to determine the meaning when the interpretation according to article 31:

(a) leaves the meaning ambiguous or obscure; or

(b) leads to a result which is manifestly absurd or unreasonable.

Article 33. Interpretation of treaties authenticated in two or more languages

1. When a treaty has been authenticated in two or more languages, the text is equally authoritative in each language, unless the treaty provides or the parties agree that, in case of divergence, a particular text shall prevail.

2. A version of the treaty in a language other than one of those in which the text was authenticated shall be considered an authentic text only if the treaty so provides or the parties so agree.

3. The terms of the treaty are presumed to have the same meaning in each authentic text.

4. Except where a particular text prevails in accordance with paragraph 1, when a comparison of the authentic texts discloses a difference of meaning which the application of articles 31 and 32 does not remove, the meaning which best reconciles the texts, having regard to the object and purpose of the treaty, shall be adopted.

SECTION 4. TREATIES AND THIRD STATES

Article 34. General rule regarding third States

A treaty does not create either obligations or rights for a third State without its consent.

Article 35. Treaties providing for obligations for third States

An obligation arises for a third State from a provision of a treaty if the parties to the treaty intend the provision to be the means of establishing the obligation and the third State expressly accepts that obligation in writing.

Article 36. Treaties providing for rights for third States

1. A right arises for a third State from a provision of a treaty if the parties to the treaty intend the provision to accord that right either to the third State, or to a group of States to which it belongs, or to all States, and the third State assents thereto. Its assent shall be presumed so long as the contrary is not indicated, unless the treaty otherwise provides.

2. A State exercising a right in accordance with paragraph 1 shall comply with the conditions for its exercise provided for in the treaty or established in conformity with the treaty.

Article 37. Revocation or modification of obligations or rights of third States

1. When an obligation has arisen for a third State in conformity with article 35, the obligation may be revoked or modified only with the consent of the parties to the treaty and of the third State, unless it is established that they had otherwise agreed.

2. When a right has arisen for a third State in conformity with article 36, the right may not be revoked or modified by the parties if it is established that the right was intended not to be revocable or subject to modification without the consent of the third State.

Article 38. Rules in a treaty becoming binding on third States through international custom

Nothing in articles 34 to 37 precludes a rule set forth in a treaty from becoming binding upon a third State as a customary rule of international law, recognized as such.

PART IV: AMENDMENT AND MODIFICATION OF TREATIES

Article 39. General rule regarding the amendment of treaties

A treaty may be amended by agreement between the parties. The rules laid down in Part II apply to such an agreement except in so far as the treaty may otherwise provide.

Article 40. Amendment of multilateral treaties

1. Unless the treaty otherwise provides, the amendment of multilateral treaties shall be governed by the following paragraphs.

2. Any proposal to amend a multilateral treaty as between all the parties must be notified to all the contracting States, each one of which shall have the right to take part in:

(a) the decision as to the action to be taken in regard to such proposal;

(b) the negotiation and conclusion of any agreement for the amendment of the treaty.

3. Every State entitled to become a party to the treaty shall also be entitled to become a party to the treaty as amended.

4. The amending agreement does not bind any State already a party to the treaty which does not become a party to the amending agreement; article 30, paragraph 4(b), applies in relation to such State.

5. Any State which becomes a party to the treaty after the entry into force of the amending agreement shall, failing an expression of a different intention by that State:

(a) be considered as a party to the treaty as amended; and

(b) be considered as a party to the unamended treaty in relation to any party to the treaty not bound by the amending agreement.

Article 41. Agreements to modify multilateral treaties between certain of the parties only

1. Two or more of the parties to a multilateral treaty may conclude an agreement to modify the treaty as between themselves alone if:

(a) the possibility of such a modification is provided for by the treaty; or

(b) the modification in question is not prohibited by the treaty and:

(i) does not affect the enjoyment by the other parties of their rights under the treaty or the performance of their obligations;

(ii) does not relate to a provision, derogation from which is incompatible with the effective execution of the object and purpose of the treaty as a whole.

2. Unless in a case falling under paragraph 1(a) the treaty otherwise provides, the parties in question shall notify the other parties of their intention to conclude the agreement and of the modification to the treaty for which it provides.

PART V: INVALIDITY, TERMINATION AND SUSPENSION OF THE OPERATION OF TREATIES

SECTION 1. GENERAL PROVISIONS

Article 42. Validity and continuance in force of treaties

1. The validity of a treaty or of the consent of a State to be bound by a treaty may be impeached only through the application of the present Convention.

2. The termination of a treaty, its denunciation or the withdrawal of a party, may take place only as a result of the application of the provisions of the treaty or of the present Convention. The same rule applies to suspension of the operation of a treaty.

Article 43. Obligations imposed by international law independently of a treaty

The invalidity, termination or denunciation of a treaty, the withdrawal of a party from it, or the suspension of its operation, as a result of the application of the present Convention or of the provisions of the treaty, shall not in any way impair the duty of any State to fulfil any obligation embodied in the treaty to which it would be subject under international law independently of the treaty.

Article 44. Separability of Treaty Provisions

1. A right of a party, provided for in a treaty or arising under article 56, to denounce, withdraw from or suspend the operation of the treaty may be exercised only with respect to the whole treaty unless the treaty otherwise provides or the parties otherwise agree.

2. A ground for invalidating, terminating, withdrawing from or suspending the operation of a treaty recognized in the present Convention may be invoked only with respect to the whole treaty except as provided in the following paragraphs or in article 60.

3. If the ground relates solely to particular clauses, it may be invoked only with respect to those clauses where:

(a) the said clauses are separable from the remainder of the treaty with regard to their application;

(b) it appears from the treaty or is otherwise established that acceptance of those clauses was not an essential basis of the consent of the other party or parties to be bound by the treaty as a whole; and

(c) continued performance of the remainder of the treaty would not be unjust.

4. In cases falling under articles 49 and 50 the State entitled to invoke the fraud or corruption may do so with respect either to the whole treaty or, subject to paragraph 3, to the particular clauses alone.

5. In cases falling under articles 51, 52 and 53, no separation of the provisions of the treaty is permitted.

Article 45. Loss of a right to invoke a ground for invalidating, terminating, withdrawing from or suspending the operation of a treaty

A State may no longer invoke a ground for invalidating, terminating, withdrawing from or suspending the operation of a treaty under articles 46 to 50 or articles 60 and 62 if, after becoming aware of the facts:

(a) it shall have expressly agreed that the treaty is valid or remains in force or continues in operation, as the case may be; or

(b) it must by reason of its conduct be considered as having acquiesced in the validity of the treaty or in its maintenance in force or in operation, as the case may be.

SECTION 2. INVALIDITY OF TREATIES

Article 46. Provisions of internal law regarding competence to conclude treaties

1. A State may not invoke the fact that its consent to be bound by a treaty has been expressed in violation of a provision of its internal law regarding competence to conclude treaties as invalidating its consent unless that violation was manifest and concerned a rule of its internal law of fundamental importance.

2. A violation is manifest if it would be objectively evident to any State conducting itself in the matter in accordance with normal practice and in good faith.

Article 47. Specific restrictions on authority to express the consent of a State

If the authority of a representative to express the consent of a State to be bound by a particular treaty has been made subject to a specific restriction, his omission to observe that restriction may not be invoked as invalidating the consent expressed by him unless the restriction was notified to the other negotiating States prior to his expressing such consent.

Article 48. Error

1. A State may invoke an error in a treaty as invalidating its consent to be bound by the treaty if the error relates to a fact or situation which was assumed by that State to exist at the time when the treaty was concluded and formed an essential basis of its consent to be bound by the treaty.

2. Paragraph 1 shall not apply if the State in question contributed by its own conduct to the error or if the circumstances were such as to put that State on notice of a possible error.

3. An error relating only to the wording of the text of a treaty does not affect its validity; article 79 then applies.

Article 49. Fraud

If a State has been induced to conclude a treaty by the fraudulent conduct of another negotiating State, the State may invoke the fraud as invalidating its consent to be bound by the treaty.

Article 50. Corruption of a representative of a State

If the expression of a State's consent to be bound by a treaty has been procured through the corruption of its representative directly or indirectly by another negotiating State, the State may invoke such corruption as invalidating its consent to be bound by the treaty.

Article 51. Coercion of a representative of a State

The expression of a State's consent to be bound by a treaty which has been procured by the coercion of its representative through acts or threats directed against him shall be without any legal effect.

Article 52. Coercion of a State by the threat or use of force

A treaty is void if its conclusion has been procured by the threat or use of force in violation of the principles of international law embodied in the Charter of the United Nations.

Article 53. Treaties conflicting with a peremptory norm of general international law (jus cogens)

A treaty is void if, at the time of its conclusion, it conflicts with a peremptory norm of general international law. For the purposes of the present Convention, a peremptory norm of general international law is a norm accepted and recognized by the international community of States as a whole as a norm from which no derogation is permitted and which can be modified only by a subsequent norm of general international law having the same character.

SECTION 3. TERMINATION AND SUSPENSION OF THE OPERATION OF TREATIES

Article 54. Termination of or withdrawal from a treaty under its provisions or by consent of the parties

The termination of a treaty or the withdrawal of a party may take place:

(a) in conformity with the provisions of the treaty; or

(b) at any time by consent of all the parties after consultation with the other contracting States.

Article 55. Reduction of the parties to a multilateral treaty below the number necessary for its entry into force

Unless the treaty otherwise provides, a multilateral treaty does not terminate by reason only of the fact that the number of the parties falls below the number necessary for its entry into force.

Article 56. Denunciation of or withdrawal from a treaty containing no provision regarding termination, denunciation or withdrawal

1. A treaty which contains no provision regarding its termination and which does not provide for denunciation or withdrawal is not subject to denunciation or withdrawal unless:

(a) it is established that the parties intended to admit the possibility of denunciation or withdrawal; or

(b) a right of denunciation or withdrawal may be implied by the nature of the treaty.

2. A party shall give not less than twelve months' notice of its intention to denounce or withdraw from a treaty under paragraph 1.

Article 57. Suspension of the operation of a treaty under its provisions or by consent of the parties

The operation of a treaty in regard to all the parties or to a particular party may be suspended:

(a) in conformity with the provisions of the treaty; or

(b) at any time by consent of all the parties after consultation with the other contracting States.

Article 58. Suspension of the operation of a multilateral treaty by agreement between certain of the parties only

1. Two or more parties to a multilateral treaty may conclude an agreement to suspend the operation of provisions of the treaty, temporarily and as between themselves alone, if:

(a) the possibility of such a suspension is provided for by the treaty; or

(b) the suspension in question is not prohibited by the treaty and:

(i) does not affect the enjoyment by the other parties of their rights under the treaty or the performance of their obligations;

(ii) is not incompatible with the object and purpose of the treaty.

2. Unless in a case falling under paragraph 1(a) the treaty otherwise provides, the parties in question shall notify the other parties of their intention to conclude the agreement and of those provisions of the treaty the operation of which they intend to suspend.

Article 59. Termination or suspension of the operation of a treaty implied by conclusion of a later treaty

1. A treaty shall be considered as terminated if all the parties to it conclude a later treaty relating to the same subject- matter and:

(a) it appears from the later treaty or is otherwise established that the parties intended that the matter should be governed by that treaty; or

(b) the provisions of the later treaty are so far incompatible with those of the earlier one that the two treaties are not capable of being applied at the same time.

2. The earlier treaty shall be considered as only suspended in operation if it appears from the later treaty or is otherwise established that such was the intention of the parties.

Article 60. Termination or suspension of the operation of a treaty as a consequence of its breach

1. A material breach of a bilateral treaty by one of the parties entitles the other to invoke the breach as a ground for terminating the treaty or suspending its operation in whole or in part.

2. A material breach of a multilateral treaty by one of the parties entitles:

(a) the other parties by unanimous agreement to suspend the operation of the treaty in whole or in part or to terminate it either:

(i) in the relations between themselves and the defaulting State, or

(ii) as between all the parties;

(b) a party specially affected by the breach to invoke it as a ground for suspending the operation of the treaty in whole or in part in the relations between itself and the defaulting State;

(c) any party other than the defaulting State to invoke the breach as a ground for suspending the operation of the treaty in whole or in part with respect to itself if the treaty is of such a character that a material breach of its provisions by one party radically changes the position of every party with respect to the further performance of its obligations under the treaty.

3. A material breach of a treaty, for the purposes of this article, consists in:

(a) a repudiation of the treaty not sanctioned by the present Convention; or

(b) the violation of a provision essential to the accomplishment of the object or purpose of the treaty.

4. The foregoing paragraphs are without prejudice to any provision in the treaty applicable in the event of a breach.

5. Paragraphs 1 to 3 do not apply to provisions relating to the protection of the human person contained in treaties of a humanitarian character, in particular to provisions prohibiting any form of reprisals against persons protected by such treaties.

Article 61. Supervening impossibility of performance

1. A party may invoke the impossibility of performing a treaty as a ground for terminating or withdrawing from it if the impossibility results from the permanent disappearance or destruction of an object indispensable for the execution of the treaty. If the impossibility is temporary, it may be invoked only as a ground for suspending the operation of the treaty.

2. Impossibility of performance may not be invoked by a party as a ground for terminating, withdrawing from or suspending the operation of a treaty if the impossibility is the result of a breach by that party either of an obligation under the treaty or of any other international obligation owed to any other party to the treaty.

Article 62. Fundamental change of circumstances

1. A fundamental change of circumstances which has occurred with regard to those existing at the time of the conclusion of a treaty, and which was not foreseen by the parties, may not be invoked as a ground for terminating or withdrawing from the treaty unless:

(a) the existence of those circumstances constituted an essential basis of the consent of the parties to be bound by the treaty; and

(b) the effect of the change is radically to transform the extent of obligations still to be performed under the treaty.

2. A fundamental change of circumstances may not be invoked as a ground for terminating or withdrawing from a treaty:

(a) if the treaty establishes a boundary; or

(b) if the fundamental change is the result of a breach by the party invoking it either of an obligation under the treaty or of any other international obligation owed to any other party to the treaty.

3. If, under the foregoing paragraphs, a party may invoke a fundamental change of circumstances as a ground for terminating or withdrawing from a treaty it may also invoke the change as a ground for suspending the operation of the treaty.

Article 63. Severance of diplomatic or consular relations

The severance of diplomatic or consular relations between parties to a treaty does not affect the legal relations established between them by the treaty except in so far as the existence of diplomatic or consular relations is indispensable for the application of the treaty.

Article 64. Emergence of a new peremptory norm of general international law (jus cogens)

If a new peremptory norm of general international law emerges, any existing treaty which is in conflict with that norm becomes void and terminates.

SECTION 4. PROCEDURE

Article 65. Procedure to be followed with respect to invalidity, termination, withdrawal from or suspension of the operation of a treaty

1. A party which, under the provisions of the present Convention, invokes either a defect in its consent to be bound by a treaty or a ground for impeaching the validity of a treaty, terminating it, withdrawing from it or suspending its operation, must notify the other parties of its claim. The notification shall indicate the measure proposed to be taken with respect to the treaty and the reasons therefor.

2. If, after the expiry of a period which, except in cases of special urgency, shall not be less than three months after the receipt of the notification, no party has raised any objection, the party making the notification may carry out in the manner provided in article 67 the measure which it has proposed.

3. If, however, objection has been raised by any other party, the parties shall seek a solution through the means indicated in article 33 of the Charter of the United Nations.

4. Nothing in the foregoing paragraphs shall affect the rights or obligations of the parties under any provisions in force binding the parties with regard to the settlement of disputes.

5. Without prejudice to article 45, the fact that a State has not previously made the notification prescribed in paragraph 1 shall not prevent it from making such notification in answer to another party claiming performance of the treaty or alleging its violation.

Article 66. Procedures for judicial settlement, arbitration and conciliation

If, under paragraph 3 of article 65, no solution has been reached within a period of 12 months following the date on which the objection was raised, the following procedures shall be followed:

(a) any one of the parties to a dispute concerning the application or the interpretation of articles 53 or 64 may, by a written application, submit it to the International Court of Justice for a decision unless the parties by common consent agree to submit the dispute to arbitration;

(b) any one of the parties to a dispute concerning the application or the interpretation of any of the other articles in Part V of the present Convention may set in motion the procedure specified in the Annexe to the Convention by submitting a request to that effect to the Secretary-General of the United Nations.

Article 67. Instruments for declaring invalid, terminating, withdrawing from or suspending the operation of a treaty

1. The notification provided for under article 65 paragraph 1 must be made in writing.

2. Any act declaring invalid, terminating, withdrawing from or suspending the operation of a treaty pursuant to the provisions of the treaty or of paragraphs 2 or 3 of article 65 shall be carried out through an instrument communicated to the other parties. If the instrument is not signed by the Head of State, Head of Government or Minister for Foreign Affairs, the representative of the State communicating it may be called upon to produce full powers.

Article 68. Revocation of notifications and instruments provided for in articles 65 and 67

A notification or instrument provided for in articles 65 or 67 may be revoked at any time before it takes effect.

SECTION 5. CONSEQUENCES OF THE INVALIDITY, TERMINATION OR SUSPENSION OF THE OPERATION OF A TREATY

Article 69. Consequences of the invalidity of a treaty

1. A treaty the invalidity of which is established under the present Convention is void. The provisions of a void treaty have no legal force.

2. If acts have nevertheless been performed in reliance on such a treaty:

(a) each party may require any other party to establish as far as possible in their mutual relations the position that would have existed if the acts had not been performed;

(b) acts performed in good faith before the invalidity was invoked are not rendered unlawful by reason only of the invalidity of the treaty.

3. In cases falling under articles 49, 50, 51 or 52, paragraph 2 does not apply with respect to the party to which the fraud, the act of corruption or the coercion is imputable.

4. In the case of the invalidity of a particular State's consent to be bound by a multilateral treaty, the foregoing rules apply in the relations between that State and the parties to the treaty.

Article 70. Consequences of the termination of a treaty

1. Unless the treaty otherwise provides or the parties otherwise agree, the termination of a treaty under its provisions or in accordance with the present Convention:

(a) releases the parties from any obligation further to perform the treaty;

(b) does not affect any right, obligation or legal situation of the parties created through the execution of the treaty prior to its termination.

2. If a State denounces or withdraws from a multilateral treaty, paragraph 1 applies in the relations between that State and each of the other parties to the treaty from the date when such denunciation or withdrawal takes effect.

Article 71. Consequences of the invalidity of a treaty which conflicts with a peremptory norm of general international law

1. In the case of a treaty which is void under article 53 the parties shall:

(a) eliminate as far as possible the consequences of any act performed in reliance on any provision which conflicts with the peremptory norm of general international law; and

(b) bring their mutual relations into conformity with the peremptory norm of general international law.

2. In the case of a treaty which becomes void and terminates under article 64, the termination of the treaty:

(a) releases the parties from any obligation further to perform the treaty;

(b) does not affect any right, obligation or legal situation of the parties created through the execution of the treaty prior to its termination; provided that those rights, obligations or situations may thereafter be maintained only to the extent that their maintenance is not in itself in conflict with the new peremptory norm of general international law.

Article 72. Consequences of the suspension of the operation of a treaty

1. Unless the treaty otherwise provides or the parties otherwise agree, the suspension of the operation of a treaty under its provisions or in accordance with the present Convention:

(a) releases the parties between which the operation of the treaty is suspended from the obligation to perform the treaty in their mutual relations during the period of the suspension;

(b) does not otherwise affect the legal relations between the parties established by the treaty.

2. During the period of the suspension the parties shall refrain from acts tending to obstruct the resumption of the operation of the treaty.

PART VI: MISCELLANEOUS PROVISIONS

Article 73. Cases of State succession, State responsibility and outbreak of hostilities

The provisions of the present Convention shall not prejudge any question that may arise in regard to a treaty from a succession of States or from the international responsibility of a State or from the outbreak of hostilities between States.

Article 74. Diplomatic and consular relations and the conclusion of treaties

The severance or absence of diplomatic or consular relations between two or more States does not prevent the conclusion of treaties between those States The conclusion of a treaty does not in itself affect the situation in regard to diplomatic or consular relations.

Article 75. Case of an aggressor State

The provisions of the present Convention are without prejudice to any obligation in relation to a treaty which may arise for an aggressor State in consequence of measures taken in conformity with the Charter of the United Nations with reference to that State's aggression.

PART VII: DEPOSITARIES, NOTIFICATIONS, CORRECTIONS AND REGISTRATION

Article 76. Depositaries of treaties

1. The designation of the depositary of a treaty may be made by the negotiating States, either in the treaty itself or in some other manner.

The depositary may be one or more States, an international organization or the chief administrative officer of the organization.

2. The functions of the depositary of a treaty are international in character and the depositary is under an obligation to act impartially in their performance. In particular, the fact that a treaty has not entered into force between certain of the parties or that a difference has appeared between a State and a depositary with regard to the performance of the latter's functions shall not affect that obligation.

Article 77. Functions of depositaries

1. The functions of a depositary, unless otherwise provided in the treaty or agreed by the contracting States, comprise in particular:

(a) keeping custody of the original text of the treaty and of any full powers delivered to the depositary;

(b) preparing certified copies of the original text and preparing any further text of the treaty in such additional languages as may be required by the treaty and transmitting them to the parties and to the States entitled to become parties to the treaty;

(c) receiving any signatures to the treaty and receiving and keeping custody of any instruments, notifications and communications relating to it;

(d) examining whether the signature or any instrument, notification or communication relating to the treaty is in due and proper form and, if need be, bringing the matter to the attention of the State in question;

(e) informing the parties and the States entitled to become parties to the treaty of acts, notifications and communications relating to the treaty;

(f) informing the States entitled to become parties to the treaty when the number of signatures or of instruments of ratification, acceptance, approval or accession required for the entry into force of the treaty has been received or deposited;

(g) registering the treaty with the Secretariat of the United Nations;

(h) performing the functions specified in other provisions of the present Convention.

2. In the event of any difference appearing between a State and the depositary as to the performance of the latter's functions, the depositary shall bring the question to the attention of the signatory States and the contracting States or, where appropriate, of the competent organ of the international organization concerned.

Article 78. Notifications and communications

Except as the treaty or the present Convention otherwise provide, any notification or communication to be made by any State under the present Convention shall:

(a) if there is no depositary, be transmitted direct to the States for which it is intended, or if there is a depositary, to the latter;

(b) be considered as having been made by the State in question only upon its receipt by the State to which it was transmitted or, as the case may be, upon its receipt by the depositary;

(c) if transmitted to a depositary, be considered as received by the State for which it was intended only when the latter State has been informed by the depositary in accordance with article 77, paragraph 1(e).

Article 79. Correction of errors in texts or in certified copies of treaties

1. Where, after the authentication of the text of a treaty, the signatory States and the contracting States are agreed that it contains an error, the error shall, unless they decide upon some other means of correction, be corrected:

(a) by having the appropriate correction made in the text and causing the correction to be initialled by duly authorized representatives;

(b) by executing or exchanging an instrument or instruments setting out the correction which it has been agreed to make; or

(c) by executing a corrected text of the whole treaty by the same procedure as in the case of the original text.

2. Where the treaty is one for which there is a depositary, the latter shall notify the signatory States and the contracting States of the error and of the proposal to correct it and shall specify an appropriate time-limit within which objection to the proposed correction may be raised.

If, on the expiry of the time-limit:

(a) no objection has been raised, the depositary shall make and initial the correction in the text and shall execute a proc rectification of the text and communicate a copy of it to the parties and to the States entitled to become parties to the treaty;

(b) an objection has been raised, the depositary shall communicate the objection to the signatory States and to the contracting States.

3. The rules in paragraphs 1 and 2 apply also where the text has been authenticated in two or more languages and it appears that there is a lack of concordance which the signatory States and the contracting States agree should be corrected.

4. The corrected text replaces the defective text ab initio, unless the signatory States and the contracting States otherwise decide.

5. The correction of the text of a treaty that has been registered shall be notified to the Secretariat of the United Nations.

6. Where an error is discovered in a certified copy of a treaty, the depositary shall execute a proc communicate a copy of it to the signatory States and to the contracting Slates.

Article 80. Registration and publication of treaties

1. Treaties shall, after their entry into force, be transmitted to the Secretariat of the United Nations for registration or filing and recording, as the case may be, and for publication.

2. The designation of a depositary shall constitute authorization for it to perform the acts specified in the preceding paragraph.

PART VIII: FINAL PROVISIONS

Article 81. Signature

The present Convention shall be open for signature by all States Members of the United Nations or of any of the specialized agencies or of the International Atomic Energy Agency or parties to the Statute of the International Court of Justice, and by any other State invited by the General Assembly of the United Nations to become a party to the Convention, as follows: until 30 November 1969, at the Federal Ministry for Foreign Affairs of the Republic of Austria, and subsequently, until 30 April 1970, at United Nations Headquarters, New York.

Article 82. Ratification

The present Convention is subject to ratification. The instruments of ratification shall be deposited with the Secretary-General of the United Nations.

Article 83. Accession

The present Convention shall remain open for accession by any State belonging to any of the categories mentioned in article 81. The instruments of accession shall be deposited with the Secretary-General of the United Nations.

Article 84. Entry into force

1. The present Convention shall enter into force on the thirtieth day following the date of deposit of the thirty-fifth instrument of ratification or accession.

2. For each State ratifying or acceding to the Convention after the deposit of the thirty-fifth instrument of ratification or accession, the Convention shall enter into force on the thirtieth day after deposit by such State of its instrument of ratification or accession.

Article 85. Authentic texts

The original of the present Convention, of which the Chinese, English, French, Russian and Spanish texts are equally authentic, shall be deposited with the Secretary-General of the United Nations.